American Casebook Series
Hornbook Series and Basic Legal Texts
Black Letter Series and Nutshell Series

of

WEST PUBLISHING COMPANY
P.O. Box 64526
St. Paul, Minnesota 55164–0526

Accounting

FARIS' ACCOUNTING AND LAW IN A NUT-SHELL, 377 pages, 1984. Softcover. (Text)

FIFLIS, KRIPKE AND FOSTER'S TEACHING MATERIALS ON ACCOUNTING FOR BUSINESS LAWYERS, Third Edition, 838 pages, 1984. (Casebook)

SIEGEL AND SIEGEL'S ACCOUNTING AND FINANCIAL DISCLOSURE: A GUIDE TO BASIC CONCEPTS, 259 pages, 1983. Softcover. (Text)

Administrative Law

BONFIELD AND ASIMOW'S STATE AND FEDERAL ADMINISTRATIVE LAW, 826 pages, 1989. (Casebook)

GELLHORN AND BOYER'S ADMINISTRATIVE LAW AND PROCESS IN A NUTSHELL, Second Edition, 445 pages, 1981. Softcover. (Text)

MASHAW AND MERRILL'S CASES AND MATERIALS ON ADMINISTRATIVE LAW—THE AMERICAN PUBLIC LAW SYSTEM, Second Edition, 976 pages, 1985. (Casebook) 1989 Supplement.

ROBINSON, GELLHORN AND BRUFF'S THE ADMINISTRATIVE PROCESS, Third Edition, 978 pages, 1986. (Casebook)

Admiralty

HEALY AND SHARPE'S CASES AND MATERIALS ON ADMIRALTY, Second Edition, 876 pages, 1986. (Casebook)

MARAIST'S ADMIRALTY IN A NUTSHELL, Second Edition, 379 pages, 1988. Softcover.

(Text)

SCHOENBAUM'S HORNBOOK ON ADMIRALTY AND MARITIME LAW, Student Edition, 692 pages, 1987 with 1989 pocket part. (Text)

Agency—Partnership

FESSLER'S ALTERNATIVES TO INCORPORATION FOR PERSONS IN QUEST OF PROFIT, Second Edition, 326 pages, 1986. Softcover. Teacher's Manual available. (Casebook)

HENN'S CASES AND MATERIALS ON AGENCY, PARTNERSHIP AND OTHER UNINCORPORATED BUSINESS ENTERPRISES, Second Edition, 733 pages, 1985. Teacher's Manual available. (Casebook)

REUSCHLEIN AND GREGORY'S HORNBOOK ON THE LAW OF AGENCY AND PARTNERSHIP, Second Edition, Approximately 750 pages, October, 1989 Pub. (Text)

SELECTED CORPORATION AND PARTNERSHIP STATUTES, RULES AND FORMS. Softcover. Approximately 700 pages, 1989.

STEFFEN AND KERR'S CASES ON AGENCY-PARTNERSHIP, Fourth Edition, 859 pages, 1980. (Casebook)

STEFFEN'S AGENCY-PARTNERSHIP IN A NUTSHELL, 364 pages, 1977. Softcover. (Text)

Agricultural Law

MEYER, PEDERSEN, THORSON AND DAVIDSON'S AGRICULTURAL LAW: CASES AND MATERIALS, 931 pages, 1985. Teacher's Manual available. (Casebook)

Alternative Dispute Resolution

KANOWITZ' CASES AND MATERIALS ON ALTER-

Alternative Dispute Resolution—Cont'd

NATIVE DISPUTE RESOLUTION, 1024 pages, 1986. Teacher's Manual available. (Casebook)

RISKIN AND WESTBROOK'S DISPUTE RESOLUTION AND LAWYERS, 468 pages, 1987. Teacher's Manual available. (Casebook)

RISKIN AND WESTBROOK'S DISPUTE RESOLUTION AND LAWYERS, Abridged Edition, 223 pages, 1987. Softcover. Teacher's Manual available. (Casebook)

TEPLE AND MOBERLY'S ARBITRATION AND CONFLICT RESOLUTION, (The Labor Law Group). 614 pages, 1979. (Casebook)

American Indian Law

CANBY'S AMERICAN INDIAN LAW IN A NUTSHELL, Second Edition, 336 pages, 1988. Softcover. (Text)

GETCHES AND WILKINSON'S CASES AND MATERIALS ON FEDERAL INDIAN LAW, Second Edition, 880 pages, 1986. (Casebook)

Antitrust—see also Regulated Industries, Trade Regulation

FOX AND SULLIVAN'S CASES AND MATERIALS ON ANTITRUST, Approximately 1100 pages, 1989. (Casebook)

GELLHORN'S ANTITRUST LAW AND ECONOMICS IN A NUTSHELL, Third Edition, 472 pages, 1986. Softcover. (Text)

HOVENKAMP'S BLACK LETTER ON ANTITRUST, 323 pages, 1986. Softcover. (Review)

HOVENKAMP'S HORNBOOK ON ECONOMICS AND FEDERAL ANTITRUST LAW, Student Edition, 414 pages, 1985. (Text)

OPPENHEIM, WESTON AND MCCARTHY'S CASES AND COMMENTS ON FEDERAL ANTITRUST LAWS, Fourth Edition, 1168 pages, 1981. (Casebook) 1985 Supplement.

POSNER AND EASTERBROOK'S CASES AND ECONOMIC NOTES ON ANTITRUST, Second Edition, 1077 pages, 1981. (Casebook) 1984–85 Supplement.

SULLIVAN'S HORNBOOK OF THE LAW OF ANTITRUST, 886 pages, 1977. (Text)

Appellate Advocacy—see Trial and Appellate Advocacy

Architecture and Engineering Law

SWEET'S LEGAL ASPECTS OF ARCHITECTURE, ENGINEERING AND THE CONSTRUCTION PROCESS, Fourth Edition, 889 pages, 1989. Teacher's Manual available. (Casebook)

Art Law

DUBOFF'S ART LAW IN A NUTSHELL, 335 pages, 1984. Softcover. (Text)

Banking Law

LOVETT'S BANKING AND FINANCIAL INSTITUTIONS LAW IN A NUTSHELL, Second Edition, 464 pages, 1988. Softcover. (Text)

SYMONS AND WHITE'S TEACHING MATERIALS ON BANKING LAW, Second Edition, 993 pages, 1984. Teacher's Manual available. (Casebook) 1987 Supplement.

Business Planning—see also Corporate Finance

PAINTER'S PROBLEMS AND MATERIALS IN BUSINESS PLANNING, Second Edition, 1008 pages, 1984. (Casebook) 1987 Supplement.

See also Selected Corporation and Partnership Statutes, Rules and Forms

SELECTED CORPORATION AND PARTNERSHIP STATUTES, RULES AND FORMS. Approximately 700 pages, 1989. Softcover.

Civil Procedure—see also Federal Jurisdiction and Procedure

AMERICAN BAR ASSOCIATION SECTION OF LITIGATION—READINGS ON ADVERSARIAL JUSTICE: THE AMERICAN APPROACH TO ADJUDICATION, 217 pages, 1988. Softcover. (Coursebook)

CLERMONT'S BLACK LETTER ON CIVIL PROCEDURE, Second Edition, 332 pages, 1988. Softcover. (Review)

COUND, FRIEDENTHAL, MILLER AND SEXTON'S CASES AND MATERIALS ON CIVIL PROCEDURE, Fifth Edition, Approximately 1280 pages, 1989. Teacher's Manual available. (Casebook)

COUND, FRIEDENTHAL, MILLER AND SEXTON'S CIVIL PROCEDURE SUPPLEMENT. Approximately 450 pages, 1989. Softcover. (Casebook Supplement)

FEDERAL RULES OF CIVIL PROCEDURE—EDUCATIONAL EDITION. Softcover. Approximately 600 pages, 1989.

Civil Procedure—Cont'd

FRIEDENTHAL, KANE AND MILLER'S HORNBOOK ON CIVIL PROCEDURE, 876 pages, 1985. (Text)

KANE AND LEVINE'S CIVIL PROCEDURE IN CALIFORNIA: STATE AND FEDERAL Approximately 500 pages, 1989. Softcover. Casebook Supplement.

KANE'S CIVIL PROCEDURE IN A NUTSHELL, Second Edition, 306 pages, 1986. Softcover. (Text)

KOFFLER AND REPPY'S HORNBOOK ON COMMON LAW PLEADING, 663 pages, 1969. (Text)

MARCUS, REDISH AND SHERMAN'S CIVIL PROCEDURE: A MODERN APPROACH, 1027 pages, 1989. Teacher's Manual available. (Casebook)

MARCUS AND SHERMAN'S COMPLEX LITIGATION–CASES AND MATERIALS ON ADVANCED CIVIL PROCEDURE, 846 pages, 1985. Teacher's Manual available. (Casebook) 1989 Supplement.

PARK'S COMPUTER-AIDED EXERCISES ON CIVIL PROCEDURE, Second Edition, 167 pages, 1983. Softcover. (Coursebook)

SIEGEL'S HORNBOOK ON NEW YORK PRACTICE, 1011 pages, 1978, with 1987 pocket part. (Text)

Commercial Law

BAILEY AND HAGEDORN'S SECURED TRANSACTIONS IN A NUTSHELL, Third Edition, 390 pages, 1988. Softcover. (Text)

EPSTEIN, MARTIN, HENNING AND NICKLES' BASIC UNIFORM COMMERCIAL CODE TEACHING MATERIALS, Third Edition, 704 pages, 1988. Teacher's Manual available. (Casebook)

HENSON'S HORNBOOK ON SECURED TRANSACTIONS UNDER THE U.C.C., Second Edition, 504 pages, 1979, with 1979 pocket part. (Text)

MURRAY'S COMMERCIAL LAW, PROBLEMS AND MATERIALS, 366 pages, 1975. Teacher's Manual available. Softcover. (Coursebook)

NICKLES' BLACK LETTER ON COMMERCIAL PAPER, 450 pages, 1988. Softcover. (Review)

NICKLES, MATHESON AND DOLAN'S MATERIALS FOR UNDERSTANDING CREDIT AND PAYMENT SYSTEMS, 923 pages, 1987. Teacher's Manual available. (Casebook)

NORDSTROM, MURRAY AND CLOVIS' PROBLEMS AND MATERIALS ON SALES, 515 pages, 1982. (Casebook)

NORDSTROM, MURRAY AND CLOVIS' PROBLEMS AND MATERIALS ON SECURED TRANSACTIONS, 594 pages, 1987. (Casebook)

RUBIN AND COOTER'S THE PAYMENT SYSTEM: CASES, MATERIALS AND ISSUES, Approximately 885 pages, 1989. (Casebook)

SELECTED COMMERCIAL STATUTES. Softcover. Approximately 1600 pages, 1989.

SPEIDEL'S BLACK LETTER ON SALES AND SALES FINANCING, 363 pages, 1984. Softcover. (Review)

SPEIDEL, SUMMERS AND WHITE'S COMMERCIAL LAW: TEACHING MATERIALS, Fourth Edition, 1448 pages, 1987. Teacher's Manual available. (Casebook)

SPEIDEL, SUMMERS AND WHITE'S COMMERCIAL PAPER: TEACHING MATERIALS, Fourth Edition, 578 pages, 1987. Reprint from Speidel et al., Commercial Law, Fourth Edition. Teacher's Manual available. (Casebook)

SPEIDEL, SUMMERS AND WHITE'S SALES: TEACHING MATERIALS, Fourth Edition, 804 pages, 1987. Reprint from Speidel et al., Commercial Law, Fourth Edition. Teacher's Manual available (Casebook)

SPEIDEL, SUMMERS AND WHITE'S SECURED TRANSACTIONS: TEACHING MATERIALS, Fourth Edition, 485 pages, 1987. Reprint from Speidel et al., Commercial Law, Fourth Edition. Teacher's Manual available. (Casebook)

STOCKTON'S SALES IN A NUTSHELL, Second Edition, 370 pages, 1981. Softcover. (Text)

STONE'S UNIFORM COMMERCIAL CODE IN A NUTSHELL, Third Edition, Approximately 540 pages, 1989. Softcover. (Text)

UNIFORM COMMERCIAL CODE, OFFICIAL TEXT WITH COMMENTS. Softcover. 1155 pages, 1987.

WEBER AND SPEIDEL'S COMMERCIAL PAPER IN A NUTSHELL, Third Edition, 404 pages,

Commercial Law—Cont'd
1982. Softcover. (Text)

WHITE AND SUMMERS' HORNBOOK ON THE UNIFORM COMMERCIAL CODE, Third Edition, Student Edition, 1386 pages, 1988. (Text)

Community Property
MENNELL AND BOYKOFF'S COMMUNITY PROPERTY IN A NUTSHELL, Second Edition, 432 pages, 1988. Softcover. (Text)

VERRALL AND BIRD'S CASES AND MATERIALS ON CALIFORNIA COMMUNITY PROPERTY, Fifth Edition, 604 pages, 1988. (Casebook)

Comparative Law
BARTON, GIBBS, LI AND MERRYMAN'S LAW IN RADICALLY DIFFERENT CULTURES, 960 pages, 1983. (Casebook)

GLENDON, GORDON AND OSAKWE'S COMPARATIVE LEGAL TRADITIONS: TEXT, MATERIALS AND CASES ON THE CIVIL LAW, COMMON LAW AND SOCIALIST LAW TRADITIONS, 1091 pages, 1985. (Casebook)

GLENDON, GORDON AND OSAKWE'S COMPARATIVE LEGAL TRADITIONS IN A NUTSHELL. 402 pages, 1982. Softcover. (Text)

LANGBEIN'S COMPARATIVE CRIMINAL PROCEDURE: GERMANY, 172 pages, 1977. Softcover. (Casebook)

Computers and Law
MAGGS AND SPROWL'S COMPUTER APPLICATIONS IN THE LAW, 316 pages, 1987. (Coursebook)

MASON'S USING COMPUTERS IN THE LAW: AN INTRODUCTION AND PRACTICAL GUIDE, Second Edition, 288 pages, 1988. Softcover. (Coursebook)

Conflict of Laws
CRAMTON, CURRIE AND KAY'S CASES–COMMENTS–QUESTIONS ON CONFLICT OF LAWS, Fourth Edition, 876 pages, 1987. (Casebook)

HAY'S BLACK LETTER ON CONFLICT OF LAWS, Approximately 325 pages, 1989. Softcover. (Review)

SCOLES AND HAY'S HORNBOOK ON CONFLICT OF LAWS, Student Edition, 1085 pages, 1982, with 1989 pocket part. (Text)

SEIGEL'S CONFLICTS IN A NUTSHELL, 470

pages, 1982. Softcover. (Text)

Constitutional Law—Civil Rights—see also Foreign Relations and National Security Law
ABERNATHY'S CASES AND MATERIALS ON CIVIL RIGHTS, 660 pages, 1980. (Casebook)

BARRON AND DIENES' BLACK LETTER ON CONSTITUTIONAL LAW, Second Edition, 310 pages, 1987. Softcover. (Review)

BARRON AND DIENES' CONSTITUTIONAL LAW IN A NUTSHELL, 389 pages, 1986. Softcover. (Text)

ENGDAHL'S CONSTITUTIONAL FEDERALISM IN A NUTSHELL, Second Edition, 411 pages, 1987. Softcover. (Text)

FARBER AND SHERRY'S HISTORY OF THE AMERICAN CONSTITUTION, Approximately 476 pages, August, 1989 Pub. Softcover. (Text)

GARVEY AND ALEINIKOFF'S MODERN CONSTITUTIONAL THEORY: A READER, Approximately 494 pages, 1989. Softcover. (Reader)

LOCKHART, KAMISAR, CHOPER AND SHIFFRIN'S CONSTITUTIONAL LAW: CASES–COMMENTS–QUESTIONS, Sixth Edition, 1601 pages, 1986. (Casebook) 1989 Supplement.

LOCKHART, KAMISAR, CHOPER AND SHIFFRIN'S THE AMERICAN CONSTITUTION: CASES AND MATERIALS, Sixth Edition, 1260 pages, 1986. Abridged version of Lockhart, et al., Constitutional Law: Cases–Comments–Questions, Sixth Edition. (Casebook) 1989 Supplement.

LOCKHART, KAMISAR, CHOPER AND SHIFFRIN'S CONSTITUTIONAL RIGHTS AND LIBERTIES: CASES AND MATERIALS, Sixth Edition, 1266 pages, 1986. Reprint from Lockhart, et al., Constitutional Law: Cases–Comments–Questions, Sixth Edition. (Casebook) 1989 Supplement.

MARKS AND COOPER'S STATE CONSTITUTIONAL LAW IN A NUTSHELL, 329 pages, 1988. Softcover. (Text)

NOWAK, ROTUNDA AND YOUNG'S HORNBOOK ON CONSTITUTIONAL LAW, Third Edition, 1191 pages, 1986 with 1988 pocket part. (Text)

ROTUNDA'S MODERN CONSTITUTIONAL LAW:

Constitutional Law—Civil Rights—Cont'd

CASES AND NOTES, Third Edition, 1085 pages, 1989. (Casebook) 1989 Supplement.

VIEIRA'S CIVIL RIGHTS IN A NUTSHELL, 279 pages, 1978. Softcover. (Text)

WILLIAMS' CONSTITUTIONAL ANALYSIS IN A NUTSHELL, 388 pages, 1979. Softcover. (Text)

Consumer Law—see also Commercial Law

EPSTEIN AND NICKLES' CONSUMER LAW IN A NUTSHELL, Second Edition, 418 pages, 1981. Softcover. (Text)

SELECTED COMMERCIAL STATUTES. Softcover. Approximately 1600 pages, 1989.

SPANOGLE AND ROHNER'S CASES AND MATERIALS ON CONSUMER LAW, 693 pages, 1979. Teacher's Manual available. (Casebook) 1982 Supplement.

Contracts

CALAMARI, AND PERILLO'S BLACK LETTER ON CONTRACTS, 397 pages, 1983. Softcover. (Review)

CALAMARI AND PERILLO'S HORNBOOK ON CONTRACTS, Third Edition, 1049 pages, 1987. (Text)

CALAMARI, PERILLO AND BENDER'S CASES AND PROBLEMS ON CONTRACTS, Second Edition, approximately 846 pages, 1989. Teacher's Manual Available. (Casebook)

CORBIN'S TEXT ON CONTRACTS, One Volume Student Edition, 1224 pages, 1952. (Text)

FESSLER AND LOISEAUX'S CASES AND MATERIALS ON CONTRACTS—MORALITY, ECONOMICS AND THE MARKET PLACE, 837 pages, 1982. Teacher's Manual available. (Casebook)

FRIEDMAN'S CONTRACT REMEDIES IN A NUTSHELL, 323 pages, 1981. Softcover. (Text)

FULLER AND EISENBERG'S CASES ON BASIC CONTRACT LAW, Fourth Edition, 1203 pages, 1981 (Casebook)

HAMILTON, RAU AND WEINTRAUB'S CASES AND MATERIALS ON CONTRACTS, 830 pages, 1984. (Casebook)

JACKSON AND BOLLINGER'S CASES ON CONTRACT LAW IN MODERN SOCIETY, Second Edition, 1329 pages, 1980. Teacher's Manual available. (Casebook)

KEYES' GOVERNMENT CONTRACTS IN A NUTSHELL, 423 pages, 1979. Softcover. (Text)

SCHABER AND ROHWER'S CONTRACTS IN A NUTSHELL, Second Edition, 425 pages, 1984. Softcover. (Text)

SUMMERS AND HILLMAN'S CONTRACT AND RELATED OBLIGATION: THEORY, DOCTRINE AND PRACTICE, 1074 pages, 1987. Teacher's Manual available. (Casebook)

Copyright—see Patent and Copyright Law

Corporate Finance

HAMILTON'S CASES AND MATERIALS ON CORPORATION FINANCE, Second Edition, approximately 1177 pages, 1989. (Casebook)

Corporations

HAMILTON'S BLACK LETTER ON CORPORATIONS, Second Edition, 513 pages, 1986. Softcover. (Review)

HAMILTON'S CASES ON CORPORATIONS—INCLUDING PARTNERSHIPS AND LIMITED PARTNERSHIPS, Third Edition, 1213 pages, 1986. Teacher's Manual available. (Casebook) 1986 Statutory Supplement.

HAMILTON'S THE LAW OF CORPORATIONS IN A NUTSHELL, Second Edition, 515 pages, 1987. Softcover. (Text)

HENN'S TEACHING MATERIALS ON THE LAW OF CORPORATIONS, Second Edition, 1204 pages, 1986. Teacher's Manual available. (Casebook)

See Selected Corporation and Partnership Statutes

HENN AND ALEXANDER'S HORNBOOK ON LAWS OF CORPORATIONS, Third Edition, Student Edition, 1371 pages, 1983, with 1986 pocket part. (Text)

SELECTED CORPORATION AND PARTNERSHIP STATUTES, RULES AND FORMS. Softcover. Approximately 650 pages, 1989.

SOLOMON, SCHWARTZ AND BAUMAN'S MATERIALS AND PROBLEMS ON CORPORATIONS: LAW AND POLICY, Second Edition, 1391 pages, 1988. Teacher's Manual available. (Casebook)

See also Selected Corporation and Partnership Statutes

Corrections

KRANTZ' CASES AND MATERIALS ON THE LAW OF CORRECTIONS AND PRISONERS' RIGHTS, Third Edition, 855 pages, 1986. (Casebook) 1988 Supplement.

KRANTZ' THE LAW OF CORRECTIONS AND PRISONERS' RIGHTS IN A NUTSHELL, Third Edition, 407 pages, 1988. Softcover. (Text)

POPPER'S POST-CONVICTION REMEDIES IN A NUTSHELL, 360 pages, 1978. Softcover. (Text)

ROBBINS' CASES AND MATERIALS ON POST-CONVICTION REMEDIES, 506 pages, 1982. (Casebook)

Creditors' Rights

BANKRUPTCY CODE, RULES AND FORMS, LAW SCHOOL EDITION. Approximately 820 pages, 1989. Softcover.

EPSTEIN'S DEBTOR-CREDITOR RELATIONS IN A NUTSHELL, Third Edition, 383 pages, 1986. Softcover. (Text)

EPSTEIN, LANDERS AND NICKLES' CASES AND MATERIALS ON DEBTORS AND CREDITORS, Third Edition, 1059 pages, 1987. Teacher's Manual available. (Casebook)

LOPUCKI'S PLAYER'S MANUAL FOR THE DEBTOR-CREDITOR GAME, 123 pages, 1985. Softcover. (Coursebook)

NICKLES AND EPSTEIN'S BLACK LETTER ON CREDITORS' RIGHTS AND BANKRUPTCY, 576 pages, 1989. (Review)

RIESENFELD'S CASES AND MATERIALS ON CREDITORS' REMEDIES AND DEBTORS' PROTECTION, Fourth Edition, 914 pages, 1987. (Casebook)

WHITE'S CASES AND MATERIALS ON BANKRUPTCY AND CREDITORS' RIGHTS, 812 pages, 1985. Teacher's Manual available. (Casebook) 1987 Supplement.

Criminal Law and Criminal Procedure—see also Corrections, Juvenile Justice

ABRAMS' FEDERAL CRIMINAL LAW AND ITS ENFORCEMENT, 866 pages, 1986. (Casebook) 1988 Supplement.

AMERICAN CRIMINAL JUSTICE PROCESS: SELECTED RULES, STATUTES AND GUIDELINES. Approximately 700 pages, 1989. Softcover.

CARLSON'S ADJUDICATION OF CRIMINAL JUSTICE: PROBLEMS AND REFERENCES, 130 pages, 1986. Softcover. (Casebook)

DIX AND SHARLOT'S CASES AND MATERIALS ON CRIMINAL LAW, Third Edition, 846 pages, 1987. (Casebook)

GRANO'S PROBLEMS IN CRIMINAL PROCEDURE, Second Edition, 176 pages, 1981. Teacher's Manual available. Softcover. (Coursebook)

HEYMANN AND KENETY'S THE MURDER TRIAL OF WILBUR JACKSON: A HOMICIDE IN THE FAMILY, Second Edition, 347 pages, 1985. (Coursebook)

ISRAEL, KAMISAR AND LAFAVE'S CRIMINAL PROCEDURE AND THE CONSTITUTION: LEADING SUPREME COURT CASES AND INTRODUCTORY TEXT, Approximately 735 pages, Revised 1989 Edition. Softcover. (Casebook)

ISRAEL AND LAFAVE'S CRIMINAL PROCEDURE—CONSTITUTIONAL LIMITATIONS IN A NUTSHELL, Fourth Edition, 461 pages, 1988. Softcover. (Text)

JOHNSON'S CASES, MATERIALS AND TEXT ON CRIMINAL LAW, Third Edition, 783 pages, 1985. Teacher's Manual available. (Casebook)

JOHNSON'S CASES AND MATERIALS ON CRIMINAL PROCEDURE, 859 pages, 1988. (Casebook) 1989 Supplement.

KAMISAR, LAFAVE AND ISRAEL'S MODERN CRIMINAL PROCEDURE: CASES, COMMENTS AND QUESTIONS, Sixth Edition, 1558 pages, 1986. (Casebook) 1989 Supplement.

KAMISAR, LAFAVE AND ISRAEL'S BASIC CRIMINAL PROCEDURE: CASES, COMMENTS AND QUESTIONS, Sixth Edition, 860 pages, 1986. Softcover reprint from Kamisar, et al., Modern Criminal Procedure: Cases, Comments and Questions, Sixth Edition. (Casebook) 1989 Supplement.

LAFAVE'S MODERN CRIMINAL LAW: CASES, COMMENTS AND QUESTIONS, Second Edition, 903 pages, 1988. (Casebook)

LAFAVE AND ISRAEL'S HORNBOOK ON CRIMINAL PROCEDURE, Student Edition, 1142 pages, 1985, with 1988 pocket part. (Text)

LAFAVE AND SCOTT'S HORNBOOK ON CRIMINAL LAW, Second Edition, 918 pages, 1986.

Criminal Law and Criminal Procedure—
Cont'd

(Text)

LANGBEIN'S COMPARATIVE CRIMINAL PROCEDURE: GERMANY, 172 pages, 1977. Softcover. (Casebook)

LOEWY'S CRIMINAL LAW IN A NUTSHELL, Second Edition, 321 pages, 1987. Softcover. (Text)

LOW'S BLACK LETTER ON CRIMINAL LAW, 433 pages, 1984. Softcover. (Review)

SALTZBURG'S CASES AND COMMENTARY ON AMERICAN CRIMINAL PROCEDURE, Third Edition, 1302 pages, 1988. Teacher's Manual available. (Casebook) 1989 Supplement.

UVILLER'S THE PROCESSES OF CRIMINAL JUSTICE: INVESTIGATION AND ADJUDICATION, Second Edition, 1384 pages, 1979. (Casebook) 1979 Statutory Supplement. 1986 Update.

VORENBERG'S CASES ON CRIMINAL LAW AND PROCEDURE, Second Edition, 1088 pages, 1981. Teacher's Manual available. (Casebook) 1987 Supplement.

Decedents' Estates—see Trusts and Estates

Domestic Relations

CLARK'S CASES AND PROBLEMS ON DOMESTIC RELATIONS, Third Edition, 1153 pages, 1980. Teacher's Manual available. (Casebook)

CLARK'S HORNBOOK ON DOMESTIC RELATIONS, Second Edition, Student Edition, 1050 pages, 1988. (Text)

KRAUSE'S BLACK LETTER ON FAMILY LAW, 314 pages, 1988. Softcover. (Review)

KRAUSE'S CASES, COMMENTS AND QUESTIONS ON FAMILY LAW, Third Edition, approximately 1200 pages, October, 1989 Pub. (Casebook)

KRAUSE'S FAMILY LAW IN A NUTSHELL, Second Edition, 444 pages, 1986. Softcover. (Text)

KRAUSKOPF'S CASES ON PROPERTY DIVISION AT MARRIAGE DISSOLUTION, 250 pages, 1984. Softcover. (Casebook)

Economics, Law and—see also Antitrust, Regulated Industries

GOETZ' CASES AND MATERIALS ON LAW AND ECONOMICS, 547 pages, 1984. (Casebook)

Education Law

ALEXANDER AND ALEXANDER'S THE LAW OF SCHOOLS, STUDENTS AND TEACHERS IN A NUTSHELL, 409 pages, 1984. Softcover. (Text)

Employment Discrimination—see also Women and the Law

JONES, MURPHY AND BELTON'S CASES AND MATERIALS ON DISCRIMINATION IN EMPLOYMENT, (The Labor Law Group). Fifth Edition, 1116 pages, 1987. (Casebook)

PLAYER'S CASES AND MATERIALS ON EMPLOYMENT DISCRIMINATION LAW, Second Edition, 782 pages, 1984. Teacher's Manual available. (Casebook)

PLAYER'S FEDERAL LAW OF EMPLOYMENT DISCRIMINATION IN A NUTSHELL, Second Edition, 402 pages, 1981. Softcover. (Text)

PLAYER'S HORNBOOK ON EMPLOYMENT DISCRIMINATION LAW, Student Edition, 708 pages, 1988. (Text)

Energy and Natural Resources Law—see also Oil and Gas

LAITOS' CASES AND MATERIALS ON NATURAL RESOURCES LAW, 938 pages, 1985. Teacher's Manual available. (Casebook)

SELECTED ENVIRONMENTAL LAW STATUTES—EDUCATIONAL EDITION. Softcover. Approximately 850 pages, 1989.

Environmental Law—see also Energy and Natural Resources Law; Sea, Law of

BONINE AND McGARITY'S THE LAW OF ENVIRONMENTAL PROTECTION: CASES—LEGISLATION—POLICIES, 1076 pages, 1984. Teacher's Manual available. (Casebook)

FINDLEY AND FARBER'S CASES AND MATERIALS ON ENVIRONMENTAL LAW, Second Edition, 813 pages, 1985. (Casebook) 1988 Supplement.

FINDLEY AND FARBER'S ENVIRONMENTAL LAW IN A NUTSHELL, Second Edition, 367 pages, 1988. Softcover. (Text)

RODGERS' HORNBOOK ON ENVIRONMENTAL LAW, 956 pages, 1977, with 1984 pocket

Environmental Law—Cont'd

part. (Text)

SELECTED ENVIRONMENTAL LAW STATUTES—EDUCATIONAL EDITION. Softcover. Approximately 850 pages, 1989.

Equity—see Remedies

Estate Planning—see also Trusts and Estates; Taxation—Estate and Gift

LYNN'S AN INTRODUCTION TO ESTATE PLANNING IN A NUTSHELL, Third Edition, 370 pages, 1983. Softcover. (Text)

Evidence

BROUN AND BLAKEY'S BLACK LETTER ON EVIDENCE, 269 pages, 1984. Softcover. (Review)

BROUN, MEISENHOLDER, STRONG AND MOSTELLER'S PROBLEMS IN EVIDENCE, Third Edition, 238 pages, 1988. Teacher's Manual available. Softcover. (Coursebook)

CLEARY, STRONG, BROUN AND MOSTELLER'S CASES AND MATERIALS ON EVIDENCE, Fourth Edition, 1060 pages, 1988. (Casebook)

FEDERAL RULES OF EVIDENCE FOR UNITED STATES COURTS AND MAGISTRATES. Softcover. 378 pages, 1989.

GRAHAM'S FEDERAL RULES OF EVIDENCE IN A NUTSHELL, Second Edition, 473 pages, 1987. Softcover. (Text)

KIMBALL'S PROGRAMMED MATERIALS ON PROBLEMS IN EVIDENCE, 380 pages, 1978. Softcover. (Coursebook)

LEMPERT AND SALTZBURG'S A MODERN APPROACH TO EVIDENCE: TEXT, PROBLEMS, TRANSCRIPTS AND CASES, Second Edition, 1232 pages, 1983. Teacher's Manual available. (Casebook)

LILLY'S AN INTRODUCTION TO THE LAW OF EVIDENCE, Second Edition, 585 pages, 1987. (Text)

McCORMICK, SUTTON AND WELLBORN'S CASES AND MATERIALS ON EVIDENCE, Sixth Edition, 1067 pages, 1987. (Casebook)

McCORMICK'S HORNBOOK ON EVIDENCE, Third Edition, Student Edition, 1156 pages, 1984, with 1987 pocket part. (Text)

ROTHSTEIN'S EVIDENCE IN A NUTSHELL: STATE AND FEDERAL RULES, Second Edition,

514 pages, 1981. Softcover. (Text)

Federal Jurisdiction and Procedure

CURRIE'S CASES AND MATERIALS ON FEDERAL COURTS, Third Edition, 1042 pages, 1982. (Casebook) 1985 Supplement.

CURRIE'S FEDERAL JURISDICTION IN A NUTSHELL, Second Edition, 258 pages, 1981. Softcover. (Text)

FEDERAL RULES OF CIVIL PROCEDURE—EDUCATIONAL EDITION. Softcover. Approximately 600 pages, 1989.

REDISH'S BLACK LETTER ON FEDERAL JURISDICTION, 219 pages, 1985. Softcover. (Review)

REDISH'S CASES, COMMENTS AND QUESTIONS ON FEDERAL COURTS, Second Edition, 1122 pages, 1989. (Casebook)

VETRI AND MERRILL'S FEDERAL COURTS PROBLEMS AND MATERIALS, Second Edition, 232 pages, 1984. Softcover. (Coursebook)

WRIGHT'S HORNBOOK ON FEDERAL COURTS, Fourth Edition, Student Edition, 870 pages, 1983. (Text)

Foreign Relations and National Security Law

FRANCK AND GLENNON'S FOREIGN RELATIONS AND NATIONAL SECURITY LAW, 941 pages, 1987. (Casebook)

Future Interests—see Trusts and Estates

Health Law—see Medicine, Law and

Human Rights—see International Law

Immigration Law

ALEINIKOFF AND MARTIN'S IMMIGRATION PROCESS AND POLICY, 1042 pages, 1985. (Casebook) 1987 Supplement.

WEISSBRODT'S IMMIGRATION LAW AND PROCEDURE IN A NUTSHELL, 345 pages, 1984, Softcover. (Text)

Indian Law—see American Indian Law

Insurance Law

DEVINE AND TERRY'S PROBLEMS IN INSURANCE LAW, Approximately 230 pages, 1989. Softcover. Teacher's Manual available. (Course book)

Insurance Law—Cont'd

DOBBYN'S INSURANCE LAW IN A NUTSHELL, Second Edition, approximately 285 pages, 1989. Softcover. (Text)

KEETON'S CASES ON BASIC INSURANCE LAW, Second Edition, 1086 pages, 1977. Teacher's Manual available. (Casebook)

KEETON AND WIDISS' INSURANCE LAW, Student Edition, 1359 pages, 1988. (Text)

WIDISS AND KEETON'S COURSE SUPPLEMENT TO KEETON AND WIDISS' INSURANCE LAW, 502 pages, 1988. Softcover. (Casebook)

YORK AND WHELAN'S CASES, MATERIALS AND PROBLEMS ON GENERAL PRACTICE INSURANCE LAW, Second Edition, 787 pages, 1988. Teacher's Manual available. (Casebook)

International Law—see also Sea, Law of

BUERGENTHAL'S INTERNATIONAL HUMAN RIGHTS IN A NUTSHELL, 283 pages, 1988. Softcover. (Text)

BUERGENTHAL AND MAIER'S PUBLIC INTERNATIONAL LAW IN A NUTSHELL, 262 pages, 1985. Softcover. (Text)

FOLSOM, GORDON AND SPANOGLE'S INTERNATIONAL BUSINESS TRANSACTIONS—A PROBLEM-ORIENTED COURSEBOOK, 1160 pages, 1986. Teacher's Manual available. (Casebook) 1989 Documents Supplement.

FOLSOM, GORDON AND SPANOGLE'S INTERNATIONAL BUSINESS TRANSACTIONS IN A NUTSHELL, Third Edition, 509 pages, 1988. Softcover. (Text)

HENKIN, PUGH, SCHACHTER AND SMIT'S CASES AND MATERIALS ON INTERNATIONAL LAW, Second Edition, 1517 pages, 1987. (Casebook) Documents Supplement.

JACKSON AND DAVEY'S CASES, MATERIALS AND TEXT ON LEGAL PROBLEMS OF INTERNATIONAL ECONOMIC RELATIONS, Second Edition, 1269 pages, 1986. (Casebook) 1989 Documents Supplement.

KIRGIS' INTERNATIONAL ORGANIZATIONS IN THEIR LEGAL SETTING, 1016 pages, 1977. Teacher's Manual available. (Casebook) 1981 Supplement.

WESTON, FALK AND D'AMATO'S INTERNATIONAL LAW AND WORLD ORDER—A PROBLEM-ORIENTED COURSEBOOK, 1195 pages, 1980. Teacher's Manual available. (Casebook)

Documents Supplement.

Interviewing and Counseling

BINDER AND PRICE'S LEGAL INTERVIEWING AND COUNSELING, 232 pages, 1977. Teacher's Manual available. Softcover. (Coursebook)

SHAFFER AND ELKINS' LEGAL INTERVIEWING AND COUNSELING IN A NUTSHELL, Second Edition, 487 pages, 1987. Softcover. (Text)

Introduction to Law—see Legal Method and Legal System

Introduction to Law Study

DOBBYN'S SO YOU WANT TO GO TO LAW SCHOOL, Revised First Edition, 206 pages, 1976. Softcover. (Text)

HEGLAND'S INTRODUCTION TO THE STUDY AND PRACTICE OF LAW IN A NUTSHELL, 418 pages, 1983. Softcover (Text)

KINYON'S INTRODUCTION TO LAW STUDY AND LAW EXAMINATIONS IN A NUTSHELL, 389 pages, 1971. Softcover. (Text)

Jurisprudence

CHRISTIE'S JURISPRUDENCE—TEXT AND READINGS ON THE PHILOSOPHY OF LAW, 1056 pages, 1973. (Casebook)

Juvenile Justice

FOX'S CASES AND MATERIALS ON MODERN JUVENILE JUSTICE, Second Edition, 960 pages, 1981. (Casebook)

FOX'S JUVENILE COURTS IN A NUTSHELL, Third Edition, 291 pages, 1984. Softcover. (Text)

Labor Law—see also Employment Discrimination, Social Legislation

FINKIN, GOLDMAN AND SUMMERS' LEGAL PROTECTION OF INDIVIDUAL EMPLOYEES, (The Labor Law Group). Approximately 1000 pages, December, 1989 Pub. (Casebook)

GORMAN'S BASIC TEXT ON LABOR LAW—UNIONIZATION AND COLLECTIVE BARGAINING, 914 pages, 1976. (Text)

GRODIN, WOLLETT AND ALLEYNE'S COLLECTIVE BARGAINING IN PUBLIC EMPLOYMENT, (The Labor Law Group). Third Edition, 430 pages, 1979. (Casebook)

Labor Law—Cont'd

LESLIE'S LABOR LAW IN A NUTSHELL, Second Edition, 397 pages, 1986. Softcover. (Text)

NOLAN'S LABOR ARBITRATION LAW AND PRACTICE IN A NUTSHELL, 358 pages, 1979. Softcover. (Text)

OBERER, HANSLOWE, ANDERSEN AND HEINSZ' CASES AND MATERIALS ON LABOR LAW—COLLECTIVE BARGAINING IN A FREE SOCIETY, Third Edition, 1163 pages, 1986. (Casebook) Statutory Supplement.

RABIN, SILVERSTEIN AND SCHATZKI'S LABOR AND EMPLOYMENT LAW: PROBLEMS, CASES AND MATERIALS IN THE LAW OF WORK, (The Labor Law Group). 1014 pages, 1988. Teacher's Manual available. (Casebook) 1988 Statutory Supplement.

Land Finance—Property Security—see Real Estate Transactions

Land Use

CALLIES AND FREILICH'S CASES AND MATERIALS ON LAND USE, 1233 pages, 1986. (Casebook) 1988 Supplement.

HAGMAN AND JUERGENSMEYER'S HORNBOOK ON URBAN PLANNING AND LAND DEVELOPMENT CONTROL LAW, Second Edition, Student Edition, 680 pages, 1986. (Text)

WRIGHT AND GITELMAN'S CASES AND MATERIALS ON LAND USE, Third Edition, 1300 pages, 1982. Teacher's Manual available. (Casebook) 1987 Supplement.

WRIGHT AND WRIGHT'S LAND USE IN A NUTSHELL, Second Edition, 356 pages, 1985. Softcover. (Text)

Legal History—see also Legal Method and Legal System

PRESSER AND ZAINALDIN'S CASES AND MATERIALS ON LAW AND JURISPRUDENCE IN AMERICAN HISTORY, Second Edition, approximately 1092 pages, 1989. Teacher's Manual available. (Casebook)

Legal Method and Legal System—see also Legal Research, Legal Writing

ALDISERT'S READINGS, MATERIALS AND CASES IN THE JUDICIAL PROCESS, 948 pages, 1976. (Casebook)

BERCH AND BERCH'S INTRODUCTION TO LEGAL METHOD AND PROCESS, 550 pages, 1985. Teacher's Manual available. (Casebook)

BODENHEIMER, OAKLEY AND LOVE'S READINGS AND CASES ON AN INTRODUCTION TO THE ANGLO-AMERICAN LEGAL SYSTEM, Second Edition, 166 pages, 1988. Softcover. (Casebook)

DAVIES AND LAWRY'S INSTITUTIONS AND METHODS OF THE LAW—INTRODUCTORY TEACHING MATERIALS, 547 pages, 1982. Teacher's Manual available. (Casebook)

DVORKIN, HIMMELSTEIN AND LESNICK'S BECOMING A LAWYER: A HUMANISTIC PERSPECTIVE ON LEGAL EDUCATION AND PROFESSIONALISM, 211 pages, 1981. Softcover. (Text)

KELSO AND KELSO'S STUDYING LAW: AN INTRODUCTION, 587 pages, 1984. (Coursebook)

KEMPIN'S HISTORICAL INTRODUCTION TO ANGLO-AMERICAN LAW IN A NUTSHELL, Second Edition, 280 pages, 1973. Softcover. (Text)

REYNOLDS' JUDICIAL PROCESS IN A NUTSHELL, 292 pages, 1980. Softcover. (Text)

Legal Research

COHEN'S LEGAL RESEARCH IN A NUTSHELL, Fourth Edition, 452 pages, 1985. Softcover. (Text)

COHEN, BERRING AND OLSON'S HOW TO FIND THE LAW, Ninth Edition, approximately 800 pages, October, 1989 Pub. (Coursebook)

Legal Research Exercises, 3rd Ed., for use with Cohen, Berring and Olson, 229 pages, 1989. Teacher's Manual available.

COHEN, BERRING AND OLSON'S FINDING THE LAW, approximately 565 pages, 1989. Softcover reprint from Cohen, Berring and Olson's How to Find the Law, Ninth Edition. (Coursebook)

ROMBAUER'S LEGAL PROBLEM SOLVING—ANALYSIS, RESEARCH AND WRITING, Fourth Edition, 424 pages, 1983. Teacher's Manual with problems available. (Coursebook)

STATSKY'S LEGAL RESEARCH AND WRITING, Third Edition, 252 pages, 1986. Softcover. (Coursebook)

TEPLY'S PROGRAMMED MATERIALS ON LEGAL RESEARCH AND CITATION, Third Edition, ap-

Legal Research—Cont'd

proximately 450 pages, 1989. Softcover. (Coursebook)

Student Library Exercises, 3rd ed., 391 pages, 1989. Answer Key available.

Legal Writing

CHILD'S DRAFTING LEGAL DOCUMENTS: MATERIALS AND PROBLEMS, 286 pages, 1988. Softcover. Teacher's Manual available. (Coursebook)

DICKERSON'S MATERIALS ON LEGAL DRAFTING, 425 pages, 1981. Teacher's Manual available. (Coursebook)

FELSENFELD AND SIEGEL'S WRITING CONTRACTS IN PLAIN ENGLISH, 290 pages, 1981. Softcover. (Text)

GOPEN'S WRITING FROM A LEGAL PERSPECTIVE, 225 pages, 1981. (Text)

MELLINKOFF'S LEGAL WRITING—SENSE AND NONSENSE, 242 pages, 1982. Softcover. Teacher's Manual available. (Text)

PRATT'S LEGAL WRITING: A SYSTEMATIC APPROACH, Approximately 412 pages, 1989. Teacher's Manual available. (Coursebook)

RAY AND RAMSFIELD'S LEGAL WRITING: GETTING IT RIGHT AND GETTING IT WRITTEN, 250 pages, 1987. Softcover. (Text)

SQUIRES AND ROMBAUER'S LEGAL WRITING IN A NUTSHELL, 294 pages, 1982. Softcover. (Text)

STATSKY AND WERNET'S CASE ANALYSIS AND FUNDAMENTALS OF LEGAL WRITING, Third Edition, 424 pages, 1989. (Text)

WEIHOFEN'S LEGAL WRITING STYLE, Second Edition, 332 pages, 1980. (Text)

Legislation

DAVIES' LEGISLATIVE LAW AND PROCESS IN A NUTSHELL, Second Edition, 346 pages, 1986. Softcover. (Text)

ESKRIDGE AND FRICKEY'S CASES AND MATERIALS ON LEGISLATION: STATUTES AND THE CREATION OF PUBLIC POLICY, 937 pages, 1988. Teacher's Manual available. (Casebook)

NUTTING AND DICKERSON'S CASES AND MATERIALS ON LEGISLATION, Fifth Edition, 744 pages, 1978. (Casebook)

STATSKY'S LEGISLATIVE ANALYSIS AND

DRAFTING, Second Edition, 217 pages, 1984. Teacher's Manual available. (Text)

Local Government

FRUG'S CASES AND MATERIALS ON LOCAL GOVERNMENT LAW, 1005 pages, 1988. (Casebook)

MCCARTHY'S LOCAL GOVERNMENT LAW IN A NUTSHELL, Second Edition, 404 pages, 1983. Softcover. (Text)

REYNOLDS' HORNBOOK ON LOCAL GOVERNMENT LAW, 860 pages, 1982, with 1987 pocket part. (Text)

VALENTE'S CASES AND MATERIALS ON LOCAL GOVERNMENT LAW, Third Edition, 1010 pages, 1987. Teacher's Manual available. (Casebook) 1989 Supplement.

Mass Communication Law

GILLMOR AND BARRON'S CASES AND COMMENT ON MASS COMMUNICATION LAW, Fifth Edition, approximately 1068 pages, September 1989 Pub. Teacher's Manual available. (Casebook)

GINSBURG'S REGULATION OF BROADCASTING: LAW AND POLICY TOWARDS RADIO, TELEVISION AND CABLE COMMUNICATIONS, 741 pages, 1979 (Casebook) 1983 Supplement.

ZUCKMAN, GAYNES, CARTER AND DEE'S MASS COMMUNICATIONS LAW IN A NUTSHELL, Third Edition, 538 pages, 1988. Softcover. (Text)

Medicine, Law and

FURROW, JOHNSON, JOST AND SCHWARTZ' HEALTH LAW: CASES, MATERIALS AND PROBLEMS, 1005 pages, 1987. Teacher's Manual available. (Casebook)

KING'S THE LAW OF MEDICAL MALPRACTICE IN A NUTSHELL, Second Edition, 342 pages, 1986. Softcover. (Text)

SHAPIRO AND SPECE'S CASES, MATERIALS AND PROBLEMS ON BIOETHICS AND LAW, 892 pages, 1981. (Casebook)

SHARPE, FISCINA AND HEAD'S CASES ON LAW AND MEDICINE, 882 pages, 1978. (Casebook)

Military Law

SHANOR AND TERRELL'S MILITARY LAW IN A NUTSHELL, 378 pages, 1980. Softcover.

Military Law—Cont'd

(Text)

Mortgages—see Real Estate Transactions

Natural Resources Law—see Energy and Natural Resources Law, Environmental Law

Negotiation

GIFFORD'S LEGAL NEGOTIATION: THEORY AND APPLICATIONS, 225 pages, 1989. Softcover. (Text)

PECK'S CASES AND MATERIALS ON NEGOTIATION, (The Labor Law Group). Second Edition, 280 pages, 1980. (Casebook)

WILLIAMS' LEGAL NEGOTIATION AND SETTLEMENT, 207 pages, 1983. Softcover. Teacher's Manual available. (Coursebook)

Office Practice—see also Computers and Law, Interviewing and Counseling, Negotiation

HEGLAND'S TRIAL AND PRACTICE SKILLS IN A NUTSHELL, 346 pages, 1978. Softcover (Text)

STRONG AND CLARK'S LAW OFFICE MANAGEMENT, 424 pages, 1974. (Casebook)

Oil and Gas—see also Energy and Natural Resources Law

HEMINGWAY'S HORNBOOK ON OIL AND GAS, Second Edition, Student Edition, 543 pages, 1983, with 1989 pocket part. (Text)

KUNTZ, LOWE, ANDERSON AND SMITH'S CASES AND MATERIALS ON OIL AND GAS LAW, 857 pages, 1986. Teacher's Manual available. (Casebook) Forms Manual. Revised.

LOWE'S OIL AND GAS LAW IN A NUTSHELL, Second Edition, 465 pages, 1988. Softcover. (Text)

Partnership—see Agency—Partnership

Patent and Copyright Law

CHOATE, FRANCIS, AND COLLINS' CASES AND MATERIALS ON PATENT LAW, INCLUDING TRADE SECRETS, COPYRIGHTS, TRADEMARKS, Third Edition, 1009 pages, 1987. (Casebook)

MILLER AND DAVIS' INTELLECTUAL PROPERTY—PATENTS, TRADEMARKS AND COPYRIGHT IN A NUTSHELL, 428 pages, 1983. Softcover.

(Text)

NIMMER'S CASES AND MATERIALS ON COPYRIGHT AND OTHER ASPECTS OF ENTERTAINMENT LITIGATION ILLUSTRATED—INCLUDING UNFAIR COMPETITION, DEFAMATION AND PRIVACY, Third Edition, 1025 pages, 1985. (Casebook) 1989 Supplement.

Products Liability

FISCHER AND POWERS' CASES AND MATERIALS ON PRODUCTS LIABILITY, 685 pages, 1988. Teacher's Manual available. (Casebook)

NOEL AND PHILLIPS' CASES ON PRODUCTS LIABILITY, Second Edition, 821 pages, 1982. (Casebook)

PHILLIPS' PRODUCTS LIABILITY IN A NUTSHELL, Third Edition, 307 pages, 1988. Softcover. (Text)

Professional Responsibility

ARONSON, DEVINE AND FISCH'S PROBLEMS, CASES AND MATERIALS IN PROFESSIONAL RESPONSIBILITY, 745 pages, 1985. Teacher's Manual available. (Casebook)

ARONSON AND WECKSTEIN'S PROFESSIONAL RESPONSIBILITY IN A NUTSHELL, 399 pages, 1980. Softcover. (Text)

MELLINKOFF'S THE CONSCIENCE OF A LAWYER, 304 pages, 1973. (Text)

PIRSIG AND KIRWIN'S CASES AND MATERIALS ON PROFESSIONAL RESPONSIBILITY, Fourth Edition, 603 pages, 1984. Teacher's Manual available. (Casebook)

ROTUNDA'S BLACK LETTER ON PROFESSIONAL RESPONSIBILITY, Second Edition, 414 pages, 1988. Softcover. (Review)

SCHWARTZ AND WYDICK'S PROBLEMS IN LEGAL ETHICS, Second Edition, 341 pages, 1988. (Coursebook)

SELECTED STATUTES, RULES AND STANDARDS ON THE LEGAL PROFESSION. Softcover. Approximately 450 pages, 1989.

SUTTON AND DZIENKOWSKI'S CASES AND MATERIALS ON PROFESSIONAL RESPONSIBILITY FOR LAWYERS, Approximately 800 pages, 1989. Teacher's Manual available. (Casebook)

WOLFRAM'S HORNBOOK ON MODERN LEGAL ETHICS, Student Edition, 1120 pages, 1986. (Text)

Property—see also Real Estate Transactions, Land Use, Trusts and Estates

BERNHARDT'S BLACK LETTER ON PROPERTY, 318 pages, 1983. Softcover. (Review)

BERNHARDT'S REAL PROPERTY IN A NUTSHELL, Second Edition, 448 pages, 1981. Softcover. (Text)

BOYER'S SURVEY OF THE LAW OF PROPERTY, Third Edition, 766 pages, 1981. (Text)

BROWDER, CUNNINGHAM, NELSON, STOEBUCK AND WHITMAN'S CASES ON BASIC PROPERTY LAW, Fifth Edition, approximately 1200 pages, 1989. (Casebook)

BRUCE, ELY AND BOSTICK'S CASES AND MATERIALS ON MODERN PROPERTY LAW, Second Edition, 953 pages, 1989. Teacher's Manual available. (Casebook)

BURKE'S PERSONAL PROPERTY IN A NUTSHELL, 322 pages, 1983. Softcover. (Text)

CUNNINGHAM, STOEBUCK AND WHITMAN'S HORNBOOK ON THE LAW OF PROPERTY, Student Edition, 916 pages, 1984, with 1987 pocket part. (Text)

DONAHUE, KAUPER AND MARTIN'S CASES ON PROPERTY, Second Edition, 1362 pages, 1983. Teacher's Manual available. (Casebook)

HILL'S LANDLORD AND TENANT LAW IN A NUTSHELL, Second Edition, 311 pages, 1986. Softcover. (Text)

KURTZ AND HOVENKAMP'S CASES AND MATERIALS ON AMERICAN PROPERTY LAW, 1296 pages, 1987. Teacher's Manual available. (Casebook) 1988 Supplement.

MOYNIHAN'S INTRODUCTION TO REAL PROPERTY, Second Edition, 239 pages, 1988. (Text)

UNIFORM LAND TRANSACTIONS ACT, UNIFORM SIMPLIFICATION OF LAND TRANSFERS ACT, UNIFORM CONDOMINIUM ACT, 1977 OFFICIAL TEXT WITH COMMENTS. Softcover. 462 pages, 1978.

Psychiatry, Law and

REISNER'S LAW AND THE MENTAL HEALTH SYSTEM, CIVIL AND CRIMINAL ASPECTS, 696 pages, 1985. (Casebook) 1987 Supplement.

Real Estate Transactions

BRUCE'S REAL ESTATE FINANCE IN A NUTSHELL, Second Edition, 262 pages, 1985. Softcover. (Text)

MAXWELL, RIESENFELD, HETLAND AND WARREN'S CASES ON CALIFORNIA SECURITY TRANSACTIONS IN LAND, Third Edition, 728 pages, 1984. (Casebook)

NELSON AND WHITMAN'S BLACK LETTER ON LAND TRANSACTIONS AND FINANCE, Second Edition, 466 pages, 1988. Softcover. (Review)

NELSON AND WHITMAN'S CASES ON REAL ESTATE TRANSFER, FINANCE AND DEVELOPMENT, Third Edition, 1184 pages, 1987. (Casebook)

NELSON AND WHITMAN'S HORNBOOK ON REAL ESTATE FINANCE LAW, Second Edition, 941 pages, 1985 with 1989 pocket part. (Text)

OSBORNE'S CASES AND MATERIALS ON SECURED TRANSACTIONS, 559 pages, 1967. (Casebook)

Regulated Industries—see also Mass Communication Law, Banking Law

GELLHORN AND PIERCE'S REGULATED INDUSTRIES IN A NUTSHELL, Second Edition, 389 pages, 1987. Softcover. (Text)

MORGAN, HARRISON AND VERKUIL'S CASES AND MATERIALS ON ECONOMIC REGULATION OF BUSINESS, Second Edition, 666 pages, 1985. (Casebook)

Remedies

DOBBS' HORNBOOK ON REMEDIES, 1067 pages, 1973. (Text)

DOBBS' PROBLEMS IN REMEDIES. 137 pages, 1974. Teacher's Manual available. Softcover. (Coursebook)

DOBBYN'S INJUNCTIONS IN A NUTSHELL, 264 pages, 1974. Softcover. (Text)

FRIEDMAN'S CONTRACT REMEDIES IN A NUTSHELL, 323 pages, 1981. Softcover. (Text)

LEAVELL, LOVE AND NELSON'S CASES AND MATERIALS ON EQUITABLE REMEDIES, RESTITUTION AND DAMAGES, Fourth Edition, 1111 pages, 1986. Teacher's Manual available. (Casebook)

MCCORMICK'S HORNBOOK ON DAMAGES, 811 pages, 1935. (Text)

Remedies—Cont'd

O'CONNELL'S REMEDIES IN A NUTSHELL, Second Edition, 320 pages, 1985. Softcover. (Text)

YORK, BAUMAN AND RENDLEMAN'S CASES AND MATERIALS ON REMEDIES, Fourth Edition, 1029 pages, 1985. Teacher's Manual available. (Casebook)

Sea, Law of

SOHN AND GUSTAFSON'S THE LAW OF THE SEA IN A NUTSHELL, 264 pages, 1984. Softcover. (Text)

Securities Regulation

HAZEN'S HORNBOOK ON THE LAW OF SECURITIES REGULATION, Student Edition, 739 pages, 1985, with 1988 pocket part. (Text)

RATNER'S MATERIALS ON SECURITIES REGULATION, Third Edition, 1000 pages, 1986. Teacher's Manual available. (Casebook) 1989 Supplement.

See Selected Securities and Business Planning Statutes

RATNER'S SECURITIES REGULATION IN A NUTSHELL, Third Edition, 316 pages, 1988. Softcover. (Text)

SELECTED SECURITIES AND BUSINESS PLANNING STATUTES, RULES AND FORMS. Softcover. 493 pages, 1987.

Social Legislation

HOOD AND HARDY'S WORKERS' COMPENSATION AND EMPLOYEE PROTECTION IN A NUTSHELL, 274 pages, 1984. Softcover. (Text)

LAFRANCE'S WELFARE LAW: STRUCTURE AND ENTITLEMENT IN A NUTSHELL, 455 pages, 1979. Softcover. (Text)

MALONE, PLANT AND LITTLE'S CASES ON WORKERS' COMPENSATION AND EMPLOYMENT RIGHTS, Second Edition, 951 pages, 1980. Teacher's Manual available. (Casebook)

Sports Law

SCHUBERT, SMITH AND TRENTADUE'S SPORTS LAW, 395 pages, 1986. (Text)

Tax Practice and Procedure

GARBIS, STRUNTZ AND RUBIN'S CASES AND MATERIALS ON TAX PROCEDURE AND TAX FRAUD, Second Edition, 687 pages, 1987. (Casebook)

Taxation—Corporate

KAHN AND GANN'S CORPORATE TAXATION, Third Edition, approximately 978 pages, 1989. Teacher's Manual available. (Casebook)

WEIDENBRUCH AND BURKE'S FEDERAL INCOME TAXATION OF CORPORATIONS AND STOCKHOLDERS IN A NUTSHELL, Third Edition, 309 pages, 1989. Softcover. (Text)

Taxation—Estate & Gift—see also Estate Planning, Trusts and Estates

MCNULTY'S FEDERAL ESTATE AND GIFT TAXATION IN A NUTSHELL, Fourth Edition, 496 pages, 1989. Softcover. (Text)

PENNELL'S CASES AND MATERIALS ON INCOME TAXATION OF TRUSTS, ESTATES, GRANTORS AND BENEFICIARIES, 460 pages, 1987. Teacher's Manual available. (Casebook)

Taxation—Individual

DODGE'S THE LOGIC OF TAX, Approximately 330 pages, September, 1989 Pub. Softcover. (Text)

GUNN AND WARD'S CASES, TEXT AND PROBLEMS ON FEDERAL INCOME TAXATION, Second Edition, 835 pages, 1988. Teacher's Manual available. (Casebook)

HUDSON AND LIND'S BLACK LETTER ON FEDERAL INCOME TAXATION, Second Edition, 396 pages, 1987. Softcover. (Review)

KRAGEN AND MCNULTY'S CASES AND MATERIALS ON FEDERAL INCOME TAXATION—INDIVIDUALS, CORPORATIONS, PARTNERSHIPS, Fourth Edition, 1287 pages, 1985. (Casebook)

MCNULTY'S FEDERAL INCOME TAXATION OF INDIVIDUALS IN A NUTSHELL, Fourth Edition, 503 pages, 1988. Softcover. (Text)

POSIN'S HORNBOOK ON FEDERAL INCOME TAXATION, Student Edition, 491 pages, 1983, with 1989 pocket part. (Text)

ROSE AND CHOMMIE'S HORNBOOK ON FEDERAL INCOME TAXATION, Third Edition, 923 pages, 1988, with 1989 pocket part. (Text)

SELECTED FEDERAL TAXATION STATUTES AND REGULATIONS. Softcover. Approximately 1550 pages, 1990.

SOLOMON AND HESCH'S PROBLEMS, CASES AND MATERIALS ON FEDERAL INCOME TAXATION OF INDIVIDUALS, 1068 pages, 1987.

Trial and Appellate Advocacy—Cont'd

PELLATE PRACTICE AND PROCEDURE, 565 pages, 1987. (Casebook)

NOLAN'S CASES AND MATERIALS ON TRIAL PRACTICE, 518 pages, 1981. (Casebook)

SONSTENG, HAYDOCK AND BOYD'S THE TRIALBOOK: A TOTAL SYSTEM FOR PREPARATION AND PRESENTATION OF A CASE, 404 pages, 1984. Softcover. (Coursebook)

Trusts and Estates

ATKINSON'S HORNBOOK ON WILLS, Second Edition, 975 pages, 1953. (Text)

AVERILL'S UNIFORM PROBATE CODE IN A NUTSHELL, Second Edition, 454 pages, 1987. Softcover. (Text)

BOGERT'S HORNBOOK ON TRUSTS, Sixth Edition, Student Edition, 794 pages, 1987. (Text)

CLARK, LUSKY AND MURPHY'S CASES AND MATERIALS ON GRATUITOUS TRANSFERS, Third Edition, 970 pages, 1985. (Casebook)

DODGE'S WILLS, TRUSTS AND ESTATE PLANNING—LAW AND TAXATION, CASES AND MATERIALS, 665 pages, 1988. (Casebook)

KURTZ' PROBLEMS, CASES AND OTHER MATERIALS ON FAMILY ESTATE PLANNING, 853 pages, 1983. Teacher's Manual available. (Casebook)

MCGOVERN'S CASES AND MATERIALS ON WILLS, TRUSTS AND FUTURE INTERESTS: AN INTRODUCTION TO ESTATE PLANNING, 750 pages, 1983. (Casebook)

MCGOVERN, KURTZ AND REIN'S HORNBOOK ON WILLS, TRUSTS AND ESTATES—INCLUDING TAXATION AND FUTURE INTERESTS, 996 pages, 1988. (Text)

MENNELL'S WILLS AND TRUSTS IN A NUTSHELL, 392 pages, 1979. Softcover. (Text)

SIMES' HORNBOOK ON FUTURE INTERESTS, Second Edition, 355 pages, 1966. (Text)

TURANO AND RADIGAN'S HORNBOOK ON NEW YORK ESTATE ADMINISTRATION, 676 pages, 1986. (Text)

UNIFORM PROBATE CODE, OFFICIAL TEXT WITH COMMENTS. 578 pages, 1987. Softcover.

WAGGONER'S FUTURE INTERESTS IN A NUTSHELL, 361 pages, 1981. Softcover. (Text)

WATERBURY'S MATERIALS ON TRUSTS AND ESTATES, 1039 pages, 1986. Teacher's Manual available. (Casebook)

Water Law—see also Energy and Natural Resources Law, Environmental Law

GETCHES' WATER LAW IN A NUTSHELL, 439 pages, 1984. Softcover. (Text)

SAX AND ABRAMS' LEGAL CONTROL OF WATER RESOURCES: CASES AND MATERIALS, 941 pages, 1986. (Casebook)

TRELEASE AND GOULD'S CASES AND MATERIALS ON WATER LAW, Fourth Edition, 816 pages, 1986. (Casebook)

Wills—see Trusts and Estates

Women and the Law—see also Employment Discrimination

KAY'S TEXT, CASES AND MATERIALS ON SEX–BASED DISCRIMINATION, Third Edition, 1001 pages, 1988. (Casebook)

THOMAS' SEX DISCRIMINATION IN A NUTSHELL, 399 pages, 1982. Softcover. (Text)

Workers' Compensation—see Social Legislation

CIVIL PROCEDURE
CASES AND MATERIALS

Fifth Edition

By

John J. Cound
Professor of Law, University of Minnesota

Jack H. Friedenthal
Dean, The National Law Center, George Washington University

Arthur R. Miller
Bruce Bromley Professor of Law, Harvard University

John E. Sexton
Dean and Professor of Law, New York University

AMERICAN CASEBOOK SERIES ®

WEST PUBLISHING CO.
ST. PAUL, MINN., 1989

COPYRIGHT © 1968, 1974, 1980, 1985 By COUND, FRIEDENTHAL and MILLER
COPYRIGHT © 1989 By COUND, FRIEDENTHAL, MILLER and SEXTON
                    WEST PUBLISHING CO.
                    50 West Kellogg Boulevard
                    P.O. Box 64526
                    St. Paul, MN 55164–0526

Library of Congress Cataloging-in-Publication Data

   Civil procedure : cases and materials / by John J. Cound...[et al.].
 — 5th ed.
      p.   cm. — (American casebook series)
   Includes index.
   ISBN 0–314–54586–7
   1. Civil procedure—United States—Cases. I. Cound, John J.
 II. Series.
   KF8839.C45   1989
   347.73′5—dc20
   [347.3075]

ISBN 0–314–54586–7

To Richard H. Field and Benjamin Kaplan of the Harvard Law School, who first unlocked the door for us and who will not be surprised if we seem, on occasion, to have mislaid the key.

*

Preface

This Fifth Edition, which has been prepared by Jack H. Friedenthal, Arthur R. Miller, and John E. Sexton, has had the benefit of many comments of colleagues from the large number of schools in which the first four editions have been used. These responses have been gratifying in confirming our own conclusion that the book is a highly successful teaching tool, regardless of the precise form of the civil procedure course being taught or of the specific material covered in it. As a result, this Fifth Edition preserves the same basic format and much of the material found in the earlier editions.

Why then is a new edition necessary? Certainly a revision cannot be justified simply to achieve relatively trivial improvements or merely to replace the original text with more recent matter of similar substantive content. The reason for this volume is that since publication of the Fourth Edition there have been important developments in several areas of procedure (for example, jurisdiction over persons and property), which give rise to intellectually stimulating questions and policy considerations that require inclusion in a contemporary casebook. Thus, the chapter on jurisdiction has been reconceptualized and updated in light of the recent Supreme Court decisions and other developments. The chapter on summary judgment has been substantially reworked and expanded; the chapter on res judicata and collateral estoppel has been reworked completely; and new sections, reflecting the recent amendments to relevant statutes and to the Federal Rules of Civil Procedure, have been added to other chapters.

We have looked for modern cases in which the facts are interesting, in which the conflicting policies seem to be in equipoise, or in which the context has extrinsic fascination, rather than for cases whose opinions offer tight little monographs on various aspects of procedure. After all, a student's preparation and participation in class discussion frequently are in direct proportion to the extent to which the materials are interesting and involving.

The notes and questions that follow nearly every principal case have been designed for the most part to encourage deeper analysis of the problems raised in the principal cases rather than to fill the student with additional detail. At the same time, we have tried to provide sufficient and selective references to secondary sources for the student who wishes to look further.

We have not aimed at a "hard" book. Civil procedure is sufficiently mysterious to law students that its ability to challenge survives best when presented in a clear and simple environment. The danger is not of patronizing students, but of losing them. In the textual survey in Chapter

One, in the long note on "the nature of the trial process" in Chapter Eleven and in briefer introductions to other sections of the book, we have tried to tell students where they are going, and through extensive cross-referencing and questions we have tried to force them to review where they have been.

We have not concentrated on the law of any one jurisdiction, although there is substantial emphasis on the operation of the Federal Rules of Civil Procedure, which have served as a model and focal point for serious discussion and implementation of procedural reform in a large majority of the states. In general the book operates on a comparative basis, except in contexts in which this approach has more limited utility than an in-depth exploration of a single system.

A careful attempt has been made to strike a balance between exploration of underlying philosophical problems and analysis of day-to-day matters that arise frequently in office practice or in the courts. Our theory is that a mixture of both is necessary to give students a comprehensive understanding of procedure. How else can they learn why, even today, after so many years of study, revision, and reform, major proposals for alteration of adjective law are still being made, and, undoubtedly, will continue to be made in the years to come? In addition, considerable use has been made of historical material, not only when it is directly relevant to today's system, as in the study of the right to jury trial, but also in contexts in which it is necessary for a true grasp of the basic problems.

Because courses in civil procedure vary greatly not only as to the hours allotted but also as to whether they are mandatory or optional and as to the year during which students are expected to take them, the materials in this edition are designed to provide maximum pedagogical flexibility. The cases and subjects covered have been selected primarily for a comprehensive, year-long course beginning in the first term of the law student's first year; yet they may easily be divided into two or more quite different subjects to be given either as preliminary or advanced courses.

The first chapter of this casebook sets forth a basic, textual statement of a procedural system's framework, without which an understanding of any particular part of the system is difficult, if not impossible. This initial discussion defines those procedural terms necessary for comprehending legal opinions, whether they be of a procedural or substantive character. This we believe, is an important function of a course in procedure, especially when it forms part of the first year curriculum. The textual analysis, which can be assigned for study with little or no class discussion, is followed by a series of illustrative cases designed to raise the basic problems of a procedural system, to illustrate the interplay among its various aspects, and to highlight many of the points in the earlier text. An effort has been made to select cases that can be handled with relative dispatch so that the introduction does not become a de facto study of the entire course. In general, Chapter One is intended to let students form some idea as to the nature of the litigation "forest" before attempting to make them master of any of its "trees."

After the first chapter, the structure of the book proceeds in a chronological fashion. The authors believe that this is the most logical way to teach civil procedure because it permits students to see the evolution and maturation of the litigation process. Furthermore, by putting personal and subject-matter jurisdiction and the materials dealing with the history of civil procedure before such subjects as pleading, joinder, and discovery, first year students are given some "breathing time" in which to absorb enough substantive law from torts, contracts, and property courses to enable them to grasp the significance of such matters as "pleading a cause of action," "contributory negligence," and "joint and several interests." Finally, the authors have concluded that despite its conceptual difficulty, personal jurisdiction is a much more teachable and exhilarating introduction to civil procedure than is pleading.

The chapter on jurisdiction includes an extensive treatment of the federal courts. An investigation of a single system in detail seems the best way to impress students with the significance attached by courts to the concept of jurisdiction over the subject matter. The length of this material is greater than is customary in a civil procedure book, but part of it may readily be treated at the end of the course or be eliminated. We believe that without a working knowledge of such concepts as diversity of citizenship and ancillary jurisdiction, the procedural ramifications of the Erie doctrine and such indisputably procedural problems as joinder cannot be properly understood.

We have concluded that to omit a plenary section on common-law pleading, the forms of action, equity, and the nineteenth century reforms (as many procedure casebooks do) would only lead to the introduction of this material in driblets by lecture during the study of modern pleading and other subjects with no substantial saving in time and probably at a cost in comprehension. At the same time we have eschewed the temptation to overcompensate for the disappearance of courses in equity; we have not attempted to cover the substantive doctrines of that discipline in a historical note. Although we believe history is invaluable to the study of modern procedure, the modern pleading chapter has been planned as a choate whole, and does not require the coverage of the earlier background chapter.

The materials in this volume refer to and are augmented by a Supplement, which contains not only the federal statutes and rules governing procedure, as is traditional, but also comparative state provisions. In some cases other materials, such as notes of Advisory Committees, also are included. Thus at a glance students are able to see the different solutions put forth for particular procedural problems and are induced to explore the reasons why one rule has not been universally acclaimed as "superior" and adopted by all jurisdictions. Use of the Supplement has the added advantage of permitting teachers and students to keep abreast of interesting alterations in the oftenchanging statutes and rules governing civil procedure, without constant revision of the casebook itself. Our practice has been to revise and reissue the Supplement every two years, adding recent significant cases, thereby achieving considerable flexibility at a minimal cost to students.

All teachers of civil procedure are well aware of how difficult it is for students to grapple with problems in the abstract; for example in the field of pleading they may have only a vague notion of what a pleading looks like. The Supplement therefore also contains a litigation time-chart and an illustrative problem, showing how a case develops in practice and samples of the documents that might actually have formed a portion of the record. It is important to note that these samples are not designed as models to be emulated. To the contrary, they often contain defects intended to induce students to criticize them in light of knowledge they have obtained from the cases and classroom discussion.

The cases and excerpts from other materials obviously have been extensively edited in order to shorten them and clarify issues for discussion. Except in a few situations, the materials from the Fourth Edition have not been significantly shortened in preparing the Fifth Edition. With regard to footnotes: the same numbering appears in the casebook as appears in the original sources; editor's footnotes are indicated by letters.

The authors are deeply grateful to a host of people who have helped us in the preparation of this volume, the earlier editions, and the Supplement. Among our students deserving special mention for the aid they provided in preparing one or more of the editions of the book are Prudence Beatty Abram, Sam L. Abram, Richard B. Bernstein, (Professor) Barry B. Boyer, William M. Burns, Bertram Carp, (Professor) Sanford Caust-Ellenbogen, Stephanie Cohen, Steven Cohen, Diane Costa, Gary Eisenberg, Lisa Fair, Raymond Fisher, Jo Anne Friedenthal, Lisa E. Goldberg, Edward Hartnett, Wendy B. Jacobs, (Professor) Joseph J. Kalo, (Professor) Mary Kay Kane, Maureen P. Manning, Matthew McGrath, Kiran H. Mehta, Marcy Oppenheimer, Jennifer Pariser, Christopher Reich, (Professor) Linda J. Silberman, Donna Silverberg, Jacqueline Veit, and Gail Zweig. A special word of thanks is due to David D. Drueding, a dear friend and practicing attorney, who spent dozens of hours discussing and implementing the changes in the Fourth and Fifth Editions. And, finally, a very special word of thanks is due to Daniel D. Chazin, another dear friend and practicing attorney, who read the entire manuscript more than once in order to remove inconsistencies (and, occasionally, inanities) and who constantly provided insights that improved the book; Dan's untiring efforts were extraordinary, and we are deeply indebted to him.

We also are grateful to the following people for their great assistance in handling the manuscript, proofs, and a variety of other operations, Michael Broyde, Grant H. Franks, Robert H. Goldman, Kevin A. Griffin, Frederick W. Lambert, Frederick Mandler, Christopher Mahon, John J. McGonagle, Franklin N. Meyer, Norman A. Platt, Martin C. Recchuite, and Marc Schuback. Nor should we overlook the enormous secretarial assistance provided by Dede Jensen and Shirley Gray, as well as the numerous helpful suggestions offered to us by our colleagues Professors Barbara Babcock, Stephen B. Burbank, Oscar Chase, Edward H. Cooper, Samuel Estreicher, Mary Kay Kane, Andreas Lowenfeld, Thomas Rowe, Linda J. Silberman, Ellen Sward, and Charles W. Wolfram.

J. H. F.

A. R. M.

J. E. S.

May, 1989

*

Summary of Contents

*

Table of Contents

*

Table of Cases

The principal cases are in bold type. Cases cited or discussed in the text are roman type. References are to pages. Cases cited in principal cases and within other quoted materials are not included.

Chapter 1

A SURVEY OF THE CIVIL ACTION

SECTION A. THE CONCERN AND CHARACTER OF PROCEDURE

The law of procedure is the body of rules that governs or provides the framework of the judicial process. The judicial process, in turn, guides the operation of courts in the determination of legal controversies, or as Wigmore defined the process, the decision "by an agent of state power, [of] a controversy existing between two individuals (or the State and an individual), by rational (not merely personal) considerations, purporting to rest on justice and law (i.e. the community's general sense of order)." [a] These definitions are terribly inadequate, and they contain question-begging elements that need definition themselves. But further explication would lead into endless philosophical debate. As stated, these definitions will serve our purpose at this time if you understand from them the following points: (1) The judicial process deals not with abstract questions or hypothetical situations but with actual controversies between real parties. (2) These controversies are such that the community will direct its collective force to their resolution. (3) This resolution proceeds not arbitrarily but according to some standards of general application. (4) These standards are applied in a proceeding that follows some fixed lines set out by a system of rules known as procedure.

A distinctive element of the procedure for resolving legal controversies is the *adversary system.* This element is indeed central to the whole subject, and unless it is understood it becomes well nigh impossible to explain, much less to justify, most of our procedural law. It means that the responsibility for beginning suit, for shaping the issues, and for producing evidence rests almost entirely upon the parties to the controversy; the court takes almost no active part, it does not do its own investigating, it rarely even asks a question. Contrasted with the methods of scientific or historical research, this system of finding answers seems sometimes to reduce the whole operation to a game. Yet although

a. Wigmore, *The Judicial Function,* in *Science of Legal Method* xxvi, xxviii (1917).

the adversary system certainly is not the only possible approach to dispute resolution, it remains a significant element of most judicial systems.

There are, of course, many degrees between the antipodes of complete control by the parties and complete control by the court, and most systems of procedure fall somewhere between these extremes. In recent times there has been a trend toward increasing the affirmative or active functions of the court that reflects the larger trend away from the "sporting" or "game" theory of litigation. Nonetheless, it cannot be questioned that in the United States the primary responsibility and control over almost all phases of the judicial process continue to reside in the parties.

The reasons for the prevalence of the adversary system are manifold, but four postulates are certainly among the most important: (1) A truer decision will be reached as the result of a contest directed by interested parties. (2) The parties, who after all are the persons principally interested in the resolution of the controversy, should bear the major burden of the time and energy required. (3) Although impartial investigation may be better when no final decision need be reached, setting up sides makes easier the type of yes-or-no decision that is thought to be necessary in a lawsuit. (4) Since resort to law has replaced the resort to force that characterized primitive ages, the atavistic instinct to do battle is better satisfied by a means of settling disputes that is very much in the hands of the parties.

It is by no means clear that these arguments, or others that may be advanced, justify the extent to which the responsibility for directing legal contests is conferred upon the parties under our rules. The fact that every civilized state has seen fit to furnish an official method for the settlement of private disputes indicates that there is more than a merely personal interest in their resolution. When one reflects on the fact that the adversary system often means that victory will turn on considerations other than the justice or true merits of the cause, there is reason to believe that we have permitted it to take an exaggerated place in our judicial scheme. But the system remains and its presence will color every facet of this course. Full understanding of the materials in this book will require your constant attention to its existence as well as critical analysis of its shortcomings.

There is but one test of a good system of procedure: *Does it tend to the just and efficient determination of legal controversies?* In this connection you must understand one thing: despite the fact that this course is only an introduction to procedure, you are not to assume that your function simply is to digest uncritically the law you read. It is a part of your process of learning to examine, "to wash in cynical acid," each rule, each form, each principle you learn. But while doing so keep in mind that many, diverse, and complex are the aspects of both justice and efficiency.

SECTION B. AN OUTLINE OF THE PROCEDURE IN A CIVIL ACTION

The first step in a lawsuit strictly speaking is not a matter of law, certainly not a matter of the law of civil procedure. As already suggested, lawsuits do not begin themselves. Someone must first decide to sue someone else. If this decision is made intelligently, the person choosing to sue must have weighed several matters, among which at least three are basic.

A potential litigant obviously feels aggrieved or would not be thinking of a lawsuit. But he or she must further consider whether the grievance is one for which the law furnishes relief. There are a great many hurts a person may feel that the law will not redress. He loses his girlfriend to another suitor; she is offended by the paint on her neighbor's house; he has worked for weeks to persuade a grocer to buy his brand of peas, and sees the sale go to a competitor; she has been holding a plot of ground for speculation expecting industry to move in and the area is zoned for residential use; he slips on a spot of grease in the county courthouse but the county is immune from suit. If the injury is among those not redressable by a court of law, litigation would be a fruitless and wasteful exercise.

Even if he concludes that his grievance is one for which the courts will grant relief, a potential litigant must consider the probability of winning a lawsuit. He must ask whether he can find and bring into court the person who has injured him; whether he can produce the witnesses and documents that will prove his case; whether this proof will be believed; whether his adversary can justify his conduct or establish any defenses to the action; and whether his (or rather his attorney's) estimate of the law will turn out to be correct.

Then, and perhaps most important of all, he must consider whether what is won will be worth the time, the effort, and the expense it will cost, and he must weigh against this the alternatives to suit, among them settlement, arbitration, self-help, and letting matters rest. What form will the relief take? Most frequently it will be restricted to a judgment for damages. If this is true he must decide whether his injury is one for which a monetary payment will be satisfactory. Assuming it is, will defendant be rich enough to pay? How difficult will a judgment be to collect? How expensive? Will he end up with enough to pay his lawyer and the other litigation expenses that undoubtedly will be incurred? Even in a context in which the court may grant specific relief—for example, an order directing the opposing party to do something or to stop doing something—will compliance by defendant be possible? Worthwhile? Sufficient? In the same vein, he also must consider whether there are risks not directly tied to the suit: Will he acquire the reputation of a crank? Will he antagonize people whose goodwill he needs? Will the action publicize an error of judgment on his part or open his private affairs to public gaze?

Only after he has thoughtfully resolved these and similar questions will the prospective plaintiff be ready for the steps that follow. Let us now consider those steps in the light of a relatively uncluttered hypothetical case:

Aikins, while crossing the street in front of her private home, was struck and seriously injured by an automobile driven by Beasley. On inquiry, Aikins found that the automobile was owned by Cecil and that Beasley apparently had been in Cecil's employ. Beasley was predictably without substantial assets and a judgment against him for Aikins' injuries promised little material compensation. But Cecil was wealthy, and Aikins was advised that if she could establish that Beasley had indeed been working for Cecil and had been negligent, she then could recover from Cecil. Aikins decided to sue Cecil for $60,000.

1. SELECTING A PROPER COURT

Aikins initially must determine in which court to bring the action. She probably will have some choice, but it will be a limited one. This is true because the court selected must have *jurisdiction over the subject matter* (that is, the constitution and statutes under which the court operates must have conferred upon it power to decide this type of case) and must also have *jurisdiction over the person* of Cecil (that is, Cecil must be subject or amenable to suit in the state in which the court is located).

Aikins probably will bring suit in a state court, for as we shall shortly see the subject-matter jurisdiction of the federal courts is severely limited. If the court organization of Aikins' state is typical, there will be courts of *original jurisdiction* in which cases are brought and tried, and one court of *appellate jurisdiction* that sits, with rare exceptions, only to review the decisions of lower courts. (In most states there will also be a group of intermediate courts of appellate jurisdiction.) The courts of original jurisdiction probably consist of one set of courts of *general jurisdiction* and several sets of courts of *inferior jurisdiction*. The courts of general jurisdiction are organized into districts comprising for the most part several counties, although the largest or most populous counties each may constitute single districts. These district courts hear cases of many kinds and are competent to grant every kind of relief, but in order to bring a case in one of them plaintiff must have a claim for more than a specific amount, perhaps two or three thousand dollars. The courts of inferior jurisdiction will include municipal courts, whose jurisdiction resembles that of the district courts except that the claims they hear are of less importance; justice-of-the-peace courts, which hear very minor matters; and specialized tribunals such as the traffic courts. Since Aikins' injuries are quite serious and her claim correspondingly large, she will, if she sues in a state court, bring the action in one of the district courts.

The federal government of course also operates a system of courts. The principal federal courts are the United States District Courts, courts of original jurisdiction of which there is at least one in every state; the thirteen United States Courts of Appeals, each of which reviews the decisions of federal district courts in the several states within its circuit (with the exception of the Courts of Appeals for the District of Columbia

Circuit and the Federal Circuit); and the Supreme Court of the United States, which not only reviews the decisions of federal courts but also reviews decisions of state courts that turn on an issue of federal law.

The jurisdiction over the subject-matter of the United States District Courts extends to many, but by no means all, cases involving federal law, and also to many cases, similar to Aikins', that do not involve federal law; the latter are cases in which there is *diversity of citizenship* (the parties are citizens of different states or one of them is a citizen of a foreign country) and the required *amount in controversy* (more than $50,000) is at stake. Diversity jurisdiction, in common with most of the federal courts' jurisdiction, is not *exclusive;* the state courts also are competent to hear these cases. But if Cecil is not a citizen of Aikins' state, Aikins may bring an action for $60,000 in a federal court. Indeed, in these circumstances, if Aikins sued Cecil in a state court in Aikins' home state Cecil could *remove* the action from the state court in which it was commenced to the federal district court in that state.[b]

It is not enough that the court selected by Aikins has jurisdiction over the subject-matter, however. That court, whether state or federal, must be one in which Cecil can be required to appear. This generally means that Cecil must reside or be found in the state in which the court sits. But the restrictions on a court's jurisdiction over the person have expanded in recent decades, and if Cecil is not present in Aikins' state but he directed Beasley to drive there, Aikins probably will be able to bring the action in that state. (Even in the event that these facts cannot be established, and Cecil cannot be found in Aikins' state, it may be possible to sue him there, if he owns property in that state, but the judgment will be limited to the value of that property.)

Not every court that has jurisdiction over the subject-matter and jurisdiction over the person of defendant will hear a case. It also is necessary that an action be brought in a court having proper *venue.* Thus, although every court in Aikins' state could assert personal jurisdiction over Cecil if he was within its boundaries, that state's statutes typically will provide that the case should be brought in a court whose district includes the county in which either Aikins or Cecil lives. Similarly, although Cecil might be found in a number of states, he can be sued in a federal court only in a district in which he or Aikins resides or where the claim arose.

Jurisdiction over the subject-matter is jealously guarded, and cannot be waived. If Aikins and Cecil are both citizens of the same state, a federal court will refuse to hear the action even though both are anxious that it do so. Jurisdiction over the person and venue, on the other hand, essentially are protections for defendant, who may waive them if he wishes.

b. If Cecil is not a citizen of Aikins' state and Beasley is, then one of the considerations Aikins will have in deciding to join Beasley as a defendant is the effect on the availability of subject-matter jurisdiction in the federal courts. If Aikins wants to be in the federal court, she should not join Beasley; if Aikins wants to begin and stay in a state court, she should join him. In the latter case, there will not be complete diversity between the plaintiff on the one side and the defendants on the other.

2. COMMENCING THE ACTION

After the court has been selected, Aikins must give notice to Cecil by *service of process.* The process typically consists of a *summons,* which directs defendant to appear and defend under penalty of *default;* that is, unless defendant answers the summons, a judgment will be entered against him. Service of process generally is achieved by *personal service;* the summons is physically delivered to the defendant or is left at his home, sometimes by the plaintiff or her attorney, sometimes by a public official such as a sheriff or a United States marshal. If Cecil lives in another state, but the circumstances are such that a court in Aikins' state may assert jurisdiction over Cecil, the summons may be personally delivered to him, or some form of *substituted service,* such as sending the papers by registered mail or delivering the summons to his agent within Aikins' state, may be employed. Even if Cecil cannot be located, service in yet another form, usually by *publication* in a newspaper for a certain length of time, may be allowed, although the validity of this kind of service in the type of case Aikins is bringing against Cecil is unlikely to be upheld. The United States Supreme Court repeatedly has emphasized that service must be of a kind reasonably calculated to bring the action to defendant's notice, and from this perspective service by publication is rarely sufficient.

3. PLEADING AND PARTIES

With the summons, Aikins usually will serve on Cecil the first of the *pleadings,* commonly called the *complaint.* This is a written statement that will contain Aikins' claim against Cecil. What should be required of such a statement? Obviously it may vary from a simple assertion that Cecil owes her $60,000, to a second-by-second narration of the accident, closely describing the scene and the conduct of each party, followed by a gruesome recital of Aikins' medical treatment and her prognosis for recovery. No procedural system insists upon either of these extremes, but systems do vary greatly in the detail required in the pleadings. The degree of detail required largely reflects the purposes that the pleadings are expected to serve. These purposes are many, but three objectives are particularly relevant and to the extent that a procedural system regards one rather than another as crucial, we may expect to find differing amounts of detail required.

First, the system may desire the pleadings to furnish a basis for identifying and separating the legal and factual contentions involved so that the legal issues—and hopefully through them the entire case—may be disposed of at an early stage. Thus, suppose that Cecil's liability for Beasley's driving depends upon the degree of independence with which Beasley was working at the time of the accident. A dispute on this issue might exist on either or both of two elements. The parties might disagree as to what Beasley's duties were, and they might disagree as to whether those duties put Beasley so much under the control of Cecil that the law will impose liability on Cecil for Beasley's actions. The first disagreement would be a question of fact, and there would be no alternative to trying the suit and letting the finder of fact (usually the jury) decide the truth. But if there was agreement on that first element, a question of law would be presented by the second issue, which could be determined by the judge without a trial. The objective of which we are speaking would be fully served in such a case only if the pleadings set forth exactly what Beasley's job required him to do. It would be very inadequately served if the complaint stated only that "Beasley was driving the car on Cecil's business."

Second, the pleadings may be intended to establish in advance what a party proposes to prove at trial so that his opponent will know what contentions he must prepare to meet. If this objective is regarded as very important it will not be enough for the complaint to state that Beasley was negligent, or that Aikins suffered serious bodily injuries. It must say that Beasley was speeding, or was not keeping a proper look-out, or had inadequate brakes, or describe some other act of negligence and say that Aikins suffered a concussion, or a broken neck, or fractures of three ribs, or other injuries.

Third, the pleadings may be intended to give each party only a general notice of his opponent's contentions, in which event the system would rely upon subsequent stages of the lawsuit to identify the legal and factual contentions of the parties and to enable each to prepare to meet the opponent's case. In such a case a complaint similar to that in Form 9 of the Federal Rules would be sufficient.

Obviously each of the first two objectives is desirable. It is a waste of everybody's time to try lawsuits when the underlying legal claim is inadequate to support a judgment, and it is only fair that a person called upon to defend a judicial proceeding should know what he is alleged to have done. But to achieve the first objective fully may require pleading after pleading in order to expose and sharpen the issues; if detail is insisted upon, a long time may be consumed in producing it. Moreover, a single pleading oversight may eliminate a contention necessary to one party's case that easily could have been proven, but which will be held to have been waived. To achieve the second objective through the pleadings will mean that the parties must take rigid positions as to their factual contentions at the very beginning when they do not know what they will learn about their cases by the time trial begins. Either the first or second objective, if fully pursued, requires that the parties adhere to the positions taken in the pleadings. They could not be permitted to introduce evidence in conflict with the pleadings or to change them. For to the extent that *variances* between pleading and proof or *amendments* to the pleadings are permitted, the objectives will be lost. The court frequently will find itself forced either to depart from these objectives or to tolerate cases turning on the skill of the lawyers rather than on the merits of the controversy.

4. THE RESPONSE

Following the service of Aikins' complaint, Cecil must respond. He may challenge the complaint by a *motion to dismiss*. This motion may challenge the court's jurisdiction over the subject-matter or Cecil's person, the service of process, or venue. It also may be a *motion to dismiss for failure to state a claim or cause of action* (or a *demurrer*). For the purpose of this motion, the facts alleged in the complaint are accepted as true, and the court considers whether, on this assumption, plaintiff has shown that the pleader is entitled to legal relief.

There are three general situations in which such a motion might be granted. First, the complaint may clearly show that the injury is one for which the law furnishes no redress; for example, when plaintiff simply alleges that "defendant has made faces at me." Second, plaintiff may have failed to include an allegation on a necessary part of the case; for example, Aikins might have alleged the accident, her injuries, and Beasley's negligence, and have forgotten to allege that Beasley was Cecil's servant. Third, the complaint may be so general or so confused that the court finds that it does not give adequate notice of what plaintiff's claim is; this would be true, for example, of a complaint in which Aikins merely said, "Cecil injured me and owes me $60,000," although complaints far more specific have fallen on this ground. Obviously, the extent to which motions to dismiss will be granted on the second and third grounds will vary with the degree of detail that the particular system requires of its pleadings.

If the motion to dismiss is denied, or if none is made, Cecil must file an *answer*. In this pleading, he must admit or deny the allegations made by Aikins in the complaint. Moreover if Cecil wishes to rely on certain contentions called *affirmative defenses,* he must plead them in the answer. Thus, if he wishes to contend that Aikins was negligent in the manner in which she tried to cross the street and that this negligence was also a cause of the accident, he must in many states plead this in the answer; if the answer only denied the allegations in Aikins' complaint, Cecil may not advance at trial the contention that Aikins' negligence caused the accident.

There may be further pleadings, particularly a *reply* by Aikins. But the tendency today is to close the pleadings after the answer, and if Cecil has raised new matters in his answer, they automatically are taken as denied by Aikins. There is one major exception: if Cecil has a claim against Aikins, particularly one that arises out of the same occurrence being sued upon by Aikins, Cecil may plead this claim as a *counterclaim* as part of the answer. This is in essence a complaint by Cecil, and Aikins will have to respond to it just as Cecil had to respond to the original complaint.

The original action between Aikins and Cecil may expand in terms of the number of parties, and this frequently will occur at the pleading stage. For example, although Aikins decided not to sue Beasley, Cecil might *implead* Beasley, asking that Beasley be held liable to him for whatever amount he may be found liable to Aikins, since his liability depends upon Beasley having been at fault. Cecil will decide whether to do this in light of a number of practical concerns, including the effect Beasley's presence will have on the Aikins v. Cecil suit.

5. OBTAINING INFORMATION PRIOR TO TRIAL

In our discussion of the objectives of pleading, it was noted that some procedural systems do not regard the pleadings as the appropriate vehicle for enabling the parties to prepare for trial. The procedure viewed as primarily charged with this function is pretrial *discovery*. This is a generic term for several methods of obtaining information from an opposing party or from witnesses.

The chief method is to take *depositions* of parties and witnesses. In this procedure, the person whose deposition is to be taken is questioned by lawyers for each side through direct and cross-examination; the *deponent's* statements are taken down and transcribed. The device is useful in finding information that is relevant to the case, including unearthing leads as to other witnesses or documents; it also is useful in laying a basis for impeaching a witness who attempts to change his story at trial. The two parties almost certainly will want depositions taken of each other, as well as of Beasley; the depositions of Aikins and Cecil will be particularly important because they are treated as admissions, and can be used by their adversaries as evidence at trial. In some circumstances, even the deposition of a nonparty witness who is unavailable at trial may be used in place of live testimony.

Another device especially adapted to probing the content of an opponent's case is *written interrogatories,* which usually may be addressed only to a party to the suit. (The availability of interrogatories may be one reason why Aikins might join Beasley as a defendant with Cecil or why Cecil might implead Beasley.) These interrogatories are answered by the party with counsel's aid, and the answers will not be as spontaneous as they would be on a deposition; on the other hand, interrogatories will require him to supply some information that he does not carry in his head but can get, and may be even more valuable than the deposition in finding out what he will try to prove. Thus, information regarding Beasley's employment that Cecil cannot be expected to have in his mind may best be exposed in this way.

Other discovery devices include *orders for the production of documents,* such as the service record of Cecil's automobile, and *requests for admissions,* which will remove uncontested issues from the case. A particularly useful device for Cecil will be a court order directing Aikins to submit to a *physical examination* by a physician of Cecil's choice so that he may determine the real extent of Aikins' alleged injuries.

The availability of discovery, now increasing in scope and use throughout the country, has had its effect on the philosophy of pleadings. This is not simply because it enables parties to prepare for trial better than pleadings ever did. Of more significance perhaps is the fact that if broad discovery is allowed, it is senseless to make parties take rigid positions with respect to the issues at the very beginning of the lawsuit before they have had the chance to utilize these very useful devices for obtaining information. In addition, the availability of discovery does much to make summary judgment, which is discussed below, a viable and fair procedure, since it enables a party to ascertain those issues on which the opposing party has no evidence, and it also gives the opponent a real chance to develop such evidence.

6. SUMMARY JUDGMENT

One of the basic difficulties with attempting to resolve cases at the pleading stage is that the allegations of the parties must be accepted as true for the purpose of ruling on a motion to dismiss. Thus, if the plaintiff tells a highly unlikely but possible story in the complaint, the court cannot dismiss the complaint even though it does not believe the allegations or think that the plaintiff will be able to prove the tale. The judge is not the person and the pleading stage is not the time to resolve questions of fact.

But in some cases it will be possible to supplement the pleadings with additional documents to show that an apparent issue that is decisive of the case is spurious. This is done by a motion for *summary judgment*. This motion can be supported by demonstrating that the crucial issue will have to be resolved in the mover's favor at trial, because the opposing party will be unable to produce any admissible evidence in support of his position on the issue. For example, suppose that it is Cecil's position that prior to the accident he had fired Beasley, but that Beasley had secreted keys to Cecil's automobile and had taken Cecil's car without permission shortly before the accident. On the face of the pleadings, we have only an allegation that Beasley was Cecil's employee and a denial of that allegation; thus, the pleadings seem to present a question of credibility that cannot be resolved at this stage. Cecil now moves for summary judgment, alleging that this issue is not a genuine one; he accompanies his motion with affidavits of his own and two other witnesses that he had fired Beasley; a deposition of the garage attendant indicating that he had been instructed not to allow Beasley to have the car, and that it was taken without Cecil's knowledge; and a deposition of Beasley to the effect that he had been fired, but wanted to use the car once more for his own purposes. It is now incumbent upon Aikins to show that the issue is genuine; Aikins cannot rely simply upon her own assertion that all this is not so; after all, she has no personal knowledge of the facts. Aikins must convince the court that she has admissible evidence that Beasley still was acting as Cecil's employee in driving the car at the time of the accident. If Aikins fails to do so, judgment will be entered against her.

It should be noted that in ruling on a motion for summary judgment the judge does not decide which side is telling the truth. If Aikins presents an affidavit of a witness who says that he was present when Cecil claims he fired Beasley, and says further that Cecil told Beasley that this was only a subterfuge and that he wanted him to continue to work for him but to pretend to steal the car, summary judgment will not be appropriate even though the judge is firmly convinced that Aikins' affiant is lying.

7. SETTING THE CASE FOR TRIAL

After discovery is completed, and if the case has not been terminated by dismissal, summary judgment, or settlement, it must be set for *trial*.

Typically either party may file a *note of issue,* at which time the case will be given a number and placed on a *trial calendar.* These calendars have become extremely long in many courts, and the case may have to wait a year, three years, or more before it is called for trial, especially if a jury trial has been requested.

8. THE JURY AND ITS SELECTION

In most actions for damages, the parties have a right to have the facts tried by a *jury.* This right is assured in the federal courts by the Seventh Amendment to the Constitution, and is protected in the courts of most states by similar constitutional provisions. If there is a right to a trial by jury, either party may assert it, but if neither wishes to do so, a judge will try the facts as well as the law. Largely for historical reasons growing out of a division of authority in the English court structure, there are many civil actions in which neither party has a right to a jury trial; these include most cases in which plaintiff wants an order directing or prohibiting specified action by defendant rather than a judgment for damages—a so-called *equitable* remedy.

If a jury has been demanded, the first order of business at trial will be to impanel the jurors. A large number of people, selected in an impartial manner from various lists, tax rolls, or street directories, will have been ordered to report to the courthouse for jury duty at a given term of court. The prospective jurors will be questioned—usually by the judge but sometimes by the lawyers—as to their possible biases. If one of the persons called has prior knowledge of the case or is a personal friend of one of the parties, he or she probably will be successfully *challenged for cause* and excused. But suppose Aikins is an architect and her lawyer finds that one of the jury panel has recently constructed a house and believes that he was greatly overcharged for its design and construction; this will likely not be enough to persuade the judge to excuse him, but fearing the juror may be prejudiced against his client, Aikins' lawyer will probably exercise one of the small number of *peremptory challenges* allowed for which no reason need be given. Ultimately, a panel of twelve, or, with increasing frequency, a panel of less than twelve, hopefully unbiased jurors will be selected.

9. THE TRIAL

After the jurors have been sworn, plaintiff's lawyer will make an *opening statement,* in which he will describe for the jury what the case is about, what contentions he will make, and how he will prove them. Defendant's lawyer also may make an opening statement at this time, but he may reserve the right to do so until he is ready to present his own case. Following the opening statement, plaintiff's lawyer calls his witnesses one by one. Each witness is first questioned by the lawyer who has called that witness—this is the *direct examination;* then the lawyer for the other side has the opportunity to *cross-examine* him; this may be followed by *re-direct* and *re-cross* examination, and even further stages. The judge maintains some control over the length and tenor of the examination, and in particular will see to it that the stages beyond cross-examination are not prolonged.

Just as the primary responsibility for introducing evidence is on the lawyers, so too is the responsibility for objecting to evidence that is thought to be inadmissible under the rules of evidence. Suppose that Aikins' lawyer asks: "What happened while you were lying on the ground after the accident?" To which Aikins replies: "The driver of the car came over and said that he had been going too fast and he was sorry." Aikins' answer is objectionable because it contains *hearsay evidence;* that is, it repeats what someone else has said for the purpose of proving the truth of what was said. The judge will not raise this issue himself, however; it is up to Cecil's counsel to object, and then the judge must rule on the objection. This particular issue is not an easy one, for Aikins' answer may well come within one of the exceptions to the rule excluding hearsay evidence. This kind of issue will recur continually throughout the trial and the judge must be prepared to make instantaneous rulings if the trial is to proceed with dispatch. Small wonder that evidentiary rulings form a major source of the errors raised on appeal, but at the same time appellate courts are very reluctant to disturb the trial judge's determination. What happens if the judge rules that Aikins' answer is inadmissible? He will instruct the jury to disregard it. Can a juror who has heard such an important confession totally drive it from his or her mind?

Documents, pictures, and other tangible items may be put into evidence, but unless their admissibility has been stipulated in advance, they will be introduced through witnesses. For example, if Aikins' lawyer has had pictures taken of the accident scene and wishes to get them to the jury, he will call the photographer as a witness, have her testify that she took pictures of the scene, and then show them to the photographer who will identify them as the pictures she took. At this point they may be formally introduced into evidence.

When plaintiff's lawyer has called all of his witnesses, and their examinations are over, plaintiff will *rest.* At this point, defendant's lawyer may ask for a *directed verdict* for defendant on the ground that plaintiff has not established a prima facie case; the thrust of the motion is that plaintiff has not introduced enough evidence to permit the jury to find in her favor. If the motion is denied, defendant may rest and choose to rely on the jury's agreeing with him, but in almost all cases he will proceed to present witnesses of his own and these witnesses will be exposed to the same process of direct and cross-examination. When defendant has rested, plaintiff may present additional evidence to meet any new matter raised by defendant's witnesses. In turn, defendant, after plaintiff rests, may meet any new matter presented by plaintiff. This procedure will continue until both parties rest. Again, the trial judge will maintain considerable control to prevent the protraction of these latter stages.

When both parties have rested, either or both may move for a directed verdict. Again, this motion asks the trial judge to rule that under the evidence presented, viewed most favorably to the nonmoving party, the jury cannot find in his or her favor. If these motions are denied, the case must be submitted to the jury.

10. SUBMITTING THE CASE TO THE JURY

At this stage the judge and the lawyers will confer out of the jury's hearing with regard to the content of the judge's *instructions* or *charge* to the jury. Each lawyer may submit proposed instructions, which the trial judge will grant or deny, but the judge is under a duty to charge the jury on the basic aspects of the case in any event. If a party's lawyer has neither requested a particular instruction nor objected to the judge's charge, however, he will generally not be permitted to claim on appeal that the charge was erroneous.

Ordinarily the lawyers will make their final arguments to the jury before the judge delivers the charge. The lawyers will review the evidence from their own points of view, and may suggest how the jury should weigh certain items and resolve specific issues, but it is improper for the lawyers to discuss a matter that has been excluded or has never been introduced. In other words, they are arguing, not testifying.

In the instructions the judge will summarize the facts and issues, tell the jury about the substantive law to be applied on each issue, give general information on determining the credibility of witnesses, and state who has the *burden of persuasion* on each issue of fact. The burden of persuasion in a civil case ordinarily requires that one party prove his contention on a given issue by a preponderance of the evidence. On most issues Aikins will carry this burden but on an affirmative defense such as contributory negligence the burden probably will be on Cecil. What the burden means is that if a juror is unable to resolve an issue in her mind, she should find on that issue against the party who has the burden. In the federal courts and in some states, the judge may comment on the evidence, as long as he emphasizes that his comments represent his own opinion and that the jurors should not feel bound by it; judicial comment is rare, however, and in many states it is not permitted at all.

Following the charge, the jury retires to reach its *verdict*. The verdict, the jury's decision, will be of a type chosen by the judge. There are three types, of which by far the most common is the *general verdict*. This verdict permits the jurors to determine the facts and apply the law on which they have been charged to those facts; it is simple in form in that only the conclusion as to who prevails, and the amount of the damages, if that party is a claimant, is stated. A second type is the *general verdict with interrogatories,* which combines the form of the general verdict with several key questions that are designed to test the jury's understanding of the issues. Suppose that the accident occurred five miles away from Beasley's appointed route. Aikins' evidence is that Beasley detoured to have the vehicle's brakes fixed; Cecil's is that Beasley was going to visit his sweetheart. The judge might charge the jury that in the former event, but not in the latter, Beasley was acting within the scope of his employment and Cecil would be liable for his negligence, and he might direct the jury, in addition to rendering a verdict for Aikins or for Cecil, to answer the question, "Why did Beasley depart from his route?" If the general verdict was for Aikins, but the jury's answer was that Beasley was driving to his sweetheart's home, the judge would order judgment for Cecil, for if the answer is inconsistent with the verdict, the answer controls. The third type of verdict is the *special verdict,* in which all of the factual issues in the case are submitted to the jury as questions without instructions as to their legal effect; the judge applies the law to the jury's answers and determines which party prevails.

Traditionally, only a unanimous jury verdict has been effective. In many states, and by consent of the parties in the federal courts, a nonunanimous verdict by the jurors may stand in a civil action. If the minimum number of jurors required for a verdict are unable to reach agreement, the jury is said to be *hung,* and a new trial before a different jury is necessary.

11. POST-TRIAL MOTIONS

After the jury has returned its verdict, judgment will be entered thereon, but the losing party will have an opportunity to make certain post-trial motions. There may be a motion for a *judgment notwithstanding the verdict* (commonly called a *judgment n.o.v.,* from the Latin non obstante veredicto); this motion raises the same question as a motion for a directed verdict. The losing party also may move for a *new trial;* the grounds for this motion are many, and may include assertions that the judge erred in admitting certain evidence, that the charge was defective, that attorneys, parties, or jurors have been guilty of misconduct, that the damages awarded are excessive, or that the jury's verdict is against the clear weight of the evidence. Should these motions fail, it is sometimes possible to reopen a judgment, even several months after the trial, on the grounds of clerical mistake, newly discovered evidence, or fraud, but the occasions on which relief is granted are very rare.

12. THE JUDGMENT AND ITS ENFORCEMENT

The *judgment* is the final determination of the lawsuit, absent an appeal. Judgment may be rendered on default when the defendant does not appear; or following the granting of a demurrer, a motion to dismiss, or a motion for summary judgment; or upon the jury's verdict, or the findings of fact and conclusions of law of the trial judge in a nonjury case. The judgment may be in the form of an award of money to plaintiff, a declaration of rights between the parties, specific recovery of property, or an order requiring or prohibiting some future activity. When defendant has prevailed, the judgment generally will not be "for" anything nor will it order anything; it simply will provide that plaintiff takes nothing by her complaint.

In most cases a judgment for plaintiff will not order defendant to do anything; typically it will simply state that plaintiff shall recover a sum of money from defendant. This does not necessarily mean that defendant will pay. It is up to plaintiff to collect the money. *Execution* is the common method of forcing the losing party to satisfy a money judgment, if the loser does not do so voluntarily. A *writ of execution* is issued by the court commanding an officer—usually the sheriff—to seize property of the losing party and, if necessary, to sell it at public sale and use the proceeds to satisfy plaintiff's judgment.

When plaintiff's recovery takes the form of an *injunction* requiring defendant to do something or to stop doing something, the judgment (in this context typically called the *decree*) is said to operate against defendant's person (in personam). Its sanction is direct, and if defendant fails to obey, he may be held in *contempt of court* and punished by fine or imprisonment.

Costs provided by statute and certain out-of-pocket disbursements are awarded the prevailing party and included in the judgment. Usually these costs are nominal in relation to the total expense of litigation and include only such items as the clerk's fee and witnesses' mileage. In the United States, in contrast to England, attorney's fees are not recoverable as costs in ordinary litigation.

13. APPEAL

Every judicial system provides for review by an appellate court of the decisions of the trial court. Generally a party has the right to appeal any judgment to at least one higher court. When the system contains two levels of appellate courts, appeal usually lies initially to one of the intermediate courts; review at the highest level is only at the discretion of that court except in certain classes of cases. Thus, in the federal courts, district-court decisions are reviewed by the courts of appeals, but review in the United States Supreme Court must be sought in most cases by a *petition for a writ of certiorari,* which that Court may deny as a matter of discretion without reaching any conclusion as to the merits of the case.[c] The discretion of a higher-level appellate court generally is exercised so that only cases whose legal issues are of broad importance are taken.

The *record* on appeal will contain the pleadings, at least a portion of the *transcript of the trial* (the court reporter's verbatim record of the trial), and the orders and rulings relevant to the appeal. The parties present their contentions to the appellate court by written *briefs* and in addition, in most cases, by *oral argument.* The appellate court may review any ruling of law by the trial judge, although frequently it will limit the scope of its review by holding that particular matters were within the trial judge's discretion or that the error if any was not prejudicial, that is, it did not substantially affect the outcome of the case. There are constitutional limits to the review of a jury's verdict, but even when these limits do not apply—for example, when the judge has sat without a jury—an appellate court rarely will re-examine a question of fact, for a cold record does not convey the nuances of what the trier observed, notably the demeanor of the witnesses.

c. In a few cases, a direct appeal lies from the district court to the Supreme Court.

The appellate court has the power to *affirm, reverse,* or *modify* the judgment of the trial court. If it reverses, it may order that judgment be entered or it may *remand* the case to the trial court for a new trial or other proceedings not inconsistent with its decision. The decision of an appellate court usually is accompanied by a written *opinion,* signed by one of the judges hearing the appeal, there always being more than one judge deciding an appeal. Concurring and dissenting opinions also may be filed. The opinions of a court are designed to set forth the reasons for a decision and to furnish guidance to lower courts, lawyers, and the public. You will spend much of your time in law school—and afterwards—reading the opinions of appellate courts. Although trial courts frequently deliver opinions when ruling on motions or sitting without a jury, except in federal courts these usually are not published.

There is an important distinction between the *reviewability* of a particular ruling of a trial judge and its *appealability.* For example, a trial judge's ruling excluding certain evidence at trial as hearsay is reviewable; that is, when the judgment is appealed, that ruling may be assigned as error and the appellate court will consider whether it was correct. But trial would be impossible if an appeal could be taken from every ruling. Thus, appeals lie only from judgments and from certain orders made in the course of litigation when immediate review is deemed so important that a delay in the action during appeal can be tolerated. Judicial systems differ in the extent to which *interlocutory orders* can be appealed. In the federal system, very little other than a final judgment can be taken to the courts of appeals; in some states, on the other hand, many kinds of orders can be appealed.

A good example of the contrast between the two approaches can be seen by looking at the consequences of an order denying a motion to dismiss. Suppose that Cecil moves to dismiss Aikins' complaint on the grounds that even on Aikins' view of the facts Cecil is not responsible for the conduct of Beasley, and this motion is denied. In the federal courts such an order would not be appealable, since it does not terminate the lawsuit. Indeed, the disposition of the motion means that the action will continue. In many states, however, this question could be taken immediately to a higher court for a ruling, while the other stages of the litigation waited.

The question as to which system is better is not easy to answer. One may argue in favor of the federal practice that everything should be done at one level before going to the next, that too much time is taken in waiting for appellate courts to decide these questions serially, and that no appeal may ever be necessary, since Cecil may prevail anyway. But on the other hand, if the appellate court holds at this early stage that Aikins has no claim against Cecil we will save the time necessary for discovery and trial.

One point worth noting is that the resolution of the question of the appealability of interlocutory orders has an important bearing on the procedural developments within a given system. In the case of motions to dismiss, for example, if denials are not appealable, the law on this subject will be made largely in the trial courts. The trial judge who is in doubt may tend to deny such motions rather than to grant them, and his decision generally will not be disturbed; even though the ruling theoretically is reviewable after final judgment, by that time the significance of the ruling on the pleadings may have been displaced by more substantive questions. If the denial is appealable, a tactical consideration is added and such motions will be resorted to more frequently, inasmuch as they will afford defendant an additional opportunity to delay trial and thus to wear down his opponent. With respect to other procedural rulings—as in the discovery area—the absence of an interlocutory appeal will strengthen the hand of the trial judge; he will in fact, if not in theory, be given a wider discretion because fewer of his rulings will come before the appellate courts and when they do they will be enmeshed in a final judgment, which will make it easy to conclude that any error was not prejudicial.

14. THE CONCLUSIVENESS OF JUDGMENTS

After the appeal and whatever further proceedings may take place, or, if no appeal is taken, when the time for appeal expires, the judgment is final. It cannot be challenged in another proceeding. It is *res judicata*, a thing decided, and now at rest. Defining the scope and effect of this finality is one of the most complex tasks in the entire law of procedure.

SECTION C. A NOTE ON MOTION PRACTICE

Throughout the previous Section the word "motion" is used frequently, and for good reason. What a motion is, how one makes a motion, and when one should make a motion are all questions of "motion practice." A motion is the procedural device by which a litigant asks a court for an order. For example, a request for an order to dismiss a complaint for failure to state a claim, a request for an order granting a summary judgment, and a request for an order granting a new trial all are formally made to a court through a motion.

A litigant generally must make a motion in writing. Two exceptions to this rule are when the court is recording a hearing verbatim or when a trial is taking place. A motion generally must state with particularity the reasons or grounds supporting the motion and the relief sought. The written motion also must appear in a proper form, which usually is determined by local court rules.

The litigant also must serve the motion on her adversary. In addition, a notice of hearing regarding the motion, a brief or memorandum of law in support of the motion, a proposed order, and affidavits, if necessary, generally accompany a motion. Briefs usually have a maximum page limit (and quite often are not brief). Not all courts require the movant to submit a proposed order. Only certain motions require affidavits.

All motions in federal court require the signature of the litigant's attorney or the litigant. This signature also attests that the attorney or litigant has read the motion papers and that the motion has sufficient grounds and is made in good faith. If a court decides that any of these are not true, the court may sanction the attorney or the litigant. Sanctions have been imposed more frequently in recent years.

A party served with a motion may answer and usually must do so within a time period specified by the rules. A party also may move for an extension of time, either to make a cross-motion, to extend the time to respond to the motion, or both. In addition, making a motion may defer the next stage of litigation. Finally, making a particular motion may preserve other legal rights.

It is this interrelationship between motions, their intended effects, their secondary effects, and their effects on the other side that determine how a party utilizes motion practice. A motion such as summary judgment is usually designed to win the lawsuit. A successful motion to exclude certain material from discovery may convince an adversary that he cannot obtain the information necessary to establish his case and thus may induce him to end the lawsuit early without an unfavorable judgment. A motion to bring a third party into the lawsuit may help convince an adversary that the lawsuit will be more time consuming and costly than expected. A lawyer deciding to make a motion must consider carefully what benefits will accrue to the movant and what obstacles will be imposed on her adversary as a result of the motion.

But a motion may have negative aspects. One of these drawbacks may be the time and expense of making the motion, including drafting and serving multiple copies of papers, spending hours preparing the brief, and taking resources from other more fruitful pursuits. Repeated, unsuccessful motions will result in expense and delay that may reduce client satisfaction.

In addition, poor motion practice may leave the judge with the impression that the lawyer is sloppy, shoddy, and disorganized. Arguing motions at a hearing that the attorneys could have settled without a hearing may convince the judge that the movant is contentious by nature. In short, an unwise use of a motion may do more harm in the long run than not making the motion at all, even if the motion is granted.

In sum, motion practice is a central part of a litigator's arsenal. When a particular motion can be made, how it must be made, and what its effect will be are questions that can be answered by studying the applicable procedural rules. When a motion *should* be made and how it can affect the course of the lawsuit are matters of judgment and experience.

SECTION D. A NOTE ON REMEDIES

The remedies that may be obtained in a modern civil action should principally be viewed as a part of the substantive law: contract law, tort law, commercial law, labor law, and so forth. Yet because the goal of a lawsuit is the remedy and the means of securing it is procedural, there necessarily is a close relationship between them. For example, the range of available remedies in a case may be limited by the manner in which plaintiff has pleaded, and on the other hand certain procedural aspects of the case, such as whether it is tried to a judge or a jury, may be determined by the remedy that is being sought; again, whether a person may be joined as a party may depend on the relief that is being sought, and conversely certain remedies may be available only if all interested persons can be joined.

Without question, the most important relationship between procedure and remedies grows out of the existence in English law of two great branches of jurisprudence administered in different courts: common law and equity; the latter was envisioned as complementary to the former. There are two special facts about equity that are important for our purpose. First, already alluded to, it had no jury. Second, the injunction was a creature of equity and remained in its sole custody so long as the two branches remained distinct. From this heritage two consequences of immense significance for the law of procedure result. One, the right of a trial by jury in the United States today, especially in the federal courts, is determined by inquiring whether the matter in question was a subject of legal or equitable cognizance in 1791—the date of the Seventh Amendment—and to some extent this question depends on the remedy sought, since the availability of injunctive relief was one font of equity's jurisdiction. Two, just as equity was regarded as a special kind of law to be resorted to only when the common law was inadequate, so too the injunction—and most forms of specific relief, even in those limited circumstances in which it is available at law—has been and still is regarded as a form of exceptional relief, to be allowed only when the ordinary remedy of damages is inadequate.

The most important types of relief that a court may award in a civil action fall into three categories: *declarative, specific,* and *compensatory.* Declarative relief consists simply in a court's defining the rights and duties of the parties in a particular legal context. Suppose a person believes that an agreement he has entered into is not a valid contract and that he is under no obligation to perform it; however, he is afraid to act on this belief in the face of another's insistence that he perform, because if the contract is enforceable the damages for the nonperformance will be great. In these circumstances he may seek a declaratory judgment asking the court to determine whether he is under a duty to perform. This type of relief is not as common as those discussed below and its availability often is limited by statute. In numerous situations, however, it is invaluable.

Specific relief consists generally of an order directing conduct. Defendant may be commanded to return a jewel he has taken from plaintiff, to stop operating a pig farm in a residential neighborhood, to deliver a car he has contracted to sell, or to refrain from opening a barbershop next door to a person to whom he has just sold his former barbershop. Obviously, specific relief is not possible in all cases. For example, no kind of specific relief will compensate or cure Aikins in our hypothetical case; Beasley cannot retroactively be ordered not to run into her. On the other hand, in some kinds of cases specific relief is available almost as a matter of course. A person who has contracted to sell a house or a piece of land ordinarily will be ordered to perform the agreement, for the law regards each bit of real property as unique. But beyond the real-property context, specific relief will be given only if damages would be completely inadequate. Thus, if you order a tuxedo from a tailor who fails to perform his promise to deliver it, it is unlikely that any remedy except damages will be forthcoming. The reasons for this are not purely historical. There is a burden on the court in ordering and supervising performance of a decree of specific performance that is avoided if a simple judgment for money damages is entered; moreover, specific performance might impose a hardship or at least an indignity on the tailor not commensurate with the advantage to be gained by your receiving this tailor's garment rather than one from another tailor. But it may well be asked whether our courts today are not being too reluctant to grant that form of relief that will most adequately redress plaintiff's grievance.

Compensatory relief calls for a judgment that defendant pay plaintiff a certain sum of money. But you should recognize that when we speak of compensation—of the remedy of damages—although we are speaking of one form of relief, it can be computed in accordance with many measures. In your action against the tailor, for example, if you had struck a good bargain, you might claim the difference between the price you agreed to pay and the value the tuxedo would have had if the tailor had performed the promise; or you might claim only the money you had advanced as a down payment; or you might claim the amount you paid for opera tickets you were unable to use without the tuxedo. In many contexts the difference in amount that could be collected under these theories might be substantial.

Again, there is a considerable difference in the process of measuring the damages sustained in losing 100 shares of General Motors stock, your leg, your reputation, or your peace of mind. Although it frequently is said that damages are recoverable only if they can be measured with a reasonable degree of certainty, this rule has come to require little more than a demonstration of as much certainty as the subject being measured permits. The fertile minds of lawyers and judges never cease in their quest for new immeasurables.

There is a final point to be considered in evaluating the adequacy of any judicial remedy: how much of it will be consumed by the cost of litigation? As we have noted, the costs awarded to a successful plaintiff will not, in most cases, reimburse him for the fees of his lawyer or for many other substantial costs of a suit, such as the expense of investigation or the fees of expert witnesses. It is not possible to give any meaningful figure for the cost of an average trial, but it can be assumed that as the stakes rise the fees will be correspondingly higher and indeed, some top attorneys charge upward of $300 an hour for their services.

In most personal-injury actions plaintiff's cost of recovery must be computed differently because the attorney will be litigating the case under a contingent-fee agreement; that is, the attorney will receive a percentage—one-third is common—of plaintiff's judgment. Thus, in a real sense, an adequate legal remedy is not one that simply compensates plaintiff for a loss but is one that covers both the loss and the cost of recovering it. This distinction has not been ignored by many triers of fact. Indeed, it has been suggested that damages for pain and suffering are "a make-weight to help personal-injury-plaintiffs pay attorney fees and other expenses of litigation." Morris, *Liability for Pain and Suffering,* 59 Colum.L.Rev. 476, 477 (1959).

SECTION E. ILLUSTRATIVE CASES

The cases that follow have been selected to illustrate many of the basic concepts, doctrines, and devices about which you have just read. This group of cases is designed to furnish examples of a broad spectrum of procedural problems, and it has been arranged for the most part to present these problems in the order in which they were discussed in the preceding text. Three factors have dominated the choice of the cases: First, each focuses on a specific issue that is typical of a range of problems involving a particular principle and at the same time throws some light on the policies that underlie the principle itself. Second, none of the cases is a "sitting duck"; in each instance strong reasons can be advanced for and against the court's result. Third, each case arises in a context that you can understand and presents an issue about which you should be able to form an opinion, however hesitant it may be. Another purpose of these cases is to help you develop a familiarity with procedural language and a feeling for procedural problems. You must, of course, consider the cases from the perspective of the courts that decided them, seeking to understand not only their rulings but why they were made, asking what other options were before them, and thinking through the consequences of those possibilities. But if the full pedagogical objectives of these cases are to be achieved, you also must regard each of them as a practical lawyer's problem—or rather a problem presenting difficulties and opportunities to the lawyers on the opposite sides. You must inquire why they acted as they did and what else they might have done; finally, you must ask in what position the decision has left them and what if anything they should do next.

1. THE AUTHORITY OF THE COURT TO PROCEED WITH THE ACTION

The plaintiff, having decided to sue, must determine in what court to bring the action. A court must be chosen that has jurisdiction over the subject matter of the suit and in which jurisdiction over the person of the defendant may be obtained. In the following case, the word "jurisdiction" is used without either of these modifiers. But from the context and from the information you have been given above you should be able to identify the kind of jurisdiction involved.

CAPRON v. VAN NOORDEN

Supreme Court of the United States, 1804.
6 U.S. (2 Cranch) 126, 2 L.Ed. 229.

Error to the [United States] circuit court of North Carolina. The proceedings stated Van Noorden to be late of Pitt county [North Carolina], but did not allege Capron, the plaintiff, to be an alien, nor a citizen of any state, nor the place of his residence.

Upon the general issue, in an action of trespass on the case, a verdict was found for the defendant, Van Noorden, upon which judgment was rendered.

The writ of error was sued out by Capron, the plaintiff below, who assigned for error, among other things, first, "that the circuit court aforesaid is a court of limited jurisdiction, and that by the record aforesaid it doth not appear, as it ought to have done, that either the said George Capron, or the said Hadrianus Van Noorden, was an alien at the time of the commencement of said suit, or at any other time, or that one of the said parties was at that or any other time, a citizen of the state of North Carolina where the suit was brought, and the other a citizen of another state; or that they the said George and Hadrianus were, for any cause whatever, persons within the jurisdiction of the said court, and capable of suing and being sued there." And, secondly, "that by the record aforesaid it manifestly appeareth that the said circuit court had not any jurisdiction of the cause aforesaid, nor ought to have held plea thereof or given judgment therein, but ought to have dismissed the same, whereas the said court hath proceeded to final judgment therein."

Harper, for the plaintiff in error, stated the only question to be whether the plaintiff had a right to assign for error the want of jurisdiction in that court to which he had chosen to resort. * * *

The defendant in error did not appear, but the citation having been duly served, the judgment was reversed.

Notes and Questions

1. The Supreme Court obviously regarded the defect in this case as extremely serious. Does the fact that it was the plaintiff who brought the case to the Supreme Court make this particularly clear? Why? Why is such significance attached to an error of this kind?

2. Read Article III, Section 2, of the United States Constitution, which is set out in the Supplement. What specific language in that Section is pertinent to the Supreme Court's opinion in *Capron?*

3. The Supreme Court reversed the judgment of the lower court. What was the effect of this reversal? Does it mean that Capron wins the lawsuit? If not, why had he sought review in the appellate court?

4. Those of you who have studied American government or political science may recall that one year before *Capron* was decided by the Supreme Court, the broad issue of the case had been involved in MARBURY v.

MADISON, 5 U.S. (1 Cranch) 137, 2 L.Ed. 60 (1803), the case that is the cornerstone of judicial review in the United States.

––––––––

Unlike the federal courts, which only exercise the limited subject-matter jurisdiction bestowed by the Constitution, as further restricted by acts of Congress, state courts of general jurisdiction have jurisdiction over the subject matter of a very broad spectrum of lawsuits. Indeed, questions of the competence of those courts to decide a particular kind of case rarely arise. But before any court may proceed, it also must have the power to require the appearance of the defendant. In the next case, the court must decide whether it has that power, and whether it will exercise it.

TICKLE v. BARTON

Supreme Court of Appeals of West Virginia, 1956.
142 W.Va. 188, 95 S.E.2d 427.

HAYMOND, JUDGE. The plaintiff, Richard Tickle, an infant, who sues by his next friend, instituted this action of trespass on the case in the Circuit Court of McDowell County in March, 1955, to recover damages from the defendants, Raymond Barton, a resident of Austinville, Virginia, and Lawrence Coleman, for personal injuries inflicted upon him by a motor vehicle, owned by the defendant Raymond Barton and operated by his agent the defendant Lawrence Coleman, * * * in that county which the plaintiff alleges were caused by the negligence of the defendants.

* * * [A first attempt to serve Barton had been made and the validity of this service was still undecided at the time the instant decision was rendered.]

On December 5, 1955, one of the attorneys for the plaintiff caused an alias process to be issued against the defendants * * * and delivered it to a deputy sheriff for service upon the defendant Barton in McDowell County; and in the evening of December 6, 1955, that process was served by the deputy upon the defendant Barton in person at the War Junior High School in the town of War in that county where he appeared to attend a banquet which was held there at that time.

By his amended plea in abatement No. 2, the defendant Barton challenged the validity of the service of the alias process upon him on the ground that he had been induced to come to that place in McDowell County by trickery, artifice and deceit practiced upon him by the attorney for the plaintiff.

The circuit court overruled the demurrer of the plaintiff to the amended plea in abatement and * * * certified its ruling upon the demurrer to this Court on the joint application of the plaintiff and the defendant Barton.

After reciting the prior proceedings in this case, the amended plea in abatement alleges in substance that after procuring alias process for the purpose of causing it to be served upon the defendant Barton in McDowell County, and inducing him to come to the Junior High School in the town of War in that county, an attorney representing the plaintiff in this action, in the evening of December 5, 1955, called by telephone the defendant Barton at his home in Austinville, Virginia, and wrongfully and deceitfully represented that, in behalf of the sponsors of a banquet honoring a championship high school football team to be held at the Junior High School in the town of War, * * * he extended an invitation to the defendant Barton, whose son had been a member of an earlier football team of that school, to attend the banquet; that during that telephone conversation between them the attorney, though requested to do so by the defendant Barton, did not disclose his identity except to say that he called him in behalf of the sponsors to extend the defendant Barton a special invitation to attend the banquet; that the defendant Barton before being so invited did not know that the banquet would be held and did not intend to attend it; that he did not know or suspect the identity of the attorney, or realize that the telephone call was a trick or device to entice, induce and inveigle him to come into McDowell County to be served with process in this action; that the attorney was not connected with any of the sponsors of the banquet and was not authorized by them to invite the defendant Barton to attend it; that the attorney called the defendant Barton and invited him to the banquet solely for the purpose of tricking, deceiving and inveigling him to come to the town of War in order to obtain personal service * * * upon him * * *; that the defendant Barton, believing that the invitation was extended in good faith, by a person authorized to extend it, and not suspecting the real purpose of the telephone call, accepted the invitation and informed the attorney that he would be present at the banquet and on December 6, 1955, left Austinville, Virginia, and went to the town of War with the intention of attending it; that, when he entered the high school where the banquet was held * * * he was served by the deputy sheriff with the alias process * * *; that the service of the alias process upon the defendant Barton, having been procured by trickery, deceit and subterfuge which was not realized or suspected by him, is, for that reason, null and void and of no force or effect and does not confer upon the Circuit Court of McDowell County jurisdiction of the person of the defendant Barton in this action.

The amended plea in abatement also alleges, on information and belief, that after the defendant Barton had left his home * * * the attorney for the plaintiff * * * made a telephone call to the residence of the defendant Barton, or caused some other person to make such call, and inquired of the wife of the defendant Barton if he intended to attend the banquet and was informed by her that he had left his home to attend it * * *.

The amended plea in abatement further avers that * * * the attorney for the plaintiff denied that he had made, or procured any person to make, either of the foregoing telephone calls, and denied that he had any knowledge whatsoever of either of them.

The question certified to this Court for decision is whether the allegations of the amended plea in abatement, which insofar as they are material and are well pleaded must be considered as true upon demurrer, are sufficient to render invalid the personal service of process upon the defendant Barton * * *.

* * * In 42 Am.Jur., Process, Section 35, the general principle is stated thus:

* * * "[I]f a person resident outside the jurisdiction of the court and the reach of its process is inveigled, enticed, or induced, by any false representation, deceitful contrivance, or wrongful device for which the plaintiff is responsible, to come within the jurisdiction of the court for the purpose of obtaining service of process on him in an action brought against him in such court, process served upon him through such improper means is invalid, and upon proof of such fact the court will, on motion, set it aside." * * *

The foregoing principle applies to the party when such service is procured by his agent or by someone acting for and in his behalf. * * *

In Economy Electric Company v. Automatic Electric Power and Light Plant, 185 N.C. 534, 118 S.E. 3, the court, discussing service of process by fraudulent means, used this language: "Where service of process is procured by fraud, that fact may be shown, and, if shown seasonably, the court will refuse to exercise its jurisdiction and turn the plaintiff out of court. The law will not lend its sanction or support to an act, otherwise lawful, which is accomplished by unlawful means. * * * Such a fraud is one affecting the court itself and the integrity of its process. * * * The objection, strictly, is not that the court is without jurisdiction, but that it ought not, by reason of the alleged fraud, to take or to hold jurisdiction of the action. * * *"

Under the material allegations of the amended plea in abatement which, as already indicated, must be considered as true upon demurrer, the defendant Barton was induced or enticed to come into McDowell County by the unauthorized invitation extended to him by the attorney for the plaintiff whose purpose at the time was to obtain personal service upon the defendant Barton * * *; the defendant Barton knew that the present action against him was pending in the circuit court by reason of the service of the original process upon him * * * but he did not suspect or realize that he would be served with process while present in McDowell County to attend the banquet; he was induced to come into that county by the invitation to the banquet; and he would not have come into that jurisdiction if the attorney for the plaintiff had disclosed his identity and his real purpose in extending the invitation, all of which he concealed from the defendant Barton.

* * *

The amended plea in abatement is sufficient on demurrer and the action of the circuit court in overruling the demurrer was correct.

It should perhaps be emphasized that, as the factual allegations of the amended plea in abatement have not been denied at this stage of this action by any pleading filed by the plaintiff, the question of the truth or the falsity of those allegations is not before this Court * * *.

Ruling affirmed.

GIVEN, JUDGE (dissenting).

My disagreement with the majority is not as to the rule of law laid down. I think the rule a salutary one, and masterfully stated. I do not believe, however, that the facts properly pleaded, and the inferences which may be rationally drawn therefrom, bring the facts of this case within the influence of the rule.

Stripped of all explanatory language, and of many allegations of conclusions of fact, * * * the plea in abatement charges no more than that the attorney, by telephone, inquired at defendant's home whether defendant intended to attend a certain social function to be held in McDowell County, to which defendant was then invited by the attorney; that the attorney, though requested to give his name, did not do so; that the attorney later, or someone for him, again by telephone, inquired whether defendant had decided to attend the social function, and was advised that defendant had made arrangements to attend; and that the attorney caused process to be served on defendant while attending the social function. * * * The principal, if not only, fact of wrongdoing, if wrongdoing, alleged against the attorney was his failure to inform defendant of the identity of the telephone caller. * * * It seems to me that the facts properly alleged can not be held to establish fraud or wrongdoing. At most, they would simply show that the attorney took advantage of an opportunity, the holding of the social function in McDowell County and the interest of defendant's son in the holding of the function, to try to obtain proper service of process, which was no more than a duty owed his client. In considering the questions arising, it should be kept in mind that defendant had full knowledge of the institution of the action against him in McDowell County, of the fact that he had questioned the validity of the service of other process issued in that action, and of the fact that the alleged cause of action arose in McDowell County, where ordinarily it would have been triable.

* * *

Notes and Questions

1. Did the court in this case decide that West Virginia courts did not have jurisdiction over the person of the defendant (assuming his story were true), or that those courts should not exercise jurisdiction in these circumstances even though they had it?

2. When should a court be able to demand that a person appear before it and defend an action? In what circumstances should this demand be permitted against a nonresident? Why should a nonresident be subject to suit if he is served with process within the state? Insofar as these reasons are concerned, should it make any difference why he is present in the state?

3. In thinking about the cases you read, you should consider how the court might approach the problem presented by a particular case with certain facts changed. For example, should service in West Virginia in the following situations be treated in the same way as it was under the facts alleged in the principal case? (a) Tickle had asked Barton to appear as a witness in a suit

against a third party involved in the accident; (b) Tickle had asked Barton to come to West Virginia to discuss settling the case; (c) Tickle had telephoned Barton and falsely told him that his son lay critically injured in a West Virginia hospital; (d) Tickle (like the Sheriff of Nottingham) had scheduled a football banquet in West Virginia that he knew Barton (like Robin Hood) would be unable to resist attending, although he did not personally invite him.

4. When the case is reconsidered by the West Virginia Circuit Court on remand, Barton's lawyer must prove his allegations if Barton is to avoid trial in West Virginia. What problems do you foresee in his being able to prove them, and how should he proceed to do so?

5. You will later become familiar with state statutes that confer upon their courts power to summon out-of-state motorists to defend actions arising out of their operating automobiles within the state. Tickle had first sought to serve Barton under a statute of this type, but because the accident had occurred on private property rather than a West Virginia public highway, a serious question as to the statute's application existed; this uncertainty prompted the second attempt at service discussed in the case.

2. DEFINING AND DETERMINING THE CASE BEFORE TRIAL

At this point, you should re-read the part of the Outline of a Civil Action that deals with pleading, especially the portion that discusses the "three general situations" in which a motion to dismiss for failure to state a claim might be granted. Is the court in the following case saying that the plaintiff has not properly pleaded its case or that it has no case at all?

CASE v. STATE FARM MUTUAL AUTOMOBILE INSURANCE CO.

United States Court of Appeals, Fifth Circuit, 1961.
294 F.2d 676.

CAMERON, CIRCUIT JUDGE. Appellant Case filed this action against the three insurance companies named as appellees for damages growing out of the termination of his representation of the three Companies as local agent. He charged in his complaint that he was appointed agent by a written contract attached as an exhibit to his complaint, which he charged, and the parties agree, constituted him an independent contractor for all purposes and provided that he was not required to "devote all of his working time to any one of the Companies;" that he represented the three Companies "through the years 1954, 1955, 1956, 1957 and 1958, and up until March 28, 1959," on which date the appellees "began to and did meddle and interfere with the plaintiff's work as agent of [the three Companies] in disregard of the agreement between the defendants and the plaintiff." [1]

1. The meddling and interference upon which appellant lays so much stress before us is stated in the complaint in these words:

"That on or about March 1, 1959, that he, the Plaintiff, publicly announced his candidacy for the office of Supervisor of District Five (5) of Adams County, Missis-

sippi, and Plaintiff shows further that on or about March 28, 1959, the Defendants, * * * began to and did meddle and interfere with the Plaintiff's work as agent of the State Farm Insurance Companies in disregard of the agreement between the Defendants and the Plaintiff. The Plain-

Properly construed in connection with the remaining allegations of the complaint,[2] appellant stated nothing in his pleading except an action based upon what he conceived to be the malicious and wrongful cancellation of the written contract between him and appellees, and on that alone. So construed, every word in the complaint related to the alleged wrongful termination of the written contract between the parties. That writing gave either party the right to terminate it with or without cause, and the charges in the complaint relating to meddling and interference make sense only when construed in the light of the allegations that the appellees expressed the purpose not to continue the contractual relationship with appellant unless he would agree to abjure the seeking and holding of the public office of county supervisor. Their efforts to induce him to follow the course which alone would permit the continuation of that contractual relationship related manifestly to the termination which finally took place. The contract gave the appellees the right to cancellation "with or without cause," and in terminating it the appellees acted entirely within their rights.

Appellant argues the case as if it were one in tort for interference with his civil rights. The allegations of the pleadings do not support such an argument. * * *

It is clear also that the complaint does not set forth an independent claim for damages based upon meddling and interference by appellees with appellant's performance of the contract. Appellant invokes the oft repeated statement of the courts that a complaint should not be dismissed

tiff was informed orally and by letter by representatives of his principals that his agency would have to be handled in a particular manner and he was directed as to when, how and why his work should be done in a certain manner and was orally informed as well as by letter that he would have to submit his decision as to whether he would be a candidate for the office of supervisor or have his contract or appointment with State Farm Insurance Companies terminated as of May 1, 1959, all of which was done wrongfully in malicious and wanton disregard of the Plaintiff's rights according to his appointment as agent of the Defendants, State Farm Insurance Companies, with the intention of coercing the Plaintiff into withdrawing from the political race and devoting his full time as an employee in the master and servant relationship to the performance of his service for said Defendants.

* * *

"Plaintiff charges and avers that the malicious intentional and wrongful direction as to his activities as agent of the Defendants was such a breach and repudiation of his contract or agreement with him as set out in Exhibit I as to entitle him, the Plaintiff to damages for the loss due to the breach or repudiation of the said agreement listed as Exhibit I."

2. E.g., immediately following the language quoted in Footnote 1, supra, the complaint charges the following:

"Plaintiff further shows unto the Court that at the time of the said repudiation or breach of contract by the Defendants, that the Plaintiff's income from the Defendants for the previous year was nine thousand seventy-three ($9,073.00) dollars and that the Plaintiff's life expectancy at his present age of 45 was 25.21 years according to the C.S.O. Mortality table, and that but for the wrongful breach, repudiation and termination of the Plaintiff's contract of agency with the Defendants, the Plaintiff would have been entitled to continued remuneration from the Defendants for the sum of two hundred twenty-six thousand, seven hundred twenty-five ($226,725.00) dollars and that but for the malicious, wanton meddling and interfering and wrongful breach, repudiation and cancellation of the Plaintiff's contract the Plaintiff is entitled to punitive damages in the sum of two hundred thousand ($200,000) dollars."

The judgment demanded against the three defendants, appellees, was the sum of the two figures mentioned above.

if it charges facts upon which a court could possibly grant relief. * * * What the courts have said does not mean that it is the duty of the trial court or the appellate court to create a claim which appellant has not spelled out in his pleading.

The court below was faced with a complaint and a motion to dismiss. Its duty was to judge the complaint by the language used in it. The only damages claimed by the appellant were those based entirely upon his claim that the written contract was wrongfully terminated, and the language concerning the meddling and interference is reasonably construed as referring to appellees' indication to appellant that he would have to give up his quest of public office if he desired to retain his contractual relationship with appellees. We are called upon here merely to test whether the court below erred in interpreting the meaning of language which was, viewed as a whole, clear and unambiguous. We do not think that it did.

If appellant had desired to pursue a charge that appellees had wrongfully interfered with the running of his business in violation of the terms of the written contract, it would have been quite simple for him to file an amended complaint. Doubtless the court below would have permitted this even after the order of dismissal had been granted. But aside from that, appellant had an absolute right to amend his complaint once, no responsive pleading having been filed. * * *

It is apparent that the complaint charged that appellees did nothing more than to exercise the right of termination given them by the explicit terms of the contract exhibited with appellant's complaint. * * * This being true, and since appellant claims no damages whatever except such as would flow from the wrongful termination of the contract, we think the court below correctly granted the motion to dismiss. Its judgment is

Affirmed.

Notes and Questions

1. Which of the three objectives of pleading discussed in the Outline of a Civil Action, in connection with the content of a complaint, was most significantly involved in this case?

2. Suppose a valid legal theory did exist that would have entitled Case to some relief, but that Case neglected to invoke it in his pleading. Would the court have been justified in dismissing the complaint on the principle that "it is [not] the duty of the trial court or the appellate court to create a claim which appellant has not spelled out in his pleading"? Wouldn't that simply punish Case for his lawyer's sloppy pleading?

3. In ROSEN v. TEXAS CO., 161 F.Supp. 55 (S.D.N.Y.1958), on a motion to dismiss under Federal Rule of Civil Procedure 12(b)(6), Judge Dimock said:

Under a system of procedure where the function of pleading was to reach and define the issues or to develop the facts a glance would suffice to demonstrate the insufficiency of the complaint. * * *

Even after a score of years of experience it is still doubtful just how much a complaint must state to avoid dismissal. * * * The principle is now expressed by many courts by the statement that a complaint will not be dismissed for failure to state a claim on which relief can be granted "unless it appears to a certainty that plaintiff is entitled to no relief under any state of facts which could be proved in support of the claim."

* * *

This would seem to mean that all a plaintiff need state is what he wants from the court, but the Advisory Committee on the Rules seems to cling to the words of Rule 8(a) that the pleader must show that he is entitled to relief. In the Advisory Committee's Report * * * the Committee stated its opinion that Rule 8(a) "requires the pleader to disclose adequate information as to the basis of his claim for relief as distinguished from a bare averment that he wants relief and is entitled to it".

* * *

These motions have, all to no purpose, consumed a large amount of time of counsel for defendant in making them, of counsel for plaintiff in opposing them and of the court in considering and determining them and the progress of the litigation has been correspondingly delayed. It is my personal belief that the profession would do well to accept the fact that little can be accomplished by motions on the pleadings. The very uncertainty as to what constitutes a statement of a "claim upon which relief can be granted" demonstrates the unimportance of the question. We all should realize that the place of pleadings and motions thereon has been taken by interrogatories, depositions and discovery.

4. In deciding the motion to dismiss in *Case,* should any significance have been given to the availability of discovery procedures to the parties? Of what relevance is the availability or nonavailability of other pretrial motions, such as summary judgment, that also might terminate the litigation before trial?

5. What was the effect of the dismissal in *Case?* Should the plaintiff have been permitted to amend the complaint and start again? Could the plaintiff interpose a new and slightly altered complaint that would survive another motion to dismiss?

6. Suppose that after the motion to dismiss had been granted Case discovered a letter agreement dated after the contract and signed by all of the parties stipulating that the insurance agency agreement could be terminated only for "good cause." Should he be able to amend his complaint and sue again in federal court? In state court?

Disputes often involve more than two people. The following case explores the question whether all those who are interested in a controversy must be made parties to a lawsuit. If the answer is no, should they at least have the option of voluntarily entering it?

NEW ENGLAND PATRIOTS FOOTBALL CLUB, INC. v. UNIVERSITY OF COLORADO

United States Court of Appeals, First Circuit, 1979.
592 F.2d 1196.

ALDRICH, SENIOR CIRCUIT JUDGE. In 1973 one Charles L. Fairbanks contracted with plaintiff New England Patriots Football Club, a professional football organization and member of the National Football League, to act as its manager and head coach. By later agreement the employment was to continue until January, 1983. The contract contained a provision that Fairbanks was not to provide services connected with football to any entity other than plaintiff, or to perform services of any kind for anyone, without plaintiff's permission, during the period of employment. In November, 1978 Fairbanks was approached by various persons, defendants herein, some of whom were officially, and some sentimentally, attached to the University of Colorado. Defendants' objective was to persuade Fairbanks to quit the Patriots and become head football coach at the University. Their successful initiation of this endeavor, at first behind the Patriots' back, and, later, over its vigorous opposition, resulted in the present action where, following a hearing, the district court entered a preliminary injunction enjoining defendant regents, defendant president, defendant athletic director, and defendant Vickers, a Colorado football fan and angel, from causing the University to employ Fairbanks as the University's coach. Fairbanks is not a party to the suit, and has not been enjoined.

Defendants appeal. In connection with the appeal, they moved for a stay pending resolution. This we denied. At the same time, in response to the representation by counsel for defendants that time was of the essence because of the nature of the employment, we agreed to expedite the hearing. We also acceded to Fairbanks' request, tendered through counsel for defendants, to file an amicus brief.

Although this is not our first experience with the athletic mileau's response to legal embroilment engendered by contract jumping, we set out the factual contentions in some detail in order to get in the mood. For this opportunity we are primarily indebted to the Fairbanks amicus brief.[3]

The extension of the contract to January 26, 1983 was agreed to on June 6, 1977. The briefs are silent as to this date, an understandable reticence in view of the fact that by that time Fairbanks had, apparently, already decided he might not keep his word.

> For a number of years, Fairbanks was extremely unhappy with remaining in professional football * * * Fairbanks believed the health of his family, and a reassessment of career objectives, *mandated a change.* Accordingly, for a number of years, he had been investigating business opportunities outside football, * * * (Amicus br. 8) (Emphasis suppl.)

---

3. In granting permission we had assumed, wrongly, it proved, that counsel knew what an amicus is, namely, one who, * * * for the assistance of the court gives information of some matter of law in regard to which the court is doubtful or mistaken, * * * rather than one who gives a highly partisan, ("eloquent," according to defendants) account of the facts.

[Since these] changes [were] * * * unconnected with professional football, [Fairbanks believed they] "should present no problem." (Amicus br. 6–7) This justification for nonperformance so satisfied Fairbanks that it was followed by a footnote expressing indignation at the court's refusal to recognize it.

Nor was this the only mantle of protection. Because in 1973 the Patriots allegedly had lured Fairbanks from the University of Oklahoma, inducing him to break his contract there, defendants conclude that the Patriots are barred from relief by the doctrine of unclean hands. We disagree. Both parties may have done the University of Oklahoma dirt, but that does not mean unclean hands with respect to "the controversy in issue." * * * The precedential effect of a court's extending this doctrine to [this case] * * * staggers the imagination.

* * *

Money does create some problems, however, quite apart from inducing Fairbanks to sign for an engagement that he had little intention of keeping. If ascertainable money damages could fully compensate the Patriots, under familiar principles there would be no basis for injunctive relief. The district court, however, found that ascertainment would be difficult. It further found that Fairbanks' services were unique, and that, accordingly, the loss of his services would occasion the Patriots irreparable harm.

Fairbanks was insufficiently modest to dispute this last. However, the cause was taken up by the defendants. They dispute both findings, offering reasons which, to put the matter in its kindest light, we may be too unsophisticated to understand. Then, in a turnabout for which, perhaps apprehending our shortcomings, no reasons are even offered, defendants state,

> In contrast, the continuation of the preliminary injunction which prevents Fairbanks from signing with Colorado does irreparably harm the University. (Defendants' br. 40)

While we are attempting to reconcile these conclusions, there comes the final drive.

> Fairbanks' departure may have no effect or, even possibly a beneficial effect, on the Patriots' performance and attendance in the future. (Defendants' br. 42).

The injunction is an ungracious, even an ungrateful, act.

Somehow it seems as if there were an extra man on the field.

Whatever may be thought rules elsewhere, the legal rules are clear. A contract is not avoided by crossed fingers behind one's back on signing, nor by unsupported, and at once inconsistently self-deprecating and self-serving protests that the breach was to the other party's benefit. Equally, we are not taken by Fairbanks' claim that because, when he told Sullivan that he was leaving at the end of the season and Sullivan responded that he was "suspended," it was Sullivan who broke the contract.

The simple fact is that Fairbanks was fired. (Amicus br. 11)

Whatever may be thought the meaning in the trade of suspension, as distinguished from its commonly understood meaning, it is a novel concept that a contract-breaker had the option to require the other party to accept his choice of dates. At least until Fairbanks withdrew his unlawful announcement, the Patriots had a right not to accept the services of an unfaithful servant, or, as Sullivan put it to him at the time, one who had "his body in Foxboro [d] and his heart in Colorado." [7]

In this circumstance defendants are * * * [left to argue] that the court lacks jurisdiction because Fairbanks, who was not joined, is an indispensable party * * *.

[The] * * * principle that we need not finally resolve all possibly debatable questions of law is fully sufficient to dispose of defendants' claim that Fairbanks is an indispensable party, F.R.Civ.P. 19(a) and (b). The standard steps which here lead us to the ultimate question of fairness [with regard to who must be joined] are too familiar to require repeating. What is fair is, basically, a subjective question. Some courts in inducing-breach-of-contract cases have regarded the question as too insubstantial to require comment, and have allowed the case to proceed without the other contracting party in silence. * * * Indeed, defendants cite no persuasive authority the other way. It is to be borne in mind that any issue of fairness is only fairness to Fairbanks; defendants can suggest no unfairness to themselves resulting from his absence. They do say that it would be unfair to Fairbanks if, due to possibly divergent interests, they omitted points he might have made. Having been exposed, through his amicus brief, to the points that Fairbanks might personally make here, it might be difficult to be moved by this contention even if, in the abstract, it were a valid one. More important, on the single issue in this case, we perceive no different interests. On the broader questions, general rights of Fairbanks and the Patriots under the contract, the decision will have no effect because Fairbanks is not a party, and for the further reason that it could not seemingly affect them even if he were.

It is a conceded fact that in a pending judicial proceeding brought by Fairbanks in the state of Colorado in which the Patriots is a defendant, Fairbanks has been ordered to respect the contract provision and arbitrate his dispute before the Commissioner of the National Football League. This seems a complete answer to defendants' claim that by plaintiff's failure to join Fairbanks as a party, plaintiff is engaging in "piecemeal litigation." Rather, plaintiff appears to have no justiciable claim against him in a court of law. We reject the claim that Fairbanks is an indispensable party.

* * *

Affirmed.

d. The town in Massachusetts where the Patriots play.

7. The district court's finding that a valid contract existed between Fairbanks and the Patriots and that Sullivan's suspension of Fairbanks was not a breach are not clearly erroneous and, at this stage, must be accepted. Of course, Fairbanks, not a party to the suit, is not bound by these, or any other findings.

Notes and Questions

1. Why do you think Fairbanks was not named as a party by the Patriots originally? Would it have been improper to do so? What would have been the claims against Fairbanks? What relief could the Patriots have sought?

2. Read Rule 19. Why doesn't Fairbanks fit within the persons who should be joined under that rule? Wasn't the validity of Fairbanks's contract with the Patriots an issue in which Fairbanks had an interest? Suppose that Fairbanks is a citizen of Massachusetts and that the Patriots are a Massachusetts corporation. Can you now give a reason why Fairbanks was not joined under Rule 19(a)?

3. Examine footnote 7 of the opinion. Why shouldn't the finding of a valid contract be binding on Fairbanks? Suppose that, in a subsequent litigation between the Patriots and Fairbanks, the suspension of Fairbanks by the Patriots is found to constitute a breach of contract. Could the University of Colorado seek Fairbanks's services at that time? Or, is it prevented from doing so by the injunction?

The purposes of discovery are many. The most important are the obtaining of evidence for one's own case and the ferreting out of weaknesses in the opponent's. Usually the party seeking discovery is asking about something of which he is ignorant or uncertain, but sometimes he seeks information about a matter within his own knowledge. In reading the next case, you should ask why the plaintiff is so determined to obtain the answers and why the defendant is equally determined that she shall not have them.

BOLDT v. SANDERS

Supreme Court of Minnesota, 1961.
261 Minn. 160, 111 N.W.2d 225.

OTIS, JUSTICE. This matter comes before the court on the petition of defendant * * * for a writ of prohibition to enjoin the trial court from enforcing its order requiring defendant to answer certain of plaintiffs' interrogatories. The action here involved is one for damages arising out of personal injuries which plaintiffs allege Ella Boldt experienced as a passenger in a car which collided with one driven by defendant * * *. In their complaint plaintiffs allege that the injuries Mrs. Boldt received are permanent and disabling. Defendant admits the accident but denies plaintiffs have been injured or damaged as alleged in their complaint.

On April 1, 1960, the deposition of Mrs. Boldt was taken by defendant. She then testified that she had never had any previous automobile accident, accidental fall, or any other kind of accident, and that she had suffered no previous injuries. On November 25, 1960, plaintiffs submitted to defendant under Rules 26.02 and 33 * * *[e] the following interrogatories, among others:

> 4. Do you have information indicating that the plaintiff Ella Boldt was injured at any time prior to the accident described in Plaintiffs' Complaint?

> 5. If your answer to No. 4 is "Yes," then give the following information relative to each accident:

> a. Give the date upon which the injury occurred;

> b. Identify the place where the injury occurred;

> c. Give the name and address of each person known to you having information relative to the accident or circumstances causing the injury;

> d. Give the name and address of each physician or other person who rendered treatment to the plaintiff Ella Boldt in connection with the injury.

In response defendant stated:

> 4. We decline to answer this question on the ground that it is not pertinent to the issues in the above litigation, is known to the plaintiff, if any other accidents occurred and would serve in the event of a trial of this action only for impeachment.

> 5. See answer to No. 4.

Thereupon, the motion of plaintiffs to compel defendant to answer these interrogatories * * * was granted * * * following which our alternative writ of prohibition was issued.

Defendant earnestly contends that the information plaintiffs seek to elicit is exempt from discovery because it is known to plaintiffs and its use is contemplated only for impeachment purposes. Defendant cites in support of his position Bogatay v. Montour R. Co., D.C.W.D.Pa., 177 F.Supp. 269, where the trial court held that the defendant railroad was not required to disclose any evidence it had marshalled concerning the physical activities of plaintiff subsequent to the date of the accident. The court stated that the observations of witnesses and the existence of movies or pictures constituted potential impeaching evidence, the disclosure of which would subvert the spirit of a local rule protecting such evidence from discovery. The court further observed that the evidence could be revealed to the court at pretrial so that the judge might determine whether it was of a substantive nature or merely impeachment. * * *

In * * * [*Discovery and Pre-trial Procedure in Federal Courts*, 12 Okla.L.Rev. 321, 324 (1959)], Judge Stephen S. Chandler * * * had this to say about divulging impeachment material:

> * * * "In his court, the writer requires that all signed statements taken from witnesses, moving pictures to show malingering, in fact all evidence, including that intended for purposes of possible impeachment or rebuttal, be furnished to opposing counsel. This is a cardinal requirement for the reason that if any instrument or fact remains undisclosed,

---

e. So far as pertinent, these rules were the same as Federal Rules of Civil Procedure 26(b) and 33 before 1970. Their substance now appears in Federal Rules 26(b)(1) and 33(a) and (b).

the lawyer concealing it feels he has an advantage. While such a situation exists, the whole picture presented by the lawsuit is distorted and obscured because the true situation is not apparent to all."

* * * Defendant's entire argument proceeds on the premise that defendant's evidence which plaintiffs seek to elicit constitutes the unblemished truth which, if prematurely disclosed, will prevent defendant from revealing to the jury the sham and perjury inherent in plaintiffs' claims. While defendant disclaims such assumption, it is implicit in his position that witnesses whose testimony is designed to impeach invariably have a monopoly on virtue and that evidence to which the attempted impeachment is directed is, without exception, fraudulent.

Let us assume hypothetically that a claimant has sustained injuries for which he seeks to recover damages and that he has been in no previous accident and has suffered no prior disability or illness and has been incapacitated solely as a result of the accident in question. The hypothetical defendant, on the other hand, has resorted to fraud and perjury in fabricating pictures of what purport to be plaintiff's physical activities subsequent to the accident, and has manufactured evidence to prove that plaintiff sustained his injuries in prior accidents. It is the defendant's position that under the assumed circumstances plaintiff is foreclosed from discovering the perjured testimony which is about to be foisted upon him because it is essentially impeachment. In other words, the defendant would have us adopt a rule that no opportunity may be afforded either party to impeach evidence which is itself impeachment, but both must await the uncertain fate which befalls litigants when confronted for the first time in the courtroom with surprise testimony for which they are wholly unprepared.

For us to revert to this philosophy would be judicial retrogression undermining the whole purpose of the rules of civil procedure. It would inevitably lead us back to the "poker hand" concept of litigation, rewarding artifice and camouflage. We do not believe the rights of the parties should be determined in such a murky atmosphere. It is essential to the achievement of justice that all of the admissible evidence be brought to light in time for both parties to evaluate it and adequately prepare for trial or settlement with full knowledge of the facts.

Not only may impeaching testimony be the subject of impeachment itself, but in this case the information which plaintiff seeks bears on the fundamental issue of the nature and extent of the injuries which Mrs. Boldt sustained in this accident. She is entitled to know what evidence defendant will produce on this issue in view of his denial that her condition is serious or is attributable to this accident.

* * *

We therefore hold that no evidence which will be admissible at the trial is exempt from discovery under Rules 26.02 and 33 unless the affected party invokes a valid privilege. We do not decide, however, whether such party may thereafter waive his privilege at the trial and introduce such testimony, nor do we suggest that pretrial discovery is limited to what is admissible in evidence.

*   *   *

The writ of prohibition is therefore discharged.

Notes and Questions

1.   *   *   * [T]he common law *   *   * *recognized no rule requiring prior notice* of intended evidence to be given to the opponent or furnishing legal process for obtaining such information *   *   *.

It might be supposed that, in the court of Chancery, a bill for discovery served as a means of evading the strict common-law rule, and that thereby a notice could be compulsorily obtained of the evidence intended to be produced by the opponent. But there was here no radical departure from the established doctrine of the common law; it was a policy, not of one Court rather than another Court, but of the whole legal system *   *   * [of England].

*   *   * It is true that, to a limited extent *   *   * the result of a bill of discovery would usually be the revelation of some portion of information not before known to the applicant. But the general theory remained, and the rule was strictly enforced, that the adversary's own evidence was not to be revealed on a bill for discovery.

In short, equitable discovery involved no more than the negation of the party's privilege at common-law trials not to testify *against* his own cause, and was not intended to give relief against the common-law principle which refused to exact before trial a disclosure of the tenor of the evidence intended to be given *for* his cause.

6 Wigmore, *Evidence* §§ 1845, 1846, at 378, 380 (3d ed. 1940).

2. Why did plaintiff in *Boldt* use Rule 33 interrogatories rather than Rule 30 depositions?

3. What is a writ of prohibition? Why was it used in the circumstances of this case? Reread pp. 15–17, supra.

4. The issue raised by the principal case is discussed in Note, *Pre-Trial Discovery of Impeachment Evidence: A Need to Reexamine Arizona's New Rule,* 7 Ariz.L.Rev. 283 (1966), in which it is suggested that in the case of evidence as to matters within the knowledge of the inquiring party, the party interrogated be allowed to determine whether he will use the evidence for impeachment purposes only, in which event it will not be subject to discovery. Would this be a good rule?

In ruling on a motion to dismiss for failure to state a claim as in Case v. State Farm Mutual Automobile Ins. Co., p. 27, supra, the judge must accept as true the allegations in the complaint. If the defendant files an answer denying those allegations, the denials are only assertions of the defendant and do not demonstrate whose story is correct. The motion for summary judgment enables a party to show that there is admissible evidence to support his allegations and to call for a similar showing by the opposing party. The judge will not try to decide a factual dispute when each party has shown that he has evidence on an issue. But if it becomes clear that one party cannot begin to prove his allegations, there is no "genuine issue" and a futile trial may be avoided by granting the motion.

ALDERMAN v. BALTIMORE & OHIO R. CO.

United States District Court, Southern District of West Virginia, 1953.
113 F.Supp. 881.

MOORE, CHIEF JUDGE. Plaintiff * * * brings this action against defendant, * * * to recover for personal injuries sustained by her as a result of the derailment of one of defendant's trains near Adrian, West Virginia, on February 14, 1952.

Plaintiff was not a fare-paying passenger. She was traveling on a trip pass, which afforded her free transportation * * *. The following conditions were printed on the pass: "In consideration of the issuance of this free pass, I hereby assume all risk of personal injury and loss of or of damage to property from whatever causes arising, and release the company from liability therefor, and I hereby declare that I am not prohibited by law from receiving free transportation and that this pass will be lawfully used."

Plaintiff in her original complaint charged defendant with negligence in the maintenance of its tracks and the operation of its train. After a pre-trial conference, at which the legal effect of the release from liability contained in the pass was discussed, plaintiff filed an amended complaint charging defendant with wilful or wanton conduct.

On the basis of the amended pleadings and supporting affidavits filed by defendant, defendant moved for summary judgment under Rule 56 * * *.

It is undisputed that the derailment was caused by a break in one of the rails as the train was passing over the track. It is also shown by defendant's affidavits, and not denied, that the break in the rail was due to a transverse fissure inside the cap of the rail, which broke vertically under the weight of the train; that such a fissure is not visible upon inspection; that such defects occur in both new and old rails; and that a visual inspection was in fact made of this particular rail the day preceding the accident and the defect was not discovered.

Since plaintiff was an intrastate passenger, and since the accident occurred in West Virginia, the law of West Virginia governs both the effect to be given to the release and the degree of care which defendant owed plaintiff. * * *

However, counsel have been unable to direct the Court's attention to, and the Court has not found, any West Virginia decision which has determined the effect which a release from liability contained in a pass has upon the carrier's duty to the holder of such a pass. * * *

Since the Federal statute and the West Virginia statute authorizing the issuance of free passes are similar, 49 U.S.C.A. § 1(7), and W.Va.Code, Ch. 24, Art. 3, § 4, it is pertinent to examine the United States Supreme Court decisions construing the Federal statute. The Supreme Court has held that a carrier may contract against liability for negligent injury to one who accepts a free pass * * *; but that for reasons of public policy it cannot relieve itself of liability for wilful or wanton acts. * * *

I am therefore of opinion that the sole duty imposed upon defendant under the facts of this case was to refrain from wilfully or wantonly injuring plaintiff.

In Kelly v. Checker White Cab, Inc., 131 W.Va. 816 at page 822; 50 S.E.2d 888 at page 892, the West Virginia court, quoting from 29 Cyc. 510 said:

> In order that one may be held guilty of wilful or wanton conduct, it must be shown that he was conscious of his conduct, and conscious, from his knowledge of existing conditions, that injury would likely or probably result from his conduct, and that with reckless indifference to consequences he consciously and intentionally did some wrongful act or omitted some known duty which produced the injurious result. * * *

The substance of plaintiff's contention that defendant wilfully injured her is that defendant used old and obsolescent rails in its tracks, knowing that the use of these rails made derailments reasonably probable. It is charged that defendant used old rails because the cost of derailments was less than the cost of replacing the old rails, and that for this reason defendant was willing to take the risk of derailments.

I am of opinion that the complaint fails to state sufficient facts to substantiate a charge of wilfulness, as that term is defined by the West Virginia court. It is clear that plaintiff has stated a charge of negligence; but that is not the test in this case. To establish wilfulness it would be necessary to charge that defendant knew of this particular defect in the rail; that the defect would probably result in a break in the rail if the train were run over it, causing a derailment of the train; and that defendant, with this knowledge of existing conditions, and the likelihood or probability of an injury resulting from its conduct, intentionally drove its train over the defective rail with an indifference to the consequences. The undenied affidavits of defendant show clearly that plaintiff cannot establish these facts.

At the hearing of this motion, counsel for plaintiff moved for a continuance of the hearing to enable him to substantiate a newspaper report to the effect that defendant was using old and obsolescent rails in its tracks because the cost of derailments was cheaper than the cost of replacing the rails. The motion was denied since this contention, even if it were true, merely has a bearing on an issue of negligence, and not upon the question of wilful conduct. Plaintiff does not contend that she can establish that defendant knew of the particular defect in the rail that caused the derailment.

For the reasons stated above, defendant's motion for summary judgment will be sustained. * * *

Notes and Questions

1. If very specific allegations of all of the facts giving rise to the plaintiff's cause of action were required to be set forth in the complaint, would

it have been possible to handle the *Alderman* case by a motion to dismiss or a demurrer? To the extent that this would have been possible, does the case present a strong argument for more specific pleading of facts? In this connection, consider whether the court should have ruled as it did if the motion for summary judgment had been made immediately upon the service of the complaint and before plaintiff had an opportunity to utilize the discovery process. What provision does Federal Rule of Civil Procedure 56 make for this contingency? Analytically, the motion for summary judgment can be thought of as a demurrer-plus. You should not forget, however, that if summary judgment is to be a fair and effective device, it must frequently be preceded by discovery, so that each party will have an opportunity to disclose the gaps in her opponent's case and to cure any defects in her own.

2. What advantage did the defendant gain in *Alderman* by moving for summary judgment, rather than moving to dismiss? Reread the third paragraph of the case. Should a plaintiff be able to amend a complaint in this situation? Was her amendment made merely to prolong litigation in the hope of forcing a settlement?

3. Should a court always grant a motion for summary judgment if the requirements of Rule 56 are met? In KENNEDY v. SILAS MASON CO., 334 U.S. 249, 256–57, 68 S.Ct. 1031, 1034, 92 L.Ed. 1347, 1350–51 (1948), Justice Jackson, speaking for the Court, said:

> * * * [S]ummary procedures, however salutary where issues are clear-cut and simple, present a treacherous record for deciding issues of far-flung import, on which this Court should draw inferences with caution from complicated courses of legislation, contracting and practice.

> We consider it the part of good judicial administration to withhold decision of the ultimate questions involved in this case until this or another record shall present a more solid basis of findings based on litigation or on a comprehensive statement of agreed facts. While we might be able, on the present record, to reach a conclusion that would decide the case, it might well be found later to be lacking in the thoroughness that should precede judgment of this importance and which it is the purpose of the judicial process to provide.

4. A motion for summary judgment may be useful even though the moving party believes it will be unsuccessful. For what reasons, other than a hope of obtaining judgment, might a defendant in a case like *Alderman* make such a motion?

3. JUDGE AND JURY

You probably will be surprised (and perhaps dismayed) by the comparatively small part of a Civil Procedure course devoted to the actual process of trial. It is true that the trial, if one occurs, is the most important and most interesting stage of a lawsuit. But most of the "law" about trials is the subject-matter of the course in Evidence. The most important aspect of trial with which this course is concerned is the division of functions between judge and jury and the various ways in which the judge acts to insure that the jury performs its proper function. In this section, we look at four of those ways: the instruction of the jury as to the law it shall apply, the form that the verdict takes, judicial control over the matters the jury may consider, and the taking from the jury of its power to decide a case when the evidence is inadequate.

a. Instructing the Jury

Broadly stated, it is a function of the judge to decide questions of law and a function of the jury to decide questions of fact. But in most cases the jury's final decision will be that one or the other party is entitled to judgment and the jury must apply the law to the facts to reach this decision. Therefore the jury must be told what the law is. The vehicle for this is the judge's charge to the jury, which comes at the end of the trial, immediately before the jury retires to consider its verdict.

An important issue concerning these instructions is how far the adversary system should extend to this stage of the lawsuit. Counsel for both parties may request that particular instructions be given to the jury, and when there is a dispute between them as to the law, they ordinarily will submit conflicting requests. The judge must resolve such conflicts, and it is the court's duty in any event to instruct the jury whether or not the parties make specific requests. The judge, even though an expert on the law, may err. To what extent is it the responsibility of counsel to attempt to correct the trial judge? The next case involves not only this question, but it also introduces you to the question of allocating the burden of proof (or burden of persuasion). Why is there any rule that says one party or the other has this burden?

ALEXANDER v. KRAMER BROS. FREIGHT LINES, INC.

United States Court of Appeals, Second Circuit, 1959.
273 F.2d 373.

SWAN, CIRCUIT JUDGE. The present action is a sequel to a collision between two tractor-trailer trucks on the Pennsylvania Turnpike in or near Somerset, Pennsylvania. It occurred * * * about six o'clock in the morning, when there was spotty fog on the Turnpike. The corporate plaintiff owned one of the trucks. It was badly damaged and its operator, the plaintiff Alexander, sustained serious injuries. The other truck was owned by the defendant corporation. Its answer to the complaint denied any negligence on its part and set up the defense of contributory negligence on the part of the plaintiffs. The jury found a verdict for the plaintiffs. * * *

Because of the character of the questions raised, a very brief statement concerning the testimony will suffice. The only eye witnesses to the accident were drivers of the two trucks. The drivers' stories were contradictory and raised issues as to the exact location of the accident and the manner in which it occurred. Both trucks were proceeding westerly. Alexander testified that the collision occurred where there was an entrance to the Turnpike from the right, that defendant's truck cut in ahead of him, and that the fog was such that he could not see the entering truck in time to avoid hitting it. Holman, defendant's driver, denied that he entered from the right and claimed that plaintiff's truck had been following for some time before it ran into the rear end of his truck. Thus the issues of negligence and contributory negligence raised questions of credibility for the jury.

The first question for consideration is whether the judgment should be reversed because of the court's erroneous charge as to the burden of proof of contributory negligence, despite defendant's failure to request a charge on that subject or to object or take exception to the charge given, as required by Rule 51 ＊ ＊ ＊. Appellant contends that he is excused from complying with the Rule by what occurred in colloquy with the court near the close of the plaintiffs' case. In the colloquy, the court stated that "the burden of proof of contributory negligence is on the defendant." Counsel for plaintiffs expressed agreement with the statement, and counsel for defendant said, "I take an exception," to which the court replied, "Yes, I give you that exception." The plaintiff then rested, and defendant proceeded to put in its case.

＊ ＊ ＊ Under the [applicable law] the plaintiffs in an action where death has not resulted ＊ ＊ ＊ carry the burden of proving freedom from contributory negligence. The cases now relied upon by appellant to prove the charge wrong were never brought to the trial court's attention either in the colloquy or at the time when counsel submitted numerous requests to charge on other matters. Had they been, it seems probable that Judge Inch would have changed the view he expressed in colloquy. The obvious purpose of the requirement in Rule 51 that objection must be made to matters in the charge in order to assign them as error, is to permit the trial judge to evaluate the objection and correct his charge if further thought persuades him of its error. This purpose is not fulfilled by taking an exception to a statement made by the judge several days prior to the time for charging the jury when nothing was before the judge requiring a ruling in respect to the statement made in colloquy. Certainly an exception under such circumstances does not meet the literal requirement of Rule 51 and, in our opinion, it is an insufficient excuse for failure to object or except to the charge.

The cases relied upon by the appellant deal either with situations where an exception was taken at the time of the charge and the question is whether the exception was sufficiently explicit, or to cases involving evidentiary rulings where exception was taken at the time of the ruling but no further exception was taken at the time of the charge. ＊ ＊ ＊ Nor do we think the instant case of the exceptional character in which an appellate court will sometimes correct an error in the charge in the absence of objection or exception. See Troupe v. Chicago, D. & G. Bay Transit Co., 2 Cir., 234 F.2d 253, 260.

＊ ＊ ＊

Judgment affirmed.

Notes and Questions

1. The opinion in this case speaks of the "burden of proof of contributory negligence." In this book, we use the term "burden of persuasion" when we are referring to the kind of burden involved in *Alexander*. There is another

kind of burden—the burden of initially putting in evidence on an issue, without which the issue is not in the case at all. This kind of burden we call the "burden of production." The two kinds of burden are distinct, but the term "burden of proof" often is used to mean either of them. For this reason we avoid it. Ordinarily the burden of production and the burden of persuasion on an issue are placed on the same party. But not always. For example, when a defense is one that is seldom raised, it might be a waste of time to require the plaintiff in every case to introduce evidence refuting it; the burden of production would be placed on the defendant. But once there is enough evidence on the issue to go to the jury, the court might rule that the plaintiff should have the burden of persuasion—that is, establishing that the defense is not valid—as the plaintiff does on most issues.

2. What factors should be considered in determining whether the burden of persuasion on the issue of contributory negligence should be placed on plaintiff or defendant? Are these the same factors that should be involved in deciding who shall be required to plead on the issue of contributory negligence? Why might the two burdens be placed differently?

3. In the *Troupe* case, cited at the end of the principal case, Judge Frank, in a concurring opinion, said, at 234 F.2d 260–61:

> On the negligence issue, the judge, at defendant's request, charged, "It is enough if the steps and paint are commonly used and accepted in the industry at the time." This was as obvious an error, on a material matter, as one can imagine. For the Supreme Court, this court and others have often held that usual practices, by others in the same industry or trade, similar to a defendant's practices, do not constitute a defense in a negligence action.

> My colleagues indicate that, were it not for our reversal on the unseaworthiness issue, they would probably have disregarded this error. I cannot agree. My colleagues refer to Rule 51 and the fact that, before the jury retired, plaintiffs' counsel did not state distinctly that he objected and the grounds of the objection. My colleagues concede that, in an exceptional case, we may review errors not "saved" by a proper objection. They suggest this is not an exceptional case, relying on a statement in United States v. Atkinson, 297 U.S. 157, 160, 56 S.Ct. 391, 392, 80 L.Ed. 555. There the Supreme Court, set forth, in the disjunctive, two grounds for reviewing such errors:

> (1) "the errors are obvious

> *or*

> (2) they otherwise seriously affect the fairness, integrity, or public reputation of judicial proceedings."

> My colleagues stress the second ground. But the first ground alone suffices, as the cases make clear. And here, as observed above, the error was magnificently obvious. A litigant surely has the right to assume that a federal trial judge knows the elementary substantive legal rules, long established by the precedents, and that therefore the judge will act accordingly, without prompting by the litigant's lawyer.

Was the trial judge's error in *Alexander* "obvious"? What factors are relevant to this question?

b. *The Form of the Verdict*

In most cases, the jury is asked to return a "general verdict." In substance, the jury simply says, "We find for the plaintiff and fix damages at *x* dollars" or "We find for the defendant." But as previously discussed in the Outline, pp. 13-14, supra, there are two variations on the general verdict. One is the special verdict, in which the jury is asked to answer questions as to the facts; the judge then applies the law to the facts as found by the jury. The other is the general verdict with interrogatories; the jury is told to return a verdict in the same form as a general verdict, but in addition it is told to answer certain questions about the facts of the case. If those answers are not consistent with the general verdict, the answers control. There are a number of reasons for using the special verdict or the general verdict with interrogatories. For example, in a complicated case, the special verdict obviates the necessity of instructing the jury about the law and permits it to concentrate on determining the facts. But you should bear in mind that both of these forms of verdict also are devices for controlling the jury—for preventing the jury from ignoring the law and simply deciding the case for the party the jurors want to win.

DINIERO v. UNITED STATES LINES CO.

United States Court of Appeals, Second Circuit, 1961.
288 F.2d 595, certiorari denied 368 U.S. 831, 82 S.Ct. 54, 7 L.Ed.2d 34.

MEDINA, CIRCUIT JUDGE. * * * Julio Diniero, a Junior Third Assistant Engineer aboard the S.S. Pioneer Land, owned by United States Lines Company, claimed to have suffered such repeated strains in his back in the performance of his duties as to cause a ruptured disc with resultant pain and suffering, culminating some years later in a fusion operation and the removal of the disc. According to Diniero's testimony, there was a blow-down valve located below a floor plate * * *. There was a slot in the floor plate and normally the valve could be opened or closed as circumstances required by using a reach rod. For a variety of reasons * * * which include the absence of a reach rod and defects in the valve, Diniero said the only way he could operate the valve was by removing the deck plate, crouching down and moving the wheel of the valve by the use of a wrench. He claimed the injuries to his back were the effect of repeatedly operating the valve under these difficult conditions. The shipowner * * * claimed there was nothing wrong with the valve, nor any necessity to remove the floor plate or to use a wrench. The eight day trial was devoted to * * * the controverted issue of liability, and there was also considerable medical proof on the general subject of whether Diniero's trouble was due to a long continued condition caused by a degenerative disc disease and having no relation whatever to the operation of the blow-down valve * * *.

At the close of the evidence the trial judge submitted the case to the jury in a wholly unexceptionable charge. In an endeavor to assist the jury in its deliberations, however, * * * he submitted eight questions to be signed and returned as the verdict of the jury. The last two were in the form of a general verdict for plaintiff or defendant, questions 2 to 6 [related] * * * to unseaworthiness, negligence, contributory negligence and proximate cause. The trouble was caused by question number 1, as follows:

> Did the plaintiff injure himself aboard the Pioneer Land because in operating the blow-down valve he had to remove the floor plates, then crouch and exert physical effort with a wrench and not his hand to stop it from leaking?

> Answer yes or no.

After some hours of deliberation and the receipt of a number of communications from the jury, the trial judge withdrew all the questions, told the jury to disregard them and bring in a general verdict in the usual form; and, after further deliberations the jury brought in a verdict in favor of the seaman for $46,150. * * *

The position of the shipowner is that * * * Rule 49(b) authorizes the submission of written interrogatories but does not authorize the withdrawal of such interrogatories, after they have once been submitted and the jury has commenced its deliberations thereon. The shipowner further argues that question number 1 related to "one or more issues of fact the decision of which is necessary to a verdict," and that * * * it was a clear abuse of discretion to withdraw a proper and material interrogatory, relating to an issue that must necessarily be decided in plaintiff's favor, if plaintiff was to recover any damages whatever. To permit such withdrawal, the shipowner claims, would defeat the very purpose of * * * Rule 49(b), and smooth the way for a reluctant jury, unable to agree on the facts basic to recovery, to do "popular justice" through the medium of "an old-fashioned verdict."

* * *

The jury commenced their deliberations at 2:45 p.m. At 5:40 p.m. the trial judge received a note from the jury reading: "Your Honor, could we ask for your interpretation of the word 'had' in the second line, first question? Did the plaintiff injure himself?"

Appellant's counsel assures us that the question and the explanation given by the trial judge is just as simple as * * * whether he was injured in the manner described by him in his testimony. What the trial judge said, however, is as follows:

> What I was trying to find out by the first question was whether or not plaintiff injured himself on board this ship, assuming that he had to remove the plates, assuming that he had to crouch down, and assuming he exerted this pressure with the wrench instead of his hand?

> So in answer to your specific question as to the interpretation of the word "had" it means that I assumed that he had to remove the plates, and had to do this, and he had to do that. I didn't mean to take away from you the question as to whether he did in fact have to do that. In other words, the purpose of the question is to find out whether the plaintiff injured himself on board the ship in the manner that he described. The defendant claims that he did not. So the first question

that I wanted answered was did he injure himself aboard the ship by doing what he said he did?

If you find that he didn't remove the plates or he didn't bend down, or he didn't crouch, or he didn't have to, or he didn't do it, those questions will be answered as you go on further down by your answers to the other questions.

But in my first question I assumed as a fact, accepted the plaintiff's testimony, that he had to bend down, that he had to crouch, that he had to remove the plates.

What I wanted to find out was, assuming all of that, did he injure himself on board the Pioneer Land.

Now I hope that is clear. If it isn't you can write me another note.

The jury retired again at 5:50 p.m. and returned with another note at 6:40 p.m. * * * as follows: "Your Honor, we cannot agree on question one. It appears there is no chance for agreement." Thereupon the trial judge withdrew all the questions from the consideration of the jury and asked them to see if they could not agree on a general verdict.

* * * [T]he jury still could not soon reach agreement. At 9:22 p.m. the jury informed the trial judge that "it finds it impossible to arrive at a unanimous agreement in this case." The trial judge thereupon read a quotation from Allen v. United States, 1896, 164 U.S. 492, 501, 17 S.Ct. 154, 41 L.Ed. 528, and returned the jury for further deliberations at 9:30 p.m. * * * At 10:30 p.m. the verdict was announced and the jury polled.

There was an inherent ambiguity in question one, and it is plain enough that the explanation failed to remove the ambiguity. Under these circumstances we think it was not an abuse of discretion to withdraw the questions and give the jury an opportunity to agree upon a general verdict. * * * It was a matter of judgment whether to attempt some further elucidation of the question, or to declare a mistrial, or to withdraw all the questions and authorize a general verdict. We cannot say the decision made here under the circumstances of this case was wrong, particularly as the jury continued its deliberations from about 6:45 p.m. until 10:30 p.m., after the withdrawal of the questions.

* * *

Other cases present the problem in its simplest form. After the submission of material and proper interrogatories, there is a delay of a few hours and the trial judge of his own motion, or on the application of plaintiff's counsel, calls in the jury, withdraws the questions, tells the jury to bring in a general verdict over the objection of defendant's counsel, and shortly thereafter the jury returns a verdict for the plaintiff. This has been held to be an abuse of discretion and ground for reversal. * * * The reason is that the action of the trial judge would probably be prejudicial to defendant. * * * This is a good general rule, and we agree with it. But it has no application to the case before us now, as the interrogatory causing all the difficulty here was unclear and ambiguous. The withdrawal of all the questions was for the purpose of eliminating the confusion caused by the formulation of an improper question. And it is to be noted that a confusing and improperly worded interrogatory cannot fairly be considered a "material" question, or one the answer to which "is necessary to a verdict." Under the circumstances it was, we think, good judgment to withdraw all the questions. Certainly we cannot say to do so was an abuse of discretion.

Affirmed.

Notes and Questions

1. Do you believe the interrogatory as first given to the jury was ambiguous? What are the possible meanings of the question? Could the jury answer the question "No" under any of these meanings and still find for plaintiff? If the jury had answered the interrogatory "No," and a reviewing court found that there was no evidence at all to support a finding that Diniero was *not* required to remove the plate, crouch down, and turn the valve with a wrench, but that a genuine issue existed on the question whether his condition was caused by this work, would the reviewing court be required to reverse a verdict for defendant that was based on the answer to the first interrogatory?

2. Could the judge simply have rewritten the interrogatory in clearer language and resubmitted it? What reasons mitigate against allowing such a practice?

3. Could the jury have properly reached a decision for plaintiff without resolving the issue that the judge said in his explanation he intended the interrogatory to present? If it could not, was it proper to withdraw the interrogatory altogether and say to the jury: "What I am going to do, in an effort to see whether you can agree, I am going to ask you to forget all of the questions I gave you and see whether you can't agree on a general verdict. * * * I think that might relieve the situation some. I hope you can come to some agreement." (Judge's Instruction, quoted from the Petition for a Writ of Certiorari, p. 11.)

4. Do you think the judge's explanation of the interrogatory was clear? Read it again very carefully before you decide. Then reflect upon the fact that it was delivered orally to the jurors, even though the interrogatories themselves were in writing. When the jury is asked to return a general verdict, the charge, frequently including very complex instructions on the law, is given orally, and although the jurors may ask to have parts of it repeated, they usually are not given a copy. From the experience in this case do you think written instructions would be a better idea?

5. The use of special verdicts and general verdicts with interrogatories is sometimes criticized as atomizing the jury's deliberations and making a unanimous result more difficult to reach. Assume that in an ordinary automobile accident case, three members of the jury believe that the defendant was going too fast but the other three believe that he was not; moreover, the latter group of jurors believes that the defendant was not looking where he was going, but the first group believes that the defendant was. Could the jury return a unanimous verdict for the plaintiff? For defendant? Would the problem be aggravated by the use of a special verdict or a general verdict with interrogatories? For a perceptive discussion of the general problem, see Ginsburg, *Special Findings and Jury Unanimity in the Federal Courts*, 65 Colum.L.Rev. 256 (1965).

6.   ALLEN v. UNITED STATES, 164 U.S. 492, 17 S.Ct. 154, 41 L.Ed. 528 (1896), which the trial court in *Diniero* quoted to the jury, involved a variation on what has come to be called the "dynamite charge," an instruction which is sometimes given in the principal charge but more frequently is given only to a jury that has been unable to reach a unanimous verdict for either party after a substantial period of time. In *Allen* this charge was given some time after the main charge. Its content was,

> in substance, that in a large proportion of cases absolute certainty could not be expected; that, although the verdict must be the verdict of each individual juror, and not a mere acquiescence in the conclusion of his fellows, yet they should examine the question submitted with candor, and with a proper regard and deference to the opinions of each other; that it was their duty to decide the case if they could conscientiously do so; that they should listen, with a disposition to be convinced, to each other's arguments; that, if much the larger number were for conviction, a dissenting juror should consider whether his doubt was a reasonable one which made no impression upon the minds of so many men, equally honest, equally intelligent with himself. If, upon the other hand, the majority were for acquittal, the minority ought to ask themselves whether they might not reasonably doubt the correctness of a judgment which was not concurred in by the majority.

Id. at 501, 17 S.Ct. at 157, 41 L.Ed. at 530–31. The United States Supreme Court said:

> While, undoubtedly, the verdict of the jury should represent the opinion of each individual juror, it by no means follows that opinions may not be changed by conference in the jury room. The very object of the jury system is to secure unanimity by a comparison of views, and by arguments among the jurors themselves. It certainly cannot be the law that each juror should not listen with deference to the arguments, and with a distrust of his own judgment, if he finds a large majority of the jury taking a different view of the case from what he does himself. It cannot be that each juror should go to the jury room with a blind determination that the verdict shall represent his opinion of the case at that moment, or that he should close his ears to the arguments of men who are equally honest and intelligent as himself.

Id. at 501, 17 S.Ct. at 157, 41 L.Ed. at 530. Does this opinion adequately answer the objections that may be made to such a charge?

c. The Jury's Deliberation

After the judge completes the charge, the jury retires to deliberate in private. Extensive precautions are taken to insure that the jury is undisturbed and unheard during this period. The jury will have been instructed to decide the case in accordance with the law as explained by the judge and on only the evidence that has been brought forward in the trial. It clearly is improper for the jury to ignore what the judge has said about the law or to speculate about what evidence that was not introduced might have proved. It also is improper for the jurors to decide the case on the basis of their own personal knowledge of the facts of the case. Indeed, if a juror has specific knowledge of the facts, it should be disclosed at the beginning of the trial, and that juror probably will be excused from serving. But a more difficult question is presented by a juror's more general knowledge and experience as it relates to the case. A strength of the jury system is thought to be that it brings together a cross-section of community standards and experienced judgments. At the same time, the parties are not able to meet the special knowledge of jurors of which they are unaware. How should the line between general experience and special knowledge be drawn?

TEXAS EMPLOYERS' INS. ASS'N v. PRICE

Court of Civil Appeals of Texas, Eastland, 1960.
336 S.W.2d 304.

COLLINGS, JUSTICE. Loyal Grant Price brought suit * * * to set aside an award of the Industrial Accident Board * * *. The defendant Texas Employers' Insurance Association answered by general denial and specifically pleaded that plaintiff's alleged injury did not result in total or permanent incapacity, but that any injury plaintiff may have received resulted only in partial and temporary incapacity, or resulted from other injuries and diseases or a combination thereof. * * *

The case was tried before a jury which found that plaintiff received an accidental injury while working for the Port Houston Iron Works, Inc.; * * * that such injury was the producing cause of total disability; that total disability began November 27, 1957; that such disability was permanent and was not partial * * *. Judgment was entered for the plaintiff for $13,415.96 in a lump sum with interest thereon at the legal rate. * * *

In appellant's first four points it is contended that there was no evidence, and in the alternative that the evidence was insufficient to support the findings that any total incapacity sustained by appellee was permanent and the finding that appellee sustained total and permanent incapacity was so against the great weight and preponderance of the evidence as to be clearly wrong and unjust. * * *

In support of its contention in this respect, appellant further urges that appellee's own doctor testified that his back had been improved by the operation and stated that he "would estimate his (appellee's) partial permanent disability as approximately twenty percent as applied to general deficiency." This testimony is not consistent with the finding of the jury and the testimony of appellee to the effect that he has sustained total and permanent incapacity. It is the province of the jury, however, to determine the weight to be given evidence and to reconcile conflicts or inconsistencies therein. * * * The matter under consideration was not one for experts and skilled witnesses alone. Appellee testified that he could not work without pain, that his back was getting worse, that he was having to wear a brace with which he had previously been fitted by Dr. Brelsford. Dr. Brelsford testified that appellee had sustained permanent incapacity although not total, but that he would not pass him to follow his trade. The fact that appellee's testimony was in conflict with expert opinion testimony concerning the extent of his disability did not, under the circumstances, render it insufficient to support the verdict. * * *

Appellant further urges that the court erred in refusing to grant a new trial on the ground of jury misconduct. The evidence concerning some of the alleged jury misconduct was conflicting and would support a finding that such misconduct did not occur. The implied findings of the court in support of the order overruling appellant's motion for a new trial, which findings have support in the evidence, are binding on us. * * *

The existence of one of the alleged acts of jury misconduct is shown conclusively and in our opinion constitutes reversible error. The question whether the incapacity of appellee was total and permanent or only permanent partial was close, as already indicated. It is our opinion that the evidence supports the finding of total permanent incapacity and that such finding is not against the great weight and preponderance of the evidence. But it is further noted that appellee's own doctor testified, in effect, that his disability was approximately twenty percent partial. It is undisputed that one of the jurors related his personal experiences to persuade the jury that appellee was totally and permanently incapacitated. The witness stated to the jury as follows:

> I said it has been my experience that in employment that if a man has an injury and it is obvious, such as, a scar on his back if he is being examined by a doctor for employment that he would want a statement from that man concerning that injury, and if he mentioned a back injury I doubted very much if he would get employment. The reason that came out was we were discussing whether or not the injury was partial or total.

The juror testified that he got this experience in union work; that he had read a letter from his company concerning back injuries showing that the company wanted to be more careful in hiring people with such injuries and that he told the jury about this experience. He testified that, in making the above statements to the jury, he was attempting to persuade a juror to come over to his side of the case; that he felt it was proper to give the jury the benefit of his personal knowledge and experience; and that was what he did. He further stated that he knew from experience that appellee could not get a job with Rohm and Haas, Shell Oil Company, Sinclair, or any other company that has a union contract or employee benefits and so advised the jury. He stated his opinion to the jury that appellee should receive total and permanent disability because he could not pass the physical examination he would be required to take; that it had been his experience that companies were very strict about whom they hire and that prospective employees were required to pass a most rigid physical examination. In this connection the juror testified that he also stated to the jury that there might be some jobs that appellee could handle but that he had a doubt whether appellee "could compete favorably on the labor market." The above evidence is undisputed. It shows that a juror related his personal experiences to the jury concerning the practice of company employers in hiring and employing workmen, and that the purpose and effect of such statements was to show that appellee was totally incapacitated. It was misconduct for the juror to relate to the other jurors his own personal experience as original evidence of material facts to be considered in their deliberation. * * * Considered in connection with the entire record, we are of the opinion that the misconduct shown was material and that it reasonably appears that injury probably resulted to appellant. * * *

For the reasons stated the judgment of the trial court is reversed and the cause is remanded.

Notes and Questions

1. Why is it misconduct for a juror "to relate to the other jurors his own personal experience as original evidence of material facts to be considered in their deliberation"? In HEAD v. HARGRAVE, 105 U.S. (15 Otto) 45, 49–50, 26 L.Ed. 1028, 1030 (1881), a case involving the value of legal services, Justice Field said:

> It was the province of the jury to weigh the testimony of the attorneys as to the value of the services, by reference to their nature, the time occupied in their performance, and other attending circumstances, and by applying to it their own experience and knowledge of the character of such services. To direct them to find the value of the services from the testimony of the experts alone, was to say to them that the issue should be determined by the opinions of the attorneys, and not by the exercise of their own judgment of the facts on which those opinions were given. * * * So far from laying aside their own general knowledge and ideas, the jury should have applied that knowledge and those ideas to the matters of fact in evidence in determining the weight to be given to the opinions expressed * * *. While they cannot act in any case upon particular facts material to its disposition resting in their private knowledge, but should be governed by the evidence adduced, they may, and to act intelligently they must, judge of the weight and force of that evidence by their own general knowledge of the subject of inquiry. If, for example, the question were as to the damages sustained by a plaintiff from a fracture of his leg by the carelessness of a defendant, the jury would ill perform their duty and probably come to a wrong conclusion, if, controlled by the testimony of the surgeons, not merely as to the injury inflicted, but as to the damages sustained, they should ignore their own knowledge and experience of the value of a sound limb. Other persons besides professional men have knowledge of the value of professional services; and, while great weight should always be given to the opinions of those familiar with the subject, they are not to be blindly received * * *.

Can the principal case be reconciled with this language?

2. The issue of jury misconduct is complicated by the doctrine, recognized in most jurisdictions but enforced with varying strictness, that a jury verdict may not be impeached by evidence that comes from the jurors themselves. Texas, in which the *Price* case arose, goes much further than most states in allowing inquiry into the jury's deliberations. See Pope, *The Mental Operations of Jurors*, 40 Texas L.Rev. 849 (1962). In KILGORE v. GREYHOUND CORP., 30 F.R.D. 385, 388 (E.D.Tenn.1962), in which the issue

concerned an unsupervised and unauthorized study of the scene of the accident by a juror and his report thereon to his fellows, it was said:

> Any time a new trial is sought on the basis of the misconduct of a juror, or the receipt and consideration by a jury of improper evidence which may have had prejudicial effect on the jurors, the Court is forced to choose between the possibility that a party litigant may have been done an injustice, and, on the other hand, the possibility that the Court will inflict a public injury which will result if jurors are permitted to testify regarding what happened in the jury room.

What is the possible "public injury" of which this court speaks? Why are jurors generally prohibited from impeaching their verdict? Is one reason a fear that if the jury's processes are too closely examined, the theoretical underpinnings of the system may be impaired?

3. The question of the extent to which jurors may rely on their own experience and knowledge may arise in contexts other than jury misconduct. In Head v. Hargrave, Note 1, supra, the issue was the denial of a requested instruction that the jury was not bound by the expert testimony. Again, the issue may be raised in terms of a question whether there is sufficient evidence to sustain a particular verdict. Compare Holt v. Pariser, 161 Pa.Super. 315, 54 A.2d 89 (1947) (holding that a jury could properly find reasonable a very long delay in the repair of a truck in light of a wartime shortage of parts, although no evidence of the reason for the delay had been introduced), with Harris v. Pounds, 185 Miss. 688, 187 So. 891 (1939) (holding that a jury in a timber-growing county could not properly find that a hardwood log 15 feet in length and 12 inches in diameter was too heavy to be safely carried by six men over rough, uneven ground in the absence of evidence as to its weight).

d. Taking the Case From the Jury

The most direct and drastic example of jury control occurs in those cases in which it is held that there is no evidence on which a reasonable jury could find for a particular party (usually the plaintiff, but sometimes the defendant). If the judge makes this determination at the close of the evidence, she will direct the jury to return a verdict for the other party. Even after the jury has returned a verdict for one party, the judge in most systems may order that judgment be entered for the other party "notwithstanding the verdict," if she decides that the case should not have been submitted to the jury. The judge also has the power to set aside the verdict and order a new trial on the ground that the verdict is against the great weight of the evidence or because of mistakes or erroneous rulings during trial.

So also, an appellate court may determine, even in the face of a jury verdict, that no reasonable jury could have reached the result announced. Clearly when these devices are used, the jury is more than "controlled"; it is eliminated from the process. If such devices were not available, the jury could decide a case any way it wanted without respect to the evidence or the law. But if the devices are not very severely restricted, the right to a jury trial can be negated.

LAVENDER v. KURN

Supreme Court of the United States, 1946.
327 U.S. 645, 66 S.Ct. 740, 90 L.Ed. 916.

On Writ of Certiorari to the Supreme Court of the State of Missouri.

MR. JUSTICE MURPHY delivered the opinion of the Court.

*   *   *

Petitioner, the administrator of the estate of L.E. Haney, brought this suit under the [Federal Employers' Liability] Act against the respondent trustees of the St. Louis-San Francisco Railway Company (Frisco) and the respondent Illinois Central Railroad Company. It was charged that Haney, while employed as a switch-tender by the respondents in the switchyard of the Grand Central Station in Memphis, Tennessee, was killed as a result of respondents' negligence. Following a trial * * *, the jury returned a verdict in favor of petitioner and awarded damages in the amount of $30,000. * * * On appeal, however, the Supreme Court of Missouri reversed the judgment, holding that there was no substantial evidence of negligence to support the submission of the case to the jury. *   *   *

[Haney was employed by the Illinois Central which owned the yards; Frisco's trains used the yards, and part of Haney's wages were paid by Frisco.]

The Illinois Central tracks run north and south directly past and into the Grand Central Station. About 2700 feet south of the station the Frisco tracks cross at right angles to the Illinois Central tracks. A westbound Frisco train wishing to use the station must stop some 250 feet or more west of this crossing and back into the station over a switchline curving east and north. The events in issue center about the switch several feet north of the main Frisco tracks at the point where the switch line branches off. This switch controls the tracks at this point.

It was very dark on the evening of December 21, 1939. At about 7:30 p.m. a westbound interstate Frisco passenger train stopped on the Frisco main line, its rear some 20 or 30 feet west of the switch. Haney, in the performance of his duties, threw or opened the switch to permit the train to back into the station. The respondents claimed that Haney was then required to cross to the south side of the track before the train passed the switch; and the conductor of the train testified that he saw Haney so cross. But there was also evidence that Haney's duties required him to wait at the switch north of the track until the train had cleared, close the switch, return to his shanty near the crossing and change the signals from red to green to permit trains on the Illinois Central tracks to use the crossing. The Frisco train cleared the switch, backing at the rate of 8 or 10 miles per hour. But the switch remained open and the signals still were red. Upon investigation Haney was found north of the track near the switch lying face down on the ground, unconscious. An ambulance was called, but he was dead upon arrival at the hospital.

Haney had been struck in the back of the head, causing a fractured skull from which he died. There were no known eye-witnesses to the fatal blow. Although it is not clear there is evidence that his body was extended north and south, the head to the south. Apparently he had fallen forward to the south; his face was bruised on the left side from hitting the ground and there were marks indicating that his toes had dragged a few inches southward as he fell. His head was about 5½ feet north of the Frisco tracks. Estimates ranged from 2 feet to 14 feet as to how far west of the switch he lay.

The injury to Haney's head was evidenced by a gash about two inches long from which blood flowed. The back of Haney's white cap had a corresponding black mark about an inch and a half long and an inch wide, running at an angle downward to the right of the center of the back of the head. A spot of blood was later found at a point 3 or 4 feet north of the tracks. The conclusion following an autopsy was that Haney's skull was fractured by "some fast moving small round object." One of the examining doctors testified that such an object might have been attached to a train backing at the rate of 8 or 10 miles per hour. But he also admitted that the fracture might have resulted from a blow from a pipe or club or some similar round object in the hands of an individual.

Petitioner's theory is that Haney was struck by the curled end or tip of a mail hook hanging down loosely on the outside of the mail car of the backing train. This curled end was 73 inches above the top of the rail, which was 7 inches high. The overhang of the mail car in relation to the rails was about 2 to 2½ feet. The evidence indicated that when the mail car swayed or moved around a curve the mail hook might pivot, its curled end swinging out as much as 12 to 14 inches. The curled end could thus be swung out to a point 3 to 3½ feet from the rail and about 73 inches above the top of the rail. Both east and west of the switch, however, was an uneven mound of cinders and dirt rising at its highest points 18 to 24 inches above the top of the rails. Witnesses differed as to how close the mound approached the rails, the estimates varying from 3 to 15 feet. But taking the figures most favorable to the petitioner, the mound extended to a point 6 to 12 inches north of the overhanging side of the mail car. If the mail hook end swung out 12 to 14 inches it would be 49 to 55 inches above the highest parts of the mound. Haney was 67½ inches tall. If he had been standing on the mound about a foot from the side of the mail car he could have been hit by the end of the mail hook, the exact point of contact depending upon the height of the mound at the particular point. His wound was about 4 inches below the top of his head, or 63½ inches above the point where he stood on the mound—well within the possible range of the mail hook end.

Respondents' theory is that Haney was murdered. They point to the estimates that the mound was 10 to 15 feet north of the rail, making it impossible for the mail hook end to reach a point of contact with Haney's head. Photographs were placed in the record to support the claim that the ground was level north of the rail for at least 10 feet. * * * It also appears that many hoboes and tramps frequented the area at night in order to get rides on freight trains. Haney carried a pistol to protect himself. This pistol was found loose under his body by those who came to his rescue. It was testified, however that the pistol had apparently slipped out of his pocket or scabbard as he fell. Haney's clothes were not disarranged and there was no evidence of a struggle or fight. No rods, pipes or weapons of any kind, except Haney's own pistol, were found near the scene. Moreover, his gold watch and diamond ring were still on him after he was struck. Six days later his unsoiled billfold was found on a high board fence about a block from the place where Haney was struck and near the point where he had been placed in an ambulance. It contained his social security card and other effects, but no money. His wife testified that he "never carried much money, not very much more than $10." Such were the facts in relation to respondents' theory of murder.

Finally, one of the Frisco foremen testified that he arrived at the scene shortly after Haney was found injured. He later examined the fireman's side of the train very carefully and found nothing sticking out or in disorder. In explaining why he examined this side of the train so carefully he stated that while he was at the scene of the accident "someone said they thought that train No. 106 backing in to Grand Central Station is what struck this man" and that Haney "was supposed to have been struck by something protruding on the side of the train." The foreman testified that these statements were made by an unknown Illinois Central switchman standing near the fallen body of Haney. The foreman admitted that the switchman "didn't see the accident." This testimony was admitted by the trial court over the strenuous objections of respondents' counsel that it was mere hearsay falling outside the *res gestae* rule.

The jury was instructed that Frisco's trustees were liable if it was found that they negligently permitted a rod or other object to extend out from the side of the train as it backed past Haney and that Haney was killed as the direct result of such negligence, if any. The jury was further told that Illinois Central was liable if it was found that the company negligently maintained an unsafe and dangerous place for Haney to work, in that the ground was high and uneven and the light insufficient and inadequate, and that Haney was injured and killed as a direct result of the said place being unsafe and dangerous. This latter instruction as to Illinois Central did not require the jury to find that Haney was killed by something protruding from the train.

The Supreme Court, in upsetting the jury's verdict against both the Frisco trustees and the Illinois Central, admitted that "It could be inferred from the facts that Haney could have been struck by the mail hook knob *if* he were standing on the south side of the mound and the mail hook extended out as far as 12 or 14 inches." * * * But it held that "all reasonable minds would agree that it would be mere speculation and conjecture to say that Haney was struck by the mail hook" and that "plaintiff failed to make a submissible case on that question." It also ruled that there "was no substantial evidence that the uneven ground and insufficient light were causes or contributing causes of the death of Haney." Finally, the Supreme Court held that the testimony of the foreman as to the statement made to him by the unknown switchman was inadmissible under the *res gestae* rule since the switchman spoke from what he had heard rather than from his own knowledge.

* * *

The evidence we have already detailed demonstrates that there was evidence from which it might be inferred that the end of the mail hook struck Haney in the back of the head, an inference that the Supreme Court admitted could be drawn. That inference is not rendered unreasonable by the fact that Haney apparently fell forward toward the main Frisco track so that his head was 5½ feet north of the rail. He may well have been struck and then wandered in a daze to the point where he fell forward. The testimony as to blood marks some distance away from his head lends credence to that possibility, indicating that he did not fall immediately upon being hit. When that is added to the evidence most favorable to the petitioner as to the height and swing-out of the hook, the height and location of the mound and the nature of Haney's duties, the inference that Haney was killed by the hook cannot be said to be unsupported by probative facts or to be so unreasonable as to warrant taking the case from the jury.

It is true that there is evidence tending to show that it was physically and mathematically impossible for the hook to strike Haney. And there are facts from which it might reasonably be inferred that Haney was murdered. But such evidence has become irrelevant upon appeal, there being a reasonable basis in the record for inferring that the hook struck Haney. The jury having made that inference, the respondents were not free to relitigate the factual dispute in a reviewing court. Under these circumstances it would be an undue invasion of the jury's historic function for an appellate court to weigh the conflicting evidence, judge the credibility of witnesses and arrive at a conclusion opposite from the one reached by the jury. * * *

It is no answer to say that the jury's verdict involved speculation and conjecture. Whenever facts are in dispute or the evidence is such that fair-minded men may draw different inferences, a measure of speculation and conjecture is required on the part of those whose duty it is to settle the dispute by choosing what seems to them to be the most reasonable inference. Only when there is a complete absence of probative facts to support the conclusion reached does a reversible error appear. But where, as here, there is an evidentiary basis for the jury's verdict, the jury is free to discard or disbelieve whatever facts are inconsistent with its conclusion. And the appellate court's function is exhausted when that evidentiary basis becomes apparent. * * *

We are unable, therefore, to sanction a reversal of the jury's verdict against Frisco's trustees. Nor can we approve any disturbance in the verdict as to Illinois Central. The evidence was uncontradicted that it was very dark at the place where Haney was working and the surrounding ground was high and uneven. The evidence also showed that this

area was entirely within the domination and control of Illinois Central
* * *. It was not unreasonable to conclude that these conditions
constituted an unsafe and dangerous working place * * *.

In view of the foregoing disposition of the case, it is unnecessary to
decide whether the allegedly hearsay testimony was admissible under the
res gestae rule. Rulings on the admissibility of evidence must normally be
left to the sound discretion of the trial judge in actions under the Federal
Employers' Liability Act. But inasmuch as there is adequate support in
the record for the jury's verdict apart from the hearsay testimony, we
need not determine whether that discretion was abused in this instance.

The judgment of the Supreme Court of Missouri is reversed and the
case is remanded for whatever further proceedings may be necessary not
inconsistent with this opinion.

THE CHIEF JUSTICE and MR. JUSTICE FRANKFURTER concur in the result.

MR. JUSTICE REED dissents.

Notes and Questions

1. Why does a trial judge or an appellate court have the power to take a
case away from the jury or to set aside its verdict? Could a court effectively
exercise this control if the rule regarding a jury's inability to use its own
knowledge were different than as stated in Texas Employers' Ins. Ass'n v.
Price, p. 49, supra?

2. In PENNSYLVANIA R. CO. v. CHAMBERLAIN, 288 U.S. 333, 339,
53 S.Ct. 391, 393, 77 L.Ed. 819, 822–23 (1933), the Supreme Court, in approving a directed verdict for defendant, said:

> * * * At most there was an inference to that effect drawn from
> observed facts which gave equal support to the opposite inference * * *.
>
> We, therefore, have a case belonging to that class of cases where
> proven facts give equal support to each of two inconsistent inferences; in
> which event, neither of them being established, judgment, as a matter of
> law, must go against the party upon whom rests the necessity of sus-
> taining one of these inferences as against the other, before he is entitled
> to recover.

Is this language consistent with the opinion of the Court in the principal case?
Is there a difference between cases in which the evidence simply fails to point
one way or the other, and cases in which the evidence on one side is
overwhelming, in terms of taking a case away from the jury? Would *Lavender* have been decided in the same way if the evidence that Haney was
murdered was much stronger than it was?

3. When the *Lavender* case is remanded to the Missouri Supreme Court,
what should that court do? In this connection, do you agree with the United
States Supreme Court that it was unnecessary to determine whether evidence
of the statement of the unknown switchman was improperly admitted?

4. APPEAL

The grounds for appeal are chiefly mistakes of law—an erroneous
ruling that the court had jurisdiction, an improper admission of evidence,

or an incorrect instruction to the jury. Even if an error of law has been committed, the appellate court must be convinced that the error was prejudicial, and that the case probably would not have come out the same if the error had not occurred. In the event of an erroneous ruling on jurisdiction the prejudice is obvious. But appellate courts are reluctant to reverse merely because an error has been committed during the trial.

An appellate court rarely will reverse a decision on the ground that a question of fact was decided improperly. If there has been a jury, the constitutional right to jury trial itself is involved in such a ruling by an appellate court. See Amendment VII to the United States Constitution, which is set out in the Supplement. When there has been no jury, no constitutional problem is involved, but it may be asked whether a broad scope of review of the trial judge's findings of fact will not encourage needless appeals and denigrate the function of the trial judge.

HICKS v. UNITED STATES

United States Court of Appeals, Fourth Circuit, 1966.
368 F.2d 626.

SOBELOFF, CIRCUIT JUDGE. This action was brought under the Federal Tort Claims Act, 28 U.S.C. § 1346, to recover damages for the death of Carol Greitens. The plaintiff, administrator of her estate, alleges that death was due to the negligence of the doctor on duty at the dispensary of the United States Naval Amphibious Base, Little Creek, Virginia, in diagnosing and treating her illness. The District Court, concluding that the evidence was insufficient to establish that the doctor was negligent, or that his concededly erroneous diagnosis and treatment was the proximate cause of her death, dismissed the complaint. * * *

The decedent, 25 years of age, had been a diabetic since the age of 13, although the condition was under control. * * * Mrs. Greitens' husband brought her to the dispensary at about 4 a.m. on August 25, 1963, suffering from intense abdominal pain and continual vomiting which had begun suddenly an hour before. The corpsman on duty in the examining room procured her medical records, obtained a brief history, took her blood pressure, pulse, temperature, and respiration and summoned the doctor on duty, then asleep in his room at the dispensary. The doctor arrived 15 or 20 minutes later and after questioning the patient concerning her symptoms, felt her abdomen and listened to her bowel sounds with the aid of a stethoscope. Recording his diagnosis on the chart as gastroenteritis, he told Mrs. Greitens that she had a "bug" in her stomach, prescribed some drugs for the relief of pain, and released her with instructions to return in eight hours. The examination took approximately ten minutes.

The patient returned to her home, and after another episode of vomiting, took the prescribed medicine and lay down. At about noon, she arose and drank a glass of water, vomited immediately thereafter and fell to the floor unconscious. She was rushed to the dispensary, but efforts to revive her were unsuccessful. She was pronounced dead at 12:48 p.m. and an autopsy revealed that she had a high obstruction, diagnosed formally as an abnormal congenital peritoneal hiatus with internal herniation into this malformation of some of the loops of the small intestine. Death was due to a massive hemorrhagic infarction of the intestine resulting from its strangulation.

I

The plaintiff contends that the doctor at the dispensary did not meet the requisite standard of care and skill demanded of him by the law of Virginia. Compliance with this standard, the plaintiff maintains, would have required a more extended examination and immediate hospitalization. More specifically, plaintiff's expert witnesses, two general practitioners in the Norfolk-Virginia Beach area, testified that, according to prevailing practice in the community, the doctor should have inquired whether the patient had had diarrhea and should have made a rectal examination to determine whether the patient was suffering from an obstruction rather than from gastroenteritis. While the latter condition does not ordinarily require immediate radical treatment, a high obstruction is almost invariably lethal unless promptly operated upon. Plaintiff's experts further testified that on observing the symptoms manifested by Mrs. Greitens, the procedure of general practitioners in the community would have been to order immediate hospitalization. * * *

The standard of care which Virginia law exacts from a physician, in this case a general practitioner, is * * * [such that] if he uses ordinary care in reaching his diagnosis, and thereafter acts upon it, he incurs no liability, even if the diagnosis proves to be a mistake in judgment.

It is undisputed that the symptoms of high obstruction and of gastroenteritis are quite similar. The District Court placed great emphasis on this fact as an indication that the doctor's erroneous diagnosis was not negligent, but was merely an error of judgment. It would seem, however, that where the symptoms are consistent with either of two possible conditions, one lethal if not attended to promptly, due care demands that a doctor do more than make a cursory examination and then release the patient. * * * The fact that an intestinal obstruction is a rare occurrence, and that some form of gastroenteritis is the more likely of the two conditions, does not excuse the failure to make inquiries and perform recognized additional tests that might have served to distinguish the one condition from the other. The dispensary doctor himself, as well as the experts for both sides, agreed that an inquiry as to diarrhea and a rectal examination were the "proper procedure" and "the accepted standard" in order to be able to rule out gastroenteritis and to make a definite diagnosis of high intestinal obstruction. If he had made the inquiry which he admits was the accepted standard, he would at least have been alerted to the fact that the case was one calling for close observation with a view to immediate surgical intervention if the graver diagnosis were confirmed. In these circumstances, failure to make this investigation constitutes a lack of due care on the part of the physician. * * * Only if a patient is adequately examined, is there no liability for an erroneous diagnosis.

Our conclusion that the physician was negligent in his diagnosis and treatment of the patient is not inconsistent with * * * [Rule] 52(a), which declares that the trial judge's findings of fact are not to be disturbed unless clearly erroneous. This Rule comes into play primarily where the trial judge as fact finder has had to reconcile conflicting testimony. Where the veracity of witnesses is in issue, the decision is for the judge who has had the opportunity to see and evaluate the witnesses' demeanor. * * * But we are dealing here with the testimony of expert witnesses who are not in controversy as to the basic facts; thus, the opportunity of the trial court to observe the witnesses is of limited significance. It has often been held that where the trial court's conclusions are based on undisputed facts, they are not entitled to the finality customarily accorded basic factual findings under Rule 52(a). * * *

The question before us is not one of fact in the usual sense, but rather whether the undisputed facts manifest negligence. Although the absence of a factual dispute does not *always* mean that the conclusion is a question of law, it becomes so *here* since the ultimate conclusion to be drawn from the basic facts, i.e., the existence or absence of negligence, is actually a question of law. For this reason, the general rule has been that when a judge sitting without a jury makes a determination of negligence his conclusion, as distinguished from the evidentiary findings leading to it, is freely reviewable on appeal. * * * The determination of negligence involves not only the formulation of the legal standard, but more particularly in this case, its application to the evidentiary facts as established; and since these are uncontested, there is no basis for applying the "clearly erroneous" rule. * * *

The government's expert opined that the dispensary physician exercised "average judgment," but analysis of his entire testimony points unavoidably to the opposite conclusion. Revealing are his statements that it was wrong not to inquire about diarrhea, conceding that "that is one question that one usually asks," and that given a patient with abdominal pain of one hour's duration, it is too soon "to expect anybody to come up with a proper diagnosis." Furthermore, his opinion was predicated upon a factual assumption not permissible in this case. His assumption was that the dispensary physician had made only a "working" or "tentative" diagnosis * * *. However, the uncontradicted evidence indicates that this was not a "tentative" diagnosis.

The examining doctor himself testified that he had already considered and ruled out at the beginning of his examination the possibility of an obstruction without making the additional differentiating diagnostic tests. He said that his only reason for asking the patient to return eight hours later was because her diabetic condition could become complicated by a case of gastroenteritis. * * * By releasing the patient, the dispensary physician made his diagnosis final, allowing no further opportunity for revision * * *.

On careful scrutiny, therefore, the government's expert is seen to have demonstrated that the examiner did *not* conform to the required standard of care. Coupled with the explicit testimony of the plaintiff's experts, the government's testimony leads us inevitably to the conclusion that the doctor was negligent as a matter of law. We think that the District Court gave undue weight to the purely conclusory opinion of the government witness. The District Court is not bound by his statement that "average judgment" had been exercised, nor are we bound by it. Only the standard of care is to be established by the testimony of experts. If under the undisputed facts the defendant failed to meet that standard it is not for the expert but for the court to decide whether there was negligence.

* * *

Judgment reversed and cause remanded for the determination of damages.

Notes and Questions

1. Would the Court of Appeals have reached the same result if the judgment appealed from had been based on the verdict of a jury rather than the findings of a judge? Why is there any difference between the standard enunciated in Lavender v. Kurn and that in Federal Rule of Civil Procedure 52(a)?

2. Is the question whether certain conduct is negligent one of law or of fact? Legal scholars have long debated the issue without resolution. In any event, the issue ordinarily is left to the jury. Why? Are the reasons for giving the issue to the jury any less persuasive when the finder of fact is a judge sitting without a jury? Is there a difference if the standard of care to be applied by the judge sitting without a jury must be derived from the testimony of experts? Why?

3. In ANDERSON v. CITY OF BESSEMER CITY, 470 U.S. 564, 105 S.Ct. 1504, 84 L.Ed.2d 518 (1985), the Supreme Court, in interpreting Rule 52(a), said: "Where there are two permissible views of the evidence, the factfinder's choice between them cannot be clearly erroneous." The Court added:

This is so even when the district court's findings do not rest on credibility determinations, but are based instead on physical or documentary evidence or inferences from other facts. To be sure, various Courts of Appeals have on occasion asserted the theory that an appellate court may exercise *de novo* review over findings not based on credibility determinations * * *.

The rationale for deference to the original finder of fact is not limited to the superiority of the trial judge's position to make determinations of credibility. The trial judge's major role is the determination of fact, and with experience in fulfilling that role comes expertise. Duplication of the trial judge's efforts in the court of appeals would very likely contribute only negligibly to the accuracy of fact determination at a huge cost in diversion of judicial resources * * *. As the Court has stated in a different context, the trial on the merits should be "the 'main event' * * * rather than a 'tryout on the road.'"

Id. at 574, 105 S.Ct. at 1511–12, 84 L.Ed.2d at 528–29. Does *Anderson* undermine the basis of the Fourth Circuit's holding in *Hicks*? Does *Anderson* overrule *Hicks*?

5. CONCLUSIVENESS OF JUDGMENTS

Lawsuits are designed to settle disputes. An idealist might argue that nothing should be considered settled until it is settled *right*. A pragmatist could counter that nothing is settled at all unless it is settled *finally*. Cosmic questions may be debated endlessly, but controversies between individuals that are expected to result in enforceable judgments for damages or orders that must be obeyed under penalty of contempt must come to an end if the judicial process is to work at all. Res judicata requires that occasionally we let a judgment stand even when we become convinced that it was wrongly decided. A doctrine that only correct decisions have res judicata effect would furnish no finality at all.

The following case decided almost 300 years ago raises the same doubts that res judicata cases raise today: Is the decision fair to the plaintiff? Would an opposite decision be fair to the defendant?

———

FETTER v. BEALE, 1 Ld.Raym. 339, 91 Eng.Rep. 1122 (King's Bench 1697). Plaintiff had brought an action for battery against defendant and recovered £11. Subsequently "part of his skull by reason of the said battery came out of his head," and plaintiff brought another action. Plaintiff's counsel argued that "this action differed from the nature of the former * * * because the recovery in the former action was only for the bruise and battery, but here there is a maihem by the loss of the skull."

> And per totam Curiam, the jury in the former action considered the nature of the wound, and gave damages for all the damages that it had done to the plaintiff; and therefore a recovery in the said action is good here. And it is the plaintiff's fault, for if he had not been so hasty, he might have been satisfied for this loss of the skull also. Judgment for the defendant * * *.

A particularly difficult question of res judicata is presented when it is alleged that the first decision—now advanced as conclusive—was rendered by a court that lacked jurisdiction over the subject matter. This group of Illustrative Cases began with a decision that demonstrated the grave concern of the United States Supreme Court to keep the federal courts from deciding cases outside their constitutional and statutory jurisdiction. Res judicata was not involved in Capron v. Van Noorden; the trial court's decision was reversed in the ordinary course of appellate review. What if the plaintiff in that case had not sought a writ of error but had permitted the decision to become final and then instituted another action?

DES MOINES NAVIGATION & R. CO. v. IOWA HOMESTEAD CO.

Supreme Court of the United States, 1887.
123 U.S. 552, 8 S.Ct. 217, 31 L.Ed. 202.

Error to the Supreme Court of the State of Iowa.

Mr. Chief Justice Waite delivered the opinion of the court.

This suit was brought by the Iowa Homestead Company against the Des Moines Navigation and Railroad Company to recover the same taxes for the years 1864 to 1871, both inclusive, which formed part of the subject matter of the litigation between the same parties in Homestead Co. v. Valley Railroad, 17 Wall. 153 * * *. The Railroad Company set up the decree in its favor in that suit as a bar to the present action, and to this the Homestead Company replied "that the decree or judgment referred to is null and void, for the reason that the courts of the United States had no jurisdiction of said suit, and no legal power or authority to render said decree or judgment."

* * * It must be conceded that the Homestead Company and the Navigation and Railroad Company were both Iowa corporations, and, therefore, in law, citizens of the same State; but the defendants * * * who caused the removal to be made [from the Iowa state court to the United States Circuit Court], were citizens of the State of New York. After the removal was effected, all the above named defendants, as well as * * * the Navigation and Railroad Company, appeared, filed answers, and defended the action. The Homestead Company took issue on all the answers, and actually contested the matters in dispute with the Navigation and Railroad Company, as well as the other defendants, in the Circuit Court, and in this court on appeal, without taking any objection to the jurisdiction.

The precise question we have now to determine is whether the adjudication by this court, under such circumstances, of the matters then and now at issue between the Homestead Company and the Navigation and Railroad Company was absolutely void for want of jurisdiction. The point is not whether it was error in the Circuit Court to take jurisdiction of the suit, or of so much of it as related to the Navigation and Railroad Company, originally, but as to the binding effect of the decree of this court so long as it remains in force, and is not judicially annulled, vacated, or set aside.

* * *

It was settled by this court at a very early day, that, although the judgments and decrees of the Circuit Courts might be erroneous, if the records failed to show the facts on which the jurisdiction of the court rested, such as that the plaintiffs were citizens of different States from the defendants, yet that they were not nullities, and would bind the parties until reversed or otherwise set aside. * * * In * * * McCormick v. Sullivant, 10 Wheat. 192 [(1825)] * * * this court held on appeal that "the courts of the United States are courts of *limited,* but not of *inferior,* jurisdiction. If the jurisdiction be not alleged in the proceedings, their judgments and decrees may be reversed for that cause on a writ of error or appeal; but until reversed they are conclusive between the parties and their privies." "But they are not nullities." There has never been any departure from this rule.

It is said, however, that these decisions apply only to cases where the record simply fails to show jurisdiction. Here it is claimed that the record shows there could be no jurisdiction, because it appears affirmatively that the Navigation and Railroad Company, one of the defendants, was a citizen of the same State with the plaintiff. But the record shows, with equal distinctness, that all the parties were actually before the court, and made no objection to its jurisdiction. The act of 1867, under which the removal was had, provided that when a suit was pending in a state court "in which there is a controversy between a citizen of the State in which the suit is brought and a citizen of another State, * * * such citizen of another State, * * * if he will make and file an affidavit stating that he has reason to and does believe that, from prejudice or local influence, he will not be able to obtain justice in such state court, may * * * file a petition in such state court for the removal of the suit" into the Circuit Court of the United States, and, when all things have been done that the act requires, "it shall be * * * the duty of the state court to * * * proceed no further with the suit," and, after the record is entered in the Circuit Court, "the suit shall then proceed in the same manner as if it had been brought there by original process." [f]

In the suit now under consideration there was a separate and distinct controversy between the plaintiff, a citizen of Iowa, and each of the citizens of New York, who were defendants. Each controversy related to the several tracts of land claimed by each defendant individually, and not as joint owner with the other defendants. Three of the citizens of New York caused to be made and filed the necessary affidavit and petition for removal, and thereupon, by common consent apparently, the suit as an entirety was transferred to the Circuit Court for final adjudication as to all the parties. * * * Whether in such a case the suit could be removed was a question for the Circuit Court to decide when it was called on to take jurisdiction. If it kept the case when it ought to have been remanded, or if it proceeded to adjudicate upon matters in dispute between two citizens of Iowa, when it ought to have confined itself to those between the citizens of Iowa and the citizens of New York, its final decree in the suit could have been reversed, on appeal, as erroneous, but the decree would not have been a nullity. To determine whether the suit was removable in whole or in part or not, was certainly within the power of the Circuit Court. The decision of that question was the exercise and the rightful exercise of jurisdiction, no matter whether in favor of or against taking the cause. Whether its decision was right, in this or any other respect, was to be finally determined by this court on appeal. As the Circuit Court entertained the suit, and this court, on appeal, impliedly recognized its right to do so, and proceeded to dispose of the case finally on its merits, certainly our decree cannot, in the light of prior adjudications on the same general question, be deemed a nullity. It was, at the time of the trial in the present case in the court below, a valid and subsisting prior adjudication of the matters in controversy, binding on these parties, and a bar to this action. In refusing so to decide, the court failed to give full faith and credit to the decree of this court * * * and this was error.

*   *   *

f. The Judiciary Act of 1789 had been interpreted by the Supreme Court to require complete diversity of citizenship (all the plaintiffs being of a citizenship different from that of any defendant) for removal. It was widely argued that the 1867 statute referred to in the *Des Moines* case, because of a difference in language, did not have the same requirement. The Supreme Court held that the 1867 statute did require complete diversity, Case of the Sewing Machine Companies, 85 U.S. (18 Wall.) 553, 21 L.Ed. 914 (1874), but this decision came a year *after* the Court's decision in the Homestead Company's first suit in which the issue had not been raised.

Notes and Questions

1. When a court has rendered a judgment in a contested action, the judgment precludes the parties from litigating the question of the court's subject-matter jurisdiction in subsequent litigation except if:

(1) The subject matter of the action was so plainly beyond the court's jurisdiction that its entertaining the action was a manifest abuse of authority; or

(2) Allowing the judgment to stand would substantially infringe upon the authority of another tribunal or agency of government; or

(3) The judgment was rendered by a court lacking capability to make an adequately informed determination of a question concerning its own jurisdiction and as a matter of procedural fairness the party seeking to avoid the judgment should have opportunity belatedly to attack the court's subject matter jurisdiction.

Restatement (Second), Judgments § 12 (1982). What factors should a court regard as important in deciding such questions as what is "a manifest abuse of authority," or when a judgment "substantially" infringes a tribunal's authority, or when a court lacks "capability to make an adequately informed determination"?

2. Was it critical to the Supreme Court's opinion in this case that the first case had been heard and determined by the Supreme Court itself? Would the case have been decided differently if no review had been sought in the first case at all?

3. Was the fact that the question of jurisdiction was a doubtful one at the time the first *Homestead Company* case arose relevant to the Supreme Court's decision in the second case?

4. Suppose that the issue of jurisdiction is raised in a case and erroneously decided. Is this a factor arguing for or against the application of res judicata in a second action?

5. Since it is clear in the principal case that in the suit before the Court there was no diversity of citizenship and the writ of error was to the Supreme Court of Iowa, what was the basis for appellate jurisdiction in the United States Supreme Court?

Chapter 2

SELECTING THE PROPER COURT

SECTION A. JURISDICTION OVER THE PARTIES

1. THE TRADITIONAL BASES FOR JURISDICTION

PENNOYER v. NEFF

Supreme Court of the United States, 1877.
95 U.S. (5 Otto) 714, 24 L.Ed. 565.

Error to the Circuit Court of the United States for the District of Oregon.

MR. JUSTICE FIELD delivered the opinion of the court.

This is an action to recover the possession of a tract of land, of the alleged value of $15,000, situated in the State of Oregon. The plaintiff asserts title to the premises by a patent of the United States issued to him in [March] 1866, under the Act of Congress of September 27th, 1850, 9 Stat. at L., 496, usually known as the Donation Law of Oregon. The defendant claims to have acquired the premises under a sheriff's deed, made upon a sale of the property on execution issued upon a judgment recovered against the plaintiff in one of the circuit courts of the State. The case turns upon the validity of this judgment.

It appears from the record that the judgment was rendered in February, 1866, in favor of J.H. Mitchell, for less than $300, including costs, in an action brought by him upon a demand for services as an attorney; that, at the time the action was commenced and the judgment rendered, the defendant therein, the plaintiff here, was a non-resident of the State; that he was not personally served with process, and did not appear therein; and that the judgment was entered upon his default in not answering the complaint, upon a constructive service of summons by publication.

The Code of Oregon provides for such service when an action is brought against a non-resident and absent defendant, who has property within the State. It also provides, where the action is for the recovery of money or damages, for the attachment of the property of the non-resident. And it also declares that no natural person is subject to the jurisdiction of a court of the State, "unless he appear in the court, or be found within the State, or be a resident thereof, or have property therein; and in the last case, only to the extent of such property at the time the jurisdiction attached." Construing this latter provision to mean that, in an action for money or damages where a defendant does not appear in the court, and is not found within the State, and is not a resident thereof, but has property therein, the jurisdiction of the court extends only over such property, the declaration expresses a principle of general, if not universal, law. The authority of every tribunal is necessarily restricted by the territorial limits of the State in which it is established. Any attempt to exercise authority beyond those limits would be deemed in every other forum, as has been said by this court, an illegitimate assumption of power, and be resisted as mere abuse. * * * In the case against the plaintiff, the property here in controversy sold under the judgment rendered was not attached, nor in any way brought under the jurisdiction of the court. Its first connection with the case was caused by a levy of the execution. It was not, therefore, disposed of pursuant to any adjudication, but only in enforcement of a personal judgment, having no relation to the property, rendered against a non-resident without service of process upon him in the action, or his appearance therein. The court below did not consider that an attachment of the property was essential to its jurisdiction or to the validity of the sale, but held that the judgment was invalid from defects in the affidavit upon which the order of publication was obtained, and in the affidavit by which the publication was proved.

There is some difference of opinion among the members of this court as to the rulings upon these alleged defects. The majority are of opinion that, inasmuch as the statute requires, for an order of publication, that certain facts shall appear by affidavit *to the satisfaction of the court or judge,* defects in such affidavit can only be taken advantage of on appeal, or by some other direct proceeding, and cannot be urged to impeach the judgment collaterally. The majority of the court are also of opinion that the provision of the statute requiring proof of the publication in a newspaper to be made by the "affidavit of the printer, or his foreman, or his principal clerk," is satisfied when the affidavit is made by the editor of the paper. * * *

If, therefore, we were confined to the rulings of the court below upon the defects in the affidavits mentioned, we should be unable to uphold its decision. But it was also contended in that court, and is insisted upon here, that the judgment in the State Court against the plaintiff was void for want of personal service of process on him, or of his appearance in the action in which it was rendered, and that the premises in controversy could not be subjected to the payment of the demand of a resident creditor except by a proceeding *in rem;* that is, by a direct proceeding against the property for that purpose. If these positions are sound, the ruling of the Circuit Court as to the invalidity of that judgment must be sustained, notwithstanding our dissent from the reasons upon which it was made. And that they are sound would seem to follow from two well established principles of public law respecting the jurisdiction of an independent State over persons and property. The several States of the Union are not, it is true, in every respect independent, many of the rights and powers which originally belonged to them being now vested in the government created by the Constitution. But, except as restrained and limited by that instrument, they possess and exercise the authority of independent States, and the principles of public law to which we have referred are applicable to them. One of these principles is, that every State possesses exclusive jurisdiction and sovereignty over persons and property within its territory. As a consequence, every State has the power to determine for itself the civil *status* and capacities of its inhabitants; to prescribe the subjects upon which they may contract, the forms and solemnities with which their contracts shall be executed, the rights and obligations arising from them, and the mode in which their validity shall be determined and their obligations enforced; and also to regulate the manner and conditions upon which property situated within such territory, both personal and real, may be acquired, enjoyed and transferred. The other principle of public law referred to follows from the one mentioned; that is, that no State can exercise direct jurisdiction and authority over persons or property without its territory. * * * The several States are of equal dignity and authority, and the independence of one implies the exclusion of power from all others. And so it is laid down by jurists, as an elementary principle, that the laws of one State have no operation outside of its territory, except so far as is allowed by comity; and that no tribunal established by it can extend its process beyond that territory so as to subject either persons or property to its decisions. * * *

But as contracts made in one State may be enforceable only in another State, and property may be held by non-residents, the exercise of the jurisdiction which every State is admitted to possess over persons and property within its own territory will often affect persons and property without it. To any influence exerted in this way by a State affecting persons resident or property situated elsewhere, no objection can be justly taken; whilst any direct exertion of authority upon them, in an attempt to give exterritorial operation to its laws, or to enforce an ex-territorial jurisdiction by its tribunals, would be deemed an encroachment upon the independence of the State in which the persons are domiciled or the property is situated, and be resisted as usurpation.

Thus the State, through its tribunals, may compel persons domiciled within its limits to execute, in pursuance of their contracts respecting property elsewhere situated, instruments in such form and with such solemnities as to transfer the title, so far as such formalities can be complied with; and the exercise of this jurisdiction in no manner interferes with the supreme control over the property by the State within which it is situated. * * *

So the State, through its tribunals, may subject property situated within its limits owned by non-residents to the payment of the demand of its own citizens against them; and the exercise of this jurisdiction in no respect infringes upon the sovereignty of the State where the owners are domiciled. Every State owes protection to its own citizens; and, when non-residents deal with them, it is a legitimate and just exercise of authority to hold and appropriate any property owned by such non-residents to satisfy the claims of its citizens. It is in virtue of the State's jurisdiction over the property of the non-resident situated within its limits that its tribunals can inquire into that non-resident's obligations to its own citizens, and the inquiry can then be carried only to the extent necessary to control the disposition of the property. If the non-resident have no property in the State, there is nothing upon which the tribunals can adjudicate.

    * * * If, without personal service, judgments *in personam,* obtained *ex parte* against non-residents and absent parties, upon mere publication of process, which, in the great majority of cases, would never be seen by the parties interested, could be upheld and enforced, they would be the constant instruments of fraud and oppression. Judgments for all sorts of claims upon contracts and for torts, real or pretended, would be thus obtained, under which property would be seized, when the evidence of the transactions upon which they were founded, if they ever had any existence, had perished.

    Substituted service by publication, or in any other authorized form, may be sufficient to inform parties of the object of proceedings taken where property is once brought under the control of the court by seizure or some equivalent act. The law assumes that property is always in the possession of its owner, in person or by agent; and it proceeds upon the theory that its seizure will inform him, not only that it is taken into the custody of the court, but that he must look to any proceedings authorized by law upon such seizure for its condemnation and sale. * * * In other words, such service may answer in all actions which are substantially proceedings *in rem.* But where the entire object of the action is to determine the personal rights and obligations of the defendants, that is, where the suit is merely *in personam,* constructive service in this form upon a non-resident is ineffectual for any purpose. Process from the tribunals of one State cannot run into another State, and summon parties there domiciled to leave its territory and respond to proceedings against them. Publication of process or notice within the State where the tribunal sits cannot create any greater obligation upon the non-resident to appear. Process sent to him out of the State, and process published within it, are equally unavailing in proceedings to establish his personal liability.

    The want of authority of the tribunals of a State to adjudicate upon the obligations of non-residents, where they have no property within its limits, is not denied by the court below; but the position is assumed that, where they have property within the State, it is immaterial whether the property is in the first instance brought under the control of the court by attachment or some other equivalent act, and afterwards applied by its judgment to the satisfaction of demands against its owner; or such demands be first established in a personal action, and the property of the non-resident be afterwards seized and sold on execution. But the answer to this position has already been given in the statement, that the jurisdiction of the court to inquire into and determine his obligations at all is only

incidental to its jurisdiction over the property. Its jurisdiction in that respect cannot be made to depend upon facts to be ascertained after it has tried the cause and rendered the judgment. If the judgment be previously void, it will not become valid by the subsequent discovery of property of the defendant, or by his subsequent acquisition of it. The judgment, if void when rendered, will always remain void; it cannot occupy the doubtful position of being valid if property be found, and void if there be none. Even if the position assumed were confined to cases where the non-resident defendant possessed property in the State at the commencement of the action, it would still make the validity of the proceedings and judgment depend upon the question whether, before the levy of the execution, the defendant had or had not disposed of the property. If, before the levy, the property should be sold, then, according to this position, the judgment would not be binding. This doctrine would introduce a new element of uncertainty in judicial proceedings. The contrary is the law; the validity of every judgment depends upon the jurisdiction of the court before it is rendered, not upon what may occur subsequently.
*   *   *

The force and effect of judgments rendered against non-residents without personal service of process upon them, or their voluntary appearance, have been the subject of frequent consideration in the courts of the United States and of the several States, as attempts have been made to enforce such judgments in States other than those in which they were rendered, under the provision of the Constitution requiring that "Full faith and credit shall be given in each State to the public Acts, records and judicial proceedings of every other State;" and the Act of Congress providing for the mode of authenticating such Acts, records and proceedings, and declaring that, when thus authenticated, "They shall have such faith and credit given to them in every court within the United States as they have by law or usage in the courts of the State from which they are or shall be taken." In the earlier cases, it was supposed that the Act gave to all judgments the same effect in other States which they had by law in the State where rendered. But this view was afterwards qualified so as to make the Act applicable only when the court rendering the judgment had jurisdiction of the parties and of the subject-matter, and not to preclude an inquiry into the jurisdiction of the court in which the judgment was rendered, or the right of the State itself to exercise authority over the person or the subject-matter. *   *   *

Since the adoption of the 14th Amendment to the Federal Constitution, the validity of such judgments may be directly questioned, and their enforcement in the State resisted, on the ground that proceedings in a court of justice to determine the personal rights and obligations of parties over whom that court has no jurisdiction do not constitute due process of law. Whatever difficulty may be experienced in giving to those terms a definition which will embrace every permissible exertion of power affecting private rights, and exclude such as is forbidden, there can be no doubt of their meaning when applied to judicial proceedings. They then mean a course of legal proceedings according to those rules and principles which have been established in our systems of jurisprudence for the protection and enforcement of private rights. To give such proceedings any validity, there must be a tribunal competent by its constitution—that is, by the law of its creation—to pass upon the subject-matter of the suit; and, if that involves merely a determination of the personal liability of the defendant, he must be brought within its jurisdiction by service of process within the State, or his voluntary appearance.

Except in cases affecting the personal *status* of the plaintiff, and cases in which that mode of service may be considered to have been assented to in advance as hereinafter mentioned, the substituted service of process by publication allowed by the law of Oregon and by similar laws in other States, where actions are brought against non-residents, is effectual only where, in connection with process against the person for commencing the action, property in the State is brought under the control of the court, and subjected to its disposition by process adapted to that purpose, or where the judgment is sought as a means of reaching such property or affecting some interest therein; in other words, where the action is in the nature of a proceeding *in rem*.   *   *   *

It is true that, in a strict sense, a proceeding *in rem* is one taken directly against property, and has for its object the disposition of the property, without reference to the title of individual claimants; but, in a larger and more general sense, the terms are applied to actions between parties, where the direct object is to reach and dispose of property owned by them, or of some interest therein. Such are cases commenced by attachment against the property of debtors, or instituted to partition real estate, foreclose a mortgage, or enforce a lien. So far as they affect property in the State, they are substantially proceedings *in rem* in the broader sense which we have mentioned.

*   *   *

It follows from the views expressed that the personal judgment recovered in the State Court of Oregon against the plaintiff herein, then a non-resident of the State, was without any validity, and did not authorize a sale of the property in controversy.

To prevent any misapplication of the views expressed in this opinion, it is proper to observe that we do not mean to assert, by anything we have said, that a State may not authorize proceedings to determine the *status* of one of its citizens towards a non-resident, which would be binding within the State, though made without service of process or personal notice to the non-resident. The jurisdiction which every State possesses to determine the civil *status* and capacities of all its inhabitants involves authority to prescribe the conditions on which proceedings affecting them may be commenced and carried on within its territory. The State, for example, has absolute right to prescribe the conditions upon which the marriage relation between its own citizens shall be created, and the causes for which it may be dissolved. One of the parties guilty of acts for which, by the law of the State, a dissolution may be granted, may have removed to a State where no dissolution is permitted. The complaining party would, therefore, fail if a divorce were sought in the State of the defendant; and if application could not be made to the tribunals of the complainant's domicil in such case, and proceedings be there instituted without personal service of process or personal notice to the offending party, the injured citizen would be without redress. * * *

Neither do we mean to assert that a State may not require a non-resident entering into a partnership or association within its limits, or making contracts enforceable there, to appoint an agent or representative in the State to receive service of process and notice in legal proceedings instituted with respect to such partnership, association or contracts, or to designate a place where such service may be made and notice given, and provide, upon their failure, to make such appointment or to designate such place that service may be made upon a public officer designated for that purpose, or in some other prescribed way, and that judgments rendered upon such service may not be binding upon the non-residents both within and without the State. * * * Nor do we doubt that a State, on creating corporations or other institutions for pecuniary or charitable purposes, may provide a mode in which their conduct may be investigated, their obligations enforced, or their charters revoked, which shall require other than personal service upon their officers or members. * * *

In the present case, there is no feature of this kind and, consequently, no consideration of what would be the effect of such legislation in enforcing the contract of a non-resident can arise. * * *

Judgment affirmed.

[The dissenting opinion of JUSTICE HUNT is omitted.]

Notes and Questions

1. Traditional analysis distinguishes three types of jurisdiction. In a proceeding in personam, the court exercises its power to render a judgment for or against a person by virtue of his presence within the state's territory or his citizenship there. In a proceeding in rem, the court exercises its power to determine the status of property located within its territory, and the determination of the court is binding with respect to all possible interest holders in that property. In a proceeding quasi-in-rem, the court renders a judgment for or against a person but recovery is limited to the value of property that is within the jurisdiction and thus subject to the court's authority. The dispute that gives rise to an action quasi-in-rem may be related to the property or unrelated to it. In an action quasi-in-rem, the property may be used to satisfy any judgment assessed in the action.

2. The concepts of jurisdiction found in the *Pennoyer* opinion were derived from nineteenth century international law. In the traditional international model, a citizen of Country A might have been injured by a citizen of Country B in Country A. The citizen of Country A seeking relief had three options: proceed against the citizen of Country B in personam in Country A (with the likelihood that the paper called a judgment would be worthless because the courts of Country B would not enforce it against citizens of Country B); proceed against the citizen of Country B quasi-in-rem in Country A (with the advantage that the property of the citizen of Country B in Country A would be available to satisfy at least part of the judgment); or proceed against the citizen of Country B in the courts of Country B (in the

hope of winning a judgment enforceable in Country B). Given these choices, it is understandable that the citizen of Country A would probably prefer the courts of Country A to the courts of Country B, the latter being farther away and possibly more disposed to find in favor of the citizen of Country B, or to sue quasi-in-rem in Country A, so at least partial payment would be assured.

Do the same factors warrant applying these distinctions in jurisdiction in the context of the American federal system? Does not the Full Faith and Credit Clause of the Constitution require states to recognize and enforce valid judgments by other states? Do the states have the same kind of interest in adjudicating claims brought by their citizens when the stake is state sovereignty rather than national sovereignty?

3. In order for a judgment to be valid, personal jurisdiction must exist under the applicable jurisdictional statutes as well as under relevant constitutional standards. Was the defect in *Pennoyer* statutory or constitutional?

4. Does the length of time the defendant is in the jurisdiction matter in an in personam action? Does the reason why the person is in the jurisdiction make a difference? In Grace v. MacArthur, 170 F.Supp. 442 (E.D.Ark.1959), service of the complaint was made on the defendant while he was a passenger on a commercial flight from Tennessee to Texas when the plane was over Arkansas. The court upheld the exercise of jurisdiction by the federal district court sitting in Arkansas. See also Peabody v. Hamilton, 106 Mass. 217, 220 (1870) ("When the party is in the state, however transiently, and the summons is actually served upon him there, the jurisdiction of the court is complete, as to the person of the defendant.").

5. Can a court assert jurisdiction over a citizen who is absent from the jurisdiction? In BLACKMER v. UNITED STATES, 284 U.S. 421, 438–39, 52 S.Ct. 252, 255, 76 L.Ed. 375, 383 (1932), petitioner, an American citizen, sought reversal of a contempt conviction resulting from his refusal to comply with a subpoena issued by an American court and served upon him in France in connection with a proceeding that grew out of the Teapot Dome Scandal. Service was authorized by federal statute. The Supreme Court concluded that no violation of due process had taken place because

> the jurisdiction of the United States over its absent citizen, so far as the binding effect of its legislation is concerned, is a jurisdiction in personam, as he is personally bound to take notice of the laws that are applicable to him and to obey them. * * * The question of the validity of the provision for actual service of the subpoena in a foreign country is one that arises solely between the * * * United States and the citizen. The mere giving of such a notice to the citizen in the foreign country of the requirement of his government that he shall return is in no sense an invasion of any right of the foreign government and the citizen has no standing to invoke any such supposed right.

The *Blackmer* principle was applied to state-court litigation in MILLIKEN v. MEYER, 311 U.S. 457, 462–63, 61 S.Ct. 339, 342–43, 85 L.Ed. 278, 283 (1940). Milliken sued Meyer, a Wyoming resident, in a Wyoming state court. Personal service was effected in Colorado under a Wyoming statute that permitted such service, in lieu of service by publication, on absent residents. Meyer did not appear and an in personam judgment was entered against him. Four years later Meyer asked a Colorado court to restrain Milliken's enforcement of the Wyoming judgment. The United States Supreme Court held the

Wyoming judgment valid and entitled to full faith and credit. According to the Court:

> * * * Domicile in the state is alone sufficient to bring an absent defendant within the reach of the state's jurisdiction for purposes of a personal judgment by means of appropriate substituted service. * * * [T]he authority of a state over one of its citizens is not terminated by the mere fact of his absence from the state. The state which accords him privileges and affords protection to him and his property by virtue of his domicile may also exact reciprocal duties.

The Court's opinion made no attempt to distinguish among "resident," "domicile," and "citizen." What factors are relevant in deciding whether defendant's relationship with the forum state is sufficient to invoke the *Milliken* doctrine? Does Section 1 of the Fourteenth Amendment help answer the question by defining what it means to be a citizen of a state? Do *Blackmer* and *Milliken* fall within the scope of the statement in *Pennoyer* that "every State has the power to determine for itself the civil *status* and capacities of its inhabitants," or do they involve a different basis of jurisdiction?

6. Suppose a plaintiff brings suit in a forum with which she has no other connection. Should that forum be able to entertain a suit *against* the plaintiff? Consider ADAM v. SAENGER, 303 U.S. 59, 67–68, 58 S.Ct. 454, 458, 82 L.Ed. 649, 654–55 (1938). The Beaumont Export & Import Co., a Texas corporation, brought suit against Montes in a California state court. In accordance with California procedure, Montes filed a cross-action against the corporation. The corporation then defaulted, its suit was dismissed, and Montes obtained a default judgment on his cross-action. Montes later assigned his judgment to Adam, who sought to enforce it in a Texas court. The Texas court refused to recognize the California judgment, holding that California law did not permit service of the complaint in the cross-action on the corporation's attorney, and that the corporation had not been otherwise "present" in California for purposes of jurisdiction. The United States Supreme Court reversed, holding that the method of service in the cross-action was authorized by California law and the judgment was entitled to full faith and credit:

> There is nothing in the Fourteenth Amendment to prevent a state from adopting a procedure by which a judgment *in personam* may be rendered in a cross-action against a plaintiff in its courts, upon service of process or of appropriate pleading upon his attorney of record. The plaintiff having, by his voluntary act in demanding justice from the defendant, submitted himself to the jurisdiction of the court, there is nothing arbitrary or unreasonable in treating him as being there for all purposes for which justice to the defendant requires his presence. It is the price which the state may exact as the condition of opening its courts to the plaintiff.

Would it matter whether or not the action is between the same two parties? Suppose a third party had instituted suit in California against Beaumont in an action unrelated to the suit with Montes. Would the California court have had jurisdiction? If there was jurisdiction, would it be based on Beaumont's presence in the state or on some other notion? In this regard, what is the significance of the Court's reference to the fact that Beaumont voluntarily acted to invoke the authority of the California courts?

Should a state be permitted to condition the use of its courts on consent to the jurisdiction of those courts for purposes unrelated to the initial lawsuit?

7. The civil-law tradition with regard to personal jurisdiction is somewhat different from our own. Whereas the cornerstone of the common-law's concept of jurisdiction historically has been defendant's presence, domicile has been the key in The Netherlands and Switzerland, plaintiff's nationality has been of great importance in France, and domicile and the situs of property have been of major significance in Germany. "In this area of law, differences among civil-law countries are as great as differences between given civil-law and common-law countries." de Vries & Lowenfeld, *Jurisdiction in Personal Actions—A Comparison of Civil Law Views,* 44 Iowa L.Rev. 306, 344 (1959).

2. EXPANDING THE BASES OF PERSONAL JURISDICTION

Increased interstate travel in the early twentieth century, particularly as a result of the growing popularity of the automobile, brought with it increased interstate litigation. In order to ensure that transient drivers not be beyond jurisdiction when they drove into another state, some states came to condition the use of their roads by out-of-state drivers on consent to the jurisdiction of the state's courts over matters arising from a party's activity within the state. In Kane v. New Jersey, 242 U.S. 160, 37 S.Ct. 30, 61 L.Ed. 222 (1916), the Supreme Court held that New Jersey could require an out-of-state motorist to file a formal instrument appointing a New Jersey agent to receive process prior to using the state's highways. Eventually, some states moved beyond express consent.

HESS v. PAWLOSKI
Supreme Court of the United States, 1927.
274 U.S. 352, 47 S.Ct. 632, 71 L.Ed. 1091.

In Error to the Superior Court of Worcester County, Massachusetts.

MR. JUSTICE BUTLER delivered the opinion of the Court.

This action was brought by defendant in error to recover damages for personal injuries. The declaration alleged that plaintiff in error negligently and wantonly drove a motor vehicle on a public highway in Massachusetts, and that by reason thereof the vehicle struck and injured defendant in error. Plaintiff in error is a resident of Pennsylvania. No personal service was made on him, and no property belonging to him was attached. The service of process was made in compliance with chapter 90, General Laws of Massachusetts, as amended by Stat.1923, c. 431, § 2, the material parts of which follow:

> The acceptance by a nonresident of the rights and privileges conferred by section three or four, as evidenced by his operating a motor vehicle thereunder, or the operation by a nonresident of a motor vehicle on a public way in the commonwealth other than under said sections, shall be deemed equivalent to an appointment by such nonresident of the registrar or his successor in office, to be his true and lawful attorney upon whom may be served all lawful processes in any action or proceeding against him, growing out of any accident or collision in which said nonresident may be involved while operating a motor vehicle on such a

way, and said acceptance or operation shall be a signification of his agreement that any such process against him which is so served shall be of the same legal force and validity as if served on him personally. Service of such process shall be made by leaving a copy of the process with a fee of two dollars in the hands of the registrar, or in his office, and such service shall be sufficient service upon the said nonresident: Provided, that notice of such service and a copy of the process are forthwith sent by registered mail by the plaintiff to the defendant, and the defendant's return receipt and the plaintiff's affidavit of compliance herewith are appended to the writ and entered with the declaration. * * *

Plaintiff in error appeared specially for the purpose of contesting jurisdiction, and filed an answer in abatement and moved to dismiss on the ground that the service of process, if sustained, would deprive him of his property without due process of law, in violation of the Fourteenth Amendment. The court overruled the answer in abatement and denied the motion. The Supreme Judicial Court held the statute to be a valid exercise of the police power, and affirmed the order. * * * At the trial the contention was renewed and again denied. Plaintiff in error excepted. The jury returned a verdict for defendant in error. The exceptions were overruled by the Supreme Judicial Court. * * * Thereupon the superior court entered judgment. The writ of error was allowed by the Chief Justice of that court.

The question is whether the Massachusetts enactment contravenes the due process clause of the Fourteenth Amendment.

The process of a court of one state cannot run into another and summon a party there domiciled to respond to proceedings against him. Notice sent outside the state to a nonresident is unavailing to give jurisdiction in an action against him personally for money recovery. Pennoyer v. Neff * * *. There must be actual service within the state of notice upon him or upon some one authorized to accept service for him. * * * A personal judgment rendered against a nonresident, who has neither been served with process nor appeared in the suit, is without validity. McDonald v. Mabee, 243 U.S. 90, 37 S.Ct. 343, 61 L.Ed. 608, L.R.A.1917F, 458. The mere transaction of business in a state by nonresident natural persons does not imply consent to be bound by the process of its courts. Flexner v. Farson, 248 U.S. 289, 39 S.Ct. 97, 63 L.Ed. 250. The power of a state to exclude foreign corporations, although not absolute, but qualified, is the ground on which such an implication is supported as to them. * * * But a state may not withhold from nonresident individuals the right of doing business therein. The privileges and immunities clause of the Constitution (section 2, art. 4), safeguards to the citizens of one state the right "to pass through, or to reside in any other state for purposes of trade, agriculture, professional pursuits, or otherwise." And it prohibits state legislation discriminating against citizens of other states. * * *

Motor vehicles are dangerous machines, and, even when skillfully and carefully operated, their use is attended by serious dangers to persons and property. In the public interest the state may make and enforce regulations reasonably calculated to promote care on the part of all, residents and nonresidents alike, who use its highways. The measure in question operates to require a nonresident to answer for his conduct in the state where arise causes of action alleged against him, as well as to provide for a claimant a convenient method by which he may sue to enforce his rights. Under the statute the implied consent is limited to proceedings growing out of accidents or collisions on a highway in which the nonresident may be involved. It is required that he shall actually receive and receipt for notice of the service and a copy of the process. And it contemplates such continuances as may be found necessary to give reasonable time and opportunity for defense. It makes no hostile discrimination against nonresidents, but tends to put them on the same footing as residents. Literal and precise equality in respect of this matter is not attainable; it is not required. * * * The state's power to regulate the use of its highways extends to their use by nonresidents as well as by residents. * * * And, in advance of the operation of a motor vehicle on its highway by a nonresident, the state may require him to appoint one of its officials as his agent on whom process may be served in proceedings growing out of such use. Kane v. New Jersey * * *. That case recognizes power of the state to exclude a nonresident until the formal appointment is made. And, having the power so to exclude, the state may declare that the use of the highway by the nonresident is the equivalent of the appointment of the registrar as agent on whom process may be served. * * * The difference between the formal and implied appointment is not substantial, so far as concerns the application of the due process clause of the Fourteenth Amendment.

Judgment affirmed.

Notes and Questions

1. Would a nonresident-motorist statute that purported to assert jurisdiction over any cause of action that arises out of the presence of defendant's vehicle within the state, or over people other than the driver of the vehicle, be constitutional? Would it be wise? Could the implied consent to jurisdiction created by driving within a state be employed to support jurisdiction over the defendant in a matter unrelated to her conduct within the state?

2. The idea of implied consent has been used in other contexts as well. In HENRY L. DOHERTY & CO. v. GOODMAN, 294 U.S. 623, 55 S.Ct. 553, 79 L.Ed. 1097 (1935), the Supreme Court upheld Iowa's right to apply a similar concept to assert jurisdiction over a nonresident who was selling securities in Iowa regarding controversies arising out of those sales.

3. THE PROBLEM OF CORPORATIONS

The jurisdictional bases developed in *Pennoyer*—presence and citizenship—are not easily applied to corporations. A corporation, after all, is a fiction. It exists on paper and acts through its employees, directors, and shareholders. Nonetheless, as corporations grew beyond state boundaries, courts were forced to develop ways to apply the jurisdictional principles of *Pennoyer* to them.

KURLAND, THE SUPREME COURT, THE DUE PROCESS CLAUSE
AND THE IN PERSONAM JURISDICTION OF STATE COURTS—FROM
PENNOYER TO DENCKLA: A REVIEW, 25 U.Chi.L.Rev. 569, 577–86
(1958):

A domestic corporation is subject to suit in the courts of the state of
its incorporation, whether because it is a creature of that state and
therefore necessarily subject to its control, or because it is "domiciled"
there, or because it is "present" there.

Foreign corporations have proved more difficult to fit into the concepts which underlie the principles of personal jurisdiction relating to
individuals, for it has been thought necessary to speak in "fictive" terms
whether the term used is the corporation's "citizenship," its "domicile," its
"consent," or its "presence." "Until toward the middle of the [nineteenth]
century, the idea seems to have been widely prevalent that foreign
attachment was the only process available against them." In some
measure the difficulties flowed from a notion phrased by Mr. Chief Justice
Taney in Bank of Augusta v. Earle [38 U.S. (13 Pet.) 519, 588, 10 L.Ed.
274, 308 (1839)]:

> * * * a corporation can have no legal existence out of the bundaries
> [sic] of the sovereignty by which it is created. It exists only in contempla-
> tion of law, and by force of the law; and where that law ceases to operate,
> and is no longer obligatory, the corporation can have no existence. It
> must dwell in the place of its creation; and cannot migrate to another
> sovereignty.

This apparently did not mean that a corporation was precluded from
engaging in activities beyond the borders of the state of its incorporation,
but only that any activity which it conducted outside the state of its
incorporation was dependent upon the permission of the government
within whose jurisdiction it desired to operate. * * *

As the corporate form of business became more and more the common
method of carrying on economic activity, it became incumbent on the
courts to make provision for suits by and against such entities in foreign
states. Two major theories evolved and merged into a third, none of
which proved satisfactory. The first was the "consent" theory, which
quickly prevailed in the Supreme Court. The second was a theory of
"presence," which became necessary in order to fill the gaps which the
"consent" theory did not cover, but which required the rejection of the
Taney dictum in Bank of Augusta v. Earle. The third was the "doing
business" notion.

1. *"Consent."* The consent thesis rested on the proposition that,
since a foreign corporation could not carry on business within a state
without the permission of that state, the state could impose as a condition
of engaging in business within its borders a requirement that the corporation appoint an agent to receive service of process within the state.
* * * The important limitations on the conditions which could be
imposed by the state were set forth * * * by Mr. Justice Field in St.
Clair v. Cox [106 U.S. 350, 356, 1 S.Ct. 354, 360, 27 L.Ed. 222, 225 (1882)]:

The State may, therefore, impose as a condition upon which a foreign corporation shall be permitted to do business within her limits, that it shall stipulate that in any litigation *arising out of its transactions in the State,* it will accept as sufficient the service of process on its agents or persons specially designated; and the condition would be eminently fit and just. And such condition and stipulation may be implied as well as expressed.

Field reiterated the primary limitation that "the corporation be engaged in business in the State, and the agent be appointed to act there." The Court later made it clear, too, that the agent must be one who would be likely to inform the corporation of the receipt and content of the process and if service were made on an official or person designated by the state that such person be required to forward notice of the suit to the defendant. The "consent" which a state could demand was held to be a valid base for jurisdiction of the federal courts within that state as well as of state courts.

One of the questions resulting from the adoption of this thesis was whether, if implied consent was confined to cases arising out of transactions within the state as stated in St. Clair v. Cox, the consent secured by the actual appointment of an agent by the corporation was similarly limited. Three of America's greatest jurists [Cardozo, Hand, and Holmes] answered the question in the negative. * * * One may wonder how, in rejecting the fiction of consent for the corporations which have not appointed agents, these three could have found "a true consent" in the appointment of an agent in conformity with statutes, especially when the statutes have not suggested different treatment for extorted actual consent and the equally unwilling implied consent. * * * One may wonder, too, why, if it is the Due Process Clause—or a "principle of natural justice"—which denied the power of the state to imply consent to suit on claims arising out of transactions occurring elsewhere than within the state, it did not also deny to the state the power to extort such a consent in writing. Certainly the *St. Clair* case on which these cases are predicated drew no such distinction.

There was still another major difficulty with the consent thesis. The Privileges and Immunities Clause did not prohibit a state from excluding a foreign corporation. This point was made pellucidly in Paul v. Virginia [75 U.S. (8 Wall.) 168, 19 L.Ed. 357 (1868)] in language quite reminiscent of Taney's in Bank of Augusta v. Earle * * *. But insurance, which was the subject of the business involved in that case, was not then considered "interstate commerce." And it soon became established law that a foreign corporation could not be prevented by a state from carrying on interstate commerce within its borders. It would seem to follow that if the state's power to exact consent to be sued depended on its power to exclude, and it could not exclude, it could not exact such consent. Nonetheless, the Court continued to hold that foreign corporations were subject to the jurisdiction of state courts, even if the business they carried on within the state was interstate commerce.

* * *

2. *"Presence."* The presence doctrine afforded an equally defective pattern, for it necessarily rejected the theme of *Bank of Augusta* and Paul v. Virginia, that a corporation cannot exist beyond the limits of the state which created it. From time to time, however, the Supreme Court spoke as though the issue were one of presence rather than consent. Thus, Mr. Justice Brandeis said in Philadelphia and Reading R.R. v. McKibbin [243 U.S. 264, 265, 37 S.Ct. 280, 61 L.Ed. 710, 711–12 (1917)], "A foreign corporation is amenable to process to enforce a personal liability, in the absence of consent, only if it is doing business within the State in such manner and to such extent as to warrant the inference that it is present there." And very distinguished authorities in other courts adopted this approach to the problem. The presence theory, unlike the consent doctrine, would sustain jurisdiction against corporations on claims which did not arise out of the business done within the state, a position which the Supreme Court never openly espoused. On the other hand, under that doctrine, the departure from the state by the corporation by ceasing to do business therein would preclude later assertion of jurisdiction even as to claims which grew out of the business it had once done there. The implied consent theory would sustain jurisdiction under such circumstances.

In the same fashion in which he had removed the mask of the consent theory, Judge Hand exposed the false face of the presence thesis. In Hutchinson v. Chase and Gilbert [45 F.2d 139, 141 (2d Cir.1930)], he wrote for a court made up of three of the most capable judges ever to sit on any American bench:

It scarcely advances the argument to say that a corporation must be 'present' in the foreign state, if we define that word as demanding such dealings as will subject it to jurisdiction, for then it does no more than put the question to be answered. * * *

When we say therefore, that a corporation may be sued only where it is 'present,' we understand that the word is used, not literally, but as shorthand for something else. It might indeed be argued that it must stand suit upon any controversy arising out of legal transactions entered into where the suit was brought, but that would impose upon it too severe a burden. On the other hand, it is not plain that it ought not, upon proper notice, to defend suits arising out of foreign transactions, if it conducts a continuous business in the state of the forum. * * * But a single transaction is certainly not enough * * *. There must be some continuous dealings in the state of the forum; enough to demand trial away from its home.

This last appears to us to be really the controlling consideration, expressed shortly by the word 'presence,' but involving an estimate of the inconveniences which would result from requiring it to defend, where it has been sued. We are to inquire whether the extent and continuity of what it has done in the state in question makes it reasonable to bring it before one of its courts. Nor is it anomalous to make the question of jurisdiction depend upon a practical test. * * * This does not indeed avoid the uncertainties, for it is as hard to judge what dealings make it just to subject a foreign corporation to local suit, as to say when it is 'present,' but at least it puts the real question, and that is something. * * *

In his conclusion, Judge Hand once again foreshadowed the doctrine which the Supreme Court would later adopt:

> In the end there is nothing more to be said than that all the defendant's local activities, taken together, do not make it reasonable to impose such a burden upon it. It is fairer that the plaintiffs should go to Boston than that the defendant should come here. Certainly such a standard is no less vague than any that the courts have hitherto set up; one may look from one end of the decisions to the other and find no vade mecum.

[45 F.2d at 142]

3. *"Doing Business."* The courts thus came round to using either the consent thesis or the presence thesis, depending largely upon which would support jurisdiction over the nonresident corporation. No notice was taken of the underlying inconsistency between the two doctrines. The application of either created difficulties, for whichever was chosen it became necessary to determine whether the foreign corporation was "doing business" within the state, either to decide whether its "consent" could properly be "implied," or to discover whether the corporation was "present." The law reports became cluttered with decisions as to what constituted "doing business." The cases drew fine lines which made little sense in terms of either theory. * * *

The real difficulty underlying these attempts to work out a rationale for personal jurisdiction lay in the fact that the doctrines were borrowed from laws relating to wholly independent sovereignties which were not relevant to jurisdictions joined in a federation. The basic premise for such decisions was "that a judgment * * * is necessarily something to be enforced and that a state which is physically impotent to enforce its judgments should be treated as legally incompetent to adjudicate. * * *" But with the Full Faith and Credit Clause as an overriding principle, such a premise only puts the question; it does not answer it. The real question becomes not whether a state could itself enforce a judgment, but rather under what circumstances the national power should be used to assist the extraterritorial enforcement of a state's judicial decrees. The great importance of Pennoyer v. Neff is that it identified the test under the Full Faith and Credit Clause with the test under the Due Process Clause, making a judgment which would not be enforceable beyond the borders of the state unenforceable within its boundaries. If there are reasons, concerned with the state's relationship with the litigation, why a judgment is not entitled to extrastate enforcement, those reasons should be sufficient to sustain attack within the state. Although *Pennoyer* suggested this principle, there remained the necessity for fixing criteria for determining when the absence of the state's physical power would be supplemented by the command of the national sovereign, criteria which must necessarily change with the basic changes in our methods of carrying on economic activity and with the changes in means of transportation and communication. * * *

With doctrine in so bad a state of disrepair, the time had long since passed for the Supreme Court to acknowledge the truth of Holmes' dictum that "[t]he Constitution is not to be satisfied with a fiction." International Shoe Co. v. Washington afforded the Court an opportunity to begin to set its house in order in this field.

4. A NEW THEORY OF JURISDICTION

INTERNATIONAL SHOE CO. v. WASHINGTON

Supreme Court of the United States, 1945.
326 U.S. 310, 66 S.Ct. 154, 90 L.Ed. 95.

Appeal from the Supreme Court of the State of Washington.

MR. CHIEF JUSTICE STONE delivered the opinion of the Court.

The questions for decision are (1) whether, within the limitations of the due process clause of the Fourteenth Amendment, appellant, a Delaware corporation, has by its activities in the State of Washington rendered itself amenable to proceedings in the courts of that state to recover unpaid contributions to the state unemployment compensation fund exacted by state statutes, * * * and (2) whether the state can exact those contributions consistently with the due process clause of the Fourteenth Amendment.

The statutes in question set up a comprehensive scheme of unemployment compensation, the costs of which are defrayed by contributions required to be made by employers to a state unemployment compensation fund. The contributions are a specified percentage of the wages payable annually by each employer for his employees' services in the state. The assessment and collection of the contributions and the fund are administered by respondents. Section 14(c) of the Act, Wash.Rev.Stat.1941 Supp., § 9998—114c, authorizes respondent Commissioner to issue an order and notice of assessment of delinquent contributions upon prescribed personal service of the notice upon the employer if found within the state, or, if not so found, by mailing the notice to the employer by registered mail at his last known address. That section also authorizes the Commissioner to collect the assessment by distraint if it is not paid within ten days after service of the notice. * * *

In this case notice of assessment for the years in question was personally served upon a sales solicitor employed by appellant in the State of Washington, and a copy of the notice was mailed by registered mail to appellant at its address in St. Louis, Missouri. Appellant appeared specially before the office of unemployment and moved to set aside the order and notice of assessment on the ground that the service upon appellant's salesman was not proper service upon appellant; that appellant was not a corporation of the State of Washington and was not doing business within the state; that it had no agent within the state upon whom service could be made; and that appellant is not an employer and does not furnish employment within the meaning of the statute.

The motion was heard on evidence and a stipulation of facts by the appeal tribunal which denied the motion and ruled that respondent

Commissioner was entitled to recover the unpaid contributions. That action was affirmed by the Commissioner; both the Superior Court and the Supreme Court affirmed. * * * Appellant in each of these courts assailed the statute as applied, as a violation of the due process clause of the Fourteenth Amendment, and as imposing a constitutionally prohibited burden on interstate commerce.

* * * Appellant is a Delaware corporation, having its principal place of business in St. Louis, Missouri, and is engaged in the manufacture and sale of shoes and other footwear. It maintains places of business in several states, other than Washington, at which its manufacturing is carried on and from which its merchandise is distributed interstate through several sales units or branches located outside the State of Washington.

Appellant has no office in Washington and makes no contracts either for sale or purchase of merchandise there. It maintains no stock of merchandise in that state and makes there no deliveries of goods in intrastate commerce. During the years from 1937 to 1940, now in question, appellant employed eleven to thirteen salesmen under direct supervision and control of sales managers located in St. Louis. These salesmen resided in Washington; their principal activities were confined to that state; and they were compensated by commissions based upon the amount of their sales. The commissions for each year totaled more than $31,000. Appellant supplies its salesmen with a line of samples, each consisting of one shoe of a pair, which they display to prospective purchasers. On occasion they rent permanent sample rooms, for exhibiting samples, in business buildings, or rent rooms in hotels or business buildings temporarily for that purpose. The cost of such rentals is reimbursed by appellant.

The authority of the salesmen is limited to exhibiting their samples and soliciting orders from prospective buyers, at prices and on terms fixed by appellant. The salesmen transmit the orders to appellant's office in St. Louis for acceptance or rejection, and when accepted the merchandise for filling the orders is shipped f.o.b. from points outside Washington to the purchasers within the state. All the merchandise shipped into Washington is invoiced at the place of shipment from which collections are made. No salesman has authority to enter into contracts or to make collections.

The Supreme Court of Washington was of opinion that the regular and systematic solicitation of orders in the state by appellant's salesmen, resulting in a continuous flow of appellant's product into the state, was sufficient to constitute doing business in the state so as to make appellant amenable to suit in its courts. But it was also of opinion that there were sufficient additional activities shown to bring the case within the rule frequently stated, that solicitation within a state by the agents of a foreign corporation plus some additional activities there are sufficient to render the corporation amenable to suit brought in the courts of the state to enforce an obligation arising out of its activities there. * * * The court found such additional activities in the salesmen's display of samples sometimes in permanent display rooms, and the salesmen's residence within the state, continued over a period of years, all resulting in a substantial volume of merchandise regularly shipped by appellant to purchasers within the state. The court also held that the statute as applied did not invade the constitutional power of Congress to regulate interstate commerce and did not impose a prohibited burden on such commerce.

Appellant's argument, renewed here, that the statute imposes an unconstitutional burden on interstate commerce need not detain us.

* * *

Appellant also insists that its activities within the state were not sufficient to manifest its "presence" there and that in its absence the state courts were without jurisdiction, that consequently it was a denial of due process for the state to subject appellant to suit. It refers to those cases in which it was said that the mere solicitation of orders for the purchase of goods within a state, to be accepted without the state and filled by shipment of the purchased goods interstate, does not render the corporation seller amenable to suit within the state. * * * And appellant further argues that since it was not present within the state, it is a denial of due process to subject it to taxation or other money exaction. It thus denies the power of the state to lay the tax or to subject appellant to a suit for its collection.

Historically the jurisdiction of courts to render judgment in personam is grounded on their de facto power over the defendant's person. Hence his presence within the territorial jurisdiction of a court was prerequisite to its rendition of a judgment personally binding him. Pennoyer v. Neff * * *. But now that the capias ad respondendum has given way to personal service of summons or other form of notice, due process requires only that in order to subject a defendant to a judgment in personam, if he be not present within the territory of the forum, he have certain minimum contacts with it such that the maintenance of the suit does not offend "traditional notions of fair play and substantial justice." Milliken v. Meyer * * *. See Holmes, J., in McDonald v. Mabee, 243 U.S. 90, 91, 37 S.Ct. 343, 61 L.Ed. 608, L.R.A.1917F, 458. * * *

Since the corporate personality is a fiction, although a fiction intended to be acted upon as though it were a fact * * *, it is clear that unlike an individual its "presence" without, as well as within, the state of its origin can be manifested only by activities carried on in its behalf by those who are authorized to act for it. To say that the corporation is so far "present" there as to satisfy due process requirements, for purposes of taxation or the maintenance of suits against it in the courts of the state, is to beg the question to be decided. For the terms "present" or "presence" are used merely to symbolize those activities of the corporation's agent within the state which courts will deem to be sufficient to satisfy the demands of due process. L. Hand, J., in Hutchinson v. Chase & Gilbert * * *. Those demands may be met by such contacts of the corporation with the state of the forum as make it reasonable, in the context of our federal system of government, to require the corporation to defend the particular suit which is brought there. An "estimate of the inconve-

niences" which would result to the corporation from a trial away from its "home" or principal place of business is relevant in this connection.
*   *   *

"Presence" in the state in this sense has never been doubted when the activities of the corporation there have not only been continuous and systematic, but also give rise to the liabilities sued on, even though no consent to be sued or authorization to an agent to accept service of process has been given. *   *   * Conversely it has been generally recognized that the casual presence of the corporate agent or even his conduct of single or isolated items of activities in a state in the corporation's behalf are not enough to subject it to suit on causes of action unconnected with the activities there. *   *   * To require the corporation in such circumstances to defend the suit away from its home or other jurisdiction where it carries on more substantial activities has been thought to lay too great and unreasonable a burden on the corporation to comport with due process.

While it has been held in cases on which appellant relies that continuous activity of some sorts within a state is not enough to support the demand that the corporation be amenable to suits unrelated to that activity *   *   *, there have been instances in which the continuous corporate operations within a state were thought so substantial and of such a nature as to justify suit against it on causes of action arising from dealings entirely distinct from those activities. *   *   *

Finally, although the commission of some single or occasional acts of the corporate agent in a state sufficient to impose an obligation or liability on the corporation has not been thought to confer upon the state authority to enforce it, Rosenberg Bros. & Co. v. Curtis Brown Co., 260 U.S. 516, 43 S.Ct. 170, 67 L.Ed. 372, other such acts, because of their nature and quality and the circumstances of their commission, may be deemed sufficient to render the corporation liable to suit. Cf. Kane v. New Jersey *   *   *; Hess v. Pawloski *   *   *. True, some of the decisions holding the corporation amenable to suit have been supported by resort to the legal fiction that it has given its consent to service and suit, consent being implied from its presence in the state through the acts of its authorized agents. *   *   * But more realistically it may be said that those authorized acts were of such a nature as to justify the fiction. *   *   *

It is evident that the criteria by which we mark the boundary line between those activities which justify the subjection of a corporation to suit, and those which do not, cannot be simply mechanical or quantitative. The test is not merely, as has sometimes been suggested, whether the activity, which the corporation has seen fit to procure through its agents in another state, is a little more or a little less. *   *   * Whether due process is satisfied must depend rather upon the quality and nature of the activity in relation to the fair and orderly administration of the laws which it was the purpose of the due process clause to insure. That clause does not contemplate that a state may make binding a judgment in personam against an individual or corporate defendant with which the state has no contacts, ties, or relations. *   *   *

But to the extent that a corporation exercises the privilege of conducting activities within a state, it enjoys the benefits and protection of the laws of that state. The exercise of that privilege may give rise to obligations; and, so far as those obligations arise out of or are connected with the activities within the state, a procedure which requires the corporation to respond to a suit brought to enforce them can, in most instances, hardly be said to be undue. * * *

Applying these standards, the activities carried on in behalf of appellant in the State of Washington were neither irregular nor casual. They were systematic and continuous throughout the years in question. They resulted in a large volume of interstate business, in the course of which appellant received the benefits and protection of the laws of the state, including the right to resort to the courts for the enforcement of its rights. The obligation which is here sued upon arose out of those very activities. It is evident that these operations establish sufficient contacts or ties with the state of the forum to make it reasonable and just according to our traditional conception of fair play and substantial justice to permit the state to enforce the obligations which appellant has incurred there. Hence we cannot say that the maintenance of the present suit in the State of Washington involves an unreasonable or undue procedure.

We are likewise unable to conclude that the service of the process within the state upon an agent whose activities establish appellant's "presence" there was not sufficient notice of the suit, or that the suit was so unrelated to those activities as to make the agent an inappropriate vehicle for communicating the notice. It is enough that appellant has established such contacts with the state that the particular form of substituted service adopted there gives reasonable assurance that the notice will be actual. * * *

Appellant having rendered itself amenable to suit upon obligations arising out of the activities of its salesmen in Washington, the state may maintain the present suit in personam to collect the tax laid upon the exercise of the privilege of employing appellant's salesmen within the state. For Washington has made one of those activities, which taken together establish appellant's "presence" there for purposes of suit, the taxable event by which the state brings appellant within the reach of its taxing power. The state thus has constitutional power to lay the tax and to subject appellant to a suit to recover it. The activities which establish its "presence" subject it alike to taxation by the state and to suit to recover the tax. * * *

Affirmed.

MR. JUSTICE JACKSON took no part in the consideration or decision of this case.

MR. JUSTICE BLACK delivered the following opinion.

* * *

I believe that the Federal Constitution leaves to each State, without any "ifs" or "buts," a power to tax and to open the doors of its courts for its citizens to sue corporations whose agents do business in those States.

Believing that the Constitution gave the States that power, I think it a judicial deprivation to condition its exercise upon this Court's notion of "fair play," however appealing that term may be. Nor can I stretch the meaning of due process so far as to authorize this Court to deprive a State of the right to afford judicial protection to its citizens on the ground that it would be more "convenient" for the corporation to be sued somewhere else.

There is a strong emotional appeal in the words "fair play," "justice," and "reasonableness." But they were not chosen by those who wrote the original Constitution or the Fourteenth Amendment as a measuring rod for this Court to use in invalidating State or Federal laws passed by elected legislative representatives. No one, not even those who most feared a democratic government, ever formally proposed that courts should be given power to invalidate legislation under any such elastic standards. Express prohibitions against certain types of legislation are found in the Constitution, and under the long settled practice, courts invalidate laws found to conflict with them. This requires interpretation, and interpretation, it is true, may result in extension of the Constitution's purpose. But that is no reason for reading the due process clause so as to restrict a State's power to tax and sue those whose activities affect persons and businesses within the State, provided proper service can be had.

* * *

Notes and Questions

1. *International Shoe* has been described as part of a "dual trend in jurisdictional decisions: in defining the court with jurisdiction, a trend from the court with immediate power over the defendant to the court where the parties may most conveniently settle their dispute; and in defining due process of law, a trend from the emphasis on territorial limitations of courts to emphasis on providing notice and an opportunity to be heard." SMYTH v. TWIN STATE IMPROVEMENT CORP., 116 Vt. 569, 80 A.2d 664 (1951). Do you agree?

2. Did the subject matter of the dispute in *International Shoe* provide a reason to find jurisdiction over the corporation? After all, Washington was suing to collect state taxes. Doesn't every state have an especially strong interest in enforcing its tax laws? It is probable that wherever the action was brought the substantive law to be applied would be Washington law. What interest would another state, such as Delaware, International Shoe's state of incorporation, have in adjudicating this dispute?

3. *International Shoe* uses contacts with the forum in two different ways. A corporation may have sufficient contact with the forum—that is, it may engage in sufficient business within the state—to warrant asserting jurisdiction over it for all matters. This is termed "general jurisdiction." On the other hand, a corporation may have sufficient contact with the forum to warrant asserting jurisdiction over it for matters related to its activity within the forum without having sufficient contact with the forum to warrant general jurisdiction. In such a case, the jurisdiction is termed "specific jurisdiction." Whether a corporation is subject to specific or general jurisdiction, however, depends on the nature and number of contacts it has with the

forum. Determining what constitutes sufficient business within the state, or what matters are related to activity within it, often are uncertain questions that may blur the distinction between general and specific jurisdiction. See Brilmayer, *Related Contacts and Personal Jurisdiction,* 101 Harv.L.Rev. 1444 (1988).

4. In PERKINS v. BENGUET CONSOLIDATED MINING CO., 342 U.S. 437, 446, 72 S.Ct. 413, 418, 96 L.Ed. 485, 493 (1952), the defendant, a Philippine corporation doing systematic and continuous business in Ohio during the Japanese occupation of the Philippines, was sued by a nonresident of Ohio in an Ohio state court on a cause of action that had arisen outside the state. The Ohio courts quashed service, and the United States Supreme Court, relying on *International Shoe,* held:

> The instant case takes us one step further to a proceeding *in personam* to enforce a cause of action not arising out of the corporation's activities in the state of the forum. * * * [W]e find no requirement of federal due process that either *prohibits* Ohio from opening its courts to the cause of action here presented or *compels* Ohio to do so. (Emphasis in original.)

On remand the Ohio courts refused to quash the summons. 158 Ohio St. 145, 107 N.E.2d 203 (1952).

Consider the following cases in light of the Supreme Court's decision in *Perkins.* In FISHER GOVERNOR CO. v. SUPERIOR COURT, 53 Cal.2d 222, 225–26, 1 Cal.Rptr. 1, 3–4, 347 P.2d 1, 3–4 (1959), a wrongful death action growing out of an explosion in Idaho, plaintiffs served defendant, an Iowa corporation, by delivering the papers to a California manufacturers' agent who sold defendant's products. The California Supreme Court ordered the process quashed. In his opinion for the court, Justice Traynor said:

> Although a foreign corporation may have sufficient contacts with a state to justify an assumption of jurisdiction over it to enforce causes of action having no relation to its activities in that state * * *, more contacts are required for the assumption of such extensive jurisdiction than sales and sales promotion within the state by independent nonexclusive sales representatives. * * * To hold otherwise would subject any corporation that promotes the sales of its goods on a nationwide basis to suit anywhere in the United States without regard to other considerations bearing on "the fair and orderly administration of the laws which it was the purpose of the due process clause to insure." * * * Accordingly, we must look beyond defendant's sales activities in this state to determine whether jurisdiction may constitutionally be assumed.

> The interest of the state in providing a forum for its residents * * * or in regulating the business involved * * *; the relative availability of evidence and the burden of defense and prosecution in one place rather than another * * *; the ease of access to an alternative forum * * *; the avoidance of multiplicity of suits and conflicting adjudications * * *; and the extent to which the cause of action arose out of defendant's local activities * * * are all relevant to this inquiry. * * *

> None of these considerations supports an assumption of jurisdiction in plaintiffs' actions.

In RATLIFF v. COOPER LABORATORIES, INC., 444 F.2d 745 (4th Cir.), certiorari denied 404 U.S. 948, 92 S.Ct. 271, 30 L.Ed.2d 265, rehearing denied 404 U.S. 1006, 92 S.Ct. 561, 30 L.Ed.2d 559 (1971), the court held that South Carolina could not assert personal jurisdiction over the defendants, two drug manufacturing companies incorporated in Delaware with principal places of business in Connecticut and New York, because their contacts with South Carolina were insufficient to satisfy due process requirements. The court placed great significance on the facts that the plaintiffs were nonresidents of South Carolina who chose the forum for its long statute of limitations, that the allegedly defective drugs were both manufactured and consumed outside the forum, and that the cause of action was unrelated to defendants' activities in the forum.

And, in HELICOPTEROS NACIONALES DE COLOMBIA, S.A. v. HALL, 466 U.S. 408, 104 S.Ct. 1868, 80 L.Ed.2d 404 (1984), the survivors of four Americans killed in a helicopter crash in Peru sued a foreign defendant ("Helicol"), which had contracted with a Texas joint venture to provide helicopter service for the joint venture's project in Peru. The Texas Supreme Court held that Texas' long-arm statute authorized jurisdiction over Helicol. The company had some contact with Texas—much, if not all of which, was unrelated to the accident in Peru. Nonetheless, the Texas court found that the minimum contacts requirement of the Due Process Clause was satisfied. The United States Supreme Court reversed. Justice Blackmun, writing for the Court, said:

> All parties to the present case concede that respondents' claims against Helicol did not "arise out of," and are not related to, Helicol's activities within Texas. We thus must explore the nature of Helicol's contacts with the State of Texas to determine whether they constitute the kind of continuous and systematic general business contacts the Court found to exist in Perkins [v. Benguet Consolidated Mining Co., p. 88, supra]. We hold that they do not.

> It is undisputed that Helicol does not have a place of business in Texas and never has been licensed to do business in the State. Basically, Helicol's contacts with Texas consisted of sending its chief executive officer to Houston for a contract-negotiation session; accepting into its New York bank account checks drawn on a Houston bank; purchasing helicopters, equipment, and training services from Bell Helicopter for substantial sums; and sending personnel to Bell's facilities in Fort Worth for training.

> The one trip to Houston by Helicol's chief executive officer for the purpose of negotiating the transportation-services contract with [the joint venture] cannot be described or regarded as a contact of a "continuous and systematic" nature, as *Perkins* described it, * * * and thus cannot support an assertion of *in personam* jurisdiction over Helicol by a Texas court. Similarly, Helicol's acceptance from [the joint venture] of checks drawn on a Texas bank is of negligible significance for purposes of determining whether Helicol had sufficient contacts in Texas. There is no indication that Helicol ever requested that the checks be drawn on a Texas bank or that there was any negotiation between Helicol and [the joint venture] with respect to the location or identity of the bank on which checks would be drawn. Common sense and everyday experience

suggest that, absent unusual circumstances, the bank on which a check is drawn is generally of little consequence to the payee and is a matter left to the discretion of the drawer. Such unilateral activity of another party or a third person is not an appropriate consideration when determining whether a defendant has sufficient contacts with a forum State to justify an assertion of jurisdiction. * * *

The Texas Supreme Court focused on the purchases and the related training trips in finding contacts sufficient to support an assertion of jurisdiction. We do not agree with that assessment, for the Court's opinion in Rosenberg Bros. & Co. v. Curtis Brown Co., 260 U.S. 516, 43 S.Ct. 170, 67 L.Ed. 372 (1923) (Brandeis, J., for a unanimous tribunal), makes clear that purchases and related trips, standing alone, are not a sufficient basis for a State's assertion of jurisdiction.

Id. at 415–17, 104 S.Ct. at 1872–74, 80 L.Ed.2d at 411–13.

5. In FRUMMER v. HILTON HOTELS INTERNATIONAL, INC., 19 N.Y.2d 533, 281 N.Y.S.2d 41, 227 N.E.2d 851 (1967), a New York tourist who fell and injured himself while taking a shower in the London Hilton brought a personal injury action against the hotel (an English corporation) in New York. Jurisdiction was upheld on the basis of the activities of the Hilton Reservation Service, a separate corporation. Although separate, the interlocking ownership of the two corporations and other facts persuaded New York's highest court that an agency relationship existed between them. It thus held that London Hilton did business in New York by "do[ing] all the business which [the principal] could do were it [in New York] by its own officials."

6. The degree of "contacts" necessary to justify exercising general jurisdiction has been stated variously (often in terms of "doing business"), but the common denominator is that the corporation is operating within the state "not occasionally or casually, but with a fair measure of permanence and continuity." Tauza v. Susquehanna Coal Co., 220 N.Y. 259, 115 N.E. 915 (1917).

5. SPECIFIC JURISDICTION AND STATE LONG–ARM LAWS

a. The Development of Long-Arm Laws

The Supreme Court's decision in Hess v. Pawloski, p. 75, supra, encouraged states to utilize their police powers to enact a number of statutes asserting jurisdiction based not only on the operation of automobiles within a state but also on engaging in a variety of other hazardous activities or enterprises. As time progressed and liberal judicial construction and emboldened state legislatures gave broader scope to these statutes, the usefulness of the technique suggested by the nonresident motorist statutes became even more apparent.

The Court's decision in *International Shoe*—with its emphasis on contacts with the forum state—further encouraged states to expand their jurisdictional reach and led to efforts on the part of many state legislatures to conform their statutory pattern to the Supreme Court's latest view as to when personal jurisdiction could be asserted consistently with the Constitution. This spate of legislative activity came largely in the form of "long-arm" or "single-act" statutes, which predicated jurisdiction over nonresidents upon the defendant's general activity in the state, or the commission of any one of a series of enumerated acts within the jurisdiction, or, in some cases, the commission of a certain act outside the jurisdiction causing consequences within it. The theory supporting the assertion of jurisdiction in these circumstances flowed naturally from the Court's decision in *International Shoe* and its emphasis on the quantum and quality of the defendant's activity in the forum state.

The first truly comprehensive long-arm statute was enacted in Illinois and it was used as a model by a number of states. According to the Illinois Supreme Court, the statute was an attempt to assert jurisdiction to the fullest permissible constitutional limits. Under the Illinois act an individual or a corporation, whether a citizen or noncitizen of Illinois, is said to be amenable to the jurisdiction of the state's courts if he transacts any business within the state; commits a tort within the state; owns, uses, or possesses any real estate within the state; or contracts to insure any person, property, or risk located within the state. Several years after its enactment, the Illinois statute was amended to include jurisdiction over claims involving alimony, support, and property division against former residents. Other states soon followed Illinois' lead in expanding the jurisdictional reach of their courts.

Contemporary long-arm statutes run the gamut from very broad ones that permit states to assert jurisdiction up to the limits allowed by the Constitution, to narrow ones that only carve out small parts of their constitutionally permitted authority. The Rhode Island long-arm statute is an example of a broad long-arm statute. It permits Rhode Island courts to assert jurisdiction over any foreign corporations, nonresident individuals (or their executors or administrators), and partnerships or associations amenable to suit within the state and having the necessary minimum contacts required by the Constitution.

Other state long-arm statutes are more limited in application, requiring the doing of business or an act or omission within the state. Many long-arm statutes apply only to corporate defendants and some states have enacted separate statutes for individuals and corporations. Several long-arm statutes are available only to resident plaintiffs. One limitation that generally is placed on the use of long-arm statutes is that they apply only to suits brought in the courts of the state in which the jurisdictional act occurs or in the federal courts sitting in that state. Despite the textual similarities of many of these statutes, judicial construction of them often differs.

Read the selected state jurisdiction statutes in the Supplement.

GRAY v. AMERICAN RADIATOR & STANDARD SANITARY CORP.

Supreme Court of Illinois, 1961.
22 Ill.2d 432, 176 N.E.2d 761.

KLINGBIEL, JUSTICE. Phyllis Gray appeals from a judgment of the circuit court of Cook County dismissing her action for damages. The issues are concerned with the construction and validity of our statute providing for substituted service of process on nonresidents. Since a constitutional question is involved, the appeal is direct to this court.

The suit was brought against the Titan Valve Manufacturing Company and others, on the ground that a certain water heater had exploded and injured the plaintiff. The complaint charges, *inter alia*, that the Titan company, a foreign corporation, had negligently constructed the safety valve; and that the injuries were suffered as a proximate result thereof. Summons issued and was duly served on Titan's registered agent in Cleveland, Ohio. The corporation appeared specially, filing a motion to quash on the ground that it had not committed a tortious act in Illinois. Its affidavit stated that it does no business here; that it has no agent physically present in Illinois; and that it sells the completed valves to defendant, American Radiator & Standard Sanitary Corporation, outside Illinois. The American Radiator & Standard Sanitary Corporation (also made a defendant) filed an answer in which it set up a cross claim against Titan, alleging that Titan made certain warranties to American Radiator, and that if the latter is held liable to the plaintiff it should be indemnified and held harmless by Titan. The court granted Titan's motion, dismissing both the complaint and the cross claim.

Section 16 of the Civil Practice Act provides that summons may be personally served upon any party outside the State; and that as to nonresidents who have submitted to the jurisdiction of our courts, such service has the force and effect of personal service within Illinois. (Ill. Rev.Stat.1959, chap. 110, par. 16.) Under section 17(1)(b) a nonresident who, either in person or through an agent, commits a tortious act within this State submits to jurisdiction. * * * The questions in this case are (1) whether a tortious act was committed here, within the meaning of the statute, despite the fact that the Titan corporation had no agent in Illinois; and (2) whether the statute, if so construed, violates due process of law.

The first aspect to which we must direct our attention is one of statutory construction. Under section 17(1)(b) jurisdiction is predicated on the committing of a tortious act in this State. It is not disputed, for the purpose of this appeal, that a tortious act was committed. The issue depends on whether it was committed in Illinois, so as to warrant the assertion of personal jurisdiction by service of summons in Ohio.

The wrong in the case at bar did not originate in the conduct of a servant physically present here, but arose instead from acts performed at the place of manufacture. Only the consequences occurred in Illinois. It is well established, however, that in law the place of a wrong is where the last event takes place which is necessary to render the actor liable. Restatement, Conflict of Laws, sec. 377. A second indication that the place of injury is the determining factor is found in rules governing the time within which an action must be brought. In applying statutes of limitation our court has computed the period from the time when the injury is done. * * * We think it is clear that the alleged negligence in manufacturing the valve cannot be separated from the resulting injury; and that for present purposes, like those of liability and limitations, the tort was committed in Illinois.

Titan seeks to avoid this result by arguing that instead of using the word "tort," the legislature employed the term "tortious act"; and that the latter refers only to the act or conduct, separate and apart from any consequences thereof. We cannot accept the argument. To be tortious an act must cause injury. The concept of injury is an inseparable part of the phrase. In determining legislative intention courts will read words in their ordinary and popularly understood sense. * * * We think the intent should be determined less from technicalities of definition than from considerations of general purpose and effect. To adopt the criteria urged by defendant would tend to promote litigation over extraneous issues concerning the elements of a tort and the territorial incidence of each, whereas the test should be concerned more with those substantial elements of convenience and justice presumably contemplated by the legislature. As we observed in Nelson v. Miller, 11 Ill.2d 378, 143 N.E.2d 673, the statute contemplates the exertion of jurisdiction over nonresident defendants to the extent permitted by the due-process clause.

The Titan company contends that if the statute is applied so as to confer jurisdiction in this case it violates the requirement of due process of law. The precise constitutional question thus presented has not heretofore been considered by this court. * * *

Under modern doctrine the power of a State court to enter a binding judgment against one not served with process within the State depends upon two questions: first, whether he has certain minimum contacts with the State * * * and second, whether there has been a reasonable method of notification. See International Shoe Co. v. State of Washington * * *. In the case at bar there is no contention that section 16 provides for inadequate notice or that its provisions were not followed. Defendant's argument on constitutionality is confined to the proposition that applying section 17(1)(b), where the injury is defendant's only contact with the State, would exceed the limits of due process.

A proper determination of the question presented requires analysis of those cases which have dealt with the quantum of contact sufficient to warrant jurisdiction. Since the decision in Pennoyer v. Neff * * * the power of a State to exert jurisdiction over nonresidents has been greatly expanded, particularly with respect to foreign corporations. * * * [In International Shoe Co. v. Washington,] the court pointed out that the activities of the corporation in Washington were not only continuous and systematic but also gave rise to the liability sued on. It was observed that such operations, which resulted in a large volume of business, established "sufficient contacts or ties with the state of the forum to make it reasonable and just according to our traditional conception of fair play and substantial justice to permit the state to enforce the obligations which appellant has incurred there." * * *

Where the business done by a foreign corporation in the State of the forum is of a sufficiently substantial nature, it has been held permissible for the State to entertain a suit against it even though the cause of action arose from activities entirely distinct from its conduct within the State. Perkins v. Benguet Consolidated Mining Co. * * *. But where such business or other activity is not substantial, the particular act or transaction having no connection with the State of the forum, the requirement of "contact" is not satisfied. * * *

In the case at bar the defendant's only contact with this State is found in the fact that a product manufactured in Ohio was incorporated in Pennsylvania, into a hot water heater which in the course of commerce was sold to an Illinois consumer. The record fails to disclose whether defendant has done any other business in Illinois, either directly or indirectly; and it is argued, in reliance on the International Shoe test, that since a course of business here has not been shown there are no "minimum contacts" sufficient to support jurisdiction. We do not think, however, that doing a given volume of business is the only way in which a nonresident can form the required connection with this State. Since the International Shoe case was decided the requirements for jurisdiction have been further relaxed, so that at the present time it is sufficient if the act or transaction itself has a substantial connection with the State of the forum.

In McGee v. International Life Insurance Co., 355 U.S. 220, 78 S.Ct. 199, 201, 2 L.Ed.2d 223 (1957), suit was brought in California against a foreign insurance company on a policy issued to a resident of California. The defendant was not served with process in that State but was notified by registered mail at its place of business in Texas, pursuant to a statute permitting such service in suits on insurance contracts. The contract in question was delivered in California, the premiums were mailed from there and the insured was a resident of that State when he died, but defendant had no office or agent in California nor did it solicit any business there apart from the policy sued on. After referring briefly to the International Shoe case the court held that "it is sufficient for purposes of due process that the suit was based on *a contract* which had substantial connection" with California. (Emphasis supplied.)

In Smyth v. Twin State Improvement Corp. * * * the court discussed the principal authorities on the question and concluded, *inter alia,* that "continuous activity within the state is not necessary as a prerequisite to jurisdiction."

In Nelson v. Miller * * * the commission of a single tort within this State was held sufficient to sustain jurisdiction under the present statute. The defendant in that case, a resident of Wisconsin, was engaged in the business of selling appliances. It was alleged that in the process of delivering a stove in Illinois, an employee of the defendant negligently caused injury to the plaintiff. In holding that the defendant was not denied due process by being required to defend in Illinois, this court observed * * *: "The defendant sent his employee into Illinois in the advancement of his own interests. While he was here, the employee and the defendant enjoyed the benefit and protection of the laws of Illinois, including the right to resort to our courts. In the course of his stay here the employee performed acts that gave rise to an injury. The law of Illinois will govern the substantive rights and duties stemming from the incident. Witnesses, other than the defendant's employee, are likely to be found here, and not in Wisconsin. In such circumstances, it is not unreasonable to require the defendant to make his defense here."

Whether the type of activity conducted within the State is adequate to satisfy the requirement depends upon the facts in the particular case. * * * The question cannot be answered by applying a mechanical formula or rule of thumb but by ascertaining what is fair and reasonable in the circumstances. In the application of this flexible test the relevant inquiry is whether defendant engaged in some act or conduct by which he may be said to have invoked the benefits and protections of the law of the forum. * * * The relevant decisions since Pennoyer v. Neff show a development of the concept of personal jurisdiction from one which requires service of process within the State to one which is satisfied either if the act or transaction sued on occurs there or if defendant has engaged in a sufficiently substantial course of activity in the State, provided always that reasonable notice and opportunity to be heard are afforded. * * * [T]he trend in defining due process of law is away from the emphasis on territorial limitations and toward emphasis on providing adequate notice and opportunity to be heard: from the court with immediate power over the defendant, toward the court in which both parties can most conveniently settle their dispute.

In the McGee case the court commented on the trend toward expanding State jurisdiction over nonresidents, observing that: "In part this is attributable to the fundamental transformation of our national economy over the years. Today many commercial transactions touch two or more States and may involve parties separated by the full continent. With this increasing nationalization of commerce has come a great increase in the amount of business conducted by mail across state lines. At the same time modern transportation and communication have made it much less burdensome for a party sued to defend himself in a State where he engages in economic activity."

It is true that courts cannot "assume that this trend heralds the eventual demise of all restrictions on the personal jurisdiction of state courts." Hanson v. Denckla * * *. An orderly and fair administration of the law throughout the nation requires protection against being compelled to answer claims brought in distant States with which the defendant has little or no association and in which he would be faced with an undue burden or disadvantage in making his defense. It must be remembered that lawsuits can be brought on frivolous demands or groundless claims as well as on legitimate ones, and that procedural rules must be designed and appraised in the light of what is fair and just to both sides in the dispute. * * *

In the case at bar defendant does not claim that the present use of its product in Illinois is an isolated instance. While the record does not disclose the volume of Titan's business or the territory in which appliances incorporating its valves are marketed, it is a reasonable inference that its commercial transactions, like those of other manufacturers, result in substantial use and consumption in this State. To the extent that its business may be directly affected by transactions occurring here it enjoys benefits from the laws of this State, and it has undoubtedly benefited, to a degree, from the protection which our law has given to the marketing of hot water heaters containing its valves. Where the alleged liability arises, as in this case, from the manufacture of products presumably sold in contemplation of use here, it should not matter that the purchase was made from an independent middleman or that someone other than the defendant shipped the product into this State.

With the increasing specialization of commercial activity and the growing interdependence of business enterprises it is seldom that a manufacturer deals directly with consumers in other States. The fact that the benefit he derives from its laws is an indirect one, however, does not make it any the less essential to the conduct of his business; and it is not unreasonable, where a cause of action arises from alleged defects in his product, to say that the use of such products in the ordinary course of commerce is sufficient contact with this State to justify a requirement that he defend here.

As a general proposition, if a corporation elects to sell its products for ultimate use in another State, it is not unjust to hold it answerable there for any damage caused by defects in those products. Advanced means of distribution and other commercial activity have made possible these modern methods of doing business, and have largely effaced the economic significance of State lines. By the same token, today's facilities for transportation and communication have removed much of the difficulty and inconvenience formerly encountered in defending lawsuits brought in other States.

* * *

The principles of due process relevant to the issue in this case support jurisdiction in the court where both parties can most conveniently settle their dispute. The facts show that the plaintiff, an Illinois resident, was injured in Illinois. The law of Illinois will govern the substantive questions, and witnesses on the issues of injury, damages and other elements relating to the occurrence are most likely to be found here. Under such circumstances the courts of the place of injury usually provide the most convenient forum for trial. * * * In Travelers Health Association v. Commonwealth of Virginia, 339 U.S. 643, 70 S.Ct. 927, 94 L.Ed. 1154, a Nebraska insurance corporation was held subject to the jurisdiction of a Virginia regulatory commission although it had no paid agents within the State and its only contact there was a mail-order business operated from its Omaha office. The court observed, by way of *dictum,* that "suits on alleged losses can be more conveniently tried in Virginia where witnesses would most likely live and where claims for losses would presumably be investigated. Such factors have been given great weight in applying the doctrine of *forum non conveniens.* * * * And prior decisions of this Court have referred to the unwisdom, unfairness and injustice of permitting policyholders to seek redress only in some distant state where the insurer is incorporated. The Due Process Clause does not forbid a state to protect its citizens from such injustice." 339 U.S. at page 649, 70 S.Ct. at page 930, 94 L.Ed. 1161–1162. * * *

     * * * We conclude accordingly that defendant's association with this State is sufficient to support the exercise of jurisdiction.

* * *

Reversed and remanded, with directions.

Notes and Questions

     1. As *Gray* illustrates, the application of long-arm statutes often entails difficult questions of statutory construction. In FEATHERS v. McLUCAS, 15 N.Y.2d 443, 463–64, 261 N.Y.S.2d 8, 23–24, 209 N.E.2d 68, 79–80, certiorari denied 382 U.S. 905, 86 S.Ct. 241, 15 L.Ed.2d 158 (1965), the New York court was asked to construe a New York statute which, like the Illinois statute involved in *Gray,* authorized jurisdiction over a non-domiciliary "if, in person or through an agent, he * * * commits a tortious act within the state." In the New York case, plaintiffs were injured by the explosion of a tractor-drawn tank of liquid propane gas on a highway near their home in New York. The tank had been manufactured in Kansas and sold to a Missouri corporation, "presumably with knowledge that the latter would mount the tank on a wheelbase and then sell it to * * * a Pennsylvania corporation, which operated as a licensed interstate carrier." The New York court refused to assert jurisdiction over the Kansas manufacturer. In reaching this result, it criticized the conclusion in *Gray* that a tort had been committed in Illinois for purposes of that state's jurisdiction statute:

     * * * It certainly does not follow that, if the "place of wrong" for purposes of conflict of laws is a particular state, the "place of the commission of a tortious act" is also that same state for purposes of interpreting a statute conferring jurisdiction, on that basis, over nonresidents. * * * Moreover, the place of the "tort" is not necessarily the same as the place of the defendant's commission of the "tortious act."
     * * *

     In sum, then, it is our conclusion, based not only on the plain language of the statute but on its legislative history, that * * * [the New York statute] covers only a tortious act committed (by a nondomiciliary) in this State. * * *

In 1966, the New York legislature amended its jurisdictional statute (C.P.L.R. § 302) to reach defendants in cases like *Feathers.* Is the text of the current New York provision, which is set out in the Supplement, broader or narrower than the Illinois act? In what ways?

     2. In GREEN v. ADVANCE ROSS ELECTRONICS CORP., 86 Ill.2d 431, 437–38, 439–40, 56 Ill.Dec. 657, 427 N.E.2d 1203, 1206–08 (1981), the issue was whether Advance Ross, a Delaware corporation with headquarters in Illinois,

in an action claiming breaches of fiduciary duty, could gain jurisdiction over Green, a Texas resident, who once served as president of two of its affiliates. All of Green's corporate responsibilities, including the acts that allegedly injured the corporation, were performed outside Illinois. Nonetheless, Advance Ross argued that, under Section 17(1)(b) of Illinois' long-arm statute, an out-of-state resident submits to the jurisdiction of the Illinois courts when he commits a tort that causes a diminution of the funds of a corporation organized or headquartered in Illinois. The Illinois Supreme Court, distinguishing *Gray*, refused to read Section 17(1)(b) to establish jurisdiction:

> As in *Gray* * * *, for the purpose of disposing of the propriety of long-arm jurisdiction there is no dispute that tortious acts were committed. To be resolved is whether their commission was "within this State" as those words are used in section 17(1)(b).
>
> * * * [Advance Ross'] theory is that although the misconduct of Green, Sr., took place outside Illinois, the consequences of his misconduct were felt in Illinois. They * * * contend that the misconduct alleged resulted in a drain upon those assets in Illinois. But the consequences upon which [Advance Ross relies] are too remote from the misconduct of Green, Sr., to support the conclusion that the tortious acts complained of were committed in Illinois. The situs of the last event whose happening was necessary to hold Green, Sr., liable was in Texas.

In support of its conclusion, the Illinois court noted:

> [A]cceptance of the theory of long-arm jurisdiction advanced by [Advance Ross] would be tantamount to permitting a corporation operating nationwide to sue employees, suppliers, customers and perhaps others, at the company's State of incorporation or at its headquarters no matter how far away they lived and worked or their contact with the corporation was. Any interpretation of the Illinois long-arm statute which would permit that result is neither fair nor wise as a matter of policy. The meaning [which Advance Ross] ask[s] us to give the words "within this State" takes us too easily out of this State to be acceptable. Dealing by a Texas resident with an Illinois corporation only in Texas is too remote from Illinois to regard any part of the action as occurring in Illinois.

3. Section 3(c) of Massachusetts' long-arm statute, M.G.L.A., ch. 223A, gives to that state's courts jurisdiction over parties who cause "tortious injury by an act or omission in this commonwealth." This language is derived from the Uniform Interstate and International Procedure Act and represents an effort to resolve, legislatively, the type of conflict over the meaning of the term "tortious act within this state" that developed between the Illinois (*Gray*) and the New York (*Feathers*) courts. The Massachusetts courts have read Section 3(c) to apply only when the act causing the injury occurs within the Commonwealth.

4. Courts have interpreted the words "within the state" more liberally when the relevant act is an alleged intentional tort. Thus, for example, in MURPHY v. ERWIN–WASEY, INC., 460 F.2d 661, 664 (1st Cir.1972), an action for fraud, deceit, and breach of contract, Murphy alleged that the defendant had misrepresented the true amount of its billings, thereby depriving him of commissions. Murphy sought to base jurisdiction on Section 3(c), arguing that when the defendant, in New York, communicated by mail or telephone false statements to him in Massachusetts, the act causing the injury

occurred within the Commonwealth. The First Circuit agreed, in part on the basis of a distinction between intentional and unintentional tort cases:

> [W]hile sending a defective tool to a dealer * * * merely creates the condition from which damage might later arise, sending a libel into a state is indistinguishable from "the frequently hypothesized but rarely encountered gunman firing across a state line."

> We believe that the same is true of the mailing of a fraudulent misrepresentation into a state. We would be closing our eyes to the realities of modern business practices were we to hold that a corporation subjects itself to the jurisdiction of another state by sending a personal messenger into that state bearing a fraudulent misrepresentation but not when it follows the more ordinary course of employing the United States Postal Service as its messenger. Where a defendant knowingly sends into a state a false statement, intending that it should there be relied upon to the injury of a resident of that state, he has, for jurisdictional purposes, acted within that state.

5. The Notes thus far, like *Gray* itself, have involved long-arm provisions designed to cover tort claims. It often is possible, of course, to assert jurisdiction over a defendant in a tort case on the authority of a long-arm provision not designed expressly to cover tort claims. For example, in GRIMANDI v. BEECH AIRCRAFT CORP., 512 F.Supp. 764 (D.Kan.1981), French plaintiffs brought a product liability suit for damages resulting from an airplane crash in France. They named as one of the defendants a Canadian corporation that regularly sold airplane engines (up to 30 million dollars in sales annually) to the Kansas-based manufacturer of the ill-fated plane. The plaintiffs asserted jurisdiction in Kansas under a provision of that state's statute authorizing jurisdiction over a defendant when the cause of action arises from the transaction of any business within the state.

Because the engine in the plane that crashed was a replacement engine that had been installed in Canada and that never had been sold to the Kansas manufacturer or sent to Kansas, there was some doubt whether the claim "arose from" the defendant's transaction of business in Kansas as required by the statute. The court resolved the doubt in the plaintiff's favor, however, and found jurisdiction. It ruled that the "arising from" requirement could be met by "but for" causation and that if it had not been for the Canadian manufacturer's business with the Kansas company, it would not have had the occasion to install the replacement engine in Canada.

6. Long-arm provisions authorizing jurisdiction over a defendant on the basis of the defendant's business within the forum often require that the plaintiff's cause of action "be related to" or "arise from" the business transacted within the state. Under these provisions, jurisdiction will not exist when the cause of action is unrelated to the defendant's contacts with the forum.

For example, in JIM FOX ENTERPRISES, INC. v. AIR FRANCE, 664 F.2d 63 (5th Cir.1981), a Texas corporation brought a breach-of-warranty action against Air France, a foreign corporation, to recover the costs of repairing a defective navigation system as well as consequential damages. The plaintiff sought to establish jurisdiction under the Texas long-arm statute, Article 2031b of the Texas Revised Civil Statutes, which provides that jurisdiction exists when a foreign corporation has engaged in business in

Texas and the action is one "arising out of such business." Air France's considerable business in Texas notwithstanding, the District Court dismissed the action for want of personal jurisdiction, and the Fifth Circuit affirmed. Judge Brown, writing for the Court of Appeals, pointed to Air France's "thriving business in Texas" (and to the fact that at least one member of the court had flown the airline to Paris), but concluded:

> [T]he Texas long-arm statute requires some nexus between the cause of action and the defendant's contacts with Texas. This requirement means that Texas does not reach nearly as far as Due Process would permit. Fox concedes that its claim does not relate to Air France's business in Texas. As a result of this anachronistic but made-in-Texas statutory provision, Air France, a foreign corporation that undoubtedly does substantial business in Texas and has "minimum contacts" galore, * * * nonetheless, under the Texas statute, slips through the fingers at the end of the Long-arm.

Id. at 63–64.

7. In the *Jim Fox Enterprises* case, a federal court was construing Texas' long-arm statute. Subsequently, the Supreme Court of Texas had occasion to examine the same provision in HALL v. HELICOPTEROS NACIONALES DE COLOMBIA, S.A., 638 S.W.2d 870 (Tex.1982), reversed 466 U.S. 408, 104 S.Ct. 1868, 80 L.Ed.2d 404 (1984), which was described at pp. 89–90, supra in the context of general jurisdiction.

The defendant Helicol did not maintain an office in Texas, was not authorized to do business, performed no helicopter operations, and did not recruit workers there. The contract between Helicol and the joint venture was negotiated in Houston, however; and, Helicol did purchase substantially all of its helicopters in Texas, spent an average of $50,000 a month there for parts, sent pilots to Texas to pick up helicopters, sent pilots and maintenance personnel there for training, had employees there on a year-round rotation basis, and maintained a New York bank account that received roughly $5,000,000 in payments in the form of checks drawn upon the joint venture's Texas account.

On these facts, the Texas Supreme Court concluded that jurisdiction was authorized by Texas' transacting-business provision. Indeed, it held that the Texas provision reaches as far as the constitutional requirements of the Due Process Clause will permit. In examining the statutory requirement that the cause of action arise out of the contacts of the defendant with Texas, the court said:

> * * * [The "arising out of" test] is useful in any fact situation in which a jurisdiction question exists; and is a necessary requirement where the nonresident defendant only maintained single or few contacts with the forum. However, the [test] is unnecessary when the nonresident defendants presence in the forum through numerous contacts is of such a nature, as in this case, so as to satisfy the demands of the ultimate test of due process. * * *

638 S.W.2d at 872. The court went on to hold that the Due Process Clause did not bar the assertion of jurisdiction in the case before it. The United States Supreme Court subsequently disagreed.

After the Texas Supreme Court rendered its decision in the *Helicopteros* case, the Fifth Circuit, on a petition for rehearing in the *Jim Fox Enterprises* case, Note 6, above, indicated that the interpretation of Texas' long-arm statute offered in its initial opinion in *Jim Fox Enterprises* was no longer in accord with Texas authority. It therefore approved the assertion of jurisdiction over Air France. Jim Fox Enterprises, Inc. v. Air France, 705 F.2d 738 (5th Cir.1983).

8. Many state courts have adopted the view, articulated in *Gray* and echoed in the Texas Supreme Court's decision in *Helicopteros,* that a seemingly limited long-arm provision was intended to extend to the limits of the Due Process Clause. Does this effectively transform statutes of the Illinois, New York, or Texas type into statutes of the California or Rhode Island type? Is it desirable to make every decision on jurisdiction a constitutional one? This approach to enumerated-act statutes has been criticized in Taylor v. Portland Paramount Corp., 383 F.2d 634, 640 (9th Cir.1967): "In effect, what these courts have done is to abdicate their duty to construe the statutes of their own states and to turn it over to the Supreme Court of the United States, which is the ultimate interpreter of the Constitution ＊ ＊ ＊."

b. *Due Process and Long-Arm Statutes*

As is illustrated by the decision of the Illinois Supreme Court in *Gray,* interpreting the relevant long-arm statute is only half of the job. Once the meaning of the statute has been determined, it must be asked whether the statute, as interpreted, is consistent with the Due Process Clause of the Constitution.

McGEE v. INTERNATIONAL LIFE INSURANCE CO., 355 U.S. 220, 222–24, 78 S.Ct. 199, 200–01, 2 L.Ed.2d 223, 225–26 (1957). The plaintiff, McGee, was the beneficiary of a life insurance policy issued by the Empire Mutual Insurance Co., an Arizona corporation, to one Lowell Franklin, a resident of California. In 1948, the defendant, International Life Insurance Co., assumed Empire Mutual's insurance obligations. Franklin and International Life transacted business by mail until Franklin's death in 1950. Neither Empire Mutual nor International Life ever had any office or agent in California, and International Life never solicited or did any insurance business in California other than the policy with Franklin.

When International Life refused to pay McGee upon Franklin's death, she sued in a California state court, basing jurisdiction on the California Unauthorized Insurer's Process Act. The Act subjects foreign corporations to suit on insurance contracts with in-state residents. After recovering a judgment in California, McGee sought to enforce the judgment in Texas. The Texas court refused to enforce the judgment, holding it to be void under the Fourteenth Amendment on the ground that the California courts could not assume jurisdiction over International Life without service of process within its boundaries. The Supreme Court held that the exercise of jurisdiction by California was proper.

The Court noted that, with increased "nationalization of commerce," the tremendous growth "in the amount of business conducted by mail across state lines" and the frequency with which "commercial transactions touch two or more States," there had developed "a trend * * * clearly discernible toward expanding the permissible scope of state jurisdiction over foreign corporations and other nonresidents."

* * * [W]e think it apparent that the Due Process Clause did not preclude the California court from entering a judgment binding on respondent. It is sufficient * * * that the suit was based on a contract which had substantial connection with that State. * * * The contract was delivered in California, the premiums were mailed from there and the insured was a resident of that state when he died. * * * California has a manifest interest in providing effective means of redress for its residents when their insurers refuse to pay claims. These residents would be at a severe disadvantage if they were forced to follow the insurance company to a distant state in order to hold it legally accountable. When claims were small or moderate individual claimants frequently could not afford the cost of bringing an action in a foreign forum—thus in effect making the company judgment proof. Often the crucial witnesses—as here on the company's defense of suicide—will be found in the insured's locality. Of course there may be inconvenience to the insurer if it is held amenable to suit in California * * * but certainly nothing which amounts to a denial of due process. * * * There is no contention that respondent did not have adequate notice of the suit or sufficient time to prepare its defenses and appear.

Notes and Questions

1. Did the *McGee* Court modify the *International Shoe* test? Is *McGee* consistent with *International Shoe*?

2. The *McGee* opinion seems to focus on the interests of California and the plaintiff in having the suit heard in California. But isn't the issue to be determined whether the defendant's due process rights have been violated? That question appears to be independent of countervailing factors supporting the exercise of jurisdiction in California. Is it fair to characterize the *McGee* Court as using a two-step approach? The first is to determine whether sufficient minimum contacts exist so as to make the exercise of personal jurisdiction permissible. The second is to balance the interests of the plaintiff, defendant, and the forum to determine if exercising jurisdiction is desirable. Or is the thrust of *McGee* that the number of contacts between the defendant and the forum that normally would be required for jurisdiction are reduced when the interests of the forum state and plaintiff strongly support jurisdiction?

3. The Court said in *McGee* that improvements in transportation and communication make it less burdensome for out-of-state litigants to defend suits. Does this observation sufficiently justify making the defendant travel to the forum chosen by the plaintiff? Do advances in transportation and communication make it easier for plaintiffs to sue out of state? For an extremely useful discussion of the influence of social attitudes and developments on judicial principles, see Kalo, *Jurisdiction as an Evolutionary Process: The Development of Quasi In Rem and In Personam Principles,* 1978 Duke L.J. 1147.

HANSON v. DENCKLA, 357 U.S. 235, 78 S.Ct. 1228, 2 L.Ed.2d 1283 (1958). Dora Donner, a resident of Pennsylvania, established a trust in Delaware, naming a Delaware bank as trustee. By the terms of the trust, during her lifetime the income from the trust would go to her and, upon her death, the remainder would pass to whomever she had appointed as beneficiaries. Mrs. Donner retained the power to change the appointed beneficiaries at any time.

Later, Mrs. Donner moved to Florida, and, several years before her death, she executed her last will and testament, leaving most of her estate, exclusive of the Delaware trust, to two of her daughters. On the same day, she executed (for the last time) her power to change the appointed beneficiaries under the trust—this time, she designated two of her grandchildren (the children of a third daughter) beneficiaries of most of the trust's assets.

After Mrs. Donner's death, the two daughters named in the will brought an action in Florida claiming that the appointment of their sister's children as beneficiaries of the trust had been ineffective. If that were true, the assets of the trust would pass under the will to the two daughters, as legatees.

The defendants argued that the suit could not go forward because the Florida court could not assert jurisdiction over the Delaware trustee, an indispensable party under Florida law.

The Florida court found that it had jurisdiction over the trustee for the purpose of the action, concluded that the trust was invalid and that the exercise of the power of appointment was ineffective to pass title, and held that the trust property therefore passed under the will. Before the Florida judgment was rendered, an action was commenced in Delaware to determine who was entitled to share the trust assets, which were situated in Delaware. With minor exceptions, the parties were the same as in the Florida action. When the Florida judgment was rendered, the legatees under the will unsuccessfully urged it as res judicata of the Delaware action. The Delaware court ultimately held the trust and the exercise of the power of appointment valid under Delaware law.

Accepting both cases for review, a divided Supreme Court found that because the trustee's contacts with Florida had been less than minimal, that state could not assert personal jurisdiction over it. Since Florida had not obtained personal jurisdiction over an indispensable party to the action, the trustee, Delaware was justified in refusing full faith and credit to the Florida decree. Writing for a majority of five, Chief Justice Warren explained that:

> * * * [T]he requirements for personal jurisdiction over nonresidents have evolved from the rigid rule of Pennoyer v. Neff * * * to the flexible standard of International Shoe Co. v. State of Washington * * *. But it is a mistake to assume that this trend heralds the eventual demise of all restrictions on the personal jurisdiction of state courts. * * * Those restrictions are more than a guarantee of immunity from inconvenient or distant litigation. They are a consequence of territorial limitations on the power of the respective States. However

minimal the burden of defending in a foreign tribunal, a defendant may not be called upon to do so unless he has had the "minimal contacts" with that State that are a prerequisite to its exercise of power over him. * * *

We fail to find such contacts in the circumstances of this case. The defendant trust company has no office in Florida, and transacts no business there. None of the trust assets has ever been held or administered in Florida, and the record discloses no solicitation of business in that State either in person or by mail. * * *

The cause of action in this case is not one that arises out of an act done or transaction consummated in the forum State. * * * Consequently, this suit cannot be said to be one to enforce an obligation that arose from a privilege the defendant exercised in Florida. * * *

* * * The unilateral activity of those who claim some relationship with a nonresident defendant cannot satisfy the requirement of contact with the forum State. The application of that rule will vary with the quality and nature of the defendant's activity, but it is essential in each case that there be some act by which the defendant purposefully avails itself of the privilege of conducting activities within the forum State, thus invoking the benefits and protections of its laws. * * *

* * * As we understand [Florida's] law, the trustee is an indispensable party over whom the court must acquire jurisdiction before it is empowered to enter judgment in a proceeding affecting the validity of a trust. It does not acquire that jurisdiction by being the "center of gravity" of the controversy, or the most convenient location for litigation. The issue is personal jurisdiction, not choice of law. * * *

Id. at 251–54, 78 S.Ct. at 1238–40, 2 L.Ed.2d at 1296–98.

Justice Black's dissent stands in sharp contrast to the Chief Justice's perception of personal jurisdiction.

In light of the * * * circumstances it seems quite clear to me that there is nothing in the Due Process Clause which denies Florida the right to determine whether [the] appointment was valid as against its statute of wills. * * * Not only was the appointment made in Florida by a domiciliary of Florida, but the primary beneficiaries also lived in that State. In my view it could hardly be denied that Florida had sufficient interest so that a court with jurisdiction might properly apply Florida law, if it chose, to determine whether the appointment was effectual. * * * True, the question whether the law of a State can be applied to a transaction is different from the question whether the courts of that State have jurisdiction to enter a judgment, but the two are often closely related and to a substantial degree depend upon similar considerations. It seems to me that where a transaction has as much relationship to a State as * * * [this] appointment had to Florida its courts ought to have power to adjudicate controversies arising out of that transaction, unless litigation there would impose such a heavy and disproportionate burden on a nonresident defendant that it would offend what this Court has referred to as "traditional notions of fair play and substantial justice." * * * Florida, the home of the principal contenders * * *, was a reasonably convenient forum for all. Certainly there is nothing fundamentally unfair in subjecting the corporate trustee to the jurisdiction of the Florida courts. It chose to maintain business relations with [the settlor] in that State for eight years, regularly communicating with her with respect to the business of the trust including the very appointment in question.

Florida's interest in the validity of [the] appointment is made more emphatic by the fact that her will is being administered in that State. It has traditionally been the rule that the State where a person is domiciled at the time of his death is the proper place to determine the validity of his will, to construe its provisions and to marshal and distribute his personal property. Here Florida was seriously concerned with winding up [this] estate and with finally determining what property was to be distributed under her will. * * *

Id. at 258–59, 78 S.Ct. at 1242–43, 2 L.Ed.2d at 1300–01.

Notes and Questions

1. The primary beneficiaries under the last appointment of the trust, the children of Mrs. Donner's daughter Elizabeth, would have received about $400,000 from the trust. Mrs. Donner's other two daughters, the residual legatees under the will, would have received over $1,000,000 from estate sources other than the trust. The Florida decision invalidated the last appointment over the trust, defeated Mrs. Donner's estate plan, and added $400,000 to the amount received by Elizabeth's sisters at the expense of Elizabeth's family.

2. In EMPIRE ABRASIVE EQUIP. CORP. v. H.H. WATSON, INC., 567 F.2d 554, 557 (3d Cir.1977), Judge Gibbons described the concerns for state sovereignty that underlie limits on the exercise of in personam jurisdiction:

[O]ut of respect for values of federalism, the due process clause [forbids] a state to exercise its adjudicatory authority in a manner that would encroach upon the sovereignty of a sister state. A state must have some palpable interest—rationally connected with public policy—in adjudicating a dispute within its borders for jurisdiction to be lawfully acquired. * * * Although some other sovereign state may have a superior interest in having the controversy finally adjudged in its courts, our system of federalism has recognized that such conflicts between states will often arise, and has concluded that as long as the forum's interest in opening its courts to the litigants is of due process dimensions, the sovereign rights of a sister state are not unconstitutionally abridged.

How much of an interest must the forum state have to justify its exercise of sovereign authority to decide a dispute to the exclusion of other potentially interested states? Does the Due Process Clause define a rather low level of state interest? Or does due process require the forum state's interests to outweigh the interests of other states? Compare California's interests in *McGee*, in which jurisdiction was upheld, with Florida's interests in *Hanson*, in which jurisdiction was denied.

3. Could the *Hanson* decision be justified on the ground that Delaware, as the state where the trust was validly established (at least under Delaware law), had a stronger interest in the disposition of the trust's funds than Florida? Delaware's interest certainly is sufficient to support jurisdiction in

Delaware. Is Delaware's interest sufficient to preclude jurisdiction in Florida? Could it be that the result in this case is a function of the fact that the Court had before it two conflicting judgments and that it could not accord full faith and credit to both?

4. What defines a state "interest" sufficient to support jurisdiction? Is a legislative desire to provide a forum enough? Every long-arm statute manifests a legislative desire to extend jurisdiction in a given class of cases, yet we subject these statutes to scrutiny under the Due Process Clause and sometimes invalidate them. Does a state's desire to provide a forum for its residents constitute an interest? Surely, the residence of the plaintiff is not sufficient by itself to provide a basis for depriving a defendant of her property. Does the fact that a state has contacts with the events giving rise to the litigation, regardless of whether those contacts are attributable to the defendant, create an "interest" sufficient to support jurisdiction? In *Hanson,* Florida had contacts with the litigation, and the Court denied its courts jurisdiction. Should state substantive regulation of a particular class of cases influence the decision on personal jurisdiction? In *McGee,* jurisdiction over the nonresident insurance company may have been justified by California's regulation of the insurance industry. Is a state's substantive regulation of an area the only interest relevant to jurisdiction? See generally Brilmayer, *How Contacts Count: Due Process Limitations on State Court Jurisdiction,* 1980 Sup.Ct.Rev. 77; Carrington & Martin, *Substantive Interests and the Jurisdiction of State Courts,* 66 Mich.L.Rev. 227 (1967); Drobak, *The Federalism Theme in Personal Jurisdiction,* 68 Iowa L.Rev. 1015 (1983); Lewis, *The "Forum State Interest" Factor in Personal Jurisdiction: Home Court Horses Hauling Constitutional Carts,* 33 Mercer L.Rev. 769 (1982).

5. In their opinions in *Hanson,* the Chief Justice and Justice Black agree that the question whether a court may apply its own law to a controversy is to be decided by a standard that differs from that used to decide the question whether the court can adjudicate the controversy at all. That is, the constitutional power to apply local law is of a different dimension from the constitutional power to assert jurisdiction. Can this difference be justified?

6. Consider the following argument:

> The *Hanson* Court's implication * * * is that more contacts with the forum state are needed for jurisdiction than for choice of law. I suggest that this implication is counterintuitive. The impact of a conflict of laws decision more seriously affects the rights of the parties than a decision on jurisdiction, which merely directs the parties to an appropriate forum in which to litigate their case. * * * I am confident that, given the choice, the Florida plaintiffs would rather have litigated in a Delaware Court applying Florida law than in a Florida court applying Delaware law.

Silberman, *Shaffer v. Heitner: The End of an Era,* 53 N.Y.U.L.Rev. 33, 82–83 (1978). Given a choice of fora with different substantive rules, it is obvious that the plaintiff would prefer one and the defendant another. But, should jurisdiction turn on the interests of the parties? Is it the state's interest that is relevant? Is the state's interest the only relevant interest?

7. Might it be appropriate to allow a court to adjudicate any controversy to which it might apply local law under the applicable choice-of-law rule? In ALLSTATE INS. CO. v. HAGUE, 449 U.S. 302, 312–13, 101 S.Ct. 633, 640, 66

L.Ed.2d 521, 531 (1981), the plurality opinion held that "for a State's substantive law to be selected in a constitutionally permissible manner, that State must have a significant contact or significant aggregation of contacts, creating state interests, such that choice of its law is neither arbitrary nor fundamentally unfair." Under this test, the plurality upheld Minnesota's decision to apply its own law in an action by a former Wisconsin resident who moved to Minnesota just prior to filing suit to collect proceeds under an automobile insurance policy made in Wisconsin covering vehicles owned by a Wisconsin resident who had been killed in an accident in Wisconsin. After *Hague* it seems clear that the Due Process Clause allows states extraordinary latitude in developing choice-of-law rules. The due process restrictions on state jurisdiction are considerably greater than those on choice of law.

WORLD–WIDE VOLKSWAGEN CORP. v. WOODSON

Supreme Court of the United States, 1980.
444 U.S. 286, 100 S.Ct. 559, 62 L.Ed.2d 490.

Certiorari to the Supreme Court of Oklahoma.

MR. JUSTICE WHITE delivered the opinion of the Court.

The issue before us is whether, consistently with the Due Process Clause of the Fourteenth Amendment, an Oklahoma court may exercise *in personam* jurisdiction over a nonresident automobile retailer and its wholesale distributor in a products liability action, when the defendants' only connection with Oklahoma is the fact that an automobile sold in New York to New York residents became involved in an accident in Oklahoma.

I

Respondents Harry and Kay Robinson purchased a new Audi automobile from petitioner Seaway Volkswagen, Inc. (Seaway) in Massena, N.Y., in 1976. The following year the Robinson family, who resided in New York, left that State for a new home in Arizona. As they passed through the State of Oklahoma, another car struck their Audi in the rear, causing a fire which severely burned Kay Robinson and her two children.

The Robinsons subsequently brought a products liability action in the District Court for Creek County, Okla., claiming that their injuries resulted from defective design and placement of the Audi's gas tank and fuel system. They joined as defendants the automobile's manufacturer, Audi NSU Auto Union Aktiengesellschaft (Audi); its importer, Volkswagen of America, Inc. (Volkswagen); its regional distributor, petitioner World-Wide Volkswagen Corporation (World-Wide); and its retail dealer, petitioner Seaway. Seaway and World-Wide entered special appearances, claiming that Oklahoma's exercise of jurisdiction over them would offend the limitations on the State's jurisdiction imposed by the Due Process Clause of the Fourteenth Amendment.

The facts presented to the District Court showed that World-Wide is incorporated and has its business office in New York. It distributes vehicles, parts, and accessories, under contract with Volkswagen, to retail dealers in New York, New Jersey, and Connecticut. Seaway, one of these retail dealers, is incorporated and has its place of business in New York.

Insofar as the record reveals, Seaway and World-Wide are fully independent corporations whose relations with each other and with Volkswagen and Audi are contractual only. Respondents adduced no evidence that either World-Wide or Seaway does any business in Oklahoma, ships or sells any products to or in that State, has an agent to receive process there, or purchases advertisements in any media calculated to reach Oklahoma. In fact, * * * there was no showing that any automobile sold by World-Wide or Seaway has ever entered Oklahoma with the single exception of the vehicle involved in the present case.

Despite the apparent paucity of contacts between petitioners and Oklahoma, the District Court rejected their constitutional claim and reaffirmed that ruling in denying petitioners' motion for reconsideration. Petitioners then sought a writ of prohibition in the Supreme Court of Oklahoma to restrain the District Judge, respondent Charles S. Woodson, from exercising *in personam* jurisdiction over them. They renewed their contention that, because they had no "minimal contacts" * * * with the State of Oklahoma, the actions of the District Judge were in violation of their rights under the Due Process Clause.

The Supreme Court of Oklahoma denied the writ, * * * holding that personal jurisdiction over petitioners was authorized by Oklahoma's "long-arm" statute, Okla.Stat., Tit. 12, § 1701.03(a)(4) (1971).[7] Although the court noted that the proper approach was to test jurisdiction against both statutory and constitutional standards, its analysis did not distinguish these questions, probably because § 1701.03(a)(4) has been interpreted as conferring jurisdiction to the limits permitted by the United States Constitution. The court's rationale was contained in the following paragraph * * *:

> In the case before us, the product being sold and distributed by the petitioners is by its very design and purpose so mobile that petitioners can foresee its possible use in Oklahoma. This is especially true of the distributor, who has the exclusive right to distribute such automobile in New York, New Jersey and Connecticut. The evidence presented below demonstrated that goods sold and distributed by the petitioners were used in the State of Oklahoma, and under the facts we believe it reasonable to infer, given the retail value of the automobile, that the petitioners derive substantial income from automobiles which from time to time are used in the State of Oklahoma. This being the case, we hold that under the facts presented, the trial court was justified in concluding that the petitioners derive substantial revenue from goods used or consumed in this State.

We granted certiorari * * * to consider an important constitutional question with respect to state-court jurisdiction and to resolve a conflict between the Supreme Court of Oklahoma and the highest courts of at least four other States. We reverse.

---

7. This subsection provides:

"A court may exercise personal jurisdiction over a person, who acts directly or by an agent, as to a cause of action or claim for relief arising from the person's * * * causing tortious injury in this state by an act or omission outside this state if he regularly does or solicits business or engages in any other persistent course of conduct, or derives substantial revenue from goods used or consumed or services rendered, in this state * * *." * * *

II

* * *

As has long been settled, and as we reaffirm today, a state court may exercise personal jurisdiction over a nonresident defendant only so long as there exist "minimum contacts" between the defendant and the forum State. International Shoe Co. v. Washington * * *. The concept of minimum contacts, in turn, can be seen to perform two related, but distinguishable, functions. It protects the defendant against the burdens of litigating in a distant or inconvenient forum. And it acts to ensure that the States, through their courts, do not reach out beyond the limits imposed on them by their status as coequal sovereigns in a federal system.

The protection against inconvenient litigation is typically described in terms of "reasonableness" or "fairness." We have said that the defendant's contacts with the forum State must be such that maintenance of the suit "does not offend 'traditional notions of fair play and substantial justice.'" * * * The relationship between the defendant and the forum must be such that it is "reasonable * * * to require the corporation to defend the particular suit which is brought there." * * * Implicit in this emphasis on reasonableness is the understanding that the burden on the defendant, while always a primary concern, will in an appropriate case be considered in light of other relevant factors, including the forum State's interest in adjudicating the dispute * * *; the plaintiff's interest in obtaining convenient and effective relief, * * * at least when that interest is not adequately protected by the plaintiff's power to choose the forum * * *; the interstate judicial system's interest in obtaining the most efficient resolution of controversies; and the shared interest of the several States in furthering fundamental substantive social policies * * *.

The limits imposed on state jurisdiction by the Due Process Clause, in its role as a guarantor against inconvenient litigation, have been substantially relaxed over the years. As we noted in McGee v. International Life Ins. Co., * * * this trend is largely attributable to a fundamental transformation in the American economy:

> Today many commercial transactions touch two or more States and may involve parties separated by the full continent. With this increasing nationalization of commerce has come a great increase in the amount of business conducted by mail across state lines. At the same time modern transportation and communication have made it much less burdensome for a party sued to defend himself in a State where he engages in economic activity.

The historical developments noted in *McGee*, of course, have only accelerated in the generation since that case was decided.

Nevertheless, we have never accepted the proposition that state lines are irrelevant for jurisdictional purposes, nor could we, and remain faithful to the principles of interstate federalism embodied in the Constitution. * * * [T]he Framers * * * intended that the States retain many essential attributes of sovereignty, including, in particular, the sovereign power to try causes in their courts. The sovereignty of each

State, in turn, implied a limitation on the sovereignty of all of its sister States—a limitation express or implicit in both the original scheme of the Constitution and the Fourteenth Amendment.

Hence, even while abandoning the shibboleth that "[t]he authority of every tribunal is necessarily restricted by the territorial limits of the State in which it is established," Pennoyer v. Neff, * * * we emphasized that the reasonableness of asserting jurisdiction over the defendant must be assessed "in the context of our federal system of government," International Shoe Co. v. Washington, * * * and stressed that the Due Process Clause ensures not only fairness, but also the "orderly administration of the laws," id. As we noted in Hanson v. Denckla * * *:

> As technological progress has increased the flow of commerce between the States, the need for jurisdiction over nonresidents has undergone a similar increase. At the same time, progress in communications and transportation has made the defense of a suit in a foreign tribunal less burdensome. In response to these changes, the requirements for personal jurisdiction over nonresidents have evolved from the rigid rule of Pennoyer v. Neff * * * to the flexible standard of International Shoe Co. v. Washington. * * * But it is a mistake to assume that this trend heralds the eventual demise of all restrictions on the personal jurisdiction of state courts. * * * Those restrictions are more than a guarantee of immunity from inconvenient or distant litigation. They are a consequence of territorial limitations on the power of the respective States.

Thus, the Due Process Clause "does not contemplate that a state may make binding a judgment *in personam* against an individual or corporate defendant with which the state has no contacts, ties, or relations." International Shoe Co. v. Washington * * *. Even if the defendant would suffer minimal or no inconvenience from being forced to litigate before the tribunals of another State; even if the forum State has a strong interest in applying its law to the controversy; even if the forum State is the most convenient location for litigation, the Due Process Clause, acting as an instrument of interstate federalism, may sometimes act to divest the State of its power to render a valid judgment. Hanson v. Denckla * * *.

III

Applying these principles to the case at hand, we find in the record before us a total absence of those affiliating circumstances that are a necessary predicate to any exercise of state-court jurisdiction. Petitioners carry on no activity whatsoever in Oklahoma. They close no sales and perform no services there. They avail themselves of none of the privileges and benefits of Oklahoma law. They solicit no business there either through salespersons or through advertising reasonably calculated to reach the State. Nor does the record show that they regularly sell cars at wholesale or retail to Oklahoma customers or residents or that they indirectly, through others, serve or seek to serve the Oklahoma market. In short, respondents seek to base jurisdiction on one, isolated occurrence and whatever inferences can be drawn therefrom: the fortuitous circumstance that a single Audi automobile, sold in New York to New York residents, happened to suffer an accident while passing through Oklahoma.

It is argued, however, that because an automobile is mobile by its very design and purpose it was "foreseeable" that the Robinsons' Audi would cause injury in Oklahoma. Yet "foreseeability" alone has never been a sufficient benchmark for personal jurisdiction under the Due Process Clause. In Hanson v. Denckla * * * it was no doubt foreseeable that the settlor of a Delaware trust would subsequently move to Florida and seek to exercise a power of appointment there; yet we held that Florida courts could not constitutionally exercise jurisdiction over a Delaware trustee that had no other contacts with the forum State. * * *

If foreseeability were the criterion, a local California tire retailer could be forced to defend in Pennsylvania when a blowout occurs there, * * * a Wisconsin seller of a defective automobile jack could be haled before a distant court for damage caused in New Jersey, * * * or a Florida soft-drink concessionaire could be summoned to Alaska to account for injuries happening there * * *. Every seller of chattels would in effect appoint the chattel his agent for service of process. His amenability to suit would travel with the chattel. * * *

This is not to say, of course, that foreseeability is wholly irrelevant. But the foreseeability that is critical to due process analysis is not the mere likelihood that a product will find its way into the forum State. Rather, it is that the defendant's conduct and connection with the forum State are such that he should reasonably anticipate being haled into court there. * * * The Due Process Clause, by ensuring the "orderly administration of the laws," * * * gives a degree of predictability to the legal system that allows potential defendants to structure their primary conduct with some minimum assurance as to where that conduct will and will not render them liable to suit.

When a corporation "purposefully avails itself of the privilege of conducting activities within the forum State," * * * it has clear notice that it is subject to suit there, and can act to alleviate the risk of burdensome litigation by procuring insurance, passing the expected costs on to customers, or, if the risks are too great, severing its connection with the State. Hence if the sale of a product of a manufacturer or distributor such as Audi or Volkswagen is not simply an isolated occurrence, but arises from the efforts of the manufacturer or distributor to serve, directly or indirectly, the market for its product in other States, it is not unreasonable to subject it to suit in one of those States if its allegedly defective merchandise has there been the source of injury to its owner or to others. The forum State does not exceed its powers under the Due Process Clause if it asserts personal jurisdiction over a corporation that delivers its products into the stream of commerce with the expectation that they will be purchased by consumers in the forum State. Cf. Gray v. American Radiator & Standard Sanitary Corp. * * *.

But there is no such or similar basis for Oklahoma jurisdiction over World-Wide or Seaway in this case. Seaway's sales are made in Massena, N.Y. World-Wide's market, although substantially larger, is limited to dealers in New York, New Jersey, and Connecticut. There is no evidence of record that any automobiles distributed by World-Wide are sold to retail customers outside this tristate area. It is foreseeable that the purchasers of automobiles sold by World-Wide and Seaway may take them to Oklahoma. But the mere "unilateral activity of those who claim some relationship with a nonresident defendant cannot satisfy the requirement of contact with the forum State." Hanson v. Denckla * * *.

In a variant on the previous argument, it is contended that jurisdiction can be supported by the fact that petitioners earn substantial revenue from goods used in Oklahoma. * * * While this inference seems less than compelling on the facts of the instant case, we need not question the court's factual findings in order to reject its reasoning.

This argument seems to make the point that the purchase of automobiles in New York, from which the petitioners earn substantial revenue, would not occur *but for* the fact that the automobiles are capable of use in distant States like Oklahoma. Respondents observe that the very purpose of an automobile is to travel, and that travel of automobiles sold by petitioners is facilitated by an extensive chain of Volkswagen service centers throughout the country, including some in Oklahoma. However, financial benefits accruing to the defendant from a collateral relation to the forum State will not support jurisdiction if they do not stem from a constitutionally cognizable contact with that State. * * * In our view, whatever marginal revenues petitioners may receive by virtue of the fact that their products are capable of use in Oklahoma is far too attenuated a contact to justify that State's exercise of *in personam* jurisdiction over them.

Because we find that petitioners have no "contacts, ties, or relations" with the State of Oklahoma, International Shoe Co. v. Washington, * * * the judgment of the Supreme Court of Oklahoma is

Reversed.

[The dissenting opinions of JUSTICE MARSHALL and JUSTICE BLACKMUN are omitted.]

MR. JUSTICE BRENNAN, dissenting.

* * *

I

The Court's opinions focus tightly on the existence of contacts between the forum and the defendant. In so doing, they accord too little weight to the strength of the forum State's interest in the case and fail to explore whether there would be any actual inconvenience to the defendant. The essential inquiry in locating the constitutional limits on state-court jurisdiction over absent defendants is whether the particular exercise of jurisdiction offends " 'traditional notions of fair play and substantial justice.' " * * * The clear focus in *International Shoe* was on fairness and reasonableness. * * * The Court specifically declined to establish a mechanical test based on the quantum of contacts between a State and the defendant * * *. The existence of contacts, so long as there were some, was merely one way of giving content to the determination of fairness and reasonableness.

Surely *International Shoe* contemplated that the significance of the contacts necessary to support jurisdiction would diminish if some other consideration helped establish that jurisdiction would be fair and reasonable. The interests of the State and other parties in proceeding with the case in a particular forum are such considerations. McGee v. International Life Ins. Co., * * * for instance, accorded great importance to a State's "manifest interest in providing effective means of redress" for its citizens. * * *

Another consideration is the actual burden a defendant must bear in defending the suit in the forum. * * * Because lesser burdens reduce the unfairness to the defendant, jurisdiction may be justified despite less significant contacts. The burden, of course, must be of constitutional dimension. Due process limits on jurisdiction do not protect a defendant from all inconvenience of travel * * *. Instead, the constitutionally significant "burden" to be analyzed relates to the mobility of the defendant's defense. For instance, if having to travel to a foreign forum would hamper the defense because witnesses or evidence or the defendant himself were immobile, or if there were a disproportionately large number of witnesses or amount of evidence that would have to be transported at the defendant's expense, or if being away from home for the duration of the trial would work some special hardship on the defendant, then the Constitution would require special consideration for the defendant's interests.

That considerations other than contacts between the forum and the defendant are relevant necessarily means that the Constitution does not require that trial be held in the State which has the "best contacts" with the defendant. * * * The defendant has no constitutional entitlement to the best forum or, for that matter, to any particular forum. Under even the most restrictive view of *International Shoe,* several States could have jurisdiction over a particular cause of action. We need only determine whether the forum States in these cases satisfy the constitutional minimum.

II

* * * I would find that the forum State has an interest in permitting the litigation to go forward, the litigation is connected to the forum, the defendant is linked to the forum, and the burden of defending is not unreasonable. Accordingly, I would hold that it is neither unfair nor unreasonable to require these defendants to defend in the forum State.

* * *

* * * [T]he interest of the forum State and its connection to the litigation is strong. The automobile accident underlying the litigation occurred in Oklahoma. The plaintiffs were hospitalized in Oklahoma when they brought suit. Essential witnesses and evidence were in Oklahoma. * * * The State has a legitimate interest in enforcing its laws

designed to keep its highway system safe, and the trial can proceed at least as efficiently in Oklahoma as anywhere else.

The petitioners are not unconnected with the forum. Although both sell automobiles within limited sales territories, each sold the automobile which in fact was driven to Oklahoma where it was involved in an accident. It may be true, as the Court suggests, that each sincerely intended to limit its commercial impact to the limited territory, and that each intended to accept the benefits and protection of the laws only of those States within the territory. But obviously these were unrealistic hopes that cannot be treated as an automatic constitutional shield.

An automobile simply is not a stationary item or one designed to be used in one place. An automobile is *intended* to be moved around. Someone in the business of selling large numbers of automobiles can hardly plead ignorance of their mobility or pretend that the automobiles stay put after they are sold. It is not merely that a dealer in automobiles foresees that they will move. * * * The dealer actually intends that the purchasers will use the automobiles to travel to distant States where the dealer does not directly "do business." The sale of an automobile does *purposefully* inject the vehicle into the stream of interstate commerce so that it can travel to distant States. * * *

The Court accepts that a State may exercise jurisdiction over a distributor which "serves" that State "indirectly" by "deliver[ing] its products into the stream of commerce with the expectation that they will be purchased by consumers in the forum State." * * * It is difficult to see why the Constitution should distinguish between a case involving goods which reach a distant State through a chain of distribution and a case involving goods which reach the same State because a consumer, using them as the dealer knew the customer would, took them there. In each case the seller purposefully injects the goods into the stream of commerce and those goods predictably are used in the forum State.

* * *

III

It may be that affirmance of the judgments in these cases would approach the outer limits of *International Shoe*'s jurisdictional principle. But that principle, with its almost exclusive focus on the rights of defendants, may be outdated. * * *

International Shoe inherited its defendant focus from Pennoyer v. Neff * * * and represented the last major step this Court has taken in the long process of liberalizing the doctrine of personal jurisdiction. Though its flexible approach represented a major advance, the structure of our society has changed in many significant ways since *International Shoe* was decided in 1945. * * * As the Court acknowledges, * * * both the nationalization of commerce and the ease of transportation and communication have accelerated in the generation since 1957. The model of society on which the *International Shoe* Court based its opinion is no longer accurate. Business people, no matter how local their businesses, cannot assume that goods remain in the business' locality. Customers and goods can be anywhere else in the country usually in a matter of hours and always in a matter of a very few days.

In answering the question whether or not it is fair and reasonable to allow a particular forum to hold a trial binding on a particular defendant, the interests of the forum State and other parties loom large in today's world and surely are entitled to as much weight as are the interests of the defendant. The "orderly administration of the laws" provides a firm basis for according some protection to the interests of plaintiffs and States as well as of defendants. Certainly, I cannot see how a defendant's right to due process is violated if the defendant suffers no inconvenience. * * *

The conclusion I draw is that constitutional concepts of fairness no longer require the extreme concern for defendants that was once necessary. Rather, * * * minimum contacts must exist "among the *parties,* the contested transaction, and the forum State."[15] The contacts between any two of these should not be determinative. * * *

In effect the Court is allowing defendants to assert the sovereign rights of their home States. The expressed fear is that otherwise all limits on personal jurisdiction would disappear. But the argument's premise is wrong. I would not abolish limits on jurisdiction or strip state boundaries of all significance * * *; I would still require the plaintiff to demonstrate sufficient contacts among the parties, the forum, and the litigation to make the forum a reasonable State in which to hold the trial.

I would also, however, strip the defendant of an unjustified veto power over certain very appropriate fora—a power the defendant justifiably enjoyed long ago when communication and travel over long distances were slow and unpredictable and when notions of state sovereignty were impractical and exaggerated. * * *

The plaintiffs * * * brought suit in a forum with which they had significant contacts and which had significant contacts with the litigation. I am not convinced that the defendants would suffer any "heavy and disproportionate burden" in defending the suits. Accordingly, I would hold that the Constitution should not shield the defendants from appearing and defending in the plaintiffs' chosen fora.

Notes and Questions

1. Neither Audi nor Volkswagen of America objected to jurisdiction. How would they have fared had they contested it? Is it likely that specific jurisdiction would exist with regard to them? General jurisdiction? Both?

Considering the deep pockets of Audi and Volkswagen, why were the plaintiffs so interested in gaining jurisdiction over Seaway and World–Wide? To answer the question, you must consider trial tactics as well as the rules of personal jurisdiction. Both Seaway and World–Wide were incorporated and had their places of business in New York. For diversity purposes, the Robinsons were New York citizens at the time the action was commenced.

---

15. In some cases, the inquiry will resemble the inquiry commonly undertaken in determining which State's law to apply. That it is fair to apply a State's law to a nonresi-dent defendant is clearly relevant in determining whether it is fair to subject the defendant to jurisdiction in that State. * * *

With Seaway and World–Wide as defendants, there would be incomplete diversity jurisdiction, and the Robinsons would not have to worry about removal to federal court. Is it possible that the fight really was about whether the case would be tried in state court or federal court in Oklahoma? Would it help you answer the question if you knew that, at the time, federal juries in Oklahoma were awarding smaller damages on claims like the Robinsons' than were their state counterparts?

See generally Lowenfeld, *Conflict of Laws* 565 (1986). Professor Lowenfeld reports:

> In the end, the forum shopping calculations of both sides proved accurate. Once the Supreme Court decided that World–Wide and Seaway could not be sued in Oklahoma, the principal defendants * * * removed the case to the U.S. Court for the Northern District of Oklahoma. Following discovery under the federal rules, the case was tried to a jury, which in January 1982 returned a verdict for defendants.

2. In the course of its *World-Wide Volkswagen* opinion, the Court employs both notions of sovereignty (like those emphasized in *Hanson*) and of convenience (like those emphasized in *McGee*). Is there a tension between these two notions? Is the Court promulgating a two-part test with a "sovereignty branch" and a "convenience branch"? Is this a new test or a refinement of the "minimum contacts" test announced in *International Shoe*?

In INSURANCE CORP. OF IRELAND v. COMPAGNIE DES BAUXITES DE GUINEE, 456 U.S. 694, 102 S.Ct. 2099, 72 L.Ed.2d 492 (1982), Justice White, the author of *World-Wide Volkswagen,* wrote for eight Justices. He described the personal jurisdiction requirement imposed by the Due Process Clause as one that "recognizes and protects an individual liberty interest." His opinion further elaborated this thought in a footnote that expressly addressed his opinion in *World-Wide Volkswagen.*

> It is true that we have stated that the requirement of personal jurisdiction, as applied to state courts, reflects an element of federalism and the character of state sovereignty vis-a-vis other states. [Justice White then quoted from *World-Wide Volkswagen*] * * *. The restriction on state sovereign power described in *World-Wide Volkswagen Corp.,* however, must be seen as ultimately a function of the individual liberty interest preserved by the Due Process Clause. That clause is the only source of the personal jurisdiction requirement and the clause itself makes no mention of federalism concerns. Furthermore, if the federalism concept operated as an independent restriction on the sovereign power of the court, it would not be possible to waive the personal jurisdiction requirement: Individual actions cannot change the powers of sovereignty, although the individual can subject himself to powers from which he may otherwise be protected.

456 U.S. at 702 n. 10, 102 S.Ct. at 2104–05 n. 10, 72 L.Ed.2d at 501 n. 10. Does this footnote transform the "sovereignty branch" of the *World-Wide Volkswagen* test? Do the Due Process Clause limitations on personal jurisdiction serve state sovereignty merely as a by-product of the protection of litigants' rights? Certainly the "minimum contacts" requirement assures that only those states sufficiently connected with the defendant may litigate the dispute. Is it possible to say that the Court's opinion in *World-Wide Volkswagen* demonstrates that protection of interstate federalism is a reason for including

in the test for personal jurisdiction a requirement of pre-litigation contact with the forum, but that the Court's use of its test shows that the protection of federalism is not an independent component of the test? How could a defendant waive the requirement of minimum contacts (as he can) if the protection of federalism created an independent restriction on the power of a court? For thoughtful discussions of this issue, see Stein, *Styles of Argument and Interstate Federalism in the Law of Personal Jurisdiction,* 65 Texas L.Rev. 689, 725 (1987), and Knudson, *Keeton, Calder, Helicopteros and Burger King— International Shoe's Most Recent Progeny,* 39 U.Miami L.Rev. 309 (1985).

3. How would *Volkswagen* have been decided if the Robinsons had been Oklahoma residents and had bought the ill-fated car while in New York on vacation? What if the driver of the other car sued World-Wide and Seaway for injuries resulting from the exploding gas tank? What if that driver never had been outside the state of Oklahoma?

4. Does *World-Wide Volkswagen* invalidate assertions of jurisdiction such as Gray v. American Radiator & Standard Sanitary Corp., p. 92, supra? In BODINE'S INC. v. SUNNY–O, INC., 494 F.Supp. 1279, 1283 (N.D.Ill.1980), the same long-arm statute that was interpreted in *Gray* was at issue. Bodine's sued Sunny-O for breach of warranty and fraud in connection with a delivery by Sunny-O of orange juice concentrate to Bodine's. Personal jurisdiction was based upon the Illinois long-arm statute providing for jurisdiction over causes of action arising from the commission of a tortious act within the state. Sunny-O contested jurisdiction, arguing that the exercise of jurisdiction would be inappropriate under *World-Wide Volkswagen.* The District Court upheld jurisdiction:

> Rather than suggesting the invalidity of the exercise of personal jurisdiction under Section 17(1)(b) herein, the decision in *World-Wide Volkswagen* only supports further the Court's view that such jurisdiction is proper. Unlike *World-Wide Volkswagen,* this case does not involve the sale of a product by a foreign corporation to a foreign resident. Nor can the presence of defendant's product in Illinois be termed a "fortuitous circumstance." Rather, the sale of the orange juice concentrate to plaintiff arose from defendant's effort to serve, directly or indirectly, the market for its products in various states, including Illinois.

Does the passage quoted completely dispose of the due process issue? What of *World-Wide Volkswagen's* "convenience branch"?

5. In KEETON v. HUSTLER MAGAZINE, INC., 465 U.S. 770, 104 S.Ct. 1473, 79 L.Ed.2d 790 (1984), Kathy Keeton, a resident of New York, brought a libel suit against Hustler Magazine, an Ohio corporation, in federal court in New Hampshire. Keeton chose the New Hampshire court because New Hampshire was the only state where the action was not time-barred when it was filed. She argued that jurisdiction existed under New Hampshire's long-arm statute because Hustler sold 10,000 to 15,000 magazines a month in the state. Keeton herself had only one connection to New Hampshire: a magazine that she helped to produce was circulated there.

The District Court dismissed Keeton's suit for lack of jurisdiction, and the First Circuit affirmed, holding that Keeton's lack of contacts with New Hampshire rendered the state's interest in redressing the libel to the plaintiff too attenuated to support jurisdiction over a suit necessarily involving nationwide damages. In the Circuit Court's words, "the New Hampshire tail is too small to wag so large an out-of-state dog."

The Supreme Court unanimously reversed, saying:

> [R]egular monthly sales of thousands of magazines cannot by any stretch of the imagination be characterized as random, isolated, or fortuitous. It is, therefore, unquestionable that New Hampshire jurisdiction over a complaint based on those contacts could ordinarily satisfy the requirement of the Due Process Clause that a State's assertion of personal jurisdiction over a nonresident defendant be predicated on "minimum contacts" between the defendant and the State. And, as the Court of Appeals acknowledged, New Hampshire has adopted a "long-arm" statute authorizing service of process on nonresident corporations whenever permitted by the Due Process Clause. Thus, all the requisites for personal jurisdiction over Hustler Magazine, Inc., in New Hampshire are present.

Id. at 774–75, 104 S.Ct. at 1478, 79 L.Ed.2d at 797. Is the key to the Court's decision in *Keeton* that the defendants intentionally acted in the forum? Does the *Keeton* Court apply both the "sovereignty branch" and the "convenience branch" of *World-Wide Volkswagen*?

What of Hustler's argument that the plaintiff's contacts with New Hampshire were minimal? Is that argument relevant to the sovereignty branch? Or the convenience branch? In discussing the argument, the Supreme Court said:

> * * * [I]mplicit in the Court of Appeals' analysis of New Hampshire's interest is an emphasis on the extremely limited contacts of the *plaintiff* with New Hampshire. But we have not to date required a plaintiff to have "minimum contacts" with the forum State before permitting that State to assert personal jurisdiction over a nonresident defendant. On the contrary, we have upheld the assertion of jurisdiction where such contacts were entirely lacking. * * *

Id. at 779, 104 S.Ct. at 1480–81, 79 L.Ed.2d at 800. The Court went on to say, however, that "[t]he plaintiff's residence is not, of course, completely irrelevant to the jurisdiction inquiry." The Court noted, for example, that a plaintiff's residence in the forum, because of the defendant's relationship with the plaintiff, may enhance the defendant's contacts with the forum.

What of the argument that it was unfair to allow suit to be brought in the only state where it was not time-barred? Is that relevant to the jurisdictional inquiry? The Court did not believe that it was:

> * * * [A]ny potential unfairness in applying New Hampshire's statute of limitations to all aspects of this nationwide suit has nothing to do with the jurisdiction of the Court to adjudicate the claims. "The issue is personal jurisdiction, not choice of law." Hanson v. Denckla * * *. The question of the applicability of New Hampshire's statute of limitations to claims for out-of-state damages presents itself in the course of litigation only after jurisdiction over respondent is established, and we do not think that such choice of law concerns should complicate or distort the jurisdictional inquiry.

Id. at 778, 104 S.Ct. at 1480, 79 L.Ed.2d at 800.

6. A defendant may have contacts with the forum state that are related or unrelated to the controversy that has come to court. In applying *World-Wide Volkswagen,* it is important to keep this distinction between related and unrelated contacts in mind. Related contacts are weighed more heavily in favor of jurisdiction than unrelated ones. Unrelated contacts—if continuous and substantial—may support general jurisdiction, but even a single contact may support jurisdiction when the cause of action arises out of the contact.

Suppose that World-Wide Volkswagen had maintained an agent in Oklahoma and had advertised there. These contacts with Oklahoma would have been unrelated to the Robinsons' accident in that state, since they had bought their car in New York. Suppose also that World-Wide's contacts with the state were insufficient to support general jurisdiction. What, if any, weight should be given to World-Wide's unrelated contacts with Oklahoma in assessing, under the Due Process Clause, the propriety of Oklahoma's attempt to assert jurisdiction over World-Wide in *Robinson v. World-Wide Volkswagen?* See Helicopteros Nacionales de Colombia, S.A. v. Hall, p. 89, supra.

————

KULKO v. SUPERIOR COURT, 436 U.S. 84, 98 S.Ct. 1690, 56 L.Ed.2d 132 (1978), was a suit for modification of a child support agreement by a California citizen against her ex-husband, a New Yorker. The couple's two children lived with their father in New York under the original separation agreement. However, when the daughter told defendant that she wanted to live with her mother, he assented and bought her a one-way plane ticket to California. The other child also joined his mother in California, after receiving a one-way ticket from her, without defendant's knowledge.

The California Supreme Court upheld jurisdiction over the defendant husband under the California long-arm statute, which authorized the exercise of jurisdiction "on any basis not inconsistent with the Constitution." The court concluded that it was "fair and reasonable" for the New York defendant to be subject to personal jurisdiction in California because by purchasing his daughter's airline ticket, he had committed a "purposeful act" outside the state that caused an effect within the state. The United States Supreme Court reversed:

> * * * We cannot accept the proposition that appellant's acquiescence in Ilsa's desire to live with her mother conferred jurisdiction over appellant in the California courts in this action. A father who agrees, in the interests of family harmony and his children's preferences, to allow them to spend more time in California than was required under a separation agreement can hardly be said to have "purposefully availed himself" of the "benefits and protections" of California's laws. * * *

> Nor can we agree with the assertion of the court below that the exercise of *in personam* jurisdiction here was warranted by the financial benefit appellant derived from his daughter's presence in California for nine months of the year. * * * [T]his circumstance, even if true, does not support California's assertion of jurisdiction here. Any diminution in

appellant's household costs resulted, not from the child's presence in California, but rather from her absence from appellant's home.

Id. at 94–95, 98 S.Ct. at 1698, 56 L.Ed.2d at 142–43.

The Court also noted that the California court's reliance on the "effects" test was misplaced because that approach applies only to wrongful activity without the state causing injury within it or to commercial activity affecting state residents, when that application would not be "unreasonable." Merely causing an effect within the forum state without purposeful availment will not support jurisdiction.

> The circumstances in this case clearly render "unreasonable" California's assertion of personal jurisdiction. There is no claim that appellant has visited physical injury on either property or persons within the State of California. The cause of action herein asserted arises, not from the defendant's commercial transactions in interstate commerce, but rather from his personal, domestic relations. * * * Furthermore, the controversy between the parties arises from a separation that occurred in the State of New York * * *.

> Finally, basic considerations of fairness point decisively in favor of appellant's State of domicile as the proper forum for adjudication of this case, whatever the merits of appellee's underlying claim. It is appellant who has remained in the State of the marital domicile, whereas it is appellee who has moved across the continent. * * * [Exercising jurisdiction] would impose an unreasonable burden on family relations, and one wholly unjustified by the "quality and nature" of appellant's activities in or relating to the State of California. * * *

Id. at 96–98, 98 S.Ct. at 1699–1700, 56 L.Ed.2d at 144–45.

Notes and Questions

1. Why is the Court emphasizing "the" proper forum as opposed to "a" proper forum. Do not the cases from *International Shoe* to *World-Wide Volkswagen* admit that jurisdiction can be proper in more than one forum? Does the switch in emphasis have to do with the type of action involved?

2. Before 1984, some cases suggested that the First Amendment imposed a significant limitation upon the exercise of jurisdiction over defendants whose rights of expression might thereby be compromised. See, e.g., New York Times Co. v. Connor, 365 F.2d 567 (5th Cir.1966). In 1984, however, the Supreme Court rejected this line of cases. In CALDER v. JONES, 465 U.S. 783, 790–91, 104 S.Ct. 1482, 1487–88, 79 L.Ed.2d 804, 813 (1984), a professional entertainer who lived and worked in California brought suit in California Superior Court, claiming that she had been libeled in an article published in the National Enquirer, a national magazine having its largest circulation in California. The plaintiff sued the writer and editor of the article, both residents of Florida, as well as the magazine. The writer and the editor moved to quash service of process for lack of personal jurisdiction, and the Superior Court granted the motion on the ground that First Amendment concerns weighed against an assertion of jurisdiction otherwise proper under the Due Process Clause. Ultimately, the United States Supreme Court disagreed, saying: "We also reject the suggestion that First Amendment concerns enter into jurisdictional analysis. The infusion of such concerns

would needlessly complicate an already imprecise inquiry." Given that the writer and editor had acted intentionally to produce an article for dissemination in California, the Court had no trouble finding that they could foresee being haled into court there. See also Keeton v. Hustler Magazine, Inc., 465 U.S. 770, 780 n. 12, 104 S.Ct. 1473, 1481 n. 12, 79 L.Ed.2d 790, 801 n. 12 (1984), p. 117, supra ("[W]e reject categorically the suggestion that invisible radiations from the First Amendment may defeat jurisdiction otherwise proper under the Due Process Clause.").

3. In addition to the limitations on jurisdiction derived from the Due Process Clause, other limitations derived from other parts of the Constitution may exist. For example, in DAVIS v. FARMERS' CO–OP. EQUITY CO., 262 U.S. 312, 43 S.Ct. 556, 67 L.Ed. 996 (1923), the Supreme Court ruled that a Minnesota court was barred by the Commerce Clause from asserting jurisdiction over a Kansas railroad in a suit brought by a Kansas corporation for damages resulting from the loss of grain shipped from one point in Kansas to another. Since the potential burden on interstate commerce is a factor that can be considered under the "minimum contacts" test, however, Commerce Clause objections to jurisdiction are rare today. But see Bendix Autolite Corp. v. Midwesco Enterprises, Inc., ___ U.S. ___, 108 S.Ct. 2218, 100 L.Ed.2d 896 (1988) (Ohio statute tolling the state's statute of limitations for any period that a person or corporation is not "present" in Ohio violates the commerce clause).

BURGER KING CORP. v. RUDZEWICZ

Supreme Court of the United States, 1985.
471 U.S. 462, 105 S.Ct. 2174, 85 L.Ed.2d 528.

[Burger King is a Florida corporation whose principal offices are in Miami. Franchisees are licensed to use its trademarks and service marks in leased standardized restaurant facilities for a period of 20 years. The governing contracts provide that the franchise relationship is established in Miami and governed by Florida law, and call for payment of all required monthly fees and forwarding of all relevant notices to the Miami headquarters. The Miami headquarters sets policy and works directly with the franchisees in attempting to resolve major problems. Day-to-day monitoring of franchisees, however, is conducted through district offices that in turn report to the Miami headquarters. John Rudzewicz is a Michigan resident who, along with another Michigan resident (Brian MacShara), entered into a 20-year franchise contract with Burger King to operate a restaurant in Michigan. Subsequently, when the restaurant's patronage declined, the franchisees fell behind in their monthly payments. Burger King then brought a diversity action in Federal District Court in Florida, alleging that the franchisees had breached their franchise obligations and requesting damages and injunctive relief. The franchisees claimed that, because they were Michigan residents and because Burger King's claim did not "arise" within Florida, the District Court lacked personal jurisdiction over them. But the court held that the franchisees were subject to personal jurisdiction pursuant to Florida's long-arm statute, which extends jurisdiction to any person, whether or not a citizen or resident of the State, who breaches a contract in the State by failing to perform acts that the contract requires to be performed there. Thereafter, the court entered judgment against the franchisees on the merits. The Court of Appeals reversed, holding that "[j]urisdiction under these circumstances would offend the fundamental fairness which is the touchstone of due process," but the Supreme Court disagreed.]

Appeal from the United States Court of Appeals for the Eleventh Circuit.

JUSTICE BRENNAN delivered the opinion of the Court.

[After a lengthy presentation of the facts, Justice Brennan began Part II of his opinion by rehearsing the basic jurisdictional rules. In that context, he turned to the requirement that the defendant "purposefully direct" his activity toward the forum state.]

We have noted several reasons why a forum legitimately may exercise personal jurisdiction over a nonresident who "purposefully directs" his activities toward forum residents. A State generally has a "manifest interest" in providing its residents with a convenient forum for redressing injuries inflicted by out-of-state actors. * * * Moreover, where individuals "purposefully derive benefit" from their interstate activities, * * * it may well be unfair to allow them to escape having to account in other States for consequences that arise proximately from such activities; the Due Process Clause may not readily be wielded as a territorial shield to avoid interstate obligations that have been voluntarily assumed. And because "modern transportation and communications have made it much less burdensome for a party sued to defend himself in a State where he engages in economic activity," it usually will not be unfair to subject him to the burdens of litigating in another forum for disputes relating to such activity. McGee v. International Life Insurance Co. * * *.

Notwithstanding these considerations, the constitutional touchstone remains whether the defendant purposefully established "minimum contacts" in the forum State. * * * Although it has been argued that foreseeability of causing *injury* in another State should be sufficient to establish such contacts there when policy considerations so require, the Court has consistently held that this kind of foreseeability is not a "sufficient benchmark" for exercising personal jurisdiction. * * * Instead, "the foreseeability that is critical to due process analysis * * * is that the defendant's conduct and connection with the forum State are such that he should reasonably anticipate being haled into court there." * * *

This "purposeful availment" requirement ensures that a defendant will not be haled into a jurisdiction solely as a result of "random," "fortuitous," or "attenuated" contacts, * * * or of the "unilateral activity of another party or a third person" * * *. Jurisdiction is proper, however, where the contacts proximately result from actions by the defendant *himself* that create a "substantial connection" with the forum State. * * * Thus where the defendant "deliberately" has engaged in significant activities within a State, * * * or has created "continuing obligations" between himself and residents of the forum, * * * he manifestly has availed himself of the privilege of conducting business there, and because his activities are shielded by "the benefits and protections" of the forum's laws it is presumptively not unreasonable to require him to submit to the burdens of litigation in that forum as well. * * *

Once it has been decided that a defendant purposefully established minimum contacts within the forum State, these contacts may be considered in light of other factors to determine whether the assertion of personal jurisdiction would comport with "fair play and substantial justice." * * * Thus courts in "appropriate case[s]" may evaluate "the burden on the defendant," "the forum State's interest in adjudicating the dispute," "the plaintiff's interest in obtaining convenient and effective relief," "the interstate judicial system's interest in obtaining the most efficient resolution of controversies," and the "shared interest of the several States in furthering fundamental substantive social policies." * * * These considerations sometimes serve to establish the reasonableness of jurisdiction upon a lesser showing of minimum contacts than would otherwise be required. * * * On the other hand, where a defendant who purposefully has directed his activities at forum residents seeks to defeat jurisdiction, he must present a compelling case that the presence of some other considerations would render jurisdiction unreasonable. Most such considerations usually may be accommodated through means short of finding jurisdiction unconstitutional. For example, the potential clash of the forum's law with the "fundamental substantive social policies" of another State may be accommodated through application of the forum's choice-of-law rules. Similarly, a defendant claiming substantial inconvenience may seek a change of venue. Nevertheless, minimum requirements inherent in the concept of "fair play and substantial justice" may defeat the reasonableness of jurisdiction even if the defendant has purposefully engaged in forum activities. * * * As we previously have noted, jurisdictional rules may not be employed in such a way as to make litigation "so gravely difficult and inconvenient" that a party unfairly is at a "severe disadvantage" in comparison to his opponent. * * *

B

(1)

Applying these principles to the case at hand, we believe there is substantial record evidence supporting the District Court's conclusion that the assertion of personal jurisdiction over Rudzewicz in Florida for the alleged breach of his franchise agreement did not offend due process. At the outset, we note a continued division among lower courts respecting whether and to what extent a contract can constitute a "contact" for purposes of due process analysis. If the question is whether an individual's contract with an out-of-state party *alone* can automatically establish sufficient minimum contacts in the other party's home forum, we believe the answer clearly is that it cannot. The Court long ago rejected the notion that personal jurisdiction might turn on "mechanical" tests, or on "conceptualistic * * * theories of the place of contracting or of performance" * * *. Instead, we have emphasized the need for a "highly realistic" approach that recognizes that a "contract" is "ordinarily but an intermediate step serving to tie up prior business negotiations with future consequences which themselves are the real object of the business transaction." * * * It is these factors—prior negotiations and contemplated future consequences, along with the terms of the contract and the parties' actual course of dealing—that must be evaluated in determining whether the defendant purposefully established minimum contacts within the forum.

In this case, no physical ties to Florida can be attributed to Rudzewicz other than MacShara's brief training course in Miami.[22] Rudzewicz did not maintain offices in Florida and, for all that appears from the record, has never even visited there. Yet this franchise dispute grew directly out of "a contract which had a *substantial* connection with that State." McGee v. International Life Insurance Co. * * *. Eschewing the option of operating an independent local enterprise, Rudzewicz deliberately "reach[ed] out beyond" Michigan and negotiated with a Florida corporation for the purchase of a long-term franchise and the manifold benefits that would derive from affiliation with a nationwide organization. * * * Upon approval, he entered into a carefully structured 20-year relationship that envisoned continuing and wide-reaching contacts with Burger King in Florida. In light of Rudzewicz's voluntary acceptance of the long-term and exacting regulation of his business from Burger King's Miami headquarters, the "quality and nature" of his relationship to the company in Florida can in no sense be viewed as "random," "fortuitous," or "attenuated." * * * Rudzewicz's refusal to make the contractually required payments in Miami, and his continued use of Burger King's trademarks and confidential business information after his termination, caused foreseeable injuries to the corporation in Florida. For these reasons it was, at the very least, presumptively reasonable for Rudzewicz to be called to account there for such injuries.

The Court of Appeals concluded, however, that in light of the supervision emanating from Burger King's district office in Birmingham [Michigan], Rudzewicz reasonably believed that "the Michigan office was for all intents and purposes the embodiment of Burger King" and that he therefore had no "reason to anticipate a Burger King suit outside of Michigan." * * * This reasoning overlooks substantial record evi-

---

22. The Eleventh Circuit held that MacShara's presence in Florida was irrelevant to the question of Rudzewicz's minimum contacts with that forum, reasoning that "Rudzewicz and MacShara never formed a partnership" and "signed the agreements in their individual capacities." * * * The two did jointly form a corporation through which they were seeking to conduct the franchise, however. * * * They were required to decide which one of them would travel to Florida to satisfy the training requirements so that they could commence business, and Rudzewicz participated in the decision that MacShara would go there. We have previously noted that when commercial activities are "carried on in behalf of" an out-of-state party those activities may sometimes be ascribed to the party, * * * at least where he is a "primary participan[t]" in the enterprise and has acted purposefully in directing those activities. * * * Because MacShara's matriculation at Burger King University is not pivotal to the disposition of this case, we need not resolve the permissible bounds of such attribution.

dence indicating that Rudzewicz most certainly knew that he was affiliating himself with an enterprise based primarily in Florida. The contract documents themselves emphasize that Burger King's operations are conducted and supervised from the Miami headquarters, that all relevant notices and payments must be sent there, and that the agreements were made in and enforced from Miami. * * * Moreover, the parties' actual course of dealing repeatedly confirmed that decisionmaking authority was vested in the Miami headquarters and that the district office served largely as an intermediate link between the headquarters and the franchisees. When problems arose over building design, site development fees, rent computation, and the defaulted payments, Rudzewicz and Mac-Shara learned that the Michigan office was powerless to resolve their disputes and could only channel their communications to Miami. Throughout these disputes, the Miami headquarters and the Michigan franchisees carried on a continuous course of direct communications by mail and by telephone, and it was the Miami headquarters that made the key negotiating decisions out of which the instant litigation arose.

Moreover, we believe the Court of Appeals gave insufficient weight to provisions in the various franchise documents providing that all disputes would be governed by Florida law. The franchise agreement, for example, stated:

> This Agreement shall become valid when executed and accepted by BKC at Miami, Florida, it shall be deemed made and entered into in the State of Florida and shall be governed and construed under and in accordance with the laws of the State of Florida. The choice of law designation does not require that all suits concerning this Agreement be filed in Florida.

* * * The Court of Appeals reasoned that choice-of-law provisions are irrelevant to the question of personal jurisdiction, relying on Hanson v. Denckla for the proposition that "the center of gravity for choice-of-law purposes does not necessarily confer the sovereign prerogative to assert jurisdiction." * * * This reasoning misperceives the import of the quoted proposition. The Court in *Hanson* and subsequent cases has emphasized that choice-of-law *analysis*—which focuses on all elements of a transaction, and not simply on the defendant's conduct—is distinct from minimum-contacts jurisdictional analysis—which focuses at the threshold solely on the defendant's purposeful connection to the forum. Nothing in our cases, however, suggests that a choice-of-law *provision* should be ignored in considering whether a defendant has "purposefully invoked the benefits and protections of a State's laws" for jurisdictional purposes. Although such a provision standing alone would be insufficient to confer jurisdiction, we believe that, when combined with the 20-year interdependent relationship Rudzewicz established with Burger King's Miami headquarters, it reinforced his deliberate affiliation with the forum State and the reasonable foreseeability of possible litigation there. * * * Rudzewicz "purposefully availed himself of the benefits and protections of Florida's laws" by entering into contracts expressly providing that those laws would govern franchise disputes. * * *

(2)

Nor has Rudzewicz pointed to other factors that can be said persuasively to outweigh the considerations discussed above and to establish the *unconstitutionality* of Florida's assertion of jurisdiction. We cannot conclude that Florida had no "legitimate interest in holding [Rudzewicz] answerable on a claim related to" the contacts he had established in that State. [See] McGee v. International Life Insurance Co. * * * (noting that State frequently will have a "manifest interest in providing effective means of redress for its residents").[25] Moreover, although Rudzewicz has argued at some length that Michigan's Franchise Investment Law * * * governs many aspects of this franchise relationship, he has not demonstrated how Michigan's acknowledged interest might possibly render jurisdiction in Florida *unconstitutional.*[26] Finally, the Court of Appeals' assertion that the Florida litigation "severely impaired [Rudzewicz's] ability to call Michigan witnesses who might be essential to his defense and counterclaim" * * * is wholly without support in the record. And even to the extent that it is inconvenient for a party who has minimum contacts with a forum to litigate there, such considerations most frequently can be accommodated through a change of venue. * * * Although the Court has suggested that inconvenience may at some point become so substantial as to achieve *constitutional* magnitude, McGee v. International Life Insurance Co., * * * this is not such a case.

The Court of Appeals also concluded, however, that the parties' dealings involved "a characteristic disparity of bargaining power" and "elements of surprise," and that Rudzewicz "lacked fair notice" of the potential for litigation in Florida because the contractual provisions suggesting to the contrary were merely "boilerplate declarations in a lengthy printed contract." * * * Rudzewicz presented many of these arguments to the District Court, contending that Burger King was guilty of misrepresentation, fraud, and duress; that it gave insufficient notice in its dealings with him; and that the contract was one of adhesion. * * * After a 3-day bench trial, the District Court found that Burger King had made no misrepresentations, that Rudzewicz and MacShara "were and are experienced and sophisticated businessmen," and that "at no time" did they "ac[t] under economic duress or disadvantage imposed by" Burger King. * * * Federal Rule of Civil Procedure 52(a) requires that "[f]indings of fact shall not be set aside unless clearly erroneous," and

25. Complaining that "when Burger King is the plaintiff, you won't 'have it your way' because it sues all franchisees in Miami," * * * Rudzewicz contends that Florida's interest in providing a convenient forum is negligible given the company's size and ability to conduct litigation anywhere in the country. We disagree. Absent compelling considerations, cf. McGee v. International Life Insurance Co., * * * a defendant who has purposefully derived commercial benefit from his affiliations in a forum may not defeat jurisdiction there simply because of his adversary's greater net wealth.

26. Rudzewicz has failed to show how the District Court's exercise of jurisdiction in this case might have been at all inconsistent with Michigan's interests. * * * In any event, minimum-contacts analysis presupposes that two or more States may be interested in the outcome of a dispute, and the process of resolving potentially conflicting "fundamental substantive social policies" * * * can usually be accommodated through choice-of-law rules rather than through outright preclusion of jurisdiction in one forum. * * *

neither Rudzewicz nor the Court of Appeals have pointed to record evidence that would support a "definite and firm conviction" that the District Court's findings are mistaken. * * *

III

Notwithstanding these considerations, the Court of Appeals apparently believed that it was necessary to reject jurisdiction in this case as a prophylactic measure, reasoning that an affirmance of the District Court's judgment would result in the exercise of jurisdiction over "out-of-state consumers to collect payments due on modest personal purchases" and would "sow the seeds of default judgments against franchisees owing smaller debts." * * * We share the Court of Appeals' broader concerns and therefore reject any talismanic jurisdictional formulas; "the facts of each case must [always] be weighed" in determining whether personal jurisdiction would comport with "fair play and substantial justice." * * * The "quality and nature" of an interstate transaction may sometimes be so "random," "fortuitous," or "attenuated" that it cannot fairly be said that the potential defendant "should reasonably anticipate being haled into court" in another jurisdiction. * * * We also have emphasized that jurisdiction may not be grounded on a contract whose terms have been obtained through "fraud, undue influence, or overweening bargaining power" and whose application would render litigation "so gravely difficult and inconvenient that [a party] will for all practical purposes be deprived of his day in court." * * * Just as the Due Process Clause allows flexibility in ensuring that commercial actors are not effectively "judgment proof" for the consequences of obligations they voluntarily assume in other States, McGee v. International Life Insurance Co., * * * so too does it prevent rules that would unfairly enable them to obtain default judgments against unwitting customers. * * *

For the reasons set forth above, however, these dangers are not present in the instant case. Because Rudzewicz established a substantial and continuing relationship with Burger King's Miami headquarters, received fair notice from the contract documents and the course of dealing that he might be subject to suit in Florida, and has failed to demonstrate how jurisdiction in that forum would otherwise be fundamentally unfair, we conclude that the District Court's exercise of jurisdiction * * * did not offend due process. The judgment of the Court of Appeals is accordingly reversed, and the case is remanded for further proceedings consistent with this opinion.

JUSTICE POWELL took no part in the consideration or decision of this case.

JUSTICE STEVENS, with whom JUSTICE WHITE joins, dissenting.

In my opinion there is a significant element of unfairness in requiring a franchisee to defend a case of this kind in the forum chosen by the franchisor. It is undisputed that respondent maintained no place of business in Florida, that he had no employees in that State, and that he was not licensed to do business there. Respondent did not prepare his french fries, shakes, and hamburgers in Michigan, and then deliver them into the stream of commerce "with the expectation that they [would] be purchased by consumers in" Florida. * * * To the contrary, respondent did business only in Michigan, his business, property, and payroll taxes were payable in that State, and he sold all of his products there.

Throughout the business relationship, respondent's principal contacts with petitioner were with its Michigan office. Notwithstanding its disclaimer, * * * the Court seems ultimately to rely on nothing more than standard boilerplate language contained in various documents * * * to establish that respondent " 'purposefully availed himself of the benefits and protections of Florida's laws.' " * * * Such superficial analysis creates a potential for unfairness not only in negotiations between franchisors and their franchisees but, more significantly, in the resolution of the disputes that inevitably arise from time to time in such relationships.

Judge Vance's opinion for the Court of Appeals for the Eleventh Circuit adequately explains why I would affirm the judgment of that court. I particularly find the following more persuasive than what this Court has written today:

> Nothing in the course of negotiations gave Rudzewicz reason to anticipate a Burger King suit outside of Michigan. The only face-to-face or even oral contact Rudzewicz had with Burger King throughout months of protracted negotiations was with representatives of the Michigan office. Burger King had the Michigan office interview Rudzewicz and MacShara, appraise their application, discuss price terms, recommend the site which the defendants finally agreed to, and attend the final closing ceremony. There is no evidence that Rudzewicz ever negotiated with anyone in Miami or even sent mail there during negotiations. He maintained no staff in the state of Florida, and as far as the record reveals, he has never even visited the state.

> The contracts contemplated the startup of a local Michigan restaurant whose profits would derive solely from food sales made to customers in Drayton Plains. The sale, which involved the use of an intangible trademark in Michigan and occupancy of a Burger King facility there, required no performance in the state of Florida. Under the contract, the local Michigan district office was responsible for providing all of the services due Rudzewicz, including advertising and management consultation. Supervision, moreover, emanated from that office alone. To Rudzewicz, the Michigan office was for all intents and purposes the embodiment of Burger King. He had reason to believe that his working relationship with Burger King began and ended in Michigan, not at the distant and anonymous Florida headquarters. * * *

> Given that the office in Rudzewicz' home state conducted all of the negotiations and wholly supervised the contract, we believe that he had reason to assume that the state of the supervisory office would be the same state in which Burger King would file suit. Rudzewicz lacked fair notice that the distant corporate headquarters which insulated itself from direct dealings with him would later seek to assert jurisdiction over him in the courts of its own home state. * * *

Just as Rudzewicz lacked notice of the possibility of suit in Florida, he was financially unprepared to meet its added costs. The franchise relationship in particular is fraught with potential for financial surprise. The device of the franchise gives local retailers the access to national trademark recognition which enables them to compete with better-financed, more efficient chain stores. This national affiliation, however, does not alter the fact that the typical franchise store is a local concern serving at best a neighborhood or community. Neither the revenues of a local business nor the geographical range of its market prepares the average franchise owner for the cost of distant litigation. * * *

The particular distribution of bargaining power in the franchise relationship further impairs the franchisee's financial preparedness. In a franchise contract, "the franchisor normally occupies [the] dominant role". * * *

We discern a characteristic disparity of bargaining power in the facts of this case. There is no indication that Rudzewicz had any latitude to negotiate a reduced rent or franchise fee in exchange for the added risk of suit in Florida. He signed a standard form contract whose terms were non-negotiable and which appeared in some respects to vary from the more favorable terms agreed to in earlier discussions. In fact, the final contract required a minimum monthly rent computed on a base far in excess of that discussed in oral negotiations. Burger King resisted price concessions, only to sue Rudzewicz far from home. In doing so, it severely impaired his ability to call Michigan witnesses who might be essential to his defense and counterclaim.

In sum, we hold that the circumstances of the Drayton Plains franchise and the negotiations which led to it left Rudzewicz bereft of reasonable notice and financially unprepared for the prospect of franchise litigation in Florida. Jurisdiction under these circumstances would offend the fundamental fairness which is the touchstone of due process. * * *

Accordingly, I respectfully dissent.

Notes and Questions

1. Some courts have distinguished between nonresident buyers and sellers, exhibiting a reluctance to sustain jurisdiction over nonresident purchasers while asserting jurisdiction over foreign sellers who ship their goods into the forum state. For example, many of these courts have concluded that a single sale contract may be sufficient to support long-arm jurisdiction (usually under a "transaction of business" provision) over a nonresident seller, but not over a buyer. See, e.g., Leoni v. Wells, 264 N.W.2d 646 (Minn.1978); Darby v. Superior Supply Co., 224 Tenn. 540, 458 S.W.2d 423 (1970). Justice White, the author of *World-Wide Volkswagen,* has noted that, even after that decision, "the disarray among federal and state courts on the issue of minimal contacts based on contractual dealings continues unabated." Baxter v. Mouzavires, 455 U.S. 1006, 102 S.Ct. 1643, 71 L.Ed.2d 875 (1982) (White, J., joined by Powell, J., dissenting from the denial of certiorari).

In ALCHEMIE INTERNATIONAL, INC. v. METAL WORLD, INC., 523 F.Supp. 1039, 1050 (D.N.J.1981), the defendant, Metal World, was a nonresident seller. The court upheld jurisdiction, even though Metal World maintained no office in New Jersey and had sent no personnel into the state: it was enough that Metal World, by numerous mail and telephone contacts with a New Jersey corporation, had solicited, executed, and allegedly breached a substantial commercial contract. The goods never entered New Jersey; and there was no evidence indicating the parties anticipated that the goods were to be taken into New Jersey. Nor was there any evidence of other contacts with the forum, unrelated to the contract at issue. Nonetheless, the district judge ruled that the assertion of jurisdiction was consistent with due process. He stated:

> I see little to distinguish a corporation's using the telephone and mail to solicit or negotiate a contract the size of that at issue here from that same corporation sending an agent into the state in pursuit of the identical contract from the identical buyer. * * * Indeed, a refusal to acknowledge the fashion in which modern business is conducted and the increasingly dominant role played in that conduct by mail and telephone communications is as much a return to the shibboleths of Pennoyer v. Neff, long abandoned by the Court, and the "magical and medieval concepts of presence and power" that typified that era as would resurrection of the notion that a defendant must be present within the territorial jurisdiction of a court before its judgment will bind him. I therefore count defendant's calls and mail communications to plaintiff as significant contacts with the State of New Jersey.

2. Doesn't *World-Wide Volkswagen* teach that the key question—at least for the "sovereignty branch"—is whether the defendant purposefully availed herself of the protection and benefits of the forum? The buyer-seller distinction is usually linked to stereotypical notions of the profiting, actively involved seller and the passive, unknowing buyer. Surely, it is argued, we would not want to permit Sears Roebuck to sue the world in Illinois. But, there are many cases in which the parties are of relatively even bargaining strength—and in which the buyer plays the more active role in creating the deal. In such cases, would it not be consistent with *Volkswagen* to permit a state to assert jurisdiction over the nonresident buyer? Is *Burger King* such a case?

Some of the cases that have found jurisdiction over nonresident buyers have placed weight on the fact that the purchaser physically came to the forum to negotiate or finalize the deal. Is the judge in *Alchemie International* correct that giving weight to such presence is a throwback to *Pennoyer*? Or is the purchaser's presence in the forum an indication that she is playing an active rather than a passive role in the transaction and that she is thus more likely to be purposefully availing herself of the protection and benefits of the forum? For a general discussion, see Note, *Minimum Contacts in Contract Cases: A Forward Looking Evaluation*, 58 Notre Dame L.Rev. 635 (1983).

ASAHI METAL INDUSTRY CO. v. SUPERIOR COURT

Supreme Court of the United States, 1987.
480 U.S. 102, 107 S.Ct. 1026, 94 L.Ed.2d 92.

Certiorari to the Supreme Court of California.

JUSTICE O'CONNOR announced the judgment of the Court and delivered the unanimous opinion of the Court with respect to Part I, the opinion of the Court with respect to Part II–B, in which THE CHIEF JUSTICE, JUSTICE BRENNAN, JUSTICE WHITE, JUSTICE MARSHALL, JUSTICE BLACKMUN, JUSTICE POWELL, and JUSTICE STEVENS join, and an opinion with respect to Parts II–A and III, in which THE CHIEF JUSTICE, JUSTICE POWELL, and JUSTICE SCALIA join.

This case presents the question whether the mere awareness on the part of a foreign defendant that the component it manufactured, sold, and delivered outside the United States would reach the forum state in the stream of commerce constitutes "minimum contacts" between the defendant and the forum state such that the exercise of jurisdiction "does not offend 'traditional notions of fair play and substantial justice.'" * * *

I

On September 23, 1978, on Interstate Highway 80 in Solano County, California, Gary Zurcher lost control of his Honda motorcycle and collided with a tractor. Zurcher was severely injured, and his passenger and wife, Ruth Ann Moreno, was killed. In September 1979, Zurcher filed a product liability action in the Superior Court of the State of California in and for the County of Solano. Zurcher alleged that the 1978 accident was caused by a sudden loss of air and an explosion in the rear tire of the motorcycle, and alleged that the motorcycle tire, tube, and sealant were defective. Zurcher's complaint named, *inter alia*, Cheng Shin Rubber Industrial Co., Ltd. (Cheng Shin), the Taiwanese manufacturer of the tube. Cheng Shin in turn filed a cross-complaint seeking indemnification from its codefendants and from petitioner, Asahi Metal Industry Co., Ltd. (Asahi), the manufacturer of the tube's valve assembly. Zurcher's claims against Cheng Shin and the other defendants were eventually settled and dismissed, leaving only Cheng Shin's indemnity action against Asahi.

California's long-arm statute authorizes the exercise of jurisdiction "on any basis not inconsistent with the Constitution of this state or of the United States." * * * Asahi moved to quash Cheng Shin's service of summons arguing the State could not exert jurisdiction over it consistent with the Due Process Clause of the Fourteenth Amendment.

In relation to the motion, the following information was submitted by Asahi and Cheng Shin. Asahi is a Japanese corporation. It manufactures tire valve assemblies in Japan and sells the assemblies to Cheng Shin, and to several other tire manufacturers, for use as components in finished tire tubes. Asahi's sales to Cheng Shin took place in Taiwan. The shipments from Asahi to Cheng Shin were sent from Japan to Taiwan. Cheng Shin bought and incorporated into its tire tubes 150,000 Asahi valve assemblies in 1978; 500,000 in 1979; 500,000 in 1980; 100,000 in 1981; and 100,000 in 1982. Sales to Cheng Shin accounted for 1.24 percent of Asahi's income in 1981 and 0.44 percent in 1982. Cheng Shin alleged that approximately 20 percent of its sales in the United States are in California. Cheng Shin purchases valve assemblies from other suppliers as well, and sells finished tubes throughout the world.

In 1983 an attorney for Cheng Shin conducted an informal examination of the valve stems of the tire tubes sold in one cyclery in Solano County. The attorney declared that of the approximately 115 tire tubes in the store, 97 were purportedly manufactured in Japan or Taiwan, and of those 97, 21 valve stems were marked with the circled letter "A", apparently Asahi's trademark. Of the 21 Asahi valve stems, 12 were incorporated into Cheng Shin tire tubes. The store contained 41 other Cheng Shin tubes that incorporated the valve assemblies of other manufacturers. * * * An affidavit of a manager of Cheng Shin whose duties included the purchasing of component parts stated: " 'In discussions with Asahi regarding the purchase of valve stem assemblies the fact that my Company sells tubes throughout the world and specifically the United States has been discussed. I am informed and believe that Asahi was fully aware that valve stem assemblies sold to my Company and to others would end up throughout the United States and in California.' " * * * An affidavit of the president of Asahi, on the other hand, declared that Asahi " 'has never contemplated that its limited sales of tire valves to Cheng Shin in Taiwan would subject it to lawsuits in California.' " * * * The record does not include any contract between Cheng Shin and Asahi. * * *

Primarily on the basis of the above information, the Superior Court denied the motion to quash summons, stating that "Asahi obviously does business on an international scale. It is not unreasonable that they defend claims of defect in their product on an international scale." Order Denying Motion to Quash Summons * * *.

The Court of Appeal of the State of California issued a peremptory writ of mandate commanding the Superior Court to quash service of summons. The court concluded that "it would be unreasonable to require Asahi to respond in California solely on the basis of ultimately realized foreseeability that the product into which its component was embodied would be sold all over the world including California." * * *

The Supreme Court of the State of California reversed and discharged the writ issued by the Court of Appeal. * * * The court observed that "Asahi has no offices, property or agents in California. It solicits no business in California and has made no direct sales [in California]." * * * Moreover, "Asahi did not design or control the system of distribution that carried its valve assemblies into California." * * * Nevertheless, the court found the exercise of jurisdiction over Asahi to be consistent with the Due Process Clause. It concluded that Asahi knew that some of the valve assemblies sold to Cheng Shin would be incorporated into tire tubes sold in California, and that Asahi benefited indirectly from the sale in California of products incorporating its components. The court considered Asahi's intentional act of placing its components into the stream of commerce—that is, by delivering the components to Cheng Shin in Taiwan—coupled with Asahi's awareness that some of the components would eventually find their way into California, sufficient to form the basis for state court jurisdiction under the Due Process Clause.

We granted certiorari * * * and now reverse.

II

A

The Due Process Clause of the Fourteenth Amendment limits the power of a state court to exert personal jurisdiction over a nonresident defendant. * * * Most recently we have reaffirmed the oft-quoted reasoning of Hanson v. Denckla * * * that minimum contacts must have a basis in "some act by which the defendant purposefully avails itself of the privilege of conducting activities within the forum State, thus invoking the benefits and protections of its laws." *Burger King* * * *. "Jurisdiction is proper * * * where the contacts proximately result from actions by the defendant *himself* that create a 'substantial connection' with the forum State." Ibid., quoting McGee v. International Life Insurance Co. * * * (emphasis in original).

Applying the principle that minimum contacts must be based on an act of the defendant, the Court in World–Wide Volkswagen Corp. v. Woodson * * * rejected the assertion that a *consumer's* unilateral act of bringing the defendant's product into the forum State was a sufficient constitutional basis for personal jurisdiction over the defendant. It had been argued in *World–Wide Volkswagen* that because an automobile retailer and its wholesale distributor sold a product mobile by design and purpose, they could foresee being haled into court in the distant States into which their customers might drive. The Court rejected this concept of foreseeability as an insufficient basis for jurisdiction under the Due Process Clause. * * * The Court disclaimed, however, the idea that "foreseeability is wholly irrelevant" to personal jurisdiction, concluding that "[t]he forum State does not exceed its powers under the Due Process Clause if it asserts personal jurisdiction over a corporation that delivers its products into the stream of commerce with the expectation that they will be purchased by consumers in the forum State." * * *.

* * *

In *World–Wide Volkswagen* itself, the state court sought to base jurisdiction not on any act of the defendant, but on the foreseeable unilateral actions of the consumer. Since *World–Wide Volkswagen,* lower courts have been confronted with cases in which the defendant acted by placing a product in the stream of commerce, and the stream eventually swept defendant's product into the forum State, but the defendant did nothing else to purposefully avail itself of the market in the forum state. Some courts have understood the Due Process Clause, as interpreted in *World–Wide Volkswagen,* to allow an exercise of personal jurisdiction to be based on no more than the defendant's act of placing the product in the stream of commerce. Other courts have understood the Due Process Clause and the above-quoted language in *World–Wide Volkswagen* to require the action of the defendant to be more purposefully directed at the forum State than the mere act of placing a product in the stream of commerce.

The reasoning of the Supreme Court of California in the present case illustrates the former interpretation of *World–Wide Volkswagen.* The Supreme Court of California held that, because the stream of commerce eventually brought some valves Asahi sold Cheng Shin into California, Asahi's awareness that its valves would be sold in California was sufficient to permit California to exercise jurisdiction over Asahi consistent with the requirements of the Due Process Clause. The Supreme Court of California's position was consistent with those courts that have held that mere foreseeability or awareness was a constitutionally sufficient basis for personal jurisdiction if the defendant's product made its way into the forum State while still in the stream of commerce. * * *

Other courts, however, have understood the Due Process Clause to require something more than that the defendant was aware of its product's entry into the forum State through the stream of commerce in order for the state to exert jurisdiction over the defendant. In the present case, for example, the State Court of Appeal did not read the Due Process Clause, as interpreted by *World–Wide Volkswagen,* to allow "mere foreseeability that the product will enter the forum state [to] be enough by itself to establish jurisdiction over the distributor and retailer." * * *

We now find this latter position to be consonant with the requirements of due process. The "substantial connection" * * * between the defendant and the forum State necessary for a finding of minimum contacts must come about by *an action of the defendant purposefully directed toward the forum State.* * * * The placement of a product into the stream of commerce, without more, is not an act of the defendant purposefully directed toward the forum State. Additional conduct of the defendant may indicate an intent or purpose to serve the market in the forum State, for example, designing the product for the market in the forum State, advertising in the forum State, establishing channels for providing regular advice to customers in the forum State, or marketing the product through a distributor who has agreed to serve as the sales agent in the forum State. But a defendant's awareness that the stream of commerce may or will sweep the product into the forum State does not convert the mere act of placing the product into the stream into an act purposefully directed toward the forum State.

Assuming, *arguendo,* that respondents have established Asahi's awareness that some of the valves sold to Cheng Shin would be incorporated into tire tubes sold in California, respondents have not demonstrated any action by Asahi to purposefully avail itself of the California market. Asahi does not do business in California. It has no office, agents, employees, or property in California. It does not advertise or otherwise solicit business in California. It did not create, control, or employ the distribution system that brought its valves to California. * * * There is no evidence that Asahi designed its product in anticipation of sales in California. * * * On the basis of these facts, the exertion of personal jurisdiction over Asahi by the Superior Court of California exceeds the limits of due process.

B

The strictures of the Due Process Clause forbid a state court from exercising personal jurisdiction over Asahi under circumstances that would offend "traditional notions of fair play and substantial justice."
* * *

We have previously explained that the determination of the reasonableness of the exercise of jurisdiction in each case will depend on an evaluation of several factors. A court must consider the burden on the defendant, the interests of the forum state, and the plaintiff's interest in obtaining relief. It must also weigh in its determination "the interstate judicial system's interest in obtaining the most efficient resolution of controversies; and the shared interest of the several States in furthering fundamental substantive social policies." * * *

A consideration of these factors in the present case clearly reveals the unreasonableness of the assertion of jurisdiction over Asahi, even apart from the question of the placement of goods in the stream of commerce.

Certainly the burden on the defendant in this case is severe. Asahi has been commanded by the Supreme Court of California not only to traverse the distance between Asahi's headquarters in Japan and the Superior Court of California in and for the County of Solano, but also to submit its dispute with Cheng Shin to a foreign nation's judicial system. The unique burdens placed upon one who must defend oneself in a foreign legal system should have significant weight in assessing the reasonableness of stretching the long arm of personal jurisdiction over national borders.

When minimum contacts have been established, often the interests of the plaintiff and the forum in the exercise of jurisdiction will justify even the serious burdens placed on the alien defendant. In the present case, however, the interests of the plaintiff and the forum in California's assertion of jurisdiction over Asahi are slight. All that remains is a claim for indemnification asserted by Cheng Shin, a Taiwanese corporation, against Asahi. The transaction on which the indemnification claim is based took place in Taiwan; Asahi's components were shipped from Japan to Taiwan. Cheng Shin has not demonstrated that it is more convenient for it to litigate its indemnification claim against Asahi in California rather than in Taiwan or Japan.

Because the plaintiff is not a California resident, California's legitimate interests in the dispute have considerably diminished. The Supreme Court of California argued that the State had an interest in "protecting its consumers by ensuring that foreign manufacturers comply with the state's safety standards." * * * The State Supreme Court's definition of California's interest, however, was overly broad. The dispute between Cheng Shin and Asahi is primarily about indemnification rather than safety standards. Moreover, it is not at all clear at this point that California law should govern the question whether a Japanese corporation should indemnify a Taiwanese corporation on the basis of a sale made in Taiwan and a shipment of goods from Japan to Taiwan. * * * The possibility of being haled into a California court as a result of an accident involving Asahi's components undoubtedly creates an additional deterrent to the manufacture of unsafe components; however, similar pressures will be placed on Asahi by the purchasers of its components as long as those who use Asahi components in their final products, and sell those products in California, are subject to the application of California tort law.

World–Wide Volkswagen also admonished courts to take into consideration the interests of the "several States," in addition to the forum state, in the efficient judicial resolution of the dispute and the advancement of substantive policies. In the present case, this advice calls for a court to consider the procedural and substantive policies of other *nations* whose interests are affected by the assertion of jurisdiction by the California court. The procedural and substantive interests of other nations in a state court's assertion of jurisdiction over an alien defendant will differ from case to case. In every case, however, those interests, as well as the Federal interest in its foreign relations policies, will be best served by a careful inquiry into the reasonableness of the assertion of jurisdiction in the particular case, and an unwillingness to find the serious burdens on an alien defendant outweighed by minimal interests on the part of the plaintiff or the forum State. "Great care and reserve should be exercised when extending our notions of personal jurisdiction into the international field." * * *

Considering the international context, the heavy burden on the alien defendant, and the slight interests of the plaintiff and the forum State, the exercise of personal jurisdiction by a California court over Asahi in this instance would be unreasonable and unfair.

III

Because the facts of this case do not establish minimum contacts such that the exercise of personal jurisdiction is consistent with fair play and substantial justice, the judgment of Supreme Court of California is reversed, and the case is remanded for further proceedings not inconsistent with this opinion.

It is so ordered.

JUSTICE BRENNAN, with whom JUSTICE WHITE, JUSTICE MARSHALL, and JUSTICE BLACKMUN join, concurring in part and in the judgment.

I do not agree with the plurality's interpretation of the stream-of-commerce theory, nor with its conclusion that Asahi did not "purposely avail itself of the California market." * * * I do agree, however, with the Court's conclusion in Part II–B that the exercise of personal jurisdiction over Asahi in this case would not comport with "fair play and substantial justice" * * *. This is one of those rare cases in which "minimum requirements inherent in the concept of 'fair play and substantial justice' . . . defeat the reasonableness of jurisdiction even [though] the defendant has purposefully engaged in forum activities." * * * I therefore join Parts I and II–B of the Court's opinion, and write separately to explain my disagreement with Part II–A.

The plurality states that "a defendant's awareness that the stream of commerce may or will sweep the product into the forum State does not convert the mere act of placing the product into the stream into an act purposefully directed toward the forum State." * * * The plurality would therefore require a plaintiff to show "[a]dditional conduct" directed toward the forum before finding the exercise of jurisdiction over the defendant to be consistent with the Due Process Clause. * * * I see no need for such a showing, however. The stream of commerce refers not to unpredictable currents or eddies, but to the regular and anticipated flow of products from manufacture to distribution to retail sale. As long as a participant in this process is aware that the final product is being marketed in the forum State, the possibility of a lawsuit there cannot come as a surprise. Nor will the litigation present a burden for which there is no corresponding benefit. A defendant who has placed goods in the stream of commerce benefits economically from the retail sale of the final product in the forum State, and indirectly benefits from the State's laws that regulate and facilitate commercial activity. These benefits accrue regardless of whether that participant directly conducts business in the forum State, or engages in additional conduct directed toward that State. Accordingly, most courts and commentators have found that jurisdiction premised on the placement of a product into the stream of commerce is consistent with the Due Process Clause, and have not required a showing of additional conduct.

* * *

Notes and Questions

1. Given the division among the Justices, which opinion states the law as it now stands?

2. The Supreme Court did not disturb the California court's finding that "Asahi knew that some of the valve assemblies sold to Cheng Shin would be incorporated into tire tubes sold in California." Under Justice O'Connor's plurality opinion, this knowledge alone could not serve as a basis for jurisdiction unless Asahi had taken some further action "purposefully directed toward the forum state." What is the rationale for requiring additional conduct? The effect is to allow manufacturers to organize their operations so as to avoid California's jurisdiction and, therefore, its safety standards. Is this option something Asahi is entitled to under the Due Process Clause?

3. In NELSON BY CARSON v. PARK INDUS., INC., 717 F.2d 1120 1125–26 (7th Cir.1983), cited in *Asahi*, a minor, who had suffered severe burns when the cotton flannel shirt she was wearing ignited, sued the retailer (F.W. Woolworth) and its insurance company as well as the purchasing agent for the flannel shirt and the manufacturer of the shirt in a federal court in Wisconsin. Interpreting *World–Wide Volkswagen* as limiting the reach of Wisconsin's long-arm statute, the District Court granted the motions of the purchasing agent and the manufacturer, both Hong Kong corporations, to dismiss the complaints against them for lack of personal jurisdiction. The manufacturer produced 100% of the cotton flannel shirts purchased by Woolworth for sale

in the United States, but it had no direct commercial relationship with Woolworth. All contacts between the two companies were made through the purchasing agent. The agent had a relationship with Woolworth dating back to World War II. The Seventh Circuit reversed the District Court and found that jurisdiction might properly be asserted:

> The *World–Wide Volkswagen* Court's recognition of a distinction among the various entities that might compose a distribution system of a product is pivotal to the decision in this case. The two defendants in *World–Wide Volkswagen* who were not amenable to Oklahoma jurisdiction were at the end of the automobile's distribution system. The scope of the foreseeable market served by those defendants and of the benefits those defendants derived from the sale of the product was narrow. In contrast, the relevant scope is generally broader with respect to manufacturers and primary distributors of products who are at the start of a distribution system and who thereby serve, directly or indirectly, and derive economic benefit from a wider market. Such manufacturers and distributors purposely conduct their activities to make their product available for purchase in as many forums as possible. For this reason, a manufacturer or primary distributor may be subject to a particular forum's jurisdiction when a secondary distributor and retailer are not, because the manufacturer and primary distributor have intended to serve a broader market and they derive direct benefits from serving that market.

Did the Seventh Circuit correctly apply *World–Wide Volkswagen*? If it did, is it possible to argue that the Hong Kong manufacturer had any more control over the whereabouts of the flannel shirt than Seaway had over the whereabouts of the Robinsons' car? Would the case be decided the same way after *Asahi*?

4. For further discussions, see Weber, *Purposeful Availment*, 39 S.C.L. Rev. 815 (1988); Maltz, *Unraveling the Conundrum of the Law of Personal Jurisdiction: A Comment on Asahi Metal Industry Co. v. Superior Court of California*, 1987 Duke L.Rev. 669.

---

6. JURISDICTIONAL REACH OF THE FEDERAL DISTRICT COURTS

Read Federal Rule of Civil Procedure 4 and the accompanying materials in the Supplement.

The United States has by statute or rule imposed a number of restrictions upon the exercise of personal jurisdiction by federal courts. Rule 4(f) of the Federal Rules of Civil Procedure limits the service of process to defendants who can be found within the territory of the state in which the district court sits. However, the Rule provides three exceptions to this limitation. First, Congress in some instances expressly has authorized nationwide, or even worldwide, service of process. See, e.g., Federal Interpleader Act, 28 U.S.C. § 2361; Clayton Act, 15 U.S.C. § 22; Securities Exchange Act of 1934, 15 U.S.C. § 78aa. Second, Rule 4(e) authorizes the federal courts to use the forum state's statutes for serving process outside the state. And, third, Rule 4(f) as amended in 1963 permits service outside the forum state (but within 100 miles of the place where the action is commenced or is to be tried) if such service is necessary to add a third-party defendant under Rule 14, or to join, under Rule 19, an indispensable party to an action or a counterclaim or cross-claim therein.

Are there constitutional limitations on the exercise of personal jurisdiction by the federal court? If there are, they are not to be found in the Fourteenth Amendment, which applies only to the states, but in the Fifth Amendment. To what extent, if any, does the Fifth Amendment require the application of the "minimum contacts" standard developed in *International Shoe?* Is there a difference between the concept of due process as applied to the states and as applied to the federal government?

OMNI CAPITAL INTERNATIONAL v. RUDOLF WOLFF & CO., LTD.

Supreme Court of the United States, 1987.
484 U.S. 97, 108 S.Ct. 404, 98 L.Ed.2d 415.

[Two New York corporations (collectively called "Omni") marketed an investment program involving commodity-futures trades on the London Metals Exchange. The corporations employed a British corporation with its offices in London as a broker to handle trades on that Exchange. An individual who was a citizen and a resident of the United Kingdom represented the British company in soliciting the New York corporations' business. When the United States Internal Revenue Service disallowed income tax deductions claimed by the participants in the investment program, some of the participants sued the New York corporations in the United States District Court for the Eastern District of Louisiana, charging that they were fraudulently induced to participate in the investment program, in violation of various federal securities laws. The New York corporations impleaded the British corporation (Wolff) and its representative (Gourlay), contending that the New York corporations' liability, if any, was caused by the British parties' improper trading activities. After the United States Supreme Court handed down a decision recognizing an implied private cause of action under the Commodity Exchange Act (CEA), the plaintiffs amended their complaints to allege violations of this statute. The District Court held that it lacked personal jurisdiction over the British parties because the Commodity Exchange Act was silent about service of process for private causes of action and the requirements of the Louisiana long-arm statute were not met. The United States Court of Appeals for the Fifth Circuit affirmed.]

JUSTICE BLACKMUN delivered the opinion of the Court.

This case presents questions concerning the prerequisites to a federal court's exercise of in personam jurisdiction.

* * *

II

Omni's primary and fundamental contention is that in a suit under the CEA, the only limits on a District Court's power to exercise personal jurisdiction derive from the Due Process Clause of the Fifth Amendment. The objection of the Court of Appeals, and of Wolff and Gourlay before this Court, is that, even if an exercise of personal jurisdiction would comport with that Due Process Clause,[5] the District Court cannot exercise personal jurisdiction over Wolff and Gourlay because they are not amenable to service of summons in the absence of a statute or rule authorizing such service.

Omni attempts to meet this objection in a variety of ways. First, Omni argues that the District Court may exercise personal jurisdiction because Wolff and Gourlay have constitutionally sufficient contacts with the forum and, as well, have notice of the suits. Second, Omni contends that even if a rule authorizing service is a prerequisite to effective service and thus to the exercise of personal jurisdiction, Congress implicitly authorized nationwide service for private causes of action under the CEA. Third, Omni presses upon us the view of the Fifth Circuit dissenters that, even if authorization for service of process is required and cannot be found in a statute or rule, such authorization should be created by fashioning a remedy to fill a gap in the Federal Rules of Civil Procedure. We examine these contentions in turn.

III

A

Omni argues that the jurisdictional limits that Art. III of the Constitution places on the federal courts relate to subject-matter jurisdiction only. In this view, although Art. III, § 1, leaves it to Congress to "ordain and establish" inferior federal courts, the only limits on those courts, once established, in their exercise of personal jurisdiction, relate to due process. Thus, Omni contends, the District Court may exercise personal jurisdiction over Wolff and Gourlay if the Due Process Clause of the Fifth Amendment does not forbid it.

Omni's argument that Art. III does not itself limit a court's personal jurisdiction is correct. "The requirement that a court have personal jurisdiction flows not from Art. III, but from the Due Process Clause. * * * It represents a restriction on judicial power not as a matter of sovereignty, but as a matter of individual liberty." Insurance Corp. of Ireland v. Compagnie des Bauxites de Guinee, 456 U.S. 694, 702, 102 S.Ct. 2099, 2104, 72 L.Ed.2d 492 (1982). Omni's argument fails, however, because there are other prerequisites to a federal court's exercise of personal jurisdiction.

---

5. Under Omni's theory, a federal court could exercise personal jurisdiction, consistent with the Fifth Amendment, based on an aggregation of the defendant's contacts with the Nation as a whole, rather than on its contacts with the State in which the federal court sits. As was the case in *Asahi* * * *, "[w]e have no occasion" to consider the constitutional issues raised by this theory. * * *

Before a federal court may exercise personal jurisdiction over a defendant, the procedural requirement of service of summons must be satisfied. "[S]ervice of summons is the procedure by which a court having venue and jurisdiction of the subject matter of the suit asserts jurisdiction over the person of the party served." *Mississippi Publishing Corp. v. Murphree,* 326 U.S. 438, 444–445, 66 S.Ct. 242, 245–246, 90 L.Ed. 185 (1946). Thus, before a court may exercise personal jurisdiction over a defendant, there must be more than notice to the defendant and a constitutionally sufficient relationship between the defendant and the forum. There also must be a basis for the defendant's amenability to service of summons. Absent consent, this means there must be authorization for service of summons on the defendant.

B

The next question, then, is whether there is authorization to serve summons in this litigation. Today, service of process in a federal action is covered generally by Rule 4 of the Federal Rules of Civil Procedure. Rule 4(f) describes where process "may be served." It authorizes service in the State in which the action is brought, or anywhere else authorized by a federal statute or by the Rules.

The "most obvious reference" of this last provision is to Rule 4(e). The first sentence of the rule speaks to the ability to serve summons on an out-of-state defendant when a federal statute authorizes such service. The second sentence, as an additional method, authorizes service of summons "under the circumstances" prescribed in a state statute or rule. Thus, under Rule 4(e), a federal court normally looks either to a federal statute or to the long-arm statute of the State in which it sits to determine whether a defendant is amenable to service, a prerequisite to its exercise of personal jurisdiction.

Omni argues that Wolff and Gourlay are amenable to service under Rule 4(e) because the CEA implicitly "provides for service *   *   * upon a party not an inhabitant of or found within the state." Omni points out that, prior to this Court's recognition *   *   * of an implied private cause of action, all other civil actions under the CEA explicitly authorized nationwide service of process. *   *   * Omni contends that this broad avenue for service is mandated by the importance of futures trading to the Nation as a whole. Since this Court concluded that a private right of action was intended as a "tool for enforcement," *   *   * it must be given the same "dignity" as other enforcement provisions. Accordingly, Omni contends, nationwide service of process is also authorized for the implied private cause of action under the CEA.

Neither the majority nor the dissent in the Court of Appeals found that the CEA contained an implied provision for nationwide service of process in a private cause of action. We, too, decline to draw that inference. *   *   * Section 22 is silent as to service of process. This contrasts sharply with the other enforcement provisions of the CEA, on which Omni asks us to rely. We find it significant that Congress expressly provided for nationwide service of process in those sections but did not do so in the new § 22. It would appear that Congress knows how to authorize nationwide service of process when it wants to provide for it. That Congress failed to do so here argues forcefully that such authorization was not its intention.

* * *

Since the CEA does not authorize service of summons on Wolff and Gourlay, we look to the second sentence of Rule 4(e), which points to the long-arm statute of the State in which the District Court sits—here, Louisiana. The District Court held that the requirements of the Louisiana long-arm statute were not met in this litigation. * * * Because the terms of the Louisiana statute were not met, the District Court considered a due process analysis unnecessary. Before us, Omni has not contended that Wolff and Gourlay may be reached under the Louisiana long-arm statute. Indeed, Omni has conceded that they may not. Thus, neither part of Rule 4(e) authorizes the service of summons on Wolff and Gourlay.

C

The dissenters in the Court of Appeals argued that even if authorization to serve process is necessary and cannot be found in Rule 4(e), the federal courts should act to fill the "interstices in the law inadvertently left by legislative enactment" by creating their own rule authorizing service of process in this litigation. * * * We decline to embark on that adventure.

As an initial matter, it is unclear at this time whether it is open to us to fashion a rule authorizing service of process. At common law, a court lacked authority to issue process outside its district, and Congress made this same restriction the general rule when it enacted the Judiciary Act of Sept. 24, 1789 * * *. Thus, specific legislative authorization of extraterritorial service of summons was required for a court to exercise personal jurisdiction over a person outside the district. Even were we to conclude that the bases for the rule * * * are no longer valid, we would not necessarily have the power to create service-of-process rules. We would have to decide that the provisions of Rules 4(e) and 4(f), in authorizing service in certain circumstances, were not intended to prohibit service in all other circumstances. We would also have to find adequate authority for common-law rulemaking. We need not decide these questions, however, since we would not fashion a rule for service in this litigation even if we had the power to do so.

We would consider it unwise for a court to make its own rule authorizing service of summons. It seems likely that Congress has been acting on the assumption that federal courts cannot add to the scope of service of summons Congress has authorized. This Court in the past repeatedly has stated that a legislative grant of authority is necessary.

The strength of this long-standing assumption, and the network of statutory enactments and judicial decisions tied to it, argue strongly against devising common-law service of process provisions at this late date for at least two reasons. First, since Congress concededly has the power to limit service of process, circumspection is called for in going beyond what Congress has authorized. Second, as statutes and rules have always provided the measures for service, courts are inappropriate forums for deciding whether to extend them. Legislative rulemaking better ensures proper consideration of a service rule's ramifications within the pre-existing structure and is more likely to lead to consistent application.

Nothing about this case impels us to a different conclusion. If we do not create a rule here, the only harm to federal interests is the inability of a private litigant to bring a CEA action in the United States against an alien defendant who is not within the reach of the state long-arm statute. Since the CEA authorizes broader service of process in other enforcement actions, aliens cannot consider themselves immune from the Act's provisions. Also, a British court may be willing to enforce the CEA itself, if Omni brings suit against Wolff and Gourlay there.

We are not blind to the consequences of the inability to serve process on Wolff and Gourlay. A narrowly tailored service of process provision, authorizing service on an alien in a federal-question case when the alien is not amenable to service under the applicable state long-arm statute, might well serve the ends of the CEA and other federal statutes. It is not for the federal courts, however, to create such a rule as a matter of common law. That responsibility, in our view, better rests with those who propose the Federal Rules of Civil Procedure and with Congress.

IV

In summary, the District Court may not exercise jurisdiction over Wolff and Gourlay without authorization to serve process. That authorization is not found in either the CEA or the Louisiana long-arm statute to which we look under Rule 4(e). We reject the suggestion that we should create a common-law rule authorizing service of process, since we would consider that action unwise, even were it within our power.

The judgment of the Court of Appeals is affirmed.

It is so ordered.

Notes and Questions

1. The Advisory Committee on Rules is considering the following amendment to Rule 4:

> With respect to a claim arising under federal law or subject to the federal interpleader jurisdiction, service of a summons pursuant to this rule shall be effective to establish jurisdiction over the person of the defendant, unless the Constitution or a statute of the United States otherwise provides. With respect to other claims, service of a summons shall not be effective to establish jurisdiction over the person or property of a defendant who is not subject to the jurisdiction of a court of general jurisdiction in the state in which the district court is held, except that a party joined under Rule 14 or Rule 19 shall also be subject to the jurisdiction of the court if served at a place within a judicial district of the United States and not more than 100 miles from the place from which the summons issues.

How would such a provision have affected the outcome of *Omni*?

2.   Even if nationwide service of process were provided for by the CEA or Rule 4, would the plaintiffs in *Omni* have been able to establish jurisdiction over Omni?   Over Wolff and Gourlay?   Consider the effect of due process limitations on the jurisdiction of federal courts hearing federal-question cases discussed below.

FEDERAL TRADE COMMISSION v. **JIM WALTER CORP.**, 651 F.2d 251 (5th Cir.1981).   Jim Walter Corporation (JWC) is a holding company providing "corporate services" for several wholly-owned subsidiaries engaged in the construction and marketing of new homes.   The corporation's headquarters are located in Tampa, Florida, and all of its employees are based in Florida.   Jim Walter Homes, Inc., a subsidiary that builds and sells homes, does business throughout the South and Southwest and has an office in Dallas.   In the course of investigating complaints about Jim Walter Homes from consumers in Texas and adjacent states, the Federal Trade Commission attempted to subpoena some records of the Florida parent.   When JWC refused to comply, the FTC sought enforcement in the District Court for the Northern District of Texas.   Service outside Texas was made pursuant to Section 9 of the Federal Trade Commission Act, 15 U.S.C. § 49.   But JWC argued that nationwide service of process violates due process guarantees when the entity served has no relationship with the district in which the relevant federal district court sits.

* * * Subject *only* to the regulation of Congress, each federal court exercises the "judicial Power of the United States," not a judicial power constitutionally limited by the boundaries of a particular district. * * * Because the district court's jurisdiction is always potentially, and, in this case, actually co-extensive with the boundaries of the United States, due process requires only that a defendant in a federal suit have minimum contacts with the United States, "the sovereign that has created the court" * * *.   JWC, as a resident United States corporation, necessarily has sufficient contacts with the United States to satisfy the requirements of due process. * * *

Anticipating our analysis, JWC argues that we should not focus on the concept of "minimum contacts" *per se*, but should instead determine whether requiring JWC to defend in a distant forum offends "traditional notions of fair play and substantial justice."   Undoubtedly, one of the "functions" of due process limitations on jurisdiction is to prevent "distant or inconvenient" litigation. * * * [However, when] minimum contacts exist with the relevant sovereign, due process no longer protects a defendant from distant litigation because the location of permissible venues is a matter of sovereign prerogative. * * * Article III grants Congress plenary power to organize the jurisdiction and venue of federal courts. * * * Whether due process imposes any limit on congressional exercise of its regulatory power under Article III is still an open question * * *.   In analyzing this issue, we do not look to the "fairness" of the regulation.   "Fairness" is a component of the jurisdictional test, but has no relevance to determining the constitutionality of Congressional regulation, given the magnitude of Congressional discretion in this area.   The regulation must deprive the litigant of process actually due; the quality of justice must indeed be strained.

JWC has failed to demonstrate such deprivation. JWC is protected by the same procedural and substantive safeguards whether it defends this suit in the Northern District of Texas or the Middle District of Florida. JWC's true complaint is that it is more expensive and inconvenient to defend a suit in a distant forum, but Congress has no constitutional obligation to make litigation as inexpensive as possible. Moreover, if the ability of one litigant to impose inordinate expense on another violated due process, major segments of our system of civil litigation might be rendered unconstitutional, rather than merely distressing. While the Alaska Supreme Court has suggested that, under certain circumstances, the inordinate expense imposed by state-wide service of process in suits involving small claims could effectively deny indigent defendants access to the courts, there is no indication here that JWC has been denied access to the courts by the expense of defending this suit in a distant venue.

The Northern District of Texas is a proper venue under Section 9. Nationwide service of process is authorized under Rule 4(e) and does not violate due process. We hold that the district court properly exercised jurisdiction over JWC.

Id. at 256–58.

Notes and Questions

1. Is *Jim Walter* consistent with *Omni?* Does the opinion in *Jim Walter* fairly construe the line of decisions beginning with *International Shoe?* Does the opinion err by over-emphasizing concerns of sovereignty? Defending a suit in Michigan is equally inconvenient, and hence unfair, for a resident of Arizona whether she has to appear before a Michigan court or a United States District Court sitting in Michigan. Should the Due Process Clause of the Fifth Amendment protect citizens from the arbitrary exercise of personal jurisdiction by federal courts just as the Due Process Clause of the Fourteenth Amendment protects citizens from such action by state courts?

2. In a thoughtful opinion by Judge Becker in OXFORD FIRST CORP. v. PNC LIQUIDATING CORP., 372 F.Supp. 191 (E.D.Pa.1974), the court concluded that, although federal statutes authorizing extra-district service of process are not constrained by the constitutional strictures defined in *International Shoe,* their application is limited by fundamental notions of "fairness" derived from the Due Process Clause of the Fifth Amendment. Among the factors identified as being relevant to the "fairness" inquiry were: (1) the extent of the defendant's contacts with the place where the action was brought, (2) the inconvenience of defending in a distant forum, (3) judicial economy, (4) the probable locus of discovery, and (5) the interstate character and impact of defendant's activities. Applying these standards to the case, the court upheld the exercise of jurisdiction.

Those courts that have considered the question, however, have refused to adopt the *Oxford* factors as a test of whether an assertion of personal jurisdiction by a federal court complies with due process. "The 'fairness' measured by these factors does not relate to the fairness of the exercise of

power by a particular sovereign ＊ ＊ ＊ but instead to the fairness of imposing the burdens of litigation in a particular forum. As such, these factors are
more appropriately used [in determining whether venue is properly laid in a
particular district], and we decline to import them into determination of the
constitutionality of exercise of personal jurisdiction." Fitzsimmons v. Barton,
589 F.2d 330 (7th Cir.1979). See Haile v. Henderson Nat. Bank, 657 F.2d 816
(6th Cir.1981), certiorari denied 455 U.S. 949, 102 S.Ct. 1450, 71 L.Ed.2d 663
(1982).

3. The "minimum contacts" standard of *International Shoe* does apply
when a federal court, pursuant to Rule 4(e), resorts to the law of the forum
state to serve process on an out-of-state defendant. The rule authorizes
service "under the circumstances" prescribed in the state statute, and this
language has been construed to mean that a federal court can use a state long-
arm statute only to reach those parties whom a court of the state could also
reach. This construction is consistent with the apparent intent of the draftsmen of Rule 4(e) to use state provisions for service in order to permit the
federal courts in a state to hear those cases that could be brought in the
state's own courts when a basis for asserting federal subject-matter jurisdiction exists. See DeMelo v. Toche Marine, Inc., 711 F.2d 1260 (5th Cir.1983);
Gemini Enterprises, Inc. v. WFMY Television Corp., 470 F.Supp. 559 (M.D.
N.C.1979).

4. The growth of international commerce has resulted in an increased
number of claims against alien defendants brought in American courts. If a
federal statute authorizes world-wide service of process, a federal court apparently may exercise in personam jurisdiction based on the alien's aggregate
contacts with the United States. Texas Trading & Milling Corp. v. Federal
Republic of Nigeria, 647 F.2d 300, 314 (2d Cir.1981), certiorari denied 454 U.S.
1148, 102 S.Ct. 1012, 71 L.Ed.2d 301 (1982). But if a federal court must rely
on a state long-arm statute, it can exercise in personam jurisdiction based
only on the alien's contacts with the forum state, even if the alien's aggregate
contacts with the United States as a whole would satisfy due process requirements mandated by the Fifth Amendment. DeJames v. Magnificence Carriers, Inc., 491 F.Supp. 1276 (D.N.J.1980), affirmed 654 F.2d 280 (3d Cir.),
certiorari denied 454 U.S. 1085, 102 S.Ct. 642, 70 L.Ed.2d 620 (1981); Superior
Coal Co. v. Ruhrkohle, A.G., 83 F.R.D. 414 (E.D.Pa.1979). This apparent
anomaly is discussed in Lilly, *Jurisdiction over Domestic and Alien Defen-*
dants, 69 Va.L.Rev. 85 (1983); Note, *National Contacts as a Basis for In*
Personam Jurisdiction over Aliens in Federal Question Suits, 70 Calif.L.Rev.
686 (1982); Note, *Alien Corporations and Aggregate Contacts: A Genuinely*
Federal Jurisdictional Standard, 95 Harv.L.Rev. 470 (1981).

5. The amenability of a party to service in the federal courts when
federal law governs is discussed in Berger, *Acquiring In Personam Jurisdic-*
tion in Federal Question Cases: Procedural Frustration Under Federal Rule of
Civil Procedure 4, 1982 Utah L.Rev. 285; Foster, *Judicial Economy, Fairness*
and Convenience of Place of Trial: Long-Arm Jurisdiction in the District
Courts, 47 F.R.D. 73 (1968); Green, *Federal Jurisdiction In Personam of*
Corporations and Due Process, 14 Vand.L.Rev. 967 (1961). The question
whether state or federal law governs amenability in diversity cases is an
aspect of the general choice-of-law problem discussed in Chapter 3, infra.

SECTION B. JURISDICTION BASED UPON POWER OVER PROPERTY

Reread Pennoyer v. Neff, p. 66, supra.

TYLER v. JUDGES OF THE COURT OF REGISTRATION, 175 Mass. 71, 55 N.E. 812 (1900), writ of error dismissed 179 U.S. 405, 21 S.Ct. 206, 45 L.Ed. 252 (1900). Petitioner sought a writ of prohibition against the judges of the Court of Registration to prevent their passing upon an application to register title to a parcel of land in which petitioner claimed an interest. The basis of the petition was that the act establishing the court violated due process because it deprived all persons except the registered owner of any interest in the land, and it provided for insufficient notice to persons having adverse claims.

The statute in question established a procedure and court for registering and confirming titles to land. It provided that the decree of registration "shall bind the land and quiet the title thereto," and "shall be conclusive upon and against all persons" whether named in the proceedings or not. It further required that notice of the proposed registration be published in a newspaper, posted on the land, and mailed to adjoining owners and all persons known to have an adverse interest. Chief Justice Holmes, writing for the majority, denied the petition and upheld the act as constitutional, but cautioned that it ought to be amended to insure actual notice:

If it does not satisfy the constitution, a judicial proceeding to clear titles against all the world hardly is possible; for the very meaning of such a proceeding is to get rid of unknown as well as known claims,— indeed, certainty against the unknown may be said to be its chief end,— and unknown claims cannot be dealt with by personal service upon the claimant. * * *

Looked at either from the point of view of history or of the necessary requirements of justice, a proceeding in rem, dealing with a tangible res, may be instituted and carried to judgment without personal service upon claimants within the state, or notice by name to those outside of it, and not encounter any provision of either constitution. Jurisdiction is secured by the power of the court over the res. * * *

But it is said that this is not a proceeding "in rem." It is certain that no phrase has been more misused. * * * If the technical object of the suit is to establish a claim against some particular person, with a judgment which generally in theory, at least, binds his body, or to bar some individual claim or objection, so that only certain persons are entitled to be heard in defense, the action is in personam, although it may concern the right to, or possession of, a tangible thing. * * * If, on the other hand, the object is to bar indifferently all who might be minded to make an objection of any sort against the right sought to be established, and if any one in the world has a right to be heard on the strength of alleging facts which, if true, show an inconsistent interest, the proceeding is in rem. * * * All proceedings, like all rights, are really against persons. Whether they are proceedings or rights in rem depends on the number of persons affected. Hence the res need not be personified, and made a party defendant * * *. It need not even be a tangible thing at all * * *. Personification and naming the res as defendant are mere symbols, not the essential matter. They are fictions, conveniently expressing the nature of the process and the result; nothing more. * * *

Id. at 73, 75–76, 55 N.E. at 813–14.

PENNINGTON v. FOURTH NATIONAL BANK, 243 U.S. 269, 271–72, 37 S.Ct. 282, 282–83, 61 L.Ed. 713 (1917):

The 14th Amendment did not, in guarantying due process of law, abridge the jurisdiction which a state possessed over property within its borders, regardless of the residence or presence of the owner. That jurisdiction extends alike to tangible and to intangible property. Indebtedness due from a resident to a nonresident—of which bank deposits are an example—is property within the state. * * * It is, indeed, the species of property which courts of the several states have most frequently applied in satisfaction of the obligations of absent debtors. * * * Substituted service on a nonresident by publication furnishes no legal basis for a judgment in personam. * * * But garnishment or foreign attachment is a proceeding quasi in rem. * * * The thing belonging to the absent defendant is seized and applied to the satisfaction of his obligation. The Federal Constitution presents no obstacle to the full exercise of this power.

* * * The power of the state to proceed against the property of an absent defendant is the same whether the obligation sought to be enforced is an admitted indebtedness or a contested claim. * * * It is likewise immaterial that the claim is, at the commencement of the suit, inchoate, to be perfected only by time or the action of the court. The only essentials to the exercise of the state's power are presence of the res within its borders, its seizure at the commencement of proceedings, and the opportunity of the owner to be heard.

Notes and Questions

1. What is the situs of corporate stock for purposes of attachment—the corporation's place of incorporation, the domicile of the shareholder, or the state in which the stock certificates actually are located? See generally Note, *Attachment of Corporate Stock: The Conflicting Approaches of Delaware and the Uniform Stock Transfer Act*, 73 Harv.L.Rev. 1579 (1960).

2. Prior to 1963, the federal courts had no general original quasi-in-rem jurisdiction. This was a curious limitation since the federal courts permitted the removal of actions initially commenced in a state court by attachment. See Rorick v. Devon Syndicate, Ltd., 307 U.S. 299, 59 S.Ct. 877, 83 L.Ed. 1303 (1939). In 1963 this inconsistency was eliminated by the amendment of Federal Rule 4(e). Full discussions of this topic are found in Carrington, *The Modern Utility of Quasi in Rem Jurisdiction*, 76 Harv.L.Rev. 303 (1962); Currie, *Attachment and Garnishment in the Federal Courts*, 59 Mich.L.Rev.

337 (1961). See also 4 Wright & Miller, *Federal Practice and Procedure: Civil* §§ 1119–23 (1969).

Quasi-in-rem jurisdiction in the federal courts also is specifically provided for in 28 U.S.C. § 1655 in connection with certain types of claims to land when defendant cannot be served personally within the state. See Blume, *Actions Quasi in Rem Under Section 1655, Title 28, U.S.C.,* 50 Mich.L.Rev. 1 (1951).

———————

HARRIS v. BALK, 198 U.S. 215, 25 S.Ct. 625, 49 L.Ed. 1023 (1905). Harris, a citizen of North Carolina, owed Balk, also of North Carolina, $180. Epstein, a Maryland citizen, claimed that Balk owed him $344. On August 6, 1896, while Harris was visiting Baltimore, Epstein instituted a garnishee proceeding in a Maryland court, attaching the debt due Balk from Harris. Harris was personally served with the writ of attachment and summons, and notice of the suit was posted at the courthouse door, as required by Maryland law. Harris consented to the entry of judgment against him and paid the $180 to Epstein. On August 11, 1896, Balk commenced an action against Harris in a North Carolina court to recover the $180. Harris asserted that he no longer owed Balk the $180, having paid that sum to Epstein in partial satisfaction of Balk's debt to Epstein, since the Maryland judgment and his payment thereof was valid in Maryland, and was therefore entitled to full faith and credit in the courts of North Carolina. The trial court ruled in favor of Balk and the North Carolina Supreme Court affirmed on the ground that the Maryland court had no jurisdiction over Harris to attach the debt because Harris was only temporarily in the state, and the situs of the debt was in North Carolina. The Supreme Court reversed:

> * * * We do not see how the question of jurisdiction *vel non* can properly be made to depend upon the so-called original situs of the debt, or upon the character of the stay of the garnishee, whether temporary or permanent, in the state where the attachment is issued. Power over the person of the garnishee confers jurisdiction on the courts of the state where the writ issues. * * * If, while temporarily there, his creditor might sue him there and recover the debt, then he is liable to process of garnishment, no matter where the situs of the debt was originally. We do not see the materiality of the expression "situs of the debt," when used in connection with attachment proceedings. If by situs is meant the place of the creation of the debt, that fact is immaterial. If it be meant that the obligation to pay the debt can only be enforced at the situs thus fixed, we think it plainly untrue. The obligation of the debtor to pay his debt clings to and accompanies him wherever he goes. He is as much bound to pay his debt in a foreign state when therein sued upon his obligation by his creditor, as he was in the state where the debt was contracted.
> * * * It would be no defense to such suit for the debtor to plead that he was only in the foreign state casually or temporarily. * * * It is nothing but the obligation to pay which is garnished or attached. This obligation can be enforced by the courts of the foreign state after personal service of process therein, just as well as by the courts of the domicil of the debtor. * * *

Id. at 222, 25 S.Ct. at 626, 49 L.Ed. at 1026. The Court indicated in dictum that the result might have been different if Balk had not been given notice of the attachment and an opportunity to defend in the Maryland action.

Notes and Questions

1. Professor Andreas Lowenfeld provides the following information concerning Harris, Balk, and Epstein. Epstein was an importer of goods who regularly did business with Balk, a retailer. The $344 debt was for money owed on shipments of goods by Epstein to Balk. Harris was a dry goods merchant from the same town as Balk, and had borrowed money from Balk on several occasions, including a $10 loan just before the fateful trip to Baltimore. Harris carried with him on that trip a message from Balk to Epstein saying that Balk would be coming to Baltimore soon. Lowenfeld, *In Search of the Intangible: A Comment on Shaffer v. Heitner,* 53 N.Y.U.L.Rev. 102, 104–06 (1978).

If this case were to occur today, could Epstein have sued Balk in personam, assuming a long-arm statute similar to Rhode Island's? Could Epstein have served Harris as Balk's agent?

2. For purposes of determining whether or not quasi-in-rem jurisdiction may be asserted, does it matter why Harris was in Baltimore? Consider the following variations:

   (a) Balk sends Harris into Maryland to conduct some business for him.

   (b) Harris goes into Maryland with Balk's knowledge, but to do business unrelated to Balk.

   (c) Harris goes into Maryland without Balk's knowledge.

   (d) Harris goes to Maryland at Epstein's request who promised Harris "it'll be worth your while."

SHAFFER v. HEITNER

Supreme Court of the United States, 1977.
433 U.S. 186, 97 S.Ct. 2569, 53 L.Ed.2d 683.

On Appeal from the Supreme Court of Delaware.

MR. JUSTICE MARSHALL delivered the opinion of the Court.

* * *

I

Appellee Heitner, a nonresident of Delaware, is the owner of one share of stock in the Greyhound Corp., a business incorporated under the laws of Delaware with its principal place of business in Phoenix, Ariz. On May 22, 1974, he filed a shareholder's derivative suit in the Court of Chancery for New Castle County, Del., in which he named as defendants Greyhound, its wholly owned subsidiary Greyhound Lines, Inc.,[1] and 28 present or former officers or directors of one or both of the corporations. In essence, Heitner alleged that the individual defendants had violated

---

1. Greyhound Lines, Inc., is incorporated in California and has its principal place of business in Phoenix, Ariz.

their duties to Greyhound by causing it and its subsidiary to engage in actions that resulted in the corporations being held liable for substantial damages in a private antitrust suit and a large fine in a criminal contempt action. The activities which led to these penalties took place in Oregon.

Simultaneously with his complaint, Heitner filed a motion for an order of sequestration of the Delaware property of the individual defendants pursuant to Del.Code Ann., Tit. 10, § 366 (1975). This motion was accompanied by a supporting affidavit of counsel which stated that the individual defendants were nonresidents of Delaware. The affidavit identified the property to be sequestered as [shares of Greyhound Corporation stock and stock options] * * *. The requested sequestration order was signed the day the motion was filed. Pursuant to that order, the sequestrator "seized" approximately 82,000 shares of Greyhound common stock belonging to 19 of the defendants, and options belonging to another 2 defendants. These seizures were accomplished by placing "stop transfer" orders or their equivalents on the books of the Greyhound Corp. So far as the record shows, none of the certificates representing the seized property was physically present in Delaware. The stock was considered to be in Delaware, and so subject to seizure, by virtue of Del.Code Ann., Tit. 8, § 169 (1975), which makes Delaware the situs of ownership of all stock in Delaware corporations.

All 28 defendants were notified of the initiation of the suit by certified mail directed to their last known addresses and by publication in a New Castle County newspaper. The 21 defendants whose property was seized (hereafter referred to as appellants) responded by entering a special appearance for the purpose of moving to quash service of process and to vacate the sequestration order. They contended that the *ex parte* sequestration procedure did not accord them due process of law and that the property seized was not capable of attachment in Delaware. In addition, appellants asserted that under the rule of International Shoe Co. v. Washington, 326 U.S. 310, 66 S.Ct. 154, 90 L.Ed. 95 (1945), they did not have sufficient contacts with Delaware to sustain the jurisdiction of that State's courts.

The Court of Chancery rejected these arguments * * *.

On appeal, the Delaware Supreme Court affirmed the judgment of the Court of Chancery. * * * Most of the Supreme Court's opinion was devoted to rejecting appellants' contention that the sequestration procedure is inconsistent with the due process analysis developed in the *Sniadach* [v. Family Finance Corp., 395 U.S. 337, 89 S.Ct. 1820, 23 L.Ed.2d 349 (1969), pp. 209–27, infra] line of cases. The court based its rejection of that argument in part on its agreement with the Court of Chancery that the purpose of the sequestration procedure is to compel the appearance of the defendant, a purpose not involved in the *Sniadach* cases. The court also relied on what it considered the ancient origins of the sequestration procedure and approval of that procedure in the opinions of this Court,[10]

---

10. The court relied * * * on our decision in Ownbey v. Morgan, 256 U.S. 94, 41   S.Ct. 433, 65 L.Ed. 837 (1921) * * *. The only question before the Court in *Ownbey*

Delaware's interest in asserting jurisdiction to adjudicate claims of mismanagement of a Delaware corporation, and the safeguards for defendants that it found in the Delaware statute. * * *

Appellants' claim that the Delaware courts did not have jurisdiction to adjudicate this action received much more cursory treatment. * * * [12] We reverse.

II

The Delaware courts rejected appellants' jurisdictional challenge by noting that this suit was brought as a *quasi in rem* proceeding. Since *quasi in rem* jurisdiction is traditionally based on attachment or seizure of property present in the jurisdiction, not on contacts between the defendant and the State, the courts considered appellants' claimed lack of contacts with Delaware to be unimportant. This categorical analysis assumes the continued soundness of the conceptual structure founded on the century-old case of Pennoyer v. Neff * * *.

[The Court's description of *Pennoyer* is omitted.] * * *

From our perspective, the importance of *Pennoyer* is not its result, but the fact that its principles and corollaries derived from them became the basic elements of the constitutional doctrine governing state-court jurisdiction. * * * As we have noted, under *Pennoyer* state authority to adjudicate was based on the jurisdiction's power over either persons or property. This fundamental concept is embodied in the very vocabulary which we use to describe judgments. If a court's jurisdiction is based on its authority over the defendant's person, the action and judgment are denominated "*in personam*" and can impose a personal obligation on the defendant in favor of the plaintiff. If jurisdiction is based on the court's power over property within its territory, the action is called "*in rem*" or "*quasi in rem*." The effect of a judgment in such a case is limited to the property that supports jurisdiction and does not impose a personal liability on the property owner, since he is not before the court.[17] In *Pennoyer*'s terms, the owner is affected only "indirectly" by an *in rem* judgment adverse to his interest in the property subject to the court's disposition.

[Justice Marshall's historical analysis of the expansion of in personam jurisdiction is omitted.] * * *

was the constitutionality of a requirement that a defendant whose property has been attached file a bond before entering an appearance. We do not read the recent references to *Ownbey* as necessarily suggesting that *Ownbey* is consistent with more recent decisions interpreting the Due Process Clause.

* * *

12. Under Delaware law, defendants whose property has been sequestered must enter a general appearance, thus subjecting themselves to *in personam* liability, before they can defend on the merits. * * *

17. "A judgment *in rem* affects the interest of all persons in designated property. A judgment *quasi in rem* affects the interests of particular persons in designated property. The latter is of two types. In one the plaintiff is seeking to secure a pre-existing claim in the subject property and to extinguish or establish the non-existence of similar interests of particular persons. In the other the plaintiff seeks to apply what he concedes to be the property of the defendant to the satisfaction of a claim against him. Restatement, Judgments, 5–9." Hanson v. Denckla, 357 U.S. 235, 246 n. 12, 78 S.Ct. 1228, 1235, 2 L.Ed.2d 1283 [1958].

As did the Court in *Hanson*, we will for convenience generally use the term "*in rem*" in place of "*in rem* and *quasi in rem*."

No equally dramatic change has occurred in the law governing jurisdiction *in rem*. There have, however, been intimations that the collapse of the *in personam* wing of *Pennoyer* has not left that decision unweakened as a foundation for *in rem* jurisdiction. Well-reasoned lower court opinions have questioned the proposition that the presence of property in a State gives that State jurisdiction to adjudicate rights to the property regardless of the relationship of the underlying dispute and the property owner to the forum. * * * The overwhelming majority of commentators have also rejected *Pennoyer*'s premise that a proceeding "against" property is not a proceeding against the owners of that property. Accordingly, they urge that the "traditional notions of fair play and substantial justice" that govern a State's power to adjudicate *in personam* should also govern its power to adjudicate personal rights to property located in the State. * * *

Although this Court has not addressed this argument directly, we have held that property cannot be subjected to a court's judgment unless reasonable and appropriate efforts have been made to give the property owners actual notice of the action. * * * This conclusion recognizes, contrary to *Pennoyer*, that an adverse judgment *in rem* directly affects the property owner by divesting him of his rights in the property before the court. * * * Moreover, in *Mullane* we held that Fourteenth Amendment rights cannot depend on the classification of an action as *in rem* or *in personam* * * *.

It is clear, therefore, that the law of state-court jurisdiction no longer stands securely on the foundation established in *Pennoyer*. We think that the time is ripe to consider whether the standard of fairness and substantial justice set forth in *International Shoe* should be held to govern actions *in rem* as well as *in personam*.

III

The case for applying to jurisdiction *in rem* the same test of "fair play and substantial justice" as governs assertions of jurisdiction *in personam* is simple and straightforward. It is premised on recognition that "[t]he phrase, 'judicial jurisdiction over a thing', is a customary elliptical way of referring to jurisdiction over the interests of persons in a thing." Restatement (Second) of Conflict of Laws § 56, Introductory Note * * *. This recognition leads to the conclusion that in order to justify an exercise of jurisdiction *in rem*, the basis for jurisdiction must be sufficient to justify exercising "jurisdiction over the interests of persons in a thing." The standard for determining whether an exercise of jurisdiction over the interests of persons is consistent with the Due Process Clause is the minimum-contacts standard elucidated in *International Shoe*.

This argument, of course, does not ignore the fact that the presence of property in a State may bear on the existence of jurisdiction by providing contacts among the forum State, the defendant, and the litigation. For example, when claims to the property itself are the source of the underlying controversy between the plaintiff and the defendant, it would be unusual for the State where the property is located not to have jurisdiction. In such cases, the defendant's claim to property located in the State would normally indicate that he expected to benefit from the State's protection of his interest. The State's strong interests in assuring the marketability of property within its borders and in providing a procedure for peaceful resolution of disputes about the possession of that property would also support jurisdiction, as would the likelihood that important records and witnesses will be found in the State. The presence of property may also favor jurisdiction in cases, such as suits for injury suffered on the land of an absentee owner, where the defendant's ownership of the property is conceded but the cause of action is otherwise related to rights and duties growing out of that ownership.

It appears, therefore, that jurisdiction over many types of actions which now are or might be brought *in rem* would not be affected by a holding that any assertion of state-court jurisdiction must satisfy the *International Shoe* standard. For the type of *quasi in rem* action typified by Harris v. Balk and the present case, however, accepting the proposed analysis would result in significant change. These are cases where the property which now serves as the basis for state-court jurisdiction is completely unrelated to the plaintiff's cause of action. Thus, although the presence of the defendant's property in a State might suggest the existence of other ties among the defendant, the State, and the litigation, the presence of the property alone would not support the State's jurisdiction. If those other ties did not exist, cases over which the State is now thought to have jurisdiction could not be brought in that forum.

Since acceptance of the *International Shoe* test would most affect this class of cases, we examine the arguments against adopting that standard as they relate to this category of litigation. Before doing so, however, we note that this type of case also presents the clearest illustration of the argument in favor of assessing assertions of jurisdiction by a single standard. For in cases such as *Harris* and this one, the only role played by the property is to provide the basis for bringing the defendant into court. Indeed, the express purpose of the Delaware sequestration procedure is to compel the defendant to enter a personal appearance. In such cases, if a direct assertion of personal jurisdiction over the defendant would violate the Constitution, it would seem that an indirect assertion of that jurisdiction should be equally impermissible.

The primary rationale for treating the presence of property as a sufficient basis for jurisdiction to adjudicate claims over which the State would not have jurisdiction if *International Shoe* applied is that a wrong-doer

> should not be able to avoid payment of his obligations by the expedient of removing his assets to a place where he is not subject to an in personam suit. Restatement [(Second) of Conflicts] § 66, Comment a.

* * * This justification, however, does not explain why jurisdiction should be recognized without regard to whether the property is present in the State because of an effort to avoid the owner's obligations. Nor does it support jurisdiction to adjudicate the underlying claim. At most, it suggests that a State in which property is located should have jurisdiction to attach that property, by use of proper procedures, as security for a

judgment being sought in a forum where the litigation can be maintained consistently with *International Shoe.* * * * Moreover, we know of nothing to justify the assumption that a debtor can avoid paying his obligations by removing his property to a State in which his creditor cannot obtain personal jurisdiction over him. The Full Faith and Credit Clause, after all, makes the valid *in personam* judgment of one State enforceable in all other States.

It might also be suggested that allowing *in rem* jurisdiction avoids the uncertainty inherent in the *International Shoe* standard and assures a plaintiff of a forum.[37] * * * We believe, however, that the fairness standard of *International Shoe* can be easily applied in the vast majority of cases. Moreover, when the existence of jurisdiction in a particular forum under *International Shoe* is unclear, the cost of simplifying the litigation by avoiding the jurisdictional question may be the sacrifice of "fair play and substantial justice." That cost is too high.

We are left, then, to consider the significance of the long history of jurisdiction based solely on the presence of property in a State. Although the theory that territorial power is both essential to and sufficient for jurisdiction has been undermined, we have never held that the presence of property in a State does not automatically confer jurisdiction over the owner's interest in that property. This history must be considered as supporting the proposition that jurisdiction based solely on the presence of property satisfies the demands of due process * * *, but it is not decisive. * * * The fiction that an assertion of jurisdiction over property is anything but an assertion of jurisdiction over the owner of the property supports an ancient form without substantial modern justification. Its continued acceptance would serve only to allow state-court jurisdiction that is fundamentally unfair to the defendant.

We therefore conclude that all assertions of state-court jurisdiction must be evaluated according to the standards set forth in *International Shoe* and its progeny.

IV

The Delaware courts based their assertion of jurisdiction in this case solely on the statutory presence of appellants' property in Delaware. Yet that property is not the subject matter of this litigation, nor is the underlying cause of action related to the property. Appellants' holdings in Greyhound do not, therefore, provide contacts with Delaware sufficient to support the jurisdiction of that State's courts over appellants. If it exists, that jurisdiction must have some other foundation.[40]

37. This case does not raise, and we therefore do not consider, the question whether the presence of a defendant's property in a State is a sufficient basis for jurisdiction when no other forum is available to the plaintiff.

40. Appellants argue that our determination that the minimum contacts standard of *International Shoe* governs jurisdiction here makes unnecessary any consideration of the existence of such contacts. * * * They point out that they were never personally served with a summons, that Delaware has no long-arm statute which would authorize such service, and that the Delaware Supreme Court has authoritatively held that the existence of contacts is irrelevant to jurisdiction under Del.Code Ann., Tit. 10, § 366 (1975). As part of its sequestration order, however, the Court of Chancery di-

Appellee Heitner did not allege and does not now claim that appellants have ever set foot in Delaware. Nor does he identify any act related to his cause of action as having taken place in Delaware. Nevertheless, he contends that appellants' positions as directors and officers of a corporation chartered in Delaware provide sufficient "contacts, ties, or relations" * * * with that State to give its courts jurisdiction over appellants in this stockholder's derivative action. This argument is based primarily on what Heitner asserts to be the strong interest of Delaware in supervising the management of a Delaware corporation. That interest is said to derive from the role of Delaware law in establishing the corporation and defining the obligations owed to it by its officers and directors. In order to protect this interest, appellee concludes, Delaware's courts must have jurisdiction over corporate fiduciaries such as appellants.

This argument is undercut by the failure of the Delaware Legislature to assert the state interest appellee finds so compelling. Delaware law bases jurisdiction, not on appellants' status as corporate fiduciaries, but rather on the presence of their property in the State. Although the sequestration procedure used here may be most frequently used in derivative suits against officers and directors, * * * the authorizing statute evinces no specific concern with such actions. Sequestration can be used in any suit against a nonresident * * * and reaches corporate fiduciaries only if they happen to own interests in a Delaware corporation, or other property in the State. But as Heitner's failure to secure jurisdiction over seven of the defendants named in his complaint demonstrates, there is no necessary relationship between holding a position as a corporate fiduciary and owning stock or other interests in the corporation. If Delaware perceived its interest in securing jurisdiction over corporate fiduciaries to be as great as Heitner suggests, we would expect it to have enacted a statute more clearly designed to protect that interest.

Moreover, even if Heitner's assessment of the importance of Delaware's interest is accepted, his argument fails to demonstrate that Delaware is a fair forum for this litigation. The interest appellee has identified may support the application of Delaware law to resolve any controversy over appellants' actions in their capacities as officers and directors. But we have rejected the argument that if a State's law can properly be applied to a dispute, its courts necessarily have jurisdiction over the parties to that dispute. * * *

Appellee suggests that by accepting positions as officers or directors of a Delaware corporation, appellants performed the acts [sufficient to justify the assertion of jurisdiction by Delaware courts under] Hanson v. Denckla. He notes that Delaware law provides substantial benefits to corporate officers and directors, and that these benefits were at least in part the

rected its clerk to send each appellant a copy of the summons and complaint by certified mail. The record indicates that those mailings were made and contains return receipts from at least 19 of the appellants. None of the appellants has suggested that he did not actually receive the summons which was directed to him in compliance with a Delaware statute designed to provide jurisdiction over non-residents. In these circumstances, we will assume that the procedures followed would be sufficient to bring appellants before the Delaware courts, if minimum contacts existed.

incentive for appellants to assume their positions. It is, he says, "only fair and just" to require appellants, in return for these benefits, to respond in the State of Delaware when they are accused of misusing their power. * * *

But like Heitner's first argument, this line of reasoning establishes only that it is appropriate for Delaware law to govern the obligations of appellants to Greyhound and its stockholders. It does not demonstrate that appellants have "purposefully avail[ed themselves] of the privilege of conducting activities within the forum State," Hanson v. Denckla * * *, in a way that would justify bringing them before a Delaware tribunal. Appellants have simply had nothing to do with the State of Delaware. Moreover, appellants had no reason to expect to be haled before a Delaware court. Delaware, unlike some States, has not enacted a statute that treats acceptance of a directorship as consent to jurisdiction in the State. And "[i]t strains reason * * * to suggest that anyone buying securities in a corporation formed in Delaware 'impliedly consents' to subject himself to Delaware's * * * jurisdiction on any cause of action." Folk & Moyer, [*Sequestration in Delaware: A Constitutional Analysis*, 73 Colum.L.Rev. 749, 785 (1973)] * * *. Appellants, who were not required to acquire interests in Greyhound in order to hold their positions, did not by acquiring those interests surrender their right to be brought to judgment only in States with which they had had "minimum contacts."

* * * Delaware's assertion of jurisdiction over appellants in this case is inconsistent with that constitutional limitation on state power. The judgment of the Delaware Supreme Court must, therefore, be reversed.

It is so ordered.

MR. JUSTICE REHNQUIST took no part in the consideration or decision of this case.

MR. JUSTICE POWELL, concurring.

* * *

I would explicitly reserve judgment * * * on whether the ownership of some forms of property whose situs is indisputably and permanently located within a State may, without more, provide the contacts necessary to subject a defendant to jurisdiction within the State to the extent of the value of the property. In the case of real property, in particular, preservation of the common law concept of *quasi in rem* jurisdiction arguably would avoid the uncertainty of the general *International Shoe* standard without significant cost to " 'traditional notions of fair play and substantial justice.' " * * *

Subject to the foregoing reservation, I join the opinion of the Court.

MR. JUSTICE STEVENS, concurring in the judgment.

* * *

One who purchases shares of stock on the open market can hardly be expected to know that he has thereby become subject to suit in a forum remote from his residence and unrelated to the transaction. As a practical matter, the Delaware sequestration statute creates an unacceptable risk of judgment without notice. Unlike the 49 other States, Delaware treats the place of incorporation as the situs of the stock, even though both the owner and the custodian of the shares are elsewhere. Moreover, Delaware denies the defendant the opportunity to defend the merits of the suit unless he subjects himself to the unlimited jurisdiction of the court. Thus, it coerces a defendant either to submit to personal jurisdiction in a forum which could not otherwise obtain such jurisdiction or to lose the securities which have been attached. If its procedure were upheld, Delaware would, in effect, impose a duty of inquiry on every purchaser of securities in the national market. For unless the purchaser ascertains both the State of incorporation of the company whose shares he is buying, and also the idiosyncrasies of its law, he may be assuming an unknown risk of litigation. I therefore agree with the Court that on the record before us no adequate basis for jurisdiction exists and that the Delaware statute is unconstitutional on its face.

How the Court's opinion may be applied in other contexts is not entirely clear to me. I agree with MR. JUSTICE POWELL that it should not be read to invalidate *in rem* jurisdiction where real estate is involved. I would also not read it as invalidating other long-accepted methods of acquiring jurisdiction over persons with adequate notice of both the particular controversy and the fact that their local activities might subject them to suit. My uncertainty as to the reach of the opinion, and my fear that it purports to decide a great deal more than is necessary to dispose of this case, persuade me merely to concur in the judgment.

MR. JUSTICE BRENNAN, concurring in part and dissenting in part.

I join Parts I–III of the Court's opinion. I fully agree that the minimum-contacts analysis * * * represents a far more sensible construct for the exercise of state-court jurisdiction than the patchwork of legal and factual fictions that has been generated from the decision in Pennoyer v. Neff * * *. It is precisely because the inquiry into minimum contacts is now of such overriding importance, however, that I must respectfully dissent from Part IV of the Court's opinion.

I

The primary teaching of Parts I–III of today's decision is that a State, in seeking to assert jurisdiction over a person located outside its borders, may only do so on the basis of minimum contacts among the parties, the contested transaction, and the forum state. The Delaware Supreme Court could not have made plainer, however, that its sequestration statute * * * does not operate on this basis, but instead is strictly an embodiment of *quasi in rem* jurisdiction, a jurisdictional predicate no longer constitutionally viable * * *. This state-court ruling obviously comports with the understanding of the parties, for the issue of the existence of minimum contacts was never pleaded by appellee, made the subject of discovery, or ruled upon by the Delaware courts. These facts notwithstanding, the Court in Part IV reaches the minimum-contacts question and finds such contacts lacking as applied to appellants. Succinctly stated, once having properly and persuasively decided that the *quasi in rem* statute that Delaware admits to having enacted is invalid, the Court then proceeds to find that a minimum-contacts law that Delaware express-ly *denies* having enacted also could not be constitutionally applied in this case.

In my view, a purer example of an advisory opinion is not to be found. True, appellants do not deny having received actual notice of the action in question. * * * But notice is but one ingredient of a proper assertion of state-court jurisdiction. The other is a statute authorizing the exercise of the State's judicial power along constitutionally permissible grounds—which henceforth means minimum contacts. As of today, § 366 is not such a law.[1] Recognizing that today's decision fundamentally alters the relevant jurisdictional ground rules, I certainly would not want to rule out the possibility that Delaware's courts might decide that the legislature's overriding purpose of securing the personal appearance in state courts of defendants would best be served by reinterpreting its statute to permit state jurisdiction of the basis of constitutionally permissible contacts rather than stock ownership. Were the state courts to take this step, it would then become necessary to address the question of whether mini-mum contacts exist here. But in the present posture of this case, the Court's decision of this important issue is purely an abstract ruling.

My concern with the inappropriateness of the Court's action is high-lighted by two other considerations. First, an inquiry into minimum contacts inevitably is highly dependent on creating a proper factual foundation detailing the contacts between the forum state and the contro-versy in question. Because neither the plaintiff-appellee nor the state courts viewed such an inquiry as germane in this instance, the Court today is unable to draw upon a proper factual record in reaching its conclusion; moreover, its disposition denies appellee the normal opportu-nity to seek discovery on the contacts issue. Second, it must be remem-bered that the Court's ruling is a constitutional one and necessarily will affect the reach of the jurisdictional laws of all 50 States. Ordinarily this would counsel restraint in constitutional pronouncements. * * * Cer-tainly it should have cautioned the Court against reaching out to decide a question that, as here, has yet to emerge from the state courts ripened for review on the federal issue.

II

Nonetheless, because the Court rules on the minimum-contacts ques-tion, I feel impelled to express my view. While evidence derived through discovery might satisfy me that minimum contacts are lacking in a given case, I am convinced that as a general rule a state forum has jurisdiction to adjudicate a shareholder derivative action centering on the conduct and policies of the directors and officers of a corporation chartered by that State. Unlike the Court, I therefore would not foreclose Delaware from

---

1. Indeed, the Court's decision to proceed to the minimum-contacts issue treats Dela-ware's sequestration statute as if it were the equivalent of Rhode Island's long-arm law, which specifically authorizes its courts to assume jurisdiction to the limit permitted by the Constitution, R.I.Gen.Laws Ann. § 9–5–33 (1970), thereby necessitating judicial con-sideration of the frontiers of minimum con-tacts in every case arising under that stat-ute.

asserting jurisdiction over appellants were it persuaded to do so on the basis of minimum contacts.

It is well settled that a derivative lawsuit as presented here does not inure primarily to the benefit of the named plaintiff. Rather, the primary beneficiaries are the corporation and its owners, the shareholders.
* * *

Viewed in this light, the chartering State has an unusually powerful interest in insuring the availability of a convenient forum for litigating claims involving a possible multiplicity of defendant fiduciaries and for vindicating the State's substantive policies regarding the management of its domestic corporations. I believe that our cases fairly establish that the State's valid substantive interests are important considerations in assessing whether it constitutionally may claim jurisdiction over a given cause of action.

In this instance, Delaware can point to at least three interrelated public policies that are furthered by its assertion of jurisdiction. First, the State has a substantial interest in providing restitution for its local corporations that allegedly have been victimized by fiduciary misconduct, even if the managerial decisions occurred outside the State. The importance of this general state interest in assuring restitution for its own residents previously found expression in cases that went outside the then-prevailing due process framework to authorize state-court jurisdiction over nonresident motorists who injure others within the State. * * * More recently, it has led States to seek and to acquire jurisdiction over nonresident tortfeasors whose purely out-of-state activities produce domestic consequences. * * * Second, state courts have legitimately read their jurisdiction expansively when a cause of action centers in an area in which the forum State possesses a manifest regulatory interest. * * * Only this Term we reiterated that the conduct of corporate fiduciaries is just such a matter in which the policies and interests of a domestic forum are paramount. * * * Finally, a State like Delaware has a recognized interest in affording a convenient forum for supervising and overseeing the affairs of an entity that is purely the creation of that State's law. For example, even following our decision in *International Shoe,* New York courts were permitted to exercise complete judicial authority over nonresident beneficiaries of a trust created under state law, even though, unlike appellants here, the beneficiaries personally entered into no association whatsoever with New York. Mullane v. Central Hanover Bank & Trust Co., 339 U.S. 306, 313, 70 S.Ct. 652, 656, 94 L.Ed. 865 (1950) * * *.

To be sure, the Court is not blind to these considerations. It notes that the State's interests "may support the application of Delaware law to resolve any controversy over appellants' actions in their capacities as officers and directors." * * * But this, the Court argues, pertains to choice of law, not jurisdiction. I recognize that the jurisdictional and choice-of-law inquiries are not identical. * * * But I would not compartmentalize thinking in this area quite so rigidly as it seems to me the Court does today, for both inquiries "are often closely related and to a substantial degree depend upon similar considerations." [Hanson v.

Denckla, 357 U.S.] at 258, 78 S.Ct. at 1242 (Black, J., dissenting). * * * At the minimum, the decision that it is fair to bind a defendant by a State's laws and rules should prove to be highly relevant to the fairness of permitting that same State to accept jurisdiction for adjudicating the controversy.

Furthermore, I believe that practical considerations argue in favor of seeking to bridge the distance between the choice-of-law and jurisdictional inquiries. Even when a court would apply the law of a different forum, as a general rule it will feel less knowledgeable and comfortable in interpretation, and less interested in fostering the policies of that foreign jurisdiction, than would the courts established by the State that provides the applicable law. * * * Obviously, such choice-of-law problems cannot entirely be avoided in a diverse legal system such as our own. Nonetheless, when a suitor seeks to lodge a suit in a State with a substantial interest in seeing its own law applied to the transaction in question, we could wisely act to minimize conflicts, confusion, and uncertainty by adopting a liberal view of jurisdiction, unless considerations of fairness or efficiency strongly point in the opposite direction.

This case is not one where, in my judgment, this preference for jurisdiction is adequately answered. Certainly nothing said by the Court persuades me that it would be unfair to subject appellants to suit in Delaware. The fact that the record does not reveal whether they "set foot" or committed "acts related to [the] cause of action" in Delaware * * * is not decisive, for jurisdiction can be based strictly on out-of-state acts having foreseeable effects in the forum State. * * * I have little difficulty in applying this principle to nonresident fiduciaries whose alleged breaches of trust are said to have substantial damaging effect on the financial posture of a resident corporation. Further, I cannot understand how the existence of minimum contacts in a constitutional sense is at all affected by Delaware's failure statutorily to express an interest in controlling corporate fiduciaries. * * * To me this simply demonstrates that Delaware did not elect to assert jurisdiction to the extent the Constitution would allow. Nor would I view as controlling or even especially meaningful Delaware's failure to exact from appellants their consent to be sued. * * * Once we have rejected the jurisdictional framework created in Pennoyer v. Neff, I see no reason to rest jurisdiction on a fictional outgrowth of that system such as the existence of a consent statute, expressed or implied.

I, therefore, would approach the minimum-contacts analysis differently than does the Court. Crucial to me is the fact that appellants voluntarily associated themselves with the State of Delaware, "invoking the benefits and protections of its laws," * * * by entering into a long-term and fragile relationship with one of its domestic corporations. They thereby elected to assume powers and to undertake responsibilities wholly derived from that State's rules and regulations, and to become eligible for those benefits that Delaware law makes available to its corporations' officials. E.g., Del.Code Ann., Tit. 8, § 143 (1975) (interest-free loans); § 145 (1975 ed. and Supp.1976) (indemnification). While it is possible that countervailing issues of judicial efficiency and the like might clearly favor a different forum, they do not appear on the meager record before us; and, of course, we are concerned solely with "minimum" contacts, not the "best" contacts. *   *   *

Notes and Questions

1. Within thirteen days after the decision in *Shaffer,* the Delaware legislature amended its laws to provide that every nonresident who is elected or appointed a director of a Delaware corporation after September 1, 1977, shall "be deemed" to have consented to the appointment of the corporation's registered agent in Delaware, or, if there is no registered agent, of the Secretary of State of Delaware, as his agent for service of process in any Delaware action based on violation of the director's duties as director after September 1, 1977. 10 Del.Code § 3114. The constitutionality of the section was upheld by the Supreme Court of Delaware in Armstrong v. Pomerance, 423 A.2d 174 (Del.1980), a suit against nonresidents whose sole contact with Delaware was their status as directors of a Delaware corporation. See also Stearn v. Malloy, 89 F.R.D. 421 (E.D.Wis.1981) (reaching the same conclusion under a similar Wisconsin statute). See Comment, *Constitutional Analysis of the New Delaware Director-Consent-to-Service Statute,* 70 Geo.L.J. 1209 (1983). In PESTOLITE, INC. v. CORDURA CORP., 449 A.2d 263 (Del.Super.1982), the court held that the statute allowed suits against directors for breach of the fiduciary duties they owed to the corporation or its shareholders, but not for consumer actions in tort or contract arising from the sale of the corporation's products. But see In re Mid-Atlantic Toyota Antitrust Litigation, 525 F.Supp. 1265, modified 541 F.Supp. 62 (D.Md.1981).

Greyhound Corporation, shortly after the enactment of the Delaware directors-consent-to-service statute, sought and obtained the approval of its shareholders to reincorporate in Arizona, where Greyhound also has its principal headquarters. A stated reason was that "it would be an unreasonable burden upon directors, not resident in Delaware, several of whom reside in Arizona and California, to be required to journey to Delaware to defend a case there when they have no contact with that state." Ratner & Schwartz, *The Impact of Shaffer v. Heitner on the Substantive Law of Corporations,* 45 Brooklyn L.Rev. 641, 653–54 (1979).

2. Does *Shaffer* preclude a state from rendering a judgment in a pure in rem action that is binding against the world? In this regard, is footnote 37 of Justice Marshall's opinion relevant?

3. In RHOADES v. WRIGHT, 622 P.2d 343 (Utah 1980), certiorari denied 454 U.S. 897, 102 S.Ct. 397, 70 L.Ed.2d 212 (1981), the court upheld the attachment for jurisdictional purposes of farm land in Utah owned by the defendant, a resident of Colorado, who was being sued for the wrongful death of a Utah resident killed outside Utah. The court considered the presence of the land (as distinguished from the kind of intangible and movable property involved in *Shaffer*), together with the fact that the Colorado defendant actively used the land, sufficient contacts with Utah to satisfy due process requirements for the exercise of quasi-in-rem jurisdiction.

4. Does *Shaffer* overturn Harris v. Balk? In FEDER v. TURKISH AIRLINES, 441 F.Supp. 1273 (S.D.N.Y.1977), quasi-in-rem jurisdiction was

upheld based on the attachment of the defendant's New York bank account. The bank account, established by the airline to pay for aircraft parts and components, was the airline's only contact with the forum. The action was a wrongful-death suit stemming from an accident that occurred in Turkey. The plaintiffs were New York residents. Is the result in *Feder* consistent with *Shaffer?*

5. Can an insurance obligation be attached? In SEIDER v. ROTH, 17 N.Y.2d 111, 269 N.Y.S.2d 99, 216 N.E.2d 312 (1966), the plaintiffs attached the obligation of an automobile insurance company to indemnify an out-of-state policy holder, and jurisdiction was upheld. New York's highest court held that the contractual obligation constituted a debt that was subject to attachment.

After *Shaffer,* the Second Circuit concluded that "[t]he fall of Harris v. Balk * * * does not necessarily topple *Seider.*" O'CONNOR v. LEE–HY PAVING CORP., 579 F.2d 194, 199 (2d Cir.), certiorari denied 439 U.S. 1034, 99 S.Ct. 639, 58 L.Ed.2d 696 (1978). The court distinguished *Shaffer* and *Harris* as cases in which the property that furnished the basis for quasi-in-rem jurisdiction was completely unrelated to plaintiff's claim, while in *O'Connor* the attached property was an insurance policy that was purchased to protect against the type of liability that was the subject of the lawsuit.

The United States Supreme Court laid the *Seider* doctrine to rest in RUSH v. SAVCHUK, 444 U.S. 320, 100 S.Ct. 571, 62 L.Ed.2d 516 (1980). In finding the attachment of an insurance policy to effect quasi-in-rem jurisdiction unconstitutional, the Court separated the contacts between the defendant and the forum from the contacts between the insurer and the forum. Having done so, the Court held that sufficient contacts between the defendant and the forum did not exist and that the Due Process Clause forbade assertion of jurisdiction.

6. Can a federal admiralty court after *Shaffer* exercise jurisdiction based on an attachment of property in the district when the defendant otherwise lacks contacts with the forum? In AMOCO OVERSEAS OIL CO. v. COMPAGNIE NATIONALE ALGERIENNE DE NAVIGATION, 605 F.2d 648, 655 (2d Cir.1979), the court upheld jurisdiction based on the attachment of a foreign corporation's bank account in New York. The court distinguished *Shaffer* stressing, in part, the special history of admiralty jurisdiction:

> * * * *Shaffer* did not consider assertion of jurisdiction over property in the admiralty context. Because the perpetrators of maritime injury are likely to be peripatetic, Ex Parte Louisville Underwriters, 134 U.S. 488, 493, 10 S.Ct. 587, 33 L.Ed. 991 (1890), and since the constitutional power of the federal courts is separately derived in admiralty, U.S. Constitution Art. III § 2, suits under admiralty jurisdiction involve separate policies to some extent. This tradition suggests not only that jurisdiction by attachment of property should be accorded special deference in the admiralty context, but also that maritime actors must reasonably expect to be sued where their property may be found.

The court also considered it relevant to the jurisdictional issue that the property attached was related to the matter in controversy and that, if jurisdiction was not exercised, defendant might not be amenable to suit at all in the United States. Is this a satisfactory explanation for depriving due process rights?

7. Some state long-arm statutes may be less inclusive than the constitutional grant of jurisdiction under the Due Process Clause. In BANCO AMBROSIANO v. ARTOC BANK & TRUST LTD., 62 N.Y.2d 65, 476 N.Y.S.2d 64, 464 N.E.2d 432 (1984), a New York court, although finding the defendant, a bank organized under the laws of the Bahamas, had minimum contacts, declined to assert in personam jurisdiction over the defendant. The court, however, did exercise quasi-in-rem jurisdiction over the defendant with respect to an account it kept in a New York bank that was reasonably related to the dispute brought before it.

8. In light of *Shaffer*, reconsider the holding in Grace v. MacArthur, p. 73, supra. The opinions in *Shaffer* implicitly suggest that a majority of the Court (all but Justices Powell and Stevens) would not uphold a state's exercise of in personam jurisdiction over a transient individual, with no other contacts with the state, based solely on the individual's presence in the forum and service of process upon the individual while there. But some of the relatively few post-*Shaffer* courts that explicitly have considered the question have upheld the exercise of jurisdiction. Amusement Equipment, Inc. v. Mordelt, 779 F.2d 264 (5th Cir.1985); Driver v. Helms, 577 F.2d 147 (1st Cir.1978), certiorari denied 439 U.S. 1114, 99 S.Ct. 1016, 59 L.Ed.2d 72 (1979); Opert v. Schmid, 535 F.Supp. 591 (S.D.N.Y.1982); Cariaga v. Karatz, ___ Nev. ___, 762 P.2d 886 (1988); Humphrey v. Langford, 246 Ga. 732, 273 S.E.2d 22 (1980); Oxmans' Erwin Meat Co. v. Blacketer, 86 Wis.2d 683, 273 N.W.2d 285 (1979). Is the explanation for the persistence of this view the fact that personal presence in a state is per se sufficient contact with the state to satisfy due process requirements?

In HUMPHREY v. LANGFORD, 246 Ga. 732, 273 S.E.2d 22 (1980), the parties made a contract in South Carolina that was to be executed in that state. Subsequently, Humphrey moved to Georgia and sued in a Georgia state court for breach of contract. Langford was "tagged" while competing in a bowling tournament in Georgia. The court exercised jurisdiction based solely on the service of process in Georgia:

> We are aware the various commentators have suggested that *Shaffer* represented the end of jurisdiction merely by personal service on a transient within the forum. We, however, believe that there are compelling reasons to uphold such jurisdiction rather than strike it down based upon cases which do not mandate such a result. We believe it is not practical to have classifications of sojourners in the state. Where does a court draw the line between sojourners here for an evening of bowling and sojourners who commute to the state on a daily basis?

Id. at 734, 273 S.E.2d at 24. Is the court refusing to do precisely the kind of line drawing that the minimum contacts test mandates?

In MAISON LAYARD ET COMPAGNIE v. BECKER, (unreported) (S.D. Cal.1984), the plaintiff "tagged" Becker, both individually and as an agent of other German defendants, while he was in San Diego attending a convention. The defendants challenged jurisdiction, citing *Shaffer* as requiring an assessment of contacts with the jurisdiction even when a defendant has been tagged therein. The court accepted the defendants' argument and ruled that jurisdiction did not exist.

> If one is to read the mandate of *Shaffer* as anything other than loose lips that sink ships, the court meant what it said; that in fact there

should be an analysis of minimum contacts to this particular defendant.
* * *

Commentators have long insisted that it is foolhardy to continue to apply the presence doctrine of *Pennoyer* to cases where a person instead of property is present in a state. Logically, it makes no sense to stick to the *Pennoyer* rationale when you require a minimum contacts test for *in rem jurisdiction.* * * *

I [therefore] hold that simply being handed service of process in a forum is not an action sufficient to overcome the problems associated with subjecting a non-resident to suit in a forum the defendant has no other relationship with.

9. For an excellent discussion of *Shaffer,* see Silberman, *Shaffer v. Heitner: The End of an Era,* 53 N.Y.U.L.Rev. 33 (1978). Further commentary is found in symposia on the impact of *Shaffer* in 45 Brooklyn L.Rev. 493 (1979); 1978 Wash.U.L.Q. 273. See also Maltz, *Reflections on a Landmark: Shaffer v. Heitner Viewed From a Distance,* 1986 B.Y.U.L.Rev. 1043; Nordenberg, *State Courts, Personal Jurisdiction and the Evolutionary Process,* 54 Notre Dame Law. 587 (1979); Riesenfeld, *Shaffer v. Heitner: Holding, Implications, Forebodings,* 30 Hastings L.J. 1183 (1979); Smit, *The Enduring Utility of In Rem Rules: A Lasting Legacy of Pennoyer v. Neff,* 43 Brooklyn L.Rev. 600 (1977).

SECTION C. OTHER BASES OF JURISDICTION: CONSENT AND NECESSITY

1. CONSENT

Earlier we saw that even under the regime of Pennoyer v. Neff, p. 66, supra, a defendant could consent to personal jurisdiction. In the simplest case, a defendant consents to personal jurisdiction either by expressly agreeing to submit to the court or by performing certain acts that constitute a waiver of objections to personal jurisdiction. For example, Rule 12(h)(1) of the Federal Rules provides that a defendant who fails to raise an objection to personal jurisdiction in the answer or in an initial motion under Rule 12 is subsequently precluded from raising the issue. Not all consent cases are "simple," however. As you read the following case, note that it seems that a defendant can consent to varying levels of involvement in a lawsuit.

INSURANCE CORP. OF IRELAND v. COMPAGNIE DES BAUXITES DE GUINEE, 456 U.S. 694, 102 S.Ct. 2099, 72 L.Ed.2d 492 (1982). The plaintiff, Compagnie des Bauxites de Guinee (CBG), a bauxite producer incorporated in Delaware but doing business only in the Republic of Guinea, had purchased business-interruption insurance from a domestic insurer in Pennsylvania and from a group of foreign insurance companies through a London brokerage house. When a mechanical failure forced a halt in production, CBG filed a multi-million dollar claim, which the insurers refused to pay. CBG then sued in federal court in Pennsylvania, but most of the foreign insurance companies contested personal jurisdiction. CBG attempted to use discovery to establish the essential jurisdictional facts. After the companies failed to comply with the court's orders for production of the requested information and after repeated warnings, the District Court, pursuant to Rule 37(b)(2)(A), imposed a sanction consisting of a presumptive finding that the insurers were subject to the jurisdiction of the court because of their business contacts in Pennsylvania. The Supreme Court upheld the sanction.

* * * The requirement that a court have personal jurisdiction flows not from Art. III, but from the Due Process Clause. * * *

Because the requirement of personal jurisdiction represents first of all an individual right, it can, like other such rights, be waived. * * *

* * * By submitting to the jurisdiction of the court for the limited purpose of challenging jurisdiction, the defendant agrees to abide by that court's determination on the issue of jurisdiction * * *, [and] the manner in which the court determines whether it has personal jurisdiction may include a variety of legal rules and presumptions, as well as straightforward factfinding. * * *

CBG was seeking through discovery to respond to [the insurers'] contention that the District Court did not have personal jurisdiction. Having put the issue in question, [the insurers] did not have the option of blocking the reasonable attempt of CBG to meet its burden of proof. [They] surely did not have this option once the court had overruled [their] objections. Because of [the insurers'] failure to comply with the discovery orders, CBG was unable to establish the full extent of the contacts between [the insurers] and Pennsylvania, the critical issue in proving personal jurisdiction. [Their] failure to supply the requested information as to [their] contacts with Pennsylvania supports "the presumption that the refusal to produce evidence * * * was but an admission of the want of merit in the asserted defense." * * * The sanction took as established the facts—contacts with Pennsylvania—that CBG was seeking to establish through discovery.

Id. at 702–09, 102 S.Ct. at 2104–08, 72 L.Ed.2d at 501–05.

Notes and Questions

1. In *Ireland*, the defendants appeared to contest jurisdiction. Is it not clear that by making the special appearance they at least consented to the adjudication of that issue by the district court? Does that obligate them to abide by the rules—including the discovery rules—laid down by the court to govern determination of the issue? Was it necessary to base the holding in *Ireland* on concepts of waiver and consent? Isn't the authority of a federal court to determine its jurisdiction implicit in the grant of limited jurisdiction? And, if a court always has jurisdiction to determine whether it has jurisdiction, doesn't that mean that it has authority to force the parties, including the defendant, to cooperate in helping it to resolve that question?

2. Is the imposition of burdens of production in a distant place one of the core elements of unfairness that the due process cases from *International Shoe* to *World-Wide Volkswagen* sought to avoid? It is small comfort to the defendant that the cost is being imposed only for the purpose of determining whether or not the court has the authority to impose it. Does the Due

Process Clause require the plaintiff to make a showing of any kind before the defendant can be forced to produce documents and witnesses for discovery in a distant forum? What if the defendant could make a prima facie showing both of absence of minimum contacts related to the claim and of absence of continuous and substantial forum presence?

3. We have seen earlier that consent to personal jurisdiction often will be implied from the defendant's conduct preceding the lawsuit. See pages 75–77, supra. In most states a foreign corporation that registers as a condition of doing business in a state is regarded as having consented to suit in the courts of that state even as to actions unconnected with the corporation's activities in the forum. See, e.g., N.Y. Bus. Corp. Law §§ 304, 1306; Schreiber v. Allis-Chalmers Corp., 611 F.2d 790 (10th Cir.1979); Springle v. Cottrell Eng'r Corp., 40 Md.App. 267, 391 A.2d 456 (1978). But is it true that the consent extracted from a foreign corporation as a condition of doing business in a state, as Justice Holmes observed, is a "mere fiction," Flexner v. Farson, 248 U.S. 289, 39 S.Ct. 97, 63 L.Ed. 250 (1919), and that under general due process principles the fiction should not be invoked unless the requisite "minimum contacts" exist? In RATLIFF v. COOPER LABS., INC., 444 F.2d 745 (4th Cir.), certiorari denied 404 U.S. 948, 92 S.Ct. 271, 30 L.Ed.2d 265 (1971), the Court of Appeals held that a foreign corporation that had qualified to do business in South Carolina and regularly sent salesmen into the state could not be sued in South Carolina by plaintiffs from Florida and Indiana who purchased and consumed in their home states drugs manufactured by the defendant, and who sued in South Carolina because of that state's relatively long statute of limitations: "Applying for the privilege of doing business is one thing, but the actual exercise of that privilege is quite another. * * * The principles of due process require a firmer foundation than mere compliance with state domestication statutes." See also In re Mid-Atlantic Toyota Antitrust Litigation, 525 F.Supp. 1265, modified 541 F.Supp. 62 (D.Md.1981).

4. If a foreign corporation, not authorized, and not doing business in a state, represents to the plaintiff that it is so authorized, may the corporation be estopped from denying jurisdiction over it in a subsequent lawsuit? In FARMINGDALE STEER–INN, INC. v. STEER INN REALTY CORP., 51 Misc. 2d 986, 274 N.Y.S.2d 379 (Sup.Ct.1966), the New York court concluded that it would be unfair to permit a defendant, which had represented that it was authorized to do business in New York, to assert later on that it was not subject to jurisdiction. The facts in the *Steer Inn* case were particularly egregious, since the corporation represented not merely that it was doing business in New York, but that it was in fact authorized by the Secretary of State to do business.

How far can this notion of estoppel be pushed? Suppose that the National Widget Corporation bills itself in its advertising as "a manufacturer servicing the nation's need for widgets." In fact, National Widget, a Montana Corporation, never has sold a widget to anyone outside of the northwestern United States. Can National Widget be sued in New York on the ground that it has consented to jurisdiction anywhere in the United States by virtue of its advertisement? Can it be prevented from contesting jurisdiction by virtue of its prior statement? Would it matter if it could be shown that a market for widgets only exists west of the Mississippi?

The possibility of jurisdiction by consent is not limited to situations in which a defendant, in one form or another, consents to jurisdiction in an ongoing action. Frequently, in forming a contract, the parties will draft an express agreement to submit to personal jurisdiction. Sometimes they will agree to submit to the jurisdiction of a designated court for any action arising out of the transaction. Sometimes they will agree to submit to the jurisdiction of a designated court—to the exclusion of all others—for any action arising out of the transaction. And, sometimes they will agree to submit to the jurisdiction of *any* court for any action arising out of the transaction. Consider the agreement and resulting dispute in the case that follows.

THE BREMEN v. ZAPATA OFF–SHORE CO., 407 U.S. 1, 92 S.Ct. 1907, 32 L.Ed.2d 513 (1972). Plaintiff Zapata, a Houston-based American corporation, contracted with Unterweser, a German corporation, to tow Zapata's drilling rig from Louisiana to Italy. The contract contained a provision that all disputes were to be litigated before the "London Court of Justice." The Bremen was the ship Unterweser used to tow the drilling rig. In the course of the towing, the rig was damaged in a storm off Florida, and was towed to Tampa. Zapata commenced suit against Unterweser in a federal court in Florida. Unterweser, citing the forum-selection clause in the contract, moved to dismiss, or, alternatively, to stay the action pending the submission of the dispute to the High Court of Justice in London. Simultaneously, Unterweser sued Zapata for breach of contract in the English court.

The District Court refused to dismiss or stay the American action, and the Court of Appeals affirmed. But the Supreme Court reversed:

> We hold * * * that far too little weight and effect were given to the forum clause in resolving this controversy. * * * The expansion of American business and industry will hardly be encouraged if, notwithstanding solemn contracts, we insist on a parochial concept that all disputes must be resolved under our laws and in our courts. * * * We cannot have trade and commerce in world markets and international waters exclusively on our terms, governed by our laws, and resolved in our courts.

Id. at 8–9, 92 S.Ct. at 1912–13, 32 L.Ed.2d at 519–20.

Notes and Questions

1. The *Zapata* Court indicates that forum-selection clauses will be enforced "unless enforcement is shown by the resisting parties to be 'unreasonable' under the circumstances." What factors should enter a trial court's assessment of the reasonableness of the stipulated forum? The bargaining power of the parties to the contract? The identity of the party who drafted the contract? The relative convenience of litigating the case where it was brought as opposed to the stipulated forum? The substantive law that would apply?

2. In evaluating whether or not to give force to a forum-selection clause, to what extent should the court consider its interest in adjudicating the dispute? For example, in *Zapata,* did the district court have an interest in regulating activity in the territorial waters of the United States? What about the sovereign's interest in providing a forum for its citizens? To what extent

does the Supreme Court balance these interests against the interests of business people who want to know that contractual provisions will be enforced?

3.   Suppose a plaintiff sues a defendant for breach of contract, choosing a forum other than the one demanded by a forum-selection clause in the contract.   The defendant, invoking the forum-selection clause, objects to jurisdiction.   Is *Zapata* dispositive in all cases?

4.   See generally Gruson, *Forum-Selection Clauses in International and Interstate Commercial Agreements,* 1982 U.Ill.L.Rev. 133.

2. NECESSITY

Given *Shaffer,* the pure in rem action might be viewed as a situation in which the court takes jurisdiction over the parties by necessity.   The typical in rem action entails a court determining the ownership of a res that is binding with respect to all other potential claim holders.   See, e.g., Tyler v. Judges of the Court of Registration, p. 147, supra.   Since some of the potential claim holders are unknown, and many probably lack the requisite minimum contacts with the forum, it appears that the exercise of jurisdiction by any court would violate *Shaffer.*   However, it is important to the smooth functioning of society that the title holders of property be identified, and it is vital that persons be able to purchase property without risking loss of the title in subsequent suits.   Consequently, actions to quiet title appear to have survived *Shaffer,* as a form of jurisdiction by necessity.

Other situations may exist when no one forum is capable of exercising jurisdiction over all of the litigants.   In that regard, consider MULLANE v. CENTRAL HANOVER BANK & TRUST CO., 339 U.S. 306, 70 S.Ct. 652, 94 L.Ed. 865 (1950), which involved a challenge to provisions of the New York Banking Law authorizing the creation of "common trusts."

A little background information is necessary.   Because mounting overhead had made the administration of small trusts undesirable to corporate trustees (thereby depriving donors and testators of small trusts of the service of corporate fiduciaries), several states (including New York) passed legislation permitting the pooling of small trust estates into one fund for investment administration.   Under the New York act, a trust company could establish a common fund and, within prescribed limits, invest in it the assets of an unlimited number of estates, trusts, or other funds of which it was trustee.   Each participating trust shared ratably in the common fund, but exclusive management and control was in the trust company as trustee.   Provision was made for an accounting twelve to fifteen months after the establishment of the fund and triennially thereafter.   The decree in each judicial settlement of accounts was made binding and conclusive as to any matter set forth in the account upon everyone having any interest in the common fund or in any participating estate, trust or fund.

In January, 1946, the Central Hanover Bank and Trust Company established a common fund in accordance with these provisions, and in March, 1947, it petitioned the Surrogate's Court for settlement of its first account as common trustee. During the accounting period a total of 113 trusts, approximately half *inter vivos* and half testamentary, participated in the common trust fund, the gross capital of which was nearly three million dollars. The record does not show the number or residence of the beneficiaries, but they were many and it is clear that some of them were not residents of New York.

Upon the filing of the petition for the settlement of accounts, Mullane was appointed special guardian and attorney for all persons known or unknown not otherwise appearing who had or might thereafter have any interest in the income of the common trust fund; and another attorney was appointed to represent those similarly interested in the principal. There were no other appearances on behalf of anyone interested in either interest or principal.

Mullane appeared specially, objecting that the court was without jurisdiction to render a final and binding decree. The Surrogate rejected his jurisdictional argument, however, and entered a final decree accepting the accounts. The Appellate Division and the Court of Appeals affirmed. The effect of this decree was to settle "all questions respecting the management of the common fund." Every right that beneficiaries otherwise would have against the trust company, either as trustee of the common fund or as trustee of any individual trust, for improper management of the common trust fund during the period covered by the accounting was sealed and wholly terminated by the decree.

Mullane appealed to the United States Supreme Court. The Court found no problem with the assertion of jurisdiction by the New York courts. Writing for the Court, Justice Jackson said:

> We are met at the outset with a challenge to the power of the State— the right of its courts to adjudicate at all as against those beneficiaries who reside without the State of New York. It is contended that the proceeding is one *in personam* in that the decree affects neither title to nor possession of any *res,* but adjudges only personal rights of the beneficiaries to surcharge their trustee for negligence or breach of trust. Accordingly, it is said, under the strict doctrine of Pennoyer v. Neff * * * the Surrogate is without jurisdiction as to nonresidents upon whom personal service of process was not made.

> Distinctions between actions *in rem* and those *in personam* are ancient and originally expressed in procedural terms what seems really to have been a distinction in the substantive law of property under a system quite unlike our own. * * * The legal recognition and rise in economic importance of incorporeal or intangible forms of property have upset the ancient simplicity of property law and the clarity of its distinctions, while new forms of proceedings have confused the old procedural classification. American courts have sometimes classed certain actions as *in rem* because personal service of process was not required, and at other times have held personal service of process not required because the action was *in rem.* * * *

> Judicial proceedings to settle fiduciary accounts have been sometimes termed *in rem,* or more indefinitely *quasi in rem,* or more vaguely still,

"in the nature of a proceeding *in rem.*" It is not readily apparent how the courts of New York did or would classify the present proceeding, which has some characteristics and is wanting in some features of proceedings both *in rem* and *in personam.* But in any event we think that the requirements of the Fourteenth Amendment to the Federal Constitution do not depend upon a classification for which the standards are so elusive and confused generally and which, being primarily for state courts to define, may and do vary from state to state. Without disparaging the usefulness of distinctions between actions *in rem* and those *in personam* in many branches of law, or on other issues, or the reasoning which underlies them, we do not rest the power of the State to resort to constructive service in this proceeding upon how its courts or this Court may regard this historic antithesis. It is sufficient to observe that, whatever the technical definition of its chosen procedure, the interest of each state in providing means to close trusts that exist by the grace of its laws and are administered under the supervision of its courts is so insistent and rooted in custom as to establish beyond doubt the right of its courts to determine the interests of all claimants, resident or nonresident, provided its procedure accords full opportunity to appear and be heard.

Id. at 311–13, 70 S.Ct. at 656, 94 L.Ed. at 872.

Notes and Questions

1. Why was jurisdiction in *Mullane* an issue at all? Hadn't the trustees and beneficiaries of the individual trusts consented to having the account settled in New York by joining a common trust established in New York under New York's laws?

2. The *Mullane* decision seems to suggest that jurisdiction may sometimes be exercised in an action involving multiple and indeterminate parties because practical necessity requires that at least one forum have the power to adjudicate the conflicting claims. The argument appears strongest in the typical in rem action, in which the rights of all potential claimants to the property are settled. Is necessity a better explanation for the exercise of jurisdiction in these cases than the protean concept of "minimum contacts"? See generally Fraser, *Jurisdiction by Necessity—An Analysis of the Mullane Case,* 100 U.Pa.L.Rev. 305 (1951).

3. What interests are sufficiently compelling to justify the forum's exercise of personal jurisdiction over nonresidents out of a sense of necessity? The decision in *World-Wide Volkswagen* indicates, does it not, that jurisdiction by necessity is not justified by a desire to afford complete relief to the parties or to avoid the possibility of conflicting results that inheres in piecemeal litigation? Is it relevant that in *World-Wide Volkswagen* jurisdiction over all the parties was available under conventional standards in New York? In HELICOPTEROS NACIONALES DE COLOMBIA, S.A. v. HALL, 466 U.S. 408, 419 n. 13, 104 S.Ct. 1868, 1874 n. 13, 80 L.Ed.2d 404, 414 n. 13 (1984), see p. 89, supra, the Court was asked to permit Texas to assume jurisdiction over three defendants—a Colombian corporation with its principal place of business in Colombia (Helicol), a Peruvian alter ego of a Texas joint venture, and a helicopter manufacturer that did substantial business in Texas—on the basis of necessity. The Court said:

As an alternative to traditional minimum contacts analysis, respondents suggest that the Court hold that the State of Texas had personal jurisdiction over Helicol under a doctrine of "jurisdiction by necessity." * * * We conclude, however, that respondents failed to carry their burden of showing that all three defendants could not be sued together in a single forum. It is not clear from the record, for example, whether suit could have been brought against all three defendants in either Colombia or Peru. We decline to consider adoption of a doctrine of jurisdiction by necessity—a potentially far-reaching modification of existing law—in the absence of a more complete record.

4. In WESTERN UNION TEL. CO. v. PENNSYLVANIA, 368 U.S. 71, 82 S.Ct. 199, 7 L.Ed.2d 139 (1961), the Supreme Court stated:

> * * * [W]hen a state court's jurisdiction purports to be based, as here, on the presence of property within the State, the holder of such property is deprived of due process of law if he is compelled to relinquish it without assurance that he will not be held liable again in another jurisdiction or in a suit brought by a claimant who is not bound by the first judgment. * * *

Id. at 75, 82 S.Ct. at 201, 7 L.Ed.2d at 142. Does a court have to dismiss a suit by a resident claimant against the stakeholder if there are potential nonresident claimants who cannot be brought within the jurisdiction of the court? Is necessity a function of the stakeholder's due process rights?

5. In NEW YORK LIFE INSURANCE CO. v. DUNLEVY, 241 U.S. 518, 36 S.Ct. 613, 60 L.Ed. 1140 (1916), the Supreme Court affirmed a judgment of the United States District Court in California requiring an insurance company to pay the full cash surrender value of a life insurance policy to the assignee of the policyholder, despite a prior Pennsylvania judgment in favor of the assignor rendered in a suit to which the assignee could not be joined under the notions of jurisdiction prevailing at the time. Partially in response to the *Dunlevy* decision, Congress passed the Federal Interpleader Act in 1917. The statute was successively broadened in 1926 and 1936 and was reconstituted in 1948 as part of the United States Judicial Code. It now appears as 28 U.S.C. §§ 1335, 1397, 2361. The present Interpleader Act manifests a congressional intent to avoid the imposition of double liability occasioned by constitutional limits on the jurisdiction of state courts. Section 2361 permits a federal district court to serve process nationwide in order to reach all of the claimants. Does the presence of the Federal Interpleader Act make it easier or harder to justify jurisdiction by a state court based on necessity?

6. ATKINSON v. SUPERIOR COURT, 49 Cal.2d 338, 342–43, 345–48, 316 P.2d 960, 963–66 (1957), certiorari denied 357 U.S. 569, 78 S.Ct. 1381, 2 L.Ed.2d 1546 (1958). Plaintiff musicians attacked the validity of certain collective bargaining and related trust agreements between their employers and the American Federation of Musicians. Plaintiffs' theory was that the union had violated its duty as collective bargaining agent in agreeing that certain royalty payments, allegedly wages, be diverted to a trust created to further the public's knowledge and appreciation of music. At the commencement of this suit, the plaintiffs moved for the appointment of a receiver to collect the payments and preliminary injunctions to prevent the employers from making the payments to the trustee. The union and the employers were personally served in California; the trustee was served in New York pursuant

to a court order, but did not appear. The lower court held that it had no jurisdiction over the trustee, who was an indispensable party to the action. The California Supreme Court, however, upheld quasi-in-rem jurisdiction in an opinion by Justice Traynor:

> In the present case, since the trustee is not and has not been a resident of California, section 417 of the Code of Civil Procedure precludes the entry of a personal judgment against him, and it is therefore unnecessary to determine whether his activities as trustee have sufficient connection with this state constitutionally to justify an assumption of personal jurisdiction without service of process here. The relevant contacts with this state are significant, however, in deciding whether due process permits exercising a more limited or quasi in rem jurisdiction to determine his and plaintiffs' interests in the intangibles in question.

> * * * The obligation plaintiffs seek to enforce grows out of their employment by defendants here. The payments involved are alleged to be consideration for work performed in this state. The Federation defendant is before the court. Under these circumstances, fairness to plaintiffs demands that they be able to reach the fruits of their labors before they are removed from the state. Moreover, fairness to the defendants who are personally before the court also demands that the conflicting claims of the trustee be subject to final adjudication. Even if we were to hold that his absence prevents the granting of the provisional remedies here sought, plaintiffs would not be foreclosed thereby from asserting that payment to him did not discharge the employers' obligation to them and that the Federation was independently liable for damages for breach of its fiduciary duty. The evil of exposing the obligor to actions to enforce the same obligation in two jurisdictions with the attendant risk of double liability would not be obviated. It was just such double liability that was sustained in the Dunlevy case and gave impetus to the passage of federal interpleader legislation. * * * It is doubtful whether today the United States Supreme Court would deny to a state court the interstate interpleader jurisdiction that federal courts may exercise. A remedy that a federal court may provide without violating due process of law does not become unfair or unjust because it is sought in a state court instead.

Can it be said that California had jurisdiction by necessity in *Atkinson*? In what sense was jurisdiction necessary to protect the rights of the plaintiff musicians? It was after all the employers who faced the risk of multiple payments. Is jurisdiction necessary because under California procedure the trustee was an indispensable party without whom the case could not proceed? Can a state bootstrap itself into jurisdiction by its rules governing the necessary joinder of a party?

7. Under the principle of "continuing jurisdiction," once a state obtains jurisdiction over a party to an action, jurisdiction continues throughout all subsequent stages of the litigation. The "extent to which jurisdiction continues * * * depends upon two factors: the needs of judicial administration and fairness to the defendant." Restatement (Second), Conflict of Laws § 26, comment *a* (1971). The classic statement of the principle is found in Justice

Holmes' opinion in MICHIGAN TRUST CO. v. FERRY, 228 U.S. 346, 353, 33 S.Ct. 550, 552, 57 L.Ed. 867, 874 (1913). Ferry had been appointed executor of an estate by a Michigan court in 1867, and moved to Utah in 1878. The Michigan court in 1903, at the behest of the beneficiaries under the will, removed Ferry as executor and decreed that he owed the estate nearly a million dollars. The Supreme Court held that the Michigan court's decree was owed full faith and credit, and had to be enforced by the courts of Utah.

> * * * [I]f a judicial proceeding is begun with jurisdiction over the person of the party concerned it is within the power of a State to bind him by every subsequent order in the cause. * * * This is true not only of ordinary actions but of proceedings like the present. It is within the power of a State to make the whole administration of the estate a single proceeding, to provide that one who has undertaken it within the jurisdiction shall be subject to the order of the court in the matter until the administration is closed by distribution * * *.

Is the exercise of continuing jurisdiction consistent with due process if none of the parties to the original suit retains any further connection with the forum state? The problem has been discussed in a number of domestic relations cases, in which the principle of continuing jurisdiction is most often invoked.

SECTION D. THE REQUIREMENT OF REASONABLE NOTICE

We have seen that the Due Process Clause limits the power of courts to assume adjudicatory authority over the parties to an action. In this section, we focus on another requirement imposed by the Due Process Clause: the requirement that the parties be given reasonable notice of the lawsuit. This section will emphasize the constitutional dimension of the notice requirement. Sections E and F, which follow, will treat the more mechanical issues raised by service of process.

As you think about notice, ask whether the definition of adequate notice should take into account the distinction between in personam actions and in rem actions. Should there be more stringent requirements when jurisdiction is asserted pursuant to a long-arm statute? What if jurisdiction is based upon implied consent, as in *Hess*? Do the improvements in transportation and communication highlighted in *McGee* suggest that we need to worry less about notice?

MULLANE v. CENTRAL HANOVER BANK & TRUST CO.

Supreme Court of the United States, 1950.
339 U.S. 306, 70 S.Ct. 652, 94 L.Ed. 865.

Appeal from the Court of Appeals of New York.

MR. JUSTICE JACKSON delivered the opinion of the Court.

This controversy questions the constitutional sufficiency of notice to beneficiaries on judicial settlement of accounts by the trustee of a common trust fund established under the New York Banking Law * * *. The New York Court of Appeals considered and overruled objections that the statutory notice contravenes requirements of the Fourteenth Amendment * * *. The case is here on appeal * * *.

[Reread the basic facts of the case, which are set out on pages 169–70, supra.] * * *

The only notice given beneficiaries of this specific application [for judicial settlement of the account] was by publication in a local newspaper [for four successive weeks] in strict compliance with the minimum requirements of N.Y. Banking Law § 100–c(12) * * *. Thus the only notice required, and the only one given, was by newspaper publication setting forth merely the name and address of the trust company, the name and the date of establishment of the common trust fund, and a list of all participating estates, trusts or funds.

At the time the first investment in the common fund was made on behalf of each participating estate, however, the trust company, pursuant to the requirements of § 100–c(9), had notified by mail each person of full age and sound mind whose name and address was then known to it and who was "entitled to share in the income therefrom * * * [or] * * * who would be entitled to share in the principal if the event upon which such estate, trust or fund will become distributable should have occurred at the time of sending such notice." Included in the notice was a copy of those provisions of the Act relating to the sending of the notice itself and to the judicial settlement of common trust fund accounts.

Upon the filing of the petition for the settlement of accounts, appellant was, by order of the court pursuant to § 100–c(12), appointed special guardian and attorney for all persons known or unknown not otherwise appearing who had or might thereafter have any interest in the income of the common trust fund; and appellee Vaughan was appointed to represent those similarly interested in the principal. There were no other appearances on behalf of any one interested in either interest or principal.

Appellant appeared specially, objecting that notice and the statutory provisions for notice to beneficiaries were inadequate to afford due process under the Fourteenth Amendment, and therefore that the court was without jurisdiction to render a final and binding decree. Appellant's objections were entertained and overruled [by] the Surrogate * * *. A final decree accepting the accounts has been entered, affirmed by the Appellate Division of the Supreme Court * * * and by the Court of Appeals of the State of New York * * *.

The effect of this decree, as held below, is to settle "all questions respecting the management of the common fund." We understand that every right which beneficiaries would otherwise have against the trust company, either as trustee of the common fund or as trustee of any individual trust, for improper management of the common trust fund during the period covered by the accounting is sealed and wholly terminated by the decree. * * *

[The Court's discussion of jurisdiction is omitted. It appears on pages 170–71, supra.] * * *

Quite different from the question of a state's power to discharge trustees is that of the opportunity it must give beneficiaries to contest. Many controversies have raged about the cryptic and abstract words of the Due Process Clause but there can be no doubt that at a minimum they require that deprivation of life, liberty or property by adjudication be preceded by notice and opportunity for hearing appropriate to the nature of the case.

In two ways this proceeding does or may deprive beneficiaries of property. It may cut off their rights to have the trustee answer for negligent or illegal impairments of their interests. Also, their interests are presumably subject to diminution in the proceeding by allowance of fees and expenses to one who, in their names but without their knowledge, may conduct a fruitless or uncompensatory contest. Certainly the proceeding is one in which they may be deprived of property rights and hence notice and hearing must measure up to the standards of due process.

Personal service of written notice within the jurisdiction is the classic form of notice always adequate in any type of proceeding. But the vital interest of the State in bringing any issues as to its fiduciaries to a final settlement can be served only if interests or claims of individuals who are outside of the State can somehow be determined. A construction of the Due Process Clause which would place impossible or impractical obstacles in the way could not be justified.

Against this interest of the State we must balance the individual interest sought to be protected by the Fourteenth Amendment. This is defined by our holding that "The fundamental requisite of due process of law is the opportunity to be heard." Grannis v. Ordean, 234 U.S. 385, 394, 34 S.Ct. 779, 783, 58 L.Ed. 1363. This right to be heard has little reality or worth unless one is informed that the matter is pending and can choose for himself whether to appear or default, acquiesce or contest.

The Court has not committed itself to any formula achieving a balance between these interests in a particular proceeding or determining when constructive notice may be utilized or what test it must meet. Personal service has not in all circumstances been regarded as indispensable to the process due to residents, and it has more often been held unnecessary as to nonresidents. * * *

An elementary and fundamental requirement of due process in any proceeding which is to be accorded finality is notice reasonably calculated, under all the circumstances, to apprise interested parties of the pendency of the action and afford them an opportunity to present their objections. * * * The notice must be of such nature as reasonably to convey the required information * * * and it must afford a reasonable time for those interested to make their appearance * * *. But if with due regard for the practicalities and peculiarities of the case these conditions are reasonably met the constitutional requirements are satisfied. * * *

But when notice is a person's due, process which is a mere gesture is not due process. The means employed must be such as one desirous of actually informing the absentee might reasonably adopt to accomplish it. The reasonableness and hence the constitutional validity of any chosen method may be defended on the ground that it is in itself reasonably certain to inform those affected * * *, or, where conditions do not reasonably permit such notice, that the form chosen is not substantially less likely to bring home notice than other of the feasible and customary substitutes.

It would be idle to pretend that publication alone, as prescribed here, is a reliable means of acquainting interested parties of the fact that their rights are before the courts. It is not an accident that the greater number of cases reaching this Court on the question of adequacy of notice have been concerned with actions founded on process constructively served through local newspapers. Chance alone brings to the attention of even a local resident an advertisement in small type inserted in the back pages of a newspaper, and if he makes his home outside the area of the newspaper's normal circulation the odds that the information will never reach him are large indeed. The chance of actual notice is further reduced when as here the notice required does not even name those whose attention it is supposed to attract, and does not inform acquaintances who might call it to attention. In weighing its sufficiency on the basis of equivalence with actual notice we are unable to regard this as more than a feint.

Nor is publication here reinforced by steps likely to attract the parties' attention to the proceeding. It is true that publication traditionally has been acceptable as notification supplemental to other action which in itself may reasonably be expected to convey a warning. The ways of an owner with tangible property are such that he usually arranges means to learn of any direct attack upon his possessory or proprietary rights. Hence, libel of a ship, attachment of a chattel or entry upon real estate in the name of law may reasonably be expected to come promptly to the owner's attention. When the state within which the owner has located such property seizes it for some reason, publication or posting affords an additional measure of notification. A state may indulge the assumption that one who has left tangible property in the state either has abandoned it, in which case proceedings against it deprive him of nothing * * *, or that he has left some caretaker under a duty to let him know that it is being jeopardized. * * *

In the case before us there is, of course, no abandonment. On the other hand these beneficiaries do have a resident fiduciary as caretaker of their interest in this property. But it is their caretaker who in the accounting becomes their adversary. Their trustee is released from giving notice of jeopardy, and no one else is expected to do so. Not even the special guardian is required or apparently expected to communicate with his ward and client, and, of course, if such a duty were merely transferred from the trustee to the guardian, economy would not be served and more likely the cost would be increased.

This Court has not hesitated to approve of resort to publication as a customary substitute in another class of cases where it is not reasonably possible or practicable to give more adequate warning. Thus it has been recognized that, in the case of persons missing or unknown, employment of an indirect and even a probably futile means of notification is all that the situation permits and creates no constitutional bar to a final decree foreclosing their rights. * * *

Those beneficiaries represented by appellant whose interests or whereabouts could not with due diligence be ascertained come clearly within this category. As to them the statutory notice is sufficient. However great the odds that publication will never reach the eyes of such unknown parties, it is not in the typical case much more likely to fail than any of the choices open to legislators endeavoring to prescribe the best notice practicable.

Nor do we consider it unreasonable for the State to dispense with more certain notice to those beneficiaries whose interests are either conjectural or future or, although they could be discovered upon investigation, do not in due course of business come to knowledge of the common trustee. Whatever searches might be required in another situation under ordinary standards of diligence, in view of the character of the proceedings and the nature of the interests here involved we think them unnecessary. We recognize the practical difficulties and costs that would be attendant on frequent investigations into the status of great numbers of beneficiaries, many of whose interests in the common fund are so remote as to be ephemeral; and we have no doubt that such impracticable and extended searches are not required in the name of due process. The expense of keeping informed from day to day of substitutions among even current income beneficiaries and presumptive remaindermen, to say nothing of the far greater number of contingent beneficiaries, would impose a severe burden on the plan, and would likely dissipate its advantages. These are practical matters in which we should be reluctant to disturb the judgment of the state authorities.

Accordingly we overrule appellant's constitutional objections to published notice insofar as they are urged on behalf of any beneficiaries whose interests or addresses are unknown to the trustee.

As to known present beneficiaries of known place of residence, however, notice by publication stands on a different footing. Exceptions in the name of necessity do not sweep away the rule that within the limits of practicability notice must be such as is reasonably calculated to reach interested parties. Where the names and post office addresses of those affected by a proceeding are at hand, the reasons disappear for resort to means less likely than the mails to apprise them of its pendency.

The trustee has on its books the names and addresses of the income beneficiaries represented by appellant, and we find no tenable ground for dispensing with a serious effort to inform them personally of the accounting, at least by ordinary mail to the record addresses. * * * Certainly sending them a copy of the statute months and perhaps years in advance does not answer this purpose. The trustee periodically remits their income to them, and we think that they might reasonably expect that with or apart from their remittances word might come to them personally that steps were being taken affecting their interests.

We need not weigh contentions that a requirement of personal service of citation on even the large number of known resident or nonresident beneficiaries would, by reasons of delay if not of expense, seriously interfere with the proper administration of the fund. Of course personal service even without the jurisdiction of the issuing authority serves the end of actual and personal notice, whatever power of compulsion it might lack. However, no such service is required under the circumstances. This type of trust presupposes a large number of small interests. The individual interest does not stand alone but is identical with that of a class. The rights of each in the integrity of the fund and the fidelity of the trustee are shared by many other beneficiaries. Therefore notice reasonably certain to reach most of those interested in objecting is likely to safeguard the interests of all, since any objections sustained would inure to the benefit of all. We think that under such circumstances reasonable risks that notice might not actually reach every beneficiary are justifiable. * * *

The statutory notice to known beneficiaries is inadequate, not because in fact it fails to reach everyone, but because under the circumstances it is not reasonably calculated to reach those who could easily be informed by other means at hand. However it may have been in former times, the mails today are recognized as an efficient and inexpensive means of communication. Moreover, the fact that the trust company has been able to give mailed notice to known beneficiaries at the time the common trust fund was established is persuasive that postal notification at the time of accounting would not seriously burden the plan.

We hold the notice of judicial settlement of accounts required by the New York Banking Law § 100–c(12) is incompatible with the requirements of the Fourteenth Amendment as a basis for adjudication depriving known persons whose whereabouts are also known of substantial property rights. * * *

Reversed.

MR. JUSTICE DOUGLAS took no part in the consideration or decision of this case.

[The dissenting opinion of JUSTICE BURTON is omitted.]

Notes and Questions

1. *Mullane* seems to require notice that is reasonably calculated to succeed. Does this mean that the method *most likely* to succeed is not required? How does *Mullane* justify this? What role should cost play in determining what is reasonable? Does *Mullane* justify applying different notice requirements for small claims than for large claims?

2. In McDONALD v. MABEE, 243 U.S. 90, 92, 37 S.Ct. 343, 344, 61 L.Ed. 608, 609–10 (1917), suit was brought against Mabee, a domiciliary of Texas, upon a promissory note. Although his family was residing in the state, he had left Texas to establish a domicile elsewhere. Service was attempted through publication in a local newspaper once a week for four successive weeks after Mabee's departure from the state. Mabee never appeared in the action.

The United States Supreme Court, reversing the Texas Supreme Court, held that the Texas judgment was void under the Fourteenth Amendment:

> There is no dispute that service by publication does not warrant a personal judgment against a nonresident. * * * When the former suit was begun, Mabee, although technically domiciled in Texas, had left the state intending to establish his home elsewhere. Perhaps in view of his technical position and the actual presence of his family in the state a summons left at his last and usual place of abode would have been enough. But it appears to us that an advertisement in a local newspaper is not sufficient notice to bind a person who has left a state intending not to return. To dispense with personal service the substitute that is most likely to reach the defendant is the least that ought to be required if substantial justice is to be done.

How does *Mullane* affect *Mabee*? Would service at the last and usual place of abode be reasonably calculated to succeed? Would publication in a local newspaper be sufficient if Mabee were still in Texas? What if Mabee had moved to a different part of Texas?

3. If personal service is impossible or impractical, what methods of service become reasonable? In DOBKIN v. CHAPMAN, 21 N.Y.2d 490, 289 N.Y.S.2d 161, 236 N.E.2d 451 (1968), the New York Court of Appeals upheld court-ordered substitute service in three automobile accident cases (by ordinary mail to defendant's last known address and publication in a local newspaper), when the whereabouts of the defendants were unknown and service in the manner attempted was the best the plaintiffs could do in these "situations in which insistence on actual notice, or even on the high probability of actual notice, would be both unfair to plaintiffs and harmful to the public interest." The court stressed that if the defendants failed to get notice it was their fault since they either had failed to furnish the plaintiff a correct address at the scene of the accident, as required by New York law, or had failed to leave a forwarding address.

4. *Mullane* states that attachment of a chattel or real estate, together with publication, may provide adequate notice, under the theory that property owners are usually aware of and concerned about the status of their property. Is this consistent with Justice Jackson's insistence that jurisdiction labels, such as in personam and in rem, should not be important? In later cases, the Court held that the manner of notice used in state condemnation proceedings did not meet due process requirements when the only notice to the property owners was by publication in a local newspaper, Walker v. City of Hutchinson, 352 U.S. 112, 77 S.Ct. 200, 1 L.Ed.2d 178 (1956), or by publication coupled with signs posted on trees, Schroeder v. City of New York, 371 U.S. 208, 83 S.Ct. 279, 9 L.Ed.2d 255 (1962). In both cases the names and addresses of the owners were known or ascertainable from public records.

In MENNONITE BOARD OF MISSIONS v. ADAMS, 462 U.S. 791, 103 S.Ct. 2706, 77 L.Ed.2d 180 (1983), the Court held that notice by publication and posting did not provide a mortgagee of real property with adequate notice of a proceeding to sell the mortgaged property for nonpayment of taxes. "When the mortgagee is identified in a mortgage that is publicly recorded, constructive notice by publication must be supplemented by notice mailed to the mortgagee's last known available address, or by personal service. But unless the mortgagee is not reasonably identifiable, constructive notice alone does not satisfy the mandate of *Mullane*." Id. at 798, 103 S.Ct. at 2711, 77 L.Ed.2d at 187. The Court observed that personal service or mailed notice is required even though the mortgagee may have known of the delinquency in the payment of taxes, or as a sophisticated creditor had the means to discover that the taxes had not been paid and that a tax sale proceeding was therefore likely to be initiated.

In light of these decisions are there any instances in which it is safe to say that attachment plus publication is a sufficient procedure to establish jurisdiction?

5. Should the fact that a state has a significant interest in the speedy and final termination of particular disputes relating to property have an effect on the constitutionality of the notice given to potential claimants? In GREENE v. LINDSEY, 456 U.S. 444, 102 S.Ct. 1874, 72 L.Ed.2d 249 (1982), the Supreme Court considered a Kentucky statute that provided, in forcible entry and detainer actions, for service of process by posting a summons on the door of a tenant's apartment. A group of tenants in a public housing project, each of whom faced eviction, sought a declaration from a federal court that the notice procedure employed as a predicate to the eviction proceedings did not satisfy the *Mullane* standard. They claimed never to have seen the posted summonses, and that they did not learn of the eviction proceedings until they were served with writs of possession, executed after default judgments had been entered against them, and after their opportunity for appeal had lapsed. The Supreme Court, in an opinion by Justice Brennan, found the notice insufficient to satisfy the Due Process Clause.

The empirical basis of the presumption that notice posted upon property is adequate to alert the owner or occupant of property of the pendency of legal proceedings would appear to make the presumption particularly well-founded where notice is posted at a residence. With respect to claims affecting the continued possession of that residence, the application of this presumption seems particularly apt: If the tenant has a continuing interest in maintaining possession of the property for his use and occupancy, he might reasonably be expected to frequent the premises; if he no longer occupies the premises, then the injury that might result from his not having received actual notice as a consequence of the posted notice is reduced. Short of providing personal service, then, posting notice on the door of a person's home would, in many or perhaps most instances, constitute not only a constitutionally acceptable means of service, but indeed a singularly appropriate and effective way of ensuring that a person who cannot conveniently be served personally is actually apprised of proceedings against him.

But whatever the efficacy of posting in many cases, it is clear that, in the circumstances of this case, merely posting notice on an apartment door does not satisfy minimum standards of due process. In a significant number of instances, reliance on posting pursuant to the provisions of * * * [the statute] results in a failure to provide actual notice to the tenant concerned. Indeed, appellees claim to have suffered precisely such a failure of actual notice. As the process servers were well aware, notices posted on apartment doors in the area where these tenants lived were "not infrequently" removed by children or other tenants before they could have their intended effect. Under these conditions, notice by posting on the apartment door cannot be considered a "reliable means of acquainting interested parties of the fact that their rights are before the courts."

456 U.S. at 452–54, 102 S.Ct. at 1879–80, 72 L.Ed.2d at 257–58. Justice Brennan conceded that the reasonableness of the notice provided must be tested with reference to the existence of feasible alternatives and supplements to the form of notice chosen, but he concluded that, given the danger that posted notice alone would not succeed in the circumstances before the Court, the Due Process Clause required that the posting be supplemented by notice through the mails.

Justice O'Connor, joined by Chief Justice Burger and Justice Rehnquist, dissented.

> The Court * * * holds that notice via the mails is so far superior to posted notice that the difference is of constitutional dimension. How the Court reaches this judgment remains a mystery, especially since the Court is unable, on the present record, to evaluate the risks that notice mailed to public housing projects might fail due to loss, misdelivery, lengthy delay, or theft. Furthermore, the advantages of the mails over posting, if any, are far from obvious. It is no secret, after all, that unattended mailboxes are subject to plunder by thieves. Moreover, unlike the use of the mails, posting notices at least gives assurance that the notice has gotten as far as the tenant's door.

456 U.S. at 459–60, 102 S.Ct. at 1883, 72 L.Ed.2d at 261. Did Justice Brennan find that notice by mail was, as a matter of constitutional law, superior to notice posted upon the apartment door?

In *Greene,* did Justice Brennan use the *Mullane* standard or did he employ a higher standard? Upon whom did he impose the burden of proof on the issue of reasonableness? How can that burden be carried? Remember, the method of notice challenged in *Greene* had been approved by the Kentucky state legislature.

Should the constitutional standard used to judge the reasonableness of notice vary according to the type of action or the nature of issue at stake? In her dissent, Justice O'Connor suggested that the need for swift action in eviction proceedings might justify a lower standard for notice. Shouldn't the issue at stake, though, be phrased as the tenants' right to possess the apartment?

6. Consider TULSA PROFESSIONAL COLLECTION SERVICES, INC. v. POPE, 485 U.S. 478, 108 S.Ct. 1340, 99 L.Ed.2d 565 (1988). Under the nonclaim provision of Oklahoma's probate code, creditors' claims against an estate generally are barred unless presented to the executor or executrix within two months of the publication of notice of the commencement of probate proceedings. Jeanne Pope, an executrix, published the required notice in compliance with the terms of the nonclaim statute and a probate court order, but Tulsa Professional Collection Services, Inc., failed to file a timely claim. For this reason, the probate court denied appellant's application for payment, and both the Oklahoma Court of Appeals and Supreme Court affirmed, rejecting appellant's contention that, in failing to require more than publication notice, the nonclaim statute violated due process.

The United States Supreme Court reversed, holding that if Tulsa Professional's identity as a creditor was known or "reasonably ascertainable" by Pope (a fact the Court said could not be determined from the record before it), the Due Process Clause of the Fourteenth Amendment required that the collection agency be given notice by mail or such other means as is certain to ensure actual notice.

The Court rejected Pope's argument that the nonclaim statute was simply a self-executing statute of limitations. Rather, it reasoned, the probate court's intimate involvement throughout the probate proceedings—particularly the court's activation of the statute's time bar by the appointment of an executor—constituted state action adversely affecting protected property interests, since untimely claims, such as the claim of Tulsa Professional Collection Services, were completely extinguished.

Given this view of the nonclaim provision, the Court went on to say that, on balance, satisfying creditors' substantial practical need for actual notice in the probate setting is not so cumbersome or impracticable as to burden unduly the state's undeniably legitimate interest in the expeditious resolution of the proceedings, since mail service (which already is routinely provided at several points in the probate process) is inexpensive, efficient, and reasonably calculated to provide actual notice, and since publication notice will suffice for creditors whose identities are not ascertainable by reasonably diligent efforts or whose claims merely are conjectural.

7. In COVEY v. TOWN OF SOMERS, 351 U.S. 141, 146–47, 76 S.Ct. 724, 727, 100 L.Ed. 1021, 1026 (1956), the Court held that notice by mail of a proceeding to foreclose a lien for delinquent taxes on realty, although ordinarily sufficient, would not satisfy due process requirements where it was mailed to someone known to have been adjudged insane and committed to a hospital, and who is without the protection of a guardian.

8. In WUCHTER v. PIZZUTTI, 276 U.S. 13, 48 S.Ct. 259, 72 L.Ed. 446 (1928), the Supreme Court invalidated a New Jersey nonresident-motorist statute similar to the one involved in Hess v. Pawloski, p. 75, supra, because it did not expressly require the Secretary of State to communicate notice of the commencement of the action to the nonresident. In fact, notice actually was given by the Secretary of State. According to the Supreme Court: "Every statute of this kind * * * should require the plaintiff bringing the suit to show in the summons to be served the post office address or residence of the defendant being sued, and should impose either on the plaintiff himself or upon the official receiving service or some other, the duty of communication by mail or otherwise with the defendant."

Why did the Supreme Court invalidate service even though the defendant received actual notice of the action? One commentator has suggested the following explanation: "Apart from the defendant's personal constitutional right to notice, the due process clause also imposes restrictions on how a state must act when it imposes unique burdens on persons. One such restriction, *Wuchter* seems to say, is that the steps that can lead to the imposition of such a burden must be formally and officially predetermined and declared rather than determined ad hoc." Casad, Book Review, 80 Mich.L.Rev. 644, 670 (1982). Is this explanation consistent with the apparent flexibility the courts seem to have in devising other methods of service when personal service is impractical or impossible?

9. If service is attempted in a case under a statutory method that is likely to give actual notice, but the statutory method is not strictly followed, will jurisdiction be proper if the defendant gets actual notice? Although some states insist upon strict compliance with the prescribed procedure, see, e.g., Pete Singh Produce, Inc. v. Macias, 608 S.W.2d 822 (Tex.Civ.App.1980), others are satisfied with "substantial compliance if the defendant actually receives notice," see, e.g., Buena Vista Manor v. Century Mfg. Co., 221 N.W.2d 286 (Iowa 1974). The general attitude of the federal courts is that the provisions of Rule 4 should be liberally construed in the interest of doing substantial justice and that the propriety of service in each case should turn on its own facts within the limits of the flexibility provided by the rule itself. See 4A Wright & Miller, *Federal Practice and Procedure: Civil 2d* § 1083 (1987). The problem almost always has been treated by both state and federal courts as a matter of statutory construction. How is it that a defective attempt at service under a valid statute does not contravene the Due Process Clause?

10. The means of communicating notice differ from the prescribed content of the notice. Is the Due Process Clause also concerned with the content of the notice given? The Restatement (Second), Judgments § 2 (1982) states that notice is adequate only if the notice is "official in tenor."

Rule 4(b) generally prescribes the contents of the summons to be used in federal actions, and the Supreme Court has approved an illustrative form of summons, Official Form 1, which is reproduced in the Supplement. If a party fails to comply with the form of summons prescribed in Rule 4(b), the liberal amendment process policy expressed in Rule 4(b) can be used to alleviate errors of a technical nature in the form of the summons that are not misleading or prejudicial to the recipient. See 4A Wright & Miller, *Federal Practice and Procedure: Civil 2d* §§ 1088, 1131 (1987).

SECTION E. THE MECHANICS OF GIVING NOTICE

Read Federal Rule of Civil Procedure 4 and the comparable state statutes set out in the Supplement.

1. INTRODUCTION

Notice of a suit is given by the service of process upon the defendant. Each jurisdiction has a set of rules governing the correct methods of making service. Traditionally, process consists of a copy of the plaintiff's complaint, together with a summons directing the defendant to answer. Service of process is made by personal delivery of the summons and complaint to the defendant. Other methods of service, such as delivery by mail, have assumed greater importance since the advent of long-arm statutes.

The procedure governing service of process in federal actions was changed significantly in 1983. In 1982, the Supreme Court proposed but Congress rejected an amendment to the Rules that would have permitted service by registered or certified mail, return receipt, with delivery restricted to the addressee. It was contended that the use of certified mail causes problems when, for example, the signature on the return receipt is illegible or the name signed differs somewhat from that of the defendant, or when it is difficult to determine whether mail has been "refused" or "unclaimed." It also was contended that the result of relying on the mail for service of process would be entry of many more unnecessary and unfair default judgments, which would have to be reopened when challenged. Other objections were directed to the provision restricting delivery: mail carriers could easily deliver process to the wrong person or fail to make the necessary inquiries to find the proper person. See Cong. Record, December 15, 1982, at H9848–H9856, reproduced in 96 F.R.D. at 116–35.

Congress chose instead a system of service by mail modeled on the one used in California. See Cal.Code Civ.Pro. § 415.30. The summons and complaint can be sent by ordinary first class mail, together with a form for acknowledging receipt of service. If the defendant returns the acknowledgment form to the sender within 20 days after the initial mailing, the sender files it with the court and service is complete. If the acknowledgment form is not returned, plaintiff must effect service through some other means authorized by the Rules. In order to encourage defendants to execute and return the form, the Rule directs the court to order a defendant who does not cooperate to pay the costs incurred by the plaintiff in making personal service, unless the defendant can show good cause for failing to return the acknowledgment form. Fed.R.Civ.P. 4(c)(2)(C)(ii) & (D). As to state statutes authorizing service by mail, see generally Annot., 95 A.L.R.2d 1033 (1984); Note, *Service of Process by Mail,* 74 Mich.L.Rev. 381 (1975).

The specific means of making personal service on, among others, individuals, corporations, partnerships, and other associations subject to suit under a common name are set out in the several subdivisions of Rule 4(d). In addition, Rule 4(c)(2)(C)(i) provides an alternative to these methods by broadly authorizing the use in federal courts of the procedures governing the manner of service prescribed by the law of the state in which the district court is sitting. And Rule 4(e) specifically provides for the use of state procedures to effect service on a party "not an inhabitant of or found within the state in which the district court is held," thus enabling federal courts to take advantage of state long-arm statutes. See 4A Wright & Miller, *Federal Practice and Procedure: Civil 2d* §§ 1112–16, 1119–23 (1987); Foster, *Long-Arm Jurisdiction in Federal Courts,* 1969 Wis.L.Rev. 9; Foster, *Judicial Economy; Fairness and Convenience of Place of Trial: Long-Arm Jurisdiction in District Courts,* 47 F.R.D. 73 (1969).

Note should be made of the elaborate provision for service of process in a foreign country in Federal Rule 4(i). A comparable provision is found in § 2.01 of the Uniform Interstate and International Procedure Act. 9B Uniform Laws Ann. 305, 315–18 (1966). The intention of these provisions is to provide American attorneys with an extremely flexible framework to permit accommodation to the widely divergent procedures for service of process employed by the various nations of the world. This accommodation is necessary in order to avoid violating the sovereignty of other countries by committing acts within their borders that they may consider to be "official" and to maximize the likelihood that the judgment rendered in the action in this country will be recognized and enforced abroad. Service of process in a foreign country and other procedural aspects of civil litigation having multi-national incidents are discussed in Miller, *International Cooperation in Litigation Between the United States and Switzerland: Unilateral Procedural Accommodation in a Test Tube,* 49 Minn.L.Rev. 1069, 1075–86 (1965); Comment, *Revitalization of the International Judicial Assistance Procedures of the United States: Service of Documents and Taking of Testimony,* 62 Mich.L.Rev. 1375, 1377–86 (1964). See also 4A Wright & Miller, *Federal Practice and Procedure: Civil 2d* §§ 1133–36 (1987).

2. SPECIFIC APPLICATIONS OF THE SERVICE PROVISIONS

a. *Service by Mail*

REPORT OF THE COMMITTEE ON FEDERAL COURTS OF THE NEW YORK STATE BAR ASSOCIATION ON SERVICE OF PROCESS BY MAIL PURSUANT TO RULE 4(c)(2)(C)(II) OF THE FEDERAL RULES OF CIVIL PROCEDURE

116 F.R.D. 169, 172–74 (1987).

EFFECT OF FAILURE TO ACKNOWLEDGE: FOLLOW-UP SERVICE BY FEDERAL METHOD ONLY

Rule 4(c)(2)(C)(ii) and Rule 4(c)(2)(D) require the person served by mail to return within 20 days a copy of the notice and acknowledgment form that accompanied the summons and complaint. (Return of the acknowledgment does not waive the defendant's right to contest improper service—for example, use of mail service outside the state.) Under subparagraph (C)(ii), "[i]f no acknowledgment of service * * * is received by the sender within 20 days after the date of mailing, service of such summons and complaint shall be made under subparagraph (A) or (B) of this paragraph in the manner prescribed by subdivision (d)(1) or (d)(3)." Therefore, follow-up service may *not* be made under state law pursuant to Rule 4(c)(2)(C)(i) or by a second attempt at mail service under C(ii) itself. That prohibition, when coupled with the restriction of mail service to use within the forum state, "places the plaintiff in a 'Catch 22' situation in that [plaintiff] may never obtain effective service of process on these out-of-state defendants because [plaintiff] is precluded from employing the [state] long-arm statute due to [plaintiff's] first attempting service by mail according to the Federal Rules." Pittsburgh Terminal Corp., 110 F.R.D. at 8.

The legislative history of the Act is silent on the reason for not permitting follow-up service under state law, except for indications in the report, accompanying the bill to postpone the effective date of the Supreme Court's proposed amendments, that the drafters of the Act simply followed the California mail procedure, which requires that follow-up service be personal. No such limitation appears necessary. Perhaps the drafters of the Act wished only to preclude follow-up service by mail-only methods; but if it is thought that follow-up mail service is insufficient— although it is the plaintiff who is wasting his own time while the 120-day clock of Rule 4(j) is running—then the Rule should be amended to permit follow-up service by any method that was available to the plaintiff at the time of the mail service, including state law methods but excluding a second attempt at service under (C)(ii).

Such an amendment would allow state methods for follow-up service without permitting the plaintiff to circumvent Rule 4(e)'s restrictions on the extraterritorial use of federal service methods by simply first attempting service under (C)(ii). If the state in which the action is pending, such as California, has a mail service statute, then the plaintiff will have a second bite at the mail service apple; but if that mail service also fails, he will be constrained to make follow-up service as provided in that state's mail service law.

EFFECT OF FAILURE TO ACKNOWLEDGE: VALIDITY OF SERVICE

The Third and Fourth Circuits have held that, when a defendant fails to return the acknowledgment form, even if that failure is deliberate, the service is invalid; and plaintiff must effect valid follow-up service in order to obtain personal jurisdiction over the defendant. The Second Circuit disagrees, holding that return of the acknowledgment form only goes to *proof* of service under Rule 4(g) and that received, but unacknowledged, mail service is effective—and thus will stop the statute of limitations from running in states, like New York, which require *service* within the statute of limitations period. Judge Weinfeld of the Southern District of New York has gone so far as to hold that, even if the plaintiff does not include the acknowledgment form, his service by mail is still effective; the defect can be cured by an admission or other proof that defendant in fact received the summons and complaint. Lee v. Carlson, 645 F.Supp. 1430, 1432–33 (S.D.N.Y.1986).

Although the Second Circuit view may sometimes require the holding of an evidentiary hearing to determine if and when the defendant actually received the summons and complaint, thereby producing the very delay and expense that mail service was in part meant to alleviate, "[t]here is * * * no rationale for allowing a properly served defendant deliberately and willfully to postpone the ending of limitations by simply refusing to do what the rule calls upon him to do." [Morse v. Elmira Country Club, 752 F.2d 35, 40 (2d Cir.1984).] Accordingly, Rule 4(c)(2)(C)(ii) should be amended to provide that failure to acknowledge the mail service does not affect the validity of the service. Use of the acknowledgment form would then be regarded as a means of insuring easier proof of service, not as a predicate to effective service.

Such an amendment would not encourage plaintiffs to ignore the requirement that the acknowledgment form be sent with the summons and complaint, for, on any motion by defendant contending that the summons and complaint were never received, plaintiff would still bear the burden of proving effective service. Moreover, even if plaintiff met that burden, he would not obtain the attorneys fees that (as proposed by this Report) would have been available under Rule 4(c)(2)(D) had he enclosed the acknowledgment form. Furthermore, the amendment would eliminate the wide disparity between cases such as *Morse*, which requires no acknowledgement at all for effective service, and those * * * which held an acknowledged mailing inadequate because the acknowledgment form was not signed but merely stamped by defendant's mailroom. However, in order to ensure actual notice, especially since (C)(ii) does not require that the summons and complaint be mailed to defendant's residence or business address, the service should only be effective if, and when, it is actually received by the defendant.

————

In COMBS v. NICK GARIN TRUCKING, 825 F.2d 437 (D.C.Cir.1987), the plaintiff attempted mail service on the defendant pursuant to Rule 4(c)(2)(C)(ii). The acknowledgment form was not returned by the defendant, however; instead, a postal return receipt, apparently bearing the defendant's signature, was returned to plaintiff. Arguing that the state process provisions required only a postal return receipt, the plaintiff asked that the District Court enter a default judgment. In support of the judgment, the plaintiff provided an affidavit stating that "the complaint and summons in this action were served upon the defendant via registered or certified mail." When the clerk of the District Court entered the judgment, the defendant appealed.

The United States Court of Appeals for the District of Columbia Circuit reversed the default judgment, holding that when service clearly is attempted pursuant to the federal mail service provision (in particular, by including the acknowledgment form) and the service is not completed, the plaintiff may not claim that service nevertheless is proper pursuant to the state provision.

What interest do the federal courts have in preventing a plaintiff from benefitting from a less restrictive state rule in instances when the plaintiff easily could have used that rule at the outset?

b. Personal Delivery on Natural Persons

McKELWAY, PROFILES—PLACE AND LEAVE WITH, New Yorker, August 24, 1935, at 23–26:

* * * In a little frame house near the intersection of Rogers and Flatbush Avenues in Brooklyn there lived until a few years ago an old lady named Mrs. Katherina Schnible. She was seventy-two and a little lame. She owned the house and rented out the first two floors as apartments, but there were mortgages and she had not met the payments. She knew the bank that held the mortgages was about to foreclose * * *. Her son, who lived with her, went out to work at eight in the morning and did not return until six, so from eight till six every day, except Sunday, Mrs. Schnible stayed in her room on the third floor and

refused to open the door, no matter who knocked. Came a day when she heard a heavy footfall on the first landing, heard somebody running frantically up the first flight of stairs, heard a man's voice shouting something. Then the footsteps came closer, up the second flight of stairs, and right outside her door she heard yelled the word "Fire!" Mrs. Schnible opened her door and hobbled hurriedly into the hall. "Hello, Mrs. Schnible," said a man standing there. "Here's a summons for you." He handed her the papers, and the proceedings were begun which eventually put Mrs. Schnible out of her house.

Harry Grossman, who was the man in the hall, is regarded by those who employ him as the champion process-server of the day. He is an instrument of justice and his profession is a corner-stone of civil law, but not many of the people he serves appreciate that. * * * Grossman has been cursed by hundreds of defendants, many of them distinguished citizens. Defendants have thrown him down flights of stairs and shoved him off porches. He has been pinched, slapped, punched, and kicked by scores of individuals, and he was beaten up one time by a family of seven.

* * *

"Place and leave with" is the legal phrase for what a process-server must do with a summons when he goes out to serve papers on a defendant, but the courts never have explained precisely what that means. Where the process-server must place the papers is still a nice legal question. A process-server once threw a summons-and-complaint at James Gordon Bennett and hit him in the chest with it, but the courts held that this was not a proper service. Another famous case in the lawbooks tells of a defendant named Martin, who in 1893 hid himself under his wife's petticoats and refused to receive the papers. The process-server saw him crouching there, so he put the papers on what seemed to be the defendant's shoulder, and went away. The Supreme Court rendered a decision which held that "where a person, to avoid service of summons, shelters himself in his wife's petticoats, the laying of the papers on his shoulder will be a sufficient service." * * *

Grossman has never bothered to look up legal precedents for his actions; he simply places the papers in the hands of the defendant and leaves them there. On innumerable occasions he has had to use ingenuity in order to get close enough to the defendant to do this, and only once has he been forced to depart from a literal interpretation of the legal phrase. That was in the case of an elderly lady, who, like Mrs. Schnible, was trying to hide from him. This lady, whose name was Mrs. Mahoney, refused to leave her apartment in the East Side tenement she owned, and Grossman's routine tricks * * * failed to budge her. He knew she was there, because he had wheedled his way into a flat across the court from her and had seen her sitting at her kitchen table in front of an open window, peeling potatoes. Grossman went home to his own apartment in Brooklyn and thought for a while, and then began to practice throwing the summons. He put rubber bands around the paper to make it compact, placed a salad bowl on the dining-room table, and practiced all that afternoon, throwing the subpoena into the bowl from the middle of the living-room. He went back next morning to the flat across the court from Mrs. Mahoney's kitchen. She came into the kitchen a little before noon, puttered around for a while, and then sat down at the table with a bowl of potatoes in front of her and began placidly to peel them. Grossman leaned out of his window and tossed the subpoena. The papers landed in the bowl just as the old lady reached into it. "There you are, Mrs. Mahoney!" Grossman shouted. "There's a foreclosure paper for you!" The courts never questioned his method of placing these papers, and Mrs. Mahoney lost her property.

Tens of thousands of papers have to be served in the course of a year in this city, and the majority of them are handled for the law firms by process-serving agencies, which rely for their profits on quantity and a quick turnover. * * * Cases involving expert dodgers or stubborn hug-the-hearths usually are turned over to private detective agencies, and the detective agencies usually hire Grossman to serve the papers. When the Electrical Research Product Institute sued the Fox Film Corporation for $15,000,000 in 1930, the lawyers for the plaintiff, naturally, surmised that it would be difficult to "place and leave with" William Fox, Winfield Sheehan, and other defendants, the papers summoning them to come to court. Grossman received the assignment through a detective agency. He got in to see Fox by having a telegram sent from Boston saying that Mr. Grossman had "closed the theatre deal" and would call on Fox at eleven o'clock the next morning. When Grossman reached Fox's office, the film executive's secretary told him Mr. Fox had received the wire but was not sure what deal it was that had been closed. "My God," said Grossman, "the theatre deal—that's what deal! If this is the way I am to be received, never mind—to hell with it!" He started out, and the secretary called him back. "Just wait one moment," she said. "I'll tell Mr. Fox." She opened a door marked "Private" and went into an inner office. Grossman followed her and handed Fox the subpoena. Fox started up from his desk indignantly, but Grossman's indignation expressed itself first. "You, a multi-millionaire!" Grossman shouted. "Is it decent, is it nice, for a multi-millionaire who can be sued for fifteen million dollars to hide from me? Why don't you take the papers like a man?" This so flabbergasted Fox that he sank back in his chair, and Grossman went through the corporation's offices unimpeded and served papers on Sheehan, two vice-presidents, the secretary, and the treasurer.

* * * Harry established a reputation as an adroit private detective before he was old enough to serve subpoenas. * * * But after he had passed his eighteenth birthday and had begun to serve summonses and subpoenas, it was evident to his employer, and to everybody else who knew him, that he had found a vocation in which he might expect to excel. During his first year he served Maude Adams by posing as a youthful adorer. When she came out of the stage entrance at the Empire Theatre after a performance one evening, Grossman stepped in front of her holding in his left hand a bouquet of jonquils. "Are you Maude Adams?" he asked. "Oh, are those really for me?" she exclaimed, reaching for the flowers, "No, but this is," said Grossman, jerking back the bouquet. With his right hand he served her with a summons. He still remembers that

he had paid fifty cents for the jonquils and that he was able to sell them back to the florist for twenty.

His ability to become more indignant at the attitude of defendants than defendants are at his actions has saved Grossman from bodily injury on many occasions. One of his early triumphs involved Gutzon Borglum. The sculptor was at that time modelling life-size figures in a studio in the Gramercy Park section. Grossman entered by means of what he calls the rush act. A maid opened the door and Grossman rushed past her, saying perfunctorily "Is Mr. Borglum in?" Borglum was chipping stone on a nearly completed nude. "Here's a summons for you, Mr. Borglum," said Grossman. "Of all the effrontery," began the sculptor. "You * * * you * * * you ought to be * * *." Then Grossman began to shout. "How about you?" he asked. "Shouldn't you maybe be ashamed of yourself? You and your naked women!" He went out spluttering with indignation, leaving Borglum speechless, clutching the summons in his hand.

c. Service on a Person Residing in Defendant's Dwelling House or Usual Place of Abode

As an alternative to personal delivery, Rule 4(d)(1) permits service of process to be made upon an individual by leaving a copy of the summons and complaint at his "dwelling house or usual place of abode with some person of suitable age and discretion then residing therein." Despite the length of time these words have been a part of federal practice, the decisions do not make clear precisely what they mean, and the facts of a particular case often prove to be crucial.

ROVINSKI v. ROWE, 131 F.2d 687, 689 (6th Cir.1942). Rowe brought suit against Rovinski in a Michigan state court, service of process being effected under the state's nonresident motorist statute. Rovinski moved to dismiss on the ground that he was a resident of Michigan, and hence not amenable to service under the statute. After the action was dismissed, Rowe commenced a diversity action against Rovinski in a federal court. Service of process was made under Federal Rule of Civil Procedure 4(d)(1) by leaving a copy of the summons and complaint with Rovinski's mother at the address that he had given as his residence in an affidavit supporting his motion to dismiss in the prior state action. Rovinski again challenged the propriety of service, contending that his "dwelling place and usual place of abode" had been in Minnesota for the past two years, and that he had returned to his mother's house only to visit, even though he considered it his legal residence. The District Court held the service of process valid, and the Sixth Circuit affirmed:

> In construing * * * Rule 4(d)(1) liberally, the district court effectuated the declared purpose of the Supreme Court Advisory Committee in submitting a service of process rule, which would provide "a good deal of freedom and flexibility in service." * * * That the rule should be liberally construed seems logical, when consideration is given to the fact that uncertainty of its applicability to varying situations would be increased by strict construction. This is apparent from the irreconcilable conflict among state courts upon the meaning and interpretation of the expression "usual place of abode." * * *

The wide diversity of opinion may be illustrated by two examples. On the one hand, delivery of process to defendant's wife at an apartment in Miami Beach, Florida, where his family had been living for about two months and where he had previously visited them, but from which he had departed to his permanent home in another state, was held *sufficient* under a Florida statute * * *. On the other hand, delivery of service of process to the father of a minor defendant at the family home where the defendant had lived up to the time of his enlistment in the United States Army less than one month previously was held *insufficient* under a New Jersey statute * * *.

The only pertinent reported Federal decision is Skidmore v. Green, D.C.N.Y., 33 F.Supp. 529, 530, wherein service was upheld under Rule 4(d)(1) against a peregrinating policeman, who, after retiring from the New York force, spent most of his time traveling about the country in an automobile and trailer. Process had been delivered at the home of defendant's brother which, in the application for his New York automobile license, defendant had given as his address. In his application for his South Carolina automobile license, he had stated that he was a resident of New York. The district judge commented that "so far as the migratory nature of his life" permitted of any place of abode or dwelling house, that place was his brother's home.

Notes and Questions

1. In FIRST NAT. BANK & TRUST CO. OF TULSA v. INGERTON, 207 F.2d 793, 796 (10th Cir.1953), defendants, who were horse owners, appeared to change their residence whenever their horses moved to a new race track. Their furniture was stored in a warehouse in Raton, New Mexico, and some of their possessions were left at a hotel there, at which they continued to receive mail. Process was served on defendants' daughter at a furnished home that they had rented for one month in Denver, Colorado. The trial court later quashed the service on the ground that defendants' usual place of abode was Raton. The appellate court affirmed but Judge Murrah dissented, noting that "the record clearly shows that as race horse owners, the Ingertons' usual place of abode was wherever their horses happened to be running."

2. To what extent should it be relevant that a defendant actually received the summons and complaint at the particular place where it was served? In KARLSSON v. RABINOWITZ, 318 F.2d 666, 668 (4th Cir.1963), the Fourth Circuit validated service that was left with the defendant's wife in Maryland even though the family was in the process of moving and the defendant already had left for Arizona, with no intent ever to return. On facts similar to *Karlsson,* the District of Columbia Circuit held that service was invalid because the papers were left with defendant's estranged wife and he did not receive the summons and complaint until three years after default judgment was entered against him. Williams v. Capital Transit Co., 215 F.2d 487 (D.C.Cir.1954). Does this reliance on actual receipt of service create a "double" standard for construing the language of Rule 4(d)(1)? Does this make sense? Under what circumstances should actual notice not be required? See Blackhawk Heating & Plumbing Co. v. Turner, 50 F.R.D. 144 (D.Ariz. 1970).

d. Delivery to an Agent Authorized by Appointment

A third method of effecting personal service on an individual under Rule 4(d)(1) is by delivering a copy of the summons and complaint to an agent of the defendant. The cases dealing with agency by appointment indicate that an actual appointment for the specific purpose of receiving process normally is expected. Consistent with this judicial construction of "appointment," the courts have held that claims by an agent that he has authority to receive process or the fact that an agent actually accepts process is not enough to bind defendant; there must be evidence that defendant himself intended to confer such authority upon the agent.

NATIONAL EQUIPMENT RENTAL, LTD. v. SZUKHENT

Supreme Court of the United States, 1964.
375 U.S. 311, 84 S.Ct. 411, 11 L.Ed.2d 354.

Certiorari to the United States Court of Appeals for the Second Circuit.

Mr. Justice Stewart delivered the opinion of the Court.

* * * The petitioner is a corporation with its principal place of business in New York. It sued the respondents, residents of Michigan, in a New York federal court, claiming that the respondents had defaulted under a farm equipment lease. The only question now before us is whether the person upon whom the summons and complaint were served was "an agent authorized by appointment" to receive the same, so as to subject the respondents to the jurisdiction of the federal court in New York.

The respondents obtained certain farm equipment from the petitioner under a lease executed in 1961. The lease was on a printed form less than a page and a half in length, and consisted of 18 numbered paragraphs. The last numbered paragraph, appearing just above the respondents' signatures and printed in the same type used in the remainder of the instrument, provided that "the Lessee hereby designates Florence Weinberg, 47–21 Forty-first Street, Long Island City, N.Y., as agent for the purpose of accepting service of any process within the State of New York." The respondents were not acquainted with Florence Weinberg.

In 1962 the petitioner commenced the present action by filing in the federal court in New York a complaint which alleged that the respondents had failed to make any of the periodic payments specified by the lease. The Marshal delivered two copies of the summons and complaint to Florence Weinberg. That same day she mailed the summons and complaint to the respondents, together with a letter stating that the documents had been served upon her as the respondents' agent for the purpose of accepting service of process in New York, in accordance with the agreement contained in the lease. The petitioner itself also notified the respondents by certified mail of the service of process upon Florence Weinberg.

Upon motion of the respondents, the District Court quashed service of the summons and complaint, holding that, although Florence Weinberg had promptly notified the respondents of the service of process and mailed copies of the summons and complaint to them, the lease agreement itself had not explicitly required her to do so, and there was therefore a "failure of the agency arrangement to achieve intrinsic and continuing reality." * * * The Court of Appeals affirmed * * * and we granted certiorari * * *.

We need not and do not in this case reach the situation where no personal notice has been given to the defendant. Since the respondents did in fact receive complete and timely notice of the lawsuit pending against them, no due process claim has been made. The case before us is therefore quite different from cases where there was no actual notice * * *. Similarly, as the Court of Appeals recognized, this Court's decision in Wuchter v. Pizzutti * * * is inapposite here. * * * *Wuchter* dealt with the limitations imposed by the Fourteenth Amendment upon a statutory scheme by which a State attempts to subject nonresident individuals to the jurisdiction of its courts. The question presented here, on the other hand, is whether a party to a private contract may appoint an agent to receive service of process within the meaning of Federal Rule of Civil Procedure 4(d)(1), where the agent is not personally known to the party, and where the agent has not expressly undertaken to transmit notice to the party.

The purpose underlying the contractual provision here at issue seems clear. The clause was inserted by the petitioner and agreed to by the respondents in order to assure that any litigation under the lease should be conducted in the State of New York. The contract specifically provided that "This agreement shall be deemed to have been made in Nassau County, New York, regardless of the order in which the signatures of the parties shall be affixed hereto, and shall be interpreted, and the rights and liabilities of the parties here determined, in accordance with the laws of the State of New York." And it is settled, as the courts below recognized, that parties to a contract may agree in advance to submit to the jurisdiction of a given court, to permit notice to be served by the opposing party, or even to waive notice altogether. * * *

Under well-settled general principles of the law of agency, Florence Weinberg's prompt acceptance and transmittal to the respondents of the summons and complaint pursuant to the authorization was itself sufficient to validate the agency, even though there was no explicit previous promise on her part to do so. * * *

We deal here with a Federal Rule, applicable to federal courts in all 50 States. But even if we were to assume that this uniform federal standard should give way to contrary local policies, there is no relevant concept of state law which would invalidate the agency here at issue. In Michigan, where the respondents reside, the statute which validates service of process under the circumstances present in this case contains no provision requiring that the appointed agent expressly undertake to notify the principal of the service of process. Similarly, New York law, which it was agreed should be applicable to the lease provisions, does not require any such express promise by the agent in order to create a valid agency for receipt of process.   *   *   *

It is argued, finally, that the agency sought to be created in this case was invalid because Florence Weinberg may have had a conflict of interest. This argument is based upon the fact that she was not personally known to the respondents at the time of her appointment and upon a suggestion in the record that she may be related to an officer of the petitioner corporation. But such a contention ignores the narrowly limited nature of the agency here involved. Florence Weinberg was appointed the respondents' agent for the single purpose of receiving service of process. An agent with authority so limited can in no meaningful sense be deemed to have had an interest antagonistic to the respondents, since both the petitioner and the respondents had an equal interest in assuring that, in the event of litigation, the latter be given that adequate and timely notice which is a prerequisite to a valid judgment.

A different case would be presented if Florence Weinberg had not given prompt notice to the respondents, for then the claim might well be made that her failure to do so had operated to invalidate the agency. We hold only that, prompt notice to the respondents having been given, Florence Weinberg was their "agent authorized by appointment" to receive process within the meaning of Federal Rule of Civil Procedure 4(d)(1).

*   *   *

Judgment of Court of Appeals reversed and case remanded.

MR. JUSTICE BLACK, dissenting.

*   *   * I disagree with *   *   * [the Court's] holding, believing that (1) whether Mrs. Weinberg was a valid agent upon whom service could validly be effected under Rule 4(d)(1) should be determined under New York law and that we should accept the holdings of the federal district judge and the Court of Appeals sitting in New York that under that State's law the purported appointment of Mrs. Weinberg was invalid and ineffective; (2) if however, Rule 4(d)(1) is to be read as calling upon us to formulate a new federal definition of agency for purposes of service of process, I think our formulation should exclude Mrs. Weinberg from the category of an "agent authorized by appointment *   *   * to receive service of process"; and (3) upholding service of process in this case raises serious questions as to whether these Michigan farmers have been denied due process of law in violation of the Fifth and Fourteenth Amendments.

*   *   *

The end result of today's holding is not difficult to foresee. Clauses like the one used against the Szukhents—clauses which companies have not inserted, I suspect, because they never dreamed a court would uphold them—will soon find their way into the "boilerplate" of everything from an equipment lease to a conditional sales contract. Today's holding gives a green light to every large company in this country to contrive contracts which declare with force of law that when such a company wants to sue someone with whom it does business, that individual must go and try to defend himself in some place, no matter how distant, where big business enterprises are concentrated, like, for example, New York, Connecticut, or Illinois, or else suffer a default judgment. In this very case the Court holds that by this company's carefully prepared contractual clause the Szukhents must, to avoid a judgment rendered without a fair and full hearing, travel hundreds of miles across the continent, probably crippling their defense and certainly depleting what savings they may have, to try to defend themselves in a court sitting in New York City. I simply cannot believe that Congress, when by its silence it let Rule 4(d)(1) go into effect, meant for that rule to be used as a means to achieve such a far-reaching, burdensome, and unjust result. Heretofore judicial good common sense has, on one ground or another, disregarded contractual provisions like this one, not encouraged them. It is a long trip from San Francisco—or from Honolulu or Anchorage—to New York, Boston, or Wilmington. And the trip can be very expensive, often costing more than it would simply to pay what is demanded. The very threat of such a suit can be used to force payment of alleged claims, even though they be wholly without merit. This fact will not be news to companies exerting their economic power to wangle such contracts. * * *

MR. JUSTICE BRENNAN, with whom THE CHIEF JUSTICE and MR. JUSTICE GOLDBERG join, dissenting.

I would affirm. In my view, federal standards and not state law must define who is "an agent authorized by appointment" within the meaning of Rule 4(d)(1). * * * In formulating these standards I would, *first,* construe Rule 4(d)(1) to deny validity to the appointment of a purported agent whose interests conflict with those of his supposed principal * * *. *Second,* I would require that the appointment include an explicit condition that the agent after service transmit the process forthwith to the principal. Although our decision in Wuchter v. Pizzutti * * * dealt with the constitutionality of a state statute, the reasoning of that case is persuasive that, in fashioning a federal agency rule, we should engraft the same requirement upon Rule 4(d)(1). *Third,* since the corporate plaintiff prepared the printed form contract, I would not hold the individual purchaser bound by the appointment without proof, in addition to his mere signature on the form, that the individual understandingly consented to be sued in a State not that of his residence. * * * It offends common sense to treat a printed form which closes an installment sale as embodying terms to all of which the individual knowingly assented. The sales pitch aims solely at getting the signature on the form and wastes no time explaining or even mentioning the print. * * *

Notes and Questions

1. In BUDGET MARKETING, INC. v. TOBACK, 88 F.R.D. 705 (D.Iowa 1981), a franchisee successfully moved to dismiss a franchisor's suit against him on the ground that he never was served in a manner permitted by law. The District Court held that service was improper when pursuant to a provision in a loan agreement, the franchisor caused a copy of the summons and complaint to be delivered to its own vice-president (the designated agent

of the franchisee for service of process) and the vice-president mailed (certified mail, return receipt requested) a copy of the summons and complaint to the franchisee at its last known address. The court ruled that the agency for receiving service of process was invalid per se and could not be validated by forwarding the papers. Is the result in *Toback* consistent with *Szukhent?* Does *Toback* turn on the fact that the plaintiff itself was the agent? Would it have made a difference if, instead of appointing the plaintiff's vice-president as its agent, the defendant had appointed the vice-president's husband? After all, in *Szukhent,* Florence Weinberg was possibly "related to an officer of the [plaintiff] corporation." If *Szukhent* and *Toback* are inconsistent, which of the two makes more sense?

2. Like jurisdiction, notice and service of process requirements may be waived by a party at trial or even in advance of litigation. For example, under the provisions of a cognovit note, a debtor may agree to submit to the jurisdiction of any court chosen by the creditor for an action to collect the debt and even may empower the creditor or any attorney to appear in the suit and confess judgment. Typically, by a cognovit note, the debtor waives objection to jurisdiction, notice, and service of process. In D.H. OVERMYER CO. v. FRICK CO., 405 U.S. 174, 92 S.Ct. 775, 31 L.Ed.2d 124 (1972), the Supreme Court considered the constitutionality of cognovit provisions and ruled that they were not per se violative of the Due Process Clause. Such agreements must be judged on a case-by-case basis, with particular sensitivity to whether there was inequality of bargaining power or lack of consideration. If cognovit notes are constitutionally acceptable, could the appointment in *Toback* be unconstitutional per se? Shouldn't the question in *Toback* have been whether the negotiation leading to the appointment was between parties with equal power? Or, is *Overmyer* wrongly decided?

Many state courts have invalidated cognovit notes and other "consent to judgment" provisions. See, e.g., Isbell v. County of Sonoma, 21 Cal.3d 61, 145 Cal.Rptr. 368, 577 P.2d 188, certiorari denied 349 U.S. 996, 99 S.Ct. 597, 58 L.Ed.2d 669 (1978). They rarely are employed outside of Pennsylvania, Delaware, Ohio, and Illinois.

e. Service on Artificial Entities: Corporations, Partnerships, and Unincorporated Associations

Rule 4(d)(3) authorizes service upon corporations, partnerships, and unincorporated associations that are subject to suit under a common name. The most frequently invoked portion of the rule is the part permitting service by delivery of process to an officer, a managing agent, or a general agent.

In INSURANCE CO. OF NORTH AMERICA v. S/S "HELLENIC CHALLENGER," 88 F.R.D. 545 (S.D.N.Y.1980), a United States Marshal deposited the summons and complaint with a claims adjuster at the office of defendant. The complaint stated an admiralty and maritime claim for nondelivery, shortage, loss, and damage relating to pickled sheepskins shipped to New York aboard defendant's vessel.

The adjuster who had accepted service of the summons and complaint was not expressly authorized by defendant to accept process; the only employees endowed with express authority to do so on behalf of defendant were all titled officers and the claims manager. At the time of service of the summons and complaint, the claims manager was absent due to illness and the adjuster, an assistant to the claims manager, accepted service.

Since the adjuster misplaced the summons and complaint, defendant remained unaware of the pendency of the lawsuit until its bank informed it that its account had been attached by the plaintiff. Only then did the defendant learn that the plaintiff's counsel had filed a default judgment and that a writ of execution had been issued. The court denied the defendant's motion to set aside the judgment on the basis of improper service of process.

Rule 4(d)(3) has been liberally construed by the courts and, as interpreted, does not require rigid formalism. To be valid, service of process is not limited solely to officially designated officers, managing agents or agents appointed by law for the receipt of process. Rather, "[r]ules governing service of process [are] to be construed in a manner reasonably calculated to effectuate their primary purpose: to give the defendant adequate notice that an action is pending. * * * [T]he rule does not require that service be made solely on a restricted class of formally titled officials, but rather permits it to be made 'upon a representative so integrated with the organization that he will know what to do with the papers. Generally, service is sufficient when made upon an individual who stands in such a position as to render it fair, reasonable and just to imply the authority on his part to receive services.'" * * *

Plaintiff's method of service of the summons and complaint was indeed "reasonably calculated" to alert defendants to the initiation of the suit. * * * [T]he adjuster served with the summons and complaint, can be categorized as a representative of defendant "well-integrated" into the organization and quite familiar with the formalities associated with the receipt of service of summonses and complaints. He had accepted service of summonses and complaints on behalf of defendant on at least two previous occasions * * * in connection with his ordinary duties of receiving and investigating new claims against defendant. Furthermore, it may be inferred from the facts presented on this motion that [the adjuster] had easy access to * * * the claims manager officially authorized to accept service of process, since the two men are separated from each other only by [the claims manager's] glass-walled office. [The adjuster's] familiarity with service of process negates any and all suspicion that the U.S. Marshal delivered the summons and complaint to a representative of defendant who had infrequent contact with summonses and complaints and whose unfamiliarity with service of process increased the risk of careless or improper handling. * * *

In the case at hand, the * * * adjuster's loss of the summons and complaint is a mistake in the ordinary course of the internal operations of defendant's business and thus does not merit remedial relief * * *.

Id. at 547–48.

Notes and Questions

1. Is the court's willingness to disregard labels and conclusory terms such as "general" and "managing" agent consistent with the clear require-

ments of Rule 4(d)(3)? Should the court simply have held that the claims adjuster could be regarded as a "managing" agent of the defendant?

2. Could the court reasonably have reached the same result by finding that the claims adjuster was an agent authorized by appointment to receive process? In FASHION PAGE, LTD. v. ZURICH INS. CO., 50 N.Y.2d 265, 270–73, 428 N.Y.S.2d 890, 892–94, 406 N.E.2d 747, 749–51 (1980), the process-server went to the defendant's office where he was greeted by a receptionist. The receptionist told him to proceed down a certain corridor and to "see the girl sitting down there." Following instructions, the process-server went to the executive secretary of the vice president in charge of the New York office. She asked to see the papers and after perusing them said, "Okay, leave it with me. * * * I'll take it." When the process-server questioned her authority, she responded, "I can take it."

There was doubt that the executive secretary possessed sufficient discretionary authority to be a "managing agent" for purposes of service. The New York Court of Appeals, however, refused to be drawn into that issue, finding instead that the executive secretary was an "agent authorized by appointment * * * to receive service." The executive secretary testified that she had regularly accepted summonses for at least five years whenever the vice president was not in the office. During that period about half of the summonses brought to his office had been accepted by her.

> Thus a corporation may assign the task of accepting process and may establish procedures for insuring that the papers are directed to those ultimately responsible for defending its interests. * * * The corporation however cannot escape the consequences of establishing alternative procedures which it may prefer. * * * Reliance may be based on the corporate employees to identify the proper person to accept service.
>
> * * *

3. RETURN OF SERVICE

After the process-server has delivered the papers, she must file a return, which should disclose enough facts to demonstrate that defendant actually has been served and given notice that he is required to appear in court. Thus, although the actual service of process and not the proof of that act is a prerequisite to the court assuming jurisdiction, it has been held that a proper return ordinarily is necessary in order for the trial court to conclude it has jurisdiction. The specific form that proof of service must take varies from state to state, as well as according to the method of service used. An affidavit executed by the person who performed the acts constituting service, or the sworn statement of the officer—the marshal, sheriff, or deputy—who made the service, is the usual proof.

Should the process-server's return of service be considered conclusive or merely presumptive evidence that service has been effected? Consider the rationale advanced by the Supreme Court in MIEDREICH v. LAUENSTEIN, 232 U.S. 236, 34 S.Ct. 309, 58 L.Ed. 584 (1914), in which plaintiff sought to vacate a mortgage foreclosure judgment rendered in a prior suit. She was not a resident of the county in which the action was brought, was not served with process, and had no knowledge of the prior proceeding;

the sheriff had made a false return of summons. The Supreme Court upheld the prior judgment:

> In the present case the * * * original party in the foreclosure proceeding did all that the law required in the issue of and attempt to serve process; and, without fraud or collusion, the sheriff made a return to the court that service had been duly made. * * * [A]lthough contrary to the fact, in the absence of any attack upon it, the court was justified in acting upon such return as upon a true return. If the return is false the law of the State * * * permitted a recovery against the sheriff upon his bond. We are of the opinion that this system of jurisprudence, with its provisions for safeguarding the rights of litigants, is due process of law. It may result, unfortunately, * * * that the recovery upon the sheriff's bond will not be an adequate remedy, but statutes must be framed and laws administered so as to protect * * * all litigants and other persons who derive rights from the judgments of courts. * * * [T]he purchaser at the sheriff's sale had a right to rely upon the record * * *.

Id. at 246, 34 S.Ct. at 312, 58 L.Ed. at 591. Is it significant that *Miedreich* involved a collateral attack on the sheriff's return? Would the result have been the same if a direct attack in the original proceeding had been involved?

In most American jurisdictions, the return of service is considered strong evidence of the facts stated, but it is not conclusive and may be controverted by proof that the return is inaccurate. However, the defendant's own testimony generally will not be sufficient to impeach the return unless it is corroborated by other evidence. See 4A Wright & Miller, *Federal Practice and Procedure: Civil 2d* § 1130, at 349–52 (1987).

"Sewer" Service

In UNITED STATES v. BRAND JEWELERS, INC., 318 F.Supp. 1293 (S.D.N.Y.1970), noted in 37 Brooklyn L.Rev. 426, 84 Harv.L.Rev. 1930, 46 N.Y.U.L.Rev. 367, 20 J.Pub.L. 337, 24 Vand.L.Rev. 829, 17 Wayne L.Rev. 1287, 1971 Wis.L.Rev. 665, it was held that the United States had standing to seek an injunction preventing defendant from systematically obtaining default judgments against economically disadvantaged defendants by utilizing so-called "sewer" service techniques, by which the process-server simply disposes of the papers and makes a false affidavit of service. The actions were for the purchase price of consumer goods sold on "easy credit terms" by door-to-door salesmen. The court reasoned that continuously failing to make proper service of process or preparing false affidavits of service imposed "a burden on interstate commerce." Moreover, defendants' alleged conduct was held to be "state action" so that the United States had standing to sue to end a widespread unconstitutional deprivation of property without due process of law.

In 1972, the case was settled, and a consent decree issued. It vacated the default judgments obtained by Brand Jewelers from 1969 to 1971, established procedures to notify defendants that they could proceed to a trial on the merits, and placed upon Brand Jewelers' attorney the duty of ensuring that future service of process would be fair and in good faith. What are the advantages and disadvantages of placing that duty on an attorney? See Federal Rule 11 for an example of relying on an attorney's good faith in a different context.

Responding to the mounting criticism of "sewer service," in 1970 New York radically changed the requirements of personal service. Until then, delivery of a summons to a person other than the defendant was not permitted unless the process-server had first exercised due diligence to locate the defendant. The burden of this requirement was viewed as the single most important cause of "sewer service." The revision adopted by the legislature allows service by leaving one copy of the summons with a person of suitable age and discretion at the place where the defendant actually works, dwells, or usually abides and by mailing a second copy to defendant's last known address. N.Y.C.P.L.R. § 308(2). In 1973, the legislature took the additional step of requiring process-servers to make more detailed statements relating to how the process was served. N.Y. C.P.L.R. § 306.

4. SERVICE OF PROCESS AND STATUTES OF LIMITATIONS

All states have statutes of limitations that fix specific time limits within which various categories of actions must be brought. They are supplemented by bodies of law that define when various causes of action are said to "accrue," the point when the limitations clock begins to run on an action, and the circumstances in which the running of the clock is suspended or "tolled" because a plaintiff for some reason has been prevented from timely asserting her rights. See generally *Developments in the Law—Statutes of Limitations,* 63 Harv.L.Rev. 1177 (1950). Although statutes of limitations generally are deemed "procedural," their impact decidedly is "substantive"—a plaintiff loses the opportunity to invoke the assistance of the courts to obtain relief for an otherwise valid claim. Almost the first duty of a lawyer for a potential plaintiff is to determine, by the most conservative estimates, the latest possible day for commencing an action.

When is a suit "commenced" for purposes of a statute of limitations? In some states, an action is not deemed "commenced" until process is served on the defendant. In these states, a defect in service can be fatal to the plaintiff's claim, because the statute of limitations may have run before the plaintiff has a chance to correct his error.

Consider MARKOFF v. SOUTH NASSAU COMMUNITY HOSP., 61 N.Y.2d 283, 473 N.Y.S.2d 766, 461 N.E.2d 1253 (1984), a medical malpractice action by decedent's executrix against a hospital and three physicians. The plaintiff experienced difficulty in personally serving the physicians, and just before the limitations period was to expire obtained an ex parte order permitting her to leave the summonses at the defendant hospital, where they were apparently received by the physicians. However, the physicians were successful in having the action dismissed on the ground that the service was improper. Plaintiff later succeeded in personally delivering a summons to each of the doctors, effectively starting a new action against them on the same claim. Defendants moved to dismiss the second action as well, this time asserting the bar of the statute of limitations. And the action clearly was barred unless plaintiff could invoke the New York "saving" statute, which permits a party six months to reinstitute an action that was timely when originally commenced and was terminated other than on the merits. The Court of Appeals held that an action dismissed for a defect of service has not been "commenced" for the purposes of the "saving" statute, and therefore cannot make timely a second action brought on the same claim.

In other states, an action is deemed "commenced" for purposes of the statute of limitations merely by filing the complaint with the court. In California, an action is "commenced" once the plaintiff files the complaint—though, after filing, the plaintiff may take up to three years to serve process, Cal.Code Civ.Proc. §§ 4411.10, 583.210, and the California courts have suggested that they even have discretion to extend the time further.

In federal court, when the underlying cause of action is based on federal law, Rule 3 governs when the action is commenced. Thus, the suit is commenced when a copy of the complaint is filed with the district court. West v. Conrail, 481 U.S. 35, 107 S.Ct. 1538, 95 L.Ed.2d 32 (1987). However, when the underlying cause of action is based on state law, state law will govern when the action is commenced. See Walker v. Armco Steel Corp., 446 U.S. 740, 100 S.Ct. 1978, 64 L.Ed.2d 659 (1980).

As a separate matter, it is noteworthy that new Rule 4(j), adopted in 1983, requires a federal court to dismiss without prejudice an action when the defendant has not been served within 120 days of the filing of the complaint, if the plaintiff fails to show "good cause" for not completing service within that time. If the statute of limitations expires during that period, and if the plaintiff's action is dismissed, can the plaintiff refile the complaint and thus still maintain the action? See Burks v. Griffith, 100 F.R.D. 491 (N.D.N.Y.1984) (attempt at refiling civil rights action met with a successful statute of limitations challenge; court observed that the problem could have been avoided had plaintiff utilized Rule 6(b) and requested an extension of time to serve her summons and complaint).

If service is promptly attempted but improperly made, should a federal court dismiss the action without prejudice, or should it merely quash service and order the plaintiff to re-serve? The general view has been that the court has discretion in this matter—discretion that is exercised with an eye toward the circumstances of the case. Courts dismiss when the plaintiff has little likelihood of effecting proper service. In cases in which the plaintiff cannot hope to acquire jurisdiction over the defendant through proper service, keeping the action alive unnecessarily burdens the courts. On the other hand, when the plaintiff can make proper service quickly, courts generally quash the faulty service without prejudice to the plaintiff to serve again. See, e.g., Alexander v. Unification Church of America, 634 F.2d 673, 675 (2d Cir.1980), in which the court approved an order by the district court refusing to dismiss when plaintiff could re-serve, and Grammenos v. Lemos, 457 F.2d 1067, 1071 (2d

Cir.1972), in which the court reversed the district court's dismissal because plaintiff could conceivably have effected service.

SECTION F. IMMUNITY FROM PROCESS AND ETIQUETTE OF SERVICE

1. IMMUNITY FROM PROCESS

A court sometimes will immunize a party from service of process, despite the fact that the constitutional and statutory conditions governing personal jurisdiction and service of process have been met. In such cases, the grant of immunity usually is justified as promoting the administration of justice. Thus, although the doctrine may help a party avoid suit, it does so not for the benefit of the party, but for the benefit of the court. For example, witnesses, parties, and attorneys who come to a state to participate in a lawsuit often are granted immunity from service of process in other suits.

STATE EX REL. SIVNKSTY v. DUFFIELD

Supreme Court of Appeals of West Virginia, 1952.
137 W.Va. 112, 71 S.E.2d 113.

[On June 30, 1951, while vacationing in Gilmer County, West Virginia, petitioner Sivnksty's automobile struck and injured two children who were walking along the highway. He was arrested on charges of reckless driving, and, being unable to post bond, was incarcerated in the county jail until his trial on July 2. While he was in jail awaiting trial, Sivnksty was served with process in a tort action brought by one of the children in the Circuit Court of Gilmer County. Sivnksty was found guilty of the criminal charge and his appeals from that conviction failed.

Sivnksty made a special appearance in the civil action and filed a plea in abatement, alleging that the court was without jurisdiction because at the time of service he was a nonresident of the county and a prisoner in the county jail. The court sustained a demurrer to the plea in abatement, whereupon Sivnksty petitioned the Supreme Court of Appeals of West Virginia for a writ of prohibition against the judge of the trial court. A stipulation was filed with the appellate court stating that Sivnksty had entered Gilmer County on June 30, 1951, with the intention of remaining there through the Fourth of July holiday and that he left the county immediately upon his release on appeal bond following his conviction on July 2, 1951.]

RILEY, PRESIDENT. * * *

The sole question presented by this record is: In the circumstances of this case was the petitioner immune from civil process at the time he was served with process in the civil action? Petitioner asserts here that the mere fact that he intended, when he came into Gilmer County, to remain for a period of a few days could not render his continuing presence in Gilmer County, after he was arrested, one of a voluntary status, when he was, in fact, incarcerated in the county jail there against his will.

The original and prime purpose for which the privilege of immunity from civil process on nonresidents of a county or state charged with crime therein was the protection of the court itself from interference with its judicial processes. Thus, originally the rule was asserted as the privilege of the court to secure the administration of justice free from outside interference or influence. Later the rule was enlarged for the protection of suitors, witnesses, jurors, and court officials from process, both in civil and criminal cases. Whited v. Phillips, 98 W.Va. 204, 205, 206, 126 S.E. 916, 917, 40 A.L.R. 83. In the Whited case the Court said: "It is well said that, if there is ever a time when a man should be relieved of all other concerns, and when he should be permitted to use unhampered his every faculty, it is when he is on trial under charge of a crime. Judicial reasoning also recognizes the right of a man, ordinarily, to be tried by a jury in the vicinity in which he resides, so that he may have such advantage and safeguard there as his conduct and character shall merit."

In addition the privilege of immunity from civil process of a nonresident of a county or state, charged with crime therein, has underlying it the public policy that a person charged with crime in a county of which he is a nonresident will not be deterred from appearing before the courts of that county or state by the threat of civil or other process; and thus a person so charged with crime because of the immunity extended will be encouraged to return to the county or state in which he is charged with crime to respond to the criminal process.

* * *

In the syllabus to Whited v. Phillips, supra, perhaps the leading case in this jurisdiction, bearing on the instant subject matter, this Court held: "A non-resident of West Virginia, who voluntarily and without compulsion of law, submits himself to the jurisdiction of a state court, in answer to an indictment therein against him, and who is not at the time a fugitive from justice, is privileged while attending court from service of process in a civil suit." In this jurisdiction the immunity rule has been applied to a case in which a defendant in a civil action was served with process while he was in a county, of which he was not a resident, in obedience to a citation from a member of the Department of Public Safety to answer a criminal charge. Morris v. Calhoun, 119 W.Va. 603, pt. 3 syl., 195 S.E. 341. It has also been applied to a case in which a person charged with a criminal offense in a county of which he was a nonresident, was arrested therefor in that county and later released on bond on his own recognizance, and who, in pursuance of such recognizance, returned to the county to answer the charge on the day set for trial. Lang v. Shaw, 113 W.Va. 628, syl., 169 S.E. 444. But in the case of State ex rel. Godby v. Chambers, 130 W.Va. 115, pt. 2 syl., 42 S.E.2d 255, 256, * * * the Court refused the writ of prohibition on the ground that after petitioner's conviction, sentence, and incarceration on a misdemeanor charge, the reason for the application of the immunity rule was not present, and that in that case there was no criminal process within the meaning of the immunity rule. * * *

In the instant case the petitioner went to Gilmer County of his own volition: he did not enter the county in response to a criminal process, because at the time of his entry therein he had committed no crime, and there was pending against him no criminal case. * * * In Crusco v. Strunk Steel Co., 365 Pa. 326, 74 A.2d 142, 20 A.L.R.2d 160, the Pennsylvania Supreme Court held that a defendant residing outside of a county in which a civil action had been commenced, and who was arrested on a warrant issued on an information of the plaintiff in the civil action and brought within the county, was not immune from civil process merely because of his status as a criminal defendant. * * * In 72 C.J.S., Process, § 82, the rule is well stated as follows: "A person confined in jail on a criminal charge or imprisoned on conviction for such charge is subject to service of civil process, irrespective of the question of residence, at least if he was voluntarily in the jurisdiction at the time of the arrest and confinement." * * *

As the petitioner did not come and was not brought into Gilmer County under criminal process, the reason for the application of the immunity rule is not present, and he is not entitled to the writ of prohibition prayed for.

Writ denied.

LOVINS, JUDGE (dissenting). * * *

In this jurisdiction there is no statute dealing with the subject of immunity from service of judicial process to a person to whom the rule applies. The law on the subject will be found in the opinion of this court in Whited v. Phillips, supra, and cases subsequently decided by this court hereinafter cited. This court in the Whited case used the following language: "Judicial reasoning also recognizes the right of a man, ordinarily, to be tried by a jury in the vicinity in which he resides, so that he may have such advantage and safeguard there as his conduct and character shall merit. An additional argument for the extension of the rule is that a person should not ordinarily be drawn into a foreign jurisdiction 'and there be exposed to entanglements in litigation far from home, which means he shall be attended with augmented expense.'" * * *

The specific question here considered is: May a defendant in a criminal charge, confined in jail on such charge and unable to furnish bail bond, be served with process commencing a civil action based on the same facts as those involved in the criminal prosecution?

An examination of the various authorities will disclose that the courts of last resort which have considered this question are not in accord and that the authorities are in confusion with respect to the same. * * *

In the instant case, Sivnksty came into Gilmer County voluntarily for the purpose of fishing. While there, he had an accident and thereafter was incarcerated in the jail. His presence in Gilmer County, originally voluntary, became involuntary. * * * I think whether Sivnksty came into Gilmer County voluntarily or otherwise has no pertinency to the question here presented.

Sivnksty will be forced to trial in a county far from his residence, among strangers. Even though he may have led an exemplary life and may have had a good reputation in the county of his residence, he would derive little or no benefit from those factors. In addition, he was harassed in his defense of the criminal charge by the institution of the civil suit against him while the criminal charge was still pending. This case is dissimilar from State ex rel. Godby v. Chambers, supra. In that case, the defendant had already been convicted.

Another element enters into this case. It is a matter of common knowledge that in this day and age there is much travel by motor vehicles. Under the rule laid down in the majority opinion, the luckless motorist, who has the misfortune to have an accident injuring persons or property in a county or state far from his residence, may be arrested and incarcerated in jail on a criminal charge, based on a real or fancied violation of an ordinance or statute having no connection with the accident, and while so incarcerated, the person suffering the injury would immediately commence an action in his own home county for the recovery of alleged damages. This could and may lead to widespread abuse of judicial process.

*   *   *

Notes and Questions

1. Although immunity from process serves legitimate goals, when carried to extremes it ignores the resident plaintiff's desire to litigate in a local forum. What limitations could be imposed on a witness' immunity from process in order to reach some form of balance between the competing interests? Should immunity be denied when the witness furthers some personal goal by entering the state to testify, or would such a test be too evanescent to enforce? See St. John v. Superior Court, 178 Cal.App.2d 794, 3 Cal.Rptr. 535 (2d Dist.1960); Franklin v. Superior Court, 98 Cal.App.2d 292, 220 P.2d 8 (1st Dist.1950). Should a nonresident attorney be exempt from process while in a state representing a client on a matter unrelated to the suit in which he is served? What if it is related? See State ex rel. Johnson v. Tautges, 146 Neb. 439, 20 N.W.2d 232 (1945). Should immunity depend upon whether the forum is a "convenient" one for defendant? What would be the ingredients of such a standard? See Note, *Immunity of Non-Resident Participants in a Judicial Proceeding from Service of Process—A Proposal for Renovation*, 26 Ind.L.J. 459 (1951). Under what circumstances should a court deny immunity to a witness or governmental official as a matter of discretion? See Lamb v. Schmitt, 285 U.S. 222, 52 S.Ct. 317, 76 L.Ed. 720 (1932); 61 Colum.L. Rev. 278 (1961). See generally 4 Wright & Miller, *Federal Practice and Procedure: Civil* §§ 1076–81 (1969).

2. In many instances immunity from process is governed by statute. For example, 22 U.S.C. §§ 254a–d and 288d(b) grant immunity to certain representatives of foreign governments, their families, and members of their households. What justification is there for giving these people immunity?

3. Does it make any sense to grant a defendant who can be reached outside the state under a long-arm statute immunity from process when she is within the state for a purpose that otherwise would qualify for immunity?

California and New York have abrogated immunity in these cases. Severn v. Adidas Sportschuhfabriken, 33 Cal.App.3d 754, 109 Cal.Rptr. 328 (1st Dist. 1973); Merigone v. Seaboard Capital Corp., 85 Misc.2d 965, 381 N.Y.S.2d 749 (Sup.Ct.1976).

2. ETIQUETTE OF SERVICE

WYMAN v. NEWHOUSE

United States Circuit Court of Appeals, Second Circuit, 1937.
93 F.2d 313.

MANTON, CIRCUIT JUDGE. This appeal is from a judgment entered dismissing the complaint on motion before trial. The action is on a judgment entered by default in a Florida state court, a jury having assessed the damages. The recovery there was for money loaned, money advanced for appellee, and for seduction under promise of marriage.

* * *

Appellant and appellee were both married, but before this suit appellant's husband died. They had known each other for some years and had engaged in meretricious relations.

The affidavits submitted by the appellee * * * established that he was a resident of New York and never lived in Florida. On October 25, 1935, while appellee was in Salt Lake City, Utah, he received a telegram from the appellant, which read: "Account illness home planning leaving. Please come on way back. Must see you." Upon appellee's return to New York he received a letter from appellant stating that her mother was dying in Ireland; that she was leaving the United States for good to go to her mother; that she could not go without seeing the appellee once more; and that she wanted to discuss her affairs with him before she left. Shortly after the receipt of this letter, they spoke to each other on the telephone, whereupon the appellant repeated, in a hysterical and distressed voice, the substance of her letter. Appellee promised to go to Florida in a week or ten days and agreed to notify her when he would arrive. This he did, but before leaving New York by plane he received a letter couched in endearing terms and expressing love and affection for him, as well as her delight at his coming. Before leaving New York, appellee telegraphed appellant, suggesting arrangements for their accommodations together while in Miami, Fla. She telegraphed him at a hotel in Washington, D.C., where he was to stop en route, advising him that the arrangements requested had been made. Appellee arrived at 6 o'clock in the morning at the Miami Airport and saw the appellant standing with her sister some 75 feet distant. He was met by a deputy sheriff who, upon identifying appellee, served him with process in a suit for $500,000. A photographer was present who attempted to take his picture. Thereupon a stranger introduced himself and offered to take appellee to his home, stating that he knew a lawyer who was acquainted with the appellant's attorney. The attorney whom appellee was advised to consult came to the stranger's home and seemed to know about the case. The attorney invited appellee to his office, and upon his arrival he found one of the lawyers for the appellant there. Appellee did not retain the Florida attorney to represent him. He returned to New York by plane that evening and consulted his New York counsel, who advised him to ignore the summons served in Florida. He did so, and judgment was entered by default. * * *

These facts and reasonable deductions therefrom convincingly establish that the appellee was induced to enter the jurisdiction of the state of Florida by a fraud perpetrated upon him by the appellant in falsely representing her mother's illness, her intention to leave the United States, and her love and affection for him, when her sole purpose and apparent thought was to induce him to come within the Florida jurisdiction so as to serve him in an action for damages. * * *

This judgment is attacked for fraud perpetrated upon the appellee which goes to the jurisdiction of the Florida court over his person. A judgment procured fraudulently, as here, lacks jurisdiction and is null and void. * * * A fraud affecting the jurisdiction is equivalent to a lack of jurisdiction. * * * The appellee was not required to proceed against the judgment in Florida. His equitable defense in answer to a suit on the judgment is sufficient. A judgment recovered in a sister state, through the fraud of the party procuring the appearance of another, is not binding on the latter when an attempt is made to enforce such judgment in another state. * * *

The appellee was not required to make out a defense on the merits to the suit in Florida. * * * An error made in entering judgment against a party over whom the court had no jurisdiction permits a consideration of the jurisdictional question collaterally. The complaint was properly dismissed.

Judgment affirmed.

Notes and Questions

1. Reread Tickle v. Barton, p. 23, supra. Which case presents a stronger case for quashing service—*Wyman* or *Tickle?* Why? Would the result have been the same in *Wyman* if Mr. Newhouse had been in Florida and the trickery had been used to "flush him out of hiding"? In Gumperz v. Hofmann, 245 App.Div. 622, 283 N.Y.S. 823 (1st Dep't 1935), affirmed 271 N.Y. 544, 2 N.E.2d 687 (1936), the court distinguished between actions designed to induce a party into a jurisdiction and actions calculated to facilitate service on a party already in the jurisdiction. In upholding service obtained by using trickery on a party who voluntarily was in New York, the court found a duty on the part of the party to accept service of process. The trickery, although reprehensible, did not lead to a quashing of service, since it merely was used to enforce a duty.

2. Instances in which a plaintiff will resort to tactics such as fraud, force, and artifice surely must be rare in an age when legitimate means of obtaining jurisdiction and serving process readily are available under long-arm statutes. Are the doctrines just examined obsolete? Are these rules justified simply because, even in the rare case, they will deter plaintiffs from doing such things?

SECTION G.   OPPORTUNITY TO BE HEARD

The Due Process Clause defines several conditions that must exist before a court may render a valid judgment. We already have seen that the court must have jurisdiction over the parties and issues before it. And we have seen that the parties must have adequate notice of the action. Yet another condition is imposed by the Due Process Clause: the parties must have an adequate opportunity to present their side of the case to the court.

In simple terms, a defendant has an adequate opportunity to be heard when—in light of the interests at stake in the litigation—she is able to develop the facts and legal issues in the case. Depending on the interests involved, a proper hearing may suffice, or a full trial may be required, or something in between may pass muster. One common requirement is that the defendant must be informed of the action (that is, must receive notice) long enough in advance of the time when she is required to respond so as to allow her to obtain counsel and prepare a defense. Thus, when, in ROLLER v. HOLLY, 176 U.S. 398, 20 S.Ct. 410, 44 L.Ed. 520 (1900), the defendant had been served in Virginia with process requiring him to defend an action in Texas only five days after the service was made, the Supreme Court held that the Due Process Clause had been violated. Consequently, Federal Rule 12(a) and state statutes generally allow defendants twenty days or more after service in which to respond.

The so-called "provisional remedies"—temporary restraining orders, preliminary injunctions, pre-action attachments and the like—represent important exceptions to the ordinary requirements associated with the constitutionally required opportunity to be heard. See Chapter 12, infra. For that reason, they present the most difficult problems in this area. The following cases examine the extent to which the Due Process Clause imposes limitations on the use of provisional remedies because they do not provide an adequate opportunity to be heard.

FUENTES v. SHEVIN

Supreme Court of the United States, 1972.
407 U.S. 67, 92 S.Ct. 1983, 32 L.Ed.2d 556, rehearing denied 409 U.S. 902, 93
S.Ct. 177, 34 L.Ed.2d 165.

Appeal from the United States District Court for the Southern District of Florida.

Mr. Justice Stewart delivered the opinion of the Court.

* * *

I

The appellant in No. 5039, Margarita Fuentes, is a resident of Florida. She purchased a gas stove and service policy from the Firestone Tire and Rubber Company (Firestone) under a conditional sales contract calling for monthly payments over a period of time. A few months later, she purchased a stereophonic phonograph from the same company under the same sort of contract. The total cost of the stove and stereo was about

$500, plus an additional financing charge of over $100. Under the contracts, Firestone retained title to the merchandise, but Mrs. Fuentes was entitled to possession unless and until she should default on her installment payments.

For more than a year, Mrs. Fuentes made her installment payments. But then, with only about $200 remaining to be paid, a dispute developed between her and Firestone over the servicing of the stove. Firestone instituted an action in a small claims court for repossession of both the stove and the stereo, claiming that Mrs. Fuentes had refused to make her remaining payments. Simultaneously with the filing of that action and before Mrs. Fuentes had even received a summons to answer its complaint, Firestone obtained a writ of replevin ordering a sheriff to seize the disputed goods at once.

* * *

Shortly thereafter, Mrs. Fuentes instituted the present action in a federal district court, challenging the constitutionality of the Florida prejudgment replevin procedures under the Due Process Clause of the Fourteenth Amendment. She sought declaratory and injunctive relief against continued enforcement of the procedural provisions of the state statutes that authorize prejudgment replevin.

The appellants in No. 5138 filed a very similar action in a federal district court in Pennsylvania, challenging the constitutionality of that State's prejudgment replevin process. Like Mrs. Fuentes, they had had possessions seized under writs of replevin. Three of the appellants had purchased personal property—a bed, a table, and other household goods—under installment sales contracts like the one signed by Mrs. Fuentes; and the sellers of the property had obtained and executed summary writs of replevin, claiming that the appellants had fallen behind in their installment payments. The experience of the fourth appellant, Rosa Washington, had been more bizarre. She had been divorced from a local deputy sheriff and was engaged in a dispute with him over the custody of their son. Her former husband, being familiar with the routine forms used in the replevin process, had obtained a writ that ordered the seizure of the boy's clothes, furniture, and toys.

In both No. 5039 and No. 5138, three-judge district courts were convened to consider the appellants' challenges to the constitutional validity of the Florida and Pennsylvania statutes. The courts in both cases upheld the constitutionality of the statutes. * * *

II

Under the Florida statute challenged here, "[a]ny person whose goods or chattels are wrongfully detained by any other person * * * may have a writ of replevin to recover them * * *." Fla.Stats. § 78.01, F.S.A. There is no requirement that the applicant make a convincing showing before the seizure that the goods are, in fact, "wrongfully detained." Rather, Florida law * * * requires only that the applicant file a complaint, initiating a court action for repossession and reciting in conclusory fashion that he is "lawfully entitled to the possession" of the property, and that he file a security bond ＊ ＊ ＊. On the sole basis of the complaint and bond, a writ is issued "command[ing] the officer to whom it may be directed to replevy the goods and chattels in possession of defendant ＊ ＊ ＊ and to summon the defendant to answer the complaint." Fla.Stats. § 78.08. If the goods are "in any dwelling house or other building or enclosure," the officer is required to demand their delivery; but if they are not delivered, "he shall cause such house, building or enclosure to be broken open and shall make replevin according to the writ ＊ ＊ ＊." Fla.Stats. § 78.10, F.S.A.

Thus, at the same moment that the defendant receives the complaint seeking repossession of property through court action, the property is seized from him. He is provided no prior notice and allowed no opportunity whatever to challenge the issuance of the writ. *After* the property has been seized, he will eventually have an opportunity for a hearing, as the defendant in the trial of the court action for repossession, which the plaintiff is required to pursue. And he is also not wholly without recourse in the meantime. For under the Florida statute, the officer who seizes the property must keep it for three days, and during that period the defendant may reclaim possession of the property by posting his own security bond in double its value. But if he does not post such a bond, the property is transferred to the party who sought the writ, pending a final judgment in the underlying action for repossession. ＊ ＊ ＊

The Pennsylvania law differs, though not in its essential nature, from that of Florida. As in Florida, a private party may obtain a prejudgment writ of replevin through a summary process of *ex parte* application, although a prothonotary rather than a court clerk issues the writ. As in Florida, the party seeking the writ may simply post with his application a bond in double the value of the property to be seized. ＊ ＊ ＊ There is no opportunity for a prior hearing and no prior notice to the other party. On this basis, a sheriff is required to execute the writ by seizing the specified property. Unlike the Florida statute, however, the Pennsylvania law does not require that there *ever* be opportunity for a hearing on the merits of the conflicting claims to possession of the replevied property. The party seeking the writ is not obliged to initiate a court action for repossession. Indeed, he need not even formally allege that he is lawfully entitled to the property. ＊ ＊ ＊ If the party who loses property through replevin seizure is to get even a postseizure hearing, he must initiate a lawsuit himself. He may also, as under Florida law, post his own counterbond within three days after the seizure to regain possession. ＊ ＊ ＊

III

＊ ＊ ＊ [Prejudgment replevin statutes] are most commonly used by creditors to seize goods allegedly wrongfully detained—not wrongfully taken—by debtors. At common law, if a creditor wished to invoke state power to recover goods wrongfully detained, he had to proceed through the action of debt or detinue. These actions, however, did not provide for a return of property before final judgment. And, more importantly, on the occasions when the common law did allow prejudgment seizure by state power, it provided some kind of notice and opportunity to be heard to the party then in possession of the property, and a state official made at least a summary determination of the relative rights of the disputing parties before stepping into the dispute and taking goods from one of them.

IV

For more than a century the central meaning of procedural due process has been clear: "Parties whose rights are to be affected are entitled to be heard; and in order that they may enjoy that right they must be notified." Baldwin v. Hale, 68 U.S. 223, 1 Wall. 223, 17 L.Ed. 531. * * * It is equally fundamental that the right to notice and an opportunity to be heard "must be granted at a meaningful time and in a meaningful manner." Armstrong v. Manzo, 380 U.S. 545, 552, 85 S.Ct. 1187, 1191, 14 L.Ed.2d 62.

The primary question in the present cases is whether these state statutes are constitutionally defective in failing to provide for hearings "at a meaningful time." The Florida replevin process guarantees an opportunity for a hearing after the seizure of goods, and the Pennsylvania process allows a post-seizure hearing if the aggrieved party shoulders the burden of initiating one. But neither the Florida nor Pennsylvania statute provides for notice or an opportunity to be heard *before* the seizure. * * *

The constitutional right to be heard is a basic aspect of the duty of government to follow a fair process of decisionmaking when it acts to deprive a person of his possessions. The purpose of this requirement is not only to ensure abstract fair play to the individual. Its purpose, more particularly, is to protect his use and possession of property from arbitrary encroachment—to minimize substantively unfair or mistaken deprivations of property, a danger that is especially great when the State seizes goods simply upon the application of and for the benefit of a private party. So viewed, the prohibition against the deprivation of property without due process of law reflects the high value, embedded in our constitutional and political history, that we place on a person's right to enjoy what is his, free of governmental interference. * * *

The requirement of notice and an opportunity to be heard raises no impenetrable barrier to the taking of a person's possessions. But the fair process of decision-making that it guarantees works, by itself, to protect against arbitrary deprivation of property. For when a person has an opportunity to speak up in his own defense, and when the State must listen to what he has to say, substantively unfair and simply mistaken deprivations of property interests can be prevented. It has long been recognized that "fairness can rarely be obtained by secret, one-sided determination of facts decisive of rights. * * * [And n]o better instrument has been devised for arriving at truth than to give a person in jeopardy of serious loss notice of the case against him and opportunity to meet it." Joint Anti-Fascist Refugee Committee v. McGrath, 341 U.S. 123, 170–172, 71 S.Ct. 624, 647, 95 L.Ed. 817 (Frankfurter, J., concurring).

If the right to notice and a hearing is to serve its full purpose, then, it is clear that it must be granted at a time when the deprivation can still be prevented. At a later hearing, an individual's possessions can be returned to him if they were unfairly or mistakenly taken in the first place. Damages may even be awarded to him for the wrongful deprivation. But no later hearing and no damage award can undo the fact that the arbitrary taking that was subject to the right of procedural due process has already occurred. "This Court has not * * * embraced the general proposition that a wrong may be done if it can be undone." Stanley v. Illinois, 405 U.S. 645, 647, 92 S.Ct. 1208, 1210, 31 L.Ed.2d 551.

This is no new principle of constitutional law. The right to a prior hearing has long been recognized by this Court under the Fourteenth and Fifth Amendments. Although the Court has held that due process tolerates variances in the *form* of a hearing "appropriate to the nature of the case," Mullane v. Central Hanover Tr. Co., * * * and "depending upon the importance of the interests involved and the nature of the subsequent proceedings [if any]," Boddie v. Connecticut, 401 U.S. 371, 378, 91 S.Ct. 780, 786, 28 L.Ed.2d 113, the Court has traditionally insisted that, whatever its form, opportunity for that hearing must be provided before the deprivation at issue takes effect. * * * "That the hearing required by due process is subject to waiver, and is not fixed in form does not affect its root requirement that an individual be given an opportunity for a hearing *before* he is deprived of any significant property interest, except for extraordinary situations where some valid governmental interest is at stake that justifies postponing the hearing until after the event." Boddie v. Connecticut, supra, 401 U.S., at 378–379, 91 S.Ct., at 786 (emphasis in original).

The Florida and Pennsylvania prejudgment replevin statutes fly in the face of this principle. To be sure, the requirements that a party seeking a writ must first post a bond, allege conclusorily that he is entitled to specific goods, and open himself to possible liability in damages if he is wrong, serve to deter wholly unfounded applications for a writ. But those requirements are hardly a substitute for a prior hearing, for they test no more than the strength of the applicant's own belief in his rights.[13] Since his private gain is at stake, the danger is all too great that his confidence in his cause will be misplaced. Lawyers and judges are familiar with the phenomenon of a party mistakenly but firmly convinced that his view of the facts and law will prevail, and therefore quite willing to risk the costs of litigation. Because of the understandable, self-interested fallibility of litigants, a court does not decide a dispute until it has had an opportunity to hear both sides—and does not generally take even tentative action until it has itself examined the support for the plaintiff's position. The Florida and Pennsylvania statutes do not even require the official issuing a writ of replevin to do that much.

---

13. They may not even test that much. For if an applicant for the writ knows that he is dealing with an uneducated, uninformed consumer with little access to legal help and little familiarity with legal procedures, there may be a substantial possibility that a summary seizure of property—however unwarranted—may go unchallenged, and the applicant may feel that he can act with impunity.

The minimal deterrent effect of a bond requirement is, in a practical sense, no substitute for an informed evaluation by a neutral official. More specifically, as a matter of constitutional principle, it is no replacement for the right to a prior hearing that is the only truly effective safeguard against arbitrary deprivation of property. While the existence of these other, less effective, safeguards may be among the considerations that affect the form of hearing demanded by due process, they are far from enough by themselves to obviate the right to a prior hearing of some kind.

V

The right to a prior hearing, of course, attaches only to the deprivation of an interest encompassed within the Fourteenth Amendment's protection. In the present cases, the Florida and Pennsylvania statutes were applied to replevy chattels in the appellants' possession. The replevin was not cast as a final judgment; most, if not all, of the appellants lacked full title to the chattels; and their claim even to continued possession was a matter in dispute. Moreover, the chattels at stake were nothing more than an assortment of household goods. Nonetheless, it is clear that the appellants were deprived of possessory interests in those chattels that were within the protection of the Fourteenth Amendment.

A

* * * The Florida and Pennsylvania statutes do not require a person to wait until a post-seizure hearing and final judgment to recover what has been replevied. Within three days after the seizure, the statutes allow him to recover the goods if he, in return, surrenders other property—a payment necessary to secure a bond in double the value of the goods seized from him.[14] But it is now well settled that a temporary, nonfinal deprivation of property is nonetheless a "deprivation" in the terms of the Fourteenth Amendment. * * *

* * * The Fourteenth Amendment draws no bright lines around three-day, 10-day or 50-day deprivations of property. Any significant taking of property by the State is within the purview of the Due Process Clause. While the length and consequent severity of a deprivation may be another factor to weigh in determining the appropriate form of hearing, it is not decisive of the basic right to a prior hearing of some kind.

B

The appellants who signed conditional sales contracts lacked full legal title to the replevied goods. The Fourteenth Amendment's protection of "property," however, has never been interpreted to safeguard only the

---

14. The appellants argue that this opportunity for quick recovery exists only in theory. They allege that very few people in their position are able to obtain a recovery bond, even if they know of the possibility. Appellant Fuentes says that in her case she was never told that she could recover the stove and stereo and that the deputy sheriff seizing them gave them at once to the Firestone agent, rather than holding them for three days. She further asserts that of 442 cases of prejudgment replevin in small claims courts in Dade County, Florida, in 1969, there was not one case in which the defendant took advantage of the recovery provision.

rights of undisputed ownership. Rather, it has been read broadly to extend protection to "any significant property interest" * * *.

The appellants were deprived of such an interest in the replevied goods—the interest in continued possession and use of the goods. * * * They had acquired this interest under the conditional sales contracts that entitled them to possession and use of the chattels before transfer of title. In exchange for immediate possession, the appellants had agreed to pay a major financing charge beyond the basic price of the merchandise. Moreover, by the time the goods were summarily repossessed, they had made substantial installment payments. Clearly, their possessory interest in the goods, dearly bought and protected by contract, was sufficient to invoke the protection of the Due Process Clause.

Their ultimate right to continued possession was, of course, in dispute. If it were shown at a hearing that the appellants had defaulted on their contractual obligations, it might well be that the sellers of the goods would be entitled to repossession. But even assuming that the appellants had fallen behind in their installment payments, and that they had no other valid defenses, that is immaterial here. The right to be heard does not depend upon an advance showing that one will surely prevail at the hearing. * * *

they may lose but still have right to hearing

C

Nevertheless, the district courts rejected the appellants' constitutional claim on the ground that the goods seized from them—a stove, a stereo, a table, a bed, and so forth—were not deserving of due process protection, since they were not absolute necessities of life. The courts based this holding on a very narrow reading of Sniadach v. Family Finance Corp., [395 U.S. 337, 89 S.Ct. 1820, 23 L.Ed.2d 349 (1969)] * * * and Goldberg v. Kelly, * * * [397 U.S. 254, 90 S.Ct. 1011, 25 L.Ed.2d 287 (1970)], in which this Court held that the Constitution requires a hearing before prejudgment wage garnishment and before the termination of certain welfare benefits. They reasoned that Sniadach and Goldberg, as a matter of constitutional principle, established no more than that a prior hearing is required with respect to the deprivation of such basically "necessary" items as wages and welfare benefits.

This reading of Sniadach and Goldberg reflects the premise that those cases marked a radical departure from established principles of procedural due process. They did not. Both decisions were in the mainstream of past cases, having little or nothing to do with the absolute "necessities" of life but establishing that due process requires an opportunity for a hearing before a deprivation of property takes effect. * * * While Sniadach and Goldberg emphasized the special importance of wages and welfare benefits, they did not convert that emphasis into a new and more limited constitutional doctrine.

* * *

VI

There are "extraordinary situations" that justify postponing notice and opportunity for a hearing. Boddie v. Connecticut, supra, 401 U.S., at

379, 91 S.Ct., at 786. These situations, however, must be truly unusual. Only in a few limited situations has this Court allowed outright seizure [23] without opportunity for a prior hearing. First, in each case, the seizure has been directly necessary to secure an important governmental or general public interest. Second, there has been a special need for very prompt action. Third, the State has kept strict control over its monopoly of legitimate force; the person initiating the seizure has been a government official responsible for determining, under the standards of a narrowly drawn statute, that it was necessary and justified in the particular instance. Thus, the Court has allowed summary seizure of property to collect the internal revenue of the United States, to meet the needs of a national war effort, to protect against the economic disaster of a bank failure, and to protect the public from misbranded drugs and contaminated food.

The Florida and Pennsylvania prejudgment replevin statutes serve no such important governmental or general public interest. They allow summary seizure of a person's possessions when no more than private gain is directly at stake.[29] * * *

Nor do the broadly drawn Florida and Pennsylvania statutes limit the summary seizure of goods to special situations demanding prompt action. There may be cases in which a creditor could make a showing of immediate danger that a debtor will destroy or conceal disputed goods. But the statutes before us are not "narrowly drawn to meet any such unusual condition." Sniadach v. Family Finance Corp., supra, 395 U.S. at 339, 89 S.Ct. at 1821. And no such unusual situation is presented by the facts of these cases.

The statutes, moreover, abdicate effective state control over state power. Private parties, serving their own private advantage, may unilaterally invoke state power to replevy goods from another. No state official

23. * * * In three cases, the Court has allowed the attachment of property without a prior hearing. In one, the attachment was necessary to protect the public against the same sort of immediate harm involved in the seizure cases—a bank failure. Coffin Bros. & Co. v. Bennett, 277 U.S. 29, 48 S.Ct. 422, 72 L.Ed. 768. Another case involved attachment necessary to secure jurisdiction in state court—clearly a most basic and important public interest. Ownbey v. Morgan, 256 U.S. 94, 41 S.Ct. 433, 65 L.Ed. 837. It is much less clear what interests were involved in the third case, decided with an unexplicated per curiam opinion simply citing Coffin Bros. and Ownbey. McKay v. McInnes, 279 U.S. 820, 49 S.Ct. 344, 73 L.Ed. 975. As far as essential procedural due process doctrine goes, McKay cannot stand for any more than was established in the Coffin Bros. and Ownbey cases on which it relied completely.

* * *

29. By allowing repossession without an opportunity for a prior hearing, the Florida and Pennsylvania statutes may be intended specifically to reduce the costs for the private party seeking to seize goods in another party's possession. Even if the private gain at stake in repossession actions were equal to the great public interests recognized in this Court's past decisions, * * * the Court has made clear that the avoidance of the ordinary costs imposed by the opportunity for a hearing is not sufficient to override the constitutional right. * * *

[The] * * * cost of an opportunity to be heard before repossession should not be exaggerated. For we deal here only with the right to an opportunity to be heard. Since the issues and facts decisive of rights in repossession suits may very often be quite simple, there is a likelihood that many defendants would forgo their opportunity, sensing the futility of the exercise in the particular case. And, of course, no hearing need be held unless the defendant, having received notice of his opportunity, takes advantage of it.

participates in the decision to seek a writ; no state official reviews the basis for the claim to repossession; and no state official evaluates the need for immediate seizure. There is not even a requirement that the plaintiff provide any information to the court on these matters. The State acts largely in the dark.

VII

Finally, we must consider the contention that the appellants who signed conditional sales contracts thereby waived their basic procedural due process rights. The contract signed by Mrs. Fuentes provided that "in the event of default of any payment or payments, Seller at its option may take back the merchandise ∗ ∗ ∗." The contracts signed by the Pennsylvania appellants similarly provided that the seller "may retake" or "repossess" the merchandise in the event of a "default in any payment." These terms were parts of printed form contracts, appearing in relatively small type and unaccompanied by any explanations clarifying their meaning.

∗ ∗ ∗ For a waiver of constitutional rights in any context must, at the very least, be clear. The contractual language relied upon must, on its face, amount to a waiver.

The conditional sales contracts here simply provided that upon a default the seller "may take back," "may retake" or "may repossess" merchandise. The contracts included nothing about the waiver of a prior hearing. They did not indicate *how* or *through what process*—a final judgment, self-help, prejudgment replevin with a prior hearing, or prejudgment replevin without a prior hearing—the seller could take back the goods. Rather, the purported waiver provisions here are no more than a statement of the seller's right to repossession upon occurrence of certain events. ∗ ∗ ∗

VIII

We hold that the Florida and Pennsylvania prejudgment replevin provisions work a deprivation of property without due process of law insofar as they deny the right to a prior opportunity to be heard before chattels are taken from their possessor. Our holding, however, is a narrow one. We do not question the power of a State to seize goods before a final judgment in order to protect the security interests of creditors so long as those creditors have tested their claim to the goods through the process of a fair prior hearing. The nature and form of such prior hearings, moreover, are legitimately open to many potential variations and are a subject, at this point, for legislation—not adjudication. ∗ ∗ ∗

Vacated and remanded.

Mr. Justice Powell and Mr. Justice Rehnquist did not participate in the consideration or decision of these cases.

Mr. Justice White, with whom The Chief Justice and Mr. Justice Blackmun join, dissenting.

* * * [The dissenters first noted that state proceedings were in progress when these actions were commenced so that jurisdiction should have been refused because there was an adequate remedy at law.]

Second: * * *.

The narrow issue, as the Court notes, is whether it comports with due process to permit the seller, pending final judgment, to take possession of the property through a writ of replevin served by the sheriff without affording the buyer opportunity to insist that the seller establish at a hearing that there is reasonable basis for his claim of default. The interests of the buyer and seller are obviously antagonistic during this interim period: the buyer wants the use of the property pending final judgment; the seller's interest is to prevent further use and deterioration in his security. By the Florida and Pennsylvania law the property is for all intents and purposes placed in custody and immobilized during this time. The buyer loses use of the property temporarily but is protected against loss; the seller is protected against deterioration of the property but must undertake by bond to make the buyer whole in the event the latter prevails.

In considering whether this resolution of conflicting interests is unconstitutional, much depends on one's perceptions of the practical considerations involved. The Court holds it constitutionally essential to afford opportunity for a probable cause hearing prior to repossession. Its stated purpose is "to prevent unfair and mistaken deprivations of the property." But in these typical situations, the buyer-debtor has either defaulted or he has not. If there is a default, it would seem not only "fair," but essential, that the creditor be allowed to repossess; and I cannot say that the likelihood of a mistaken claim of default is sufficiently real or recurring to justify a broad constitutional requirement that a creditor do more than the typical state law requires and permits him to do. Sellers are normally in the business of selling and collecting the price for their merchandise. I could be quite wrong, but it would not seem in the creditor's interest for a default occasioning repossession to occur; as a practical matter it would much better serve his interests if the transaction goes forward and is completed as planned. Dollar and cents considerations weigh heavily against false claims of default as well as against precipitate action that would allow no opportunity for mistakes to surface and be corrected. Nor does it seem to me that creditors would lightly undertake the expense of instituting replevin actions and putting up bonds.

* * * Viewing the issue before us in this light, I would not construe the Due Process Clause to require the creditors to do more than they have done in these cases to secure possession pending final hearing. Certainly, I would not ignore, as the Court does, the creditor's interest in preventing further use and deterioration of the property in which he has substantial interest. Surely under the Court's own definition, the creditor has a "property" interest as deserving of protection as that of the debtor. At least the debtor, who is very likely uninterested in a speedy resolution that could terminate his use of the property, should be required to make

those payments, into court or otherwise, upon which his right to possession is conditioned. * * *

Third: The Court's rhetoric is seductive, but in end analysis, the result it reaches will have little impact and represents no more than ideological tinkering with state law. It would appear that creditors could withstand attack under today's opinion simply by making clear in the controlling credit instruments that they may retake possession without a hearing, or, for that matter, without resort to judicial process at all. Alternatively, they need only give a few days' notice of a hearing, take possession if hearing is waived or if there is default; and if hearing is necessary merely establish probable cause for asserting that default has occurred. It is very doubtful in my mind that such a hearing would in fact result in protections for the debtor substantially different from those the present laws provide. On the contrary, the availability of credit may well be diminished or, in any event, the expense of securing it increased.

[handwritten margin note: Still have procedure regardless of effective = nature of procedural safeguards.]

None of this seems worth the candle to me. The procedure which the Court strikes down is not some barbaric hangover from bygone days. The respective rights of the parties in secured transactions have undergone the most intensive analysis in recent years. * * *

Notes and Questions

1. As the Court in *Fuentes* noted, its holding as to replevin statutes was an application of its earlier decision in SNIADACH v. FAMILY FINANCE CORP., 395 U.S. 337, 89 S.Ct. 1820, 23 L.Ed.2d 349 (1969), which struck down a Wisconsin prejudgment wage garnishment procedure as violative of due process guarantees:

> A prejudgment garnishment of the Wisconsin type is a taking which may impose tremendous hardship on wage earners with families to support. Until a recent act of Congress, * * * which forbids discharge of employees on the ground that their wages have been garnished, garnishment often meant the loss of a job. Over and beyond that was the great drain on family income.
>
> * * * [P]rejudgment garnishment of the Wisconsin type may as a practical matter drive a wage-earning family to the wall. Where the taking of one's property is so obvious, it needs no extended argument to conclude that absent notice and a prior hearing * * * this prejudgment garnishment procedure violates the fundamental principles of due process.

Id. at 340–42, 89 S.Ct. at 1822, 23 L.Ed.2d at 353–54.

2. How sound is the dissent's argument that creditors can avoid the restrictions of *Fuentes* by providing in their financing contracts that they may retake possession of property without a hearing? Reconsider D.H. Overmyer Co. v. Frick Co., p. 197, supra, in which the Court held that a clause authorizing a creditor upon default to use a confession-of-judgment procedure and secure the entry of judgment against a debtor without service of process or notice was not per se violative of the Fourteenth Amendment requirements of prejudgment notice and a hearing. Then, consider KOSCHES v. NICHOLS,

68 Misc.2d 795, 327 N.Y.S.2d 968 (N.Y.City Civ.Ct.1971), in which the court stated:

> * * * The court also recognizes that, in these adhesion agreements where the buyer has no alternative but to purchase on credit, the parties are not in equal bargaining position. The era of the company store where the purchaser had no place else to go may not be dead. * * * Needless to say, the clauses giving the seller the right to enter a debtor's residence and seize the goods without a court order are unconscionable.

Id. at 797, 327 N.Y.S.2d at 970. See also Hopson, *Cognovit Judgments: An Ignored Problem of Due Process and Full Faith and Credit*, 29 U.Chi.L.Rev. 111 (1961).

MITCHELL v. W.T. GRANT CO., 416 U.S. 600, 601, 604–07, 611, 614–15, 617–20, 94 S.Ct. 1895, 1897–1900, 1902, 1904–06, 40 L.Ed.2d 406, 410, 412–13, 415, 418–20 (1974) (White, J.):

In this case, a state trial judge in Louisiana ordered the sequestration of personal property on the application of a creditor who had made an installment sale of the goods to petitioner and whose affidavit asserted delinquency and prayed for sequestration to enforce a vendor's lien under state law. The issue is whether the sequestration violated the Due Process Clause of the Fourteenth Amendment because it was ordered *ex parte*, without prior notice or opportunity for a hearing. * * *

Plainly enough, this is not a case where the property sequestered by the court is exclusively the property of the defendant debtor. The question is not whether a debtor's property may be seized by his creditors, *pendente lite*, where they hold no present interest in the property sought to be seized. The reality is that both seller and buyer had current, real interests in the property, and the definition of property rights is a matter of state law. Resolution of the due process question must take account not only of the interests of the buyer of the property but those of the seller as well.

* * *

Louisiana statutes provide for sequestration where "one claims the ownership or right to possession of property, or a mortgage, lien, or privilege thereon * * * if it is within the power of the defendant to conceal, dispose of, or waste the property or the revenues therefrom, or remove the property from the parish, during the pendency of the action." Art. 3571. The writ, however, will not issue on the conclusory allegation of ownership or possessory rights. Article 3501 provides that the writ of sequestration shall issue "only when the nature of the claim and the amount thereof, if any, and the grounds relied upon for the issuance of the writ clearly appear from specific facts" shown by a verified petition or affidavit. In the parish where this case arose, the clear showing required must be made to a judge, and the writ will issue only upon his authorization and only after the creditor seeking the writ has filed a sufficient bond to protect the vendee against all damages in the event the sequestration is shown to have been improvident. Arts. 3501 and 3574.

The writ is obtainable on the creditor's *ex parte* application, without notice to the debtor or opportunity for a hearing, but the statute entitles the debtor immediately to seek dissolution of the writ, which must be ordered unless the creditor "proves the grounds upon which the writ was issued," Art. 3506, the existence of the debt, lien, and delinquency, failing which the court may order return of the property and assess damages in favor of the debtor, including attorney's fees.

The debtor, with or without moving to dissolve the sequestration, may also regain possession by filing his own bond to protect the creditor against interim damage to him should he ultimately win his case and have judgment against the debtor for the unpaid balance of the purchase price which was the object of the suit and of the sequestration. Arts. 3507 and 3508.

* * *

Petitioner asserts that his right to a hearing before his possession is in any way disturbed is nonetheless mandated by a long line of cases in this Court, culminating in Sniadach v. Family Finance Corp. * * * and Fuentes v. Shevin * * *.

* * * The suing creditor in *Sniadach* had no prior interest in the property attached, and the opinion did not purport to govern the typical case of the installment seller who brings a suit to collect an unpaid balance and who does not seek to attach wages pending the outcome of the suit but to repossess the sold property on which he had retained a lien to secure the purchase price. * * * [The *Fuentes*] holding is the mainstay of petitioner's submission here. But we are convinced that *Fuentes* was decided against a factual and legal background sufficiently different from that now before us and that it does not require the invalidation of the Louisiana sequestration statute, either on its face or as applied in this case.

* * * In Florida and Pennsylvania property was only to be replevied in accord with state policy if it had been "wrongfully detained." This broad "fault" standard is inherently subject to factual determination and adversarial input. * * * [I]n *Fuentes* this fault standard for replevin was thought ill-suited for preliminary *ex parte* determination. In Louisiana, on the other hand, the facts relevant to obtaining a writ of sequestration are narrowly confined. As we have indicated, documentary proof is particularly suited for questions of the existence of a vendor's lien and the issue of default. There is thus far less danger here that the seizure will be mistaken and a corresponding decrease in the utility of an adversary hearing which will be immediately available in any event.

* * * Our conclusion is that the Louisiana standards regulating the use of the writ of sequestration are constitutional. Mitchell was not deprived of procedural due process in this case. The judgment of the Supreme Court of Louisiana is affirmed.

Notes and Questions

1. Justice Powell concurred with the majority in a separate opinion. Justices Stewart, Douglas, and Marshall dissented on the grounds that (1) the

Louisiana affidavit requirement was little more than a standardized form that only tested the creditor-applicant's own belief in his rights, (2) replacing the court clerk with a judge would have no effect on the assessment of the affidavit or the issuance of the writ, (3) the factual issues in *Mitchell* were no different from those in *Fuentes,* and (4) the majority had unjustifiably disregarded *stare decisis* in overruling *Fuentes.* Justice Brennan agreed with the dissenters that *Fuentes* required the reversal of the judgment of the Supreme Court of Louisiana.

2. Are you, as was the majority, "convinced that *Fuentes* was decided against a factual and legal background sufficiently different" to justify the result in *Mitchell*? Can *Fuentes* and *Mitchell* be reconciled or was Justice Stewart's dissenting opinion correct in its assessment that *Mitchell*

> has unmistakably overruled a considered decision of this Court that is barely two years old, without pointing to any change in either societal perceptions or basic constitutional understandings that might justify this total disregard of *stare decisis.*

Id. at 635, 94 S.Ct. at 1913, 40 L.Ed.2d at 429.

3. In the majority opinion, Justice White wrote: "In our view, this statutory procedure effects a constitutional accommodation of the conflicting interests of the parties." Although the Louisiana statute required the creditor to make more specific allegations than did the Florida and Pennsylvania statutes, can this requirement adequately replace the debtor's opportunity for a prior hearing? Is it of constitutional significance that the official who signs the writ after the ex parte application is a judge rather than a court clerk?

NORTH GEORGIA FINISHING, INC. v. DI–CHEM, INC., 419 U.S. 601, 601–08, 95 S.Ct. 719, 720–23, 42 L.Ed.2d 751, 754–58 (1975) (White, J.):

Under the statutes of the State of Georgia, plaintiffs in pending suits are "entitled to the process of garnishment." Ga.Code Ann. § 46–101. To employ the process, plaintiff or his attorney must make an affidavit before "some officer authorized to issue an attachment, or the clerk of any court of record in which the said garnishment is being filed or in which the main case is filed, stating the amount claimed to be due in such action * * * and that he has reason to apprehend the loss of the same or some part thereof unless process of garnishment shall issue." § 46–102. To protect defendant against loss or damage in the event plaintiff fails to recover, that section also requires plaintiff to file a bond in a sum double the amount sworn to be due. Section 46–401 permits the defendant to dissolve the garnishment by filing a bond "conditioned for the payment of any judgment that shall be rendered on said garnishment." Whether these provisions satisfy the Due Process Clause of the Fourteenth Amendment is the issue before us in this case.

* * * [The Court proceeded to explain the background of the case. Respondent had filed suit against petitioner, alleging that petitioner owed it $51,279 for goods sold and delivered. Before petitioner received service of the complaint, respondent filed an affidavit and bond for garnishing petitioner's bank account. Petitioner responded first by filing its own bond to discharge the bank as garnishee and then by filing a motion to

discharge its bond on the ground that the statute unconstitutionally failed to provide notice and hearing prior to the garnishment. The Georgia Supreme Court upheld the constitutionality of the statute.]

The Georgia court recognized that Sniadach v. Family Finance Corp. * * * had invalidated a statute permitting the garnishment of wages without notice and opportunity for hearing, but considered that case to have done nothing more than to carve out an exception, in favor of wage earners, "to the general rule of legality of garnishment statutes." * * * The garnishment of other assets or properties pending the outcome of the main action * * * was apparently thought not to implicate the Due Process Clause.

This approach failed to take account of Fuentes v. Shevin * * *. Because the official seizures had been carried out without notice and without opportunity for a hearing or other safeguard against mistaken repossession, they were held to be in violation of the Fourteenth Amendment.

The Georgia statute is vulnerable for the same reasons. Here, a bank account, surely a form of property, was impounded and, absent a bond, put totally beyond use during the pendency of the litigation on the alleged debt, all by a writ of garnishment issued by a court clerk without notice or opportunity for an early hearing and without participation by a judicial officer.

Nor is the statute saved by the more recent decision in Mitchell v. W.T. Grant Co. * * *.

The Georgia garnishment statute has none of the saving characteristics of the Louisiana statute. The writ of garnishment is issuable on the affidavit of the creditor or his attorney, and the latter need not have personal knowledge of the facts. § 46–103. The affidavit, like the one filed in this case, need contain only conclusory allegations. The writ is issuable, as this one was, by the court clerk, without participation by a judge. Upon service of the writ, the debtor is deprived of the use of the property in the hands of the garnishee. Here a sizable bank account was frozen, and the only method discernible on the face of the statute to dissolve the garnishment was to file a bond to protect the plaintiff creditor. There is no provision for an early hearing at which the creditor would be required to demonstrate at least probable cause for the garnishment. Indeed, it would appear that without the filing of a bond the defendant debtor's challenge to the garnishment will not be entertained, whatever the grounds may be.

Respondent also argues that neither *Fuentes* nor *Mitchell* is apposite here because each of those cases dealt with the application of due process protections to consumers who are victims of contracts of adhesion and who might be irreparably damaged by temporary deprivation of household necessities, whereas this case deals with its application in the commercial setting to a case involving parties of equal bargaining power. * * * It is asserted in addition that the double bond posted here gives assurance to petitioner that it will be made whole in the event the garnishment turns out to be unjustified. It may be that consumers deprived of household appliances will more likely suffer irreparably than corporations deprived of bank accounts, but the probability of irreparable injury in the latter case is sufficiently great so that some procedures are necessary to guard against the risk of initial error. We are no more inclined now than we have been in the past to distinguish among different kinds of property in applying the Due Process Clause.   *   *   *

Enough has been said, we think, to require the reversal of the judgment of the Georgia Supreme Court. The case is remanded to that court for further proceedings not inconsistent with this opinion.

Notes and Questions

1. Although the Court in *Di-Chem* claimed to have relied on *Fuentes* in declaring the Georgia garnishment statute unconstitutional, did the Court actually insist that the Georgia statute provide an opportunity for a pre-seizure hearing? Would the Georgia statute have been acceptable if it had provided for an immediate post-seizure hearing, as did the Louisiana statute in *Mitchell?* What did the Court mean by the words "or other safeguard against mistaken repossession" on page 223, supra?

2. Has the *Di-Chem* Court reconciled its earlier decisions in *Sniadach, Fuentes,* and *Mitchell?* What is left of *Fuentes* after *Di-Chem?* Of *Mitchell?* Has *Mitchell* become an exception to the *Fuentes* case or has *Mitchell* become the new standard? See Catz & Robinson, *Due Process and Creditor's Remedies: From Sniadach and Fuentes to Mitchell, North Georgia and Beyond,* 28 Rutgers L.Rev. 541 (1975); Recent Decisions, 14 Duq.L.Rev. 494 (1975).

3. Might the result in *Di-Chem* have been different if the creditor had a pre-existing property interest in the property garnished, as did the creditor in *Mitchell?*

4. For a discussion of these four cases, see generally Kay & Lubin, *Making Sense of the Prejudgment Seizure Cases,* 64 Ky.L.J. 705 (1976); Comment, *A Confusing Course Made More Confusing: The Supreme Court, Due Process, and Summary Creditor Remedies,* 70 Nw.U.L.Rev. 331 (1975).

5. To what other types of situations might the *Sniadach* line of cases apply? Consider, for example, the provisions of Federal Rule 65(b) authorizing issuance of temporary restraining orders without notice or a hearing. Note that Rule 65(b) provides that a TRO is effective only for a period of 10 days. During that time, a hearing may be held to determine whether or not a preliminary injunction should issue. If a preliminary injunction is granted, it remains in effect until a final judgment is rendered. Do the procedures outlined in Rule 65(b) satisfy the Due Process Clause as interpreted in *Sniadach* and its progeny? Which of those procedures are constitutionally required?

6. The preceding cases dealt with pre-action attachment to secure property pending litigation. Of course, attachment often is effected for reasons other than security—for example, to create quasi-in-rem jurisdiction. In light of the cases you have just read (especially *Fuentes*), what is the status of pre-action attachment to effect quasi-in-rem jurisdiction? Is the availability of in personam jurisdiction relevant to your answer? At least one court has held that quasi-in-rem attachment procedure cannot be used if the defendant is subject to in personam jurisdiction. McQueeny v. J.W. Fergusson & Sons,

Inc., 527 F.Supp. 728 (D.N.J.1981). Is this decision correct? If quasi-in-rem is the only way to assert jurisdiction over the defendant, would jurisdictional attachment be one of those "extraordinary situations," referred to by the Court in *Fuentes*, that "justify postponing notice and opportunity for a hearing"? See generally Jonnet v. Dollar Sav. Bank, 530 F.2d 1123 (3d Cir. 1976); Bourne, *The Demise of Foreign Attachment*, 21 Creighton L.Rev. 141 (1987); Silberman, *Shaffer v. Heitner: The End of an Era*, 53 N.Y.U.L.Rev. 33, 53–62 (1978). Does it make any difference, in answering the previous question, if quasi-in-rem is the only available jurisdictional basis solely because the state's long-arm statute, which might have provided in personam jurisdiction, is a restrictive one?

Suppose that property is attached to effect quasi-in-rem jurisdiction. Can the defendant consent to in personam jurisdiction and demand that the attachment be lifted? In UNITECH USA, INC. v. PONSOLDT, 91 A.D.2d 903, 457 N.Y.S.2d 526 (1st Dep't 1983), a New York court read that state's quasi-in-rem statute to say that the mere fact that an unlicensed foreign corporation whose assets have been attached appears in an action and submits to in personam jurisdiction does not mean the attachment automatically must be vacated. The New York court found that the state's attachment provision was designed to provide security as well as jurisdiction. Was the court correct in introducing the security interest while examining a jurisdiction statute?

In BRASTEX CORP. v. ALLEN INTERNATIONAL, INC., 702 F.2d 326 (2d Cir.1983), the Second Circuit examined the same statute, but required that the attachment be lifted once the defendant had submitted to in personam jurisdiction. An order of attachment was signed against a foreign corporation that had no license to do business in New York. Two weeks before the oral argument of the motion to confirm the attachment order, the defendant qualified to do business in New York. Denying the plaintiff's motion to confirm the order of attachment, the Second Circuit held that whether an order of attachment is proper must be decided as of the date an attack is made on it. The plaintiff argued that denying its motion would give defendants the power to pull the attachment rug from under a plaintiff at any time. The court refused to hold that the attachment could continue in force because the corporation did not file its qualification papers "in the normal course of business."

In ELTON LEATHER CORP. v. FIRST GENERAL RESOURCES CO., 138 A.D.2d 132, 529 N.Y.S.2d 769 (1st Dep't 1988), the New York Appellate Division rejected the *Brastex* court's conclusion that a foreign corporation's post-attachment, pre-confirmation application to do business in New York removes the statutory basis for attachment. Instead, it cited favorably the Second Circuit's subsequent decision in ITC Entertainment, Ltd. v. Nelson Film Partners, 714 F.2d 217 (2d Cir. 1983). In this latter opinion, the Second Circuit construed the New York statute more broadly:

> New York's nonresident attachment statute is designed to serve two independent purposes: obtaining jurisdiction over and securing judgments against nondomiciliaries residing without the state. New York courts have long recognized that provisions for attachment against nonresidents are based on the assumption that "[t]here is much more propriety in requiring a debtor, whose domicile is without the state, to give security for the debt than one whose domicile is within."

Id. at 220. Does the Due Process Clause permit New York to take this approach to attachment?

7. In PERALTA v. HEIGHTS MEDICAL CENTER, INC., 485 U.S. 80, 108 S.Ct. 896, 99 L.Ed.2d 75 (1988), the Supreme Court considered attachment in another context. In *Peralta,* a default judgment was entered in a suit by a hospital against Peralta to recover a medical bill owed by one of Peralta's employees and guaranteed by him. A writ of attachment was issued and Peralta's property was sold to satisfy the judgment.

Later, Peralta brought an action to set aside the default judgment and void the sale. In this later action, he alleged that the return of service in the first action showed that it was not timely, and that he in fact had not been served personally. The Texas courts denied his requests, holding that in order to have a default judgment reversed there must be a showing of a meritorious defense. But the United States Supreme Court held that requiring a party seeking to vacate a judgment to show a meritorious defense violated the Due Process Clause. Justice White wrote:

> The Texas courts * * * held, as appellee urged them to do, that to have the judgment set aside, appellant was required to show that he had a meritorious defense, apparently on the ground that without a defense, the same judgment would again be entered on retrial and hence appellant had suffered no harm from the judgment entered without notice. But this reasoning is untenable. As appellant asserts, had he had notice of the suit, he might have impleaded the employee whose debt had been guaranteed, worked out a settlement, or paid the debt. He would also have preferred to sell his property himself in order to raise funds rather than to suffer it sold at a constable's auction.

> Nor is there any doubt that the entry of the judgment itself had serious consequences. It is not denied that the judgment was entered on the county records, became a lien on appellant's property, and was the basis for issuance of a writ of execution under which appellant's property was promptly sold, without notice. Even if no execution sale had yet occurred, the lien encumbered the property and impaired appellant's ability to mortgage or alienate it; and state procedures for creating and enforcing such liens are subject to the strictures of due process. * * * Here, we assume that the judgment against him and the ensuing consequences occurred without notice to appellant, notice at a meaningful time and in a meaningful manner that would have given him an opportunity to be heard.

Id. at ___, 108 S.Ct. at 899, 99 L.Ed.2d at 81.

8. In FINBERG v. SULLIVAN, 634 F.2d 50 (3d Cir.1980), the court, sitting en banc, held that Pennsylvania's postjudgment garnishment procedure violated the Due Process Clause. Beatrice Finberg was a sixty-eight year old widow entirely dependent on social security for her income. A discount company obtained a default judgment against her and sought to execute the judgment pursuant to Pennsylvania practice permitting the seizure of assets, without notice or opportunity for a hearing, upon a judgment creditor's petition (to a clerk or magistrate) for a writ of execution. Under this procedure, the plaintiff garnished Finberg's bank accounts, which contained the proceeds of her social security benefits. The critical fact was that all of the garnished money was exempt from seizure because federal law proscribes

the seizure of social security benefits and Pennsylvania law provides a $300 cash exemption to debtors in Mrs. Finberg's position. The *Finberg* court held the Pennsylvania practice unconstitutional because it failed to require the creditor to inform the debtor of existing exemptions and because it did not provide prompt post-seizure adjudication of claims to exemption. Is the Third Circuit's decision correct? Does the proceeding underlying the judgment satisfy the requirements of due process? In *Finberg*, the underlying proceeding produced a default judgment. Would it make a difference if there had been a full trial? Or, is something beyond liability at stake here?

9. When, as in *Mitchell*, a pre-action attachment is sought to secure property pending a disposition, what should the focus of the inquiry be? Should the party seeking attachment be required to show a likelihood that the property to be attached will be removed from the jurisdiction or destroyed? Should she be required to show a likelihood that she will prevail on the merits? If the party seeking attachment is not required to demonstrate a need to secure the property and a likelihood of success on the merits, wouldn't there be a serious danger that the pre-action attachment procedure would be used to harass?

When an attachment is sought, not for security purposes, but to establish quasi-in-rem jurisdiction, should the substantive focus of the inquiry be the same as for security attachments? When a jurisdictional attachment is sought, is there any reason why the need for security should militate for or against an attachment? Aren't the only relevant concerns in assessing the propriety of a jurisdictional attachment the likelihood that the plaintiff will prevail on the merits and the existence or non-existence of minimum contacts sufficient to satisfy *Shaffer*?

When, as in *Finberg*, a post-action attachment is sought to enforce a judgment, should the substantive focus of the inquiry be the same as for other types of attachments? Surely, the plaintiff should not have to demonstrate that the property is in danger. And, after a judgment has been obtained, the likelihood that the plaintiff will prevail on the merits has been demonstrated. Is the only issue the existence or non-existence of exempted property, as in *Finberg*?

As noted earlier, the process that is constitutionally mandated in a given situation turns, in part, on the interests at stake in that situation. Some of the strongest interests that can be advanced to justify shortcuts in process are so-called "public interests." Consider the following case in light of that fact and the *Sniadach* line of cases.

PATTERSON v. CRONIN

Supreme Court of Colorado, 1982.
650 P.2d 531.

ERICKSON, JUSTICE.

The appellant, City and County of Denver (Denver), has appealed from a decision of the Denver District Court which held that service of a summons for a parking violation by affixing a summons and complaint to an unattended automobile is invalid. The district court concluded that the method of service of process * * * was defective because it did not comply with the methods of service required by Rule 206(f) of the Colorado Municipal Court Rules of Procedure (Municipal Court Rules). We affirm the district court judgment but upon different grounds.

I.

Prior to August 17, 1977, Stephen Patterson's Checker automobile was illegally parked in Denver on seven separate occasions. In each instance, a summons and complaint was affixed to the windshield of his automobile. The summons ordered Patterson to appear before the Denver Traffic Violations Bureau within seven days to answer the alleged violation of the Municipal Code for illegal parking. Additionally, each summons contained the following warning:

> IMPORTANT: FAILURE TO RESPOND WITHIN 30 DAYS OF ISSUE DATE WILL SUBJECT THE VIOLATOR TO SUCH OTHER PENALTIES AS PRESCRIBED BY LAW, INCLUDING THE IMPOUNDING OF THE VEHICLE INVOLVED AND THE ISSUANCE OF A WARRANT FOR THE ARREST OF THE VIOLATOR.

In each of the seven instances, Patterson failed to respond. Accordingly, the Denver Traffic Violations Bureau issued an order that his automobile be immobilized in accordance with the provisions of section 505.11–1(15) of the Denver Municipal Code. Pursuant to the order, a "boot" was attached to the automobile on August 17, 1977, by a member of the Denver Sheriff's Department. In addition, an immobilization notice was affixed to the vehicle which provided in pertinent part:

> RELEASE:

> Release can be obtained at the Clerk's Office of the county court, Room 106, City and County Building, * * *. Arrangements for the release must be made within 72 hours after the installation of this device or the vehicle will be removed from the street and impounded pursuant to section 505.11–1(15). NO CHECKS ACCEPTED IN PAYMENT OF FINES.

The boot was removed the following day when Patterson appeared before the traffic bureau and paid his accumulated fines and a ten dollar "boot" fee.

On August 30, 1977, Patterson filed a civil rights action in the Denver District Court alleging that the City's failure to provide a hearing before immobilizing his automobile violated his right to due process of law as guaranteed by the Fourteenth Amendment to the United States Constitution and Article II, section 25 of the Colorado Constitution. He sought damages pursuant to 42 U.S.C. § 1983 and 42 U.S.C. § 1985 for the alleged unconstitutional deprivation of the use of his automobile. In ruling on the complaint, the trial court did not reach the issue of whether due process required a predeprivation hearing before a motor vehicle may be immobilized. Instead, the court concluded that because the service of the individual parking summonses by affixing them to Patterson's automobile did not comply with the notice requirements of C.M.C.R. 206(f), Patterson was not required to respond to the parking violation charges.

Accordingly, the subsequent immobilization of his vehicle pursuant to section 505.11–1(15) constituted a taking of property without due process of law. The court then concluded that Patterson failed to prove actual damage resulting from the immobilization of his vehicle but that Patterson was entitled to nominal damages in the sum of $250.

II.

Initially, we disagree with the trial court's conclusion that Denver's practice of affixing a summons and complaint to the windshield of an unattended motor vehicle is improper notice of a parking violation. Although the method of service in issue here is not specifically sanctioned by C.M.C.R. 206(f), we hold that it is sufficient for the limited purpose of notifying the owner of an unattended motor vehicle of a parking violation.

* * * Denver issues over 650,000 summonses for illegal parking each year. * * * A requirement of personal service for such violations would be impracticable and unduly burdensome on Denver's law enforcement resources and would unreasonably delay the resolution of the charges. Prima facie responsibility for an unlawfully parked motor vehicle may be imposed upon the registered owner by a municipality's use of its police power in the enactment of traffic ordinances. * * *

We do not believe that fundamental principles of due process require personal service of parking summonses. In Mullane v. Central Hanover Bank and Trust Co., * * * the United States Supreme Court set forth the * * * test to be applied in determining whether the method of service utilized to provide notice satisfies the requirements of due process * * *. Applying the *Mullane* test to the method of service now under review, we conclude that the practice of affixing summonses and complaints to illegally parked vehicles which are left unattended is a method of service reasonably certain to provide notice of the violation. Although a summons so served may not always be received due to outside forces, due process does not require that the adopted method of service be absolutely certain to provide notice in every instance. * * * In addition, if no response to the summons is received by the Traffic Violations Bureau within seven days, section 505.5 of the Denver Municipal Code provides that a subsequent notice of the violation shall be mailed to the violator.

We therefore hold that the fundamental principles of due process are satisfied by the methods of service and the notice of parking violations currently provided by Denver. Accordingly, we reverse the decision of the trial court on the issue of service.

III.

Patterson claims that the immobilization of his vehicle without notice and the right to a hearing violated his right to due process of law guaranteed by the Fourteenth Amendment to the United States Constitution and Article II, section 25 of the Colorado Constitution. We agree.

Procedural due process requires that a person with a possessory interest in property seized by the state must be afforded an opportunity for a hearing and adequate notice of the hearing. North Georgia Finishing, Inc. v. Di-Chem, Inc. * * *. As now enforced, the property interests deprived by the immobilization procedure of section 505.11–1(15) of the Denver Municipal Code are twofold: (1) an interest in and use of the immobilized vehicle; and (2) an interest in the "boot" fee collected by Denver for the removal of the immobilization device. Both interests may be significant to the individual involved.

First, an owner's right to the continued possession and uninterrupted use of his vehicle is protected by the constitutional provisions of due process. A person's ability to make a living as well as access to both the necessities and amenities of life may depend on the availability of an automobile when needed. * * * While the owner's interest may only be temporarily restricted before the boot is removed upon payment of the accumulated parking fines and a "boot" fee, it does not diminish the fact that a deprivation has occurred in violation of due process * * *.

Secondly, the individual's interest in the money used to pay the "boot" fee collected by Denver for the removal of the immobilization device itself is also constitutionally protected. * * * Inasmuch as the ordinance now under review provides no mechanism whereby the owner of the automobile can challenge the immobilization procedure as improper, the deprivation which results from the payment of the "boot" fee must be considered final.[11] Therefore, because constitutionally protected private interests are involved when an automobile is immobilized pursuant to section 505.11–1(15) of the Denver Municipal Code, we conclude that the due process requirements of a hearing and adequate notice of the hearing must be provided.

Once a property or liberty deprivation is shown, the fundamental procedural due process safeguards of notice and an opportunity to be heard "at a meaningful time and in a meaningful manner" are absolute. However, the specific procedures required will vary depending upon the nature of each case. * * * In determining what procedures must be afforded to satisfy constitutional due process requirements in a particular case, the United States Supreme Court has formulated a balancing test which weighs the following three factors: (1) the kind of private interest at stake; (2) the risk of an erroneous deprivation of that interest and the probable value of additional or substitute procedures in reducing the risk; and (3) the public or governmental interest involved and the fiscal and administrative burden additional procedural requirements would entail.
* * *

A balancing of the three factors is generally the approach used to determine the timing of the required hearing. * * * The United States Supreme Court has long recognized an exception to the general rule that the deprivation of property requires a pre-deprivation hearing in extraordinary circumstances where a valid governmental interest is at stake which justifies postponing the hearing until after the event. * * * In

---

11. Our conclusion is not altered by Denver's contention that, should the immobilization be improper, it "stands ready to answer in damages for said error." A subsequent action for damages does not cure the due process infirmity which results from the failure to provide a hearing in compliance with the requirements of due process.

such cases, the balancing approach recognizes that the fiscal and administrative burden of a pre-deprivation hearing may outweigh the incremental benefits in fairness and accuracy resulting from such a hearing, especially in cases which occur in large numbers or involve relatively little risk of error or temporary deprivations. * * *

In this case, the magnitude of the private interest at stake is the temporary loss of the use of the automobile and any funds paid for the release of the vehicle. Although these are clearly property interests sufficient to mandate due process protection, they are minimal and of limited duration. * * * Moreover, the risk of erroneous deprivation is also minimal here. It is a simple procedure to determine that a parking violation has occurred. * * *

Under the system presently used in Denver, the violator has already had an opportunity to contest the validity of each ticket he receives. Those instances in which some administrative error has occurred could satisfactorily be resolved at a post-immobilization hearing.

In contrast, the governmental interest in enforcing parking ordinances is an important one for the safety of the public. Denver authorities issue over 650,000 summonses for illegal parking each year. Because vehicles are, by their nature, movable, and because the violators subject to the immobilization procedure have a history of failing to respond to summonses, the "boot" has proved a practical method of insuring a violator's presence before the proper authorities and the disposition of overdue summonses. In light of the vast number of violations involved, the requirement of personal service and an opportunity for a prior hearing might well overwhelm the administrative machinery in place to deal with traffic violations. On the contrary, if the vast majority of violators chose to ignore the notice informing them of the possibility that their vehicle would be "booted," just as they have ignored all prior notices, the prior hearing requirement would fail to serve the due process purpose for which it is intended.

We therefore conclude that a hearing is not constitutionally mandated prior to the immobilization of a motor vehicle, so long as a prompt and adequate proceeding is available upon demand after the immobilization has occurred. Under the procedures currently followed in Denver, however, no post-deprivation hearing is so provided to persons whose vehicles have been immobilized by the "boot." As stated in the immobilization notice affixed to the immobilized vehicle, release can be obtained only after the owner pays a "boot" fee and all accumulated fines registered against the vehicle. No provision exists in the ordinance for obtaining release of the vehicle by posting a bond while a deprivation hearing is pending. * * * Nor is there any provision which would mitigate the loss if the detention of the vehicle is improper. * * * Moreover, the ordinance as written and enforced lacks any procedure whereby the owner of the vehicle can subsequently challenge the immobilization as unjustified. * * * Because no opportunity is given under the present scheme to contest Denver's action immobilizing a motor vehicle at a prompt post-deprivation hearing, we conclude that the immobilization of Patterson's vehicle violated his right to due process of law. * * *

ROVIRA, JUSTICE, concurring in part and dissenting in part:

* * *

I respectfully disagree with the analysis and conclusions of that part of Section III which holds that Patterson is entitled to a hearing after immobilization (booting) of his vehicle. * * *

Patterson's argument that he was denied due process of law rises or falls on whether the notice that he received was adequate and provided him an opportunity to contest the charge of illegal parking. * * *

Patterson failed, in each of seven instances, to avail himself of the opportunity to contest the charge of illegal parking and therefore by his own acts, or failure to act, placed himself in jeopardy of having his automobile "booted."

In my view, the summonses and complaints he received were sufficient notice of his right to a hearing and the possible penalty of impoundment to permit the booting. Having been given notice of and the opportunity for a hearing at a meaningful time and in a meaningful manner, the requirements of procedural due process have been met. * * *

Patterson had ample opportunity to challenge the charge of illegal parking which was the basis of the original booting and failed to do so. He is not entitled, nor does due process require, another opportunity to challenge the booting as unjustified.

In essence, the majority opinion countenances the acts of a citizen in ignoring the law and rewards the scoff law who habitually violates parking regulations and ignores tickets placed on his car.

I would reverse the judgment of the district court.

Notes and Questions

1. The majority views the "booting" of an automobile as a provisional remedy that, once invoked, must be followed by a hearing on the merits. The dissent views the booting as a final remedy flowing from default judgments on previous tickets. Which view is correct? If the dissenting judge is correct, could Denver auction off the car to pay for the parking fines?

2. When a parking violation is alleged, service normally is accomplished by placing a citation on the car. Is this notice constitutionally sufficient? What if a defendant could demonstrate that passersby often remove tickets from cars?

3. What kind of post-seizure hearing would cure the defect in Patterson v. Cronin? Would the car owner be barred from arguing the merits of alleged violations as a matter of res judicata?

4. Consider the common practice of towing cars that are thought to be illegally parked. Does that violate due process? Can the practice be justified because illegally parked cars threaten public safety?

SECTION H. CHALLENGING A COURT'S EXERCISE OF JURISDICTION OVER THE PERSON OR PROPERTY

1. RAISING THE JURISDICTIONAL ISSUE DIRECTLY

Read Federal Rules of Civil Procedure 12(b), (g), and (h) and the accompanying material in the Supplement.

The term "special appearance" refers to the procedure at common law by which a defendant presented a challenge to the court's exercise of personal jurisdiction without submitting to the court's jurisdiction for any other purpose. The rules varied from state to state on the technical requirements for making a special appearance. A defendant generally had to designate the appearance "special" and limit himself to raising the jurisdictional defense. If he did anything else, such as argue the merits in any way, the defendant would be deemed to have made a "general appearance," constituting a voluntary submission to the court's jurisdiction and a waiver of any defects in the court's jurisdiction. Although substantial variation still may be encountered among different systems of state procedure, the general rules regarding objections to personal jurisdiction are illustrated by the federal scheme.

Assuming that the jurisdictional issue is timely raised, what procedures should a trial court follow to resolve the issue when the relevant facts are sharply disputed by the parties? Consider the discussion in DATA DISC, INC. v. SYSTEMS TECHNOLOGY ASSOCIATES, INC., 557 F.2d 1280, 1285–86 & n. 2 (9th Cir.1977):

A defendant may move, prior to trial, to dismiss the complaint for lack of personal jurisdiction. Fed.R.Civ.P. 12(b)(2). Because there is no statutory method for resolving this issue, the mode of its determination is left to the trial court. * * * The limits which the district judge imposes on the pre-trial proceedings will affect the burden which the plaintiff is required to meet.

If the court determines that it will receive only affidavits or affidavits plus discovery materials, these very limitations dictate that a plaintiff must make only a prima facie showing of jurisdictional facts through the submitted materials in order to avoid a defendant's motion to dismiss. Any greater burden—such as proof by a preponderance of the evidence— would permit a defendant to obtain a dismissal simply by controverting the facts established by a plaintiff through his own affidavits and supporting materials. Thus a plaintiff could not meet a burden of proof requiring a preponderance of the evidence without going beyond the written materials. Accordingly, if a plaintiff's proof is limited to written materials, it is necessary only for these materials to demonstrate facts which support a finding of jurisdiction in order to avoid a motion to dismiss.

* * *

If a plaintiff make [sic] such a showing, however, it does not necessarily mean that he may then go to trial on the merits. If the pleadings and other submitted materials raise issues of credibility or disputed questions of fact with regard to jurisdiction, the district court has the discretion to take evidence at a preliminary hearing in order to resolve the contested issues. * * * In this situation, where plaintiff is put to his full proof, plaintiff must establish the jurisdictional facts by a preponderance of the evidence, just as he would have to do at trial. * * *

In a footnote, the court observed:

Where the jurisdictional facts are intertwined with the merits, a decision on the jurisdictional issues is dependent on a decision of the merits. In such a case, the district court could determine its jurisdiction in a plenary pretrial proceeding. * * * However, it is preferable that this determination be made at trial, where a plaintiff may present his case in a coherent, orderly fashion and without the risk of prejudicing his case on the merits. * * * Accordingly, where the jurisdictional facts are enmeshed with the merits, the district court may decide that the plaintiff should not be required in a Rule 12(d) preliminary proceeding to meet the higher burden of proof which is associated with the presentation of evidence at a hearing, but rather should be required only to establish a prima facie showing of jurisdictional facts with affidavits and perhaps discovery materials. * * * Of course, at any time when the plaintiff avoids a preliminary motion to dismiss by making a prima facie showing of jurisdictional facts, he must still prove the jurisdictional facts at trial by a preponderance of the evidence.

Notes and Questions

1. *Data Disc* suggests that trial courts have broad leeway in determining the procedures they will follow in resolving the jurisdictional issue. Is this degree of discretion consistent with due process considerations? Should a court have to determine the jurisdictional issue at the earliest possible stage of the proceeding by the most expeditious means? Is early resolution of the jurisdictional issue required to protect the defendant's constitutional right not to have to defend in a forum that does not have jurisdiction over her?

2. Occasionally the issue upon which jurisdiction depends is also an issue related to the merits of the claim. For example, in H.V. ALLEN CO. v. QUIP-MATIC, INC., 47 N.C.App. 40, 266 S.E.2d 768, review denied, 301 N.C. 85, 273 S.E.2d 298 (1980), the plaintiff brought an action against a nonresident defendant alleging a breach of an oral contract. The plaintiff argued that jurisdiction was proper under North Carolina's long-arm statute, which authorized jurisdiction over defendants who had entered into contracts to be performed in the state. The defendant moved to dismiss for lack of personal jurisdiction and simultaneously sought summary judgment on the ground that there was no contract. In a case like *Quip-Matic*, what standard of proof must the plaintiff meet to establish jurisdiction? Would requiring proof by a preponderance of the evidence effectively create a trial on the merits? Would it be better to require the plaintiff to prove only a reasonable likelihood of success on the merits in order to establish jurisdiction and, if that standard is met, to put the jurisdictional issue to rest? A "reasonable likelihood" standard would avoid the anomalous result produced by a dismissal for lack of

jurisdiction (an action that has no res judicata effect) after the merits have been fully litigated and decided by a jury in favor of defendant.

In *Quip-Matic,* the trial court denied the motion to dismiss for lack of jurisdiction, but granted the motion for summary judgment. When both parties appealed, the court of appeals ruled that the trial court should have dismissed for want of jurisdiction. Does this favor the plaintiff, since it can reinstitute the action in another forum as if there had been no ruling that no contract existed?

2. COLLATERAL ATTACK ON PERSONAL JURISDICTION

If a defendant contests a court's exercise of personal jurisdiction and loses, may he challenge jurisdiction again in a later action to enforce the judgment? Consider BALDWIN v. IOWA STATE TRAVELING MEN'S ASS'N, 283 U.S. 522, 51 S.Ct. 517, 75 L.Ed. 1244 (1931), in which respondent attempted to attack a judgment rendered against it in a Missouri federal district court. The company had made a special appearance in the prior suit and had moved to set aside service and dismiss the case for a lack of personal jurisdiction, alleging that (1) it was an Iowa corporation, (2) it had never been present in Missouri, and (3) the person who had been served was not a proper agent for receiving process. The motion was overruled after a full hearing on affidavits and briefs. The company failed to plead on the merits, and judgment was entered against it. No appeal was taken. Suit then was brought in Iowa to enforce the judgment. In rejecting the respondent's attempt to attack the first judgment collaterally, the Supreme Court stated:

> * * * It is of no moment that the appearance was a special one expressly saving any submission to such jurisdiction. That fact would be important upon appeal from the judgment, and would save the question of the propriety of the court's decision on the matter, even though, after the motion had been overruled, the respondent had proceeded, subject to a reserved objection and exception, to a trial on the merits. * * * The special appearance gives point to the fact that the respondent entered the Missouri court for the very purpose of litigating the question of jurisdiction over its person. It had the election not to appear at all. * * * It had also the right to appeal from the decision of the Missouri District Court. * * *

> Public policy dictates that there be an end of litigation; that those who have contested an issue shall be bound by the result of the contest; and that matters once tried shall be considered forever settled as between parties. We see no reason why this doctrine should not apply in every case where one voluntarily appears, presents his case and is fully heard, and why he should not, in the absence of fraud, be thereafter concluded by the judgment of the tribunal to which he has submitted his cause.

Id. at 524–26, 51 S.Ct. at 517–18, 75 L.Ed. at 1245.

The *Baldwin* opinion repeats the persisting rule that a defendant who makes no appearance whatsoever remains free to challenge a default judgment for want of personal jurisdiction. The principle that a court has power to determine its own personal jurisdiction is limited to defendants who submit the question for resolution in that court. Would it be unthinkable to require a defendant to raise the jurisdictional objection in the initial forum or lose the opportunity to contest personal jurisdiction?

3. THE LIMITED–APPEARANCE PROBLEM

Can a defendant in an action commenced on a quasi-in-rem basis appear for the limited purpose of defending his interest in the attached property without submitting to the full in personam jurisdiction of the court? Is it fair to force a defendant in such an action to choose between appearing, and thereby risking the possibility of an in personam judgment in excess of the value of the attached property, or not appearing, thereby, as a practical matter, suffering the forfeiture of his property? Is it a violation of due process because it imposes an unconstitutional condition on a defendant's ability to protect his property? See *Developments in the Law—State Court Jurisdiction,* 73 Harv.L.Rev. 909, 954 (1960). How satisfactory is the answer given in U.S. INDUSTRIES, INC. v. GREGG, 58 F.R.D. 469, 479–80 (D.Del.1973), a case in which a Florida resident whose property had been sequestered in Delaware was refused the right to make a limited appearance and told that any judgment the court might enter in favor of the plaintiff would be an in personam one.

There is * * * a legitimate public interest behind the general appearance rule. If a state or federal court is required by a defendant's response to a complaint to try and determine all of the issues upon which an *in personam* claim turns, there is a public interest in having that expenditure of judicial resources settle the rights of the parties with respect to that claim and in not leaving open the possibility of subsequent, duplicative litigation in the same court or another. This interest is similar to, though stronger, than, the one reflected in compulsory counterclaim rules.

One must still ask, however, whether the price which a general appearance rule extracts from a defendant is excessive despite the countervailing public interest. Gregg suggests that it is because the forum, by definition, is one with which his only contact is the presence of his property within its jurisdiction. Requiring him to litigate in such a forum, he says, imposes an unconscionable burden. This Court has already held, however, that the acquisition of quasi-in-rem jurisdiction by sequestration is constitutional. Given the right of a court to require that a defendant whose property is seized defend on the merits or default, it is difficult to see what additional litigation burden a general appearance rule imposes upon a defendant. If he defaults recovery will be limited to the property seized. If he defends on the merits the trouble and expense of litigation will be no different whether a general or limited appearance rule is applied.

Also unpersuasive is Gregg's argument that a general appearance rule gives a plaintiff an unfair advantage by allowing him to bring suit on a large claim in a jurisdiction where the original basis for jurisdiction is the presence of property having a comparatively small value. Any such unfairness does not rise to constitutional proportions. A similar phenomenon frequently occurs under compulsory counterclaim rules.

Put in Gregg's "contact" terminology, if he defends upon the merits he has created an additional relationship with the forum jurisdiction; he is present in the forum court to litigate the factual and legal issues upon which a claim turns. This is sufficient contact to permit the court to adjudicate that very claim once and for all. ＊ ＊ ＊

Notes and Questions

1. Does the limited appearance have a constitutional basis after Shaffer v. Heitner, p. 150, supra? Of course, limited appearances still may be desirable as a matter of state law. For example, suppose that the state long-arm statute does not permit the exercise of personal jurisdiction to the full extent of the Due Process Clause, but that the statute for quasi-in-rem jurisdiction does. Without a limited-appearance provision, defendants would be forced either to forego litigation on the merits or to accept full in personam liability—this, even when the long-arm statute would not allow in personam litigation. The trend has been toward permitting defendants the right of a "limited appearance." See, e.g., Dry Clime Lamp Corp. v. Edwards, 389 F.2d 590 (5th Cir.1968); Harvard Trust Co. v. Bray, 138 Vt. 199, 413 A.2d 1213 (1980).

2. In SALMON FALLS MFG. CO. v. MIDLAND TIRE & RUBBER CO., 285 Fed. 214, 217 (6th Cir.1922), a case originally commenced in an Ohio state court and then removed to a federal court, the court permitted a limited appearance with the following caveat: "[H]ad defendant, while protesting against the court's jurisdiction to render personal judgment without reference to the value of the attached property, yet asked relief on the merits beyond that value, whether before or in connection with the making of its protest, [he] would be deemed to have appeared generally, and so to have waived lack of personal jurisdiction." But see Norris, Inc. v. M.H. Reed & Co., 278 Fed. 19 (5th Cir.1922); Grant v. Kellogg Co., 3 F.R.D. 229 (S.D.N.Y.1943), affirmed on other grounds 154 F.2d 59 (2d Cir.1946). Should a federal court exercising original quasi-in-rem jurisdiction under Rule 4(e) permit a limited appearance or should it follow the practice of the state in which it is sitting? See generally 4 Wright & Miller, *Federal Practice and Procedure: Civil* § 1123 (1969).

SECTION I. JURISDICTION OVER THE SUBJECT MATTER OF THE ACTION— THE COURT'S COMPETENCY

1. BASIC PRINCIPLES

As was described briefly in Chapter One, pp. 4–5, supra, most Anglo-American jurisdictions have distributed judicial power to hear disputes among a variety of courts. In many instances this is accomplished by segregating certain types of controversies from the mainstream of litigation and giving special courts subject-matter jurisdiction over them, as usually is done with domestic relations and probate matters, and formerly was true of "actions at law" and "suits in equity." As described by one commentator:

* * * In practically all states * * * there are separate courts for large and small cases with an arbitrary line of division between them. There are usually separate courts of first instance and of review. Separate courts of probate, criminal courts, courts of equity, and courts for causes arising in certain localities are common. Jurisdiction of the same kind is often apportioned among several different courts, each exercising only a designated and restricted part of it, as where certain appeals must be taken to one reviewing court and other appeals to another. Sometimes different courts with concurrent jurisdiction in certain classes of cases and exclusive jurisdiction in others are established. It is not uncommon to find a large number of municipal courts in the various cities of the same state, no two of which exercise the same jurisdiction. And as a final complication, the legislature is constantly shifting and changing the jurisdiction of the various courts, practically every change involving litigation to construe the meaning and ascertain the effect of the legislative act.

Sunderland, *Problems Connected with the Operation of a State Court System,* 1950 Wis.L.Rev. 585, 585–86. As you gain familiarity with the materials in this Section, give some thought to the extent to which historical allocations of subject-matter jurisdiction over matters such as probate, divorce, disputes involving land, and patents continue to make sense.

Probably the most common method of limiting judicial power is by providing that the court only can adjudicate controversies involving more than a certain minimum or less than a stated maximum amount of money, or its equivalent. These rules often are designed to direct the quantitative and qualitative flow of litigation into the various courts within a jurisdiction. Thus, for example, it is provided by statute, 28 U.S.C. § 1332, that cases in the federal courts based solely on diversity of citizenship must involve more than $50,000. If a dispute does not, it cannot be instituted in a federal court and must be brought in a state court. Amount-in-controversy restrictions also are common in state systems. These often provide that a plaintiff cannot bring his action in a particular court—typically called a court of inferior, limited, or special jurisdiction—if the amount involved exceeds a statutorily established jurisdictional maximum. What factors are relevant in choosing appropriate jurisdictional amount figures? Are the same factors relevant for both the state and federal courts?

2. SUBJECT–MATTER JURISDICTION IN STATE COURTS

LACKS v. LACKS

New York Court of Appeals, 1976.
41 N.Y.2d 71, 390 N.Y.S.2d 875, 359 N.E.2d 384.

BREITEL, CHIEF JUDGE. * * * The parties were married in New York in 1938. After an apparently turbulent marriage, marked since 1953 by a series of bitter litigations, the husband, on August 10, 1965, began this action for a separation on the ground of cruelty. After nonjury trial, Supreme Court, on June 28, 1967, dismissed the complaint, but, on

March 26, 1968, the Appellate Division reversed, and ordered a new trial. At the second trial, plaintiff husband, in reliance upon the then recent liberalizing changes in the divorce law, added a prayer for a judgment of absolute divorce, on the same allegations and proof as the earlier cause for separation. The husband was granted a judgment of divorce on March 16, 1970, and, after modifications not now relevant, the judgment was affirmed by the Appellate Division on October 26, 1972. Leave to appeal to the Court of Appeals was denied by both the Appellate Division and this court. The final judgment was thus beyond further review.

Then, nearly two years later, defendant, through her most recently retained lawyer, moved to vacate the judgment, contending that the court had been without subject matter jurisdiction to entertain the divorce action. She argued that the husband had not been a resident of New York for a full year preceding the commencement of the original action, and that the court had thus erroneously granted a divorce judgment in violation of the provisions of section 230. * * *

The confusion [in this case], if there be confusion, starts with a line of decisions dating back to the last century and continuing into the present in which this court has said with less than perfect meticulousness that "jurisdiction" of New York courts in matrimonial cases is limited to the powers conferred by statute * * *. Jurisdiction is a word of elastic, diverse, and disparate meanings * * *.

A statement that a court lacks "jurisdiction" to decide a case may, in reality, mean that elements of a cause of action are absent * * *. Similarly, questions of mootness and standing of parties may be characterized as raising questions of subject matter jurisdiction * * *. But these are not the kinds of judicial infirmities to which CPLR 5015 * * * is addressed. That provision is designed to preserve objections so fundamental to the power of adjudication of a court that they survive even a final judgment or order * * *.

In Thrasher v. United States Liab. Ins. Co., * * * this court, in discussing subject matter jurisdiction, drew a clear distinction between a court's competence to entertain an action and its power to render a judgment on the merits * * *. Absence of competence to entertain an action deprives the court of "subject matter jurisdiction"; absence of power to reach the merits does not.

* * * [I]t has often been said: "the Supreme Court is a court of original, unlimited and unqualified jurisdiction" and "competent to entertain all causes of action unless its jurisdiction has been specifically proscribed" * * *.

Against the State Constitution's broad grant of jurisdiction to the Supreme Court, defendant offers the language of section 230 of the Domestic Relations Law. It provides merely that "[a]n action * * * for divorce on separation may be maintained only when" the residence requirements are met. Not even the catchall word "jurisdiction" appears in the statute, much less an explicit limitation on the court's competence to entertain the action. In no way do these limitations on the cause of action circumscribe the power of the court in the sense of competence to adjudicate causes in the matrimonial categories. That a court has no "right" to adjudicate erroneously is no circumscription of its power to decide, rightly or wrongly.

* * *

The court has never before considered the unlikely question, until this case, whether the judicial error on an essential element of the cause of action was so fundamental as to permit vacatur of a final judgment, collaterally or after final judgment beyond ordinary appellate review. Had that ever been the problem unlikely until this case, perhaps the need for a less elastic and encompassing term than the word "jurisdiction" would have been apparent.

* * *

Hence, any error of law or fact which might have been committed in the divorce action did not deprive the court of jurisdiction to adjudicate the case, CPLR 5015 * * * is inapplicable, and Special Term erroneously vacated the final judgment.

In sum, the overly stated principle that lack of subject matter jurisdiction makes a final judgment absolutely void is not applicable to cases which, upon analysis, do not involve jurisdiction, but merely substantive elements of a cause for relief. To do so would be to undermine significantly the doctrine of *res judicata,* and to eliminate the certainty and finality in the law and in litigation which the doctrine is designed to protect.

In concluding the jurisdiction-competence issue it is not assumed that the courts in the action made any error of law or fact in determining the durational or initial residence requirements to maintain an action for a separation or a divorce. Nor is it assumed that the same courts did not consider and determine the issues of residence, whether or not raised by the wife. On the contrary, there was considerable evidence of residence by the husband, and the court obviously determined that the husband had some residence even if not of the duration to satisfy the matrimonial statutes. The point is that the litigation having gone to final judgment, the right to review by appeal having been exhausted, that is and should be the end of the matter.

On the foregoing analysis it has been unnecessary to dissect the elements of subject matter jurisdiction, because it turns out that the contentions of the wife are not addressed to bases for subject matter jurisdiction. Rather, despite her characterization of subject matter jurisdiction in order to invoke CPLR 5015 * * * to undo a final judgment of four years' standing, the defects to which she points relate only to substantive elements in a cause of action adjudicable by the Supreme Court, a court competent to decide all the substantive issues.

Accordingly, the order of the Appellate Division should be affirmed, without costs.

Notes and Questions

1. A state court of general jurisdiction is presumably permitted and may be under a constitutional duty to hear a cause of action arising under the laws of another state. In HUGHES v. FETTER, 341 U.S. 609, 71 S.Ct. 980, 95

L.Ed. 1212 (1951), the Supreme Court held that the Full Faith and Credit Clause, U.S. Const. Art. IV, § 1, precluded Wisconsin from closing its courts to a suit under the Illinois wrongful-death act in the absence of a valid Wisconsin policy to weigh against the national interest favoring the availability of a Wisconsin forum. "[A state] * * * cannot escape [its] constitutional obligation to enforce the rights and duties validly created under the laws of other states by the simple device of removing jurisdiction from courts otherwise competent." *Hughes* has not been construed as a bar to a state applying its own law to vindicate policies related to the conduct of litigation in its courts. For example, a state may apply its own statute of limitations even though the claim would be timely under the law of the state under which the cause of action arose. See Wells v. Simonds Abrasive Co., 345 U.S. 514, 73 S.Ct. 856, 97 L.Ed. 1211 (1953).

    2. Unless Congress has made federal jurisdiction exclusive, a state court may entertain an action even though it is based entirely on federal law.

        * * * This rule is premised on the relation between the States and the National Government within our federal system. See The Federalist No. 82 (Hamilton). The two exercise concurrent sovereignty, although the Constitution limits the powers of each and requires the States to recognize federal law as paramount. Federal law confers rights binding on state courts, the subject-matter jurisdiction of which is governed in the first instance by state laws.

        * * * Congress, however, may confine jurisdiction to the federal courts either explicitly or implicitly. Thus, the presumption of concurrent jurisdiction can be rebutted by an explicit statutory directive, by unmistakable implication from legislative history, or by a clear incompatibility between state-court jurisdiction and federal interests.

GULF OFFSHORE CO. v. MOBIL OIL CORP., 453 U.S. 473, 478, 101 S.Ct. 2870, 2875, 69 L.Ed.2d 784, 791 (1981).

    3. If a state court can hear a case arising under federal law, must it do so? In McKNETT v. ST. LOUIS & SAN FRANCISCO RY. CO., 292 U.S. 230, 234, 54 S.Ct. 690, 692, 78 L.Ed. 1227, 1229 (1934), a unanimous Supreme Court held unconstitutional an Alabama statute that, as construed, precluded its courts from hearing a claim under the Federal Employers' Liability Act that arose outside the state. The Alabama court would have had jurisdiction if the accident had occurred in Alabama, or if the plaintiff had sued under the law of Tennessee, where the injury occurred. "The denial of jurisdiction by the Alabama court is based solely upon the source of law sought to be enforced. The plaintiff is cast out because he is suing to enforce a federal act. A state may not discriminate against rights arising under federal laws."

3. THE SUBJECT–MATTER JURISDICTION OF THE FEDERAL COURTS—FEDERAL QUESTIONS

MISHKIN, THE FEDERAL "QUESTION" IN THE DISTRICT COURTS, 53 Colum.L.Rev. 157, 157–59 (1953):

Although the framers of our Constitution could not agree upon whether there should be any federal trial courts at all, it was generally conceded at the Convention that the national judicial power should, in some form, extend to cases arising under the laws of the new government.

However, though the first Congress did exercise its option to establish a system of "inferior" national tribunals, it did not assign to them general jurisdiction over cases of that type. With the exception of an extremely shortlived statute enacted just after the end of the eighteenth century, it was not until 1875 that the federal courts were given initial cognizance of all types of federal question cases. * * *

Whatever may have been the circumstances and needs during the first century of our country's history, there seems to be little doubt that today, with the expanding scope of federal legislation, the exercise of power over cases of this sort constitutes one of the major purposes of a full independent system of national trial courts. The alternative would be to rely entirely upon United States Supreme Court review of state court decisions. But, at least in our present judicial system, Supreme Court pronouncements as to any particular segment of national law are comparatively few. Consequently, sympathetic handling of the available Supreme Court rulings assumes a role of substantial importance in achieving widespread, uniform effectuation of federal law. Presumably judges selected and paid by the central government, with tenure during good behavior—and that determined by the Congress—and probably even somewhat insulated by a separate building, are more likely to give full scope to any given Supreme Court decision, and particularly ones unpopular locally, than are their state counterparts. By the same token, should a district judge fail, or err, a more sympathetic treatment of Supreme Court precedents can be expected from federal circuit judges than from state appellate courts.

Thus, the exercise of federal question jurisdiction by lower federal tribunals presumably permits the Supreme Court to confine itself (insofar as any such distinction can be drawn) to the solving of new problems rather than the policing of old solutions, without the loss that might otherwise be entailed in the effectuation of national rights. Further, the fact that the lower federal bench is chosen by officials of the national government under the same procedure as the members of the high Court suggests a greater similarity in the interpretation of national law, even on first impression, among the several parts of the national system than between the Supreme Court and any state system, or among the various state tribunals themselves. Insofar as this is true, it also promotes a more uniform, correct application of federal law in that significant group of cases where, either because of the novelty of the question, disproportionate expense or for other reasons, recourse to the Supreme Court has previously either not been attempted or been precluded. Finally, it might even be argued that the very existence of an alternative forum stimulates state courts to give a more attentive treatment to claims of federal right.

These factors suggest that it is desirable that Congress be competent to bring to an initial national forum all cases in which the vindication of federal policy may be at stake. However, it does not follow from this that at any given time all such cases should in fact be brought before the federal courts. There are other considerations which must enter into any decision as to the actual use of the national judiciary. For example, there are limits on the volume of litigation which they can handle without an expansion which might not be warranted by the advantages to be gained; the hardships which the geographic location of these courts may impose on the litigants and a willingness to trust that a party's self-interest will lead him to bring or remove an appropriate case to the federal courts might well justify the current rule that federal question jurisdiction is, for the most part, shared by the local courts; in some circumstances, such as where the validity of state action may be at issue, it may avoid friction and wasted effort, without sacrificing national authority, to allow the initial adjudication to be made by the state's tribunals subject to ultimate review by the United States Supreme Court. Other factors could easily be added. * * *

Read 28 U.S.C. §§ 1331, 1334, 1337, 1338, 1343, 1345, and 1346, which are in the Supplement.

GULLY v. FIRST NAT. BANK IN MERIDIAN, 299 U.S. 109, 112–13, 117–18, 57 S.Ct. 96, 97–98, 100, 81 L.Ed. 70, 72, 74–75 (1936):

How and when a case arises "under the Constitution or laws of the United States" has been much considered in the books. Some tests are well established. To bring a case within the statute, a right or immunity created by the Constitution or laws of the United States must be an element, and an essential one, of the plaintiff's cause of action. * * * The right or immunity must be such that it will be supported if the Constitution or laws of the United States are given one construction or effect, and defeated if they receive another. * * * A genuine and present controversy, not merely a possible or conjectural one, must exist with reference thereto * * * and the controversy must be disclosed upon the face of the complaint, unaided by the answer or by the petition for removal. * * *

This Court has had occasion to point out how futile is the attempt to define a "cause of action" without reference to the context. * * * To define broadly and in the abstract "a case arising under the Constitution or laws of the United States" has hazards of a kindred order. What is needed is something of that common-sense accommodation of judgment to kaleidoscopic situations which characterizes the law in its treatment of problems of causation. One could carry the search for causes backward, almost without end. * * * Instead, there has been a selective process which picks the substantial causes out of the web and lays the other ones aside. As in problems of causation, so here is the search for the underlying law. If we follow the ascent far enough, countless claims of right can be discovered to have their source or their operative limits in the provisions of a federal statute or in the Constitution itself with its circumambient restrictions upon legislative power. To set bounds to the pursuit, the courts have formulated the distinction between controversies that are basic and those that are collateral, between disputes that are necessary and those that are merely possible. We shall be lost in a maze if we put that compass by.

T.B. HARMS CO. v. ELISCU

United States Court of Appeals, Second Circuit, 1964.
339 F.2d 823.

FRIENDLY, CIRCUIT JUDGE. A layman would doubtless be surprised to learn that an action wherein the purported sole owner of a copyright alleged that persons claiming partial ownership had recorded their claim in the Copyright Office and had warned his licensees against disregarding their interests was not one "arising under any Act of Congress relating to * * * copyrights" over which 28 U.S.C. § 1338 gives the federal courts exclusive jurisdiction. Yet precedents going back for more than a century teach that lesson and lead us to affirm Judge Weinfeld's dismissal of the complaint.

The litigation concerns four copyrighted songs. * * * The music for the songs was composed by Vincent Youmans for use in a motion picture, "Flying Down to Rio," pursuant to a contract made in 1933 with RKO Studios, Inc. He agreed to assign to RKO the recordation and certain other rights relating to the picture during the existence of the copyrights and any renewals. RKO was to employ a writer of the lyrics and to procure the publishing rights in these for Youmans, who was "to pay said lyric writer the usual and customary royalties on sheet music and mechanical records." Subject to this, Youmans could assign the publication and small performing rights to the music and lyrics as he saw fit. In fact RKO employed two lyric writers, Gus Kahn and the defendant Edward Eliscu, who agreed to assign to RKO certain rights described in a contract dated as of May 25, 1933. Max Dreyfus, principal stockholder of the plaintiff Harms, which has succeeded to his rights, acquired Youmans' reserved rights to the music and was his designee for the assignment with respect to the lyrics. Allegedly—and his denial of this is a prime subject of dispute—Eliscu then entered into an agreement dated June 30, 1933, assigning his rights to the existing and renewal copyrights to Dreyfus in return for certain royalties.

When the copyrights were about to expire, proper renewal applications were made by the children of Youmans, by the widow and children of Kahn, and by Eliscu. The two former groups executed assignments of their rights in the renewal copyrights to Harms. But Eliscu, by an instrument dated February 19, 1962, recorded in the Copyright Office, assigned his rights in the renewal copyrights to defendant Ross Jungnickel, Inc., subject to a judicial determination of his ownership. Thereafter Eliscu's lawyer advised ASCAP and one Harry Fox—respectively the agents for the small performing rights and the mechanical recording license fees—that Eliscu had become vested with a half interest in the renewal copyrights and that any future payments which failed to reflect his interest would be made at their own risk; at the same time he demanded an accounting from Harms. Finally, Eliscu brought an action in the New York Supreme Court for a declaration that he owned a one-third interest in the renewal copyrights and for an accounting.

Harms then began the instant action in the District Court for the Southern District of New York for equitable and declaratory relief against Eliscu and Jungnickel. Jurisdiction was predicated on 28 U.S.C. § 1338; plaintiff alleged its own New York incorporation and did not allege the citizenship of the defendants, which concededly is in New York. Defendants moved to dismiss the complaint for failure to state a claim on which relief can be granted and for lack of federal jurisdiction; voluminous affidavits were submitted. The district court dismissed the complaint for want of federal jurisdiction * * *.

In line with what apparently were the arguments of the parties, Judge Weinfeld treated the jurisdictional issue as turning solely on whether the complaint alleged any act or threat of copyright infringement. He was right in concluding it did not. Infringement, as used in copyright law, does not include everything that may impair the value of the copyright; it is doing one or more of those things which * * * the Act * * * reserves exclusively to the copyright owner. * * *

Although Chief Justice Marshall, construing the "arising under" language in the context of Article III of the Constitution, indicated in Osborn v. Bank of the United States * * * that the grant extended to every case in which federal law furnished a necessary ingredient of the claim even though this was antecedent and uncontested, the Supreme Court has long given a narrower meaning to the "arising under" language in statutes defining the jurisdiction of the lower federal courts. * * * If the ingredient theory of Article III had been carried over to the general grant of federal question jurisdiction now contained in 28 U.S.C. § 1331, there would have been no basis—to take a well-known example—why federal courts should not have jurisdiction as to all disputes over the many western land titles originating in a federal patent, even though the controverted questions normally are of fact or of local land law. Quite sensibly, such extensive jurisdiction has been denied. * * *

The cases dealing with statutory jurisdiction over patents and copyrights have taken the same conservative line. * * * Just as with western land titles, the federal grant of a patent or copyright has not been thought to infuse with any national interest a dispute as to ownership or contractual enforcement turning on the facts or on ordinary principles of contract law. Indeed, the case for an unexpansive reading of the provision conferring exclusive jurisdiction with respect to patents and copyrights has been especially strong since expansion would entail depriving the state courts of any jurisdiction over matters having so little federal significance.

In an endeavor to explain precisely what suits arose under the patent and copyright laws, Mr. Justice Holmes stated that "[a] suit arises under the law that creates the cause of action"; in the case *sub judice,* injury to a business involving slander of a patent, he said, "whether it is a wrong or not depends upon the law of the State where the act is done" so that the suit did not arise under the patent laws. American Well Works Co. v.

Layne & Bowler Co.   *   *   * The Holmes "creation" test explains the taking of federal jurisdiction in a great many cases, notably copyright and patent infringement actions, both clearly authorized by the respective federal acts, * * * and thus unquestionably within the scope of 28 U.S.C. § 1338; indeed, in the many infringement suits that depend only on some point of fact and require no construction of federal law, no other explanation may exist.

Harms' claim is not within Holmes' definition. The relevant statutes create no explicit right of action to enforce or rescind assignments of copyrights, nor does any copyright statute specify a cause of action to fix the locus of ownership. To be sure, not every federal cause of action springs from an express mandate of Congress; federal civil claims have been "inferred" from federal statutes making behavior criminal or otherwise regulating it. * * * Such statutes invariably impose a federal duty and usually create some express remedy as well, while the relevant copyright provision merely authorizes an assignment by written instrument, 17 U.S.C. § 28. * * *

It has come to be realized that Mr. Justice Holmes' formula is more useful for inclusion than for the exclusion for which it was intended. Even though the claim is created by state law, a case may "arise under" a law of the United States if the complaint discloses a need for determining the meaning or application of such a law. * * * But Harms likewise does not meet this test. The crucial issue is whether or not Eliscu executed the assignment to Dreyfus; possibly the interpretation of the initial May, 1933, contract is also relevant, but if any aspect of the suit requires an interpretation of the Copyright Act, the complaint does not reveal it.

*   *   *

Mindful of the hazards of formulation in this treacherous area, we think that an action "arises under" the Copyright Act if and only if the complaint is for a remedy expressly granted by the Act, e.g., a suit for infringement or for the statutory royalties for record reproduction, * * * or asserts a claim requiring construction of the Act, * * * or, at the very least and perhaps more doubtfully, presents a case where a distinctive policy of the Act requires that federal principles control the disposition of the claim. The general interest that copyrights, like all other forms of property, should be enjoyed by their true owner is not enough to meet this last test.

*   *   *

Affirmed.

Notes and Questions

1. What types of cases should be heard in the federal courts? In formulating your thoughts on the subject, keep in mind that the character of federal litigation has changed dramatically in the past two decades. To a large degree this stems from fundamental rethinking of the role of the federal government in assuring justice, proper resource allocation, and individual rights. Often these changes are reflected in legislation that provides for

public or private actions to vindicate statutory policies. For example, the Civil Rights Act of 1964 and the Voting Rights Act of 1965 have spawned a multitude of cases challenging racial and sex-based discrimination; similarly, the Truth in Lending and Fair Credit Reporting Acts exemplify the federal statutes that have led to the growth of consumer protection litigation. Other incentives to sue have been generated by the federal courts recognizing private rights of action under federal statutes, particularly in the securities and antitrust fields, as well as by showing an increasing sensitivity to due process concerns. What effect should these changes in federal litigation have on the distribution of federal judicial resources?

2. As Judge Friendly points out, the same words—"arising under"—have been understood to have a different meaning in Article III of the Constitution than in various jurisdictional statutes. Does this make sense? To what extent might this be a function of the fact that Congress, if faced with a judicial interpretation of "arising under" in Article III that it did not prefer, would find it easier to pass a new jurisdictional statute than to amend the Constitution?

3. SMITH v. KANSAS CITY TITLE & TRUST CO., 255 U.S. 180, 41 S.Ct. 243, 65 L.Ed. 577 (1921), provides an example of a claim that, although created by state law, "arises under" a law of the United States by virtue of requiring a determination of the meaning or application of such law. In *Kansas City Title,* a shareholder sued to enjoin the Trust Company, a Missouri corporation, from investing in certain federal bonds on the ground that the Act of Congress authorizing their issuance was unconstitutional. The plaintiff claimed that under Missouri law an investment in securities the issuance of which had not been authorized by a valid law was *ultra vires* and enjoinable. The cause of action was thus state-created. Nonetheless, the Supreme Court held that the action "arose under" federal law.

> The general rule is that where it appears from the bill or statement of the plaintiff that the right to relief depends upon the construction or application of the Constitution or laws of the United States, and that such federal claim is not merely colorable, and rests upon a reasonable foundation, the District Court has jurisdiction. * * *

Id. at 199, 41 S.Ct. at 245, 65 L.Ed. at 585.

4. Should all causes of action created by federal law confer federal-question jurisdiction? The Supreme Court addressed this question in SHOSHONE MINING CO. v. RUTTER, 177 U.S. 505, 20 S.Ct. 726, 44 L.Ed. 864 (1900). Congress had established a system which allowed miners to file patents on their claims, and which set up a scheme for settling the conflicting claims of miners. The federal statute provided that the right to possession was to be determined by the "local customs or rules of miners in the several mining districts, so far as the same are applicable and not inconsistent with the laws of the United States." The Court determined:

> Inasmuch * * * as the "adverse suit" to determine the right of possession may not involve any question as to the construction or effect of the Constitution or laws of the United States, but may present simply a question of fact as to the time of the discovery of mineral, the location of the claim on the ground, or a determination of the meaning and effect of certain local rules and customs prescribed by the miners of the district, or

the effect of state statutes, it would seem to follow that it is not one which necessarily arises under the Constitution and laws of the United States.

Id. at 509, 20 S.Ct. at 727, 44 L.Ed. at 866.

The situation in *Shoshone* is the reverse of *Smith*: *Smith* arose from a state-created cause of action that turned on issues of federal law, *Shoshone* arose from a federally-created cause of action that turned on issues of state law.

5. The question whether a case is one "arising under" the Constitution or laws of the United States often is difficult to resolve, and a variety of standards has been advanced. Professor Cohen argues that the search for "a single, all-purpose, neutral analytical concept which marks out federal question jurisdiction" is futile. He suggests a "pragmatic" test that would include consideration of the extent of the effect on the court's caseload if jurisdiction is recognized, the extent to which a class of cases is likely to turn on issues of state or federal law, the extent to which the federal courts would have expertise in the area, and the extent to which a sympathetic federal tribunal is necessary. Cohen, *The Broken Compass: The Requirement that a Case Arise "Directly" Under Federal Law,* 115 U.Pa.L.Rev. 890 (1967). See also Shapiro, *Jurisdiction and Discretion,* 60 N.Y.U.L.Rev. 543 (1985).

6. Areas in which Congress has given the federal courts exclusive jurisdiction include, *inter alia,* bankruptcy, 28 U.S.C. § 1334, patents and copyrights, 28 U.S.C. § 1338(a), actions against foreign consuls and vice-consuls, 28 U.S.C. § 1351, actions to recover a fine, penalty, or forfeiture under federal law, 28 U.S.C. § 1355, and actions involving certain seizures, 28 U.S.C. § 1356. What factors should motivate Congress in choosing between a grant of concurrent or exclusive jurisdiction? See Note, *Exclusive Jurisdiction of the Federal Courts in Private Civil Actions,* 70 Harv.L.Rev. 509 (1957).

7. As suggested in *Harms,* the notion that a federal court has exclusive jurisdiction often means less than it seems to say. Consider disputes involving patents. In LUCKETT v. DELPARK, INC., 270 U.S. 496, 510–11, 46 S.Ct. 397, 402, 70 L.Ed. 703, 708–09 (1926), the patentee apparently could have sued for infringement of his patent but chose instead to sue for breach of contract. The District Court dismissed for want of jurisdiction, and the Supreme Court affirmed.

> [W]here a patentee complainant makes his suit one for recovery of royalties under a contract of license or assignment, or for damages for a breach of its covenants, or for a specific performance thereof, or asks the aid of the Court in declaring a forfeiture of the license or in restoring an unclouded title to the patent, he does not give the federal district court jurisdiction of the cause as one arising under the patent laws.

What is the point of the grant of exclusive jurisdiction if a plaintiff by artful pleading can choose whether the claim is to be heard in state or federal court?

8. A federal court must dismiss a claim arising under federal law for want of subject-matter jurisdiction if the claim is "so attenuated and unsubstantial as to be absolutely devoid of merit." Hagans v. Lavine, 415 U.S. 528, 536, 94 S.Ct. 1372, 1379, 39 L.Ed.2d 577, 587 (1974). It similarly must dismiss for want of jurisdiction if the claim clearly is foreclosed by prior decisions of the Supreme Court. Levering & Garrigues Co. v. Morrin, 289 U.S. 103, 105, 53 S.Ct. 549, 550, 77 L.Ed. 1062, 1064 (1933). The test for dismissal is a

rigorous one and, if there is any foundation of plausibility to the claim, federal jurisdiction exists.

LOUISVILLE & NASHVILLE R. CO. v. MOTTLEY

Supreme Court of the United States, 1908.
211 U.S. 149, 29 S.Ct. 42, 53 L.Ed. 126.

Appeal from the Circuit Court of the United States for the Western District of Kentucky * * *.

The appellees (husband and wife), being residents and citizens of Kentucky, brought this suit in equity in the circuit court of the United States for the western district of Kentucky against the appellant, a railroad company and a citizen of the same state. * * *

The bill alleged that in September, 1871, plaintiffs, while passengers upon the defendant railroad, were injured by the defendant's negligence, and released their respective claims for damages in consideration of the agreement for transportation during their lives, expressed in the contract. It is alleged that the contract was performed by the defendant up to January 1, 1907, when the defendant declined to renew the passes. The bill then alleges that the refusal to comply with the contract was based solely upon that part of the act of Congress of June 29, 1906 (34 Stat. at L. 584, chap. 3591, U.S.Comp.Stat.Supp.1907, p. 892), which forbids the giving of free passes or free transportation. The bill further alleges: First, that the act of Congress referred to does not prohibit the giving of passes under the circumstances of this case; and, second, that, if the law is to be construed as prohibiting such passes, it is in conflict with the 5th Amendment of the Constitution, because it deprives the plaintiffs of their property without due process of law. The defendant demurred to the bill. The judge of the circuit court overruled the demurrer, entered a decree for the relief prayed for, and the defendant appealed directly to this court.

MR. JUSTICE MOODY, after making the foregoing statement, delivered the opinion of the court:

Two questions of law were raised by the demurrer to the bill, were brought here by appeal, and have been argued before us. They are, first, whether * * * the act of Congress of June 29, 1906 * * * makes it unlawful to perform a contract for transportation of persons who, in good faith, before the passage of the act, had accepted such contract in satisfaction of a valid cause of action against the railroad; and, second, whether the statute, if it should be construed to render such a contract unlawful, is in violation of the 5th Amendment of the Constitution of the United States. We do not deem it necessary, however, to consider either of these questions, because, in our opinion, the court below was without jurisdiction of the cause. Neither party has questioned that jurisdiction, but it is the duty of this court to see to it that the jurisdiction of the circuit court, which is defined and limited by statute, is not exceeded. * * *

There was no diversity of citizenship, and it is not and cannot be suggested that there was any ground of jurisdiction, except that the case was a "suit * * * arising under the Constitution or laws of the United

States." 25 Stat. at L. 434, chap. 866, U.S.Comp.Stat.1901, p. 509. It is the settled interpretation of these words, as used in this statute, conferring jurisdiction, that a suit arises under the Constitution and laws of the United States only when the plaintiff's statement of his own cause of action shows that it is based upon those laws or that Constitution. It is not enough that the plaintiff alleges some anticipated defense to his cause of action, and asserts that the defense is invalidated by some provision of the Constitution of the United States. Although such allegations show that very likely, in the course of the litigation, a question under the Constitution would arise, they do not show that the suit, that is, the plaintiff's original cause of action, arises under the Constitution. In Tennessee v. Union & Planters' Bank, 152 U.S. 454, 38 L.Ed. 511, 14 S.Ct. Rep. 654, the plaintiff, the state of Tennessee, brought suit in the circuit court of the United States to recover from the defendant certain taxes alleged to be due under the laws of the state. The plaintiff alleged that the defendant claimed an immunity from the taxation by virtue of its charter, and that therefore the tax was void, because in violation of the provision of the Constitution of the United States, which forbids any state from passing a law impairing the obligation of contracts. The cause was held to be beyond the jurisdiction of the circuit court, the court saying, by Mr. Justice Gray (p. 464): "A suggestion of one party, that the other will or may set up a claim under the Constitution or laws of the United States, does not make the suit one arising under that Constitution or those laws." Again, in Boston & M. Consol. Copper & S. Min. Co. v. Montana Ore Purchasing Co., 188 U.S. 632, 47 L.Ed. 626, 23 S.Ct.Rep. 434, the plaintiff brought suit in the circuit court of the United States for the conversion of copper ore and for an injunction against its continuance. The plaintiff then alleged, for the purpose of showing jurisdiction, in substance, that the defendant would set up in defense certain laws of the United States. The cause was held to be beyond the jurisdiction of the circuit court, the court saying, by Mr. Justice Peckham (pp. 638, 639):

It would be wholly unnecessary and improper, in order to prove complainant's cause of action, to go into any matters of defense which the defendants might possibly set up, and then attempt to reply to such defense, and thus, if possible, to show that a Federal question might or probably would arise in the course of the trial of the case. To allege such defense and then make an answer to it before the defendant has the opportunity to itself plead or prove its own defense is inconsistent with any known rule of pleading, so far as we are aware, and is improper.

The rule is a reasonable and just one that the complainant in the first instance shall be confined to a statement of its cause of action, leaving to the defendant to set up in his answer what his defense is, and, if anything more than a denial of complainant's cause of action, imposing upon the defendant the burden of proving such defense.

Conforming itself to that rule, the complainant would not, in the assertion or proof of its cause of action, bring up a single Federal question. The presentation of its cause of action would not show that it was one arising under the Constitution or laws of the United States.

* * *

* * * The application of this rule to the case at bar is decisive against the jurisdiction of the circuit court.

It is ordered that the judgment be reversed and the case remitted to the circuit court with instructions to dismiss the suit for want of jurisdiction.

Notes and Questions

1. What justifications are there for the Supreme Court's disposition of *Mottley?* Why should subject-matter jurisdiction depend on technical pleading rules and the content of the complaint? Following the Court's decision, the Mottleys commenced an action in a Kentucky state court. The case ultimately was brought to the United States Supreme Court by appeal from the highest court in Kentucky on the question of the validity and construction of the 1906 Act; three years after the Supreme Court dismissed the federal action it examined the merits of the Mottleys' contentions and decided in favor of the railroad. In light of this history, what was gained by the original dismissal? Consider the proposal of the American Law Institute, *Study of the Division of Jurisdiction Between State and Federal Courts* § 1312(d) (1969), which provides that a federal court may retain subject-matter jurisdiction even when the complaint does not present a claim within its original jurisdiction if defendant introduces a federal defense or counterclaim. See also Doernberg, *There's No Reason for It; It's Just Our Policy: Why the Well-Pleaded Complaint Rule Sabotages the Purposes of Federal Question Jurisdiction,* 38 Hastings L.J. 597 (1987).

2. Would there have been jurisdiction in the principal case if the railroad had sought, as it can today, a judicial declaration, see pp. 18–21, supra, under the Declaratory Judgment Act, 28 U.S.C. §§ 2201–02, to the effect that the 1906 Act had rendered the passes invalid? See SKELLY OIL CO. v. PHILLIPS PETROLEUM CO., 339 U.S. 667, 673–74, 70 S.Ct. 876, 880, 94 L.Ed. 1194, 1200–01 (1950), in which suit was brought for a declaration that certain contracts had not been terminated. The effectiveness of an attempted termination by defendant depended on whether the Federal Power Commission had issued a certificate of public convenience and necessity under the Federal Natural Gas Act. In denying jurisdiction, the Court said: "To sanction suits for declaratory relief as within the jurisdiction of the District Courts merely because, as in this case, artful pleading anticipates a defense based on federal law would contravene the whole trend of jurisdictional legislation by Congress, disregard the effective functioning of the federal judicial system and distort the limited procedural purposes of the Declaratory Judgment Act." How would the assertion of jurisdiction in *Skelly* have done all of those things?

FRANCHISE TAX BD. v. CONSTRUCTION LABORERS VACATION TRUST

Supreme Court of the United States, 1983.
463 U.S. 1, 103 S.Ct. 2841, 77 L.Ed.2d 420.

Certiorari to the United States Court of Appeals for the Ninth Circuit.

JUSTICE BRENNAN delivered the opinion of the Court.

The principal question in dispute between the parties is whether the Employee Retirement Income Security Act of 1974 (ERISA) * * * permits state tax authorities to collect unpaid state income taxes by levying on funds held in trust for the taxpayers under an ERISA-covered vacation benefit plan. The issue is an important one, which affects thousands of federally regulated trusts and all nonfederal tax collection systems, and it must eventually receive a definitive, uniform resolution. Nevertheless, for reasons involving perhaps more history than logic, we hold that the lower federal courts had no jurisdiction to decide the question in the case before us, and we vacate the judgment and remand the case with instructions to remand it to the state court from which it was removed.

I

* * *

In June 1980, the Franchise Tax Board filed a complaint in state court against [Construction Laborers Vacation Trust (CLVT)] and its trustees. Under the heading "First Cause of Action," appellant alleged that CLVT had failed to comply with three [tax] levies issued under [California law] * * *. Under the heading "Second Cause of Action," appellant incorporated its previous allegations and added:

> There was at the time of the levies alleged above and continues to be an actual controversy between the parties concerning their respective legal rights and duties. The Board * * * contends that defendants [CLVT] are obligated and required by law to pay over to the Board all amounts held * * * in favor of the Board's delinquent taxpayers. On the other hand, defendants contend that * * * ERISA preempts state law and that the trustees lack the power to honor the levies made upon them by the State of California.

> [D]efendants will continue to refuse to honor the Board's levies in this regard. Accordingly, a declaration by this court of the parties' respective rights is required to fully and finally resolve this controversy. * * *

In a prayer for relief, appellant requested damages for defendants' failure to honor the levies and a declaration that defendants are "legally obligated to honor all future levies by the Board." * * *

CLVT removed the case to the United States District Court for the Central District of California, and the court denied the Franchise Tax Board's motion for remand to the state court. On the merits, the District Court ruled that ERISA did not preempt the State's power to levy on funds held in trust by CLVT. CLVT appealed, and the Court of Appeals reversed. * * * We now hold that this case was not within the removal jurisdiction conferred by 28 U.S.C. § 1441, and therefore we do not reach the merits of the pre-emption question.

II

The jurisdictional structure at issue in this case has remained basically unchanged for the past century. With exceptions not relevant here, "any civil action brought in a State court of which the district courts of the United States have original jurisdiction, may be removed by the defendant or the defendants, to the district court of the United States for the district and division embracing the place where such action is pending." If it appears before final judgment that a case was not properly removed, because it was not within the original jurisdiction of the United States district courts, the district court must remand it to the state court from which it was removed. * * * For this case—as for many cases where there is no diversity of citizenship between the parties—the propriety of removal turns on whether the case falls within the original "federal question" jurisdiction of the United States district courts: "The district courts shall have original jurisdiction of all civil actions arising under the Constitution, laws, or treaties of the United States." * * *

Since the first version of § 1331 was enacted * * *, the statutory phrase "arising under the Constitution, laws, or treaties of the United States" has resisted all attempts to frame a single, precise definition for determining which cases fall within, and which cases fall outside, the original jurisdiction of the district courts. * * *

One powerful doctrine has emerged, however—the "well-pleaded complaint" rule—which as a practical matter severely limits the number of cases in which state law "creates the cause of action" that may be initiated in or removed to federal district court, thereby avoiding more-or-less automatically a number of potentially serious federal-state conflicts.

* * * For better or worse, under the present statutory scheme as it has existed since 1887, a defendant may not remove a case to federal court unless the *plaintiff's* complaint establishes that the case "arises under" federal law. "[A] right or immunity created by the Constitution or laws of the United States must be an element, and an essential one, of the plaintiff's cause of action." Gully v. First National Bank in Meridian, 299 U.S. 109, 112, 57 S.Ct. 96, 97, 81 L.Ed. 70 (1936).

For many cases in which federal law becomes relevant only insofar as it sets bounds for the operation of state authority, the well-pleaded complaint rule makes sense as a quick rule of thumb. * * *

The rule, however, may produce awkward results, especially in cases in which neither the obligation created by state law nor the defendant's factual failure to comply are in dispute, and both parties admit that the only question for decision is raised by a federal pre-emption defense. Nevertheless, it has been correctly understood to apply in such situations. As we said in *Gully:* "By unimpeachable authority, a suit brought upon a state statute does not arise under an act of Congress or the Constitution of the United States because prohibited thereby." * * *

III

* * *

A

Even though state law creates appellant's causes of action, its case might still "arise under" the laws of the United States if a well-pleaded complaint established that its right to relief under state law requires resolution of a substantial question of federal law in dispute between the parties. For appellant's first cause of action—to enforce its levy—* * *

a straightforward application of the well-pleaded complaint rule precludes original federal-court jurisdiction. California law establishes a set of conditions, without reference to federal law, under which a tax levy may be enforced; federal law becomes relevant only by way of a defense to an obligation created entirely by state law, and then only if appellant has made out a valid claim for relief under state law. The well-pleaded complaint rule was framed to deal with precisely such a situation.

* * *

Appellant's declaratory judgment action poses a more difficult problem. Whereas the question of federal pre-emption is relevant to appellant's first cause of action only as a potential defense, it is a necessary element of the declaratory judgment claim. Under [California's statute], a party with an interest in property may bring an action for a declaration of another party's legal rights and duties with respect to that property upon showing that there is an "actual controversy relating to the legal rights and duties" of the parties. The only questions in dispute between the parties in this case concern the rights and duties of CLVT and its trustees under ERISA. Not only does appellant's request for a declaratory judgment under California law clearly encompass questions governed by ERISA, but appellant's complaint identifies no other questions as a subject of controversy between the parties. Such questions must be raised in a well-pleaded complaint for a declaratory judgment. Therefore, it is clear on the face of its well-pleaded complaint that appellant may not obtain the relief it seeks in its second cause of action * * * without a construction of ERISA and/or an adjudication of its pre-emptive effect and constitutionality—all questions of federal law.

Appellant argues that original federal-court jurisdiction over such a complaint is foreclosed by our decision in Skelly Oil Co. v. Phillips Petroleum Co., 339 U.S. 667, 70 S.Ct. 876, 94 L.Ed. 1194 (1950). As we shall see, however, *Skelly Oil* is not directly controlling.

In *Skelly Oil,* Skelly Oil and Phillips had a contract, for the sale of natural gas, that entitled the seller—Skelly Oil—to terminate the contract at any time after December 1, 1946, if the Federal Power Commission had not yet issued a certificate of convenience and necessity to a third party, a pipeline company to whom Phillips intended to resell the gas purchased from Skelly Oil. Their dispute began when the Federal Power Commission informed the pipeline company on November 30 that it would issue a conditional certificate, but did not make its order public until December 2. By this time Skelly Oil had notified Phillips of its decision to terminate their contract. Phillips brought an action in United States District Court under the federal Declaratory Judgment Act * * * seeking a declaration that the contract was still in effect.

There was no diversity between the parties, and we held that Phillips' claim was not within the federal-question jurisdiction conferred by § 1331. We reasoned:

" '[T]he operation of the Declaratory Judgment Act is procedural only.' Aetna Life Ins. Co. v. Haworth, 300 U.S. 227, 240 [57 S.Ct. 461, 463–464, 81 L.Ed. 617]. Congress enlarged the range of remedies available in the federal courts but did not extend their jurisdiction. When concerned as we are with the power of the inferior federal courts to entertain litigation within the restricted area to which the Constitution and Acts of Congress confine them, 'jurisdiction' means the kinds of issues which give right of entrance to federal courts. Jurisdiction in this sense was not altered by the Declaratory Judgment Act. Prior to that Act, a federal court would entertain a suit on a contract only if the plaintiff asked for an immediately enforceable remedy like money damages or an injunction, but such relief could only be given if the requisites of jurisdiction, in the sense of a federal right or diversity, provided foundation for resort to the federal courts. The Declaratory Judgment Act allowed relief to be given by way of recognizing the plaintiff's right even though no immediate enforcement of it was asked. But the requirements of jurisdiction—the limited subject matters which alone Congress had authorized the District Courts to adjudicate—were not impliedly repealed or modified." * * *

We then observed that, under the well-pleaded complaint rule, an action by Phillips to enforce its contract would not present a federal question. * * * *Skelly Oil* has come to stand for the proposition that "if, but for the availability of the declaratory judgment procedure, the federal claim would arise only as a defense to a state created action, jurisdiction is lacking." * * *

1. As an initial matter, we must decide whether the doctrine of *Skelly Oil* limits original federal-court jurisdiction under § 1331—and by extension removal jurisdiction under § 1441—when a question of federal law appears on the face of a well-pleaded complaint for a state-law declaratory judgment. * * *

Our interpretation of the federal Declaratory Judgment Act in *Skelly Oil* does not apply of its own force to *state* declaratory judgment statutes, many of which antedate the federal statute * * *.

Yet while *Skelly Oil* itself is limited to the federal Declaratory Judgment Act, fidelity to its spirit leads us to extend it to state declaratory judgment actions as well. If federal district courts could take jurisdiction, either originally or by removal, of state declaratory judgment claims raising questions of federal law, without regard to the doctrine of *Skelly Oil*, the federal Declaratory Judgment Act—with the limitations *Skelly Oil* read into it—would become a dead letter. * * *

2. The question, then, is whether a federal district court could take jurisdiction of appellant's declaratory judgment claim had it been brought under 28 U.S.C. § 2201. The application of *Skelly Oil* to such a suit is somewhat unclear. Federal courts have regularly taken original jurisdiction over declaratory judgment suits in which, if the declaratory judgment defendant brought a coercive action to enforce its rights, that suit would necessarily present a federal question. Section 502(a)(3) of ERISA specifically grants trustees of ERISA-covered plans like CLVT a cause of action for injunctive relief when their rights and duties under ERISA are at issue, and that action is exclusively governed by federal law. If CLVT could have sought an injunction under ERISA against application to it of

state regulations that require acts inconsistent with ERISA, does a declaratory judgment suit by the State "arise under" federal law?

* * * There are good reasons why the federal courts should not entertain suits by the States to declare the validity of their regulations despite possibly conflicting federal law. States are not significantly prejudiced by an inability to come to federal court for a declaratory judgment in advance of a possible injunctive suit by a person subject to federal regulation. They have a variety of means by which they can enforce their own laws in their own courts, and they do not suffer if the pre-emption questions such enforcement may raise are tested there. The express grant of federal jurisdiction in ERISA is limited to suits brought by certain parties * * * as to whom Congress presumably determined that a right to enter federal court was necessary to further the statute's purposes. It did not go so far as to provide that any suit *against* such parties must also be brought in federal court when they themselves did not choose to sue. The situation presented by a State's suit for a declaration of the validity of state law is sufficiently removed from the spirit of necessity and careful limitation of district court jurisdiction that informed our statutory interpretation in *Skelly Oil* and *Gully* to convince us that, until Congress informs us otherwise, such a suit is not within the original jurisdiction of the United States district courts. Accordingly, the same suit brought originally in state court is not removable either.

B

CLVT also argues that appellant's "causes of action" are, in substance, federal claims. * * *

CLVT's best argument stems from our decision in Avco Corp. v. Aero Lodge No. 735 * * *. In that case, the petitioner filed suit in state court alleging simply that it had a valid contract with the respondent, a union, under which the respondent had agreed to submit all grievances to binding arbitration and not to cause or sanction any "work stoppages, strikes, or slowdowns." The petitioner further alleged that the respondent and its officials had violated the agreement by participating in and sanctioning work stoppages, and it sought temporary and permanent injunctions against further breaches. It was clear that, had petitioner invoked it, there would have been a federal cause of action under § 301 of the Labor Management Relations Act * * * and that, even in state court, any action to enforce an agreement within the scope of § 301 would be controlled by federal law. It was also clear, however, under the law in effect at the time, that independent limits on federal jurisdiction made it impossible for a federal court to grant the injunctive relief petitioner sought. * * *

The Court of Appeals held * * * and we affirmed * * * that the petitioner's action "arose under" § 301, and thus could be removed to federal court, although the petitioner had undoubtedly pleaded an adequate claim for relief under the state law of contracts and had sought a remedy available *only* under state law. The necessary ground of decision was that the pre-emptive force of § 301 is so powerful as to displace entirely any state cause of action "for violation of contracts between an employer and a labor organization." Any such suit is purely a creature of federal law, notwithstanding the fact that state law would provide a cause of action in the absence of § 301. *Avco* stands for the proposition that if a federal cause of action completely pre-empts a state cause of action any complaint that comes within the scope of the federal cause of action necessarily "arises under" federal law.

CLVT argues by analogy that ERISA, like § 301, was meant to create a body of federal common law, and that "any state court action which would require the interpretation or application of ERISA to a plan document 'arises under' the laws of the United States." * * * ERISA contains provisions creating a series of express causes of action in favor of participants, beneficiaries, and fiduciaries of ERISA-covered plans, as well as the Secretary of Labor. * * * It may be that, as with § 301 as interpreted in *Avco,* any state action coming within the scope of § 502(a) of ERISA would be removable to federal district court, even if an otherwise adequate state cause of action were pleaded without reference to federal law. It does not follow, however, that either of appellant's claims in this case comes within the scope of one of ERISA's causes of action.

The phrasing of § 502(a) is instructive. Section 502(a) specifies which persons—participants, beneficiaries, fiduciaries, or the Secretary of Labor—may bring actions for particular kinds of relief. It neither creates nor expressly denies any cause of action in favor of state governments, to enforce tax levies or for any other purpose. It does not purport to reach every question relating to plans covered by ERISA. Furthermore, § 514(b)(2)(A) of ERISA * * * makes clear that Congress did not intend to pre-empt entirely every state cause of action relating to such plans. * * *

Against this background, it is clear that a suit by state tax authorities under a statute like § 18818 does not "arise under" ERISA. Unlike the contract rights at issue in *Avco,* the State's right to enforce its tax levies is not of central concern to the federal statute. For that reason, as in *Gully* * * *, on the face of a well-pleaded complaint there are many reasons completely unrelated to the provisions and purposes of ERISA why the State may or may not be entitled to the relief it seeks. Furthermore, ERISA does not provide an alternative cause of action in favor of the State to enforce its rights, while § 301 expressly supplied the plaintiff in *Avco* with a federal cause of action to replace its pre-empted state contract claim. Therefore, even though the Court of Appeals may well be correct that ERISA precludes enforcement of the State's levy in the circumstances of this case, an action to enforce the levy is not itself pre-empted by ERISA.

Once again, appellant's declaratory judgment cause of action presents a somewhat more difficult issue. The question on which a declaration is sought—that of the CLVT trustees' "power to honor the levies made upon them by the State of California" * * *—is undoubtedly a matter of concern under ERISA. It involves the meaning and enforceability of provisions in CLVT's trust agreement forbidding the trustees to assign or otherwise to alienate funds held in trust, * * * and thus comes within the class of questions for which Congress intended that federal courts create federal common law. Under § 502(a)(3)(B) of ERISA, a participant, beneficiary, or fiduciary of a plan covered by ERISA may bring a declaratory judgment action in federal court to determine whether the plan's trustees may comply with a state levy on funds held in trust. Nevertheless, CLVT's argument that appellant's second cause of action arises under ERISA fails for the second reason given above. ERISA carefully enumerates the parties entitled to seek relief under § 502; it does not provide anyone other than participants, beneficiaries, or fiduciaries with an express cause of action for a declaratory judgment on the issues in this case. A suit for similar relief by some other party does not "arise under" that provision.

*   *   *

Notes and Questions

1. The trustees of CLVT could have brought an action in federal court to enjoin the state officials from collecting the tax based on a claim that ERISA preempted the state statute. If this suit could have been brought in federal court anyway, why not permit the Franchise Tax Board to seek a declaratory judgment in federal court? Is this anomaly the reason Justice Brennan says the holding in the case is "for reasons involving perhaps more history than logic?"

2. In MERRELL DOW PHARMACEUTICALS INC. v. THOMPSON, 478 U.S. 804, 106 S.Ct. 3229, 92 L.Ed.2d 650 (1986), the parents of two children born with multiple deformities sued the manufacturer of the drug Bendectin in the Ohio Court of Common Pleas. They alleged that the complications attending the pregnancies had resulted from the mothers' ingestion of Bendectin during pregnancy and sought recovery on common-law theories of negligence, breach of warranty, strict liability, fraud, and gross negligence. The plaintiffs also alleged that the drug Bendectin was "misbranded" in violation of the Federal Food, Drug, and Cosmetic Act (FDCA), because its labeling did not provide adequate warning that its use was potentially dangerous. They further alleged that the violation of the FDCA "in the promotion" of Bendectin "constitutes a rebuttable presumption of negligence"—and that Merrell Dow's alleged violations of the FDCA "directly and proximately caused the injuries suffered" by the two infants.

Merrell Dow sought to remove the case to the Federal District Court, alleging that the action was "founded, in part, on an alleged claim arising under the laws of the United States." After removal, the District Court held that the complaint alleged a cause of action arising under federal law and denied the plaintiffs' motion to remand. The Court of Appeals for the Sixth Circuit reversed, and the Supreme Court affirmed that reversal.

Justice Stevens wrote for the majority. Noting that both parties agreed that there is no federal cause of action for FDCA violations, he assumed *arguendo* that Congress did not intend a private federal remedy for violations of the statute that it had enacted. Based on this premise, he concluded:

> The significance of the necessary assumption that there is no federal private cause of action thus cannot be overstated. For the ultimate import of such a conclusion, as we have repeatedly emphasized, is that it

would flout congressional intent to provide a private federal remedy for the violation of the federal statute. We think it would similarly flout, or at least undermine, congressional intent to conclude that the federal courts might nevertheless exercise federal-question jurisdiction and provide remedies for violations of that federal statute solely because the violation of the federal statute is said to be a "rebuttable presumption" or a "proximate cause" under state law, rather than a federal action under federal law.

Id. at 812, 106 S.Ct. at 3234–35, 92 L.Ed.2d at 660–61.

Dissenting for himself and three others, Justice Brennan rejected the major premise advanced by Justice Stevens:

     * * * Why should the fact that Congress chose not to create a private federal *remedy* mean that Congress would not want there to be federal *jurisdiction* to adjudicate a state claim that imposes liability for violating the federal law? Clearly, the decision not to provide a private federal remedy should not affect federal jurisdiction unless the reasons Congress withholds a federal remedy are also reasons for withholding federal jurisdiction. * * *

               * * *

     It may be that a decision by Congress not to create a private remedy is intended to preclude all private enforcement. If that is so, then a state cause of action that makes relief available to private individuals for violation of the FDCA is pre-empted. But if Congress' decision not to provide a private federal remedy does *not* pre-empt such a state remedy, then, in light of the FDCA's clear policy of relying on the federal courts for enforcement, it also should not foreclose federal jurisdiction over that state remedy. Both § 1331 and the enforcement provisions of the FDCA reflect Congress' strong desire to utilize the federal courts to interpret and enforce the FDCA, and it is therefore at odds with both these statutes to recognize a private state-law remedy for violating the FDCA but to hold that this remedy cannot be adjudicated in the federal courts.

     The Court's contrary conclusion requires inferring from Congress' decision not to create a private federal remedy that, while some private enforcement is permissible in state courts, it is "bad" if that enforcement comes from the *federal* courts. But that is simply illogical. * * *

Id. at 824, 831–32, 106 S.Ct. at 3242, 3245, 92 L.Ed.2d at 669–70, 673–74.

4. THE SUBJECT–MATTER JURISDICTION OF THE FEDERAL COURTS—DIVERSITY OF CITIZENSHIP

Article III, Section 2 of the United States Constitution extends the judicial power of the United States to controversies "between Citizens of different States * * * and between a State, or the Citizens thereof, and Foreign States, Citizens or Subjects." [a] The current scope of the diversity jurisdiction granted to the federal courts by Congress is set out in 28 U.S.C. § 1332. One of the most important limitations on federal diversity jurisdiction is the rule of "complete diversity" announced by Chief Justice

---

   a. Controversies between a citizen of a state and an alien technically are denominated "alienage cases," but may be considered as diversity cases for purposes of this Section.

Marshall in STRAWBRIDGE v. CURTISS, 7 U.S. (3 Cranch) 267, 2 L.Ed. 435 (1806). The rule provides in effect that there is no diversity jurisdiction if any plaintiff is a citizen of the same state as any defendant, no matter how many parties are involved in the litigation. The precise status of the complete diversity doctrine has been a subject of considerable debate because until recently it was not clear that the *Strawbridge* decision was intended by Chief Justice Marshall as simply a construction of the diversity statute then in force rather than as a constitutional limitation on federal-court jurisdiction. See also pp. 631–32, infra.

The origin and purposes of diversity-of-citizenship jurisdiction have long been the subject of vigorous debate. The most widely accepted rationale was offered by Chief Justice Marshall in BANK OF THE UNITED STATES v. DEVEAUX, 9 U.S. (5 Cranch) 61, 87, 3 L.Ed. 38, 45 (1809):

> However true the fact may be, that the tribunals of the states will administer justice as impartially as those of the nation, * * * it is not less true that the constitution itself either entertains apprehensions on this subject, or views with such indulgence the possible fears and apprehensions of suitors, that it has established national tribunals for the decision of controversies * * * between citizens of different states.

Another argument that has been advanced to justify diversity jurisdiction is that the availability of a federal tribunal during our nation's formative period afforded some measure of security to investors developing the southern and western portions of the country. Analyses of the historical origins of the diversity jurisdiction can be found in Frank, *Historical Bases of the Federal Judicial System,* 13 Law & Contemp.Prob. 1 (1948); Friendly, *The Historic Basis of the Diversity Jurisdiction,* 41 Harv.L.Rev. 483 (1928); and Phillips & Christenson, *The Historical and Legal Background of the Diversity Jurisdiction,* 46 A.B.A.J. 959 (1960).

Assuming that diversity jurisdiction was created to protect out-of-state litigants against local prejudice and that it has helped speed the economic growth of the country, are these realistic or meaningful bases for continuing diversity jurisdiction today? Statistical data on the actual existence of local prejudice against out-of-state parties, or whether an attorney's belief in the existence of such prejudice is a factor influencing forum choice, is sparse and inconclusive. Compare Summers, *Analysis of Factors that Influence Choice of Forum in Diversity Cases,* 47 Iowa L.Rev. 933 (1962), with Note, *The Choice Between State and Federal Court in Diversity Cases in Virginia,* 51 Va.L.Rev. 178 (1965). Are there other reasons that are more persuasive for retaining or even enlarging the scope of diversity jurisdiction? In what ways should the existing diversity scheme be modified to make it more rational and responsive to current conditions? In this regard, examine American Law Institute, *Study of the Division of Jurisdiction Between State and Federal Courts* §§ 1301–02, and comments at pp. 111–34 (1969). For a detailed analysis of the proposal, see Currie, *The Federal Courts and the American Law Institute,* 36 U.Chi. L.Rev. 1, 268 (1968–69).

More than 70,000 diversity cases were filed in the federal district courts in the year ending December 31, 1988. This figure represents approximately 22.3% of the total number of federal civil cases filed during that year. In view of the amount of federal judicial time and energy devoted to diversity cases, it is not surprising that the utility of diversity jurisdiction has been the subject of sharp debate. Proposals to curtail or abolish diversity jurisdiction have been made in Congress since the 1920's.

The Terms of the Debate

The arguments against the continued existence of any diversity jurisdiction concentrate primarily on five problems resulting from the creation of that jurisdiction. The first, often noted by Justice Frankfurter, is the congestion diversity cases allegedly cause in the federal courts. Second, the rule of Erie Railroad Co. v. Tompkins, which requires the application of state law to substantive issues in diversity cases, has been thought by many to make the handling of diversity cases by federal judges unnecessary, wasteful, and inappropriate. The reasoning behind this argument is that only the state courts are considered to be authoritative on matters of substantive law and the federal courts therefore are unable to exercise their creative function and are performing an unneeded service in avowedly aiming to project state-court decisions. Third, it is argued that judicial and legislative authority should be coextensive, and that for federal courts to decide cases arising under state law is an undesirable interference with state autonomy. A fourth and related problem is the effect that the diversion of litigation to federal courts may have in retarding the development of state law. Fifth, and finally, it is said that the continuation of diversity jurisdiction diminishes the incentives for state court reform by those influential professional groups who, by virtue of diversity jurisdiction, are able to avoid litigation in the state courts.

Although each of these arguments has some merit, they do not make a case for the total abolition of diversity jurisdiction if it can be shown that diversity jurisdiction in fact serves some useful purpose in the federal system. Thus we are left with the ultimate question. Of what utility is diversity jurisdiction today?

It is remarkable how little justification is offered in the literature, even by those who are friendly to diversity jurisdiction. Since this jurisdiction "is at least as traditionally federal as the Flag and the 4th of July," many of the writers who support diversity content themselves with asserting that the burden of proof is on those who would limit or abolish it. This approach, of course, avoids, if indeed it does not beg, the question. Other defenders of diversity do undertake to justify its present value, but their arguments rarely rise beyond the level of mere assertion.

The most common explanation for the creation of diversity jurisdiction was a fear that state courts would be prejudiced against out-of-state parties. Those who favor the retention of diversity jurisdiction contend that this prejudice still exists. But in a society infinitely more mobile than the one that existed at the time the Constitution was framed, it is difficult to believe that prejudice against a litigant based upon his being a citizen of a different state is a significant factor. Regrettably, prejudice may take a number of different forms but diversity jurisdiction has no bearing on most of them.

Another argument, with respectable historical antecedents, is that diversity jurisdiction is necessary in order to implement the constitutional guarantee that the citizens of each State shall be entitled to all the privileges and immunities of citizens of the several States. This argument has been characterized as specious, on the ground that abridgement of the privileges and immunities clause is in itself sufficient for federal question jurisdiction, and that diversity jurisdiction is not needed for this purpose. In this connection, it is worthy to note that other federal systems have flourished without anything comparable to diversity jurisdiction, although meaningful comparison of federal systems is very difficult.

A further argument, again going back to Hamilton, is that the federal courts qualitatively are so superior to the state courts that it is desirable to channel as many cases as possible to the federal courts, or at least that out-of-state litigants, who have no opportunity to work for the improvement of the state courts, should be spared exposure to them. There may be merit to this argument. Federal judges enjoy life tenure, they are free to comment on the evidence, and they sit with juries selected from a broader geographical area than most state tribunals. Not all lawyers would agree, however, that these differences lead to better justice, and even though the prestige of the federal courts generally has been high, there have been long periods when procedural differences have led to suspicion of the federal courts as rich people's courts or defendants' courts. Furthermore, arguments stemming from a supposed inferiority of state justice are insusceptible of proof and hardly politic to advance.

There is, however, a somewhat related argument to the effect that the existence of concurrent state and federal jurisdiction creates a competition between the two that acts as a spur to higher standards of justice in each court system. It is hard to believe that already crowded state courts will feel a strong incentive in order to keep the comparative handful of cases in which diversity exists and in which, therefore, the litigants have a choice of forum. In any event, concurrent jurisdiction exists over many federal-question cases, and whatever benefits concurrent judicial power may be thought to confer can be had from that phase of jurisdiction.

In addition, regardless of the supposed inferiority of the state courts, as long as diversity exists the choice of forum undoubtedly will be utilized for tactical purposes by particular litigants in particular cases, who think they may obtain an advantage from one forum or the other. To the extent this type of forum shopping exists, as it surely does, it seems more an abuse of concurrent jurisdiction than an argument for the retention of diversity jurisdiction.

Proponents of diversity jurisdiction also contend that the interaction between state and federal courts that results from the existence of concurrent jurisdiction in areas of substantive law practiced by substantial segments of the bar has resulted in improvements in the procedures followed by both state and federal courts. According to this theory, the large number and variety of cases litigated in federal courts because of diversity jurisdiction are essential to maintain this flow of ideas. However, even if diversity jurisdiction were restricted or abolished, a substantial number of cases involving significant state matters still would be adjudicated in federal courts, and the exchange of ideas would not come to an end.

Finally, it has been argued that the fear on the part of investors that local prejudice may exist provides a justification for diversity jurisdiction. This argument at one time was endorsed by the Judicial Conference of the United States.

If it is true that diversity jurisdiction is an indispensable condition to the free flow of capital from one part of the nation to another, then it should be retained. At first glance it might seem that the merit of this argument is dependent on the other arguments for diversity, which we have seen are of doubtful validity. If local prejudice will not be a significant factor and if state courts are as competent as federal courts, then there is no apparent reason why the decisions of entrepreneurs to invest their funds in other parts of the country should be affected by the availability of recourse to the federal courts. On reflection, however, this response is insufficient, as most of those who have put forward the flow-of-capital argument point out. The key question is not whether out-of-state investors in fact will receive fair treatment from state courts, but whether they think they will. If the abolition, or significant curtailment, of diversity jurisdiction would give rise to irrational fears by investors, and inhibit their willingness to invest in different parts of the country, then diversity serves a useful purpose and should be retained.

It may be that investors are now sufficiently national-minded, and accustomed enough to investing abroad where they enjoy no protection from the federal courts, that they no longer have fears of state courts, rational or irrational, that require the retention of diversity jurisdiction to comfort them. But it is hard to know how this can be proved short of the heroic experiment of its abolition.

It is unfortunate that the future of diversity jurisdiction is not likely to be resolved by an objective consideration of the arguments for and against it. Any proposal to modify diversity meets immediate organized opposition from those who believe that they have a vested interest in preserving, for their own advantage, the widest possible choice of forum.

Notes and Questions

1. Various views on the diversity jurisdiction debate can be found in Frankfurter, *Distribution of Judicial Power Between United States and State Courts*, 13 Cornell L.Q. 499 (1928); Marbury, *Why Should We Limit Federal Diversity Jurisdiction?*, 36 A.B.A.J. 379 (1960); Moore & Weckstein, *Diversity Jurisdiction: Past, Present and Future*, 43 Texas L.Rev. 1 (1964); Shapiro, *Federal Diversity Jurisdiction: A Survey and Proposal*, 91 Harv.L.Rev. 317 (1977); Rowe, *Abolishing Diversity Jurisdiction: Positive Side Effects and*

Potential for Further Reforms, 92 Harv.L.Rev. 963 (1979). For an empirical study, see Bass, *A Preliminary Empirical Inquiry,* 9 J.Legal Studies 93 (1980).

2. There are two important areas, domestic relations cases and probate matters, in which judge-made exceptions to the statute provide that the federal courts will not act even though diversity is present. These two exceptions were first developed at a time when the diversity statute granted jurisdiction of "suits of a civil nature in law or in equity," and it was thought that domestic relations and probate cases, being matters that would have been heard in the ecclesiastical courts, did not fit this description. The 1948 Judicial Code substituted the term "civil action" for the phrase used in the older statutes, but the exceptions have persisted. Today the exceptions may more rationally be defended on the ground that these are areas of the law in which the states have an especially strong interest and a well-developed competence for dealing with them.

The probate matters exception is far from absolute. It turns, instead, on unclear distinctions of the utmost subtlety. For example, a federal court may not probate a will nor undertake the administration of an estate, but if diversity or some other basis for jurisdiction is present, the federal court can entertain actions against administrators, executors, and other claimants in which plaintiffs seek to establish their claims against an estate so long as the federal court does not interfere with the probate proceedings or assume general jurisdiction of the probate or control of the property in the custody of the state court. The federal action in such a case will establish the claimant's right in a fashion that will be binding in the state proceedings, but the federal court cannot order actual distribution of property in the custody of the state court nor give execution on its judgment.

a. Determining Citizenship

MAS v. PERRY

United States Court of Appeals, Fifth Circuit, 1974.
489 F.2d 1396, certiorari denied 419 U.S. 842, 95 S.Ct. 74, 42 L.Ed.2d 70.

AINSWORTH, CIRCUIT JUDGE:

* * *

Appellees Jean Paul Mas, a citizen of France, and Judy Mas were married at her home in Jackson, Mississippi. Prior to their marriage, Mr. and Mrs. Mas were graduate assistants, pursuing coursework as well as performing teaching duties, for approximately nine months and one year, respectively, at Louisiana State University in Baton Rouge, Louisiana. Shortly after their marriage, they returned to Baton Rouge to resume their duties as graduate assistants at LSU. They remained in Baton Rouge for approximately two more years, after which they moved to Park Ridge, Illinois. At the time of the trial in this case, it was their intention to return to Baton Rouge while Mr. Mas finished his studies for the degree of Doctor of Philosophy. Mr. and Mrs. Mas were undecided as to where they would reside after that.

Upon their return to Baton Rouge after their marriage, appellees rented an apartment from appellant Oliver H. Perry, a citizen of Louisiana. This appeal arises from a final judgment entered on a jury verdict awarding $5,000 to Mr. Mas and $15,000 to Mrs. Mas for damages incurred by them as a result of the discovery that their bedroom and bathroom contained "two-way" mirrors and that they had been watched through them by the appellant during three of the first four months of their marriage.

At the close of the appellees' case at trial, appellant made an oral motion to dismiss for lack of jurisdiction. The motion was denied by the district court. Before this Court, appellant challenges the final judgment below solely on jurisdictional grounds, contending that appellees failed to prove diversity of citizenship among the parties and that the requisite jurisdictional amount is lacking with respect to Mr. Mas. Finding no merit to these contentions, we affirm. Under section 1332(a)(2), the federal judicial power extends to the claim of Mr. Mas, a citizen of France, against the appellant, a citizen of Louisiana. Since we conclude that Mrs. Mas is a citizen of Mississippi for diversity purposes, the district court also properly had jurisdiction under section 1332(a)(1) of her claim.

It has long been the general rule that complete diversity of parties is required in order that diversity jurisdiction obtain; that is, no party on one side may be a citizen of the same State as any party on the other side. Strawbridge v. Curtiss * * *. This determination of one's State citizenship for diversity purposes is controlled by federal law, not by the law of any State. * * * As is the case in other areas of federal jurisdiction, the diverse citizenship among adverse parties must be present at the time the complaint is filed. * * * Jurisdiction is unaffected by subsequent changes in the citizenship of the parties. * * * The burden of pleading the diverse citizenship is upon the party invoking federal jurisdiction * * * and if the diversity jurisdiction is properly challenged, that party also bears the burden of proof.

To be a citizen of a State within the meaning of section 1332, a natural person must be both a citizen of the United States * * * and a domiciliary of that State. * * * For diversity purposes, citizenship means domicile; mere residence in the State is not sufficient. * * *

A person's domicile is the place of "his true, fixed, and permanent home and principal establishment, and to which he has the intention of returning whenever he is absent therefrom * * *." * * * A change of domicile may be effected only by a combination of two elements: (a) taking up residence in a different domicile with (b) the intention to remain there. * * *

It is clear that at the time of her marriage, Mrs. Mas was a domiciliary of the State of Mississippi. While it is generally the case that the domicile of the wife—and, consequently, her State citizenship for purposes of diversity jurisdiction—is deemed to be that of her husband, * * * we find no precedent for extending this concept to the situation here, in which the husband is a citizen of a foreign state but resides in the United States. Indeed, such a fiction would work absurd results on the facts before us. If Mr. Mas were considered a domiciliary of France—as he would be since he had lived in Louisiana as a student-teaching assistant prior to filing this suit * * *—then Mrs. Mas would also be deemed a domiciliary, and thus, fictionally at least, a citizen of France. She would not be a citizen of any State and could not sue in a federal court on that basis; nor could she invoke the alienage jurisdiction to bring her claim in federal court, since she is not an alien. * * * On the other hand, if Mrs. Mas's domicile were Louisiana, she would become a Louisiana citizen for diversity purposes and could not bring suit with her husband against appellant, also a Louisiana citizen, on the basis of diversity jurisdiction. These are curious results under a rule arising from the theoretical identity of person and interest of the married couple. * * *

An American woman is not deemed to have lost her United States citizenship solely by reason of her marriage to an alien. 8 U.S.C. § 1489. Similarly, we conclude that for diversity purposes a woman does not have her domicile or State citizenship changed solely by reason of her marriage to an alien.

Mrs. Mas's Mississippi domicile was disturbed neither by her year in Louisiana prior to her marriage nor as a result of the time she and her husband spent at LSU after their marriage, since for both periods she was a graduate assistant at LSU. * * * Though she testified that after her marriage she had no intention of returning to her parents' home in Mississippi, Mrs. Mas did not effect a change of domicile since she and Mr. Mas were in Louisiana only as students and lacked the requisite intention to remain there. Until she acquires a new domicile, she remains a domiciliary, and thus a citizen of Mississippi. * * *

[The court's discussion of the jurisdictional amount is omitted.]

Thus the power of the federal district court to entertain the claims of appellees in this case stands on two separate legs of diversity jurisdiction: a claim by an alien against a State citizen; and an action between citizens of different States. We also note, however, the propriety of having the federal district court entertain a spouse's action against a defendant, where the district court already has jurisdiction over a claim, arising from the same transaction, by the other spouse against the same defendant. * * * In the case before us, such a result is particularly desirable. The claims of Mr. and Mrs. Mas arise from the same operative facts, and there was almost complete interdependence between their claims with respect to the proof required and the issues raised at trial. Thus, since the district court had jurisdiction of Mr. Mas's action, sound judicial administration militates strongly in favor of federal jurisdiction of Mrs. Mas's claim.

Affirmed.

Notes and Questions

1. The court equates citizenship with domicile for purposes of diversity jurisdiction but distinguishes domicile from residence. If the goal of diversity jurisdiction is to protect out-of-staters from bias in suits against in-staters, does it make sense to disregard residence in defining citizenship for diversity purposes?

2. The party asserting the existence of diversity jurisdiction has the burden of proving its existence. How could a party prove citizenship for

diversity purposes? Does it make sense for Perry to bear the burden of proof in this case, or are the Mases in a superior position to come forward with evidence?

3. Is an alien, who also is a stateless person, a citizen or subject of a foreign state under the diversity statute? In BLAIR HOLDINGS CORP. v. RUBINSTEIN, 133 F.Supp. 496 (S.D.N.Y.1955), the defendant was described in the complaint as "not [being] a citizen of the United States." The plaintiff argued that it was not incumbent upon it to establish that the defendant was a citizen or subject of a particular foreign state. The court disagreed, and interpreted 28 U.S.C. § 1332(a)(2) to require a showing that the defendant was a citizen of a foreign state. Since that showing had not been made, suit could not be maintained in federal court. One reason that the plaintiff had not made the required showing in *Rubinstein* was that the defendant, Serge Rubinstein, had been issued a so-called "Nansen" passport (a passport given to stateless persons) by the League of Nations and had registered as a stateless person with the United States Department of Justice.

4. A corporation is deemed a citizen of the states in which it is incorporated *and* in which it has its principal place of business. What if the corporation is incorporated in more than one state?

5. It generally is accepted that a corporation can have only one principal place of business for purposes of applying 28 U.S.C. § 1332. How does a court determine what that is? Is it where the stockholders or board of directors meet, where operational policy is fixed, where the greatest amount of corporate property or employees are located, or where the largest amount of revenue is earned? What other factors might be relevant? See J.A. Olson Co. v. City of Winona, 818 F.2d 401 (5th Cir.1987) ("total activity" test); Kelly v. United States Steel Corp., 284 F.2d 850 (3d Cir.1960) ("place of activity" test); Scot Typewriter Co. v. Underwood Corp., 170 F.Supp. 862 (S.D.N.Y.1959) ("nerve center" test). See generally 13B Wright, Miller & Cooper, *Federal Practice and Procedure: Jurisdiction and Related Matters 2d* § 3625 (1984).

6. In general, courts have held that an unincorporated association is not treated as a citizen for purposes of federal diversity jurisdiction, but instead, courts consider the citizenship of its members. Why are corporations treated differently from unincorporated associations? See United Steelworkers of America v. R.H. Bouligny, Inc., 382 U.S. 145, 86 S.Ct. 272, 15 L.Ed.2d 217 (1965).

Read 28 U.S.C. § 1359 in the Supplement.

KRAMER v. CARIBBEAN MILLS, INC.

Supreme Court of the United States, 1969.
394 U.S. 823, 89 S.Ct. 1487, 23 L.Ed.2d 9.

Certiorari to the United States Court of Appeals for the Fifth Circuit.

MR. JUSTICE HARLAN delivered the opinion of the Court.

The sole question presented by this case is whether the Federal District Court in which it was brought had jurisdiction over the cause, or

whether that court was deprived of jurisdiction by 28 U.S.C. § 1359.
* * *

The facts were these. Respondent Caribbean Mills, Inc. (Caribbean) is a Haitian corporation. In May 1959 it entered into a contract with an individual named Kelly and the Panama and Venezuela Finance Company (Panama), a Panamanian Corporation. The agreement provided that Caribbean would purchase from Panama 125 shares of corporate stock, in return for payment of $85,000 down and an additional $165,000 in 12 annual installments.

No installment payments ever were made, despite requests for payment by Panama. In 1964, Panama assigned its entire interest in the 1959 contract to petitioner Kramer, an attorney in Wichita Falls, Texas. The stated consideration was $1. By a separate agreement dated the same day, Kramer promised to pay back to Panama 95% of any net recovery on the assigned cause of action, "solely as a Bonus."

Kramer soon thereafter brought suit against Caribbean for $165,000 in the United States District Court for the Northern District of Texas, alleging diversity of citizenship between himself and Caribbean. The District Court denied Caribbean's motion to dismiss for want of jurisdiction. The case proceeded to trial, and a jury returned a $165,000 verdict in favor of Kramer.

On appeal, the Court of Appeals for the Fifth Circuit reversed, holding that the assignment was "improperly or collusively made" within the meaning of 28 U.S.C. § 1359, and that in consequence the District Court lacked jurisdiction. We granted certiorari * * *. For reasons which follow, we affirm the judgment of the Court of Appeals.

I.

The issue before us is whether Kramer was "improperly or collusively made" a party "to invoke the jurisdiction" of the District Court, within the meaning of 28 U.S.C. § 1359. We look first to the legislative background.

Section 1359 has existed in its present form only since the 1948 revision of the Judicial Code. Prior to that time, the use of devices to create diversity was regulated by two federal statutes. The first [was] known as the "assignee clause" * * *.

II.

* * * Because the approach of the former assignee clause was to forbid the grounding of jurisdiction upon *any* assignment, regardless of its circumstances or purpose, decisions under that clause are of little assistance. However, decisions of this Court under the other predecessor statute, 28 U.S.C. § 80 (1940 ed.), seem squarely in point. These decisions, together with the evident purpose of § 1359, lead us to conclude that the Court of Appeals was correct in finding that the assignment in question was "improperly or collusively made."

The most compelling precedent is Farmington Village Corp. v. Pillsbury * * *. There Maine holders of bonds issued by a Maine village desired to test the bonds' validity in the federal courts. In an effort to accomplish this, they cut the coupons from their bonds and transferred them to a citizen of Massachusetts, who gave in return a nonnegotiable two-year note for $500 and a promise to pay back 50% of the net amount recovered above $500. The jurisdictional question was certified to this Court, which held that there was no federal jurisdiction because the plaintiff had been "improperly or collusively" made a party within the meaning of the predecessor statute to 28 U.S.C. § 80 (1940 ed.). The Court pointed out that the plaintiff could easily have been released from his nonnegotiable note, and found that apart from the hoped-for creation of federal jurisdiction the only real consequence of the transfer was to enable the Massachusetts plaintiff to "retain one-half of what he collects for the use of his name and his trouble in collecting." * * * The Court concluded that "the transfer of the coupons was 'a mere contrivance, a pretense, the result of a collusive arrangement to create'" federal jurisdiction. * * *

We find the case before us indistinguishable from *Farmington* and other decisions of like tenor. When the assignment to Kramer is considered together with his total lack of previous connection with the matter and his simultaneous reassignment of a 95% interest back to Panama, there can be little doubt that the assignment was for purposes of collection, with Kramer to retain 5% of the net proceeds "for the use of his name and his trouble in collecting." If the suit had been unsuccessful, Kramer would have been out only $1, plus costs. Moreover, Kramer candidly admits that the "assignment was in substantial part motivated by a desire by [Panama's] counsel to make diversity jurisdiction available * * *."

The conclusion that this assignment was "improperly or collusively made" within the meaning of § 1359 is supported not only by precedent but also by consideration of the statute's purpose. If federal jurisdiction could be created by assignments of this kind, which are easy to arrange and involve few disadvantages for the assignor, then a vast quantity of ordinary contract and tort litigation could be channeled into the federal courts at the will of one of the parties. Such "manufacture of Federal jurisdiction" was the very thing which Congress intended to prevent when it enacted § 1359 and its predecessors.

III.

Kramer nevertheless argues that the assignment to him was not "improperly or collusively made" within the meaning of § 1359, for two main reasons. First, he suggests that the undisputed legality of the assignment under Texas law necessarily rendered it valid for purposes of federal jurisdiction. We cannot accept this contention. The existence of federal jurisdiction is a matter of federal, not state law. * * * Under the predecessor section * * * this Court several times held that an assignment could be "improperly or collusively made" even though binding under state law, and nothing in the language or legislative history of § 1359 suggests that a different result should be reached under that statute. Moreover, to accept this argument would render § 1359 largely incapable of accomplishing its purpose; this very case demonstrates the ease with which a party may "manufacture" federal jurisdiction by an assignment which meets the requirements of state law.

Second, Kramer urges that this case is significantly distinguishable from earlier decisions because it involves diversity jurisdiction under 28 U.S.C. § 1332(a)(2), arising from the alienage of one of the parties, rather than the more common diversity jurisdiction based upon the parties' residence in different States. We can perceive no substance in this argument: by its terms, § 1359 applies equally to both types of diversity jurisdiction, and there is no indication that Congress intended them to be treated differently.

* * *

Affirmed.

Notes and Questions

1. In PRUDENTIAL OIL CORP. v. PHILLIPS PETROLEUM CO., 546 F.2d 469 (2d Cir.1976), Prudential Equities, a Delaware corporation, assigned its claims against Phillips Petroleum, also a Delaware corporation, to Prudential Oil, a wholly-owned subsidiary incorporated in New York. Prudential Oil was engaged in no business other than the prosecution of these claims. The Second Circuit held that the assignment was a presumptively improper attempt to invoke the federal court's jurisdiction through the manufacture of diversity. Would the result have been the same if the assignment had been for a valid business reason?

2. In 1988, Congress added to Section 1332(c) a provision that "the legal representative of the estate of a decedent shall be deemed to be a citizen only of the same State as the decedent, and the legal representative of an infant or incompetent shall be deemed to be a citizen only of the same State as the infant or incompetent." In so doing, Congress articulated a rule which prevented the appointment of administrators to create (or destroy) diversity. See, e.g., Mecom v. Fitzsimmons Drilling Co., 284 U.S. 183, 52 S.Ct. 84, 76 L.Ed. 233 (1931); Vaughan v. Southern Railway Co., 542 F.2d 641 (4th Cir. 1976).

b. Amount in Controversy

BURNS v. ANDERSON

United States Court of Appeals, Fifth Circuit, 1974.
502 F.2d 970.

JOHN R. BROWN, CHIEF JUDGE:

The question on this appeal is whether a district court may dismiss a personal injury diversity suit where it appears "to a legal certainty" that the claim was "really for less than the jurisdictional amount."

The suit grew out of an auto accident in which plaintiff Burns' automobile was struck amidships by that of defendant Anderson. Burns' principal injury was a broken thumb. He brought the action in the Eastern District of Louisiana, claiming $1,026.00 in lost wages and medical expenses and another $60,000.00 for pain and suffering. After a pretrial conference and considerable discovery, the District Court dismissed for want of jurisdiction. Plaintiff appeals.

The test for jurisdictional amount was established by the Supreme Court in St. Paul Mercury Indemnity Co. v. Red Cab Co. There, the Court held that the determinant is plaintiff's good faith claim and that to justify dismissal it must appear to a legal certainty that the claim is really for less than the jurisdictional amount. There is no question but that this is a test of liberality, and it has been treated as such by this Court. This does not mean, however, that Federal Courts must function as small claims courts. The test is an objective one and, once it is clear that as a matter of law the claim is for less than $10,000.00, the Trial Judge is required to dismiss.

In the instant case, the District Judge dismissed only after examination of an extensive record. This record included the testimony of three doctors who treated Burns, as well as his own deposition. The accident occurred on May 26. The evidence is without contradiction that by the middle of August only very minimal disability remained. By December, even this minor condition had disappeared. Burns' actions speak even more strongly than the medical testimony. In his deposition he testified that he took a job as a carpenter's assistant on June 21 or 22—less than a month after the accident. He did heavy manual labor for the remainder of the summer with absolutely no indication of any difficulty with his thumb. It is equally clear that any pain he suffered was not of very great magnitude or lasting duration. Burns admitted that by the end of July there was no pain whatsoever. As a matter of fact, the evidence reveals that the only medication he ever received was a single prescription on the day of the accident for Empirin, a mild aspirin compound. Nor did his special damages take him a significant way down the road to the $10,000.00 minimum. His total medical bills were less than $250.00. Although he claims $800.00 in lost wages, it is difficult to see how this could have amounted to even $300.00 at Burns' rate of pay that summer.[5]

The point of this fact recitation is that it really does appear to a legal certainty that the amount in controversy is less than $10,000. This is no * * * case where dismissal was based on "bare bones pleadings" alone. The present situation differs from that case also in that this dismissal was for lack of subject matter jurisdiction not for failure to state a claim. Here the Trial Court examined an extensive record and determined as a matter of law that the requisite amount in controversy was not present. Indeed, had the case gone to trial and had the jury returned an award of $10,000, a * * * Judge would have been compelled as a matter of law to order a remittitur. He would have inescapably found that the verdict was "so inordinately large as obviously to exceed the maximum of the reasonable range within which the jury may properly operate." Of course, we decline to make any more precise determination of plaintiff's loss since to do so might prejudice his right to a trial in another court.

5. Burns was making the minimum wage, $1.65 an hour. Four forty-hour work weeks at this wage grosses $264.00.

Neither are we affected by plaintiff's plaintive plea that he is being deprived of a jury trial. The question in this case is not whether Burns is entitled to a trial by jury but rather where that trial is to be. We hold only that the case cannot be tried in the Federal Court because competence over it has not been granted to that Court by Congress.

Affirmed.

Notes and Questions

1. Until 1980, 28 U.S.C. § 1331 contained an amount-in-controversy requirement for federal-question cases. In that year, the requirement was deleted. The amendment makes it unnecessary in most cases to rely on the specific statutes conferring federal-question jurisdiction without regard to any jurisdictional amount. Jurisdictional amount is now an issue only in diversity cases and in some rare federal-question cases (actions brought under the Consumer Product Safety Act, for example) when a statute expressly requires that the federal question present a given amount in controversy.

2. In 1988, Congress amended 28 U.S.C. § 1332 to raise the jurisdictional amount from $10,000 to $50,000. The increase was a compromise between those who wished to abolish diversity jurisdiction and those who wished to maintain the rights of litigants to choose between the state and federal courts. Is it possible that plaintiffs simply will increase the amount of damages sought and undermine the purpose of the amendment?

In ARNOLD v. TROCCOLI, 344 F.2d 842 (2d Cir.1965), plaintiff's personal-injury action for $15,000, which originally had been brought for $6,000 in a state court, was dismissed as a colorable claim asserted for the sole purpose of conferring federal jurisdiction. There appeared to be no justification for the increase in claimed damages, and plaintiff's counsel admitted that the switch from state to federal court was made because of the congested condition of the state courts. In the course of its opinion, the Second Circuit examined statistics prepared by New York's Judicial Conference showing that 97% of all accident claims in New York result in settlements or judgments of less than $10,000. Of what relevance is this statistic in determining whether plaintiff's claim is "in excess of $10,000"? What if plaintiff discovers new facts during pretrial proceedings that show that any possible recovery cannot reach the jurisdictional amount, and his attorney files a written stipulation to that effect? Must the action be dismissed or is it saved by the fact that the original claim was made in "good faith"? See National Sur. Corp. v. City of Excelsior Springs, 123 F.2d 573 (8th Cir.1941).

3. If a question of jurisdictional amount is raised as in *Burns,* what types of evidence and information should the court be allowed to consider in ruling on a motion to dismiss? To what extent may the court examine the merits to determine the jurisdiction question? May the court hear argument on the question whether the elements of plaintiff's purported injuries are compensable under the governing law? See McDonald v. Patton, 240 F.2d 424 (4th Cir. 1957). Should alleged punitive damages be included in determining amount in controversy?

4. The liberal joinder provisions of the Federal Rules raise a number of questions as to whether "aggregation" can be used to meet the jurisdictional amount. See Wright, *Federal Courts* § 36 (4th ed.1983); 14A Wright, Miller

& Cooper, *Federal Practice and Procedure: Jurisdiction and Related Matters 2d* §§ 3704–06 (1985). See also Zahn v. International Paper Co., 414 U.S. 291, 94 S.Ct. 505, 38 L.Ed.2d 511 (1973), in which the Court held that each claim in a federal class-action suit must independently satisfy the jurisdictional amount requirement. Consider whether a federal court can assert jurisdiction in the following situations:

(a) One plaintiff sues one defendant claiming $10,000 property damage and $45,000 personal injury resulting from the same accident.

(b) One plaintiff sues one defendant on two unrelated claims, one for $10,000 and the other for $45,000.

(c) Two plaintiffs sue one defendant each seeking $30,000 in damages.

(d) Two plaintiffs sue one defendant jointly seeking $60,000 in damages.

(e) One plaintiff sues seeking $30,000 from each of two defendants.

(f) Two plaintiffs sue one defendant on the same issue. One plaintiff seeks $40,000 in damages; the other seeks $20,000.

In general, single plaintiffs can aggregate claims against single defendants. Two plaintiffs may not aggregate if they have separate and distinct claims. If there is a single indivisible harm, plaintiffs may aggregate. Does this make any sense? To what extent do these rules follow from a plain reading of Section 1332 and to what extent are they motivated by concerns of judicial economy? Why should the rules distinguish between cases with single plaintiffs and defendants and those with multiple parties?

5. Determining the amount in controversy, for jurisdictional purposes, in diversity cases seeking injunctive relief poses a difficult problem for federal courts. In McCARTY v. AMOCO PIPELINE CO., 595 F.2d 389, 391–93 (7th Cir.1979), Judge Swygert described this task as follows:

Valuation of the matter in controversy in suits for declaratory or injunctive relief is a complex task. The court must not only undertake to evaluate intangible rights as opposed to objects commonly found in the marketplace, but it must decide what rights are involved in the controversy and from whose viewpoint their value is to be measured. * * *

Some courts have resolved the difficulty by adopting the rule that only the value to the plaintiff may be used to determine the jurisdictional amount. Support for this interpretation is principally garnered from the Supreme Court's opinion in Glenwood Light & Water Co. v. Mutual Light, Heat & Power Co. * * *.

Although supportive of the "plaintiff viewpoint" rule, the holding in *Glenwood* is only that jurisdiction is present if the value to the plaintiff exceeds the required amount regardless of the value to the defendant. The *Glenwood* case does not exclude the possibility that jurisdiction would be present in a case where the value required was present from the defendant's viewpoint but not from the plaintiff's. * * *

Another approach taken by some courts is to view the amount in controversy from the point of view of the party seeking to invoke federal jurisdiction. Under this rule, the court would look to the plaintiff's viewpoint in a case brought originally in federal court and to the defendant's viewpoint in a case removed to federal court from a state court.

Although this rule has certain attractive features such as tying the controlling viewpoint to the burden of proof as to jurisdiction, two problems with it arise. The first is the possibility of anomalous results. Under the rule, if a case originally brought in federal court were dismissed for failure to meet the jurisdictional amount from the plaintiff's viewpoint, it could yet end up in federal court if the plaintiff reinstituted the case in state court and the defendant—from whose point of view the required amount was present—then removed it. * * *

There is yet a third rule which a number of courts have adopted and which may be termed the "either viewpoint" rule. Under this rule, as the court stated it in Ronzio v. Denver & R.G.W.R. Co. * * *:

> In determining the matter in controversy, we may look to the object sought to be accomplished by the plaintiffs' complaint; the test for determining the amount in controversy is the pecuniary result to either party which the judgment would directly produce.

* * *

5. SUBJECT–MATTER JURISDICTION OF THE FEDERAL COURTS—PENDENT AND ANCILLARY CLAIMS

Sometimes a federal court may decide matters that, if presented independently, would not provide a basis for federal subject-matter jurisdiction. The doctrines of pendent and ancillary jurisdiction describe two such situations. The term "pendent jurisdiction" is used when the plaintiff, in her complaint, seeks to append a claim lacking an independent basis for federal subject-matter jurisdiction to a claim possessing such a basis. The term "ancillary jurisdiction" is used when either a plaintiff or a defendant injects a claim lacking an independent basis for jurisdiction by way of a counterclaim, cross-claim, or third-party complaint. In short, although the doctrines have developed independently, they are two species of the same generic problem: Under what circumstances may a federal court hear and decide a claim for which there is no independent basis for federal subject-matter jurisdiction? What are the constitutional barriers to asserting jurisdiction over these claims? What nonconstitutional factors should a federal court consider in determining whether or not to exercise its power to hear a pendent or ancillary claim?

UNITED MINE WORKERS OF AMERICA v. GIBBS

Supreme Court of the United States, 1966.
383 U.S. 715, 86 S.Ct. 1130, 16 L.Ed.2d 218.

Certiorari to the United States Court of Appeals for the Sixth Circuit.

MR. JUSTICE BRENNAN delivered the opinion of the Court.

Respondent Paul Gibbs was awarded compensatory and punitive damages in this action against petitioner United Mine Workers of America (UMW) for alleged violations of § 303 of the Labor Management Relations Act, 1947, and of the common law of Tennessee. The case grew out of the rivalry between the United Mine Workers and the Southern Labor Union over representation of workers in the southern Appalachian coal fields. Tennessee Consolidated Coal Company, not a party here, laid off 100 miners of the UMW's Local 5881 when it closed one of its mines in southern Tennessee during the spring of 1960. Late that summer, Grundy Company, a wholly owned subsidiary of Consolidated, hired respondent as mine superintendent to attempt to open a new mine on Consolidated's property at nearby Gray's Creek through use of members of the Southern Labor Union. As part of the arrangement, Grundy also gave respondent a contract to haul the mine's coal to the nearest railroad loading point.

On August 15 and 16, 1960, armed members of Local 5881 forcibly prevented the opening of the mine, threatening respondent and beating an organizer for the rival union. The members of the local believed Consolidated had promised them the jobs at the new mine; they insisted that if anyone would do the work, they would. * * * George Gilbert, the UMW's field representative for the area including Local 5881, * * * [had] explicit instructions from his international union superiors to establish a limited picket line, to prevent any further violence, and to see to it that the strike did not spread to neighboring mines. There was no further violence at the mine site * * *.

Respondent lost his job as superintendent, and never entered into performance of his haulage contract. He testified that he soon began to lose other trucking contracts and mine leases he held in nearby areas. Claiming these effects to be the result of a concerted union plan against him, he sought recovery not against Local 5881 or its members, but only against petitioner, the International. The suit was brought in the United States District Court for the Eastern District of Tennessee, and jurisdiction was premised on allegations of secondary boycotts under § 303. The state law claim, for which jurisdiction was based upon the doctrine of pendent jurisdiction, asserted "an unlawful conspiracy and an unlawful boycott aimed at him and [Grundy] to maliciously, wantonly and willfully interfere with his contract of employment and with his contract of haulage."

* * * The jury's verdict was that the UMW had violated both § 303 and state law. Gibbs was awarded $60,000 as damages under the employment contract and $14,500 under the haulage contract; he was also awarded $100,000 punitive damages. On motion, the trial court set aside the award of damages with respect to the haulage contract on the ground that damage was unproved. It also held that union pressure on Grundy to discharge respondent as supervisor would constitute only a primary dispute with Grundy, as respondent's employer, and hence was not cognizable under § 303. Interference with employment was cognizable as a state claim, however, and a remitted award was sustained on the state law claim. * * * The Court of Appeals for the Sixth Circuit affirmed. * * * We granted certiorari. * * *

I.

A threshold question is whether the District Court properly entertained jurisdiction of the claim based on Tennessee law. * * *

* * * The Court held in Hurn v. Oursler, 289 U.S. 238, 53 S.Ct. 586, 77 L.Ed. 1148, that state law claims are appropriate for federal court

determination if they form a separate but parallel ground for relief also sought in a substantial claim based on federal law. The Court distinguished permissible from non-permissible exercises of federal judicial power over state law claims by contrasting "a case where two distinct grounds in support of a single cause of action are alleged, one only of which presents a federal question, and a case where two separate and distinct causes of action are alleged, one only of which is federal in character. In the former, where the federal question averred is not plainly wanting in substance, the federal court, even though the federal ground be not established, may nevertheless retain and dispose of the case upon the nonfederal *ground;* in the latter it may not do so upon the nonfederal *cause of action.*" 289 U.S., at 246, 53 S.Ct., at 589. The question is into which category the present action fell.

Hurn was decided in 1933, before the unification of law and equity by the Federal Rules of Civil Procedure. At the time, the meaning of "cause of action" was a subject of serious dispute * * *. The Court in *Hurn* identified what it meant by the term by citation of Baltimore S.S. Co. v. Phillips, 274 U.S. 316, 47 S.Ct. 600, 71 L.Ed. 1069, a case in which "cause of action" had been used to identify the operative scope of the doctrine of *res judicata.* In that case the Court had noted that " 'the whole tendency of our decisions is to require a plaintiff to try his whole cause of action and his whole case at one time,' " 274 U.S., at 320, 47 S.Ct., at 602, and stated its holding in the following language, quoted in part in the *Hurn* opinion:

> Upon principle, it is perfectly plain that the respondent [a seaman suing for an injury sustained while working aboard ship] suffered but one actionable wrong, and was entitled to but one recovery, whether his injury was due to one or the other of several distinct acts of alleged negligence, or to a combination of some or all of them. In either view, there would be but a single wrongful invasion of a single primary right of the plaintiff, namely, the right of bodily safety, whether the acts constituting such invasion were one or many, simple or complex.

> A cause of action does not consist of facts, but of the unlawful violation of a right which the facts show. The number and variety of the facts alleged do not establish more than one cause of action so long as their result, whether they be considered severally or in combination, is the violation of but one right by a single legal wrong. The mere multiplication of grounds of negligence alleged as causing the same injury does not result in multiplying the causes of action. "The facts are merely the means, and not the end. They do not constitute the cause of action, but they show its existence by making the wrong appear." Id., at 321, 47 S.Ct. at 602.

Had the Court found a jurisdictional bar to reaching the state claim in *Hurn,* we assume that the doctrine of *res judicata* would not have been applicable in any subsequent state suit. But the citation of *Baltimore S.S. Co.* shows that the Court found that the weighty policies of judicial economy and fairness to parties reflected in *res judicata* doctrine were in themselves strong counsel for the adoption of a rule which would permit federal courts to dispose of the state as well as the federal claims.

With the adoption of the Federal Rules of Civil Procedure and the unified form of action * * * much of the controversy over "cause of action" abated. The phrase remained as the keystone of the *Hurn* test, however, and * * * has been the source of considerable confusion. Under the Rules, the impulse is toward entertaining the broadest possible scope of action consistent with fairness to the parties; joinder of claims, parties and remedies are strongly encouraged. Yet because the *Hurn* question involves issues of jurisdiction as well as convenience, there has been some tendency to limit its application to cases in which the state and federal claims are, as in *Hurn,* "little more than the equivalent of different epithets to characterize the same group of circumstances." 289 U.S., at 246, 53 S.Ct. at 590.

This limited approach is unnecessarily grudging. Pendent jurisdiction, in the sense of judicial *power,* exists whenever there is a claim "arising under [the] Constitution, the Laws of the United States, and Treaties made, or which shall be made, under their Authority * * *," U.S. Const., Art. III, § 2, and the relationship between that claim and the state claims made in the complaint permits the conclusion that the entire action before the court comprises but one constitutional "case." The federal claim must have substance sufficient to confer subject matter jurisdiction on the court. Levering & Garrigues Co. v. Morrin, 289 U.S. 103, 53 S.Ct. 549, 77 L.Ed. 1062. The state and federal claims must derive from a common nucleus of operative fact. But if, considered without regard for their federal or state character, a plaintiff's claims are such that he would ordinarily be expected to try them all in one judicial proceeding, then, assuming substantiality of the federal issues, there is *power* in federal courts to hear the whole.

That power need not be exercised in every case in which it is found to exist. It has consistently been recognized that pendent jurisdiction is a doctrine of discretion, not of plaintiff's right. Its justification lies in considerations of judicial economy, convenience and fairness to litigants; if these are not present a federal court should hesitate to exercise jurisdiction over state claims, even though bound to apply state law to them, Erie R. Co. v. Tompkins * * * [p. 346, infra]. Needless decisions of state law should be avoided both as a matter of comity and to promote justice between the parties, by procuring for them a surer-footed reading of applicable law. Certainly, if the federal claims are dismissed before trial, even though not insubstantial in a jurisdictional sense, the state claims should be dismissed as well. Similarly, if it appears that the state issues substantially predominate, whether in terms of proof, of the scope of the issues raised, or of the comprehensiveness of the remedy sought, the state claims may be dismissed without prejudice and left for resolution to state tribunals. There may, on the other hand, be situations in which the state claim is so closely tied to questions of federal policy that the argument for exercise of pendent jurisdiction is particularly strong. In the present case, for example, the allowable scope of the state claim implicates the federal doctrine of pre-emption; while this interrelationship does not create statutory federal question jurisdiction, Louisville & N.R. Co. v. Mottley, * * * its existence is relevant to the exercise of discretion. Finally, there may be reasons independent of jurisdictional considerations, such as the likelihood of jury confusion in treating divergent legal theories of relief, that would justify separating state and federal claims for trial, Fed.Rule Civ.Proc. 42(b). If so, jurisdiction should ordinarily be refused.

The question of power will ordinarily be resolved on the pleadings. But the issue whether pendent jurisdiction has been properly assumed is one which remains open throughout the litigation. Pretrial procedures or even the trial may reveal a substantial hegemony of state law claims, or likelihood of jury confusion, which could not have been anticipated at the pleading stage. Although it will of course be appropriate to take account in this circumstance of the already completed course of the litigation, dismissal of the state claim might even then be merited. For example, it may appear that the plaintiff was well aware of the nature of his proofs and the relative importance of his claims; recognition of a federal court's wide latitude to decide ancillary questions of state law does not imply that it must tolerate a litigant's effort to impose upon it what is in effect only a state law case. Once it appears that a state claim constitutes the real body of a case, to which the federal claim is only an appendage, the state claim may fairly be dismissed.

We are not prepared to say that in the present case the District Court exceeded its discretion in proceeding to judgment on the state claim.
*   *   *

It is true that the § 303 claims ultimately failed and that the only recovery allowed respondent was on the state claim. We cannot confidently say, however, that the federal issues were so remote or played such a minor role at the trial that in effect the state claim only was tried. Although the District Court dismissed as unproved the claims that petitioner's secondary activities included attempts to induce coal operators other than Grundy to cease doing business with respondent, the court submitted the § 303 claims relating to Grundy to the jury. The jury returned verdicts against petitioner on those § 303 claims, and it was only on petitioner's motion for a directed verdict and a judgment *n.o.v.* that the verdicts on those claims were set aside. * * * Although there was some risk of confusing the jury in joining the state and federal claims— especially since, as will be developed, differing standards of proof of UMW involvement applied—the possibility of confusion could be lessened by employing a special verdict form, as the District Court did. * * *

[The Court went on to hold that the plaintiff could not recover damages for conspiracy under Tennessee common law on the basis of the record.]

Reversed.

THE CHIEF JUSTICE took no part in the decision of this case.

[A concurring opinion by JUSTICE HARLAN, joined by JUSTICE CLARK, is omitted.]

Notes and Questions

1. To what extent are Hurn v. Oursler and United Mine Workers of America v. Gibbs inconsistent with the notion that the subject-matter jurisdiction of the federal courts is limited by Article III of the Constitution and whatever enabling legislation Congress chooses to enact? Surely convenience and judicial administration, although admirable goals, cannot always be used to override basic tenets regarding the distribution of judicial business in a federal system. In this connection, consider the following passage:

> * * * [T]he exercise of pendent jurisdiction must be judged by whether it furthers some federal policy. Measured by that test pendent jurisdiction serves two purposes. First, it ensures that litigants will not be dissuaded from maintaining their federal rights in a federal court solely because they can dispose of all claims by one litigation in the state but not the federal forum. When jurisdiction over the federal claim is exclusive in the federal judiciary, only pendent jurisdiction makes possible a complete remedy for vindication of the plaintiff's rights. Second, assuming that the litigants are in a federal forum, pendent jurisdiction serves the interest of avoiding piecemeal litigation, thus promoting judicial economy and greater expedition for the litigants. In respect to judicial economy, one must reject the idea * * * of a dichotomy between the state and federal judicial systems; rather they are copartners in the judicial endeavor to effectuate justice throughout the nation with the least burden on national and individual resources.

Note, *The Evolution and Scope of the Doctrine of Pendent Jurisdiction in the Federal Courts,* 62 Colum.L.Rev. 1018, 1044 (1962). See also Note, *Problems of Parallel State and Federal Remedies,* 71 Harv.L.Rev. 513 (1958); Note, *Pendent Jurisdiction: An Expanding Concept in Federal Court Jurisdiction,* 51 Iowa L.Rev. 151 (1965). The principal case is discussed in Note, *UMW v. Gibbs and Pendent Jurisdiction,* 81 Harv.L.Rev. 657 (1968), and is criticized in Shakman, *The New Pendent Jurisdiction of the Federal Courts,* 20 Stan.L.Rev. 262 (1968). For a general discussion of pendent jurisdiction, see 13B Wright, Miller & Cooper, *Federal Practice and Procedure: Jurisdiction and Related Matters 2d* § 3567 (1984).

2. The aspect of *Hurn* that caused the most interpretive difficulties was the requirement that the state and federal claims merely be two distinct grounds of a "single cause of action" rather than "two separate and distinct causes of action." What considerations are relevant to the question whether two claims are but aspects of a "single cause of action"? See Armstrong Paint & Varnish Works v. Nu-Enamel Corp., 305 U.S. 315, 59 S.Ct. 191, 83 L.Ed. 195 (1938); Kleinman v. Betty Dain Creations, Inc., 189 F.2d 546 (2d Cir.1951). See generally Comment, *Discretionary Federal Jurisdiction Over the Pendent Cause,* 46 Ill.L.Rev. 646 (1951). What is the test for pendency that emerges from *Gibbs*? Is it any easier to apply than the *Hurn* test?

3. Should the considerations of judicial economy and party convenience underlying pendent subject-matter jurisdiction also allow the court to assert pendent personal jurisdiction for purposes of adjudicating the nonfederal claim? For example, if jurisdiction over defendant has been effected pursuant to a federal statute providing for nationwide service of process, but defendant would not be subject to process in the forum state for purposes of the joined

state claim, must the court dismiss the latter? See Robinson v. Penn Central Co., 484 F.2d 553 (3d Cir.1973); Price v. United Mine Workers of America, 336 F.2d 771 (6th Cir.1964), certiorari denied 380 U.S. 913, 85 S.Ct. 899, 13 L.Ed.2d 799 (1965).

4. When is the federal question that forms the basis for a claim of pendent jurisdiction "plainly wanting in substance"? Is an adequate answer provided by the "sufficient substance" test for federal claims in general articulated in Levering & Garrigues Co. v. Morrin, 289 U.S. 103, 53 S.Ct. 549, 77 L.Ed. 1062 (1933), see p. 248, supra, which was decided shortly before *Hurn* and is cited in *Gibbs*? The Court in *Levering* noted that a federal question may be plainly insubstantial either because it is "obviously without merit" or because "its unsoundness so clearly results from previous decisions of this court." A number of federal courts apply a somewhat different test and deny pendent jurisdiction when the federal claim is dismissed on the pleadings. See, e.g., Strachman v. Palmer, 177 F.2d 427 (1st Cir.1949); Walters v. Shari Music Publishing Corp., 193 F.Supp. 307 (S.D.N.Y.1961). What are the advantages, if any, of this test? Is it more or less permissive than the one suggested in *Levering*?

5. *Gibbs* defines the court's power to hear a pendent claim, but says that this power need not be exercised in every case. Should this choice depend upon whether jurisdiction is concurrent or exclusive? What factors should a court consider in deciding whether or not to exercise its power?

Jurisdiction Over Pendent Parties

In *Gibbs,* the plaintiff joined federal and state claims against a single defendant. What if a federal claim is asserted against one defendant and a closely related state claim is asserted against another, whose presence in the action would destroy complete diversity of citizenship? In the years following *Gibbs,* many lower federal courts recognized "pendent party" jurisdiction in such situations. See Mobil Oil Corp. v. Kelley, 493 F.2d 784 (5th Cir.1974); Schulman v. Huck Finn, Inc., 472 F.2d 864 (8th Cir.1973); Astor-Honor, Inc. v. Grosset & Dunlap, Inc., 441 F.2d 627 (2d Cir.1971).

However, in ALDINGER v. HOWARD, 427 U.S. 1, 96 S.Ct. 2413, 49 L.Ed.2d 276 (1976), the Supreme Court refused to apply pendent jurisdiction to an additional party with respect to whom no independent basis of federal jurisdiction existed. The suit was brought by a citizen of Washington against several officers of Spokane County, Washington, and alleged violations of the Civil Rights Act (42 U.S.C. § 1983). Plaintiff sought to join the county itself as an additional defendant, but under the construction given the federal statute at the time, counties were not considered to be subject to it.[b] Therefore, plaintiff was forced to sue the county under state law, and argue that a federal court could hear her claim under its pendent jurisdiction, despite the absence of diversity, since her two claims met the *Gibbs* "common nucleus of operative fact" test. The Supreme Court rejected the argument and distinguished *Gibbs* on two grounds:

b. Municipalities and other governmental units since have been held to be amenable to suit under the Civil Rights Act. See Monell v. Department of Social Servs. of City of New York, 436 U.S. 658, 98 S.Ct. 2018, 56 L.Ed.2d 611 (1978).

* * * From a purely factual point of view, it is one thing to authorize two parties, already present in federal court by virtue of a case over which the court has jurisdiction, to litigate in addition to their federal claim a state-law claim over which there is no independent basis of federal jurisdiction. But it is quite another thing to permit a plaintiff, who has asserted a claim against one defendant with respect to which there is federal jurisdiction, to join an entirely different defendant on the basis of a state-law claim over which there is no independent basis of federal jurisdiction, simply because his claim against the first defendant and his claim against the second defendant "derive from a common nucleus of operative fact." * * * True, the same considerations of judicial economy would be served * * *. But the addition of a completely new party would run counter to the well-established principle that federal courts, as opposed to state trial courts of general jurisdiction, are courts of limited jurisdiction marked out by Congress. * * *

There is also a significant legal difference. In * * * *Gibbs* Congress was silent on the extent to which the defendant, already properly in federal court under a statute, might be called upon to answer nonfederal questions or claims; the way was thus left open for the Court to fashion its own rules under the general language of Art. III. But the extension of *Gibbs* to this kind of "pendent party" jurisdiction—bringing in an additional defendant at the behest of the plaintiff—presents rather different statutory jurisdictional considerations. Petitioner's contention that she should be entitled to sue Spokane County as a new third party, and then to try a wholly state-law claim against the county, all of which would be "pendent" to her federal claim against respondent county treasurer, must be decided, not in the context of congressional silence or tacit encouragement, but in quite the opposite context. The question here, which it was not necessary to address in *Gibbs* * * *, is whether by virtue of the statutory grant of subject-matter jurisdiction, upon which petitioner's principal claim against the treasurer rests, Congress has addressed itself to the *party* as to whom jurisdiction pendent to the principal claim is sought. And it undoubtedly has done so.

* * *

Resolution of a claim of pendent-party jurisdiction, therefore, calls for careful attention to the relevant statutory language. As we have indicated, we think a fair reading of the language used in [the relevant statutes] * * * requires a holding that the joinder of a municipal corporation, like the county here, for purposes of asserting a state-law claim not within federal diversity jurisdiction, is without the statutory jurisdiction of the district court.

Id. at 14–18, 96 S.Ct. at 2420–22, 49 L.Ed.2d at 286–88.

However, the Court carefully refused to lay down any "sweeping pronouncement upon the existence or exercise of [pendent party] jurisdiction":

* * * Other statutory grants and other alignments of parties and claims might call for a different result. When the grant of jurisdiction to a federal court is exclusive, for example, as in the prosecution of tort claims against the United States * * *, the argument of judicial econo-

my and convenience can be coupled with the additional argument that *only* in a federal court may all of the claims be tried together. * * *

Id. at 18, 96 S.Ct. at 2422, 49 L.Ed.2d at 288. District courts also were instructed that before they could conclude that pendent-party jurisdiction existed, they must ask if "Congress in the statutes conferring jurisdiction has not expressly or by implication negated its existence."

OWEN EQUIPMENT & ERECTION CO. v. KROGER

Supreme Court of the United States, 1978.
437 U.S. 365, 98 S.Ct. 2396, 57 L.Ed.2d 274.

Certiorari to the United States Court of Appeals for the Eighth Circuit.

MR. JUSTICE STEWART delivered the opinion of the Court.

In an action in which federal jurisdiction is based on diversity of citizenship, may the plaintiff assert a claim against a third-party defendant when there is no independent basis for federal jurisdiction over that claim? The Court of Appeals for the Eighth Circuit held in this case that such a claim is within the ancillary jurisdiction of the federal courts. We granted certiorari * * * because this decision conflicts with several recent decisions of other Courts of Appeals.

I

On January 18, 1972, James Kroger was electrocuted when the boom of a steel crane next to which he was walking came too close to a high tension electric power line. The respondent (his widow, who is the administratrix of his estate) filed a wrongful death action in the United States District Court for the District of Nebraska against the Omaha Public Power District (OPPD). Her complaint alleged that OPPD's negligent construction, maintenance and operation of the power line had caused Kroger's death. Federal jurisdiction was based on diversity of citizenship, since the respondent was a citizen of Iowa and OPPD was a Nebraska corporation.

OPPD then filed a third-party complaint pursuant to Fed.Rule Civ. Proc. 14(a) against the petitioner, Owen Equipment and Erection Company (Owen), alleging that the crane was owned and operated by Owen, and that Owen's negligence had been the proximate cause of Kroger's death. OPPD later moved for summary judgment on the respondent's complaint against it. While this motion was pending, the respondent was granted leave to file an amended complaint naming Owen as an additional defendant. Thereafter, the District Court granted OPPD's motion for summary judgment in an unreported opinion. The case thus went to trial between the respondent and the petitioner alone.

The respondent's amended complaint alleged that Owen was "a Nebraska corporation with its principal place of business in Nebraska." Owen's answer admitted that it was "a corporation organized and existing under the Laws of the State of Nebraska," and denied every other allegation of the complaint. On the third day of trial, however, it was disclosed that the petitioner's principal place of business was in Iowa, not

Nebraska,[5] and that the petitioner and the respondent were thus both citizens of Iowa. The petitioner then moved to dismiss the complaint for lack of jurisdiction. The District Court reserved decision on the motion, and the jury thereafter returned a verdict in favor of the respondent. In an unreported opinion issued after the trial, the District Court denied the petitioner's motion to dismiss the complaint.

The judgment was affirmed on appeal. * * * The Court of Appeals held that under this Court's decision in Mine Workers v. Gibbs * * * the District Court had jurisdictional power, in its discretion, to adjudicate the respondent's claim against the petitioner because that claim arose from the "core of 'operative facts' giving rise to both [respondent's] claim against OPPD and OPPD's claim against Owen." * * *

II

It is undisputed that there was no independent basis of federal jurisdiction over the respondent's state-law tort action against the petitioner, since both are citizens of Iowa. And although Fed.Rule Civ.Proc. 14(a) permits a plaintiff to assert a claim against a third-party defendant, * * * it does not purport to say whether or not such a claim requires an independent basis of federal jurisdiction. Indeed, it could not determine that question, since it is axiomatic that the Federal Rules of Civil Procedure do not create or withdraw federal jurisdiction.[7]

In affirming the District Court's judgment, the Court of Appeals relied upon the doctrine of ancillary jurisdiction, whose contours it believed were defined by this Court's holding in Mine Workers v. Gibbs, supra. The *Gibbs* case differed from this one in that it involved pendent jurisdiction, which concerns the resolution of a plaintiff's federal and state law claims against a single defendant in one action. By contrast, in this case there was no claim based upon substantive federal law, but rather state-law tort claims against two different defendants. Nonetheless, the Court of Appeals was correct in perceiving that *Gibbs* and this case are two species of the same generic problem: Under what circumstances may a federal court hear and decide a state-law claim arising between citizens of the same State? But we believe that the Court of Appeals failed to understand the scope of the doctrine of the *Gibbs* case.

* * *

It is apparent that *Gibbs* delineated the constitutional limits of federal judicial power. But even if it be assumed that the District Court in the present case had constitutional power to decide the respondent's lawsuit against the petitioner,[10] it does not follow that the decision of the

---

5. The problem apparently was one of geography. Although the Missouri River generally marks the boundary between Iowa and Nebraska, Carter Lake, Iowa, where the accident occurred and where Owen had its main office, lies west of the river, adjacent to Omaha, Neb. Apparently the river once avulsed at one of its bends, cutting Carter Lake off from the rest of Iowa.

7. Fed.Rule Civ.Proc. 82 * * *.

10. Federal jurisdiction in *Gibbs* was based upon the existence of a question of federal law. The Court of Appeals in the present case believed that the "common nucleus of operative fact" test also determines the outer boundaries of constitutionally permissible federal jurisdiction when that jurisdiction is based upon diversity of citizenship. We may assume without deciding that the Court of Appeals was correct in this regard.

* * *

Court of Appeals was correct. Constitutional power is merely the first hurdle that must be overcome in determining that a federal court has jurisdiction over a particular controversy. For the jurisdiction of the federal courts is limited not only by the provisions of Art. III of the Constitution, but by Acts of Congress. * * *

That statutory law as well as the Constitution may limit a federal court's jurisdiction over nonfederal claims [11] is well illustrated by * * * Aldinger v. Howard, 427 U.S. 1, 96 S.Ct. 2413, 49 L.Ed.2d 276 * * *.

The *Aldinger* * * * [case] thus make[s] clear that a finding that federal and nonfederal claims arise from a "common nucleus of operative fact," the test of *Gibbs,* does not end the inquiry into whether a federal court has power to hear the nonfederal claims along with the federal ones. Beyond this constitutional minimum, there must be an examination of the posture in which the nonfederal claim is asserted and of the specific statute that confers jurisdiction over the federal claim, in order to determine whether "Congress in [that statute] has * * * expressly or by implication negated" the exercise of jurisdiction over the particular nonfederal claim. * * *

III

The relevant statute in this case, 28 U.S.C. § 1332(a)(1), * * * and its predecessors have consistently been held to require complete diversity of citizenship. That is, diversity jurisdiction does not exist unless *each* defendant is a citizen of a different State from *each* plaintiff. Over the years Congress has repeatedly re-enacted or amended the statute conferring diversity jurisdiction, leaving intact this rule of complete diversity. Whatever may have been the original purposes of diversity of citizenship jurisdiction, this subsequent history clearly demonstrates a congressional mandate that diversity jurisdiction is not to be available when any plaintiff is a citizen of the same State as any defendant. * * * [16]

Thus it is clear that the respondent could not originally have brought suit in federal court naming Owen and OPPD as codefendants, since citizens of Iowa would have been on both sides of the litigation. Yet the identical lawsuit resulted when she amended her complaint. Complete diversity was destroyed just as surely as if she had sued Owen initially. * * *

It is a fundamental precept that federal courts are courts of limited jurisdiction. The limits upon federal jurisdiction, whether imposed by the

---

11. As used in this opinion, the term "nonfederal claim" means one as to which there is no independent basis for federal jurisdiction. Conversely, a "federal claim" means one as to which an independent basis for federal jurisdiction exists.

16. Notably, Congress enacted § 1332 as part of the Judicial Code of 1948, 62 Stat. 930, shortly after Rule 14 was amended in 1946. When the Rule was amended, the Advisory Committee noted that "in any case where the plaintiff could not have joined the third party originally because of jurisdictional limitations such as lack of diversity of citizenship, the majority view is that any attempt by the plaintiff to amend his complaint and assert a claim against the impleaded third party would be unavailing." 28 U.S.C.App., p. 7752. The subsequent re-enactment without relevant change of the diversity statute may thus be seen as evidence of congressional approval of that "majority view."

Constitution or by Congress, must be neither disregarded nor evaded. Yet under the reasoning of the Court of Appeals in this case, a plaintiff could defeat the statutory requirement of complete diversity by the simple expedient of suing only those defendants who were of diverse citizenship and waiting for them to implead nondiverse defendants.[17] If, as the Court of Appeals thought, a "common nucleus of operative fact" were the only requirement for ancillary jurisdiction in a diversity case, there would be no principled reason why the respondent in this case could not have joined her cause of action against Owen in her original complaint as ancillary to her claim against OPPD. Congress' requirement of complete diversity would thus have been evaded completely.

It is true, as the Court of Appeals noted, that the exercise of ancillary jurisdiction over nonfederal claims has often been upheld in situations involving impleader, cross-claims or counterclaims. But in determining whether jurisdiction over a nonfederal claim exists, the context in which the nonfederal claim is asserted is crucial. See Aldinger v. Howard * * *. And the claim here arises in a setting quite different from the kinds of nonfederal claims that have been viewed in other cases as falling within the ancillary jurisdiction of the federal courts.

First, the nonfederal claim in this case was simply not ancillary to the federal one in the same sense that, for example, the impleader by a defendant of a third-party defendant always is. A third-party complaint depends at least in part upon the resolution of the primary lawsuit. * * * Its relation to the original complaint is thus not mere factual similarity but logical dependence. * * * The respondent's claim against the petitioner, however, was entirely separate from her original claim against OPPD, since the petitioner's liability to her depended not at all upon whether or not OPPD was also liable. Far from being an ancillary and dependent claim, it was a new and independent one.

Second, the nonfederal claim here was asserted by the plaintiff, who voluntarily chose to bring suit upon a state-law claim in a federal court. By contrast, ancillary jurisdiction typically involves claims by a defending party haled into court against his will, or by another person whose rights might be irretrievably lost unless he could assert them in an ongoing action in a federal court. A plaintiff cannot complain if ancillary jurisdiction does not encompass all of his possible claims in a case such as this one, since it is he who has chosen the federal rather than the state forum and must thus accept its limitations. "[T]he efficiency plaintiff seeks so avidly is available without question in the state courts." * * *

It is not unreasonable to assume that, in generally requiring complete diversity, Congress did not intend to confine the jurisdiction of federal courts so inflexibly that they are unable to protect legal rights or effectively to resolve an entire, logically entwined lawsuit. Those practical needs are the basis of the doctrine of ancillary jurisdiction. But neither the convenience of litigants nor considerations of judicial economy can

17. This is not an unlikely hypothesis, since a defendant in a tort suit such as this one would surely try to limit his liability by impleading any joint tortfeasors for indemnity or contribution. * * *

suffice to justify extension of the doctrine of ancillary jurisdiction to a plaintiff's cause of action against a citizen of the same State in a diversity case. Congress has established the basic rule that diversity jurisdiction exists * * * only when there is complete diversity of citizenship. * * * To allow the requirement of complete diversity to be circumvented as it was in this case would simply flout the congressional command.

Accordingly, the judgment of the Court of Appeals is reversed.

It is so ordered.

MR. JUSTICE WHITE, with whom MR. JUSTICE BRENNAN joins, dissenting.

* * *

In Mine Workers v. Gibbs, * * * we held that once a claim has been stated that is of sufficient substance to confer subject-matter jurisdiction on the federal district court, the court has judicial power to consider a nonfederal claim if it and the federal claim are derived from "a common nucleus of operative fact." Although the specific facts of that case concerned a state claim that was said to be pendent to a federal-question claim, the Court's language and reasoning were broad enough to cover the instant factual situation * * *. In the present case, Mrs. Kroger's claim against Owen and her claim against OPPD derived from a common nucleus of fact; this is necessarily so because in order for a plaintiff to assert a claim against a third-party defendant, Fed.Rule Civ.Proc. 14(a) requires that it "aris[e] out of the transaction or occurrence that is the subject matter of the plaintiff's claim against the third-party plaintiff * * *." Furthermore, the substantiality of the claim Mrs. Kroger asserted against OPPD is unquestioned. Accordingly, as far as Art. III of the Constitution is concerned, the District Court had power to entertain Mrs. Kroger's claim against Owen.

The majority correctly points out, however, that the analysis cannot stop here. As Aldinger v. Howard * * * teaches, the jurisdictional power of the federal courts may be limited by Congress, as well as by the Constitution. * * *

In the present case, the only indication of congressional intent that the Court can find is that contained in the diversity jurisdictional statute, 28 U.S.C. § 1332(a) * * *. Because this statute has been interpreted as requiring complete diversity of citizenship between each plaintiff and each defendant, Strawbridge v. Curtiss * * *, the Court holds that the District Court did not have ancillary jurisdiction over Mrs. Kroger's claim against Owen. In so holding, the Court unnecessarily expands the scope of the complete-diversity requirement while substantially limiting the doctrine of ancillary jurisdiction.

The complete-diversity requirement, of course, could be viewed as meaning that in a diversity case, a federal district court may adjudicate only those claims that are between parties of different States. Thus, in order for a defendant to implead a third-party defendant, there would have to be diversity of citizenship; the same would also be true for cross-claims between defendants and for a third-party defendant's claim against a plaintiff. Even the majority, however, refuses to read the complete-diversity requirement so broadly; it recognizes with seeming approval the exercise of ancillary jurisdiction over nonfederal claims in situations involving impleader, cross-claims, and counterclaims. * * * Given the Court's willingness to recognize ancillary jurisdiction in these contexts, despite the requirements of § 1332(a), I see no justification for the Court's refusal to approve the District Court's exercise of ancillary jurisdiction in the present case.

It is significant that a plaintiff who asserts a claim against a third-party defendant is not seeking to add a new party to the lawsuit. In the present case, for example, Owen had already been brought into the suit by OPPD, and, that having been done, Mrs. Kroger merely sought to assert against Owen a claim arising out of the same transaction that was already before the court. * * *

* * * [Thus] considerations of judicial economy, convenience, and fairness to the litigants—the factors relied upon in *Gibbs,* supra—support the recognition of ancillary jurisdiction here. * * *

The majority, however, brushes aside such considerations * * * because it concludes that recognizing ancillary jurisdiction over a plaintiff's claim against a third-party defendant would permit the plaintiff to circumvent the complete-diversity requirement and thereby "flout the congressional command." Since the plaintiff in such a case does not bring the third-party defendant into the suit, however, there is no occasion for deliberate circumvention of the diversity requirement, absent collusion with the defendant. In the case of such collusion, of which there is absolutely no indication here, the court can dismiss the action under the authority of 28 U.S.C. § 1359. In the absence of such collusion, there is no reason to adopt an absolute rule prohibiting the plaintiff from asserting those claims that he may properly assert against the third-party defendant pursuant to Fed.Rule Civ.Proc. 14(a). The plaintiff in such a situation brings suit against the defendant only with absolutely no assurance that the defendant will decide or be able to implead a particular third-party defendant. Since the plaintiff has no control over the defendant's decision to implead a third party, the fact that he could not have originally sued that party in federal court should be irrelevant. Moreover, the fact that a plaintiff in some cases may be able to foresee the subsequent chain of events leading to the impleader does not seem to me to be a sufficient reason to declare that a district court does not have the *power* to exercise ancillary jurisdiction over the plaintiff's claims against the third-party defendant.

* * * [I]t seems to me appropriate to view § 1332 as requiring complete diversity only between the plaintiff and those parties he actually brings into the suit. Beyond that, I would hold that in a diversity case the District Court has power, both constitutional and statutory, to entertain all claims among the parties arising from the same nucleus of operative fact as the plaintiff's original, jurisdiction-conferring claim against the defendant. * * *

Notes and Questions

1. Should ancillary jurisdiction apply to a claim by the third-party defendant against the original defendant or the original plaintiff? See Revere Copper & Brass, Inc. v. Aetna Cas. & Sur. Co., 426 F.2d 709, 715–17 (5th Cir. 1970), p. 611, infra, which says that ancillary jurisdiction should apply. Compare Heintz & Co. v. Provident Tradesmens Bank & Trust Co., 30 F.R.D. 171 (E.D.Pa.1962), with James King & Son, Inc. v. Indemnity Ins. Co., 178 F.Supp. 146 (S.D.N.Y.1959). Note that even in *Kroger* the Supreme Court seemed to approve ancillary jurisdiction in the context of cross-claims, counterclaims, or impleader. What are the relevant considerations in these situations? In what other contexts might ancillary jurisdiction be appropriate? See 13 Wright, Miller & Cooper, *Federal Practice and Procedure: Jurisdiction and Related Matters 2d* § 3523 (1984); Fraser, *Jurisdiction of the Federal Courts of Actions Involving Multiple Claims,* 76 F.R.D. 525 (1978).

2. Note that the main claim in *Kroger* (plaintiff v. original defendant) was based on diversity-of-citizenship jurisdiction. Given the current pressure to abolish or curtail diversity jurisdiction, would the result in *Kroger* have been different if the main claim had been within the court's federal-question jurisdiction? Would it make any difference whether the case was within the federal court's concurrent or exclusive jurisdiction? Ortiz v. United States Government, 595 F.2d 65 (1st Cir.1979), involved a claim under the Federal Tort Claims Act, along with the ancillary claim. The court noted that jurisdiction under the diversity statute tends to be narrowly construed but claims under the FTCA are liberally construed. It then allowed the ancillary claim so long as it was within the common nucleus of operative facts as the main claim.

Mrs. Kroger's attempted ancillary claim (plaintiff v. third-party defendant) also was state based. Would ancillary jurisdiction be recognized over a claim by a plaintiff against a third-party defendant when the main claim was based on concurrent or exclusive federal-question jurisdiction and the plaintiff v. third-party defendant claim satisfied diversity of citizenship but lacked the requisite jurisdictional amount?

FINLEY v. UNITED STATES

Supreme Court of the United States, 1989.
___ U.S. ___, 109 S.Ct. 52, 102 L.Ed.2d 31.

Certiorari to the United States Court of Appeals for the Ninth Circuit.

JUSTICE SCALIA delivered the opinion of the Court.

On the night of November 11, 1983, a twin-engine plane carrying petitioner's husband and two of her children struck electric transmission lines during its approach to a San Diego, California, airfield. No one survived the resulting crash. Petitioner brought a tort action in state court, claiming that San Diego Gas and Electric Company had negligently positioned and inadequately illuminated the transmission lines, and that the city of San Diego's negligent maintenance of the airport's runway lights had rendered them inoperative the night of the crash. When she later discovered that the Federal Aviation Administration (FAA) was in fact the party responsible for the runway lights, petitioner filed the present action against the United States in the United States District Court for the Southern District of California. The complaint based jurisdiction upon the Federal Tort Claims Act (FTCA), 28 U.S.C. § 1346(b), alleging negligence in the FAA's operation and maintenance of the runway lights and performance of air traffic control functions. Almost a year later, she moved to amend the federal complaint to include claims against the original state-court defendants, as to which no independent basis for federal jurisdiction existed. The District Court granted petitioner's motion and asserted "pendent" jurisdiction under Mine Workers v. Gibbs, 383 U.S. 715, 86 S.Ct. 1130, 16 L.Ed.2d 218 (1966), finding it "clear" that "judicial economy and efficiency" favored trying the actions together, and concluding that they arose "from a common nucleus of operative facts." * * * The District Court certified an interlocutory appeal to the Court of Appeals for the Ninth Circuit under 28 U.S.C. § 1292(b). That court summarily reversed * * *. We granted certiorari * * *.

* * *

In 1807 Chief Justice Marshall wrote for the Court that "courts which are created by written law, and whose jurisdiction is defined by written law, cannot transcend that jurisdiction. It is unnecessary to state the reasoning on which this opinion is founded, because it has been repeatedly given by this court; and with the decisions heretofore rendered on this point, no member of the bench has, even for an instant, been dissatisfied." Ex parte Bollman, 8 U.S. (4 Cranch) 75, 93, 2 L.Ed. 554 (1807). It remains rudimentary law that "[a]s regards all courts of the United States inferior to this tribunal, two things are necessary to create jurisdiction, whether original or appellate. The Constitution must have given to the court the capacity to take it, *and an act of Congress must have supplied it* * * *. To the extent that such action is not taken, the power lies dormant." The Mayor v. Cooper, 73 U.S. (6 Wall.) 247, 252, 18 L.Ed. 851 (1868) (emphasis added); accord, Christianson v. Colt Industries Operating Co., 486 U.S. ___, ___, 108 S.Ct. 2166, ___, 100 L.Ed.2d 811 (1988); Firestone Tire & Rubber Co. v. Risjord, 449 U.S. 368, 379–380, 101 S.Ct. 669, 676–677, 66 L.Ed.2d 571 (1981); Kline v. Burke Construction Co., 260 U.S. 226, 233–234, 43 S.Ct. 79, 82–83, 67 L.Ed. 226 (1922); Case of the Sewing Machine Companies, 85 U.S. (18 Wall.) 553, 577, 578, 586–587, 21 L.Ed. 914 (1874); Sheldon v. Sill, 49 U.S. (8 How.) 441, 449, 12 L.Ed. 1147 (1850); Cary v. Curtis, 44 U.S. (3 How.) 236, 245, 11 L.Ed. 576 (1845); McIntire v. Wood, 11 U.S. (7 Cranch) 504, 506, 3 L.Ed. 420 (1813).

Despite this principle, in a line of cases by now no less well established we have held, without specific examination of jurisdictional statutes, that federal courts have "pendent" claim jurisdiction—that is, jurisdiction over nonfederal claims between parties litigating other matters properly before the court—to the full extent permitted by the Constitution. Mine Workers v. Gibbs, 383 U.S. 715, 86 S.Ct. 1130, 16 L.Ed.2d 218 (1966); Hurn v. Oursler, 289 U.S. 238, 53 S.Ct. 586, 77 L.Ed. 1148 (1933); Siler v. Louisville & Nashville R. Co., 213 U.S. 175, 29 S.Ct. 451, 53 L.Ed. 753 (1909). * * * The requisite relationship exists, *Gibbs* said, when the federal and nonfederal claims "derive from a common nucleus of operative fact" and are such that a plaintiff "would ordinarily be expected to try them in one judicial proceeding." * * * Petitioner contends that the same criterion applies here, leading to the result that her state-law claims against San Diego Gas and Electric Company and the city of San Diego may be heard in conjunction with her FTCA action against the United States.

Analytically, petitioner's case is fundamentally different from *Gibbs* in that it brings into question what has become known as pendent-*party* jurisdiction, that is, jurisdiction over parties not named in any claim that is independently cognizable by the federal court. We may assume, without deciding, that the constitutional criterion for pendent-party jurisdiction is analogous to the constitutional criterion for pendent-claim jurisdiction, and that petitioner's state-law claims pass that test. Our cases show, however, that with respect to the addition of parties, as opposed to the addition of only claims, we will not assume that the full constitutional power has been congressionally authorized, and will not read jurisdictional statutes broadly. In Zahn v. International Paper Co., 414 U.S. 291, 301, 94 S.Ct. 505, 512, 38 L.Ed.2d 511 (1973), we refused to allow a plaintiff pursuing a diversity action worth less than the jurisdictional minimum of $10,000 to append his claim to the jurisdictionally adequate diversity claims of other members of a plaintiff class—even though all of the *claims* would together have amounted to a single "case" under *Gibbs*, see Owen Equipment & Erection Co. v. Kroger, 437 U.S. 365, 372, 98 S.Ct. 2396, 2401, 57 L.Ed.2d 274 (1978). We based this holding upon "the statutes defining the jurisdiction of the District Court" * * * and did not so much as mention *Gibbs*.

Two years later, the nontransferability of *Gibbs* to pendent-party claims was made explicit. In Aldinger v. Howard, 427 U.S. 1, 96 S.Ct. 2413, 49 L.Ed.2d 276 (1976), the plaintiff brought federal claims under 42 U.S.C. § 1983 against individual defendants, and sought to append to them a related state claim against Spokane County, Washington. * * * We specifically disapproved application of the *Gibbs* mode of analysis, finding a "significant legal difference." * * * We held in *Aldinger* that the jurisdictional statute under which suit was brought, 28 U.S.C. § 1343, which conferred district court jurisdiction over civil actions of certain types "authorized by law to be commenced," did not mean to include as "authorized by law" a state-law claim against a party that had been statutorily insulated from similar federal suit. The county had been "*excluded* from liability in § 1983, and therefore by reference in the grant of jurisdiction under § 1343(3)." * * *

We reaffirmed and further refined our approach to pendent-party jurisdiction in Owen Equipment & Erection Co. v. Kroger * * *. We held that the jurisdiction which § 1332(a)(1) confers over a "matter in controversy" between a plaintiff and defendant of diverse citizenship cannot be read to confer pendent jurisdiction over a different, nondiverse defendant, even if the *claim* involving that other defendant meets the *Gibbs* test. "*Gibbs*," we said, "does not end the inquiry into whether a federal court has power to hear the nonfederal claims along with the federal ones. Beyond this constitutional minimum, there must be an examination of the posture in which the nonfederal claim is asserted and of the specific statute that confers jurisdiction over the federal claim" * * *.

The most significant element of "posture" or of "context" * * * in the present case (as in *Zahn, Aldinger* and *Kroger*) is precisely that the added claims involve added parties over whom no independent basis of jurisdiction exists. * * * As in *Kroger*, the relationship between petitioner's added claims and the original complaint is one of "mere factual similarity," which is of no consequence since "neither the convenience of the litigants nor considerations of judicial economy can suffice to justify extension of the doctrine of ancillary jurisdiction" * * *. It is true that here, unlike in *Kroger*, * * * the party seeking to bring the added claims had little choice but to be in federal rather than state court, since the FTCA permits the Federal Government to be sued only there. But that alone is not enough, since we have held that suits against the United States under the Tucker Act, 24 Stat. 505 (which can of course be brought only in federal court, see 28 U.S.C. §§ 1346(a)(2), 1491(a)(1)) cannot include private defendants. United States v. Sherwood, 312 U.S. 584, 61 S.Ct. 767, 85 L.Ed. 1058 (1941).

The second factor invoked by *Kroger*, the text of the jurisdictional statute at issue, likewise fails to establish petitioner's case. The FTCA, § 1346(b), confers jurisdiction over "civil actions on claims against the United States." It does not say "civil actions on claims that include requested relief against the United States," nor "civil actions in which there is a claim against the United States"—formulations one might expect if the presence of a claim against the United States constituted merely a minimum jurisdictional requirement, rather than a definition of the permissible scope of FTCA actions. Just as the statutory provision "between * * * citizens of different States" has been held to mean citizens of different States and no one else, * * * so also here we conclude that "against the United States" means against the United States and no one else. * * *

Petitioner contends, however, that an affirmative grant of pendent-party jurisdiction is suggested by changes made to the jurisdictional grant of the FTCA as part of the comprehensive 1948 revision of the Judicial Code. * * * In its earlier form, the FTCA had conferred upon district courts "exclusive jurisdiction to hear, determine, and render judgment *on any claim* against the United States" for specified torts. * * * In the 1948 revision, this provision was changed to "exclusive jurisdiction of *civil actions on claims* against the United States." * * * Petitioner argues that this broadened the scope of the statute, permitting the assertion of jurisdiction over any "civil action," so long as that action *includes* a claim against the United States. We disagree.

Under established canons of statutory construction, "it will not be inferred that Congress, in revising and consolidating the laws, intended to change their effect, unless such intention is clearly expressed." * * * Concerning the 1948 recodification of the Judicial Code in particular, we have stated that "no changes in law or policy are to be presumed from changes of language in the revision unless an intent to make such changes is clearly expressed." * * * We have found no suggestion, much less a clear expression, that the minor rewording at issue here imported a substantive change.

The change from "claim against the United States" to "civil actions on claims against the United States" would be a strange way to express the substantive revision asserted by the petitioner—but a perfectly understandable way to achieve another objective. The 1948 recodification came relatively soon after the adoption of the Federal Rules of Civil Procedure, which provide that "[t]here shall be one form of action to be known as 'civil action.'" * * * Consistent with this new terminology, the 1948 revision inserted the expression "civil action" throughout the provisions governing district-court jurisdiction. * * *

Reliance upon the 1948 recodification also ignores the fact that the concept of pendent-party jurisdiction was not considered remotely viable until *Gibbs* liberalized the concept of pendent-claim jurisdiction—nearly 20 years later. * * * Indeed, in 1948 even a relatively limited substantive expansion of pendent-*claim* jurisdiction with respect to unfair competition actions provoked considerable discussion, * * * and was described by the chief reviser as one of a dozen "major changes of law" effected by his handiwork * * *. That change, in the already accepted realm of pendent-*claim* jurisdiction, was accomplished by wording that could not be mistaken, referring to "any civil action asserting a claim of unfair competition when joined with a substantial and related claim under the copyright, patent, or trademark laws." * * * It is inconceivable that the much more radical change of adopting pendent-party jurisdiction would have been effected by the minor and obscure change of wording at issue here—especially when that revision is more naturally understood as stylistic.

Because the FTCA permits the Government to be sued only in federal court, our holding that parties to related claims cannot necessarily be sued there means that the efficiency and convenience of a consolidated action will sometimes have to be forgone in favor of separate actions in state and federal courts. We acknowledged this potential consideration in *Aldinger*, * * * but now conclude that the present statute permits no other result.

* * *

As we noted at the outset, our cases do not display an entirely consistent approach with respect to the necessity that jurisdiction be explicitly conferred. The *Gibbs* line of cases was a departure from prior practice, and a departure that we have no intent to limit or impair. But *Aldinger* indicated that the *Gibbs* approach would not be extended to the pendent-party field, and we decide today to retain that line. Whatever we say regarding the scope of jurisdiction conferred by a particular statute can of course be changed by Congress. What is of paramount importance is that Congress be able to legislate against a background of clear interpretive rules, so that it may know the effect of the language it adopts. All our cases—*Zahn, Aldinger,* and *Kroger*—have held that a grant of jurisdiction over claims involving particular parties does not itself confer jurisdiction over additional claims by or against different parties. Our decision today reaffirms that interpretive rule; the opposite would sow confusion.

For the foregoing reasons, the judgment of the Court of Appeals is Affirmed.

JUSTICE BLACKMUN, dissenting.

If Aldinger v. Howard, 427 U.S. 1, 96 S.Ct. 2413, 49 L.Ed.2d 276 (1976), required us to ask whether the Federal Tort Claims Act embraced "an affirmative grant of pendent-party jurisdiction," * * * I would agree with the majority that no such specific grant of jurisdiction is present. But, in my view, that is not the appropriate question under *Aldinger*. I read the Court's opinion in that case, rather, as requiring us to consider whether Congress has demonstrated an intent to *exempt* "the party as to whom jurisdiction pendent to the principal claim" is asserted from being haled into federal court. * * * And, as those of us in dissent in *Aldinger* observed, the *Aldinger* test would be rendered meaningless if the required intent could be found in the failure of the relevant jurisdictional statute to mention the type of party in question, "because all instances of asserted pendent-party jurisdiction will by definition involve a party as to whom Congress has impliedly 'addressed itself' by not expressly conferring subject-matter jurisdiction on the federal courts." * * *

In *Aldinger*, the Court found the requisite intent to exclude municipalities from the relevant jurisdictional statute, because (the Court then thought) municipalities had been affirmatively excluded by Congress from the scope of § 1983. In such a case, the Court barred the use of the pendent-party doctrine, for otherwise the doctrine would permit an end-run around an express congressional limitation of federal power. * * *

In the present case, I find no such substantive limitation. Nor, in my view, is there any other expression of congressional intent to exclude private defendants from federal tort claims litigation. United States v. Sherwood, 312 U.S. 584, 61 S.Ct. 767, 85 L.Ed. 1058 (1941), is not to the contrary. There, this Court held that Congress did not intend under the Tucker Act to permit the district courts to adjudicate any cause of action that could not have been brought in the Court of Claims, an Article I court in which no private party could be a defendant. *Sherwood* did not turn solely on a canon of "conservatism which is appropriate in the case of a waiver of sovereign immunity." * * * It turned also upon "the history of the Court of Claims' jurisdiction." * * * There is no equivalent history of adjudication of tort claims against the United States in a tribunal without power to litigate the liability of private tortfeasors; thus, *Sherwood* does not require the result the Court reaches today.

In a case not controlled by any express intent to limit the scope of a constitutional "case," *Aldinger* suggests that the appropriateness of pendent-party jurisdiction might turn on the "alignmen[t] of parties and claims," and that one significant factor is whether "the grant of jurisdiction to [the] federal court is exclusive," * * * as is the situation here.

Where, as here, Congress' preference for a federal forum for a certain category of claims makes the federal forum the *only* possible one in which the constitutional case may be heard as a whole, the sensible result is to permit the exercise of pendent-party jurisdiction. *Aldinger* imposes no obstacle to that result, and I would not reach out to create one. I therefore dissent.

JUSTICE STEVENS, with whom JUSTICE BRENNAN and JUSTICE MARSHALL join, dissenting.

The Court's holding is not faithful to our precedents and casually dismisses the accumulated wisdom of our best judges. * * *

* * *

The case before us today is one in which the United States is a party. Given the plain language of Article III, there is not even an arguable basis for questioning the federal court's constitutional power to decide it. Moreover, by enacting the Federal Tort Claims Act (FTCA) in 1946, 28 U.S.C. § 1346(b), Congress unquestionably authorized the District Court to accept jurisdiction of "civil actions on claims against the United States." Thus, it is perfectly clear that the District Court has both constitutional and statutory power to decide this case.

It is also undisputed that this power will not be defeated by the joinder of two private defendants. Rule 14(a) of the Federal Rules of Civil Procedure expressly authorizes the defendant to implead joint tortfeasors, and this Rule is applicable to FTCA cases. Moreover, if the claim against nonfederal defendants had been properly brought in a federal court, those defendants could require the United States to defend their claim for contribution in that action. The dispute between all the parties derives from a common nucleus of operative fact. There is accordingly ample basis for regarding this entire three-cornered controversy as a single "case" and for allowing petitioners to assert additional claims against the nonfederal defendants as they are authorized to do by Rule 20(a) of the Federal Rules.

* * *

The Court's contrary conclusion rests on an insufficient major premise, a failure to distinguish between diversity and federal question cases, and an implicit reliance on a narrow view of the waiver of sovereign immunity in the Federal Tort Claims Act.

The Court treats the absence of an affirmative grant of jurisdiction by Congress as though it constituted the kind of implicit rejection of pendent jurisdiction that we found in *Aldinger*, supra. Its opinion laboriously demonstrates that the FTCA "defines jurisdiction in a manner that does not reach defendants other than the United States," * * * and that the language of the statute cannot be construed as "adopting pendent party jurisdiction." * * * That, of course, is always the predicate for the question whether a federal court may rely on the doctrine of ancillary or pendent jurisdiction to fill a gap in the relevant jurisdictional statute. If the Court's demonstration were controlling, *Gibbs*, *Hurn*, and *Moore*, as well as a good many other cases, were incorrectly decided.

In *Aldinger*, we adopted a rule of construction that assumed the existence of pendent jurisdiction unless "Congress in the statutes conferring jurisdiction has * * * expressly or by implication negated its existence" * * *. We rejected the assertion of pendent-party jurisdiction there because it arose "not in the context of congressional silence or tacit encouragement, but in quite the opposite context." * * * Congress' exclusion of municpal corporations from the definition of persons under § 1983, we concluded, evinced an intent to preclude the exercise of federal-court jurisdiction over them. If congressional silence were sufficient to defeat pendent jurisdiction, the careful reasoning in our *Aldinger* opinion was wholly unnecessary, for obviously the civil rights statutes do not affirmatively authorize the joinder of any state-law claims.

A similar approach, focusing on a legislative intent to bar a party from federal court, guided our analysis in Zahn v. International Paper Co., 414 U.S. 291, 94 S.Ct. 505, 38 L.Ed.2d 511 (1973), and Owen Equipment & Erection Co. v. Kroger, 437 U.S. 365, 98 S.Ct. 2396, 57 L.Ed.2d 274 (1978). In *Zahn*, we surveyed the "firmly rooted" law that "multiple plaintiffs with separate and distinct claims must each satisfy the jurisdictional-amount requirement for suit in federal courts" * * * and refused to adopt a rule that would allow putative plaintiffs who could not meet the jurisdictional amount to assert claims pendent to jurisdictionally sufficient claims. We noted that adoption of such a rule "would undermine the purpose and intent of Congress in providing that plaintiffs in diversity cases must present claims in excess of the specified jurisdictional amount" and would depart from "the historic construction of the jurisdictional statutes, left undisturbed by Congress over these many years." * * * In *Kroger*, the rule at issue was the requirement that a plaintiff invoking diversity jurisdiction plead complete diversity. After noting the historical evidence demonstrating "a congressional mandate that diversity jurisdiction is not to be available when any plaintiff is a citizen of the same State as any defendant," * * * we held that that jurisdictional requirement could not be circumvented through the exercise of pendent jurisdiction.

The Court today adopts a sharply different approach. Without even so much as acknowledging our statement in *Aldinger* that before a federal court may exercise pendent party jurisdiction it must satisfy itself that Congress "has not expressly or by implication negated its existence," * * * it now instructs that "a grant of jurisdiction over claims involving particular parties does not itself confer jurisdiction over additional claims by or against different parties." * * *

The Court's reliance on cases within the diversity jurisdiction also loses sight of the purpose behind the principle of pendent jurisdiction. The doctrine of pendent jurisdiction rests in part on a recognition that forcing a federal plaintiff to litigate his or her case in both federal and state courts impairs the ability of the federal court to grant full relief. * * * "The courts, by recognizing pendent jurisdiction, are effectuating Congress' decision to provide the plaintiff with a federal forum for litigating a jurisdictionally sufficient claim." Miller, Ancillary and Pendent Jurisdiction, 26 So.Tex.L.Rev. 1, 4 (1985). This is especially the case when, by virtue of the grant of exclusive federal jurisdiction, "*only* in a federal court may all of the claims be tried together." * * * In such circumstances, in which Congress has unequivocally indicated its intent that the federal right be litigated in a federal forum, there is reason to believe that Congress did not intend that the substance of the federal right be diminished by the increased costs in efficiency and convenience of litigation in two forums. * * * No such special federal interest is present when federal jurisdiction is invoked on the basis of the diverse citizenship of the parties and the state-law claims may be litigated in a state forum. * * * To be sure "[w]hatever we say regarding the scope of jurisdiction conferred by a particular statute can . . . be changed by Congress," * * * but that does not relieve us of our responsibility to be faithful to the congressional design. The Court is quite incorrect to presume that because Congress did not sanction the exercise of pendent-party jurisdiction in the diversity context, it has not permitted its exercise with respect to claims within the exclusive federal jurisdiction.

* * *

6. THE SUBJECT–MATTER JURISDICTION OF THE FEDERAL COURTS—REMOVAL

Read 28 U.S.C. § 1441 in the Supplement.

Removal is an anomalous form of jurisdiction. It gives a defendant who has been sued in a state court of competent jurisdiction the right to substitute a forum of his or her own choosing for that originally selected by the plaintiff, although the defendant's choice is limited. Removal jurisdiction is not mentioned in the Constitution. Nevertheless, the removal of cases from state to federal courts has been provided for ever since the original Judiciary Act of 1789.

SHAMROCK OIL & GAS CORP. v. SHEETS, 313 U.S. 100, 105–09, 61 S.Ct. 868, 871–72, 85 L.Ed. 1214, 1217–19 (1941), presented the question whether a plaintiff could remove a state-court action to the federal courts because defendant had interposed a counterclaim. Justice Stone, writing for a unanimous Court, held no:

> Section 12 of the Judiciary Act of 1789 * * * declared that "if a suit be commenced in any state court against an alien * * * or * * * against a citizen of another state, and the matter in dispute exceeds" the jurisdictional amount "and the defendant shall, at the time of entering his appearance in such state court, file a petition for the removal of the cause," it shall be removable to the circuit court. In West v. Aurora City, 6 Wall. 139, 18 L.Ed. 819, this Court held that removal of a cause from a state to a federal court could be effected under § 12 only by a defendant against whom the suit is brought by process served upon him. Consequently a non-citizen plaintiff in the state court, against whom the citizen-defendant had asserted in the suit a claim by way of counterclaim

which, under state law, had the character of an original suit, was not entitled to remove the cause. The Court ruled that the plaintiff, having submitted himself to the jurisdiction of the state court, was not entitled to avail himself of a right of removal conferred only on a defendant who has not submitted himself to the jurisdiction.

By § 3 of the Act of 1875 * * * the practice on removal was greatly liberalized. It authorized "either party, or any one or more of the plaintiffs or defendants entitled to remove any suit" from the state court to do so upon petition in such suit to the state court "before or at the term at which said cause could be first tried and before the trial thereof." These provisions were continued until the adoption of the provisions of the present statute so far as now material by the Act of 1887 * * *.

We cannot assume that Congress, in thus revising the statute, was unaware of the history which we have just detailed, or certainly that it regarded as without significance the omission from the earlier act of the phrase "either party," and the substitution for it of the phrase authorizing removal by the "defendant or defendants" in the suit, or the like omission of the provision for removal at any time before the trial, and the substitution for it of the requirement that the removal petition be filed by the "defendant" at or before the time he is required to plead in the state court.

* * *

Not only does the language of the Act of 1887 evidence the Congressional purpose to restrict the jurisdiction of the federal courts on removal, but the policy of the successive acts of Congress regulating the jurisdiction of federal courts is one calling for the strict construction of such legislation. * * *

Notes and Questions

1. Why should Section 1441(b) permit a defendant to remove a federal-question action when plaintiff has commenced it in a state court of competent jurisdiction and presumably is content to have it adjudicated in a local forum? Is defendant's right of removal consistent with the denial of original or removal jurisdiction when plaintiff anticipates or defendant raises a federal defense, as in the *Mottley* case? See Wechsler, *Federal Jurisdiction and the Revision of the Judicial Code,* 13 Law & Contemp.Prob. 216, 233–34 (1948).

2. After defendant removes, can plaintiff amend her complaint to ask for less than the jurisdictional amount in an attempt to destroy the federal court's jurisdiction? See St. Paul Mercury Indem. Co. v. Red Cab Co., 303 U.S. 283, 58 S.Ct. 586, 82 L.Ed. 845 (1938). Is it permissible for plaintiff to seek recovery for "no more than $50,000" in order to defeat defendant's right of removal? See Capps v. New Jellico Coal Co., 87 F.Supp. 369 (E.D.Tenn.1950). For a discussion of the jurisdictional amount in the context of removal, see 14A Wright, Miller & Cooper, *Federal Practice and Procedure: Jurisdiction and Related Matters 2d* § 3725 (1985). May plaintiff prevent an out-of-state defendant from removing by joining an in-state defendant? Section 1304(b) of the American Law Institute, *Study of the Division of Jurisdiction Between State and Federal Courts* 141–47 (1969), suggests that an out-of-state defendant may remove the entire action if she could have done so had she been sued alone.

3. To what extent should the determination of jurisdiction be different in the initial and removal contexts? In the initial context, the plaintiff is seeking to invoke the jurisdiction of the court. She controls the selection of the court and the selection of the parties to the suit. In the removal context, though, it is the defendant who seeks to invoke the court's jurisdiction. To what extent should we require him to be governed by the plaintiff's choices of court and parties?

4. The removal procedure is set out in 28 U.S.C. § 1446, which is in the Supplement. Prior to 1948, an application for removal was made in the state court, which frequently led to a federal-state conflict over the case. Once the case has been removed it is governed by federal procedure. See Freeman v. Bee Machine Co., 319 U.S. 448, 63 S.Ct. 1146, 87 L.Ed. 1509 (1943).

5. If a case is removed erroneously, a federal court must remand it to the state court. See 28 U.S.C. § 1447(c). Note that a remand order is not reviewable. Section 1447(d). In THERMTRON PRODS., INC. v. HERMANSDORFER, 423 U.S. 336, 96 S.Ct. 584, 46 L.Ed.2d 542 (1976), the district judge had remanded a properly removed action because his docket was overcrowded, reasoning that the litigants would receive a speedier adjudication of the case in the state courts. Review was sought by the extraordinary writ of mandamus. The Court of Appeals for the Sixth Circuit held that it had no jurisdiction to review the order or to issue the writ because of Section 1447(d). The Supreme Court, dividing five to three, reversed. The Court held that Sections 1447(c) and (d) should be read together so that remand may be directed only if it is based on the grounds specified in subsection (c)—removal was improvident and without jurisdiction—and only an order invoking these reasons is immune from review under subsection (d).

Read 28 U.S.C. § 1441(c) in the Supplement.

Section 1441(c) has provoked considerable discussion among courts and commentators. In AMERICAN FIRE & CAS. CO. v. FINN, 341 U.S. 6, 71 S.Ct. 534, 95 L.Ed. 702 (1951), the Supreme Court rendered what is still the most important interpretation of Section 1441(c). Finn, a Texan, sued two foreign insurance companies and their local agent, also a Texan, in a Texas state court. The complaint contained alternative claims for recovery for a fire loss suffered by plaintiff alleging that one or the other insurer had issued policies that covered the loss or that the local agent was liable for having failed to keep plaintiff's property insured. The foreign insurance companies removed the entire case to the appropriate federal court, relying on Section 1441(c). A jury trial was held and ultimately a judgment was entered for the amount of the plaintiff's loss against one of the insurers and in favor of the other company and the agent. The company against which judgment had been entered then sought to vacate the judgment on the ground that the action had been improperly removed and that the federal court lacked jurisdiction. The Supreme Court agreed, reading the Reviser's Notes to the 1948 amendments to the Judicial Code as evidencing a congressional objective to restrict removal. The Court explained:

Of course, "separate cause of action" restricts removal more than "separable controversy." In a suit covering multiple parties or issues based on a single claim, there may be only one cause of action and yet be separable controversies. The addition of the word "independent" gives emphasis to congressional intention to require more complete disassociation between the federally cognizable proceedings and those cognizable only in state courts before allowing removal.

Id. at 12, 71 S.Ct. at 539, 95 L.Ed. at 707. The Court then attempted to define the elusive concept of "cause of action," using the passage from Baltimore S.S. Co. v. Phillips, quoted in *Gibbs,* which appears at page 276, supra. Id. at 13, 71 S.Ct. at 539–40, 95 L.Ed. at 708.

TWENTIETH CENTURY–FOX FILM CORP. v. TAYLOR

United States District Court, Southern District of New York, 1965.
239 F.Supp. 913.

WEINFELD, DISTRICT JUDGE. The plaintiff, Twentieth Century-Fox Film Corporation, moves to remand this action to the New York State Supreme Court whence it was removed to this Court on the petition of the defendant Richard Burton. The action is one of a series of litigations arising out of the production of the motion picture "Cleopatra," in which Burton and Elizabeth Taylor, now husband and wife, play principal roles. Twentieth Century-Fox seeks to recover substantial damages based upon five separate causes of action, the first and fifth of which are against Taylor individually, the second against Burton individually, and the third and fourth against them severally and jointly.

Plaintiff, a Delaware corporation, alleges its principal place of business is New York. Taylor is a citizen of the United States, but is not a citizen of any state. Burton is a British subject, not resident in any state of the United States.

I. REMOVAL OF THE SECOND CAUSE OF ACTION

Had Burton, an alien, been named as the sole defendant, removability could not be questioned, since the case would be within the original diversity jurisdiction of this Court. And so, too, it is beyond challenge that had Taylor been named as the sole defendant, the action would have been non-removable. However, the joinder of the claims against them enabled Burton to remove the entire case to this Court upon his allegation that the second cause of action, pleaded solely against him, came within the purview of 28 U.S.C. § 1441(c) * * *.

The section, with its "separate and independent claim or cause of action" removability standard, was enacted in 1948, according to the revisers of the Judicial Code, to avoid the confusion which had beset the earlier "separable controversy" test and also in the hope that it would "somewhat decrease the volume of Federal litigation." The new provision had its first, and thus far only, consideration by the Supreme Court in American Fire & Cas. Co. v. Finn. * * * The Court, in upholding an

attack upon removal jurisdiction by the very defendant which had successfully invoked it in the courts below but had failed in the action itself, held:

> * * * where there is a single wrong to plaintiff, for which relief is
> sought, arising from an interlocked series of transactions, there is no
> separate and independent claim or cause of action under § 1441(c).

In applying the test to the case before it, the Court attached significant weight to the circumstances that "[t]he single wrong for which relief
is sought is the failure to pay compensation for the loss on the property";
that the "facts in each portion of the complaint" involved the local agent,
plaintiff's co-citizen; that the damages arose from a single incident; and
that each of the three claims asserted involved "substantially the same
facts and transactions," and consequently concluded that removal was
improper.

Twentieth Century-Fox, relying heavily upon Finn, contends that the
acts and conduct of the two defendants set forth in the first four causes of
action are so interlaced that in substantial measure they give rise to and
establish the two individual causes of action for breach of each respective
employment agreement, as well as the two causes of action, one for the
inducement of the breach, and the other for tortious interference—that, as
in Finn, in plaintiff's words, "one 'fire' both induced and resulted in the
simultaneous breach of two employment contracts so as to render this
action [the second cause of action] not removable as a 'separate and
independent cause of action' for breach of one of the agreements."

The statutory test is more easily stated than applied. When multiple
defendants are alleged to have contributed concurrently or jointly to a
single tortious impact and claims are stated against alternative defendants, removal is uniformly denied. But the courts are split as to
removability where one defendant is accused of breach of contract and
another is charged with inducing or exploiting the breach, and where co-
insurers are sued on separate contracts covering a single loss. The
present case, however, fits none of these categories. Having examined the
judicial gloss which Finn and other decisions have put on section 1441(c),
the Court concludes that the "second cause of action," the basis of
Burton's removal petition, constitutes "a separate and independent claim
or cause of action" within the statute. * * *

The first cause of action is against Taylor individually for breach of
her contract, and specifies a series of acts and conduct which gives rise to
the claim. These include allegations that she failed to perform her
services with diligence, care and attention; that she reported for work in
an unfit condition; that she allowed herself to become unphotographable
and unfit to perform her services; that she failed to report for work; that
she failed to report on time; that she suffered herself to be held up to
scorn, ridicule and unfavorable publicity by her public conduct; and that
she conspired with and induced others to breach their agreements with
plaintiff.

The second cause of action against Burton for breach of his employment contract contains allegations of conduct identical to those charged

against Taylor. There are, however, allegations that he breached the contract in other respects.

The third cause of action against Taylor and Burton, individually and jointly, charges that each induced the other, and others, to breach the respective employment agreements as set forth in the first and second causes of action; this cause of action specifies that each induced the other:

> 30.(a) * * * to engage in conduct with each other although each was to public knowledge at these times, married to another, so as to hold the other up to public scorn and ridicule;

> 30.(b) * * * not to abide by and observe reasonable and customary rules, directives, regulations and orders for conduct and deportment during the course of production * * *.

The fourth cause of action against Taylor and Burton, individually and jointly, charges interference with and injury to plaintiff's business and property rights by the acts and conduct complained of in the prior causes of action.

The fifth cause of action is solely against Taylor and alleges that she is the alter ego of MCL Films, S.A., and seeks a declaratory judgment that any money due from Twentieth Century-Fox to MCL may be set off against any judgment against Taylor.

The hard core of the rationale of the Finn holding is that the plaintiff suffered a single wrong arising out of the fire, which entitled him to but one recovery, sought alternatively against one of the three defendants. The situation here is quite unlike that. Basically there are two separate and distinct employment contracts, one with each defendant, for services of a highly specialized and individual nature. This circumstance at once negates rather than supports plaintiff's position that individual breaches of the two separate contracts give rise to a single wrong and a single claim for damages.

The contracts were entered into on different dates. Taylor performed services almost a year before Burton entered into his agreement. Each alleged breach, predicated upon individual acts, gives rise to a separate wrong and a separate claim for damages unrelated to the breach of the employment contract with the other defendant. The fact that the services were to be rendered by each performer in the production of one film does not coalesce violations of the two separate contracts into a single wrong. While it is true that the same kind or type of conduct is asserted to constitute the breach of each separate contract, it does not follow that the acts resulted, as plaintiff charges, in the "simultaneous breach of two employment agreements." For example, it is alleged that each defendant rendered himself or herself unfit to perform required services; failed to report for work; to report on time; and refused to follow directions. But it is not alleged, and it does not appear from the complaint, that one defendant's violation of contractual duty is necessarily related to the other; that their alleged absences from work or tardiness in appearing, or refusal to follow directions occurred simultaneously, at the same place or under similar circumstances. Moreover, as already noted, there are some allegations of breaches different in the one cause of action from the other.

Thus, Taylor is charged with having permitted herself to become un-photographable. No such claim is made against Burton. On the other hand, charges are made against him that are not made against her—to wit, that he disabled himself from performing in the manner directed and at times and places required; that he failed or refused to perform to the best of his ability with due regard to the efficient production of the picture; that he circulated and disseminated news stories and issued other publicity without prior approval contrary to his agreement.

It is true that the individual acts alleged in support of the respective claims against each defendant for breach of his or her contract serve, upon additional allegations of joint conduct, as the basis for the third and fourth causes of action—the tort claims. However, these allegations of joint conduct which underlie the tort claims do not destroy the independent character of the cause of action against Burton for breach of his individual agreement—the single wrong attributed to Burton still remains one of the plaintiff's separate claims.

The claim against him individually is not governed by the operative facts required to establish, nor does it turn upon, any other cause of action. The amount of damages claimed from Burton for his alleged breach is $5,000,000; that sought from Taylor for her alleged breach is $20,000,000. A recovery by Twentieth Century-Fox in its suit against her for breach of her contract will not foreclose recovery against Burton for breach of his, and vice versa. * * * Similarly with respect to the tort actions, a disposition of them will not necessarily be dispositive of the second cause of action against Burton. First, one cannot be charged with inducing a breach of his own contract. Then, should it be found there was no breach of the agreement, it would end any claim of inducement, and even should it be found that there has been a breach, it would not necessarily follow that it was the result of tortious conduct or inducement on the part of any third person. In sum, plaintiff here charges more than a single wrong; it seeks more than a single recovery.

* * * And finally, in no respect has the second cause of action any relationship whatsoever to the fifth cause of action involving the status of Taylor and a Swiss corporation. The motion to remand on the ground that the suit was not removable under Section 1441(c) is denied.

II. The Remaining Causes of Action

The plaintiff further moves, in the event the second cause of action is deemed separate and independent, that the Court remand the other four claims, nonremovable in and of themselves, to the State Court. It urges that such a course is constitutionally compelled and, if not, is justified as a matter of discretion. Neither ground is persuasive.

Plaintiff's constitutional contention may be summarized as follows: Article III, Section 2, of the Constitution authorizes the Federal courts to adjudicate only those controversies arising between parties of diverse citizenship or cases involving Federal questions; Twentieth Century-Fox and defendant Taylor are not of diverse citizenship within the meaning of the Article; the claims or causes of action asserted against Taylor clearly raise no Federal question; therefore they cannot be carried into the Federal courts on the coattails of the separate and independent cause of action which plaintiff brought against defendant Burton; to the extent Section 1441(c) authorizes the transfer of the separate nondiversity, nonfederal question claims against Taylor, it confers jurisdiction upon the Federal courts in excess of the judicial power authorized in Article III, Section 2. The unconstitutionality of this grant of jurisdiction, argues plaintiff, is underscored by the fact that the 1948 requirement of a separate and independent cause of action as a predicate for removal necessarily means that such a claim or cause of action is so "unrelated," "disassociated," or "isolated" from the joined and otherwise nonremovable claims as to foreclose the application of pendant and ancillary jurisdiction doctrines to justify Federal retention of such claims. * * *

First, the presumption of constitutionality which cloaks all legislation is, in this instance, strengthened by nearly a century of usage and judicial decision upholding the jurisdiction of Federal courts to remove not only a controversy between diverse citizens, but the entire case, including nonfederal, nondiversity claims of other citizens. * * *

The plaintiff's basic position is that the rule of Strawbridge v. Curtiss, requiring diversity of citizenship between all plaintiffs and all defendants, expresses a limitation inherent in Article III, Section 2, rather than a construction of the Judiciary Act of 1789. Chief Justice Marshall's decision in Strawbridge clearly purported only to construe "The words of the act of congress." There is nothing in the opinion to justify attributing to Marshall, who was after all profoundly aware of the difference between construing a statute and expounding the Constitution, any purpose to impose an inflexible, narrow view upon the grant of jurisdiction contained in Article III. The Supreme Court has never so read his opinion. * * * In Finn, the Supreme Court itself noted that the revisers carefully provided "an opportunity" for state courts to adjudicate nonfederal causes of action, implying that such claims may be federally retained. * * * In numerous other contexts the Federal courts have declined to apply the rule of complete diversity. * * *

Finally, and wholly apart from the foregoing analysis, Section 1441(c) finds support in Congressional power under the "necessary and proper" clause of Article I, Section 8. Since 1875 Congress has manifested concern lest the removal jurisdiction result in the fragmentation of litigation. * * * Although Congress in 1948 narrowed the category of removable claims, requiring of them a greater degree of disassociation than was true of the "separable controversies" * * *, it still retained power to effectuate a policy against fragmentation of litigation. * * * Where considerations of convenience and economy of litigation dictated, the expansive "necessary and proper" clause frequently has been relied upon to sustain judicial power beyond the strict limits of Article III, assuming arguendo that the Article commands complete diversity. * * * And the whole notion of removal, nowhere provided for in the Constitution, is itself a creature of Congressional power "[t]o make all Laws which shall be necessary and proper for carrying into Execution * * * all Powers vested by this Constitution." * * * To the extent that "separate and independent" claims relate to the same transaction or series of transactions and thus involve overlapping items of proof, as in the instant case, retention of them by this Court places no greater strain on Article III than do many accepted applications of the ancillary jurisdiction doctrine. Since the power of Congress to make a Federal forum available to a diversity litigant in Burton's position is unquestioned, this Court is of the view that Congress has the concomitant power to provide that, once the litigant exercises his right to remove, he may be relieved of the burden of multiple trials in different jurisdictions, at least where some degree of duplication is involved. * * *

As to plaintiff's alternative motion addressed to the Court's discretion, it is abundantly clear that, despite the "separate and independent" quality of the second cause of action, at least the first four claims have some common problems. Items of proof may overlap and the same witnesses may be called to testify with relation to all four claims. To splinter the case and to require a separate trial in this Court, and another in the State Court as to those claims, would needlessly waste the time and effort of all concerned—litigants, witnesses, counsel and courts. The parties are already embroiled in enough litigation here and in California; it would be unreasonable further to proliferate the litigation. Accordingly, the alternative motion to remand the first, third and fourth causes of action is denied. As to the fifth cause of action for a declaratory judgment against Taylor alone, this has no relationship of any kind to the individual claims against Burton, or for that matter to the claims asserted against him and Taylor jointly and severally. The motion for remand of the fifth claim is granted.

Notes and Questions

1. What policies underlie the removability of (a) "a separate and independent claim or cause of action" and (b) "the entire case," including "otherwise non-removable claims or causes of action," when a removable separate and independent claim is present? See generally 14A Wright, Miller & Cooper, *Federal Practice and Procedure: Jurisdiction and Related Matters 2d* § 3724 (1985).

2. In Hurn v. Oursler, quoted at length in United Mine Workers v. Gibbs, pp. 275–77, supra, the Supreme Court limited pendent jurisdiction by saying that "the rule does not go so far as to permit a federal court to assume jurisdiction of a separate and distinct non-federal cause of action because it is joined in the same complaint with a federal cause of action." How is this consistent with the requirement in Section 1441(c) that a federal claim must be "separate and independent" before the otherwise nonremovable claims can be heard in a federal court? See generally Cohen, *Problems in the Removal of a "Separate and Independent Claim or Cause of Action,"* 46 Minn.L.Rev. 1 (1961); Lewin, *The Federal Courts' Hospitable Back Door—Removal of "Separate and Independent" Non-Federal Causes of Action,* 66 Harv.L.Rev. 423 (1953); Moore & Van Dercreek, *Multi-Party, Multi-Claim Removal Problems: The Separate and Independent Claim Under Section 1441(c),* 46 Iowa L.Rev.

489 (1961); Comment, *Diversity Removal Where the Federal Court Would Not Have Original Jurisdiction: A Suggested Reform*, 114 U.Pa.L.Rev. 709 (1966).

3.   A suit is brought in state court. The defendant properly removes the action and impleads a third-party defendant.   The original plaintiff now wishes to assert a transactionally related claim against the third-party defendant, but there is no independent basis for federal jurisdiction over the claim. Does the Supreme Court's holding in Owen Equipment & Erection Co. v. Kroger, p. 282, supra, prevent a federal district court from exercising ancillary jurisdiction over the claim? See Steinman, *Removal, Remand, and Review in Pendent Claim and Pendent Party Cases*, 41 Vand.L.Rev. 923 (1988).

SECTION J. CHALLENGING THE SUBJECT–MATTER JURISDICTION OF THE COURT

1. DIRECT ATTACK ON A COURT'S LACK OF SUBJECT–MATTER JURISDICTION

———

Read Federal Rules of Civil Procedure 8(a)(1), 12(b)(1) and (h)(3), 60(b) (4), and Official Form 2, and 28 U.S.C. § 1653 in the Supplement.

———

As we repeatedly have seen, in the federal courts a lack of subject-matter jurisdiction may be asserted at any time by any interested party, either in the answer, or in the form of a suggestion to the court prior to final judgment or on appeal. And it is axiomatic that the parties may not create the jurisdiction of a federal court by agreement or by consent. See, e.g., Mansfield, C. & L.M. R. Co. v. Swan, 111 U.S. 379, 4 S.Ct. 510, 28 L.Ed. 462 (1884). To what extent is this required because the objection arguably goes to the power of a court of limited jurisdiction to hear and decide a case?

Notes and Questions

1.   Are there situations in which defects in subject-matter jurisdiction should be immune from direct attack? In Di FRISCHIA v. NEW YORK CENTRAL R. CO., 279 F.2d 141, 144 (3d Cir.1960), the defendants initially objected to the jurisdiction of the court, asserting lack of diversity, but then filed a stipulation withdrawing the objection. After extensive pretrial preparations, and after the statute of limitations had run on any state-court action, the defendant reasserted its jurisdictional objection. The District Court dismissed the action, but the Third Circuit reversed, refusing to permit defendant to "play fast and loose with the judicial machinery and deceive the courts." Accord, American Law Institute, *Study of the Division of Jurisdiction Between State and Federal Courts* § 1386, at 64–66, 366–74 (1969). See Dobbs, *Beyond Bootstrap: Foreclosing the Issue of Subject-Matter Jurisdiction Before Final Judgment*, 51 Minn.L.Rev. 491 (1967). *Di Frischia* has not been followed by other courts. See, e.g., Sadat v. Mertes, 615 F.2d 1176, 1189 (7th Cir.1980); Eisler v. Stritzler, 535 F.2d 148, 151–52 (1st Cir.1976). And it was at least implicitly disapproved by the Supreme Court in Owen Equipment & Erection Co. v. Kroger, p. 282, supra.

2. In UNITED STATES v. UNITED MINE WORKERS, 330 U.S. 258, 67 S.Ct. 677, 91 L.Ed. 884 (1947), the District Court issued a temporary restraining order to prevent a strike in mines that earlier had been seized by the government. The union and its officers disobeyed the order, and subsequently were held in contempt of court, notwithstanding the defendants' contention that under the Norris-LaGuardia Act the District Court lacked jurisdiction to issue injunctions in labor disputes. A divided Supreme Court held that the order had to be obeyed until set aside, and that the defendants could not raise the asserted lack of jurisdiction as a defense to the contempt charges. Justice Frankfurter, concurring in the result only, emphasized the power of a federal court to determine its jurisdiction:

> Only when a court is so obviously traveling outside its orbit as to be merely usurping judicial forms and facilities, may an order issued by a court be disobeyed and treated as though it were a letter to a newspaper. Short of an indisputable want of authority on the part of a court, the very existence of a court presupposes its power to entertain a controversy, if only to decide, after deliberation, that it has no power over the particular controversy.

Id. at 309–10, 67 S.Ct. at 704, 91 L.Ed. at 921. Subsequent decisions suggest a general principle that obedience to a temporary restraining order is required, even though the issuing court may lack subject-matter jurisdiction or otherwise may have based its decision on an incorrect view of the law, unless there is no opportunity for effective appellate review of the decree. See United States v. Dickinson, 465 F.2d 496, 509 (5th Cir.1972); 11 Wright & Miller, *Federal Practice and Procedure: Civil* § 2960 (1975).

3. After a judgment has been entered and time for appeal has passed, must the rendering court reopen the case and set aside the judgment if it appears that it lacked subject-matter jurisdiction? Rule 60(b)(4) authorizes relief from "void judgments," and a judgment is void if the rendering court lacked jurisdiction over the subject matter. However, an erroneous determination by a court of its jurisdiction does not render the judgment void. Consider HONNEUS v. DONOVAN, 691 F.2d 1 (1st Cir.1982), in which the defendant initially appeared in the action, but subsequently failed to participate and as a result a default judgment was entered. Several years later, he moved for relief from the judgment, pursuant to Rule 60(b), alleging that the plaintiff fraudulently had alleged diversity. The District Court denied the motion. It found that, although plaintiff had not been a resident of Florida at the time he filed suit and therefore diversity was lacking, he had not committed fraud because he had not intended to deceive the court. The court further said that even though its conclusion that it had jurisdiction may have been erroneous, it was not void because the complaint, which defendant Donovan never answered, sufficiently alleged diversity. The First Circuit affirmed.

2. COLLATERAL ATTACK ON A JUDGMENT FOR LACK OF SUBJECT–MATTER JURISDICTION

If neither the parties nor the court notice the absence of subject-matter jurisdiction at any time during the original proceeding, can defendant successfully raise the lack of jurisdiction as a defense to a subsequent proceeding by plaintiff to enforce the decree? Would it make any difference for purposes of collateral attack if the issue of jurisdiction had been raised and litigated in the original action and it had been decided that the court did have power to proceed? In grappling with this problem, reconsider Capron v. Van Noorden, p. 22, supra, and Des Moines Navigation & R. Co. v. Iowa Homestead Co., p. 62, supra, and recall that one of the oldest pieces of jurisdiction dogma is the maxim that a judgment rendered by a court that lacked jurisdiction over the subject matter (or the "cause," to use the older terminology) is void and a nullity. See, e. g., The Case of the Marshalsea, 10 Co.Rep. 68b, 77 Eng.Rep. 1027 (K.B. 1613); Elliott v. Piersol, 26 U.S. (1 Pet.) 328, 7 L.Ed. 164 (1828). Of course, the subject is considerably more complex than the dogma would indicate, and *Des Moines* demonstrates that collateral attack is not always an available technique for challenging a judgment on the ground that the rendering court lacked subject-matter jurisdiction.

Section 10 of the first *Restatement of Judgments* analyzed the question of the availability of collateral attack in terms of balancing the policies underlying res judicata and finality of judgments, which are treated in detail in Chapter Fourteen, against the policy of prohibiting a court from exceeding the powers conferred upon it by the legislature or the jurisdiction's organic law. It stated that if the court in the original action determined that it had subject-matter jurisdiction, the permissibility of collateral attack depended on weighing a non-exclusive list of factors:

(a) the lack of jurisdiction over the subject matter was clear;

(b) the determination as to jurisdiction depended upon a question of law rather than of fact;

(c) the court was one of limited and not of general jurisdiction;

(d) the question of jurisdiction was not actually litigated;

(e) the policy against the court's acting beyond its jurisdiction is strong.

The *Restatement (Second), Judgments* § 12, 69 (1982) takes the approach that the judgment in a contested action, whether or not the question of subject-matter jurisdiction actually was litigated, is beyond collateral attack unless there are no justifiable interests of reliance that must be protected, and:

(1) The subject matter of the action was so plainly beyond the court's jurisdiction that its entertaining the action was a manifest abuse of authority; or

(2) Allowing the judgment to stand would substantially infringe the authority of another tribunal or agency of government; or

(3) The judgment was rendered by a court lacking capability to make an adequately informed determination of a question concerning its own jurisdiction and as a matter of procedural fairness the party seeking to avoid the judgment should have opportunity belatedly to attack the court's subject-matter jurisdiction.

In addition, the second *Restatement* generally permits collateral attack on the original court's subject-matter jurisdiction, as well as on personal jurisdiction and inadequate notice, in default judgment situations. Id. § 65. Does this approach go far enough, or too far, toward giving preclusive effect to the original court's judgment?

The Supreme Court has had to deal with problems of collateral attack on numerous occasions. In CHICOT COUNTY DRAINAGE DIST. v. BAXTER STATE BANK, 308 U.S. 371, 60 S.Ct. 317, 84 L.Ed. 329 (1940), parties who had notice but chose not to appear in the original action attempted to attack collaterally a judgment rendered by a district court sitting as a court of bankruptcy under a statute that was later declared unconstitutional. The Supreme Court refused to allow the attack:

> * * * If the general principles governing the defense of *res judicata* are applicable, [respondents], having the opportunity to raise the question of invalidity, were not the less bound by the decree because they failed to raise it. * * *

> * * * The lower federal courts are all courts of limited jurisdiction, that is, with only the jurisdiction which Congress has prescribed. But none the less they are courts with authority * * * to determine whether or not they have jurisdiction to entertain the cause and for this purpose to construe and apply the statute under which they are asked to act. Their determinations of such questions, while open to direct review, may not be assailed collaterally.

Id. at 375–76, 60 S.Ct. at 319, 84 L.Ed. at 333.

But collateral attack was allowed by the Court in KALB v. FEUER-STEIN, 308 U.S. 433, 60 S.Ct. 343, 84 L.Ed. 370 (1940), decided the same day as *Chicot*. The questions for decision in *Kalb* were whether a state court had jurisdiction to render a judgment confirming a foreclosure sale while the mortgagor's petition under the Bankruptcy Act was pending in a bankruptcy court, and, if not, whether the mortgagor was prohibited from attacking the state-court judgment collaterally. The Court answered both questions in the negative:

> It is generally true that a judgment by a court of competent jurisdiction bears a presumption of regularity and is not thereafter subject to collateral attack. But Congress, because its power over the subject of bankruptcy is plenary, may by specific bankruptcy legislation create an exception to that principle and render judicial acts taken with respect to the person or property of a debtor whom the bankruptcy law protects nullities and vulnerable collaterally. * * *

> We think the language and broad policy of the * * * Act conclusively demonstrate that Congress intended to, and did deprive the Wisconsin County Court of the power and jurisdiction to continue or maintain in any manner the foreclosure proceedings against appellants without the consent * * * of the bankruptcy court * * *.

Id. at 438–40, 60 S.Ct. at 346, 84 L.Ed. at 374–75.

Which of the categories in the two *Restatements* seems determinative of the *Kalb* case? Are *Chicot* and *Kalb* reconcilable? A fuller discussion of *Chicot* and *Kalb* can be found in Boskey & Braucher, *Jurisdiction and Collateral Attack: October Term, 1939,* 40 Colum.L.Rev. 1006 (1940).

DURFEE v. DUKE, 375 U.S. 106, 84 S.Ct. 242, 11 L.Ed.2d 186 (1963), involved a dispute over title to a tract of bottom land on the Missouri River, which forms the boundary between Nebraska and Missouri. A Missouri federal district court allowed collateral attack on a Nebraska judgment quieting title, on the ground that considerations of territorial sovereignty outweighed the policies of res judicata. The Nebraska court's subject-matter jurisdiction depended on whether the land was within Nebraska, which "depended entirely upon a factual question—whether a shift in the river's course had been caused by avulsion or accretion." The question had been fully litigated in the Nebraska action. The Supreme Court reversed:

> * * * [W]hile it is established that a court in one State, when asked to give effect to the judgment of a court in another State, may constitutionally inquire into the foreign court's jurisdiction to render that judgment, the modern decisions of this Court have carefully delineated the permissible scope of such an inquiry. From these decisions there emerges the general rule that a judgment is entitled to full faith and credit—even as to questions of jurisdiction—when the second court's inquiry discloses that those questions have been fully and fairly litigated and finally decided in the court which rendered the original judgment. * * *

> To be sure, the general rule of finality of jurisdictional determinations is not without exceptions. Doctrines of federal preemption or sovereign immunity may in some contexts be controlling. Kalb v. Feuerstein * * *. But no such overriding considerations are present here.

Id. at 111–14, 84 S.Ct. at 245–47, 11 L.Ed.2d at 191–93. The decision in *Durfee* was followed in Underwriters Nat. Assurance Co. v. North Carolina Life & Acc. Ins. Guar. Ass'n, 455 U.S. 691, 102 S.Ct. 1357, 71 L.Ed.2d 558 (1982).

A more recent example of the Supreme Court's attitude toward collateral attack can be found in UNITED STATES CATHOLIC CONFERENCE v. ABORTION RIGHTS MOBILIZATION, INC., ___ U.S. ___, 108 S.Ct. 2268, 101 L.Ed.2d 69 (1988). In the underlying action, Abortion Rights Mobilization (ARM) sued to revoke the tax-exempt status of the Roman Catholic Church because of the church's intervention in favor of political candidates who support the church's position on abortion. ARM served the Conference with a subpoena seeking extensive documentary evidence to support its claims. The Conference refused to comply with the subpoena and was held in civil contempt with a fine of $50,000 per day for further noncompliance. The Supreme Court held that a non-party witness, the Conference, could challenge the court's lack of subject-matter jurisdiction in defense of a civil contempt citation. The Court reasoned:

> * * * The distinction between subject-matter jurisdiction and waivable defenses is not a mere nicety of legal metaphysics. It rests instead on the central principle of a free society that courts have finite bounds of authority, some of constitutional origin, which exist to protect citizens from the very wrong asserted here, the excessive use of judicial power.

The courts, no less than the political branches of the government, must respect the limits of their authority.

Id. at ___, 108 S.Ct. at 2271, 101 L.Ed.2d at 77.

See generally 18 Wright, Miller & Cooper, *Federal Practice and Procedure: Jurisdiction and Related Matters* § 4428 (1981 & Supp.1988); Dobbs, *The Validation of Void Judgments: The Bootstrap Principle, Part I,* 53 Va.L.Rev. 1003 (1967); Note, *Filling the Void: Judicial Power and Jurisdictional Attacks on Judgments,* 87 Yale L.J. 164 (1977).

SECTION K. VENUE, TRANSFER, AND FORUM NON CONVENIENS

1. VENUE

a. General Principles

STEVENS, VENUE STATUTES: DIAGNOSIS AND PROPOSED CURE, 49 Mich.L.Rev. 307, 307–15 (1951):

Venue * * * means the place of trial in an action within a state. Given a cause of action, and having decided what court has jurisdiction over the subject matter, the lawyer must lay the venue, that is, select the place of trial. In making this decision, the lawyer in every state of the United States turns in the first instance, not to common law, but to statute, constitutional provision or rule of court. And he finds that the "proper" venue of his action depends upon the theory of his claim, the subject matter of his claim, the parties involved, or a combination of these factors.

Most codes make provision for the place of trial in local actions, and all codes provide in one way or another for venue in transitory actions arising both within and without the state. Many states make special provision for divorce actions, actions against executors, and actions for the specific recovery of personal property. Most states also provide for venue in actions against residents, against nonresidents, against corporations, domestic and foreign, against partnerships, associations and individuals doing business in the state, and against the state, or a county, or a city or public officers generally or specifically. The nature of the plaintiff, as a resident or nonresident, corporation, domestic or foreign, or political entity, is another factor frequently considered and provided for. * * *

A comparative study of contemporary venue provisions reveals some thirteen different fact situations upon which venue statutes are predicated.

A. *Where the subject of action or part thereof is situated.* The common law concept of actions which were local because the facts could have occurred only in a particular place still persists. As might well be expected, the proper venue for such actions is the county where the subject of the action is situated. There is, however, considerable variation from state to state as to what types of cases are local and fall into this category. * * *

This type of venue * * * is based upon the idea that the court of the county in which the res, which is the subject matter of the suit, is located is best able to deal with the problem. The local sheriff can attach, deliver or execute upon the property. The local clerk can make the necessary entries with a minimum of red tape where title to land is affected. Trial convenience is served where "a view" is necessary or of value in reaching a determination. Third parties can readily ascertain, at a logical point of inquiry, the status of a res in which they may be interested.

It is submitted that these factors are of sufficient importance in this type of case to outweigh other considerations such as convenience of parties or witnesses in the selection of place of trial. * * *

B. *Where the cause of action, or part thereof, arose or accrued.* Convenience of witnesses is the most logical reason for venue provisions allowing the action to be brought in the county where the cause of action, or part thereof, arose or accrued. And since convenience of witnesses is a very practical problem in the trial of a law suit, one would expect to find venue based upon the place where the cause of action arose or accrued a rather common, and general, provision. * * *

The idea behind this type of venue provision * * * is sound and popular. * * * However, its usefulness has been somewhat impaired by difficulties arising out of problems of statutory interpretation. First, what do the words "arose" and "accrued" mean? Second, what is the difference, if any, between "arose" and "accrued"? And, third, what is the meaning of the phrase "or part thereof"? * * *

C. *Where some fact is present or happened.* There is a sizeable group of statutes which provide for trial of the action in the county where some particular fact or fact situation related to, but no part of, the cause of action is present or happened. * * *

If the purpose of venue is trial convenience, either of parties, or witnesses, or the court or court officials, then it is hard to find any real justification for this group of venue provisions. Most if not all of them are examples of singling out certain specific types of actions for special treatment where a need for special treatment is not or at least no longer [is] apparent. * * *

D. *Where the defendant resides.* Convenience of the defendant is the reason usually given for venue statutes which provide for the place of trial in the county where the defendant resides—the theory probably being, as suggested by Professor E.R. Sunderland, "that since the plaintiff controls the institution of the suit he might behave oppressively toward the defendant unless restrained." * * *

E. *Where the defendant is doing business.* * * * Convenience of the defendant, and of witnesses, appears to be the reason behind such provisions where they are tied to causes of action arising out of the doing of business in the state. Convenience of the defendant, and even more clearly, convenience of the plaintiff, by providing a county in which to lay the venue against a nonresident individual, partnership, company or corporation without undue inconvenience to defendant, is served by the

broader type of provision—against certain classes of defendants generally.
* * *

F. *Where defendant has an office or place of business, or an agent, or representative, or where an agent or officer of defendant resides.* [These venue statutes] * * * are quite common where a corporation, company or some other type of business organization is the defendant. Convenience of the plaintiff, rather than the defendant, is the moving consideration behind such statutes in most instances. * * *

G. *Where the plaintiff resides.* * * *

Convenience of the plaintiff is the obvious reason behind venue statutes of this nature. Convenience of plaintiff's witnesses may or may not be served, depending upon the nature of the action. * * * In certain types of cases against certain classes of defendants—such as an action on a foreign cause of action against a nonresident—this type of provision is both logical and practical. * * *

H. *Where the plaintiff is doing business.* * * * Obviously the convenience of the plaintiff is the sole consideration behind such a provision. It is submitted that other factors of trial convenience such as convenience of witnesses and of the defendant are more important, and that in view of the number of adherents to this ground of venue, it would be wise to advocate its abandonment. * * *

I. *Where the defendant may be found.* Venue based upon the county where the defendant may be found is in accord with the common law doctrine that the right of action follows the person. * * *

It is difficult to find any sound reason for venue based upon where the defendant may be found. It serves no useful purpose—no trial convenience of either witnesses or parties. It is a good example of a historical hang-over—a type of provision which has long since outlived its usefulness. The problem which this type of provision was designed to solve was and is not one of venue but of service of process. * * *

J. *Where the defendant may be summoned or served.* Another group of statutes, also based upon the common law doctrine that the right of action follows the person, provides that venue may be laid in the county where the defendant may be summoned, or served with process. * * *

The comments which were made with respect to venue based upon where the defendant may be found apply with equal force to this type of provision. * * *

K. *In the county designated in the plaintiff's complaint.* * * *

Venue provisions of this type give the plaintiff an unnecessary economic advantage not warranted by convenience of parties or witnesses. In the interests of justice and trial convenience they should be eliminated.

L. *In any county.* The broadest venue provision on the books is that which provides that the plaintiff may lay the venue in any county.
* * *

M. *Where the seat of government is located.* * * *

Statutes of this sort have a sound and practical reason behind them. With one exception, this type of provision is reserved for actions by or against governmental units or agencies. Convenience of the government appears to be the controlling factor. * * *

Notes and Questions

1. See also Blume, *American Civil Procedure* 309–10 (1955); Report of the Temporary Commission on the Courts of the State of New York, *First Preliminary Report of the Advisory Committee on Practice and Procedure* 495– 552 (1957).

2. What should be the underlying goals of a venue system? Is it really necessary to superimpose notions of venue on a soundly conceived jurisdictional system, especially one with a long-arm statute? What statistics and empirical data do you think are relevant to deciding where contract, tort, and property actions should be brought? Indeed, should venue depend on the nature of the plaintiff's action at all? In what ways should the venue system for the federal courts differ from the ways in which the states allocate judicial business among their courts?

b. Local and Transitory Actions

REASOR–HILL CORP. v. HARRISON

Supreme Court of Arkansas, 1952.
220 Ark. 521, 249 S.W.2d 994.

GEORGE ROSE SMITH, JUSTICE. Petitioner asks us to prohibit the circuit court of Mississippi County from taking jurisdiction of a cross-complaint filed by D.M. Barton. In the court below the petitioner moved to dismiss the cross-complaint for the reason that it stated a cause of action for injury to real property in the state of Missouri. When the motion to dismiss was overruled the present application for prohibition was filed in this court.

The suit below was brought by the Planters Flying Service to collect an account for having sprayed insecticide upon Barton's cotton crop in Missouri. In his answer Barton charged that the flying service had damaged his growing crop by using an adulterated insecticide, and by cross-complaint he sought damages from the petitioner for its negligence in putting on the market a chemical unsuited to spraying cotton. The petitioner is an Arkansas corporation engaged in manufacturing insecticides and is not authorized to do business in Missouri.

The question presented is one of first impression: May the Arkansas courts entertain a suit for injuries to real property situated in another State? For the respondent it is rightly pointed out that if the suit is not maintainable Barton has no remedy whatever. The petitioner cannot be served with summons in Missouri; so unless it is subject to suit in Arkansas it can escape liability entirely by staying out of Missouri until the statute of limitations has run. * * * The petitioner answers this argument by showing that with the exception of the Supreme Court of

Minnesota every American court that has passed upon the question (and there have been about twenty) has held that jurisdiction does not exist.

We agree that the weight of authority is almost unanimously against the respondent, although in some States the rule has been changed by statute and in others it has been criticized by the courts and restricted as narrowly as possible. But before mechanically following the majority view we think it worthwhile to examine the origin of the rule and the reasons for its existence.

The distinction between local and transitory actions was recognized at the beginning of the fourteenth century in the common law of England. Before then all actions had to be brought where the cause of action arose, because the members of the jury were required to be neighbors who would know something of the litigants and of the dispute as well. But when cases were presented that involved separate incidents occurring in different communities the reason for localizing the action disappeared, for it was then impossible to obtain a jury who knew all the facts. Consequently the courts developed the distinction between a case that might have arisen anywhere, which was held to be transitory, and one that involved a particular piece of land, which was held to be local. * * *

As between judicial districts under the same sovereign the rule has many advantages and has been followed in America. As between counties our statutes in Arkansas require that actions for injury to real estate be brought where the land lies. * * * But we permit the defendant to be served anywhere in the State * * *; so that plaintiff is not denied a remedy even though the defendant is a resident of another county.

The English courts, in developing the law of local and transitory actions, applied it also to suits for injuries to real property lying outside England. If, for example, there had been a trespass upon land in France, the courts would not permit the plaintiff to bring suit in England, even though the defendant lived in England and could not be subjected to liability in France. The American courts, treating the separate States as independent sovereigns, have followed the English decisions.

In the United States the leading case is unquestionably Livingston v. Jefferson * * *. That suit was a part of the famous litigation between Edward Livingston and Thomas Jefferson * * *. The case was heard by Marshall as circuit justice and Tyler as district judge. Both agreed that the suit, which was for a wrongful entry upon land in Louisiana, could not be maintained in Virginia. In Marshall's concurring opinion he examined the English precedents and concluded that the law was so firmly established that the court was bound to follow it, though Marshall expressed his dissatisfaction with a rule which produced "the inconvenience of a clear right without a remedy."

Since then the American courts have relied almost uniformly upon the Livingston case in applying the rule to interstate litigation in this country. At least three reasons have been offered to justify the rule, but it is easy to show that each reason is more applicable to international controversies than to interstate disputes.

First, the ground most frequently relied upon is that the courts are not in a position to pass upon the title to land outside the jurisdiction. As between nations this reasoning may be sound. The members of this court have neither the training nor the facilities to investigate questions involving the ownership of land in France, in Russia, or in China. But the same difficulties do not exist with respect to land in another State. In our library we have the statutes and decisions of every other State, and it seldom takes more than a few hours to find the answer to a particular question. Furthermore, the American courts do not hesitate to pass upon an out-of-state title when the issue arises in a transitory action. If, for example, Barton had charged that this petitioner converted a mature crop in Missouri and carried it to Arkansas, our courts would decide the case even though it became necessary to pass upon conflicting claims of title to the land in Missouri. Again, a suit for damages for nonperformance of a contract to purchase land is transitory and may be maintained in another State, even though the sole issue is the validity of the seller's title. To put an extreme example, suppose that two companion suits, one local and one transitory, were presented to the same court together. In those States where the courts disclaim the ability to pass upon questions of title in local actions it might be necessary for the court to dismiss the local action for that reason and yet to decide the identical question in the allied transitory case.

Second, it has been argued that since the tort must take place where the land is situated the plaintiff should pursue his remedy before the defendant leaves the jurisdiction. This argument, too, has merit when nations are concerned. A sovereign, by its control of passports and ports of entry, may detain those who wish to cross its borders. But the citizens of the various States have a constitutional right to pass freely from one jurisdiction to another. * * * In the case at bar * * * Barton could hardly be expected to discover the damage and file an attachment suit before the pilot returned to his landing field in Arkansas.

Third, there is an understandable reluctance to subject one's own citizens to suits by aliens, especially if the other jurisdiction would provide no redress if the situation were reversed. * * * One may have some sympathy for this position in international disputes, but it has no persuasive effect when the States are involved. We do not feel compelled to provide a sanctuary in Arkansas for those who have willfully and wrongfully destroyed property, torn down houses, uprooted crops, polluted streams, and inflicted other injuries upon innocent landowners in our sister States. Yet every jurisdiction which follows the rule of the Livingston case affords that refuge to any person—whether one of its citizens or not—who is successful in fleeing from the scene of such misdeeds.

The truth is that the majority rule has no basis in logic or equity and rests solely upon English cases that were decided before America was discovered and in circumstances that are not even comparable to those existing in our Union. Basic principles of justice demand that wrongs should not go unredressed. * * * Under the majority rule we should have to tell Barton that he would have been much better off had the petitioner stolen his cotton outright instead of merely damaging it. And the only reason we could give for this unfortunate situation would be that English juries in the thirteenth century were expected to have personal knowledge of the disputes presented to them. We prefer to afford this litigant his day in court.

Writ denied.

GRIFFIN SMITH, C.J., concurs.

MCFADDIN and WARD, JJ., dissent.

MCFADDIN, JUSTICE (dissenting).

* * *

In the first place, the majority says that we have ample facilities to determine the land laws of other States in the United States. * * * This statement about the size of the law library seems rather weak, because land actions are tried in lower courts and not in the Supreme Court library. Just because we have a fine law library does not mean that we are prepared to determine the title to lands in Texas,[4] Missouri, Vermont, or any other State. But if we have the jurisdiction which the majority claims, then we could determine ejectment actions involving ownership of lands in other States. We might undertake to do this, but the Full Faith and Credit clause of the U.S. Constitution would not require the Sister State to recognize our judgment. * * *

Secondly, the majority says that the rule, requiring that an action be brought in the jurisdiction in which the land is situated, is a good rule between Nations, but is not good as between States in the American Union. For answer to this, I say: I have always understood that each of the American States is Sovereign; that the Federal Government is a government of delegated powers; and that all powers not delegated to the Federal Government are retained by the States and the People. Surely the majority is not attempting to reduce our American States to the level of mere local administrative units. Yet such, unfortunately, is the natural conclusion to which the majority opinion would carry us, when it concedes one rule for Nations and another for States.

Thirdly, the majority says that it does not desire to afford Arkansas Citizens a sanctuary from damage actions by citizens of other States. This is an argument that should be made—if at all—in the Legislative branch of Government, rather than in a judicial opinion. It is for the Legislative Department to determine when and where actions may be prosecuted. * * *

* * * [M]any, many cases * * * have considered the question here involved; and each Court—with the sole exception of Minnesota—has seen fit to follow the great weight of authority which has come down to us from the common law. In matters affecting real property particularly, we should leave undisturbed the ancient landmarks. * * *

4. The writer knows by experience that only one skilled in Texas Land Law can successfully handle an action of Trespass to Try Title in the State of Texas.

Questions

In those jurisdictions following the "majority" or "local action" rule, can the parties consent to a waiver of the venue objection to actions involving foreign land? See, e.g., Taylor v. Sommers Bros. Match Co., 35 Idaho 30, 204 P. 472 (1922). If not, doesn't the local-transitory action distinction really raise a more serious problem than simply a defect in venue? Why does the dissenting opinion in *Reasor-Hill* say that a judgment in ejectment rendered by the Arkansas courts involving lands in other states would not be entitled to full faith and credit?

c. Venue in the Federal Courts

————

Read 28 U.S.C. § 1391 in the Supplement.

————

LEROY v. GREAT WESTERN UNITED CORP.

Supreme Court of the United States, 1979.
443 U.S. 173, 99 S.Ct. 2710, 61 L.Ed.2d 464.

Appeal from the United States Court of Appeals for the Fifth Circuit.

MR. JUSTICE STEVENS delivered the opinion of the Court.

An Idaho statute imposes restrictions on certain purchasers of stock in corporations having substantial assets in Idaho. The questions presented by this appeal are whether the state agents responsible for enforcing the statute may be required to defend its constitutionality in a Federal District Court in Texas and, if so, whether the statute conflicts with the Williams Act amendments to the Securities Exchange Act of 1934, or with the Commerce Clause of the United States Constitution.

Sunshine Mining and Metal Co. (Sunshine) is a "target company" within the meaning of the Idaho Corporate Takeover Act—a statute designed to regulate takeovers of corporations that have certain connections to the State. Sunshine's principal business is a silver mining operation in the Coeur d'Alene Mining District in Idaho. Its executive offices and most of its assets are located in the State. Sunshine is also engaged in business in New York and, through a subsidiary, in Maryland. Its stock is traded over the New York Stock Exchange, and its shareholders are dispersed throughout the country. * * * It is a Washington corporation. * * *

Great Western United Corp. (Great Western) is an "offeror" within the meaning of the Idaho statute. Great Western is a publicly owned Delaware corporation with executive headquarters in Dallas, Tex., and corporate offices in Denver, Colo. * * * In early 1977, Great Western decided to make a public offer to purchase 2 million shares of Sunshine stock for a premium price. Because consummation of the proposed tender offer would cause Great Western to own more than 5% of Sunshine's outstanding shares, Great Western was required to comply with certain provisions of the Williams Act and arguably also to comply with the Idaho

Corporate Takeover Act as well as with similar provisions of New York and Maryland.

On March 21, 1977, Great Western publicly announced its intent to make a tender offer for 2 million shares of Sunshine, and its representatives took simultaneous steps to implement the proposed tender offer. * * *

On March 28, 1977, Great Western filed this action in the United States District Court for the Northern District of Texas, naming as defendants the state officials responsible for enforcing the Idaho, New York, and Maryland takeover laws. The complaint prayed for a declaration that the state laws were invalid insofar as they purported to apply to interstate cash tender offers to purchase securities traded on the national exchange. * * * The claims against the Maryland and New York defendants were dismissed because the former did not attempt to enforce their statute against Great Western and the latter expressly stated that they would not assert jurisdiction over the proposed tender offer. * * * The two Idaho defendants—McEldowney, the Director of Finance, and Wayne Kidwell, then Attorney General of the State—appeared specially to contest jurisdiction and venue, and later filed an answer contesting the merits of the claim.

The District Court found four separate statutory bases for federal jurisdiction. It held that personal jurisdiction over the Idaho defendants had been obtained by service pursuant to the Texas long-arm statute. It concluded, however, that venue was improper under the general federal venue statute, 28 U.S.C. § 1391(b), because the defendants obviously did not reside in Texas and the claim arose in Idaho rather than in Texas. Nonetheless, it decided that venue could be sustained under the special venue provision in § 27 of the Securities Exchange Act of 1934 (1934 Act). * * *

A divided panel of the Court of Appeals for the Fifth Circuit affirmed. * * *

We noted probable jurisdiction of the appeal. * * * Without reaching either the merits or the constitutional question arising out of the attempt to assert personal jurisdiction over appellants, we now reverse because venue did not lie in the Northern District of Texas.

[In Parts I and II of its opinion, the Court explains that there is no statutory basis in Section 27 of the Securities Exchange Act of 1934 for venue in this case.]

III

Nor * * * is venue available under § 1391(b). The first test of venue under that provision—the residence of the defendants—obviously points to Idaho rather than Texas. The Court of Appeals reasoned, however, under the second relevant test that the claim arose in Dallas because that is the place where the Idaho officials "invalidly prevented Great Western from initiating a tender offer for Sunshine." * * * The court buttressed its conclusion by noting that a single action against the officials of New York, Maryland, and Idaho could not have been instituted in any one place unless the claim was treated as having arisen in Dallas. * * *

The easiest answer to this latter argument is that Great Western's complaint did not in fact raise justiciable claims against any officials save those in Idaho. But that is not the only answer. Although the legal issues raised in the complaint challenging the constitutionality of the statutes of three different States were similar, and the convenience of Great Western would obviously be served by consolidating the three claims for trial in one district, the general venue statute does not authorize the plaintiff to rely on either of those reasons to justify its choice of forum.

In most instances, the purpose of statutorily specified venue is to protect the *defendant* against the risk that a plaintiff will select an unfair or inconvenient place of trial. For that reason, Congress has generally not made the residence of the plaintiff a basis for venue in nondiversity cases. But cf. 28 U.S.C. § 1391(e). The desirability of consolidating similar claims in a single proceeding may lead defendants, such perhaps as the New York and Maryland officials in this case, to waive valid objections to otherwise improper venue. But that concern does not justify reading the statute to give the plaintiff the right to select the place of trial that best suits his convenience. So long as the plain language of the statute does not open the severe type of "venue gap" that the amendment giving plaintiffs the right to proceed in the district where the claim arose was designed to close, there is no reason to read it more broadly on behalf of plaintiffs.

Moreover, the plain language of § 1391(b) will not bear the Court of Appeals' interpretation. The statute allows venue in "the judicial district * * * in which the claim arose." Without deciding whether this language adopts the occasionally fictive assumption that a claim may arise in only one district, it is absolutely clear that Congress did not intend to provide for venue at the residence of the plaintiff or to give that party an unfettered choice among a host of different districts. * * * Rather, it restricted venue either to the residence of the defendants or to "a place which may be more convenient to the litigants"—*i.e.,* both of them—"or to the witnesses who are to testify in the case." * * * In our view, therefore, the broadest interpretation of the language of § 1391(b) that is even arguably acceptable is that in the unusual case in which it is not clear that the claim arose in only one specific district, a plaintiff may choose between those two (or conceivably even more) districts that with approximately equal plausibility—in terms of the availability of witnesses, the accessibility of other relevant evidence, and the convenience of the defendant (but *not* of the plaintiff)—may be assigned as the locus of the claim. * * *

This case is not, however, unusual. For the claim involved has only one obvious locus—the District of Idaho. Most importantly, it is action that was taken in Idaho by Idaho residents—the enactment of the statute by the legislature, the review of Great Western's filing, the forwarding of the comment letter by Deputy Administrator Baptie, and the entry of the order postponing the effective date of the tender by Finance Director McEldowney—as well as the future action that may be taken in the State by its officials to punish or to remedy any violation of its law, that provides the basis for Great Western's federal claim. For this reason, the bulk of the relevant evidence and witnesses—apart from employees of the plaintiff, and securities experts who come from all over the United States—is also located in the State. Less important, but nonetheless relevant, the nature of this action challenging the constitutionality of a state statute makes venue in the District of Idaho appropriate. The merits of Great Western's claims may well depend on a proper interpretation of the State's statute, and federal judges sitting in Idaho are better qualified to construe Idaho law, and to assess the character of Idaho's probable enforcement of that law, than are judges sitting elsewhere.

* * *

We therefore reject the Court of Appeals' reasoning that the "claim arose" in Dallas because that is where Great Western proposed to initiate its tender offer, and that is where Idaho's statute had its impact on Great Western. Aside from the fact that these "contacts" between the "claim" and the Texas District fall far short of those connecting the claim and the Idaho District, we note that this reasoning would subject the Idaho officials to suit in almost every district in the country. For every prospective offeree—be he in New York, Los Angeles, Miami, or elsewhere, rather than in Dallas—could argue with equal force (or Great Western could argue on his behalf) that he had intended to direct his local broker to accept the tender and was frustrated in that desire by the Idaho law. As we noted above, however, such a reading of § 1391(b) is inconsistent with the underlying purpose of the provision, for it would leave the venue decision entirely in the hands of plaintiffs, rather than making it "primarily a matter of convenience of litigants and witnesses." In short, the District of Idaho is the only one in which "the claim arose" within the meaning of § 1391(b).

The judgment of the Court of Appeals is reversed.

[A dissenting opinion by JUSTICE WHITE, joined by JUSTICE BRENNAN and JUSTICE MARSHALL, is omitted.]

Notes and Questions

1. Is venue proper if A, a resident of X, brings a diversity action against B, a resident of Y, and C, a resident of Z, in a federal court sitting in Z on a cause of action that did not arise in Z? Would the court's venue be proper if the action were based on federal-question jurisdiction? Suppose A, a resident of X, sues B, a resident of Y, in a state court in Z. If B attempts to remove the action to the federal court in Z on the ground that diversity jurisdiction exists, can A defeat removal by asserting a lack of venue? See 28 U.S.C. § 1441(a).

2. In *Leroy,* the Supreme Court specifically left open whether there can be more than one district with sufficient contacts with the events giving rise to a lawsuit to qualify as a district "where the claim arose." For example, NOVEL v. GARRISON, 294 F.Supp. 825 (N.D.Ill.1969), involved an alleged libel by the District Attorney of New Orleans, Jim Garrison, in an interview

Garrison gave to Playboy Magazine. Garrison gave the interview in New Orleans, and clearly a strong argument could be made that the claim arose there; yet, the District Court found that the claim arose in Illinois because many phone calls were made to Garrison from Playboy's Chicago office and because the magazine was published and printed in that city. Would venue have been proper in the district court in New Orleans?

3.   Changes in the statute governing venue in the federal courts, 28 U.S.C. § 1391, reflect the need to conform venue to the expanding notions of jurisdiction. In 1939, when the Supreme Court decided NEIRBO CO. v. BETHLEHEM SHIPBUILDING CORP., 308 U.S. 165, 60 S.Ct. 153, 84 L.Ed. 167 (1939), the general venue statute required that diversity actions be brought "in the district of the residence of either the plaintiff or the defendant." In *Neirbo*, defendant Bethlehem objected to venue in New York on the ground that it was not incorporated under the laws of that state. Prior cases had held that "residence" meant "state of incorporation" in the case of corporations. The Supreme Court held that Bethlehem's appointment of an agent to receive service of process in New York, an act required by the laws of that state as a condition of doing business there, was a "voluntary act" that gave "actual consent by Bethlehem to be sued in the courts of New York, federal as well as state."

A similar argument was advanced by plaintiff in OLBERDING v. ILLINOIS CENT. R. CO., 346 U.S. 338, 74 S.Ct. 83, 98 L.Ed. 39 (1953). The railroad, an Illinois corporation, brought suit in a Kentucky district court against Olberding, a citizen of Indiana and owner of a truck that had caused the derailment of an Illinois Central train by striking a railroad overpass in Kentucky. Jurisdiction over Olberding was asserted under a nonresident-motorist statute similar to the one upheld in Hess v. Pawloski, p. 75, supra. The venue statute enacted in 1948 required that a diversity action be brought "only in the judicial district where all plaintiffs or all defendants reside." Plaintiff argued, on the basis of *Hess* and *Neirbo*, that Olberding had impliedly consented to a waiver of his federal venue objection by driving into Kentucky. This contention was rejected by Justice Frankfurter:

> * * * In point of fact * * *, jurisdiction in these cases does not rest on consent at all. * * * The potentialities of damage by a motorist, in a population as mobile as ours, are such that those whom he injures must have opportunities of redress against him provided only that he is afforded an opportunity to defend himself. We have held that this is a fair rule of law * * * and that the requirements of due process are therefore met. Hess v. Pawloski * * *. But to conclude from this holding that the motorist, who never consented to anything and whose consent is altogether immaterial, has actually agreed to be sued and has thus waived his federal venue rights is surely to move in the world of Alice in Wonderland.

Id. at 341, 74 S.Ct. at 85–86, 98 L.Ed. at 43. *Neirbo* was distinguished as involving "actual consent." Justice Reed dissented, saying: "I see no difference of substance between the signing of a paper under the New York statute upon which *Neirbo* is based and the acceptance, by action in driving a motor car, of the privilege of using state highways under the Kentucky statute." Id. at 345, 74 S.Ct. at 87, 98 L.Ed. at 45.

Olberding was legislatively overruled in 1963 by the addition of a new Section 1391(f), providing for venue in tort claims "arising out of the manufacture, assembly, repair, ownership, maintenance, use or operation of an automobile * * * in the judicial district wherein the act or omission complained of occurred." This section was repealed in 1966, and the phrase "where the claim for relief arose" was added to subsections (a) and (b).

4. In 1988, Congress amended § 1391(c) to make a corporation a citizen, for venue purposes, of any judicial district in which it is subject to personal jurisdiction at the time the action is commenced. In a state with more than one judicial district, a corporation is deemed to reside in any district within which its contacts would be sufficient to subject it to personal jurisdiction if that district were a separate state. Do the considerations which justify the "minimum contacts" test for personal jurisdiction apply with equal force for venue?

The interrelationship between venue and personal jurisdiction has also been recognized in § 1391(e), which is a broad venue provision for suits against federal officials and agencies, allowing nationwide service of process by registered mail. The Supreme Court has narrowed the reach of § 1391(e) in holding that Congress intended it to apply only in actions that "are nominally against an individual officer but are in reality against the Government." Stafford v. Briggs, 444 U.S. 527, 542, 100 S.Ct. 774, 783, 63 L.Ed.2d 1, 14 (1980). In an action for damages against a government official in her individual capacity, the venue rules in suits against private individuals will normally apply. Therefore, if the claim arose in a district in a state without a long-arm statute, the district court might not be able to secure jurisdiction over the defendant.

5. For diversity jurisdiction, a natural person is a citizen of only one state. Should the term "residence" in the venue statute be restricted in the same way? See 15 Wright, Miller & Cooper, *Federal Practice and Procedure 2d* § 3805 (1986).

6. For venue purposes, should an unincorporated association be held to "reside" in any state in which one of its members resides, only in the state in which all of its members reside, in any state in which the association is doing business, or only in the state in which the association has its principal place of business? This question was resolved by the Supreme Court in DENVER & R.G.W.R. CO. v. BROTHERHOOD OF RAILROAD TRAINMEN, 387 U.S. 556, 559–62, 87 S.Ct. 1746, 1748–50, 18 L.Ed.2d 954, 958–59 (1967):

> * * * [W]e think that the question of the proper venue for such a defendant * * * should be determined by looking to the residence of the association itself rather than that of its individual members. Otherwise, § 1391(b) would seem to require either holding the association not suable at all where its members are residents of different States, or holding that the association "resides" in any State in which any of its members resides. The first alternative * * * removes federal-question litigation from the federal courts unnecessarily; the second is patently unfair to the association when it is remembered that venue is primarily a matter of convenience of litigants and witnesses.
>
>   * * *
>
> We think it most nearly approximates the intent of Congress to recognize the reality of the multi-state, unincorporated association such

as a labor union and to permit suit against that entity, like the analogous corporate entity, wherever it is "doing business."

7.   Various questions arise in applying the venue requirements when an action involves multiple claims or multiple parties.   For example, can a properly impleaded third-party defendant secure a dismissal of the third-party claim for lack of venue if the venue in the principal action is proper?   Would it make any difference if the subject-matter jurisdiction over the third-party claim is merely ancillary to the jurisdiction over the principal action?   See Brandt v. Olson, 179 F.Supp. 363 (N.D.Iowa 1959).   See also Note, *Ancillary Process and Venue in the Federal Courts,* 73 Harv.L.Rev. 1164 (1960).

8.   Can the parties contractually agree on a forum for litigating any action arising out of their contract?   Can they designate a place other than those provided in the general venue statutes?   See National Equipment Rental, Ltd. v. Szukhent, p. 193, supra.   What are some of the factors the court should consider in deciding whether to uphold the stipulation?   Compare The Bremen v. Zapata Off-Shore Co., p. 168, supra, with Leasewell, Ltd. v. Jake Shelton Ford, Inc., 423 F.Supp. 1011 (S.D.W.Va.1976).

9.   Do we need venue provisions at all, given the kind of convenience analysis that *World-Wide Volkswagen* constitutionally requires?   See Clermont, *Refuting Territorial Jurisdiction and Venue for State and Federal Courts,* 66 Cornell L.Rev. 411 (1981).

2. TRANSFER OF VENUE IN FEDERAL COURTS

HOFFMAN v. BLASKI

Supreme Court of the United States, 1960.
363 U.S. 335, 80 S.Ct. 1084, 4 L.Ed.2d 1254.

Certiorari to the United States Court of Appeals for the Seventh Circuit.

MR. JUSTICE WHITTAKER delivered the opinion of the Court.

* * *

The instant cases present the question whether a District Court, in which a civil action has been properly brought, is empowered by § 1404(a) to transfer the action, on the motion of the defendant, to a district in which the plaintiff did not have a *right* to bring it.

Respondents, Blaski and others, residents of Illinois, brought this patent infringement action in the United States District Court for the Northern District of Texas against one Howell and a Texas corporation controlled by him, alleging that the defendants are residents of, and maintain their only place of business in, the City of Dallas, in the Northern District of Texas, where they are infringing respondents' patents.   After being served with process and filing their answer, the defendants moved, under § 1404(a), to transfer the action to the United States District Court for the Northern District of Illinois.   Respondents objected to the transfer on the ground that, inasmuch as the defendants did not reside, maintain a place of business, or infringe the patents in, and could not have been served with process in, the Illinois district, the courts of that district lacked venue over the action and ability to command jurisdiction over the defendants; that therefore that district was not a forum in

which the respondents had a right to bring the action, and, hence, the court was without power to transfer it to that district. Without mentioning that objection or the question it raised, the District Court found that "the motion should be granted for the convenience of the parties and witnesses in the interest of justice," and ordered the case transferred to the Illinois district. Thereupon, respondents moved in the Fifth Circuit for leave to file a petition for a writ of mandamus directing the vacation of that order. That court, holding that "[t]he purposes for which § 1404(a) was enacted would be unduly circumscribed if a transfer could not be made 'in the interest of justice' to a district where the defendants not only waive venue but to which they seek the transfer," denied the motion.
* * *

Upon receipt of a certified copy of the pleadings and record, the Illinois District Court assigned the action to Judge Hoffman's calendar. Respondents promptly moved for an order remanding the action on the ground that the Texas District Court did not have power to make the transfer order and, hence, the Illinois District Court was not thereby vested with jurisdiction of the action. After expressing his view that the "weight of reason and logic" favored "retransfer of this case to Texas," Judge Hoffman, with misgivings, denied the motion. Respondents then filed in the Seventh Circuit a petition for a writ of mandamus directing Judge Hoffman to reverse his order. After hearing and rehearing, the Seventh Circuit, holding that "[w]hen Congress provided [in § 1404(a)] for transfer [of a civil action] to a district 'where it might have been brought,' it is hardly open to doubt but that it referred to a district where the plaintiff * * * had a right to bring the case," and that respondents did not have a *right* to bring this action in the Illinois district, granted the writ, one judge dissenting. * * *

Petitioners' "thesis" and sole claim is that § 1404(a), being remedial, * * * should be broadly construed, and, when so construed, the phrase "where it might have been brought" should be held to relate not only to the time of the bringing of the action but also to the time of the transfer; and that "if at such time the transferee forum has the power to adjudicate the issues of the action, it is a forum in which the action might *then* have been brought." (Emphasis added.) They argue that in the interim between the bringing of the action and the filing of a motion to transfer it, the defendants may move their residence to, or, if corporations, may begin the transaction of business in, some other district, and, if such is done, the phrase "where it might have been brought" should be construed to empower the District Court to transfer the action, on motion of the defendants, to such other district; and that, similarly, if, as here, the defendants move to transfer the action to some other district and consent to submit to the jurisdiction of such other district, the latter district should be held one "in which the action might *then* have been brought." (Emphasis added.)

We do not agree. * * *

It is not to be doubted that the transferee courts, like every District Court, had jurisdiction to entertain actions of the character involved, but it is obvious that they did not acquire jurisdiction over these particular actions when they were brought in the transferor courts. The transferee courts could have acquired jurisdiction over these actions only if properly brought in those courts, or if validly transferred thereto under § 1404(a). Of course, venue, like jurisdiction over the person, may be waived. A defendant, properly served with process by a court having subject matter jurisdiction, waives venue by failing seasonably to assert it, or even simply by making default. * * * But the power of a District Court under § 1404(a) to transfer an action to another district is made to depend not upon the wish or waiver of the defendant but, rather, upon whether the transferee district was one in which the action "might have been brought" by the plaintiff.

The thesis urged by petitioners would not only do violence to the plain words of § 1404(a), but would also inject gross discrimination. That thesis, if adopted, would empower a District Court, upon a finding of convenience, to transfer an action to any district desired by the *defendants* and in which they were willing to waive their statutory defenses as to venue and jurisdiction over their persons, regardless of the fact that such transferee district was not one in which the action "might have been brought" by the plaintiff. Conversely, that thesis would not permit the court, upon motion of the *plaintiffs* and a like showing of convenience, to transfer the action to the same district, without the consent and waiver of venue and personal jurisdiction defenses by the defendants. Nothing in § 1404(a), or in its legislative history, suggests such a unilateral objective and we should not, under the guise of interpretation, ascribe to Congress any such discriminatory purpose.

* * *

Inasmuch as the respondents (plaintiffs) did not have a right to bring these actions in the respective transferee districts, it follows that the judgments of the Court of Appeals were correct and must be affirmed.

Affirmed.

[A concurring opinion by JUSTICE STEWART and a dissenting opinion by JUSTICES FRANKFURTER, HARLAN, and BRENNAN have been omitted. Both of these opinions pertained only to Hoffman v. Blaski.]

MR. JUSTICE FRANKFURTER, whom MR. JUSTICE HARLAN and MR. JUSTICE BRENNAN join, dissenting.*

The problem in this case is of important concern to the effective administration of justice in the federal courts. * * * Section 1404(a) was devised to avoid needless hardship and even miscarriage of justice by empowering district judges to recognize special circumstances calling for special relief. It provides that an action, although begun in a place falling within the normally applicable venue rubric may be sent by the District Court to go forward in another district much more appropriate when judged by the criteria of judicial justice.

* * *

* This opinion applies only to [the companion case of] Sullivan v. Behimer [which raised the same question as Hoffman v. Blaski]. [Footnote by the Court.]

The part of § 1404(a) the meaning of which is at issue here is its last phrase * * *. The significance of this phrase is this: even though a place be found to be an overwhelmingly more appropriate forum from the standpoint of "convenience" and "justice," the litigation may not be sent to go forward there unless it is a place where the action "might have been brought." Upon the scope to be given this phrase thus depends almost entirely the effectiveness of § 1404(a) to insure an appropriate place of trial, when the action is begun in an oppressive forum.

One would have to be singularly unmindful of the treachery and versatility of our language to deny that as a mere matter of English the words "where it might have been brought" may carry more than one meaning. * * * On the face of its words alone, the phrase may refer to * * * venue, amenability to service, or period of limitations, to all of them or to none of them, or to others as well. * * *

Surely, the Court creates its own verbal prison in holding that "the plain words" of § 1404(a) dictate that transfer may not be made in this case although transfer concededly was in the interest of "convenience" and "justice." Moreover, the Court, while finding the statutory words "plain," decides the case by applying, not the statutory language, but a formula of words found nowhere in the statute, namely, whether plaintiffs had "a right to bring these actions in the respective transferee districts." This is the Court's language, not that of Congress. * * * There can be expected to be very few, if any, alternative forums in a given case where the plaintiff has a "right" to sue, considering that that means places of unobjectionable venue where the defendant is amenable to service of process and where there are no other impediments such as a statute of limitations which the defendant can rely on to defeat the action.

* * * At the crux of the business, as I see it, is the realization that we are concerned here not with a question of a limitation upon the power of a federal court but with the place in which that court may exercise its power. We are dealing, that is, not with the jurisdiction of the federal courts, which is beyond the power of litigants to confer, but with the locality of a lawsuit, the rules regulating which are designed mainly for the convenience of the litigants. * * *

In light of the nature of rules governing the place of trial in the federal system * * *, what are the competing considerations here? The transferee court in this case plainly had and has jurisdiction to adjudicate this action with the defendant's acquiescence. As the defendant, whose privilege it is to object to the place of trial, has moved for transfer, and has acquiesced to going forward with the litigation in the transferee court, it would appear presumptively, unless there are strong considerations otherwise, that there is no impediment to effecting the transfer so long as "convenience" and "justice" dictate that it be made. It does not counsel otherwise that here the plaintiff is to be sent to a venue to which he objects, whereas ordinarily, when the defendant waives his privilege to object to the place of trial, it is to acquiesce in the plaintiff's choice of forum. This would be a powerful argument if, under § 1404(a), a transfer were to be made whenever requested by the defendant. Such is not the case, and this bears emphasis. A transfer can be made under § 1404(a) to a place where the action "might have been brought" only when "convenience" and "justice" so dictate, not whenever the defendant so moves. A legitimate objection by the plaintiff to proceeding in the transferee forum will presumably be reflected in a decision that the interest of justice does not require the transfer, and so it becomes irrelevant that the proposed place of transfer is deemed one where the action "might have been brought." * * *

On the other hand, the Court's view restricts transfer, when concededly warranted in the interest of justice, to protect no legitimate interest on the part of the plaintiff. And by making transfer turn on whether the defendant could have been served with process in the transferee district on the day the action was brought, the Court's view may create difficult problems in ascertaining that fact, especially in the case of non-corporate defendants. These are problems which have no conceivable relation to the proper administration of a provision meant to assure the most convenient and just place for trial.

* * *

The relevant legislative history of § 1404(a) is found in the statement in the Reviser's Notes, accompanying the 1948 Judicial Code, that § 1404(a) "was drafted in accordance with the doctrine of forum non conveniens." Under that doctrine, the remedy for an inconvenient forum was not to transfer the action, but to dismiss it. In Gulf Oil Corp. v. Gilbert * * * we held that "[i]n all cases in which the doctrine of *forum non conveniens* comes into play, it presupposes at least two forums in which the defendant is amenable to process; the doctrine furnishes criteria for choice between them." It is entirely "in accordance" with this view of the doctrine of *forum non conveniens* to hold that transfer may be made at the instance of the defendant regardless of the plaintiff's right as an original matter to sue him in the transferee court, so long as the defendant stipulates to going forward with the litigation there. Indeed, to hold otherwise as the Court does is to limit § 1404(a) to a much narrower operation than the nonstatutory doctrine of *forum non conveniens.*
* * *

The only consideration of the Court not resting on the "plain meaning" of § 1404(a) is that it would constitute "gross discrimination" to permit transfer to be made with the defendant's consent and over the plaintiff's objection to a district to which the plaintiff could not similarly obtain transfer over the defendant's objection. * * * Transfer cannot be made under this statute unless it is found to be in the interest of "convenience" and in the interest of "justice." Whether a party is in any sense being "discriminated" against through a transfer is certainly relevant to whether the interest of justice is being served. If the interest of justice is being served, as it must be for a transfer to be made, how can it be said that there is "discrimination" in any meaningful sense? Moreover, the transfer provision cannot be viewed in isolation in finding "discrimination." It, after all, operates to temper only to a slight degree the enormous "discrimination" inherent in our system of litigation, whereby the sole choice of forum, from among those where service is possible and venue unobjectionable, is placed with the plaintiff.   *   *   *

Notes and Questions

1. To what extent does the decision in *Blaski* favor plaintiffs at the expense of defendants? How does the transferor court determine whether defendant is amenable to service in the transferee district? Does *Blaski* require the movant to demonstrate conclusively that defendant was amenable to process in the transferee district court at the time the action was commenced, or should a lesser showing be sufficient? See Dill v. Scuka, 198 F.Supp. 808 (E.D.Pa.1961); Comment, *The Requirement of Personal Jurisdiction When Transferring an Action Under Section 1404(a)*, 57 Nw.U.L.Rev. 456 (1962).

2. The Ninth Circuit has upheld a transfer from California to Delaware on the ground that the action could have been brought as a permissive counterclaim in an action between the parties already underway in Delaware. A.J. INDUSTRIES, INC. v. UNITED STATES DISTRICT COURT, 503 F.2d 384 (9th Cir.1974). The court stated that Hoffman v. Blaski has been widely criticized, and that there was no reason to "extend it unnecessarily."

3. Is the fact that the action would be barred by the statute of limitations in the transferee district relevant to the decision of a motion under Section 1404(a)? To what extent should the transferee court attempt to reach the same result on the merits that would have been rendered by the transferor court? Must the transferee court apply the law of the transferor court? See generally Van Dusen v. Barrack, 376 U.S. 612, 84 S.Ct. 805, 11 L.Ed.2d 945 (1964), which held that, in diversity cases, the law applicable in the transferor forum follows the transfer. At least one federal court recently declined to follow the *Van Dusen* rule with regard to transferred federal claims. See In re Korean Air Lines Disaster of September 1, 1983, 829 F.2d 1171 (D.C.Cir.1987), certiorari granted ___ U.S. ___, 108 S.Ct. 1288, 99 L.Ed.2d 499 (1988), in which the court held that the law of the transferor forum on federal questions merits close consideration but does not have stare decisis effect in a transferee forum situated in another circuit. But see In re Plumbing Fixtures Litigation, 342 F.Supp. 756 (J.P.M.D.L.1972) (*Van Dusen* rule applies to transferred federal claims). See also Marcus, *Conflict Among Circuits and Transfers Within Federal Judicial System*, 93 Yale L.J. 677, 721 (1984); Steinman, *Law of the Case: A Judicial Puzzle in Consolidated and Transferred Cases and in Multidistrict Litigation*, 135 U.Pa.L.Rev. 595, 662– 706 (1987).

4. Can plaintiffs as well as defendants transfer an action under Section 1404(a)? What circumstances might motivate a plaintiff to request a transfer of venue? See generally Torres v. Walsh, 221 F.2d 319 (2d Cir.), certiorari denied 350 U.S. 836, 76 S.Ct. 72, 100 L.Ed. 746 (1955); Philip Carey Mfg. Co. v. Taylor, 286 F.2d 782 (6th Cir.1961); Korbel, *The Law of Federal Venue and Choice of the Most Convenient Forum*, 15 Rutgers L.Rev. 607 (1961).

5. Should the defendant be able to obtain a transfer under Section 1404(a) of a quasi-in-rem action? If transfer is permitted, what should happen to the property that was attached? To what degree does the availability of transfer under 28 U.S.C. § 1404(a) mitigate the inconvenience to defendants that might be caused by the assertion of quasi-in-rem jurisdiction? Is this

relevant to the application of Shaffer v. Heitner, p. 150, supra, in federal-court actions? See Note, *Transfer of Quasi in Rem Actions Under 28 U.S.C. § 1404(a): A Study in the Interpretation of "Civil Action,"* 31 U.Chi.L.Rev. 373 (1964).

6. Section 1406(a) permits the district court to dismiss "or if it be in the interest of justice" to transfer a case to any district in which it could have been brought when it was brought initially in a court in which venue was improper. This provision should be distinguished from Section 1404(a), which presupposes that venue in the district of commencement is proper.

One of the more interesting cases involving Section 1406(a) is GOLD-LAWR, INC. v. HEIMAN, 369 U.S. 463, 82 S.Ct. 913, 8 L.Ed.2d 39 (1962), a treble-damage action under the antitrust laws commenced in the Eastern District of Pennsylvania against a number of defendants. On motion, the District Court found both a lack of personal jurisdiction and improper venue and transferred the case to the Southern District of New York, where venue was proper and defendants could be reached by process. The New York federal court, however, dismissed the case on the ground that the Pennsylvania court could not transfer the action because it lacked personal jurisdiction. The Supreme Court reversed.

> * * * The problem which gave rise to the enactment of the section was that of avoiding the injustice which had often resulted to plaintiffs from dismissal of their actions merely because they had made an erroneous guess with regard to the existence of some elusive fact of the kind upon which venue provisions often turn. Indeed, this case is itself a typical example of the problem sought to be avoided, for dismissal here would have resulted in plaintiff's losing a substantial part of its cause of action under the statute of limitations merely because it made a mistake in thinking that the respondent corporations could be "found" or that they "transact * * * business" in the Eastern District of Pennsylvania. The language and history of § 1406(a) * * * show a congressional purpose to provide as effective a remedy as possible to avoid precisely this sort of injustice.
>
> The language of § 1406(a) is amply broad enough to authorize the transfer of cases, however wrong the plaintiff may have been in filing his case as to venue, whether the court in which it was filed had personal jurisdiction over the defendants or not. The section is thus in accord with the general purpose which has prompted many of the procedural changes of the past few years—that of removing whatever obstacles may impede an expeditious and orderly adjudication of cases and controversies on their merits. When a lawsuit is filed, that filing shows a desire on the part of the plaintiff to begin his case and thereby toll whatever statutes of limitation would otherwise apply. The filing itself shows the proper diligence on the part of the plaintiff which such statutes of limitation were intended to insure. If by reason of the uncertainties of proper venue a mistake is made, Congress, by the enactment of § 1406(a), recognized that "the interest of justice" may require that the complaint not be dismissed but rather that it be transferred in order that the plaintiff not be penalized * * *.

Id. at 466–67, 82 S.Ct. at 915–16, 8 L.Ed.2d at 42. Justice Harlan and Justice Stewart dissented for the following reasons:

The notion that a District Court may deal with an *in personam* action in such a way as possibly to affect a defendant's substantive rights without first acquiring jurisdiction over him is not a familiar one in federal jurisprudence. No one suggests that Congress was aware that * * * § 1406(a) might be so used when it enacted that statute. The "interest of justice" of which the statute speaks * * * is assuredly not a one-way street. And it is incongruous to consider, as the Court's holding would seem to imply, that in the "interest of justice" Congress sought in § 1406(a) to deal with the transfer of cases where *both* venue and jurisdiction are lacking in the district where the action is commenced, while neglecting to provide any comparable alleviative measures for the plaintiff who selects a district where venue is proper but where personal jurisdiction cannot be obtained.

Id. at 467–68, 82 S.Ct. at 916, 8 L.Ed.2d at 43.

The *Goldlawr* decision leaves open a number of questions that raise doubts as to its soundness. Suppose that plaintiff commences an action in a district court that patently lacks personal jurisdiction one day before the expiration of the applicable statute of limitations and ten days later moves to transfer the action to a district in which venue and jurisdiction are proper. If plaintiff is permitted to transfer, hasn't defendant lost the benefit of the statute of limitations? Put another way, shouldn't plaintiff be required to institute an action in a district having personal jurisdiction over defendant prior to the end of the limitations period? Furthermore, shouldn't defendant be guaranteed an opportunity to contest the transfer motion? If the court lacks personal jurisdiction over her, how will defendant know that the action has been instituted and a transfer motion made? An even broader question is to what extent *Goldlawr* results in plaintiff abdicating the obligation to choose an appropriate forum in which defendant is amenable to suit and foisting that task upon the federal courts. Read 28 U.S.C. § 1631, added by the Federal Courts Improvement Act of 1982. What is the impact of this statute on *Goldlawr?*

The ramifications of the *Goldlawr* case are discussed in Note, *Change of Venue in Absence of Personal Jurisdiction Under 28 U.S.C. §§ 1404(a) and 1406(a),* 30 U.Chi.L.Rev. 735 (1963); Comment, *Personal Jurisdiction Requirements Under Federal Change of Venue Statutes,* 1962 Wis.L.Rev. 342.

7. One significant development in federal venue procedure has been the enactment of 28 U.S.C. § 1407, which provides for the temporary transfer to one district of complex cases such as multidistrict antitrust actions. Such transfer is appropriate when the cases involve common questions of fact and law and when it would be for the convenience of the parties and witnesses and in the interests of justice. This provision has frequently been used to take advantage of coordinated pretrial discovery, for example. A panel on multidistrict litigation, composed of seven courts of appeals and district judges appointed by the Chief Justice, makes decisions on whether or not cases should be transferred. See 15 Wright, Miller & Cooper, *Federal Practice and Procedure: Jurisdiction and Related Matters 2d* § 3862 (1986).

3. FORUM NON CONVENIENS

PIPER AIRCRAFT CO. v. REYNO

Supreme Court of the United States, 1981.
454 U.S. 235, 102 S.Ct. 252, 70 L.Ed.2d 419.

Certiorari to the United States Court of Appeals for the Third Circuit.

JUSTICE MARSHALL delivered the opinion of the Court.

* * *

I

A

In July 1976, a small commercial aircraft crashed in the Scottish highlands during the course of a charter flight from Blackpool to Perth. The pilot and five passengers were killed instantly. The decedents were all Scottish subjects and residents, as are their heirs and next of kin. There were no eyewitnesses to the accident. At the time of the crash the plane was subject to Scottish air traffic control.

The aircraft, a twin-engine Piper Aztec, was manufactured in Pennsylvania by petitioner Piper Aircraft Co. (Piper). The propellers were manufactured in Ohio by petitioner Hartzell Propeller, Inc. (Hartzell). At the time of the crash the aircraft was registered in Great Britain and was owned and maintained by Air Navigation and Trading Co., Ltd. (Air Navigation). It was operated by McDonald Aviation, Ltd. (McDonald), a Scottish air taxi service. Both Air Navigation and McDonald were organized in the United Kingdom. The wreckage of the plane is now in a hangar in Farnsborough, England.

The British Department of Trade investigated the accident several months after it occurred. A preliminary report found that the plane crashed after developing a spin, and suggested that mechanical failure in the plane or the propeller was responsible. At Hartzell's request, this report was reviewed by a three-member Review Board, which held a 9-day adversary hearing attended by all interested parties. The Review Board found no evidence of defective equipment and indicated that pilot error may have contributed to the accident. The pilot, who had obtained his commercial pilot's license only three months earlier, was flying over high ground at an altitude considerably lower than the minimum height required by his company's operations manual.

In July 1977, a California probate court appointed respondent Gaynell Reyno administratrix of the estates of the five passengers. Reyno is not related to and does not know any of the decedents or their survivors; she was a legal secretary to the attorney who filed this lawsuit. Several days after her appointment, Reyno commenced separate wrongful death actions against Piper and Hartzell in the Superior Court of California, claiming negligence and strict liability. Air Navigation, McDonald, and the estate of the pilot are not parties to this litigation. The survivors of the five passengers whose estates are represented by Reyno filed a separate action in the United Kingdom against Air Navigation, McDonald, and the pilot's estate. Reyno candidly admits that the action against Piper and Hartzell was filed in the United States because its laws regarding liability, capacity to sue, and damages are more favorable to her position than are those of Scotland. Scottish law does not recognize strict liability in tort. Moreover, it permits wrongful death actions only when brought by a decedent's relatives. The relatives may sue only for "loss of support and society."

On petitioners' motion, the suit was removed to the United States District Court for the Central District of California. Piper then moved for transfer to the United States District Court for the Middle District of Pennsylvania, pursuant to 28 U.S.C. § 1404(a). Hartzell moved to dismiss for lack of personal jurisdiction, or in the alternative, to transfer.[5] In December 1977, the District Court quashed service on Hartzell and transferred the case to the Middle District of Pennsylvania. Respondent then properly served process on Hartzell.

B

In May 1978, after the suit had been transferred, both Hartzell and Piper moved to dismiss the action on the ground of *forum non conveniens.* The District Court granted these motions in October 1979. It relied on the balancing test set forth by this Court in Gulf Oil Corp. v. Gilbert [p. 338, infra] * * *.

* * * [T]he District Court analyzed the facts of [this case]. It began by observing that an alternative forum existed in Scotland; Piper and Hartzell had agreed to submit to the jurisdiction of the Scottish courts and to waive any statute of limitations defense that might be available. It then stated that plaintiff's choice of forum was entitled to little weight. The court recognized that a plaintiff's choice ordinarily deserves substantial deference. It noted, however, that Reyno "is a representative of foreign citizens and residents seeking a forum in the United States because of the more liberal rules concerning products liability law," and that "the courts have been less solicitous when the plaintiff is not an American citizen or resident, and particularly when the foreign citizens seek to benefit from the more liberal tort rules provided for the protection of citizens and residents of the United States." * * *

The District Court next examined several factors relating to the private interests of the litigants, and determined that these factors strongly pointed towards Scotland as the appropriate forum. Although evidence concerning the design, manufacture, and testing of the plane and propeller is located in the United States, the connections with Scotland are otherwise "overwhelming." * * * The real parties in interest are citizens of Scotland, as were all the decedents. Witnesses who could testify regarding the maintenance of the aircraft, the training of the pilot, and the investigation of the accident—all essential to the defense—are in Great Britain. Moreover, all witnesses to damages are located in Scotland. Trial would be aided by familiarity with Scottish topography, and by easy access to the wreckage.

5. The District Court concluded that it could not assert personal jurisdiction over Hartzell consistent with due process. However, it decided not to dismiss Hartzell because the corporation would be amenable to process in Pennsylvania.

The District Court reasoned that because crucial witnesses and evidence were beyond the reach of compulsory process, and because the defendants would not be able to implead potential Scottish third-party defendants, it would be "unfair to make Piper and Hartzell proceed to trial in this forum." * * * The survivors had brought separate actions in Scotland against the pilot, McDonald, and Air Navigation. "[I]t would be fairer to all parties and less costly if the entire case was presented to one jury with available testimony from all relevant witnesses." * * * Although the court recognized that if trial were held in the United States, Piper and Hartzell could file indemnity or contribution actions against the Scottish defendants, it believed that there was a significant risk of inconsistent verdicts.

The District Court concluded that the relevant public interests also pointed strongly towards dismissal. The court determined that Pennsylvania law would apply to Piper and Scottish law to Hartzell if the case were tried in the Middle District of Pennsylvania.[8] As a result, "trial in this forum would be hopelessly complex and confusing for a jury." * * * In addition, the court noted that it was unfamiliar with Scottish law and thus would have to rely upon experts from that country. The court also found that the trial would be enormously costly and time-consuming; that it would be unfair to burden citizens with jury duty when the Middle District of Pennsylvania has little connection with the controversy; and that Scotland has a substantial interest in the outcome of the litigation.

In opposing the motions to dismiss, respondent contended that dismissal would be unfair because Scottish law was less favorable. The District Court explicitly rejected this claim. * * *

C

On appeal, the * * * Third Circuit reversed and remanded for trial. The decision to reverse appears to be based on two alternative grounds. First, the Court held that the District Court abused its discretion in conducting the *Gilbert* analysis. Second, the Court held that dismissal is never appropriate where the law of the alternative forum is less favorable to the plaintiff.

The Court of Appeals began its review of the District Court's *Gilbert* analysis by noting that the plaintiff's choice of forum deserved substantial weight, even though the real parties in interest are nonresidents. It then rejected the District Court's balancing of the private interests. It found

8. Under Klaxon v. Stentor Electric Mfg. Co., 313 U.S. 487, 61 S.Ct. 1020, 85 L.Ed. 1477 (1941), a court ordinarily must apply the choice-of-law rules of the State in which it sits. However, where a case is transferred pursuant to 28 U.S.C. § 1404(a), it must apply the choice-of-law rules of the State from which the case was transferred. Van Dusen v. Barrack * * *. Relying on these two cases, the District Court concluded that California choice-of-law rules would apply to Piper, and Pennsylvania choice-of-law rules would apply to Hartzell. It further concluded that California applied a "governmental interests" analysis in resolving choice-of-law problems, and that Pennsylvania employed a "significant contacts" analysis. The court used the "governmental interests" analysis to determine that Pennsylvania liability rules would apply to Piper, and the "significant contacts" analysis to determine that Scottish liability rules would apply to Hartzell.

that Piper and Hartzell had failed adequately to support their claim that key witnesses would be unavailable if trial were held in the United States: they had never specified the witnesses they would call and the testimony these witnesses would provide. The Court of Appeals gave little weight to the fact that Piper and Hartzell would not be able to implead potential Scottish third-party defendants, reasoning that this difficulty would be "burdensome" but not "unfair" * * *. Finally, the court stated that resolution of the suit would not be significantly aided by familiarity with Scottish topography, or by viewing the wreckage.

The Court of Appeals also rejected the District Court's analysis of the public interest factors. It found that the District Court gave undue emphasis to the application of Scottish law: "the fact that the court is called upon to determine and apply foreign law does not present a legal problem of the sort which would justify the dismissal of a case otherwise properly before the court." * * * In any event, it believed that Scottish law need not be applied. After conducting its own choice-of-law analysis, the Court of Appeals determined that American law would govern the actions against both Piper and Hartzell. The same choice-of-law analysis apparently led it to conclude that Pennsylvania and Ohio, rather than Scotland, are the jurisdictions with the greatest policy interests in the dispute, and that all other public interest factors favored trial in the United States.

In any event, it appears that the Court of Appeals would have reversed even if the District Court had properly balanced the public and private interests. The court stated:

"[I]t is apparent that the dismissal would work a change in the applicable law so that the plaintiff's strict liability claim would be eliminated from the case. But * * * a dismissal for forum non conveniens, like a statutory transfer, 'should not, despite its convenience, result in a change in the applicable law.' Only when American law is not applicable, or when the foreign jurisdiction would, as a matter of its own choice of law, give the plaintiff the benefit of the claim to which she is entitled here, would dismissal be justified." 630 F.2d, at 163–164 (footnote omitted) (quoting DeMateos v. Texaco, Inc., 562 F.2d 895, 899 (CA3 1977), cert. denied, 435 U.S. 904, 98 S.Ct. 1449, 55 L.Ed.2d 494 (1978)).

In other words, the court decided that dismissal is automatically barred if it would lead to a change in the applicable law unfavorable to the plaintiff.

We granted certiorari in these cases to consider the questions they raise concerning the proper application of the doctrine of *forum non conveniens.* * * *

II

The Court of Appeals erred in holding that plaintiffs may defeat a motion to dismiss on the ground of *forum non conveniens* merely by showing that the substantive law that would be applied in the alternative forum is less favorable to the plaintiffs than that of the present forum. The possibility of a change in substantive law should ordinarily not be given conclusive or even substantial weight in the *forum non conveniens* inquiry.

* * *

In fact, if conclusive or substantial weight were given to the possibility of a change in law, the *forum non conveniens* doctrine would become virtually useless. Jurisdiction and venue requirements are often easily satisfied. As a result, many plaintiffs are able to choose from among several forums. Ordinarily, these plaintiffs will select that forum whose choice-of-law rules are most advantageous. Thus, if the possibility of an unfavorable change in substantive law is given substantial weight in the *forum non conveniens* inquiry, dismissal would rarely be proper.

* * *

The Court of Appeals' approach is not only inconsistent with the purpose of the *forum non conveniens* doctrine, but also poses substantial practical problems. If the possibility of a change in law were given substantial weight, deciding motions to dismiss on the ground of *forum non conveniens* would become quite difficult. Choice-of-law analysis would become extremely important, and the courts would frequently be required to interpret the law of foreign jurisdictions. First, the trial court would have to determine what law would apply if the case were tried in the chosen forum, and what law would apply if the case were tried in the alternative forum. It would then have to compare the rights, remedies, and procedures available under the law that would be applied in each forum. Dismissal would be appropriate only if the court concluded that the law applied by the alternative forum is as favorable to the plaintiff as that of the chosen forum. The doctrine of *forum non conveniens,* however, is designed in part to help courts avoid conducting complex exercises in comparative law. As we stated in *Gilbert,* the public interest factors point towards dismissal where the court would be required to "untangle problems in conflict of laws, and in law foreign to itself." * * *

Upholding the decision of the Court of Appeals would result in other practical problems. At least where the foreign plaintiff named an American manufacturer as defendant, a court could not dismiss the case on grounds of *forum non conveniens* where dismissal might lead to an unfavorable change in law. The American courts, which are already extremely attractive to foreign plaintiffs, would become even more attractive. The flow of litigation into the United States would increase and further congest already crowded courts.

* * *

We do not hold that the possibility of an unfavorable change in law should *never* be a relevant consideration in a *forum non conveniens* inquiry. Of course, if the remedy provided by the alternative forum is so clearly inadequate or unsatisfactory that it is no remedy at all, the unfavorable change in law may be given substantial weight; the district court may conclude that dismissal would not be in the interests of justice.[22] In these cases, however, the remedies that would be provided by

---

22. At the outset of any *forum non conveniens* inquiry, the court must determine whether there exists an alternative forum.

Ordinarily, this requirement will be satisfied when the defendant is "amenable to process" in the other jurisdiction. *Gilbert*

the Scottish courts do not fall within this category. Although the relatives of the decedents may not be able to rely on a strict liability theory, and although their potential damages award may be smaller, there is no danger that they will be deprived of any remedy or treated unfairly.

III

The Court of Appeals also erred in rejecting the District Court's *Gilbert* analysis. The Court of Appeals stated that more weight should have been given to the plaintiff's choice of forum, and criticized the District Court's analysis of the private and public interests. However, the District Court's decision regarding the deference due plaintiff's choice of forum was appropriate. Furthermore, we do not believe that the District Court abused its discretion in weighing the private and public interests.

A

The District Court acknowledged that there is ordinarily a strong presumption in favor of the plaintiff's choice of forum, which may be overcome only when the private and public interest factors clearly point towards trial in the alternative forum. It held, however, that the presumption applies with less force when the plaintiff or real parties in interest are foreign.

The District Court's distinction between resident or citizen plaintiffs and foreign plaintiffs is fully justified. * * * When the home forum has been chosen, it is reasonable to assume that this choice is convenient. When the plaintiff is foreign, however, this assumption is much less reasonable. Because the central purpose of any *forum non conveniens* inquiry is to ensure that the trial is convenient, a foreign plaintiff's choice deserves less deference.

B

The *forum non conveniens* determination is committed to the sound discretion of the trial court. It may be reversed only when there has been a clear abuse of discretion; where the court has considered all relevant public and private interest factors, and where its balancing of these factors is reasonable, its decision deserves substantial deference. * * * Here, the Court of Appeals expressly acknowledged that the standard of review was one of abuse of discretion. In examining the District Court's analysis of the public and private interests, however, the Court of Appeals seems to have lost sight of this rule, and substituted its own judgment for that of the District Court.

(1)

In analyzing the private interest factors, the District Court stated that the connections with Scotland are "overwhelming." * * * This characterization may be somewhat exaggerated. Particularly with re-

---

* * *. In rare circumstances, however, where the remedy offered by the other forum is clearly unsatisfactory, the other forum may not be an adequate alternative, and the initial requirement may not be satisfied. Thus, for example, dismissal would not be appropriate where the alternative forum does not permit litigation of the subject matter of the dispute. * * *

spect to the question of relative ease of access to sources of proof, the private interests point in both directions. As respondent emphasizes, records concerning the design, manufacture, and testing of the propeller and plane are located in the United States. She would have greater access to sources of proof relevant to her strict liability and negligence theories if trial were held here. However, the District Court did not act unreasonably in concluding that fewer evidentiary problems would be posed if the trial were held in Scotland. A large proportion of the relevant evidence is located in Great Britain.

The Court of Appeals found that the problems of proof could not be given any weight because Piper and Hartzell failed to describe with specificity the evidence they would not be able to obtain if trial were held in the United States. It suggested that defendants seeking *forum non conveniens* dismissal must submit affidavits identifying the witnesses they would call and the testimony these witnesses would provide if the trial were held in the alternative forum. Such detail is not necessary. Piper and Hartzell have moved for dismissal precisely because many crucial witnesses are located beyond the reach of compulsory process, and thus are difficult to identify or interview. Requiring extensive investigation would defeat the purpose of their motion. Of course, defendants must provide enough information to enable the District Court to balance the parties' interests. Our examination of the record convinces us that sufficient information was provided here. Both Piper and Hartzell submitted affidavits describing the evidentiary problems they would face if the trial were held in the United States.

The District Court correctly concluded that the problems posed by the inability to implead potential third party defendants clearly supported holding the trial in Scotland. Joinder of the pilot's estate, Air Navigation, and McDonald is crucial to the presentation of petitioners' defense. If Piper and Hartzell can show that the accident was caused not by a design defect, but rather by the negligence of the pilot, the plane's owners, or the charter company, they will be relieved of all liability. It is true, of course, that if Hartzell and Piper were found liable after a trial in the United States, they could institute an action for indemnity or contribution against these parties in Scotland. It would be far more convenient, however, to resolve all claims in one trial. The Court of Appeals rejected this argument. Forcing petitioners to rely on actions for indemnity or contributions would be "burdensome" but not "unfair." * * * Finding that trial in the plaintiff's chosen forum would be burdensome, however, is sufficient to support dismissal on grounds of *forum non conveniens.*

(2)

The District Court's review of the factors relating to the public interest was also reasonable. On the basis of its choice-of-law analysis, it concluded that if the case were tried in the Middle District of Pennsylvania, Pennsylvania law would apply to Piper and Scottish law to Hartzell. It stated that a trial involving two sets of laws would be confusing to the jury. It also noted its own lack of familiarity with Scottish law. Consideration of these problems was clearly appropriate under *Gilbert;* in that case we explicitly held that the need to apply foreign law pointed towards dismissal. The Court of Appeals found that the District Court's choice-of-law analysis was incorrect, and that American law would apply to both Hartzell and Piper. Thus, lack of familiarity with foreign law would not be a problem. Even if the Court of Appeals' conclusion is correct, however, all other public interest factors favored trial in Scotland.

Scotland has a very strong interest in this litigation. The accident occurred in its airspace. All of the decedents were Scottish. Apart from Piper and Hartzell, all potential plaintiffs and defendants are either Scottish or English. As we stated in *Gilbert,* there is "a local interest in having localized controversies decided at home." * * * Respondent argues that American citizens have an interest in ensuring that American manufacturers are deterred from producing defective products, and that additional deterrence might be obtained if Piper and Hartzell were tried in the United States, where they could be sued on the basis of both negligence and strict liability. However, the incremental deterrence that would be gained if this trial were held in an American court is likely to be insignificant. The American interest in this accident is simply not sufficient to justify the enormous commitment of judicial time and resources that would inevitably be required if the case were to be tried here.

* * *

Reversed.

[JUSTICE POWELL and JUSTICE O'CONNOR took no part in the decision of this case. JUSTICE WHITE concurred in part and dissented in part. JUSTICE STEVENS, with whom JUSTICE BRENNAN joined, dissented.]

Notes and Questions

1. GULF OIL CORP. v. GILBERT, 330 U.S. 501, 67 S.Ct. 839, 91 L.Ed. 1055 (1947), which is relied upon heavily by Justice Marshall, delineated the factors to be considered in deciding a motion based upon the principle of forum non conveniens:

The principle of *forum non conveniens* is simply that a court may resist imposition upon its jurisdiction even when jurisdiction is authorized by the letter of a general venue statute. These statutes are drawn with a necessary generality and usually give a plaintiff a choice of courts, so that he may be quite sure of some place in which to pursue his remedy. But the open door may admit those who seek not simply justice but perhaps justice blended with some harassment. A plaintiff sometimes is under temptation to resort to a strategy of forcing the trial at a most inconvenient place for an adversary, even at some inconvenience to himself.

Many of the states have met misuse of venue by investing courts with a discretion to change the place of trial on various grounds, such as the convenience of witnesses and the ends of justice. The federal law contains no such express criteria to guide the district court in exercising its power. But the problem is a very old one affecting the administration of the courts as well as the rights of litigants, and both in England and in this country the common law worked out techniques and criteria for dealing with it.

* * *

If the combination and weight of factors requisite to given results are difficult to forecast or state, those to be considered are not difficult to name. An interest to be considered, and the one likely to be most pressed, is the private interest of the litigant. Important considerations are the relative ease of access to sources of proof; availability of compulsory process for attendance of unwilling, and the cost of obtaining attendance of willing witnesses; possibility of view of premises, if view would be appropriate to the action; and all other practical problems that make trial of a case easy, expeditious and inexpensive. There may also be questions as to the enforcibility of a judgment if one is obtained. The court will weigh relative advantages and obstacles to fair trial. It is often said that the plaintiff may not, by choice of an inconvenient forum, "vex," "harass," or "oppress" the defendant by inflicting upon him expense or trouble not necessary to his own right to pursue his remedy. But unless the balance is strongly in favor of the defendant, the plaintiff's choice of forum should rarely be disturbed.

Factors of public interest also have place in applying the doctrine. Administrative difficulties follow for courts when litigation is piled up in congested centers instead of being handled at its origin. Jury duty is a burden that ought not to be imposed upon the people of a community which has no relation to the litigation. In cases which touch the affairs of many persons, there is reason for holding the trial in their view and reach rather than in remote parts of the country where they can learn of it by report only. There is a local interest in having localized controversies decided at home. There is an appropriateness, too, in having the trial of a diversity case in a forum that is at home with the state law that must govern the case, rather than having a court in some other forum untangle problems in conflict of laws, and in law foreign to itself.

Id. at 507–09, 67 S.Ct. at 842–43, 91 L.Ed. at 1062–63.

2. Does *Piper Aircraft* convert forum non conveniens into forum conveniens? Justice Marshall seems to be evaluating whether Scotland is a better forum than the United States. Is the relevant inquiry whether the United States is an inconvenient forum? As Justice Marshall points out, there are some reasons for having a trial in the United States. The aircraft, for example, was manufactured in the United States and records pertaining to manufacture are contained here.

3. What if the injured parties in *Piper Aircraft* had been American? Would the United States still be an inappropriate forum? If the answer is no, what does this say about the doctrine of forum non conveniens? Is it a doctrine aimed at protecting the courts from suits they have no interest in adjudicating? Is forum non conveniens being used in this case as an excuse to protect a domestic corporation from the application of a harsh law? Should we evaluate a plaintiff's interest in litigating in a particular forum differently depending on whether that plaintiff is a citizen of the jurisdiction or not?

4. In part, the doctrine of forum non conveniens operates to ameliorate the burden imposed upon a defendant when jurisdictional rules would permit a plaintiff to force her to litigate in an especially inconvenient forum.

However, the doctrine does not relieve the court of the burden of deciding whether it has jurisdiction to hear the lawsuit. For example, in DE CEDENO v. AROSA MERCANTILE, S.A., 91 Misc.2d 577, 398 N.Y.S.2d 250 (Sup.Ct. 1977), the defendants urged the court to decide their forum non conveniens motion before their challenges to personal and subject-matter jurisdiction, arguing that discovery on the jurisdictional issues should be avoided when it is abundantly clear that the forum is an inconvenient one. The trial judge disagreed and held that the jurisdictional issues *must* be decided first: "A motion to dismiss [on the basis of forum non conveniens] is addressed to the court's discretion to refuse to retain and entertain an action, *otherwise properly before it*, [and] * * * therefore, 'presupposes the existence of a valid jurisdiction.' " Id. at 579, 398 N.Y.S.2d at 252 (emphasis in original).

5. Inconvenience to the defendant is, of course, one of the factors considered in determining whether an exercise of jurisdiction over a defendant violates due process. But inconvenience to the defendant of less magnitude than that required to invoke due process may be sufficient to justify granting a motion to dismiss under the doctrine of forum non conveniens. There are important conditions precedent to the application of the doctrine in such situations, however.

One important requirement is that there must exist another more convenient forum where the plaintiff can obtain adequate relief. Need this forum have been available to the plaintiff when she commenced the action? Should the court grant a forum non conveniens motion if personal jurisdiction could not have been obtained over the defendant in any other jurisdiction at the start of the lawsuit but the defendant is now willing to waive his objection to personal jurisdiction in a more convenient forum? What if the statute of limitations has run in the more convenient forum (but not in the forum where the motion is made) but the defendant is willing to stipulate that he will waive the defense? Courts often have based their willingness to grant motions to dismiss for forum non conveniens on a stipulation from the defendant accepting these conditions. Thus, for example, even though a state court does not have the authority to transfer a suit to another state, it may use its ability to shape the form of the dismissal to obtain the same result.

Notwithstanding the considerable latitude available to courts to grant forum non conveniens motions, however, it remains the case that courts are loathe to cede jurisdiction once obtained and that motions based upon forum non conveniens arguments are not granted with great frequency. See Stewart, *Forum Non Conveniens: A Doctrine in Search of a Role,* 74 Cal.L.Rev. 1259 (1986).

6. In ISLAMIC REPUBLIC OF IRAN v. PAHLAVI, 62 N.Y.2d 474, 478 N.Y.S.2d 597, 467 N.E.2d 245 (1984), the Islamic Republic of Iran sued the Shah and his wife to recover $35 billion dollars in Iranian funds, which they allegedly had misappropriated. Iran asked the New York court to impress a constructive trust on the defendants' assets located throughout the world. The Shah was served at New York Hospital where he was undergoing cancer therapy, and the Empress was served at the same time at the New York home of the Shah's sister. The trial court granted the defendants' motion to dismiss the action on forum non conveniens grounds, concluding that the parties had no connection with New York other than a claim that the Shah had deposited some funds in a New York bank. The intermediate appellate court affirmed,

even though it appeared from the record that no alternative forum was available to the plaintiff, because of the political situation in Iran.

The New York Court of Appeals affirmed, finding that the application of the doctrine of forum non conveniens is a matter of discretion for the lower courts and that those courts had not abused that discretion. The Court of Appeals concluded that New York's courts were not required to entertain litigation that had no connection with the state—especially when, as here, the burden on the state's courts would be tremendous. The court noted the plaintiff's argument that the availability of an alternative forum was a precondition to dismissal on forum non conveniens grounds, and acknowledged the language in Gulf Oil v. Gilbert (quoted in *Piper Aircraft*) supporting the plaintiff's view. But it dismissed the passage in *Gulf Oil* as dicta (because there was an alternative forum in that case) and found that the availability of another forum was just a "most important" factor to be considered.

Is this decision correct? Is it relevant that the plaintiff asked the New York court to provide sweeping review of the political and financial management of the Iranian government during the Shah's regime?

7. A forum non conveniens motion is not the only remedy available to a defendant who objects to plaintiff's choice of forum. Defendant also may institute a suit in another court to enjoin plaintiff from proceeding in the objectionable form. See generally Comment, *Injunctions Against Suits In Foreign Jurisdictions*, 10 La.L.Rev. 302, 302–12 (1950). However, defendant usually must demonstrate that plaintiff chose the forum to gain some form of advantage or to harass defendant.

> * * * This requirement, which is not part of the doctrine of forum non conveniens, may have arisen from judicial concern about the disruptive effect of injunctions against suit on interstate relations. * * *

> Occasionally, injunctions are issued without regard either for the criteria of trial convenience or the propriety of plaintiff's motive, but rather to promote interests local to the enjoining forum. Some courts, for example, have sought to prevent the "exportation" of particular classes of claims arising within the state; others have issued injunctions in order to guarantee the application of local law to controversies based on domestic incidents.

> * * *

> But a choice between the two remedies is not always available. * * * Many states reject the doctrine [of forum non conveniens] entirely;[c] and of those in which it is applied, relief is unlikely if either party is a resident of the forum state.

Comment, *Forum Non Conveniens, Injunctions Against Suit and Full Faith and Credit*, 29 U.Chi.L.Rev. 740, 747–50 (1962).

> The principal defect of injunctions to restrain parties from proceeding in another court is the fact that frequently they are unenforceable; if the enjoining court cannot subject plaintiff or his property to its control, the threat of contempt proceedings may be ineffective. Moreover the original forum occasionally will issue a counterinjunction to restrain defendant from enforcing the injunction purporting to direct the parties to refrain from

---

c. E.g., Missouri, State ex rel. Southern Ry. v. Mayfield, 362 Mo. 101, 240 S.W.2d 106, certiorari denied 342 U.S. 871, 72 S.Ct. 107, 96 L.Ed. 655 (1951).

proceeding in the original action. See, e.g., James v. Grand Trunk W.R. Co., 14 Ill.2d 356, 152 N.E.2d 858 (1958). This procedure obviously may have a detrimental effect on the relations among state courts or between federal and state courts. See generally Note, *State Injunction of Proceedings in Federal Courts,* 75 Yale L.J. 150 (1965).

Another approach to the problem of the inconvenient forum already has been mentioned—the court may grant a motion by defendant to stay the proceedings on the condition that defendant make himself available in the alternative forum. How does this procedure differ from the forum non conveniens practice? What are the respective merits of dealing with the inconvenient-forum problem by dismissal, injunction, or stay? To what extent must the court investigate the availability of jurisdiction in the alternative forum when it employs each of these techniques?

Chapter 3

ASCERTAINING THE APPLICABLE LAW

Civil actions involving citizens of a single state and a transaction that occurred entirely within the boundaries of that state do not present any problems of choosing the proper body of substantive law to be applied in determining the rights and liabilities of the parties. However, as soon as the litigation touches two or more states, one is likely to be confronted with the serious question of choosing between two or more sources of law. For example, suppose plaintiff and defendant, both citizens of State X, are involved in an automobile accident or agree to perform a contract or engage in a transfer of property in State Y. Should questions pertaining to defendant's alleged negligence or failure to perform the contract or the ownership of the property be decided under the law of State X or the law of State Y? Should the choice be made in the same way in tort, contract, and property actions? The complexity of these questions increases if plaintiff and defendant are citizens of different states and the event, relationship, or property that forms the predicate of the controversy can be traced to a third, and perhaps a fourth or fifth, state. The student will be exposed to problems of this type on numerous occasions during the civil procedure course and must learn to recognize them. However, formal education in the philosophy of choosing among the laws of two or more states must be postponed until the course in conflict of laws.

This Chapter is devoted to choice-of-law problems of a somewhat different dimension. Let us suppose that plaintiff is a citizen of State X and defendant is a citizen of State Y and that plaintiff has decided to litigate a tort or contract claim against defendant in a federal district court in State Y. What law should the federal court apply to adjudicate this action? The law of State X? Of State Y? Federal law? Would the answer be different if, assuming personal jurisdiction could be acquired, the action was commenced in a federal district court in State X? The problem of choosing between federal and state law also is present when a state court is called upon to decide cases arising under federal statutes or cases in which federal rights and liabilities are in issue. As one might surmise, the process of choosing between the law of two states and that of choosing between federal and state law are analogous. In some situations, particularly diversity cases, they are intertwined. This Chapter will explore some of the problems created by the application of state law in the federal courts and the role of federal law in the state courts.

A final observation before beginning: If the law applied by one court differs materially from that applied by another, an attorney interested in achieving a particular result for a client obviously may wish to steer the lawsuit, if the jurisdiction and venue rules permit, to a particular tribunal. To what extent should a court take account of this type of forum manipulation in choosing the law to be applied?

SECTION A. STATE LAW IN THE FEDERAL COURTS

1. THE RULE OF SWIFT v. TYSON

Although Article III of the Constitution sets limits on the jurisdiction of the federal court system, it does not establish any lower federal courts. The power to establish those "inferior" courts was left to Congress, which quickly used it. The Judiciary Act of 1789 established a lower federal court system and promulgated rules governing its jurisdiction and operation. Among those rules, in Section 34 of the Judiciary Act, was the so-called Rules of Decision Act. The modern version of this Act is found in 28 U.S.C. § 1652 and reads:

> The laws of the several states, except where the Constitution or treaties of the United States or Acts of Congress otherwise require or provide, shall be regarded as rules of decision in civil actions in the courts of the United States, in cases where they apply.

For nearly one hundred years, the Supreme Court's decision in SWIFT v. TYSON, 41 U.S. (16 Pet.) 1, 10 L.Ed. 865 (1842), provided the basic interpretation of the language of the Rules of Decision Act. In *Swift*, some Maine land speculators sold land that they did not own to some New Yorkers. Although the speculators planned to use the New Yorkers' money to purchase the land, the New Yorkers thought that the speculators already owned the land. Some New Yorkers, including George W. Tyson, gave the speculators negotiable instruments instead of money to pay for their investments. Tyson "accepted" a bill of exchange in return for a six-month postponement in his payments on the land contract.

One of the speculators gave Tyson's note to Joseph Swift, a Maine banker, in satisfaction of a preexisting debt. When Swift sought payment from Tyson, Tyson refused to pay on the ground that his obligation was unenforceable since he had been induced to "accept" the bill by the speculator's fraud. Swift sued Tyson in federal court in New York based upon diversity jurisdiction. The principal question before the court was whether the case should be governed by New York contract law, under which the fraud tainting the transaction provided a defense for Tyson, or by the new law of negotiable instruments that was developing in recent English decisions, under which Tyson would have to pay Swift if Swift had accepted the instrument without notice of the fraud.

Whether New York law applied or not turned upon the meaning of the phrase "laws of the several states" in the Rules of Decision Act. If the phrase encompassed both the statutory and the decisional law of the states (that is, if the Act commanded federal courts to follow both state statutes and state court decisions in cases in which they covered the controversy), then the New York rule (which was judge-made, not part of a statute) had to be applied. If, on the other hand, the phrase encompassed only statutory law (that is, if the Act commanded federal courts to follow the state rule *only* if it was in a state statute), then the federal court in *Swift* was free to use the emerging rule or any other it felt was best. Justice Story, writing for a unanimous Court, concluded that the Act commanded federal courts to follow simply the statutory law of the states.

It is observable that the Courts of New York do not found their decisions upon this point upon any local statute, or positive, fixed, or ancient local usage: but they deduce the doctrine from the general principles of commercial law. It is, however, contended, that the thirty-fourth section of the judiciary act of 1789, ch. 20, furnishes a rule obligatory upon this Court to follow the decisions of the state tribunals in all cases to which they apply. * * * In order to maintain the argument, it is essential, therefore, to hold, that the word "laws," in this section, includes within the scope of its meaning the decisions of the local tribunals. In the ordinary use of language it will hardly be contended that the decisions of Courts constitute laws. They are, at most, only evidence of what the laws are, and are not of themselves laws. They are often reexamined, reversed, and qualified by the Courts themselves, whenever they are found to be either defective, or ill-founded, or otherwise incorrect. The laws of a state are more usually understood to mean the rules and enactments promulgated by the legislative authority thereof, or long established local customs having the force of laws. In all the various cases, which have hitherto come before us for decision, this Court have uniformly supposed, that the true interpretation of the thirty-fourth section limited its application to state laws strictly local, that is to say, to the positive statutes of the state, and the construction thereof adopted by the local tribunals, and to rights and titles to things having a permanent locality, such as the rights and titles to real estate, and other matters immovable and intraterritorial in their nature and character. It never has been supposed by us, that the section did apply, or was designed to apply, to questions of a more general nature, not at all dependent upon local statutes or local usages of a fixed and permanent operation, as, for example, to the construction of ordinary contracts or other written instruments and especially to questions of general commercial law, where the state tribunals are called upon to perform the like functions as ourselves, that is, to ascertain upon general reasoning and legal analogies, what is the true exposition of the contract or instrument, or what is the just rule furnished by the principles of commercial law to govern the case. And we have not now the slightest difficulty in holding, that this section, upon its true intendment and construction, is strictly limited to local statutes and local usages of the character before stated, and does not extend to contracts and other instruments of a commercial nature, the true interpretation and effect whereof are to be sought, not in the decisions of the local tribunals, but in the general principles and doctrines of commercial jurisprudence. * * *

Id. at 18–19, 10 L.Ed. at 871.

Is Justice Story correct when he asserts that "[i]n the ordinary use of language it will hardly be contended that the decisions of Courts constitute laws"? Does it make sense to have the federal courts promulgate general, uniformly applied commercial laws? Why should a person suing in federal court in Oklahoma not receive the same remedy as a person suing in federal court in Vermont? On the other hand, if a federal court sitting in diversity is forced to apply the forum state's court decisions, what advantage would a party have in going to federal court?

The *Swift* decision must be evaluated in the context in which it was decided. First, *Swift* was decided in the heyday of "the common law." Justice Story believed that judges were responsible for finding "the truth" by examining all of the available authorities. In commercial matters, such as contracts, Story saw no need to adhere to the decisions of a single jurisdiction: Since the nature of commercial contracts is universal, the principles that should guide them are universal and are to be found by tapping the wisdom and experience of humankind.

Second, the federal government, including the judiciary, were seeking greater uniformity and stability in interstate commerce and, in this specific context, wanted to encourage businessmen to trust out-of-state negotiable instruments. On the other hand, the states' attitudes were guided by provincial concerns, such as trying to protect local debtors from foreign creditors. Thus, the *Swift* decision helped simplify commercial law and simultaneously encouraged the nationalist goals of the federal government.

2. THE *ERIE* DOCTRINE: THE RULES OF DECISION ACT AND THE RULES ENABLING ACT

ERIE R. CO. v. TOMPKINS

Supreme Court of the United States, 1938.
304 U.S. 64, 58 S.Ct. 817, 82 L.Ed. 1188.

[Slightly after midnight on July 27, 1934, Harry James Tompkins was walking home along a well-trodden footpath running parallel to the Erie Railroad tracks in Hughestown, Pennsylvania, when he was struck by "a black object that looked like a door" protruding from a passing train. Tompkins' right arm was severed.

Under Pennsylvania law, a traveler like Tompkins on a parallel (or "longitudinal") path was regarded as a trespasser to whom the railroad merely owes a duty to avoid wanton negligence. The majority rule in most states, however, was that a railroad owes a duty of ordinary care to a traveler on a parallel footpath.

Tompkins' lawyers were well aware of the rule in *Swift* that, absent state statutory law, federal courts apply "general law," and thus they tried to avoid the harsh Pennsylvania rule by suing the New York-based railroad in federal court. As anticipated, the District Court applied "general law," the majority rule, and the jury awarded Tompkins $30,000 in damages.

The Court of Appeals affirmed, holding that

upon questions of general law the federal courts are free, in absence of a local statute, to exercise their independent judgment as to what the law is; and it is well settled that the question of the responsibility of a railroad for injuries caused by its servants is one of general law. * * * Where the public has made open and notorious use of a railroad right of way for a long period of time and without objection, the company owes to persons on such permissive pathway a duty of care in the operation of its trains. * * * It is likewise generally recognized law that a jury may find that negligence exists toward a pedestrian using a permissive path on the railroad right of way if he is hit by some object projecting from the side of the train.

The Supreme Court granted certiorari. After hearing the opening arguments, Chief Justice Hughes declared: "If we wish to overrule Swift v. Tyson, here is our opportunity."]

Certiorari to the Circuit Court of Appeals for the Second Circuit.

MR. JUSTICE BRANDEIS delivered the opinion of the Court.

* * *

First. Swift v. Tyson * * * held that federal courts exercising jurisdiction on the ground of diversity of citizenship need not, in matters of general jurisprudence, apply the unwritten law of the state as declared by its highest court; that they are free to exercise an independent judgment as to what the common law of the state is—or should be * * *.

* * * The federal courts assumed, in the broad field of "general law," the power to declare rules of decision which Congress was confessedly without power to enact as statutes. Doubt was repeatedly expressed as to the correctness of the construction given section 34, and as to the soundness of the rule which it introduced. But it was the more recent research of a competent scholar, who examined the original document, which established that the construction given to it by the Court was erroneous; and that the purpose of the section was merely to make certain that, in all matters except those in which some federal law is controlling, the federal courts exercising jurisdiction in diversity of citizenship cases would apply as their rules of decision the law of the state, unwritten as well as written.[5]

Criticism of the doctrine became widespread after the decision of Black & White Taxicab & Transfer Co. v. Brown & Yellow Taxicab & Transfer Co., 276 U.S. 518, 48 S.Ct. 404, 72 L.Ed. 681, 57 A.L.R. 426. There, Brown & Yellow, a Kentucky corporation owned by Kentuckians, and the Louisville & Nashville Railroad, also a Kentucky corporation, wished that the former should have the exclusive privilege of soliciting passenger and baggage transportation at the Bowling Green, Ky., railroad

5. Charles Warren, New Light on the History of the Federal Judiciary Act of 1789 (1923) 37 Harv.L.Rev. 49, 51–52, 81–88, 108.

station; and that the Black & White, a competing Kentucky corporation, should be prevented from interfering with that privilege. Knowing that such a contract would be void under the common law of Kentucky, it was arranged that the Brown & Yellow reincorporate under the law of Tennessee, and that the contract with the railroad should be executed there. The suit was then brought by the Tennessee corporation in the federal court for Western Kentucky to enjoin competition by the Black & White; an injunction issued by the District Court was sustained by the Court of Appeals; and this Court, citing many decisions in which the doctrine of Swift v. Tyson had been applied, affirmed the decree.

Second. Experience in applying the doctrine of Swift v. Tyson, had revealed its defects, political and social; and the benefits expected to flow from the rule did not accrue. Persistence of state courts in their own opinions on questions of common law prevented uniformity; and the impossibility of discovering a satisfactory line of demarcation between the province of general law and that of local law developed a new well of uncertainties.

On the other hand, the mischievous results of the doctrine had become apparent. Diversity of citizenship jurisdiction was conferred in order to prevent apprehended discrimination in state courts against those not citizens of the state. Swift v. Tyson introduced grave discrimination by noncitizens against citizens. It made rights enjoyed under the unwritten "general law" vary according to whether enforcement was sought in the state or in the federal court; and the privilege of selecting the court in which the right should be determined was conferred upon the noncitizen. Thus, the doctrine rendered impossible equal protection of the law. In attempting to promote uniformity of law throughout the United States, the doctrine had prevented uniformity in the administration of the law of the state.

The discrimination resulting became in practice far-reaching. This resulted in part from the broad province accorded to the so-called "general law" as to which federal courts exercised an independent judgment. In addition to questions of purely commercial law, "general law" was held to include the obligations under contracts entered into and to be performed within the state, the extent to which a carrier operating within a state may stipulate for exemption from liability for his own negligence or that of his employee; the liability for torts committed within the state upon persons resident or property located there, even where the question of liability depended upon the scope of a property right conferred by the state; and the right to exemplary or punitive damages. Furthermore, state decisions construing local deeds, mineral conveyances, and even devises of real estate, were disregarded.

In part the discrimination resulted from the wide range of persons held entitled to avail themselves of the federal rule by resort to the diversity of citizenship jurisdiction. Through this jurisdiction individual citizens willing to remove from their own state and become citizens of another might avail themselves of the federal rule. And, without even change of residence, a corporate citizen of the state could avail itself of the federal rule by reincorporating under the laws of another state, as was done in the Taxicab Case.

The injustice and confusion incident to the doctrine of Swift v. Tyson have been repeatedly urged as reasons for abolishing or limiting diversity of citizenship jurisdiction. Other legislative relief has been proposed. If only a question of statutory construction were involved, we should not be prepared to abandon a doctrine so widely applied throughout nearly a century. But the unconstitutionality of the course pursued has now been made clear, and compels us to do so.

Third. Except in matters governed by the Federal Constitution or by acts of Congress, the law to be applied in any case is the law of the state. And whether the law of the state shall be declared by its Legislature in a statute or by its highest court in a decision is not a matter of federal concern. There is no federal general common law. Congress has no power to declare substantive rules of common law applicable in a state whether they be local in their nature or "general," be they commercial law or a part of the law of torts. And no clause in the Constitution purports to confer such a power upon the federal courts. As stated by Mr. Justice Field when protesting in Baltimore & Ohio R.R. Co. v. Baugh, 149 U.S. 368, 401, 13 S.Ct. 914, 927, 37 L.Ed. 772, against ignoring the Ohio common law of fellow-servant liability: "I am aware that what has been termed the general law of the country—which is often little less than what the judge advancing the doctrine thinks at the time should be the general law on a particular subject—has been often advanced in judicial opinions of this court to control a conflicting law of a state. I admit that learned judges have fallen into the habit of repeating this doctrine as a convenient mode of brushing aside the law of a state in conflict with their views. And I confess that, moved and governed by the authority of the great names of those judges, I have, myself, in many instances, unhesitatingly and confidently, but I think now erroneously, repeated the same doctrine. But, notwithstanding the great names which may be cited in favor of the doctrine, and notwithstanding the frequency with which the doctrine has been reiterated, there stands, as a perpetual protest against its repetition, the constitution of the United States, which recognizes and preserves the autonomy and independence of the states,—independence in their legislative and independence in their judicial departments. Supervision over either the legislative or the judicial action of the states is in no case permissible except as to matters by the constitution specifically authorized or delegated to the United States. Any interference with either, except as thus permitted, is an invasion of the authority of the state, and, to that extent, a denial of its independence."

The fallacy underlying the rule declared in Swift v. Tyson is made clear by Mr. Justice Holmes.[23] The doctrine rests upon the assumption that there is "a transcendental body of law outside of any particular State but obligatory within it unless and until changed by statute," that federal

23. Kuhn v. Fairmont Coal Co., 215 U.S. 349, 370–372, 30 S.Ct. 140, 54 L.Ed. 228; Black & White Taxicab, etc., Co. v. Brown & Yellow Taxicab, etc., Co., 276 U.S. 518, 532–536, 48 S.Ct. 404, 408, 409, 72 L.Ed. 681, 57 A.L.R. 426.

courts have the power to use their judgment as to what the rules of common law are; and that in the federal courts "the parties are entitled to an independent judgment on matters of general law":

> But law in the sense in which courts speak of it today does not exist without some definite authority behind it. The common law so far as it is enforced in a State, whether called common law or not, is not the common law generally but the law of that State existing by the authority of that State without regard to what it may have been in England or anywhere else. * * *

> The authority and only authority is the State, and if that be so, the voice adopted by the State as its own [whether it be of its Legislature or of its Supreme Court] should utter the last word.

Thus the doctrine of Swift v. Tyson is, as Mr. Justice Holmes said, "an unconstitutional assumption of powers by the Courts of the United States which no lapse of time or respectable array of opinion should make us hesitate to correct." In disapproving that doctrine we do not hold unconstitutional section 34 of the Federal Judiciary Act of 1789 or any other act of Congress. We merely declare that in applying the doctrine this Court and the lower courts have invaded rights which in our opinion are reserved by the Constitution to the several states.

Fourth. The defendant contended that by the common law of Pennsylvania * * * the only duty owed to the plaintiff was to refrain from willful or wanton injury. The plaintiff denied that such is the Pennsylvania law. In support of their respective contentions the parties discussed and cited many decisions of the Supreme Court of the State. The Circuit Court of Appeals ruled that the question of liability is one of general law; and on that ground declined to decide the issue of state law. As we hold this was error, the judgment is reversed and the case remanded to it for further proceedings in conformity with our opinion.

Reversed.

MR. JUSTICE CARDOZO took no part in the consideration or decision of this case.

MR. JUSTICE BUTLER (dissenting).

* * *

Defendant's petition for writ of certiorari presented two questions: Whether its duty toward plaintiff should have been determined in accordance with the law as found by the highest court of Pennsylvania, and whether the evidence conclusively showed plaintiff guilty of contributory negligence. Plaintiff contends that, as always heretofore held by this Court, the issues of negligence and contributory negligence are to be determined by general law against which local decisions may not be held conclusive * * *.

No constitutional question was suggested or argued below or here. And as a general rule, this Court will not consider any question not raised below and presented by the petition. * * * Here it does not decide either of the questions presented, but, changing the rule of decision in force since the foundation of the government, remands the case to be adjudged according to a standard never before deemed permissible.

* * *

The doctrine of * * * [Swift v. Tyson] has been followed by this Court in an unbroken line of decisions. So far as appears, it was not questioned until more than 50 years later, and then by a single judge.[1] Baltimore & O. Railroad Co. v. Baugh, 149 U.S. 368, 390, 13 S.Ct. 914, 37 L.Ed. 772. * * *

And since that decision, the division of opinion in this Court has been of the same character as it was before. In 1910, Mr. Justice Holmes, speaking for himself and two other Justices, dissented from the holding that a court of the United States was bound to exercise its own independent judgment in the construction of a conveyance made before the state courts had rendered an authoritative decision as to its meaning and effect. Kuhn v. Fairmont Coal Co., 215 U.S. 349, 30 S.Ct. 140, 54 L.Ed. 228. But that dissent accepted * * * as "settled" the doctrine of Swift v. Tyson, and insisted * * * merely that the case under consideration was by nature and necessity peculiarly local.

* * *

So far as appears, no litigant has ever challenged the power of Congress to establish the rule as construed. It has so long endured that its destruction now without appropriate deliberation cannot be justified. There is nothing in the opinion to suggest that consideration of any constitutional question is necessary to a decision of the case. * * * Against the protest of those joining in this opinion, the Court declines to assign the case for reargument. It may not justly be assumed that the labor and argument of counsel for the parties would not disclose the right conclusion and aid the Court in the statement of reasons to support it. Indeed, it would have been appropriate to give Congress opportunity to be heard before divesting it of power to prescribe rules of decision to be followed in the courts of the United States. * * *

The course pursued by the Court in this case is repugnant to the Act of Congress of August 24, 1937, 50 Stat. 751, 28 U.S.C.A. §§ 17 and note, 349a, 380a and note, 401. It declares that: "Whenever the constitutionality of any Act of Congress affecting the public interest is drawn in question in any court of the United States in any suit or proceeding to which the United States, or any agency thereof, or any officer or employee thereof, as such officer or employee, is not a party, the court having jurisdiction of the suit or proceeding shall certify such fact to the Attorney General. In any such case the court shall permit the United States to intervene and become a party for presentation of evidence * * * and argument upon the question of the constitutionality of such Act. * * *" If defendant had applied for and obtained the writ of certiorari upon the claim that, as now held, Congress has no power to prescribe the rule of decision, section 34 as construed, it would have been the duty of this Court to issue the prescribed certificate to the Attorney General in

---

1. Mr. Justice Field filed a dissenting opinion.

order that the United States might intervene and be heard on the constitutional question. * * * Congress intended to give the United States the right to be heard in every case involving constitutionality of an act affecting the public interest. In view of the rule that, in the absence of challenge of constitutionality, statutes will not here be invalidated on that ground, the Act of August 24, 1937 extends to cases where constitutionality is first "drawn in question" by the Court. * * *

I am of opinion that the constitutional validity of the rule need not be considered, because under the law, as found by the courts of Pennsylvania and generally throughout the country, it is plain that the evidence required a finding that plaintiff was guilty of negligence that contributed to cause his injuries, and that the judgment below should be reversed upon that ground.

MR. JUSTICE MCREYNOLDS concurs in this opinion.

MR. JUSTICE REED (concurring in part).

I concur in the conclusion reached in this case, in the disapproval of the doctrine of Swift v. Tyson, and in the reasoning of the majority opinion, except in so far as it relies upon the unconstitutionality of the "course pursued" by the federal courts.

The "doctrine of Swift v. Tyson," as I understand it, is that the words "the laws," as used in section 34 of the Federal Judiciary Act of September 24, 1789, do not include in their meaning "the decisions of the local tribunals." * * *

To decide the case now before us and to "disapprove" the doctrine of Swift v. Tyson requires only that we say that the words "the laws" include in their meaning the decisions of the local tribunals. As the majority opinion shows, by its reference to Mr. Warren's researches and the first quotation from Mr. Justice Holmes, that this Court is now of the view that "laws" includes "decisions," it is unnecessary to go further and declare that the "course pursued" was "unconstitutional," instead of merely erroneous.

The "unconstitutional" course referred to in the majority opinion is apparently the ruling in Swift v. Tyson that the supposed omission of Congress to legislate as to the effect of decisions leaves federal courts free to interpret general law for themselves. I am not at all sure whether, in the absence of federal statutory direction, federal courts would be compelled to follow state decisions. There was sufficient doubt about the matter in 1789 to induce the first Congress to legislate. No former opinions of this Court have passed upon it. * * * If the opinion commits this Court to the position that the Congress is without power to declare what rules of substantive law shall govern the federal courts, that conclusion also seems questionable. The line between procedural and substantive law is hazy, but no one doubts federal power over procedure. * * * The Judiciary Article, 3, and the "necessary and proper" clause of article 1, § 8, may fully authorize legislation, such as this section of the Judiciary Act.

* * *

Notes and Questions

1. Is *Erie* a constitutional decision or does it rest on other grounds? What constitutional provision could provide the basis for Justice Brandeis' opinion? Is he claiming that the result in *Swift* was unconstitutional because a regime of federal common law making is not authorized by any constitutional provision? Or is he claiming that federal courts cannot make common law for traditionally state causes of action, such as contracts, torts, and property?

The constitutional discussion in *Erie* is sometimes referred to as "dicta." Is Justice Brandeis' reference to the Constitution merely a way of bolstering his interpretation of the Rules of Decision Act? See Clark, *State Law in the Federal Courts: The Brooding Omnipresence of Erie v. Tompkins*, 55 Yale L.J. 267, 278 (1946).

2. If discrimination against in-state defendants really is a problem, could it not be solved by allowing in-state defendants to remove to federal court? Does it make sense to require federal courts to apply state law in diversity cases simply out of a desire for parity between in-state defendants who cannot remove and out-of-state defendants who can?

Justice Brandeis uses the *Black & White Taxicab* case to illustrate the evils resulting from *Swift*. But could not the problem presented in that case be handled without overruling *Swift* by preventing reincorporation solely to assert diversity jurisdiction? Reread 28 U.S.C. § 1359, set out in the Supplement. Would that have alleviated the problem?

3. In the article referred to at footnote 5 of the Court's opinion, Professor Charles Warren revealed a previously unknown draft of what became the Rules of Decision Act of 1789. The draft read:

> And be it further enacted, That the Statute law of the several States in force for the time being and their unwritten or common law now in use, whether by adoption from the common law of England, the ancient statutes of the same or otherwise, except where the Constitution, treaties or statutes of the United States shall otherwise require or provide, shall be regarded as rules of decision in the trials at common law in the courts of the United States in cases where they apply.

Did Justice Brandeis properly interpret the Rules of Decision Act given this legislative history? Or, did the shorter final version reflect congressional intent to limit the definition of "laws of the several states" to statutory laws, thus expanding the federal common law making power of the federal courts in diversity cases?

4. Reactions to the *Erie* decision voiced shortly after it was handed down include Shulman, *The Demise of Swift v. Tyson*, 47 Yale L.J. 1336 (1938); Tunks, *Categorization and Federalism: "Substance" and "Procedure" After Erie Railroad v. Tompkins*, 34 Ill.L.Rev. 271 (1939). More recent treatments of the subject are found in Gelfand & Abrams, *Putting Erie on the Right Track*, 49 U.Pitt.L.Rev. 937 (1988); Friendly, *In Praise of Erie—And of the New Federal Common Law*, 39 N.Y.U.L.Rev. 383 (1964); Hill, *The Erie Doctrine and the Constitution*, 53 Nw.U.L.Rev. 427, 541 (1958); Kurland, *Mr. Justice Frankfurter, the Supreme Court and the Erie Doctrine in Diversity Cases*, 67 Yale L.J. 187 (1957); Note, *The Law Applied in Diversity Cases: The Rules of Decision Act and the Erie Doctrine*, 85 Yale L.J. 678 (1976). Perhaps

the strongest attack on the *Erie* doctrine in the literature is found in Keeffe, Gilhooley, Bailey & Day, *Weary Erie,* 34 Cornell L.Q. 494 (1949). For an interesting debate on the meaning of *Erie,* see Redish & Phillips, *Erie and the Rules of Decision Act: In Search of the Appropriate Dilemma,* 91 Harv.L.Rev. 356 (1977); Westen & Lehman, *Is There Life for Erie After the Death of Diversity?,* 78 Mich.L.Rev. 311 (1981); Redish, *Continuing the Erie Debate: A Response to Westen and Lehman,* 78 Mich.L.Rev. 959 (1982); Westen, *After "Life for Erie"—A Reply,* 78 Mich.L.Rev. 971 (1982).

* * *

GUARANTY TRUST CO. v. YORK

Supreme Court of the United States, 1945.
326 U.S. 99, 65 S.Ct. 1464, 89 L.Ed. 2079.

[The Guaranty Trust Company served as trustee for some of the noteholders of Van Sweringen Corporation. In October 1930, Guaranty loaned money to corporations affiliated with and controlled by Van Sweringen. By October 1931, it was evident that the corporation was having trouble meeting its financial obligations. Guaranty and several other banks worked out a plan by which Guaranty would offer to purchase the notes by paying $500 and twenty shares of Van Sweringen stock for each $1,000 note.

Respondent York received $6,000 of the notes from a donor who had not accepted Guaranty's offer. York brought a diversity suit alleging that Guaranty had breached its fiduciary duties. York's complaint involved allegations of fraud and misrepresentation, relief for which was governed by equitable principles. On appeal, the Circuit Court of Appeals, one judge dissenting, found that in a suit brought on the equity side of a federal district court the court was not required to apply the state statute of limitations that would govern similar suits in state courts, even though the exclusive basis of federal jurisdiction was diversity of citizenship. The Supreme Court granted review in order to decide whether federal courts should apply state statutes of limitations in such cases.]

Certiorari to the Circuit Court of Appeals for the Second Circuit.

MR. JUSTICE FRANKFURTER delivered the opinion of the Court.

* * *

Our starting point must be the policy of federal jurisdiction which Erie R. Co. v. Tompkins * * * embodies. In overruling Swift v. Tyson * * * Erie R. Co. v. Tompkins did not merely overrule a venerable case. It overruled a particular way of looking at law which dominated the judicial process long after its inadequacies had been laid bare. * * * Law was conceived as a "brooding omnipresence" of Reason, of which decisions were merely evidence and not themselves the controlling formulations. Accordingly, federal courts deemed themselves free to ascertain what Reason, and therefore Law, required wholly independent of authoritatively declared State law, even in cases where a legal right as the basis for relief was created by State authority and could not be created by federal authority and the case got into a federal court merely because it was "between Citizens of different States" under Art. III, § 2 of the Constitution * * *.

In exercising their jurisdiction on the ground of diversity of citizenship, the federal courts, in the long course of their history, have not differentiated in their regard for State law between actions at law and suits in equity. Although § 34 of the Judiciary Act of 1789 * * * directed that the "laws of the several States * * * shall be regarded as rules of decision in trials of common law * * *," this was deemed, consistently for over a hundred years, to be merely declaratory of what would in any event have governed the federal courts and therefore was equally applicable to equity suits. * * * Indeed, it may fairly be said that the federal courts gave greater respect to State-created "substantive rights," Pusey & Jones Co. v. Hanssen, 261 U.S. 491, 498, 43 S.Ct. 454, 456, 67 L.Ed. 763, in equity than they gave them on the law side, because rights at law were usually declared by State courts and as such increasingly flouted by extension of the doctrine of Swift v. Tyson, while rights in equity were frequently defined by legislative enactment and as such known and respected by the federal courts. * * *

Partly because the States in the early days varied greatly in the manner in which equitable relief was afforded and in the extent to which it was available, * * * Congress provided that "the forms and modes of proceeding in suits * * * of equity" would conform to the settled uses of courts of equity. * * * But this enactment gave the federal courts no power that they would not have had in any event when courts were given "cognizance," by the first Judiciary Act, of suits "in equity." From the beginning there has been a good deal of talk in the cases that federal equity is a separate legal system. And so it is, properly understood. The suits in equity of which the federal courts have had "cognizance" ever since 1789 constituted the body of law which had been transplanted to this country from the English Court of Chancery. * * * In giving federal courts "cognizance" of equity suits in cases of diversity jurisdiction, Congress never gave, nor did the federal courts ever claim, the power to deny substantive rights created by State law or to create substantive rights denied by State law.

This does not mean that whatever equitable remedy is available in a State court must be available in a diversity suit in a federal court, or conversely, that a federal court may not afford an equitable remedy not available in a State court. * * * State law cannot define the remedies which a federal court must give simply because a federal court in diversity jurisdiction is available as an alternative tribunal to the State's courts. Contrariwise, a federal court may afford an equitable remedy for a substantive right recognized by a State even though a State court cannot give it. Whatever contradiction or confusion may be produced by a medley of judicial phrases severed from their environment, the body of adjudications concerning equitable relief in diversity cases leaves no doubt that the federal courts enforced State-created substantive rights if the mode of proceeding and remedy were consonant with the traditional body of equitable remedies, practice and procedure, and in so doing they were enforcing rights created by the States and not arising under any inherent or statutory federal law.

*   *   *

And so this case reduces itself to the narrow question whether, when no recovery could be had in a State court because the action is barred by the statute of limitations, a federal court in equity can take cognizance of the suit because there is diversity of citizenship between the parties. Is the outlawry, according to State law, of a claim created by the States a matter of "substantive rights" to be respected by a federal court of equity when that court's jurisdiction is dependent on the fact that there is a State-created right, or is such statute of "a mere remedial character," *   *   * which a federal court may disregard?

Matters of "substance" and matters of "procedure" are much talked about in the books as though they defined a great divide cutting across the whole domain of law. But, of course, "substance" and "procedure" are the same keywords to very different problems. Neither "substance" nor "procedure" represents the same invariants. Each implies different variables depending upon the particular problem for which it is used. *   *   * And the different problems are only distantly related at best, for the terms are in common use in connection with situations turning on such different considerations as those that are relevant to questions pertaining to ex post facto legislation, the impairment of the obligations of contract, the enforcement of federal rights in the State courts and the multitudinous phases of the conflict of laws. *   *   *

Here we are dealing with a right to recover derived not from the United States but from one of the States. When, because the plaintiff happens to be a non-resident, such a right is enforceable in a federal as well as in a State court, the forms and mode of enforcing the right may at times, naturally enough, vary because the two judicial systems are not identic. But since a federal court adjudicating a state-created right solely because of the diversity of citizenship of the parties is for that purpose, in effect, only another court of the State, it cannot afford recovery if the right to recover is made unavailable by the State nor can it substantially affect the enforcement of the right as given by the State.

And so the question is not whether a statute of limitations is deemed a matter of "procedure" in some sense. The question is whether such a statute concerns merely the manner and the means by which a right to recover, as recognized by the State, is enforced, or whether such statutory limitation is a matter of substance in the aspect that alone is relevant to our problem, namely, does it significantly affect the result of a litigation for a federal court to disregard a law of a State that would be controlling in an action upon the same claim by the same parties in a State court?

It is therefore immaterial whether statutes of limitation are characterized either as "substantive" or "procedural" in State court opinions in any use of those terms unrelated to the specific issue before us. Erie R. Co. v. Tompkins was not an endeavor to formulate scientific legal terminology. It expressed a policy that touches vitally the proper distribution of judicial power between State and federal courts. In essence, the intent of that decision was to insure that, in all cases where a federal court is exercising jurisdiction solely because of the diversity of citizenship of the parties, the outcome of the litigation in the federal court should be substantially the same, so far as legal rules determine the outcome of a litigation, as it would be if tried in a State court. The nub of the policy that underlies Erie R. Co. v. Tompkins is that for the same transaction the accident of a suit by a non-resident litigant in a federal court instead of in a State court a block away, should not lead to a substantially different result. * * * A policy so important to our federalism must be kept free from entanglements with analytical or terminological niceties.

Plainly enough, a statute that would completely bar recovery in a suit if brought in a State court bears on a State-created right vitally and not merely formally or negligibly. As to consequences that so intimately affect recovery or non-recovery a federal court in a diversity case should follow State law. * * *

Diversity jurisdiction is founded on assurance to non-resident litigants of courts free from susceptibility to potential local bias. The Framers of the Constitution, according to Marshall, entertained "apprehensions" lest distant suitors be subjected to local bias in State courts, or, at least, viewed with "indulgence the possible fears and apprehensions" of such suitors. Bank of the United States v. Deveaux, 5 Cranch 61, 87, 3 L.Ed. 38. And so Congress afforded out-of-State litigants another tribunal, not another body of law. The operation of a double system of conflicting laws in the same State is plainly hostile to the reign of law. Certainly, the fortuitous circumstance of residence out of a State of one of the parties to a litigation ought not to give rise to a discrimination against others equally concerned but locally resident. The source of substantive rights enforced by a federal court under diversity jurisdiction, it cannot be said too often, is the law of the States. * * *

The judgment is reversed and the case is remanded for proceedings not inconsistent with this opinion.

So ordered.

Reversed.

MR. JUSTICE ROBERTS and MR. JUSTICE DOUGLAS took no part in the consideration or decision of this case.

[JUSTICE RUTLEDGE dissented in an opinion in which JUSTICE MURPHY joined.]

Notes and Questions

1. Does the Rules of Decision Act apply to a federal court sitting as an equity court in the same way that it does to a federal court sitting as a court of law? If a New York State equity court would not have granted a remedy to York for whatever reason, should a federal court sitting in diversity nevertheless grant a remedy? In answering this question, consider Justice Frankfurter's discussion of the difference between recognizing a state-created right and providing a remedy for infringement of that right. Could not it be argued that available remedies actually define the scope of the underlying rights?

2. Almost any legal rule, whether labelled as procedural or substantive, has the potential to affect the outcome of litigation. Does this mean that, after *York*, a federal court in a diversity case must apply every state legal rule that, if enforced, would affect the outcome of litigation? Does this include housekeeping rules like rules about the size of briefs or the color of paper used? Did Justice Frankfurter mean any rule that could affect the outcome, or would he say that only rules that influence a lawyer's choice of forum at the time she is choosing a forum are "outcome determinative"?

3. To what extent does *York* require the displacement of a Federal Rule of Civil Procedure in favor of a contrary state practice?

Shortly after *York,* the Supreme Court considered a trio of cases all decided by the Court on the same day. RAGAN v. MERCHANTS' TRANS-FER & WAREHOUSE CO., 337 U.S. 530, 69 S.Ct. 1233, 93 L.Ed. 1520 (1949), grew out of a highway accident that occurred on October 1, 1943. On September 4, 1945, Ragan filed a diversity action in a federal court in Kansas. However, service was not made on the defendant until December 28. Kansas had a two-year statute of limitations on tort claims. Ragan claimed that according to Rule 3 of the Federal Rules, the suit was commenced (and hence the statute tolled) by the filing of the complaint. The defendant countered that Kansas law dictated that service had to have been made within the two-year period. The Supreme Court held that Rule 3 was not intended to govern questions concerning the tolling of statutes of limitations, and, therefore, state law would determine in diversity when the statute was tolled.

In COHEN v. BENEFICIAL INDUSTRIAL LOAN CORP., 337 U.S. 541, 69 S.Ct. 1221, 93 L.Ed. 1528 (1949), the Court held that a federal court must apply a New Jersey statute requiring a plaintiff in a shareholder derivative suit to post a security-for-expenses bond—even though what is now Federal Rule 23.1, which ostensibly governs such cases, did not require a bond. The Court found that whether the New Jersey statute was classified as procedural or substantive, it created substantive liabilities for expenses. In the Court's view, Rule 23.1 did not contradict the New Jersey statute, but was addressed to independent concerns.

And, finally, in WOODS v. INTERSTATE REALTY CO., 337 U.S. 535, 69 S.Ct. 1235, 93 L.Ed. 1524 (1949), the Court held that a Tennessee corporation that had not qualified to do business in Mississippi could not maintain a diversity action in a federal court in that state if, by virtue of its failure to qualify, the Mississippi state courts were closed to it.

Strong dissents were filed in all three cases. Justice Rutledge, dissenting in *Cohen,* argued that these cases were a perversion of the *Erie* doctrine. To him, *Erie* involved an issue that clearly was substantive, while these cases presented issues that were at least arguably procedural. What do you think? See 19 Wright, Miller & Cooper, *Federal Practice and Procedure: Jurisdiction and Related Matters* § 4510 (1982).

4. Evaluate the following passage:

The *York* case, of necessity, spelled death to the hope for a completely uniform federal procedure. When its doctrine is logically applied, each important step in a diversity action must be examined in the light of two systems of law—first, under the Federal Rules, and then under the law of the state in which the federal court sits. In one state, a particular Rule might not clash with a local law or decision which significantly bears upon the outcome of a litigation. Under such circumstances, the Rule should prevail, although the determination as to its applicability is actually made under state law. In another state, the same Rule might conflict in some substantial way with that state's policy or law. In such instances, state law, and not the Rule, will govern a federal court's decision.

Merrigan, *Erie to York to Ragan—A Triple Play on the Federal Rules*, 3 Vand. L.Rev. 711, 717 (1950).

BYRD v. BLUE RIDGE RURAL ELECTRIC COOPERATIVE, INC.

Supreme Court of the United States, 1958.
356 U.S. 525, 78 S.Ct. 893, 2 L.Ed.2d 953.

Certiorari to the United States Court of Appeals for the Fourth Circuit.

MR. JUSTICE BRENNAN delivered the opinion of the Court.

This case was brought in the District Court for the Western District of South Carolina. Jurisdiction was based on diversity of citizenship. * * * The petitioner, a resident of North Carolina, sued respondent, a South Carolina corporation, for damages for injuries allegedly caused by the respondent's negligence. He had judgment on a jury verdict. The Court of Appeals for the Fourth Circuit reversed and directed the entry of judgment for the respondent. * * *

The respondent is in the business of selling electric power to subscribers in rural sections of South Carolina. The petitioner was employed as a lineman in the construction crew of a construction contractor. The contractor, R.H. Bouligny, Inc., held a contract with the respondent * * * for the building of some * * * power lines, the reconversion to higher capacities of * * * existing lines, and the construction of 2 new substations and a breaker station. The petitioner was injured while connecting power lines to one of the new substations.

One of respondent's affirmative defenses was that under the South Carolina Workmen's Compensation Act, the petitioner—because the work contracted to be done by his employer was work of the kind also done by the respondent's own construction and maintenance crews—had the status of a statutory employee of the respondent and was therefore barred from suing the respondent at law because obliged to accept statutory compensation benefits as the exclusive remedy for his injuries. Two questions concerning this defense are before us: (1) whether the Court of Appeals erred in directing judgment for respondent without a remand to give petitioner an opportunity to introduce further evidence; and (2) whether petitioner, state practice notwithstanding, is entitled to a jury determination of the factual issues raised by this defense.

* * *

[The Supreme Court initially decided to remand the case to the trial court to provide the petitioner an opportunity to introduce evidence on the question of whether the respondent was a statutory employer.]

A question is also presented as to whether on remand the factual issue is to be decided by the judge or by the jury. The respondent argues on the basis of the decision of the Supreme Court of South Carolina in Adams v. Davison-Paxon Co., 230 S.C. 532, 96 S.E.2d 566, that the issue of immunity should be decided by the judge and not by the jury. That was a negligence action brought in the state trial court against a store owner by an employee of an independent contractor who operated the store's millinery department. The trial judge denied the store owner's motion for a directed verdict made upon the ground that [South Carolina Code, 1952] § 72–111 barred the plaintiff's action. The jury returned a verdict for the plaintiff. The South Carolina Supreme Court reversed, holding that it was for the judge and not the jury to decide on the evidence whether the owner was a statutory employer, and that the store owner had sustained his defense. * * *

The respondent argues that this state-court decision governs the present diversity case and "divests the jury of its normal function" to decide the disputed fact question of the respondent's immunity under § 72–111. This is to contend that the federal court is bound under Erie R. Co. v. Tompkins * * * to follow the state court's holding to secure uniform enforcement of the immunity created by the State.

First. It was decided in Erie R. Co. v. Tompkins that the federal courts in diversity cases must respect the definition of state-created rights and obligations by the state courts. We must, therefore, first examine the rule in Adams v. Davison-Paxon Co. to determine whether it is bound up with these rights and obligations in such a way that its application in the federal court is required. * * *

The Workmen's Compensation Act is administered in South Carolina by its Industrial Commission. The South Carolina courts hold that, on judicial review of actions of the Commission under § 72–111, the question whether the claim of an injured workman is within the Commission's jurisdiction is a matter of law for decision by the court, which makes its own findings of fact relating to that jurisdiction. The South Carolina Supreme Court states no reasons in Adams v. Davison-Paxon Co. why, although the jury decides all other factual issues raised by the cause of action and defenses, the jury is displaced as to the factual issue raised by the affirmative defense under § 72–111. * * * A State may, of course, distribute the functions of its judicial machinery as it sees fit. The decisions relied upon, however, furnish no reason for selecting the judge rather than the jury to decide this single affirmative defense in the negligence action. They simply reflect a policy * * * that administrative determination of "jurisdictional facts" should not be final but subject to judicial review. The conclusion is inescapable that the Adams holding is grounded in the practical consideration that the question had theretofore come before the South Carolina courts from the Industrial Commission and the courts had become accustomed to deciding the factual issue of immunity without the aid of juries. We find nothing to suggest that this rule was announced as an integral part of the special relationship created by the statute. Thus the requirement appears to be merely a form and mode of enforcing the immunity ＊ ＊ ＊ and not a rule intended to be bound up with the definition of the rights and obligations of the parties. ＊ ＊ ＊

Second. But cases following *Erie* have evinced a broader policy to the effect that the federal courts should conform as near as may be—in the absence of other considerations—to state rules even of form and mode where the state rules may bear substantially on the question whether the litigation would come out one way in the federal court and another way in the state court if the federal court failed to apply a particular local rule. E.g., Guaranty Trust Co. of New York v. York, supra; Bernhardt v. Polygraphic Co., 350 U.S. 198, 76 S.Ct. 273, 100 L.Ed. 199. Concededly the nature of the tribunal which tries issues may be important in the enforcement of the parcel of rights making up a cause of action or defense, and bear significantly upon achievement of uniform enforcement of the right. It may well be that in the instant personal-injury case the outcome would be substantially affected by whether the issue of immunity is decided by a judge or a jury. Therefore, were "outcome" the only consideration, a strong case might appear for saying that the federal court should follow the state practice.

But there are affirmative countervailing considerations at work here. The federal system is an independent system for administering justice to litigants who properly invoke its jurisdiction. An essential characteristic of that system is the manner in which, in civil common-law actions, it distributes trial functions between judge and jury and, under the influence—if not the command—of the Seventh Amendment, assigns the decisions of disputed questions of fact to the jury. ＊ ＊ ＊ The policy of uniform enforcement of state-created rights and obligations ＊ ＊ ＊ cannot in every case exact compliance with a state rule—not bound up with rights and obligations—which disrupts the federal system of allocating functions between judge and jury. ＊ ＊ ＊ Thus the inquiry here is whether the federal policy favoring jury decisions of disputed fact questions should yield to the state rule in the interest of furthering the objective that the litigation should not come out one way in the federal court and another way in the state court.

We think that in the circumstances of this case the federal court should not follow the state rule. It cannot be gainsaid that there is a strong federal policy against allowing state rules to disrupt the judge-jury relationship in the federal courts. In Herron v. Southern Pacific Co., [283 U.S. 91, 51 S.Ct. 383, 75 L.Ed. 857 (1931),] ＊ ＊ ＊ the trial judge in a personal-injury negligence action brought in the District Court for Arizona on diversity grounds directed a verdict for the defendant when it appeared as a matter of law that the plaintiff was guilty of contributory negligence. The federal judge refused to be bound by a provision of the Arizona Constitution which made the jury the sole arbiter of the question of contributory negligence. This Court sustained the action of the trial judge, holding that "state laws cannot alter the essential character or function of a federal court" because that function "is not in any sense a local matter, and state statutes which would interfere with the appropriate performance of that function are not binding upon the federal court under either the Conformity Act or the 'Rules of Decision' Act." * * * Perhaps even more clearly in light of the influence of the Seventh Amendment, the function assigned to the jury "is an essential factor in the process for which the Federal Constitution provides." * * * Concededly the *Herron* case was decided before Erie R. Co. v. Tompkins, but even when Swift v. Tyson * * * was governing law and allowed federal courts sitting in diversity cases to disregard state decisional law, it was never thought that state statutes or constitutions were similarly to be disregarded. * * * Yet *Herron* held that state statutes and constitutional provisions could not disrupt or alter the essential character or function of a federal court.[14]

Third. We have discussed the problem upon the assumption that the outcome of the litigation may be substantially affected by whether the issue of immunity is decided by a judge or a jury. But clearly there is not present here the certainty that a different result would follow * * * or even the strong possibility that this would be the case * * *. There are factors present here which might reduce that possibility. The trial judge in the federal system has powers denied the judges of many States to comment on the weight of evidence and credibility of witnesses, and discretion to grant a new trial if the verdict appears to him to be against the weight of the evidence. We do not think the likelihood of a different result is so strong as to require the federal practice of jury determination of disputed factual issues to yield to the state rule in the interest of uniformity of outcome.[15]

* * *

Reversed and remanded.

* * *

[JUSTICE WHITTAKER concurred in Part I of the Court's opinion but dissented from Part II on the ground that the South Carolina rule requiring "its courts—not juries—to determine whether jurisdiction over the subject matter of cases like this is vested in its Industrial Commission" should be honored by a federal court. JUSTICE FRANKFURTER and JUSTICE HARLAN dissented on the ground that the evidence required the district court to direct a verdict for the respondent.]

Notes and Questions

1. What does Justice Brennan mean when he writes that "the influence—if not the command—of the Seventh Amendment" determined the

---

14. Diederich v. American News Co., 10 Cir., 128 F.2d 144, decided after Erie R. Co. v. Tompkins, held that an almost identical provision of the Oklahoma Constitution, art. 23, § 6, O.S.1951 was not binding on a federal judge in a diversity case.

15. Stoner v. New York Life Ins. Co., 311 U.S. 464, 61 S.Ct. 336, 85 L.Ed. 284, is not contrary. It was there held that the federal court should follow the state rule defining the evidence sufficient to raise a jury question whether the state-created right was es-

tablished. But the state rule did not have the effect of nullifying the function of the federal judge to control a jury submission as did the Arizona constitutional provision which was denied effect in *Herron.* The South Carolina rule here involved affects the jury function as the Arizona provision affected the function of the judge: The rule entirely displaces the jury without regard to the sufficiency of the evidence to support a jury finding of immunity.

result in *Byrd?* If the Seventh Amendment provides a rule of decision for *Byrd,* isn't the Rules of Decision Act inapplicable by its own terms? Indeed, if the Seventh Amendment "commands" that a federal court utilize a jury to decide who is a statutory employee, could the Rules of Decision Act dictate a contrary result? On the other hand, if the Seventh Amendment does not "command" the result in *Byrd,* why should it "influence" the result?

In this light, consider the following excerpt from SIMLER v. CONNER, 372 U.S. 221, 222, 83 S.Ct. 609, 610–11, 9 L.Ed.2d 691, 693 (1963):

> The federal policy favoring jury trials is of historic continuing strength. * * * Only through a holding that the jury-trial right is to be determined according to federal law can the uniformity in its exercise which is demanded by the Seventh Amendment be achieved. In diversity cases, of course, the substantive dimension of the claim asserted finds its source in state law, * * * but the characterization of that state-created claim as legal or equitable for purposes of whether a right to jury trial is indicated must be made by recourse to federal law.

2. Is Justice Brennan correct in asserting that the South Carolina rule at issue in *Byrd* is "merely a form and mode of enforcing the immunity * * * and not a rule intended to be bound up with the definition of the rights and obligations of the parties"? Most states have adopted their worker compensation schemes only after carefully balancing the equities involved in the typical workplace accident. These statutes are complex and detailed and often are the result of a political compromise. Does it seem likely, then, that South Carolina randomly would have appropriated to the judge the function of defining a statutory employee?

3. In *Byrd,* Justice Brennan proposes what appears to be a balancing test for determining *Erie* questions. Does the balancing test in *Byrd* replace the outcome-determinative test of *York?* Whether it replaces the outcome-determinative test or not, how does Justice Brennan's balancing test work? If a state rule is "bound up with the definition of the rights and obligations of the parties," does a federal court still engage in balancing? How do we determine whether a state rule is "bound up with the definition of the rights and obligations of the parties"?

4. Once it begins to engage in the balancing process dictated in *Byrd,* how does a federal court identify and then weigh the competing state and federal policies? What sources should it examine in pursuing this inquiry? In ALLSTATE INS. CO. v. CHARNESKI, 286 F.2d 238 (7th Cir.1960), the court dismissed an action for judgment declaring an insurance company's nonliability. The court, after reviewing the major *Erie*-doctrine cases and concluding that a Wisconsin court would dismiss the declaratory-judgment action before it, employed the following reasoning:

> First, as to the State of Wisconsin. This is not a case where a federal declaratory judgment action is filed in a state which has no statute providing for such relief. Wisconsin has passed a general statute providing declaratory relief. However, this statute was held not applicable * * * [by the Wisconsin Supreme Court] because it conflicted with the Wisconsin state policy of providing direct actions against insurance companies. This is a declaration of the *substantive* law of Wisconsin. The Wisconsin Supreme Court held that to allow declaratory relief in such circumstances would undercut its policy of direct actions against an

insurance company and thereby concluding the action—defining the rights of the insurer, the insured, and the injured party—in a single suit. This holding represents a legitimate and proper implementation of Wisconsin policy. * * *

    The federal interest to be served here is slight. There is the general interest of a court controlling its own procedure. There is the general policy evidenced by the federal Declaratory Judgments Act. However, no right to jury trial, guaranteed by the Seventh Amendment, is involved here, as in Byrd. The cause of action arising from the accident, the issue of coverage of the policy, and the rights of the insured, the insurer and the injured parties are intimately connected with Wisconsin law and have no connection with the federal government except that the latter provides a fair and orderly forum in which to try the diversity case. Finally, relief under the Federal act is expressly discretionary. Such relief is permissive and not absolute. Declaratory relief "may" be granted, and need not be when it would create an unnecessary federal-state conflict.

286 F.2d at 244. Is the court's analysis of the Wisconsin and federal policies adequate? Is it persuasive?

    5. In BERNHARDT v. POLYGRAPHIC CO. OF AMERICA, INC., 350 U.S. 198, 203, 76 S.Ct. 273, 276, 100 L.Ed. 199, 205 (1956), plaintiff brought an action in a Vermont state court for damages resulting from his discharge by defendant. Defendant removed the action to a federal district court and moved for a stay pending arbitration in New York pursuant to the contract. The District Court denied the stay, ruling that under *Erie* the arbitration provision was governed by Vermont law, which permitted revocation of an agreement to arbitrate any time before an award was made. The Second Circuit reversed on the ground that arbitration merely relates to the form of the trial. The Supreme Court disagreed and reversed and remanded, stating:

    * * * If the federal court allows arbitration where the state court would disallow it, the outcome of litigation might depend on the courthouse where suit is brought. For the remedy by arbitration, whatever its merits or shortcomings, substantially affects the cause of action created by the State. The nature of the tribunal where suits are tried is an important part of the parcel of rights behind a cause of action. The change from a court of law to an arbitration panel may make a radical difference in ultimate result. Arbitration carries no right to trial by jury that is guaranteed both by the Seventh Amendment and by Ch. 1, Art. 12th, of the Vermont Constitution. Arbitrators do not have the benefit of judicial instruction on the law; they need not give their reasons for their results; the record of their proceedings is not as complete as it is in a court trial; and judicial review of an award is more limited than judicial review of a trial * * *.

After *Byrd,* would *Bernhardt* be decided the same way? Is state law governing arbitration bound up with the definition of the parties' rights and obligations?

    6. Between 1960 and 1965, one of the most debated subjects in procedural circles was whether a federal court in a diversity action should employ a federal or state standard to determine the existence or nonexistence of in personam jurisdiction over a foreign corporation. By and large the post-*Byrd* cases appear to have opted for the state standard. E.g., Arrowsmith v. United

Press Int'l, 320 F.2d 219 (2d Cir.1963) (en banc), apparently overruling a contrary two-to-one decision in Jaftex Corp. v. Randolph Mills, Inc., 282 F.2d 508 (2d Cir.1960). See 4 Wright & Miller, *Federal Practice and Procedure: Civil* § 1075 (1969).

If *Erie* is constitutionally based, does Congress or do the federal courts have the power to establish jurisdictional standards for diversity actions? Putting the question another way, are jurisdictional rules substantive or procedural within the meaning of *Erie* and *York* or don't they fall entirely within either category? Would a federal test for personal jurisdiction promote or discourage forum-shopping? Assuming federal power, have either Congress or the federal courts established a clear test for amenability to suit in a federal court? Is the standard in International Shoe Co. v. Washington, p. 82, supra, relevant? What about Federal Rule of Civil Procedure 4 or 28 U.S.C. §§ 1391, 1693? A lengthy dialogue on these questions is offered by the late Judges Clark and Friendly in the *Jaftex* and *Arrowsmith* cases.

In 1934, Congress passed 28 U.S.C. § 2072, commonly known as the Rules Enabling Act. Read the current version of this Act, which is in the Supplement.

HANNA v. PLUMER
Supreme Court of the United States, 1965.
380 U.S. 460, 85 S.Ct. 1136, 14 L.Ed.2d 8.

Certiorari to the United States Court of Appeals for the First Circuit.

MR. CHIEF JUSTICE WARREN delivered the opinion of the Court.

The question to be decided is whether, in a civil action where the jurisdiction of the United States District Court is based upon diversity of citizenship between the parties, service of process shall be made in the manner prescribed by state law or that set forth in Rule 4(d)(1) of the Federal Rules of Civil Procedure.

On February 6, 1963, petitioner, a citizen of Ohio, filed her complaint in the District Court for the District of Massachusetts, claiming damages in excess of $10,000 for personal injuries resulting from an automobile accident in South Carolina, allegedly caused by the negligence of one Louise Plumer Osgood, a Massachusetts citizen deceased at the time of the filing of the complaint. Respondent, Mrs. Osgood's executor and also a Massachusetts citizen, was named as defendant. On February 8, service was made by leaving copies of the summons and the complaint with respondent's wife at his residence, concededly in compliance with Rule 4(d)(1) * * *. Respondent filed his answer on February 26, alleging, *inter alia*, that the action could not be maintained because it had been brought "contrary to and in violation of the provisions of Massachusetts General Laws (Ter.Ed.) Chapter 197, Section 9." That section provides:

> Except as provided in this chapter, an executor or administrator shall not be held to answer to an action by a creditor of the deceased which is not commenced within one year from the time of his giving bond for the performance of his trust, or to such an action which is commenced within said year unless before the expiration thereof the writ in such action has

been served by delivery in hand upon such executor or administrator or service thereof accepted by him or a notice stating the name of the estate, the name and address of the creditor, the amount of the claim and the court in which the action has been brought has been filed in the proper registry of probate. * * *

On October 17, 1963, the District Court granted respondent's motion for summary judgment, citing Ragan v. Merchants Transfer & Warehouse Co. * * * and Guaranty Trust Co. of New York v. York * * * in support of its conclusion that the adequacy of the service was to be measured by § 9, with which, the court held, petitioner had not complied. On appeal, petitioner * * * argued that Rule 4(d)(1) defines the method by which service of process is to be effected in diversity actions. The Court of Appeals for the First Circuit, finding that "[r]elatively recent amendments [to § 9] evince a clear legislative purpose to require personal notification within the year," [1] concluded that the conflict of state and federal rules was over "a substantive rather than a procedural matter," and unanimously affirmed. * * *

We conclude that the adoption of Rule 4(d)(1), designed to control service of process in diversity actions, neither exceeded the congressional mandate embodied in the Rules Enabling Act nor transgressed constitutional bounds, and that the Rule is therefore the standard against which the District Court should have measured the adequacy of the service. Accordingly, we reverse the decision of the Court of Appeals.

* * * Under the cases construing the scope of the Enabling Act, Rule 4(d)(1) clearly passes muster. Prescribing the manner in which a defendant is to be notified that a suit has been instituted against him, it relates to the "practice and procedure of the district courts." * * *

> The test must be whether a rule really regulates procedure,—the judicial process for enforcing rights and duties recognized by substantive law and for justly administering remedy and redress for disregard or infraction of them. Sibbach v. Wilson & Co., [p. 373, infra] * * *.

In Mississippi Pub. Corp. v. Murphree, 326 U.S. 438, 66 S.Ct. 242, 90 L.Ed. 185, this Court upheld Rule 4(f), which permits service of a summons anywhere within the State (and not merely the district) in which a district court sits:

1. Section 9 is in part a statute of limitations, providing that an executor need not "answer to an action * * * which is not commenced within one year from the time of his giving bond * * *." This part of the statute, the purpose of which is to speed the settlement of estates, * * * is not involved in this case, since the action clearly was timely commenced. (Respondent filed bond on March 1, 1962; the complaint was filed February 6, 1963; and the service—the propriety of which is in dispute—was made on February 8, 1963.) * * *.

Section 9 also provides for the manner of service. Generally, service of process must be made by "delivery in hand." * * * The purpose of this part of the statute, which is involved here, is, as the court below noted, to insure that executors will receive actual notice of claims. * * * Actual notice is of course also the goal of Rule 4(d)(1); however, the Federal Rule reflects a determination that this goal can be achieved by a method less cumbersome than that prescribed in § 9. In this case the goal seems to have been achieved; although the affidavit filed by respondent in the District Court asserts that he had neither been served in hand nor accepted service, it does not allege lack of actual notice.

We think that Rule 4(f) is in harmony with the Enabling Act ∗   ∗   ∗. Undoubtedly most alterations of the rules of practice and procedure may and often do affect the rights of litigants.   Congress' prohibition of any alteration of substantive rights of litigants was obviously not addressed to such incidental effects as necessarily attend the adoption of the prescribed new rules of procedure upon the rights of litigants who, agreeably to rules of practice and procedure, have been brought before a court authorized to determine their rights.   ∗   ∗   ∗ The fact that the application of Rule 4(f) will operate to subject petitioner's rights to adjudication by the district court for northern Mississippi will undoubtedly affect those rights.   But it does not operate to abridge, enlarge or modify the rules of decision by which that court will adjudicate its rights.   Id., at 445–446, 66 S.Ct. at 246.

Thus were there no conflicting state procedure, Rule 4(d)(1) would clearly control.   National Equipment Rental, Ltd. v. Szukhent ∗   ∗   ∗ [p. 193, supra].   However, respondent, focusing on the contrary Massachusetts rule, calls to the Court's attention another line of cases, a line which—like the Enabling Act—had its birth in 1938.   Erie R. Co. v. Tompkins, ∗   ∗   ∗ overruling Swift v. Tyson, ∗   ∗   ∗ held that federal courts sitting in diversity cases, when deciding questions of "substantive" law, are bound by state court decisions as well as state statutes.   The broad command of *Erie* was therefore identical to that of the Enabling Act: federal courts are to apply state substantive law and federal procedural law.   However, as subsequent cases sharpened the distinction between substance and procedure, the line of cases following *Erie* diverged markedly from the line construing the Enabling Act.   ∗   ∗   ∗

Respondent, by placing primary reliance on *York* and *Ragan*, suggests that the *Erie* doctrine acts as a check on the Federal Rules of Civil Procedure, that despite the clear command of Rule 4(d)(1), *Erie* and its progeny demand the application of the Massachusetts rule.   Reduced to essentials, the argument is: (1) *Erie*, as refined in *York*, demands that federal courts apply state law whenever application of federal law in its stead will alter the outcome of the case.   (2) In this case, a determination that the Massachusetts service requirements obtain will result in immediate victory for respondent.   If, on the other hand, it should be held that Rule 4(d)(1) is applicable, the litigation will continue, with possible victory for petitioner.   (3) Therefore, *Erie* demands application of the Massachusetts rule.   The syllogism possesses an appealing simplicity, but is for several reasons invalid.

In the first place, it is doubtful that, even if there were no Federal Rule making it clear that in hand service is not required in diversity actions, the *Erie* rule would have obligated the District Court to follow the Massachusetts procedure.   "Outcome determination" analysis was never intended to serve as a talisman.   Byrd v. Blue Ridge Rural Elec. Cooperative ∗   ∗   ∗.   Indeed, the message of *York* itself is that choices between state and federal law are to be made not by application of any automatic, "litmus paper" criterion, but rather by reference to the policies underlying the *Erie* rule.   Guaranty Trust Co. of New York v. York ∗   ∗   ∗.

The *Erie* rule is rooted in part in a realization that it would be unfair for the character or result of a litigation materially to differ because the suit had been brought in a federal court. * * * The decision was also in part a reaction to the practice of "forum-shopping" which had grown up in response to the rule of Swift v. Tyson. * * * That the *York* test was an attempt to effectuate these policies is demonstrated by the fact that the opinion framed the inquiry in terms of "substantial" variations between state and federal litigation. * * * Not only are nonsubstantial, or trivial, variations not likely to raise the sort of equal protection problems which troubled the Court in *Erie*; they are also unlikely to influence the choice of a forum. The "outcome-determination" test therefore cannot be read without reference to the twin aims of the *Erie* rule: discouragement of forum-shopping and avoidance of inequitable administration of the laws.[9]

The difference between the conclusion that the Massachusetts rule is applicable, and the conclusion that it is not, is of course at this point "outcome-determinative" in the sense that if we hold the state rule to apply, respondent prevails, whereas if we hold that Rule 4(d)(1) governs, the litigation will continue. But in this sense *every* procedural variation is "outcome-determinative." For example, having brought suit in a federal court, a plaintiff cannot then insist on the right to file subsequent pleadings in accord with the time limits applicable in state courts, even though enforcement of the federal timetable will, if he continues to insist that he must meet only the state time limit, result in determination of the controversy against him. So it is here. Though choice of the federal or state rule will at this point have a marked effect upon the outcome of the litigation, the difference between the two rules would be of scant, if any, relevance to the choice of a forum. Petitioner, in choosing her forum, was not presented with a situation where application of the state rule would wholly bar recovery; rather, adherence to the state rule would have resulted only in altering the way in which process was served.[11] Moreover, it is difficult to argue that permitting service of defendant's wife to

9. The Court of Appeals seemed to frame the inquiry in terms of how "important" Section 9 is to the State. In support of its suggestion that Section 9 serves some interest the State regards as vital to its citizens, the court noted that something like Section 9 has been on the books in Massachusetts a long time, that Section 9 has been amended a number of times, and that Section 9 is designed to make sure that executors receive actual notice. * * * The apparent lack of relation among these three observations is not surprising, because it is not clear to what sort of question the Court of Appeals was addressing itself. One cannot meaningfully ask how important something is without first asking "important for what purpose?" *Erie* and its progeny make clear that when a federal court sitting in a diversity case is faced with a question of whether or not to apply state law, the importance of a state rule is indeed relevant, but only in the context of asking whether application of the rule would make so important a difference to the character or result of the litigation that failure to enforce it would unfairly discriminate against citizens of the forum State, or whether application of the rule would have so important an effect upon the fortunes of one or both of the litigants that failure to enforce it would be likely to cause a plaintiff to choose the federal court.

11. * * * We cannot seriously entertain the thought that one suing an estate would be led to choose the federal court because of a belief that adherence to Rule 4(d)(1) is less likely to give the executor actual notice than Section 9, and therefore more likely to produce a default judgment. Rule 4(d)(1) is well designed to give actual notice, as it did in this case. * * *

take the place of in hand service of defendant himself alters the mode of enforcement of state-created rights in a fashion sufficiently "substantial" to raise the sort of equal protection problems to which the *Erie* opinion alluded.

There is, however, a more fundamental flaw in respondent's syllogism: the incorrect assumption that the rule of Erie R. Co. v. Tompkins constitutes the appropriate test of the validity and therefore the applicability of a Federal Rule of Civil Procedure. The *Erie* rule has never been invoked to void a Federal Rule. It is true that there have been cases where this Court has held applicable a state rule in the face of an argument that the situation was governed by one of the Federal Rules. But the holding of each such case was not that *Erie* commanded displacement of a Federal Rule by an inconsistent state rule, but rather that the scope of the Federal Rule was not as broad as the losing party urged, and therefore, there being no Federal Rule which covered the point in dispute, *Erie* commanded the enforcement of state law. * * * (Here, of course, the clash is unavoidable; Rule 4(d)(1) says—implicitly, but with unmistakable clarity—that in hand service is not required in federal courts.) At the same time, in cases adjudicating the validity of Federal Rules, we have not applied the *York* rule or other refinements of *Erie*, but have to this day continued to decide questions concerning the scope of the Enabling Act and the constitutionality of specific Federal Rules in light of the distinction set forth in *Sibbach*. * * *

Nor has the development of two separate lines of cases been inadvertent. The line between "substance" and "procedure" shifts as the legal context changes. * * * It is true that both the Enabling Act and the *Erie* rule say, roughly, that federal courts are to apply state "substantive" law and federal "procedural" law, but from that it need not follow that the tests are identical. For they were designed to control very different sorts of decisions. When a situation is covered by one of the Federal Rules, the question facing the court is a far cry from the typical, relatively unguided *Erie* choice: the court has been instructed to apply the Federal Rule, and can refuse to do so only if the Advisory Committee, this Court, and Congress erred in their prima facie judgment that the Rule in question transgresses neither the terms of the Enabling Act nor constitutional restrictions.

We are reminded by the *Erie* opinion that neither Congress nor the federal courts can, under the guise of formulating rules of decision for federal courts, fashion rules which are not supported by a grant of federal authority contained in Article I or some other section of the Constitution; in such areas state law must govern because there can be no other law. But the opinion in *Erie*, which involved no Federal Rule and dealt with a question which was "substantive" in every traditional sense * * *, surely neither said nor implied that measures like Rule 4(d)(1) are unconstitutional. For the constitutional provision for a federal court system (augmented by the Necessary and Proper Clause) carries with it congressional power to make rules governing the practice and pleading in those courts, which in turn includes a power to regulate matters which, though falling within the uncertain area between substance and procedure, are rationally capable of classification as either. * * * Neither *York* nor the cases following it ever suggested that the rule there laid down for coping with situations where no Federal Rule applies is coextensive with the limitation on Congress to which *Erie* had adverted. Although this Court has never before been confronted with a case where the applicable Federal Rule is in direct collision with the law of the relevant State, courts of appeals faced with such clashes have rightly discerned the implications of our decisions.

> One of the shaping purposes of the Federal Rules is to bring about uniformity in the federal courts by getting away from local rules. This is especially true of matters which relate to the administration of legal proceedings, an area in which federal courts have traditionally exerted strong inherent power, completely aside from the powers Congress expressly conferred in the Rules. The purpose of the *Erie* doctrine, even as extended in *York* and *Ragan*, was never to bottle up federal courts with "outcome-determinative" and "integral-relations" stoppers—when there are "affirmative countervailing [federal] considerations" and when there is a Congressional mandate (the Rules) supported by constitutional authority. Lumbermen's Mutual Casualty Co. v. Wright, 322 F.2d 759, 764 (C.A.5th Cir.1963).[16]

Erie and its offspring cast no doubt on the long-recognized power of Congress to prescribe housekeeping rules for federal courts even though some of those rules will inevitably differ from comparable state rules. * * * Thus, though a court, in measuring a Federal Rule against the standards contained in the Enabling Act and the Constitution, need not wholly blind itself to the degree to which the Rule makes the character and result of the federal litigation stray from the course it would follow in state courts, * * * it cannot be forgotten that the *Erie* rule, and the guidelines suggested in *York*, were created to serve another purpose altogether. To hold that a Federal Rule of Civil Procedure must cease to function whenever it alters the mode of enforcing state-created rights would be to disembowel either the Constitution's grant of power over federal procedure or Congress' attempt to exercise that power in the Enabling Act. Rule 4(d)(1) is valid and controls the instant case.

Reversed.

MR. JUSTICE BLACK concurs in the result.

MR. JUSTICE HARLAN, concurring.

* * *

Erie was something more than an opinion which worried about "forum-shopping and avoidance of inequitable administration of the laws," * * * although to be sure these were important elements of the decision. I have always regarded that decision as one of the modern cornerstones of our federalism, expressing policies that profoundly touch the allocation of judicial power between the state and federal systems. *Erie*

16. To the same effect, see D'Onofrio Construction Co. v. Recon Co., 255 F.2d 904, 909–910 (C.A.1st Cir.1958).

recognized that there should not be two conflicting systems of law controlling the primary activity of citizens, for such alternative governing authority must necessarily give rise to a debilitating uncertainty in the planning of everyday affairs. And it recognized that the scheme of our Constitution envisions an allocation of law-making functions between state and federal legislative processes which is undercut if the federal judiciary can make substantive law affecting state affairs beyond the bounds of congressional legislative powers in this regard. * * *

The shorthand formulations which have appeared in some past decisions are prone to carry untoward results that frequently arise from oversimplification. The Court is quite right in stating that the "outcome-determinative" test of Guaranty Trust Co. of New York v. York * * * if taken literally, proves too much, for any rule, no matter how clearly "procedural," can affect the outcome of litigation if it is not obeyed. In turning from the "outcome" test of *Guaranty* back to the unadorned forum-shopping rationale of *Erie*, however, the Court falls prey to like oversimplification, for a simple forum-shopping rule also proves too much; litigants often choose a federal forum merely to obtain what they consider the advantages of the Federal Rules of Civil Procedure or to try their cases before a supposedly more favorable judge. To my mind the proper line of approach in determining whether to apply a state or a federal rule, whether "substantive" or "procedural," is to stay close to basic principles by inquiring if the choice of rule would substantially affect those primary decisions respecting human conduct which our constitutional system leaves to state regulation. If so, *Erie* and the Constitution require that the state rule prevail, even in the face of a conflicting federal rule.

The Court weakens, if indeed it does not submerge, this basic principle by finding, in effect, a grant of substantive legislative power in the constitutional provision for a federal court system * * *, and through it, setting up the Federal Rules as a body of law inviolate. * * * So long as a reasonable man could characterize any duly adopted federal rule as "procedural," the Court, unless I misapprehend what is said, would have it apply no matter how seriously it frustrated a State's substantive regulation of the primary conduct and affairs of its citizens. Since the members of the Advisory Committee, the Judicial Conference, and this Court who formulated the Federal Rules are presumably reasonable men, it follows that the integrity of the Federal Rules is absolute. Whereas the unadulterated outcome and forum-shopping tests may err too far towards honoring state rules, I submit that the Court's "arguably procedural, *ergo* constitutional" test moves too fast and far in the other direction.

The courts below relied upon this Court's decisions in Ragan v. Merchants Transfer & Warehouse Co. * * * and Cohen v. Beneficial Indus. Loan Corp. * * *. Those cases deserve more attention than this Court has given them, particularly *Ragan* which, if still good law, would in my opinion call for affirmance of the result reached by the Court of Appeals. * * *

* * * I think that the [*Ragan*] decision was wrong. At most, application of the Federal Rule would have meant that potential Kansas

tort defendants would have to defer for a few days the satisfaction of knowing that they had not been sued within the limitations period. The choice of the Federal Rule would have had no effect on the primary stages of private activity from which torts arise, and only the most minimal effect on behavior following the commission of the tort. In such circumstances the interest of the federal system in proceeding under its own rules should have prevailed.

* * * [A statute like the one in *Cohen*] is not "outcome determinative"; the plaintiff can win with or without it. The Court now rationalizes the case on the ground that the statute might affect the plaintiff's choice of forum * * * but as has been pointed out, a simple forum-shopping test proves too much. The proper view of *Cohen* is in my opinion, that the statute was meant to inhibit small stockholders from instituting "strike suits," and thus it was designed and could be expected to have a substantial impact on private primary activity. Anyone who was at the trial bar during the period when *Cohen* arose can appreciate the strong state policy reflected in the statute. I think it wholly legitimate to view Federal Rule 23 as not purporting to deal with the problem. But even had the Federal Rules purported to do so, and in so doing provided a substantially less effective deterrent to strike suits, I think the state rule should still have prevailed. * * *

It remains to apply what has been said to the present case. * * * The evident intent of [the Massachusetts] statute is to permit an executor to distribute the estate which he is administering without fear that further liabilities may be outstanding for which he could be held personally liable. If the Federal District Court in Massachusetts applies Rule 4(d) (1) of the Federal Rules of Civil Procedure instead of the Massachusetts service rule, what effect would that have on the speed and assurance with which estates are distributed? As I see it, the effect would not be substantial. It would mean simply that an executor would have to check at his own house or the federal courthouse as well as the registry of probate before he could distribute the estate with impunity. As this does not seem enough to give rise to any real impingement on the vitality of the state policy which the Massachusetts rule is intended to serve, I concur in the judgment of the Court.

Notes and Questions

1. How are procedural rules formally included in the Federal Rules of Civil Procedure different from procedural rules adopted by a court on its own? Chief Justice Warren seems to give the Federal Rules of Civil Procedure special status. Why? Reread the Rules Enabling Act and the Rules of Decision Act. How do these statutes interact? Are they consistent? If not, how can the inconsistencies be resolved? Upon which of these two statutes is the holding in *Hanna* based?

2. The distinction between substance and procedure is important in both the Rules Enabling Act and the Rules of Decision Act. The second sentence of the Rules Enabling Act says that no Federal Rule may "abridge, enlarge, or modify any substantive right," and of course the distinction between sub-

stance and procedure is at the core of the line of cases interpreting the Rules of Decision Act. How does Chief Justice Warren treat the distinction between substance and procedure in *Hanna*? How does he define that distinction for purposes of the Rules Enabling Act? For purposes of the Rules of Decision Act? Are the definitions the same?

In SIBBACH v. WILSON & CO., 312 U.S. 1, 61 S.Ct. 422, 85 L.Ed. 479 (1941), plaintiff sued defendant in an Illinois federal district court for damages inflicted in Indiana. The Supreme Court affirmed the District Court's order that plaintiff undergo a physical examination pursuant to Federal Rule 35, despite an Illinois policy forbidding compulsory physical examinations. The Court concluded that the promulgation of Rule 35 was within the ambit of congressional power, since Rule 35 does not "abridge, enlarge, [or] modify substantive rights, in the guise of regulating procedure." Moreover, the Court rejected plaintiff's argument that a rule regulating procedure still could so affect a substantial personal right as to violate the Rules Enabling Act. In an opinion written by Justice Roberts, the Court held:

> * * * If we were to adopt the suggested criterion of the importance of the alleged right we should invite endless litigation and confusion * * *. The test must be whether a rule really regulates procedure—the judicial process for enforcing rights and duties recognized by substantive law and for justly administering remedy and redress for disregard or infraction of them. That the rules in question are such is admitted.

In dissent, Justice Frankfurter maintained that Rule 35, which provides for "the invasion of the person," is quite different from other rules of procedure. He noted, furthermore, that the Rules are effective automatically absent a veto by Congress.

> * * * [T]o draw any inference of tacit approval from non-action by Congress is to appeal to unreality. And so I conclude that to make the drastic change that Rule 35 sought to introduce would require explicit legislation.

Is the distinction in *Sibbach* usable to interpret the distinction between substance and procedure as that distinction is embodied in the Rules of Decision Act?

3. After *Hanna*, did *Byrd* fly away? Is there a new *York* analysis? Is the entire discussion of the *Erie* question in *Hanna* merely dicta?

4. Chief Justice Warren asserts that "the *Erie* rule is rooted in part in a realization that it would be unfair for the character or result of a litigation materially to differ because the suit had been brought in federal court [and] in part a reaction to the practice of forum-shopping." Has he abandoned part of Justice Brandeis' argument in *Erie*? Was not *Erie* based in important part on notions of state and federal relations?

5. What is the effect of *Hanna* on state statutes that close the doors of the state courts to suits by foreign corporations that have not registered to do business in the state? Can the Diversity Clause in Article III of the Constitution be said to exude a federal policy that there be a forum in every state for the protection of foreign corporations? Does anything turn on the nature of the policies underlying the state statute? See Szantay v. Beech Aircraft Corp., 349 F.2d 60 (4th Cir.1965). Compare the earlier decisions in Angel v.

Bullington, 330 U.S. 183, 67 S.Ct. 657, 91 L.Ed. 832 (1947), and Woods v. Interstate Realty Co., p. 358, supra.

6. In MARSHALL v. MULRENIN, 508 F.2d 39 (1st Cir.1974), the First Circuit challenged the Supreme Court's interpretation of the Massachusetts statute applied in *Hanna* and held the Massachusetts rule for amendments changing the party against whom a claim is asserted to be controlling over Federal Rule 15(c). The decision meant that the plaintiff could maintain the action against the substituted defendants even though these defendants had not received actual notice of the institution of the action within the applicable statute of limitations as required by Rule 15(c)(1) and (2) because the Massachusetts rule allows any amendment "which may enable the plaintiff to sustain the action for the cause for which it was intended to be brought." Given *Hanna,* is the *Marshall* decision correct? Can these two cases be explained by the fact that both permitted an adjudication on the merits? For an analysis of *Marshall* and its relationship to *Hanna,* see Comment, *Federal Rules of Civil Procedure—The Erie Doctrine—State Relation-Back Provision Found Controlling Over Rule 15(c)—Marshall v. Mulrenin,* 50 N.Y.U.L.Rev. 952 (1975).

Since *Hanna,* commentators have been attempting to define precisely the test to be used to answer *Erie* questions. Consider the following:

* * * [T]he indiscriminate mixture of all questions respecting choices between federal and state law in diversity cases, under the single rubric of "the Erie doctrine" or "the Erie problem," has served to make a major mystery out of what are really three distinct and rather ordinary problems of statutory and constitutional interpretation. Of course there will be occasions with respect to all three on which reasonable persons will differ, but that does not make the problems mysterious or even very unusual. The United States Constitution, I shall argue, constitutes the relevant text only where Congress has passed a statute creating law for diversity actions, and it is in this situation alone that *Hanna's* "arguably procedural" test controls. Where a nonstatutory rule is involved, the Constitution necessarily remains in the background, but it is functionally irrelevant because the applicable statutes are significantly more protective of the prerogatives of state law. Thus, where there is no relevant Federal Rule of Civil Procedure or other Rule promulgated pursuant to the Enabling Act and the federal rule in issue is therefore wholly judge-made, whether state or federal law should be applied is controlled by the Rules of Decision Act, the statute construed in *Erie* and *York.* Where the matter in issue is covered by a Federal Rule, however, the Enabling Act— and not the Rules of Decision Act itself or the line of cases construing it— constitutes the relevant standard. To say that, however, and that is one of the things *Hanna* said, is by no means to concede the validity of all Federal Rules, for the Enabling Act contains significant limiting language of its own. The Court has correctly sensed that that language cannot be construed to protect state prerogatives as strenuously as the Rules of Decision Act protects them in the absence of a Federal Rule. However, the Court's recent appreciation that the Enabling Act constitutes the only check on the Rules—that "Erie" does not stand there as a backstop—

should lead it in an appropriate case to take the Act's limiting language more seriously than it has in the past.

Ely, *The Irrepressible Myth of Erie,* 87 Harv.L.Rev. 693, 697–98 (1974).

Compare Professor Ely's analysis with the following:

If a valid and pertinent federal rule exists, then of course it applies, notwithstanding any state rule to the contrary. The supremacy clause says so. The real task under *Erie,* therefore, is not to choose between federal law and state law, but rather to decide if there really is a valid federal rule on the issue. * * * [T]he Rules of Decision Act is an explicit grant of authority: It directs the federal courts to apply state law with regard to any issue that is not governed by a pertinent and valid federal rule. It reminds the federal courts that if a valid federal rule exists—whether constitutional, statutory, or judge-made—the federal rule shall govern. * * *

To understand how *Erie* operates in diversity cases, it is important to distinguish between the pertinence of federal rules and their validity. To say a federal rule is "pertinent" means that it was intended or designed to govern the issue at hand—that the rule's purposes would be served by applying it. To say a rule is "valid" means that it has been adopted in conformity with the legal norms controlling the creation of federal law— that it is consistent with the Constitution and other organic statutes regulating the formation of federal law. These combined qualities of pertinence and validity are necessary and sufficient for the proper application of a federal rule: If either quality is absent, a federal rule cannot be lawfully applied; if both are present, the federal rule must be applied.

* * *

Federal rules of civil procedure should be analyzed in the same way as federal statutes, except the rules must satisfy an additional standard of validity. The pertinence analysis is precisely the same for rules as it is for other laws. The court must determine whether the framers of a rule intended that it govern the issue at hand; if so (and if the rule is valid), the rule applies; if not, state law applies.

Weston & Lehman, *Is There Life for Erie After the Death of Diversity?,* 78 Mich.L.Rev. 311, 314–15, 342, 359 (1981).

With these conflicting explanations of *Hanna* in mind, consider the following case:

On August 22, 1975, Fred Walker suffered an injury when a nailhead fragmented and hit his right eye. Later, he sued Armco Steel Corporation, the manufacturer of the nail, alleging that it was defective. His complaint was filed in the Clerk's Office of the United States District Court for the Western District of Oklahoma on August 19, 1977. A summons was issued the next day; but process was not served on Armco until December 1, 1977. Armco filed a motion to dismiss Walker's complaint, asserting that the statute of limitations barred the action. Armco argued that the question was controlled by an Oklahoma statute that required service be carried out within 60 days of date of issuance, provided the summons issued within the limitations period. Although Walker's summons was issued on time, the service was not completed

within 60 days. Therefore, Walker's only hope was that a federal procedural provision would be ruled applicable. He therefore argued that,
pursuant to Federal Rule 3, his action had commenced when he filed his
complaint with the court.

In arguing that the Oklahoma statute controlled, Armco cited the
Supreme Court's decision in Ragan v. Merchants' Transfer & Warehouse
Co., p. 358, supra. In arguing that Rule 3 controlled, Walker cited *Hanna*.
Although it felt constrained to follow *Ragan* until the Supreme Court
expressly overturned it, the Tenth Circuit clearly thought Walker had the
better argument.

> The Supreme Court's decision in *Hanna* * * * gave promise that
> the corner had been turned, so to speak, as far as *Guaranty* and *Ragan*
> continuing to dominate where the question is one of pure procedure such
> as we have here. *Hanna* construed a Massachusetts statute which had
> the same kind of complicated statute with respect to mode of service of
> process as we find here. In *Hanna,* as here, the application of the
> outcome test would have resulted in the state law being applied and in
> the defendant prevailing. In the opinion which was written by Chief
> Justice Warren, the outcome determinative test was rejected and the
> Federal Rules of Civil Procedure were ruled applicable. However, the
> Court in a footnote distinguished *Ragan* even though *Ragan* had applied
> the outcome determinative test which the Court was engaged in rejecting
> at least to the extent that pure procedural questions were being decided.
> The *Hanna* opinion observed that every procedural variation is in fact
> outcome determinative. The Court acknowledged that the outcome deter-
> minative test would have a marked effect on the outcome of litigation
> before it. It said, however, that the test was not to be regarded as a
> talisman. Inasmuch as *Ragan* is based entirely upon the *Guaranty Trust*
> conception that outcome determinative is the answer, the refusal of the
> court to apply this result in the *Hanna* decision is irreconcilable with that
> in *Ragan.*

Walker v. Armco Steel Corp., 592 F.2d 1133, 1135–36 (10th Cir.1979).

When the case reached the Supreme Court, however, the Supreme
Court unanimously reaffirmed its decision in *Ragan*. Justice Marshall,
writing for the Court, observed:

> This Court in *Hanna* distinguished *Ragan* rather than overruled it,
> and for good reason. Application of the *Hanna* analysis is premised on a
> "direct collision" between the Federal Rule and the state law. * * * In
> *Hanna* itself the "clash" between Rule 4(d)(1) and the state in-hand
> service requirement was "unavoidable." * * * The first question must
> therefore be whether the scope of the Federal Rule in fact is sufficiently
> broad to control the issue before the Court. It is only if that question is
> answered affirmatively that the *Hanna* analysis applies.

> * * * There is no indication that * * * Rule [3] was intended to toll a
> state statute of limitations, much less that it purported to displace state
> tolling rules for purposes of state statutes of limitations. In our view, in
> diversity actions Rule 3 governs the date from which various timing
> requirements of the Federal Rules begin to run, but does not affect state
> statutes of limitations. * * *

In contrast to Rule 3, the Oklahoma statute is a statement of a substantive decision by that State that actual service on, and accordingly actual notice by, the defendant is an integral part of the several policies served by the statute of limitations. * * * The statute of limitations establishes a deadline after which the defendant may legitimately have peace of mind; it also recognizes that after a certain period of time it is unfair to require the defendant to attempt to piece together his defense to an old claim. A requirement of actual service promotes both of those functions of the statute. * * * It is these policy aspects which make the service requirement an "integral" part of the statute of limitations both in this case and in *Ragan*. As such, the service rule must be considered part and parcel of the statute of limitations. Rule 3 does not replace such policy determinations found in state law. Rule 3 and [the Oklahoma statute] can exist side by side, therefore, each controlling its own intended sphere of coverage without conflict.

Since there is no direct conflict between the Federal Rule and the state law, the *Hanna* analysis does not apply. Instead, the policies behind *Erie* and *Ragan* control the issue whether, in the absence of a federal rule directly on point, state service requirements which are an integral part of the state statute of limitations should control in an action based on state law which is filed in federal court under diversity jurisdiction. * * *

Walker v. Armco Steel Corp., 446 U.S. 740, 749–52, 100 S.Ct. 1978, 1985–86, 64 L.Ed.2d 659, 667–69 (1980).

Walker v. Armco Steel Corp. is not the final word on the meaning of *Hanna*. In BURLINGTON NORTHERN R. CO. v. WOODS, 480 U.S. 1, 107 S.Ct. 967, 94 L.Ed.2d 1 (1987), Woods had obtained a jury verdict against Burlington Northern in a personal injury action prosecuted in an Alabama federal district court. After the verdict had been affirmed on appeal without modification, the Court of Appeals assessed the penalty (10% of the damages) prescribed by Alabama law for all unsuccessful appeals of money judgments. Burlington Northern objected, arguing that Rule 38 of the Federal Rules of Appellate Procedure controlled the case— and that, under Rule 38, penalties were appropriate only if, in the judgment of the appellate court, the appeal was frivolous.

The Supreme Court held that Rule 38 controlled. Justice Marshall, writing for the Court, reasoned:

In *Hanna* * * * we set forth the appropriate test for resolving conflicts between state law and Federal Rules. The initial step is to determine whether, when fairly construed, the scope of Federal Rule 38 is "sufficiently broad" to cause a "direct collision" with the state law or, implicitly, to "control the issue" before the court, thereby leaving no room for the operation of that law. * * * The Rule must then be applied if it represents a valid exercise of Congress' rule-making authority, which originates in the Constitution and has been bestowed on this Court by the Rules Enabling Act. * * *

* * * Rule 38 affords a Court of Appeals plenary discretion to assess "just damages" in order to penalize an appellant who takes a frivolous appeal and to compensate the injured appellee for the delay and added expense of defending the District Court's judgment. Thus, the

Rule's discretionary mode of operation unmistakably conflicts with the mandatory provision of Alabama's affirmance penalty statute. Moreover, the purposes underlying the Rule are sufficiently co-extensive with the asserted purposes of the Alabama statute to indicate that the Rule occupies the statute's field of operation so as to preclude its application in federal diversity actions.

Petitioner nevertheless argues that, because Alabama has a similar Appellate Rule which may be applied in state court alongside the affirmance penalty statute, * * * a federal court sitting in diversity could impose the mandatory penalty and likewise remain free to exercise its discretionary authority under Federal Rule 38. This argument, however, ignores the significant possibility that a Court of Appeals may, in any given case, find a limited justification for imposing penalties in an amount *less than* 10% of the lower court's judgment. Federal Rule 38 adopts a case-by-case approach to identifying and deterring frivolous appeals; the Alabama statute precludes any exercise of discretion within its scope of operation. Whatever circumscriptive effect the mandatory affirmance penalty statute may have on the state court's exercise of discretion under Alabama's Rule 38, that Rule provides no authority for defining the scope of discretion allowed under Federal Rule 38.

Federal Rule 38 regulates matters which can reasonably be classified as procedural, thereby satisfying the constitutional standard for validity. Its displacement of the Alabama statute also satisfies the statutory constraints of the Rules Enabling Act. The choice made by the drafters of the Federal Rules in favor of a discretionary procedure affects only the process of enforcing litigants' rights and not the rights themselves.

480 U.S. at 4–8, 107 S.Ct. at 969–71, 94 L.Ed.2d at 7–9.

STEWART ORGANIZATION, INC. v. RICOH CORP.

Supreme Court of the United States, 1988.
—— U.S. ——, 108 S.Ct. 2239, 101 L.Ed.2d 22.

Certiorari to the United States Court of Appeals for the Eleventh Circuit.

JUSTICE MARSHALL delivered the opinion of the Court.

This case presents the issue whether a federal court sitting in diversity should apply state or federal law in adjudicating a motion to transfer a case to a venue provided in a contractual forum-selection clause.

I

The dispute underlying this case grew out of a dealership agreement that obligated petitioner, an Alabama corporation, to market copier products of respondent, a nationwide manufacturer with its principal place of business in New Jersey. The agreement contained a forum-selection clause providing that any dispute arising out of the contract could be brought only in a court located in Manhattan. Business relations between the parties soured under circumstances that are not relevant here. In September 1984, petitioner brought a complaint in United States

District Court for the Northern District of Alabama. The core of the complaint was an allegation that respondent had breached the dealership agreement, but petitioner also included claims for breach of warranty, fraud, and antitrust violations.

Relying on the contractual forum-selection clause, respondent moved the District Court either to transfer the case to the Southern District of New York under 28 U.S.C. § 1404(a) or to dismiss the case for improper venue under 28 U.S.C. § 1406. The District Court denied the motion. * * * It reasoned that the transfer motion was controlled by Alabama law and that Alabama looks unfavorably upon contractual forum-selection clauses. The court certified its ruling for interlocutory appeal, * * * and the Court of Appeals for the Eleventh Circuit accepted jurisdiction.

On appeal, a divided panel of the Eleventh Circuit reversed the District Court. The panel concluded that questions of venue in diversity actions are governed by federal law, and that the parties' forum-selection clause was enforceable as a matter of federal law. * * * The panel therefore reversed the order of the District Court and remanded with instructions to transfer the case to a Manhattan court. After petitioner successfully moved for rehearing en banc, the full Court of Appeals proceeded to adopt the result, and much of the reasoning, of the panel opinion. * * * We now affirm under somewhat different reasoning.

II

Both the panel opinion and the opinion of the full Court of Appeals referred to the difficulties that often attend "the sticky question of which law, state or federal, will govern various aspects of the decisions of federal courts sitting in diversity." * * * A District Court's decision whether to apply a federal statute such as § 1404(a) in a diversity action, however, involves a considerably less intricate analysis than that which governs the "relatively unguided *Erie* choice." * * * Our cases indicate that when the federal law sought to be applied is a congressional statute, the first and chief question for the District Court's determination is whether the statute is "sufficiently broad to control the issue before the Court." * * * This question involves a straightforward exercise in statutory interpretation to determine if the statute covers the point in dispute.[4]

If the District Court determines that a federal statute covers the point in dispute, it proceeds to inquire whether the statute represents a valid exercise of Congress' authority under the Constitution. * * * If Congress intended to reach the issue before the District Court, and if it enacted its intention into law in a manner that abides with the Constitution, that is the end of the matter; "[f]ederal courts are bound to apply

---

4. Our cases at times have referred to the question at this stage of the analysis as an inquiry into whether there is a "direct collision" between state and federal law. * * * Logic indicates, however, and a careful reading of the relevant passages confirms, that this language is not meant to mandate that federal law and state law be perfectly coextensive and equally applicable to the issue at hand; rather, the "direct collision" language, at least where the applicability of a federal statute is at issue, expresses the requirement that the federal statute be sufficiently broad to cover the point in dispute. * * * It would make no sense for the supremacy of federal law to wane precisely because there is no state law directly on point.

rules enacted by Congress with respect to matters * * * over which it has legislative power" * * *.[6] Thus, a District Court sitting in diversity must apply a federal statute that controls the issue before the court and that represents a valid exercise of Congress' constitutional powers.

III

Applying the above analysis to this case persuades us that federal law, specifically 28 U.S.C. § 1404, governs the parties' venue dispute. * * *

B

* * * Under the analysis outlined above, we first consider whether § 1404(a) is sufficiently broad to control the issue before the court. That issue is whether to transfer the case to a court in Manhattan in accordance with the forum-selection clause. We believe that the statute, fairly construed, does cover the point in dispute.

Section 1404(a) is intended to place discretion in the District Court to adjudicate motions for transfer according to an "individualized, case-by-case consideration of convenience and fairness." * * * A motion to transfer under § 1404(a) thus calls on the District Court to weigh in the balance a number of case-specific factors. The presence of a forum-selection clause such as the parties entered into in this case will be a significant factor that figures centrally in the District Court's calculus. In its resolution of the § 1404(a) motion in this case, for example, the District Court will be called on to address such issues as the convenience of a Manhattan forum given the parties' expressed preference for that venue, and the fairness of transfer in light of the forum selection clause and the parties' relative bargaining power. The flexible and individualized analysis Congress prescribed in § 1404(a) thus encompasses consideration of the parties' private expression of their venue preferences.

Section 1404(a) may not be the only potential source of guidance for the District Court to consult in weighing the parties' private designation of a suitable forum. The premise of the dispute between the parties is that Alabama law may refuse to enforce forum-selection clauses providing for out-of-state venues as a matter of state public policy. If that is so, the District Court will have either to integrate the factor of the forum-selection clause into its weighing of considerations as prescribed by Congress, or else to apply, as it did in this case, Alabama's categorical policy disfavoring forum-selection clauses. Our cases make clear that, as between these two choices in a single "field of operation," * * * the instructions of Congress are supreme. * * *

It is true that § 1404(a) and Alabama's putative policy regarding forum-selection clauses are not perfectly coextensive. Section 1404(a) directs a District Court to take account of factors other than those that

---

6. If no federal statute or Rule covers the point in dispute, the District Court then proceeds to evaluate whether application of federal judge-made law would disserve the so-called "twin aims of the *Erie* rule: discouragement of forum-shopping and avoid- ance of inequitable administration of the laws." * * * If application of federal judge-made law would disserve these two policies, the District Court should apply state law. * * *

bear solely on the parties' private ordering of their affairs. The District Court also must weigh in the balance the convenience of the witnesses and those public-interest factors of systemic integrity and fairness that, in addition to private concerns, come under the heading of "the interest of justice." It is conceivable in a particular case, for example, that because of these factors a District Court acting under § 1404(a) would refuse to transfer a case notwithstanding the counterweight of a forum-selection clause, whereas the coordinate state rule might dictate the opposite result. * * * But this potential conflict in fact frames an additional argument for the supremacy of federal law. Congress has directed that multiple considerations govern transfer within the federal court system, and a state policy focusing on a single concern or a subset of the factors identified in § 1404(a) would defeat that command. Its application would impoverish the flexible and multifaceted analysis that Congress intended to govern motions to transfer within the federal system. The forum-selection clause, which represents the parties' agreement as to the most proper forum, should receive neither dispositive consideration (as respondent might have it) nor no consideration (as Alabama law might have it), but rather the consideration for which Congress provided in § 1404(a). * * * This is thus not a case in which state and federal rules "can exist side by side * * * each controlling its own intended sphere of coverage without conflict." * * *

Because section 1404(a) controls the issue before the District Court, it must be applied if it represents a valid exercise of Congress's authority under the Constitution. The constitutional authority of Congress to enact section 1404(a) is not subject to serious question. As the Court made plain in *Hanna*, "the constitutional provision for a federal court system * * * carries with it congressional power to make rules governing the practice and pleading in those courts, which in turn includes a power to regulate matters which, though falling within the uncertain area between substance and procedure, are rationally capable of classification as either." * * * Section 1404(a) is doubtless capable of classification as a procedural rule, and indeed, we have so classified it in holding that a transfer pursuant to § 1404(a) does not carry with it a change in the applicable law. * * * It therefore falls comfortably within Congress's powers under Article III as augmented by the Necessary and Proper Clause. * * *

We hold that federal law, specifically 28 U.S.C. § 1404(a), governs the District Court's decision whether to give effect to the parties' forum-selection clause and transfer this case to a court in Manhattan. * * * The case is remanded so that the District Court may determine in the first instance the appropriate effect under federal law of the parties' forum-selection clause on respondent's § 1404(a) motion.

It is so ordered.

SECTION B. THE PROBLEM OF ASCERTAINING STATE LAW

1. DETERMINING WHICH STATE'S LAW GOVERNS

In *Erie,* the parties—and the courts—appear to have assumed that if state law applied, Pennsylvania tort law would govern—even though the action was being tried in a federal court in New York. Why did they make this assumption? Was the federal court free to choose the most appropriate state law to govern the dispute? Or was it that New York's choice-of-law rules pointed to an application of Pennsylvania law?

———

KLAXON CO. v. STENTOR ELECTRIC MFG. CO., 313 U.S. 487, 61 S.Ct. 1020, 85 L.Ed. 1477 (1941). The Supreme Court held that in order to promote the desired uniform application of substantive law within a state, federal courts must apply the conflicts-of-laws rules of the states in which they sit. The Court explained:

> * * * Whatever lack of uniformity this may produce between federal courts in different states is attributable to our federal system, which leaves to a state, within the limits permitted by the Constitution, the right to pursue local policies diverging from those of its neighbors. It is not for the federal courts to thwart such local policies by enforcing an independent "general law" of conflict of laws. * * * [T]he proper function of [a] federal court is to ascertain what the state law is, not what it ought to be.

Id. at 496–97, 61 S.Ct. at 1022, 85 L.Ed. at 1480–81.

Notes and Questions

1. Could Congress enact a statute specifying choice-of-law rules for federal courts in diversity cases? In answering this question, remember that, although it is true today that every state contains at least one federal judicial district, there is no constitutional provision that compels this. What if Congress had established only regional courts? Under such a scheme, would Congress or the courts have been forced to establish their own choice-of-law rules?

2. The states have been allowed great leeway in establishing choice-of-law rules. In ALLSTATE INS. CO. v. HAGUE, pp. 106–07, supra, the Supreme Court held that a state could apply its substantive law in a case, so long as the state had significant contacts or a significant aggregation of contacts with the parties and the transaction. Doesn't *Hague* encourage plaintiffs to forum shop and *Klaxon* seal the defendant's fate?

3. If a diversity case is transferred under 28 U.S.C. § 1404(a), what law should the transferee court apply? Does it matter whether the plaintiff or the defendant moved to transfer? In VAN DUSEN v. BARRACK, 376 U.S. 612, 639, 84 S.Ct. 805, 820, 821, 11 L.Ed.2d 945, 962–63 (1964), defendants sought to transfer the action from federal court in Pennsylvania to federal court in Massachusetts, where the state law was more favorable to their case. The Supreme Court rejected a wooden reading of *Erie,* which would require the

transferee court to apply the law of the state in which it sits—that is, Massachusetts law. Rather, the Court determined that the "critical identity" is between the federal court that decides the case and the courts of the state in which the action was filed. According to the Court: "A change of venue under § 1404(a) generally should be, with respect to state law, but a change of courtrooms."

The Court speaks of not letting the "accident" of federal diversity jurisdiction affect the outcome of the lawsuit. Yet, it appears that *Van Dusen* makes it possible for a suit to be filed in federal court in one state and then transferred to a different state with the result that the law applied will differ from the law that would have applied if the suit had been filed initially in the transferee court. Isn't the real policy behind *Van Dusen* simply to prevent the defendant from forum shopping?

4. Which court's law should apply if a plaintiff seeks a transfer of venue? In CARSON v. U–HAUL CO., 434 F.2d 916 (6th Cir.1970), the plaintiff transferred the action from federal court in Georgia to federal court in Kentucky. At the time the suit was brought, the action was time barred in Kentucky, but not in Georgia. The court held that, after transfer, Kentucky became the new forum state and that its statute of limitations controlled.

2. ASCERTAINING THE STATE LAW
McKENNA v. ORTHO PHARMACEUTICAL CORP.
United States Court of Appeals, Third Circuit, 1980.
622 F.2d 657, certiorari denied 449 U.S. 976, 101 S.Ct. 387, 66 L.Ed.2d 237.

ADAMS, CIRCUIT JUDGE.

* * *

I.

James and Sondra McKenna brought this suit for negligence, misrepresentation, and products liability against Ortho Pharmaceutical Corporation (Ortho). The plaintiffs charged that Mrs. McKenna suffered severe personal injury and permanent disability as a result of ingesting Ortho-Novum, an oral contraceptive manufactured and marketed by Ortho. * * * [I]n March 1972, she suffered a catastrophic cerebrovascular stroke that left her severely and permanently paralyzed.

One year and nine months thereafter, in November 1973, the McKennas commenced this action in a Pennsylvania state court by a praecipe for a writ of trespass.[2] On Ortho's motion, the suit was removed to the federal district court in Pittsburgh, where it was ultimately tried. * * *

Prior to trial, the district court denied Ortho's motion for summary judgment on the ground that a genuine issue of material fact existed as to whether the McKennas knew, or reasonably should have known, more than two years prior to the commencement of the suit, that Mrs. McKenna's injuries resulted from the ingestion of Ortho-Novum. During the four weeks of jury trial, the McKennas introduced expert witnesses who

---

2. The district court noted that inasmuch as the plaintiffs' counsel is a Pittsburgh attorney, "it was natural" that suit was brought in Pennsylvania.

testified that the cerebrovascular stroke was the ultimate result of either vessel-wall damage or high blood pressure, and that both of these conditions, as well as the headaches and transient ischemia attacks, were caused by Mrs. McKenna's ingestion of Ortho-Novum. At the close of trial, but prior to submission of the case to the jury, the district court granted Ortho's motion for a directed verdict on the ground that the action was barred under Ohio's statute of limitations. The district court concluded that the Ohio statute began to run, at the latest, in 1969 when Mrs. McKenna developed high blood pressure, and that the cause of action was accordingly barred because it was filed more than two years after that time. It is this conclusion that we review here.

II.

Although Pennsylvania courts ordinarily apply the statute of limitations of the forum state,[3] the Pennsylvania "borrowing statute" in effect when the case was tried provided a statutory exception to this rule. It declared:

> When a cause of action has been fully barred by the law of the state in which it arose, such bar shall be a complete defense to an action thereon in any of the courts of this Commonwealth.

The district court, in granting Ortho's motion for a directed verdict, reasoned that the Pennsylvania statute borrowed not only Ohio's two-year limitations period, but also Ohio's law governing the determination when the cause of action arises. In their appeal, the McKennas contend that this was error; they argue that even though the Pennsylvania statute "borrows" the law of Ohio regarding the length of the applicable limitations period, the question when that limitations period begins to run must be determined not by Ohio but by Pennsylvania law.

* * *

We are persuaded, rather, that the apparent purpose of the Pennsylvania "borrowing statute" requires us to look to the law of the state where the cause of action arose to determine not only the prescribed period of limitations but also the point at which the statute begins to run. By its terms, the "borrowing statute" bars a plaintiff from suing in Pennsylvania "when [the] cause of action has been fully barred by the laws of the state * * * in which it arose * * *." In our view, the essential question posed under the "borrowing statute" is whether the action in question is precluded by the laws of the state in which it accrued, and the answer to that question also must be based on the law of the state in which the claim arose. To do otherwise might well revive an action which is "fully barred by the laws" of another state. Accordingly, because the McKennas' cause of action arose in Ohio, we must look to Ohio law to determine when Ohio's statute of limitations commenced to run. And the question for decision, then, is whether Ohio's statute of limitations commenced to run prior to the date Mrs. McKenna knew, or

3. * * * Inasmuch as all of the significant events pertinent to this action occurred in Ohio, it is not disputed that the cause of action arose in Ohio and that under Pennsylvania's conflict of law rules * * * the substantive law of Ohio governs this action.

reasonably should have discovered, that her injuries were caused by Ortho-Novum.

III.

Given that Ohio law governs the question for decision, the task remains to determine what the pertinent Ohio law is and then to apply it to this controversy. The question of how a federal court is to ascertain and apply state decisional law to a particular case has provoked considerable comment from courts and commentators alike. As some have noted, the concept that a federal court must determine state law is somewhat misleading inasmuch as it implies the existence of a readily accessible and easily understood body of state law. On the contrary, the law of a state is frequently "dynamic rather than static," and consists of a working body of rules, which find expression in a number of sources. It is this working body of rules to which a federal court must look in order to ascertain the state law that governs in a particular case.

In those few instances in which the highest state court has recently spoken to the precise question at issue in a particular setting, the duty of the federal court to determine and apply state law is easily met. After all, "[t]he State's highest court is the best authority on its own law." The problem of ascertainment arises when, as here, the highest state court has not yet authoritatively addressed the critical issue. Recent opinions of this Court make clear that our disposition of such cases must be governed by a prediction of how the state's highest court would decide were it confronted with the problem. Although some have characterized this assignment as speculative or crystal-ball gazing, nonetheless it is a task which we may not decline.

An accurate forecast of Ohio's law, as it would be expressed by its highest court, requires an examination of all relevant sources of that state's law in order to isolate those factors that would inform its decision. The primary source that must be analyzed of course, is the decisional law of the Ohio Supreme Court. In the absence of authority directly on point, decisions by that court in analogous cases provide useful indications of the court's probable disposition of a particular question of law. * * * In determining state law, a federal tribunal should be careful to avoid the "danger" of giving "a state court decision a more binding effect than would a court of that state under similar circumstances." Rather, relevant state precedents must be scrutinized with an eye toward the broad policies that informed those adjudications, and to the doctrinal trends which they evince.

Considered dicta by the state's highest court may also provide a federal court with reliable indicia of how the state tribunal might rule on a particular question. * * * [H]owever, a federal court should be circumspect in surrendering its own judgment concerning what the state law is on account of dicta. * * * Of somewhat less importance to a prognostication of what the highest state court will do are decisions of lower state courts and other federal courts. Such decisions should be accorded "proper regard" of course, but not conclusive effect. Thus, the Supreme Court has held that although the decision of a lower state court "should be 'attributed some weight * * * the decision [is] not controlling * * *' where the highest court of the State has not spoken on the point. * * * Thus, under some conditions, federal authority may not be bound even by an intermediate state appellate court ruling." Additionally, federal courts may consider scholarly treatises, the Restatement of Law, and germane law review articles * * *.

IV.

In support of its conclusion that Ohio's statutes of limitation bar the McKennas' actions, the district court relied, as does the dissent here, primarily on Wyler v. Tripi,[31] decided nine years ago by the Ohio Supreme Court. The central dispute in that case concerned the date on which a cause of action for medical malpractice accrued. Expressly following the rule announced in a series of prior decisions, *Wyler* held that the cause of action came into existence at the latest, at the time the physician-patient relationship terminated, and not when the plaintiff discovered the injury.

The "termination of treatment" concept was developed very early in Ohio law as an exception to the traditional rule that statutes of limitation commenced to run at the time an individual sustained injury as the result of the tortious act of another. It was designed, as the *Wyler* court observed, "to avoid the harsh results of the traditional rule" by tolling the applicable statute of limitations until the conclusion of the physician-patient relationship. Although this doctrine represents a "marked departure from the general rule," it "affords little relief in cases where the injury is one which requires a long developmental period before becoming dangerous and discoverable." * * *

It was this kind of issue with which the Ohio Supreme Court was confronted in *Wyler*. The plaintiff there alleged that improper treatment by her physician ultimately resulted in the manifestation of asceptic necrosis, necessitating the replacement of her hip and the subsequent removal of her leg. Because the plaintiff failed to discover the alleged negligence within a year after she left the care of her physician, application of either the traditional rule or the "termination of treatment" exception would not prevent what the *Wyler* majority itself termed "the unconscionable result that the injured party's right to recovery can be barred by the statute of limitations before [s]he is even aware of its existence." Troubled by this result, the Ohio court examined the laws of various jurisdictions and the growing trend away from the traditional rule and towards adoption of the discovery rule. According to this approach, the statute of limitations does not begin to run until the plaintiff actually discovers, or with due diligence should have discovered, the negligence alleged.

Although the court's examination of the cases persuaded it that "there is much to recommend the adoption of the discovery rule," a bare majority nonetheless "reluctantly conclud[ed]" that "the courts of Ohio should not decree such an adoption." The sole justification for refusing to

31. 25 Ohio St.2d 164, 267 N.E.2d 419 (1971).

adopt the discovery rule was that such action should be left to the legislature. * * * Referring to the legislature's failure to adopt the discovery rule by legislation, the court concluded: "In consideration of the obvious and repeated disinclination of the General Assembly to amend its malpractice statute of limitations, we are compelled to adhere to our former decisions on the question and refrain from judicially adopting that which has so clearly been legislatively rejected."

Notwithstanding this extensive pronouncement of the court's position, this same court during the following year employed the discovery rule in Melnyk v. Cleveland Clinic.[43] The plaintiff there alleged that a physician employed by the Clinic had negligently left a metallic forceps and a nonabsorbent sponge in his abdomen. Even though the plaintiff failed to discover the negligence until more than one year after he left the care of the physician, the Ohio Supreme Court refused to bar his action, and held that the applicable one-year statute of limitations was tolled "until such time as the patient discovers, or by exercise of reasonable diligence should have discovered, the negligent act."

* * *

Melnyk's implicit rejection of the Wyler rationale—that only the state legislature may properly decide whether to apply the discovery rule—appears well justified. * * * The legislature left unresolved when a cause of action arises and when the statute commences to run. And, in Ohio, these kinds of determinations have always been the product of "judicial interpretation, not legislative promulgation." Consequently, application of the discovery rule to the facts of this case in no way intrudes on the authority of the state legislature. * * *

* * * [T]he Ohio Supreme Court in Melnyk distinguished its decision in Wyler as speaking only to the question of when a cause of action arises, and not to the determination whether the running of the statute of limitations is, for some reason, tolled. It then proceeded to hold that the running of the statute of limitations on Melnyk's cause of action was tolled until such time as he discovered, or by the exercise of reasonable diligence should have discovered, the negligent act, even though his cause of action accrued, under Wyler, at the termination of the patient-physician relationship. On this analysis, the holding in Wyler determines only when the McKennas' cause of action accrued; it is inapposite to the question whether the action was tolled until such time as the McKennas could know how Mrs. McKenna's injuries occurred.

It is claimed, nonetheless, that "Melnyk does not overrule Wyler," but "merely carves out a very specific and narrow exception" to the termination rule when, as in that case, surgical instruments are left in a patient's body. For this reason, the dissent would not apply the discovery rule to the circumstances of this case. In its view, we are improperly modifying a "decadent" and "unenlightened" doctrine of state law simply because we disagree with it. On the contrary, however, we fully recognize our responsibility to accurately apply the pertinent Ohio law. Indeed, we do

43. 32 Ohio St.2d 198, 290 N.E.2d 916 (1972).

not dispute that federal courts must faithfully adhere to state substantive law in non-federal matters. But, as commentators have emphasized, such adherence should be wise and discerning. This Court has noted only recently that "while a federal diversity court must not fashion a wholly independent federal standard with which to determine matters of substantive right, it likewise must not conceive of its role as applying the state decisional law to the case at hand in a narrow and mechanical fashion." Rather, a federal court must "be sensitive to the doctrinal trends of the state whose law it applies, and the policies which inform the prior adjudications by the state courts."

In our view, the Ohio Supreme Court's decision in *Melnyk* not only abandoned the sole justification proffered for its opposition in *Wyler* to the adoption of the discovery rule, but also manifested a recognition that this approach alone avoids the harsh and inequitable results of applying the traditional rule in such cases. * * * A fair scrutiny of the relevant Ohio precedents, with an eye toward the principles and policies underlying them, strongly indicates that the Ohio Supreme Court would extend the discovery rule set forth in *Melnyk* to include the type of personal injury action present here.

The task of a federal court sitting in diversity is often difficult, for it must forsake its own expertise and assume that of the foreign state. Required as we are to predict how the Ohio Supreme Court would decide the present case, however, we believe that the Court would hold that the applicable statutes of limitation in this case were tolled until the McKennas knew, or by the exercise of reasonable diligence should have discovered, the cause of Mrs. McKenna's injuries. Accordingly, we reverse the judgment of the district court, and remand for further proceedings consistent with this opinion.

SUPPLEMENTAL OPINION SUR THE DENIAL OF THE PETITION FOR REHEARING

ADAMS, CIRCUIT JUDGE.

Shortly after the opinions in this matter were filed, Counsel for Ortho Pharmaceutical Corporation brought to the attention of the Court the fact that the Governor of Ohio on March 13, 1980, signed into law a bill amending § 2305.10 of the Ohio Rev. Code. * * *

Prior to the amendment in question, § 2305.10 required that an action for bodily injury "shall be brought within two years after the cause thereof arose." Regarding the question *when* a cause of action arises, however the statute was silent. In amending this provision, the legislature specifically stipulated that a cause of action for bodily injury caused by exposure to asbestos or to chromium arises upon the date on which the plaintiff is informed or reasonably should have become aware that he was injured by the exposure.

Ortho argues that this amendment represents a clear legislative pronouncement that the "Ohio courts are to apply a discovery rule in the two enumerated categories of cases and none other."

* * * In our view, the cautious and more reasonable construction of the amendment, a[s] [sic] well as the one we believe the Ohio Supreme Court would embrace, is that it was not meant to preclude judicial adoption of the discovery rule in appropriate circumstances. Adoption of the contrary construction would effectively abrogate that court's well-established principle, expressly reaffirmed in Wyler v. Tripi, * * * that a cause of action for medical malpractice arises, at the latest, when the physician-patient relationship terminates. We believe the Ohio Supreme Court would hold that if the legislature had intended, by its passage of this amendment, not merely to extend greater protection to victims of asbestos and chromium poisoning but at the same time to deprive victims of medical malpractice of the protection they currently enjoy under the Ohio Supreme Court's decisional law, it would have done so expressly and not by implication.

Even if the amendment to § 2305.10 does—by indicating specifically when a cause of action arises in cases of asbestos or chromium poisoning— effectively establish just when a cause of action must arise in all other cases, however, that would not affect our decision here. * * * [W]e held that the Ohio Supreme Court would decide that the applicable statutes of limitation were tolled until the McKenna's knew, or by the exercise of reasonable diligence should have discovered, the cause of Mrs. McKenna's injuries. In so doing, we expressly followed the distinction drawn by the Ohio Supreme Court in *Melnyk* between the question *when* a cause of action arises and the determination *whether* the statute of limitations may, for some reason, be tolled on such action. Since the amendment at issue, even if it implicates the question when a cause of action for bodily injury from birth control pills arises, does not affect the determination whether the statute of limitations respecting that action may be tolled, we adhere to our prior opinion.

JUDGE HUNTER joins in this opinion.

A. LEON HIGGINBOTHAM, JR., CIRCUIT JUDGE, dissenting.

* * *

Ohio courts have long held that the plaintiff's inability to discover the tortious act of the defendant has no relevance to the running of the applicable statute of limitations. * * * This doctrine was reaffirmed by the Ohio Supreme Court in Wyler v. Tripi in 1971 and applied to medical malpractice actions. In Wyler v. Tripi, the court rejected an explicit request of the plaintiff to overrule that harsh precedent. * * *

In spite of this explicit statement the majority declines to follow *Wyler.* It argues that the *Wyler* rationale would be abandoned in a 1980 decision of the Ohio Supreme Court and thus it feels free to include the discovery rule in its decision. I do not agree. None of the materials the majority cites persuades me that an abandonment of the *Wyler* rationale is in the wind, nor have I unearthed any materials that foretell such an event.

The primary source of the majority's view is Melnyk v. The Cleveland Clinic, * * * a decision of the Ohio Supreme Court, decided one year after *Wyler.* * * *

Melnyk does not overrule *Wyler*; it merely carves out a very specific and narrow exception: when surgical instruments are left in a patient's body a discovery period tolls the running of the statute of limitations. The *Melnyk* court did not "abando[n] the rationale" of *Wyler* when it created this exception. * * * The court held that the case before it did not disturb the legislative judgment. Justice Herbert noted that the limitations period in most malpractice cases reflected a balancing of the interests of physicians and patients and that the Ohio legislature had struck the balance in favor of physicians because of the difficulties of proof in most malpractice cases. The court argued that in a "foreign-objects" case the plaintiff's proof of the physician's negligence, once the existence of the foreign object was established, was irrefutable, and therefore the court felt free to include a discovery period in the "foreign objects" cases. * * * The *Melnyk* court carefully noted that it did not "need to disturb the holding in *Wyler*, nor interfere in the affairs of our sister branch government, in order to accord this rule of law the viability we have determined it must have." * * *

Finally, I am convinced that the majority reading of the *Melnyk* decision is incorrect because every state or federal court decision in Ohio on this question has rejected that reading, * * * including those courts that have considered claims for injuries allegedly resulting from birth control pills. * * *

Notes and Questions

1. Judge Adams quoted the Supreme Court in Commissioner v. Bosch's Estate, 387 U.S. 456, 87 S.Ct. 1776, 18 L.Ed.2d 886 (1967), for the proposition that decisions of lower state courts, although entitled to some weight, do not control a federal diversity court's reading of state law. Does such a rule invite a federal judge to circumvent the rule in *Erie?* If intermediate state courts consistently reach the same conclusion on a matter of state law and the state's highest court has not addressed the issue, should not a federal court be obligated to find that the intermediate state courts have determined accurately what the state law is?

Many states' highest courts, like the United States Supreme Court, have considerable descretion in deciding which cases to hear. Should not a federal court view the state's highest court's refusal to hear those cases as an implicit acknowledgement that the lower courts have articulated the state law accurately?

2. Should a federal court sitting in diversity jurisdiction accord an *unreported* state decision any weight? Would a federal court be bound by a state statute that provided: "Only such cases as are hereafter reported in accordance with the provisions of this section shall be recognized by and receive the official sanction of any court within the state"? See Gustin v. Sun Life Assur. Co., 154 F.2d 961 (6th Cir.), certiorari denied 328 U.S. 866, 66 S.Ct. 1374, 90 L.Ed. 1636 (1946).

3. What should a federal court do when the courts of the state in which it is sitting have not considered the particular problem before the federal court? Should it stay its own proceeding and allow the litigants to seek a declaratory judgment from a state court? See United Services Life Ins. Co. v.

Delaney, 328 F.2d 483 (5th Cir.1964). What problems are created by such a procedure? See Agata, *Delaney, Diversity and Delay: Abstention or Abdication?,* 4 Houston L.Rev. 422 (1966). May a federal diversity court refuse to accept jurisdiction over such a case? See Meredith v. City of Winter Haven, 320 U.S. 228, 64 S.Ct. 7, 88 L.Ed. 9 (1943); Daily v. Parker, 152 F.2d 174 (7th Cir.1945).

4. Several states have adopted certification procedures that permit federal courts to petition a state's highest court to rule on an issue of state law upon which the state's highest court has not spoken. Illinois Supreme Court Rule 20, which is set forth in your Supplement, is representative of such statutes. What is the interrelationship between the *Erie* doctrine and such a rule? If the state's highest court may choose not to answer a certified question, may a federal court choose not to employ this procedure? If the rule required the state court to answer such questions, would a federal court be required to resort to this procedure every time it was applicable?

5. In POMERANTZ v. CLARK, 101 F.Supp. 341, 345–46 (D.Mass.1951), a diversity action by policyholders against directors of an insurance company to retrieve for the company certain sums allegedly improvidently and illegally loaned, Judge Wyzanski held that no action was maintainable under Massachusetts law and stated:

> In considering whether ＊ ＊ ＊ [to create] an exception to the Massachusetts rule that before bringing a derivative suit a member must first lay his case before the body of members, the never-to-be-forgotten caution is that this Court is not free to render such decision as seems to it equitable, just and in accordance with public policy and responsive to all those jurisprudential criteria which so often enter into what Justice Cardozo called "The Nature of the Judicial Process." A federal judge sitting in a diversity jurisdiction case has not a roving commission to do justice or to develop the law according to his, or what he believes to be the sounder, views. His problem is less philosophical and more psychological. His task is to divine the views of the state court judges. ＊ ＊ ＊

> The eminence of the Massachusetts Supreme Judicial Court, an eminence not surpassed by any American tribunal, is in large measure due to its steadiness, learning and understanding of the durable values long prized in this community. Subtle variations and blurred lines are not characteristic of that court. Principles are announced and adhered to in broad magisterial terms. The emphasis is on precedent and adherence to the older ways, not on creating new causes of action or encouraging the use of novel judicial remedies that have sprung up in less conservative communities. Here abides the ancient faith in the right of men to choose their own associates, make their own arrangements, govern themselves and thus grow in responsibility without much in the way of either hindrance or help from the state. This basic philosophy permeates the Massachusetts rules governing derivative suits ＊ ＊ ＊.

Compare Judge Friendly's observation in Nolan v. Transocean Air Lines, 276 F.2d 280, 281 (2d Cir.1960): "Our principal task, in this diversity of citizenship case, is to determine what the New York courts would think the California courts would think on an issue about which neither has thought." See generally 19 Wright, Miller & Cooper, *Federal Practice and Procedure: Jurisdiction and Related Matters* § 4507 (1982).

6. Judge Adams wrote in *McKenna* that, when a state's highest court has not directly addressed a particular legal question, a federal court may analyze that state court's decisions in analogous areas to determine the state court's "probable disposition" of the legal question at issue. Suppose, however that recent personnel changes in the state court give a federal court strong reason to believe that older, yet still valid, decisions from analogous areas no longer are adequate indicators. Suppose further that the federal judge believes nonetheless that the best rule is provided by the law previously announced in the analogous areas. How should the federal judge interpret the state law?

7. In FACTORS ETC., INC. v. PRO ARTS, INC., 652 F.2d 278 (2d Cir. 1981), certiorari denied 456 U.S. 927, 102 S.Ct. 1973, 72 L.Ed.2d 442 (1982), a federal court sitting in New York was required to apply Tennessee law to the question of whether Elvis Presley's right of publicity survived his death. Tennessee state courts had never addressed that issue, but the Sixth Circuit (the circuit encompassing Tennessee) had decided a similar case. The Second Circuit held that the District Court, in such a circumstance, was bound by the Sixth Circuit's view of Tennessee law. The court reasoned that the Sixth Circuit was more familiar with Tennessee law since it frequently was required to interpret Tennessee law.

The dissent argued that there was no reason to follow the Sixth Circuit's views when they were not derived from the laws or decisions of the state. Since the Sixth Circuit was only espousing what it considered the preferable common-law rule, its decision should be accorded no greater deference than that given to any circuit court's views. The dissent also pointed out that, considering the physical size of the circuit and the relatively small number of diversity cases appealed to the court, the Sixth Circuit was unlikely to have any special familiarity with Tennessee law.

Which position is correct? Or are both incorrect in that the relevant question is not what Tennessee's law is, but, rather, what would a New York state court think that Tennessee's law is? If the relevant view is that of a New York state court, is it not likely that, in the absence of a Tennessee precedent, New York would find a way to justify using New York's rule on the issue? See Note, *Circuit Court of Appeals Must Accord Conclusive Deference to Another Circuit: Factors Etc., Inc. v. Pro Arts, Inc.*, 67 Cornell L.Rev. 415 (1982).

By the time the District Court heard the case on remand from the Second Circuit, a Tennessee court had addressed the issue. Accordingly, the District Court applied the Tennessee court's holding to the facts of the case. See 562 F.Supp. 304 (S.D.N.Y.1983).

8. Mass tort disasters easily can become unmanageable for a federal court sitting in diversity. Should a federal court, in the interest of judicial economy, develop one general law to cover the situation? Would it have the authority under either Article III or statute to do so?

In IN RE "AGENT ORANGE" PRODUCT LIABILITY LITIGATION, 580 F.Supp. 690 (E.D.N.Y.1984), the court considered the problem of a nationwide tort disaster involving veterans from all over the country who alleged injury resulting from the use of toxic defoliants in Viet Nam. It concluded that every state court that would have adjudicated an Agent Orange class action involving plaintiffs from many states would have decided that a national rule of decision would have been adopted by all other state courts adjudicating this type of case. The need for a uniform rule of decision, the unique relationship between the United States and its servicemen, and the special relationship between the United States and its defense would have compelled such adoption.

* * * [A] state court passing on the claims of an individual or a group of veterans might well recognize the unfairness in treating differently legally identical claims involving servicemen who fought a difficult foreign war shoulder-to-shoulder and were exposed to virtually identical risks. As the Supreme Court stated in a related context, because "the Armed Services perform a unique, nationwide function in protecting the security of the United States," it makes "little sense for the Government's liability to members of the Armed Services [to be] dependent on the fortuity of where the soldier happened to be stationed at the time of his injury." * * *

It quickly becomes apparent that it is impossible through sensible application of Restatement (Second) choice of law doctrine or analysis to identify the interest of any one state as being sufficiently greater than that of any others to a degree sufficient to justify the application of that state's law in resolving the issues in this litigation. Any narrow and mechanical state choice of law system simply collapses under the weight of the multiplicity of contacts, policies and unarticulated or conflicting state interests in this unique case. A state court, therefore, because of its inability to identify and select any other state's law to be applied as the rule of decision and because of the need for uniformity across the country, would seek to divine what the national rule of decision with regard to product liability law would be so that such law would appropriately reflect the national and international characteristics of this case. By contrast, the application of an individual state's law rather than a federal law or a national consensus law would be irrational and unfair.

* * *

The policies of the United States, broadly speaking, parallel the states': on the one hand, it has a policy of compensating servicemen who are injured in the course of military service. On the other hand, there is the policy expressed by the government contract defense of insulating defense contractors who merely produced military equipment according to the specifications set forth by the government. * * * How the balance should be struck in this case between those two conflicting policies need not be decided at this point. What is important is that these federal policies are far more specific than those of the states and the national interest in this litigation is far greater than that of any individual state.

* * *

580 F.Supp. at 703.

SECTION C. FEDERAL "COMMON LAW"

1. THE TRADITIONAL BASES OF FEDERAL COMMON LAW

MELTZER, STATE COURT FORFEITURES OF FEDERAL RIGHTS

99 Harv.L.Rev. 1128, 1167–71 (1986).

Despite *Erie*'s declaration that "[t]here is no federal general common law," courts have fashioned what Judge Friendly has termed "specialized federal common law" to govern a broad range of areas. Unlike the "spurious" federal common law of the era of Swift v. Tyson, this new federal common law is binding under the supremacy clause in the state courts.

The proper scope of federal common lawmaking is a matter of considerable uncertainty. If *Erie* held that federal court jurisdiction does not in itself provide the power to fashion common law, then some more specialized source must be found for each example of judicial lawmaking. The lawmaking power of federal courts has been viewed as far more limited than that of Congress, for two reasons extrapolated from the constitutional structure. The first is the idea of separation of powers and the supremacy (in matters not governed by the Constitution) of Congress. But perhaps more important is the view that federal law is and should be interstitial, operating against a background of existing bodies of state law. Restricted federal common lawmaking reduces the number of agencies broadly fashioning federal rules of decision, and preserves the primary role for Congress, in which the interests of the states are more strongly represented—and in which inertia is more powerful. Hence, state law is presumptively operative, and if it is to be displaced, ordinarily it must be Congress that does so.

But these structural concerns do not indicate whether federal common law should be considered altogether illegitimate or simply restricted in scope. And important countervailing arguments support the existence of some common law power in the federal courts. Numerous cases raise issues implicating important federal interests that are not specifically governed by a statutory or constitutional rule. Congress could have enacted a rule governing the issue, but may not have done so, because it lacked time, foresight, or a political consensus. The Court has, accordingly, recognized that federal common law may be a " 'necessary expedient.' " Nor does Congress's failure to specify a view on a particular subject indicate that Congress preferred that state rules be followed. Here, as elsewhere, congressional inaction is hardly a clear-cut guide for determining congressional intent, and a failure by a court to make law is itself an important and controversial decision.

Thus, legislative inertia and the political safeguards of federalism are ultimately a double-edged sword. They help explain why the authority to make federal common law is nowhere near so broad as congressional authority to legislate, but also argue that federal common lawmaking may be necessary to fill in the interstices of congressional and constitutional mandates or otherwise to deal with matters of important national concern. Despite extensive discussion in the cases and commentary, no clear standard for judging the appropriateness of federal common law has emerged. [Nonetheless, some general points are] * * * accepted by most cases and commentators.

To begin with, there must be a strong need for the formulation of federal common law in order to justify displacing otherwise operative state rules. Moreover, federal common law, perhaps even more than federal law generally, should be interstitial, building upon the total "corpus juris" of the states. Federal common law fits most easily when it supplements federal constitutional or statutory provisions, providing rules of decision that implement or safeguard the norms embodied in such provisions.

Even where federal interests are implicated, it is often possible, and desirable, to rely upon extant state law for the rule of decision. Such reliance eliminates the need for (and possible difficulties in) fashioning a new rule from scratch, and also promotes intrastate uniformity, which may be of great value. Thus, the decision to formulate federal common law is one of judicial policy, in which a court must find that the advantages of borrowing state law are outweighed by either the need for national uniformity or the inconsistency of state law (either of states generally or of the particular state involved) with federal interests.

Regardless of how the balance is struck in particular states, it is clear that there is a distinctive body of federal common law, and recognized and defensible authority for its creation. * * *

Federal common law has developed in two broad situations. First, federal common law is used to resolve cases involving peculiarly important federal interests. These strong federal interests have emerged in several contexts. When interstate disputes have erupted, federal common law has been adopted where it would be unfair to apply the statutes or decisional law from either state. See, e.g., Hinderlider v. La Plata River & Cherry Creek Ditch Co., 304 U.S. 92, 58 S.Ct. 803, 82 L.Ed. 1202 (1938) (dispute over the apportionment of the water of an interstate stream). Similarly, federal common law has become firmly established in admiralty and maritime cases, where the desire for a uniform body of substantive law has long been considered of primary importance. See, e.g., Kossick v. United Fruit Co., 365 U.S. 731, 81 S.Ct. 886, 6 L.Ed.2d 56 (1961). And, cases implicating the international relations of the United States have provided another occasion for resort to federal common law, including cases involving commercial disputes between United States citizens and foreign parties. See, e.g., Banco Nacional de Cuba v. Sabbatino, 376 U.S. 398, 84 S.Ct. 923, 11 L.Ed.2d 804 (1964).

An interesting and confusing use of federal common law occurs in cases involving the legal activities of the United States. These cases often invoke issues concerning the federal government's contract rights, tort liabilities, rights to collect loans and proceeds due to it, or the management of United States bonds and securities.

CLEARFIELD TRUST CO. v. UNITED STATES

Supreme Court of the United States, 1943.
318 U.S. 363, 63 S.Ct. 573, 87 L.Ed. 838.

[A check issued by the United States had been mailed, but was not received by its intended recipient. An unknown person, who presumably had stolen the check, cashed the check at a J.C. Penney store, endorsing it by signing the name of the intended recipient. J.C. Penney in turn endorsed the check to Clearfield Trust, which accepted it. Clearfield then endorsed the check with a guaranty of all prior endorsements, collected the amount of the check from the Federal Reserve and paid it to J.C. Penney. Neither Penney nor Clearfield had suspected forgery. Federal officials did not inform any of the interested parties of the forgery until eight months after they had learned that the intended recipient had not received the check.

The United States sued Clearfield on Clearfield's express guaranty of prior endorsements. The District Court held that the rights of the parties were to be determined by the law of Pennsylvania. Since the United States had unreasonably delayed giving notice of the forgery, it was barred from recovery under Pennsylvania law and the District Court dismissed the complaint. The Court of Appeals for the Third Circuit reversed.]

Certiorari to the Circuit Court of Appeals for the Third Circuit.

MR. JUSTICE DOUGLAS delivered the opinion of the Court.

* * *

We agree with the Circuit Court of Appeals that the rule of Erie R. Co. v. Tompkins * * * does not apply to this action. The rights and duties of the United States on commercial paper which it issues are governed by federal rather than local law. When the United States disburses its funds or pays its debts, it is exercising a constitutional function or power. This check was issued for services performed under the Federal Emergency Relief Act of 1935 * * *. The authority to issue the check had its origin in the Constitution and the statutes of the United States and was in no way dependent on the laws of Pennsylvania or of any other state. * * * The duties imposed upon the United States and the rights acquired by it as a result of the issuance find their roots in the same federal sources.[2] * * * In absence of an applicable Act of Congress it is for the federal courts to fashion the governing rule of law according to their own standards. * * *

In our choice of the applicable federal rule we have occasionally selected state law. * * * But reasons which may make state law at

---

2. Various Treasury Regulations govern the payment and endorsement of government checks and warrants and the reimbursement of the Treasurer of the United States by Federal Reserve banks and member bank depositories on payment of checks or warrants bearing a forged endorsement. * * * Forgery of the check was an offense against the United States. * * *

times the appropriate federal rule are singularly inappropriate here. The issuance of commercial paper by the United States is on a vast scale and transactions in that paper from issuance to payment will commonly occur in several states. The application of state law, even without the conflict of laws rules of the forum, would subject the rights and duties of the United States to exceptional uncertainty. It would lead to great diversity in results by making identical transactions subject to the vagaries of the laws of the several states. The desirability of a uniform rule is plain. And while the federal law merchant developed for about a century under the regime of Swift v. Tyson * * * represented general commercial law rather than a choice of a federal rule designed to protect a federal right, it nevertheless stands as a convenient source of reference for fashioning federal rules applicable to these federal questions.

United States v. National Exchange Bank * * * falls in that category. The Court held that the United States could recover as drawee from one who presented for payment a pension check on which the name of the payee had been forged, in spite of a protracted delay on the part of the United States in giving notice of the forgery. * * *

The *National Exchange Bank* case went no further than to hold that prompt notice of the discovery of the forgery was not a condition precedent to suit. It did not reach the question whether lack of prompt notice might be a defense. We think it may. If it is shown that the drawee on learning of the forgery did not give prompt notice of it and that damage resulted, recovery by the drawee is barred. * * * The fact that the drawee is the United States and the laches those of its employees are not material. * * * The United States as drawee of commercial paper stands in no different light than any other drawee. As stated in United States v. National Exchange Bank * * *, "The United States does business on business terms." It is not excepted from the general rules governing the rights and duties of drawees "by the largeness of its dealings and its having to employ agents to do what if done by a principal in person would leave no room for doubt." * * * But the damage occasioned by the delay must be established and not left to conjecture. Cases * * * place the burden on the drawee of giving prompt notice of the forgery—injury to the defendant being presumed by the mere fact of delay. * * * But we do not think that he who accepts a forged signature of a payee deserves that preferred treatment. It is his neglect or error in accepting the forger's signature which occasions the loss. * * * He should be allowed to shift that loss to the drawee only on a clear showing that the drawee's delay in notifying him of the forgery caused him damage. * * * No such damage has been shown by Clearfield Trust Co. who so far as appears can still recover from J.C. Penney Co. The only showing on the part of the latter is contained in the stipulation to the effect that if a check cashed for a customer is returned unpaid or for reclamation a short time after the date on which it is cashed, the employees can often locate the person who cashed it. It is further stipulated that when J.C. Penney Co. was notified of the forgery in the present case none of its employees was able to remember anything about the transaction or check in question. The inference is that the more prompt the notice the more likely the detection of the forger. But that falls short of a showing that the delay caused a manifest loss. * * * It is but another way of saying that mere delay is enough.

Affirmed.

MR. JUSTICE MURPHY and MR. JUSTICE RUTLEDGE did not participate in the consideration or decision of this case.

Notes and Questions

1. Why doesn't the *Clearfield* Court mention the Rules of Decision Act?

2. Once a court has decided to use federal common law, how does the court determine what the appropriate federal law should be? In UNITED STATES v. KIMBELL FOODS, INC., 440 U.S. 715, 99 S.Ct. 1448, 59 L.Ed.2d 711 (1979), the question arose whether federal or state rules should be used for Small Business Administration and Farmers Home Administration loans in order to determine whether the federal government or a private creditor would be able to collect first on a loan. In addressing this issue, the Court embarked upon a two-step analysis. First, the Court interpreted *Clearfield* broadly as permitting federal courts to develop federal law for "questions involving the rights of the United States arising under nationwide federal programs." Thus, the Court held that "the priority of liens stemming from federal lending programs must be determined with reference to federal law" and that the "SBA and FHA unquestionably perform federal functions within the meaning of *Clearfield.*"

Having decided that federal law controlled, the Court turned to the second and more challenging task of determining the content of the federal law.

> Controversies directly affecting the operations of federal programs, although governed by federal law, do not inevitably require resort to uniform federal rules. * * * Whether to adopt state law or to fashion a nationwide federal rule is a matter of judicial policy "dependent upon a variety of considerations always relevant to the nature of the specific governmental interests and to the effects upon them of applying state law." * * *

> Undoubtedly, federal programs that "by their nature are and must be uniform in character throughout the Nation" necessitate formulation of controlling federal rules. * * * Conversely, when there is little need for a nationally uniform body of law, state law may be incorporated as the federal rule of decision. Apart from considerations of uniformity, we must also determine whether application of state law would frustrate specific objectives of the federal programs. If so, we must fashion special rules solicitous of those federal interests. Finally, our choice-of-law inquiry must consider the extent to which application of a federal rule would disrupt commercial relationships predicated on state law. * * *

Id. at 727–30, 99 S.Ct. at 1458–59, 59 L.Ed.2d at 723–25.

After weighing these factors with respect to priority rules for the SBA and FHA loans, the Court held that there was no need for an independent federal rule. Thus, the Court chose to adopt the state rule as federal law rather than to develop a separate federal rule.

If a federal court chooses to adopt state law as the federal law in a given situation, should the method for determining state law differ from the process outlined in *Ortho Pharmaceutical*, p. 383, supra?

3. The *Clearfield* decision has been criticized for adopting federal common law in a situation in which there were insufficient considerations to justify a uniform federal rule. As one commentator explains, the presence of a federal function, the issuance of commercial paper, merely signals that federal law may be appropriate. A federal interest in uniformity does not follow automatically:

> * * * [T]his interest in uniformity [in the law of commercial paper] is open to serious question. The Government cannot be overly inconvenienced in issuing commercial paper when dozens of major corporations issue it on a nationwide scale, apparently without varying state law causing undue difficulties. The Treasury has never broached the subject of facilitating its operations with uniform national rules. And the work of the Treasury is left unchanged by *Clearfield* since it is only through negligence that it will fail to give warning of a known forgery.
>
> The attainability of uniform rules is often ignored just as the importance of them is overstated. The Supreme Court lacks the time to erect common law principles governing everything from the construction of government contracts to the issuance of United States commercial paper. The barriers to uniformity resulting from divergence of opinion among courts of appeals may be intensified when state courts exercise their concurrent jurisdiction over these cases. Some state courts treat lower federal court rulings as binding and may follow its interpretation of the federal common law, but some do not. Nor is a state court bound by the interpretation of its local circuit; thus a general lack of uniformity may be complicated by a situation conflicting with the policy of *Erie* in which the federal common law applicable depends upon the forum in which suit was brought.
>
> [Another] interest in uniformity which generally cuts against the creation of federal common law is that of individuals who would prefer to look to but one source of law to govern the same or similar transactions. The failure to consider this interest is a further problem with the *Clearfield* decision. As Judge Friendly has noted, it is far from clear why the convenience uniform rules afforded the Treasury should be placed ahead of the inconvenience to Pennsylvanians of having two systems of law govern similar commercial paper moving through identical channels.

Note, *Federal Common Law*, 82 Harv.L.Rev. 1512, 1530–31 (1969).

4. Courts have not perceived a need for federal common law in every case involving commercial paper. In BANK OF AMERICA NATIONAL TRUST & SAVINGS ASSOCIATION v. PARNELL, 352 U.S. 29, 77 S.Ct. 119, 1 L.Ed.2d 93 (1956), the Bank of America brought a diversity action alleging that two individual defendants (Parnell and Rocco) and two corporate defendants (First National Bank of Indiana and Federal Reserve Bank of Cleveland) had converted 73 Home Owners' Loan Corporation bonds which belonged to Bank of America. The bonds were bearer bonds with payment guaranteed by

the United States. They carried interest coupons calling for semi-annual payment. They were due to mature May 1, 1952, but pursuant to their terms, had been called on or about May 1, 1944. On May 2, 1944, the bonds disappeared while petitioner was getting them ready for presentation to the Federal Reserve Bank for payment. In 1948 they were presented to the First National Bank for payment by Parnell on behalf of Rocco. The First National Bank forwarded them to the Federal Reserve Bank of Cleveland. It cashed them and paid the First National Bank, which issued cashier's checks to Parnell. Parnell then turned the proceeds over to Rocco less a fee—there was conflicting testimony as to whether the fee was nominal or substantial.

The principal issue at the trial was whether the defendants took the bonds in good faith, without knowledge or notice of the defect in title. On this issue the trial judge charged the jury based on state law. The jury brought in verdicts for Bank of America against the defendants.

On appeal, the Court of Appeals for the Third Circuit, sitting *en banc,* reversed. It held that the District Court had erred in treating the case as an ordinary diversity case and in regarding state law as governing the rights of the parties and the burden of proof. It considered *Clearfield Trust* controlling and held that federal law placed the burden of proof on Bank of America to show notice and lack of good faith on the part of the defendants. As the Third Circuit saw it, there was no evidence of bad faith by the First National Bank since the bonds were not "overdue" as a matter of federal law when presented to it; the court therefore directed entry of judgment for First National. On the other hand, the Circuit Court concluded that there was evidence of bad faith on the part of Parnell; thus, it ordered a new trial because of the erroneous instructions.

The Supreme Court reversed, saying:

> Securities issued by the Government generate immediate interests of the Government. * * * But they also radiate interests in transactions between private parties. The present litigation is purely between private parties and does not touch the rights and duties of the United States. The only possible interest of the United States in a situation like the one here, exclusively involving the transfer of Government paper between private persons, is that the floating of securities of the United States might somehow or other be adversely affected by the local rule of a particular State regarding the liability of a converter. This is far too speculative, far too remote a possibility to justify the application of federal law to transactions essentially of local concern.
>
> We do not mean to imply that litigation with respect to Government paper necessarily precludes the presence of a federal interest, to be governed by federal law, in all situations merely because it is a suit between private parties, or that it is beyond the range of federal legislation to deal comprehensively with Government paper. We do not of course foreclose such judicial or legislative action in appropriate situations by concluding that this controversy over burden of proof and good faith represents too essentially a private transaction not to be dealt with by the local law of Pennsylvania where the transactions took place. Federal law of course governs the interpretation of the nature of the rights and obligations created by the Government bonds themselves. A decision with respect to the "overdueness" of the bonds is therefore a

matter of federal law, which, in view of our holding, we need not elucidate.

This conclusion requires reversal of the judgments of the Court of Appeals but not reinstatement of the judgments of the District Court. The Court of Appeals did not originally consider all the points raised by respondents. Moreover, since the Court of Appeals misconceived the applicable law, it is for that court to review the judgments of the District Court in the light of the controlling state law. The Court of Appeals has not decided what the governing state law on burden of proof is, and it is the court which should so decide. Likewise, if state law casts the burden on respondents to demonstrate their good faith, it is for the Court of Appeals to assess the evidence in light of that standard.

The majority view did not go unchallenged. Justices Black and Douglas dissented:

We believe that the "federal law merchant," which Clearfield Trust Co. v. United States * * * held applicable to transactions in the commercial paper of the United States, should be applicable to all transactions in that paper. * * * Not until today has a distinction been drawn between suits by the United States on that paper and suits by other parties to it. But the Court does not stop there. Because this is "essentially a private transaction," it is to be governed by local law. Yet the nature of the rights and obligations created by commercial paper of the United States Government is said to be controlled by federal law. Thus, federal law is to govern some portion of a dispute between private parties, while that portion of the dispute which is "essentially of local concern" is to be governed by local law. The uncertainties which inhere in such a dichotomy are obvious. * * *

The virtue of a uniform law governing bonds, notes, and other paper issued by the United States is that it provides a certain and definite guide to the rights of all parties rather than subjecting them to the vagaries of the laws of many States. The business of the United States will go on without that uniformity. But the policy surrounding our choice of laws is concerned with the convenience, certainty, and definiteness in having one set of rules governing the rights of all parties to government paper, as contrasted to multiple rules. If the rule of the *Clearfield Trust* case is to be abandoned as to some parties, it should be abandoned as to all and we should start afresh on this problem.

MIREE v. DeKALB COUNTY

Supreme Court of the United States, 1977.
433 U.S. 25, 97 S.Ct. 2490, 53 L.Ed.2d 557.

Certiorari to the United States Court of Appeals for the Fifth Circuit.

Mr. Justice Rehnquist delivered the opinion of the Court.

These consolidated cases arise out of the 1973 crash of a Lear Jet shortly after takeoff from the DeKalb–Peachtree Airport. The United States Court of Appeals for the Fifth Circuit, en banc, affirmed the dismissal of petitioners' complaint against respondent DeKalb County (hereafter respondent), holding that principles of federal common law were applicable to the resolution of petitioners' breach-of-contract claim. We granted certiorari to consider whether federal or state law should have been applied to that claim; we conclude that the latter should govern.

I

Petitioners are, respectively, the survivors of deceased passengers, the assignee of the jet aircraft owner, and a burn victim. They brought separate lawsuits, later consolidated, against respondent in the United States District Court for the Northern District of Georgia. The basis for federal jurisdiction was diversity of citizenship, 28 U.S.C. § 1332, and the complaints asserted that respondent was liable on three independent theories: negligence, nuisance, and breach of contract. The District Court granted respondent's motion to dismiss each of these claims. The courts below have unanimously agreed that the negligence and nuisance theories are without merit; only the propriety of the dismissal of the contract claims remains in the cases.

Petitioners seek to impose liability on respondent as third-party beneficiaries of contracts between it and the Federal Aviation Administration (FAA). Their complaints allege that respondent entered into six grant agreements with the FAA. * * * Under the terms of the contracts respondent agreed to

> take action to restrict the use of land adjacent to or in the immediate vicinity of the Airport to activities and purposes compatible with normal airport operations including landing and takeoff of aircraft. * * *

Petitioners assert that respondent breached the FAA contracts by owning and maintaining a garbage dump adjacent to the airport, and that the cause of the crash was the ingestion of birds swarming from the dump into the jet engines of the aircraft.

Applying Georgia law, the District Court found that petitioners' claims as third-party beneficiaries under the FAA contracts were barred by the county's governmental immunity, and dismissed the complaints under Fed.Rule Civ.Proc. 12(b)(6). A divided panel of the Court of Appeals decided that under state law petitioners could sue as third-party beneficiaries and that governmental immunity would not bar the suit. * * * The dissenting judge argued that the court should have applied federal rather than state law; he concluded that under the principles of federal common law the petitioners in this case did not have standing to sue as third-party beneficiaries of the contracts. Sitting en banc, the Court of Appeals reversed the panel on the breach-of-contract issue and adopted the panel dissent on this point as its opinion. * * * Judge Morgan, who had written the panel opinion, argued for five dissenters that there was no identifiable federal interest in the outcome of this diversity case, and thus that federal common law had no applicability.

II

Since the only basis of federal jurisdiction alleged for petitioners' claim against respondent is diversity of citizenship, the case would unquestionably be governed by Georgia law, Erie R. Co. v. Tompkins, * * * but for the fact that the United States is a party to the contracts in question, entered into pursuant to federal statute. * * * The en banc majority of the Court of Appeals adopted, by reference, the view that, given these factors, application of federal common law was required * * *.

We do not agree with the conclusion of the Court of Appeals. The litigation before us raises no question regarding the liability of the United States or the responsibilities of the United States under the contracts. The relevant inquiry is a narrow one: whether petitioners as third-party beneficiaries of the contracts have standing to sue respondent. While federal common law may govern even in diversity cases where a uniform national rule is necessary to further the interests of the Federal Government, Clearfield Trust Co. v. United States * * *, the application of federal common law to resolve the issue presented here would promote no federal interests even approaching the magnitude of those found in *Clearfield Trust.* * * *

* * * [I]n this case, the resolution of petitioners' breach-of-contract claim against respondent will have no direct effect upon the United States or its Treasury. The Solicitor General, waiving his right to respond in these cases, advised us:

> In the course of the proceedings below, the United States determined that its interests would not be directly affected by the resolution of these issue[s] and therefore did not participate in briefing or argument in the court of appeals. In view of these considerations, the United States does not intend to respond to the petitions unless it is requested to do so by the Court.

The operations of the United States in connection with FAA grants such as these are undoubtedly of considerable magnitude. However, we see no reason for concluding that these operations would be burdened or subjected to uncertainty by variant state-law interpretations regarding whether those with whom the United States contracts might be sued by third-party beneficiaries to the contracts. Since only the rights of private litigants are at issue here, we find the *Clearfield Trust* rationale inapplicable.

We think our conclusion that these cases do not fit within the *Clearfield Trust* rule follows from the Court's later decision in Bank of America Nat. Trust & Sav. Assn. v. Parnell, 352 U.S. 29, 77 S.Ct. 119, 1 L.Ed.2d 93 (1956), in which the Court declined to apply that rule in a fact situation analogous to this one. * * *

* * *

The parallel between *Parnell* and these cases is obvious. The question of whether petitioners may sue respondent does not require decision under federal common law since the litigation is among private parties and no substantial rights or duties of the United States hinge on its outcome. On the other hand, nothing we say here forecloses the applicability of federal common law in interpreting the rights and duties of the United States under federal contracts.

Nor is the fact that the United States has a substantial interest in regulating aircraft travel and promoting air travel safety sufficient, given the narrow question before us, to call into play the rule of *Clearfield Trust.* * * * The question of whether private parties may, as third-party beneficiaries, sue a municipality for breach of the FAA contracts involves this federal interest only insofar as such lawsuits might be thought to advance federal aviation policy by inducing compliance with FAA safety provisions. However, even assuming the correctness of this notion, we adhere to the [view] that the issue of whether to displace state law on an issue such as this is primarily a decision for Congress. Congress has chosen not to do so in this case.[5] Actually the application of federal common law, as interpreted by the Court of Appeals here would frustrate this federal interest *pro tanto,* since that court held that this breach-of-contract lawsuit would not lie under federal law. On the other hand, at least in the opinion of the majority of the panel below, Georgia law would countenance the action. * * * We conclude that any federal interest in the outcome of the question before us "is far too speculative, far too remote a possibility to justify the application of federal law to transactions essentially of local concern." Parnell, 352 U.S., at 33–34, 77 S.Ct., at 121.

Although we have determined that Georgia law should be applied to the question raised by respondent's motion to dismiss, we shall not undertake to decide the correct outcome under Georgia law. * * * We therefore vacate the judgment and remand to the Court of Appeals for consideration of the claim under applicable Georgia law.

* * *

[CHIEF JUSTICE BURGER concurred in the judgment.]

Notes and Questions

1. In KOHR v. ALLEGHENY AIRLINES, INC., 504 F.2d 400 (7th Cir. 1974), certiorari denied sub nom. Forth Corp. v. Allegheny Airlines, Inc., 421 U.S. 978, 95 S.Ct. 1980, 44 L.Ed.2d 470 (1975), an Allegheny Airlines jet and an aircraft owned by a corporation and operated by a student pilot were involved in a mid-air collision. The crash took place over Indiana. The collision totally destroyed both aircraft and killed all 83 occupants. The United States was involved because at the time of the crash the Allegheny jet was adhering to air traffic control radar directions from an employee of the Federal Aviation Administration.

Separate actions were filed in various federal district courts on behalf of the estates of almost all of the passengers against the corporation, the estate of the student pilot, Allegheny Airlines, and the United States. Although not all of the suits had been commenced in Indiana, the Judicial Panel on Multidistrict Litigation consolidated the suits in the Indiana district court. The United States and Allegheny filed cross claims seeking indemnity and contribution from the corporation and the estate of the student pilot.

5. The Congress has considered, but not passed, a bill to provide for a federal cause of   action arising out of aircraft disasters. * * *

The District Court held that Indiana law governed the indemnity and contribution claims, and that this law precluded recovery. The court arrived at this holding by the standard practice of applying the choice-of-law rule of the state in which it sat (Indiana, in this case). That rule in turn referred the court to Indiana substantive law. The Court of Appeals reversed in part and remanded the case, holding that federal law governed:

> The basis for imposing a federal law of contribution and indemnity is what we perceive to be the predominant, indeed almost exclusive, interest of the federal government in regulating the affairs of the nation's airways. Moreover, the imposition of a federal rule of contribution and indemnity serves a second purpose of eliminating inconsistency of result in similar collision occurrences as well as within the same occurrence due to the application of differing state laws on contribution and indemnity. Given the prevailing federal interest in uniform air law regulation, we deem it desirable that a federal rule of contribution and indemnity be applied.

> * * * With the passage of the Federal Aviation Act of 1958, 49 U.S.C. § 1301 et seq., Congress expressed the view that the control of aviation should rest exclusively in the hands of the federal government. * * * The explicit objective of the Act is to foster the development of air commerce. 49 U.S.C. § 1346. To that end, it has been recognized that the principal purpose of the Act is to create one unified system of flight rules and to centralize in the Administrator of the Federal Aviation Administration the power to promulgate rules for the safe and efficient use of the country's airspace. * * * When the notion of federal preemption over aviation is viewed in combination with the fact that this litigation ensues from a mid-air collision occurring in national airspace, the Government is a party to the action pursuant to the Federal Tort Claims Act (28 U.S.C. § 1346(b) et seq.) and that this litigation has since its inception been subject to the supervision of the Judicial Panel created by the Multidistrict Litigation Act (28 U.S.C. § 1407 et seq.), there is no perceptible reason why federal law should not be applied to determine the rights and liabilities of the parties involved. The interest of the state wherein the fortuitous event of the collision occurred is slight as compared to the dominant federal interest. Accordingly, the rights and liabilities of Allegheny and the United States are peculiarly federal in nature and are to be governed by a federal rule of contribution and indemnity.

Id. at 403–04. How might *Kohr* and *Miree* be reconciled? Does *Miree* overrule *Kohr*?

2. What factors persuaded the court in *Kohr* to apply federal common law? Suppose the case had involved the crash of a non-commercial plane on an intrastate flight that resulted in the deaths of four people. Would the federal interest in regulating air space demand the application of federal common law in this situation? See Smith v. Cessna Aircraft Corp., 428 F.Supp. 1285 (N.D.Ill.1977).

3. Why doesn't the Court in *Miree* use the two-step technique outlined in *Kimbell Foods,* p. 398, supra?

4. *Miree* raises the question whether plaintiffs have standing to sue as third-party beneficiaries of a federal government contract. This question

implicates both general contract law (does a third-party beneficiary of a contract have a right to sue for breach of contract?) and the interpretation of the particular contract at issue. Is the Court in *Miree* holding that state law governs both of these issues? Should it?

2. INTERSTITIAL FEDERAL COMMON LAW

One of the most challenging contexts of federal common lawmaking involves statutes that express national policy in a particular area but leave many of the specifics to the federal courts. Two questions typically arise in these cases. First, is the statutory gap at issue one that the federal courts should fill? If the answer is yes, on what sources should a federal court rely in order to derive the law? The answers to these questions can be crucial in shaping the overall national policy involved in the statute.

DelCOSTELLO v. INTERNATIONAL BROTHERHOOD OF TEAMSTERS

Supreme Court of the United States, 1983.
462 U.S. 151, 103 S.Ct. 2281, 76 L.Ed.2d 476.

Certiorari to the United States Court of Appeals for the Second Circuit.

JUSTICE BRENNAN delivered the opinion of the Court.

Each of these cases arose as a suit by an employee or employees against an employer and a union, alleging that the employer had breached a provision of a collective bargaining agreement, and that the union had breached its duty of fair representation by mishandling the ensuing grievance-and-arbitration proceedings. * * * The issue presented is what statute of limitations should apply to such suits. In United Parcel Service, Inc. v. Mitchell, 451 U.S. 56, 101 S.Ct. 1559, 67 L.Ed.2d 732 (1981), we held that a similar suit was governed by a state statute of limitations for vacation of an arbitration award, rather than by a state statute for an action on a contract. We left two points open, however. First, our holding was limited to the employee's claim against the employer; we did not address what state statute should govern the claim against the union. Second, we expressly limited our consideration to a choice between two *state* statutes of limitations; we did not address the contention that we should instead borrow a *federal* statute of limitations, namely § 10(b) of the National Labor Relations Act, 29 U.S.C. § 160(b). These cases present these two issues. We conclude that § 10(b) should be the applicable statute of limitations governing the suit, both against the employer and against the union.

* * *

As is often the case in federal civil law, there is no federal statute of limitations expressly applicable to this suit. In such situations we do not ordinarily assume that Congress intended that there be no time limit on actions at all; rather, our task is to "borrow" the most suitable statute or other rule of timeliness from some other source. We have generally concluded that Congress intended that the courts apply the most closely analogous statute of limitations under state law. "The implied absorption

of State statutes of limitation within the interstices of the federal enactments is a phase of fashioning remedial details where Congress has not
spoken but left matters for judicial determination within the general
framework of familiar legal principles." Holmberg v. Armbrecht, 327
U.S. 392, 395, 66 S.Ct. 582, 584, 90 L.Ed. 743 (1946). * * *

In some circumstances, however, state statutes of limitations can be
unsatisfactory vehicles for the enforcement of federal law. In those
instances, it may be inappropriate to conclude that Congress would choose
to adopt state rules at odds with the purpose or operation of federal
substantive law. * * *

Hence, in some cases we have declined to borrow state statutes but
have instead used timeliness rules drawn from federal law—either express
limitations periods from related federal statutes, or such alternatives as
laches. * * *

Auto Workers v. Hoosier Cardinal Corp. [383 U.S. 696, 86 S.Ct. 1107,
16 L.Ed.2d 192 (1966)] was a straightforward suit under § 301 of the Labor
Management Relations Act, 29 U.S.C. § 185, for breach of a collective-
bargaining agreement by an employer. * * * We held that the suit was
governed by Indiana's 6-year limitations period for actions on unwritten
contracts; we resisted the suggestion that we establish some uniform
federal period. Although we recognized that "the subject matter of § 301
is 'peculiarly one that calls for uniform law,' " 383 U.S., at 701, 86 S.Ct., at
1110, quoting Teamsters v. Lucas Flour Co., 369 U.S. 95, 103, 82 S.Ct. 571,
576, 7 L.Ed.2d 593 (1962), we reasoned that national uniformity is of less
importance when the case does not involve "those consensual processes
that federal labor law is chiefly designed to promote—the formation of the
collective agreement and the private settlement of disputes under it," 383
U.S., at 702, 86 S.Ct., at 1111. We also relied heavily on the obvious and
close analogy between this variety of § 301 suit and an ordinary breach-of-
contract case. We expressly reserved the question whether we would
apply state law to § 301 actions where the analogy was less direct or the
relevant policy factors different * * *.

Justice Stewart, who wrote the Court's opinion in *Hoosier*, took this
caution to heart in *Mitchell*. He concurred separately in the judgment,
arguing that the factors that compelled adoption of state law in *Hoosier*
did not apply [and that] we should apply the federal limitations period of
§ 10(b). * * * As we shall explain, we agree.

* * *

In *Mitchell*, we analogized the employee's claim against the employer
to an action to vacate an arbitration award in a commercial setting.
* * * Nevertheless, the parallel is imperfect in operation. The main
difference is that a party to commercial arbitration will ordinarily be
represented by counsel or, at least, will have some experience in matters
of commercial dealings and contract negotiation. Moreover, an action to
vacate a commercial arbitral award will rarely raise any issues not
already presented and contested in the arbitration proceeding itself. In
the labor setting, by contrast, the employee will often be unsophisticated
in collective-bargaining matters, and he will almost always be represented

solely by the union. He is called upon, within the limitations period, to evaluate the adequacy of the union's representation, to retain counsel, to investigate substantial matters that were not at issue in the arbitration proceeding, and to frame his suit. Yet state arbitration statutes typically provide very short times in which to sue for vacation of arbitration awards. Concededly, the very brevity of New York's 90-day arbitration limitations period was a major factor why, in *Mitchell*, we preferred it to the 6-year statute for breach of contract * * *; but it does not follow that because 6 years is too long, 90 days is long enough. * * *

Justice Stevens suggested an alternative solution for the claim against the union: borrowing the state limitations period for legal malpractice. * * *

The most serious objection is that it does not solve the problem caused by the too-short time in which an employee could sue his employer under borrowed state law. In a commercial setting, a party who sued his lawyer for bungling an arbitration could ordinarily recover his entire damages, even if the statute of limitations foreclosed any recovery against the opposing party to the arbitration. The same is not true in the § 301/fair representation setting, however. * * * Thus, if we apply state limitations periods, a large part of the damages will remain uncollectible in almost every case unless the employee sues within the time allotted for his suit against the employer.

Further, while application of a short arbitration period as against employers would endanger employees' ability to recover most of what is due them, application of a longer malpractice statute as against unions would preclude the relatively rapid final resolution of labor disputes favored by federal law—a problem not present when a party to a commercial arbitration sues his lawyer. * * *

These objections to the resort to state law might have to be tolerated if state law were the only source reasonably available for borrowing, as it often is. In this case, however, we have available a federal statute of limitations actually designed to accommodate a balance of interests very similar to that at stake here—a statute that is, in fact, an analogy to the present lawsuit more apt than any of the suggested state-law parallels. We refer to § 10(b) of the National Labor Relations Act, which establishes a 6-month period for making charges of unfair labor practices to the NLRB.

The NLRB has consistently held that all breaches of a union's duty of fair representation *are* in fact unfair labor practices. * * * Even if not all breaches of the duty are unfair labor practices, however, the family resemblance is undeniable, and indeed there is a substantial overlap. Many fair representation claims * * * include allegations of discrimination based on membership status or dissident views, which would be unfair labor practices * * *. Aside from these clear cases, duty of fair representation claims are allegations of unfair, arbitrary, or discriminatory treatment of workers by unions—as are virtually all unfair labor practice charges made by workers against unions. * * *

At least as important as the similarity of the rights asserted in the two contexts, however, is the close similarity of the considerations relevant to the choice of a limitations period. As Justice Stewart observed in *Mitchell:*

> In § 10(b) of the NLRA, Congress established a limitations period attuned to what it viewed as the proper balance between the national interests in stable bargaining relationships and finality of private settlements, and an employee's interest in setting aside what he views as an unjust settlement under the collective-bargaining system. That is precisely the balance at issue in this case. The employee's interest in setting aside the "final and binding" determination of a grievance through the method established by the collective-bargaining agreement unquestionably implicates "those consensual processes that federal labor law is chiefly designed to promote—the formation of the * * * agreement and the private settlement of disputes under it." *Hoosier*, 383 U.S., at 702, 86 S.Ct., at 1111. Accordingly, "[t]he need for uniformity" among procedures followed for similar claims, ibid., as well as the clear congressional indication of the proper balance between the interests at stake, counsels the adoption of § 10(b) of the NLRA as the appropriate limitations period for lawsuits such as this. 451 U.S., at 70–71, 101 S.Ct., at 1567–1568 (opinion concurring in the judgment) (footnote omitted).

We stress that our holding today should not be taken as a departure from prior practice in borrowing limitations periods for federal causes of action, in labor law or elsewhere. We do not mean to suggest that federal courts should eschew use of state limitations periods anytime state law fails to provide a perfect analogy. * * * On the contrary, as the courts have often discovered, there is not always an obvious state-law choice for application to a given federal cause of action; yet resort to state law remains the norm for borrowing of limitations periods. Nevertheless, when a rule from elsewhere in federal law clearly provides a closer analogy than available state statutes, and when the federal policies at stake and the practicalities of litigation make that rule a significantly more appropriate vehicle for interstitial lawmaking, we have not hesitated to turn away from state law. * * *

JUSTICE STEVENS, dissenting.

For the past century federal judges have "borrowed" state statutes of limitations, not because they thought it was a sensible form of "interstitial law making", but rather because they were directed to do so by the Congress of the United States.

Today the Court holds that the Rules of Decision Act does not determine the result in this case, because it believes that a separate federal law, growing out of "the policies and requirements of the underlying cause of action," "otherwise require[s] or provide[s]." The Court's opinion sets forth a number of reasons why it may make good sense to adopt a 6-month statute of limitations, but nothing in that opinion persuades me that the Constitution, treaties, or statutes of the United States "require or provide" that this particular limitations period must be applied to this case.

Congress has given us no reason to depart from our settled practice, grounded in the Rules of Decision Act, of borrowing analogous state statutes of limitation in cases such as this. * * * I believe that in a suit for a breach of the duty of fair representation, the appropriate "laws of the several states" are the statutes of limitations governing malpractice suits against attorneys. I would apply those laws to resolve the worker-union disputes in these two cases. * * *

For these reasons, I respectfully dissent.

[The dissenting opinion of JUSTICE O'CONNOR is omitted.]

Notes and Questions

1. In TEXTILE WORKERS UNION v. LINCOLN MILLS, 353 U.S. 448, 77 S.Ct. 912, 1 L.Ed.2d 972 (1957), the union brought suit to compel arbitration of various grievances. The collective bargaining agreement provided for arbitration after the other grievance procedures had been exhausted. Justice Douglas, writing for the majority, held that federal common law would govern the decision of whether the court had jurisdiction to enforce the collective bargaining agreement under § 301 of the Labor Management Relations Act of 1947. After examining the legislative history, Justice Douglas explained:

> * * * Both the Senate Report and the House Report indicate a primary concern that unions as well as employees should be bound to collective bargaining contracts. But there was also a broader concern—a concern with a procedure for making such agreements enforceable in the courts by either party. * * *

Justice Douglas added that federal common law dictated that the agreement to arbitrate would be specifically enforced:

> It seems, therefore, clear to us that Congress adopted a policy which placed sanctions behind agreements to arbitrate grievance disputes, by implication rejecting the common-law rule * * * against enforcement of executory agreements to arbitrate. We would undercut the Act and defeat its policy if we read § 301 narrowly as only conferring jurisdiction over labor organizations.

> The question then is, what is the substantive law to be applied in suits under § 301(a)? We conclude that the substantive law to apply in suits under § 301(a) is federal law, which the courts must fashion from the policy of our national labor laws. * * * The Labor Management Relations Act expressly furnishes some substantive law. It points out what the parties may or may not do in certain situations. Other problems will lie in the penumbra of express statutory mandates. Some will lack express statutory sanction but will be solved by looking at the policy of the legislation and fashioning a remedy that will effectuate that policy. The range of judicial inventiveness will be determined by the nature of the problem. * * * Federal interpretation of the federal law will govern, not state law. * * * But state law, if compatible with the purpose of § 301, may be resorted to in order to find the rule that will best effectuate the federal policy. * * * Any state law applied, however, will be absorbed as federal law and will not be an independent source of private rights.

353 U.S. at 453, 456–57, 77 S.Ct. at 916–18, 1 L.Ed.2d at 978, 980–81. In the absence of a federal statutory scheme governing labor relations in the United States, would federal courts be able to fashion common law in this area?

2. Even if a statutory scheme is silent as to a particular procedure or remedy, the federal courts will not necessarily always fashion federal common law to fill in the gaps. In TEXAS INDUSTRIES, INC. v. RADCLIFF MATERIALS, INC., 451 U.S. 630, 101 S.Ct. 2061, 68 L.Ed.2d 500 (1981), the Court held that it could not fashion federal common law in order to permit contribution among joint antitrust violators:

> In contrast to the sweeping language of §§ 1 and 2 of the Sherman Act, the remedial provisions defined in the antitrust laws are detailed and specific: (1) violations of §§ 1 and 2 are crimes; (2) Congress has expressly authorized a private right of action for treble damages, costs, and reasonable attorney's fees; (3) other remedial sections also provide for suits by the United States to enjoin violations or for injury to its "business or property," and *parens patriae* suits by state attorneys general; (4) Congress has provided that a final judgment or decree of an antitrust violation in one proceeding will serve as prima facie evidence in any subsequent action or proceeding; and (5) the remedial provisions in the antimerger field, not at issue here, are also quite detailed.

> The presumption that a remedy was deliberately omitted from a statute is strongest when Congress has enacted a comprehensive legislative scheme including an integrated system of procedures for enforcement. * * *

That presumption is strong indeed in the context of antitrust violations; the continuing existence of this statutory scheme for 90 years without amendments authorizing contribution is not without significance. There is nothing in the statute itself, in its legislative history, or in the overall regulatory scheme to suggest that Congress intended courts to have the power to alter or supplement the remedies enacted.

451 U.S. at 644–45, 101 S.Ct. at 2069, 68 L.Ed.2d at 511–12.

Many states today allow contribution among joint tortfeasors, and antitrust violators frequently are analogized to tortfeasors. Is Chief Justice Burger's decision not to allow contribution actually a decision to fashion federal common law to reach a result different from what state law would yield? Consider that in Wallis v. Pan American Petroleum Corp., 384 U.S. 63, 86 S.Ct. 1301, 16 L.Ed.2d 369 (1966), the Court intimated that Congress enacts legislation against a background of the total corpus juris of the states. If the Court could not develop federal common law in *Texas Industries,* should the prevailing state remedy have applied?

3. State law is borrowed in many areas of law. In DE SYLVA v. BALLENTINE, 351 U.S. 570, 76 S.Ct. 974, 100 L.Ed. 1415 (1956), for example, the Court looked to state law in determining who is a "child" for purposes of the Copyright Act. Justice Harlan, writing for the majority, noted that in questions of domestic relations, when there is no federal law and when the subject is largely a matter of state concern, it was reasonable to borrow the state standards. Justices Douglas and Black disagreed, arguing that a federal standard was needed in order to ensure uniformity.

Assuming that the Court were to apply a federal standard to the question of who is a child, how would it derive that standard? Most likely, there is no federal legislative history on the point. Isn't it true that the Court would have before it only the various state definitions and its own notion of the "better view"? In that case, why not simply use the state law on the point?

SECTION D. FEDERAL LAW IN THE STATE COURTS

State courts often are called upon to construe and apply federal law. Indeed, Congress has created a number of statutory causes of action, such as actions under the Federal Employers' Liability Act, that can be asserted by plaintiff in either a state or federal court but which defendant cannot remove from a state court. When a state attempts to adjudicate such a right, the Supremacy Clause, U.S. Const. Art. VI, requires the application of federal law. Ward v. Love County, 253 U.S. 17, 40 S.Ct. 419, 64 L.Ed. 751 (1920). A federally created right also may become germane to a state-court action when it is interposed as a defense to a claim based on state law. For example, in an action for royalties due under a contract licensing the use of a copyright or patent, defendant commonly will assert that the copyright or patent is invalid under the substantive tests established by the Copyright or Patent Act or that the copyright or patent has been used in violation of the federal antitrust laws. See, e.g., Sola Elec. Co. v. Jefferson Elec. Co., 317 U.S. 173, 63 S.Ct. 172, 87 L.Ed. 165 (1942). By way of further example, federal law may become relevant to a state lawsuit because of the presence of some federal interest or policy, which often springs out of its proprietary or governmental activities, or because one of the parties asserts a right protected by the United States Constitution. Finally, federal decisional law may come into play because it provides precedents bearing on issues being litigated before the state court in a nonfederal action. See generally Oakley & Coon, *The Federal Rules in State Courts: A Survey of State Court Systems of Civil Procedure*, 61 Wis.L.Rev. 1367 (1986).

TESTA v. KATT, 330 U.S. 386, 67 S.Ct. 810, 91 L.Ed. 967 (1947). Petitioner bought an automobile from respondent for $1100. The Emergency Price Control Act of 1942 set a ceiling price for such a purchase at $890. Petitioner then sued respondent under Section 205(e) of the Act in Rhode Island state court, seeking treble damages plus attorney's fees. The Act specifically provided, in Section 205(c), that the federal courts had concurrent jurisdiction with the state courts over matters arising under the Act. On appeal, the Rhode Island Supreme Court refused to enforce the statute and dismissed the action, interpreting Section 205(e) to be "a penal statute in the international sense." It reasoned that since, under widely recognized principles, state courts need not enforce the penal laws of other states or nations, they do not have to enforce the penal laws of the federal government.

The Supreme Court reversed, holding that:

* * * [W]e cannot accept the basic premise on which the Rhode Island Supreme Court held that it has no more obligation to enforce a valid penal law of the United States than it has to enforce a penal law of another state or a foreign country. Such a broad assumption flies in the face of the fact that the States of the Union constitute a nation. It disregards the purpose and effect of Article VI, § 2 of the Constitution * * *.

It cannot be assumed, the supremacy clause considered, that the responsibilities of a state to enforce the laws of a sister state are identical with its responsibilities to enforce federal laws. Such an assumption represents an erroneous evaluation of the statutes of Congress and the prior decisions of this Court in their historic setting. Those decisions establish that state courts do not bear the same relation to the United States that they do to foreign countries. * * *

* * * [W]hen in Mondou v. New York, N.H. & H.R. Co., * * * this Court was presented with a case testing the power and duty of states to enforce federal laws, it found the solution in the broad principles announced in the *Claflin* opinion.

* * * The contention that enforcement of the congressionally created right was contrary to Connecticut policy was answered as follows:

> The suggestion that the act of Congress is not in harmony with the policy of the State, and therefore that the courts of the state are free to decline jurisdiction, is quite inadmissible, because it presupposes what in legal contemplation does not exist. When Congress, in the exertion of the power confided to it by the Constitution, adopted that act, it spoke for all the people and all the states, and thereby established a policy for all. That policy is as much the policy of Connecticut as if the act had emanated from its own legislature, and should be respected accordingly in the courts of the State. * * *

The Rhode Island court in its *Robinson* decision on which it relies cites cases of this Court which have held that states are not required by the full faith and credit clause of the Constitution to enforce judgments of the courts of other states based on claims arising out of penal statutes. But those holdings have no relevance here, for this case raises no full faith and credit question. Nor need we consider in this case prior decisions to the effect that federal courts are not required to enforce state penal laws. * * * For whatever consideration they may be entitled in the field in which they are relevant, those decisions did not bring before us our instant problem of the effect of the supremacy clause on the relation of federal laws to state courts. Our question concerns only the right of a state to deny enforcement to claims growing out of a valid federal law.

It is conceded that this same type of claim arising under Rhode Island law would be enforced by that State's courts. Its courts have enforced claims for double damages growing out of the Fair Labor Standards Act * * *. Thus the Rhode Island courts have jurisdiction adequate and appropriate under established local law to adjudicate this action. Under these circumstances the State courts are not free to refuse enforcement of petitioners' claim. * * *

Id. at 389–94, 67 S.Ct. at 812–15, 91 L.Ed. at 970–72.

Questions

What are the limits on the rule announced in *Testa*? Suppose that a state does not allow suits brought by corporations not registered to do business in that state. Could they be compelled under *Testa* to hear a federal claim brought by such a corporation in its court system?

DICE v. AKRON, CANTON & YOUNGSTOWN R. CO.

Supreme Court of the United States, 1952.
342 U.S. 359, 72 S.Ct. 312, 96 L.Ed. 398.

Certiorari to the Supreme Court of Ohio.

Opinion of the Court by MR. JUSTICE BLACK, announced by MR. JUSTICE DOUGLAS.

Petitioner, a railroad fireman, was seriously injured when an engine in which he was riding jumped the track. Alleging that his injuries were due to respondent's negligence, he brought this action for damages under the Federal Employers' Liability Act, 35 Stat. 65, 45 U.S.C. § 51 et seq., in an Ohio court of common pleas. Respondent's defenses were (1) a denial of negligence and (2) a written document signed by petitioner purporting to release respondent in full for $924.63. Petitioner admitted that he had signed several receipts for payments made him in connection with his injuries but denied that he had made a full and complete settlement of all his claims. He alleged that the purported release was void because he had signed it relying on respondent's deliberately false statement that the document was nothing more than a mere receipt for back wages.

After both parties had introduced considerable evidence the jury found in favor of petitioner and awarded him a $25,000 verdict. The trial judge later entered judgment notwithstanding the verdict. In doing so he reappraised the evidence as to fraud, found that petitioner had been "guilty of supine negligence" in failing to read the release, and accordingly held that the facts did not "sustain either in law or equity the allegations of fraud by clear, unequivocal and convincing evidence." This judgment notwithstanding the verdict was reversed by the Court of Appeals of Summit County, Ohio, on the ground that under federal law, which controlled, the jury's verdict must stand because there was ample evidence to support its finding of fraud. The Ohio Supreme Court, one judge dissenting, reversed the Court of Appeals' judgment and sustained the trial court's action, holding that: (1) Ohio, not federal, law governed; (2) under that law petitioner, a man of ordinary intelligence who could read, was bound by the release even though he had been induced to sign it by the deliberately false statement that it was only a receipt for back wages; and (3) under controlling Ohio law factual issues as to fraud in the execution of this release were properly decided by the judge rather than by the jury. * * *

First. We agree with the Court of Appeals of Summit County, Ohio, and the dissenting judge in the Ohio Supreme Court and hold that validity of releases under the Federal Employers' Liability Act raises a federal question to be determined by federal rather than state law. Congress in § 1 of the Act granted petitioner a right to recover against his employer for damages negligently inflicted. State laws are not controlling in determining what the incidents of this federal right shall be. * * * Manifestly the federal rights affording relief to injured railroad employees under a federally declared standard could be defeated if states were permitted to have the final say as to what defenses could and could not be properly interposed to suits under the Act. Moreover, only if federal law controls can the federal Act be given that uniform application throughout the country essential to effectuate its purposes. * * * Releases and other devices designed to liquidate or defeat injured employees' claims play an important part in the federal Act's administration. * * * Their validity is but one of the many interrelated questions that must constantly be determined in these cases according to a uniform federal law.

Second. In effect the Supreme Court of Ohio held that * * * the negligence of an innocent worker is sufficient to enable his employer to benefit by its deliberate fraud. Application of so harsh a rule to defeat a railroad employee's claim is wholly incongruous with the general policy of the Act to give railroad employees a right to recover just compensation for injuries negligently inflicted by their employers. And this Ohio rule is out of harmony with modern judicial and legislative practice to relieve injured persons from the effect of releases fraudulently obtained. * * * We hold that the correct federal rule is that * * * a release of rights under the Act is void when the employee is induced to sign it by the deliberately false and material statements of the railroad's authorized representatives made to deceive the employee as to the contents of the release. The trial court's charge to the jury correctly stated this rule of law.

Third. Ohio provides and has here accorded petitioner the usual jury trial of factual issues relating to negligence. But Ohio treats factual questions of fraudulent releases differently. It permits the judge trying a negligence case to resolve all factual questions of fraud "other than fraud in the factum." The factual issue of fraud is thus split into fragments, some to be determined by the judge, others by the jury.

It is contended that since a state may consistently with the Federal Constitution provide for trial of cases under the Act by a nonunanimous verdict, Minneapolis & St. Louis R. Co. v. Bombolis, 241 U.S. 211, 36 S.Ct. 595, 60 L.Ed. 961, Ohio may lawfully eliminate trial by jury as to one phase of fraud while allowing jury trial as to all other issues raised. The *Bombolis* case might be more in point had Ohio abolished trial by jury in all negligence cases including those arising under the federal Act. But Ohio has not done this. It has provided jury trials for cases arising under the federal Act but seeks to single out one phase of the question of fraudulent releases for determination by a judge rather than by a jury.

* * *

We have previously held that "The right to trial by jury is 'a basic and fundamental feature of our system of federal jurisprudence'" and that it is "part and parcel of the remedy afforded railroad workers under the Employers' Liability Act." Bailey v. Central Vermont R. Co., 319 U.S. 350, 354, 63 S.Ct. 1062, 1064, 87 L.Ed. 1444. We also recognized in that case that to deprive railroad workers of the benefit of a jury trial where there is evidence to support negligence "is to take away a goodly portion of the relief which Congress has afforded them." It follows that the right to trial by jury is too substantial a part of the rights accorded by the Act to permit it to be classified as a mere "local rule of procedure" for denial in the manner that Ohio has here used. * * *

Reversed and remanded with directions.

MR. JUSTICE FRANKFURTER, whom MR. JUSTICE REED, MR. JUSTICE JACKSON and MR. JUSTICE BURTON join, concurring for reversal but dissenting from the Court's opinion.

Ohio, as do many other States, maintains the old division between law and equity as to the mode of trying issues, even though the same judge administers both. * * * [I]n all cases in Ohio, the judge is the trier of fact on this issue of fraud, rather than the jury. It is contended that the Federal Employers' Liability Act requires that Ohio courts send the fraud issue to a jury in the cases founded on that Act. To require Ohio to try a particular issue before a different fact-finder in negligence actions brought under the Employers' Liability Act from the fact-finder on the identical issue in every other negligence case disregards the settled distribution of judicial power between Federal and State courts where Congress authorizes concurrent enforcement of federally-created rights.

* * *

In 1916 the Court decided without dissent that States in entertaining actions under the Federal Employers' Liability Act need not provide a jury system other than that established for local negligence actions. States are not compelled to provide the jury required of Federal courts by the Seventh Amendment. Minneapolis & St. L.R. Co. v. Bombolis * * *. In the thirty-six years since this early decision after the enactment of the Federal Employers' Liability Act, 35 Stat. 65 (1908), the *Bombolis* case has often been cited by this Court but never questioned. Until today its significance has been to leave to States the choice of the fact-finding tribunal in all negligence actions, including those arising under the Federal Act. * * *

Although a State must entertain negligence suits brought under the Federal Employers' Liability Act if it entertains ordinary actions for negligence, it need conduct them only in the way in which it conducts the run of negligence litigation. The *Bombolis* case directly establishes that the Employers' Liability Act does not impose the jury requirements of the Seventh Amendment on the States *pro tanto* for Employers' Liability litigation. If its reasoning means anything, the *Bombolis* decision means that, if a State chooses not to have a jury at all, but to leave questions of fact in all negligence actions to a court, certainly the Employers' Liability Act does not require a State to have juries for negligence actions brought under the Federal Act in its courts. Or, if a State chooses to retain the old double system of courts, common law and equity * * *, surely there is nothing in the Employers' Liability Act that requires traditional distribution of authority for disposing of legal issues as between common law and chancery courts to go by the board. * * * So long as all negligence suits in a State are treated in the same way, by the same mode of disposing equitable, non-jury, and common law, jury issues, the State does not discriminate against Employers' Liability suits nor does it make any inroad upon substance.

Ohio and her sister States with a similar division of functions between law and equity are not trying to evade their duty under the Federal Employers' Liability Act * * *. The States merely exercise a preference in adhering to historic ways of dealing with a claim of fraud; they prefer the traditional way of making unavailable through equity an otherwise valid defense. The State judges and local lawyers who must administer the Federal Employers' Liability Act in State courts are trained in the ways of local practice; it multiplies the difficulties and confuses the administration of justice to require, on purely theoretical grounds, a hybrid of State and Federal practice in the State courts as to a single class of cases. Nothing in the Employers' Liability Act or in the judicial enforcement of the Act for over forty years forces such judicial hybridization upon the States. The fact that Congress authorized actions under the Federal Employers' Liability Act to be brought in State as well as in Federal courts seems a strange basis for the inference that Congress overrode State procedural arrangements controlling all other negligence suits in a State * * *. Such an inference is admissible, so it seems to me, only on the theory that Congress included as part of the right created by the Employers' Liability Act an assumed likelihood that trying all issues to juries is more favorable to plaintiffs. * * *

Even though the method of trying the equitable issue of fraud which the State applies in all other negligence cases governs Employers' Liability cases, two questions remain for decision: Should the validity of the release be tested by a Federal or a State standard? And if by a Federal one, did the Ohio courts in the present case correctly administer the standard? If the States afford courts for enforcing the Federal Act, they must enforce the substance of the right given by Congress. They cannot depreciate the legislative currency issued by Congress—either expressly or by local methods of enforcement that accomplish the same result. * * * In order to prevent diminution of railroad workers' nationally-uniform right to recover, the standard for the validity of a release of contested liability must be Federal. * * *

Notes and Questions

1. In what ways is the question of what law governs the right to jury trial in *Dice* the same or distinguishable from the question of the governing law in *Byrd*? Under what circumstances might a state court ignore federal law when it deems it to be inconsistent with its own law or policy? By what

method is uniform construction and application of federal law by state courts assured?

2.   Under what circumstances might a state court or legislature voluntarily incorporate or apply federal law to a state-created right? Would such an incorporation or application present a federal question for purposes of original jurisdiction in the federal district courts or appellate jurisdiction in the United States Supreme Court? See generally Hart, *The Relations Between State and Federal Law,* 54 Colum.L.Rev. 489, 536–38 (1954); Note, *Supreme Court Review of State Interpretations of Federal Law Incorporated by Reference,* 66 Harv.L.Rev. 1498 (1953). Are the federal courts bound by the state construction of the incorporated federal law?

3.   In BROWN v. WESTERN RY. OF ALABAMA, 338 U.S. 294, 70 S.Ct. 105, 94 L.Ed. 100 (1949), respondent demurred to petitioner's complaint in an action brought in a Georgia state court under the Federal Employers' Liability Act. The theory of the demurrer was that the complaint failed to "set forth a cause of action and is otherwise insufficient in law." The Georgia courts sustained the demurrer on the basis of a state practice rule requiring pleading allegations to be construed "most strongly against the pleader." The Supreme Court reversed, stating in part:

> It is contended that this construction of the complaint is binding on us. The argument is that while state courts are without power to detract from "substantive rights" granted by Congress in FELA cases, they are free to follow their own rules of "practice" and "procedure." To what extent rules of practice and procedure may themselves dig into "substantive rights" is a troublesome question at best * * *. [C]ases in this Court point up the impossibility of laying down a precise rule to distinguish "substance" from "procedure." Fortunately, we need not attempt to do so. A long series of cases previously decided, from which we see no reason to depart, makes it our duty to construe the allegations of this complaint ourselves in order to determine whether petitioner has been denied a right of trial granted him by Congress. This federal right cannot be defeated by the forms of local practice. * * *

> Strict local rules of pleading cannot be used to impose unnecessary burdens upon rights of recovery authorized by federal laws. * * * Should this Court fail to protect federally created rights from dismissal because of over-exacting local requirements for meticulous pleadings, desirable uniformity in adjudication of federally created rights could not be achieved.

Id. at 296, 298–99, 70 S.Ct. at 106, 108, 94 L.Ed. at 102–04. Of what relevance is the presence or absence under Georgia practice of a right to replead following a demurrer?

4.   Is the process of applying federal law in a state court identical to the process of applying state law in a federal court under the *Erie* doctrine? How does a state court ascertain federal law? Suppose, for example, that there is a conflict between the federal courts of appeals over what a statute means, or over an issue of federal common law. Is the state court free to adopt any position it wishes? What if the state court never has ruled on the issue? Should the state court try to figure out how the federal court might have ruled? Which federal court? How does a state court determine which aspects of federal law it must apply?

5.   May the federal government require state courts to apply the Federal Rules of Civil Procedure in order to ensure that a federally-created right is enforced with procedures which the federal government approves?   Should the federal government do so?   In FEDERAL ENERGY REGULATORY COMMISSION v. MISSISSIPPI, 456 U.S. 742, 102 S.Ct. 2126, 72 L.Ed.2d 532 (1982), the Supreme Court upheld provisions of the Public Utilities Regulatory Policies Act of 1978 (PURPA) which required state public utility commissions to observe certain federal procedures in regulating energy usage.   Justice Powell, concurring in part of the judgment and dissenting in part, wrote:

> "The general rule, bottomed deeply in belief in the importance of state control of state judicial procedure, is that federal law takes the state courts as it finds them."   Hart, The Relations Between State and Federal Law, 54 Colum.L.Rev. 489, 508 (1954).   I believe the same principle must apply to other organs of state government.   It may be true that the procedural provisions of the PURPA may not effect dramatic changes in the laws and procedures of some States.   But I know of no other attempt by the Federal Government to supplant state-prescribed procedures that in part define the nature of their administrative agencies.   If Congress may do this, presumably it has the power to pre-empt state-court rules of civil procedure and judicial review in classes of cases found to affect commerce.

Id. at 774, 102 S.Ct. at 2145, 72 L.Ed.2d at 556–57.

6.   The question of federal control over state procedures when a state court is adjudicating a federal cause of action is discussed in Meltzer, *State Court Forfeitures of Federal Rights,* 99 Harv.L.Rev. 1130 (1986); Neuborne, *Toward Procedural Parity in Constitutional Litigation,* 22 Wm. & Mary L.Rev. 725 (1981); Redish & Muench, *Adjudication of Federal Causes of Action in State Court,* 75 Mich.L.Rev. 311 (1976).   See also Steinglass, *The Emerging State Court § 1983 Action: A Procedural Review,* 38 U.Miami L.Rev. 381 (1984).

Chapter 4

THE DEVELOPMENT OF MODERN PROCEDURE

SECTION A. COMMON–LAW PLEADING

STEPHEN, THE PRINCIPLES OF PLEADING IN CIVIL ACTIONS
37, 147–50 (Tyler ed. 1882): [a]

In the course of administering justice between litigating parties there are two successive objects: to ascertain the subject for decision, and to decide. It is evident that, towards the attainment of the first of these results, there is, in a *general* point of view, only one satisfactory mode of proceeding; and that this consists in making each of the parties state his own case, and collecting, from the opposition of their statements, the points of the legal controversy. Thus far, therefore, the course of every system of judicature is the same. It is common to them all to require, on behalf of each contending party, before the decision of the cause, a statement of his case. But from this point the coincidence naturally ceases. * * *

The manner of allegation in our courts may be said to have been first methodically formed and cultivated as a science in the reign of Edward I [1272–1307]. From this time the judges began systematically to prescribe and enforce certain *rules of statement* * * *. None of them seem to have been originally of legislative enactment, or to have had any authority except usage or judicial regulation; but, from the general perception of their wisdom and utility, they acquired the character of fixed and positive institutions, and grew up into an entire and connected *system of pleading*. * * *

As the object of all pleading or judicial allegation is to ascertain the subject for decision, so the main object of that system of pleading established in the common law of England is to ascertain it by the production of an *issue;* and this appears to be peculiar to that system. * * *

The author is of opinion that this peculiarity of coming to issue took its rise in the practice of *oral* pleading. It seems a natural incident of

a. This edition is based upon Stephen's own second edition of 1827, which is the last of his editions before the reform of common-law pleading in England in 1834.

that practice, to compel the pleaders to short and terse allegations, applying to each other by way of answer, in somewhat of a logical form, and at length reducing the controversy to a precise point. For while the pleading was *merely* oral, * * * the court and the pleaders would have to rely exclusively on their memory for retaining the tenor of the discussion; and the development of some precise question or issue would then be a very convenient practice, because it would prevent the necessity of reviewing the different statements, and leave no burden on the memory but that of retaining the question itself so developed. And even after the practice of recording was introduced, the same brief and logical forms of allegation would naturally continue to be acceptable, while the pleadings were still *viva voce* * * *.

A co-operative reason for coming to issue was the variety of the modes of decision which the law assigned to different kinds of question. * * * As questions of law were decided by the *court,* and matters of fact referred to other kinds of investigation, it was, in the first place, necessary to settle whether the question in the cause or issue was a matter of *law* or *fact.* Again, if it happened to be a matter of fact, it required to be developed in a form sufficiently specific to show what was the method of trial appropriate to the case. And, unless the state of the question were thus adjusted between the parties, it is evident that they would not have known whether they were to put themselves on the judgment of the court or to go to trial; nor, in the latter case, whether they were to prepare themselves for trial by jury or for one of the other various modes of deciding [the] matter of fact.

Notes

1. The change from oral to written pleadings cannot be dated precisely. The shift began in the late fourteenth century and extended into the second half of the sixteenth. Predictably the change increased the rigor and technicality of the pleading rules.

> * * * [T]his system of oral pleading had one great advantage over the later system of written pleadings. It made for far greater freedom in the statement of the case. * * * [W]hen all objections to the writ and process had been disposed of * * * the debate between the opposing counsel, carried on subject to the advice or the rulings of the judge, allowed the parties considerable latitude in pleading to the issue. Suggested pleas will, after a little discussion, be seen to be untenable; a proposition to demur will, after a few remarks by the judge, be obviously the wrong move. The counsel feel their way towards an issue which each can accept and allow to be enrolled. * * *

3 Holdsworth, *A History of English Law* 635 (4th ed. 1935). Milsom, *Historical Foundations of the Common Law* 28–37, 39–40 (1969), contains a good description of oral pleadings as well as an excellent explanation of the Yearbooks, from which most of our knowledge of early pleading is derived; this book is a particularly valuable reference for most of the matters covered in this Chapter.

2. In this discussion we are concerned with pleading in the royal courts. It should be noted that at the time of the Norman Conquest (1066) and for a

century or more afterward the ordinary recourse of suitors was not to the royal courts but to local, or communal, courts and to feudal courts in which a lord heard cases involving his tenants. The royal courts existed primarily to try offenses against the king's laws and to hear cases involving his tenants-in-chief, which came before the king in his capacity as a feudal lord. Gradually, however, these royal courts began to absorb business from the communal and feudal courts.

A person with a grievance against another sought justice from the king, and the king issued a *writ,* ordering the sheriff to bring the other person before the king's judges to answer the complaint. In the course of the twelfth century this pattern became standardized. When it became established that the king's courts would hear a particular kind of case—for example, an action for assault, an action for debt, an action for the possession of land—the complainant in such a case could obtain a writ from the king's chief minister, the chancellor, as a matter of course. See Milsom, *Historical Foundations of the Common Law* 22–25 (1969).

The writ, strictly speaking, was simply the document that commenced the action, similar in function to the modern summons; but each writ came to embody a *form of action,* a concept that governed the method of commencing the suit, the substantive requirements of the case, the manner of trial, and the type of sanction that would attend the eventual judgment. See pp. 432–36, infra. For the present it is enough to say that there was a writ for each type of case—or form of action—that the royal courts would hear; thus, for example, there was a writ of trespass, a writ of debt, and a writ of nuisance. If plaintiff selected a writ that did not fit the case, the action would fail. If there was no writ that fit the case, and the chancellor would not draw up a new one, plaintiff could obtain no relief in the royal courts.

3. The "modes of decision" for issues of fact, referred to in the extract from Stephen, were, at an early date, "trial" by ordeal, by combat, and by oath. These were not trials in the sense in which we now understand and use that term; rather they were proofs undertaken by one of the parties (or both in the case of combat) at the direction of the court. Ordeal—proof by carrying a red-hot iron unscathed or by sinking when thrown into a pool of water [b]—disappeared in England after it was proscribed by the Lateran Council in 1215. Combat—waged by champions of the parties—was resisted as a Norman importation, and during the reign of Henry II (1154–1189) an early form of jury began to supplant it, although it was not formally abolished until 1819.

For our purpose the most important of these early methods of proof was that by oath, or as more generally known, *wager of law* or *compurgation.* It required one of the parties to swear to his case with strict and elaborate formalities, accompanied by a number of "oath-helpers," usually twelve, who swore to the truthfulness of the party's oath, or in later periods to their belief in its truth. If all went as prescribed, he prevailed; but if the party or any of the "helpers" made an error by using a wrong word, that party lost.

It is hard for us to say how this ancient procedure worked in practice, hard to tell how easy it was to get oath-helpers who would swear falsely, hard to tell how much risk there was in an ordeal. The rational element

b. See Lea, *Superstition and Force* 252, 279 (3d ed. 1878). In ordeal by water, it was thought that the water would reject the evil-doer; a rope was tied to the person making the proof in the hope that if proved innocent he could be kept from drowning.

of law must, it would seem, have asserted itself in the judgment which decided how and by whom the proof should be given; the jurisprudence of the old courts must have been largely composed of the answers to this question; * * * for example, we can see that even before the Norman Conquest the man who has been often accused has to go to the ordeal instead of being allowed to purge himself with oath-helpers.

Maitland, *Equity, Also the Forms of Action at Common Law* 310 (1909).

The importance of this procedure in legal history lies in the fact that a right to wage one's law was firmly established in certain classes of cases by the last half of the twelfth century, long before the jury began to emerge as an instrument for fact-determination. In its original form the jury, developed as a body for valuing property for taxes, decided cases on its own knowledge rather than after hearing witnesses. Even in this form suitors saw in the jury a more rational mode of trial, and sought to use forms of action such as trespass, which having developed at a relatively late period did not provide a right to wager of law.[c] Thus, as we shall see in Section B of this Chapter, judicial development of the law for four-and-a-half centuries was channeled and motivated to a substantial degree by increasingly successful attempts to avoid the older modes of trial.[d]

1. A BRIEF OVERVIEW OF COMMON–LAW PLEADING

The basic structure of common-law pleading was simple and well-calculated to bring the parties to an issue of law or of fact. It was based on the following analysis. A substantive response to a claim—other than an expression of total agreement—will fall into one of three categories: (1) A party can deny that the alleged facts, even if true, give the claimant any legal right; (2) a party can deny that the alleged facts are true; or (3) a party can say that even if the alleged facts are true and taken alone would establish a right, additional facts not mentioned by the claimant negate that right. Responses (1) and (2) raise issues of law and of fact respectively. Response (3) does not itself raise a contested issue; there is as yet no necessary disagreement between the parties. To raise the necessary issue the claimant must respond to the response, and this response also may fall into any of the three categories. If this response is again of type (3) no issue will have been raised and the process must continue. (How do the Federal Rules avoid the necessity for further pleading after a type (3) response? See Federal Rules 7(a) and 8(d).)

Of course the real process was more complex than this. Plaintiff's claim was set forth in the *declaration*. This document had to meet many formal requirements that might differ from one type of case to another. But stripped of much verbiage, and stated in modern English, it might

---

c. A similar desire to avoid trial by combat was among the causes for the desuetude of the writ of right, once the most important action. Preference for jury trial also encouraged the expanding jurisdiction of royal courts at the expense of the feudal courts since the jury was found only in the former.

d. For a time in the fourteenth century it seemed that wager of law might be denied when the facts were well known to witnesses, but this development aborted. Fifoot, *History and Sources of the Common Law—Tort and Contract* 28–29 (1949). By the last quarter of the sixteenth century, however, "a defendant proposing to wage his law was somehow examined and admonished." Milsom, *Historical Foundations of the Common Law* 292–93 (1969).

have said: "Defendant promised to deliver a horse to plaintiff and plaintiff promised to pay 100 dollars for it, but defendant has refused to deliver the horse."

At this point, defendant had to *demur* or *plead*. A demurrer would challenge the legal sufficiency of the declaration. Thus prior to STRANGBOROUGH & WARNERS CASE, 4 Leon. 3, 74 Eng.Rep. 686 (K.B. 1589), the modern language declaration set out above would have failed on demurrer, because a promise was not regarded as good consideration for a promise until that decision. A demurrer also would succeed if plaintiff had chosen the wrong writ (or form of action). There were also a great many technical sins that the declaration might commit, but by statute, 27 Eliz. 1, c. 5, § 1 (1585) and 4 Anne, c. 16, § 1 (1705), unless these defects were raised by a *special demurrer,* which precisely spelled out the faults, they were waived. If a demurrer was sustained, plaintiff was out of court, although he generally was free to begin again if he could correct the mistake, as by suing in another form of action if the original form was incorrect. If the demurrer was quashed, judgment was entered for plaintiff.

If defendant did not demur, he responded to the declaration in a *plea.* Pleas were of two types, *dilatory* and *peremptory.* Dilatory pleas did not deny the merits of plaintiff's claim, but challenged plaintiff's right to have the court hear the case; they included pleas to the jurisdiction of the court, pleas of a variance between the declaration and the writ, and pleas that the case must be suspended (when, for example, one of the parties was under age at the time of suit). A peremptory plea, or *plea in bar,* was on the merits. If defendant denied that he had promised to sell the horse, the plea was a *traverse;* a traverse terminated the pleadings and the case would go to trial to dispose of the issue raised by plaintiff's allegation and defendant's denial. But suppose defendant wanted to allege that at the time of the purported contract he was a minor; defendant would then plead by *confession and avoidance,* that is, admit the allegations of the declaration and seek to avoid them by pleading minority. If defendant followed this course, no issue would have been reached, and plaintiff would have to respond.

Plaintiff's response might be a demurrer to defendant's plea, which would raise the question whether minority was a defense to the agreement he had pleaded and defendant had confessed.[e] Or plaintiff might plead in a *replication,* either traversing defendant's allegation of his age, or confessing it, and alleging that defendant had lied about his age when making the contract. If plaintiff pleaded in confession and avoidance, defendant would again have to respond, by demurrer or by *rejoinder.* The pleas in confession and avoidance theoretically might go on indefinitely, and in some of the cases we read of a *surrejoinder,* a *rebutter,* and a *surrebutter.* Lack of formal names beyond that point suggests that even the ingenuity of the common-law pleader may have had its limits.

e. After a successful demurrer to a dilatory plea, judgment was not entered for plaintiff, but by an order *respondeat ouster,* defendant was directed to plead over.

The common-law pleading system may seem ornate to you, even after only the brief description on the preceding pages. Yet bear in mind that this is only a skeletal outline. When the outline is filled in with special instances, inexplicable exceptions, arbitrary rules, and untraversable fictions, the result is one of the most complex and snare-ridden creations ever devised by man. Let us look at a common-law record and decision. (The reporter of the case, it should be noted, is the victorious lawyer, Saunders.)

VEALE v. WARNER
Court of King's Bench, 1670.
1 Wms. Saund. 323, 326, 85 Eng.Rep. 463, 468.

Be it remembered that * * * before our lord the King at Westminster came Thomas Veale Esquire * * * and brought here * * * his certain bill against William Warner, * * * in the custody of the marshal, &c. of a plea of debt: and there are pledges of prosecution, to wit, John Doe and Richard Roe; which said bill follows in these words, * * * [Veale] complains of [Warner] * * * that he render to him 2000l., of lawful money of England, which he owes to, and unjustly detains from him; for that whereas the said William, * * * at London aforesaid, to wit, in the parish of St. Mary-le Bow in the ward of Cheap, by his certain writing obligatory, sealed * * * and to the Court of our said lord the King now here shewn, * * * acknowledged himself to be held and firmly bound to * * * [Veale] in the said 2000l. to be paid to the said Thomas when he should be thereunto requested. Nevertheless, the said William (although often requested) hath not yet paid the said 2000l. to the said Thomas, but to pay the same to him hath hitherto altogether refused, and yet refuses, to the damage of him the said Thomas of 100l.: and therefore he brings suit, &c.

And [Warner] * * * comes and defends the wrong and injury when, &c. and prays oyer of the said writing obligatory, and it is read to him, &c. He also prays oyer of the condition of the said writing, &c. and it is read to him in these words, to wit: "The condition of this obligation is such, that if * * * [Warner] shall and do in all things well and truly stand to, obey, abide, perform, fulfil, and keep the award * * * of John Coggs, gent. and John Foxwell, arbitrators * * * to arbitrate * * * and determine of and concerning all and all manner of action and actions, cause and causes of actions, suits, bills, bonds, specialties, judgments, executions, extents, quarrels, controversies, trespasses, damages, and demands whatsoever, at any time heretofore had, made, moved, brought, commenced, sued, prosecuted, done, suffered, committed, or depending by or between the said parties, * * * then this obligation to be void and of none effect, or else to remain in full force and virtue." Which being read and heard, the said William saith, that * * * [Veale] ought not to have his aforesaid action against him, because he saith that * * * the arbitrators in the said condition named, * * * made their award * * * that [Warner] * * * should satisfy, content, and pay to [Veale] * * * the full sum of 3169l. 16s. and 3d. of lawful money of England. And they further

awarded that [Warner] * * * should seal, and as his deed deliver to
[Veale] * * * a full and general release and discharge of all and all
manner of actions, and causes of actions, suits, bills, bonds, specialties,
judgments, executions, extents, quarrels, controversies, trespasses, damages, and demands whatsoever, at any time before the date of the bond
brought here into Court had, made, moved, commenced, sued, prosecuted,
committed, or depending by or between the said parties. And * * *
[Warner] further saith, that he the said William * * * paid to * * *
[Veale] the said sum * * * and also, then and there did seal, and as his
deed deliver to * * * [Veale] the said full release * * * and this he is
ready to verify: wherefore he prays judgment if the said Thomas ought to
have or maintain his said action thereof against him &c.

And * * * [Veale] saith, that he by any thing by * * * [Warner]
above in pleading alleged, ought not to be barred from having his said
action thereof against the said William, because he saith that * * *
[Warner] did not pay the said sum * * * as the said William hath above
thereof in pleading alleged; and this he prays may be inquired of by the
country, &c.

And * * * [Warner] saith that * * * [Veale] ought not to be
admitted to say that he the said William hath not paid the said sum
* * * because he saith that he the said Thomas, * * * by his certain
writing acknowledged that he the said William had paid the said sum to
the said Thomas * * * and this he is ready to verify: wherefore he
prays judgment if the said Thomas ought to be admitted, against his own
acknowledgment, to say, that he the said William hath not paid the said
sum of money, &c.

Demurrer and joinder in demurrer.

* * *

And now in this term the plaintiff moved to have judgment. And
Saunders for the defendant objected that the plaintiff could not have
judgment, because it appeared by the record that the award was void,
being all to be performed by the defendant and nothing by the plaintiff:
and, therefore, if the award is void, it is not material whether the
defendant has performed it or not, although he has pleaded a performance
of it. And now he has acknowledged the contrary by his waiver of the
issue offered by the plaintiff and pleading a bad rejoinder. And the
plaintiff and defendant have both agreed, that the award pleaded by the
defendant was the true award made by the arbitrators, which is altogeth-
'er vicious. But if the plaintiff would have helped himself, he ought to
have shewn the other part of the award before he assigned the breach,
which he has not done here; and therefore he cannot have judgment.

And of such opinion was the whole Court clearly. But they would not
give judgment for the defendant, because they conceived it was a trick in
pleading; but they gave the plaintiff leave to discontinue on payment of
costs. And Kelynge Chief Justice, reprehended Saunders for pleading so
subtly on purpose to trick the plaintiff by the omission of the other part of
the award. But it was a case of the greatest hardship on the defendant;
for the bond of submission was only in the penalty of 2000l., and the

arbitrators had awarded him to pay 3100l., being 1100l. more than the real penalty of the bond; when in truth there was nothing at all due to the plaintiff, but he was indebted to the defendant. And afterwards the defendant exhibited an English bill in the Exchequer, disclosing bad practice of the plaintiff with the arbitrators, and had relief against the bond: and so this matter was at rest. * * *

Notes and Questions

1. "[B]efore our lord the King at Westminster." Veale v. Warner was brought in the Court of King's Bench, one of the three royal common-law courts, maintaining separate existence until merged in the High Court of Justice in 1873. The others were the Court of Common Pleas and the Court of Exchequer. All three developed out of the *Curia Regis* (the King's Court), which at the time of the Norman Conquest and for a period thereafter performed administrative and judicial functions in conjunction with the king. The first offshoot was Exchequer, which originally was charged with the collection and administration of the king's finances, but by 1250 had acquired full judicial jurisdiction. Next to develop separate status was Common Pleas, established by Henry II as the primary tribunal to hear cases not involving the crown. The remaining part of the King's Court supervised Common Pleas through the writ of error, and heard matters particularly touching the king's interests, such as criminal actions and cases involving his tenants in chief; it developed into King's Bench, but the fiction was maintained that hearings before that tribunal were before the king himself. See Plucknett, *A Concise History of the Common Law* 143–51 (5th ed. 1956).

2. "[H]is * * * bill against William Warner, * * * in the custody of the marshal, &c." Common Pleas was supposed to have exclusive jurisdiction over actions of debt, such as Veale v. Warner. But the judges and lawyers of each common-law court zealously sought to expand the jurisdiction of their tribunal, and Veale v. Warner illustrates one method by which King's Bench accomplished this. Not all common-law proceedings were commenced by writ; to an undefined extent each court could proceed on a *bill,* which was a complaint addressed directly to the court. See 2 Holdsworth, *A History of English Law* 339 (3d ed. 1923). One instance in which a court clearly could proceed on a bill was an action against one of the court's officers or a person within its custody, and such a bill might be brought on a cause of action that ordinarily was not within the jurisdiction of the court. Thus, a plaintiff who desired to bring an action of debt in King's Bench would first charge defendant with trespass, and by a "bill of Middlesex" that court would order the sheriff of Middlesex to arrest defendant and deliver him to the custody of the marshal of the Marshalsea—the court's prison; once defendant was within the custody of King's Bench, plaintiff could proceed against him by bill in the action of debt. Predictably, the arrest and commitment eventually became wholly fictitious, but defendant was not permitted to challenge the allegation that they had occurred. A similar device used to expand the jurisdiction of Exchequer was the writ of *quo minus,* by which a debtor to the crown could bring suit in that court on the theory that anyone withholding money from the debtor was rendering him unable to pay what was owed the king; in time, the allegation of plaintiff's debt to the king also became

untraversable. See Plucknett, op. cit. supra at 161, 387; Milsom, *Historical Foundations of the Common Law* 53–59 (1969).

3. "[P]ledges of prosecution." The original writ in a lawsuit directed the sheriff, to whom it was addressed, to take some action, conditioned on plaintiff's "mak[ing] you secure of prosecuting his claim." Thus plaintiff had to furnish sureties, who would be liable to pay a fine that was imposed upon unsuccessful claimants. As the names of the pledges in the case suggest, the requirement became a sham.

4. "[I]n the parish of St. Mary-le Bow in the ward of Cheap." As the jury originally decided cases on its own knowledge, it was necessary that jurors be drawn from the vicinity in which a transaction had occurred; the action therefore had to be brought near the place at which it arose, and the declaration had to show this. Since an English court could not summon jurors from abroad, technically it would have been impossible to bring an action on a contract made outside England. In such cases, however, plaintiff made an untraversable allegation that the contract had been made in the aforesaid parish and ward of the city of London. See Sack, *Conflict of Laws in the History of English Law,* in *3 Law: A Century of Progress* 342, 370 (1937). Some cases actually must have arisen there, but you cannot tell from the records which they are.

5. "[T]o the Court * * * now here shewn"; "prays oyer." A plaintiff suing upon a deed or a bond made profert of the document—that is, the plaintiff formally tendered it to the court, although it was strictly speaking not a part of the pleading. If defendant wanted to get the document in the pleadings in order to raise a question of law about it, she had to demand oyer of it, which meant that defendant was entitled to read it and copy as much of it as she chose into the plea. At this point you might conclude that if defendant demurred, she would be demurring to her own pleading, but even though the document was set out in the plea, it was treated as if it were a part of the declaration. See Sutton, *Personal Actions at Common Law* 103 (1929), which is a particularly valuable introduction to common-law pleading. In what way does this process resemble the modern motion for summary judgment? See p. 10, supra.

6. "[W]herefore he prays judgment if the said Thomas ought to have or maintain his said action." This is the standard conclusion of a pleading in confession and avoidance. Compare the conclusion of plaintiff's replication in the next paragraph of the report of the case. Why was defendant's allegation that he had performed the bond treated as a matter of confession and avoidance?

7. "[W]herefore he prays judgment if the said Thomas ought to be admitted, against his own acknowledgment, to say." Plaintiff in his replication had traversed defendant's claim of payment. Thus the replication already had created an issue, and defendant's rejoinder could not be one of the three responses described in the Overview of Common-Law Pleading, pp. 423–24, supra; it is a plea of estoppel, and as stated in Saunders' argument waives the issue created by the traverse in plaintiff's replication. Why was this rejoinder "bad"? Did it allege that the award had been paid?

8. Why did Saunders, a thoroughly capable lawyer, file what he knew was an inadequate rejoinder? The answer lies in a peculiar facet of the demurrer:

> * * * *[O]n demurrer the court will consider the whole record, and give judgment for the party, who on the whole, appears to be entitled to it.* Thus, on demurrer to the replication, if the court think the replication bad, but perceive a substantial fault in the *plea,* they will give judgment, not for the defendant, but the plaintiff, provided the *declaration* be good; but if the declaration also be bad in substance, then, upon the same principle, judgment would be given for the defendant.

Stephen, *The Principles of Pleading in Civil Actions* 160 (Tyler ed. 1882). Thus, by making a rejoinder that he knew plaintiff would demur to, Saunders baited the trap he had set in his plea.

9. "[A]n English bill in the Exchequer." That part of the report of Veale v. Warner beginning, "But it was a case of the greatest hardship * * * *" is not a part of the record, but is simply the reporter's justification of his own tactics. An English bill was a bill in equity, so-called because it was written in English rather than in the Latin of the common-law courts. As we will see, many instances of fraud and overreaching did not constitute defenses at law, but when such factors were established equity would enjoin a victorious plaintiff from enforcing the judgment at law. See p. 457, infra. But how could such relief be obtained in Exchequer, which was a common-law court? The answer is that Exchequer had an equity side.

2. THE QUEST FOR A SINGLE ISSUE: PATHS AND PITFALLS

The principal aim of common-law pleading was the production of a single issue; in many ways, the most serious problems in common-law pleading grew out of this persistent drive. To achieve the goal of singleness of issue, it was necessary to prohibit *duplicity* in pleading. That term did not connote fraud, but simply meant raising more than one issue in a pleading. Thus, in our example concerning the sale of the horse, defendant might wish to deny that he had made any promise *and* to assert that he was a minor at the time *and* to contend that a promise was not good consideration for another promise. There would be nothing devious or inconsistent in claiming all three defenses, but he was not permitted to do so. The traverse, the plea in confession and avoidance, and the demurrer were mutually exclusive.

A procedure was available that, in effect, permitted a party to delay the "demurrer." After trial and verdict for plaintiff, defendant could *move to arrest the judgment,* thereby raising the question whether the pleadings could support the judgment. In the case of a verdict for defendant, plaintiff's equivalent motion was for *judgment notwithstanding the verdict*—a term that has now come to identify a motion on a quite different theory. See p. 14, supra. By following this procedure, however, a party could not escape the expense of trial (costs not being awarded to the prevailing party on such a motion), and that party assumed the risk that the defect in a pleading might be cured by a later pleading or aided by the verdict; in any event, a fault that required the use of a special demurrer would not support such a delayed motion. Nonetheless, the practice became very popular.

No such procedure was available to the party who wanted to deny his adversary's allegations and at the same time advance affirmative allegations of his own. For the plea in confession and avoidance had to give *color.* "As a term of pleading, * * * ["color"] signifies an apparent or prima facie right; and the meaning of the rule, that every pleading in confession and avoidance must give color, is, that it must admit an apparent right in the opposite party, and rely, therefore, on some new matter by which that apparent right is defeated." Stephen, *The Principles of Pleading in Civil Actions* 206–07 (Tyler ed. 1882). A plea in confession and avoidance that failed to give color was doomed, even though it revealed a defense that could have been raised by traverse. In GIBBONS v. PEPPER, 1 Ld.Raym. 38, 91 Eng.Rep. 922 (K.B. 1695), an action for running down plaintiff, defendant admitted the trespass but pleaded that his horse had become so frightened he could not control it; on demurrer the court ordered judgment for plaintiff, holding that if defendant's facts were true there had been no battery at all and the plea should have been a traverse.

Out of this rule that a party could not plead new matter without confessing the opposing party's prima-facie right grew one of the weirder formulae of common-law pleading—the giving of *express color.* Today, we mercifully are spared the necessity of learning the hoary details that surrounded this device, but a brief look at it will illustrate the complexities of the system that lay beneath the surface of our original simple outline.

Suppose that plaintiff had brought an action of trespass against defendant for entering on plaintiff's land, and that the only genuine issue in the case was the title to the land, defendant contending that although plaintiff had been in possession of the land, defendant was the true owner. If defendant denied the trespass by a traverse, she would be permitted to establish her own title as a defense. However, even if the only issue concerning her title was a question of law, there would have to be a full trial and the case would be decided by a jury under the guidance of the judge. Trial could not be avoided unless defendant somehow could introduce the new matter—her claim of title—into the pleadings and thereby permit it to be made the subject of a demurrer. Yet under the rule that required a plea in confession and avoidance to give color to plaintiff's claim, defendant could not assert new matter without confessing plaintiff's apparent right. The solution of express color was for defendant to confess the existence of a plausible, but imperfect, title in plaintiff, and then to assert her own title by way of avoidance. Having done this, plaintiff could not traverse the confession—even though it was the sheerest fiction—for that would leave two issues in the case; he had to respond to the matter pleaded in avoidance, and when the validity of defendant's claim turned on a question of law, the appropriate response would be a demurrer. You should note, however, that although giving express color enabled defendant to introduce her claim of title into the case, defendant was not able at the same time to deny that she had entered the land at all.

The insistence on arriving at a single issue also prohibited raising more than one issue of fact in a pleading. The fault could be challenged only by a special demurrer, and over a long period the strictness of the prohibition against multiple issues was relaxed, but it never ceased to pose a problem for the pleader. Originally a declaration could not state more than one cause of action; at an early date, however, plaintiffs were permitted to join causes of action arising under the same writ, and, as long as they were stated in separate counts, different versions of the same cause of action could be pleaded.[f] Defendant was permitted to plead separately to each count, and indeed might demur to one, traverse a second, and confess and avoid a third. But defendant could not plead two or more defenses to a single count and the ability to deny more than one of its allegations was severely restricted. By a statute, 4 Anne, c. 16, § 4 (1705), this was changed to allow more than one plea to a count with the court's permission, but as long as common-law pleading survived there could be no more than one replication to a plea.

As a consequence of these rules, a defendant who did not demur was safest if he could make a defense under a plea of the *general issue,* which challenged plaintiff's whole case.[g] This plea spared defendant the necessity of spelling out his defense, which meant that he did not have to divulge it to plaintiff or run the risk of misstating it. More importantly, the general issue in effect permitted defendant to traverse a number of plaintiff's allegations and, in addition, to raise defenses that ordinarily would be matters of confession and avoidance. Of course not all defenses could be raised under the general issue, and knowing which defenses had to be specially pleaded in particular forms of action was a matter of subtle learning. Although the whole theoretical structure of common-law pleading and its quest for a single issue was threatened by the general issue, inexorable pressures—particularly in the eighteenth century—gradually expanded its scope and availability. In conjunction with the common counts—a particularly cryptic form of declaration in contract, see p. 449, infra—the plea of the general issue permitted some cases to come to trial with the issues not only unnarrowed, but indeed undisclosed. A good example of the problem was stated by Henry Brougham in a seminal speech to Parliament on law reform:

> * * * The plaintiff declares, that the defendant, being indebted to him for so much money had and received to the use of the said plaintiff * * * undertook and faithfully promised to pay it, but broke his engagement; and the count is thus framed, the self-same terms being invariably used, whatever be the cause of action which can be brought into Court under this head. * * * In the first place, such is the

f. This privilege was widely used because of the strictness of the rule against *variances* between pleading and proof. A good example of the prohibition on variances is Latham v. Rutley, 2 B. & C. 20, 107 Eng.Rep. 290 (K.B. 1823). Plaintiff who had pleaded breach of a contract to carry and deliver goods safely was nonsuited because he proved a contract to carry and deliver goods safely, fire and robbery excepted, even though the verdict established that the loss was not caused by either fire or robbery.

g. Plaintiff's equivalent to the plea of the general issue, the replication *de injuria*, was less frequently available, and in most cases plaintiff was permitted to seize on only one facet of the plea. The most famous illustration is Crogate's Case, 8 Coke 66b, 77 Eng. Rep. 574 (K.B. 1608), which forms the basis for a brilliant satire on the common-law system. Hayes, *Crogate's Case: A Dialogue in Ye Shades on Special Pleading,* in 9 Holdsworth, *A History of English Law* 417 (2d ed. 1938).

declaration for money paid by one individual to another, for the use and benefit of the plaintiff; this is what alone the words of the count imply, but to express this they are rarely, indeed, made use of. 2dly, The self-same terms are used on suing for money received on a consideration that fails, and used in the same way to describe all the endless variety of cases which can occur of such failure * * *. 3dly, The same words are used * * * to recover money paid under mistake of fact. 4thly, To recover money paid by one person to a stakeholder, in consideration of an illegal contract made with another person. 5thly, Money paid to revenue officers for releasing the goods illegally detained, of the person paying. 6thly, To try the right to any office, instead of bringing an assize. 7thly, To try the liability of the landlord for rates levied on his tenant. What information, then, does such a declaration give?

* * *

In the [form of action of] *indebitatus assumpsit,* from which I took my first example, * * * under [a plea of the general issue] no less than eight different defences may be set up; as, for instance, a denial of the contract, payment, usury, gaming, infancy, coverture, accord and satisfaction, release.

Brougham, *Present State of the Law* 70–71, 73 (1828).

Thus the pleadings in the English common-law courts immediately preceding the period of reform that began in 1825 presented a strange potpourri of ornate and sinuous paths toward an elusive single issue, side by side with a series of pleading rules that fostered abstract and unilluminating statements of dispute.

SECTION B. THE FORMS OF ACTION

1. THE DEVELOPMENT OF THE FORMS—CHIEFLY OF TRESPASS

MAITLAND, EQUITY, ALSO THE FORMS OF ACTION AT COMMON LAW 296, 298–99, 304–05, 314–15, 332, 335, 342–47, 359–61 (1909):

Let it be granted that one man has been wronged by another; the first thing that he or his advisers have to consider is what form of action he shall bring. * * * This choice is not merely a choice between a number of queer technical terms, it is a choice between methods of procedure adapted to cases of different kinds.

* * * '[A] form of action' has implied a particular original process, a particular mesne process, a particular final process, a particular mode of pleading, of trial, of judgment. But further to a very considerable degree the substantive law administered in a given form of action has grown up independently of the law administered in other forms. Each procedural pigeon-hole contains its own rules of substantive law, and it is with great caution that we may argue from what is found in one to what will probably be found in another; each has its own precedents. It is quite possible that a litigant will find that his case will fit some two or three of these pigeon-holes. If that be so he will have a choice, which will often be a choice between the old, cumbrous, costly, on the one hand, the modern,

rapid, cheap, on the other. Or again he may make a bad choice, fail in his action, and take such comfort as he can from the hints of the judges that another form of action might have been more successful. * * * Lastly he may find that, plausible as his case may seem, it just will not fit any one of the receptacles provided by the courts and he may take to himself the lesson that where there is no remedy there is no wrong.

* * * So long as the forms of action were still in use, it was difficult to tell the truth about their history. * * * But now, * * * the truth might be discovered and be told, and one part of the truth is assuredly this that throughout the early history of the forms of action there is an element of struggle, of struggle for jurisdiction. In order to understand them we must not presuppose a centralized system of justice * * *; rather we must think that the forms of action, the original writs, are the means whereby justice is becoming centralized, whereby the king's court is drawing away business from other courts.

* * * I shall attempt a sketch in brief outline of the order in which the different forms of action are developed. * * *

I. 1066–1154. The first [period] * * * would end with the great reforms of Henry II. Litigation of an ordinary kind still takes place chiefly in the communal and feudal courts; even the king's court may be considered as a feudal court, a court of and for the king's tenants in chief. * * * His court is concerned chiefly with (1) the pleas of the crown, i.e. cases in which royal rights are concerned, (2) litigation between the king's tenants in chief—for such tenants it is the proper feudal court, (3) complaints of default of justice in lower courts. * * *

II. 1154–1189. The legislative activity of Henry II's reign marks a second period. Under Henry II the exceptional becomes normal. He places royal justice at the disposal of anyone who can bring his case within a certain formula. From the end of his reign we have Glanvill's book, and we see already a considerable apparatus of writs * * *; they have assumed distinct forms, forms which they will preserve until the nineteenth century * * *; each writ is the beginning of a particular form of action. * * *

As regards those claims which in after days give rise to the personal actions, those actions which, as we say, are founded on contract or founded on tort, Glanvill has but little to tell us; they are seldom prosecuted in the king's court. But the action of Debt is known there. * * *

III. 1189–1272. This, our third period, extending from the death of Henry II to the accession of Edward I, is a period of rapid growth * * *. New writs are freely invented, though towards the end of Henry III's reign this gives rise to murmurs * * *. There is now a large store of original writs which are writs of course (*brevia de cursu*), that is to say, they may be obtained from the subordinate officers of the royal chancery * * *.

Meanwhile the actions which came to be known as personal make their appearance. The oldest seems to be 'Debt-Detinue' * * *. Gradually this action divides itself into two, Detinue for a specific chattel, Debt for a sum of money—this differentiation takes place early in the thirteenth century. As in Detinue the judgment given for the plaintiff awards him either the chattel itself, or its value; and, as the defendant thus has the option of giving back the chattel or paying its value, Bracton is led to make the important remark that there is no real action for chattels—an important remark, for it is the foundation of all our talk about real and personal property. To Debt and Detinue we must now add Replevin, the action for goods unlawfully taken in distress. * * * Covenant also has appeared * * *. Gradually the judges came to the opinion that the only acceptable evidence of a covenant is a sealed writing, and one of the foundations of our law of contract is thus laid. * * *

But the most important phenomenon is the appearance of Trespass—that fertile mother of actions. Instances of what we can not but call actions of trespass are found even in John's reign, but I think it clear that the writ of trespass did not become a writ of course until very late in Henry III's reign. Now trespass * * * has its roots in criminal law * * *. The old criminal action (yes, action) was the Appeal of Felony * * *. It was but slowly supplanted by indictment—the procedure of the common accuser set going by Henry II, the appeal on the other hand being an action brought by a person aggrieved by the crime.

* * * The new phenomenon appears about the year 1250, it is an action which might be called an attenuated appeal based on an act of violence. * * * The action of trespass is founded on a breach of the king's peace:—with force and arms the defendant has assaulted and beaten the plaintiff, broken the plaintiff's close, or carried off the plaintiff's goods; he is sued for damages. The plaintiff seeks not violence but compensation, but the unsuccessful defendant will also be punished and pretty severely. In other actions the unsuccessful party has to pay an amercement for making an unjust, or resisting a just claim; the defendant found guilty of trespass is fined and imprisoned. What is more, the action for trespass shows its semi-criminal nature in the process that can be used against a defendant who will not appear—if he will not appear, his body can be seized and imprisoned; if he can not be found, he may be outlawed. We thus can see that the action of trespass is one that will become very popular with plaintiffs because of the stringent process against defendants. I very much doubt whether in Henry III's day the action could as yet be used save where there really had been what we might fairly call violence and breach of the peace; but gradually the convenience of this new action showed itself. In order to constitute a case for 'Trespass *vi et armis*,' it was to the last necessary that there should be some wrongful application of physical force to the defendant's lands or goods or person—but a wrongful step on his land, a wrongful touch to his person or chattels was held to be force enough and an adequate breach of the king's peace. This action then has the future before it.

* * *

IV. 1272–1307. The reign of 'the English Justinian' may be treated as a period by itself—a period of statutory activity. Statutes made by king and parliament now interfere with many details both of substantive law and of procedure. * * * The whole system stiffens. Men have learnt that a power to invent new remedies is a power to create new rights and duties, and it is no longer to be suffered that the chancellor or the judges should wield this power. How far the process of crystallisation had gone, how rigid the system was becoming, we learn from a section of the Statute of Westminster II, 13 Edw. I c. 24 (1285). Men have been obliged to depart from the Chancery without getting writs, because there are none which will exactly fit their cases, although these cases fall within admitted principles. It is not to be so for the future * * *. 'And whensoever from henceforth it shall fortune in the Chancery, that in one case a writ is found, and in a like case falling under like law, and requiring like remedy, is found none, the clerks of the Chancery shall agree in making the writ; or * * * let the cases be written in which they can not agree, and let them refer them until the next Parliament, and by consent of men learned in the law, a writ shall be made, lest it might happen after that the court should long time fail to minister justice unto complainants.' * * * [W]hen we say that but little use was made of this Statute there is one great exception. It is regarded as the statutory warrant for the variation of the writs of trespass so as to suit special cases, until at length—about the end of the Middle Ages—lawyers perceive that they have a new form 'Trespass upon the special case' or 'Case.' * * * It is worth noting that a writ issued by the Chancery is not necessarily a good writ. The justices may quash it as contrary to law, and in the later Middle Ages the judges are conservative * * *. At any rate the tale of common law (*i.e.* non-statutory) actions was now regarded as complete. The king's courts had come to be regarded as omnicompetent courts, they had to do all the important civil justice of the realm and to do it with the limited supply of forms of action which had been gradually accumulated in the days when feudal justice and ecclesiastical justice were serious competitors with royal justice.

V. 1307–1833. * * *

From Edward I's day onwards trespass *vi et armis* is a common action. We may notice three main varieties—unlawful force has been used against the body, the goods, the land of the plaintiff; so we have trespass in assault and battery, trespass *de bonis asportatis, trespass quare clausum fregit.* * * *

I have already said that the writ-making power wielded by the king and his Chancellor was gradually curbed by our parliamentary constitution, and in Edward I's day it has become necessary to tell the Chancery that it is not to be too pedantic, but may make variations in the old formulas when a new case falls under an old rule. * * * [T]he most important use made of this liberty consisted in some extensions of the action of trespass. Gradually during Edward III's reign we find a few writs occurring which in form are extremely like writs of trespass—and they are actually called writs of trespass—but the wrong complained of does not always consist of a direct application of unlawful physical force * * *; sometimes the words *vi et armis* do not appear. Sometimes there is no mention of the king's peace. Still they are spoken of as writs of trespass * * *. The plaintiff is said to bring an action upon his case, or upon the special case, and gradually it becomes apparent that really a new and a very elastic form of action has thus been created. I think that lawyers were becoming conscious of this about the end of the fourteenth century. Certain procedural differences have made their appearance— when there is *vi et armis* in the writ, then the defendant if he will not appear may be taken by *capias ad respondendum* or may be outlawed— this can not be if there is no talk of force and arms or the king's peace. Thus Case falls apart from Trespass—during the fifteenth century the line between them becomes always better marked. * * *

Case becomes a sort of general residuary action; much, particularly, of the modern law of negligence developed within it. Sometimes it is difficult to mark off case from trespass.

Notes and Questions

1. Case developed into a remedy not only for wrongs that were similar to those governed by trespass, but for wrongs that were much more similar to those for which the action of debt was appropriate. Yet case never lost its roots in trespass. Why didn't actions of debt on the case develop? See Kiralfy, *The Action on the Case* 3, 44 (1951).

2. Maitland's conclusions that trespass grew out of the appeal of felony and that case drew its authority from the Statute of Westminster II are debatable. Others have found the root of trespass in the assize of novel disseisin, in the proceedings of local courts, and in *queralae* ("innominate" actions without writ frequently found in the records of royal courts through- out the thirteenth century). The diversity of opinion is comprehensively reported in Fifoot, *History and Sources of the Common Law—Tort and Contract* 44–56, 66–74 (1949), a book of very great value in the study of the forms. See also Milsom, *Historical Foundations of the Common Law* 244–70 (1969).

3. In England's American colonies, the distinctions between the forms of action, although recognized, were not enforced with the rigor that character- ized the procedure of the mother country. For example, there are instances of the use of both trespass and case for the specific recovery of chattels and real property, and trover and assumpsit frequently were not distinguished from case. Ejectment, when it was still regarded as a modern improvement in England, was unused in New England because of its technicalities. See Morris, *Studies in the History of American Law* 46–59 (2d ed. 1959). Since law books were scarce in the colonies, and many of the judges were laymen, these developments were to be expected. The most technical applications of the forms of action in this country came during the first half of the nine- teenth century after the bar had grown in influence, and texts such as Blackstone had become available. See, e.g., Adams v. Hemmenway, 1 Mass. 145 (1804); Wilson v. Smith, 10 Wend. 324 (N.Y.1833).

2. THE LINES BLUR

a. Trespass or Case?

SCOTT, an Infant, by his next Friend v. SHEPHERD, an Infant, by Guardian

Court of Common Pleas, 1773.
2 Wm.Bl. 892, 96 Eng.Rep. 525.

Trespass and assault * * *. On not guilty pleaded, the cause came on to be tried before Nares, J., * * * when the jury found a verdict for the plaintiff with 100£. damages, subject to the opinion of the Court on this case: * * * [D]efendant threw a lighted squib, made of gunpowder, &c. from the street into the market-house, * * * where a large concourse of people were assembled; which lighted squib, * * * fell upon the standing of one Yates, who sold gingerbread, &c. That one Willis instantly, and to prevent injury to himself and the said wares of the said Yates, took up the said lighted squib from off the said standing, and then threw it across the said market-house, when it fell upon another standing there of one Ryal, * * * who instantly, and to save his own goods from being injured, took up the said lighted squib from off the said standing, and then threw it to another part of the said market-house, and, in so throwing it, struck the plaintiff * * * in the face therewith, and the combustible matter then bursting, put out one of the plaintiff's eyes. Qu. If this action be maintainable?

* * *

NARES, J., was of opinion, that trespass would well lie in the present case. That the natural and probable consequence of the act done by the defendant was injury to somebody, and therefore the act was illegal at common law. * * * Being therefore unlawful, the defendant was liable to answer for the consequences, be the injury mediate or immediate. * * * The principle I go upon is what is laid down in *Reynolds and Clark*, Stra. 634, that if the act in the first instance be unlawful, trespass will lie. Wherever therefore an act is unlawful at first, trespass will lie for the consequences of it. * * * [Defendant] * * * is the person, who, in the present case, gave the mischievous faculty to the squib. That mischievous faculty remained in it till the explosion. No new power of doing mischief was communicated to it by Willis or Ryal. It is like the case of a mad ox turned loose in a crowd. The person who turns him loose is answerable in trespass for whatever mischief he may do. The intermediate acts of Willis and Ryal will not purge the original tort in the defendant. * * *

BLACKSTONE, J., was of opinion, that an action of trespass did not lie for Scott against Shepherd upon this case. He took the settled distinction to be, that where the injury is immediate, an action of trespass will lie; where it is only consequential, it must be an action on the case: *Reynolds and Clarke*, Lord Raym. 1401. * * * The lawfulness or unlawfulness of the original act is not the criterion; though something of that sort is put into Lord Raymond's mouth in Stra. 635 * * *. But this cannot be the general rule; for it is held by the Court in the same case, that if I throw a log of timber into the highway, (which is an unlawful act), and another man tumbles over it, and is hurt, an action on the case only lies, it being a consequential damage; but if in throwing it I hit another man, he may bring trespass, because it is an immediate wrong. Trespass may sometimes lie for the consequences of a lawful act. If in lopping my own trees a bough accidentally falls on my neighbour's ground, and I go thereon to fetch it, trespass lies. * * * But then the entry is of itself an immediate wrong. And case will sometimes lie for the consequence of an unlawful act. If by false imprisonment I have a special damage, as if I forfeit my recognizance thereby, I shall have an action on the case. * * * Yet here the original act was unlawful, and in the nature of trespass. So that lawful or unlawful is quite out of the case; the solid distinction is between direct or immediate injuries on the one hand, and mediate or consequential on the other. And trespass never lay for the latter. If this be so, the only question will be, whether the injury which the plaintiff suffered was immediate, or consequential only; and I hold it to be the latter. The original act was, as against Yates, a trespass; not as against Ryal, or Scott. The tortious act was complete when the squib lay at rest upon Yates's stall. He, or any bystander, had, I allow, a right to protect themselves by removing the squib, but should have taken care to do it in such a manner as not to endamage others. But Shepherd, I think, is not answerable in an action of trespass and assault for the mischief done by the squib in the new motion impressed upon it, and the new direction given it, by either Willis or Ryal; who both were free agents, and acted upon their own judgment. This differs it from the cases put of turning loose a wild beast or a madman. They are only instruments in the hand of the first agent. Nor is it like diverting the course of an enraged ox, or of a stone thrown, or an arrow glancing against a tree; because there the original motion, the vis impressa, is continued, though diverted. Here the instrument of mischief was at rest, till a new impetus and a new direction are given it, not once only, but by two successive rational agents. But it is said that the act is not complete, nor the squib at rest, till after it is spent or exploded. It certainly has a power of doing fresh mischief, and so has a stone that has been thrown against my windows, and now lies still. Yet if any person gives that stone a new motion, and does farther mischief with it, trespass will not lie for that against the original thrower. No doubt but Yates may maintain trespass against Shepherd. And, according to the doctrine contended for, so may Ryal and Scott. Three actions for one single act! nay, it may be extended in infinitum. If a man tosses a football into the street, and after being kicked about by one hundred people, it at last breaks a tradesman's windows; shall he have trespass against the man who first produced it? Surely only against the man who gave it that mischievous direction. But it is said, if Scott has no action against Shepherd, against whom must he seek his remedy? I give no opinion whether case would lie against Shepherd for the consequential damage; though, as at present advised, I think, upon the circumstances, it would. But I think, in strictness of law, trespass would lie against Ryal, the immediate actor in this unhappy business. * * * The throwing it across the market-house, instead of brushing it down, or throwing [it] out of the open sides into the street, (if it was not meant to continue the sport, as it is called), was at least an unnecessary and incautious act. * * * And I admit that the defendant is answerable in trespass for all the direct and inevitable effects caused by his own immediate act. * * * But he is not responsible for the acts of other men. * * * In our case the verdict is suspended till the determination of the Court. And though after verdict the Court will not look with eagle's eyes to spy out a variance, yet, when a question is put by the jury upon such a variance, and it is made the very point of the cause, the Court will not wink against the light, and say that evidence, which at most is only applicable to an action on the case, will maintain an action of trespass. * * * The same evidence that will maintain trespass, may also frequently maintain case, but not e converso. Every action of trespass with a "per quod" includes an action on the case. I may bring trespass for the immediate injury, and subjoin a "per quod" for the consequential damages;—or may bring case for the consequential damages, and pass over the immediate injury * * *. But if I bring trespass for an immediate injury, and prove at most only a consequential damage, judgment must be for the defendant * * *.

GOULD, J., was of the same opinion with Nares, J., that this action was well maintainable.—The whole difficulty lies in the form of the action, and not in the substance of the remedy. The line is very nice between case and trespass upon these occasions: I am persuaded there are many instances wherein both or either will lie. I agree with brother Nares, that wherever a man does an unlawful act, he is answerable for all the consequences; and trespass will lie against him, if the consequence be in nature of trespass. But, exclusive of this, I think the defendant may be considered in the same view as if he himself had personally thrown the squib in the plaintiff's face. The terror impressed upon Willis and Ryal excited self-defence, and deprived them of the power of recollection. * * *

DE GREY, C.J. * * * I agree with my brother Blackstone as to the principles he has laid down, but not in his application of those principles to the present case. The real question certainly does not turn upon the lawfulness or unlawfulness of the original act; for actions of trespass will lie for legal acts when they become trespasses by accident * * *. They may also not lie for the consequences even of illegal acts, as that of casting a log in the highway, &c.—But the true question is, whether the injury is the direct and immediate act of the defendant; and I am of opinion, that in this case it is. The throwing the squib was an act unlawful and tending to affright the bystanders. So far, mischief was originally intended; not any particular mischief, but mischief indiscriminate and wanton. Whatever mischief therefore follows, he is the author of it * * *. Every one who does an unlawful act is considered as the doer of all that follows. * * * I look upon all that was done subsequent to the original throwing as a continuation of the first force and first act, which will continue till the squib was spent by bursting. And I think that any innocent person removing the danger from himself to another is justifiable; the blame lights upon the first thrower. * * * It has been urged, that the intervention of a free agent will make a difference: but I do not consider

Willis and Ryal as free agents in the present case, but acting under a compulsive necessity for their own safety and self-preservation. * * *

Postea to the plaintiff.

Notes and Questions

1. In what ways does Justice Blackstone differ from Chief Justice De Grey? From Justice Nares? On what facts might Chief Justice De Grey and Justice Nares reach a different result? Chief Justice De Grey and Justice Gould? Since Justice Blackstone believes an action in case would lie against Shepherd, is there really any substantive difference between him and his brethren? Would they have agreed with him that Scott could have maintained an action against Ryal? What would have been the nature of that action? In light of Gibbons v. Pepper, p. 430, supra, would actions of trespass lie against both Shepherd and Ryal?

2. Trials ordinarily were held at common law before a single judge and a jury. After verdict, if the losing party wanted the judgment of the entire court on a question of law that was involved in the case, that party asked for a rule *nisi*. A hearing before the court *en banc* was then held, and if that court sustained the rulings of the trial judge it denied the rule; otherwise, it made the rule *absolute*. When a verdict was taken subject to the opinion of the court *en banc*, as in Scott v. Shepherd, the ordinary procedure of applying for a rule *nisi* was unnecessary. Therefore, instead of denying a rule or making it absolute, the order of the court *en banc* was in the form of a *postea* to the prevailing party, which authorized the entry of judgment.

b. Case Captures Negligence

The close of the eighteenth century brought before the judges a great number of cases of a kind theretofore little known but which ever since have glutted our courts: running-down accidents and vehicular collisions. Echoes of Lord Raymond's distinction in Reynolds v. Clarke were less frequently heard, but the categories of direct and indirect injuries became mixed with those of wilful and negligent conduct, often in a context complicated by the involvement of servants. Matters would not stay within the simple confines that Justice Blackstone envisioned.

DAY v. EDWARDS, 5 T.R. 648, 101 Eng.Rep. 361 (K.B.1794), was an action in case against a defendant who had driven his cart "so furiously, negligently and improperly" that it "struck with great force and violence * * * against plaintiff's carriage." Plaintiff's lawyer touched on all the elements that had been or would become significant—legality, indirectness, negligence; the "act of driving * * * in consequence of which the injury arose, was a legal one in itself, although negligently exercised," he said. But Lord Kenyon merely repeated the immediate injury-consequential injury distinction, found that plaintiff "complains of the immediate act," and gave judgment for defendant.

One year later in MORLEY v. GAISFORD, 2 H.Bl. 441, 126 Eng.Rep. 639 (C.P.1795), Common Pleas held case was proper when defendant's servant was alleged to have "badly, ignorantly, and negligently" driven a cart against plaintiff's chaise, saying "it was difficult to put a case where the master could be considered as a trespasser for an act of his servant, which was not done at his command."

The *Morley* holding clearly turned on the issue of a master's liability in trespass, but when plaintiffs brought an action of case against defendants for having "so incautiously, carelessly, negligently, and inexpertly managed, steered and directed" their ship that it collided with plaintiffs' vessel, their counsel relied upon *Morley* solely for the proposition that trespass lay for wilful conduct and case for negligence, and two of the three judges accepted it. OGLE v. BARNES, 8 T.R. 188, 101 Eng.Rep. 1338 (K.B.1799). Lord Kenyon continued to insist upon the distinction between an immediate and a consequential injury, but he agreed that case was proper, since the charge was that by reason of defendants' negligence, their ship sailed against plaintiffs' vessel.

By 1803, we find defendant in LEAME v. BRAY, 3 East 593, 102 Eng. Rep. 724 (K.B.), challenging an action of trespass for a highway collision on the ground that the evidence showed his conduct to be negligent only, and that the action should therefore have been case. The court, however, reaffirmed its position in Day v. Edwards, that trespass lay for an immediate injury. Justice Lawrence, who had sat in *Ogle,* explained now that "what I principally relied on there was, that it did not appear that the mischief happened from the personal acts of the defendants: it might have happened from the operation of the wind and tide counteracting their personal efforts at the time: or indeed they might not even have been on board."

Common Pleas, which now clearly favored case for these actions, twice suggested that *Leame* be reconsidered, but King's Bench under Lord Ellenborough stood fast. In HALL v. PICKARD, 3 Camp. 187, 170 Eng. Rep. 1350 (K.B.1812), however, he raised the question whether it "may * * * be worthy of consideration, whether, in those instances where trespass may be maintained, the party may not waive the trespass, and proceed for the tort?" Later cases built on this suggestion until at last WILLIAMS v. HOLLAND, 10 Bing. 112, 131 Eng.Rep. 848 (C.P.1833), was accepted as settling the matter:

> The declaration * * * states the ground of action to be an injury occasioned by the carelessness and negligence of the Defendant in driving his own gig; * * * and the jury have found in the very terms of the declaration, that the jury [sic] was so occasioned. Under such a form of action, therefore, and with such a finding by the jury, the present objection ought not to prevail, unless some positive and inflexible rule of law, or some authority too strong to be overcome, is brought forward in its support. * * *

> But upon examining the cases cited in argument, both in support of, and in answer to, the objection, we cannot find one in which it is distinctly held, that the present form of action is not maintainable under the circumstances of this case.

> * * * [T]he late case of Moreton v. Hardern [4 B. & C. 223, 107 Eng. Rep. 1042 (K.B.1825)], appears to us to go the full length of deciding, that * * * where the injury is occasioned by the carelessness and negligence

of the Defendant, the Plaintiff is at liberty to bring an action on the case, notwithstanding the act is immediate, so long as it is not a wilful act * * *.

3. THE LOSS AND DETENTION OF PERSONAL PROPERTY

The writ of detinue lay when defendant had possession of plaintiff's personal property and refused to relinquish it. The writ would lie, for example, against a bailee who refused to redeliver bailed goods or an executor who withheld the title-deed to an heir's real property. Although the gist of the action was wrongful detention, rather than wrongful taking, detinue would lie against a thief. But in this type of case trespass *de bonis asportatis* was preferred because detinue had several drawbacks: Defendant had a right to wage his law, and could deliver up the property in lieu of paying damages, even though it was damaged, for detinue did not lie for mere harm to goods.

Not surprisingly, plaintiffs began to try to substitute an action on the case in circumstances that seemed to call for detinue. They succeeded, first in the situation in which detinue was clearly inadequate—when the goods had spoiled—and then in situations in which its remedy might be appropriate but its mode of trial was unsatisfactory. See Fifoot, *History and Sources of the Common Law—Tort and Contract* 102–04 (1949). By 1500, case was essentially an alternative to detinue, and in the course of the sixteenth century a distinct species of case developed—the action of trover. The form of this new action was predicated upon a fiction— plaintiff alleged that he had lost goods, that they had been found by defendant and were now in that party's possession, and that defendant refused to deliver them upon request. Loss and finding soon became recognized as formal allegations only, but the allegations concerning the request for return of the goods and defendant's refusal to deliver retained some significance; after all, your bailee cannot be considered to have committed a tort if you have not asked for your goods back. What might constitute a legitimate, conditional refusal to deliver—as in the case of a finder who wished to check the credentials of a claimant—became an important issue. Apart from the fact that defendant was not entitled to wage his law, trover differed from detinue in this respect: Plaintiff was under no obligation to take back the goods, and in an action against a thief was under no obligation to demand them. The essence of trover was the conversion of the goods.

What is a conversion? The term has troubled the courts for several hundred years, but the most famous definition is that of Chief Justice Holt, in BALDWIN v. COLE, 6 Mod. 212, 87 Eng.Rep. 964 (K.B.1705): "[W]hat is a conversion, but an assuming upon one's self the property and right of disposing another's goods; and he that takes upon himself to detain another man's goods from him without cause, takes upon himself the right of disposing of them * * *." Is this really helpful? Consider the following case.

BUSHEL v. MILLER

Court of King's Bench, 1718.
1 Strange 128, 93 Eng.Rep. 428.

Upon the Custom-House quay there is a hut, where particular porters put in small parcels of goods, if the ship is not ready to receive them when they are brought upon the quay. The porters, who have a right in this hut, have each particular boxes or cupboards, and as such the defendant had one. The plaintiff being one of the porters puts in goods belonging to A and lays them so that the defendant could not get to his chest without removing them. He accordingly does remove them about a yard from the place where they lay, towards the door, and without returning them into their place goes away, and the goods are lost. The plaintiff satisfies A of the value of the goods, and brings trover against the defendant. And upon the trial two points were ruled by the C.J.

1. That the plaintiff having made satisfaction to A for the goods, had thereby acquired a sufficient property in them to maintain trover.

2. That there was no conversion in the defendant. The plaintiff by laying his goods where they obstructed the defendant from going to his chest, was in that respect a wrong-doer. The defendant had a right to remove the goods, so that thus far he was in no fault. Then as to the not returning the goods to the place where he found them; if this were an action of trespass, perhaps it might be a doubt; but he was clear it could not amount to a conversion.

Notes and Questions

1. Plaintiff's goods were delivered by a ship's captain to defendant wharfingers to be held for plaintiff. The goods were then lost or stolen from defendants. Could defendants be said to have converted them? In ROSS v. JOHNSON, 5 Burrow 2825, 98 Eng.Rep. 483 (K.B.1772), Lord Mansfield said case, not trover, was the only remedy: "[I]n order to maintain trover, there must be an injurious conversion. This is not to be deemed a refusal to deliver the goods. They can't deliver them: it is not in their power to do it. It is a bare omission."

2. If defendant so negligently kept twenty barrels of plaintiff's butter that "they were become of little value," would trover lie? See Walgrave v. Ogden, 1 Leon. 224, 74 Eng.Rep. 205 (K.B.1590).

GORDON v. HARPER

Court of King's Bench, 1796.
7 T.R. 9, 101 Eng.Rep. 828.

In trover for certain goods, being household furniture * * *. [Plaintiff leased a house with the goods in question to A for a term still extant at the time of trial. While A was in possession under the lease, defendant sheriff seized the goods in execution of a judgment against B, who had sold the furniture to plaintiff sometime before the lease. Defendant after the seizure sold the goods.]

LORD KENYON, CH. J. The only point for the consideration of the Court in the case of Ward v. Macauley [4 T.R. 489, 100 Eng.Rep. 1135 (K.B.1791)] was, whether in a case like the present, the landlord could maintain an action of trespass against the sheriff for seizing goods, let with a house, under an execution against the tenant; and it was properly decided that no such action could be maintained. What was said further by me in that case, that trover was the proper remedy, was an extrajudicial opinion, to which upon further consideration I cannot subscribe. The true question is, whether when a person has leased goods in a house to another for a certain time, whereby he parts with the right of possession during the term to the tenant, and has only a reversionary interest, he can notwithstanding recover the value of the whole property pending the existence of the term in an action of trover. The very statement of the proposition affords an answer to it. If, instead of household goods, the goods here taken had been machines used in manufacture, which had been leased to a tenant, no doubt could have been made but that the sheriff might have seized them under an execution against the tenant, and the creditor would have been entitled to the beneficial use of the property during the term: the difference of the goods then cannot vary the law. * * * I forbear to deliver any opinion as to what remedy the landlord has in this case, not being at present called upon so to do: but it is clear that he cannot maintain trover.

ASHHURST, J. I have always understood the rule of law to be, that in order to maintain trover the plaintiff must have a right of property in the thing, and a right of possession, and that unless both these rights concur, the action will not lie. * * *

GROSE, J. The only question is whether trover will lie where the plaintiff had neither the actual possession of the goods taken at the time, nor the right of possession. * * * Where goods are delivered to a carrier, the owner has still a right of possession as against a tort-feasor, and the carrier is no more than his servant. But here it is clear that the plaintiff had no right of possession; and he would be a trespasser if he took the goods from the tenant: then by what authority can he recover them from any other person during the term? * * *

LAWRENCE, J. * * *. Now here if the taking of the goods by the sheriff determined the interest of the tenant in them, and revested it in the landlord, I admit that the latter might maintain trover for them * * *: but it is clearly otherwise; for here the tenant's property and interest did not determine by the sheriff's trespass, and the tenant might maintain trespass against the wrong-doer, and recover damages. * * *

Postea to the defendant.

Notes and Questions

1. Plaintiff pawned a jeweled hatband to X for 25 pounds with no certain time fixed for redemption. X delivered it to defendant, and then died. Plaintiff tendered 25 pounds to the executrix, who refused it, and then demanded the hatband of defendant. Would trover lie? See Ratcliff v. Davies, Croke Jac. 244, 79 Eng.Rep. 210 (K.B.1611).

2. Plaintiff leased a farm with cattle to Y for one year. After a few months, Y sold the cattle to defendant and absconded. What theory might be used to allow plaintiff to bring trover against defendant? See Swift v. Moseley, 10 Vt. 208 (1838).

4. THE CREATION OF CONTRACT LAW

a. *Special Assumpsit*

Glanvill said, shortly before 1200: "[I]t is not the custom of the court of the lord king to protect private agreements, nor does it concern itself with such contracts as can be considered to be like private agreements." *The treatise on the laws and customs of the realm of England commonly called Glanvill,* Bk. X [18 (Hall ed. 1965). By the middle of the fourteenth century, there remained a good deal of truth in this. Two forms of action, each with significant shortcomings, lay for breach of contract—the writs of covenant and debt. Covenant required a sealed instrument and did not lie when debt was available. Debt lay only when an agreement had been fully performed by one party and he was entitled to a sum certain, and as in the case of detinue, defendant was entitled to wage his law, unless the agreement was sealed. Again, plaintiffs resorted to case as a safety valve for the deficiencies of covenant and debt, but progress was slower than it had been in the evasion of detinue, perhaps because the effort was not so much to avoid a particular writ as to create a new area of substantive law.

By 1400, plaintiff could maintain case against a defendant who had carried out his promise so badly that plaintiff was in a worse position than before defendant made his promise. Thus in 1370 case was held to lie against a defendant who having undertaken to cure plaintiff's horse, treated it so negligently that it died. WALDON v. MARSHALL, Y.B. Mich. 43 Ed. 3, f. 33, pl. 38. Chief Justice Cavendish, in an action against a surgeon for maiming plaintiff while trying to cure him, said "this action of covenant of necessity is maintained without specialty, since for every little thing a man cannot always have a Clerk to make a specialty for him." THE SURGEON'S CASE, Y.B.Hil. 48 Ed. 3, f. 6, pl. 11 (K.B.1375). But case did not lie for nonfeasance. Through the fifteenth century there were occasional departures, but the courts seemed always to return to this rule. Then suddenly it was abandoned for good, and a new form of action developed from case and received judicial acceptance—special assumpsit. No single case seems to have established assumpsit as a remedy for nonperformance of a promise, but shortly after 1500 it had become the accepted view.

b. *General Assumpsit*

Special assumpsit filled a major gap left by the action of debt, but it did not take the place of debt, as trover substantially had taken the place of detinue. For another century, argument flared on the question whether assumpsit would lie for a debt. Gradually it was established that if a person, who already was indebted to another, made a fresh promise to pay the debt, assumpsit would lie for a breach of that promise, even though it would not have lain for the debt itself. The question then arose whether the fresh promise actually had to be made, or assumpsit would lie even when the promise was a fiction. In part, the answer lay in the desires of two courts to draw business to themselves; debt was the exclusive province of Common Pleas, while assumpsit with its background in trespass could be brought there or in King's Bench. For thirty years they squabbled over the matter.

SLADE'S CASE

Court of Exchequer Chamber, 1602.
4 Co.Rep. 92b, 76 Eng.Rep. 1074.

John Slade brought an action on the case in the King's Bench against Humphrey Morley * * * and declared, that whereas the plaintiff * * * was possessed of a close of land * * * and being so possessed, the plaintiff * * * the said close had sowed with wheat and rye, which wheat and rye * * * were grown into blades, the defendant, in consideration that the plaintiff, at the special instance and request of the said Humphrey, had bargained and sold to him the said blades of wheat and rye growing upon the said close, * * * assumed and promised the plaintiff to pay him 16l. * * *: and for non-payment thereof * * * the plaintiff brought the said action: the defendant pleaded *non assumpsit modo et forma;* and on the trial of this issue the jurors gave a special verdict, *sc.* that the defendant bought of the plaintiff the wheat and rye in blades growing upon the said close * * * and further found, that between the plaintiff and the defendant there was no other promise or assumption but only the said bargain * * *. And for the honour of the law, and for the quiet of the subject in the appeasing of such diversity of opinions * * * the case was openly argued before all the Justices of England, and Barons of the Exchequer, * * * and after many conferences between the justices and Barons, it was resolved, that the action was maintainable, and that the plaintiff should have judgment. And in this case these points were resolved:—1. That although an action of debt lies upon the contract, yet the bargainor may have an action on the case, or an action of debt at his election * * *. 3. It was resolved, that every contract executory imports in itself an *assumpsit,* for when one agrees to pay money, or to deliver anything, thereby he assumes or promises to pay, or deliver it, and therefore when one sells any goods to another, and agrees to deliver them at a day to come, and the other in consideration thereof agrees to pay so much money as such a day, in that case both parties may have an action of debt, or an action on the case on *assumpsit,* for the mutual executory agreement of both parties imports in itself reciprocal actions upon the case, as well as actions of debt * * *. 4. It was resolved, that the plaintiff in this action on the case on assumpsit should not recover only damages for the special loss (if any be) which he had, but also for the whole debt, so that a recovery or bar in this action would be a good bar in an action of debt brought upon the same contract * * *. And as to the objection which has been made, that it would be mischievous to the defendant that he should not wage his law, forasmuch as he might pay it in secret: to that it was answered, that it should be accounted his folly that he did not take sufficient witnesses with him to prove the payment he made: but the mischief would be rather on the other party, for now experience proves that men's consciences grow so large that the respect of their private advantage rather induces men (and chiefly those who have declining estates) to perjury *   *   *.

Note

You should remember in considering the demise of wager of law that at this time, and for two centuries more, parties were incompetent to testify at a trial. The enactment of the Statute of Frauds, 29 Charles 2, c. 3 (1677), which required several kinds of contracts to be in writing, is attributed by many to the problem of proof posed by the result in Slade's Case. See, e.g., Plucknett, *A Concise History of the Common Law* 648 (5th ed. 1956).

The recognition of *indebitatus assumpsit* (literally, "being indebted, he promised"), or *general assumpsit,* did more than deliver the quietus to debt. The contract-like sanction it imposed upon an obligation that did not really arise out of an actual promise provided the structure for wholly new developments. When A has delivered goods to B or has performed services for the latter, it may be presumed that A expects payment and B expects to pay; but the common law had furnished no remedy in the absence of an actual agreement. Now a new action of quantum meruit developed based upon an implied promise to pay the reasonable value of the goods or services, not unlike the imputed promise to pay the debt that furnished the basis for Slade's Case. Even more significant was the extension of this same formula into circumstances in which a promise to pay was the last thing in defendant's mind.

LAMINE v. DORRELL
Court of Queen's Bench, 1705.
2 Ld.Raym. 1216, 92 Eng.Rep. 303.

In an indebitatus assumpsit for money received by the defendant to the use of the plaintiff as administrator of J.S. on non assumpsit pleaded, upon evidence the case appeared to be, that J.S. died intestate possessed of certain Irish debentures; and the defendant pretending to a right to be administrator, got administration granted to him, and by that means got these debentures into his hands, and disposed of them: then the defendant's administration was repealed, and administration granted to the plaintiff, and he brought this action against the defendant for the money he sold the debentures for. And it being objected upon the evidence, that this action would not lie, because the defendant sold the debentures as one that claimed a title and interest in them, and therefore could not be said to receive the money for the use of the plaintiff, which indeed he received to his own use; but the plaintiff ought to have brought trover or detinue for the debentures: the point was saved to the defendant, and now the Court was moved, and the same objection made.

POWELL JUSTICE. It is clear the plaintiff might have maintained detinue or trover for the debentures *   *   *. But the plaintiff may dispense with the wrong, and suppose the sale made by his consent, and bring an action for the money they were sold for, as money received to his use.   *   *   *

HOLT CHIEF JUSTICE.   These actions have crept in by degrees.   *   *   * So the defendant in this case pretending to receive the money the debentures were sold for in the right of the intestate, why should he not be answerable for it to the intestate's administrator?   If an action of trover should be brought by the plaintiff for these debentures after judgment in this indebitatus assumpsit, he may plead this recovery in bar of the action of trover, in the same manner as it would have been a good plea in bar for the defendant to have pleaded to the action of trover, that he sold the debentures, and paid to the plaintiff in satisfaction.   *   *   * This recovery may be given in evidence upon not guilty in the action of trover, because by this action the plaintiff makes and affirms the act of the defendant in the sale of the debentures to be lawful, and consequently the sale of them is no conversion.

*   *   *

———

MOSES v. MACFERLAN, 2 Burrow 1005, 97 Eng.Rep. 676 (K.B.1760). Plaintiff had endorsed four promissory notes to defendant under a written agreement that he should not be liable thereon; in defendant's suit in a Court of Conscience (a small claims court), however, the agreement was not recognized, and plaintiff was found liable for six pounds, which he paid.   (On these facts, would Lamine v. Dorrell support an action for money had and received?)   Lord Mansfield said:

2d objection.—"That no assumpsit lies, except upon an express or implied contract: but here it is impossible to presume any contract to refund money, which the defendant recovered by an adverse suit."

Answer.   If the defendant be under an obligation, from the ties of natural justice, to refund; the law implies a debt, and gives this action, founded in the equity of the plaintiff's case, as it were upon a contract ("quasi ex contractu," as the Roman law expresses it).

*   *   *

Money may be recovered by a right and legal judgment; and yet the iniquity of keeping that money may be manifest, upon grounds which could not be used by way of defence against the judgment.

*   *   *

Suppose a man recovers upon a policy for a ship presumed to be lost, which afterwards comes home;—or upon the life of a man presumed to be dead, who afterwards appears;—or upon a representation of a risque deemed to be fair, which comes out afterwards to be grossly fraudulent.

*   *   *

One great benefit, which arises to suitors from the nature of this action, is, that the plaintiff needs not state the special circumstances from which he concludes "that, ex aequo & bono, the money received by the defendant, ought to be deemed as belonging to him:" he may declare generally, "that the money was received to his use;" and make out his case, at the trial.

*   *   *

This kind of equitable action to recover back money, which ought not in justice to be kept, is very beneficial, and therefore much encouraged. It lies only for money which, ex aequo et bono, the defendant ought to refund: it does not lie for money paid by the plaintiff, which is claimed of him as payable in point of honor and honesty, although it could not have been recovered from him by any course of law; as in payment of a debt barred by the Statute of Limitations, or contracted during his infancy, or to the extent of principal and legal interest upon an usurious contract, or, for money fairly lost at play: because in all these cases, the defendant may retain it with a safe conscience, though by positive law he was barred from recovering.

An important procedural result of the development of indebitatus assumpsit was a new manner of pleading contract actions. The declaration in money had and received, as Lord Mansfield noted in Moses v. MacFerlan, was broad in the extreme. See also p. 431, supra. The declarations in other actions derived from indebitatus assumpsit were equally broad. Pleaders seized upon this liberality to develop what became known as the "common counts," standardized allegations concealing virtually all of the particulars of an action. The principal common counts were for money had and received, for goods sold and delivered, for work done, for money lent, for money paid by plaintiff to the use of defendant, and for money due on an account stated. See Fifoot, *History and Sources of the Common Law—Tort and Contract* 369–70, 393–94 (1949).

SECTION C. THE OTHER SYSTEM: EQUITY

1. THE RISE OF CHANCERY

MAITLAND, EQUITY, ALSO THE FORMS OF ACTION AT COMMON LAW 2–10 (1909):

In Edward I's day, at the end of the thirteenth century, three great courts have come into existence * * *.

One of the three courts, namely, the Exchequer, is more than a court of law. From our modern point of view it is not only a court of law but a 'government office'. * * * What we should call the 'civil service' of the country is transacted by two great offices or 'departments'; there is the Exchequer which is the fiscal department, there is the Chancery which is the secretarial department, while above these there rises the king's permanent Council. At the head of the Chancery stands the Chancellor, usually a bishop; he is we may say the king's secretary of state for all departments, he keeps the king's great seal and all the already great mass of writing that has to be done in the king's name has to be done under his supervision.

He is not as yet a judge, but already he by himself or his subordinates has a great deal of work to do which brings him into a close connexion with the administration of justice. One of the duties of that great staff of clerks over which he presides is to draw up and issue those writs whereby actions are begun in the courts of law—such writs are sealed with the king's seal. * * *

But by another route the Chancellor is brought into still closer contact with the administration of justice. Though these great courts of law have been established there is still a reserve of justice in the king. Those who can not get relief elsewhere present their petitions to the king and his council praying for some remedy. * * * In practice a great share of this labour falls on the Chancellor. He is the king's prime minister, he is a member of the council, and the specially learned member of the council. It is in dealing with these petitions that the Chancellor begins to develop his judicial powers.

* * * Very often the petitioner requires some relief at the expense of some other person. He complains that for some reason or another he can not get a remedy in the ordinary course of justice and yet he is entitled to a remedy. He is poor, he is old, he is sick, his adversary is rich and powerful, will bribe or will intimidate jurors, or has by some trick or some accident acquired an advantage of which the ordinary courts with their formal procedure will not deprive him. The petition is often couched in piteous terms, the king is asked to find a remedy for the love of God and in the way of charity. Such petitions are referred by the king to the Chancellor. Gradually in the course of the fourteenth century petitioners, instead of going to the king, will go straight to the Chancellor * * *. Now one thing that the Chancellor may do in such a case is to invent a new writ and so provide the complainant with a means of bringing an action in a court of law. But in the fourteenth century the courts of law have become very conservative and are given to quashing writs which differ in material points from those already in use. But another thing that the Chancellor can do is to send for the complainant's adversary and examine him concerning the charge that has been made against him. Gradually a procedure is established. The Chancellor having considered the petition, or 'bill' as it is called, orders the adversary to come before him and answer the complaint. The writ whereby he does this is called a subpoena—because it orders the man to appear upon pain of forfeiting a sum of money * * *. It is very different from the old writs whereby actions are begun in the courts of law. They tell the defendant what is the cause of action against him * * *. The subpoena, on the other hand, will tell him merely that he has got to come before the Chancellor and answer complaints made against him by A.B. Then when he comes before the Chancellor he will have to answer on oath, and sentence by sentence, the bill of the plaintiff. * * *

I do not think that in the fourteenth century the Chancellors considered that they had to administer any body of substantive rules that differed from the ordinary law of the land. * * * The complaints that come before them are in general complaints of indubitable legal wrongs * * * of which the ordinary courts take cognizance, wrongs which they ought to redress. * * * However this sort of thing can not well be permitted. * * * And so the Chancellor is warned off the field of common law—he is not to hear cases which might go to the ordinary courts, he is not to make himself a judge of torts and contracts, of property in lands and goods.

But then just at this time it is becoming plain that the Chancellor is doing some convenient and useful works that could not be done, or could not easily be done by the courts of common law. He has taken to enforcing uses or trusts. * * * No doubt they were troublesome things, things that might be used for fraudulent purposes, and statutes were passed against those who employed them for the purpose of cheating their creditors or evading the law of mortmain. But I have not a doubt that they were very popular, and I think we may say that had there been no Chancery, the old courts would have discovered some method of enforcing these fiduciary obligations. That method however must have been a clumsy one. A system of law which will never compel, which will never even allow, the defendant to give evidence, a system which sends every question of fact to a jury, is not competent to deal adequately with fiduciary relationships. On the other hand the Chancellor had a procedure which was very well adapted to this end.

* * * And then there were some other matters that were considered to be fairly within his jurisdiction. An old rhyme allows him 'fraud, accident, and breach of confidence'—there were many frauds which the stiff old procedure of the courts of law could not adequately meet, and 'accident,' in particular the accidental loss of a document, was a proper occasion for the Chancellor's interference.

* * * In James I's day occurred the great quarrel between Lord Chancellor Ellesmere and Chief Justice Coke which finally decided that the Court of Chancery was to have the upper hand over the courts of law. If the Chancery was to carry out its maxims about trust and fraud it was essential that it should have a power to prevent men from going into the courts of law and to prevent men from putting in execution the judgments that they had obtained in courts of law. In fraud or in breach of trust you obtain a judgment against me in a court of law; I complain to the Chancellor, and he after hearing what you have to say enjoins you not to put in force your judgment, says in effect that if you do put your judgment in force you will be sent to prison. Understand well that the Court of Chancery never asserted that it was superior to the courts of law; it never presumed to send to them such mandates as the Court of King's Bench habitually sent to the inferior courts, telling them that they must do this or must not do that or quashing their proceedings * * *. It was addressed not to the judges, but to the party. * * * For all this, however, it was natural that the judges should take umbrage at this treatment of their judgments. Coke declared that the man who obtained such an injunction was guilty of the offence denounced by the Statutes of Praemunire, that of calling in question the judgments of the king's courts in other courts (these statutes had been aimed at the Papal curia). King James had now a wished-for opportunity of appearing as supreme over all his judges, and all his courts * * *.

ARGUMENTS Proving from ANTIQUITY the Dignity, Power, and Jurisdiction of the COURT OF CHANCERY

1 Chan.Rep. (App.) 1, 20, 23–24, 49–50, 21 Eng.Rep. 576, 581–82, 588 (1616).

* * *

His said Majesty being informed of this Difference between his two Courts of Chancery and King's Bench, * * * directed, That his Attorney General, calling to him the Rest of his Learned Counsel, should peruse the * * * Precedents, and certify his Majesty the Truth thereof with their Opinions.

* * *

And afterwards a Case was presented to his Majesty as followeth.

THE CASE.

A. hath a Judgment and Execution in the King's Bench or Common Pleas against B. in an Action of Debt of £1000, and in an *Ejectione Firmae* of the Manor of D. B. complains in the Chancery to be relieved against these Judgments according to Equity and Conscience, allowing the Judgment to be lawful and good by the Rigour and strict Rules of the Law, and the Matter in Equity to be such, as the Judges of the Common Law being no Judges of Equity, but bound by their Oaths to do the Law, cannot give any Remedy or Relief for the same, either by Error or Attaint, or by any other Means.

QUESTION.

Whether the Chancery may relieve B. in this or such like Cases, or else leave him utterly remediless and undone? And if the Chancery be restrained herein by any Statute of Praemunire, then by what Statute, and by what Words in any Statute is the Chancery so restrained, and Conscience and Equity excluded, banished and damned?

Which Case his Majesty referred again to his said Attorney and Learned Counsel * * *.

* * *

Upon which Certificate the King gave his Judgment as followeth.

Forasmuch as Mercy and Justice be the true Supporters of our Royal Throne, and that it properly belongeth unto us in our Princely Office to take Care and provide, that our Subjects have equal and indifferent Justice ministred unto them: And that where their Case deserveth to be relieved in Course of Equity by Suit in our Court of Chancery, they should not be abandoned and exposed to perish under the Rigor and Extremity of our Laws, We in our Princely Judgment * * * do approve, ratify and confirm, * * * the Practice of our Court of Chancery * * *. And do will and command that our Chancellor, or Keeper of the Great Seal for the Time being, shall not hereafter desist to give unto our Subjects, * * * such Relief in Equity (notwithstanding any Proceedings at the Common Law against them) as shall stand with the Merit and Justice of their Cause, and with the former, ancient and continued Practice and Presidency of our Chancery have done. * * *

BEALE, EQUITY IN AMERICA, 1 Cambridge L.J. 21, 22–23 (1921):

At about the time of the English Revolution colonies came to be more rigorously governed. Most of the old charters were forfeited, and a new provincial form of government was established; and from that time the Judges were appointed, through the royal governors, by the Crown, and they came to be regarded, naturally, as the enemies of popular rights and as creatures of the Crown. The situation at about the time of the American Revolution was that Judges in the North were still regarded as tools of the King and as enemies of the popular will. * * *

In the South conditions were very different. The ruling class was well satisfied with the condition of affairs in England, and, although there were popular uprisings in some parts of the South, notably in Virginia and Maryland, the power of the aristocracy on the whole was never shaken. They determined the laws, they had no distrust of Judges, and in those States there was no desire to hamper a Judge or to exalt the jury at his expense. * * *

We should not be surprised, therefore, to find that in the North at least the people were very jealous of giving any jurisdiction to the Court of Equity, there being no jury in that Court. Equity seemed to the people of America, a hundred years ago even, as a non-popular method of applying law, which it was the duty of the people alone to deal with. The Courts administering equity were, so to speak, royalist persons administering the law of an effete monarchy which had never taken foothold in the democratic part of America. The consequence was that in New England there was no equity jurisdiction and very little admixture of equity in the law. The law administered was the strictly legal portion of the law; and the books cited, when they came to cite books, were the reports of the common law Courts. In New York there was a Chancellor from the time of the original constitution; but that Chancellor was not supposed to be a Judge who administered the English system of equity. * * *

Pennsylvania never had any Court of equity. The law, however, had more of what they regarded as equitable doctrines in it than the law of Massachusetts * * *. In New Jersey and Delaware, however, and throughout the South, there was set up at the time of our Revolution a separate Court of Chancery, sitting beside the Common Law Court and administering the principles of English equity.

2. PROCEDURE IN EQUITY

BOWEN, PROGRESS IN THE ADMINISTRATION OF JUSTICE DURING THE VICTORIAN PERIOD, 1 Select Essays in Anglo-American Legal History 516, 524–27 (1907):

* * * A bill in a Chancery suit was a marvellous document, which stated the plaintiff's case at full length and three times over. There was first the part in which the story was circumstantially set forth. Then

came the part which "charged" its truth against the defendant—or, in
other words, which set it forth all over again in an aggrieved tone. Lastly
came the interrogating part, which converted the original allegations into
a chain of subtly framed inquiries addressed to the defendant, minutely
dovetailed and circuitously arranged so as to surround a slippery conscience and to stop up every earth. No layman, however intelligent, could
compose the "answer" without professional aid. It was inevitably so
elaborate and so long, that the responsibility for the accuracy of the story
shifted, during its telling, from the conscience of the defendant to that of
his solicitor and counsel, and truth found no difficulty in disappearing
during the operation. * * * [The form of the answer] often rendered
necessary a re-statement of the plaintiff's whole position, in which case an
amended bill was drawn requiring another answer, until at last the
voluminous pleadings were completed and the cause was at issue. By a
system which to lawyers in 1887 appears to savour of the Middle Ages, the
evidence for the hearing was thereupon taken by interrogatories written
down beforehand upon paper and administered to the witnesses in private
before an examiner or commissioner. At this meeting none of the parties
were allowed to be present, either by themselves or their agents, and the
examiner himself was sworn to secrecy. If cross-examined at all (for
cross-examination under such conditions was of necessity somewhat of a
farce), the witnesses could only be cross-examined upon written inquiries
prepared equally in advance by a counsel who had never had the opportunity of knowing what had been said during the examination-in-chief.
* * * On the day of the publication of the depositions copies were
furnished to the parties at their own expense; but, from that moment, no
further evidence was admissible, nor could any slip in the proofs be
repaired, except by special permission of the court, when, if such leave
was granted, a fresh commission was executed with the same formalities
and in the same secret manner as before. The expense of the pleadings,
of the preparation for the hearing, and of the other stages of the litigation
may be imagined, when we recollect that it was a necessary maxim of the
Court of Chancery that all parties interested in the result must be parties
to the suit. If, for example, relief was sought against a breach of trust, all
who were interested in the trust estate had to be joined, as well as all who
had been privy to the breach of trust itself. During the winding journey
of the cause towards its termination, whenever any death occurred, bills
of review or supplemental suits became necessary to reconstitute the
charmed circle of litigants which had been broken. On every such
catastrophe the plaintiff had again to begin wearily to weave his web,
liable on any new death to find it unravelled and undone. It was
satirically observed that a suit to which fifty defendants were necessary
parties (a perfectly possible contingency) could never hope to end at all,
since the yearly average of deaths in England was one in fifty, and a
death, as a rule, threw over the plaintiff's bill for at least a year. The
hearing in many cases could not terminate the cause. Often inquiries or
accounts were necessary, and had still to be taken under the supervision
of a master. Possibly some issue upon the disputed facts required to be
sent for trial at the assizes, or a point of law submitted to a common law

court. In such cases, the verdict of the jury, or the opinions of the court so taken, in no way concluded the conscience of the Court of Chancery. It resumed charge of the cause again, when the intermediate expedition to the common law was over, and had the power, if it saw fit, to send the same issue to a new trial, or to disregard altogether what had been the result. * * * When a cause had reached its final stage—when all inquiries had been made, all parties represented, all accounts taken, all issues tried—justice was done with vigour and exactitude. Few frauds ever in the end successfully ran the gauntlet of the Court of Chancery. But the honest suitor emerged from the ordeal victorious rather than triumphant, for too often he had been ruined by the way.

Notes and Questions

1. What differences do you find between procedure at common law and procedure in equity as it is described by Bowen? What are the differences in pleading, the manner of receiving evidence, the attitude toward singleness of issue, and the determination of questions of fact? The rules of evidence, which are chiefly concerned with the exclusion of testimony of doubtful value, were developed in the common-law courts and were never strictly applied in equity. How is this fact related to the differences in equity and common-law procedures?

2. Although the division between law and equity in the federal courts never took the form of separate courts or judges of law and equity, the two were separately administered in the federal system until 1938. From the beginning, procedure at law was conformed to that of the state in which the court was held, but—due in part to the fact that some states had no system of equity in 1789—equity procedure in the federal courts was governed by statutes of Congress and rules promulgated by the Supreme Court. In 1915, Congress provided that when "a suit at law should have been brought in equity or a suit in equity should have been brought at law, the court shall order any amendments to the pleadings which may be necessary to conform them to the proper practice," and that in "all actions at law equitable defenses may be interposed by answer, plea, or replication without the necessity of filing a bill on the equity side of the court." 38 Stat. 956.

The elements of procedure in equity discussed in the foregoing materials are significant because of their impact on the substantive and remedial doctrines of equity. Together with the method of enforcing equity decrees, which is discussed below, these elements largely determined the type of case that equity would hear and the disposition it would order. As you read the materials that follow, ask yourself how these differences between law and equity may explain the particular equitable approach in question.

3. THE UNIQUE CHARACTER OF EQUITABLE RELIEF

a. Specific Relief

The ordinary judgment of a common-law court consisted of a declaration of a legal relationship. When plaintiff prevailed in the action, this declaration in all but rare instances was that plaintiff was entitled to a sum of money from defendant. Even this declaration was not an order that defendant pay the sum; if defendant did not pay, plaintiff had to take further steps to execute the judgment. The decree in equity, on the other hand, was an order directed at defendant; imprisonment and fines were used not only to coerce compliance, but to punish disobedience. This difference between the remedies in the two systems of courts was summed up in the maxim that equity acts in personam and not in rem. The primary means by which equity acted in personam was the injunction—an order directing defendant to perform or to stop performing an act.

The injunction and other forms of specific relief shaped the substantive doctrines of equity. But it affected the common law as well in at least three important ways. First, the availability of specific relief through the injunction or specific performance when compensatory relief through a judgment for damages would be inadequate was the chief basis for drawing common-law causes into equity. As a result equity now dominates many areas of controversy originally governed by the common law, because damages are an impotent remedy in such cases; a good example is nuisance. Similarly the enforcement of contracts for the sale of real property has become principally a concern of equity, because specific performance is ordered as a matter of course. Second, the availability of specific relief in equity has effectively dampened pressures to develop common-law remedies in that direction. Third, the injunction was the means by which equity imposed its substantive doctrines on the common-law courts. As noted in the extract from Maitland, if the chancellor found that a common-law judgment had been obtained by fraud, the equity court did not purport to negate it; the chancellor simply took the equally effective step of threatening the judgment creditor with jail if the latter sought to enforce it. In similar fashion equity enjoined the bringing of suits in inconvenient fora and compelled interpleader and class actions in multiparty suits.

A plaintiff who sought specific relief also might have sustained an injury that an injunction could not cure. But there was no necessity for choosing between equitable relief and compensatory damages. A "clean-up" doctrine gave Chancery authority to accord full relief in any case of which it had cognizance even though giving such relief might mean redressing injuries for which there was an adequate remedy at law. See pp. 878–79, infra.

b. Availability of Relief

You must not think that the doctrine of the adequate remedy at law was the only restriction on the use of equitable remedies. Equity carefully husbanded its power. It was reluctant to issue orders that it might not be able to enforce or that might involve it in detailed supervision of a transaction. Traditionally, equity would not direct a party to take action outside its territorial jurisdiction or order specific performance of a building or personal services contract. For other reasons, activity that might be criminal ordinarily would not be enjoined. While the Court of

Star Chamber flourished there was no call for criminal jurisdiction in equity, and after that court was abolished in 1642, Chancery, perhaps for fear of meeting a similar fate, refrained from encroaching on this particular domain of the common-law courts. What aspects of Chancery procedure might have seemed particularly odious in criminal cases to people who celebrated the common law as the palladium of their liberty?

The availability of equitable relief also was hedged by doctrines of fairness and justice. Thus the opinions of the chancellor continually repeat that he who seeks equity must do equity, that he must come into equity with "clean hands," that equity abhors a forfeiture, and that equity will not protect one who sleeps on his rights. Is there any reason why these ideas should have been applied only in equity?

c. Fraud

Fraud often is spoken of as a fount of equitable jurisdiction. Yet the common law also permitted actions for fraud, and defenses as well. Why was protection against fraud thought to be a peculiarly equitable concern? For at least two reasons. For one thing, it was a function of equity's getting there first and going further. The common law would not recognize fraud as a defense to an action on a sealed instrument. Thus, before the rise of assumpsit, at a time when most of the agreements that were enforced by the courts were under seal, equity furnished the only remedy for fraud in the great bulk of cases. When simple contracts—to which fraud was a common-law defense—became enforceable, Chancery sustained its lead by developing the doctrine of constructive fraud, a doctrine in which the rigid technicalities of the common-law fraud concept played little part.

The second reason lay in equity's procedure. Equity implemented its concern with fraud in two ways. First, by denying its own relief to fraudulent complainants, and second, by enjoining legal suitors from pressing their claims or enforcing their judgments. The fraud concept in the latter case has come to be known as an "equitable defense," together with such doctrines as accident, undue influence, and estoppel. Of course, the term "equitable defense" does not indicate a defense in an equity suit, but connotes an effective—if not technical—defense to an action at law.

d. Discovery

Equity and the common law should not be thought of as conflicting systems. In many respects the relationship was one of cooperation, especially after the confrontation of 1616. The most important aspect of this mutual assistance, for our purposes, was discovery, by which a party at law might obtain through equity information for his case. The procedure and the limitations are set forth by Lord Chief Baron Abinger:

> * * * A party has a right to compel the production of a document in which he has an equal interest, though not equal in degree, yet to a certain extent equal, with the party who detains it from him. In that case he may file a bill of discovery, in order to have the possession of it, and the inspection of it. A party has also a right to file a bill of discovery

for the purpose of obtaining such facts as may tend to prove his case; and if those facts are either in possession of the other party, or, if they consist of documents in possession of the other party, in which he either has an interest, or which tend to prove his case, and have no relation to the case of the other party, he has a right to have them produced, and he may file a bill of discovery, in order to aid him in law or in equity, to exhibit those documents in evidence, or compel a statement of those facts. * * * Has he a right, as against the defendant, to discover the defendant's case? * * * The ground on which he files his bill, is to make the defendant discover what is material to his (the plaintiff's) case; but he has no right to say to the defendant, "Tell me what your title is—tell me what your case is—tell me how you mean to prove it—tell me the evidence you have to support it—disclose the documents you mean to make use of in support of it—tell me all these things, that I may find a flaw in your title." Surely that is not the principle of a bill of discovery.

COMBE v. CITY OF LONDON, 4 Y. & C.Ex. 139, 154, 160 Eng.Rep. 953, 959 (Exch.1840). What aspects of equitable procedure explain the availability of discovery in equity? In this connection, reread those portions of Maitland and Bowen in this Section dealing with the pleadings and the taking of evidence in equity.

SECTION D. REFORM: NEW PLEADING, ABOLITION OF THE FORMS, AND THE MERGER OF LAW AND EQUITY

1. THE EMERGENCE OF CODE PROCEDURE

The first significant reform in procedure occurred in England in the period between 1825 and 1834. Chancery practice was substantially reformed during these years. One form of writ was adopted for all three common-law courts. All but three real actions were abolished. Debt and detinue were reshaped. Wager of law was ended.

The capstone of the reform was a body of new rules of pleading, drafted by a committee that included Henry Stephen, author of the treatise cited earlier in this Chapter, and Sir James Parke, who, as a judge of the Court of Exchequer, was to become the foremost expositor of the new rules. Many of their recommendations were distinct improvements on existing practice; one—not accepted—would have permitted the joinder of counts in trespass and case, and amendments from the one form of action to the other. The principal defect the commissioners found in the existing system of pleading, however, was the ubiquitous availability of the general issue. The commissioners attributed to pleas of the general issue "the unnecessary accumulation of proof," the failure to raise questions of law by demurrer, the imposition of the duty to separate law and fact upon the busy *nisi prius* judge, and the proliferation of new trials. This position was reflected by the new rules announced under the authority of an Act of Parliament by the judges of all three common-law courts at Hilary Term, 1834, and known as the Hilary Rules; the defenses that could be proved under a plea of the general issue were greatly reduced, and special pleading was substantially restored. 2 C. & M. 1–30, 149 Eng. Rep. 651–63 (1834).

The result was a disaster. "Under the common-law system the matter was bad enough with a pleading question decided in every sixth case. But under the Hilary Rules it was worse. Every fourth case decided a question on the pleadings. Pleading ran riot." Whittier, *Notice Pleading*, 31 Harv.L.Rev. 501, 507 (1918). Fortunately, corrective action was not long in coming. The Common Law Procedure Acts of 1852, 1854, and 1860 weakened the forms of action, expanded joinder, and liberalized pleading. Finally, the Judicature Acts of 1873 and 1875 combined Chancery and the common-law courts into one Supreme Court of Judicature, fused law and equity, and abolished the forms of action. See 15 Holdsworth, *A History of English Law* 104–38 (Goodhart & Hanbury ed. 1965).

Meanwhile in the United States,[h] a new constitution in New York in 1846 abolished the Court of Chancery and directed the legislature to provide for the appointment of commissioners to "revise, reform, simplify, and abridge" the civil procedure of the state. N.Y. Const. 1846 Art. VI, § 24. The legislature implemented this directive in 1847 and expressly charged the newly-appointed commissioners to "provide for the abolition of the present forms of actions and pleadings in cases at common law; for a uniform course of proceeding in all cases whether of legal or equitable cognizance, and for the abandonment * * * of any form and proceeding not necessary to ascertain or preserve the rights of the parties." N.Y. Laws 1847, c. 59, § 8.

————

FIRST REPORT OF THE COMMISSIONERS ON PRACTICE AND PLEADINGS (New York) 73–74, 87, 123–24, 137–38, 140–41, 144 (1848):

The history of jurisprudence, both in this state and in England, * * * affords a most convincing proof of the wisdom of the measure adopted by the people of this state, in abolishing the distinction between law and equity tribunals. Notwithstanding their separate existence, they had, under the institutions of this state, but one common object, the administration of justice—depending not upon the mere discretion of the court, but ascertained by fixed and certain rules of law. And yet, while they were kept distinct, though their jurisdictions continually encroached upon each other, there were certain rules, not well defined, but yet existing, by which their powers were distinguished. It is, therefore, no matter of surprise, that the books are filled with cases, in which the injustice has been imposed upon parties, of suffering the loss of a substantial right, because of a mistake in the choice of a forum, before which its enforcement was sought. * * *

From the period [in which the forms of action developed] * * *—a period comparatively benighted and ignorant, in all that is valuable in science—to the present, these forms have been adhered to with a sort of

h. The textual discussion is limited to states with a common-law heritage. Louisiana had adopted a system based on Spanish law with only one form of action by 1812, the year it was admitted to the Union. Texas experimented briefly with separate systems but by 1845 had a unitary system based on Spanish-Mexican jurisprudence.

bigoted devotion. While the principles of legal science have expanded and adapted themselves to the exigencies of each successive age, through which they have passed, we find ourselves met with the standing argument against improvement, that the time-honored institutions of ages must be held sacred, and that these forms, which may have been well suited to the age in which they originated, must be left untouched.

* * * It seems to us, clear, that neither the forms of remedies, nor the mode in which they are stated, require the complexity, in which both are now enveloped. The embarrassments, to which they have given rise, have resulted from no difficulty in determining the real rights of parties, but simply in the means of enforcing them; and in this respect, we feel no hesitation in recommending, that the retention of forms, which serve no valuable purpose, should no longer constitute a portion of the remedial law of this state. * * *

The rules respecting parties in the courts of law, differ from those in the courts of equity. The blending of the jurisdictions makes it necessary to revise these rules, to some extent. In doing so, we have had a three-fold purpose in view: first, to do away with the artificial distinctions existing in the courts of law, and to require the real party in interest to appear in court as such: second, to require the presence of such parties as are necessary to make an end of the controversy: and third, to allow otherwise great latitude in respect to the number of parties who may be brought in.

* * *

The courts of law generally administer justice betweee [sic] those parties only who stand in the same relation to * * * [each] other; while courts of equity bring before them various parties, standing in different relations, that the whole controversy may be settled, if possible, in one suit, and others avoided. This reasonable and just rule, we would adopt for all actions. * * *

As has been already remarked, the change in the mode of pleading is the key of the reform which we propose. Without this, we should despair of any substantial and permanent improvement in our modes of legal controversy. * * *

The pleadings, we have said, are the written allegations of the parties of the cause of action on one side, and the defence on the other. Their object is three-fold: to present the facts on which the court is to pronounce the law; to present them in such a manner, as that the precise points in dispute shall be perceived, to which the proofs may be directed; and to preserve the record of the rights determined. Not one of these objects is gained by the law of pleading as it now exists in this state.

* * *

There are many treatises and books of forms, indispensable to the lawyer, on the mode of pleading and the forms of the allegations. The rules and the commentaries upon them, form one of the most technical and abstruse branches of the law * * *. We are * * * disposed to pronounce it a system of dialectics, very fit for the schoolmen with whom it originated, but unfit for the practical business of life.

So unfit has it been found, that in instances almost numberless, the legislature and the courts have departed from it and gone to the other extreme. * * * A form of plea was devised which in many cases would virtually deny every material allegation of the declaration without disclosing any particular defence. The courts from time to time have admitted new defences under these general issues, and still further to encourage them, a statute has been passed allowing the defendant to plead the general issue, and with it give notice of any defence, which he could not otherwise introduce under such issue. * * *

Besides the general issues, we have general declarations, or in technical language, common counts. These have been so contrived as to give no information of the particular demand. They also have been encouraged by the courts and numberless demands allowed to be proven under them. * * *

In truth the arguments of those who defend the present system destroy each other. One is the advantage of having the question of fact drawn out so precisely, that the court and jury may see what they have to try, and the parties be prepared with their proofs; the other is the advantage of having the facts stated in so general a form, that the allegations shall cover any state of facts that may appear on the trial, or in other words, the advantage of having no question of fact drawn out by the pleadings at all.

* * *

Disentangling the questions and separating those of fact and of law, is rarely effected by the present system of pleading at common law. * * * This is necessarily so, so long as the pleadings state the conclusions of fact, instead of the facts themselves. * * *

Following the report of the commissioners, the New York legislature enacted a Code of Civil Procedure, commonly called the Field Code after David Dudley Field, the most influential of the commissioners. N.Y.Laws 1848, c. 379. This Code proved to be the prototype for numerous state codes—at one time more than one-half the states had codes patterned to some degree after the Field Code—and the precursor of the Federal Rules. Among its most important provisions were the following:

§ 69. [§ 62] [i] The distinction between actions at law and suits in equity, and the forms of all such actions and suits, heretofore existing, are abolished; and, there shall be in this state, hereafter, but one form of action, for the enforcement or protection of private rights and the redress of private wrongs, which shall be denominated a civil action.

§ 140. [§ 118] All the forms of pleading heretofore existing, inconsistent with the provisions of this act, are abolished * * *.

§ 142. [§ 120] The complaint shall contain:

i. The New York legislature added several sections to the Code in 1849, and renumbered the provisions first enacted in 1848 with some very slight changes in language. N.Y.Laws 1849, c. 438. Because the 1849 version became the best known, it is used here. Section numbers in brackets refer to the sections of the 1848 Code.

1. * * *

2. A statement of the facts constituting the cause of action, in ordinary and concise language, without repetition, and in such a manner as to enable a person of common understanding to know what is intended;

3. A demand of the relief, to which the plaintiff supposes himself entitled. If the recovery of money be demanded, the amount thereof shall be stated.

§ 156. [§ 132] No other pleading shall be allowed than the complaint, answer, reply and demurrers.

§ 159. [§ 136] In the construction of a pleading, for the purpose of determining its effect, its allegations shall be liberally construed, with a view to substantial justice between the parties.

§ 176. [§ 151] The court shall, in every stage of an action, disregard any error, or defect in the pleadings or proceedings, which shall not affect the substantial rights of the adverse party; and no judgment shall be reversed or affected by reason of such error or defect.

Note

In 1851 the New York legislature amended Section 142(2) to read: "A plain and concise statement of the facts constituting a cause of action without unnecessary repetition." N.Y.Laws 1851, c. 479, § 1.

2. SOME OLD PROBLEMS PERSIST

Could it have been reasonably expected that the transition from the common-law system of procedure to the code system would represent a clean break with the past? Consider the following factors:

(a) The substantive law was supposed to remain unaltered, yet the substantive law had been intimately tied to the older mode of procedure. Moreover, certain procedural institutions—notably trial by jury—had acquired the character of substantive rights.

(b) The most fundamental aspects of procedure—such as the necessity of striking a balance between the function of pleading as setting the limits of the controversy and the function of trial as determining the true merits of the case—are not created by a particular system of procedure but are an integral part of an adjudicative process based upon a theory of party-presentation. Indeed it is rare that any system of procedure attempts by rigid rule to settle these issues definitively. Much will depend on the attitudes, experiences, and predispositions of those who are called upon to apply the rules.

(c) The problems presented by the change in procedure confronted a profession that had traditionally chosen precedent as its polestar, a profession comprised of people who might feel they had an interest in their established ways of proceeding and who in any event were trained in analysis under the older system. The judges who were called upon to interpret the new provisions were of course established members of this profession; indeed, if the methods of judicial selection were effective, they were lawyers who had performed quite competently under the older procedure and they understandably may have been a little impatient with complaints that this procedure was replete with snares and absurdities.

Whatever the reasons, it is clear that many courts did not view the new codes as having been written on a clean slate. Even today concepts of the common-law system occasionally seem to assume a significant role in the decision of pleading and procedure questions. We will see more of this in the next Chapter. For the present we will look at one aspect of the perseverance of common-law notions—the "theory of the pleading" doctrine and related questions.

JONES v. WINSOR

Supreme Court of South Dakota, 1908.
22 S.D. 480, 118 N.W. 716.

CORSON, J. This is an appeal by the defendant from an order overruling his demurrer to the complaint.

It is alleged in the complaint, in substance: That on or about the 1st of April, 1907, the plaintiffs, being desirous of securing a franchise for a city railway system in the city of Sioux Falls, employed the defendant to act as an attorney for them in securing or attempting to secure an ordinance from the city council granting the plaintiffs such license; that carrying out their purpose, * * * it became necessary for the plaintiffs to make a deposit with the city treasurer, and on said day the plaintiffs delivered to the defendant the sum of $2,500 to be by him deposited with the said treasurer of the city, and which money was so deposited * * *; that on or about the 4th day of April the defendant received a further sum of $130, which was to be used by the defendant for these plaintiffs in securing or attempting to secure the said franchise; that the said franchise which plaintiffs were attempting to secure from said city was not granted to these plaintiffs, and thereupon, about the 17th day of April, the city treasurer returned to the defendant the said sum of $2,500 "as money belonging to these plaintiffs and for their use and benefit"; that on or about the same day the said defendant rendered to these plaintiffs an account of all moneys received by him for and on account of these plaintiffs, with an itemized statement of all disbursements, and in connection therewith a pretended charge for his services or fee of $1,250, and with said account was a draft drawn in favor of the plaintiffs for $1,012.25; that the pretended charge of the defendant of the sum of $1,250 as shown upon said account and alleged to be for services rendered by him is unjust, unlawful, and fraudulent, and the reasonable value of the services rendered by the defendant was not and is not of the value of more than $250; that of the moneys so received by the defendant for and on behalf of these plaintiffs and for their use and benefit there remains in his hands the sum of $1,000, which he has refused and still refuses to pay over to these plaintiffs, although frequently requested so to do, and "he has wrongfully and fraudulently converted to his own use the said sum of $1,000"; that on or about the 10th day of September, 1907, the plaintiffs demanded of the said defendant payment * * * "but the said defendant then and there refused and still refuses to pay the same or any part thereof to the plaintiffs and has wrongfully converted the same to his own use." Wherefore "plaintiffs demand judgment against the said defendant for the sum of $1,000 and interest thereon from the 17th day of April, 1907, for the wrongful conversion of said property and for the costs of this action." * * *

It is contended by the appellant that the complaint does not state facts sufficient to constitute a cause of action in trover or conversion, for the reason that the complaint nowhere alleges ownership by the plaintiffs of the property alleged to have been converted at the time the action was brought; nor does it allege ownership or possession of the property in the plaintiffs at the time it is alleged to have been converted which is absolutely essential in the form of action. Assuming that the complaint in this case was intended to state an action for the conversion of this money by the defendant, it is clearly insufficient in not alleging that the plaintiffs, at the time the defendant is charged with having converted it, were the owners or in possession of the money so alleged to have been converted. * * * But it is somewhat difficult to determine from the complaint whether the plaintiffs intended that their action should be for a tort or one ex contractu, as the complaint seems to have been framed with a double aspect. Taking a general view of the allegations of the complaint, it would seem that the pleaders intended to state a cause of action as for money had and received; but looking at the complaint in another aspect, and giving effect to some of the allegations therein, it would seem that the pleaders intended it as an action in conversion, in the nature of the old action of trover.

It is contended by the respondent, in support of the ruling of the court below upon the demurrer, that the action is to recover money had and received by the plaintiffs, and that the allegations contained in the complaint alleged [sic] the fraudulent conversion of the property, etc., may be treated as surplusage. Such a complaint, framed with a double aspect or to unite distinct and incongruous causes of actions, cannot be sustained on demurrer. While our Code has abolished forms of pleading, and only requires that the facts shall be stated in a plain and concise manner without unnecessary repetition, still the distinctions between actions as they formerly existed cannot be entirely ignored. In Pierce v. Carey, 37 Wis. 232, * * * Chief Justice Ryan, quotes with approval * * * Supervisors of Kewaunee County v. Decker, 30 Wis. 624, as follows: "Dixon, C.J. It would certainly be a most anomalous and hitherto unknown condition of the laws of pleading, were it established that the plaintiff in a civil action could file and serve a complaint, the particular nature and object of which no one could tell, but which might and should be held good, as a statement of two or three or more different and inconsistent causes of action, as one in tort, one upon money demand on contract, and one in equity, all combined or fused and moulded into one count or declaration, so that the defendant must await the accidents and events of trial, and until the plaintiff's proofs are all in, before being informed with any certainty or definiteness, what he was called upon to meet. The proposition that a complaint, or any single count of it, may be so framed with a double, treble, or any number of aspects looking to so many distinct and incongruous causes of action, in order to hit the exigencies of the plaintiff's case or any possible demands of his proofs at the trial, we must say, strikes us as something exceedingly novel in the rules of pleading. We do not think it is the law * * *."

As before stated, it is contended by the respondents that these allegations for conversion, etc., may be treated as surplusage, and the complaint held good as an action in assumpsit for money had and received; but in our opinion we would not be justified in holding that these allegations constitute mere surplusage and might be disregarded by the court. To so hold would introduce into the law too much uncertainty and ambiguity in pleading which would have a tendency to mislead the courts and the opposing party. A complaint should be framed upon the theory that it is either a complaint in tort or one ex contractu, and the two theories cannot be combined in one action; neither can an action at law and an action in equity be combined in one count in the same action. As was stated in the headnote in the case of Supervisors of Kewaunee County v. Decker, supra: " * * * On demurrer to a complaint, or any count thereof, the court must determine what cause of action such complaint or count is designed to state, and then whether it states facts sufficient to constitute such a cause of action; and, if not, the demurrer must be sustained, though facts may be stated sufficient to show that plaintiff has a cause of action of a different character."

* * *

The order of the circuit court overruling the demurrer is reversed.

Notes and Questions

1. Reread the provision of the Field Code, pp. 461–62, supra, that tells what a complaint shall contain. Is there language in that provision that lends support to the decision in the principal case?

2. Is it appropriate for a court to insist that plaintiff's complaint is based on a theory that is not supported by the alleged facts, as in Jones v. Winsor, especially when the facts are adequate to support a different theory? Would your answer be different if the facts in the complaint were adequate to sustain either theory but the less apparent theory was the only one proved at trial? Is the result in *Jones* consistent with Section 159 of the Field Code, which is set out on p. 462, supra?

CONAUGHTY v. NICHOLS, 42 N.Y. 83 (1870). Plaintiff alleged that he had consigned goods to defendants for sale, that they had been sold for $690.82, and that after deducting the expenses of the sale there was due to plaintiff $618.43, that defendants had refused to pay this amount over to plaintiff and "have converted the same to their own use." After trial, plaintiff moved to amend the complaint by striking the allegation of conversion, but this motion was denied by the referee who then nonsuited plaintiff "on the ground that the cause of action stated in the complaint was for a tort, and the proof established a cause of action upon contract." The General Term reversed the judgment, and the Court of Appeals affirmed:

* * * If the words "and have converted the same to their own use" had been omitted in the complaint, it could not reasonably be contended, that the same was not adapted to the cause of action established by the evidence. The case, therefore, seems to be reduced to the proposition, whether the plaintiff, having alleged facts constituting a cause of action, and having sustained them by proof upon the trial, should have been nonsuited, because the pleading contained an allegation adapted to a complaint in an action *ex delicto,* and which was unnecessary to be stated or proved, to justify a recovery on contract. We are of opinion that no such rigid rule of construction in regard to pleading should prevail under the liberal system introduced by the Code.

* * * If the complaint in question had merely stated facts sufficient to authorize a recovery for a wrongful detention of the money, and upon the trial, the plaintiff had applied to amend by inserting facts appropriate to a cause of action on contract, and thereby changing the form and character of the action, the application should have been denied. That, however, was not the case, as the facts were fully stated, and the defendants apprized of what they were to meet upon the trial, and there was no pretense that they were surprised. If they chose to accept the complaint without moving to strike out any portion of it, or to compel the plaintiff to make it more definite, or to elect in regard to the form of action, they should not, upon the trial, have been allowed to prevent a recovery by the plaintiff of a judgment for the amount of his demand. * * * It is quite probable that the plaintiff intended, down to the trial, to recover against the defendants for a wrongful conversion of the proceeds of the sale of the property consigned to them, and doubtless the mistake should have been fatal but for the ample statement of facts contained in the complaint, which justified a recovery on contract for the amount of his demand. It does not follow that, because the parties go down to the trial upon a particular theory, which is not supported by the proof, the cause is to be dismissed, when there are facts alleged in the complaint, and sustained by the evidence, sufficient to justify a recovery upon a different theory or form of action. * * *

Questions

Is *Conaughty* consistent with Jones v. Winsor? "The reasoning of the Court in Conaughty v. Nichols that where the pleading is misleading the defendant should move to make it definite or to have the pleader elect between the possible theories, and that if he proceeds without doing so he is to be taken as fully understanding the pleading, seems very weak." Whittier, *The Theory of a Pleading,* 8 Colum.L.Rev. 523, 534 (1908). Why? If you were preparing a complaint in New York after *Conaughty,* what moral would you draw from the opinion in that case?

GARRITY v. STATE BOARD OF ADMINISTRATION

Supreme Court of Kansas, 1917.
99 Kan. 695, 162 P. 1167.

PORTER, J. * * * A demurrer to the petition was sustained; plaintiff elected to stand upon the petition and appeals.

The petition charges that in July, 1911, the board of regents of the state university, by its assistant curator of mammals, wrongfully and without plaintiff's knowledge or consent, entered upon his farm in Wallace county and removed therefrom a large and valuable fossil, the property of plaintiff, and wrongfully converted it to the use and benefit of the board of regents and its successors, depositing the fossil in the museum of the university for exhibition and scientific purposes; that the fossil was of the value of $2,500, and plaintiff had received no compensation therefor. It is alleged that the board of administration is a board created by law for the government, management, and control of the university of Kansas, * * * and is the successor of the board of regents, subrogated to the rights, duties, and responsibilities of the board of regents, and subject to its obligations and liable for its debts and contracts. * * *

1. It is the defendants' contention that both the original and the amended petition were subject to demurrer because, if they stated a cause of action at all, it was barred by the statute of limitations; that the action is one sounding in tort, and therefore barred by the two-year statute * * *. On the other hand the plaintiff claims the right to waive the tort and recover upon an implied promise to pay what the fossil is worth. We think, if [the] petition stated a cause of action against defendants, it must be held that sufficient facts were stated to authorize plaintiff to waive the tort and rely upon an implied promise to pay the value of the property converted. * * *

The two-year statute of limitations was therefore no bar to the action.

* * *

3. The principal question raised by the appeal is whether the action can be maintained against the board of administration, the original defendant. Prior to 1913 the state university was managed and controlled by a board of regents which was a body corporate created by the Legislature. It went out of existence when the act of 1913 placed the state educational institutions in control of the state board of administration, which was not made a body corporate. The act * * * provided that the board shall manage and control the property of the educational institutions named, including the state university, and conferred upon the board power "to execute trusts or other obligations now or hereafter committed to any of the said institutions * * *." The power "to execute trusts or other obligations now or hereafter committed to any of * * * said institutions" cannot be construed so as to make either the board of administration or its members liable for a tort committed by the board of regents; and the plaintiff cannot, by waiving the tort, make either the board or its members liable upon the theory of an implied promise.

* * *

The judgment is affirmed. All the Justices concurring.

Notes and Questions

1. Is *Garrity,* in either its statute-of-limitations aspect or its liability aspect, concerned with the theory of the pleading? In what way, if any, is the problem in *Garrity* different?

2. Why did the court hold that the action was in contract for purposes of the statute of limitations but in tort for purposes of deciding whether the Board was liable for the Regents' action?

3. Governments generally are immune from suit except as their immunity has been expressly waived by statute. Suits in contract are more commonly consented to than suits in tort. See 3 Davis, *Administrative Law Treatise* § 25.01 (1958). Under a statute consenting to suit in contract only, should a plaintiff be permitted to "waive" a tort and sue in "assumpsit"?

4. In a contract action, may a claim for money had and received based upon a conversion be brought as a counterclaim under a statute that provides that "in an action on contract, any other cause of action on contract" may be brought as a counterclaim? See Manhattan Egg Co. v. Seaboard Terminal & Refrig. Co., 137 Misc. 14, 242 N.Y.S. 189 (N.Y.City Ct.1929).

3. THE ARRIVAL OF MODERN PROCEDURE

Modern procedure arrived on September 16, 1938, when the Federal Rules of Civil Procedure came into effect. The adoption of the Federal Rules followed an extended period of agitation for uniform procedural rules in the federal district courts and for uniting the procedure of law and equity under one form of action. In 1934, Congress passed the Rules Enabling Act, 28 U.S.C. § 2077, authorizing the United States Supreme Court to promulgate rules of procedure for the district courts. On June 3, 1935, the Supreme Court appointed an Advisory Committee of distinguished lawyers and law professors to prepare and submit a draft of unified rules. The Committee prepared and received public comments on two published drafts. It submitted its final report to the Supreme Court in November 1937. The Supreme Court carefully reviewed and made a number of changes in the rules recommended by the Committee. The rules as adopted by the Court on December 20, 1937, were transmitted to the Attorney General and were submitted by him to the 75th Congress on January 3, 1938. Pursuant to the terms of the Rules Enabling Act, the rules came into effect when the Congress adjourned without taking action to postpone their effective date. See generally Burbank, *The Rules Enabling Act of 1934*, 130 U.Pa.L.Rev. 1015 (1982).

The chief characteristics of the Federal Rules are common sense, simplicity, and flexibility of procedure. The declared purpose of the rules is "to secure the just, speedy and inexpensive determination of every action." Fed.R.Civ.P. 1. Some of the major aspects in which the rules advanced federal practice were union of law and equity as one form of action, the simplification of pleadings and issues, pretrial procedure, discovery, and trial reforms. All of these subjects are developed in the succeeding chapters of this book.

Note

The Federal Rules have had a strong impact on court procedures in most of the states. Nonetheless, state rules of civil procedure still vary greatly. Some states had adopted code systems similar to New York's Field Code, others modeled their rules after the Federal Rules of Civil Procedure, and others maintained common-law rules. Most states have been influenced by two or more of these models and have adopted elements of each. For example, some states, such as Delaware and New Jersey, have maintained separate court systems for law and for equity, yet they have abandoned common-law pleading. For a state-by-state discussion, see Oakley & Coon, *The Federal Rules in State Courts: A Survey of State Court Systems of Civil Procedure,* 61 Wash.L.Rev. 1367 (1986).

Chapter 5

MODERN PLEADING

Chapter Four discussed the history of the pleading rules. Those rules served four functions: (1) providing notice of the nature of a claim or defense; (2) identifying baseless claims; (3) setting each party's view of the facts; and (4) narrowing the issues. Modern pleading rules are not calculated to perform the last three of these functions. Thus, Federal Rule 8(a) requires only a short and plain statement of the claim showing that the plaintiff is entitled to relief. The shift in emphasis embodied in the Federal Rules on pleading in part reflects a view of the place of litigation in the dispute-resolution process.

At the outset of a lawsuit, the court's primary interest is in deterring baseless claims that may clog its calendar. The framers of the Federal Rules were satisfied that this limited objective could be achieved by requiring a short and plain statement of the claim and a certification that the pleadings were truthful (Rule 11) and by establishing other provisions designed expressly to screen baseless claims (most notably, the motion to dismiss under Rule 12 and the motion for summary judgment under Rule 56).

As the invocation of Rules 12 and 56 makes clear, the shift in emphasis embodied in the federal pleading rules also reflects the rulemakers' intention to relegate to procedural devices other than the pleading rules the primary responsibility for serving several of the functions performed by pleading rules under earlier systems of procedure. As noted, Rules 11, 12, and 56 are designed to serve the function of screening baseless claims. Other rules are designed to serve the other functions of detailed pleadings. For example, the Federal Rules create a wide array of discovery devices that make it unnecessary for the parties to provide a detailed statement of the facts at the pleading stage. By shifting from the pleading stage to the discovery stage the attempt to set each party's view of the facts, the Rules implement their framers' conviction that parties should not be forced to take positions before they have access to facts and documents, some of which may be obtainable only from the other party.

Under the Federal Rules, there are only three pleading stages: a complaint, an answer, and a reply. The answer is designed to inform the plaintiff as to which of the allegations in the complaint the defendant will contest as well as of any counterclaims or affirmative defenses that may exist—in short, to serve the same simple notice-giving function that is served by the complaint. Like the complaint, the answer ordinarily provides little in the way of concrete information, consisting mainly of general statements. In cases in which there is counterclaim, a reply is required and serves the same function as an answer to a complaint.

SECTION A. THE COMPLAINT

1. DETAIL REQUIRED UNDER THE CODES

Read Nebraska Revised Statutes §§ 25–804, 25–806, which appear in the Supplement in conjunction with Federal Rules of Civil Procedure 8 and 12, respectively.

GILLISPIE v. GOODYEAR SERVICE STORES

Supreme Court of North Carolina, 1963.
258 N.C. 487, 128 S.E.2d 762.

The hearing below was on demurrers to the complaint.

Plaintiff alleges she and each of the four individual defendants are citizens and residents of Alamance County, North Carolina; that defendant Goodyear Tire & Rubber Company is a corporation doing business in North Carolina and having a place of business and store in Burlington, North Carolina; and that Goodyear Service Stores is a division of defendant Goodyear Tire & Rubber Company.

The remaining allegations of the complaint and the prayer for relief are as follows:

4. On or about May 5, 1959, and May 6, 1959, the defendants, without cause or just excuse and maliciously came upon and trespassed upon the premises occupied by the plaintiff as a residence, and by the use of harsh and threatening language and physical force directed against the plaintiff assaulted the plaintiff and placed her in great fear, and humiliated and embarrassed her by subjecting her to public scorn and ridicule, and caused her to be seized and exhibited to the public as a prisoner, and to be confined in a public jail, all to her great humiliation, embarrassment and harm.

5. By reason of the defendants' malicious and intentional assault against and humiliation of the plaintiff, the plaintiff was and has been damaged and injured in the amount of $25,000.00.

6. The acts of the defendants as aforesaid were deliberate, malicious, and with the deliberate intention of harming the plaintiff, and the plaintiff is entitled to recover her actual damages as well as punitive damages from the defendants and each of them.

THEREFORE, the plaintiff prays that she have and recover of the defendants the sum of $25,000.00 as damages and $10,000.00 in addition thereto as punitive damages, and that she have such other and further relief as may be just and proper.

* * *

BOBBITT, JUSTICE. * * *

ISSUE

Does the complaint state *facts* sufficient to constitute *any* cause of action?

A complaint must contain "(a) plain and concise statement of the facts constituting a cause of action * * *." G.S. § 1–122. "The cardinal requirement of this statute * * * is that the facts constituting a cause of action, rather than the conclusions of the pleader, must be set out in the complaint, so as to disclose the issuable facts determinative of the plaintiff's right to relief." Shives v. Sample, 238 N.C. 724, 79 S.E.2d 193. The cause of action consists of the facts alleged. * * * The statutory requirement is that a complaint must allege the material, essential and ultimate facts upon which plaintiff's right of action is based. * * * "The law is presumed to be known, but the facts to which the law is to be applied are not known until properly presented by the pleading and established by evidence." McIntosh, North Carolina Practice and Procedure, § 379.

The facts alleged, but not the pleader's legal conclusions, are deemed admitted when the sufficiency of the complaint is tested by demurrer. * * * Where the complaint merely alleges conclusions and not facts, it fails to state a cause of action and is demurrable. * * * However, it is well settled that a complaint must be fatally defective before it will be rejected as insufficient, and "if in any portion of it or to any extent it presents *facts* sufficient to constitute a cause of action the pleading will stand." (Our italics) Snotherly v. Jenrette, * * * 232 N.C. p. 608, 61 S.E.2d p. 711. * * *

When a complaint alleges defendant is indebted to plaintiff in a certain amount and such debt is due, but does not allege in what manner or for what cause defendant became indebted to plaintiff, it is demurrable for failure to state facts sufficient to constitute a cause of action. * * *

"In an action or defense based upon negligence, it is not sufficient to allege the mere happening of an event of an injurious nature and call it negligence on the part of the party sought to be charged. This is necessarily so because negligence is not a fact in itself, but is the legal result of certain facts. Therefore, the facts which constitute the negligence charged and also the facts which establish such negligence as the proximate cause, or as one of the proximate causes, of the injury must be alleged." Shives v. Sample, supra * * *.

Plaintiff alleges, in a single sentence, that defendant, "without cause or just excuse and maliciously," trespassed upon premises occupied by her as a residence, assaulted her and caused her to be seized and confined as a prisoner. The complaint states no facts upon which these legal conclusions may be predicated. Plaintiff's allegations do not disclose *what* occurred, *when* it occurred, *where* it occurred, *who* did *what*, the relationships between defendants and plaintiff or of defendants *inter se*, or any other factual data that might identify the occasion or describe the circumstances of the alleged wrongful conduct of defendants.

* * * When considered in the light most favorable to plaintiff, this complaint, in our opinion, falls short of minimum requirements.

In Stivers v. Baker, 10 Ky. 523, 9 S.W. 491, * * * the court, in opinion by Holt, J., points out that a statement of the facts constituting a cause of action "is not only necessary to enable the opposite party to form an issue, and to inform him of what his adversary intends to prove, but to enable the court to declare the law upon the facts stated. It cannot do so if a mere legal conclusion is stated. The term 'assault' has a legal meaning; as much so as the word 'trespass.' " * * *

The judgments sustaining the demurrers are affirmed on the ground the complaint does not state facts sufficient to constitute any cause of action. It would seem appropriate that plaintiff, in accordance with leave granted in the judgments from which she appealed, now file an amended complaint and therein allege the facts upon which she bases her right to recover.

Affirmed.

Notes and Questions

1. Is the court in *Gillispie* legitimately concerned with the inability of defendants to ascertain the claims against them in order that they might answer and prepare their defenses? Of what significance is the fact that in North Carolina one party can take a pretrial deposition of the opposing party in order to obtain information necessary to prepare a pleading and to obtain evidence for use at trial? Can it be said that the pleading in *Gillispie* is unsatisfactory because the trial judge will not know what evidence is or is not relevant?

2. To what extent might the court in *Gillispie* have been motivated by the notion that a detailed account of the facts might well show that plaintiff did not have a valid claim for relief? Is it significant that at the time of the *Gillispie* decision North Carolina did not have a provision for summary judgment? Has the North Carolina court simply followed a hard and fast line concerning the "fact" pleading requirement, quite forgetting its basic purpose as a device for pretrial communication?

3. Note the ultimate disposition in the *Gillispie* case. Suppose that plaintiff's amended complaint also is deficient. Will she be given leave to amend again? How should the right to amend affect the question of whether or not a pleading is or is not satisfactory?

McCAUGHEY v. SCHUETTE, 117 Cal. 223, 224–26, 48 P. 1088 (1897). Plaintiff alleged that he contracted to buy a piece of real estate from defendant in exchange for the cancellation of several of defendant's promissory notes held by plaintiff. Plaintiff further alleged that the notes were cancelled and the deed to the property delivered but that defendant had refused to yield physical possession of the property to plaintiff. Defendant demurred on the ground that the complaint failed to state a cause of action. The trial court overruled the demurrer and the case proceeded to trial at which a verdict was rendered for plaintiff. On appeal, the state supreme court reversed, adopting the following language from a lower appellate-court decision in the same case (46 P. 666):

> It is a fundamental rule of our code pleading that ultimate and not probative facts are to be averred in a pleading. * * *

> It will be observed that in the complaint in the present case there is no averment of seisin, or ownership, or possession, or right of possession, to the demanded premises, but the pleader contents himself with a statement of evidentiary facts, which, if proven at the trial, would authorize the court in finding the ultimate fact of ownership and right to possession in the plaintiff.

> *   *   *

> Such pleading wes [sic] bad at common law, and is none the less so under our code system.

> To uphold such a pleading is to encourage prolixity and a wide departure from that definiteness, certainty, and perspicuity which it was one of the paramount objects sought to be enforced by the code system of pleading, and that, too, with no resultant effect, except to encumber the record with verbiage and enhance the cost of litigation.

Notes and Questions

1. "Quite commonly an allegation has been held bad as a statement of law only. The stating of evidence, while subject to criticism, is not so often held to render the pleading bad, since the court itself will draw the ultimate conclusion where it is the one necessarily following from the allegations made." Clark, *Code Pleading* § 38, at 228 (2d ed. 1947). When does the ultimate conclusion "necessarily follow"? Compare ROBINSON v. MEYER, 135 Conn. 691, 693–94, 68 A.2d 142, 143 (1949), in which the court inferred title by adverse possession on the basis of allegations of "all the facts necessary to establish ouster," with O'REGAN v. SCHERMERHORN, 25 N.J. Misc. 1, 50 A.2d 10 (Sup.Ct.1946), in which the court refused to infer the defense of truth in a defamation suit when defendant alleged he believed the statement to be true and further alleged the facts on which that belief was based.

2. Should a party be able to plead an essential fact merely by referring to an exhibit in which the fact is stated? Consider ANDERSON v. CHAMBLISS, 199 Or. 400, 409, 262 P.2d 298, 302 (1953), in which the court refused to permit a lien notice attached to and referred to in the complaint to supply the necessary allegation that the notice was filed within sixty days of completion of construction. The court said: "[A]nnexing an exhibit to a pleading does not amount to an allegation that the statements contained therein are true. * * * [Hence it] cannot serve the purpose of supplying necessary and material averments." See also Lion Secor Real Estate Co. v. Westgate Village Shopping Center, Inc., 117 Ohio App. 96, 191 N.E.2d 179 (1962).

Compare STANDARD REGISTER CO. v. GREENBERG, 120 Vt. 112, 116, 132 A.2d 174, 177 (1957):

Inclusion of the exhibit as a part of the pleading does not appear to work any hardship on this defendant. Reference to the writing, coupled with its annexation to the complaint, brings the context of the agreement before the court as effectively as a recopy of the document verbatim, into the body of the complaint itself. * * * The rule permitting such method of pleading is accepted, with varying limitations, in numerous other jurisdictions. * * * And even by rigid rules of common law pleading, a writing became a part of a declaration by profert and oyer, to be considered on demurrer. * * * The written agreement of the defendant * * *, exhibited with the complaint, is to be considered in determining the sufficiency of the plaintiff's pleading.

Is the decision in *Anderson* preferable to that in *Greenberg*? Does Federal Rule 10(c), which makes a written instrument that is attached to a pleading as an exhibit "a part thereof for all purposes," raise any special problem in those situations in which the party is required to attest under oath to the truth of his pleading?

COOK, STATEMENTS OF FACT IN PLEADING UNDER THE CODES, 21 Colum.L.Rev. 416, 416–19, 422 (1921):

In a recent case in New York [California Packing Corp. v. Kelly Storage & Distributing Co., 228 N.Y. 49, 126 N.E. 269 (1920)] the plaintiff alleged in his complaint that the promise for the breach of which he was suing was made in exchange for "a valuable consideration." The case went to the Court of Appeals upon the question whether this allegation is a "statement of fact" or a "conclusion of law." [The court held it was the former.] * * * An examination of the authorities in [New York and] other code jurisdictions reveals a conflict of authority. * * *

The movement for "simplified procedure" began in this country about the middle of the last century. How comes it that after more than seventy years of discussion and judicial decision, a question of this kind can still be an open one? Why is it that eminent judges and lawyers took and still take opposite views upon this and similar questions? * * *

These [code] provisions at first sight seem simple, and probably the men who first drew them so believed. That the simplicity is not real, however, becomes clear when one reads the hundreds, not to say thousands, of decisions which have passed upon the question whether in a given case the pleader has "stated the facts" in an acceptable manner. In many cases he is told that he has pleaded "evidentiary facts" instead of the "facts constituting the cause of action"; in many others he is held to have stated merely "conclusions of law."

[Upon careful analysis] * * * it will appear at once that there is no logical distinction between statements which are grouped by the courts under the phrases "statements of fact" and "conclusions of law." It will also be found that many, although by no means all, pleadings held bad because they are said to plead "evidence" rather than "the facts constituting the cause of action" or defense really do nevertheless "state" the operative facts which the pleader will have to prove at the trial, but in a form different from that to which courts and lawyers are accustomed to recognize as a proper method of pleading.

* * *

The facts of life which compose the group of "operative facts" to which the law attaches legal consequences are always *specific* and not *generic.* * * * [I]n an action on the case for, let us say, negligently injuring the plaintiff by the operation of an automobile, the "operative" or "ultimate" facts proved at the trial will always be specific. It will appear that the defendant was driving a particular kind of automobile at some particular rate of speed, *etc., etc.* If now a plaintiff were to state the facts thus specifically in his complaint he would doubtless be told by the average court that he had "pleaded his evidence" and not the "facts constituting the cause of action." This would of course be erroneous. What is according to accepted notions the proper way to plead is merely a mode of stating the facts generically rather than specifically.

It must of course be recognized that at times a pleader really does err by "pleading evidence," i.e., by stating, generically or specifically, facts which do not form part of the group of operative facts, but are merely facts from which by some process of logical inference the existence of the operative facts can be inferred. More often, however, the "error" consists merely in pleading the operative facts more specifically than is usual.

So much for the cases involving the distinction between pleading "evidence" and "ultimate facts." Let us now examine "conclusions of law." The first thing noticed upon analysis is that a so-called "conclusion of law" is a generic statement which can be made only after some legal rule has been applied to some specific group of operative facts. Consider, for example, a statement in a pleading that "defendant owes plaintiff $500." Standing by itself in a pleading this is usually treated as a mere "conclusion of law." It can, however, be made only when one knows certain facts and also the applicable legal rule. It is, in fact, the conclusion of a logical argument: Whenever certain facts, a, b, c, *etc.,* exist, B (defendant) owes A (plaintiff) $500; facts a, b, c, *etc.,* exist; therefore B owes A $500. This being so, when the bare statement is made that "B owes A $500" we may, if we wish, regard it as a statement in generic form that all the facts necessary to create the legal duty to pay money described by the word "owe" are true as between A and B. In dealing, for example, with misrepresentation, such statements are more often than otherwise regarded in exactly this way. The same statement may, however, under proper circumstances be merely a statement as to the law applicable to facts given or known, and so be purely a statement of a "conclusion of law."

* * * How specific or how generic statements in a pleading may and must be can obviously not be settled by mere logic, but according to notions of fairness and convenience. The pleading should give the adversary and the court reasonable notice of the real nature of the claim or defense; nothing more should be required.

Notes and Questions

1. In ROBINSON v. BOARD OF COUNTY COMMISSIONERS, 262 Md. 342, 278 A.2d 71 (1971), plaintiff alleged that defendants "did then and there falsely, maliciously, and without just cause * * * arrest [plaintiff] * * * on charge[s] of disorderly conduct and resisting arrest, * * * [they took him to the police station where he was forceably imprisoned, kept, detained and restrained of his liberty * * * [but upon trial he] was acquitted * * *. [Defendants] well knew that the prosecution was false, groundless, and without probable cause * * *." The court held that this passage stated facts sufficient to constitute a cause of action. Compare this pleading with that in *Gillispie*. Is one of the pleadings more informative than the other? See also D'Auria v. Niemiec, 15 Misc.2d 449, 450, 182 N.Y.S.2d 378, 379 (Sup.Ct.1959), upholding as sufficient an allegation "That on or about July 1, 1956, on Amherst Street in the City of Buffalo, New York, the defendant assaulted, battered and beat plaintiff without any provocation or just cause." On the other hand, consider VAN DEKERKHOV v. CITY OF HERRIN, 51 Ill.2d 374, 282 N.E.2d 723 (1972), holding that an allegation that defendant "had charge of" certain construction work was a conclusion of law, thus resulting in the dismissal of the action based on a statute that imposed liability on any "person having charge of" the work in question.

2. To what extent do the problems in determining what are "facts" represent an inherent defect of the code system?

2. DETAIL REQUIRED UNDER THE FEDERAL RULES

———

Read Federal Rules of Civil Procedure 8(a) and 12(b) in the Supplement.

———

DIOGUARDI v. DURNING

United States Circuit Court of Appeals, Second Circuit, 1944.
139 F.2d 774.

CLARK, CIRCUIT JUDGE. In his complaint, obviously home drawn, plaintiff attempts to assert a series of grievances against the Collector of Customs at the Port of New York growing out of his endeavors to import merchandise from Italy "of great value," consisting of bottles of "tonics." We may pass certain of his claims as either inadequate or inadequately stated and consider only these two: (1) that on the auction day, October 9, 1940, when defendant sold the merchandise at "public custom," "he sold my merchandise to another bidder with my price of $110, and not of his price of $120," and (2) "that three weeks before the sale, two cases, of 19 bottles each case, disappeared." Plaintiff does not make wholly clear how these goods came into the collector's hands, since he alleges compliance with the revenue laws; but he does say he made a claim for "refund of merchandise which was two-thirds paid in Milano, Italy," and that the collector denied the claim. These and other circumstances alleged indicate (what, indeed, plaintiff's brief asserts) that his original dispute was with his consignor as to whether anything more was due upon the merchandise, and that the collector, having held it for a year (presumably as unclaimed merchandise under 19 U.S.C.A. § 1491), then sold it, or such part of it as was left, at public auction. For his asserted injuries plaintiff claimed $5,000 damages, together with interest and costs, against the defendant individually and as collector. This complaint was dismissed by the District Court, with leave, however, to plaintiff to amend, on motion of the United States Attorney, appearing for the defendant, on the ground that it "fails to state facts sufficient to constitute a cause of action."

Thereupon plaintiff filed an amended complaint, wherein, with an obviously heightened conviction that he was being unjustly treated, he vigorously reiterates his claims, including those quoted above and now stated as that his "medicinal extracts" were given to the Springdale Distilling Company "with my betting [bidding?] price of $110: and not their price of $120," and "It isn't so easy to do away with two cases with 37 bottles of one quart. Being protected, they can take this chance." An earlier paragraph suggests that defendant had explained the loss of the two cases by "saying that they had leaked, which could never be true in the manner they were bottled." On defendant's motion for dismissal on the same ground as before, the court made a final judgment dismissing the complaint, and plaintiff now comes to us with increased volubility, if not clarity.

It would seem, however, that he has stated enough to withstand a mere formal motion, directed only to the face of the complaint, and that here is another instance of judicial haste which in the long run makes waste. Under the new rules of civil procedure, there is no pleading requirement of stating "facts sufficient to constitute a cause of action," but only that there be "a short and plain statement of the claim showing that the pleader is entitled to relief," * * * rule 8(a) * * *; and the motion for dismissal under Rule 12(b) is for failure to state "a claim upon which relief can be granted." The District Court does not state why it concluded that the complaints showed no claim upon which relief could be granted; and the United States Attorney's brief before us does not help us, for it is limited to the prognostication—unfortunately ill founded so far as we are concerned—that "the most cursory examination" of them will show the correctness of the District Court's action.

We think that, however inartistically they may be stated, the plaintiff has disclosed his claims that the collector has converted or otherwise done away with two of his cases of medicinal tonics and has sold the rest in a manner incompatible with the public auction he had announced—and, indeed, required by 19 U.S.C.A. § 1491, above cited, and the Treasury Regulations promulgated under it, formerly 19 CFR 18.7–18.12, now 19 CFR 20.5, 8 Fed.Reg. 8407, 8408, June 19, 1943. As to this latter claim, it may be that the collector's only error is a failure to collect an additional ten dollars from the Springdale Distilling Company; but giving the plaintiff the benefit of reasonable intendments in his allegations (as we must on this motion), the claim appears to be in effect that he was actually the first bidder at the price for which they were sold, and hence was entitled to the merchandise. Of course, defendant did not need to move on the complaint alone; he could have disclosed the facts from his point of view, in advance of a trial if he chose, by asking for a pre-trial hearing or by moving for a summary judgment with supporting affidavits. But, as it stands, we do not see how the plaintiff may properly be deprived of his day in court to show what he obviously so firmly believes and what for present purposes defendant must be taken as admitting. * * *

On remand, the District Court may find substance in other claims asserted by plaintiff, which include a failure properly to catalogue the items (as the cited Regulations provide), or to allow plaintiff to buy at a discount from the catalogue price just before the auction sale (a claim whose basis is not apparent), and a violation of an agreement to deliver the merchandise to the plaintiff as soon as he paid for it, by stopping the payments. In view of plaintiff's limited ability to write and speak English, it will be difficult for the District Court to arrive at justice unless he consents to receive legal assistance in the presentation of his case. The record indicates that he refused further help from a lawyer suggested by the court, and his brief (which was a recital of facts, rather than an argument of law) shows distrust of a lawyer of standing at this bar. It is the plaintiff's privilege to decline all legal help * * *; but we fear that he will be indeed ill advised to attempt to meet a motion for summary judgment or other similar presentation of the merits without competent advice and assistance.

Judgment is reversed and the action is remanded for further proceedings not inconsistent with this opinion.

Notes and Questions

1. Dioguardi's amended complaint read as follows:

UNITED STATES DISTRICT COURT

SOUTHERN DISTRICT OF NEW YORK

JOHN DIOGUARDI

                        Plaintiff,

        -against-

HARRY M. DURNING
Individually and as Collector of Customs
at the Port of New York

                        Defendant,

Plaintiff, as and for his bill of amended complaint the defendant, respectfully alleges:

FIRST: I want justice done on the basis of my medicinal extracts which have disappeared saying that they had leaked, which could never be true in the manner they were bottled,

SECOND: Mr. E.G. Collord Clerk in Charge, promised to give me my merchandise as soon as I paid for it. Then all of a sudden payments were stopped.

THIRD: Then, he didn't want to sell me my merchandise at catalogue price with the 5% off, which was very important to me, after I had already paid $5,000 for them, beside a few other expenses.

FOURTH: Why was the medicinaly given to the Springdale Distilling Co. with my betting price of $110; and not their price of $120.

FIFTH: It isn't so easy to do away with two cases with 37 bottles of one quart. Being protected, they can take this chance.

SIXTH: No one can stop my rights upon my merchandise, because of both the duly and the entry.

WHEREFORE: Plaintiff demands judgment against the defendant, individually and as Collector of Customs at the Port of New York, in the sum of Five Thousand Dollars ($5,000) together with interest from the respective dates of payment as set forth herein, together with the costs and disbursements of this action.

2. The *Dioguardi* decision was sharply criticized in McCaskill, *The Modern Philosophy of Pleading: A Dialogue Outside the Shades,* 38 A.B.A.J. 123 (1952), and has been a focal point of opposition to the so-called liberal "notice-pleading" of the Federal Rules. How would the *Dioguardi* case have been decided in a jurisdiction that requires a statement of "facts constituting a cause of action"?

3. Does Federal Rule 8(a) have the effect of completely eliminating the requirement of detailed fact pleadings? Is *Dioguardi* typical or atypical? The Supreme Court in CONLEY v. GIBSON, 355 U.S. 41, 47–48, 78 S.Ct. 99, 103, 2 L.Ed.2d 80, 85 (1957), cited *Dioguardi* and gave its views as follows:

* * * [T]he Federal Rules of Civil Procedure do not require a claimant to set out in detail the facts upon which he bases his claim. To the contrary, all the Rules require is "a short and plain statement of the claim" that will give the defendant fair notice of what the plaintiff's claim is and the grounds upon which it rests. The illustrative forms appended to the Rules plainly demonstrate this. Such simplified "notice pleading" is made possible by the liberal opportunity for discovery and the other pretrial procedures established by the Rules to disclose more precisely the basis of both claim and defense and to define more narrowly the disputed facts and issues.

Shortly thereafter Judge Clark made the following comment:

* * * Some people love to say that all the rules require is fair notice, that pleading under the rules is only notice pleading. * * * Notice pleading is a beautiful nebulous thing. I ought not to say too much about it because there are two pretty good decisions of the Supreme Court that speak of notice pleading. One of the last was the *Conley* decision just this fall, where Justice Black for the Court speaks of modern pleading as being designed only to give fair notice. I don't use that expression—not that I object to it as such. I think it is something like the Golden Rule, which is a nice hopeful thing; but I can't find that it means much of anything and it isn't anything that we can use with any precision. What we require is a general statement of the case, and our best precedents are those that have been honored over the years, which show that we haven't done anything really violent. We do not require detail. We require a general statement. How much? Well, the answer is made in what I think is probably the most important part of the rules

so far as this particular topic is concerned, namely, the Forms. These are important because when you can't define you can at least draw pictures to show your meaning.

Clark, *Pleading Under the Federal Rules,* 12 Wyo.L.J. 177, 181 (1958).

4. Examples of the simplicity of pleading under Rule 8(a) are found in the Appendix of Forms, which are set out in the Supplement following the Federal Rules of Civil Procedure; in particular see Forms 9 and 11. Note that in 1946, Rule 84 was amended to state that the Forms were not mere guides but were themselves "sufficient under the rules." This change was intended to overcome the effect of WASHBURN v. MOORMAN MFG. CO., 25 F.Supp. 546 (S.D.Cal.1938), in which it was held that a complaint failed to state a claim for relief despite the fact that it followed one of the forms.

5. Under the Federal Rules, can a pleading be rejected for being *too* specific? Consider the following case:

> In a prolix and discursive 69 page complaint, which is anything but the simple, direct, and concise statement mandated by Fed.R.Civ.P. 8(e), plaintiff's battery of lawyers seek to charge Massey with liability for the losses sustained by class members who purchased Massey stock between 1976 and 1978. The complaint is an "everything but the kitchen sink" type of pleading which would give the plaintiff's attorneys carte blanche in the area of liberal federal discovery. Because the "in terrorem" effect of such unfettered discovery would, to say the least, be substantial, it is important that the wheat in plaintiff's pleading be separated from the chaff.

DECKER v. MASSEY–FERGUSON, LTD., 681 F.2d 111, 114–15 (2d Cir.1982).

6. Consider which, if any, of the following pleadings would, in itself, be sufficient to state a claim under Federal Rule 8(a)(2).

(a) D is legally liable to P for damages.

(b) D negligently caused P's injury.

(c) D negligently caused P's injuries on July 4, 1983, at Dreamworld Amusement Park.

(d) D negligently operated a roller coaster ride on which P was a passenger on July 4, 1983, at Dreamworld Amusement Park. As a result of this negligence, P suffered a broken arm and was otherwise injured, and P incurred hospital and other medical expenses, and was prevented from transacting business, resulting in damages of $25,000.

(e) D negligently operated a roller coaster ride on which P was a passenger on July 4, 1983, at Dreamworld Amusement Park. D was negligent because it was operating the roller coaster at excessive speed and the ride was improperly maintained. As a result of this negligence, P suffered a broken arm and was otherwise injured, and P incurred hospital and other medical expenses, and was prevented from transacting business, resulting in damages of $25,000.

(f) D negligently operated a roller coaster ride on which P was a passenger on July 4, 1983, at Dreamworld Amusement Park. D was negligent because it was operating the roller coaster at excessive speed (the roller coaster was travelling at a speed of 32 mph, exceeding the safe speed by 5 mph) and the ride was improperly maintained.

As a result of this negligence, P suffered a broken arm and was otherwise injured and P incurred hospital and other medical expenses, and was prevented from transacting business, resulting in damages of $25,000.

(g) D negligently operated a roller coaster ride on which P was a passenger on July 4, 1983, at Dreamworld Amusement Park. D was negligent because it was operating the roller coaster at excessive speed (the roller coaster was travelling at a speed of 32 mph, exceeding the safe speed by 5 mph), and the ride was improperly maintained. P was not contributorily negligent. As a result of this negligence, P suffered a broken arm and was otherwise injured and P incurred hospital and other medical expenses, and was prevented from transacting business, resulting in damages of $25,000.

Does Official Form 9 provide a benchmark for judging any of these? Which satisfy Federal Form 9? Which are too vague? Which are too specific?

––––––––

LODGE 743, INTERNATIONAL ASS'N OF MACHINISTS v. UNITED AIRCRAFT CORP., 30 F.R.D. 142 (D.Conn.1962). Plaintiff brought suit under the Labor Management Relations Act, 29 U.S.C. § 185, alleging a violation of a strike settlement contract in that defendant-employer had failed to recall strikers to work as jobs for which they were qualified became available. Defendant moved for a more definite statement under Federal Rule 12(e), demanding that plaintiff identify by name the strikers involved and specify the jobs for which they were qualified. Defendant claimed that some 2,000 registered strikers were covered by the contract and it had no knowledge of any violation.

Plaintiff contended that if the court granted the motion, it would be tantamount to a dismissal of its action because the agreement imposed the obligation to keep proper hiring lists on the defendant and thus the information sought was obtainable only from the latter's own personnel files. As the court stated:

> The overwhelming weight of authority is to the effect that a motion for a bill of particulars or a motion for more definite statement of the claim should not be granted if the complaint sets forth a cause of action with sufficient definiteness to enable the defendant to frame an answer. Additional details that the defendant needs in order to prepare for trial shall be obtained by discovery after issue is joined. Montgomery v. Kingsland, 83 U.S.App.D.C. 66, 166 F.2d 953, 955 (1948) [see Federal Rules 26–37] * * *.

In the present case, however, the [union's] allegations might be applicable to a few or as many as 2,000 registered strikers. It is the company's claim that it has no information within its possession of any instance where those allegations are applicable and is at a loss to prepare a proper defense.

The plaintiff-union contends that while it has substantial reason to believe the allegations of the complaint are true, it is not presently in a position to name the union members to whom the allegations apply nor the jobs which they claim have been unjustly and illegally filled and their members discriminated against. Under such circumstances, no good purpose could be accomplished at this time by the defendant-corporation resorting to the use of interrogatories, in order to procure more definite specifications in this regard.

* * *

The motion of the defendant for more definite statement is granted * * *. However, the plaintiff shall not be required to answer any part of said motion until its own discovery proceedings are completed. This order is without prejudice to the defendant to move for a modification of this ruling during the course of the discovery proceedings by the plaintiff, if good cause appears.

Notes and Questions

1. In WEBB v. WEBB, 32 F.R.D. 615 (W.D.Mo.1963), defendant was charged with negligence in extracting a tooth and rendering postoperative care. He moved for a more definite statement to require plaintiff to specify the acts of negligence. The court denied the motion, pointing out that the complaint clearly was sufficient under Form 9. Does the *Webb* decision in any way subvert the policy of Federal Rule 12(e)? Is *Webb* consistent with *United Aircraft*? Why shouldn't a plaintiff be required to specify the elements of defendant's alleged negligence?

2. The proper function of the Federal Rule 12(e) motion for a more definite statement is better understood in light of its history. Read the commentary accompanying Federal Rule 12(e) in the Supplement and consider the amendments that have been made in the Rule since its original promulgation. What was the purpose of these changes? Is the decision in the principal case consistent with the policies underlying the amendments? Why shouldn't the Federal Rules contain a provision for a bill of particulars as an additional method of discovery? See 5 Wright & Miller, *Federal Practice and Procedure: Civil* §§ 1374–79 (1969).

3. PLEADING THE RIGHT TO RELIEF

Read Federal Rule of Civil Procedure 8(a)(2) in the Supplement.

GARCIA v. HILTON HOTELS INTERNATIONAL, INC.

United States District Court, District of Puerto Rico, 1951.
97 F.Supp. 5.

ROBERTS, DISTRICT JUDGE. The action here is for damages for defamation brought by plaintiff, a citizen and resident of Puerto Rico, against defendant, a Delaware corporation, in the District Court of Puerto Rico and removed to this Court by defendant corporation. The complaint sets forth two causes of action and the paragraphs considered herein are identical in each cause. Defendant has moved to dismiss the complaint for failure to state a claim upon which relief can be granted and, in the alternative, to strike Paragraphs 5, 6, 7 and 8 and for a more definite statement.

In supoprt [sic] of its motion to dismiss, defendant contends that no publication of the alleged slanderous statement is alleged and that the complaint, therefore, fails to state a cause of action. This contention will be considered first with respect to Paragraph 4 of the complaint, which reads as follows: "4. On August 22, 1950, the plaintiff was violently discharged by the defendant, being falsely and slanderously accused of being engaged in bringing women from outside the Hotel and introducing them into the rooms thereof for the purpose of developing prostitution in the Hotel and that such women brought by him from outside the Hotel and introduced therein carried on acts of prostitution in said Hotel."

* * *

The controlling question here, with respect to the motion to dismiss, is whether the allegations of Paragraph 4 of the complaint, state a claim upon which relief can be granted. An examination of the authorities is persuasive that is [sic] does. It is settled, with respect to motions to dismiss for insufficiency of statement, that the complaint is to be construed in the light most favorable to the plaintiff with all doubts resolved in his favor and the allegations accepted as true. If, when a complaint is so considered, it reasonably may be anticipated that plaintiff, on the basis of what has been alleged, could make out a case at trial entitling him to some relief, the complaint should not be dismissed. * * *

In the instant case, it is true that Paragraph 4, of the complaint, fails to state, in so many words, that there was a publication of the alleged slanderous utterance and, to that extent, the cause of action is defectively stated. However, it does not follow that the allegations do not state a claim upon which relief can be granted. It is alleged that plaintiff was "violently discharged" and was "falsely and slanderously accused" of procuring for prostitution. While in a technical sense, this language states a conclusion, it is clear that plaintiff used it intending to charge publication of the slanderous utterance and it would be unrealistic for defendant to claim that it does not so understand the allegations. See, Edelman v. Locker, D.C., 6 F.R.D. 272, 274. Clearly, under such allegations it reasonably may be conceived that plaintiff, upon trial, could adduce evidence tending to prove a publication. * * *

In further support of its motion to dismiss, defendant contends that the alleged slanderous utterance was conditionally privileged. Conceding that to be so does not require that a different conclusion be reached with respect to the motion to dismiss. Rule 12(b) requires that every defense in law or fact be asserted in a responsive pleading when one is required or permitted under the rules. The rule, however, enumerates certain defenses which may be asserted by motion to dismiss, all of which go to the jurisdiction except that of failure to state a claim upon which relief can be granted, rule 12(b)(6). And this latter defense may be asserted successfully by a motion prior to responsive pleading only when it appears to a certainty that plaintiff would be entitled to no relief under any state of

fact which could be proved in support of the claim asserted by him.
* * *

The conclusiveness of privilege as a defense depends upon whether the privilege involved in [sic] absolute or conditional. When the privilege involved is absolute, it constitutes a finally determinative or conclusive defense to an action based on the utterance. Consequently, when it appears from a complaint that absolute privilege exists, the defense of failure to state a claim properly may be asserted to accomplish a dismissal on motion under rule 12(b). It is for the court to determine the existence of privilege and when absolute privilege is found, it constitutes an unassailable defense and, clearly, in such a case, the claim stated is one upon which relief cannot be granted.

But conditional privilege is not a conclusive defense to an action based on a slanderous utterance. It is but a qualified defense which may be lost to the defendant if plaintiff can prove abuse of the privilege or actual malice. * * * When from the allegations contained therein, a complaint indicates the availability of the defense of conditional privilege, it cannot be held therefrom as a matter of law, that there has been a failure to state a claim upon which relief can be granted, such as will warrant dismissal of the complaint on motion under rule 12(b)(6), for the factual question remains whether defendant abused the privilege or made the communication maliciously. * * *

As has been noted, on motion to dismiss for failure to state a claim, complaint must be construed in the light most favorable to plaintiff with all doubts resolved in his favor and the allegation taken as true. That being so, when allegations are sufficient to sustain the defense of conditional privilege they will be, generally, sufficient to permit the introduction of evidence tending to prove abuse of the privilege or actual malice. Save in some extraordinary situation, allegations which are adequate for the admission of evidence to prove the defense of qualified privilege are adequate for the admission of evidence to negative that defense. It appears from the complaint in the instant case that defendant is entitled to raise the defense of conditional privilege. But this defense may be lost to it if plaintiff proves abuse of the privilege or actual malice. And, clearly, plaintiff may introduce evidence under the allegations for the purpose of proving abuse of the privilege or actual malice. Therefore, it is concluded that defendant's motion to dismiss the complaint for failure to state a claim upon which relief can be granted should be denied.

The conclusion to deny defendant's motion to dismiss requires that consideration be given its alternative motion to strike Paragraphs 5, 6, 7 and 8 of the complaint. It is alleged in these paragraphs, in substance, that upon being discharged, plaintiff made claim with the Labor Department of Puerto Rico for severance pay and overtime as is provided for by law (Section 20, Organic Act of Labor Department of Puerto Rico, approved April 14, 1931); that during a hearing on such claim held by the Labor Department, defendant, falsely and slanderously, repeated its charge that plaintiff had been engaged in procuring for prostitution; and, that, after said hearing defendant had compromised plaintiff's claim for severance pay and overtime. As respects defendant's motion to strike, the controlling allegations are contained in Paragraph 7 of this complaint.

Section 4 of "An Act Authorizing Civil Actions to recover Damages for Libel and Slander," enacted by the Legislature of Puerto Rico and approved on February 19, 1902, (Code of Civil Procedure of Puerto Rico, Ed. 1933, page 309) provides in part as follows: "Section 4. A publication or communication shall not be held or deemed malicious when made in any legislative or judicial proceeding or in any other proceeding authorized by law. * * * "

The effect of the above quoted portions of the statute is to confer absolute privilege upon any communication made in any of the proceedings contemplated therein. If the hearing held by the Labor Department on plaintiff's claim for severance pay and overtime, referred to in Paragraph 7 of the complaint, is a proceeding within the meaning of the phrase "or any other proceeding authorized by law" as used in said Section 4 of the Act of February 19, 1902, the utterance was absolutely privileged and such privilege constitutes a conclusive defense in an action based on that utterance.

It appears that the hearing on plaintiff's claim by the Labor Department, referred to in Paragraph 7 of the complaint, is a proceeding "authorized by law" within the meaning of Section 4 of the Act of February 19, 1902. The Labor Department is authorized to hold such a hearing by Act No. 122 of the Legislature of Puerto Rico, approved April 27, 1949, which statute requires the Commissioner of Labor to enforce labor protecting laws. * * *

It appears, upon examination, that this Statute (Act No. 122) has for its purpose the protection of the welfare of the workman and the furtherance of the public good, and that when hearings are held pursuant to its terms it is necessary, if those purposes are to be effectuated, that those called upon to give evidence therein must be protected against liability, civil or criminal, for communications given in evidence at such hearings. And this without regard for the motives of the witness or the truth or falsity of his statements. For otherwise, the giving of full, free and honest testimony, essential to the enforcement of such laws, will be discouraged. Therefore, communications made by witnesses in the course of such hearings, should be absolutely privileged in the same manner and to like extent as those made in the course of a judicial proceeding.

* * *

Clearly, then, the utterance of the defendant made during the Labor Department hearing referred to in Paragraph 7 of the complaint was absolutely privileged and that Paragraph 7 is, therefore, redundant in that it fails to state a claim upon which relief can be granted. It appears then, that defendant's motion to strike Paragraphs 5, 6, 7 and 8 should be granted.

The parties have agreed on hearing in open court that Paragraph 9 of the complaint should be stricken. And this Court being of the opinion that Paragraphs 5, 6, 7 and 8 should be stricken as redundant, defendant's motion for a more definite statement need be considered only with respect to the allegations of Paragraph 4 of the complaint.

As has been noted herein, conditional privilege is an affirmative defense which properly should be raised by its assertion in a responsive pleading. Consequently, when it appears from a complaint that the defense of conditional privilege may be available to a defendant, the allegations thereof should be reasonably adequate to permit the preparation of a responsive pleading asserting such defense. But when, in an action for slander, the complaint fails to set out substantially the utterance alleged to have been slanderously made or the facts relied upon to establish a publication of such utterance, such omission constitutes vagueness such as is a ground for granting a motion for more definite statement within the contemplation of rule 12(e). Obviously, when such material allegations are insufficient, it would be unreasonable to require the defendant to prepare a responsive pleading without a more definite statement of the pertinent facts.

Considering the allegations of Paragraph 4 of the complaint, the defense of conditional privilege is indicated. However, the allegations suffer from vagueness with respect to the utterance alleged to have been slanderously made and the facts relied upon to establish a publication of the utterance. It is concluded that the defendant here is entitled to a more definite statement setting forth substantially the words alleged to have been slanderously uttered and the facts relied upon to establish a publication thereof.

Defendant's motion to dismiss the complaint for failure to state a claim upon which relief can be granted is denied. Defendant's motion to strike Paragraphs 5, 6, 7 and 8 of the complaint is granted. Defendant's motion for a more definite statement with respect to the matters prescribed in this opinion, is granted. Paragraph 9 of the complaint is ordered stricken. The decisions herein reached are hereby made applicable to the second cause of action set out in the complaint.

Notes and Questions

1. To what extent could plaintiff in *Garcia* have phrased the complaint to avoid the granting of defendant's motions? How should plaintiff alter the complaint to satisfy the court's order for a more definite statement? Can he merely eliminate some of the allegations that gave rise to the conditional privilege?

2. Suppose defendant's motion under Federal Rule 12(e) had been denied by the court. What other means might he have used to learn the details of the alleged defamatory publication? What advantage, if any, is there to a motion under Federal Rule 12(e) as opposed to these other means?

3. Assume plaintiff in *Garcia* had not included any facts in the complaint indicating either a conditional or absolute privilege. How could defendant have raised these issues? See Federal Rule 8(c). Since privilege is obviously a matter of defense, why should it be significant whether plaintiff raises it in the complaint? Shouldn't these matters simply be ignored unless defendant pursues them in the answer? Consider ELLIS v. BLACK DIA-

MOND COAL MINING CO., 265 Ala. 264, 90 So.2d 770 (1956): "Even though a complaint at law shows on its face that the cause of action is barred by the statute of limitations the defense of the statute cannot be taken by demurrer." Compare BAGGETT v. CHAVOUS, 107 Ga.App. 642, 131 S.E.2d 109 (1963) (involving the anticipated defense of accord and satisfaction in a contract action): " 'Ordinarily the plaintiff, in his petition, need not anticipate or negative a possible defense. Where, however, such defense is anticipated, it must be effectively avoided, or the complaint is bad.' " On what basis, if any, can *Ellis* and *Baggett* be reconciled? Would it be fair to say that the decision in *Garcia* is consistent with *Ellis* and inconsistent with *Baggett?*

The Burden of Pleading and the Burden of Production

The burden of pleading an issue usually is assigned to the party who has the burden of producing evidence on that issue at trial. Plaintiff has the burden of production on two types of issues. First, plaintiff must put forth evidence on certain matters basic to the action or he cannot prevail. In a slander action, for example, plaintiff must introduce evidence that the remarks were made, that they were published, and that he was injured thereby. If plaintiff rests his case without producing evidence on any one of these issues, the court will dismiss the action and enter judgment for defendant. Second, if, but only if, defendant establishes a defense, plaintiff will then have a second burden of production, this time to introduce evidence as to new facts that will avoid defendant's defense. For example, if defendant proves that allegedly slanderous statements were made to plaintiff's prospective employer under conditions that rendered the statements privileged, plaintiff must then carry the burden of producing evidence showing that the statements were made maliciously and solely with intent to injure plaintiff.

Plaintiff has the burden of pleading all matters of the first type in the complaint; that is, he is required to plead those matters on which he must introduce evidence at trial. The rationale for the rule is simple. If plaintiff cannot legitimately allege the existence of each of the basic elements of his claim, it may be assumed that he could not introduce evidence on them at trial. Since the action would have to be dismissed as soon as plaintiff rested his case, it would be an idle act to permit the trial to begin, and the action might as well be terminated at the pleading stage.

On the other hand, plaintiff normally does not have to plead matters on which defendant must introduce proof. If plaintiff were required to plead the nonexistence of every defense, not only would the pleading be long, complex, and fraught with danger for a plaintiff who omitted a remote possibility, but the pleadings would not reveal, in any direct way, precisely upon which defenses defendant actually intended to rely. By placing the burden of pleading defenses on defendant, the court and parties know exactly on which of the many possible defenses he intends to introduce evidence, thus making preparation for trial and work at trial more manageable. Obviously, plaintiff is not required to plead, in the original complaint, matters to avoid defenses, since he cannot tell which defenses will be raised until the answer is filed. In some jurisdictions plaintiff is required to set forth such matters of avoidance in a second pleading, which serves as a reply to the answer; in other jurisdictions the decision whether to require a reply is left to the trial court's discretion.

Other Considerations in Allocating the Burden of Pleading

Aside from those matters upon which he must initially introduce evidence if he is to prevail, plaintiff, in the complaint, is sometimes required to plead the nonexistence of certain defenses upon which defendant has the burden of proof, although as we have seen, such a requirement is technically illogical. The reason for these special rules is sometimes historical and sometimes practical. Consider, for example, a case in which plaintiff sues defendant on an overdue note. Payment of a note traditionally has been considered a defense to be proved by defendant, who by virtue of having a receipt usually is in a better position to put in evidence on the issue. Nevertheless, plaintiff, as part of the claim, must allege nonpayment. Without such an allegation the complaint would really say nothing; it would simply set forth the existence of the note without mentioning the nature of the breach of its terms. To inform the court and defendant as to the basis of the complaint, an allegation of nonpayment is essential. It is only when a defense, such as payment, goes to the very heart of the action, so that plaintiff should, in order to state a claim, be required to face the issue and allege in good faith that such defense does not exist, that the burden of pleading and the burden of producing evidence need not coincide. Another example occurs in the slander context in which some courts consider the truth of the remarks an absolute defense. In some of these jurisdictions, although not all, falsity is thought to be so much a part of the basic action, that plaintiff must plead it, even though defendant has the burden of introducing evidence of truth.

Because of the technical imbalance in cases in which plaintiff must plead the nonexistence of a defense in order to state a claim, some courts require defendant to raise the defense specially in the answer, rather than by simply denying plaintiff's allegation, if defendant really intends to pursue it; otherwise the defense will be waived. Thus before such an issue actually is tried, it will be pleaded twice, once in the complaint and once in the answer.

Allocation of the pleading burden sometimes is complicated by rules or statutes that specifically set forth matters that are to be considered defenses and contained in the answer. See, e.g., Federal Rule of Civil Procedure 8(c). The enumerated matters usually are those that traditionally have been treated as defenses both as to the burden of pleading and the burden of proof. Not all jurisdictions have adhered to these traditional views, however. For example, contributory negligence historically was treated as a defense, but today, in a number of jurisdictions, plaintiff, in order to prevail in a negligence case, must prove his own due care. If the pleading rule in these jurisdictions deems the issue of plaintiff's negligence to be a defense, it creates a serious anomaly, since defendant must raise the issue even though plaintiff is required to prove it. Furthermore, since a defense is waived if defendant does not plead it, the failure of defendant to raise the matter in the answer would seem to obviate plaintiff's proof of the matter, thus thwarting the express policy of the jurisdiction requiring plaintiff to prove his own due care.

Fortunately those situations in which the burden of proof and burden of pleading do not coincide are few in number and usually are well known. By following approved pleading forms and precedents covering these odd cases, most attorneys handle such cases without incident.

4. PLEADING SPECIAL MATTERS

Read Federal Rule of Civil Procedure 9 and the related materials in the Supplement.

DENNY v. CAREY

United States District Court, Eastern District of Pennsylvania, 1976.
72 F.R.D. 574.

JOSEPH S. LORD, III, CHIEF JUDGE.

Plaintiff brings this proposed class action on behalf of himself and other purchasers of First Pennsylvania Corporation ("First Penn") securities alleging violation of federal and state securities laws. * * * Defendants have not answered the complaint, but have moved to dismiss pursuant to Fed.R.Civ.P. 12(b)(6) on the ground that plaintiff's allegations fail to state the circumstances constituting the alleged fraud with sufficient particularity as required by Fed.R.Civ.P. 9(b). * * *

On information and belief, plaintiff alleges that from January 1, 1974 to January 28, 1976 defendants conspired to conceal the true picture of First Penn's financial condition by issuing false and fraudulent statements which unreasonably avoided recognition and accrual of losses and inadequately provided for loan losses and total reserves, thereby inflating First Penn's equity and net income. * * *

Specifically, plaintiff alleges, *inter alia,* that First Penn: (1) improperly included as income accruals of interest where the borrower had already defaulted; (2) engaged in sales of foreclosed properties on terms which would not have been made in good faith with arm's length bargaining ("paper sales") to avoid showing substantial losses; (3) inadequately provided for loan losses by not accounting for expected uncollectibles in real estate loans where the mortgage loans constituted a high percentage of the total cost of projects undertaken by borrowers; and (4) concealed the default of loans by entering into extensions, modifications and other arrangements with defaulting borrowers. * * *

Defendants contend that these allegations fail to state the circumstances constituting fraud with sufficient particularity to comply with Fed.R.Civ.P. 9(b), and hence, do not state a claim upon which relief can be granted. Defendants also assert that plaintiff's allegations are "conclusory"—that they are "neutral," simply track the statutory language and fail to delineate the underlying acts and transactions. * * * Defendants state that plaintiff's deficiency is exacerbated by the fact that all of the operative allegations are made on information and belief without a statement of the facts upon which plaintiff's belief is founded. * * *

Defendants believe that plaintiff's burden of pleading fraud with particularity is a "rigorous" one. They point to several rationales given for Rule 9(b) which they believe support this position. Defendants state that since fraud is easily charged and such allegations of moral turpitude may at times be advanced only for their nuisance or settlement value, Rule 9(b) serves to protect defendants. * * * Defendants also argue that Rule 9(b) shields defendants, especially accountants and other professional defendants, from lawsuits which wrongfully damage their reputations. * * *

Defendants are incorrect when they argue that Rule 9(b) places a "rigorous" burden of pleading on plaintiff. A court may become too demanding if it unduly focuses on potential harm to defendants' reputations or the possibility of a "strike" or nuisance suit. "[R]ule 9(b) does not insulate professionals from claims of fraud where a complaint alleges the fraudulent acts with particularity * * *." Felton v. Walston and Co., [508 F.2d 577, 581–82 (2d Cir.1971)] * * *. "A strict application of Rule 9(b) in class action securities fraud cases could result in substantial unfairness to persons who are the victims of fraudulent conduct." In re Caesars Palace Securities Litigation, 360 F.Supp. 366, 388 (S.D.N.Y.1973). This is especially true where many of the matters are peculiarly within the knowledge of defendants. * * * Certainly in such cases, once plaintiff has satisfied the minimum burden of Rule 9(b), plaintiff should be allowed to flesh out the allegations in the complaint through discovery. * * *

Fed.R.Civ.P. 8 requires a short and plain statement of the claim which is simple, concise and direct. Rule 9(b) must be harmonized with the notice pleading mandate of Rule 8. * * * "Rule 9(b) does not require nor make legitimate the pleading of detailed evidentiary matter." *Moore* ¶ 9.03 at 1930 * * *.

Since fraud embraces a wide variety of potential misconduct, *Wright & Miller* § 1296 at 400, Rule 9(b) requires slightly more notice than would be forthcoming under Rule 8.[5] * * * But the requirement of Rule 9(b) is met when there is sufficient identification of the circumstances constituting fraud so that the defendant can prepare an adequate answer to the allegations. * * *

---

5. *Wright & Miller* § 1300 at 425 points out: "the notion that Rule 9(b) does not actually require significantly more particularity than Rule 8 seems to be supported by the text of Official Form 13, which contains little more than a general allegation of fraud."

We find that the complaint [though not a model of perfect pleading] satisfies the requirement of Rule 9(b). * * * Before discovery, any stricter application of Rule 9(b) is especially inappropriate in a case such as this where the matters alleged are peculiarly within the knowledge of defendants. * * *

Notes and Questions

1. DENNY v. BARBER, 576 F.2d 465 (2d Cir.1978), was a case remarkably similar to Denny v. Carey. Both were brought by the same plaintiff, represented by the same counsel, and the same public accounting firm was one of the defendants in each case. The complaint, couched only in general terms, alleged, inter alia, that defendants had fraudulently concealed defendant Chase Manhattan Corporation's true financial picture by not revealing that the corporation had made "risky and speculative" investments without providing adequate reserves for losses and had delayed in writing off uncollectible loans. The court held that Rule 9(b) had not been followed:

> Plaintiff's counsel has called our attention to a number of district court decisions * * * [including Denny v. Carey] which are alleged to have sustained complaints no more specific than this. We see no profit in attempting to analyze these decisions, which may or may not be consistent and each of which necessarily rests on its particular facts. * * * [There] must be more than vague allegations that, as shown by subsequent developments, the corporation's true financial picture was not so bright in some respects as its annual reports had painted and that the defendants knew, or were reckless in failing to know, this. The admission in [plaintiff's] counsel's * * * statement [that he could provide no further facts] * * * in the absence of discovery is significant. The Supreme Court has admonished that to the extent that such discovery "permits a plaintiff with a largely groundless claim to simply take up the time of a number of other people, with the right to do so representing an *in terrorem* increment of the settlement value, rather than a reasonably founded hope that the process will reveal relevant evidence, it is a social cost rather than a benefit." Blue Chip Stamps v. Manor Drug Stores * * * 421 U.S. at 741. * * *

2. What are the policies underlying Rule 9(b), requiring particularity in pleading fraud? Is it designed to discourage nuisance suits? If so, why does not Rule 11 requiring truthful pleadings handle this problem? And in any event, why would concern about nuisance suits be more acute with regard to fraud than with regard to other causes of action? Is it because a defendant who is accused of fraud often might be harmed even if subsequently he prevails on the merits? Requiring particularity in these cases has the effect of screening out such cases early on, instead of relying on other devices, such as summary judgment.

Is the particularity requirement of Rule 9(b) justified as a means of shielding defendants from the heavy expense of complying with burdensome discovery requests in lawsuits that appear on the face of the complaint to be marginal? Would a better solution be to shift the expense of discovery in fraud cases? See Sovern, *Reconsidering Federal Civil Rule 9(b): Do We Need Particularized Pleading Requirements in Fraud Cases?*, 104 F.R.D. 143 (1985);

Richman, Lively, & Mell, *The Pleading of Fraud: Rhymes Without Reason,* 60 S.Cal.L.Rev. 959 (1987).

3. Would a defendant receive adequate notice of the particulars of the circumstances constituting the fraud case, absent the special Rule 9(b) requirement? If not, is this an additional reason for the particularity requirement?

———

Even in areas other than those delineated in Rule 9, some courts have imposed more rigorous pleading requirements in some types of cases. Consider the following excerpt from Marcus, *The Revival of Fact Pleading Under the Federal Rules of Civil Procedure,* 86 Colum.L.Rev. 433, 445–50 (1986):

> Undoubtedly, lax pleading has * * * benefitted plaintiffs. Plaintiffs have an incentive to plead vaguely in hopes that discovery will turn up material on which to base a more specific charge. Indeed, it has even been suggested that specificity inherently favors defendants. Moreover, under Conley v. Gibson [p. 480, supra] courts may be inclined to deny motions to dismiss precisely because they cannot tell enough about a plaintiff's claim from the pleadings to decide whether the plaintiff has a chance of prevailing at trial. * * * [P]laintiffs with weak claims have good reason to want to stave off dismissal in hopes of a settlement.

> A natural antidote to pro-plaintiff biases and the impulse toward vagueness is to promote pleadings decisions, and the courts have adopted this solution in areas that were viewed as particularly troubling. The Supreme Court itself, while approaching pleading issues with what has been called "appalling casualness" and continuing outwardly to adhere to *Conley,* has nevertheless provided some support for such creativity. It has suggested that "insubstantial" cases can be dismissed despite "artful pleading" and appeared receptive to using pleading motions to weed out meritless cases. In a 1983 decision reversing dismissal of an antitrust case, for example, it exhorted the district court to require plaintiff to plead with particularity, concluding that "in a case of this magnitude, a district court must retain the power to insist upon some specificity in pleading before allowing a potentially massive factual controversy to proceed."

> * * *

> Many lower courts have been even more vigorous in insisting on fact pleading. Although special pleading rules are sometimes used to accomplish a narrow policy objective, these decisions generally fit into one of three categories.

> 1. *Securities Fraud.*—Virtually unknown when the Federal Rules were adopted, securities fraud cases have since proliferated. Many courts have responded by requiring plaintiffs to plead detailed facts. To some extent this insistence can be justified by the special pleading requirements of Rule 9(b), which requires that in fraud cases "the circumstances constituting fraud * * * shall be stated with particularity." * * *

> Consistent with the general purposes of the Rules, some courts find that Rule 9(b) is designed to provide somewhat more specific notice and that it requires only "slightly more" detail than Rule 8(a)(2). However,

other courts, particularly the Second Circuit, find that Rule 9(b) serves a much more substantive purpose—to protect defendants' reputations from unfounded claims of fraud and to assure that such malodorous claims are not filed as a pretext for discovery * * *.

The stricter courts pay great attention to "conclusory" allegations about defendants' knowledge or intent. Some hold that plaintiffs may not rely on allegations based on information and belief. Some insist that the plaintiff provide specific details that support factual conclusions. For example, in Ross v. A.H. Robins Co., [607 F.2d 545 (2d Cir.1979), certiorari denied 446 U.S. 946, 100 S.Ct. 2175, 64 L.Ed.2d 802 (1980),] plaintiff shareholders sued the company and its senior officers. Plaintiffs claimed that the defendants had knowingly or recklessly failed to disclose the health risks caused by use of the Dalkon Shield intrauterine device that eventually resulted in the filing of hundreds of lawsuits against Robins, with total claims far exceeding Robins' net worth. In their complaint, plaintiffs, who bought their shares in 1973, alleged that Robins had then touted the device as a boost to the company's financial health even though in May, 1974, the company wrote 120,000 doctors across the country warning them of health hazards associated with the use of the device. To bolster their claim that defendants had known or recklessly disregarded these risks prior to plaintiffs' purchase of their shares in 1973, plaintiffs pointed to an unpublished 1972 study detailing the health hazards associated with the Dalkon Shield. Because plaintiffs did not allege Robins was aware of the study, however, the Second Circuit found the complaint inadequate for failure to "specifically plead those events which they assert give rise to a strong inference that defendants had knowledge of the facts."

2. *Civil Rights Cases.*—Like securities fraud cases, civil rights suits have since 1938 become a staple of the federal courts' civil docket. Unlike securities fraud cases, however, there is no special provision of the Federal Rules applicable to civil rights claims. Many lower federal courts have nevertheless revived fact pleading requirements in such cases.

The leader in this movement has been the Third Circuit, which is forthright about its motivation: " 'In recent years there has been an increasingly large volume of cases brought under the Civil Rights Act. * * * It is an important public policy to weed out the frivolous and insubstantial cases at an early stage in the litigation. * * *' " To achieve this objective most courts now declare that conclusory allegations are inadequate to state a civil rights claim. They require specific delineation of the facts claimed to show a violation of plaintiff's civil rights and, as in securities fraud cases, focus particularly on plaintiff's allegations about intent.

These requirements have been applied with remarkable enthusiasm. In United States v. City of Philadelphia, [644 F.2d 187 (3d Cir.1980),] for example, the Department of Justice filed a complaint alleging in part that the Philadelphia police department systematically violated the civil rights of minority persons by abusing them physically. The complaint was signed by several government lawyers, including the Attorney General. Citing, among other things, the potential that such a claim could be vexatious to local police officials, the trial court dismissed. Although it specifically disavowed any need to determine whether the claim was frivolous, the Third Circuit affirmed on the ground that the complaint did not satisfy the specificity requirement for civil rights cases, which it said was necessary to provide "fair notice" and to dispose of frivolous cases.

Notes and Questions

1. The Marcus article observes that cases brought under the Civil Rights Acts have been singled out for special treatment by some federal courts. Can this practice be justified under Federal Rule 8(a)? Why should civil rights cases be treated this way? SMITH v. AMBROGIO, 456 F.Supp. 1130, 1132, 1134, 1137 (D.Conn.1978), illustrates the judicial attitude:

> This motion presents the issue of what allegations are sufficient to state a claim of municipal liability for deprivation of constitutional rights * * *.
>
> * * * [C]onduct is the action of a town when the conduct executes or implements official policy of the town. The policy can be found in an ordinance, regulation, policy statement, or decision officially adopted by the town's officers, or in a pattern of "persistent practices" sufficiently known to and approved by town officials to constitute a custom of equivalent though unofficial authoritativeness. * * *
>
> The requirement of particularized fact pleading to state a valid conspiracy claim is equally appropriate for statement of a valid claim of municipal liability predicated on the inaction of senior officials that is tantamount to approval of unconstitutional acts by subordinates. At a minimum the pleader must specify the overt acts relied upon as a basis for the claim that a pattern of unconstitutional actions exists and that the senior officials of the town knew of the unconstitutional actions and encouraged their repetition by inaction.
>
> The standard for municipal liability predicated on inaction of senior personnel must be frankly acknowledged as difficult to meet. A claim of this sort should not be initiated unless there is a sufficient factual basis to justify the extensive litigation that such a claim entails. * * *

The Supreme Court never has approved an exception to federal notice pleading in civil rights cases—many of which are pro se complaints brought by prison inmates. To the contrary, HAINES v. KERNER, 404 U.S. 519, 520, 92 S.Ct. 594, 596, 30 L.Ed.2d 652, 654 (1972) (per curiam), militates strongly against it by holding that pro se inmate civil rights complaints are to be measured against "less stringent standards than formal pleadings drafted by lawyers."

2. An area of special concern has been the role of pleading in cases containing numerous complex factual issues, a prime example being antitrust suits in the federal courts. From time to time some federal judges have urged that a separate, more rigorous standard of pleading should apply in these cases. See, e.g., Baim & Blank, Inc. v. Warren-Connelly Co., 19 F.R.D. 108, 109–10 (S.D.N.Y.1956). Arguments of this type have become increasingly rare, however, as court after court has specifically held that the so-called "big case" cannot receive special treatment since the Federal Rules do not provide for it. See, e.g., Walker Distrib. Co. v. Lucky Lager Brewing Co., 323 F.2d 1, 3 (9th Cir.1963); Nagler v. Admiral Corp., 248 F.2d 319 (2d Cir.1957). Should

the Federal Rules be amended to require more detailed pleadings in antitrust and other complex actions? Given the variety of contexts in which difficult factual disputes may arise, what should such an amendment say? Should trial courts have discretion to require the pleading of extra detail in any case that involves complex factual issues?

For various views of the problem, see Report to the Judicial Conference of the United States, *Procedure in Antitrust and Other Protracted Cases,* 13 F.R.D. 62, 66–68 (1953); Clark, *Special Pleading in the "Big Case,"* 21 F.R.D. 45 (1958); Freund, *The Pleading and Pre-Trial of an Antitrust Claim,* 46 Cornell L.Q. 555 (1961).

5. ALTERNATIVE AND INCONSISTENT ALLEGATIONS

———

Read Federal Rule of Civil Procedure 8(e)(2) and the related materials in the Supplement.

———

In the past, some courts have held pleadings that contain inconsistent allegations defective, at least if they appeared in a single cause of action or defense. See, e.g., Pavalon v. Thomas Holmes Corp., 25 Wis.2d 540, 131 N.W.2d 331 (1964). Many of these same courts approved these allegations so long as they were contained in separately stated causes or defenses. See Bischoff v. Hutisford State Bank, 195 Wis. 312, 218 N.W. 353 (1928).

Despite occasional statements indicating that inconsistent allegations are improper, see, e.g., Katz v. Feldman, 23 Cal.App.3d 500, 504, 100 Cal. Rptr. 367, 369 (1972), virtually all courts today permit inconsistent allegations, whether separately pleaded or not, if they are made in good faith, for example, in a situation in which the pleader has been unable to ascertain all the facts prior to filing the complaint or answer. See pp. 541–45, infra. A number of states specifically have altered their pleading rules to permit inconsistent pleadings. See, e.g., Mo.Rules of Civil Procedure 55.10 (revised in 1973). Compare Ga.Code Ann. § 9–11–8(e)(2) with Republic Mortgage Co. v. Beasley, 117 Ga.App. 303, 160 S.E.2d 429 (1968) (decided under prior Georgia law).

As previously noted, see pp. 429–32, supra, under the original common-law rules, pleadings were designed to reduce every controversy to a single issue of law or fact. Alternative and hypothetical allegations would have made the search for the single issue impossible and therefore they were forbidden. See generally McDonald, *Alternative Pleading: I,* 48 Mich.L.Rev. 311 (1950). Is there any justification today for a rule prohibiting alternative allegations? To what extent does the availability of discovery, pretrial conference, and summary judgment affect your answer?

———

The Separate-Statement Requirement

Rules permitting parties to plead in the alternative usually are coupled with provisions requiring each separate cause of action or defense to be separately stated. See, e.g., Ill.Stat.Ann. ch. 110, ¶¶ 2–603(b), 2–613(a).

Federal Rule of Civil Procedure 10(b) does not contain a formal separate-statement requirement, although the Rule does express the hope that "as far as practicable" each paragraph will be limited "to a statement of a single set of circumstances." The Rule also requires separation of claims founded on different transactions "whenever separation facilitates the clear presentation of the matters set forth." One commentator argues that this type of discretionary rule coupled with Rule 8(e), which permits inconsistent allegations in a single count, may be too liberal and may encourage confusion in pleading. He goes on to state:

> * * * If consistency promotes clarity, it is no great burden upon the plaintiff for him to state his separate grounds of recovery consistently. But if his position is clear, and it is obvious that the inconsistencies arise from an attempt to press alternative interpretations of the facts, little is to be gained by striking the pleading only to have it reformed in multiple counts asserting the same grounds of recovery.

McDonald, *Alternative Pleading in the United States: I,* 52 Colum.L.Rev. 443, 464 (1952). See also O'Donnell v. Elgin, J. & E. Ry. Co., 338 U.S. 384, 70 S.Ct. 200, 94 L.Ed. 187 (1949). Is the code-system requirement of separate counts, each of which is consistent within itself, preferable to Federal Rule 10(b)?

When a party violates the separate-statement requirement, the appropriate corrective procedure may be a motion to make separate statements, see Consolidated Airborne Systems, Inc. v. Silverman, 23 A.D.2d 695, 257 N.Y.S.2d 827 (2d Dep't 1965), or a motion to strike, see Brainerd v. First Lake County Nat. Bank, 109 Ill.App.2d 251, 248 N.E.2d 542 (1969), or a special preliminary objection, see General State Authority v. Lawrie & Green, 24 Pa.Cmwlth. 407, 356 A.2d 851 (1976). In any case the party will be allowed to amend his pleading to conform to the rules. If a plaintiff refuses to amend, should the case be dismissed? See Sawyer v. Sawyer, 181 Okl. 567, 75 P.2d 423 (1937) (dismissal proper).

6. PLEADING DAMAGES

Reread Federal Rule of Civil Procedure 9(g) in the Supplement.

P/A'ee   D/A'nt

ZIERVOGEL v. ROYAL PACKING CO.
St. Louis Court of Appeals, Missouri, 1949.
225 S.W.2d 798.

McCULLEN, JUDGE. This action was brought by respondent as plaintiff against appellant as defendant to recover damages for injuries plaintiff alleged she sustained as a result of a collision between an automobile driven by her and a motor vehicle (tractor-trailer, also referred to as truck) operated by defendant's employee. A trial before the court and a jury resulted in a verdict and judgment in favor of plaintiff against defendant in the sum of $2000.00. After an unavailing motion for a new trial defendant appealed.

   * * * Describing her injuries plaintiff alleged in her petition that "Plaintiff sustained injuries to her neck, back, spine and nervous system and was otherwise injured and her earning capacity has been permanently impaired."

* * *

   For its first point defendant contends that the trial court erred in permitting plaintiff's counsel in his opening statement, over defendant's objection, to state to the jury that plaintiff's blood pressure had increased by the accident and in refusing to declare a mistrial on defendant's motion because of such statement and in permitting plaintiff to introduce evidence over defendant's objection of plaintiff's increased blood pressure and in refusing to declare a mistrial on defendant's motion because of the introduction of such evidence and also in permitting [plaintiff] over defendant's objection to present evidence of an injury to her shoulder. Defendant points out that plaintiff's petition does not allege that she was caused to develop high blood pressure or that such an existing condition was aggravated by the accident. Defendant further contends that the evidence does not establish that a continuing elevation in blood pressure is an inevitable or necessary result of the injuries averred and that the evidence of such condition was, therefore, inadmissible. In support of these contentions defendant cites a number of cases which apply the principle of law that before a plaintiff can recover for a physical condition claimed to have resulted from the negligence of another, such condition must be pleaded or the evidence must establish the condition as being the inevitable or necessary result of injuries which are particularly set out in the petition. The reason underlying such decisions is that it would be unjust to permit a plaintiff to take advantage of a defendant at the trial by presenting evidence of injuries of which the defendant did not have the kind of notice required by law, namely, through allegations in plaintiff's petition.

   It is true the evidence in this case does show, as plaintiff contends, that defendant had actual notice before trial of plaintiff's increased blood pressure, which she claimed was a result of the collision, through a statement made by plaintiff to that effect to the Claim Agent of defendant's insurer and through an examination of plaintiff made by defendant's doctor, Dr. Leo A. Will, and reported by him to said Claim Agent as well as through plaintiff's deposition which was taken by defendant. However, we are of the opinion that although it cannot be said that defendant was "surprised" when plaintiff presented evidence at the trial relating to the condition of her blood pressure, defendant nevertheless had the right to object to such evidence on the ground that it related to "special damages" which were not pleaded in plaintiff's petition. Although defendant could not have claimed "surprise" upon the introduction of such evidence, it was not required to do so and its objections at the trial to such evidence in the absence of proper allegations thereon in plaintiff's petition should have been sustained. No such special damages were pleaded by plaintiff, nor did plaintiff ask leave to amend her petition to include such special damages which she could have done on such terms, at that stage of the proceedings, as the court should order. However, plaintiff did not amend her petition, nor ask leave to amend, and defendant had the right to object to the evidence in question.

* * * [Missouri Rule of Civil Procedure 55.19] expressly provides: "When items of special damage are claimed, they shall be specifically stated." * * *

It has been held by our Supreme Court that a specific personal injury which is not the necessary or inevitable result of an injury alleged in the petition constitutes an element of "special damage" which must be specifically pleaded before evidence thereof is admissible. See State ex rel. Grisham v. Allen, 344 Mo. 66, 124 S.W.2d 1080. * * *

In the case at bar the only allegations in plaintiff's petition with respect to the injuries she suffered as the result of the collision were as follows: "Plaintiff sustained injuries to her neck, back, spine and nervous system and was otherwise injured and her earning capacity has been permanently impaired." It will be observed that not only is there no mention of increased blood pressure but no injuries are alleged from which it can reasonably be said that an increase in blood pressure was an inevitable or necessary result. Nor was there any evidence to show that the increased blood pressure was the necessary or inevitable result of the injuries alleged in the petition.

* * *

What we have said herein with respect to the evidence of plaintiff's increase of blood pressure applies with equal force to the evidence of the injury to plaintiff's shoulder. In the absence of any allegation in plaintiff's petition relating to that injury, it was error for the court to admit such evidence.

* * *

On Motion for Rehearing or, in the Alternative, to Transfer to Supreme Court.

McCULLEN, JUDGE. Plaintiff has filed an extended motion for rehearing in which she earnestly argues that this court committed error in holding that the trial court erred in permitting plaintiff to introduce evidence of her high blood pressure when no such damage was pleaded in plaintiff's petition. * * *

It is contended by plaintiff that [the Missouri rule] * * *, which provides that when "items of special damage" are claimed "they shall be specifically stated," having been copied verbatim from Rule 9(g) of the Federal Rules * * *, the "construction" given said Rule 9(g) by the Federal Courts must be given to [the Missouri rule as well] * * *.

* * *

In the lengthy argument of plaintiff she repeatedly refers to the "construction" given to Federal Rule 9(g) but nowhere is there cited any authority showing what such "construction" was in any kind of a case. * * * Plaintiff evidently has found no case in point on the facts of this case (just as we have found none) because, as we see it, the words of both

Federal Rule 9(g) and the state [rule] * * *, are so simple, plain and unambiguous that no one has even heretofore contended in a court of last resort that a party could plead only "general" damages and recover for "special" damages.

* * *

[Motion denied.]

Notes and Questions

1. In EPHREM v. PHILLIPS, 99 So.2d 257, 260–61 (Fla.App.1st Dist. 1957), a case arising out of an auto accident, plaintiff, who alleged only that she was "painfully, seriously and permanently injured, bruised and lacerated in and throughout her head, body and limbs," sought and was permitted to collect damages for a required abortion. The court held:

> Within the allegations of the complaint it is clear that plaintiff might show any change in her physical condition due to the injuries sustained, and such was the abortion. Where only such damages as may be reasonably expected to follow an injury are claimed, no allegation of special damages is required. In personal injury actions proof that the plaintiff's pain and suffering resulted in and were aggravated by an abortion is clearly admissible. So far as the abortion augments the physical injury, pain or suffering, then so far is it proper to be considered on the question of damages.

> For the foregoing reasons we hold that a claim based upon pain and anguish, suffered as a consequence of injuries sustained from the negligent act of another, is not an item of special damages merely because such pain and anguish resulted in and was aggravated by an abortion.

Can *Ziervogel* and *Ephrem* be reconciled? Did plaintiff's lawyer in *Ziervogel* hurt his client's case by pleading too much? See THACKER v. WARD, 263 N.C. 594, 140 S.E.2d 23, certiorari denied 382 U.S. 865, 86 S.Ct. 134, 15 L.Ed.2d 104 (1965), in which the court refused to permit a plaintiff who had alleged physical injuries to his body and nervous system to collect damages for unpleaded psychological disturbances that resulted from the physical injuries but had an emotional, rather than a physical, basis.

2. Should medical bills incurred as a result of personal injuries be considered special damages requiring special pleading or should they be provable as a logical and necessary result of the injuries themselves? See Sossamon v. Nationwide Mut. Ins. Co., 243 S.C. 552, 135 S.E.2d 87 (1964), which held a general allegation of damages sufficient to permit proof of doctor and hospital bills. There are many cases that take a contrary view.

Elements of special damages that must be pleaded if proof of them is to be allowed at trial also may appear in other types of actions. In contract actions, for example, special damages are those that would not normally be foreseen as the consequence of defendant's breach. Special damages can be recovered in contract actions from a defaulting party who was informed that they might result from a breach. See Bumann v. Maurer, 203 N.W.2d 434, 440–41 (N.D. 1972).

3. Although the normal consequence of failing to plead special damages is being barred from proving them at trial, it is important to note that with regard to a few types of cases the existence of special damages is an integral

part of the claim, and the failure to plead them renders the complaint subject to a demurrer or motion to dismiss. See, e.g., Paine-Erie Hospital Supply, Inc. v. Lincoln First Bank, 82 Misc.2d 432, 370 N.Y.S.2d 370 (Sup.Ct.1975). Should the degree of specificity required in pleading special damages be the same in all cases or should it depend on whether the special damages are simply added elements of injury or are an integral part of the claim? Does the fact that a distinction along these lines is drawn by the courts of the state in which the federal court is sitting have any relevance to a federal court's construction of Federal Rule 9(g)?

7. THE PRAYER FOR RELIEF

————

Read Federal Rules of Civil Procedure 8(a)(3) and 54(c) in the Supplement.

————

BAIL v. CUNNINGHAM BROTHERS, INC.

United States Court of Appeals, Seventh Circuit, 1971.
452 F.2d 182.

PELL, CIRCUIT JUDGE. * * * The final contention raised by defendant on this appeal is that the judgment against defendant should be remitted from $135,000 to $85,000.

Plaintiff's original complaint sought damages in the amount of $100,000. On the morning the trial was to begin, plaintiff presented a motion to amend the complaint requesting that the ad damnum clause in the complaint against defendant be increased from $100,000 to $250,000. The district judge denied this motion " * * * for the reason that the case is at issue, it is set for trial this date, and the defendant was not given notice of the filing of the motion."

The jury notwithstanding the complaint-contained limitation of $100,000 returned a verdict for the higher figure of $150,000. In a post-trial motion Bail sought and was granted leave to amend the complaint by increasing the ad damnum clause to $150,000. Bail had received $15,000 from another defendant originally named in the complaint in return for "a covenant not to pursue." This payment had been set off, leaving the final judgment of $135,000. It has been said that the office of the ad damnum in a pleading is to fix the amount beyond which a party may not recover on the trial of his action. Gable v. Pathfinder Irrigation District, 159 Neb. 778, 68 N.W.2d 500, 506 (1955). However, an examination of the cases reveals that the rule thus enunciated, if indeed it still be a rule, has flexibility to the virtual point of nonexistence. Thus, in *Gable* the court pointed out that there was also a general rule that amendment may be made to a pleading which did not change the issues or affect the quantum of proof as to a material fact and that no good reason was apparent for not applying this privilege of amendment to the ad damnum clause. Id. at 506.

In the case before us, even though it is a diversity case, a matter of procedure is involved and governed, therefore, entirely by the federal rules. Riggs, Ferris & Geer v. Lillibridge, 316 F.2d 60, 62 (2d Cir.1963).

*   *   *

There is substantial authority for the proposition that pursuant to Rule 54(c) a claimant may be awarded damages in excess of those demanded in his pleadings.   *   *   *

Cunningham, however, contends that the authority is not all one way *   *   * [citing, inter alia,] the case of Wyman v. Morone, 33 A.D.2d 168, 306 N.Y.S.2d 115 (1969), to the effect that under New York law the granting of the motion to increase the amount sued for, after a jury has rendered its verdict, is an abuse of discretion. We, of course, in view of Rule 54(c) are not in any way bound by the interpretation of this lower court of New York as to the law of that state but do observe that there apparently was some significance attached to the extended delay in moving to amend and in any event feel that the dissenting opinion in *Wyman* swims with the main current of judicial thinking in this particular area as opposed to the contrary movement of the majority opinion.

The difficulty, if any there be, posed here, however, lies in the fact that Bail attempted to amend the ad damnum clause in advance of trial and the right of amendment was denied by the court. In this respect the case would seem to be one of first impression as no case involving this exact factual situation has been brought to our attention. It appears to us that the motion to amend, even though on the morning of the trial, should have been granted. It not having been granted, our inquiry must be as to whether the normal rule prevailing under 54(c) should be varied. In our opinion, it should not be.

On oral argument, inquiry was directed to counsel for Cunningham as to how the conduct of the trial would have differed if the pretrial motion to amend had been granted. The thought was ventured that the attorneys might have tried the case differently, that they might have argued damages to the jury (which subject they conspicuously avoided in final argument) or they might have cross-examined more extensively. With hindsight, they may well think that they should have argued damages even if no post-trial amendment were to be permitted and the limitation on recovery were left at $100,000. In essence, however, we cannot see that the quantum of proof as to any material fact varied or that any change of issues resulted, or would have resulted, from an amendment of the ad damnum clause. Counsel competently and vigorously defended on the theory of no liability whatsoever, and we can find no basis for an assumption that $100,000 is such an insignificant amount that counsel somehow would try harder if they knew that the exposure might be $250,000.

No doubt if the ad damnum had sought some insignificant amount such as $1,000, the case would not have received the attention from trial counsel that it did. In the case before us, however, defense counsel were never confronted with an insignificant amount.

It perhaps is unfortunate that the district court did not permit the amendment as requested in advance of trial so as to eliminate the claim that the defendant somehow was prejudiced in relying on this. Finding, however, no real prejudice we will follow the rule generally prevailing to the effect that even though the party was not successful in demanding such relief in his pleadings, he was entitled thereto under the evidence. At least the jury thought that he was so entitled, and we find no basis for upsetting their determination irrespective of whether we would have reached this exact amount in assessing damages. Further, the district court who heard the evidence on a front line basis was satisfied that the amendment should be allowed on a post-trial motion.

Although Bail's counsel under the constraint of the court's ruling did confine his final argument to an amount within the unamended ad damnum clause, it is not entirely unreasonable to assume that he and his client would have been well satisfied with a verdict of $100,000 and, indeed, it does not stretch the imagination too far to conceive that a settlement could have been arrived at for less than that figure if the general practical pattern of settlements in personal injury cases had had any application here. Nevertheless, the case was not settled and inasmuch as the damages cannot be shown to be excessive, nor to have been dictated by passion and prejudice, the verdict will stand. While Cunningham finds some source of complaint in the fact that plaintiff's counsel himself argued less than $100,000 and while it may not now be much solace to Cunningham, nevertheless there was the trial advantage to the defense that plaintiff was precluded from arguing a larger sum.

What we have had to say with regard to the ad damnum clause is indicative of the anachronistic character of the clause. Indeed, there is a well publicized school of thought that it should be done away with altogether. * * * It is true that in some suits it is necessary to allege a jurisdictional amount, but ordinarily this is far less than the ad damnum prayer and can be gleaned in most instances from the pleadings and discovery procedures.

As a matter of fact in the case before us it appears from the record that the jury was in no way aware of the amount of the ad damnum in the complaint and, therefore, clearly their verdict did not reflect a conscious arrival at a figure in excess of the ad damnum.

* * *

Affirmed.

Notes and Questions

1. Is the damage prayer anachronistic as the court in *Bail* suggests? Should it be abolished? What problems would this create? Would elimination of the ad damnum clause have avoided the uncertainty upon which defendant in *Bail* based the claim of prejudice? Suppose the court had found defendant to have been unduly prejudiced by the trial court's refusal to grant plaintiff's pretrial amendment. In that case should the jury award have been reduced? What other remedy is available? See pp. 993–1025, *infra*.

A modern trend in many states is the elimination of the prayer for relief in medical malpractice cases, except that the complaint must generally allege that the amount in controversy meets the jurisdictional requirements of the court. See, e.g., Ga.Code Ann. § 9–11–8(a)(2) (1980 amendment); N.Y.C.P.L.R. 3017(c) (1980 amendment). Some courts have extended this policy to all personal injury cases. See, e.g., Cal.Code Civ.Proc. § 425.10(b) (1979 amendment); Ill.Stat.Ann. ch. 110, ¶ 2.604 (1983 amendment). Michigan has extended it to every action seeking monetary relief. Mich.Ct.R. 2.111(B)(2) (1976 amendment).

What purpose, if any, does this serve? Consider Hughes v. Children's Clinic, P.A., 269 S.C. 389, 404, 237 S.E.2d 753, 760 (1977), upholding the practice of permitting the jury to see the pleadings and allowing plaintiff's counsel to call the jurors' attention to the size of the demand.

2.   Note that under Federal Rule 54(c) relief is limited by the ad damnum clause in default cases. Why? See 10 Wright, Miller & Kane, *Federal Practice and Procedure: Civil 2d* § 2663 (1983). Why should courts permit relief to be granted that is different from or in excess of plaintiff's demand? Why should a defendant who defaults be protected by a cap on damages, but a defendant who participates be exposed to damages greater than those pleaded by the plaintiff? Although the vast majority of state courts follow Federal Rule 54(c), the Iowa courts apparently do not. See Stromberg v. Crowl, 257 Iowa 348, 353, 132 N.W.2d 462, 465 (1965).

3.   How far does the mandate found in Federal Rule 54(c) go? Suppose a party claims a certain element of damage on the basis of proof at trial despite the fact that the pleadings contained no claim or indication of a claim that would permit such recovery? In CONVERTIBLE TOP REPLACEMENT CO. v. ARO MFG. CO., 312 F.2d 52, 58 (1st Cir.1962), modified on other grounds 377 U.S. 476, 84 S.Ct. 1526, 12 L.Ed.2d 457 (1964), in which plaintiff sued for patent infringement, defendant not only answered, alleging, *inter alia,* the defense of patent misuse, but also counterclaimed for a declaratory judgment that plaintiff had misused the patent. The trial court's finding against defendant on the issue of misuse was not challenged on appeal. Defendant argued, however, that having asserted a counterclaim it could recover, under Rule 54(c), any relief to which it was entitled, and that the record in the case showed that plaintiff had violated the federal antitrust laws, which permitted defendant to recover treble damages. The court denied the claim as follows:

> * * * The short answer to this contention is that Aro has never pleaded a cause of action under the antitrust laws.

> * * * [Rule 54(c)] does not authorize a grant of the relief requested. That Rule should be liberally construed to grant a prevailing party substantial justice. But it is not to be so liberally construed as to conflict with the requirement of Rule 8(a) * * *. There is no merit whatever in this appeal.

Is this decision sound? Is it merely a return to the generally discarded theory-of-the-pleadings doctrine? See pp. 462–68, supra.

4.   In HANEY v. BURGIN, 106 N.H. 213, 208 A.2d 448 (1965), plaintiff originally brought suit for $15,000. After the first day of trial plaintiff was permitted to amend the complaint to request $25,000. Two days later, when defendant's sole witness strongly supported plaintiff's case, plaintiff was

allowed to amend to pray for $50,000 damages. Subsequently the jury returned a verdict of $87,345. Plaintiff, in order to receive the full amount of the verdict, once again was permitted to amend the prayer, this time to $100,000. The New Hampshire Supreme Court held that since defendant had not requested a continuance as a condition of granting any of the motions to amend, he could not have been prejudiced and therefore there was no error. Does the use of amendment to permit full recovery in a jurisdiction that does not allow relief in excess of that requested in the pleadings make more sense than the adoption of a provision like Federal Rule 54(c)?

5. The jurisdiction of inferior state tribunals often is limited as to the type and amount of relief that can be awarded. See pp. 237–38, supra. What if plaintiff obtains a verdict for an amount in excess of the court's jurisdictional maximum? Should plaintiff be held to have waived any excess by bringing suit in such a court? If not, should plaintiff be permitted to waive the excess? See Cal.Code Civ.Proc. § 396, which specifically provides that if plaintiff's *demand* exceeds the jurisdictional maximum of the inferior court "the excess may be *remitted* and the action may continue in the court where it is pending." [Emphasis added.] Should a waiver, if allowed, require the consent of defendant as well as of plaintiff? See Izzi v. Dolgin, 64 Misc.2d 742, 315 N.Y.S.2d 1005 (N.Y.City Civ.Ct.1970). For a general discussion of jurisdictional amount problems, reread pp. 270–74, supra.

SECTION B. RESPONDING TO THE COMPLAINT

1. THE TIME PERMITTED FOR A RESPONSE

Read Rule 12(a) and the accompanying materials in the Supplement.

Rule 12(a) gives most defendants 20 days from the service of the complaint to respond either by a motion pursuant to Rule 12 or by answering the complaint. In reality, defense counsel routinely request, and plaintiff's counsel routinely consent to, an extension of the defendant's time to answer. These agreements generally are considered a matter of courtesy among counsel, and Rule 6(a) authorizes the court to grant these extensions. Although practices vary, most judges will order an extension based upon a written stipulation of the attorneys.

2. MOTIONS TO DISMISS

Read Federal Rules of Civil Procedure 12(b), 12(c), and 12(f) and the materials accompanying them in the Supplement.

a. *Historical Antecedents*

The origins of the motion to dismiss can be traced to the common-law demurrer. As described in Chapter 4, under common-law pleading rules, a party who faced a complaint could either answer, responding to each of the claims, or demur. If the defendant demurred, he was not allowed to contest the complaint's facts if the demurrer was overruled. On the other hand, if the demurrer was sustained, the plaintiff had no right to replead or amend her complaint. Later, these harsh rules were modified to allow a party to proceed to the merits if the demurrer was overruled and to allow the plaintiff to amend her complaint if the demurrer was sustained.

The common-law demurrer was incorporated into code pleading. In most code states, a complaint could be dismissed on the pleadings for failure to state facts sufficient to constitute a cause of action, absence of subject-matter jurisdiction, and deficiencies in the form of the pleading.

The demurrer and its code equivalents elevated the importance of technicalities and produced considerable delay. Dissatisfaction frequently was expressed:

> * * * In an earlier period, when the ruling on the demurrer terminated the action, it was strategic to demur only for clear defects of form or substance. But since the ruling no longer serves to end the litigation but merely postpones the trial, the demurrer is used as a convenient means of delay by counsel with too much business or too little ambition. And where further delay is desired counsel may invoke separately the several motions which exist concurrently with the demurrer: motions to strike, expunge, elect or separate; motions to make more definite and certain or for a bill of particulars. This multiplicity of weapons has inevitably led to a host of tenuous distinctions: whether demurrer or motion is proper, what kind of demurrer, what kind of motion. By the use of successive demurrers and motions, it is possible, then, not only to delay but also to discourage altogether the party whose pleading is subjected to this barrage of objections.

Pike, *Objections to Pleadings Under the New Federal Rules of Civil Procedure,* 47 Yale L.J. 50, 51 (1937).

b. The Motion to Dismiss for Failure to State a Claim

Rule 12(b)(6), the federal system's counterpart to the common-law demurrer, must be viewed in conjunction with other federal pleading rules. For example, because Rule 8 requires only "a short and plain statement of the claim showing that the pleader is entitled to relief," few pleadings are likely to fail under Rule 12(b)(6). This does not mean, however, that the motion is useless. Pure questions of law can be tested using the motion. The availability under the Federal Rules of summary judgment and partial summary judgment, directed verdict, and judgment notwithstanding the verdict (all of which are discussed later), also diminishes the importance of using Rule 12(b)(6) to screen frivolous cases.

> * * * The salvaged minutes that may accrue from circumventing these procedures can turn to wasted hours if the appellate court feels constrained to reverse the dismissal of an action. That is one of the reasons why a motion to dismiss is viewed with disfavor in the federal courts. Another is the basic precept that the primary objective of the law is to obtain a determination of the merits of any claim; and that a case should be tried on the proofs rather than the pleadings. * * * This is not to say or imply that a motion to dismiss should never be granted. It

is obvious that there are cases which justify and indeed compel the
granting of such motion. The line between the totally unmeritorious
claims and the others cannot be drawn by scientific instruments but must
be carved out case by case by the sound judgment of trial judges. That
judgment should be exercised cautiously on such a motion.

RENNIE & LAUGHLIN, INC. v. CHRYSLER CORP., 242 F.2d 208, 213
(9th Cir.1957).

AMERICAN NURSES' ASSOCIATION v. ILLINOIS
United States Court of Appeals, Seventh Circuit, 1986.
783 F.2d 716.

POSNER, CIRCUIT JUDGE.

The class action charges the State of Illinois with sex discrimination
in employment, in violation of Title VII of the Civil Rights Act of 1964, 42
U.S.C. § 2000e, and the equal protection clause of the Fourteenth Amendment. * * * The precise allegations of the complaint will require our
careful attention later, but for now it is enough to note that they include
as an essential element the charge that the state pays workers in predominantly male job classifications a higher wage not justified by any difference in the relative worth of the predominantly male and the predominantly female jobs in the state's roster.

* * * [T]he district judge dismissed the complaint under Fed.R.Civ.
P. 12(b)(6) * * * [on the ground] that the complaint pleaded a comparable worth case and that a failure to pay employees in accordance with
comparable worth does not violate federal antidiscrimination law. The
plaintiffs appeal. They argue that their case is not (or perhaps not just) a
comparable worth case and that in characterizing the complaint as he did
the district judge terminated the lawsuit by a semantic manipulation.
* * *

* * * [A]s we understand the plaintiffs' position it is not that a
mere failure to rectify traditional wage disparities between predominantly
male and predominantly female jobs violates federal law. The circuits
that have considered this contention have rejected it. * * *

The * * * question is whether a failure to achieve comparable
worth—granted that it would not itself be a violation of law—might
permit an inference of deliberate and therefore unlawful discrimination,
as distinct from passive acceptance of a market-determined disparity in
wages. * * *

* * *

* * * Knowledge of a disparity is not the same thing as an intent to
cause or maintain it; if for example the state's intention was to pay
market wages, its knowledge that the consequence would be that men got
higher wages on average than women and that the difference might
exceed any premium attributable to a difference in relative worth would
not make it guilty of intentionally discriminating against women. Similarly, even if the failure to act on the comparable worth study could be
regarded as "reaffirming" the state's commitment to pay market wages,

this would not be enough to demonstrate discriminatory purpose. To demonstrate such a purpose the failure to act would have to be motivated at least in part by a desire to benefit men at the expense of women.

* * *

So if all that the plaintiffs in this case are complaining about is the State of Illinois' failure to implement a comparable worth study, they have no case and it was properly dismissed. We must therefore consider what precisely they are complaining about. Our task would be easier if the complaint had been drafted with the brevity that the Federal Rules of Civil Procedure envisage though do not require. * * *

[But t]he idea of "a plain and short statement of the claim" has not caught on. Few complaints follow the models in the Appendix of Forms. Plaintiffs' lawyers, knowing that some judges read a complaint as soon as it is filed in order to get a sense of the suit, hope by pleading facts to "educate" (that is to say, influence) the judge with regard to the nature and probable merits of the case, and also hope to set the stage for an advantageous settlement by showing the defendant what a powerful case they intend to prove. The pleading of facts is well illustrated by the present case. The complaint is twenty pages long and has a hundred page appendix (the comparable worth study).

A plaintiff who files a long and detailed complaint may plead himself out of court by including factual allegations which if true show that his legal rights were not invaded. * * * The district judge thought the plaintiffs had done that here. Let us see.

The key paragraph of the complaint is paragraph 9 * * *.

* * * The paragraph initially charges the state with intentional discrimination against its female employees, because of their sex; and this, standing alone, would be quite enough to state a claim under Title VII. It continues, "and because of their employment in historically female-dominated sex-segregated job classifications," and then adds a claim on behalf of male employees in those classifications. The continuation could be interpreted as an allegation that the state's failure to adopt a wage scale based on the principle of comparable worth violates Title VII, and if so fails to state a claim. But the mention of "sex-segregated" blurs the picture. If the state has deliberately segregated jobs by sex, it has violated Title VII. Anyway a complaint cannot be dismissed merely because it includes invalid claims along with a valid one. Nothing is more common.

Subparagraphs (a) through (g) present a list of particular discriminatory practices; and since they are merely illustrative ("not limited to"), the complaint would not fail even if none of them were actionable. Some are, some aren't. * * * [If subparagraph (a)] means to allege that the state has departed from the market measure on grounds of sex—not only paying higher than market wages in predominantly male job classifications and only market wages in predominantly female classifications, but keeping women from entering the predominantly male jobs ("sex-segregated")—it states a claim. Subparagraph (b) adds nothing. If the state is discriminating against women by maintaining unwarranted wage differentials between predominantly male and predominantly female jobs, any men who happen to find themselves in predominantly female jobs will be, as it were, dragged down with the women—will be incidental victims of a discrimination targeted against others.

Subparagraph (c) is an effort to fit the case to the mold of [County of Washington v. Gunther, 452 U.S. 161, 101 S.Ct. 2242, 68 L.Ed.2d 751 (1981)]. * * * But as we said earlier, the failure to accept the recommendations in a comparable worth study is not actionable. Paragraph 9(c) thus fails to state a claim—as does (d), which is the same as (c) except that it, like subparagraph (b), complains on behalf of male occupants of predominantly female jobs.

Subparagraphs (e) and (f) are inscrutable. If they complained about payment of unequal pay for the same work they would state a claim under the Equal Pay Act. But that Act is not cited in the complaint, perhaps deliberately, and the substitution of "work of equal skill" etc. for "equal work * * * of equal skill" etc. may also be deliberate. The intention may be to claim that different pay for different *but comparable* work violates Title VII—and if so this is a comparable worth claim by a different name, and fails. However, when a defendant is unclear about the meaning of a particular allegation in the complaint, the proper course is not to move to dismiss but to move for a more definite statement. * * *

That leaves subparagraph (g)—"Discrimination in classification." This could be a reprise of the comparable worth allegations or it could mean that in classifying jobs for pay purposes the responsible state officials had used the fraction of men in each job as a factor in deciding how high a wage to pay—which would be intentional discrimination.

Maybe the allegations in paragraph 9 are illuminated by subsequent paragraphs of the complaint. Paragraph 10, after summarizing the comparable worth study, says, "Defendants knew or should have known of the historical and continuing existence of patterns and practices of discrimination in compensation and classification, as documented at least in part by the State of Illinois Study." All that the study "documents," however, is that 28 percent of the employees subject to the state's personnel code are employed in 24 job classifications, in each of which at least 80 percent of the employees are of the same sex, and that based on the principles of comparable worth the 12 predominantly female job classifications are underpaid by between 29 and 56 percent. * * * These disparities are consistent, however, with the state's paying market wages, and of course the fact that the state knew that market wages do not always comport with the principles of comparable worth would not make a refusal to abandon the market actionable under Title VII. But at the very end of paragraph 10 we read, "Moreover, defendants have knowingly and *willfully* failed to take any action to correct such discrimination" (emphasis added), and in the word "willfully" can perhaps be seen the glimmerings of another theory of violation that could survive a motion to dismiss. Suppose the state has declined to act on the results of the comparable worth study not because it prefers to pay (perhaps is forced by labor-market or fiscal constraints to pay) market wages but because it thinks men deserve to be paid more than women. * * * This would be the kind of deliberate sex discrimination that Title VII forbids, once the statute is understood to allow wage disparities between dissimilar jobs to be challenged * * *.

"Willfully" is, however, a classic legal weasel word. Sometimes it means with wrongful intent but often it just means with knowledge of something or other. Willful evasion of taxes means not paying when you know you owe tax. After reading the comparable worth study the responsible state officials knew that the state's compensation system might not be consistent with the principles of comparable worth ("might" because there has been no determination that the comparable worth study is valid even on its own terms—maybe it's a lousy comparable worth study). But it would not follow that their failure to implement the study was willful in a sense relevant to liability under Title VII. They may have decided not to implement it because implementation would cost too much or lead to excess demand for some jobs and insufficient demand for others. The only thing that would make the failure a form of intentional and therefore actionable sex discrimination would be if the motivation for not implementing the study was the sex of the employees—if for example the officials thought that men ought to be paid more than women even if there is no difference in skill or effort or in the conditions of work. * * *

We have said that a plaintiff can plead himself right out of court. But the court is not to pounce on the plaintiff and by a crabbed and literal reading of the complaint strain to find that he has pleaded facts which show that his claim is not actionable, and then dismiss the complaint on the merits so that the plaintiff cannot replead. (The dismissal would preclude another suit based on any theory that the plaintiff could have advanced on the basis of the facts giving rise to the first suit.) * * * The district judge did not quite do that here, because this complaint can easily be read to allege a departure from the principles of comparable worth, and no more. But that reading is not inevitable, and the fact that it is logical and unstrained is not enough to warrant dismissal. In the system created by the Federal Rules of Civil Procedure a complaint "should not be dismissed for failure to state a claim unless it appears beyond doubt that the plaintiff can prove no set of facts in support of his claim which would entitle him to relief." Conley v. Gibson [p. 480, supra]. This language, repeated though it has been in countless later cases * * *, should not be taken literally; for taken literally it would permit dismissal only in frivolous cases. As we said earlier, if the plaintiff, though not required to do so, pleads facts, and the facts show that he is entitled to no relief, the complaint should be dismissed. There would be no point in allowing such a lawsuit to go any further; its doom is foretold. But this is not such a case. * * * A complaint that alleges intentional sex discrimination * * * cannot be dismissed just because one of the practices, indeed the principal practice, instanced as intentional sex discrimination—the employer's failure to implement comparable worth— is lawful.

Furthermore, a complaint is not required to allege all, or any, of the facts logically entailed by the claim. If Illinois is overpaying men relative to women, this must mean—unless the market model is entirely inapplicable to labor markets—that it is paying women at least their market wage (and therefore men more), for women wouldn't work for less than they could get in the market; and if so the state must also be refusing to hire women in the men's jobs, for above-market wages in those jobs would be a magnet drawing the women from their lower-paying jobs. Maybe the references in the complaint to the segregation of jobs by sex are meant to allege such refusals but if not this pleading omission would not be critical. A plaintiff does not have to plead evidence. If these plaintiffs admitted or the defendants proved that there was no steering or other method of segregating jobs by sex, the plaintiffs' theory of discrimination might be incoherent, and fail. But a complaint does not fail to state a claim merely because it does not set forth a complete and convincing picture of the alleged wrongdoing. So the plaintiffs do not have to allege steering even if it is in some sense implicit in their claim.

* * * We do not want to arouse false hopes; the plaintiffs have a tough row to hoe. They may lose eventually on summary judgment if discovery yields no more evidence than is contained in the unsupported assertions and stale and seemingly isolated incidents in the plaintiffs' exhibits. But the plaintiffs are entitled to make additional efforts to prove a case of intentional discrimination within the boundaries sketched in this opinion.

Reversed and Remanded.

Notes and Questions

1. How should a court resolve mixed questions of fact and law when deciding Rule 12(b)(6) motions? In HARTFORD ACCIDENT & INDEMNITY CO. v. MERRILL LYNCH, PIERCE, FENNER & SMITH, INC., 74 F.R.D. 357 (W.D.Okl.1976), plaintiff sued defendant for negligently failing to inform a bank that its employee was investing with defendant in margin accounts. The employee had forged signatures on certain certificates of deposit drawn from that bank that he had used as collateral to procure personal loans from other banks. When the employee defaulted, the lending banks recovered their losses from plaintiff under plaintiff's blanket fidelity bond. Plaintiff alleged that defendant's failure to inform was the proximate cause of its loss. The court dismissed plaintiff's claim:

> A Complaint should not be dismissed for failure to state a claim unless it appears beyond doubt that the plaintiff can prove no set of facts in support of his claim which would entitle him to relief." * * However, the legal effect ascribed by the pleader is not to be admitted, but is to be determined by its terms, as a matter of law. * * *

> The Oklahoma cases indicate that under proper circumstances the existence of probable cause becomes a question of law for the Court. * * * In considering the allegations of the Complaint, the Court finds that the facts contained therein are insufficient to show any causal connection between the alleged negligent acts of Merrill Lynch in failing to advise Conine's employer and obtaining said employer's permission for

him to engage in trading on margin accounts and the loss sustained by Plaintiff on its banker's fidelity bond. The Complaint fails to show the required proximate cause between the negligence alleged and the injuries complained of as a matter of law.

The facts as set out in the Complaint indicate the alleged forgeries or obtaining forged documents by the bank officer were the efficient cause which set in motion the chain of circumstances leading to the loss sustained by Plaintiff Hartford on its banker's fidelity bond. The allegation that negligent acts of Defendant Merrill Lynch permitted the continued employment of the alleged defalcating bank officer only appears to indicate a condition which permitted the acts to go undetected and possibly allowed subsequent wrongful acts to be committed by the bank officer after the first had been committed. Such condition is not any more related to the proximate cause of the loss sustained by Plaintiff than the acts of the directors of the Oklahoma State Bank who initially placed Conine in the position of employment as an officer of the bank and retained him in said position while the wrongful acts were committed.

Under the standards expressed in *American Nurses' Ass'n,* did the District Court in *Hartford* err in granting the Rule 12(b)(6) motion? Was the District Court justified in concluding that plaintiff could prove no set of facts in support of its contention as a matter of law? Does the *Erie* doctrine require the court to follow the Oklahoma courts' declaration that under proper circumstances the existence of proximate cause is a question of law?

2. The Supreme Court, in SCHEUER v. RHODES, 416 U.S. 232, 236, 94 S.Ct. 1683, 1686, 40 L.Ed.2d 90, 96 (1974), said that "[w]hen a federal court reviews the sufficiency of a complaint, * * * the issue is * * * whether the claimant is entitled to offer evidence to support the claims." Under that standard, did the District Court in *Hartford* err in granting the Rule 12(b)(6) motion?

3. Should a Rule 12(b)(6) motion be granted in a case in which the "claim" exists but the desired remedy is not available? In DOPICO v. GOLDSCHMIDT, 687 F.2d 644 (2d Cir.1982), plaintiffs, wheelchair-bound handicapped people, sued local and federal transit officials, claiming violations of federal statutes and regulations relating to making transit facilities accessible to the handicapped. The District Court dismissed the plaintiffs' complaint against the local officials for failure to state a claim upon which relief could be granted. It based its decision on a finding that the plaintiffs could not obtain the "massive relief involving extra-ordinary expenditures" that they sought. The Court of Appeals did not disagree, but reversed, saying that "[t]he extreme result of dismissing the claim would be proper only if plaintiffs would not be entitled to any relief, even if they were to prevail on the merits. We do not believe that conclusion can be reached at this preliminary stage of the law suit." Id. at 649.

4. What is the effect of a successful Rule 12(b)(6) motion? Can the plaintiff modify the complaint and re-serve the complaint, or do principles of res judicata bar that? In SHAW v. MERRITT–CHAPMAN & SCOTT CORP., 554 F.2d 786 (6th Cir.1977), certiorari denied 434 U.S. 852, 98 S.Ct. 167, 54 L.Ed.2d 122 (1977), the court held that absent specific language to the contrary by the district court, a Rule 12(b)(6) motion constitutes an adjudication on the merits, and so further actions on the same claim are barred.

5. Consider the following assessment:

[R]ule 12(b)(6), the vaunted motion to dismiss for failure to state a claim upon which relief can be granted * * *, is a wonderful tool on paper, but * * * it was last effectively used during the McKinley Administration.

Miller, *The August 1983 Amendments to the Federal Rules of Civil Procedure: Promoting Effective Case Management and Lawyer Responsibility* 7–8 (1984). In light of the cases you have read, and putting aside that McKinley was President before the adoption of the Federal Rules of Civil Procedure, is Professor Miller's observation valid?

6. In the federal system, a motion to strike, pursuant to Rule 12(f), is the mechanism for challenging the substantive sufficiency of defenses raised in an adversary's answer or other responsive pleading. A motion for judgment on the pleadings, pursuant to Rule 12(c), is a method of attacking the substantive sufficiency of an opposing party's pleading after all the pleadings have been completed. Both motions raise the same issues raised by a motion under Rule 12(b), and are dealt with by the courts in the same manner.

At common law and under the codes for "speaking demurrer," a demurrer that attempted to introduce material outside the pleadings was not permitted. Technically this is still the rule even in most modern jurisdictions. However, in most courts today a motion for summary judgment is available to challenge the factual basis of a pleading that on its face is sufficient to state a claim or defense. Under the Federal Rules and comparable state rules, the distinction between a pleading challenge and a motion for summary judgment is blurred, since a pleading challenge simply is treated as a motion for summary judgment if outside matter is introduced. The Rules were amended in 1948 to provide an express basis for courts to treat motions under Rules 12(b)(6) and 12(c) as motions for summary judgment when matters outside the pleadings are considered.

7. In addition to a Rule 12(b)(6) motion to dismiss for failure to state a claim, Rule 12(b) provides the pleader with the option of raising six other defenses by motion prior to service of a responsive pleading. The defenses in Rules 12(b)(1) through 12(b)(5) and 12(b)(7) are essentially jurisdictional. They are modern counterparts to the common-law pleas of abatement. There never was any doubt as to the court's considering extra-pleading material on these motions, and so, although Rule 12(b) as amended in 1948 expressly permits the use of extraneous matters on a Rule 12(b)(6) motion only, the practice before (and since) the amendment allows "speaking motions" in connection with these defenses. Their validity rarely is apparent on the face of the pleadings, and motions raising them generally require reference to matters outside the pleadings.

Of the six defenses, which, if any, may a party who makes a motion to dismiss under Rule 12(b) waive by not raising it in the motion? Which may a party waive by failing to raise it either by motion under Rule 12(b) or by the party's answer? When, if ever, is it too late to challenge a pleading for failure to state a claim or defense?

8. Although the seven motions specifically enumerated in Rule 12(b) theoretically are the only motions that can be made prior to service of a responsive pleading, in fact the preliminary motion practice in the federal

courts has a much broader compass. For example, although affirmative defenses under Rule 8(c) probably were intended to be raised only by responsive pleading, it is now common to allow an affirmative defense to be asserted by a motion under Rule 12(b)(6) when the validity of that defense is apparent from the face of the pleading. A complaint showing that the statute of limitations has run on the claim is the most common situation in which the affirmative defense appears on the face of the pleading. Moreover, the procedure in Rule 12(b) for converting the motion into a Rule 56 motion for summary judgment by presenting matters outside the pleadings, and the possibility of defendant moving for summary judgment prior to serving his responsive pleading, have the effect of allowing the early assertion of defenses other than those specifically enumerated in Rule 12(b).

3. OTHER MOTIONS ATTACKING PLEADINGS

One problem regarding challenges to the form of the pleadings already has been considered in connection with the *United Aircraft* and *Garcia* cases, which dealt with motions for a more definite statement. See pp. 482–88, supra.

A somewhat different challenge to the form arises when a party has included "scandalous," "impertinent," or "irrelevant" matter in a pleading. Traditionally, the remedy afforded is a motion to strike. See, e.g., Federal Rule 12(f); N.Y.C.P.L.R. 3024(b). On occasion some parties have attempted to utilize this motion to destroy or undercut their opponents' statements of valid claims or defenses. As held in GATEWAY BOTTLING, INC. v. DAD'S ROOTBEER CO., 53 F.R.D. 585, 588 (W.D.Pa.1971):

> With respect to the complaint that the material is scandalous, the question is again whether it asserts a valid and good faith defense to plaintiff's claim. To strike material as scandalous it must be obviously false and unrelated to the subject matter of the action. * * * The facts here may be unpleasant for plaintiff to have on the record and they certainly contain charges of reprehensible conduct but the same is true of many facts of life which are entitled to be pleaded as relevant to a cause of action or defense. Such, for example, are the facts concerning a divorce for adultery. These may be scandalous and annoying and prejudicial to the accused party but plaintiff or defendant is certainly entitled to plead them.

Even when allegations are not related to the subject matter of the case, the general rule today is that they will not be stricken from a complaint unless their presence will prejudice the adverse party. See Atlantic City Elec. Co. v. General Elec. Co., 207 F.Supp. 620 (S.D.N.Y. 1962). The common-law and code motions to strike allegations because they were "sham," "frivolous," "irrelevant," "redundant," "repetitious," "unnecessary," "immaterial," or "impertinent" have been eliminated, which "reflects a basic judgment that nothing is gained in the way of speedy and accurate disposition of litigation by disputes over the formal propriety of the allegations in the pleadings." 3 Weinstein, Korn & Miller, New York Civil Practice ¶ 3024.01.

The question whether allegations really are prejudicial seems to turn on whether the contents of the pleadings will be disclosed to the jury. In some instances pleadings themselves can become part of the evidence in the case and then, of course, the jury will be able to see and use them. However, such usage is strictly limited by the rules of evidence and irrelevant or prejudicial matters in the pleadings will be excluded. Hines v. Bost, 224 S.W. 698 (Tex.Civ.App.1920). Courts are divided on whether and to what extent such disclosure is proper when the pleadings are not introduced as part of the evidence in the case. What circumstances, if any, would justify a motion to strike redundant, impertinent, or scandalous material in a case tried before a judge or before a jury in a jurisdiction that does not permit the jury to see the pleadings? See Silver v. Queen's Hospital, 53 F.R.D. 223 (D.Hawaii 1971).

Yet another problem of form exists in cases in which an entire pleading is challenged, either because it was filed too late, or necessary court approval had not been obtained, or other rules or orders have not been satisfied. Traditionally, this type of defect is reached by a motion to strike the pleading or to dismiss the claims that it contains. See Buck v. Morrossis, 114 Cal.App.2d 461, 250 P.2d 270 (1st Dist.1952).

4. ANSWERING THE COMPLAINT

a. Denials

Rule 8 requires a defendant to make one of three responses to the paragraphs of plaintiff's complaint. Defendant may admit, deny, or plead insufficient information in response to each allegation. Rule 8(d) provides that all averments to which defendant does not specifically respond are deemed admitted. To avoid an unintended admission, defendants often add an all-inclusive paragraph denying each and every averment unless otherwise admitted.

A defendant under Rule 8 and most state rules also may deny generally the entire complaint, but general denials tend to defeat the purpose of pleading as a means of narrowing and focusing the issues in controversy. For this reason, the Federal Rules encourage the use of the general denial, which is supposed to be made in good faith, only in situations where everything can be denied legitimately. Using a general denial can be risky. If a court decides that a general denial does not "fairly meet the substance of the averments denied," it may deem the defendant to have admitted the plaintiff's specific averments. In addition, a general denial does not put in issue such matters as capacity or conditions precedent, which under Rule 9 must be specifically challenged.

ZIELINSKI v. PHILADELPHIA PIERS, INC.

United States District Court, Eastern District of Pennsylvania. 1956.
139 F.Supp. 408.

VAN DUSEN, DISTRICT JUDGE. Plaintiff requests a ruling that, for the purposes of this case, the motor-driven fork lift operated by Sandy Johnson on February 9, 1953, was owned by defendant and that Sandy Johnson was its agent acting in the course of his employment on that date. The following facts are established by the pleadings, interrogatories, depositions and uncontradicted portions of affidavits:

1. Plaintiff filed his complaint on April 28, 1953, for personal injuries received on February 9, 1953, while working on Pier 96, Philadelphia, for J.A. McCarthy, as a result of a collision of two motor-driven fork lifts.

2. Paragraph 5 of this complaint stated that "a motor-driven vehicle known as a fork lift or chisel, owned, operated and controlled by the defendant, its agents, servants and employees, was so negligently and carelessly managed * * * that the same * * * did come into contact with the plaintiff causing him to sustain the injuries more fully hereinafter set forth."

3. The "First Defense" of the Answer stated "Defendant * * * (c) denies the averments of paragraph 5 * * *."

4. The motor-driven vehicle known as a fork lift or chisel, which collided with the McCarthy fork lift on which plaintiff was riding, had on it the initials "P.P.I."

5. On February 10, 1953, Carload Contractors, Inc. made a report of this accident to its insurance company, whose policy No. CL 3964 insured Carload Contractors, Inc. against potential liability for the negligence of its employees contributing to a collision of the type described in paragraph 2 above.

6. By letter of April 29, 1953, the complaint served on defendant was forwarded to the above-mentioned insurance company. This letter read as follows:

Gentlemen:

* * *

We find that a fork lift truck operated by an employee of Carload Contractors, Inc. also insured by yourselves was involved in an accident with another chisel truck, which, was alleged, did cause injury to Frank Zielinski, and same was reported to you by Carload Contractors, Inc. at the time, and you assigned Claim Number OL 0153–94 to this claim.

Should not this Complaint in Trespass be issued against Carload Contractors, Inc. and not Philadelphia Piers, Inc.?

We forward for your handling.

7. Interrogatories * * * and the answers thereto, which were sworn to by defendant's General Manager on June 12, 1953, and filed on June 22, 1953, read as follows:

1. State whether you have received any information of an injury sustained by the plaintiff on February 9, 1953, South Wharves. If so, state when and from whom you first received notice of such injury. A. We were first notified of this accident on or about February 9, 1953 by Thomas Wilson.

2. State whether you caused an investigation to be made of the circumstances of said injury and if so, state who made such investigation and when it was made. A. We made a very brief investigation on February 9, 1953 and turned the matter over to (our insurance company) for further investigation.

* * *

8. At a deposition taken August 18, 1953, Sandy Johnson testified that he was the employee of defendant on February 9, 1953, and had been their employee for approximately fifteen years.

9. At a pre-trial conference held on September 27, 1955,[3] plaintiff first learned that over a year before February 9, 1953, the business of moving freight on piers in Philadelphia, formerly conducted by defendant, had been sold by it to Carload Contractors, Inc. and Sandy Johnson had been transferred to the payroll of this corporation without apparently realizing it, since the nature or location of his work had not changed.

* * *

11. Defendant now admits that on February 9, 1953, it owned the fork lift in the custody of Sandy Johnson and that this fork lift was leased to Carload Contractors, Inc. It is also admitted that the pier on which the accident occurred was leased by defendant.

12. There is no indication of action by either party in bad faith and there is no proof of inaccurate statements being made with intent to deceive. Because defendant made a prompt investigation of the accident (see answers to Interrogatories 1, 2, * * *), its insurance company has been representing the defendant since suit was brought, and this company insures Carload Contractors, Inc. also, requiring defendant to defend this suit, will not prejudice it.

Under these circumstances, and for the purposes of this action, it is ordered that the following shall be stated to the jury at the trial:

It is admitted that, on February 9, 1953, the towmotor or fork lift bearing the initials "P.P.I." was owned by defendant and that Sandy Johnson was a servant in the employ of defendant and doing its work on that date.

This ruling is based on the following principles:

1. Under the circumstances of this case, the answer contains an ineffective denial of that part of paragraph 5 of the complaint which alleges that "a motor driven vehicle known as a fork lift or chisel (was) owned, operated and controlled by the defendant, its agents, servants and employees." [See] F.R.Civ.P. 8(b) * * *.

For example, it is quite clear that defendant does not deny the averment in paragraph 5 that the fork lift came into contact with plaintiff, since it admits * * * that an investigation of an occurrence of the accident had been made and that a report dated February 10, 1953, was sent to its insurance company stating "While Frank Zielinski was riding on bumper of chisel and holding rope to secure cargo, the chisel truck collided with another chisel truck operated by Sandy Johnson causing injuries to Frank Zielinski's legs and hurt head of Sandy Johnson." Compliance with the above-mentioned rule required that defendant file a more specific answer than a general denial. A specific denial of parts of this paragraph and specific admission of other parts would have warned plaintiff that he had sued the wrong defendant.

---

3. The applicable statute of limitations prevented any suit against Carload Contrac-

tors, Inc. after February 9, 1955, 12 P.S. § 34.

* * *

Under circumstances where an improper and ineffective answer has been filed, the Pennsylvania courts have consistently held that an allegation of agency in the complaint requires a statement to the jury that agency is admitted where an attempt to amend the answer is made after the expiration of the period of limitation. * * * Although the undersigned has been able to find no federal court decisions on this point, he believes the principle of these Pennsylvania appellate court decisions may be considered in view of all the facts of this case, where jurisdiction is based on diversity of citizenship, the accident occurred in Pennsylvania, and the federal district court is sitting in Pennsylvania. * * *

2. Under the circumstances of this case, principles of equity require that defendant be estopped from denying agency because, otherwise, its inaccurate statements and statements in the record, which it knew (or had the means of knowing within its control) were inaccurate, will have deprived plaintiff of his right of action.

If Interrogatory 2 had been answered accurately by saying that employees of Carload Contractors, Inc. had turned the matter over to the insurance company, it seems clear that plaintiff would have realized his mistake. The fact that if Sandy Johnson had testified accurately, the plaintiff could have brought its action against the proper party defendant within the statutory period of limitations is also a factor to be considered, since defendant was represented at the deposition and received knowledge of the inaccurate testimony.

At least one appellate court has stated that the doctrine of equitable estoppel will be applied to prevent a party from taking advantage of the statute of limitations where the plaintiff has been misled by conduct of such party. See, Peters v. Public Service Corporation, 132 N.J.Eq. 500, 29 A.2d 189, 195 (1942). In that case, the court said, 29 A.2d at page 196:

> Of course, defendants were under no duty to advise complainants' attorney of his error, other than by appropriate pleadings, but neither did defendants have a right, knowing of the mistake, to foster it by its acts of omission.

* * *

Since this is a pre-trial order, it may be modified at the trial if the trial judge determines from the facts which then appear that justice so requires. * * *

Notes and Questions

1. In BIGGS v. PUBLIC SERV. COORDINATED TRANSP., 280 F.2d 311, 313–14 (3d Cir.1960), a diversity-of-citizenship case, the defendant generally denied plaintiff's jurisdictional allegations, including an express claim that defendant was a New Jersey corporation. The court stated:

> We cannot for a moment believe that defendant's counsel was denying in good faith that his client was a New Jersey corporation. We think the only fair interpretation of the pleading in this case is that the denial does not run to the allegation of defendant's citizenship. Therefore, that allegation must be deemed to be admitted. Fed.R.Civ.P. 8(d).

See also Vrooman Floor Covering, Inc. v. Dorsey, 267 Minn. 318, 126 N.W.2d 377 (1964) (general denial raises no defenses when entered in bad faith).

2. In the *Biggs* case defendant, in addition to the general denial, had specifically denied the allegation that the amount in controversy exceeded the minimum jurisdictional amount required in diversity cases. Does this help to explain the decision? Should a defendant who joins general and special denials in the answer be permitted to rely upon a general denial to put in issue those allegations by plaintiff that have not been specially denied? See Fawcett v. Miller, 85 Ohio L.Abs. 443, 172 N.E.2d 328 (Ct.App.1961) (failure of defendant to elect to rely on a general denial results in admissions of all facts not specially denied). Suppose a defendant's answer couples a general denial with specific admissions of facts alleged in the complaint. Should defendant be permitted to elect to stand on the denial at trial, thus forcing plaintiff to prove even those facts admitted? See Johnson v. School Dist. No. 3, 168 Neb. 547, 96 N.W.2d 623 (1959) (admissions take precedence over a general denial even though admissions were made in connection with an affirmative defense).

3. To what extent should defendant be permitted to respond that "he neither admits nor denies" plaintiff's allegations? Should it make any difference whether or not a general denial is allowed? See Rahal v. Titus, 107 Ga. App. 844, 131 S.E.2d 659 (1963). In many jurisdictions statutes specifically prohibit "evasive denials." E.g., Ill.Stat.Ann. ch. 110, ¶ 2–610(c). Compare the language of Federal Rule 8(b).

4. In California, if a complaint is verified, the answer not only must be verified but it cannot contain a general denial. See Cal.Code Civ.Proc. §§ 431.30(d) (1986 Amendment), 446. What justification is there for these provisions?

OLIVER v. SWISS CLUB TELL

California District Court of Appeal, First District, 1963.
222 Cal.App.2d 528, 35 Cal.Rptr. 324.

MOLINARI, JUSTICE. This is an appeal by plaintiffs from a summary judgment in favor of defendant "The Swiss Club Tell, an unincorporated association" [on the ground that it is nonexistent.] * * *

Plaintiffs filed no counteraffidavit. When the motion came on for hearing on September 5, 1961, plaintiffs did not appear, the motion for summary judgment was granted, and a judgment was entered pursuant thereto on September 15, 1961. * * *

Plaintiffs have devoted a considerable portion of their briefs to the assertion that the answer admits that the named defendant is an unincorporated association. The basis of this contention is that the denial in said answer, upon information and belief, of the allegation that defendant is an unincorporated association amounts to an admission of that allegation. * * * Although section 437 of the Code of Civil Procedure permits a denial in a nonpositive form based upon information and belief, or upon lack of information or belief, such denials are insufficient where the facts are presumptively within the knowledge of the defendant. * * * This rule is frequently applied to matters of public record. * * *

[A] * * * defendant ought to know whether or not it is an unincorporated association. The rule precluding the use of nonpositive denials, where matters are presumptively within the defendant's knowledge, has been applied to corporations as well as to natural persons. * * * It is evident that an unincorporated association has possession of its own records, an examination of which will disclose its status, and thus enable it to answer definitely an allegation that it is such an association. * * * Accordingly, in the instant case, the denial, purportedly based upon lack of information or belief, was to matters which would be within the actual knowledge of a defendant, and, as such, raises no issue and is in effect an admission of the truth of the allegation in the complaint "that defendant the Swiss Club Tell is an unincorporated association transacting business for the benefit of its members. * * * "

The said purported denial is defective for still another reason. The language of the denial is that "defendants do not have sufficient information to answer. * * * " Such a denial is insufficient and does not comply with section 437 of the Code of Civil Procedure, which provides in part: "If the defendant has no information or belief upon the subject sufficient to enable him to answer an allegation of the complaint, he may so state in his answer, and place his denial on that ground." * * *

Under the state of the pleadings as they stood in the present case the existence of the "Swiss Club Tell, an unincorporated association," was purportedly admitted. It appears from the pretrial conference order, however, that the issue remained in the case for adjudication. Plaintiffs not only contended at the pretrial conference that "the Swiss Clubtel [sic] *is* an unincorporated association and has been regularly served" (emphasis added), but the pretrial conference order specifically provides that "issue has been joined by the parties named above but there remains open for adjudication the nature and capacity of the Defendants Swiss Clubtel [sic]." Implicit in this issue is the question of the existence or nonexistence of defendant as an unincorporated association. The pretrial conference order controls the subsequent course of the litigation and supersedes the pleadings where inconsistent with them unless modified at or before trial. * * * Upon this posture of the case, therefore, the existence of defendant as an unincorporated association was a fact which plaintiffs were required to prove as part of their cause of action and consequently was issuable.

* * *

[Reversed.]

Notes and Questions

1. What facts are "presumptively within the knowledge" of a defendant? To what extent should defendant be obligated to ascertain facts that are easily obtainable? For example, should a corporate enterprise be charged with knowledge of representations to customers made by several of its salesmen? Does the answer depend on the size and nature of the business? See Kayser v. Railway Express Agency, 54 N.Y.S.2d 623 (Sup.Ct.1945). Suppose plaintiff's complaint alleges facts that can be ascertained only by a detailed and costly

search of defendant's records? Should defendant be required to discharge this burden prior to its answer? See Olin v. Town of North Hempstead, 194 N.Y.S.2d 979 (Sup.Ct.1959). To what extent is the response affected by the fact that under state rules defendant usually has at most 30 days in which to file an answer? See, e.g., Missouri Rule of Civil Procedure 55.25(a) (30 days); cf. Fed.Rule Civ.Proc. 12(a) (20 days). See Washington Nat. Trust Co. v. W.M. Dary Co., 116 Ariz. 171, 568 P.2d 1069 (1977) (ample opportunity to investigate exists when answer delayed until six months after complaint).

2. In *Oliver* the court held, *inter alia,* that the purported denial was ineffective because it was improperly stated. Is there any justification for this holding? Did the form of the denial create any added opportunity for untruthful or evasive pleading?

———

WINGFOOT CALIFORNIA HOMES CO. v. VALLEY NAT. BANK, 80 Ariz. 133, 294 P.2d 370 (1956). Plaintiff sued to recover on a series of notes, each of which permitted plaintiff to obtain reasonable attorneys' fees for collection thereon. Accordingly, plaintiff's complaint contained the following allegation (referred to as Paragraph VII), with respect to each of the notes: "That the sum of $150.00 is a reasonable sum to be allowed to the plaintiff as and for its attorneys' fees in this cause of action * * *." The answer merely stated that defendant "denies the allegations contained in Paragraphs VII * * *."

The plaintiff sought summary judgment on the ground that the pleading showed that no material issue of fact existed. The trial court granted the motion, awarding $100 for attorneys' fees regarding each of the notes. Defendant appealed on the ground that the denial put the matter of attorney's fees in issue. The Arizona Supreme Court upheld the decision below, stating:

> * * * [P]laintiff's argument was that this general denial that the reasonable value of attorneys' fees in each cause of action was $150, constituted a negative in that it admitted that any sum less than $150 was a reasonable sum. A negative pregnant with an admission may be defined as that form of denial which involves an affirmative implication favorable to the adversary. The general rule is that since a negative pregnant is a negative which implies an affirmative, it cannot be found in a general denial, because a general denial puts in issue every averment of the complaint which a plaintiff is required to prove to sustain his cause of action including jurisdiction. * * * But where the defendant merely denies that a debt or damage is the precise sum alleged by the plaintiff it is an admission of the value, debt or damage in a lesser amount. * * * The allegation concerning attorneys' fees is found in Paragraph VII of the complaint. The answer specifically denied Paragraph VII. This can only be interpreted to mean that defendants denied that $150 was a reasonable attorneys' fee in each cause of action for the services rendered for the plaintiff. * * * [E]mploying the use of a general specific denial as to Paragraph VII of the complaint does not invest the denial with any of the legal effects of a general denial to the entire complaint which, as above stated, is construed as denial of every allegation in the complaint. * * *

* * * Defendants did not deny that an attorneys' fee in some amount less than $150 would be a reasonable fee for the services rendered. In fact such a denial would have indicated on its face a lack of good faith on the part of the defendants in filing such a pleading. The only effect of the denial is that they contend that the sum of $150 is not reasonable. Such a denial does not fairly meet the substance of the averment in the complaint relating to attorneys' fees. If it was defendants' intention to deny that the sum of $150 was an unreasonable [sic] fee in order to form an issue on the reasonableness thereof it was incumbent on them, as above stated, to state in their pleadings the specific amount which they considered to be a maximum of the reasonable value thereof. * * *

One Justice dissented as follows:

* * * The doctrine of negative pregnant is merely a specific application of the general rule that evasive and dilatory pleadings are defective. Thus if a plaintiff sets up a certain hypothesis in his pleading and defendant denies this is [sic] the same words used, including inconsequential and qualifying facts of the complaint, then the answer is considered evasive for the reason that defendant may just as logically be denying the inconsequential qualifying facts as the primary or material ones. Therefore to *punish* such evasiveness, the doctrine states that the denial will be considered as traversing only the immaterial and admitting the material issues of fact, and the denial (or negative) is spoken of as "pregnant with admission of the material issues."

* * *

The majority opinion concedes that a negative pregnant cannot be found in a broad general denial to an entire complaint. * * * They seem to concede that if defendant had generally denied the whole complaint, no negative pregnant would exist. Yet where precisely the same effect is created by a denial of all the allegations of a specific paragraph they shut their eyes to said effect and treat the denial as defective. I submit the same reasoning whereby no negative pregnant can be found in a general denial of the whole complaint applies to the denial herein, which as to paragraph VII operated as a general denial. * * *

Notes and Questions

1. For a later and somewhat different view of the negative-pregnant doctrine in Arizona, see Frank v. Solomon, 94 Ariz. 55, 381 P.2d 591 (1963) (amendment should be permitted to eliminate negative pregnant). Compare State v. Means, 71 Nev. 340, 291 P.2d 909 (1955).

2. In JANEWAY & CARPENDER v. LONG BEACH PAPER & PAINT CO., 190 Cal. 150, 211 P. 6 (1922), plaintiff alleged that defendant "made, executed, and delivered its contract for goods to the plaintiff." Defendant denied the allegation specifically, using the identical words of the complaint. The court held that this denial was evasive and therefore admitted the existence of a contract. What arguments can be made in support of the decision? What arguments against? This type of pleading defect is termed a "conjunctive denial." To what extent does it differ from a "negative pregnant"?

b. *Affirmative Defenses*

Read Federal Rule of Civil Procedure 8(c).

Rule 8(c) lists 19 affirmative defenses that must be raised specifically. This list is not exhaustive, however. In determining whether a particular defense must be affirmatively raised, courts look to statutes in the case of federal questions, and to state practice in diversity cases. In general, defendants must raise affirmatively defenses that do not flow logically from the plaintiff's complaint. For example, a defense of the statute of frauds may not flow logically from a plaintiff's contract claim, and so it must be raised affirmatively. The function of the Rule, then, is to provide notice to the plaintiff of the existence of the defenses.

INGRAHAM v. UNITED STATES

United States Court of Appeals, Fifth Circuit, 1987.
808 F.2d 1075.

POLITZ, CIRCUIT JUDGE:

The appellees in these consolidated cases sued the United States, under the Federal Tort Claims Act, for severe injuries caused by the negligence of government physicians. In each case, after entry of adverse judgment the government moved for relief from the judgment to the extent that the damages exceeded the limit imposed on medical malpractice awards by the Medical Liability and Insurance Improvement Act of Texas * * *. The respective district courts denied these post-trial motions. Concluding that the government did not raise the issue timely before the trial courts, [and] that the issues were not preserved for appeal, * * * we affirm both judgments.

BACKGROUND

In 1977, in response to what was perceived to be a medical malpractice crisis, the Legislature of Texas, like several other state legislatures, adopted certain limitations on damages to be awarded in actions against health care providers, for injuries caused by negligence in the rendering of medical care and treatment. Of particular significance to these appeals is the $500,000 cap placed on the *ex delicto* recovery, not applicable to past and future medical expenses.

On February 12, 1979, Dwight L. Ingraham was operated on by an Air Force surgeon. During the back surgery a drill was negligently used and Ingraham's spinal cord was damaged, causing severe and permanent injuries. The court awarded Ingraham judgment for $1,264,000. This total included $364,000 for lost wages and $900,000 for pain, suffering, and disability. There is no reference to the Medical Liability and Insurance Improvement Act of Texas in the pleadings, nor was any reference made to the Act during the trial. After entry of judgment, the United States filed a notice of appeal. Thereafter, urging the Act's limitations, the government sought relief from judgment under Fed.R.Civ.P. 60(b). The district court denied that motion. * * *

Similarly, in March of 1979, Jocelyn and David Bonds, and their infant daughter Stephanie, were victims of the negligent performance by an Air Force physician. Because of the mismanagement of the 43rd week of Jocelyn Bonds's first pregnancy, and the negligent failure to perform timely a caesarian section delivery, Stephanie suffered asphyxiation *in utero.* The loss of oxygen caused extensive brain damage, resulting in spastic quadriparesis, cortical blindness, seizures, and mental retardation. In their FCTA action the court awarded Stephanie $1,814,959.70 for medical expenses and $1,675,595.90 for the other losses. Jocelyn Bonds was awarded $750,000 for her losses, including loss of the society of her daughter. As in the Ingraham case, the government did not invoke the Texas malpractice limitation in pleading or at trial. Post judgment the government filed a motion to amend the judgment under Fed.R.Civ.P. 59, but, again, there was no mention of the limitations Act. Subsequently, three months after entry of the judgment, the government filed a pleading entitled "Motion for Reconsideration," in which it advanced the malpractice Act. That motion was denied. * * *

These appeals do not challenge the courts' findings of liability, but object only to quantum, contending that damages are limited by the Medical Liability and Insurance Improvement Act * * *.

ANALYSIS

Appellees maintain that we should not consider the statutory limitation of liability invoked on appeal because it is an affirmative defense under Rule 8(c) of the Federal Rules of Civil Procedure, and the failure to raise it timely constitutes a waiver. We find this argument persuasive.

Rule 8(c) first lists 19 specific affirmative defenses, and concludes with the residuary clause "any other matter constituting an avoidance or affirmative defense." In the years since adoption of the rule, the residuary clause has provided the authority for a substantial number of additional defenses which must be timely and affirmatively pleaded. These include: exclusions from a policy of liability insurance; breach of warranty; concealment of an alleged prior undissolved marriage; voidable preference in bankruptcy; noncooperation of an insured; statutory limitation on liability; the claim that a written contract was incomplete; judgment against a defendant's joint tortfeasor; circuity of action; discharge of a contract obligation through novation or extension; re[s]cission or mutual abandonment of a contract; failure to mitigate damages; adhesion contract; statutory exemption; failure to exhaust state remedies; immunity from suit; good faith belief in lawfulness of action; the claim that a lender's sale of collateral was not commercially reasonable; a settlement agreement or release barring an action; and custom of trade or business. * * *

Determining whether a given defense is "affirmative" within the ambit of Rule 8(c) is not without some difficulty. We find the salient comments of Judge Charles E. Clark, Dean of the Yale Law School, later

Chief Judge of the United States Second Circuit Court of Appeals, and the principal author of the Federal Rules to be instructive:

> [J]ust as certain disfavored allegations made by the plaintiff * * * must be set forth with the greatest particularity, so like disfavored defenses must be particularly alleged by the defendant. These may include such matters as fraud, statute of frauds * * *, statute of limitations, truth in slander and libel * * * and so on. In other cases the mere question of convenience may seem prominent, as in the case of payment, where the defendant can more easily show the affirmative payment at a certain time than the plaintiff can the negative of nonpayment over a period of time. Again it may be an issue which may be generally used for dilatory tactics, such as the question of the plaintiff's right to sue * * * a vital question, but one usually raised by the defendant on technical grounds. These have been thought of as issues "likely to take the opposite party by surprise," which perhaps conveys the general idea of fairness or the lack thereof, though there is little real surprise where the case is well prepared in advance.

Clark, *Code Pleading*, 2d ed. 1947, § 96, at 609–10 * * *.

Also pertinent to the analysis is the logical relationship between the defense and the cause of action asserted by the plaintiff. This inquiry requires a determination (1) whether the matter at issue fairly may be said to constitute a necessary or extrinsic element in the plaintiff's cause of action; (2) which party, if either, has better access to relevant evidence; and (3) policy considerations: should the matter be indulged or disfavored? * * *

Central to requiring the pleading of affirmative defenses is the prevention of unfair surprise. A defendant should not be permitted to "lie behind a log" and ambush a plaintiff with an unexpected defense. * * * The instant cases illustrate this consideration. Plaintiffs submit that, had they known the statute would be applied, they would have made greater efforts to prove medical damages which were not subject to the statutory limit. In addition, plaintiffs maintain that they would have had an opportunity and the incentive to introduce evidence to support their constitutional attacks on the statute.

This distinction separates the present cases from our recent decision in Lucas v. United States, 807 F.2d 414 (5th Cir.1986). In *Lucas,* although the limitation of recovery issue was not pleaded, it was raised at trial. We held that the trial court was within its discretion to permit the defendant to effectively amend its pleadings and advance the defense. The treatment we accorded this issue in *Lucas* is consistent with long-standing precedent of this and other circuits that " 'where [an affirmative defense] is raised in the trial court in a manner that does not result in unfair surprise, * * * technical failure to comply with Rule 8(c) is not fatal.' " * * *

We view the limitation on damages as an "avoidance" within the intendment of the residuary clause of 8(c). Black's Law Dictionary * * * defines an avoidance in pleadings as "the allegation or statement of new matter, in opposition to a former pleading, which, admitting the facts alleged in such former pleading, shows cause why they should not have their ordinary legal effect." Applied to the present discussion, a plaintiff pleads the traditional tort theory of malpractice and seeks full damages. The defendant responds that assuming recovery is in order under the ordinary tort principles, because of the new statutory limitation, the traditional precedents "should not have their ordinary legal effect."

Considering these factors, against the backdrop and with the illumination provided by other applications of Rule 8(c), we conclude that the Texas statutory limit on medical malpractice damages is an affirmative defense which must be pleaded timely and that in the cases at bar the defense has been waived.

* * *

SECTION C. THE REPLY

Read Federal Rule of Civil Procedure 7(a) and the accompanying materials in the Supplement. Pay particular attention to Section 25–820 of the Nebraska Revised Statutes.

Notes and Questions

1. The two prevailing types of provisions governing use of the reply are represented by Federal Rule 7(a) and the Nebraska statute. In Nebraska all allegations of an affirmative defense are admitted unless they are denied in a reply. Neb.Rev.Stat. § 25–842. Even the Nebraska statute, by cutting off or severely restricting pleadings at the reply stage, see Neb.Rev.Stat. § 25–803, departs significantly from the common-law practice, which required pleadings to continue back and forth between plaintiff and defendant until disputed issues were isolated.

Is Federal Rule 7(a), when read in conjunction with Rule 8(d), consistent with Federal Rule 8(b), which requires a defendant to answer plaintiff's allegations specifically?

2. Although the text of Federal Rule 7(a) expressly provides that a court may order plaintiff to reply to allegations other than counterclaims, judges have been reluctant to do so, at least in the absence of "a clear and convincing factual showing of necessity or other extraordinary circumstances of a compelling nature." MOVIECOLOR LTD. v. EASTMAN KODAK CO., 24 F.R.D. 325, 326 (S.D.N.Y.1959). Why, given liberal discovery rules, should it ever be necessary to order a reply? Cf. Reynolds v. Needle, 132 F.2d 161 (D.C.Cir. 1942) (summary judgment granted when plaintiff's complaint revealed affirmative defense and plaintiff failed to request leave to reply or otherwise attempt to avoid the defense).

BECKSTROM v. COASTWISE LINE, 13 F.R.D. 480, 482–83 (D.Alaska 1953), provides an interesting illustration of a tactical use of the reply. Under the terms of Federal Rule 38(b), a party who wishes a trial by jury of any issue must make a demand therefor not later than 10 days after the service of the *last pleading directed to such issue.* Defendants had answered plaintiff's complaint on August 22, alleging several affirmative defenses; on October 6 plaintiff moved for leave to reply and, at the same time, made his first demand for trial by jury.

* * * Plaintiff has not shown a substantial reason for seeking permission to file a reply or for being *ordered* to do so. Accordingly, plaintiff's motion * * * must be denied.

* * * [I]n the absence of a reply now denied, [defendant's answer] was the last pleading directed to the issues between the plaintiff and the defendants in this action. The demand for jury trial as of right must therefore be denied.

What would you have done to improve plaintiff's strategy in this case? Do you consider this a proper or ethical use of the pleadings? Demand for trial by jury is discussed further at pp. 918–23, infra.

3. Allegations to which a reply is not permitted or required are considered avoided or denied and plaintiff may controvert them at trial. See Federal Rule 8(d); N.Y.C.P.L.R. 3018(a). Conversely, matters requiring a responsive pleading are taken as admitted if not denied in the reply or if a reply is not filed. See Federal Rule 8(d); Neb.Rev.Stat. § 25–842.

Suppose defendant's answer contains an allegation denominated a "counterclaim," but plaintiff believes it is properly an affirmative defense. Or suppose in a "new matter" jurisdiction, such as Nebraska, plaintiff thinks defendant's "affirmative defense" could have been raised by a simple denial. See Vevelstad v. Flynn, 230 F.2d 695, 703 (9th Cir.), certiorari denied 352 U.S. 827, 77 S.Ct. 40, 1 L.Ed.2d 49 (1956) ("a counterclaim" held to be really a denial not requiring reply); Sais v. City Elec. Co., 26 N.M. 66, 188 P. 1110 (1920) ("affirmative defense" that could have been raised by denial does not require responsive pleading). What if plaintiff does not reply and the court believes that the material in fact was a counterclaim? See Dyotherm Corp. v. Turbo Mach. Co., 39 F.R.D. 370 (E.D.Pa.1966) (plaintiff granted 10 days to file reply after court ruled against its contention that defendant's answer was not a properly denominated counterclaim). Should the court always grant plaintiff some relief? See Federal Rule 8(c).

SECTION D. AMENDMENTS

Read Federal Rule of Civil Procedure 15 and the accompanying materials in the Supplement.

MOORE v. MOORE
District of Columbia Court of Appeals, 1978.
391 A.2d 762.

FERREN, ASSOCIATE JUDGE:

Reuben and Sidney Moore, plaintiff-appellant and defendant-appellee, respectively, were married on October 19, 1968, in the District of Columbia. Their only child, Jessica Moore, was born on August 4, 1973. The marriage deteriorated [and in December, 1975] * * * Sidney Moore moved with Jessica to her parents' home in Schenectady, New York.

Reuben Moore soon initiated a custody action in New York. The court orally granted temporary custody of Jessica to Mrs. Moore, with visitation rights for Mr. Moore. On February 22, 1976, pursuant to a plan aided by a detective he had hired, Reuben Moore took Jessica from the physical custody of her maternal grandfather and brought her to Washington, D.C.

Month later *child 2 3/4*

* * * [W]hile leaving a hospital where he had been visiting his ill father on March 17, 1976, Reuben Moore was confronted and grabbed by his wife and her parents. They wrested control of the child from him and returned, with Jessica, to Schenectady.

month later

On April 2, 1976, Reuben Moore * * * filed the present action: a complaint for custody. Sidney Moore * * * answered the complaint * * * [and] the matter came to trial on October 20–21, 1976, in the Family Division of the Superior Court.

* * *

On October 27, 1976, Sidney Moore filed a motion to conform the pleadings to the evidence, Super.Ct.Dom.Rel.R. 15(b), as well as a motion for award of counsel fees. In the first motion, Mrs. Moore sought to assert a counterclaim for custody, child support, separate maintenance, and counsel fees (in connection with the District of Columbia custody litigation only). In the second motion she asked for the same counsel fees, specified the reasons for requesting them, and itemized the matters and amounts claimed.

By written order of February 28, 1977, the court *alimony* granted the motion to conform. It awarded to defendant Sidney Moore custody of Jessica, child support of $500 per month, separate maintenance of $500 per month, and counsel fees in the amount requested, $5,916.65. The court granted plaintiff Reuben Moore visitation rights, subject to the continued posting of a $7,500 bond. * * * Plaintiff Reuben Moore now appeals. * * *

Appellant now asserts, as he did at trial, that because appellee requested no affirmative relief in pretrial pleadings the court erred in affording her any relief. It is one thing, he argues, to deny his claim for custody; it is another to award custody to appellee, as well as child support, separate maintenance, and attorneys' fees. He essentially contends, therefore, that the court abused its discretion in permitting the post-trial pleading amendment under Super.Ct.Dom.Rel.R. 15(b), since he was unaware at trial that the matters ultimately stated in appellee's counterclaim were at stake; he was not prepared, nor given an adequate opportunity, to contest them.

Our treatment of this argument must begin with Rule 15(b), which is identical to Fed.R.Civ.Pro. 15(b). Our analysis is accordingly aided by authorities which have interpreted the federal rule. Rule 15(b) is an attempt to favor substance over form, i.e., "to avoid the tyranny of formalism," Rosden v. Leuthold, 107 U.S.App.D.C. 89, 92, 274 F.2d 747,

750 (1960), and thus promote the resolution of cases on their merits by permitting the amendment of pleadings to reflect the actual litigation which transpired. Wright & Miller, *Fed.Prac. & Proc., Civil* § 1491. * * * If issues not raised in pleadings are tried by express consent of the parties, there can be no question about the propriety of permitting amendment. The difficult issue arises when, as in most Rule 15(b) cases, "implied consent" is asserted.

Whether parties have impliedly contested a matter—i.e., whether parties recognize that an issue not stated by the pleadings entered the case * * *—is determined by searching the trial record for indications that the party contesting the amendment received actual notice of the injection of the unpleaded matters, as well as an adequate opportunity to litigate such matters and to cure any surprise from their introduction. * * *

The clearest indications of a party's implied consent to try an issue lie in the failure to object to evidence, or in the introduction of evidence which is clearly apposite to the new issue but not to other matters specified in the pleadings. * * * Having in mind the tension between the desire to abandon formalism and, on the other hand, the need to assure fair notice and opportunity to litigate, we turn to the facts to assess whether the trial court's grant of permission to amend and, ultimately, its resolution of the additional issues were within the purview of discretion granted under Rule 15(b).

A. CUSTODY

Although at the time of trial only appellant, and not his wife, had filed an action for custody, we conclude—without difficulty—that appellant was on timely notice that the court would decide not merely whether he was entitled to custody but, more broadly, would determine *who* was entitled to custody. Mrs. Moore asserted in her answer to appellant's complaint that "the best interests of the child" would be served by the child's being in her custody. Moreover, both parties introduced evidence supporting their respective qualifications for custodian. * * *

Appellant accordingly can claim no surprise or lack of notice or opportunity to litigate. The issue of Mrs. Moore's right to permanent custody—even if not raised by the pleadings—clearly was tried by the parties and the court. * * *

B. CHILD SUPPORT

The pretrial pleadings do not include a claim for child support. Our determination, therefore, again must be whether the issue was litigated by implied consent. For two reasons we find that it was.

First, and most germane, we believe that the resolution of child support inheres in a custody battle where the best interests of the child are the focal concern. * * * The trial judge recognized this relationship when she opined that a grant of support was required by the court's duty to afford complete relief. Second, our conclusion is bolstered by appellee's introduction of evidence of the financial needs of the child. As appellee points out, this evidence was not contested on relevance grounds; it served to put appellant on notice. * * *

In light of these two factors, we conclude that appellant received ample notice that the matter of child support would be determined and that he therefore impliedly consented. The trial court accordingly did not abuse its Rule 15(b) discretion in permitting appellee's amendment of the pleadings to raise the issue of child support.

C. VISITATION RIGHTS AND BOND

Appellant does not dispute that visitation rights are a proper subject for determination as part of the overall custody question. In her Rule 15(b) motion, appellee did not request imposition of a bond covering her husband's visits with Jessica. However, because trial courts are given broad discretion in resolving custody cases, * * * and ought to fashion relief to foster and safeguard a child's best interests, * * * we find no fault with the imposition of a bond upon a parent whose history reflected a capacity for absconding with the child. The judge was acting within the scope of her duties and powers to grant complete relief. Rule 54(c). She did not abuse her discretion.

D. ATTORNEYS' FEES

This court has determined that even though there is no specific statutory authorization for attorneys' fees awards in child custody cases, courts are empowered to award them to a parent who has enlisted legal assistance to protect the interests of the child. * * *

Although counsel fees for the assertion of a minor's interests are not as integral to a custody claim as child support, we believe that, given legal precedent, the prospect of incurring such fees would surely be within the contemplation of an opposing party. We note in this connection that evidence of expenditures for counsel fees to District of Columbia lawyers was admitted without objection. We also recognize that the trial judge initially reserved judgment on the issue, entertained a motion and opposition, and then held a hearing before awarding the fees. On this record we find no prejudicial surprise to appellant. * * *

E. SEPARATE MAINTENANCE

The grant of spousal support is a different matter. The initial pleadings did not mention a claim for separate maintenance, which is not customarily a part of a child custody suit between parents whose marital relationship had not been—and was not being—litigated. While evidence of Mrs. Moore's financial needs was admitted without objection relatively late in the proceedings, we cannot conclude that this evidence was so uniquely pertinent to her support alone, in contrast with the custody or the child support issues, that it justifies our concluding that appellant had adequate, timely notice of, and an opportunity to contest, a claim by his wife for her own support. We find no other indication of record that appellant impliedly consented to try his wife's support claim, Rule 15(b), nor can we conclude that the award was a proper, supportable element of full relief in the child custody action. Rule 54(b) [sic]. We therefore find an abuse of trial court discretion in permitting amendment of the pleadings to include separate maintenance and, thereafter, in making such an award.

* * *

[Affirmed in part, reversed in part.]

Notes and Questions

1. Notice the tactical dilemma faced by a party when the opposition seeks to introduce evidence at trial on an issue that clearly is not within the pleadings. The litigant may object and keep the evidence out, but this will induce the other side to request leave to amend, perhaps even to add an issue of which the party seeking amendment previously was not aware. On the other hand, a failure to object may be taken as implied consent to try the issue, thus permitting an amendment to conform to the proof. Whenever a party fails to object in this situation a second dilemma must be faced— whether or not to produce evidence on the point in question.

Even a party who objects to the evidence may face further problems. Suppose the court erroneously holds that the original pleadings encompass the newly introduced issue? In HAYES v. RICHFIELD OIL CORP., 38 Cal.2d 375, 382, 240 P.2d 580, 584 (1952), the court held:

> A variance between the allegations of a pleading and the proof will not be deemed material unless it has actually misled the adverse party to his prejudice * * *. If anything, Richfield's continued insistence [throughout the trial] that the issue was not presented by the pleadings indicates that it was fully aware that the [trial] court's rulings would permit recovery under * * * [the new] theory. It does not appear that Richfield has been in any way prejudiced by the variance * * *.

See also Stolz v. Franklin, 258 Ark. 999, 531 S.W.2d 1, 6–7 (1975).

2. Should the court in *Moore* have remanded the case for consideration of whether an amendment under the District of Columbia rule (identical to Federal Rule 15(a)) was appropriate on the separate maintenance issue? Such an amendment normally would require the court to reopen the case for additional evidence. Of what significance is the fact that *Moore* was not a jury case? What other factors should be considered in deciding whether an amendment after trial is proper?

Would serious prejudice to the opposing party, for example, the death of an important witness, automatically preclude the amendment, or should the court balance the alleged prejudice against the interests of the party seeking to amend? See generally Donnici, *The Amendment of Pleadings—A Study of the Operation of Judicial Discretion in the Federal Courts,* 37 S.Cal.L.Rev. 529 (1964).

BEECK v. AQUASLIDE 'N' DIVE CORP.

United States Court of Appeals, Eighth Circuit, 1977.
562 F.2d 537.

BENSON, DISTRICT JUDGE.*

This case is an appeal from the trial court's exercise of discretion on procedural matters in a diversity personal injury action.

Jerry A. Beeck was severely injured on July 15, 1972, while using a water slide. He and his wife, Judy A. Beeck, sued Aquaslide 'N' Dive Corporation (Aquaslide), a Texas corporation, alleging it manufactured the slide involved in the accident, and sought to recover substantial damages on theories of negligence, strict liability and breach of implied warranty.

Aquaslide initially admitted manufacture of the slide, but later moved to amend its answer to deny manufacture; the motion was resisted. The district court granted leave to amend. On motion of the defendant, a separate trial was held on the issue of "whether the defendant designed, manufactured or sold the slide in question." This motion was also resisted by the plaintiffs. The issue was tried to a jury, which returned a verdict for the defendant, after which the trial court entered summary judgment of dismissal of the case. Plaintiffs took this appeal, and stated the issues presented for review to be:

1. Where the manufacturer of the product, a water slide, admitted in its Answer and later in its Answer to Interrogatories both filed prior to the running of the statute of limitations that it designed, manufactured and sold the water slide in question, was it an abuse of the trial court's discretion to grant leave to amend to the manufacturer in order to deny these admissions after the running of the statute of limitations?

2. After granting the manufacturer's Motion for Leave to Amend in order to deny the prior admissions of design, manufacture and sale of the water slide in question, was it an abuse of the trial court's discretion to further grant the manufacturer's Motion for a Separate Trial on the issue of manufacture?

I. FACTS

A brief review of the facts found by the trial court in its order granting leave to amend, and which do not appear to have been in dispute, is essential to a full understanding of appellants' claims.

In 1971 Kimberly Village Home Association of Davenport, Iowa, ordered an Aquaslide product from one George Boldt, who was a local distributor handling defendant's products. The order was forwarded by Boldt to Sentry Pool and Chemical Supply Co. in Rock Island, Illinois, and Sentry forwarded the order to Purity Swimming Pool Supply in Hammond, Indiana. A slide was delivered from a Purity warehouse to Kimberly Village, and was installed by Kimberly employees. On July 15,

* The Honorable Paul Benson, Chief Judge, United States District Court for the   District of North Dakota, sitting by designation.

1972, Jerry A. Beeck was injured while using the slide at a social gathering sponsored at Kimberly Village by his employer, Harker Wholesale Meats, Inc. Soon after the accident investigations were undertaken by representatives of the separate insurers of Harker and Kimberly Village. On October 31, 1972, Aquaslide first learned of the accident through a letter sent by a representative of Kimberly's insurer to Aquaslide, advising that "one of your Queen Model # Q–3D slides" was involved in the accident. Aquaslide forwarded this notification to its insurer. Aquaslide's insurance adjuster made an on-site investigation of the slide in May, 1973, and also interviewed persons connected with the ordering and assembly of the slide. An inter-office letter dated September 23, 1973, indicates that Aquaslide's insurer was of the opinion the "Aquaslide in question was definitely manufactured by our insured." The complaint was filed October 15, 1973. Investigators for three different insurance companies, representing Harker, Kimberly and the defendant, had concluded that the slide had been manufactured by Aquaslide, and the defendant, with no information to the contrary, answered the complaint on December 12, 1973, and admitted that it "designed, manufactured, assembled and sold" the slide in question.

The statute of limitations on plaintiff's personal injury claim expired on July 15, 1974. About six and one-half months later Carl Meyer, president and owner of Aquaslide, visited the site of the accident prior to the taking of his deposition by the plaintiff. From his on-site inspection of the slide, he determined it was not a product of the defendant. Thereafter, Aquaslide moved the court for leave to amend its answer to deny manufacture of the slide.

II. LEAVE TO AMEND

Amendment of pleadings in civil actions is governed by Rule 15(a) * * *.

In Foman v. Davis, 371 U.S. 178, 83 S.Ct. 227, 9 L.Ed.2d 222 (1962), the Supreme Court had occasion to construe * * * Rule 15(a) * * *:

> Rule 15(a) declares that leave to amend "shall be freely given when justice so requires," this mandate is to be heeded. * * * If the underlying facts or circumstances relied upon by a plaintiff may be a proper subject of relief, he ought to be afforded an opportunity to test his claim on the merits. In the absence of any apparent or declared reason—such as undue delay, bad faith or dilatory motive on the part of the movant, repeated failure to cure deficiencies by amendments previously allowed, undue prejudice to the opposing party by virtue of allowance of the amendment, futility of amendment, etc.—the leave sought should, as the rules require, be "freely given." Of course, the grant or denial of an opportunity to amend is within the discretion of the District Court, * * *.

371 U.S. at 182, 83 S.Ct. at 230. * * *

This Court in Hanson v. Hunt Oil Co., 398 F.2d 578, 582 (8th Cir. 1968), held that "[p]rejudice *must be shown*." (Emphasis added). The burden is on the party opposing the amendment to show such prejudice. In ruling on a motion for leave to amend, the trial court must inquire into the issue of prejudice to the opposing party, in light of the particular facts of the case.   *   *   *

Certain principles apply to appellate review of a trial court's grant or denial of a motion to amend pleadings. First, as noted in Foman v. Davis, allowance or denial of leave to amend lies within the sound discretion of the trial court, *   *   * and is reviewable only for an abuse of discretion. *   *   * The appellate court must view the case in the posture in which the trial court acted in ruling on the motion to amend.   *   *   *

It is evident from the order of the district court that in the exercise of its discretion in ruling on defendant's motion for leave to amend, it searched the record for evidence of bad faith, prejudice and undue delay which might be sufficient to overbalance the mandate of Rule 15(a), F.R. Civ.P., and Foman v. Davis, that leave to amend should be "freely given." Plaintiffs had not at any time conceded that the slide in question had not been manufactured by the defendant, and at the time the motion for leave to amend was at issue, the court had to decide whether the defendant should be permitted to litigate a material factual issue on its merits.

In inquiring into the issue of bad faith, the court noted the fact that the defendant, in initially concluding that it had manufactured the slide, relied upon the conclusions of three different insurance companies, each of which had conducted an investigation into the circumstances surrounding the accident. This reliance upon investigations of three insurance companies, and the fact that "no contention has been made by anyone that the defendant influenced this possibly erroneous conclusion," persuaded the court that "defendant has not acted in such bad faith as to be precluded from contesting the issue of manufacture at trial." The court further found "[t]o the extent that 'blame' is to be spread regarding the original identification, the record indicates that it should be shared equally."

In considering the issue of prejudice that might result to the plaintiffs from the granting of the motion for leave to amend, the trial court held that the facts presented to it did not support plaintiffs' assertion that, because of the running of the two year Iowa statute of limitations on personal injury claims, the allowance of the amendment would sound the "death knell" of the litigation. In order to accept plaintiffs' argument, the court would have had to assume that the defendant would prevail at trial on the factual issue of manufacture of the slide, and further that plaintiffs would be foreclosed, should the amendment be allowed, from proceeding against other parties if they were unsuccessful in pressing their claim against Aquaslide. On the state of the record before it, the trial court was unwilling to make such assumptions, and concluded "[u]nder these circumstances, the Court deems that the possible prejudice to the plaintiffs is an insufficient basis on which to deny the proposed amendment." The court reasoned that the amendment would merely allow the defendant to contest a disputed factual issue at trial, and further that it would be prejudicial to the defendant to deny the amendment.

The court also held that defendant and its insurance carrier, in investigating the circumstances surrounding the accident, had not been so lacking in diligence as to dictate a denial of the right to litigate the factual issue of manufacture of the slide.

On this record we hold that the trial court did not abuse its discretion in allowing the defendant to amend its answer.

* * *

SCHIAVONE v. FORTUNE   *(After amendments 1966)*

Supreme Court of the United States, 1986.
477 U.S. 21, 106 S.Ct. 2379, 91 L.Ed.2d 18.

[Plaintiffs commenced libel actions on May 9, 1983, by filing their respective complaints in the federal District Court for the District of New Jersey. Jurisdiction was based on diversity of citizenship. Each complaint alleged that the plaintiff was libeled in a story in Fortune magazine that was published no later than May 19, 1982 and described Fortune as "a foreign corporation having its principal offices at Time and Life Building" in New York City. On May 20, the complaints were mailed to Time's registered agent in New Jersey, who received them on May 23 but refused service because Time was not named as a defendant. On July 19, 1983, each petitioner amended his complaint to name as the captioned defendant and to refer in the body of the complaint to "Fortune, also known as Time, Incorporated." The amended complaints were served on Time by certified mail on July 21. The District Court dismissed the complaints under the New Jersey statute of limitations, which requires a libel action to be commenced within one year of the publication of the libel. The court held that, although the amended complaints adequately named Time as a defendant, the amendments did not relate back, under Federal Rule 15(c), to the filing of the original complaints because it had not been shown that Time received notice of the institution of the actions within the period provided by New Jersey law. On consolidated appeals, the Third Circuit affirmed.]

Certiorari to the United States Court of Appeals for the Third Circuit.

JUSTICE BLACKMUN delivered the opinion of the Court. *affirmed*

* * * [T]he three complaints as originally drawn were filed within the limitations period; * * * service was attempted only after that period had expired; and * * * the amendment of the complaints, and the service of the complaints as so amended, also necessarily took place after the expiration of the limitations period. * * *

* * *

* * * Relation back is dependent upon four factors, all of which must be satisfied: (1) the basic claim must have arisen out of the conduct set forth in the original pleading; (2) the party to be brought in must have received such notice that it will not be prejudiced in maintaining its defense; (3) that party must or should have known that, but for a mistake concerning identity, the action would have been brought against it; and (4) the second and third requirements must have been fulfilled within the prescribed limitations period. We are not concerned here with the first factor, but we are concerned with the satisfaction of the remaining three.

The first intimation that Time had of the institution and maintenance of the three suits took place after May 19, 1983, the date the Court of Appeals said the statute ran "at the latest." * * * Only on May 20 did petitioners' counsel mail the complaints to Time's registered agent in New Jersey. Only on May 23 were those complaints received by the registered agent, and then refused. Only on July 19 did each petitioner amend his complaint. And only on July 21 were the amended complaints served on Time.

It seems to us inevitably to follow that notice to Time and the necessary knowledge did not come into being "within the period provided by law for commencing the action against" Time, as is so clearly required by Rule 15(c). That occurred only after the expiration of the applicable one-year period. This is fatal, then, to petitioners' litigation.

We do not have before us a choice between a "liberal" approach toward Rule 15(c), on the one hand, and a "technical" interpretation of the Rule, on the other hand. The choice, instead, is between recognizing or ignoring what the Rule provides in plain language. We accept the Rule as meaning what it says.

We are not inclined, either, to temper the plain meaning of the language by engrafting upon it an extension of the limitations period equal to the asserted reasonable time, inferred from Rule 4, for the service of a timely filed complaint. Rule 4 deals only with process. Rule 3 concerns the "commencement" of a civil action. Under Rule 15(c), the emphasis is upon "the period provided by law for commencing the action against" the defendant. An action is commenced by the filing of a complaint and, so far as Time is concerned, no complaint against it was filed on or prior to May 19, 1983.

Any possible doubt about this should have been dispelled 20 years ago by the Advisory Committee's 1966 Note about Rule 15(c). The Note specifically states that the Rule's phrase "within the period provided by law for commencing the action" means "within the applicable limitations period" * * *.

The linchpin is notice, and notice within the limitations period. Of course, there is an element of arbitrariness here, but that is a characteristic of any limitations period. And it is an arbitrariness imposed by the legislature and not by the judicial process. * * *

The judgments of the Court of Appeals are affirmed.

[The dissenting opinion of JUSTICE STEVENS is omitted.]

Notes and Questions

1. Reread the Advisory Committee Note to the 1966 amendments to Rule 15 in the Supplement. Could Time have been charged with constructive notice in *Schiavone,* given that Time's agent received the complaint before the

limitations period ran? After all, Time knew that it published Fortune magazine, and the complaint named Fortune as the defendant.

After the decision in *Schiavone,* how will cases against the federal government that name the wrong defendant (for example, "Health and Human Services Department" instead of its Secretary) be decided? If plaintiffs will not be able to amend their complaints in such situations, how could Rule 15 be amended to alter that result? See Brussack, *Outrageous Fortune: The Case for Amending Rule 15(c) Again,* 61 S.Cal.L.Rev. 671 (1988); Lewis, *The Excessive History of Federal Rule 15(c) and Its Lessons for Civil Rules Revision,* 85 Mich.L.Rev. 1507 (1987).

2. One of the most vexing problems in Rule 15(c) cases arises when several corporations who are potential parties to the litigation have similar names. In **MARTZ v. MILLER BROTHERS CO.,** 244 F.Supp. 246 (D.Del. 1965), plaintiff served a complaint for negligence against Miller Brothers Company arising from an accident in a Miller Brothers' furniture store two days before the statute of limitations expired. Defendant moved for summary judgment, filing an affidavit of its secretary declaring that defendant did not own the store. In fact, Miller Brothers Company of Newark was a company with the same officers as Miller Brothers Company except for the secretary, who had been served the original complaint.

Plaintiff sought to amend the complaint after the limitations period had run. The court ruled that the two companies were separate entities and thus would not permit a substitution of the name of defendant, on the ground that such permission would result in a new party being brought into an action after the limitations period had run. The court also refused to treat the original defendant's secretary as an agent of the second company, because the secretary was neither an officer nor a shareholder of the second company.

3. In **STAUFFER v. ISALY DAIRY CO.,** 4 Ohio App.2d 15, 27, 211 N.E. 2d 72, 80 (1965), plaintiff originally named and served the Isaly Dairy Company of Pittsburgh, a different corporation than the proper defendant, the Isaly Dairy Company. The two corporations maintained the same address, the person who was served was an officer of both corporations, and plaintiff had no idea that more than one corporation existed. In holding that an amendment altering the name of the defendant related back to the time the original complaint was filed, the court stated: "[W]hen intermingled corporations have intermingled officers who conduct the business and management of such corporations in such a manner that the general public is under the impression that they are all one and the same corporation, we feel that these corporations should be bound by their representations."

4. A number of states have adopted provisions, identical to Federal Rule 15(c), to permit a change of party defendant after the limitations period has run. Others have followed the California procedure, Cal.Code Civ.Proc. § 474, which allows plaintiff to name as defendants any number of "John Does" against whom the statute of limitations will then cease to run on any causes of action stated against them. When plaintiff becomes aware that he has sued a wrong defendant or has failed to sue a proper defendant, he may then merely substitute the name of the new defendant for one of the John Doe-defendants and proceed with the case. Why isn't this the most sensible way in which to handle the relation-back problem? A number of plaintiffs in federal court cases routinely have named John Doe defendants in an attempt

to allow additional parties to be joined even though the conditions of Rule 15(c) cannot be met. These efforts generally have failed because there is no Federal Rule permitting the use of fictitious defendants. See, e.g., Sassi v. Breier, 584 F.2d 234 (7th Cir.1978); Craig v. United States, 413 F.2d 854 (9th Cir.1969). But see Duisen v. Terrel, 332 F.Supp. 127 (W.D.Mo.1971). Should a state "John Doe" practice be applicable in federal court in a case governed by state law? Should it make a difference if the state treats its John Doe provision as an integral aspect of the statute of limitations itself rather than as a procedural rule dealing with relation back of amendments? See Britt v. Arvanitis, 590 F.2d 57 (3d Cir.1978).

5. In STAGGERS v. OTTO GERDAU CO., 359 F.2d 292, 297 (2d Cir. 1966), the original plaintiff, an assignee of the claim, died prior to trial. Subsequently, and after the statute of limitations on the claim had run, an amendment substituted both the original plaintiff's administrator and the assignor of the claim as parties plaintiff. The trial court held that the amendment did not relate back to the time of the original complaint. The Court of Appeals reversed:

> No matter who the plaintiffs are, the "transactions" with which we are concerned are those which led to the establishment and breach of the * * * contracts * * * set forth in the "original pleading." There is no meaningful statute of limitations problem here; the claims of all potential plaintiffs relate back to the date of the original pleading.

Does this language go too far? Are there different considerations with regard to relation back of amendments when it is a plaintiff rather than a defendant who is added? Rules and statutes such as Federal Rule 15(c) usually are oriented solely toward joinder of new defendants. When a new plaintiff is joined after the limitations period has passed, is it significant that the jurisdiction relies on a new-cause-of-action theory rather than a same-transaction-or-occurrence rule in deciding generally whether amendments relate back? See Maxson v. McElhinney, 370 Pa. 622, 88 A.2d 747 (1952) (in wrongful-death action brought by deceased's widow who had no standing to sue, an amendment substituting deceased's personal representative would state a new cause of action and would not relate back). See also Brauer v. Republic Steel Corp., 460 F.2d 801 (10th Cir.1972) (amendment naming additional plaintiffs and adding new negligence claim after limitations period had run held to relate back to original claim for breach of warranty).

In connection with the joinder of new plaintiffs under Rule 15(c), consider the 1966 amendments to Federal Rule 17(a) and the Advisory Committee's comments, which appear in the Supplement. For a thorough discussion of the interrelation between Rule 15(c) and Rule 17(a), see Unilever (Raw Materials) Ltd. v. M/T Stolt Boel, 77 F.R.D. 384 (S.D.N.Y.1977).

SECTION E. SUPPLEMENTAL PLEADINGS

Read Federal Rules of Civil Procedure 7(a) and 15(d) in the Supplement.

Notes and Questions

1. "The office of a supplemental complaint is to aid the cause of action already averred, not to enable the plaintiff to recover upon a cause of action which has accrued since the action was commenced." HALSTEAD v. HALSTEAD, 7 Misc. 23, 27 N.Y.S. 408 (C.P.1894). This passage was quoted with approval in Giglio v. Konold, 5 Ohio App.2d 250, 251, 214 N.E.2d 806, 808 (1965) (plaintiff cannot file supplemental complaint alleging defendants' refusal to obey trial court order pending appeal; proper step is to file new action for contempt). Cf. Wallace v. Hanover Ins. Co., 164 So.2d 111 (La.App.1964) (defendant cannot raise by supplemental pleading an affirmative defense of fraud when only defense relied upon in original answer was premature filing of claim). What reason, if any, is there for prohibiting a "new cause of action" in a supplemental pleading?

Compare the statement by the revisers of New York's supplemental pleadings statute, N.Y.C.P.L.R. 3025(b), which appears in the Supplement in conjunction with Federal Rule of Civil Procedure 15(d): "[This new section is] * * * intended to grant the widest possible discretion to the court in granting leave to serve supplemental pleadings and imposing terms, even if the pleader had no cause of action at the time of the original pleading but has subsequently acquired and stated one in a supplemental pleading." N.Y. Advisory Comm. on Practice & Procedure, *First Preliminary Rep.* 78 (1957). Taking its cue from the revisers' statement, the court in HERZOG v. HERZOG, 43 Misc.2d 1062, 252 N.Y.S.2d 704 (Sup.Ct.1964), permitted a wife suing for separation to add a cause of action for divorce based on alleged evidence that her husband had developed into an adulterer. The husband protested—unsuccessfully—that the supplemental complaint was being improperly used to obtain divorce jurisdiction over him in a suit that had begun as a simple separation action. Wasn't the court clearly unfair to Mr. Herzog? Does the New York rule go too far? The New York provision is further analyzed in 3 Weinstein, Korn & Miller, *New York Civil Practice* ¶¶ 3025.12, 3025.17–.25. The lower federal courts appear to be favoring the New York position. See, e.g., Vernay Laboratories, Inc. v. Industrial Electronic Rubber Co., 234 F.Supp. 161, 166–67 (N.D.Ohio 1964) (Federal Rule 15(d) permits additional infringement claims based on newer patent nearly identical to original patent). But see General Bronze Corp. v. Cupples Prods. Corp., 9 F.R.D. 269 (E.D.Mo.1949).

2. Suppose, rather than adding supplemental facts setting out a "new cause of action" to an already validly stated claim, a party seeks instead to add supplemental facts without which the original pleading is defective. Are the considerations relevant to the two situations the same? Federal Rule 15(d) provides that a supplemental pleading *may* be allowed "even though the original pleading is defective in its statement of a claim for relief or defense." Until 1963, when this provision was added, the federal courts were split as to whether curative supplemental pleadings should ever be allowed. Compare La Salle Nat. Bank v. 222 East Chestnut St. Corp., 267 F.2d 247, 252–53 (7th Cir.), certiorari denied 361 U.S. 836, 80 S.Ct. 88, 4 L.Ed.2d 77 (1959), with Friedman Elec. Co. v. Typhoon Air Conditioning Co., 31 F.R.D. 287, 290 (E.D. N.Y.1962). Under what circumstances should a court deny leave to supplement a defective pleading? What relation, if any, does the 1963 amendment

to Rule 15(d) have to the new-cause-of-action problem? See generally 6 Wright & Miller, *Federal Practice and Procedure: Civil* § 1505 (1971); 3 Moore, *Federal Practice* ¶ 15.16[2]–[3] (2d ed.).

3. "Although supplemental pleadings are treated in most respects as are amended pleadings, they are not permitted to relate back * * *." Note, *Federal Rule 15(c) and the Doctrine of Substantive Conformity*, 59 Colum.L. Rev. 648, 653–54 (1959). Why not? Consider, for example, the following case. On June 10, 1962, A files suit against B alleging that 10 days earlier A had supplied materials to B for which A had not yet paid. The action is based on a statute that stipulates that suit can be brought only after 90 days have elapsed since the date the materials were furnished; B moves to dismiss for lack of jurisdiction. A now seeks, on October 18, 1963, to file a supplemental complaint alleging that more than 90 days have elapsed and that B still has not paid. However, the statute also provides that no suit can be commenced after the expiration of one year after the day on which the materials were supplied. What argument would you make for A? For B?

————

In SECURITY INS. CO. v. UNITED STATES FOR THE USE OF HAY-DIS, 338 F.2d 444, 445–46, 449 (9th Cir.1964), the court declared:

> Appellant's argument, in substance, is this: When the complaint was filed the plaintiff had no claim for relief because the ninety-day period * * * had not expired. When the supplement to the complaint was filed, more than one year from the pertinent date had expired. A supplemental complaint alleges new matter; therefore its allegations, unlike those of an amended complaint, or of an amendment to a complaint, do not relate back so as to remove the bar of the statute of limitations. Hence the action was barred by the one year limitation * * *. Moreover, say appellants, if the allegations of the supplemental complaint can be said to relate back, then under Rule 15(c), F.R.Civ.P. they must relate back to the time when the action was filed and at that time the plaintiff had no claim for relief. Consequently, the court was and remains without jurisdiction.

> Nothing but the most compelling authority * * * would induce us to stay on this legal merry-go-round.

> * * * [R]egardless of whether the supplement to the complaint filed in the present action be considered an amendment to the complaint or a supplemental complaint, we think that the doctrine of relation back can properly be applied to prevent the one-year provision of subdivision (b) from barring the action, but that we are not required to apply the doctrine of relation back so literally as to carry it to a time within the ninety-day period specified in subdivision (a), so as to prevent the maintenance of the action in the first place.

> If the supplement to the complaint be treated as filed under Rule 15(d), we can apply the doctrine of relation back, even though that rule does not mention it * * *. If it be treated as an amendment, to which Rule 15(c) applies, then * * * [we should not] apply Rule 15(c) so literally as to defeat a decision on the merits.

Contra, Walton v. Kern County, 39 Cal.App.2d 32, 102 P.2d 531 (4th Dist. 1940).

SECTION F. PROVISIONS TO ENSURE TRUTHFUL ALLEGATIONS

Read Federal Rules of Civil Procedure 11 and 23.1 and related materials in the Supplement.

SUROWITZ v. HILTON HOTELS CORP.

Supreme Court of the United States, 1966.
383 U.S. 363, 86 S.Ct. 845, 15 L.Ed.2d 807.

Certiorari to the United States Court of Appeals for the Seventh Circuit.

MR. JUSTICE BLACK delivered the opinion of the Court.

Petitioner, Dora Surowitz, a stockholder in Hilton Hotels Corporation, brought this action in a United States District Court on behalf of herself and other stockholders charging that the officers and directors of the corporation had defrauded it of several million dollars by illegal devices and schemes designed to cheat the corporation and enrich the individual defendants. The acts charged, if true, would constitute frauds of the grossest kind against the corporation, and would be in violation of the Securities Act of 1933, the Securities Exchange Act of 1934, and the Delaware General Corporation Law. * * * The [detailed] complaint [containing more than 60 printed pages] was signed by counsel for Mrs. Surowitz in compliance with Rule 11 of the Federal Rules of Civil Procedure which provides that "The signature of an attorney constitutes a certificate by him that he has read the pleading; that to the best of his knowledge, information, and belief there is good ground to support it; and that it is not interposed for delay." [a] Also pursuant to Rule 23(b) [now Rule 23.1] of the Federal Rules, the complaint was verified by Mrs. Surowitz, the petitioner, who stated that some of the allegations in the complaint were true and that she "on information and belief" thought that all the other allegations were true.

So far as the language of the complaint and of Mrs. Surowitz's verification was concerned, both were in strict compliance with the provisions of Rule 23(b) which states that a shareholder's complaint in a secondary action must contain certain averments and be verified by the plaintiff. Notwithstanding the sufficiency of the complaint and verification under Rule 23(b), however, the court, without requiring defendants to file an answer and over petitioner's protest, granted defendants' motion to require Mrs. Surowitz to submit herself to an oral examination by the defendants' counsel. In this examination Mrs. Surowitz showed in her answers to questions that she did not understand the complaint at all, that she could not explain the statements made in the complaint, that she

---

a. The quoted language is from Rule 11 prior to its revision in 1983.

had a very small degree of knowledge as to what the lawsuit was about, that she did not know any of the defendants by name, that she did not know the nature of their alleged misconduct, and in fact that in signing the verification she had merely relied on what her son-in-law had explained to her about the facts in the case. On the basis of this examination, defendants moved to dismiss the complaint, alleging that "1. It is a sham pleading, and 2. Plaintiff, Dora Surowitz, is not a proper party plaintiff. * * *" In response, Mrs. Surowitz's lawyer, in an effort to cure whatever infirmity the court might possibly find in Mrs. Surowitz's verification in light of her deposition, filed two affidavits which shed much additional light on an extensive investigation which had preceded the filing of the complaint. Despite these affidavits the District Judge dismissed the case holding that Mrs. Surowitz's affidavit was "false," that being wholly false it was a nullity, that being a nullity it was as though no affidavit had been made in compliance with Rule 23, that being false the affidavit was a "sham" and Rule 23(b) required that he dismiss her case, and he did so, "with prejudice."

The Court of Appeals affirmed the District Court's dismissal * * * despite the fact that the charges made against the defendants were viewed as very serious and grave charges of fraud and that "many of the material allegations of the complaint are obviously true and cannot be refuted." 342 F.2d, at 607. We cannot agree with either of the courts below and reverse their judgments. * * *

Mrs. Surowitz, the plaintiff and petitioner here, is a Polish immigrant with a very limited English vocabulary and practically no formal education. For many years she has worked as a seamstress in New York where by reason of frugality she saved enough money to buy some thousands of dollars worth of stocks. She was of course not able to select stocks for herself with any degree of assurance of their value. Under these circumstances she had to receive advice and counsel and quite naturally she went to her son-in-law, Irving Brilliant. Mr. Brilliant had graduated from the Harvard Law School, possessed a master's degree in economics from Columbia University, was a professional investment advisor, and in addition to his degrees and his financial acumen, he wore a Phi Beta Kappa key. In 1957, six years before this litigation began, he bought some stock for his mother-in-law in the Hilton Hotels Corporation, paying a little more than $2,000 of her own money for it. * * *

About December 1962, Mrs. Surowitz received through the mails a notice from the Hilton Hotels Corporation announcing its plan to purchase a large amount of its own stock. Because she wanted it explained to her, she took the notice to Mr. Brilliant. Apparently disturbed by it, he straightway set out to make an investigation. Shortly thereafter he went to Chicago, Illinois, where Hilton Hotels has its home office and talked the matter over with Mr. Rockler. Mr. Brilliant and Mr. Rockler had been friends for many years. * * * The two decided to investigate further, and for a number of months both pursued whatever avenues of information that were open to them. By August of 1963 on the basis of their investigation, both of them had reached the conclusion [that defendants were engaged in a fraudulent scheme, and Mr. Brilliant explained this to Mrs. Surowitz.]   *   *   *

  *   *   * When, on the basis of this conversation, Mrs. Surowitz stated that she agreed that suit be filed in her name, Mr. Rockler prepared a formal complaint which he mailed to Mr. Brilliant. Mr. Brilliant then, according to both his affidavit and Mrs. Surowitz's testimony, read and explained the complaint to his mother-in-law before she verified it. Her limited education and her small knowledge about any of the English language, except the most ordinarily used words, probably is sufficient guarantee that the courts below were right in finding that she did not understand any of the legal relationships or comprehend any of the business transactions described in the complaint. She did know, however, that she had put over $2,000 of her hard-earned money into Hilton Hotels stock, that she was not getting her dividends, and that her son-in-law who had looked into the matter thought that something was wrong. She also knew that her son-in-law was qualified to help her and she trusted him. It is difficult to believe that anyone could be shocked or harmed in any way when, in the light of all these circumstances, Mrs. Surowitz verified the complaint, not on the basis of her own knowledge and understanding, but in the faith that her son-in-law had correctly advised her either that the statements in the complaint were true or to the best of his knowledge he believed them to be true.

  *   *   * Rule 23(b) was not written in order to bar derivative suits. Unquestionably it was originally adopted and has served since in part as a means to discourage "strike suits" by people who might be interested in getting quick dollars by making charges without regard to their truth so as to coerce corporate managers to settle worthless claims in order to get rid of them.   *   *   *

When the record of this case is reviewed in the light of the purpose of Rule 23(b)'s verification requirement, there emerges the plain, inescapable fact that this is not a strike suit or anything akin to it. Mrs. Surowitz was not interested in anything but her own investment made with her own money. Moreover, there is not one iota of evidence that Mr. Brilliant, her son-in-law and counselor, sought to do the corporation any injury in this litigation. In fact his purchases for the benefit of his family of more than $50,000 of securities in the corporation, including a $10,000 debenture, all made years before this suit was brought, manifest confidence in the corporation, not a desire to harm it in any way. The Court of Appeals in affirming the District Court's dismissal, however, indicated that whether Mrs. Surowitz and her counselors acted in good faith and whether the charges they made were truthful were irrelevant once Mrs. Surowitz demonstrated in her oral testimony that she knew nothing about the content of the suit.   *   *   *

We cannot construe Rule 23 or any other one of the Federal Rules as compelling courts to summarily dismiss, without any answer or argument at all, cases like this where grave charges of fraud are shown by the record to be based on reasonable beliefs growing out of careful investigation. The basic purpose of the Federal Rules is to administer justice through fair trials, not through summary dismissals as necessary as they may be on occasion. These rules were designed in large part to get away from some of the old procedural booby traps which common-law pleaders could set to prevent unsophisticated litigants from ever having their day in court. If rules of procedure work as they should in an honest and fair judicial system, they not only permit, but should as nearly as possible guarantee that bona fide complaints be carried to an adjudication on the merits. Rule 23(b), like the other civil rules, was written to further, not defeat the ends of justice. The serious fraud charged here, which of course has not been proven, is clearly in that class of deceitful conduct which the federal securities laws were largely passed to prohibit and protect against. There is, moreover, not one word or one line of actual evidence in this record indicating that there has been any collusive conduct or trickery by those who filed this suit except through intimations and insinuations without any support from anything any witness has said. The dismissal of this case was error. It has now been practically three years since the complaint was filed and as yet none of the defendants have even been compelled to admit or deny the wrongdoings charged. They should be. The cause is reversed and remanded to the District Court for trial on the merits.

Reversed and remanded.

MR. JUSTICE HARLAN, concurring.

Rule 23(b) directs that in a derivative suit "the complaint shall be verified by oath" but nothing dictates that the verification be that of the plaintiff shareholder. * * * In the present circumstances, it seems to me the affidavit of Walter J. Rockler, counsel for Mrs. Surowitz, amounts to an adequate verification by counsel, which I think is permitted by a reasonable interpretation of the Rule at least in cases such as this. On this premise, I agree with the decision of the Court.

Notes and Questions

1. Compare Roussel v. Tidelands Capital Corp., 438 F.Supp. 684, 688 (N.D.Ala.1977), reaffirming the dismissal of an action under Rule 23.1, because, among other things, plaintiff admitted he verified the pleading without reading it, and thus had demonstrated he was not likely to represent the shareholders fairly and adequately. Why is a dismissal ever an appropriate way of enforcing the verification provision of Rule 23.1? Shouldn't plaintiff be prosecuted for the crime of perjury instead? Of what significance is it that any recovery in a suit under Rule 23.1 goes directly to the corporation, not to plaintiff? Suppose the statute of limitations on the claim runs just before the dismissal. What additional problems would this raise?

2. Why does Rule 23.1 require verification? Why doesn't the Rule 11 procedure suffice? In those state courts in which fact pleadings generally do not have to be verified, there are certain exceptions. Some of the typical ones found in state practice are: petitions for divorce (Iowa Code Ann. § 598.7; Kan.Stat.Ann. § 60–1604(a); Okl.Stat.Ann. tit. 12, § 1273), petitions brought by the state to enjoin a nuisance (Okl.Stat.Ann. tit. 12, § 1397), and com-

plaints to obtain support of an illegitimate child (Iowa Code Ann. § 675.13). What makes these actions sufficiently distinctive to require verification?

3. To what extent should a plaintiff or defendant be excused from a verification requirement if an admission of truth might subject him to criminal prosecution? See S.C.Code, 1976, § 15–13–50 (verification excused). If no excuse is allowed, should the prosecution be barred from using the verified pleading as evidence? See DeCamp v. First Kensington Corp., 83 Cal. App.3d 268, 147 Cal.Rptr. 869 (2d Dist.1978) (prosecution barred from use of pleading and all information obtained as a result of reading it).

———

Lenient pleading rules such as those embodied in the Federal Rules and comparable state systems provide an opportunity for abuse. For example, is it appropriate for a party to institute a colorable claim with the sole intention of pressuring another party into settling? Or would it be right for a party who has been sued on a legitimate claim to interpose a counterclaim on a questionable legal theory—simply to induce the plaintiff to drop the suit?

Rule 11 (in both its 1983 form and its earlier incarnation) attempts to curb abuse of the federal pleading rules by imposing affirmative duties on attorneys and by raising the possibility of sanctions for failure to discharge them. As is clear from *Surowitz,* the pre-1983 incarnation of Rule 11 employed a subjective standard to judge attorney conduct—so long as attorneys acted in good faith, they were not subject to sanctions if it later became clear that their legal theory was faulty or that the facts did not support their claims.

Unfortunately, this pre-1983 version of Rule 11 did not work the way its framers intended—indeed, it was largely ignored, widely perceived as ineffectual, and rarely used. One study reveals that, between 1938 and 1976, there were only 23 reported cases in which a party invoked Rule 11 to strike a pleading and only nine cases in which violations were found. Risinger, *Honesty in Pleading and its Enforcement: Some "Striking" Problems with Federal Rule of Civil Procedure 11,* 61 Minn.L.Rev. 1 (1976). Consequently, the Rule was modified in 1983.

EASTWAY CONSTRUCTION CORP. v. CITY OF NEW YORK

United States Court of Appeals, Second Circuit, 1985.
762 F.2d 243.

[Eastway, a general contractor, was precluded from working on various housing reconstruction projects sponsored by the City of New York— on the ground that Eastway was an irresponsible contractor, its principals having defaulted previously on nearly eight million dollars of non-recourse loans the City made to finance the rehabilitation of apartment buildings in depressed neighborhoods. After negotiations with the City failed, Eastway brought a special proceeding against the City, but the state court held that the City's refusal to deal with Eastway was a proper exercise of its discretion. Eastway then sued the City and others in federal court, alleging violations of federal antitrust and civil rights statutes. The District Court granted the defendants' motion for summary judgment, "finding that there was not 'any basis for a civil rights claim,' and that 'the affidavits and other supporting data [do not] show any violation of the antitrust laws. * * *' [T]he most that has been shown * * * is a possible commercial tort which can be adjudicated in the state courts. * * *" 762 F.2d at 248. But the court denied the defendants' further request for attorney's fees as a sanction for Eastway having brought a frivolous action. In the court's view, the case was not frivolous.

The Second Circuit held that both the civil rights claim and the antitrust claim were properly dismissed, and indicated that they could just as easily have been dismissed pursuant to Rule 12(b)(6). The Court of Appeals then took up the City's cross-appeal from the portion of the District Court order denying it attorney's fees. The court ruled that the City was entitled under 42 U.S.C. § 1988 to recover the fees it incurred in defending against Eastway's civil rights claim. It then turned to the City's claim pursuant to Rule 11 to recover the attorney's fees it incurred in defending against Eastway's antitrust claim.]

IRVING R. KAUFMAN, CIRCUIT JUDGE.

* * *

The language of [Rule 11] which was amended in 1983, provides a striking contrast to the words of its predecessor. Prior to the 1983 amendment, the rule spoke in plainly subjective terms: An attorney's certification of a pleading was an assertion that "to the best of his knowledge, information, and belief, there [was] good ground to support it." The rule, therefore, contemplated sanctions only where there was a showing of bad faith * * * and the only proper inquiry was the subjective belief of the attorney at the time the pleading was signed.

The addition of the words "formed after a reasonable inquiry" demand that we revise our inquiry. * * * No longer is it enough for an attorney to claim that he acted in good faith, or that he personally was unaware of the groundless nature of an argument or claim. For the language of the new Rule 11 explicitly and unambiguously imposes an affirmative duty on each attorney to conduct a reasonable inquiry into the viability of a pleading before it is signed. Simply put, subjective good faith no longer provides the safe harbor it once did.

The notes of the Advisory Committee on Rules appear to support this expanded reading of the rule. The Committee was frank in admitting that, "in practice Rule 11 has not been effective in deterring abuses." * * * Thus, the drafters speak of the amended rule as an attempt to "build[ ] upon and expand[ ]" the equitable doctrine. To this end, they state, the new language is "intended to reduce the reluctance of courts to impose sanctions . . . *by emphasizing the responsibilities of the attorney*" (emphasis added). Finally, the drafters make absolutely clear that the standard is more stringent than the original good faith formula. * * *

In light of the express intent of the drafters of the new Rule 11, and the clear policy concerns underlying its amendment, we hold that a showing of subjective bad faith is no longer required to trigger the sanctions imposed by the rule. Rather, sanctions shall be imposed [7] against an attorney and/or his client when it appears that a pleading has been interposed for any improper purpose, *or where,* after reasonable inquiry, a competent attorney could not form a reasonable belief that the pleading is well grounded in fact and is warranted by existing law or a good faith argument for the extension, modification or reversal of existing law.

In framing this standard, we do not intend to stifle the enthusiasm or chill the creativity that is the very lifeblood of the law. Vital changes have been wrought by those members of the bar who have dared to challenge the received wisdom, and a rule that penalized such innovation and industry would run counter to our notions of the common law itself. Courts must strive to avoid the wisdom of hindsight in determining whether a pleading was valid when signed, and any and all doubts must be resolved in favor of the signer. But where it is patently clear that a claim has absolutely no chance of success under the existing precedents, and where no reasonable argument can be advanced to extend, modify or reverse the law as it stands, Rule 11 has been violated. Such a construction serves to punish only those who would manipulate the federal court system for ends inimicable to those for which it was created.   *   *   *

Returning to the facts of this appeal, we cannot say for a certainty that Eastway or its counsel acted in subjective bad faith in bringing or maintaining this lawsuit, or that its actual motive was to harass the City. After its travails of the preceding decade, it might just as well have been acting out of frustration or desperation. We can say, however, that its claim of an antitrust violation by non-competitors, without any allegation of an antitrust injury, was destined to fail. Moreover, a competent attorney, after reasonable inquiry, would have had to reach the same conclusion.

Accordingly, we hold that it was error for the district court to deny the municipal defendants' motion for attorneys' fees incurred in defending against the antitrust claim. On remand, the district court shall impose appropriate sanctions against the appellants-cross-appellees, their counsel or both, which shall include an order to pay the municipal defendants the amount of the reasonable expenses incurred by them in defending the antitrust claim, including a reasonable attorney's fee.

7. By employing the imperative "shall," we believe the drafters intended to stress the mandatory nature of the imposition of sanctions pursuant to the rule. Unlike the statutory provisions that vest the district court with "discretion" to award fees, Rule 11 is clearly phrased as a directive. Accordingly, where strictures of the rule have been transgressed, it is incumbent upon the district court to fashion proper sanctions.

A natural concomitant of a mandatory imposition of sanctions is a broadened scope of review by the Court of Appeals. Where the only question on appeal becomes whether, in fact, a pleading was groundless, we are in as good a position to determine the answer and, thus, we need not defer to the lower court's opinion.

At the same time, however, we note that the district courts retain broad discretion in fashioning sanctions, and apportioning fees between attorney and client. The commentary to Rule 11 sets forth a number of the factors that will be examined in arriving at an appropriate award, and in determining by whom any costs will be borne. In reviewing the specifics of an award of attorneys' fees, therefore, we shall continue to adhere to the "abuse of discretion" standard.

* * *

Notes and Questions

1.   On remand, the District Court in *Eastway* determined that $52,912.50 represented "reasonable attorney's fees."   Nonetheless it ordered a sanction of only $1000, explaining that

> heavy sanctions would be unfair because *Eastway I* is a case of first impression; there was no reason for plaintiffs or their counsel to have predicted the objective standard Rule 11 ruling of the Court of Appeals. In addition, because the case was brought in good faith, because of the otherwise exemplary conduct of plaintiff's counsel, because the pleading was only marginally frivolous, and for other reasons set forth in this opinion, attorney's fees in the amount of $1000 * * * are sufficiently punitive.

Eastway Construction Corp. v. City of New York, 637 F.Supp. 558, 584 (E.D. N.Y.1986).

The City of New York appealed this award, and the Second Circuit in *Eastway II* raised the amount of the sanction to $10,000, explaining:

> We have concluded that the award [$1000] falls below even the range within which a district judge may exercise his considerable discretion in such matters, and we therefore modify the award to the amount at the lower limit of the range appropriate for this case, $10,000.

Eastway Construction Corp. v. City of New York, 821 F.2d 121, 122 (2d Cir. 1987).   In his dissent, Judge Pratt identified the heart of the controversy:

> As intimated in the majority opinion, I do not agree that the amount of "a reasonable attorney's fee" imposed as a sanction under Rule 11 should be measured by the severity of an adversary's misconduct. * * * We should end the misleading practice of justifying what are in reality punitive fines by pretending that they represent attorney's fees.
>
> * * * [M]any courts, our own included, have over the years imposed sanctions of varying amounts under the rubric of "reasonable attorney's fees", but without any pretense at determining what compensation for the attorney of the wronged party would be reasonable.   However tolerable that kind of approach may have been in former years when sanctions were relatively uncommon, I think it now not only disserves both the language and intent of the amended Rule 11, but also perpetuates disparities in sanctions, encourages arbitrariness in the day-to-day operations of some of our district courts, and runs counter to logic.
>
> In reaching what is essentially a policy-based decision, the majority leans heavily on the punitive aspect of Rule 11 sanctions and the need for judicial discretion in calibrating the severity of a penalty; in doing so, however, the majority neglects the second purpose of Rule 11: to provide restitution to the victim of the sanctioned conduct.

Id. at 124.   Judge Pratt suggested that "reasonable attorney's fees," in the absence of special circumstances such as an inability to pay that would make the award unjust, should be calculated with reference to the actual cost burden inflicted upon the moving party by the violator's misconduct.

Should the sanctioned party's ability to pay be a consideration in determining the proper monetary sanctions? See Heimbaugh v. City and County of San Francisco, 591 F.Supp. 1573 (N.D.Cal.1984). Should the amount of the sanction be adjusted if the court determines that the attorney acted with subjective bad faith?

While the usual sanction under Rule 11 is a monetary penalty, courts have imposed other kinds of sanctions, including requiring the errant attorney to circulate the court's opinion finding him in violation of Rule 11 to every member of his firm, Huettig & Schromm, Inc. v. Landscape Contractors Council, 582 F.Supp. 1519 (N.D.Cal.1984), affirmed 790 F.2d 1421 (9th Cir. 1986); suspension or disbarment from practice, In re Disciplinary Action Curl, 803 F.2d 1004 (9th Cir.1986); or judicial reprimands in open court or through publication of a critical opinion.

2. In *Eastway I,* Judge Kaufman highlights the change from the subjective standard of the old Rule 11 to the objective standard of the new Rule 11:

> [S]anctions shall be imposed against an attorney and/or his client when it appears that a pleading has been interposed for any improper purpose, *or where,* after reasonable inquiry, a competent attorney could not form a reasonable belief that the pleading is well grounded in fact and is warranted by existing law or a good faith argument for the extension, modification or reversal of existing law.

762 F.2d at 254. Is this disjunctive reading of Rule 11 consistent with the language of the rule?

After outlining the objective standard, Judge Kaufman adds: "Such a construction serves to punish only those who would manipulate the federal court system for ends inimicable to those for which it was created." Id. Does the goal of punishing manipulators reflect a return to a subjective standard? In actuality, is the new Rule 11, which involves inherently subjective factors such as a reasonable inquiry into the facts and law and a proper purpose, any more objective than its predecessor?

3. Has an attorney made a reasonable inquiry into the underlying facts if she relies on her client's version of the facts? Is a client, the "represented party," held to the same standards of reasonable inquiry and proper purpose as the "signer"?

What is expected of an attorney who files a complaint when most of the evidence is in the defendant's possession? Does Rule 11 undermine the discovery process, which occurs after the initial papers have been filed and the purpose of which is to uncover evidence?

Should the amount of time available to the attorney before the statute of limitations expires bear on whether his factual inquiry was sufficient? What if the shortage of time was created by the attorney's own procrastination?

4. If a case can be dismissed under Rule 12(b)(6) as in *Eastway,* is this per se a violation of Rule 11 for failure to make a "reasonable inquiry" into the underlying facts? To satisfy Rule 11, must the parties state the facts in the pleadings, a requirement that would be at apparent cross-purposes with Rule 8(a), which merely requires "a short and plain statement"? Or is it enough merely to have the facts available on file? Should it be sufficient merely to establish that one has "inquired" about the facts?

5. How extensive an inquiry into the law underlying a cause of action must an attorney undertake to satisfy the Rule's requirement that the claim is "warranted by existing law"? The District Court in GOLDEN EAGLE DISTRIBUTING CORP. v. BURROUGHS CORP., 103 F.R.D. 124 (N.D.Cal. 1984), reversed 801 F.2d 1531 (9th Cir.1986), examined the Model Rules of Professional Conduct and explained that:

> A court has a right to expect that counsel will state the controlling law fairly and fully; indeed, unless that is done the court cannot perform its task properly. A lawyer must not misstate the law, fail to disclose adverse authority (not disclosed by his opponent), or omit facts critical to the application of the rule of law relied on.

Id. at 127.

In *Golden Eagle*, the plaintiff's counsel had cited a 1965 California Supreme Court case supporting its argument and had not cited a 1979 California Supreme Court opinion that was inconsistent with the 1965 case. Counsel distinguished the later case in its reply brief after it had been cited by the opposition, arguing that the 1965 case had not been overruled. Counsel did not address two intermediate court opinions that discussed the effect of the 1979 opinion on the 1965 opinion.

The District Court held that Rule 11 sanctions were appropriate for failure to cite adverse authority. The court noted that "as early as February 1984, Shepard lists [one of the intermediate court cases] under [the 1965 case] as 'distinguished'" and suggested that therefore counsel should have been aware of the case and should have cited it as adverse authority.

On appeal, the Ninth Circuit unanimously reversed. The Circuit Court conceded that new Rule 11 was designed to create an affirmative duty of investigation, both as to law and as to fact, before motions are filed. But the court went on to say that, in order to avoid chilling creativity in advocacy, courts should be careful not to hold lawyers to a standard measured by what the judge later decides. Rather, courts should measure the lawyer's performance by an objective standard, applied as of the time the lawyer was making the decision in question.

The Ninth Circuit panel opined that the objective inquiry authorized by Rule 11 does not empower district courts to assess the manner in which motions are presented. The appellate court did not quarrel with the District Court's "salutary admonitions against misstatements of the law, failure to disclose directly adverse authority, or omission of critical facts." 801 F.2d at 1539. But it concluded that Rule 11 does not envision an evaluation under ethical standards of the accuracy of a lawyer's arguments. Therefore, it reversed the imposition of Rule 11 sanctions for unethical conduct.

Is the rule promulgated by the District Court or the one promulgated by the Court of Appeals more consistent with the purposes of amended Rule 11?

6. May an attorney rely on the results of research undertaken by local counsel in an action? May an attorney rely on the results of research completed by another attorney in his own firm? See Pravic v. U.S. Industries—Clearing, 109 F.R.D. 620 (E.D.Mich.1986), in which the court imposed sanctions upon defense counsel for relying upon a memorandum of law produced by the attorney for a codefendant, stating:

* * * an attorney may not rely on a legal memorandum prepared by a second lawyer without independently verifying the reasoning of the cases cited in the memorandum and without "Shepardizing" the cases cited in the memorandum.

Id. at 623.

See also Long v. Quantex Resources, Inc., 108 F.R.D. 416 (S.D.N.Y.1985), in which sanctions were imposed on local counsel who signed papers prepared by primary counsel in a foreign jurisdiction when the local counsel withdrew the motion "in the eleventh hour," as oral arguments were about to commence.

7.   The rulemakers attempted to encourage creative advocacy by protecting from sanctions an attorney who made "a good faith argument for the extension, modification, or reversal of existing law." As the court in STORAGE TECHNOLOGY PARTNERS II v. STORAGE TECHNOLOGY CORP., 117 F.R.D. 675 (D.Colo.1987), explains, however:

[This provision] taints Rule 11 with a hue that makes judicial consideration of the provision particularly difficult. This is because different standards inevitably will govern diverse areas of the law. More open textured issues—such as constitutional questions—will be subjected to a less rigorous examination under this test than, for example, a closely knit and specific statutory scheme, such as the Bankruptcy Code.

Id. at 678. Is the court correct that the "hue" now built into Rule 11 is undesirable? As Professor Vairo has noted: "In a lot of areas, what was thought of as completely frivolous 20 years ago is now well-accepted law. * * * What would the courts have thought of a school desegregation suit 20 years before Brown v. Board of Education? It probably would have been considered completely frivolous." In the end, are we penalizing litigants and attorneys who choose to fight uphill battles?

8.   A paper may not be submitted for any "improper purpose, such as to harass or to cause unnecessary delay or needless increase in the cost of litigation." What purposes, in addition to the examples provided in the Rule, violate Rule 11?

Suppose a plaintiff included frivolous federal claims in a complaint containing valid state claims in order to fall within the jurisdiction of federal court. Is this forum shopping an "improper purpose" or is it the aggressive pursuit of all possible means of reaching the best result for a client? See Coast Mfg. Co. v. Keylon, 600 F.Supp. 696 (S.D.N.Y.1985).

Consider the following case:

Plaintiffs bring a wrongful death action in federal court. Under Texas law, every beneficiary provided for by the Texas Wrongful Death Statute must be a party to an action based on the statute, or the action must be dismissed. A decedent's children are covered under this statute.

Plaintiffs are the children of the decedent from his second marriage. Defendant files a motion to dismiss for failure to join the decedent's children from his first marriage as plaintiffs. Plaintiffs file a response to this motion, explaining that they had obtained a waiver from decedent's first wife waiving her children's rights under the statute.

Defendant learns through discovery that the decedent's first wife had signed an agreement with the plaintiffs under which her children would receive 27½% of the plaintiff's recovery as consideration for having signed the waiver. Defendant files a Rule 11 motion claiming that the response to the motion to dismiss had been filed for an improper purpose since the disclaimer had been obtained by plaintiffs in order to preserve the federal court's diversity jurisdiction. Complete diversity would have been destroyed if the children from the first marriage had been joined as plaintiffs. Should the Rule 11 motion be granted? See Hearld v. Barnes & Spectrum Emergency Care, 107 F.R.D. 17 (E.D.Tex.1985).

9. Does Rule 11 authorize a court to impose sanctions on an attorney who fails to withdraw a complaint that was colorable at the time the complaint was filed, but which has become frivolous in light of evidence disclosed during discovery? Which answer to this question is consistent with the language of the Rule? With the Advisory Committee Notes? With the purposes of Rule 11? See Note, *Rule 11 of the Federal Rules of Civil Procedure and the Duty to Withdraw a Baseless Pleading*, 56 Fordham L.Rev. 697 (1988).

10. Since its revision in 1983, Rule 11 has been the subject of extensive collateral litigation and continuing debate. For further analyses of the issues, see Schwarzer, *Rule 11 Revisited*, 101 Harv.L.Rev. 1013 (1988); Untereiner, *A Uniform Approach to Rule 11 Sanctions*, 97 Yale L.J. 901 (1988); Vairo, *Rule 11: A Critical Analysis*, 118 F.R.D. 189 (1988); Federal Procedure Committee, Litigation Section, American Bar Association, *Sanctions: Rule 11 and Other Powers* (2d ed. 1988); Nelken, *Sanctions Under Amended Federal Rule 11— Some "Chilling" Problems in the Struggle Between Compensation and Punishment*, 74 Geo.L.J. 1313 (1986); Schwarzer, *Sanctions Under the New Rule 11— A Closer Look*, 104 F.R.D. 181 (1985).

11. Rule 11 is not the only sanctioning provision available to the courts. The most notable additional provision is 28 U.S.C. § 1927, which gives courts authority to impose excess costs against attorneys who have "unreasonably and vexatiously" increased the costs of litigation by "multipl[ying] the proceeding." However, because the statute requires a determination of bad faith, it rarely is invoked. See Kiefel v. Las Vegas Hacienda, Inc., 404 F.2d 1163, 1167 (7th Cir.1968), certiorari denied 395 U.S. 908, 89 S.Ct. 1750, 23 L.Ed.2d 221 (1969) (§ 1927 applies only to a "serious and studied disregard for the orderly processes of justice"). Other statutes authorize courts in specific kinds of actions to award attorney's fees to a prevailing defendant if the plaintiff's claim is frivolous, unreasonable, or groundless. See, for example, § 706(k) of Title VII of the Civil Rights Act of 1964, 42 U.S.C. § 2000e–g(k) (1982), for employment discrimination actions. See also Christiansburg Garment Co. v. EEOC, 434 U.S. 412, 98 S.Ct. 694, 54 L.Ed.2d 648 (1978).

Chapter 6

JOINDER OF CLAIMS AND PARTIES: EXPANDING THE SCOPE OF THE CIVIL ACTION

In its simplest form, the paradigm of a lawsuit has a single plaintiff asserting a single cause of action against a single defendant. Although the equity courts were more flexible, the common-law courts, with their emphasis on the unitary civil action, rarely deviated from this model and developed rules relating to joinder along strict and formalistic lines. See generally Blume, *A Rational Theory for Joinder of Causes of Action and Defences, and for the Use of Counterclaims*, 26 Mich.L.Rev. 1 (1927); Sunderland, *Joinder of Actions*, 18 Mich.L.Rev. 571 (1920). As the complexity of society increased and more intricate disputes were generated, the need for obviating piecemeal litigation became widely recognized. The most obvious method of accomplishing this objective was by expanding the scope of civil actions by permitting the joinder of claims and parties. This Chapter will explore the various forms that this expansion has taken.

SECTION A. JOINDER OF CLAIMS

HARRIS v. AVERY

Supreme Court of Kansas, 1869.
5 Kan. 146.

VALENTINE, J. This action was brought in the court below by Avery * * *. The petition states two causes of action,—false imprisonment and slander,—and alleges that both arose out of the same transaction. Harris demurred to this petition, on the ground "that it appears on the face of the petition that several causes of action are improperly joined." The district court overruled the demurrer, and this ruling is assigned as error. The petition shows that the two causes of action are founded upon the following facts: Harris met Avery in the city of Fort Scott, and, in the presence of several other persons, called Avery a thief; said he had a stolen horse; took the horse from Avery, and kept the horse for four or five days; arrested Avery, and confined him in the county jail with felons four or five days. We think these facts, as detailed in the petition, constitute only one transaction, * * * and whether they constitute more than one cause of action, under our Code practice, may be questionable. * * * But as we have not been asked to decide the latter question, we will pass it over and treat the case as though the facts stated constitute two causes of action.

Section 89 of the Code (Comp.Laws, 138,) provides "that the plaintiff may unite several causes of action in the same petition, whether they be such as have heretofore been denominated legal or equitable, or both, when they are included in either one of the following classes: First, *the same transaction* or transactions connected with the same subject of action." This differs in many respects from the common-law rule. At common law, "where the same form of action may be adopted for several distinct injuries, the plaintiff may, in general, proceed for all in one action, though the several rights affected were derived from different titles," (1 Chit.Pl. 201; Tidd, Pr. 11;) and different forms of action may be united, "where the same plea may be pleaded and the same judgment given on all the counts of the declaration, or whenever the counts are of the same nature, and the same judgment is to be given on them, although the pleas be different." 1 Chit.Pl. 200.

In the action at bar, if Harris had arrested Avery on a warrant, which Harris had maliciously and without probable cause obtained from a court of competent jurisdiction, and had also converted the horse to his own use, then at common law Avery would have had three distinct causes of action, which he could unite in one suit: *First,* an action for the false imprisonment or malicious prosecution; *second,* an action of slander for the words spoken; and, *third,* an action of trover for the conversion of the horse. These may all be united in an action on the case, * * * trover being a species of case. Avery might, also, at common law unite with these causes of action as many other causes of action as he might have, for malicious prosecution, slander, trover, criminal conversation, nuisance, and other causes of action which may be sued in an action on the case, and although they each may have arisen out of a different transaction, and at a different time, and in a different place. But if Harris arrested Avery without any process—which was the fact in this case—and in an entirely irregular manner, then the two causes of action for false imprisonment and slander could not at common law be united, as the first would have to be sued in an action of trespass and the second in an action on the case, and it would make no difference whether they both arose out of the same transaction or not. Our Code has abolished all the common-law forms of action * * *. It follows the rules of equity more closely than it does those of the common law, one object seeming to be to avoid the multiplicity of suits, and to settle in one action, as equity did, as far as practicable, the whole subject-matter of a controversy. * * * It is probably true that the two causes of action for false imprisonment and slander cannot, under our Code, be united, unless both arise out of the same transaction, one being an injury to the person and the other being an injury to the character; but we do not know of any reason why they should not be united when both do arise out of the same transaction. * * *

The order of the district court overruling the demurrer to the petition is affirmed.

Notes and Questions

1. The typical code provision authorized joinder of claims when they fell within one of several statutory classes, which generally included the following:

(a) Contracts, express or implied;

(b) Injuries to the person;

(c) Injuries to character;

(d) Injuries to property;

(e) Actions to recover real property, with or without damages;

(f) Actions to recover chattels, with or without damages; and

(g) Actions arising out of the same transaction or transactions connected with the same subject of the action.

In what ways do these categories differ from the use of the common-law forms of action as guidelines for the joinder of claims? What is the logic of each of these classes? Is the code approach to joinder of claims as described in *Harris* any less formalistic than the common-law theory? Joinder at common law and under the codes is discussed in Clark, *Code Pleading* §§ 68–70 (2d ed. 1947); Blume, *A Rational Theory for Joinder of Causes of Action and Defences, and for the Use of Counterclaims,* 26 Mich.L.Rev. 1 (1927).

2. Read Federal Rule 18. Note that it removes all obstacles to joinder of claims and permits the joinder of both legal and equitable actions; the only restriction on the claims that may be joined is imposed by subject-matter jurisdiction requirements. What are the advantages of permitting liberal joinder of claims? Are there any disadvantages? In SPORN v. HUDSON TRANSIT LINES, 265 App.Div. 360, 38 N.Y.S.2d 512 (1st Dep't 1942), the court had before it an attempt to join five causes of action for negligence resulting in personal injuries with one cause of action for malicious prosecution. It stated:

> The causes of action for negligence and for malicious prosecution are essentially different in nature; each type involves different rules of law; each requires different testimony to establish a case and each carries a different measure of damages. If a single jury were to try both types of action at the one time, there is a strong likelihood that confusion would exist in the minds of the jurors as to the rules of law to be applied to the respective actions and they would undoubtedly entertain much difficulty in applying the various parts of testimony introduced to the appropriate cause of action. There is nothing in common to be found in the two types of action.
>
> Moreover, it is clear that if these actions were tried together jurors might, quite naturally, engender a prejudice against the appellant in the negligence actions if the proof adduced in the malicious prosecution action were to show that, in causing the arrest of one of the respondents for reckless driving, there was, as alleged in the complaint, malice and want of probable cause. In such a situation it might well be that a jury would be unduly liberal in assessing damages under the causes of action

in negligence and that they might visit upon appellant in those actions damages which were punitive rather than compensatory.

> In the interest of justice, we think there should be a severance. * * * The avoidance of a multiplicity of suits is much to be desired, but where, as here, the enforcement of such a rule might entail prejudice to appellant's substantial rights and would tend to confuse the jury, the divergent causes of action should be severed.

Id. at 361–62, 38 N.Y.S.2d at 514. Would the result in *Sporn* have been different if the action had been brought in a federal court? Read Federal Rule 42. Does the availability of severance of claims eliminate all of the objections to permitting unrestricted joinder of claims as an initial matter? To what extent does the court's power to sever claims prevent the system from achieving the objectives of a liberal joinder rule?

3. Note that Federal Rule 18 only describes the claims that a plaintiff may assert against defendant; it does not require plaintiff to join claims in a single action. Should there be compulsory joinder of all related claims existing between the litigants? See Friedenthal, *Joinder of Claims, Counterclaims and Cross-Complaints: Suggested Revision of the California Provisions,* 23 Stan.L.Rev. 1, 11–17 (1970). Michigan's joinder provision, Michigan Court Rule 2.203(A), which is in the Supplement following Federal Rule 18, is unusual in that it provides for the compulsory joinder of certain claims. See generally Honigman & Hawkins, *Michigan Court Rules Annotated,* Rule 203, Author's Comment; Meisenholder, *Joinder of Claims and Parties—The New Michigan Pre-Trial Procedural Rules—Models For Other States?,* 61 Mich.L. Rev. 1389, 1417 (1963).

4. Even though the joinder of claims by plaintiffs in the federal courts is permissive, the principles of res judicata, which prohibit the splitting of a cause of action into two or more lawsuits, often have the effect of compelling plaintiff to join all related claims. See generally Blume, *Required Joinder of Claims,* 45 Mich.L.Rev. 797 (1947). Thus, for example, if A and B are involved in an automobile accident in which A suffers both bodily injury and damage to her automobile, the risk of res judicata typically will lead A to join both claims in one action, although Federal Rule 18 does not require her to do so. See pp. 1148–54, infra.

SECTION B.   ADDITION OF CLAIMS

1.   COUNTERCLAIMS

The counterclaim in its present form did not exist at common law, although it has well-recognized precursors in set-off and recoupment and in equity practice. The philosophy underlying set-off and recoupment was the common sense view that someone should not be compelled to pay one moment what he will be entitled to recover back the next. Judge Clark outlined the development and theory of set-off and recoupment as follows:

> * * * At first * * * [recoupment] was limited to a showing of payment, or of former recovery. Later, recoupment was developed so as to allow a defendant to show for the purpose of reducing the plaintiff's recovery any facts arising out of the transaction sued upon or connected with the subject thereof, which facts might have founded an independent

action in favor of the defendant against the plaintiff. * * * It was not necessary that the opposing claims be liquidated, or that they be of the same character; i.e., a claim in "tort" could be set off against one in "contract." It was essential, however, that the claims of both plaintiff and defendant involve the same "subject-matter," or arise out of the "same transaction" * * *.

But where the defendant's claims arose out of a transaction different from that sued upon, the common-law recoupment was unavailable. The defendant, therefore, was compelled to bring a separate suit in order to satisfy his claim against the plaintiff. Equity, at an early date, relieved the defendant of this hardship by allowing a set-off of claims [growing out of a transaction different from the plaintiff's claim] * * *.

Under the set-off * * *, it was necessary that the demands either be liquidated, or arise out of contract or judgment. It was necessary, also, that the demands be due the defendant in his own right against the plaintiff, or his assignor, and be not already barred by the statute of limitations * * *.

Clark, *Code Pleading* § 100, at 634–36 (2d ed. 1947). See also Waterman, *Set-Off, Recoupment and Counterclaim* §§ 302–03 (2d ed. 1872). The utility of the common-law recoupment and set-off practice was limited because in the former situation defendant was not permitted to recover affirmative relief; the claim could be used only to reduce or "net out" plaintiff's recovery. In the case of set-off the claim had to be for a liquidated amount.

The movement for procedural reform in the mid-nineteenth century gave passing attention to the problem of defendant's claims against plaintiff; the original New York Field Code of 1848 made no provision for counterclaims. Amendments in 1852 corrected this omission and permitted as a counterclaim:

1. A cause of action arising out of the contract or transaction set forth in the complaint, as the foundation of the plaintiff's claim, or connected with the subject of the action; and

2. In an action arising on contract, any other cause of action arising on contract, and existing at the commencement of the action.

See Blume, *A Rational Theory for Joinder of Causes of Action and Defences, and for the Use of Counterclaims,* 26 Mich.L.Rev. 1, 48 (1927).

The English Judicature Act of 1873 eliminated the historic limitations on defendant's ability to assert claims against plaintiff. Then, at the beginning of this century, a number of states amended their codes to adopt the English practice. Note that the text of Federal Rule 13(a) goes beyond the English and code practice by *requiring* defendant to assert certain claims. Is this step desirable? Why? See generally Kennedy, *Counterclaims Under Federal Rule 13,* 11 Houston L.Rev. 255 (1974).

———

Read Federal Rules of Civil Procedure 13(a)–(f) and the accompanying material in the Supplement.

UNITED STATES v. HEYWARD–ROBINSON CO.

United States Court of Appeals, Second Circuit, 1970.
430 F.2d 1077.

FREDERICK VAN PELT BRYAN, DISTRICT JUDGE.*

This is an appeal from a judgment for the plaintiff entered in the United States District Court for the District of Connecticut * * *.

The action involves two subcontracts for excavation work between D'Agostino Excavators, Inc. (D'Agostino) and The Heyward–Robinson Company, Inc. (Heyward) as prime contractor on two construction jobs in Connecticut. One of the prime contracts, for the construction of barracks at the Naval Submarine Base in New London, Groton, was with the federal government (the Navy job). The other, a non-federal job, was for the construction of a plant for Stelma, Inc. at Stamford (the Stelma job).

D'Agostino brought this action against Heyward and its surety, Maryland Casualty Company (Maryland) under the Miller Act * * * to recover payments alleged to be due on the Navy job. Heyward answered, denying liability on the Navy job and counterclaiming for alleged overpayments and extra costs of completing both the Navy job and the Stelma job. In reply, D'Agostino denied liability on the Heyward counterclaims and interposed a reply counterclaim to recover from Heyward monies alleged to be due on the Stelma job.

At the trial, the two subcontracts in suit were treated together. D'Agostino claimed that Heyward had breached both subcontracts by failing to make progress payments as required and that substantial sums were owing to it from Heyward on both jobs. Heyward claimed that D'Agostino had breached both subcontracts by permitting its compensation and employee liability insurance to lapse; that, as a result, Heyward on October 19, 1965 had terminated both; and that D'Agostino was liable for overpayments and costs of completion on both.

The issue as to whether Heyward had breached the subcontracts prior to October 19, 1965, when Heyward claimed to have terminated them, was submitted to the jury as a special question. The jury found that Heyward had breached the subcontracts prior to that date.

After amendment of the complaint by D'Agostino to allege a claim in quantum meruit for the work performed on both jobs, special questions then were submitted to the jury as to the reasonable value of the work performed by D'Agostino on each project and the net amount owed by Heyward to D'Agostino on both. The jury found, in answer to these questions, that the net amount owed by Heyward to D'Agostino on both jobs was $63,988.36. Judgment against Heyward was rendered accordingly. Under a formula agreed to by the parties, it was determined that the amount due to D'Agostino on the Navy job was $40,771.46 and judgment was entered against Maryland in that sum.

* * *

* Of the Southern District of New York, sitting by designation.

I.

Appellants' initial contention is that the District Court had no jurisdiction over the counterclaims on the Stelma job. They therefore contend that the Stelma claims must be dismissed and that since D'Agostino's claims on the Navy and Stelma jobs were presented to the jury as inseparable, the judgment below must be reversed.

Appellants urge that the Stelma counterclaims are not compulsory counterclaims over which the federal court acquired jurisdiction ancillary to the jurisdiction which it had over D'Agostino's Miller Act claim stated in the complaint. They say that these are permissive counterclaims over which the court had no ancillary jurisdiction and which lacked the required independent basis of federal jurisdiction.

This jurisdictional issue is raised for the first time in this Court. In the Court below appellants affirmatively urged that the Stelma counterclaims were compulsory. Nevertheless, it is well settled that lack of federal jurisdiction may be raised for the first time on appeal, even by a party who originally asserted that jurisdiction existed or by the court sua sponte. * * * We turn, then, to the jurisdictional issue.

It is apparent from the record that there is no independent basis of federal jurisdiction over the Stelma counterclaims. Both D'Agostino and Heyward are New York corporations with offices in New York. There is thus no diversity jurisdiction. Clearly there is no jurisdiction under the Miller Act over these counterclaims since the Stelma contract did not involve public work for the federal government.

The question is whether the Stelma counterclaims are compulsory or are permissive. Under the rule in this circuit, if they are permissive there is no Federal jurisdiction over them unless they rest on independent jurisdictional grounds. * * * On the other hand, if they are compulsory counterclaims, they are ancillary to the claim asserted in the complaint and no independent basis of Federal jurisdiction is required. E.g., United Artists Corp. v. Masterpiece Productions, Inc., 221 F.2d 213 (2d Cir.1955) * * *.

Under Rule 13(a) Fed.R.Civ.P. a counterclaim is compulsory "if it arises out of the transaction or occurrence that is the subject matter of the opposing party's claim." In United Artists Corp. v. Masterpiece Productions, supra, Chief Judge Clark said:

In practice this criterion has been broadly interpreted to require not an absolute identity of factual backgrounds for the two claims, but only a logical relationship between them. Lesnik v. Public Industrials Corp., 2 Cir., 144 F.2d 968, 975, citing and quoting, inter alia, Moore v. New York Cotton Exchange, 270 U.S. 593, 610, 46 S.Ct. 367, 371, 70 L.Ed. 750, thus: " 'Transaction' is a word of flexible meaning. It may comprehend a series of many occurrences, depending not so much upon the immediateness of their connection as upon their logical relationship." * * *

Thus " * * * courts should give the phrase 'transaction or occurrence that is the subject matter' of the suit a broad realistic interpretation in the interest of avoiding a multiplicity of suits." * * * As the Supreme Court [has] said * * *:

> The requirement that counterclaims arising out of the same transaction or occurrence as the opposing party's claim "shall" be stated in the pleadings was designed to prevent multiplicity of actions and to achieve resolution in a single lawsuit of all disputes arising out of common matters. * * *

In the case at bar the counterclaims were compulsory within the meaning of Rule 13(a). There was such a close and logical relationship between the claims on the Navy and Stelma jobs that the Stelma counterclaims arose out of the same "transaction or occurrence" as those terms are now broadly defined. Both subcontracts were entered into by the same parties for the same type of work and carried on during substantially the same period. Heyward had the right to terminate both subcontracts in the event of a breach by D'Agostino of either. Heyward also had the right to withhold monies due on one to apply against any damages suffered on the other. Progress payments made by Heyward were not allocated as between jobs and were made on a lump sum basis for both as though for a single account.

A single insurance policy covered both jobs. The letters of Heyward to D'Agostino of October 8 and 19, 1965 threatening termination and terminating both jobs, allegedly because of the cancellation by D'Agostino of this joint insurance coverage and failure to properly man both projects, treated both jobs together. These letters formed the basis of one of Heyward's major claims at the trial.

The controversy between the parties which gave rise to this litigation was with respect to both jobs and arose from occurrences affecting both. Indeed, it would seem to have been impossible for Heyward to have fully litigated the claims against it on the Navy job without including the Stelma job, because the payments it made to D'Agostino could not be allocated between the two jobs.

As the appellants themselves point out in their brief, the "Stelma and Navy claims were so interwoven at the trial that they are now absolutely incapable of separation." The proof as to payments and alleged defaults in payments was made without any differentiation between the two claims and neither of the parties was able to offer any evidence of apportionment. Finally, the evidence as to the breaches of contract claimed by the respective parties related in the main to both contracts rather than to one or the other.

The jurisdictional question so belatedly raised by the appellants must be viewed in light of the record as a whole. So viewed, it is plain that the Stelma counterclaims bare [sic] a logical and immediate relationship to the claims on the Navy job. Thus they arose out of the "transaction or occurrence which is the subject matter" of the suit instituted by D'Agostino on the Navy job and are compulsory counterclaims under Rule 13(a). The Stelma counterclaims were thus ancillary to the claims asserted in the complaint over which the Federal Court had acquired jurisdiction under the Miller Act, and there is jurisdiction over them. * * * To require that the closely related Navy and Stelma claims must be litigated separately would result in fragmentation of litigation and multiplicity of suits contrary to one of the major purposes of Rule 13(a).   *   *   *

*   *   *

The judgment below is affirmed.

FRIENDLY, CIRCUIT JUDGE (concurring).

I cannot agree that, as maintained in Part I of the majority opinion, the counterclaim relating to the Stelma job was compulsory under F.R. Civ.P. 13(a). Of course, it is tempting to stretch a point when a jurisdictional objection is so belatedly raised by the very party who clamored for the exercise of jurisdiction until the decision went against it. But we must consider the question as if Heyward had not pleaded the Stelma counterclaim and proceeded to sue D'Agostino in some other court for failure to perform that subcontract, and D'Agostino then claimed that Heyward's failure to bring the Stelma transaction into this Miller Act suit barred the later action. Despite the desirability of requiring that all claims which in fact arise "out of the transaction or occurrence that is the subject of the opposing party's claim" be litigated in a single action, courts must be wary of extending these words in a way that could cause unexpectedly harsh results.

Even on a liberal notion of "logical relation," *   *   * I am unable to perceive how Heyward's claim for breach of the Stelma subcontract arose "out of the transaction or occurrence" to wit, the Navy subcontract, that was the subject matter of D'Agostino's Miller Act claim. Whatever historical interest there may be in the circumstances that the two subcontracts were entered into between the same parties for the same type of work and were carried on during substantially the same period, these facts seem to me to be lacking in legal significance. So likewise do D'Agostino's having furnished a single insurance policy to cover both jobs and Heyward's having cancelled the subcontracts in one letter rather than two. The boiler-plate in each subcontract, whereby "if one or more other contracts, now or hereafter, exist between the parties," a breach of any such contract by D'Agostino might, at Heyward's option be considered a breach of the contract at issue and Heyward might terminate any or all contracts so breached and withhold moneys due on any contract and apply these to damages on any other, might meet the test if Heyward had availed itself of these rights, but it did not.

All that is left is that, as the trial proceeded, it turned out that some of Heyward's payments were not earmarked as between the two subcontracts. However, the determination whether a counterclaim is compulsory must be made at the pleading stage. The complaint was specific on how much Heyward owed on the Navy subcontract, and the counterclaims were equally so on how much D'Agostino owed for failure to complete this and how much it owed for failure to complete the Stelma subcontract. To say that the failure to earmark some payments made it impossible to try the claims separately ignores the law on application of payments. If Heyward did not specify the application of its payments, as it could, and

D'Agostino had not made an application of them, as it could in default of specification by Heyward, the court would do this. * * *

* * *

GREAT LAKES RUBBER CORP. v. HERBERT COOPER CO.

United States Court of Appeals, Third Circuit, 1961.
286 F.2d 631.

BIGGS, CHIEF JUDGE. This is an appeal from an order of the court below dismissing a counterclaim of Great Lakes Rubber Corporation (Great Lakes), made against Herbert Cooper Co., Inc. (Cooper), on the ground that the court lacked jurisdiction of the subject matter of the counterclaim. * * *

On May 12, 1959, Great Lakes filed an amended complaint naming Cooper as defendant. Jurisdiction was allegedly based on diversity. The allegations fall roughly into three groups. First, it was alleged that Howard Cooper and Joseph Herbert had been employed by Great Lakes * * * and that they left Great Lakes' employ taking with them certain information relating to the flexible rubber tubing manufactured by Great Lakes, and lists disclosing Great Lakes' customers; that shortly thereafter they, with others, founded Cooper; that Cooper competed for and obtained customers that were, until then, customers of Great Lakes; and, that Cooper's "offering to sell, and manufacturing and selling flexible tubing made and offered for sale with utilization of knowledge and information acquired while these men [Cooper and Herbert] were in a fiduciary relationship with plaintiff" constituted "acts of unfair competition and unfair business practices."

* * * [The second allegation was that Cooper had obtained government contracts for tubing of a type that would infringe on patents licensed to Great Lakes, and that Cooper had been able to submit the lowest bid for these contracts because it was not paying patent royalties. Great Lakes claimed that Cooper "is and has been in an unfair competitive position" because of its operations as an "unlicensed infringer."]

Third, it was alleged that Cooper implied to customers of Great Lakes that the quality of the tubing manufactured by Great Lakes was inferior; that Cooper represented to the United States Air Force that no validly patented ideas, processes or inventions held by others would be utilized in fulfilling its contracts for flexible tubing, that their representations were false; and, that these acts have damaged and imminently threaten Great Lakes' business operations.

Great Lakes referred to various contracts with the United States Army and Air Force which it alleged it had failed to obtain but which Cooper did obtain, and further specified an Air Force contract on which it was then being underbid by Cooper and which it would not obtain if Cooper's acts of "unfair competition" were not enjoined. Great Lakes asked for relief in the form of an injunction, an accounting for profits and an award of damages.

On June 23, 1959, Cooper filed an answer to the amended complaint and a counterclaim which asserted that Great Lakes, Fred T. and Robert E. Roberts, * * * and various * * * companies and individuals "have been and still are * * * conspiring together and attempting both individually and in concert to restrain and monopolize interstate commerce" in violation of Sections 1 and 2 of the Sherman Act, 15 U.S.C.A. §§ 1 and 2. The conspiracy was alleged to include, without limitation, the making of false representations to certain of Cooper's material suppliers that they were guilty of contributory infringement when the conspirators knew that the supplied items were staple articles of commerce and could not be the basis of such liability.

The counterclaim also alleged, and this is of prime importance in the instant case, "the bringing of a series of unjustified lawsuits by the conspirators in bad faith and without color of right with the sole object of harassing and preventing defendant from competing in the manufacture and sale of flexible hose and thus eliminating defendant as a competitor, including this action [i.e., the action brought by the filing of the amended complaint by Great Lakes] * * *." The counterclaim asked treble damages, costs and attorneys' fees.

On July 2, 1959, Cooper moved to dismiss Great Lakes' amended complaint on the ground that there was no diversity of citizenship between the parties. By order dated December 9, 1959, the court granted Cooper's motion to dismiss. Jurisdiction of Cooper's counterclaim was retained on the ground that it had an independent basis of jurisdiction in that it asserted a claim arising under the laws of the United States. No appeal was taken from that order. * * *

On December 28, 1959, Great Lakes filed an answer and a counterclaim to Cooper's counterclaim. Great Lakes' counterclaim repeated in substance the allegations of its amended complaint. The counterclaim is distinguishable from the amended complaint only in that it is more specific and in that it * * * [contained further allegations of misconduct by Cooper].

On January 6, 1960, Cooper moved to dismiss the Great Lakes counterclaim on the ground that the court below lacked jurisdiction of the subject matter. In opposition to this motion Great Lakes contended that the court had ancillary jurisdiction of its counterclaim as a compulsory counterclaim arising out of the same transaction and occurrences that were the subject matter of Cooper's claim arising under the Federal antitrust laws. On May 5, 1960, the court granted Cooper's motion to dismiss on the ground that Great Lakes' counterclaim was not a compulsory counterclaim. This appeal followed.

A federal court has ancillary jurisdiction of the subject matter of a counterclaim if it arises out of the transaction or occurrence that is the subject matter of an opposing party's claim of which the court has jurisdiction. * * * Similarly, a counterclaim that arises out of the transaction or occurrence that is the subject matter of an opposing party's claim is a "compulsory counterclaim" within the meaning of Rule 13(a) of the Federal Rules of Civil Procedure. It is stated frequently that the determination of ancillary jurisdiction of a counterclaim in a federal court must turn on whether the counterclaim is compulsory within the meaning of Rule 13(a). Such a statement of the law relating to ancillary jurisdiction of counterclaims is not intended to suggest that Rule 13(a) extends the jurisdiction of the federal courts to entertain counterclaims for the Federal Rules of Civil Procedure cannot expand the jurisdiction of the United States courts. What is meant is that the issue of the existence of ancillary jurisdiction and the issue as to whether a counterclaim is compulsory are to be answered by the same test. It is not a coincidence that the same considerations that determine whether a counterclaim is compulsory decide also whether the court has ancillary jurisdiction to adjudicate it. The tests are the same because Rule 13(a) and the doctrine of ancillary jurisdiction are designed to abolish the same evil, viz, piecemeal litigation in the federal courts.

We have indicated that a counterclaim is compulsory if it bears a "logical relationship" to an opposing party's claim. Zion v. Sentry Safety Control Corp., 3 Cir., 1958, 258 F.2d 31. * * * The phrase "logical relationship" is given meaning by the purpose of the rule which it was designed to implement. Thus, a counterclaim is logically related to the opposing party's claim where separate trials on each of their respective claims would involve a substantial duplication of effort and time by the parties and the courts. Where multiple claims involve many of the same factual issues, or the same factual and legal issues, or where they are offshoots of the same basic controversy between the parties, fairness and considerations of convenience and of economy require that the counterclaimant be permitted to maintain his cause of action. Indeed the doctrine of *res judicata* compels the counterclaimant to assert his claim in the same suit for it would be barred if asserted separately, subsequently.

Cooper alleges that the claims originally asserted in Great Lakes' amended complaint, reiterated in substance in its counterclaim, are "unjustified" and were brought in "bad faith and without color of right with the sole object of harassing and preventing defendant [Cooper] from competing in the manufacture and sale of flexible hose." These are the only allegations set out by Cooper's counterclaim which demonstrate a relationship within the purview of Rule 13(a) to Great Lakes' amended complaint or counterclaim. But that they do demonstrate a relationship is unquestionable. It is clear that a determination that Cooper's claims that the claims asserted in Great Lakes' amended complaint and reiterated in substance in its counterclaim are harassing will entail an extensive airing of the facts and the law relating to Great Lakes' counterclaim. It follows that the court below was in error in dismissing Great Lakes' counterclaim on the ground that it was permissive. We hold that Great Lakes' counterclaim was a compulsory one within the meaning of Rule 13(a).

* * *

The judgment will be reversed * * *.

Notes and Questions

1. There is considerable disagreement as to the wisdom of the compulsory counterclaim. Consider the following arguments:

> Compulsory counterclaim rules may at first blush appear harsh. On their face they are opposed to the dominant trend in procedure today which is to get away from penalizing a party's procedural errors by an adverse judgment against an otherwise meritorious claim. Yet such rules are an important part of the movement to end a multiplicity of litigation, and thus are in the interest of both litigants and the public. Since there is never any need for a party to incur the penalty for failure to counterclaim, and since there are ample remedies for the party who has so acted through inadvertence, the actual working of the rules has not been harsh. Their salutary effect has been had with comparatively little injustice
> * * *.

Wright, *Estoppel by Rule: The Compulsory Counterclaim Under Modern Pleading,* 38 Minn.L.Rev. 423, 465 (1954).

> * * * Certainly a rule of compulsion extended to every allowable counterclaim cannot be regarded as defensible. If a compulsory rule is ever justifiable it is only when the counterclaim operates by way of defense to the principal claim. Just as a defendant may not with impunity withdraw a defense, so we may without violence to the traditional maxim deny him the right to withdraw a counterclaim if this in whole or part is of a defensive nature. * * *

Millar, *Civil Procedure of the Trial Court in Historical Perspective* 138 (1952). Is Professor Millar arguing for a return to common-law recoupment? Are there any strong arguments for going further than he suggests by not making counterclaims compulsory under any circumstances?

2. In applying Federal Rule 13(a), the critical question is: What constitutes a "transaction or occurrence"? Four tests have been suggested:

(a) Are the issues of fact and law raised by the claim and counterclaim largely the same?

(b) Would res judicata bar a subsequent suit on defendant's claim absent the compulsory counterclaim rule?

(c) Will substantially the same evidence support or refute plaintiff's claim as well as defendant's counterclaim?

(d) Is there any logical relation between the claim and the counterclaim?

The fourth of these tests has been called "the one compelling test of compulsoriness." Do you agree? What are the strengths and weaknesses of each of these tests? See 6 Wright & Miller, *Federal Practice and Procedure: Civil* § 1410 (1971).

3. The classic definition of "transaction" is found in MOORE v. NEW YORK COTTON EXCHANGE, 270 U.S. 593, 46 S.Ct. 367, 70 L.Ed. 750 (1926). Plaintiff, Moore, sought to compel defendant to install a price quotation ticker in plaintiff's place of business. Defendant counterclaimed for damages, alleging that although plaintiff had been denied permission to use quotations from defendant's exchange, plaintiff "was purloining them and giving them out."

In the course of holding defendant's counterclaim compulsory under former Equity Rule 30, the Court said:

> * * * "Transaction" is a word of flexible meaning. It may comprehend a series of many occurrences, depending not so much upon the immediateness of their connection as upon their logical relationship. The refusal to furnish the quotations is one of the links in the chain which constitutes the transaction upon which appellant here bases its cause of action. It is an important part of the transaction constituting the subject-matter of the counterclaim. It is the one circumstance without which neither party would have found it necessary to seek relief. Essential facts alleged by appellant enter into and constitute in part the cause of action set forth in the counterclaim. That they are not precisely identical, or that the counterclaim embraces additional allegations, as, for example, that appellant is unlawfully getting the quotations, does not matter. To hold otherwise would be to rob this branch of the rule of all serviceable meaning, since the facts relied upon by the plaintiff rarely, if ever, are in all particulars, the same as those constituting the defendant's counterclaim. * * *

Id. at 610, 46 S.Ct. at 371, 70 L.Ed. at 757.

4. Consider the application of the transaction-or-occurrence test in the following cases. In INTERNATIONAL UNION, UNITED AUTOMOBILE, AIRCRAFT & AGRICULTURAL IMPLEMENT WORKERS v. PIASECKI AIRCRAFT CORP., 241 F.Supp. 385 (D.Del.1965), the union brought suit against an employer for violation of a collective-bargaining agreement. Defendant counterclaimed for damages resulting from a strike by the union. The court said:

> * * * Thus, the complaint charges damages resulting to employees by reason of (1) Piasecki's alleged default in making contributions to the insurance program, (2) for the violation of seniority provisions of the contract, (3) lost wages, (4) lost union dues and (5) lost vacation benefits. On the other hand, the subject matter of the counterclaim is a common law tort action for damages * * *.
>
> While * * * there is a broad relationship between the two, nevertheless, the questions of fact relevant to alleged violence on the picket line are not common to the subject matter of the complaint and the two claims do not represent the "same basic controversy."

Id. at 389. Is the court's application of the test correct?

In GLOBE INDEM. CO. v. TEIXEIRA, 230 F.Supp. 444 (D.Haw.1963), plaintiff insurance company joined the insured and the injured parties in a declaratory-judgment action. Plaintiff disclaimed liability under the policy because at the time of the accident the insured was driving a car without the permission of the owner. The injured defendants cross- and counterclaimed for damages. The court held that the counterclaims did not arise from the same transaction or occurrence and were not compulsory because "the subject matter of the complaint herein is the liability or non-liability of plaintiff on the insurance policy," whereas "the subject matter of the counterclaims is the negligence or non-negligence of defendant." Would the result have been any different under any of the tests set forth in Note 2?

In *Globe*, defendants' counterclaims were not even permitted to stand as permissive because the insurance policy prohibited suits against the insurer until the amount of the insured's liability had been established. Can the court refuse to entertain a permissive counterclaim if there are independent jurisdictional grounds supporting it? When might the court wish to do so and what alternative does the court have to dismissing the counterclaim?

5. In ZELTZER v. CARTE BLANCHE CORP., 414 F.Supp. 1221 (W.D.Pa. 1976), the holder of a credit card brought an action against the issuer for alleged violations of the Truth in Lending Act. The court held that although the plaintiff's claim against the credit card company and the latter's debt collection counterclaim both arose out of a single occurrence, the plaintiff's purchase of airline tickets through the use of his credit card, there was not the same basic controversy between the parties but rather mere transactional identity, and the debt-collection counterclaim, rooted in state law, was not compulsory, but permissive. The court stated:

> Plaintiff brings this action exclusively under a federal statute, the Truth in Lending Act. At issue is whether Carte Blanche complied with the technical requirements of the Act, and the regulations promulgated thereunder, in terms of disclosure of required credit information in its periodic billings to plaintiff. The outcome would seem to turn upon an interpretation of federal law, as well as upon the resolution of disputed factual issues regarding the disclosures.

> Defendant's counterclaim, however, bears no relationship to these matters, but is, rather, a debt collection suit rooted in and governed by state contract law. While the two claims stem from the same underlying business transaction, they involve entirely distinct legal issues: plaintiff's claim concerns the application of the * * * Act; the counterclaim does not concern the * * * Act or any other federal law. Moreover, the factual issues are distinct. Plaintiff's claim entails proof of a limited set of facts relating to the nature of the disclosures made by defendant. The counterclaim involves proof of a contract, its validity, the record of payments and plaintiff's default. In these circumstances * * * I find that the respective claims are "offshoots" of the same basic transaction, but not the "same basic controversy between the parties," and that separate trials on each distinct claim will not involve a "substantial duplication of effort and time by the parties and the courts." The two claims are thus not logically related * * *.

Id. at 1223–24. Is the court correct? Of what significance is Congress' desire to create, by passing the Truth in Lending Act, an incentive for private attorneys general to police consumer credit practices? Should factors like this affect the application of the transaction-or-occurrence test of Federal Rule 13(a)?

6. The states have widely divergent attitudes toward compulsory counterclaims. The Minnesota compulsory-counterclaim rule, for example, is virtually identical to Federal Rule 13(a), except that the reference to "occurrence" is omitted from the rule, which has led that state's courts to read the rule restrictively. In HOUSE v. HANSON, 245 Minn. 466, 72 N.W.2d 874 (1955), the Minnesota Supreme Court held that "Rule 13.01 was approved by this court with the express understanding and intent that the omission

therefrom of the word 'occurrence' would insure that tort counterclaims would not be compulsory."

Consequences of Failing to Plead a Counterclaim

Rule 13(a) is silent as to the consequences of a failure to raise a compulsory counterclaim. It seems clear that an unasserted compulsory counterclaim cannot be raised in a subsequent suit in a federal court, see, e.g., Twin Disc, Inc. v. Lowell, 69 F.R.D. 64 (E.D.Wis.1975), although the courts differ as to the proper theory for reaching this conclusion. Some apply a res judicata principle, others use waiver; and yet another group relies on estoppel. See Scott, *Collateral Estoppel by Judgment*, 56 Harv.L. Rev. 1 (1942) (res judicata theory); Wright, *Estoppel by Rule: The Compulsory Counterclaim Under Modern Pleading*, 38 Minn.L.Rev. 423 (1954) (estoppel). Does it make any difference which theory is used?

Under what circumstances should the liberal amendment policy of Federal Rule 13(f) be used to permit the tardy assertion of a compulsory counterclaim? See Safeway Trails, Inc. v. Allentown & Reading Transit Co., 185 F.2d 918 (4th Cir.1950), in which leave to amend was granted when the excuse for failing to plead an omitted counterclaim was that defendant's lawyer had not read the federal rules! For a strict application of the barring effect of a failure to assert a compulsory counterclaim, see Keller v. Keklikian, 362 Mo. 919, 244 S.W.2d 1001 (1951). If the statute of limitations has run on a counterclaim between the filing of the original action and defendant's motion under Rule 13(f), so that the claim would be barred if asserted independently, does the filing of the counterclaim relate back to the filing of the original action under Rule 15(c)? Should the result depend on whether the counterclaim is compulsory or permissive?

Hypothesize an action in a federal court in which defendant fails to raise a compulsory counterclaim. Does the failure to bring the claim in federal court prevent defendant from raising it in a subsequent state-court action? What if defendant brings suit on the unasserted claim in a state court before the federal action is terminated? Should the state court hearing the alleged counterclaim grant a motion to dismiss based on the assertion that Federal Rule 13(a) barred the state action? What other action might it take? Should the federal court hearing plaintiff's suit restrain further proceedings in the state court?

The answer * * * depends upon a determination of whether or not Congress intended in adopting Rule 13(a) to create another statutory exception to its policy of Federal Courts' non-interference with State Court actions. [See 28 U.S.C. § 2283.] Insofar as the effect of a party's failure to plead a compulsory counterclaim * * * in a Federal action is concerned the Congressional intent is clear—said party is thereafter barred from pleading same on the ground that it is res judicata. However, insofar as the effect of such failure on a State Court action is concerned the Congressional intent is not so clear; thus, in the absence of a clearer expression than is contained in Rule 13(a) we are unwilling to say that Congress * * * intended to grant Federal Courts the authority to enjoin State Court actions * * *.

FANTECCHI v. GROSS, 158 F.Supp. 684, 687 (E.D.Pa.1957), appeal dismissed 255 F.2d 299 (3d Cir.1958).

Are the considerations any different when the situation is reversed and the first action is brought in a state court in which a compulsory-counterclaim rule is in effect and the second case is in a federal court? Can plaintiff in the state proceeding ask the state court to enjoin the parties to a federal court action from litigating what should have been a compulsory counterclaim in the state court? Should the federal court grant a motion to dismiss? Cf. Donovan v. City of Dallas, 377 U.S. 408, 84 S.Ct. 1579, 12 L.Ed.2d 409 (1964). Should one state be required to give full faith and credit to another state's compulsory-counterclaim rule?

Notes and Questions

1. In SOUTHERN CONSTRUCTION CO. v. PICKARD, 371 U.S. 57, 83 S.Ct. 108, 9 L.Ed.2d 31 (1962), the Southern Construction Company was the prime contractor on contracts with the United States for the rehabilitation of certain barracks at Fort Campbell, Tennessee, and Fort Benning, Georgia. The plumbing and heating subcontractor on both projects was the respondent Samuel J. Pickard, doing business as Pickard Engineering Company. Pickard's primary supplier on both projects was the Atlas Supply Company.

Pickard filed suit against Southern in district courts in both Georgia and Tennessee under the Miller Act for amounts due on the contracts. Defendant elected to assert its counterclaim for the amount paid in settlement to Atlas in the Tennessee suit, the second of the two suits commenced. Pickard answered that the counterclaim was barred for failure to raise it in the first suit as a compulsory counterclaim.

The Supreme Court accepted the District Court's ruling that the $35,000 settlement had not been allocated as between the Tennessee and Georgia projects and that it therefore could have been asserted in either action. It stated, however, that Rule 13(a) does not operate to prohibit its use in the later Tennessee action. The Court found the policy of preventing multiplicity of actions and achieving resolution in a single lawsuit of all disputes arising out of common matters to be inapplicable in these circumstances:

> * * * The Rule was particularly directed against one who failed to assert a counterclaim in one action and then instituted a second action in which that counterclaim became the basis of the complaint. * * *

It is readily apparent that this policy has no application here. In this instance, the plaintiff-respondent, who originally sought to combine all his claims in a single suit, correctly concluded that he was required by statute to split those claims and to bring two separate actions in two different districts. The fragmentation of these claims, therefore, was compelled by federal law, and the primary defendant in both actions was thus for the first time confronted with the choice of which of the two pending suits should be resorted to for the assertion of a counterclaim common to both. Under these circumstances, we hold that Rule 13(a) did not compel this counterclaim to be made in whichever of the two suits the first responsive pleading was filed. Its assertion in the later suit, to which Southern, not without reason, considered it more appurtenant

* * * by no means involved the circuity of action that Rule 13(a) was aimed at preventing. * * *

Should the "common-law" exception to Rule 13(a) the Supreme Court invoked in *Pickard* be limited to the situation in which the governing substantive law requires plaintiff to bring related claims in separate districts?

2. Several exceptions to the compulsory-counterclaim rule are set out in the text of Rule 13(a) itself. Consider their relevance to the following situations.

(a) In UNION PAVING CO. v. DOWNER CORP., 276 F.2d 468 (9th Cir. 1960), the court discussed the passage in Rule 13(a) providing that waiver will not result from the failure to assert a counterclaim that already is the subject of litigation pending in another court:

> * * * The purpose of this exception is seemingly to prevent one party from compelling another to try his cause of action in a court not of the latter's choosing when the same cause of action is already the subject of pending litigation in another forum, one which was probably chosen by the owner of the cause of action concerned. The language of the exception clause in Rule 13(a)—"such a claim *need not* be so stated [as a counterclaim] if at the time the action was commenced the claim was the subject of another pending action"—seems clearly permissive. [The italics are ours.] * * * It does not preclude him from electing instead to counterclaim his cause of action in the instant case.
>
> This conclusion is reinforced by the fact that under Rule 13(b) pending litigation on the same cause of action has no effect on the ability to plead a permissive counterclaim. Thus, under the district court's theory, a cause of action which did *not* arise out of the same transaction or occurrence as the main claim could be pleaded as a counterclaim under Rule 13(b) even though the counterclaim was the subject of another pending action; but a claim so closely connected with the main action that it would otherwise be a compulsory counterclaim subject to waiver under Rule 13(a) cannot be pleaded at all if it is the subject of another pending action. Such a result is wholly unreasonable. * * *

Id. at 470–71.

(b) If defendant has a claim that arises out of the same transaction or occurrence as plaintiff's claim but it can be brought only against plaintiff and a third person who is "indispensable" and over whom defendant cannot obtain jurisdiction, is assertion of the claim mandatory?

(c) If five days after defendant serves her answer she becomes the assignee of a claim against plaintiff and if the assigned claim arose out of the same transaction or occurrence as plaintiff's claim against defendant, must defendant amend her answer and assert it? Cf. Federal Rule 13(e). What if the counterclaim is acquired during the trial?

(d) If defendant is sued in one capacity (e.g., as an administrator in an action based on the negligence of an intestate) and has a counterclaim in another capacity (e.g., as a beneficiary in a wrongful-death action) that arises out of the same transaction or occurrence, is it compulsory? See Newton v. Mitchell, 42 So.2d 53 (Fla.1949).

3. Assume plaintiff commences an action within the appropriate statute of limitations and defendant has a compulsory counterclaim that would be

barred by the statute of limitations if asserted in an independent action. Should the claim be permitted? See Nathan v. McKernan, 170 Neb. 1, 101 N.W.2d 756 (1960). Does it make any difference if defendant's claim was not time-barred when plaintiff commenced the suit but became so before defendant was required to answer? Assuming that the claim would be barred if asserted as a counterclaim, should it be permitted if it otherwise qualifies as a common-law recoupment or set-off? See American Law Institute, *Study of the Division of Jurisdiction Between State and Federal Courts* 258 (1969).

4. If defendant's answer contains a counterclaim, must plaintiff assert a compulsory counterclaim to defendant's counterclaim? Does it matter whether defendant's counterclaim is compulsory or permissive? Is a counterclaim to a counterclaim likely to be so confusing that it will prevent the orderly disposition of the case? Would it make any difference if plaintiff amended the complaint to include the claim rather than asserting it as a counterclaim? See Millar, *Counterclaim Against Counterclaim,* 48 Nw.U.L.Rev. 671, 690 (1954).

2. CROSS–CLAIMS

Read Federal Rules of Civil Procedure 13(g) and (h) and the accompanying material in the Supplement.

LASA PER L'INDUSTRIA DEL MARMO SOCIETA PER AZIONI v. ALEXANDER

United States Court of Appeals, Sixth Circuit, 1969.
414 F.2d 143.

[This controversy arose out of the construction of the Memphis, Tennessee City Hall. Southern Builders, a Tennessee corporation, was retained by the City as the principal contractor. Southern Builders' performance was secured by a bond, with Continental Casualty as surety. Southern Builders subcontracted with Alexander Marble and Tile Co., a partnership comprised of Tennessee residents, and Marble International, Inc., a Texas corporation, to supply and install some marble in the new City Hall. Alexander then contracted with LASA, an Italian corporation, to supply it with marble.

LASA alleged that it had fully performed its contract with Alexander and that Alexander owed it $127,240.80 out of the $468,641.26 contract price. It sued Alexander, Marble International, Southern Builders, Continental Casualty, and the City for the balance due.

Alexander filed an answer and counterclaim in which it alleged that LASA had breached the contract by not shipping the marble on time, by shipping marble of the wrong type, by shipping damaged marble, and by failing to ship all the marble it was obligated to ship. Alexander further alleged that the contract price was only $265,050.00. It sought restitution of the amount it overpaid LASA plus damages resulting from LASA's breach of contract.

Southern Builders filed an answer and counterclaim. In its counterclaim, Southern Builders alleged that LASA failed to ship marble as agreed to Alexander, and claimed damages resulting from that breach by LASA.

Alexander filed a cross-claim against Southern Builders, Continental Casualty, and the City for money alleged to be due on its contract with Southern Builders. Southern Builders and Continental Casualty filed answers and Southern Builders filed a cross-claim against Alexander for breach of contract.

Alexander filed third-party complaints against A.L. Aydelott and Associates, Inc. and against Aydelott individually alleging that they, as architects on the project, negligently supervised the project, wrongfully required Alexander to install marble in inclement weather, wrongfully directed Southern Builders to terminate its contract with Alexander, willfully refused to approve Alexander's estimates for work done, and wrongfully and maliciously injured Alexander's business reputation. Alexander sought unliquidated actual and punitive damages as well as treble damages, under a Tennessee statute, for inducing Southern Builders to breach the subcontract.

Alexander also sued Southern Builders for actual and punitive damages resulting from the wrongful termination of its contract and for injury to the business reputation of Alexander.]

PHILLIPS, CIRCUIT JUDGE.

* * * The confusion in pleadings that can arise out of cross-claims, counterclaims and a third-party complaint, all involving the same construction project, is demonstrated by the present appeal.

* * *

Among the pleadings were a cross-claim filed by the defendant subcontractor, Alexander, against the prime contractor, its surety and the City of Memphis; a counterclaim filed by the prime contractor against Alexander; and a third-party complaint filed by Alexander against the architect. The third-party complaint was treated by the District Court as a cross-claim against the architect as was the counterclaim of the prime contractor against Alexander.

Construing Rules 13(g) and 13(h), Fed.R.Civ.P., the District Court dismissed the two cross-claims and the third-party complaint, holding that they do not arise out of the same transaction or occurrence that is the subject matter of the original action or of a counterclaim therein.

We reverse.

* * *

Under the Federal Rules of Civil Procedure the rights of all parties generally should be adjudicated in one action. Rules 13 and 14 are remedial and are construed liberally. Both Rules 13 and 14 are "intended to avoid circuity of action and to dispose of the entire subject matter arising from one set of facts in one action, thus administering complete and evenhanded justice expeditiously and economically." Blair v. Cleveland Twist Drill Co., 197 F.2d 842, 845 (7th Cir.). The aim of these rules "is facilitation not frustration of decisions on the merits." Frommeyer v. L. & R. Construction Co., 139 F.Supp. 579, 585 (D.N.J.).

A decision involving jurisdiction over cross-claims in litigation growing out of a construction project similar in some respects to the issues presented on this appeal is Glens Falls Indemnity Co. v. United States, 229 F.2d 370 (9th Cir.). In that case the Court said:

> It is well settled that a grant of jurisdiction over particular subject matter includes the power to adjudicate all matters ancillary to the particular subject matter. * * * Therefore, if either a cross-claim under Rule 13 or a third-party claim under Rule 14 does arise out of the subject matter of the original action and involves the same persons and issues, the claim is ancillary to the original action. In such cases, if the court has jurisdiction to entertain the original action, no independent basis of jurisdiction for the cross-claim or third-party claim need be alleged or proved. 229 F.2d at 373–374.

* * *

The District Court held that no part of Alexander's cross-claim against the prime contractor, his third-party complaint against the architect or of the prime contractor's cross-claim against Alexander for breach of contract arose out of the transaction or occurrence that is the subject matter of the original action or the two counterclaims. With deference to the well-written opinion of the District Judge, we disagree.

* * *

The words "transaction or occurrence" are given a broad and liberal interpretation in order to avoid a multiplicity of suits. * * *

Our reading of the pleadings in this case convinces us that there is a "logical relationship" between the cross-claims (including the third party complaint against the architect) and the "transaction or occurrence" that is the subject matter of the complaint and the two pending counterclaims. Although different subcontracts are involved, along with the prime contract and specifications, all relate to the same project and to problems arising out of the marble used in the erection of the Memphis City Hall. The recurring question presented by the various pleadings is directed to the principal issue of who is responsible for the marble problems which arose on this job. Blame is sought to be placed upon plaintiff as furnisher of the marble, upon Alexander as subcontractor, upon the prime contractor and upon the architect. Many of the same or closely related factual and legal issues necessarily will be presented under the complaint, counterclaims and cross-claims in the resolution of these issues. It seems apparent that some of the same evidence will be required in the hearing on the cross-claims and in the hearing or hearings with respect to the complaint and the two pending counterclaims.

We understand it to be the purpose of Rule 13 and the related rules that all such matters may be tried and determined in one action and to make it possible for the parties to avoid multiplicity of litigation. The intent of the rules is that all issues be resolved in one action, with all parties before one court, complex though the action may be.

In support of the decision of the District Court it is argued that, since a jury trial has been demanded, the complications and confusions of the cross-claims are such that it would be impossible to try the numerous issues before the jury in an orderly manner. The short answer to this contention is that the District Judge is authorized by Rule 42(b) to order separate trials on any cross-claim, counterclaim, other claim or issues. If on the trial of this case the District Court concludes that separate trials on one or more of the counterclaims, cross-claims or issues would be conducive to expedition and economy, Rule 42(b) provides a practical solution to this problem.

Reversed and remanded for further proceedings not inconsistent with this opinion.

McALLISTER, SENIOR CIRCUIT JUDGE (dissenting).

* * *

The questions of fact or law involved in the original suit filed by LASA, and the counterclaim for overpayment filed by Alexander, are totally different from Alexander's claim against Southern Builders, claiming damages on the ground that Southern Builders wrongfully prevented and obstructed Alexander from performing its duties; wrongfully forced Alexander off the job; wrongfully brought in an outside subcontractor to complete the job at a highly inflated price, all of which was wrongfully and illegally charged to the account of Alexander—as well as Alexander's allegation in its same cross-claim against Southern Builders charging that Southern Builders and Aydelott entered upon a course of action wrongfully injuring the business reputation of Alexander for which it claimed $250,000 in punitive damages.

Alexander's cross-claim against Aydelott for treble damages in the amount of $750,000 for wrongfully and maliciously damaging Alexander's business reputation by abuse, harassment and public blame, and wrongfully and illegally inducing and procuring by inducement, persuasion or insistence, the breach and violation of Alexander's contract with Southern Builders, was an action in tort.

The suit brought by LASA was an action in contract to recover a balance due. The cross-claim of Alexander against Southern Builders constituted an action in tort.

Neither of these two cross-claims in tort, filed by Alexander, arises out of the transaction or occurrence that is the subject matter of the original action, or counterclaim thereto, as will hereafter more fully appear.

Alexander's cross-claim against Southern Builders does not arise out of the transaction or occurrence that is the subject matter of the original action—it does not arise out of the transaction or occurrence upon which LASA's suit is based, as is required by Rule 13(g); nor does it arise out of "a counterclaim therein"—that is, out of a counterclaim to LASA's suit. As the District Court properly held: "Rule 13(g) refers to counterclaims in the original action."

In like manner, Alexander's cross-claim against Aydelott does not arise out of the transaction or occurrence that is the subject matter of the original action—it does not arise out of the transaction or occurrence upon which LASA's suit is based. Nor does it arise out of "a counter-claim *therein*"—that is, out of a counterclaim in LASA's suit.

* * *

* * * [W]e are of the opinion that the cross-claims are not related to the original claim and the counterclaims, and that there is no identity of the many factual issues involved in the original claim and counterclaims, and in the cross-claims.

The proofs in LASA's suit and in Alexander's and Southern Builders' counterclaims against LASA would be entirely different from the proofs in Alexander's cross-claim against Southern Builders and its cross-claim against Aydelott.

* * *

* * * The same issues of fact would not determine both the original action and Alexander's cross-claims. The cross-claims, therefore, do not arise out of the transaction or occurrence which is the subject matter of the original claim, or out of the counterclaims therein.

Considering appellant Alexander's claim that not only its cross-claim and its third-party claim include absolute identity of the many factual issues in the original claim of LASA and the counterclaims filed therein— a contention which we have hereinbefore found erroneous—we proceed to Alexander's argument that the cross-claim and the third-party claim against Southern Builders and Aydelott include absolute identity of the many legal issues in the original claim by LASA and the counterclaims filed therein.

* * *

There is * * * no identity of legal issues in the original claims of LASA and Alexander's and Southern Builders' counterclaims—all founded on contract and breach of contract—and Alexander's cross-claim against Southern Builders and its third-party claim against Aydelott—all founded in tort.

It seems clear then that, in this case, the proof of claim in tort would have no connection with the proof of claim in contract and that, consequently, the two different claims do not arise out of the same transaction or occurrence. * * *

The only claims in this case that arise out of the transaction or occurrence that is the subject matter of the original action *for balance due on a contract* are the counterclaims filed against LASA by Alexander and Southern Builders, *claiming breach of that contract*—not Alexander's two cross-claims against Southern Builders and Aydelott for their claimed deliberately malicious, tortious, and damaging conduct, for which Alexander claimed damages of several hundred thousand dollars.

In accordance with the foregoing, in my opinion, the judgments of the District Court should be affirmed in accordance with the opinion of Chief Judge Bailey Brown.

Notes and Questions

1. Is the reasoning of the majority or dissenting opinion more persuasive? Should the fact that different subcontracts were involved, which arguably meant that different transactions were before the court, be determinative? What ways other than dismissal could be employed to deal with the complexity of the litigation or to avoid confusion?

2. Should transactionally related cross-claims be compulsory? Generally speaking, cross-claims are permissive, and failure to raise them does not bar suit in a subsequent action. Why should this be so? Doesn't this lead to a multiplicity of suits? Isn't judicial economy fostered by hearing all transactionally related claims in one suit? Or, is it unfair to force defendants to file cross-claims in a forum not of their own choosing merely because of the actions of the plaintiff?

3. Some states have adopted a narrow definition of a transaction for cross-claim purposes. In LIEBHAUSER v. MILWAUKEE ELEC. RY. & LIGHT CO., 180 Wis. 468, 193 N.W. 522 (1923), plaintiff-passenger sued to recover for personal injuries allegedly sustained while a passenger on one of defendant-railway company's street cars when it collided with an automobile owned and driven by defendant Kroscher. Kroscher cross-claimed against the railway company alleging that the collision was due solely to the negligence of the company and seeking $150 for damages to his automobile. The Wisconsin cross-claim provision in effect at the time stated that "A defendant * * * may have affirmative relief against a codefendant * * * but in all such cases such relief must involve or in some manner affect the contract, transaction or property, which is the subject-matter of the action." The court, construing that statute, dismissed the cross-claim, saying:

> Whether or not the defendant Kroscher may set up by way of cross-complaint a cause of action and demand affirmative relief against his codefendant depends upon whether or not the relief which Kroscher asks involves the transaction which constitutes the subject-matter of plaintiff's action. * * * The subject-matter of the action, then, in this case is the plaintiff's right to have the defendants exercise the required degree of care in respect to her. Manifestly, the relief demanded by Kroscher in his cross-complaint against the company in no way involves or affects the plaintiff's main primary right. Kroscher's cause of action, if any he has, arose by reason of the failure of the company to exercise the required degree of care in respect to him, and it was entirely complete before plaintiff's cause of action arose. It cannot, therefore, be said logically that the relief demanded by Kroscher in his cross-complaint involves in any respect the transaction which is the subject-matter of the plaintiff's action or her main primary right.

> The mere fact that the two occurrences were nearly contemporaneous in time in no manner affects the question. * * *

> A careful study of the matter * * * convinces us that the revisers intended to limit the cases where cross-complaints might be filed to those where the rights of the plaintiff were necessarily involved. Underlying this is a sound public policy. Plaintiff should have a right to bring her action and obtain an adjudication of her rights without being compelled to become a mere observer in a contest between two defendants which in no

way whatever concerns her. In the present case it is conceivable that the plaintiff might establish without difficulty a right of recovery against both defendants, and be entitled to receive compensation for the injuries complained of, and yet the determination of her right might be compelled to await the issue of long litigation between the defendants, in which she was in no way concerned, and in which the act by which her main primary right was invaded was in no way involved. * * * To make the plaintiff's right to judgment dependent upon final adjudication of an independent controversy existing between the defendants is in effect to grant her the right to appeal to the courts upon a condition. This should not be. * * *

Id. at 473–74, 475–76, 481–82, 193 N.W. at 524–25, 525. Compare the reasoning of the *Liebhauser* case with Section 3019(b) of the New York Civil Practice Law, which is in the Supplement following Rule 13. In what ways do the two provisions differ? The New York statute is discussed in 3 Weinstein, Korn & Miller, *New York Civil Practice* ¶ 3019.14.

4. Can a party plaintiff cross-claim against a coplaintiff? If so, under what circumstances? In DANNER v. ANSKIS, 256 F.2d 123 (3d Cir.1958), the driver and passenger of one car sued the driver of a second car for damages arising out of a two-car collision. The passenger-plaintiff also attempted to cross-claim for her injuries against the driver-plaintiff. The trial court's dismissal of the cross-claim was affirmed:

> The purpose of Rule 13(g) is to permit a defendant to state as a cross-claim a claim against a co-defendant growing out of the same transaction or occurrence that is the subject matter of the original action * * *, and to permit a plaintiff against whom a defendant has filed a counterclaim to state as a cross-claim against a co-plaintiff a claim growing out of the transaction or occurrence that is the subject matter of the counterclaim. * * * This, we think, is the clear intent of the language of the rule. In other words, a cross-claim is intended to state a claim which is ancillary to a claim stated in a complaint or counterclaim which has previously been filed against the party stating the cross-claim. * * * Unless so limited the rule could have the effect of extending the jurisdiction of the district court to controversies not within the federal judicial power. * * * Accordingly, Rule 13(g) does not authorize a plaintiff to state as a cross-claim against a co-plaintiff a claim arising out of the transaction or occurrence which is also the subject matter of their common complaint against the defendant. * * *

Id. at 124. Is the court's approach to the question of cross-claims between coplaintiffs sound? How is the *Danner* court defining "transaction"?

5. Rule 13(h) is used to add parties not already in the suit. In order to invoke Rule 13(h), a party must be asserting a Rule 13(a), 13(b), or 13(g) claim against someone who already is a party. Note that this differs from claims under Rule 14. In *LASA*, Alexander's claim against the architect, Aydelott, originally was pleaded as a Rule 14 claim. The District Court and the Sixth Circuit treated it as if it were a motion to bring in an additional cross-defendant under Rule 13(h); the courts thus viewed Aydelott as a codefendant on the cross-claims against Southern Builders and the others. Isn't it true, therefore, that Rule 14 claims can be transformed into Rule 13(h) motions whenever defendant can assert a cross-claim against a party? Is there any

tactical advantage in doing so? Are the additional party's rights different if it is brought in under Rule 13(h) rather than Rule 14? See the discussion of Rule 14 at pp. 607–14, infra.

SECTION C. IDENTIFYING PARTIES WHO MAY SUE AND BE SUED

Read Federal Rule of Civil Procedure 17 in the Supplement.

ELLIS CANNING CO. v. INTERNATIONAL HARVESTER CO.

Supreme Court of Kansas, 1953.
174 Kan. 357, 255 P.2d 658.

PARKER, JUSTICE. * * *

In its petition plaintiff alleged that in furnishing service on its tractor defendant negligently started a fire in that vehicle resulting in damage amounting to $479.79; that plaintiff was insured in The Potomac Insurance Company against the loss, under a policy containing a subrogation clause; that it had been paid in full for the amount of its loss; and that it had commenced and was maintaining the action to recover such amount in its own name for the use and benefit of the insurance company.

Defendant's amended answer denied *seriatim* all acts of negligence * * *; admitted all allegations of that pleading respecting insurance, the amount of the loss, and the fact such loss had been fully paid by the insurance company; and then, in the third paragraph thereof, * * * alleged and charged, that since plaintiff was seeking to recover the amount paid to it by the insurer as full compensation for the loss of the tractor, the insurance company was the real party in interest and plaintiff had no legal right to maintain the action.

Plaintiff's motion to strike paragraph three of the answer and its demurrer to the same paragraph of that pleading * * * were overruled by the trial court. This appeal followed.

The appellant insists, the appellee concedes, and we agree, the sole question involved is whether the insured (appellant), after having been paid the full amount of its loss, is a real party in interest and legally entitled to maintain this action, for the use and benefit of the insurer, to recover such loss from the party (appellee), whose negligence is alleged to be responsible therefor. The question thus raised is not new in this jurisdiction and we frankly concede is one on which there is apparent conflict in our decisions.

Subject to certain exceptions, not here involved, our statute, G.S.1949, 60–401, requires that "Every action must be prosecuted in the name of the real party in interest." Given its common and accepted meaning, particularly where—as here—it must be conceded the appellant is no longer directly interested in the subject matter of the litigation, it would seem that, in and of itself, language of the statute would compel a negative answer to the question now under consideration. * * *

Notwithstanding, earlier decisions * * * holding that in the situation disclosed by the pleadings in the case at bar, the insurer is the real and only party in interest and must undertake the maintenance of the action for his reimbursement, it must and should be frankly admitted that in * * * [two decisions], as appellant contends, we held the insured might maintain the action in his own name for the use and benefit of the insurer. Be that as it may it must be conceded, that fully aware of the rule announced in those cases, we have repudiated what was there said and held with respect to such rule and now recognize and adhere to the doctrine that under the facts and circumstances disclosed by such pleadings an insured who has been fully paid for his loss is not the real party in interest * * * and hence cannot maintain an action to recover the amount of such loss in his own name for the use and benefit of the insurer. Conversely stated, the rule now recognized and applied is, that under the confronting conditions and circumstances the right of action against the alleged wrongdoer vests wholly in the insurer who * * * may, and indeed must, bring the action as the real and only party in interest if one is to be maintained. * * *

The judgment is affirmed.

Notes and Questions

1. A person is injured due to the negligence of another. She receives payment from an insurance company. The insurance company persuades the insured to sue the negligent party in her name in state court rather than the insurance company pursuing the action itself. Why would the insurance company wish to do this? Consider the following reasons:

(a) The insurance company thinks that a jury might be more sympathetic to an injured individual than to a large company.

(b) The injured party and the negligent party are not diverse. Had the insurance company pursued the action, the parties would have been diverse and the defendant (if not a citizen of the forum state) could have removed the action to federal court. The insurance company wanted the action to remain in state court, where it thought it could get a higher award.

2. Can there be more than one real party in interest to a suit? Suppose, for example, that an injured party is only partly covered by insurance. Can she sue the negligent party? Can the insurance company? Or, must the two sue jointly? In PINEWOOD GIN CO. v. CAROLINA POWER & LIGHT CO., 41 F.R.D. 221 (D.S.C.1966) the court held that the parties should be made to sue jointly, but that each had an interest in the outcome. The court, however, indicated that the result might be different if joinder of the parties would destroy diversity.

3. Is the real party in interest to be determined using a federal standard, or would a federal court adjudicating a state-based claim be bound by the rule of the state in which it sits? In R.J. REYNOLDS TOBACCO CO. v. LANEY & DUKE STORAGE WAREHOUSE CO., 39 F.R.D. 607 (M.D.Fla.1966), the court

held that a Florida rule allowing only the insured to enforce a claim against a tortfeasor, even after payment by an insurer, was procedural and not substantive. Since it did not feel bound to follow Florida law on the matter, the court felt comfortable holding that under Rule 17(a) the insurer and not the insured was the real party in interest. The court distinguished this state procedural rule, however, from a rule that determined whether a subrogee had a right to receive the proceeds of a recovery in a tort action. According to the court, this latter rule was substantive, and thus the state rule had to be applied.

4. Generally, courts have held that diversity of citizenship is to be determined by the citizenship of the real party in interest. Does this invite maneuvers designed to create or destroy diversity jurisdiction? Suppose, for example, that a nondiverse party wishes to sue in federal court. Can she assign her claim to another party so that complete diversity would exist? Alternatively, can a party assign a claim so as to defeat diversity?

When assignments or appointments are used to create diversity, 28 U.S.C. § 1359, see pp. 267–70, supra, appears to be relevant. Federal courts generally have permitted assignments or appointments to destroy diversity—in large part because of the absence of a statute like Section 1359 treating the destruction of diversity.

5. If the party designated in the original complaint is not the real party in interest, should a substitution of the proper party be given retroactive effect to the date of the original complaint for statute-of-limitations purposes? Should a motion for substitution be made under the provisions of Federal Rule 25(c), or does Rule 15(c)(2) adequately cover the situation? See Link Aviation, Inc. v. Downs, 117 U.S.App.D.C. 40, 325 F.2d 613 (D.C.Cir.1963). Federal Rule 17(a) was amended in 1966 to add the provision that no action shall be dismissed because it was not prosecuted in the name of the real party in interest until a reasonable time has been allowed for substitution. The Advisory Committee's Notes, which appear in the Supplement, specifically limit the application of this passage to cases in which the proper party to sue is difficult to ascertain or when an excusable mistake has been made. Does the court have any discretion to refuse substitution? For example, if a suit originally is brought by John Doe against an airline for personal injuries arising out of an airline crash, should the court later allow the names of all the victims of the disaster to be substituted as the real parties in interest?

6. Various authorities have advocated the abolition of the real-party-in-interest concept. Even New York, the originator of the real-party-in-interest rule, has abolished it. According to 2 Weinstein, Korn & Miller, *New York Civil Practice* ¶ 1004.01:

> * * * [I]t was unnecessary because (1) the law would be the same without any express rule, (2) it was an inept statement of an obvious principle of substantive law, (3) it misleadingly seemed to say that the action must be brought by the party to be benefited, and (4) the second part of [the former New York rule (which was similar to the second sentence of Federal Rule 17(a))] * * * was not an exception to the first part even though it was cast in the form of an exception.

The question of who has a substantive right and whether that right has been violated to the extent that an action for redress may be brought is a matter of substantive not procedural law. Where a claim is, for example, assigned before the action is commenced, the assignor lacks any substantive right against the debtor which can be enforced. Analysis is impeded by attempting to treat the problem in terms of "real party in interest."

7. In addition to the rules on real party in interest, two other concepts are relevant to determining who may sue or be sued—"capacity" and "standing." Capacity refers to the ability of an individual or corporation to enforce rights or to be sued by others. Many states, for example, have special rules to deal with suits by or against minors and mental incompetents. See Federal Rules 17(b) and 17(c).

Standing is a concept, most relevant in the federal courts, used to ensure that the parties before the court will vigorously argue the legal claims at issue. Federal standing rules, which are derived primarily from Article III, are treated in detail in Federal Courts and Constitutional Law courses. Only summary treatment may be given here. Present doctrine requires that the litigant suffer an injury, that the injury arise out of or relate to the litigation, and that the litigant have a personal stake in the outcome of the suit. See 13 & 13A Wright, Miller & Cooper, *Federal Practice and Procedure: Jurisdiction and Related Matters 2d* §§ 3531, 3531.16 (1984).

8. It is useful to contrast the three issues of capacity, real party in interest, and standing to show how they operate together. Capacity rules are designed to protect a party by ensuring that she is represented adequately. So, a representative will be appointed to advance the interests of a minor or a mental incompetent, who might not be able to understand fully the nature of the issues involved in the lawsuit.

Real-party-in-interest rules serve to protect the opposing party's interests by ensuring that only the litigant who has a true stake in the outcome can sue or be sued. This prevents situations in which a person might be sued by the person who holds the nominal title to a claim, and after successfully defending that claim, by the real party in interest.

Standing rules protect the judicial system (and persons not parties to the suit) more than the individual litigants involved in the case. These rules ensure that only bona fide disputes between adverse parties come before the courts.

It is possible, therefore, to have a case in which a real party in interest (the beneficiary of a will, for example) lacks capacity to sue (perhaps because he is a minor). Moreover, even if this hypothetical beneficiary had capacity to sue, he might not have standing to raise particular claims. So, for example, the beneficiary of the will might not be able to bring an action against the government on the ground that the estate tax is used for illegal purposes by the government since the injury suffered is of a general nature, not particular to the litigant, and hence the beneficiary lacks standing to sue.

SECTION D. CLAIMS INVOLVING MULTIPLE PARTIES

1. PERMISSIVE JOINDER OF PARTIES

Joinder of parties at common law was controlled by the substantive rules of law, often as reflected in the forms of action, rather than by notions of judicial economy and trial convenience. Plaintiffs who were asserting joint rights were compelled by these principles to join their respective claims in a single action; permissive joinder of plaintiffs, in the sense of plaintiffs having an option to join their claims when they were not joint, did not exist. The common-law rules governing joinder of defendants were slightly more flexible: joint tortfeasors and defendants whose contract obligations were both joint and several could be joined at the plaintiff's option.

The equity courts adopted a more flexible approach to permissive joinder of parties than prevailed in the common-law courts. They allowed all persons having an interest in the subject matter of the action or in the relief demanded to join in a single proceeding.

The early codes adopted the equity rule as a general provision governing joinder of parties. Many state courts read this language as imposing a two-part requirement for joinder of plaintiffs, however. As a result, joinder of plaintiffs was restricted to those cases in which all plaintiffs were interested in both the subject matter of the action and all the relief demanded. Joinder of defendants was even more restricted by code provisions relating to joinder of causes of action, which typically required all parties to be interested in each of the joined causes.

For a history of American joinder rules, see 7 Wright, Miller & Kane, *Federal Practice and Procedure: Civil 2d* § 1651 (1986); Blume, *Free Joinder of Parties, Claims, and Counterclaims*, 2 F.R.D. 250 (1943); Legislation, *Recent Trends in Joinder of Parties, Causes, and Counterclaims*, 37 Colum.L.Rev. 462 (1937). For a comparative view, see Millar, *The Joinder of Actions in Continental Civil Procedure*, 28 Ill.L.Rev. 26, 177 (1933).

———

Read Federal Rules of Civil Procedure 20, 21, and 42(a) in the Supplement.

———

RYDER v. JEFFERSON HOTEL CO.

Supreme Court of South Carolina, 1922.
121 S.C. 72, 113 S.E. 474.

MARION, J. The complaint in this action * * * alleges in substance that the plaintiff Charles A. Ryder and the plaintiff Edith C. Ryder are husband and wife; that [they] * * * became guests of the defendant Jefferson Hotel Company * * *; that thereafter, during the night * * *, the defendant S.J. Bickley, acting as the servant and agent of the defendant Jefferson Hotel Company, roused the plaintiffs by rapping upon their room door, and in a rude and angry manner insulted the plaintiff Edith C. Ryder; that as a result of the insults * * * the plaintiffs were compelled to give up the accommodations due them and leave the said hotel, and were forced at midnight and at great inconvenience and uncertainty to seek another lodging place; that by reason of such high-handed, malicious, and willful conduct, on the part of the said hotel and its servant and agent, the plaintiffs were greatly injured in their reputations, credit, and business, and that the plaintiff Charles A. Ryder has suffered great loss of custom and has been deprived of great gains and profits * * *; and that * * * the plaintiffs have been damaged in the sum of $10,000.

Defendants separately demurred to the complaint upon the ground that it appeared upon the face thereof that several causes of action had been improperly united therein, for the reason that the several causes of action united do not affect all the parties to the action. From an order overruling the demurrer, defendants appeal.

The sole question for determination is: Does the complaint contain two causes of action which may be joined in the same complaint? It is apparent, as appellants suggest, that the complaint alleges a cause of action by Charles A. Ryder against the defendants for a personal tort— that is, for a breach of duty growing out of the relationship existing between the parties, to wit, innkeeper and guest—and also a cause of action by Edith C. Ryder against the defendants for a tortious breach of duty growing out of the same relationship. It is also apparent that both of these alleged causes of action arose out of the same transaction, in the sense that the injury to each of the plaintiffs was caused by the same delict. But appellants contend that it is equally apparent from the allegations of the complaint that the rights invaded and the injuries sustained are necessarily several, and that plaintiffs cannot maintain a joint action and recover joint damages therefor. We think that contention must be sustained.

Section 218 of the Code of Procedure (1912), classifying the various causes of action which may be united in the same complaint, contains this proviso:

> But the causes of action, so united, must all belong to one of these classes, and, except in actions for the foreclosure of mortgages, must affect all the parties to the action, and not require different places of trial, and must be separately stated.

The rule applicable is thus stated by Judge Pomeroy in his work on Code Remedies (4th Ed.) p. 215:

> When a tort of a personal nature * * * is committed upon two or more, the right of action must, except in a very few special cases, be several. In order that a joint action may be possible, there must be some prior bond of legal union between the persons injured—such as partnership relation—of such a nature that the tort interferes with it, *and by virtue of that very interference* produces a wrong and consequent damage common to all. It is not every prior existing legal relation between the parties that will impress a joint character upon the injury and damage. Thus, if a husband and wife be libeled, or slandered, or beaten, although there is a close legal relation between the parties, it is not one which can be affected by such a wrong, and no joint cause of action will arise.
>
> * * *

That the rights infringed and the injuries suffered by the two plaintiffs in the case at bar are several, and not joint, would not seem open to question. To illustrate: If the two plaintiffs, husband and wife, occupying the same berth in a sleeping car, had both been physically injured in a wreck of the train, it would scarcely be contended that they could properly bring a joint action for the damages sustained by each on account of the carrier's delict. The complaint here does not state a cause of action for injuries to the wife alone * * *. Neither is the husband's alleged cause of action based upon loss of consortium and expenses incurred on behalf of the wife. The wife's cause of action as alleged does not "affect" the husband, and the husband's cause of action does not "affect" the wife, in the sense that the Code of Procedure (section 218) requires that the causes of action joined in the same complaint "must affect all parties to the action." Neither has a legal interest in the pecuniary recovery of the other, and in contemplation of law there can be no joint and common damage to both resulting from a wrong which gives rise to separate and distinct rights personal to each. * * *

At common law it seems that even the husband's cause of action for the loss of the wife's services and companionship and expenses incurred by him on account of injury to the wife could not be joined with the cause of action for injuries personal to the wife. * * * In the case at bar not only are the parties plaintiff different, and the potential elements of damage recoverable by the parties different, but neither party has the right to sue for the benefit of the other * * *.

The order of the circuit court is reversed.

GARY, C.J., and COTHRAN, J., concur.

FRASER, J. (dissenting). * * * The plaintiffs * * * were expelled from the hotel, under the allegation that they were not husband and wife. It was a denial of the joint relationship that caused the trouble.

It seems to me that the illustrations used are not appropriate to the case. When a husband and wife are injured in one railroad accident, the injuries are individual, and not joint. It seems to me that the case is somewhat like an injury to a copartnership. I do not think that it will be doubted that the copartnership can bring an action for injury to the copartnership, although the injury to the two copartners may not be the same. * * * In the joint action the other copartner may not be able to recover for the injury peculiar to himself; but the injury to the copartnership is a joint injury, and for this injury it may recover. Here the offense was against the husband and wife and affected their relation as husband and wife. This is manifestly a joint injury. * * *

For these reasons I dissent.

Notes and Questions

1. Doesn't *Ryder* emasculate the concept of permissive joinder by allowing joinder only when the parties are "united in interest" and presumably would be *compelled* to join? In this connection consider the court's reliance on Pomeroy's statement that "although there is a close legal relation between the parties, it is not one which can be *affected* by such a wrong, and no joint cause of action will arise." (Emphasis added.) If the injury *affected* a relationship, wouldn't the parties to that relationship be classified as necessary or indispensable parties and be required to join? Is the joint-interest

standard consistent with the objectives of permissive joinder? Reconsider these questions after completing the material on necessary joinder, pp. 589–606, infra.

The *Ryder* approach has been rejected in a substantial number of jurisdictions. See, e.g., Peters v. Bigelow, 137 Cal.App. 135, 30 P.2d 450 (3d Dist. 1934).

2. How would *Ryder* have been decided by a federal court? What are the factors that should be weighed under Rule 20 in deciding a permissive-joinder question? Consider the following cases. In REKEWEG v. FEDERAL MUT. INS. CO., 27 F.R.D. 431 (N.D.Ind.1961), judgment on merits affirmed 324 F.2d 150 (7th Cir.1963), certiorari denied 376 U.S. 943, 84 S.Ct. 798, 11 L.Ed.2d 767 (1964), the court permitted an injured plaintiff to join a claim against an insurance company and its agent for fraudulently inducing plaintiff's attorney to delay the filing of a personal-injury claim until after the statute of limitations had run with a claim against plaintiff's attorney for negligent delay in bringing a timely action. But in SUN–X GLASS TINTING OF MID–WISCONSIN, INC. v. SUN–X INT'L, INC., 227 F.Supp. 365 (W.D. Wis.1964), an action for fraud in which eight distributors sought to join as plaintiffs against the company for which they agreed to act as distributors, the court found that there was no single transaction or occurrence since the solicitation, negotiation, and execution of each distributor's contract was unrelated to any of the other contracts. Can these two cases be reconciled?

3. In AKELY v. KINNICUTT, 238 N.Y. 466, 144 N.E. 682 (1924), one hundred ninety-three plaintiffs joined in an action alleging that they were induced to purchase shares of stock in a corporation by defendant's prospectus. The question of fraud was common to all but separate questions relating to individual plaintiffs also were certain to arise—e.g., whether each plaintiff justifiably relied on the prospectus. Defendant objected to joinder on the grounds that (1) the presence of separate questions outweighed the advantages of joinder and (2) the claims did not arise out of the same transaction. The court upheld joinder because the fraud issue was fundamental and would involve more dispute and elicit more evidence than any other issue. The court also held that there was but one transaction, stating:

> * * * The transaction in respect of or out of which the cause of action arises is the purchase by plaintiff of his stock * * * and such purchases conducted by one plaintiff after another respectively plainly constitute a series of transactions within the meaning of the statute. The purchase by plaintiff of his stock is not robbed of its character as a "transaction" because * * * the transaction was not a dual one occurring between the plaintiff and the defendants, and the many purchases by plaintiffs respectively do not lose their character as a series of transactions because they occurred at different places and times extending through many months.

Id. at 474, 144 N.E. at 684. Compare Goodman v. H. Hentz & Co., 265 F.Supp. 440 (N.D.Ill.1967). Could plaintiffs in *Akely* have brought a class action under Federal Rule 23? See pp. 662–67, infra.

4. In LUCAS v. CITY OF JUNEAU, 15 Alaska 413, 127 F.Supp. 730 (1955), and STATE EX REL. SMITH v. WEINSTEIN, 398 S.W.2d 41 (Mo.Ct. App.1965), plaintiff's injuries were sustained through the negligence of A and were aggravated by the subsequent negligence of B, an ambulance driver,

while taking plaintiff to the hospital. In *Lucas,* the ambulance accident occurred eighteen days after the original injury to plaintiff. In both cases, the court concluded that the ambulance trips were necessitated by the original accidents and permitted joinder.

In WATTS v. SMITH, 375 Mich. 120, 134 N.W.2d 194 (1965), plaintiff was a passenger in a car that was struck from the rear twice in one day—once when plaintiff and his driver were en route to work in the morning and again when they were returning home in the afternoon. Plaintiff attempted to join the drivers of both cars which struck him in a single lawsuit. Michigan Court Rule 2.206(A) allows persons to be joined in one action as defendants (1) if there is asserted against them jointly, severally, or in the alternative, any right to relief in respect of or arising out of the same transaction, occurrence or series of transactions or occurrences, and if any question of law or fact common to all of them will arise in the action; or (2) if it appears that their presence in the action will promote the convenient administration of justice. Relying on the second provision, the Michigan court allowed joinder because separation of the causes would permit each defendant to argue that it was uncertain what injuries plaintiff sustained from each accident. Do you perceive any problems in permitting joinder in this case? See Note, *The Challenge of the Mass Trial,* 68 Harv.L.Rev. 1046 (1955).

5. Many of the tactical factors that must be considered before attempting to join multiple defendants are discussed in Friedenthal, *Whom to Sue— Multiple Defendants,* in 5 *Am.Jur. Trials* 1–25 (1966).

TANBRO FABRICS CORP. v. BEAUNIT MILLS, INC.

Supreme Court of New York, Appellate Division, First Department, 1957.
4 A.D.2d 519, 167 N.Y.S.2d 387.

BREITEL, JUSTICE.   *   *   *

The underlying business dispute spawned three lawsuits. In the first action * * *, the seller, Beaunit, sought to recover the purchase price of goods sold and delivered to Tanbro. The buyer, Tanbro, counterclaimed for breach of warranty for improper manufacture, as a result of which the goods were subject to "yarn slippage." The seller replied to the counterclaim by denying that the slippage was due to improper manufacture. A portion of the goods still being in the hands of the processor, Tanbro initiated another action * * *, in replevin, to recover these goods. The processor, Amity, counterclaimed for its charges and asserted its claim to the goods under an artisan's lien. In the exchanges that preceded and attended the bringing of these lawsuits, the buyer Tanbro received Beaunit's assertion that the yarn slippage was caused by the processor's improper handling, while with equal force the processor charged the same defect to Beaunit as a consequence of its improper manufacture.

At this juncture, Tanbro, the buyer, brought the third lawsuit * * * against Beaunit and Amity, charging the goods were defective because of yarn slippage and that such slippage was caused by either the seller, Beaunit, or alternatively the processor, Amity, or both. This is the main action before the court.

At Special Term, the buyer Tanbro moved to consolidate the three actions. Beaunit and Amity separately cross-moved to dismiss the complaint in the buyer's main action on the ground that there were prior actions pending between the parties with respect to the same cause of action. The motion to consolidate was denied and Beaunit's cross-motion to dismiss the complaint as against it was granted.

* * *

Both the seller and the processor resist consolidation. They do so on the ground that each had a separate and different relationship to the buyer, and that each was involved in a separate and independent contract. Therefore, they say, there is not involved the "same transaction or occurrence," nor any common question of law or fact to sustain either a joinder of parties or a consolidation of the actions. They stress that the buyer Tanbro wishes to pit against each other the seller and the processor on the issue of responsibility for the alleged defect, while the buyer sits back free from the obligation to prove a full case, as it would otherwise have to do in separate actions against the seller and the processor. The buyer, on the other hand, argues that what is identical to the cases are the goods and the defect, with the common question of who is responsible for the defect. The buyer concedes that it would have to prove the defect, and also prove that the defect must have been caused by either the seller or the processor or both of them; that, therefore, this involves a single transaction or occurrence and involves a common question of fact.

The controlling statute is Section 212 of the Civil Practice Act. * * * The portion pertinent to the joinder of defendants reads as follows:

> 2. All persons may be joined in one action as defendants if there is asserted against them jointly, severally, or in the alternative, any right to relief in respect of or arising out of the same transaction, occurrence, or series of transactions or occurrences and if any question of law or fact common to all of them would arise in the action. * * *

A reading of the section by itself would suggest little or no difficulty in permitting a joinder of parties in the buyer's main action or a consolidation of the three actions. However, the section has a history, which has created some confusion as to the meaning and application of the section.

The seller and the processor rely heavily on Ader v. Blau, 241 N.Y. 7, 148 N.E. 771, 41 A.L.R. 1216. The case arose under the predecessor statute permitting joinder * * *. In that case the plaintiff sought to join in one death action the person charged with having caused the accident resulting in the injuries ending in death and a treating physician who, it was charged, by his incompetence, was the cause of the decedent's death. The Court of Appeals * * * [held] that Section 258 of the Civil Practice Act, since repealed, albeit a restriction on joinder of causes of action in pleading, was a limiting factor in permitting joinder of parties. Applying the statute, it held the joinder impermissible.

In reaction to this decision * * * Section 258 was repealed in favor of a broad pleading section * * *. In making the recommendation, the Judicial Council referred to the Ader case, supra, and the fact that the court had regarded the area of joinder of parties limited by the pleading restrictions of Section 258. It added, "Complete freedom should be allowed in the joinder of causes of action as in the joinder of parties, and it is submitted that the correct approach to the joinder both of parties and of causes of action is the English one: May the matters conveniently be tried together? The problem is to combine as many matters as possible to avoid multiplicity and at the same time not unduly complicate the litigation for the jury."

The full effect of the repealer of old Section 258 has, however, not been left to speculation. The Court of Appeals, in Great Northern Telegraph Company v. Yokohama Specie Bank, 297 N.Y. 135, 76 N.E.2d 117, discussed the question frontally. It held that the *Ader* case, supra, was a result of the pleading limitation contained in the old, and now repealed, Section 258. * * * And in the *Great Northern* case, itself, joinder was allowed plaintiff against the Superintendent of Banks for payments due plaintiff, on which claim the Superintendent was asserting as a bar a time limitation provided by statute, and a correspondent Bank, which plaintiff asserted owed a duty to plaintiff to file the claim promptly with the Superintendent of Banks, in the event that it should be held that the claim was barred by lapse of time.

Notably, in the *Great Northern Telegraph* case, and in the English cases relied upon therein, there were joined, as defendants, parties that owed to plaintiff obligations under independent and separate contracts and in independent and separate relationships. In none of the cases was the "same transaction or occurrence" construed to require an identity of duty and relationship. * * *

This then is the background for the present section 212 of the Civil Practice Act. It should be beyond argument, by now, that it is no longer a bar to joinder, and, by parallel reasoning, *a fortiori,* to consolidation, that there is not an identity of duty or contract upon which to assert alternative liability. It is still necessary, of course, that there be a finding that the alternative liability arises out of a common transaction or occurrence involving common questions of fact and law. But this is not a rigid test. It is to be applied with judgment and discretion, in the balancing of convenience and justice between the parties involved * * *. Indeed, the buyer's situation prompted Special Term to comment that the buyer, Tanbro, "is in the unenviable position of not knowing possibly which of its contracting parties is responsible and in separate actions may find itself confronted with defeat in each event though the product as finally delivered may be defective."

* * *

The right of joinder and the privilege to obtain consolidation is always counterbalanced, of course, by the power of the court to grant a severance, or to deny a consolidation, if prejudice or injustice appear. In this case, the danger of separate trials, leading, perhaps, to an unjust and illogical result, is a possibility well worth avoiding. The buyer is entitled to a less hazardous adjudication of his dispute, so long as he is able to make out a prima facie case of alternative liability.

Accordingly, the order of Special Term insofar as it granted the cross motion to dismiss the complaint in the first described action as against the defendant Beaunit and denied the buyer Tanbro's motion to consolidate the three actions should be modified to deny the cross motion and to grant the motion to consolidate, and otherwise should be affirmed * * *.

All concur.

Notes and Questions

1. Where one of two persons are [sic] liable but the plaintiff is not certain he can make out a case against either, the opportunity to join them as defendants is of great tactical importance. The court should not dismiss after the close of plaintiff's case merely because the plaintiff has not shown which of the two defendants is responsible if he has shown that one of them must have been. It is not unfair to require each of the defendants to assume the risk of a failure to show that he was not responsible. Some attorneys sometimes fail to recognize that evidence supplied by one co-defendant may be used against another to support the plaintiff's case. * * * Even if the court might feel that a prima facie case has not been made out against one of the co-defendants, it should at least reserve decision on the motion to dismiss until after the defendants rest.

2 Weinstein, Korn & Miller, *New York Civil Practice* ¶ 1002.08. See also 7 Wright, Miller & Kane, *Federal Practice and Procedure: Civil 2d* § 1654 (1986).

In *Tanbro,* the buyer's motion was for consolidation. The court's opinion might convey the impression that the court assumed the New York standard for consolidation was identical to that for joinder. In fact, however, the New York consolidation provision is much broader than the New York joinder provision. The text of both have been set out in the Supplement—the former under Federal Rule 42(a) and the latter under Federal Rule 20. In comparing the Federal Rules with the New York provisions note that the Federal Rules also differentiate between joinder and consolidation. Can a discrepancy between the availability of joinder and consolidation be justified?

2. For a history of American joinder rules, see Blume, *Free Joinder of Parties, Claims, and Counterclaims,* 2 F.R.D. 250 (1943), and Legislation, *Recent Trends in Joinder of Parties, Causes, and Counterclaims,* 37 Colum.L. Rev. 462 (1937). For a comparative view, see Millar, *The Joinder of Actions in Continental Civil Procedure,* 28 Ill.L.Rev. 26, 177 (1933).

2. JOINDER OF PERSONS NEEDED FOR A JUST ADJUDICA-TION—NECESSARY AND INDISPENSABLE PARTIES

BANK OF CALIFORNIA NAT. ASS'N v. SUPERIOR COURT

Supreme Court of California, 1940.
16 Cal.2d 516, 106 P.2d 879.

GIBSON, CHIEF JUSTICE. * * *

Sara M. Boyd * * * died testate in June, 1937, leaving an estate valued at about $225,000. On July 8, 1937, * * * her will was admitted to probate, and petitioner, Bank of California, was appointed executor. The will left individual legacies and bequests amounting to $60,000 to a large number of legatees, * * * some residing in other states and in foreign countries. Petitioner, St. Luke's Hospital, was named residuary legatee and devisee, and thereby received the bulk of the estate.

On October 14, 1937, Bertha M. Smedley, a niece and legatee, brought an action to enforce the provisions of an alleged contract by which decedent agreed to leave her entire estate to the plaintiff. The complaint named as parties defendant the executor and all of the beneficiaries under the will, and prayed for a decree adjudging that plaintiff is, by virtue of the agreement, the owner of the entire estate of the decedent after payment of debts and expenses. It was further prayed that plaintiff's title to the property be quieted * * *.

Summons was served only upon petitioners, the executor and the residuary legatee. No other defendants were served, and none appeared. * * * [At trial] petitioners made a motion * * * for an order to bring in the other defendants, and to have summons issued and served upon them. The motion was made on the ground that all of the other defendants were "necessary and indispensable parties" to the action, and that the court could not proceed without them. The motion was denied by respondent court. Petitioners then applied for a writ of prohibition to restrain the trial until these other parties should be brought in.

In support of their application, petitioners point out that the complaint challenges the right of every legatee and devisee to share in the estate, and prays for an award of the entire property to plaintiff. It is contended that a trial and judgment without the absent defendants would adversely affect the rights of such parties, would result in a multiplicity of suits, and would subject the petitioning executor to inconvenience, expense and the burden of future litigation.

* * * [T]he precise issue is * * * whether the absent defendants are not only proper parties but "indispensable parties" in the sense that service upon them or their appearance is essential to the jurisdiction of the court to proceed in the action. * * *

At common law, joinder of plaintiffs was compulsory where the parties under the substantive law, were possessed of joint rights. * * * Equity courts developed another theory of compulsory joinder, to carry out the policy of avoiding piecemeal litigation and multiplicity of suits. Those persons necessary to a complete settlement of the controversy were usually required to be joined, in order that the entire matter might be concluded by a single suit. Obviously, this theory of joinder covered many situations where the substantive rights were not joint, and accordingly joinder would not have been required in an action at law. * * * Generally speaking, the modern rule under the codes carries out the established equity doctrine. Thus, section 389 of the Code of Civil Procedure states: "The court may determine any controversy between parties before it, when it can be done without prejudice to the rights of others, or by saving their rights; but when a complete determination of the controversy cannot be had without the presence of other parties, the court must then order them to be brought in * * *." * * *

But the equity doctrine as developed by the courts is loose and ambiguous in its expression and uncertain in its application. Sometimes it is stated as a mandatory rule, and at other times as a matter of discretion, designed to reach an equitable result if it is practicable to do so. * * * Bearing in mind the fundamental purpose of the doctrine, we should, in dealing with "necessary" and "indispensable" parties, be careful to avoid converting a discretionary power or a rule of fairness in procedure into an arbitrary and burdensome requirement which may thwart rather than accomplish justice. These two terms have frequently been coupled together as if they have the same meaning; but there appears to be a sound distinction, both in theory and practice, between parties deemed "indispensable" and those considered merely "necessary." * * * "* * * While necessary parties are so interested in the controversy that they should normally be made parties in order to enable the court to do complete justice, yet if their interests are separable from the rest and particularly where their presence in the suit cannot be obtained, they are not indispensable parties. The latter are those without whom the court cannot proceed." Clark[,] Code Pleading, p. 245, note 21. * * *

First, then, what parties are indispensable? There may be some persons whose interests, rights, or duties will inevitably be affected by any decree which can be rendered in the action. Typical are the situations where a number of persons have undetermined interests in the same property, or in a particular trust fund, and one of them seeks, in an action, to recover the whole, to fix his share, or to recover a portion claimed by him. The other persons with similar interests are indispensable parties. The reason is that a judgment in favor of one claimant for part of the property or fund would necessarily determine the amount or extent which remains available to the others. Hence, any judgment in the action would inevitably affect their rights. Thus, in an action by one creditor against assignees for the benefit of creditors, seeking an accounting and payment of his share of the assets, the other creditors were held indispensable * * *. * * * Where, also, the plaintiff seeks some other type of affirmative relief which, if granted, would injure or affect the interests of a third person not joined that third person is an indispensable party. Thus, in an action by a lessor against a sublessee to forfeit a parent lease because of acts of the sublessee, the sublessors (original lessees) were indispensable parties, since a decree of forfeiture would deprive them of their lease. * * *

All of these persons are, of course, "necessary" parties, but the decisions show that they come within a special classification of necessary parties, to which the term "indispensable" seems appropriate. An attempt to adjudicate their rights without joinder is futile. Many cases go so far as to say that the court would have no jurisdiction to proceed without them, and that its purported judgment would be void and subject to collateral attack. The objection being so fundamental, it need not be raised by the parties themselves; the court may, of its own motion, dismiss the proceedings, or refuse to proceed, until these indispensable parties are brought in. * * *

The other classification includes persons who are interested in the sense that they might possibly be affected by the decision, or whose interests in the subject matter or transaction are such that it cannot be finally and completely settled without them; but nevertheless their interests are so separable that a decree may be rendered between the parties before the court without affecting those others. These latter may perhaps be "necessary" parties to a complete settlement of the entire controversy or transaction, but are not "indispensable" to any valid judgment in the particular case. They should normally be joined, and the court, following the equity rule, will usually require them to be joined, in order to carry out the policy of complete determination and avoidance of multiplicity of suits. But, since the rule itself is one of equity, it is limited and qualified by considerations of fairness, convenience, and practicability. Where, for example, it is impossible to find these other persons or impracticable to bring them in, the action may proceed as to those parties who are present.

* * *

The action in these cases is against the distributee personally, and not against the estate; and it is independent of the will and the probate proceeding. Each distributee is individually held as a constructive trustee solely of the property which came to him, and none is interested in the granting or denial of similar relief as to any other. Where there are a number of legatees and devisees, they would all appear to be "necessary" parties in the sense that the main issue, the validity of the testamentary disposition of the property of decedent, affects their property interests, and the entire matter, the disposition of all of the decedent's property, cannot be finally settled without a binding adjudication for or against every legatee or devisee. Hence, the court will usually order them served and brought in unless there is some good reason for not doing so. But the absent defendants in such a case are not indispensable parties. Unlike the situations discussed above, in which any judgment would necessarily affect the rights of the absent persons, the case here is one where plaintiff may litigate her claim against the appearing defendants alone and obtain a decree which binds them alone. The absent defendants, not being before the court, will not be bound by the judgment, whether favorable or unfavorable, and their property interests will not be affected.

* * *

Only brief mention need be made of the contention that the prosecution of the action against less than all of the distributees will cause inconvenience and multiplicity of suits to the injury of the executor. These are all matters within the discretion of the court to consider in connection with its policy to settle the entire controversy in one proceeding, if possible. * * *

We have refrained from discussing the question whether the lower court's denial of the motion to bring in the absent defendants was, under the circumstances, an abuse of discretion. If they were readily available and could have been brought in without serious difficulty, it may well be that the motion should have been granted. On the other hand, if, as is asserted by respondents, many reside outside the state or the country, great difficulty might be encountered in any attempt to bring them in, and the trial might be indefinitely delayed, to the detriment of the present parties. The fact that the interests of the absent defendants are trivial as compared with that of the residuary legatee, which received over seventy-five percent of the estate, is perhaps some indication of the reason why plaintiff chose to go to trial against the latter alone. All these considerations, however, were for the trial court in the first instance, and its determination, though reviewable in the proper manner, cannot be attacked on an application for writ of prohibition.

The alternative writ, heretofore issued, is discharged, and the peremptory writ is denied.

Notes and Questions

1. SHIELDS v. BARROW, 58 U.S. (17 How.) 130, 15 L.Ed. 158 (1854), established the notion that parties could be classified as necessary or indispensable depending on the nature of their substantive rights ("joint" or "severable"). The consequences of this classification were extremely important. If an absent party who was not subject to the jurisdiction of the court or whose joinder would destroy the pre-existing diversity of citizenship was labelled indispensable, the entire action had to be dismissed. On the other hand, if the absentee merely was necessary, the court might exercise its discretion in determining whether or not to continue without that person. Because a plaintiff might have been deprived of any remedy if a party was found to be indispensable, courts often strained to avoid that conclusion. As might be suspected, this method had a debilitating effect on the standard for classification.

2. WARNER v. PACIFIC TEL. & TEL. CO., 121 Cal.App.2d 497, 263 P.2d 465 (2d Dist.1953), involved the following three successive telephone book listings: (1) Warner, Caryl atty, 639 S Spring—TUkr 9171 Woodland Hills Office, 21042 Rios—DIamnd 85761; (2) Warner, Caryl Mrs. 1600 Westrly Ter—NOrmndy 22011; and (3) Warner, Caryl Mrs. Warner Caryl atty 21042 Rios Wdlnd Hills—DIamnd 85761. The "Mrs. Caryl Warner" in the second listing was the first wife of Caryl Warner; the "Mrs. Caryl Warner" in the third listing was Caryl Warner's wife at the time of the lawsuit. After the telephone company refused to delete or change the second listing, the present Mrs. Warner brought suit against the company for damages on the ground that the existing listings injured her reputation in the community and caused her "emotional distress, humiliation, fear, vexation, annoyance, scorn and ridicule as to her marital status, rendering her sick, with recurrent asthma attacks, to her damage." Plaintiff also asserted that she owned the title "Mrs. Caryl Warner," that the name has acquired a secondary meaning by reason of the professional and social standing of Caryl Warner, that her prestige and dignity were being depreciated, that the telephone listings constitute an invasion of privacy because they depict plaintiff as a party to a bigamous marriage, and that the telephone company knew or should have known that its maintenance of the listings would cause damage to plaintiff. The telephone company demurred to plaintiff's third amended and supple-

mental complaint on the ground, *inter alia,* that plaintiff had failed to join an indispensable party—the first Mrs. Caryl Warner. In light of the *Bank of California* case, should the California Court of Appeals affirm or reverse the lower court's grant of the demurrer? Why?

3. Is the failure to join an indispensable party really a jurisdictional defect as the *Bank of California* case suggests? See Hazard, *Indispensable Party: The Historical Origin of a Procedural Phantom,* 61 Colum.L.Rev. 1254, 1255–56 (1961).

4. If the indispensable-party rule cannot be justified on the ground that the absentee's rights will be prejudiced by a judgment, are there other considerations that might induce a court to refrain from adjudicating an action when an interested party is not present? Consider MAHR v. NORWICH UNION FIRE INS. SOC'Y, 127 N.Y. 452, 28 N.E. 391 (1891), in which plaintiff brought an action to restrain an insurance company from indemnifying the insured or his assignee. The policy had been issued to Bartlett and although delivered to plaintiff as collateral for a loan, it never was formally assigned. Thereafter Bartlett assigned the policy to Kelly, an Iowa resident, who had not been made a party to the action and could not be joined because he was beyond the jurisdiction of the New York courts. The insurance company moved to dismiss, claiming that Kelly was an indispensable party, but the trial court denied the motion. The Court of Appeals reversed, expressing the fear that "payment or performance may be exacted as many times as there are separate claimants." In fact, Kelly had brought suit against the insurance company in an Iowa court. Even if the threat of an inconsistent decision is remote, shouldn't the threat of multiplicity be sufficient to excuse defendant from defending the action? See Petrogradsky M.K. Bank v. National City Bank, 253 N.Y. 23, 170 N.E. 479, certiorari denied 282 U.S. 878, 51 S.Ct. 82, 75 L.Ed. 775 (1930). Is prejudice to defendant and the possibility of inconsistent adjudications only a factor to be weighed as part of a balancing of competing interests or should the threat of multiple liability be elevated to a constitutional level?

Isn't nationwide service of process, as is now available under the Federal Interpleader Act, 28 U.S.C. § 2361, see pp. 625–37, *infra,* the most efficacious solution to the joinder-of-parties problem? Notice that a federal court can acquire jurisdiction over an absentee not within the state pursuant to any state long-arm statute, Rule 4(e), and that it also can serve persons brought in under Rule 19 if they are within 100 miles from the place where the action is commenced, whether or not the place of service is within the state in which the action is pending, Rule 4(f). Should the remaining territorial barriers be broken down?

5. PETTENGILL v. UNITED STATES, 253 F.Supp. 321 (N.D.Ill.1966), which was decided prior to the effective date of the 1966 amendment to Federal Rule 19, involved three separate tax-refund actions, one brought by the administratrix and two by heirs of the deceased, to recover taxes erroneously collected from the decedent's estate. A third heir brought an individual refund action in a Florida District Court. The United States argued that all the heirs were required to join as indispensable parties in a single action. Plaintiffs had commenced separate actions because venue barred them from bringing suit in a single court and because there is no trial by jury in the Court of Claims, an alternative forum. If the court dismissed for lack of an

indispensable party, a subsequent action would have been barred by the statute of limitations; if it did not, the government would be put to the expense of defending separate actions. What factors should the court weigh in reaching its result and what should that result be?

6. Reconsider the hypothetical concerning partial subrogation in Note 1 on p. 579, supra. In that context are the insured and the insurer necessary or indispensable parties? If one of the two refuses to join in an action, is there any way to make her a party? In INDEPENDENT WIRELESS TEL. CO. v. RADIO CORP. OF AMERICA, 269 U.S. 459, 46 S.Ct. 166, 70 L.Ed. 357 (1926), the owner of a patent refused to join with plaintiff, an exclusive licensee, in a suit to enjoin further infringement by defendant. The owner was not amenable to process and could not be made a party defendant. The court held that it was proper to treat the recalcitrant absentee as an "involuntary plaintiff" to secure "justice." The involuntary plaintiff rule is not generally available unless the absent party had a duty to allow the plaintiff to bring suit. What are the advantages of the technique employed in the *Independent Wireless* case? Its disadvantages? In EIKEL v. STATES MARINE LINES, INC., 473 F.2d 959 (5th Cir.1973), the absent plaintiff was amenable to the court's process as a defendant. The court joined him as a defendant but realigned him as a plaintiff for diversity purposes only. Was this correct?

7. In KROESE v. GENERAL STEEL CASTINGS CORP., 179 F.2d 760 (3d Cir.), certiorari denied 339 U.S. 983, 70 S.Ct. 1026, 94 L.Ed. 1386 (1950), suit was brought by a shareholder for the declaration of a dividend. Plaintiff did not serve a majority of the members of the board of directors of the corporation. Defendants argued that joinder of a majority was indispensable to the suit since in order to make the court's decree effective, if it decided that a dividend should be declared, the directors would have to be forced to act and this could be done only by binding them to the decree as parties. The court rejected this argument, stating:

> But how can the chancellor's action be made effective? To doubt its effectiveness is to doubt the power of a court wielded by a chancellor with legal imagination. It is certainly true that he cannot do anything to directors who are not subject to his jurisdiction. But he can do a great deal to the property of the corporate group which is within his jurisdiction. The Pennsylvania courts know how to sequester assets of foreign corporations when the case is such that this form of relief is appropriate and the federal courts are equally potent in this respect. If the formal act by the board of directors is necessary under the Delaware General Corporation Law to regularize the dividends to which shareholders are entitled, we cannot think that a receivership or sequestration of a foreign corporation's property will not produce the result. Equity courts have known for a long time how to impose onerous alternatives at home to the performance of affirmative acts abroad as a means of getting those affirmative acts accomplished. In other words, if there is a corporate defendant properly subject to suit within the state and the plaintiff makes out a legal right against the corporation and the corporation has property within the state * * *, the chancellor can accomplish the result the plaintiff is entitled to have accomplished.

Id. at 764–65. Does this holding have any application outside the immediate context of forcing the payment of dividends? Is it indeed any different from simply ordering the corporation to pay dividends, and ignoring the directors? Can a court control the conduct of persons not subject to its personal jurisdiction by seizing control of property they own within its jurisdiction? See Shaffer v. Heitner, p. 150, supra.

———————

Read Federal Rule of Civil Procedure 19 and the accompanying material in the Supplement.

———————

PROVIDENT TRADESMENS BANK & TRUST CO. v. PATTERSON

United States Supreme Court, 1968.
390 U.S. 102, 88 S.Ct. 733, 19 L.Ed.2d 936.

Certiorari to the Circuit Court of Appeals for the Third Circuit.

MR. JUSTICE HARLAN delivered the opinion of the Court.

This controversy, involving in its present posture the dismissal of a declaratory judgment action for nonjoinder of an "indispensable" party, began nearly 10 years ago with a traffic accident. An automobile owned by Edward Dutcher, who was not present when the accident occurred, was being driven by Donald Cionci, to whom Dutcher had given the keys. John Lynch and John Harris were passengers. The automobile crossed the median strip of the highway and collided with a truck being driven by Thomas Smith. Cionci, Lynch, and Smith were killed and Harris was severely injured.

Three tort actions were brought. Provident Tradesmens Bank, the administrator of the estate of passenger Lynch and petitioner here, sued the estate of the driver, Cionci, in a diversity action. Smith's administratrix, and Harris in person, each brought a state-court action against the estate of Cionci, Dutcher, the owner, and the estate of Lynch. These Smith and Harris actions, for unknown reasons, have never gone to trial and are still pending. The Lynch action against Cionci's estate was settled for $50,000, which the estate of Cionci, being penniless, has never paid.

Dutcher, the owner of the automobile and a defendant in the as yet untried tort actions, had an automobile liability insurance policy with Lumbermens Mutual Casualty Company, a respondent here. That policy had an upper limit of $100,000 for all claims arising out of a single accident. This fund was potentially subject to two different sorts of claims by the tort plaintiffs. First, Dutcher himself might be held vicariously liable as Cionci's "principal"; the likelihood of such a judgment against Dutcher is a matter of considerable doubt and dispute. Second, the policy by its terms covered the direct liability of any person driving Dutcher's car with Dutcher's "permission."

The insurance company had declined, after notice, to defend in the tort action brought by Lynch's estate against the estate of Cionci, believing that Cionci had not had permission and hence was not covered by the policy. The facts allegedly were that Dutcher had entrusted his car to Cionci, but that Cionci had made a detour from the errand for which Dutcher allowed his car to be taken. The estate of Lynch, armed with its $50,000 liquidated claim against the estate of Cionci, brought the present diversity action for a declaration that Cionci's use of the car had been "with permission" of Dutcher. The only named defendants were the company and the estate of Cionci. The other two tort plaintiffs were joined as plaintiffs. Dutcher, a resident of the State of Pennsylvania as were all the plaintiffs, was not joined either as plaintiff or defendant. The failure to join him was not adverted to at the trial level.

The major question of law contested at trial was a state-law question. * * * The District Court * * * directed verdicts in favor of the two estates. * * * The jury * * * found that Cionci had had permission, and hence awarded a verdict to Harris also.

Lumbermens appealed the judgment to the Court of Appeals for the Third Circuit, raising various state-law questions.[1] The Court of Appeals did not reach any of these issues. Instead, after reargument *en banc,* it decided, 5–2, to reverse on two alternative grounds neither of which had been raised in the District Court or by the appellant.

The first of these grounds was that Dutcher was an indispensable party. The court held that the "adverse interests" that had rendered Dutcher incompetent to testify under the Pennsylvania Dead Man Rule also required him to be made a party. The court did not consider whether the fact that a verdict had already been rendered, without objection to the nonjoinder of Dutcher, affected the matter. Nor did it follow the provision of Rule 19 of the Federal Rules of Civil Procedure that findings of "indispensability" must be based on stated pragmatic considerations. It held, to the contrary, that the right of a person who "may be affected" by the judgment to be joined is a "substantive" right, unaffected by the federal rules; that a trial court "may not proceed" in the absence of such a person; and that since Dutcher could not be joined as a defendant without destroying diversity jurisdiction the action had to be dismissed.

* * * Concluding that the inflexible approach adopted by the Court of Appeals in this case exemplifies the kind of reasoning that the Rule was designed to avoid, we reverse.

I.

* * *

We may assume, at the outset, that Dutcher falls within the category of persons who, under [Rule 19] (a), should be "joined if feasible." The action was for an adjudication of the validity of certain claims against a fund. Dutcher, faced with the possibility of judgments against him, had an interest in having the fund preserved to cover that potential liability. Hence there existed, when this case went to trial, at least the possibility

1. Appellants challenged the District Court's ruling on the Dead Man issue that Dutcher was incompetent to testify under Pennsylvania law against an estate if he had an adverse interest to that of the estate, the fairness of submitting the question as to Harris to a jury that had been directed to find in favor of the two estates whose position was factually indistinguishable, and certain instructions.

that a judgment might impede Dutcher's ability to protect his interest, or lead to later relitigation by him.

The optimum solution, an adjudication of the permission question that would be binding on all interested persons, was not "feasible," however, for Dutcher could not be made a defendant without destroying diversity. Hence the problem was the one to which Rule 19(b) appears to address itself: in the absence of a person who "should be joined if feasible," should the court dismiss the action or proceed without him? Since this problem emerged for the first time in the Court of Appeals, there were also two subsidiary questions. First, what was the effect, if any, of the failure of the defendants to raise the matter in the District Court? Second, what was the importance, if any, of the fact that a judgment, binding on the parties although not binding on Dutcher, had already been reached after extensive litigation? The three questions prove, on examination, to be interwoven.

We conclude, upon consideration of the record and applying the "equity and good conscience" test of Rule 19(b), that the Court of Appeals erred in not allowing the judgment to stand.

Rule 19(b) suggests four "interests" that must be examined in each case to determine whether, in equity and good conscience, the court should proceed without a party whose absence from the litigation is compelled. Each of these interests must, in this case, be viewed entirely from an appellate perspective since the matter of joinder was not considered in the trial court. First, the plaintiff has an interest in having a forum. Before the trial, the strength of this interest obviously depends upon whether a satisfactory alternative forum exists. On appeal, if the plaintiff has won, he has a strong additional interest in preserving his judgment. Second, the defendant may properly wish to avoid multiple litigation, or inconsistent relief, or sole responsibility for a liability he shares with another. After trial, however, if the defendant has failed to assert this interest, it is quite proper to consider it foreclosed.

Third, there is the interest of the outsider whom it would have been desirable to join. Of course, since the outsider is not before the court, he cannot be bound by the judgment rendered. This means, however, only that a judgment is not *res judicata* as to, or legally enforceable against, a nonparty. It obviously does not mean either (a) that a court may never issue a judgment that, in practice, affects a nonparty or (b) that (to the contrary) a court may always proceed without considering the potential effect on nonparties simply because they are not "bound" in the technical sense. Instead, as Rule 19(a) expresses it, the court must consider the extent to which the judgment may "as a practical matter impair or impede his ability to protect" his interest in the subject matter. When a case has reached the appeal stage the matter is more complex. The judgment appealed from may not in fact affect the interest of any outsider even though there existed, before trial, a possibility that a judgment affecting his interest would be rendered. When necessary, however, a court of appeals should, on its own initiative, take steps to protect the absent party, who of course had no opportunity to plead and prove his interest below.

Fourth, there remains the interest of the courts and the public in complete, consistent, and efficient settlement of controversies. We read the Rule's third criterion, whether the judgment issued in the absence of the nonjoined person will be "adequate," to refer to this public stake in settling disputes by wholes, whenever possible, for clearly the plaintiff, who himself chose both the forum and the parties defendant, will not be heard to complain about the sufficiency of the relief obtainable against them. After trial, considerations of efficiency of course include the fact that the time and expense of a trial have already been spent.

Rule 19(b) also directs a district court to consider the possibility of shaping relief to accommodate these four interests. Commentators had argued that greater attention should be paid to this potential solution to a joinder stymie, and the Rule now makes it explicit that a court should consider modification of a judgment as an alternative to dismissal. Needless to say, a court of appeals may also properly require suitable modification as a condition of affirmance.

Had the Court of Appeals applied Rule 19's criteria to the facts of the present case, it could hardly have reached the conclusion it did. We begin with the plaintiffs' viewpoint. It is difficult to decide at this stage whether they would have had an "adequate" remedy had the action been dismissed before trial for nonjoinder: we cannot here determine whether the plaintiffs could have brought the same action, against the same parties plus Dutcher, in a state court. After trial, however, the "adequacy" of this hypothetical alternative, from the plaintiffs' point of view, was obviously greatly diminished. Their interest in preserving a fully litigated judgment should be overborne only by rather greater opposing considerations than would be required at an earlier stage when the plaintiffs' only concern was for a federal rather than a state forum.

Opposing considerations in this case are hard to find. The defendants had no stake, either asserted or real, in the joinder of Dutcher. They showed no interest in joinder until the Court of Appeals took the matter into its own hands. This properly forecloses any interest of theirs, but for purposes of clarity we note that the insurance company, whose liability was limited to $100,000, had or will have full opportunity to litigate each claim on that fund against the claimant involved. Its only concern with the absence of Dutcher was and is to obtain a windfall escape from its defeat at trial.

The interest of the outsider, Dutcher, is more difficult to reckon. The Court of Appeals, concluding that it should not follow Rule 19's command to determine whether, as a practical matter, the judgment impaired the nonparty's ability to protect his rights, simply quoted the District Court's reasoning on the Dead Man issue as proof that Dutcher had a "right" to be joined:

> The subject matter of this suit is the coverage of Lumbermens' policy issued to Dutcher. Depending upon the outcome of this trial, Dutcher may have the policy all to himself or he may have to share its coverage

with the Cionci Estate, thereby extending the availability of the proceeds of the policy to satisfy verdicts and judgments in favor of the two Estate plaintiffs. Sharing the coverage of a policy of insurance with finite limits with another, and thereby making that policy available to claimants against that other person is immediately worth less than having the coverage of such policy available to Dutcher alone. By the outcome in the instant case, to the extent that the two Estate plaintiffs will have the proceeds of the policy available to them in their claims against Cionci's estate, Dutcher will lose a measure of protection. Conversely, to the extent that the proceeds of this policy are not available to the two Estate plaintiffs Dutcher will gain. * * * It is sufficient for the purpose of determining adversity [of interest] that it appears clearly that the measure of Dutcher's protection under this policy of insurance is dependent upon the outcome of this suit. That being so, Dutcher's interest in these proceedings is adverse to the interest of the two Estate plaintiffs, the parties who represent, on this record, the interests of the deceased persons in the matter in controversy.[11]

There is a logical error in the Court of Appeals' appropriation of this reasoning for its own quite different purposes: Dutcher had an "adverse" interest (sufficient to invoke the Dead Man Rule) because he would have been *benefited* by a ruling *in favor of* the insurance company; the question before the Court of Appeals, however, was whether Dutcher was *harmed* by the judgment *against* the insurance company.

The two questions are not the same. If the three plaintiffs had lost to the insurance company on the permission issue, that loss would have ended the matter favorably to Dutcher. If, as has happened, the three plaintiffs obtain a judgment against the insurance company on the permission issue, Dutcher may still claim that as a nonparty he is not estopped by that judgment from relitigating the issue. At that point it might be argued that Dutcher should be bound by the previous decision because, although technically a nonparty, he had purposely bypassed an adequate opportunity to intervene. We do not now decide whether such an argument would be correct under the circumstances of this case. If, however, Dutcher is properly foreclosed by his failure to intervene in the present litigation, then the joinder issue considered in the Court of Appeals vanishes, for any rights of Dutcher's have been lost by his own inaction.

If Dutcher is not foreclosed by his failure to intervene below, then he is not "bound" by the judgment in favor of the insurance company and, in theory, he has not been harmed. There remains, however, the practical question whether Dutcher is likely to have any need, and if so will have any opportunity, to relitigate. The only possible threat to him is that if the fund is used to pay judgments against Cionci the money may in fact have disappeared before Dutcher has an opportunity to assert his interest. Upon examination, we find this supposed threat neither large nor unavoidable.

11. 218 F.Supp. 802, 805–806, quoted at 365 F.2d, at 805.

The state-court actions against Dutcher had lain dormant for years at the pleading stage by the time the Court of Appeals acted. Petitioner asserts here that under the applicable Pennsylvania vicarious liability law there is virtually no chance of recovery against Dutcher. We do not accept this assertion as fact, but the matter could have been explored below. Furthermore, even in the event of tort judgments against Dutcher, it is unlikely that he will be prejudiced by the outcome here. The potential claimants against Dutcher himself are identical with the potential claimants against Cionci's estate. Should the claimants seek to collect from Dutcher personally, he may be able to raise the permission issue defensively, making it irrelevant that the actual monies paid from the fund may have disappeared: Dutcher can assert that Cionci did not have his permission and that therefore the payments made on Cionci's behalf out of Dutcher's insurance policy should properly be credited against Dutcher's own liability. Of course, when Dutcher raises this defense he may lose, either on the merits of the permission issue or on the ground that the issue is foreclosed by Dutcher's failure to intervene in the present case, but Dutcher will not have been prejudiced by the failure of the District Court here to order him joined.

If the Court of Appeals was unconvinced that the threat to Dutcher was trivial, it could nevertheless have avoided all difficulties by proper phrasing of the decree. The District Court, for unspecified reasons, had refused to order immediate payment on the Cionci judgment. Payment could have been withheld pending the suits against Dutcher and relitigation (if that became necessary) by him. In this Court, furthermore, counsel for petitioners represented orally that they, the tort plaintiffs, would accept a limitation of all claims to the amount of the insurance policy. Obviously such a compromise could have been reached below had the Court of Appeals been willing to abandon its rigid approach and seek ways to preserve what was, as to the parties, subject to the appellants' other contentions, a perfectly valid judgment.

The suggestion of potential relitigation of the question of "permission" raises the fourth "interest" at stake in joinder cases—efficiency. It might have been preferable, at the trial level, if there were a forum available in which both the company and Dutcher could have been made defendants, to dismiss the action and force the plaintiffs to go elsewhere. Even this preference would have been highly problematical, however, for the actual threat of relitigation by Dutcher depended on there being judgments against him and on the amount of the fund, which was not revealed to the District Court. By the time the case reached the Court of Appeals, however, the problematical preference on efficiency grounds had entirely disappeared: there was no reason then to throw away a valid judgment just because it did not theoretically settle the whole controversy.

II.

Application of Rule 19(b)'s "equity and good conscience" test for determining whether to proceed or dismiss would doubtless have led to a contrary result below. The Court of Appeals' reasons for disregarding the Rule remain to be examined. The majority of the court concluded that the Rule was inapplicable because "substantive" rights are involved, and substantive rights are not affected by the Federal Rules. Although the court did not articulate exactly what the substantive rights are, or what law determines them, we take it to have been making the following argument: (1) there is a category of persons called "indispensable parties"; (2) that category is defined by substantive law and the definition cannot be modified by rule; (3) the right of a person falling within that category to participate in the lawsuit in question is also a substantive matter, and is absolute.

With this we may contrast the position that is reflected in Rule 19. Whether a person is "indispensable," that is, whether a particular lawsuit must be dismissed in the absence of that person, can only be determined in the context of particular litigation. There is a large category, whose limits are not presently in question, of persons who, in the Rule's terminology, should be "joined if feasible," and who, in the older terminology, were called either necessary or indispensable parties. Assuming the existence of a person who should be joined if feasible, the only further question arises when joinder is not possible and the court must decide whether to dismiss or to proceed without him. To use the familiar but confusing terminology, the decision to proceed is a decision that the absent person is merely "necessary" while the decision to dismiss is a decision that he is "indispensable." The decision whether to dismiss (i.e., the decision whether the person missing is "indispensable") must be based on factors varying with the different cases, some such factors being substantive, some procedural, some compelling by themselves, and some subject to balancing against opposing interests. Rule 19 does not prevent the assertion of compelling substantive interests; it merely commands the courts to examine each controversy to make certain that the interests really exist. To say that a court "must" dismiss in the absence of an indispensable party and that it "cannot proceed" without him puts the matter the wrong way around: a court does not know whether a particular person is "indispensable" until it has examined the situation to determine whether it can proceed without him.

The Court of Appeals concluded, although it was the first court to hold, that the 19th century joinder cases in this Court created a federal, common-law, substantive right in a certain class of persons to be joined in the corresponding lawsuits. At the least, that was not the way the matter started. The joinder problem first arose in equity and in the earliest case giving rise to extended discussion the problem was the relatively simple one of the inefficiency of litigation involving only some of the interested persons. [Elmendorf v. Taylor, 23 U.S. (10 Wheat.) 152, 6 L.Ed. 289 (1825).] * * *

Following this case there arose three cases, also in equity, that the Court of Appeals here held to have declared a "substantive" right to be joined. It is true that these cases involved what would now be called "substantive" rights. This substantive involvement of the absent person with the controversy before the Court was, however, in each case simply an inescapable fact of the situation presented to the Court for adjudication. The Court in each case left the outsider with no more "rights" than it had already found belonged to him. The question in each case was simply whether, given the substantive involvement of the outsider, it was proper to proceed to adjudicate as between the parties.

* * *

The most influential of the cases in which this Court considered the question whether to proceed or dismiss in the absence of an interested but not joinable outsider is Shields v. Barrow, 17 How. 130, 15 L.Ed. 158, referred to in the opinion below. There the Court attempted, perhaps unfortunately, to stage general definitions of those persons without whom litigation could or could not proceed. In the former category were placed

> Persons having an interest in the controversy, and who ought to be made parties, in order that the court may act on that rule which requires it to decide on, and finally determine the entire controversy, and do complete justice, by adjusting all the rights involved in it. These persons are commonly termed necessary parties; but if their interests are separable from those of the parties before the court, so that the court can proceed to a decree, and do complete and final justice, without affecting other persons not before the court, the latter are not indispensable parties.

The persons in the latter category were

> Persons who not only have an interest in the controversy, but an interest of such a nature that a final decree cannot be made without either affecting that interest, or leaving the controversy in such a condition that its final termination may be wholly inconsistent with equity and good conscience.

These generalizations are still valid today, and they are consistent with the requirements of Rule 19, but they are not a substitute for the analysis required by that Rule. Indeed, the second *Shields* definition states, in rather different fashion, the criteria for decision announced in Rule 19(b). One basis for dismissal is prejudice to the rights of an absent party that *"cannot"* be avoided in issuance of a final decree. Alternatively, if the decree can be so written that it protects the interests of the absent persons, but as so written it leaves the controversy so situated that the outcome may be inconsistent with "equity and good conscience," the suit should be dismissed.

The majority of the Court of Appeals read Shields v. Barrow to say that a person whose interests "may be affected" by the decree of the court is an indispensable party, and that all indispensable parties have a "substantive right" to have suits dismissed in their absence. We are unable to read *Shields* as saying either. It dealt only with persons whose interests must, unavoidably, be affected by a decree and it said nothing about substantive rights. Rule 19(b), which the Court of Appeals dismissed as an ineffective attempt to change the substantive rights stated in *Shields,* is, on the contrary, a valid statement of the criteria for determining whether to proceed or dismiss in the forced absence of an interested person. It takes, for aught that now appears, adequate account of the very real, very substantive claims to fairness on the part of outsiders that may arise in some cases. This, however, simply is not such a case.

* * *

The judgment is vacated and the case is remanded to the Court of Appeals * * *.

Notes and Questions

1. *Provident Tradesmens* interprets the amended version of Federal Rule 19, which was promulgated in 1966. Examine the Advisory Committee's Note to Rule 19, which is set out in the Supplement. What impact does the amendment have on the distinction between necessary and indispensable parties? Given the amendment, what is the purpose of Rule 12(b)(7)? For a negative appraisal of the amended text, see Fink, *Indispensable Parties and the Proposed Amendment to Federal Rule 19,* 74 Yale L.J. 403 (1965).

2. What was the basis of the Court's finding in *Provident Tradesmens* with regard to prejudice for purposes of Rule 19(b) if Dutcher was not joined? Consider the following comments in an article written shortly after the Third Circuit decision dismissing the action and before the Supreme Court's decision.

> * * * How has Dutcher been affected? The judgment declaring that Cionci was driving with permission does not bind Dutcher legally, since he was not a party. Dutcher is free to contest the point with all, including the insurer. Be it noted that although he testified in the action, Dutcher made no attempt to intervene; as the minority suggests, he might have reasonably preferred to stay out of the action. Whereas a judgment declaring Cionci to be an insured did not bind Dutcher, a judgment the other way would very likely have inured to Dutcher's benefit * * *.

Kaplan, *Continuing Work of the Civil Committee: 1966 Amendments of the Federal Rules of Civil Procedure (I),* 81 Harv.L.Rev. 356, 373 (1967).

In what ways might the court shape relief in order to lessen any prejudice? Is the court free simply to grant a remedy other than the one originally requested—for example, by awarding money damages when specific performance might have a detrimental impact on the absentee? Of what importance is the availability of another forum in determining whether the action must be dismissed in the absence of someone whose joinder is not feasible?

3. What weight should be given to the various factors listed in Rule 19? Because there is no precise formula for determining whether a particular nonparty must be joined under Rule 19(a), the decision has to be made in light of the general policies of the Rule. Can you articulate what those policies are? For example, what is the difference between the Rule 19(a)(1) standard that in the absence of the nonparty "complete relief cannot be accorded among those already parties," and the third factor listed in Rule 19(b), "whether a judgment rendered in the person's absence will be adequate"? The second test set out in Rule 19(a) focuses on the prejudicial effect of not joining the absentee. What type of prejudice must be shown to meet this requirement? See generally Tobias, *Rule 19 and the Public Rights Exception to Party Joinder,* 65 N.C.L.Rev. 745 (1987).

4. What should be the result be when plaintiff, a citizen of Texas, sues defendant, a citizen of Arkansas, in a federal district court in Arkansas, and,

on defendant's motion, the court requires that X, a citizen of Texas, be joined as a defendant in the action?

In SCHUTTEN v. SHELL OIL CO., 421 F.2d 869 (5th Cir.1970), the plaintiff filed suit seeking an accounting for the removal of oil, gas, and other minerals from land in Plaquemines Parish, Louisiana, claiming ownership of the land. The defendant filed a motion to dismiss on the ground that its lessor, the Board of Commissioners of the Orleans Levee District, who also claimed title to the land in question, was an "indispensable party" who could not be joined since such action would destroy the District Court's diversity jurisdiction. The District Court granted the defendant's motion and dismissed the case.

After concluding that the Levee Board was a party "to be joined if feasible," the Fifth Circuit stated:

> * * * Since it is not feasible to join the Levee Board we must now consider what alternatives are available under the "equity and good conscience" standard. To do this we must apply the pragmatic criteria of subdivision (b) of Rule 19.
>
> The first factor that must be considered is the extent to which a judgment might prejudice the unjoined Levee Board or those already parties. * * * It is clear that courts should not proceed simply because the unjoined party is not "bound" in the technical sense. * * * Furthermore, one of the purposes, though not the sole purpose, of Rule 19 is the avoidance of multiple litigation of essentially the same issues.
>
> The possibility of prejudice to the Levee Board is most certainly not superficial. First, if Shell is ousted the Levee Board's royalty interest would cease in practically the same manner as if the court had decreed a cancellation of the lease. This would happen despite the fact that the Levee Board's claim of ownership would be technically unimpaired by the judgment in the sense that it would not be bound by the judgment.
>
> Second, though not technically bound a judgment would most assuredly create a cloud on the Levee Board's title and greatly diminish the value of the property. This result would be adverse to both appellants and the Board and would require yet more litigation. A judgment in favor of the appellants would in effect adjudicate the Levee Board's claim of ownership without giving them the right to present their defense and assert their own claim on its merits. While Shell does have a substantial interest in the Levee Board's claim this "interest" would not justify placing the burden of proving the Levee Board's ownership on Shell.
>
> Third, a judgment might result in inconsistent obligations for the defendant Shell Oil Company. * * * Again all of this could come about without affording the Levee Board the opportunity to defend its interests even though the Board would not be bound by the judgment.
>
> A conclusion that as a practical matter the Levee Board would be prejudiced by a judgment rendered in their absence leads us to consider the second and third "factors" of Rule 19: "the extent to which, by protective provisions in the judgment, by the shaping of relief, or other measures, the prejudice can be lessened or avoided", and whether a judgment rendered in the Levee Board's absence will be adequate. Appellants have suggested no way in which these objectives could be accom-

plished and we are unable to discover any ourselves. Since the litigation revolved around the conflicting claims of ownership, we are unable to envision a decree which would effectively settle any controversy between the appellants and the present defendant, Shell, without doing substantial practical injury to the Levee Board's unassertable claims. Any attempt to fashion a judgment which would lessen this harm would result in a meaningless decree.

* * * [Last we must] consider the fourth and final criteria of Rule 19: whether the appellant has an adequate remedy elsewhere. The answer to this question is that appellants will by no means be prejudiced themselves if forced to pursue their remedy in the courts of the State of Louisiana. Both the Levee Board and Shell are amenable to process in Louisiana. This litigation concerns land situated in Louisiana, is governed by Louisiana law and involves a claim of ownership asserted by an agency of the State of Louisiana. * * * There is, however, an even more compelling reason for appellants to seek relief in the Louisiana courts. * * * By dismissing the case now and directing the appellants to proceed in the Louisiana courts most if not all issues can be settled in one bout of litigation. As noted above, the expeditious and effective disposition of litigation is desirable if not always obtainable. In the present case it is not only desirable but obtainable and is indeed made necessary under the circumstances.

Id. at 874–75.

SECTION E. IMPLEADER

Read Federal Rule of Civil Procedure 14 and the material accompanying it in the Supplement.

JEUB v. B/G FOODS, INC.

United States District Court, District of Minnesota, 1942.
2 F.R.D. 238.

NORDBYE, DISTRICT JUDGE. The facts are briefly these: The complainants seek to recover damages from the defendant, B/G Foods, Inc., on the grounds that, in one of the restaurants operated by this defendant, they were served with certain ham which was contaminated, unwholesome, and deleterious to the health, causing complainants to become sick and distressed to their damage. * * * Prior to the service of the answer, on application of the defendant, an ex parte order was obtained, making Swift and Company a third-party defendant. The third-party complaint set forth that the ham served was canned "Swift Premium Ham", a product of Swift and Company, and purchased in a sealed can by B/G Foods the day preceding the serving of the ham to the complainants. It is asserted that B/G Foods was entirely free from any blame or negligence in connection therewith. It is further alleged in the third-party complaint that "if any of said ham was unwholesome, poisonous, deleterious or otherwise in any way unfit for human consumption, such condition was caused solely and entirely by negligence and carelessness and unlawful conduct on the part of Swift and Company." Further, that "Swift and Company is liable to indemnify and reimburse B/G Foods, Inc., for the whole amount of any recovery made by plaintiff, * * * against B/G Foods, Inc., on account of said ham being served to her in its food shop. * * *" Judgment is prayed that any recovery be against Swift and Company and not B/G Foods, Inc., and that B/G Foods, Inc., have judgment against Swift and Company for any and all sums which may be adjudged against B/G Foods, Inc., in favor of the plaintiff.

The motion to vacate the order is based on the showing that plaintiffs have not amended, and have refused to amend, their complaints to state any cause of action against Swift and Company. It is therefore the position of the third-party defendant that no relief can be granted against it in this proceeding; that [Federal] Rule 14 * * * is merely procedural and does not create any substantive rights; that no right of contribution or indemnity exists under the Minnesota law merely because a suit has been commenced; and that the party must have suffered some loss or paid more than his share of the loss before any rights will inure. It is pointed out that, as yet, the B/G Foods has suffered no loss and has made no payment growing out of the incident in question.

That the rights over and against Swift and Company, which B/G Foods may have by reason of any loss sustained by it, must be governed by the substantive laws of this State is entirely clear. The invoking of the third-party procedural practice must not do violence to the substantive rights of the parties. However, an acceleration or an expedition of the presentation of such rights does not conflict with any Minnesota law. [Federal] Rule 14 * * * permits the impleader of a party "who is or may be liable." The fact that an independent action for money recovery could not be brought at this time does not militate against B/G Foods' right to invoke a procedure which will determine rights of the parties concurrently with that of the basic proceeding, and if and when any loss has been sustained as to which Swift and Company is liable over, the laws of this State in regard thereto may be made effective. * * * Rule 14 is not restricted to the rights of indemnity or contribution which are presently enforcible * * *.

The apparent purpose of Rule 14 is to provide suitable machinery whereby the rights of all parties may be determined in one proceeding. Manifestly if Swift and Company is liable over to B/G Foods, Inc., for any or all damages sustained by reason of the tortious act alleged, no cogent reason is suggested why the original defendant should not avail itself of this rule. Otherwise, B/G Foods, Inc., would be required to await the outcome of the present suit, and then if plaintiffs recover, to institute an independent action for contribution or indemnity. The rule under consideration was promulgated to avoid this very circuity of proceeding. Neither is any good reason suggested why the determination of the entire controversy in one proceeding will prejudice the rights of any of the parties. Certainly, plaintiffs cannot complain. They have not availed themselves of the opportunity to join Swift and Company as a party defendant. To require the same jury to determine the controversy between the third-party plaintiff and third-party defendant will not harm or jeopardize their rights or position before these triers of fact. The rights of Swift and Company are likewise not prejudiced by being made a third-party defendant. If it is liable over, it is concerned with the payment by B/G Foods, Inc., of any loss or damage obtained by these plaintiffs. However, the recognition or preservation of that right presents no particular difficulty. Any judgment against it by way of contribution or indemnity may be stayed until the judgment in the original proceeding against the B/G Foods, Inc., is paid or satisfied. One jury impaneled to determine the entire controversy may not only save time and expense, but it is fair to assume that the ends of justice will be served by disposition of the entire matter through the facilities of one jury. * * *

The motion, therefore, to vacate the order making Swift and Company a third-party defendant in each of the above-entitled cases, is denied. * * *

Notes and Questions

1. In a diversity case in a state that adheres to the common-law rule prohibiting contribution among joint tortfeasors, must a federal court deny impleader of a joint tortfeasor? Note that in *Jeub* the applicable state law recognized a substantive right of action but merely failed to provide a procedural device for the acceleration or concurrent determination of the liability as part of the principal lawsuit. How might the court shape the relief on an accelerated or contingent claim to reflect the limitations of substantive state law?

2. What factors should the court consider in determining whether to allow a third-party defendant to be impleaded? May a defendant-insured in a negligence action implead the liability insurer under Rule 14 when the insurance policy contains either a "no action" clause or a provision to the effect that "nothing contained in this policy shall give any person or organization any right to join the company as a codefendant in any action against the insured to determine the latter's liability"?

3. In MISKELL v. W.T. COWN, INC., 10 F.R.D. 617 (E.D.Pa.1950), defendant moved to bring in a third party. Plaintiff opposed the motion on the ground that the third party was a sailor who might be unavailable at the time of trial or exempted from appearing under the Soldiers' and Sailors' Civil Relief Act. The court rejected plaintiff's arguments.

The plaintiff's concern is, I believe, premature. For even though the motion to implead be granted, this Court has, under the Federal Rules, ample discretion to protect the plaintiff from prejudice and inconvenience. If, at the time of trial, the third party is not required to answer, the Court may order a separate trial between plaintiff and defendant under Rule 42(b) and, under Rule 54(b) enter a separate judgment. In this manner, not only may the plaintiff be protected but the defendant may also be protected against the necessity of filing a separate suit should the situation not require it.   *   *   *

Id. at 618.

In GOODHART v. UNITED STATES LINES CO., 26 F.R.D. 163 (S.D.N.Y. 1960), plaintiff sued for personal injuries caused by defendant's employee. The court denied a motion to implead the employee:

> I feel safe in taking judicial notice of the fact that the operator of a hi-lo [defendant's employee] will not be financially able to indemnify defendant to any substantial extent. Defendant must have some other reason or reasons for seeking impleader. One of those reasons is that jurors will likely render a smaller verdict if they are required to find that an individual employee of defendant is ultimately responsible for its payment. Another is that the interest of the hi-lo operator in a verdict for his employer will be heightened.   *   *   *
>
> In seeking the first result defendant, in effect, asks me to give it the advantage of the chance that the jury will proceed upon a false supposition that the hi-lo operator will pay the judgment. In seeking the second result defendant, in effect, asks me to help him threaten the hi-lo operator with the necessity of going through bankruptcy unless he testifies favorably to defendant. Neither of these pleas recommends itself to the court as a subject for exercise of the court's discretion. Such legitimate claim as defendant may have against the hi-lo operator is amply protected by defendant's right to bring a separate suit.

Id. at 164. Would permitting impleader but granting a motion for separate trials under Rule 42(b), as suggested in *Miskell,* have adequately protected plaintiff from possible prejudice? Are there any advantages to this procedure?

HORTON v. CONTINENTAL CAN CO.
United States District Court, District of Nebraska, 1956.
19 F.R.D. 429.

[Horton was employed by Wade and Son, a construction contractor doing work for Continental Can Company. He was injured while working on a metallic scaffold owned by Continental but being used by Wade and Son in connection with its work for Continental. Wade and Son paid benefits to Horton under the Nebraska Workmen's Compensation Law. Subsequently, Horton instituted this action against Continental on the theory that the latter had negligently maintained the scaffold. Wade and Son was made a party defendant in order to protect its right to subrogation in any judgment obtained against Continental to the extent of its earlier workmen's compensation payments. Continental denied negligence and sought, by third-party complaint, to assert that if it was liable to Horton, that liability arose only by reason of the active negligence by one Elbert T. Culver, an iron workers crew foreman of Wade and Son. The answer further asserted that Wade and Son, as Culver's employer and master, was ultimately liable. In the first part of its opinion, the District Court concluded that Elbert T. Culver could be made a third-party defendant but, because of a technical defect in Continental's motion papers, a new third-party complaint was necessary. The court then went on to discuss Continental's attempt to make Wade and Son a third-party defendant.]

DELEHANT, CHIEF JUDGE. ＊ ＊ ＊

In the context of the case the motion to bring in Wade and Son as a third-party defendant presents a different question. Wade and Son is a party to the action and has been from its institution. Upon the record it is a defendant. Continental argues with some force that it should be aligned as a plaintiff along with Horton. But that point need not be determined. Whether it is substantially a defendant or a plaintiff, Wade and Son is a party to the case. It has voluntarily appeared, and has served and filed its answer praying for judgment in its behalf in the sum of its compensation payments on account of plaintiff "out of any judgment rendered against the defendant, Continental Can Company, Inc., in favor of the plaintiff," and has served and filed a designation of the place of trial.

In such a situation the pertinent language of Rule 14 needs to be recalled. ＊ ＊ ＊ For the invocation of the rule it appears ＊ ＊ ＊ to be required that the proposed additional defendant be not only one who is or may be liable to the moving defendant for all or part of plaintiff's claim against him, but, what is of present significance, also "a person not a party to the action." And it is obvious that Wade and Son is not such a person. Being already a party to the action, it appears to be quite unnecessary that it be now made a party under a new title or style. ＊ ＊ ＊ Continental would seem already to possess resources in pleading appropriate for the assertion of its claim against Wade and Son. And resort to Rule 14, seemingly not available, ought also to be quite unnecessary. ＊ ＊ ＊

An order is, therefore, being made denying and overruling the motion insofar as it seeks to make Wade and Son a third-party defendant, but without prejudice to the right of Continental to assert its claim against Wade and Son by any other appropriate procedure, in respect of which the order does not make, or this memorandum suggest, any limitation.

＊ ＊ ＊

Notes and Questions

1. The court in *Horton* states that Continental could assert its claim against Wade and Son other than under Rule 14. There are at least two possible procedures; what are they? One is dealt with in Sporia v. Pennsylvania Greyhound Lines, Inc., 143 F.2d 105 (3d Cir.1944). What difference does it make if Continental's claim is brought under Rule 14 or by some "other appropriate procedure"? Does it make any sense to conclude that a third-party claim is proper as against Culver but not as against Wade and Son? What is the logic of Rule 13(a), (b), and (g) permitting or requiring

counterclaims and cross-claims to be asserted against persons who already are parties and Rule 14(a) denying impleader in that context?

2.   *   *   *   This practice [impleader] has its roots in the common-law procedure of "vouching to warranty," whereby a person whose title to land has been attacked could notify his vendor of the attack if the latter had warranted the title. The vendor, whether or not he chose to participate, would then be bound by the prior determination in a subsequent suit by his vendee.

Developments in the Law—Multiparty Litigation in the Federal Courts, 71 Harv.L.Rev. 874, 907 (1958). In what ways does third-party practice under Federal Rule 14 differ from the common-law procedure of vouching to warranty? See Note 4 on p. 1190, infra. For a discussion of the "vouching-in" procedure, see Degnan & Barton, *Vouching to Quality Warranty: Case Law and Commercial Code,* 51 Calif.L.Rev. 471 (1963).

3.   The states take a variety of different approaches to third-party practice. Indeed, the practice in a number of states is very different from that under Federal Rule 14. Many of the reasons for this difference in practice are described in Friedenthal, *The Expansion of Joinder in Cross-Complaints by the Erroneous Interpretation of Section 442 of the California Code of Civil Procedure,* 51 Calif.L.Rev. 494 (1963).

REVERE COPPER & BRASS, INC. v. AETNA CAS. & SUR. CO., 426 F.2d 709, 715–17 (5th Cir.1970). Revere sued Aetna on a surety bond executed in connection with a construction contract, alleging that Fuller, the builder, had breached express and implied warranties and specific contract provisions, had been negligent, had made false representations, and had failed to complete its work within the prescribed time. It sought damages of $2,045,000. Aetna impleaded Fuller under Rule 14(a), claiming that the builder had agreed to indemnify Aetna for all losses sustained as a result of the suretyship. Fuller asserted a "counterclaim" against Revere seeking $1,328,880 based on the breach of certain express and implied warranties and for wanton and willful misconduct. Revere moved to dismiss Fuller's claim on the ground that there was no diversity of citizenship between Revere and Fuller; the District Court held the claim to be within its ancillary jurisdiction. On appeal, the Fifth Circuit, after discussing the six reported district court decisions dealing with the question, affirmed, holding that the claim clearly fell within the core of aggregate facts upon which the original claim rested and thus was within the court's ancillary jurisdiction. Judge Morgan, speaking for the court, stated:

> It is easily seen that Fuller's claim arises out of the aggregate of operative facts which forms the basis of Revere's claim in such a way to put their logical relationship beyond doubt. The two claims are but two sides of the same coin. The construction was not completed before the time provided in the two contracts. If Revere is not responsible for the delay, as Fuller alleges, Fuller must at least be guilty of breach of contract, not to mention the other allegations of fault in Revere's complaint. To paraphrase the Supreme Court in Moore v. New York Cotton

Exchange * * * [p. 565, supra]: so close is the connection between the case sought to be stated in Revere's complaint and that set up in Fuller's Rule 14(a) counterclaim that it only needs the failure of the former to establish the foundation for the latter.

Not only is the parallel between a Rule 14(a) counterclaim and a compulsory counterclaim under Rule 13(a) so close as to be persuasive on the question of ancillarity, the parallel between the instant case and cases dealing with the ability of an intervenor of right under Rule 24(a) to counterclaim against the original plaintiff without an independent basis of federal jurisdiction removes any substantial doubt. It is well established that a contractor who has agreed to indemnify his surety on a performance bond can intervene as a party defendant as of right in a suit on the performance bond against the surety and then assert his counterclaim against the plaintiff, even in the absence of an independent ground of federal jurisdiction. * * * It would be anomalous to hold that Fuller could have asserted its counterclaim against Revere free of any jurisdictional impediment if it had taken the initiative of intervening, and yet hold that since Fuller was brought into this action involuntarily as a third-party defendant, its counterclaim must satisfy the requirements of strict diversity and thus fail.

* * * Revere argues that since there must be an independent ground of jurisdiction to support the original plaintiff's claim against a third-party defendant, the same requirement must be met by the third-party defendant in asserting a counterclaim against the original plaintiff. Suffice it to say that the two situations are the converse of each other only superficially and that there are differences which militate against identical treatment. First of all, the plaintiff has the option of selecting the forum where he believes he can most effectively assert his claims, he has not been involuntarily brought to a forum, faced with the prospect of defending himself as best he can under the rules that forum provides, or defending himself not at all. Since a plaintiff could not initially join a non-diverse defendant, it is arguable he should not be allowed to do so indirectly by way of a fortuitous impleader. Moreover, there is the possibility, whether real or fanciful, of collusion between the plaintiff and an overly cooperative defendant impleading just the right third party. Whatever the merit or demerit of these reasons, they point to a sufficient difference to require that the application of ancillary jurisdiction to each type of claim must be decided separately. Consequently, this decision is to be strictly limited to the precise question decided.

Notes and Questions

1. The *Revere* case is discussed in 59 Ky.L.J. 506 (1970); 1970 Wash.U.L. Q. 511; and 49 N.C.L.Rev. 503 (1971). In Owen Equipment & Erection Co. v. Kroger, p. 282, supra, the Supreme Court validated the conclusion in *Revere* that a claim by the original plaintiff against the third-party defendant arising out of the transaction or occurrence that is the subject matter of plaintiff's claim against the original defendant may be interposed only if it meets independent jurisdictional requirements. Does a rereading of *Kroger* reveal any reason to doubt the conclusion in *Revere* that a claim by a third-party

defendant against the original plaintiff is within the ancillary jurisdiction of the federal courts?

2. According to the existing case law, the statutory venue limitations have no application to Rule 14 claims even if they would require the third-party proceeding to be heard in another district had it been brought as an independent action. However, should jurisdiction and venue be treated the same or differently in the context of a claim by the third-party defendant against the original plaintiff? See *Developments in the Law—Multiparty Litigation in the Federal Courts,* 71 Harv.L.Rev. 874, 911–12 (1958). Reconsider the materials on ancillary jurisdiction on p. 288, supra. See also Pennsylvania R. Co. v. Erie Ave. Warehouse Co., 302 F.2d 843 (3d Cir.1962).

3. Are there any limitations on the third-party defendant's ability to assert a claim against the third-party plaintiff? Against the original plaintiff? In HEINTZ & CO. v. PROVIDENT TRADESMENS BANK & TRUST CO., 30 F.R.D. 171 (E.D.Pa.1962), plaintiff alleged that defendant negligently permitted Kerr to open a bank account in plaintiff's name and to draw checks without plaintiff's permission. Defendant impleaded Kerr. Kerr then filed a claim against plaintiff for services rendered and materials furnished to plaintiff in connection with the establishment of a branch office managed by Kerr. The court found Kerr's claim within Rule 14 because it arose out of the same transaction as the original suit.

> * * * The only distinction between a counterclaim under Rule 13(a) and the sort of claim we have before us under Rule 14 is that defendant "must" plead his counterclaim under Rule 13(a) if it grows out of the same transaction or occurrence, whereas under Rule 14, the third party "may" plead his claim for relief. But this, we think, is a distinction without a difference. The ancillary nature of the claim is not to be determined by whether the pleader "must" or "may" assert it, but by its relation to the transaction that is the subject of the main suit.

Id. at 174. If the original plaintiff has a counterclaim arising out of the same transaction as the claim asserted by the third-party defendant, is it compulsory? Can the original plaintiff assert a permissive counterclaim against the third-party defendant?

Another problem in third-party practice is exemplified by NOLAND CO. v. GRAVER TANK & MFG. CO., 301 F.2d 43 (4th Cir.1962), which grew out of a suit originally brought by Ruscon Construction Company, a general contractor, against Noland, a subcontractor, for the difference between the cost of a water tank and the subcontractor's bid price. Noland's bid was based on estimates given to it by Graver, a water tank supplier. Noland impleaded Graver not only to obtain indemnity for his liability to Ruscon but also to recover $4,000 in contemplated profits. The District Court allowed Noland only the indemnity. The Fourth Circuit framed the issue as

> * * * whether, under Rule 14, a third-party defendant, *once made a party to an action,* can be proceeded against by the third-party plaintiff upon a claim closely related to, yet different from and for an amount in excess of, the original plaintiff's claim asserted in the primary action.

* * *

Id. at 49. The court then held:

> * * * In view of the ease with which disposition of all claims herein could be made in this one action, we conclude that Rule 14 should be construed to be sufficiently broad and flexible so as to permit the District Court, in the exercise of its sound discretion, to make such disposition.

Id. at 50. In a more recent Third Circuit opinion, SCHWAB v. ERIE LACKAWANNA R. CO., 438 F.2d 62 (3d Cir.1971), the court held that although it would be improper to allow the third-party plaintiff to bring an additional claim against the third-party defendant under Rule 14, the claim was proper under Rule 18 and came within the ancillary jurisdiction of the court. Does it make any difference under which rule the claim is asserted? Does it make any difference if the third-party plaintiff's additional claim does not have a close nexus with the ancillary claim under Rule 14? See U.S. v. United Pacific Ins. Co., 472 F.2d 792 (9th Cir.1973).

SECTION F. INTERPLEADER

Read Federal Rule of Civil Procedure 22, 28 U.S.C. §§ 1335, 1397, and 2361, and the accompanying material in the Supplement.

Interpleader is a device designed to enable a party who might be exposed to multiple claims to money or property under her control to settle the controversy in a single proceeding. For example, if two people claim that each is the sole beneficiary of a life insurance policy, the insurance company, in the absence of a joinder device such as interpleader, would be required to defend against both in two actions. Not only would the company be forced to incur the expense of additional litigation, but it would be faced with the possibility that, in separate lawsuits, *both* claimants might win.

1. HISTORICAL LIMITATIONS ON THE USE OF INTER-PLEADER

HANCOCK OIL CO. v. INDEPENDENT DISTRIBUTING CO.

Supreme Court of California, 1944.
24 Cal.2d 497, 150 P.2d 463.

EDMONDS, JUSTICE. * * *

According to the complaint [filed by two corporate lessees of certain real property], in 1936 W.L. Hopkins and Gertrude Ann Hopkins, his wife, leased certain real property to Hancock Oil Company of California and R.R. Bush Oil Company. Landowner's royalties of approximately $1,500. have accrued. It is also alleged that in 1941, Independent Distributing Co., a copartnership composed of Merritt Bloxom, Eugene E. Olwell and Murray M. Olwell, brought an action asserting that W.L. Hopkins, Gertrude Ann Hopkins, and two persons sued by fictitious names, hold the real property described in the lease in trust for them. The relief sought in the suit of Independent Distributing Co. was an accounting of the rents of the land.

The copartnership and the copartners, together with W.L. Hopkins and Gertrude Ann Hopkins, H. James Hopkins and W.L. Hopkins, trustees of Wilbur T. Hopkins Trust, and H. James Hopkins and W.L. Hopkins, trustees of the H. James Hopkins Trust, are named as the defendants in the present suit, the charge of the complaint being that the copartnership and the copartners claim to be the owners of the land described in the lease and entitled to all of the landowner's royalties accrued and to accrue under that agreement. A further assertion of the complaint is that the defendants other than the copartnership and the copartners also claim the same royalties and by reason of these conflicting claims the lessees cannot safely determine to whom the rent should be paid. * * *

To this complaint Merritt Bloxom, Eugene E. Olwell, Murray M. Olwell and Independent Distributing Co. filed an answer alleging that they are the owners of the property and entitled to all of the rents and profits from it. They also assert that the defendants named Hopkins are holding title to the property in trust for them. The defendants other than the copartners and the copartnership interposed a general demurrer and a special demurrer upon the ground of uncertainty. Each demurrer was sustained without leave to amend and the corporations' appeal is from the judgment which followed that order.

From an opinion of the trial judge, it appears that the demurrers were sustained upon the sole ground that a tenant may not question the title of his landlord at the date of the lease; accordingly, a suit by a tenant to interplead his landlord and one who claims the rent agreed to be paid in accordance with the terms of the lease by which he holds possession of the real property is in violation of this fundamental principle. The appellants assert that a suit in interpleader does not constitute a denial of the landlord's title but is simply a means by which the tenant may discharge his obligation to pay rent under the lease without becoming involved in the conflict between different claimants to the amount due and unpaid. * * *

The common law bill of interpleader had four essential elements: (1) The same thing, debt, or duty must be claimed by both or all the parties against whom the relief is demanded; (2) all of the adverse titles or claims must be dependent, or be derived from a common source; (3) the one seeking the relief must not have nor claim any interest in the subject matter; and (4) he must have incurred no independent liability to either of the claimants. See 4 Pomeroy's Equity Jurisprudence, 5th Ed.1941, § 1322, p. 906.

These requirements have been termed historical limitations upon this otherwise expeditious equitable proceeding * * *, and in 1881 section 386 of the Code of Civil Procedure was amended to broaden the remedy. The statute * * * declares * * *: "And whenever conflicting claims are or may be made upon a person for or relating to personal property, or the performance of an obligation, or any portion thereof, such person may bring an action against the conflicting claimants to compel them to interplead and litigate their several claims among themselves. The order of substitution may be made and the action of interpleader may be maintained, and the applicant or plaintiff be discharged from liability to all or any of the conflicting claimants, although their titles or claims have not a common origin, or are not identical, but are adverse to and independent of one another." The provision of this enactment, that interpleader lies "although their titles or claims have not a common origin * * * but are adverse to and independent of one another," directly abrogates the common law requirement that all the adverse titles or claims must be dependent or be derived from a common source, and it is therefore clear that privity between the conflicting claimants need not be shown to invoke the remedy under the code. * * *

Early in the history of interpleader, it was held that one who sought to maintain such a suit must show outstanding claims, identical in every respect and without the slightest degree of variation, to the same thing, debt or duty. In the case of conflicting claims to specific personal property, this rigid formalism did not seriously interfere with the effectiveness of the proceeding. But where, as is generally the situation modernly, the subject matter of the conflicting claims was an obligation, a debt or a duty, the requirement as to the identity of the defendant's demands very often prevented a stakeholder from using interpleader where he was doubly vexed with respect to one liability. For example, under the narrow rule of the common law, if one person claimed all of the fund held by a bank and another person asserted the right to only a portion of that fund, the bank could not secure a determination of its liability by means of the equitable proceeding. The Legislature has removed this restriction, yet the very rationale of interpleader compels the conclusion that the amendment does not allow the remedy where each of the claimants asserts the right to a different debt, claim or duty. If the conflicting claims are mutually exclusive, interpleader cannot be maintained, but the fact that an identical right is not asserted by each of the claimants does not preclude the use of the remedy. * * *

In the present case, the plaintiffs have alleged that each of the two groups against whom interpleader is sought claims the right to receive the rents and royalties reserved in the lease. If Independent Distributing Co. and the members of that copartnership should assert that they are entitled to the reasonable value of the use and occupation of the land leased to the plaintiffs, together with the mesne profits or damages for waste, the trial court would be required to deny the plaintiffs the right to interplead those parties with their lessors. Under such circumstances the claims of the parties would not relate to the same obligation. But as the appellants' complaint pleads that there are conflicting claims concerning their obligation to pay the rents and royalties reserved by the lease, the lessors and the third parties must answer and, if each of them agrees that his claim concerns the right to those rents and royalties, the lessees should be discharged from liability upon payment of their obligations under the lease.

As to the remaining common law principles governing a suit of interpleader, the appellants' complaint conforms with the requirement that the plaintiff in such a proceeding must stand in the position of a disinterested stakeholder. However, much of the present controversy centers about the last element which is specified as essential. Although the complaint discloses no obligation of the appellants other than under the lease, the respondents assert that the obligation to pay rent constitutes an independent liability and bars the remedy of interpleader.

＊ ＊ ＊ The rule concerning independent liability is stated in Corpus Juris as follows: "Interpleader will not lie if the stakeholder has incurred some personal obligation to either of the claimants, independent of the title or the right to possession, because such claimant would in that event have a claim against him which could not be settled in a litigation with the other claimant." 33 C.J. 439. ＊ ＊ ＊ The Supreme Court of Maine put the matter most convincingly when it said: "The mere fact that a contractual relation exists between plaintiff and one of the defendants, under which the fund is required to be paid to such claimant, does not of itself defeat the right of interpleader. ＊ ＊ ＊ If such were the law, it would be difficult to conceive of any set of facts which would enable a bank, a trustee, or other custodian of funds, or even a bailee, to maintain interpleader. The obligation referred to in the rule must be independent of the title or right of possession of the fund or property in question. ＊ ＊ ＊" First National Bank v. Reynolds, 127 Me. 340, 143 A. 266, 268, 60 A.L.R. 712. ＊ ＊ ＊

Although Professor Pomeroy declares that an independent liability "arises from the very nature of the original relation subsisting between" the landlord and tenant, he states that such a suit is proper whenever there is some privity between the claimant and the lessor, as, for example, when the relation of trustee and *cestui que trust* has been created between them. It seems, therefore, that the reason why the author asserts that the relationship of the landlord and tenant precludes interpleader by the tenant is not that, under the lease, there is an independent liability but because there is no privity between the landlord and the one joined with him as a defendant. ＊ ＊ ＊

From what has been said, then, it is clear that, in the present case, as according to the facts alleged in the complaint, the relations inter se of the respondents and the copartners are such that the decision will determine the liability of the lessees to each of them, there is no independent liability which will bar the remedy of interpleader; accordingly the appellants' complaint is sufficient with respect to those of the four common law requirements for interpleader not abolished or modified by the amendment in 1881 to section 386 of the Code of Civil Procedure. ＊ ＊ ＊

[The court went on to consider the effect of the common-law rule that a tenant may not dispute the title of his landlord at the time of the commencement of the relation.]

Notwithstanding the strict common law limitation on interpleader in landlord-tenant cases which is justified by an ancient rule of real property, the code provision concerning the remedy must be liberally construed. A remedial statute, its purpose is to avoid a multiplicity of suits and prevent vexatious litigation. * * *

* * * [I]n the absence of the right to interplead the landlord and the adverse claimant to the rent, the tenant is faced with the unfortunate alternative of forfeiting his lease or possibly paying twice. * * * And there is no action at law adequate to shield him from vexation by multiple litigation over the obligation for rent, against the risk of double liability upon the same obligation, and against insecurity of tenancy.

Furthermore, interpleader is not only of importance to the tenant; it is also of advantage to the third party claimant. If the tenant may not interplead his landlord and another under the common law rule, the third party must establish his right to rent in a separate action. During the progress of this litigation the tenant would pay the rents to the landlord. It is entirely conceivable that before judgment was rendered the tenant might become insolvent, leaving the third party without recourse, or because of financial difficulties overtaking the landlord, the tenant would be required to pay his obligation twice.

Unquestionably the landlord may suffer some disadvantage in being forced to defend a suit in interpleader. While the litigation continues the rent is withheld from him without interest. But the tenant may not maintain such a suit upon the mere pretext or suspicion of double vexation; he must allege facts showing a reasonable probability of double vexation. Without accurately appraising the rationale of interpleader, by some decisions this court has mentioned as an additional requirement that the plaintiff must allege facts showing a doubt as to which claimant he can safely pay. * * * However, to demand from a plaintiff that he express a doubt as to which adverse claimant he is liable is an admission that the basis upon which the right to interpleader rests is the avoidance of double liability. "The right to the remedy by interpleader is founded, however, not on the consideration that a man may be subjected to double liability, but on the fact that he is threatened with double vexation in respect to one liability." Pfister v. Wade, * * * 56 Cal. at page 47 * * *.

The complaint therefore states a cause of action against a general demurrer and denial of leave to amend was an abuse of discretion even if the special demurrer was well taken. * * *

The judgment is reversed.

[The dissenting opinion of JUSTICE CARTER has been omitted.]

Notes and Questions

1. Does the fact that modern interpleader is a remodeling by the equity courts of the common-law writ of interpleader explain why its availability was limited prior to statutory modification?

2. The California Supreme Court states in *Hancock* that interpleader would have been denied if Independent Oil Company had asserted a claim for profits and damages. In such a situation, the court reasoned, "the claims of

the parties [Independent and Hopkins] would not relate to the same obligation." What does the court mean by "the same obligation"? Consider the probable content of the allegations if Independent had asserted a claim for profits and damages and Hopkins had asserted a claim for the rents; would the claims have been mutually exclusive?

3. ALTON & PETERS v. MERRITT, 145 Minn. 426, 177 N.W. 770 (1920). Defendants, owners of certain real property, entered into a contract with plaintiffs, real estate brokers, under which they agreed to pay plaintiffs a commission of $500 if they produced a purchaser ready, willing, and able to pay $200 per acre for defendants' land. Two weeks after the date of that contract, defendants entered into a similar contract with Sandlin, also a real estate broker. Within the time stipulated in plaintiffs' contract, they presented to defendants a purchaser ready, willing, and able to buy the land at $200 per acre. At about the same time, Sandlin produced a different purchaser. Plaintiffs and Sandlin both claimed commissions. When plaintiffs brought suit to collect their commission, defendants sought to interplead Sandlin. The trial court's grant of the motion to interplead was reversed by the Minnesota Supreme Court. Was the appellate court's decision correct? Why? Would interpleader have been granted if the case had arisen in a jurisdiction adopting the *Hancock* approach? Would the result have been different if plaintiffs and Sandlin had found the same purchaser?

4. The typical interpleader suit has two stages. The first determines whether interpleader is proper; in it, the controversy is between the stakeholder on one side and all the claimants on the other. If interpleader is granted, the first stage ends with a decree allowing the stakeholder to withdraw from the case and enjoining the claimants from taking any further proceedings against the stakeholder. Before retiring, however, the stakeholder is required to deposit the money or property involved in the dispute with the court, generally less court costs and attorney's fees. In the second stage, the contest is among the claimants to determine their respective rights to the property or fund deposited in court. See McClintock, *Equity* § 188 (2d ed. 1948); 4 Pomeroy, *Equity Jurisprudence* § 1320 (5th ed. 1941).

5. Consider PLAZA EXPRESS CO. v. GALLOWAY, 365 Mo. 166, 280 S.W.2d 17 (1955). Galloway commenced an action claiming $20,000 for personal injuries allegedly caused by the negligence of Plaza Express. When Galloway died, his administrator was substituted as a party plaintiff. Shortly before substitution, Galloway's widow brought a separate action for $15,000 against Plaza Express. According to Missouri law, a cause of action for personal injuries other than injuries resulting in death survives in the personal representative of the injured party, whereas a cause of action for wrongful death vests in the surviving spouse of the deceased. Plaza Express was allowed to interplead the administrator and the widow under a provision similar to the one found in Federal Rule of Civil Procedure 22(1). Would the same result have been reached if the action had been brought in a jurisdiction that follows the historical restrictions on interpleader? Would interpleader have been available if the case had been brought in California after the *Hancock* decision?

6. The third requirement for interpleader mentioned in the *Hancock* case is that the party seeking interpleader must neither have nor claim any interest in the subject matter. The first case in which the requirement

appeared, Mitchell v. Hayne, 2 Simons & Stuart 63, 57 Eng.Rep. 268 (Ch.1824), cites no authority and gives no reasons for its adoption. Nevertheless, the requirement has been accepted by most American jurisdictions. See, e.g., Texas v. Florida, 306 U.S. 398, 406–07, 59 S.Ct. 563, 568, 83 L.Ed. 817, 825 (1939); Maxim v. Shotwell, 209 Mich. 79, 176 N.W. 414 (1920). For this requirement's early history, see Hazard & Moskovitz, *An Historical and Critical Analysis of Interpleader,* 52 Calif.L.Rev. 706, 744–47 (1964). At the time the *Hancock* case was decided, this requirement was still in full force in California. However, in 1951, Section 386 of California's Code of Civil Procedure, which is set out in the Supplement under Federal Rule 22, was amended to permit a defendant to interpose a claim to a portion of the property or money in dispute. Is there any reason why the right of an interested stakeholder to interplead apparently exists under the California statute only in favor of a defendant stakeholder? Can Section 386 be construed to give the same right to the plaintiff? See Note, *1951 Amendment to California Code of Civil Procedure Section 386,* 39 Calif.L.Rev. 591, 594 (1951). For a sharp attack on the no-interest-in-the-subject-matter requirement, see Chafee, *Modernizing Interpleader,* 30 Yale L.J. 814, 840–42 (1921).

7. The fourth historical requirement—that the stakeholder must not have incurred any independent liability with regard to the stake to either of the claimants—derived from the principle that the stakeholder should retire from the case once interpleader was allowed. By way of illustration, assume that a bailee who is subject to conflicting claims to the bailed article has expressly acknowledged the title of one of the claimants to it. Interpleader could not be granted because a decision awarding ownership to the other claimant might not terminate the controversy concerning the bailed item; the losing claimant still might have a cause of action against the stakeholder based on the latter's acknowledgment of title, and the stakeholder could not withdraw from the litigation at the end of the first stage of the suit. What underlies the principle that the stakeholder must be neutral, disinterested, and withdraw permanently from the suit when interpleader is allowed?

EX PARTE MERSEY DOCKS & HARBOUR BOARD, [1899] 1 Q.B. 546 (C.A.), involved a situation similar to the hypothetical above. The court permitted interpleader and concluded that if the claimant with an independent cause of action regarding the stake lost as against the other claimant, he would be allowed to assert it against the bailee in a third stage of the same suit. Compare the hardship to the claimant of two contests, first with another claimant and then with the bailee, with the hardship to the bailee of two actions and a possible double recovery. Is the solution adopted in the *Mersey* case desirable? The status of this requirement in the federal courts is discussed in Note, *The Independent Liability Rule as a Bar to Interpleader in the Federal Courts,* 65 Yale L.J. 715 (1956).

2. JURISDICTIONAL PROBLEMS

The historic territorial approach to jurisdiction over the person has raised a number of peculiar problems in the interpleader context. Occasionally, the stakeholder will not be able to obtain in personam jurisdiction over all of the claimants in any one state because of the limitations imposed by the Due Process Clause of the Fourteenth Amendment. To overcome this difficulty, courts often have characterized interpleader as an in rem or quasi-in-rem proceeding and predicated jurisdiction on the presence of the stake within the territorial reach of the court. Assuming that this is a sound approach, should it make any difference that the stake is a debt rather than a chattel or a trust fund? In the case that follows, the Supreme Court was faced with the question of whether to treat a debt as an in rem or quasi-in-rem base for interpleader. Before proceeding, it might be advisable to review the materials in Chapter 2 on jurisdiction over the person and jurisdiction over property. In particular, reread Shaffer v. Heitner, p. 150, supra.

NEW YORK LIFE INS. CO. v. DUNLEVY

Supreme Court of the United States, 1916.
241 U.S. 518, 36 S.Ct. 613, 60 L.Ed. 1140.

Certiorari to the Circuit Court of Appeals for the Ninth Circuit.

Mr. Justice McREYNOLDS delivered the opinion of the court:

Respondent, Effie J. Gould Dunlevy, instituted this suit in the superior court, Marin county, California, January 14, 1910, against petitioner and Joseph W. Gould, her father, to recover $2,479.70, the surrender value of a policy on his life which she claimed had been assigned to her in 1893, and both were duly served with process while in that state. It was removed to the United States district court, February 16, 1910, and there tried by the judge in May, 1912, a jury having been expressly waived. Judgment for amount claimed was affirmed by the Circuit Court of Appeals. * * *

The insurance company by an amended answer filed December 7, 1911, set up in defense * * * that Mrs. Dunlevy was concluded by certain judicial proceedings in Pennsylvania wherein it had been garnished and the policy had been adjudged to be the property of Gould.
* * *

In 1907 Boggs & Buhl recovered a valid personal judgment by default, after domiciliary service, against Mrs. Dunlevy, in the common pleas court at Pittsburgh, where she then resided. During 1909, "the tontine dividend period" of the life policy having expired, the insurance company became liable for $2,479.70, and this sum was claimed both by Gould, a citizen of Pennsylvania, and his daughter, who had removed to California. In November, 1909, Boggs & Buhl caused issue of an execution attachment on their judgment, and both the insurance company and Gould were summoned as garnishees. He appeared, denied assignment of the policy, and claimed the full amount due thereon. On February 5, 1910,—after this suit was begun in California,—the company answered, admitted its indebtedness, set up the conflicting claims to the fund, and prayed to be advised as to its rights. At the same time it filed a petition asking for a rule upon the claimants to show cause why they should not interplead and thereby ascertain who was lawfully entitled to the proceeds, and, further, that it might be allowed to pay amount due into court for benefit of proper party. An order granted the requested rule, and directed that notice be given to Mrs. Dunlevy in California. This was done, but she made no answer and did not appear. Later the insurance company filed a second petition, and, upon leave obtained thereunder, paid $2,479.70 into court, March 21, 1910. All parties except Mrs. Dunlevy having appeared, a feigned issue was framed and tried to determine validity of alleged transfer of the policy. The jury found, October 1, 1910, there was no valid assignment, and thereupon, under an order of court, the fund was paid over to Gould.

Beyond doubt, without the necessity of further personal service of process upon Mrs. Dunlevy, the court of common pleas at Pittsburgh had ample power through garnishment proceedings to inquire whether she held a valid claim against the insurance company, and, if found to exist, then to condemn and appropriate it so far as necessary to discharge the original judgment. Although herself outside the limits of the state, such disposition of the property would have been binding on her. * * * But the interpleader initiated by the company was an altogether different matter. This was an attempt to bring about a final and conclusive adjudication of her personal rights, not merely to discover property and apply it to debts. And unless in contemplation of law she was before the court, and required to respond to that issue, its orders and judgments in respect thereto were not binding on her. Pennoyer v. Neff * * *.

Counsel maintain that having been duly summoned in the original suit instituted by Boggs & Buhl in 1907, and notwithstanding entry of final judgment therein, "Mrs. Dunlevy was in the Pennsylvania court and was bound by every order that court made, whether she remained within the jurisdiction of that court after it got jurisdiction over her person or not;" and hence, the argument is, "When the company paid the money into court where she was, it was just the same in legal effect as if it had paid it to her." This position is supposed to be supported by our opinion in Michigan Trust Co. v. Ferry, 228 U.S. 346, 57 L.Ed. 867, 33 S.Ct. 550, where it is said (p. 353): "If a judicial proceeding is begun with jurisdiction over the person of the party concerned, it is within the power of a state to bind him by every subsequent order in the cause. * * * This is true not only of ordinary actions, but of proceedings like the present. It is within the power of a state to make the whole administration of the estate a single proceeding, to provide that one who has undertaken it within the jurisdiction shall be subject to the order of the court in the matter until the administration is closed by distribution, and, on the same principle, that he shall be required to account for and distribute all that he receives, by the order of the probate court."

Of course the language quoted had reference to the existing circumstances, and must be construed accordingly. The judgment under consideration was fairly within the reasonable anticipation of the executor when he submitted himself to the probate court. But a wholly different and intolerable condition would result from acceptance of the theory that, after final judgment, a defendant remains in court and subject to whatsoever orders may be entered under title of the cause. * * * The interpleader proceedings were not essential concomitants of the original action by Boggs & Buhl against Dunlevy, but plainly collateral; and, when summoned to respond in that action, she was not required to anticipate them. * * *

The established general rule is that any personal judgment which a state court may render against one who did not voluntarily submit to its jurisdiction, and who is not a citizen of the state, nor served with process within its borders, no matter what the mode of service, is void, because the court had no jurisdiction over his person. * * *

We are of opinion that the proceedings in the Pennsylvania court constituted no bar to the action in California, and the judgment below is accordingly affirmed.

Notes and Questions

1. Partially in response to the *Dunlevy* decision, Congress passed the Federal Interpleader Act in 1917. The statute was successively broadened in 1926 and 1936 and was reconstituted in 1948 as part of the United States Judicial Code. It now appears as 28 U.S.C. §§ 1335, 1397, 2361. The present Interpleader Act manifests a congressional intent to avoid a repetition of the *Dunlevy* decision in an action arising in a federal court. For example, Section 1397 permits venue to be laid in any judicial district in which one or more of the claimants reside and Section 2361 permits nationwide service of process in order to reach all of the claimants. Further recognition of the interstate quality of interpleader and the need for the exercise of federal judicial power in this context is the provision in Section 1335 permitting the federal courts to assert jurisdiction when the stake is worth as little as $500. In light of the principles of federal jurisdiction explored in Chapters Two and Three, can the Federal Interpleader Act be challenged on constitutional grounds? The Federal Interpleader Acts are analyzed in a series of articles by their principal proponent, the late Professor Chafee: *Interstate Interpleader,* 33 Yale L.J. 685 (1924); *Interpleader in the United States Courts,* 41 Yale L.J. 1134 (1932), 42 Yale L.J. 41 (1932); *The Federal Interpleader Act of 1936,* 45 Yale L.J. 963, 1161 (1936); *Federal Interpleader Since the Act of 1936,* 49 Yale L.J. 377 (1940).

2. Interpleader under the Federal Interpleader Act is referred to as "statutory interpleader." Interpleader under Federal Rule 22, known as "rule interpleader," is somewhat different. Although the fourfold requirements of the old equitable remedy are not necessary, the usual jurisdictional, venue, and process limitations still apply. Statutory and rule interpleader are further discussed on pp. 625–37, infra.

3. Is *Dunlevy* consistent with Shaffer v. Heitner, p. 150, supra? For a case reaching the same result as *Dunlevy,* see Hanna v. Stedman, 230 N.Y. 326, 130 N.E. 566 (1921). In view of the extent to which state judicial power over nonresidents has been extended since the *Dunlevy* decision, would the Supreme Court limit the state's power over interpleader today as it did in *Dunlevy?* Which of the cases in Chapter 2 are relevant to this question? Do the "long-arm" or "single-act" statutes render the *Dunlevy* problem moot or is there still some area in which federal interpleader can profitably function? Does the presence of the Federal Interpleader Act make it easier or harder for the Supreme Court to eliminate the *Dunlevy* limitation on state jurisdictional power? See von Mehren & Trautman, *Jurisdiction to Adjudicate: A Suggest-*

ed Analysis, 79 Harv.L.Rev. 1121, 1156–59 (1966). For a modern approach to *Dunlevy,* see *Developments in the Law—Multiparty Litigation in the Federal Courts,* 71 Harv.L.Rev. 874, 914–18 (1958).

4. Section 216 of the New York Civil Practice Law and Rules permits a stakeholder who has been sued by one claimant to apply to the court for permission to send notice of the action's pendency to another claimant who is not subject to the court's personal jurisdiction. The proceeding is then suspended and the nonresident may intervene within a year and ten days after the date the notice is sent. If the nonresident claimant does not appear within that period, the claim is barred in New York. The claim also may be barred in those states having "borrowing statutes" under which another jurisdiction's statutes of limitations are applied in certain situations rather than those of the forum. However, the stakeholder is not protected if the nonresident claimant asserts a right to the property in another jurisdiction before the statutory period has elapsed or in a jurisdiction that will not "borrow" New York's statute. Because of these risks, the New York Court of Appeals has held that the defendant stakeholder can challenge the claim of the resident claimants by asserting that title is held by a nonresident claimant. Solicitor v. Bankers Trust Co., 304 N.Y. 282, 107 N.E.2d 448 (1952). Are there any constitutional objections to the New York statute? See also 1 Weinstein, Korn & Miller, *New York Civil Practice* ¶ ¶ 216.01–.03.

5. In WESTERN UNION TEL. CO. v. PENNSYLVANIA, 368 U.S. 71, 82 S.Ct. 199, 7 L.Ed.2d 139 (1961), the Supreme Court stated:

> * * * [W]hen a state court's jurisdiction purports to be based, as here, on the presence of property within the State, the holder of such property is deprived of due process of law if he is compelled to relinquish it without assurance that he will not be held liable again in another jurisdiction or in a suit brought by a claimant who is not bound by the first judgment. * * *

Id. at 75, 82 S.Ct. at 201, 7 L.Ed.2d at 142. If this statement is applicable to individual claims, as well as to a claim by the state to a particular fund, a court would have to dismiss a suit by a resident claimant against the stakeholder when there are potential nonresident claimants who cannot be brought within the jurisdiction of the court. Does this make it unwise to extend the *Western Union* doctrine to include private claims?

6. Can a stakeholder create in rem jurisdiction by depositing a stake with the court? N.Y.C.P.L.R. § 1006(g) permits a party to pay a sum of money into court when the money is "payable in the state pursuant to a contract or claimed as damages for unlawful retention of specific real or personal property in the state." It then states: "Upon compliance with a court order permitting such deposit or retention, the sum of money shall be deemed specific property within the state * * *." Doesn't this rule confer unlimited personal jurisdiction in interpleader actions in the New York courts?

3. INTERPLEADER IN THE FEDERAL COURTS

———

Reread 28 U.S.C. §§ 1335, 1397, 2361 and Federal Rule of Civil Procedure 22.

———

PAN AMERICAN FIRE & CAS. CO. v. REVERE

United States District Court, Eastern District of Louisiana, 1960.
188 F.Supp. 474.

WRIGHT, DISTRICT JUDGE. On February 3, 1960, a * * * large tractor and trailer collided head-on with a bus carrying school children. The bus driver and three of the children were killed and 23 others were injured, some very seriously. A few moments later, compounding the disaster, another collision occurred between two cars following the bus. * * *

Alleging that three suits against it have already been filed and that numerous other claims have been made, the tractor's liability insurer has instituted this interpleader action, citing all potential claimants. It asks that they be enjoined from initiating legal proceedings elsewhere or further prosecuting the actions already filed and that they be directed to assert their claims in the present suit. Plaintiff has deposited a bond in the full amount of its policy limits, $100,000, and avers that "it has no interest" in these insurance proceeds, being merely "a disinterested stakeholder." On the other hand, the Company denies liability toward any and all claimants. This apparently contradictory position is explained by the statement of its counsel, incorporated in the record as an amendment to the complaint, that plaintiff "has no further claim" on the sum deposited with the court, but cannot technically admit "liability" since that would amount to a concession that its assured was negligent and expose him to a deficiency judgment.

The only question presented at this stage of the proceeding is whether, under the circumstances outlined, the remedy of interpleader is available to the insurer. * * *

1. *Jurisdiction.* * * *

[The court concluded that the jurisdictional amount and diversity requirements of the Interpleader Act and Federal Rule 22 had been satisfied.]

2. *Strict Interpleader or Bill in the Nature of Interpleader.* Apparently of the opinion that the answer may affect the availability of the remedy sought here, the parties have debated the question whether this is a case for "true," "strict," or "pure" interpleader or whether the present facts support only an action "in the nature of interpleader." The difference between the two is that in strict interpleader the plaintiff is a disinterested stakeholder while in the action in the nature of interpleader he is himself a claimant, whether directly or by denying the validity of some or all of the other claims. State of Texas v. State of Florida, 306 U.S. 398, 406–407, 59 S.Ct. 563, 830, 83 L.Ed. 817. Thus, if the casualty

insurer had brought in the claimants and said to them: "Gentlemen, I put before you the full amount of the policy which those of you who prove your claims must divide between you, but I deny that any of you is entitled to any portion of the fund and pray that all your demands be rejected and that the deposit be returned to me in due course," clearly this would not be a true interpleader but an action in the nature of interpleader. The problem here is whether the allegation of disinterestedness already noted changes the character of the action to one of strict interpleader. * * *

But does it matter how the action is characterized? It would seem to make no difference since both Rule 22 and the Interpleader Act expressly provide for actions in the nature of interpleader as well as strict bills, the drafters in each case voicing their intent to erase the distinction. But before so concluding, we must dispose of an old rule of equity that gave importance to the difference between "pure" and "impure" bills of interpleader.

3. *Special Equitable Ground for Bill in the Nature of Interpleader.* Though apparently known to the early common law, modern interpleader developed in the chancery courts and is today considered an equitable remedy. Hence, in theory at least, the resort to equity must be justified by the absence of an adequate remedy at law. One might suppose that exposure to unnecessary vexation by a multiplicity of suits on the same obligation were a sufficient ground for equitable relief. And so it is if the conditions of strict interpleader are met. But, for reasons that no one bothered to explain, the rule was otherwise when the plaintiff was not a mere stakeholder. It was laid down that a bill in the nature of interpleader would not lie unless supported by some special equity besides double vexation. Thus, a suit like this one which has no independent equitable basis could not be maintained unless it could be characterized as a true bill of interpleader.

Though it was perhaps more honored in the breach than the observance, such was the rule. But, inherently weak, it could not long survive the liberalizing force of the Interpleader Act of 1936 and the Rules of Civil Procedure promulgated in 1938. Indeed, once the difference between strict bills and bills in the nature of interpleader was eliminated, there remained no basis for distinguishing the requirements and demanding special equities for the action in the nature of interpleader. Henceforth, it could be assumed that the prerequisites of interpleader were the same whether the plaintiff were interested or not, and that these conditions were spelled out in the written provisions. The point was forcibly made by Judge Chesnut whose celebrated opinion in John Hancock Mut. Life Ins. Co. v. Kegan, * * * [22 F.Supp. 326 (D.Md.1938)], noted the absurdity of distinguishing between the equities required for "pure" and "impure" interpleader and held that exposure to undue harassment by a multiplicity of suits was a sufficient ground to maintain a bill in the nature of interpleader. * * *

The present law, then, is that the only equitable ground necessary for interpleader, whether the plaintiff is a disinterested stakeholder or not, is exposure to double or multiple vexation. But, of course, this does not mean that every person threatened with a multiplicity of suits is entitled to interplead. The function of interpleader is to rescue a debtor from *undue* harassment when there are several claims made against the *same fund.* It is because the aggregate demands exceed the insurer's contractual obligation that the condition is here satisfied.

Policy for interpleader satisfied here

4. *Exposure to Multiple Liability.* Though the Interpleader Act makes no such requirement, Rule 22 apparently permits interpleader only if the claims "are such that the plaintiff is or may be exposed to double or multiple *liability.*" (Emphasis added.) In theory at least, this is not necessarily the same thing as exposure to double or multiple *vexation* on a single obligation. There may be situations in which the debtor, though harassed by many suits on account of one transaction, is never in danger of being compelled to pay the same debt twice. Indeed, here, the argument is advanced that because it has fixed the limits of its liability in its policy, the insurer is not exposed to multiple liability no matter how many claims are filed, and, therefore, is not entitled to maintain interpleader, at least under the Rule.

But the requirement is not a strict one. * * * The key to the clause requiring exposure to "double or multiple liability" is in the words "may be." The danger need not be immediate; any possibility of having to pay more than is justly due, no matter how improbable or remote, will suffice. At least, it is settled that an insurer with limited contractual liability who faces claims in excess of his policy limits is "exposed" within the intendment of Rule 22, and we need go no further to find the requirement satisfied here.

5. *Adversity of Claimants.* In a somewhat overlapping objection, it is said that the present claims are not characterized by that "adversity" to one another which is a prerequisite of interpleader. It is of course true that they are identical neither in origin nor in amount and that they are, in some degree at least, independent demands. But, despite the objection of purists who would retain the old doctrine of complete "mutual exclusiveness," both Rule 22 and the Interpleader Act now expressly provide that this is no bar to the remedy. On the other hand, there remains a requirement that the claimants be "adverse" in some way. The question is whether that requirement is met when, as here, the claimants, though in theory indifferent toward each other, are in fact competing for a fund which is not large enough to satisfy them all. The answer is clear. As Judge Thompson said in Fidelity & Deposit Co. of Maryland v. A.S. Reid & Co., D.C.E.D.Pa., 16 F.2d 502, 504: "In that situation it is to the interest of each claimant to reduce or defeat altogether the claim of every other claimant. * * *"

6. *Fault of Plaintiff.* * * *

[The court here held that the plaintiff was not guilty of "unclean hands," which would have barred equitable relief.]

7. *Unliquidated Tort Claims as Justifying Interpleader.* Over and above the technical objections already disposed of, the argument is advanced that interpleader is not an appropriate method of adjudicating

unliquidated tort claims. Such a bald proposition might be rejected summarily were it not for the startling fact that there appears to be no precedent in the federal courts for granting interpleader in the present situation. * * *

At the outset, it seems clear that interpleader will lie when there are several tort claimants who have obtained judgments which aggregate more than the amount of the policy. Indeed, in that case it can make no difference whether the claims originated in tort or contract. Moreover, it is settled that interpleader is available to an insurer whose policy is insufficient to satisfy contract claims, though they have not been reduced to judgment. Why, then, should the remedy be denied to a blameless insurer faced with excessive tort claims? Three reasons have been suggested: (1) As to quantum, at least, tort claims are more conjectural than contract claims; (2) since it is not directly liable to the claimants, the insurer's exposure as to tort claims is "remote" until they have been reduced to judgment; and (3) tort claims "are peculiarly appropriate for jury trial," which would have to be denied under the equitable practice of interpleader.

The effect of the first objection is only this: that it is more difficult in the case of tort claims to determine whether the aggregate will exceed the policy limits so as to render the claimants "adverse" and expose the insurer to "multiple liability." It may be that there are few cases in which this result can be reasonably anticipated, but, clearly, this is one of them.

The second objection, though it forms the basis of the only reported decision denying interpleader to an automobile liability insurer,[36] is no better. Indeed, under the "may be exposed" clause of Rule 22 and the "may claim" clause of the Interpleader Act, it would not seem to matter how remote the danger might be. But, in any event, prematurity is no defense under the peculiar Louisiana law which allows a direct action against the automobile liability insurer.

8. *Jury Trial.* On the theory that the resort to equity defeats the right of trial by jury, it has been said that once interpleader is granted all issues in the case must be tried to the judge alone. There is, however, eminent authority to the contrary, including Judge Learned Hand, Professor Chafee, and Professor Moore, who hold that legal issues arising in an interpleader action can be tried before a jury. Whatever may be the right solution in another case, here it seems clear that the questions of liability and damages ought to be put to a jury. * * * Nothing in Rule 22 or the Interpleader Act opposes such a procedure. Indeed, the provision of the Federal Rules which permits separate trial of distinct issues invites this solution. * * * Each claimant can be given a full opportunity to prove his case before a jury, reserving to the court only the task of apportioning the fund between those who are successful if the aggregate of the verdicts exceeds the amount of the insurance proceeds.

36. American Indemnity Co. v. Hale, D.C. W.D.Mo., 71 F.Supp. 529, 533–534.

9. *Enjoining of Other Proceedings.* Usually interpleader will not be really effective unless all claimants are brought before the same court in one proceeding and restricted to that single forum in the assertion of their claims. * * * Immediately, the question arises whether Section 2283 of Title 28 of the Code presents an obstacle to enjoining state court proceedings.

As amended in 1948, that section prohibits a federal court from interfering with a pending state court action except in three situations: (1) Where such a course is "expressly authorized by Act of Congress"; (2) where the issuance of an injunction by the federal court is "necessary in aid of its jurisdiction"; and (3) where the court's action is required "to protect or effectuate its judgments." Clearly, the first exception is applicable to a suit brought under the Interpleader Act since that statute expressly empowers the court to enjoin the claimants "from instituting or prosecuting any proceeding in any State or United States court affecting the property, instrument or obligation involved in the interpleader action * * *." But the exception does not apply to an action under Rule 22, for the quoted provision authorizing stay orders is restricted to statutory interpleader. If state court proceedings can be enjoined when interpleader is brought under the Rule it must be by virtue of the second exception in Section 2283.

The question whether the court entertaining a non-statutory interpleader suit may enjoin state court proceedings on the same issues on the theory that it is "necessary in aid of its jurisdiction" is not free from doubt. * * * But * * * every indication is that, regardless of the Interpleader Act, the power of a federal court to enjoin pending state court proceedings in a case like this one will be sustained. Certainly that result is desirable, if not indispensable. * * *

10. *Venue and Service of Process.* * * * [T] here are two procedural limitations on actions under the Rule which become important whenever the claimants are not all within the territorial jurisdiction of the district court. The first is that the only proper venue for the suit when the defendants do not all reside in the same state is the residence of the plaintiff; the second, that process cannot run beyond the boundaries of the state in which the court sits. These restrictions are of course waivable, but if objection is raised by the affected defendant, they usually form an absolute bar to the action. Thus, here, if Rule 22 alone were applicable, absent a waiver of venue by Wells [a passenger in one of the cars following the bus], the suit would have to be instituted at the plaintiff's domicile in Texas, and none of the defendants could be validly served unless they were found in that state.

But the situation is different when jurisdiction exists under the statute, for the Interpleader Act specially provides that the action may be commenced in any district where one defendant resides and that process will run throughout the United States. Unfortunately, these exceptional rules apply only to statutory interpleader. The present suit, then, is maintainable only under the Interpleader Act unless the Wisconsin defendant waives venue and voluntarily appears or is found in Louisiana.

11. *Conclusion.* * * * [T]he prayer for interpleader will be granted, without, however, discharging the plaintiff who is contractually bound to resist the demands. Injunctions will issue restraining all parties from further prosecuting any pending suits against plaintiff or its assured on account of the accident described, or from instituting like proceedings before this or any other court. All defendants will be required to enter their claims by way of answer in this action within thirty days from notice of this judgment. Thereafter, upon timely demand by any one of the parties, the court will order a joint jury trial of all the claims upon the issues of liability and damages. In the event the aggregate of the verdicts should exceed the amount of plaintiff's liability, the court reserves unto itself the task of apportioning the insurance proceeds in such manner as it deems just.

The motion to dismiss will be denied.

Notes and Questions

1. If an insurance company faced with the *Pan American* situation pays the full amount of the policy to certain claimants, either by way of settlement or in satisfaction of a judgment, can it defend later actions by unpaid claimants by arguing that it has already exhausted the policy? To what extent is the answer to this question relevant in determining whether interpleader should be granted?

2. STEPHENSON v. BURDETT, 56 W.Va. 109, 117–18, 48 S.E. 846, 850 (1904):

* * * The only material difference between the two kinds of bills, pointed out by the courts and the law writers is that, in a bill in the nature of a bill of interpleader, the plaintiff may show that he has an interest in the subject matter of the controversy between the defendants. * * * There is no suggestion * * * that there is any further departure from the principles governing a pure bill of interpleader. Must not the defendants claim the same thing from the plaintiff, according to the requirement in a pure bill of interpleader? Must not a relation of privity exist between the defendants? Can a tenant require his landlord to interplead with a third person claiming under a strange and hostile title? If the plaintiff show by his bill that he is in the attitude of a wrongdoer toward one of the defendants, may he require an interpleader? The language of a definition of a bill in the nature of a bill of interpleader, found in the books, does not answer any of these questions in the affirmative, or indicate that the principles governing a pure bill of interpleader are relaxed in any of these particulars. Nor do any of the decided cases countenance such a proposition.

3. In addition to the articles by Professor Chafee cited following the *Dunlevy* case, a useful discussion of federal interpleader is found in 7 Wright, Miller & Kane, *Federal Practice and Procedure: Civil 2d* §§ 1701–21 (1986). See also *Developments in the Law—Multiparty Litigation in the Federal Courts,* 71 Harv.L.Rev. 874, 913–28 (1958).

STATE FARM FIRE & CAS. CO. v. TASHIRE
Supreme Court of the United States, 1967.
386 U.S. 523, 87 S.Ct. 1199, 18 L.Ed.2d 270.

[This case arose out of a collision between a Greyhound bus and a pickup truck in Shasta County, California in September, 1964. Two of the bus passengers were killed and 33 others were injured, as were the bus driver, the driver of the truck, and its passenger. One of the dead and 10 of the injured passengers were Canadians; the rest of the individuals were citizens of five American states.

Four of the injured passengers filed suit in California state courts seeking damages in excess of $1,000,000 and naming as defendants: Greyhound Lines, Inc.; Nauta, the bus driver; Clark, the driver of the truck; and Glasgow, the truck passenger who apparently was its owner. Each of the individual defendants was a citizen of Oregon; Greyhound was a California corporation. Before the California cases came to trial and before any other suits were filed, petitioner, State Farm Fire & Casualty Company, an Illinois corporation, brought this action in the nature of interpleader in the United States District Court for the District of Oregon.

State Farm asserted that at the time of the collision it had in force an insurance policy covering Clark, the driver of the truck, for bodily injury liability up to $10,000 per person and $20,000 per occurrence. State Farm further asserted that the aggregate damages sought in actions already filed in California and other anticipated actions far exceeded the amount of its maximum liability under the policy. Accordingly, it paid into court the sum of $20,000 and asked the court (1) to require all claimants to establish their claims against Clark and his insurer in the Oregon proceeding and in no other action, and (2) to discharge State Farm from all further obligations under its policy. Alternatively, State Farm requested a decree that the insurer owed no duty to Clark and was not liable on the policy, and asked the court to refund the $20,000 deposit. State Farm joined as defendants Clark, Glasgow, Nauta, Greyhound, and each of the prospective claimants. Jurisdiction was predicated both upon the Federal Interpleader Act and general diversity of citizenship. Personal service was effected on each of the American defendants and registered mail was employed to give notice to the 11 Canadian claimants.

The Oregon District Court issued an order requiring each of the defendants to show cause why he should not be restrained from filing or prosecuting any proceeding affecting the property or obligation involved in the interpleader action. In response, several of the defendants contended that the policy did cover the accident and advanced various arguments for the position that interpleader was inappropriate.

When a temporary injunction along the lines sought by State Farm issued, the respondents moved to dismiss and, in the alternative, sought a change of venue to the district in which the collision had occurred. After a hearing, the District Court declined to dissolve the temporary injunction but continued the motion for a change of venue. Later, the temporary injunction was broadened so that all suits against Clark, State Farm, Greyhound, and Nauta had to be prosecuted in the interpleader proceeding.

On interlocutory appeal, the Ninth Circuit reversed on the ground that in states, such as Oregon, that do not permit a "direct action" against an insurance company until a judgment is obtained against the insured, State Farm could not invoke federal interpleader until the claims against the insured had been reduced to judgment. The Court of Appeals held that prior to that time claimants with unliquidated tort claims are not "claimants" within the meaning of Section 1335 of Title 28 and are not "persons having claims against the plaintiff" within the meaning of Federal Rule 22. The Ninth Circuit directed that the temporary injunction be dissolved and the action be dismissed. The Supreme Court granted certiorari.]

Certiorari to the United States Court of Appeals for the Ninth Circuit.

MR. JUSTICE FORTAS delivered the opinion of the Court.

* * *

I.

Before considering the issues presented by the petition for certiorari, we find it necessary to dispose of a question neither raised by the parties nor passed upon by the courts below. Since the matter concerns our jurisdiction, we raise it on our own motion. * * * The interpleader statute * * * has been uniformly construed to require only "minimal diversity," that is, diversity of citizenship between two or more claimants, without regard to the circumstance that other rival claimants may be co-citizens. The language of the statute, the legislative purpose broadly to remedy the problems posed by multiple claimants to a single fund, and the consistent judicial interpretation tacitly accepted by Congress, persuade us that the statute requires no more. There remains, however, the question whether such a statutory construction is consistent with Article III of our Constitution * * *. In Strawbridge v. Curtiss, 3 Cranch 267, 2 L.Ed. 435 (1806), this Court held that the diversity of citizenship statute required "complete diversity": where co-citizens appeared on both sides of a dispute, jurisdiction was lost. But Chief Justice Marshall there purported to construe only "The words of the act of Congress," not the Constitution itself. And in a variety of contexts this Court and the lower courts have concluded that Article III poses no obstacle to the legislative extension of federal jurisdiction, founded on diversity, so long as any two adverse parties are not co-citizens. Accordingly, we conclude that the present case is properly in the federal courts.

II.

We do not agree with the Court of Appeals that, in the absence of a state law or contractual provision for "direct action" suits against the insurance company, the company must wait until persons asserting claims against its insured have reduced those claims to judgment before seeking to invoke the benefits of federal interpleader. That may have been a tenable position under the 1926[8] and 1936 interpleader statutes.[9] These statutes did not carry forward the language in the 1917 Act authorizing interpleader where adverse claimants "may claim" benefits as well as where they "are claiming" them.[10] In 1948, however, in the revision of the Judicial Code, the "may claim" language was restored.[11] Until the decision below, every court confronted by the question has concluded that the 1948 revision removed whatever requirement there might previously have been that the insurance company wait until at least two claimants reduced their claims to judgments. The commentators are in accord.

Considerations of judicial administration demonstrate the soundness of this view which, in any event, seems compelled by the language of the present statute, which is remedial and to be liberally construed. Were an insurance company required to await reduction of claims to judgment, the first claimant to obtain such a judgment or to negotiate a settlement might appropriate all or a disproportionate slice of the fund before his fellow claimants were able to establish their claims. The difficulties such a race to judgment pose for the insurer, and the unfairness which may result to some claimants, were among the principal evils the interpleader device was intended to remedy.

III.

The fact that State Farm had properly invoked the interpleader jurisdiction under § 1335 did not, however, entitle it to an order both enjoining prosecution of suits against it outside the confines of the interpleader proceeding and also extending such protection to its insured, the alleged tortfeasor. Still less was Greyhound Lines entitled to have that order expanded so as to protect itself and its driver, also alleged to be tortfeasors, from suits brought by its passengers in various state or federal courts. Here, the scope of the litigation, in terms of parties and claims, was vastly more extensive than the confines of the "fund," the deposited proceeds of the insurance policy. In these circumstances, the mere existence of such a fund cannot, by use of interpleader, be employed to accomplish purposes that exceed the needs of orderly contest with respect to the fund.

There are situations, of a type not present here, where the effect of interpleader is to confine the total litigation to a single forum and proceeding. One such case is where a stakeholder, faced with rival claims to the fund itself, acknowledges—or denies—his liability to one or the other of the claimants. In this situation, the fund itself is the target of

8. 44 Stat. 416 (1926), which added casualty companies to the enumerated categories of plaintiffs able to bring interpleader, and provided for the enjoining of proceedings in other courts.

9. 49 Stat. 1096 (1936), which authorized "bill[s] in the nature of interpleader," meaning those in which the plaintiff is not wholly disinterested with respect to the fund he has deposited in court. * * *

10. 39 Stat. 929 (1917). See Klaber v. Maryland Cas. Co., 69 F.2d 934, 938–939, 106 A.L.R. 617 (C.A.8th Cir.1934), which held that the omission in the 1926 Act of the earlier statute's "may claim" language required the denial of interpleader in the face of unliquidated claims (alternative holding).

11. * * * [I]t was widely assumed that restoration of the "may claim" language would have the effect of overruling the holding in Klaber, supra, that one may not invoke interpleader to protect against unliquidated claims. * * *

the claimants. It marks the outer limits of the controversy. It is, therefore, reasonable and sensible that interpleader, in discharge of its office to protect the fund, should also protect the stakeholder from vexatious and multiple litigation. In this context, the suits sought to be enjoined are squarely within the language of 28 U.S.C. § 2361 * * *.

But the present case is another matter. Here, an accident has happened. Thirty-five passengers or their representatives have claims which they wish to press against a variety of defendants: the bus company, its driver, the owner of the truck, and the truck driver. The circumstance that one of the prospective defendants happens to have an insurance policy is a fortuitous event which should not of itself shape the nature of the ensuing litigation. * * * [A]n insurance company whose maximum interest in the case cannot exceed $20,000 and who in fact asserts that it has no interest at all, should not be allowed to determine that dozens of tort plaintiffs must be compelled to press their claims— even those claims which are not against the insured and which in no event could be satisfied out of the meager insurance fund—in a single forum of the insurance company's choosing. There is nothing in the statutory scheme, and very little in the judicial and academic commentary upon that scheme, which requires that the tail be allowed to wag the dog in this fashion.

State Farm's interest in this case * * * receives full vindication when the court restrains claimants from seeking to enforce against the insurance company any judgment obtained against its insured, except in the interpleader proceeding itself. To the extent that the District Court sought to control claimants' lawsuits against the insured and other alleged tortfeasors, it exceeded the powers granted to it by the statutory scheme.

We recognize, of course, that our view of interpleader means that it cannot be used to solve all the vexing problems of multiparty litigation arising out of a mass tort. But interpleader was never intended to perform such a function, to be an all-purpose "bill of peace." Had it been so intended, careful provision would necessarily have been made to insure that a party with little or no interest in the outcome of a complex controversy should not strip truly interested parties of substantial rights—such as the right to choose the forum in which to establish their claims, subject to generally applicable rules of jurisdiction, venue, service of process, removal, and change of venue. None of the legislative and academic sponsors of a modern federal interpleader device viewed their accomplishment as a "bill of peace," capable of sweeping dozens of lawsuits out of the various state and federal courts in which they were brought and into a single interpleader proceeding. And only in two reported instances has a federal interpleader court sought to control the underlying litigation against alleged tortfeasors as opposed to the allocation of a fund among successful tort plaintiffs. See Commercial Union Ins. Co. of New York v. Adams, 231 F.Supp. 860 (D.C.S.D.Ind.1964) (where there was virtually no objection and where all of the basic tort suits would in any event have been prosecuted in the forum state), and Pan American Fire & Cas. Co. v. Revere * * *.

In light of the evidence that federal interpleader was not intended to serve the function of a "bill of peace" in the context of multiparty litigation arising out of a mass tort, of the anomalous power which such a construction of the statute would give the stakeholder, and of the thrust of the statute and the purpose it was intended to serve, we hold that the interpleader statute did not authorize the injunction entered in the present case. Upon remand, the injunction is to be modified consistently with this opinion.

IV.

The judgment of the Court of Appeals is reversed * * *. *Interpleader allowed*

[JUSTICE DOUGLAS dissented on the ground that the litigants were not "claimants" to the fund as required by the Federal Interpleader Act. He pointed out that the insurance policy specifically provided that no action could be brought against the company until the insured's obligation was determined. Furthermore, he argued, both California and Oregon law did not permit a direct action against the insurer until after final judgment against the insured. The Justice also took issue with the majority's construction of the words "may claim" in the Federal Interpleader Act.]

Notes and Questions

1. In TREINIES v. SUNSHINE MINING CO., 308 U.S. 66, 60 S.Ct. 44, 84 L.Ed. 85 (1939), the Supreme Court held that a federal court could constitutionally assert jurisdiction under the Federal Interpleader Act despite the cocitizenship of the stakeholder and one of the claimants. In arriving at this conclusion, the Court said that the stakeholder's "disinterestedness as between the claimants and as to the property in dispute" was demonstrated by his deposit of the fund in court and his discharge, which left the dispute to be ironed out between the adverse claimants. Id. at 72, 60 S.Ct. at 48, 84 L.Ed. at 90. Was it realistic for the Court to regard the disinterested stakeholder as a nominal party for diversity purposes? Can you reconcile the Court's conclusion with the fact that under Federal Rule 22(1) jurisdiction is proper if there is diversity between the stakeholder and the claimants, even though there is no diversity between the claimants? But what if the stakeholder in *Treinies* had asserted a claim to the money? Would the requisite diversity have existed? In other words, should the Court's reasoning also extend to bills in the nature of a bill of interpleader? See Bierman v. Marcus, 140 F.Supp. 66, 70 (D.N.J.1956), reversed on other grounds 246 F.2d 200 (3d Cir. 1957). But cf. Boice v. Boice, 135 F.2d 919, 920 (3d Cir.1943). Does *State Farm* answer this question?

2. Note that in the principal case, the stakeholder was a citizen of Illinois and defendants were citizens of California, Oregon, several other states, and Canada. A number of claimants were citizens either of the same state or Canada. Since *Treinies* only dealt with cocitizenship as between the stakeholder and a claimant, on what basis does the Supreme Court in *State Farm* cavalierly decide that cocitizenship between adverse claimants does not destroy diversity jurisdiction since there was diversity between two or more of

the claimants to the fund and between State Farm and all of the named defendants? Would the result have been different in *State Farm* if there had not been diversity between State Farm and the named defendants as well as an absence of "complete diversity" among all of the claimants?

Perhaps the leading case on the subject of diversity in statutory interpleader actions prior to *State Farm* was HAYNES v. FELDER, 239 F.2d 868 (5th Cir.1957), which involved a Texas stakeholder who brought interpleader against two rival sets of claimants consisting of a citizen of Texas on one side opposed by four joint claimants of whom three were citizens of Texas and one was a citizen of Tennessee. In an exhaustive and illuminating opinion, the Fifth Circuit held that sufficient diversity existed for purposes of the Federal Interpleader Act and seemingly adopted a test of "minimal diversity." In what ways is *State Farm* distinguishable from *Haynes*? These two cases and the subject of minimal diversity in statutory interpleader actions are discussed in 14 Wright, Miller & Cooper, *Federal Practice and Procedure: Jurisdiction and Related Matters 2d* § 3636 (1985).

3. When an action has been brought against a stakeholder in a federal court, there is some authority permitting a stakeholder to file a bill of interpleader or a bill in the nature of a bill of interpleader against plaintiff and one or more of the claimants, regardless of the citizenship of the added claimants. If the resulting interpleader suit is considered ancillary to the suit against the stakeholder, it is immaterial that the stakeholder is a cocitizen with any of the added claimants or that these claimants are themselves cocitizens. See Sherman Nat. Bank v. Shubert Theatrical Co., 238 Fed. 225 (S.D.N.Y.1916), affirmed 247 Fed. 256 (2d Cir.1917). For a discussion of ancillary jurisdiction and interpleader, see Chafee, *Interpleader in United States Courts*, 41 Yale L.J. 1134, 1145–60 (1931).

4. Consider the following situation. Decedent was a stockholder in both A and B Corporations. His stock certificates in these two corporations are in the hands of C–2, a broker, who contends that she bought the stock from decedent. C–1, decedent's executrix, says that decedent merely entrusted the stock certificates to C–2 for safekeeping. Each claimant requests that A Corporation recognize her as the owner of the stock. The corporation interpleads. In addition to responding to the interpleader, C–1's answer demands that C–2 hand over the stock in B Corporation. Ownership of both sets of certificates turns on precisely the same facts. If the interpleader suit is brought under the Federal Interpleader Act, should the court adjudicate the ownership of both the A and B stock? For an argument that an interpleader suit should permit litigation of claims between the claimants in an interpleader suit other than claims for the disputed fund, see Chafee, *Broadening the Second Stage of Interpleader*, 56 Harv.L.Rev. 541, 929 (1943).

But what about the statement in *Tashire* that "our view of interpleader means that it cannot be used to solve all the vexing problems of multiparty litigation arising out of a mass tort." 386 U.S. at 535, 87 S.Ct. at 1206, 18 L.Ed.2d at 278. Does this prohibit cross-claims between interpleader claimants, the assertion of an unrelated claim by a disinterested stakeholder against a claimant, and a counterclaim by a claimant against the stakeholder? See generally 7 Wright, Miller & Kane, *Federal Practice and Procedure: Civil 2d* § 1715 (1986).

Assume that the interpleader suit concerning the A stock is brought in New York and that C–1 is a citizen of New York and C–2 is a citizen of Illinois and was personally served in that state under the Interpleader Act. If C–1 had started a separate action for the B stock, she would have had to travel to Illinois to try the suit because she could not have served C–2 with process in New York. Can the nationwide service of process permitted by the Interpleader Act be used to assert jurisdiction over the claims to the B stock by C–1 and C–2 in the suit involving the A stock? Cf. Moreno v. United States, 120 F.2d 128 (1st Cir.1941). See also Hagen v. Central Ave. Dairy, Inc., 180 F.2d 502 (9th Cir.1950). What if C–2 had been the first party to demand the B stock in her answer in the interpleader suit?

Applicable Law in Federal Interpleader Cases

In GRIFFIN v. McCOACH, 313 U.S. 498, 61 S.Ct. 1023, 85 L.Ed. 1481 (1941), the Supreme Court held that in a statutory interpleader suit based on diversity jurisdiction a federal court is bound by the *Erie* doctrine to apply the conflict-of-law rules of the state in which it sits. The case was decided on the same day as Klaxon Co. v. Stentor Elec. Mfg. Co., p. 382, supra. Yet, in certain statutory interpleader actions, the courts of the forum state might never have been able to hear a comparable case due to Fourteenth Amendment limitations on their personal jurisdiction. For a compelling argument that federal courts should develop their own conflicts rules when a federal act extends service of process beyond what is permitted a state by the Constitution, see *Developments in the Law— Multiparty Litigation in the Federal Courts,* 71 Harv.L.Rev. 874, 924–26 (1958). Are there any other arguments to suggest the inapplicability of *Erie* and *Klaxon* in statutory interpleader cases? The *Griffin* decision has been criticized in Cook, *The Federal Courts and the Conflict of Laws,* 36 Ill.L.Rev. 493, 507–15 (1942).

Can a federal court grant interpleader under Federal Rule 22 when the state courts would deny interpleader because the stakeholder alleges a personal interest in the outcome of the case?

SECTION G. INTERVENTION

As discussed earlier in this chapter, through devices such as Federal Rules 19 and 20, the parties may add additional parties to the lawsuit under certain circumstances. These Rules, however, are devices at the disposal of parties already in the lawsuit. But suppose a person learns of a lawsuit, the result of which might affect her. Should she be allowed to enter it as an additional party?

———

Read Federal Rule of Civil Procedure 24 in the Supplement.

———

BRUNE v. McDONALD
Supreme Court of Oregon, 1938.
158 Or. 364, 75 P.2d 10.

KELLY, JUSTICE. * * *

It appears from the original complaint of plaintiff that on the 16th day of August defendant was driving his automobile, with plaintiff as his guest therein, * * * on the Mount Hood Loop Road, toward Hood river, and that, when in the vicinity of Van Horn, defendant drove his automobile off the highway, along the edge thereof, across a culvert, through a fence and into a tree, causing injuries to plaintiff.

To support the charge of gross negligence on defendant's part, plaintiff specifically alleged in her original complaint that defendant operated his automobile at an excessive rate of speed, failed to keep his automobile under control, failed to maintain a proper lookout, and failed and neglected to heed plaintiff's remonstrance against defendant's maintenance of such excessive speed. In said original complaint plaintiff also alleged that prior to said accident defendant had imbibed alcoholic liquor, and, in the face of plaintiff's positive opposition thereto, drank excessively of alcohol.

On the 19th day of December, 1936, an amended complaint was filed from which reference to defendant's use of alcohol was omitted.

On the 9th day of January, 1937, said Pacific Indemnity Company procured an order granting said company leave to file a complaint in intervention herein.

On the 15th day of January, 1937, said Pacific Indemnity Company filed its complaint in intervention, in which said company alleged * * * it insured defendant against loss by reason of the liability imposed by law upon him for damages on account of bodily injuries suffered or alleged to have been suffered by any person other than his employees as a result of the ownership, maintenance, or use for pleasure purposes of the automobile referred to in the amended complaint herein, subject to a limitation to the sum of $5,000 for bodily injuries sustained by any one person.

* * *

The intervener, in its complaint in intervention, alleges:

* * *

"V. That prior to the trip during which said accident occurred plaintiff and defendant were and had been for a long time intimate friends and associates, frequently in the company of each other, and on frequent parties together, at which intoxicating liquors were consumed, and in the consumption of which both participated, and that plaintiff was well aware of the habits of defendant with respect to the use of intoxicating liquor.

"VI. That on the afternoon of Sunday, August 16, 1936, plaintiff and defendant embarked upon a pleasure trip around the Mount Hood Loop Highway, taking with them a bottle of intoxicating liquor for consumption during the trip, and they did from time to time during said trip jointly participate in drinking said intoxicating liquor and at Government Camp on said highway jointly engaged in drinking other intoxicating liquor with other persons.

"VII. That after said accident defendant gave to this intervenor several conflicting stories about the occurrences leading up to said accident, at first alleging that, while he was operating his automobile carefully and at a moderate speed, it was forced from the highway by another automobile, and then later that both plaintiff and defendant had consumed a considerable quantity of intoxicating liquor on the trip and that the accident occurred because of a momentary lapse of attention on his part while the automobile was being operated at a moderate speed; later plaintiff and defendant learned that there could be no recovery under said policy on such allegations and then connived and conspired with each other to mulct this intervenor of damages under said insurance policy and to that end jointly agreed that plaintiff should file an action against defendant for damages on account of her personal injuries and should allege that at the time of the accident defendant was grossly intoxicated and operating his automobile at a grossly high rate of speed and that defendant should represent to this intervenor that such charges were true and should deny to this intervenor that plaintiff participated in any of the drinking done on the trip, or knew that defendant was or was becoming intoxicated, thereby presenting an appearance of liability on the part of the defendant to plaintiff where none in truth and in fact existed, and with the intent of defrauding this intervenor of a substantial part of the face of said insurance policy.

"VIII. That in pursuance of said conspiracy plaintiff caused a complaint to be filed in this cause wherein she made the charges heretofore referred to against defendant and defendant thereupon represented to intervenor that said charges were all true, and further represented that the plaintiff did not participate in the drinking of any liquor on said trip, that plaintiff was not aware that he was or was becoming intoxicated and was not aware of his habits respecting intoxicating liquor because of his peculiar ability and capacity to imbibe large quantities of intoxicating liquor without other persons being aware of the fact, all of which representations made by the defendant were false and known by him and by plaintiff to be false and were made in accordance with their joint agreement to deceive and defraud this intervenor.

"IX. That by reason of the matters aforesaid said policy of insurance is void as to the accident in which plaintiff was injured and neither plaintiff nor defendant should be permitted to look to said policy in equity and in good conscience for any reimbursement or damages growing out of said accident; that plaintiff and defendant are planning to procure the entry of a judgment in favor of plaintiff and against defendant for a sum equal to the face of said policy but have agreed that plaintiff will look solely to this intervenor for the payment of said judgment and will make no attempt to collect any part of said judgment from defendant; that plaintiff will, unless restrained by this Court, procure a judgment to be entered against defendant and will then delay action on said policy of insurance until just prior to the expiration of the period of limitation applicable thereto, by which time the witnesses to establish the facts concerning said accident and said conspiracy of plaintiff and defendant, and the fraud perpetrated on defendant will have scattered and be unavailable.

* * *

The question here is whether said complaint in intervention states facts sufficient to warrant the court in granting the relief sought by the intervener, which is an injunction restraining the prosecution of plaintiff's cause of action until it can be determined whether defendant has breached the terms and conditions of said policy of insurance, as alleged by intervener.

The view usually expressed by the courts is that originally, in jurisdictions in which the common law prevailed, intervention was unknown except that it was in use to some extent in the ecclesiastical courts, and that apparently it is derived from the civil law. Therefore, in common-law jurisdictions intervention is usually regarded as of purely statutory origin. * * *

The generally accepted rule is that the right or interest which will authorize a third person to intervene must be of such a direct and immediate character that the intervener will either gain or lose by the direct legal operation of the judgment. * * *

It is obvious that the direct legal operation of the judgment in the case at bar would not cause intervener either to gain or lose anything.

It is equally apparent that the complaint in intervention herein tenders an entirely new and different issue from those of the complaint.

* * *

It will be noted that the intervener does not seek to interpose an answer to the complaint of plaintiff upon the merits of her alleged claim at law. Tested by a demurrer, the clause, "thereby presenting an appearance of liability on the part of the defendant to plaintiff where none in truth and in fact existed," does not constitute a statement of any defense to plaintiff's legal demand against defendant.

The relief sought by intervener is equitable. Intervener prays for an injunction restraining the further prosecution of plaintiff's action against defendant, until it can be determined whether the intervener would be liable to defendant upon its policy of insurance in case plaintiff should secure a judgment against defendant herein.

The reason assigned for seeking this relief is that by the time the judgment, if any, is procured by plaintiff against defendant, and proceedings are instituted to recover on intervener's policy, the intervener's witnesses to the alleged conspiracy will have become scattered and difficult, if not impossible, to procure, and that intervener will be confronted by a woman claimant whose femininity will render it much harder for intervener than if the same issue should be tried before plaintiff's claim against defendant has been adjudicated.

No case has been cited wherein such a procedure as intervener seeks to establish has been approved. The cases cited by intervener deal with sureties and with parties in interest who have been omitted in the original proceeding.

The policy of the courts generally has been to deal with the insurer in such a case as this as not being a party in interest and on the trial to guard against any willful reference to such insurer or to the fact that defendant is insured.

* * *

In giving effect to the allegations of the complaint in intervention we must assume that in case plaintiff prevails against defendant, the intervener will not be liable to defendant in any sum on that account. No liability on intervener's part could result in case defendant prevailed. We think that the supposed embarrassment which intervener alleges it will suffer by reason of the lapse of time necessary to determine this action at law, before the question of the validity or nonvalidity of intervener's policy of insurance can be presented, is not such an interest as the statute above quoted includes.

* * *

The controversy before the court, when the complaint in intervention was filed, was based upon a charge by plaintiff against defendant of gross negligence constituting the proximate cause of personal injury to plaintiff whereby plaintiff suffered damages in the amount demanded. It is obvious that this controversy may be completely determined without any reference, to intervener's policy of insurance. Certainly an invalid, void policy of insurance could not in any way affect the issues tendered in plaintiff's complaint.

* * *

We hold that no error was committed by the circuit court in sustaining plaintiff's demurrer to the complaint in intervention.

The judgment of the circuit court is affirmed.

———

KNAPP v. HANKINS, 106 F.Supp. 43, 47–48 (E.D.Ill.1952):

It is argued that the [insurance] Company may sit idly by and let the defendant employ counsel of his own choosing to defend the action. Under the terms of the policy defendant is obligated only to cooperate with the Company in defense of the suit. It would be unfair to require defendant to defend the case at his own expense if the policy is valid, even though he might subsequently recover such expenses from the Company; it would be equally unfair to require the Company to defend Hankins if the policy is void. * * *

Lastly, the plaintiffs and the defendant contend that the intervention by the Company will introduce new issues in the controversy between plaintiffs and defendant and that the plaintiffs are not interested in the controversy between the Company and the defendant.

* * * The allowance of intervention in the suit will not change the issues between the plaintiffs and the defendant one iota, but before these issues are tried the Company and the defendant will be permitted to determine the validity of the policy. A separate trial will no doubt be had on the issues raised by the intervening petition.

WHARFF v. WHARFF, 244 Iowa 496, 502–03, 56 N.W.2d 1, 4–5 (1952). Plaintiff-husband brought a divorce action against defendant-wife. In his complaint plaintiff described certain real estate held under a tenancy in common by the parties and asked that each party be declared to have certain rights of ownership therein. In her answer, defendant alleged that the real estate had been purchased in part with money she held in trust for her children by a previous marriage. The children petitioned to intervene, claiming the existence of a trust agreement under which their mother, defendant, held the sum of $21,500 for them, part of which had been invested in the real estate in question. The intervention petition prayed for a trust to be impressed for the benefit of the children. The denial of plaintiff's motion to strike the petition of intervention was affirmed by the Supreme Court of Iowa, which said:

> * * * It is true that persons not parties to the litigation would not be bound by its result and might bring a separate action. But we think the rule that a multiplicity of suits will be avoided wherever possible has a direct application. It might also happen that if the plaintiff and defendant here should try out their action first, and intervenors be relegated to a separate suit, different and contradictory results would be reached. A division of the property of the original parties without the benefit of such evidence as the intervenors might produce could very well be inequitable, resulting, at the best, in an action to modify the divorce decree by the litigant whose rights were adversely affected by a later trial of the separate action to enforce a trust. * * * There seems every reason in policy why, if there are third parties claiming an interest in either the real or personal property, the entire matter should be decided at once. Such a course will do away with a multiplicity of suits and will enable the court to make orders concerning property rights and allowances with a full knowledge of the exact extent of the interests of the litigants. In the case at bar, if the court is not to be permitted to know the real interest of the plaintiff and defendant in the realty and personalty now owned by them, if this must be left to determination in a future and separate suit brought by the proposed intervenors, it will be greatly hampered in making a fair order. * * *

Notes and Questions

1. As *Brune* notes, intervention is a relatively new development, and is largely statutory in nature. By allowing a third person to interject himself into a lawsuit, it undercuts the traditional notion that a plaintiff is allowed to control his suit. See 7C Wright, Miller & Kane, *Federal Practice and Procedure: Civil 2d* § 1901 (1986).

2. Is the statement in *Brune* that "the direct legal operation of the judgment * * * would not cause intervenor either to gain or lose anything" accurate? Does it mean that a party will be allowed to intervene only if the judgment will bind that party by principles of res judicata or collateral

estoppel? Would the intervenors in *Wharff* have been affected by these doctrines had they not been allowed to intervene?

3. How might the *Brune* court have decided the intervention issue in *Wharff*? Can the difference in outcome in the two cases be explained by the *Wharff* court's willingness to consider the forum's interest in efficient adjudication of claims?

SMUCK v. HOBSON

United States Court of Appeals, District of Columbia Circuit, 1969.
132 U.S.App.D.C. 372, 408 F.2d 175.

[In Hobson v. Hansen, 269 F.Supp. 401 (D.D.C.1967), a class action brought on behalf of Black and poor children, the court found that the plaintiffs were being denied their constitutional rights to equal educational opportunities because the District of Columbia schools were being operated on a basis that was racially and economically discriminatory. The Board of Education voted not to appeal and ordered Dr. Carl Hansen, the Superintendent of Schools, not to appeal. Nonetheless, Dr. Hansen and Carl Smuck, one of the dissenting Board members, filed notices of appeal. In addition, motions to intervene were made in the District Court and in the Court of Appeals by Dr. Hansen and twenty parents who said they "dissent from" the court's decision. The Court of Appeals decided to hold the direct appeals in abeyance and remanded the intervention motions for a hearing. The District Court granted the motions to intervene, even though neither Hansen nor the parents had shown a substantial interest that could be protected only through intervention, "in order to give the Court of Appeals an opportunity to pass on the intervention questions raised here, and the questions to be raised by the appeal on the merits * * *." Hobson v. Hansen, 44 F.R.D. 18, 33 (D.D.C.1968). The Court of Appeals then considered the matter *en banc*.]

BAZELON, CHIEF JUDGE * * *. These appeals challenge the findings of the trial court that the Board of Education has in a variety of ways violated the Constitution in administering the District of Columbia schools. Among the facts that distinguish this case from the normal grist of appellate courts is the absence of the Board of Education as an appellant. Instead, the would-be appellants are Dr. Carl F. Hansen, the resigned superintendent of District schools, who appeals in his former official capacity and as an individual; Carl C. Smuck, a member of the Board of Education, who appeals in that capacity; and the parents of certain school children who have attempted to intervene in order to register on appeal their "dissent" from the order below.

* * * Whatever standing he might have possessed to appeal as a named defendant in the original suit * * * disappeared when Dr. Hansen left his official position. Presumably because he was aware of this, he subsequently moved to intervene under Rule 24(a) of the Rules of Civil Procedure in order to appeal as an individual. * * * He does not claim that a reversal or modification of the order by this Court would make his return to office likely. Consequently, the supposed impact of the decision upon his tenure is irrelevant insofar as an appeal is con-

cerned, since a reversal would have no effect. Dr. Hansen thus has no "interest relating to the property or transaction which is the subject of the action" sufficient for Rule 24(a), and intervention is therefore unwarranted.

We also find that Mr. Smuck has no appealable interest as a member of the Board of Education. While he was in that capacity a named defendant, the Board of Education was undeniably the principal figure and could have been sued alone as a collective entity. Appellant Smuck had a fair opportunity to participate in its defense, and in the decision not to appeal. Having done so, he has no separate interest as an individual in the litigation. The order directs the board to take certain actions. But since its decisions are made by vote as a collective whole, there is no apparent way in which Smuck as an individual could violate the decree and thereby become subject to enforcement proceedings.

The motion to intervene by the parents presents a more difficult problem requiring a correspondingly more detailed examination of the requirements for intervention of right.

* * *

The phrasing of Rule 24(a)(2) as amended parallels that of Rule 19(a)(2) concerning joinder. But the fact that the two rules are entwined does not imply that an "interest" for the purpose of one is precisely the same as for the other. The occasions upon which a petitioner should be allowed to intervene under Rule 24 are not necessarily limited to those situations when the trial court should compel him to become a party under Rule 19. And while the division of Rule 24(a) and (b) into "Intervention of Right" and "Permissible Intervention" might superficially suggest that only the latter involves an exercise of discretion by the court, the contrary is clearly the case.

The effort to extract substance from the conclusory phrase "interest" or "legally protectable interest" is of limited promise. Parents unquestionably have a sufficient "interest" in the education of their children to justify the initiation of a lawsuit in appropriate circumstances, as indeed was the case for the plaintiff-appellee parents here. But in the context of intervention the question is not whether a lawsuit should be begun, but whether already initiated litigation should be extended to include additional parties. The 1966 amendments to Rule 24(a) have facilitated this, the true inquiry, by eliminating the temptation or need for tangential expeditions in search of "property" or someone "bound by a judgment." It would be unfortunate to allow the inquiry to be led once again astray by a myopic fixation upon "interest." Rather, as Judge Leventhal recently concluded for this Court, "[A] more instructive approach is to let our construction be guided by the policies behind the 'interest' requirement. * * * [T]he 'interest' test is primarily a practical guide to disposing of lawsuits by involving as many apparently concerned persons as is compatible with efficiency and due process."[12]

12. Nuesse v. Camp, 128 U.S.App.D.C. 172, 385 F.2d 694, 700 (1967).

The decision whether intervention of right is warranted thus involves an accommodation between two potentially conflicting goals: to achieve judicial economies of scale by resolving related issues in a single lawsuit, and to prevent the single lawsuit from becoming fruitlessly complex or unending. Since this task will depend upon the contours of the particular controversy, general rules and past decisions cannot provide uniformly dependable guides. The Supreme Court, in its only full-dress examination of Rule 24(a) since the 1966 amendments, found that a gas distributor was entitled to intervention of right although its only "interest" was the economic harm it claimed would follow from an allegedly inadequate plan for divestiture approved by the Government in an antitrust proceeding.[14] While conceding that the Court's opinion granting intervention in Cascade Natural Gas Corp. v. El Paso Natural Gas Co. "is certainly susceptible of a very broad reading," the trial judge here would distinguish the decision on the ground that the petitioner "did show a strong direct economic interest, for the new company [to be created by divestiture] would be its sole supplier." Yet while it is undoubtedly true that "*Cascade* should not be read as a carte blanche for intervention by anyone at any time," there is no apparent reason why an "economic interest" should always be necessary to justify intervention. The goal of "disposing of lawsuits by involving as many apparently concerned persons as is compatible with efficiency and due process" may in certain circumstances be met by allowing parents whose only "interest" is the education of their children to intervene. In determining whether such circumstances are present, the first requirement of Rule 24(a)(2), that of an "interest" in the transaction, may be a less useful point of departure than the second and third requirements, that the applicant may be impeded in protecting his interest by the action and that his interest is not adequately represented by others.

This does not imply that the need for an "interest" in the controversy should or can be read out of the rule. But the requirement should be viewed as a prerequisite rather than relied upon as a determinative criterion for intervention. If barriers are needed to limit extension of the right to intervene, the criteria of practical harm to the applicant and the adequacy of representation by others are better suited to the task. If those requirements are met, the nature of his "interest" may play a role in determining the sort of intervention which should be allowed—whether, for example, he should be permitted to contest all issues, and whether he should enjoy all the prerogatives of a party litigant.

Both courts and legislatures have recognized as appropriate the concern for their children's welfare which the parents here seek to protect by intervention. While the artificiality of an appeal without the Board of Education cannot be ignored, neither can the importance of the constitutional issues decided below. The relevance of substantial and unsettled questions of law has been recognized in allowing intervention to perfect an appeal. And this Court has noted repeatedly, "obviously tailored to fit ordinary civil litigation, [the provisions of Rule 24] require other than

14. Cascade Natural Gas Corp. v. El Paso
Natural Gas Co., 386 U.S. 129, 132–136, 87
S.Ct. 932, 17 L.Ed.2d 814 (1967).

literal application in atypical cases." [20]   We conclude that the interests asserted by the intervenors are sufficient to justify an examination of whether the two remaining requirements for intervention are met.

* * *

[The court then determined that the disposition of the action might impair the applicants' ability to protect their interests if they were not allowed to intervene.]

The remaining requirement for intervention is that the applicant not be adequately represented by others.   No question is raised here but that the Board of Education adequately represented the intervenors at the trial below; the issue rather is whether the parents were adequately represented by the school board's decision not to appeal.   The presumed good faith of the board in reaching this decision is not conclusive.   * * * As the conditional wording of Rule 24(a)(2) suggests in permitting intervention "unless the applicant's interest is adequately represented by existing parties," "the burden [is] on those opposing intervention to show the adequacy of the existing representation."   In this case, the interests of the parents who wish to intervene in order to appeal do not coincide with those of the Board of Education.   The school board represents all parents within the District.   The intervening appellants may have more parochial interests centering upon the education of their own children.   While they cannot of course ask the Board to favor their children unconstitutionally at the expense of others, they like other parents can seek the adoption of policies beneficial to their own children.   Moreover, considerations of publicity, cost, and delay may not have the same weight for the parents as for the school board in the context of a decision to appeal.   And the Board of Education, buffeted as it like other school boards is by conflicting public demands, may possibly have less interest in preserving its own untrammeled discretion than do the parents.   It is not necessary to accuse the board of bad faith in deciding not to appeal or of a lack of vigor in defending the suit below in order to recognize that a restrictive court order may be a not wholly unwelcome haven.

* * *

Our holding that the appellants would be practically disadvantaged by a decision without appeal in this case and that they are not otherwise adequately represented necessitates a closer scrutiny of the precise nature of their interest and the scope of intervention that should accordingly be granted.   The parents who seek to appeal do not come before this court to protect the good name of the Board of Education.   Their interest is not to protect the board, or Dr. Hansen, from an unfair finding.   Their asserted interest is rather the freedom of the school board—and particularly the new school board recently elected—to exercise the broadest discretion constitutionally permissible in deciding upon educational policies.   Since this is so, their interest extends only to those parts of the order which can fairly be said to impose restraints upon the Board of Education.   And

20.   Textile Workers Union, etc. v. Allendale Co., 96 U.S.App.D.C. 401, 403, 226 F.2d 765, 767 (1955) (en banc), cert. denied, Allendale Co. v. Mitchell, 351 U.S. 909, 76 S.Ct. 699, 100 L.Ed. 1444 (1956), cited in Neusse v. Camp, 128 U.S.App.D.C. 172, 385 F.2d 694, 700 (1967).

because the school board is not a party to this appeal, review should be limited to those features of the order which limit the discretion of the old or new board.

* * *

[A partial concurring opinion by JUDGE MCGOWAN and dissenting opinions by JUDGES DANAHER and BURGER are omitted.]

Notes and Questions

1. In addition to the reasons offered in *Smuck,* typical grounds for the assertion of inadequacy of representation for purposes of intervening as of right under Rule 24(a)(2) are: the applicant's interests are not represented at all, Gaines v. Dixie Carriers, Inc., 434 F.2d 52 (5th Cir.1970); the applicant and the attorney who supposedly represents his interest are antagonistic, United States v. C.M. Lane Lifeboat Co., 25 F.Supp. 410 (E.D.N.Y.1938), but see Stadin v. Union Elec. Co., 309 F.2d 912 (8th Cir.1962), certiorari denied 373 U.S. 915, 83 S.Ct. 1298, 10 L.Ed.2d 415 (1963); and there is collusion between the representative and the adverse parties, Park & Tilford, Inc. v. Schulte, 160 F.2d 984 (2d Cir.), certiorari denied 332 U.S. 761, 68 S.Ct. 64, 92 L.Ed.2d 347 (1947). See generally Shapiro, *Some Thoughts on Intervention Before Courts, Agencies and Arbitrators,* 81 Harv.L.Rev. 721 (1968); Note, *Intervention in Government Enforcement Actions,* 89 Harv.L.Rev. 1174 (1976).

It often is held that the United States adequately represents the public interest in antitrust suits and intervention in those cases is denied absent a clear showing to the contrary. Is this approach justifiable? How does the Department of Justice determine what the public interest is?

2. What factors affect the standard for adequate representation? In APPEAL OF AMERICAN PETROLEUM INSTITUTE, 834 F.2d 60 (2d Cir. 1987), the American Petroleum Institute (API) appealed a District Court order denying its motion to intervene in a lawsuit brought by the Natural Resources Defense Council, Inc. and other groups concerned with air pollution against the New York State Department of Environmental Conservation, the United States Environmental Protection Agency, and the administrators of both agencies. The Court of Appeals affirmed:

This suit is a so-called "citizen suit". It seeks to compel the state defendants to implement four ozone pollution control strategies contained in New York's State Implementation Plan (SIP). * * * One of the ozone control strategies, known as Stage II, requires the use of equipment designed to capture gasoline vapors that escape when automobile fuel tanks are filled at gasoline stations. API, whose members own or supply some 3500 gasoline stations in New York City, asserts an interest in challenging the efficacy of the Stage II strategy * * * [T]he only issues concerning Stage II in this citizen suit are whether New York has unlawfully delayed implementation of Stage II and whether the State has a nondiscretionary duty to implement Stage II forthwith. * * * [T]he District Judge * * * ruled that API had not demonstrated a sufficient interest not already adequately represented by existing parties to the lawsuit.

* * * API contends that in this suit it too has an interest different from that of New York. API's interest, it urges, is economic, whereas the State's interest is governmental.

We think API misperceives the concept of an interest "adequately represented" within the meaning of Rule 24. A putative intervenor does not have an interest not adequately represented by a party to a lawsuit simply because it has a motive to litigate that is different from the motive of an existing party. So long as the party has demonstrated sufficient motivation to litigate vigorously and to present all colorable contentions, a district judge does not exceed the bounds of discretion by concluding that the interests of the intervenor are adequately represented. * * *

In this case API may be motivated to defend the plaintiffs' suit because of economic interests not necessarily shared by the state and federal defendants, but there has been no showing that the nature of those economic interests is related to colorable legal defenses that the public defendants would be less able to assert. * * * The fact that API wishes to advance contentions the existing defendants apparently believe are unavailing does not require API's intervention where no nexus exists between the interest asserted and the contentions sought to be put forth. * * *

Is this case consistent with *Smuck*? Why do you think the two come out differently?

3. An example of a federal statute that permits intervention is Section 902 of the Civil Rights Act of 1964, 42 U.S.C. § 2000h–2, which gives the United States an unconditional right to intervene in actions seeking relief against a denial of equal protection of the laws under the Fourteenth Amendment on account of race, color, religion, sex, or national origin. See Lemon v. Bossier Parish School Bd., 240 F.Supp. 709 (W.D.La.1965). Perhaps the single most important statutory provision permitting intervention by the United States is Section 2403(a) of the Judicial Code, which applies to actions challenging the constitutionality of an act of Congress. This provision has even enabled the United States to intervene to show that a case should be decided on nonconstitutional grounds. See Smolowe v. Delendo Corp., 36 F.Supp. 790 (S.D.N.Y.1940), affirmed on other grounds 136 F.2d 231 (2d Cir.), certiorari denied 320 U.S. 751, 64 S.Ct. 56, 88 L.Ed. 446 (1943). The government also has used it to show that the suit is collusive and there is no case or controversy before the court. See United States v. Johnson, 319 U.S. 302, 63 S.Ct. 1075, 87 L.Ed. 1413 (1943). See 7C Wright, Miller & Kane, *Federal Practice and Procedure: Civil 2d* § 1906 (1986), for a discussion of other statutes conferring an unconditional right to intervene. 28 U.S.C. § 2403(b) extends the intervention right to states in actions involving the constitutionality of state statutes.

4. Both Rule 24(a) and Rule 24(b) require that an application to intervene be "timely." As the court noted in *Smuck*, intervention after judgment will be allowed only in unique situations. One court has stated:

The rationale which seems to underlie this general principle * * * is the assumption that allowing intervention after judgment will either (1) prejudice the rights of the existing parties to the litigation or (2) substantially interfere with the orderly processes of the court.

McDONALD v. E.J. LAVINO CO., 430 F.2d 1065, 1072 (5th Cir.1970).

What factors should the court consider when determining whether a motion to intervene is timely? Should a different standard be used for deciding the timeliness of motions to intervene permissively as opposed to motions to intervene as of right? If so, why? Sullivan, *Enforcement of Government Antitrust Decrees by Private Parties: Third Party Beneficiary Rights and Intervenor Status,* 123 U.Pa.L.Rev. 822, 873–92 (1975), explores the possibility of post-judgment intervention in government antitrust suits in order to enforce the judgment.

5. Must the intervenor present an independent basis for subject-matter jurisdiction, or can the intervenor's claims be viewed as being within the ancillary jurisdiction of the court? Does it matter whether the intervention was as of right or permissive?

Generally, if the applicant has a right to intervene under Rule 24(a), no independent basis for jurisdiction is required. See Lenz v. Wagner, 240 F.2d 666 (5th Cir.1957). See also Fraser, *Ancillary Jurisdiction of Federal Courts of Persons Whose Interests May Be Impaired if Not Joined,* 62 F.R.D. 483 (1974). In general, an independent basis for jurisdiction must be shown in permissive actions. See, e.g., Reedsburg Bank v. Apollo, 508 F.2d 995 (7th Cir. 1975).

6. Can intervention as of right destroy jurisdiction? What would happen, for example, if a party sought to intervene as of right in a suit based on diversity, and permitting her to do so would destroy complete diversity?

Courts have held, in general, that intervenors may enter the suit under the theory of ancillary jurisdiction. In situations, however, in which the intervenor is an indispensable party under the tests of Rule 19, intervention has not been allowed and the suit must be dismissed. See Chance v. County Bd. of School Trustees, 332 F.2d 971 (7th Cir.1964). Is this approach sound given the principles of Owen Equipment & Erection Co. v. Kroger, p. 282, supra? Does the extension of jurisdiction to the intervenor's claims serve to undermine the statutory requirement of complete diversity? If Rule 24 undermines complete-diversity requirements, does it violate 28 U.S.C. § 1332? Would doing so violate 28 U.S.C. § 2072 and its requirement that the Federal Rules "shall not abridge, enlarge or modify any substantive right"? Would your answer depend on whether intervention is based on a right given by statute or by Rule 24 itself?

7. Can an intervenor assert additional claims, counterclaims, cross-claims, or third-party claims in the lawsuit? Should your answer depend upon whether the intervention was discretionary or as of right? Does the answer turn on the nature of the claim: compulsory or permissive? See 7C Wright, Miller & Kane, *Federal Practice and Procedure: Civil 2d* § 1917 (1986).

ATLANTIS DEVELOPMENT CORP. v. UNITED STATES

United States Court of Appeals, Fifth Circuit, 1967.
379 F.2d 818.

JOHN R. BROWN, CIRCUIT JUDGE. This case involves a little bit of nearly everything—a little bit of oceanography, a little bit of marine biology, a little bit of the tidelands oil controversy, a little bit of international law, a little bit of latter day Marco Polo exploration. But these do not command our resolution since the little bits are here controlled by the less exciting bigger, if not big, problem of intervention. The District Court declined to permit mandatory intervention as a matter of right or to allow intervention as permissive. As is so often true, a ruling made to avoid delay, complications, or expense turns out to have generated more of its own. With the main case being stayed by the District Court pending this appeal, it is pretty safe to assume that the case would long have been decided on its merits (or lack of them) had intervention of either kind been allowed. And this seems especially unfortunate since it is difficult to believe that the presence of the attempted intervenor would have added much to the litigation. All of this becomes the more ironic, if not unfortunate, since the intervenor[1] and the Government sparring over why intervention ought or ought not to have been allowed, each try to persuade us the one was bound to win, the other lose on the merits which each proceeds to argue as though the parties were before or in the court. Adding to the problem, or perhaps more accurately aiding in the solution of it, are the mid-1966 amendments to the Federal Rules of Civil Procedure including specifically those relating to intervention. We reverse.

What the jousting is all about is the ownership in, or right to control the use, development of and building on a number of coral reefs or islands comprising Pacific Reef, Ajax Reef, Long Reef, an unnamed reef and Triumph Reef which the intervenor has called the "Atlantis Group" because of the name given them by Anderson, its predecessor in interest and the supposed discoverer. * * *

Just how or in what manner these reefs were "discovered" is so far unrevealed. Some time in 1962 William T. Anderson discovered the reefs apparently by conceiving the idea of occupying them through the construction of facilities for fishing club, marina, skin diving club, a hotel, and, perhaps as the chief lure, a gambling casino. Anderson made some sort of claim to it and with facilities unavailable to the adventurous explorers of the long past, he gave public notice of this in the United States and in England by newspaper advertisements in late 1962 and early 1963. These "rights" were acquired by Atlantis Development Corporation, Ltd., the proposed intervenor. Reflecting the desire manifested now by the persistent efforts to intervene to have legal rights ascertained in a peaceful fashion through established tribunals and not by self-help or the initiation of physical activities which would precipitate counter moves,

---

1. Atlantis Development Corporation, Ltd., a Bahamian corporation, will be referred to interchangeably as either Atlantis or Intervenor.

physical or legal, or both, Atlantis (and predecessors) patiently sought permission from all governmental agencies, state and federal—just short of the United Nations—but to no avail. * * * In December 1964 on learning that the defendants in the main case had formally sought a permit from the Engineers, Atlantis notified the Government of its claim to ownership of the islands and the threatened unauthorized actions by the defendants. This precipitated further communications with the Department of Justice with Atlantis importuning, apparently successfully, the Government to initiate the present action.

It was against this background that the litigation commenced. The suit is brought by the United States against the main defendants.[5] The complaint was in two counts seeking injunctive relief. In the first the Government asserted that Triumph and Long Reefs are part of the bed of the Atlantic Ocean included in the Outer Continental Shelf subject to the jurisdiction, control and power of disposition of the United States. The action of the defendants (note 5, supra) in the erection of caissons on the reefs, the dredging of material from the seabed, and the depositing of the dredged material within the caissons without authorization was charged as constituting a trespass on government property. In the second count the Government alleged that the defendants were engaged in the erection of an artificial island or fixed structure on the Outer Continental Shelf in the vicinity of the reefs without a permit from the Secretary of the Army in violation of the Outer Continental Shelf Lands Act, 43 U.S.C.A. § 1333(f) and 33 U.S.C.A. § 403. * * *

Atlantis seeking intervention by proposed answer and cross-claim against the defendants admitted the jurisdiction of the District Court. It asserted that the United States has no territorial jurisdiction, dominion or ownership in or over the reefs and cannot therefore maintain the action for an injunction, and that conversely Atlantis has title to the property by discovery and occupation. In the cross-claim, Atlantis charged the defendants as trespassers against it. Appropriate relief was sought by the prayer.

The District Court without opinion declared in the order that intervenor "does not have such an interest in this cause as will justify its intervention, either as a matter of right or permissively." Leave was granted to appear amicus curiae.

We think without a doubt that under former F.R.Civ.P. 24(a), intervention as a matter of right was not compelled under (a)(2). The situation did not present one in which the intervenor "is or may be bound" by a decree rendered in his absence in the sense articulated most recently in *Sam Fox*[9] in terms of res judicata. Although not quite so clear, we also think it did not measure up to the notions loosely reflected in a case-by-case development under which, although res judicata was technically lacking, the decree is considered "binding" since in a very practical sense

5. Acme General Contractors, Inc., and J.H. Coppedge Company, each Florida corporations, and Louis M. Ray, a resident of Dade County, Florida.

9. Sam Fox Publishing Co. v. United States, 1961, 366 U.S. 683, 81 S.Ct. 1309, 6 L.Ed.2d 604.

it would have an immediate operative effect upon the intervenor. In none of these cases was it suggested that if the only effect of the decree in intervenor's absence would be to raise the hurdle of stare decisis, this would amount to the absentee being bound as a practical matter.

This brings us squarely to the effect of the 1966 Amendments and the new F.R.Civ.P. 24(a). * * *

In assaying the new Rule, several things stand out. The first, as the Government acknowledges, is that this amounts to a legislative repeal of the rigid *Sam Fox* * * * res judicata rule. But more important, the revision was a coordinated one to tie more closely together the related situations of joinder, F.R.Civ.P. 19, and class actions, F.R.Civ.P. 23.

As the Advisory Committee's notes reflect, there are competing interests at work in this area. On the one hand, there is the private suitor's interests in having his own lawsuit subject to no one else's direction or meddling. On the other hand, however, is the great public interest, especially in these explosive days of ever-increasing dockets, of having a disposition at a single time of as much of the controversy to as many of the parties as is fairly possible consistent with due process.

In these three Rules the Advisory Committee, unsatisfied with the former Rules which too frequently defined application in terms of rigid legal concepts such as joint, common ownership, res judicata, or the like, as well as court efforts in applying them, deliberately set out on a more pragmatic course. For the purposes of our problem, this course is reflected in the almost, if not quite, uniform language concerning a party who claims an interest relating to the subject of the action and is so situated that the disposition of the action may as a practical matter impair or impede his ability to protect that interest * * *.

Although this is question-begging and is therefore not a real test, this approach shows that the question of whether an intervention as a matter of right exists often turns on the unstated question of whether joinder of the intervenor was called for under new Rule 19. Were this the controlling inquiry, we find ample basis here to answer it in the affirmative. Atlantis—having formally informed the Government in detail of its claim of ownership to the very reefs in suit, that the defendants were trespassing against it, and having successfully urged the Government to institute suit against the defendants—seems clearly to occupy the position of a party who ought to have been joined as a defendant under new Rule 19(a) (2)(i) * * *.

This interim conclusion is, of course, a rejection of the Government's approach made for this day, case, and time only that all new Rule 24(a) was to do was to abandon the rigidity of *Sam Fox* and codify the ameliorative exceptions * * * to escape the unfortunate consequences of a rule expressed in terms of the party being "bound," i.e., res judicata. Any such narrow approach is to deprecate the painstaking work of the Advisory Committee especially the deliberate efforts to dovetail F.R.Civ.P. 19, 24 and 23 together with two of them being radically rewritten.

When approached in this light, we think that both from the terms of new Rule 24(a) and its adoption of 19(a)(2)(i) intervention of right is called for here. Of course F.R.Civ.P. 24(a)(2) requires both the existence of an interest which may be impaired as a practical matter and an absence of adequate representation of the intervenor's interest by existing parties. There can be no difficulty here about the lack of representation. On the basis of the pleadings * * * Atlantis is without a friend in this litigation. The Government turns on the defendants and takes the same view both administratively and in its brief here toward Atlantis. The defendants, on the other hand, are claiming ownership in and the right to develop the very islands claimed by Atlantis.

Nor can there be any doubt that Atlantis "claims an interest relating to the property or transaction which is the subject of the action." The object of the suit is to assert the sovereign's exclusive dominion and control over two out of a group of islands publicly claimed by Atlantis. This identity with the very property at stake in the main case and with the particular transaction therein involved (the right to build structures with or without permission of the Corps of Engineers) is of exceptional importance. For 24(a)(2) is in the conjunctive requiring both an interest relating to the property or transaction and the practical harm if the party is absent. This sharply reduces the area in which stare decisis may, as we later discuss, supply the element of practical harm.

This brings us then to the question whether these papers reflect that in the absence of Atlantis, a disposition of the main suit may as a practical matter impair or impede its ability to protect that interest—its claim to ownership and the right to control, use and develop without hindrance from the Government, the Department of Defense, or other agencies. Certain things are clear. Foremost, of course, is the plain proposition that the judgment itself as between Government and defendants cannot have any direct, immediate effect upon the rights of Atlantis, not a party to it.

But in a very real and practical sense is not the trial of this lawsuit the trial of Atlantis' suit as well? Quite apart from the contest of Atlantis' claim of sovereignty vis-a-vis the Government resulting from its "discovery" and occupation of the reefs, there are at least two basic substantial legal questions directly at issue, but not yet resolved in any Court at any time between the Government and the defendants which are inescapably present in the claim of Atlantis against the Government. One is whether these coral reefs built up by accretion of marine biology are "submerged lands" under the Outer Continental Shelf Lands Act, 43 U.S.C.A. § 1331 et seq. The second basic question is whether, assuming both from the standpoint of geographical location and their nature they constitute "lands," does the sovereignty of the United States extend to them with respect to any purposes not included in or done for the protection of the "exploring for, developing, removing, and transporting * * *" natural resources therefrom, 43 U.S.C.A. § 1333(a)(1). Another, closely related, is whether the authority of the Secretary of the Army to prevent obstruction of navigation extended by § 1333(f) to "artificial islands and fixed structures," includes structures other than those "erected thereon for the purpose of exploring for, developing, removing, and transporting" mineral resources therefrom (§ 1333(a)(1) * * *).

The Government would avoid all of these problems by urging us to rule as a matter of law on the face of the moving papers that the intervenors could not possibly win on the trial of the intervention and consequently intervention should be denied. In support it asserts that the claim that the reefs are beyond the jurisdiction of the United States is self-defeating, and under the plain meaning of the Outer Continental Shelf Lands Act and the facts revealed from the Coast and Geodetic Chart of which we must take judicial knowledge as proof of all facts shown.

The first is at least contingently answered by § 1333(b) which invests jurisdiction in the United States District Court of the nearest adjacent state. As to the others, it is, of course, conceivable that there will be some instances in which the total lack of merit is so evident from the face of the moving papers that denial of the right of intervention rests upon a complete lack of a substantial claim. But it hardly comports with good administration, if not due process, to determine the merits of a claim asserted in a pleading seeking an adjudication through an adversary hearing by denying access to the court at all. * * *

If in its claim against the defendants in the main suit these questions are answered favorably to the Government's position, the claim of Atlantis for all practical purposes is worthless. That statement assumes, of course, that such holding is either approved or made by this Court after an appeal to it and thereafter it is either affirmed, or not taken for review, on certiorari. It also assumes that in the subsequent separate trial of the claim of Atlantis against the Government the prior decision would be followed as a matter of stare decisis. Do these assumptions have a realistic basis? Anyone familiar with the history of the Fifth Circuit could have but a single answer to that query. This Court, unlike some of our sister Circuit Courts who occasionally follow a different course, has long tried earnestly to follow the practice in which a decision announced by one panel of the Court is followed by all others until such time as it is reversed, either outright or by intervening decisions of the Supreme Court, or by the Court itself en banc. That means that if the defendants in the main action do not prevail upon these basic contentions which are part and parcel of the claim of Atlantis, the only way by which Atlantis can win is to secure a rehearing en banc with a successful overruling of the prior decision or, failing in either one or both of those efforts, a reversal of the earlier decision by the Supreme Court on certiorari. With the necessarily limited number of en banc hearings in this Circuit and with the small percentage of cases meriting certiorari, it is an understatement to characterize these prospects as formidable.

That is but a way of saying in a very graphic way that the failure to allow Atlantis an opportunity to advance its own theories both of law and fact in the trial (and appeal) of the pending case will if the disposition is favorable to the Government "as a practical matter impair or impede [its] ability to protect [its] interest." That is, to be sure, a determination by us that in the new language of 24(a)(2) stare decisis may now—unlike the former days under 24(a)(2)—supply that practical disadvantage which warrants intervention of right. It bears repeating, however, that this holding does not presage one requiring intervention of right in every conceivable circumstance where under the operation of the Circuit's stare decisis practice, the formidable nature of an en banc rehearing or the successful grant of a writ of certiorari, an earlier decision might afford a substantial obstacle. We are dealing here with a conjunction of a claim to and interest in the very property and the very transaction which is the subject of the main action. When those coincide, the Court before whom the potential parties in the second suit must come must itself take the intellectually straight forward, realistic view that the first decision will in all likelihood be the second and the third and the last one. Even the possibility that the decision might be overturned by en banc ruling or reversal on certiorari does not overcome its practical effect, not just as an obstacle, but as the forerunner of the actual outcome. * * *

Reversed.

Notes and Questions

1. Early commentary on the 1966 amendment to Federal Rule 24 appears in Cohn, *The New Federal Rules of Civil Procedure*, 54 Geo.L.J. 1204, 1229–32 (1966); Kaplan, *Continuing Work of the Civil Committee: 1966 Amendments of the Federal Rules of Civil Procedure (I)*, 81 Harv.L.Rev. 356, 400–07 (1967).

2. In what ways other than those described in *Atlantis* does the amended text of Federal Rule 24 have the effect of liberalizing intervention as of right? Prior to 1966, one of the two conditions on intervention of right was a showing that the representation of the intervenor "is or may be inadequate." Under amended Rule 24(a), if the other conditions of that provision are satisfied, intervention is of right unless it is shown that the applicant's interest is adequately represented by existing parties. What is the effect of this change? Intervention classically has been viewed as having three functions: protection of nonparties, trial convenience, and protection of the original parties. In what ways has the balance among these three functions been altered by the 1966 amendments?

3. Why does Rule 24 distinguish between intervention as of right and permissive intervention? In Shreve, *Questioning Intervention of Right— Toward a New Methodology of Decisionmaking*, 74 Nw.U.L.Rev. 894 (1980), the author argues that trial court judges should be allowed to exercise their discretion in all non-statutory intervention cases. He says that intervention of right has had the effect of adding needless appellate review, resulting in inefficiencies. According to the author, a procedural device designed, in part, to improve the use of court resources has had the opposite effect in many cases.

Chapter 7

CLASS ACTIONS

Read Federal Rule of Civil Procedure 23 and the material accompanying it in the Supplement.

SECTION A. HISTORY AND PHILOSOPHY OF THE CLASS ACTION

The history of the class action can be traced to the English "bill of peace" in the seventeenth century. The "bill" was a procedural device utilized by the Courts of Chancery to allow an action to be brought by or against representative parties when (1) the number of persons involved was too large to permit joinder, (2) all the members of the group possessed a joint interest in the question being adjudicated, and (3) the named parties adequately represented the interests of those who were not present. If these three conditions were met, the judgment that ultimately was entered was binding on all the members of the represented group. An excellent summary of the history of class actions can be found in S. Yeazell, *From Medieval Group Litigation to the Modern Class Action* (1987).

Although provisions for class actions modelled after the English procedure existed in various state codes and the Federal Equity Rules, Federal Rule 23, as originally adopted in 1938, represented the first attempt to provide for class actions in a mature form. Moreover, with the adoption of the Federal Rules the class action became available in both legal and equitable actions in the federal courts.

Original Rule 23 attempted to describe when a class action was proper in a highly conceptualized way. All class actions were divided into three categories and a particular suit was assigned to one classification or another, depending on the character of the right being asserted. The differences among the various categories were important for determining questions such as whether jurisdictional requirements were met, whether the decree had binding effect, and when the statute of limitations was

656

tolled. Briefly, the categories were as follows: A so-called "true" class action was involved when the class members possessed joint and common interests in the subject matter of the action; a "hybrid" class action was present when several claims to the same property were being litigated; and what was described as a "spurious" class action existed when persons possessing independent interests joined together in the suit.

This structure proved to be confusing to apply, see 7A Wright, Miller, & Kane, *Federal Practice and Procedure: Civil 2d* § 1752 (1986), which led the Advisory Committee to rewrite Rule 23 completely to substitute functional tests for the conceptual categories and to provide some procedural guidance for the courts with regard to handling class actions. The amendment also made clear that a judgment in a class action is binding on all class members, except in those cases in which the right to opt-out under Rule 23(c)(2) applies and has been exercised. The philosophy of the 1966 amendment was aptly described by the Reporter to the Advisory Committee when he said:

> * * * [The Advisory Committee] perceived, as lawyers had for a long time, that some litigious situations affecting numerous persons "naturally" or "necessarily" called for unitary adjudication. The problem was how to elaborate this insight while avoiding the pitfalls of abstract classification on the style of 1938. Approaching rule 23, then, in much the same spirit in which it was considering rule 19, the Committee strove to sort out the factual situations or patterns that had recurred in class actions and appeared with varying degrees of convincingness to justify treatment of the class *in solido*. The revised rule was written upon the framework thus revealed * * *.

Kaplan, *Continuing Work of the Civil Committee: 1966 Amendments of the Federal Rules of Civil Procedure (I),* 81 Harv.L.Rev. 356, 386 (1967).

The evolution of the rules governing class actions parallels in part an evolution in society and in society's understanding of the role of courts. As two early commentators on the Federal Rules put it:

> Modern society seems increasingly to expose men to * * * group injuries for which individually they are in a poor position to seek legal redress, either because they do not know enough or because such redress is disproportionately expensive. If each is left to assert his rights alone if and when he can, there will at best be a random and fragmentary enforcement, if there is any at all. This result is not only unfortunate in the particular case, but it will operate seriously to impair the deterrent effect of the sanctions which underlie much contemporary law. The problem of fashioning an effective and inclusive group remedy is thus a major one.

Kalven and Rosenfield, *Function of a Class Suit,* 8 U.Chi.L.Rev. 684, 686 (1941). This state of affairs is as true 50 years later.

Class actions are justified by the assumption that the members of the class are similarly situated in some way. In many class actions the legal theories and evidence used by one member can be used by the entire class. In others, the facts applicable to one member will be applicable to all. Class actions are said to promote judicial efficiency by curtailing multiple litigation. In many cases the class-action device ensures that all plaintiffs are compensated. By contrast, if each plaintiff sued individually, the defendant might run out of money before all the claims were decided.

As you read this Chapter, it will become clear that there are two ways of viewing the modern class-action device: It can be viewed simply as another joinder device, or it can be viewed as something different—a representational device that empowers the named class representative to act on behalf of others similarly situated whether or not they could have sued independently, or even wanted to do so. See generally Hutchinson, *Class Actions: Joinder or Representational Device?,* 1984 Sup.Ct.Rev. 459. Although the 1966 amendments to Rule 23 moved in the direction of the representational model, courts (including the Supreme Court) have vacillated between the two views of the class-action device just described. As you read this Chapter, be sensitive to this vacillation—and ask yourself if the choice of models produces different results in concrete cases. And, at the close of the Chapter, ask yourself whether the class-action device is only a convenience that goes slightly beyond Rule 20, or whether the device makes possible litigation on the part of absentee class members that they otherwise would be unable to maintain.

One other general issue should engage your attention. On either of the two models just described, the rules governing class actions depart from the traditional notion that individuals can be bound by a court judgment only when they themselves have had an opportunity to have a day in court. What justifies this departure? What is there about the procedures that have been developed around the class-action device that makes it possible and fair to bind a party who has not made an appearance in court? As you consider these questions, pay special attention to the connections among the doctrines governing res judicata, notice, and adequate representation.

———

Since the 1966 amendments, even the utility of class actions has been the subject of much debate. The following excerpt summarizes the extremes of the debate and attempts to characterize and explain the experience with class actions since 1966.

———

MILLER, *OF FRANKENSTEIN MONSTERS AND SHINING KNIGHTS: MYTH, REALITY, AND THE "CLASS ACTION PROBLEM,"* 92 Harv.L.Rev. 664, 665–66, 677–81 (1979):

* * * Opinions regarding the effect of the revision range over an amazing gamut. Class action adherents would have us believe it is a panacea for a myriad of social ills, which deters unlawful conduct and compensates those injured by it. Catch phrases such as "therapeutic" or "prophylactic" and "[taking] care of the smaller guy" are frequently trumpeted. Its opponents have rallied around characterizations of the procedure as a form of "legalized blackmail" or a "Frankenstein Monster." They also have charged widespread abuse of the rule by lawyers and litigants on both sides of the "v.," including unprofessional practices

relating to attorneys' fees, "sweetheart" settlement deals, dilatory motion practice, harassing discovery, and misrepresentations to judges. Finally, some have questioned the wisdom of imposing the burdens of class actions on an already overtaxed federal judiciary. They assert that many Rule 23 cases are unmanageable and inordinately protracted by opposing counsel, creating a certain millstone or dinosaur character that diverts federal judges from matters more worthy of their energies.

Yet despite the attention that has been riveted on Rule 23, we have precious little empiric evidence as to how it actually has been functioning, in terms of either its alleged benefits or supposed blasphemies. Even if the negative effects of class actions were assumed, they would have to be balanced against the societal benefits derived from deterring socially proscribed conduct and providing small claim rectification—considerations that thus far have escaped measurement and perhaps always will.

* * *

* * * [T]he past twelve years have been characterized by radical swings in the administration of the amended rule and judicial attitudes toward it. As a result, each class action decision must be considered in terms of when it was rendered and which court issued it. The movement of the decisions has resembled that of a pendulum, and although the arc on the swings has been diminishing, the practice continues to vary. The period since the revision can be divided into three time frames, each characterized by distinctive attitudes and practices. The divisions are used to provide a generalized description of the periods. Although they may appear arbitrary to some, I offer them only as a device for structuring my impressions gleaned from a perusal of the cases and thinking about our experience under the revision.

During the first period, dating from 1964, when many members of the bench and bar actually began to invoke the new text in anticipation of its promulgation, until approximately 1969, the legal community exhibited considerable euphoria over the rule's potential. Hopes were great that the class action would prove instrumental in dispensing justice to socially or economically disadvantaged groups as well as to small claimants generally. Statements that the rule "should be given a liberal rather than a restrictive interpretation," and that "if there is to be an error made, let it be in favor and not against the maintenance of the class action," were characteristic of this first period. The possibilities for class action litigation seemed limitless.

Unfortunately, during this period of great expectations many lawyers and judges appear not to have paid sufficient attention to the prerequisites for class action treatment prescribed by the rule. Cases often were certified as class actions on the basis of rather conclusory assertions of compliance with Rule 23(a) and (b). Settlements were sometimes approved without an in-depth analysis of the underlying merits of the claim, the economics of the litigation, or the feasibility of distributing the funds to class members. In addition, fee petitions were not scrutinized as carefully as experience now suggests they should have been. Enthusiasm for the class action fed upon itself, and the procedure fell victim to overuse by its champions and misuse by some who sought to exploit it for reasons external to the merits of the case. Mistakes, in most cases honest mistakes of faith, were made. By the end of this first phase, class action practice had been given a very black eye. Unfortunately, many members of the legal community formed negative impressions of the class action during this period that continue to influence them today despite radical changes in the conditions that gave rise to the procedure's unsavory reputation.

Quite naturally a reaction developed. Numerous voices were raised condemning excessive attorneys' fees and decrying the growing burdens of class action litigation. The spotlight was cast on certain cases involving questionable conduct or seemingly inexplicable fee awards, such as the settlement in the Playboy litigation, which reportedly gave club members chits for a small number of drinks and the lawyers a six-figure fee. And, not surprisingly, opposition to class action requests in specific cases stiffened. Defendants began treating the decision under Rule 23(c)(1) as if it were Armaggedon and mounted major challenges to class action certification, inevitably producing proliferated precertification discovery and motion practice devoted to the structure of the suit rather than to the substance of the claim.

Accordingly, from 1969 to approximately 1973 or perhaps 1974, antipathy to the class action became palpable. Federal courts were much readier to deny certification; attorneys' fee applications were eviscerated; interlocutory appeals were sought, and many were accepted, to review certification questions. The defense bar developed numerous litigation techniques to make the class action venture as unattractive as possible, including attacking class counsel's professional conduct. It was a very difficult time for the class action practitioner, and the viability of the device itself was in serious doubt. The picture was made all the bleaker by the Supreme Court's restrictive decisions in Snyder v. Harris,[a] Zahn v. International Paper Co.,[b] and Eisen v. Carlisle & Jacquelin.[c]

In my judgment, the pendulum has swung again, and we are now in a third phase, which began in 1973 or 1974 in some courts, more recently in others, and perhaps not at all in still others. We probably will remain in this phase for some time, quite possibly until the end of the generation-long period Professor Kaplan envisioned. It is a period characterized by increasing sophistication, restraint, and stabilization in class action practice. The current phase is marked by great concern within the profession about the excesses of the first two periods. The shock waves sent out by *Snyder, Zahn,* and *Eisen* have encouraged many plaintiffs' lawyers to be much more precise and careful. By defining their classes and describing

a. 394 U.S. 332, 89 S.Ct. 1053, 22 L.Ed.2d 319 (1969) (individual claims of class members cannot be aggregated to meet federal court jurisdictional-amount requirements). See pp. 697–98, infra.

b. 414 U.S. 291, 94 S.Ct. 505, 38 L.Ed.2d 511 (1973) (each claim in a federal class action must independently satisfy the juris-dictional-amount requirement). See pp. 697–99, infra.

c. 417 U.S. 156, 94 S.Ct. 2140, 40 L.Ed.2d 732 (1974) (named class members must bear the costs of individual notice to each class member in a Rule 23(b)(3) class action). See pp. 683–84, infra.

the scope of their claims realistically, they are acting more responsibly than before. The result is that classes have become more reasonable aggregations of litigants, thus reducing the manageability problems created by sheer class size. In addition, plaintiffs' lawyers are beginning to recognize that there may be good reasons, such as the danger of getting trapped in the morass of giving notice and securing judicial approval of any settlement required under Rule 23, to resist the almost reflexive impulse to seek class action treatment. For their part, judges are now sensitive to the desirability of requiring counsel to make full factual presentations on questions of certification, settlement, and fees. Finally, defendants are becoming somewhat less intransigent in their opposition to requests for class certification, at least in restraining their use of boilerplate arguments against it.

One key to this third phase is that district judges are now exploiting the arsenal of procedural powers set out in subdivisions (c) and (d) of the rule, which largely went unnoticed for a number of years following Rule 23's revision. More judges are aware that there are possibilities other than an across-the-board grant or denial of certification. Instead of wielding a meat axe, courts increasingly are operating with a scalpel. As a result, district judges frequently redefine classes to improve manageability; grant partial certification when appropriate to take advantage of the economics of group adjudication on at least some issues; bifurcate the adjudication of liability from the remedy phase in certain cases to improve efficiency; insist on a high level of legal skill to improve the quality of representation, which serves to reduce the risk of collateral attack; establish subclasses when antagonisms or conflicts exist within the group; and employ efficient management techniques during the precertification period to achieve an early determination of that issue. On a more general level, the growing judicial willingness to control the discovery process and prevent its overuse is being felt in the class-action context.

———

Eight years after he wrote his *Harvard Law Review* piece, Professor Miller served as the Reporter for a study of complex litigation for the American Law Institute. In it, he wrote:

> Class actions have proven to be the most effective legal technique for avoiding piecemeal litigation and preserving legal resources. Nevertheless, the class action suit continues to be eyed with suspicion by many courts. In complex cases, the goals of the class action device have been frustrated by strict adherence to the requirements of Rule 23. Often, complex multiparty, multiforum cases are denied class action treatment. Certification of large scale tort action classes is rare. Courts deny certification based on decisions that the commonality of interest requirement is not satisfied and based on fear that the size of the class would make the litigation unwieldy and inefficient.

> Generally, present treatment of class action suits begins with an initial skepticism towards the class. Cases that involve incidents of personal injury occurring in a series of related events that may be separated by time or geography are usually denied certification. In the

case of property damage, the class may receive certification but courts are wary that the litigation may degenerate into individual suits over specific pieces of property. Courts are split as to whether mass tort cases should be certified as 23(b)(1)(B) cases. Proponents argue that certification is more beneficial when total damages requested exceeds defendant's net worth. Detractors are concerned that such certification is merely a shortcut around notice and opt-out requirements. * * *

The usefulness of the class action device for future complex litigation raises two issues concerning the suitability of class actions to modern litigation needs. The first issue is whether the scope of the class action should be broadened to include more types of litigation. The second is whether courts should increase the frequency with which they certify mandatory classes. Presently, class actions are used relatively infrequently in many multiparty, multiforum litigation contexts. With some adjustments the class action device could be made a valuable litigation tool.

American Law Institute, *Preliminary Study of Complex Litigation*, Report, 61–70 (1987).

SECTION B. OPERATION OF THE CLASS–ACTION DEVICE

1. INTRODUCTION

Because the 1966 amendments to Rule 23 had a significant impact on state class-action procedures, Federal Rule 23 provides a paradigm that can be used to study the operation of class-action statutes generally. Although there are defendant class actions as well as plaintiff class actions, the plaintiff class action (which is far more common) will be the model used. Most of the observations made about the plaintiff class action are applicable to defendant class actions as well, however.

2. INITIATION OF CLASS ACTIONS

Although Rule 23 expressly gives courts power to issue certification orders sua sponte, they normally are issued in response to a motion made by the litigant who ultimately will be class representative. Frequently, that litigant's initial complaint contains both individual and class allegations, and the motion for certification is filed concurrently with the initial complaint; it is not uncommon, however, for a litigant to move for class certification substantially after the initial filing, following an amendment of the complaint to include class allegations.

The individual who wants to initiate a class action need not get the permission of potential class members before moving for certification, and the consent of class members generally is not a prerequisite for a court's certifying a suit as a class action. In fact, potential class members often oppose the class suit, either wishing to bring their own individual suits, or preferring not to have suit brought at all. In many jurisdictions (including the federal system), the members of the class are provided an opportunity to "opt out" of the class. In other jurisdictions (several state systems, for example), individuals are not considered members of the class until they have been notified of its existence and have chosen to "opt in" to the class.

In practice, attorneys often play a critical role in causing class suits to be brought. Sometimes, attorneys simply persuade individuals who have a legal problem that the best way to obtain a remedy is by filing a class-action suit embracing the claims of others who are similarly situated. Other times, attorneys actually solicit clients for class suits. For example, in what many think is a modern version of ambulance chasing, a lawyer, upon hearing of a disaster, may contact one of the victims and may offer to serve as counsel in a class action. The Supreme Court has held that this form of solicitation—for the lawyer's personal gain—is prohibited by legal ethical rules. See Ohralik v. Ohio State Bar Association, 436 U.S. 447, 98 S.Ct. 1912, 56 L.Ed.2d 444 (1978). But there are other examples in which the solicitation of clients for class suits is permissible. For instance, during the 1960's and 1970's NAACP lawyers went to the South to inform minorities of their legal rights and to offer themselves as counsel to those who decided to bring suit. The Supreme Court has held that offers of legal services in this context are a form of political expression, and that prohibitions against solicitation are invalid on First Amendment grounds. See In re Primus, 436 U.S. 412, 98 S.Ct. 1893, 56 L.Ed.2d 417 (1978).

3. CERTIFICATION

a. The Requirements for Certification

The district judge must make seven affirmative findings before a suit can be certified, and the plaintiff has the burden of establishing all seven prerequisites. Two of them are not expressed in Rule 23 and have been developed by the courts. Four more are enumerated in Rule 23(a). The seventh is that the district judge must find that the case falls within one of the three categories of class actions described in Rule 23(b).

The first requirement is that there be a class. This may sound self-evident, and in most instances the plaintiff will describe an ascertainable group that claims to be injured—for example, recipients of a particular welfare benefit or employees of a certain company. However, occasionally the plaintiff will offer a very vague description. A class described as "all poor people" is insufficient without providing some objective factors that determine who is poor for purposes of class membership. Conversely, the plaintiff's description of the class can err by being too specific. In TIJERINA v. HENRY, 48 F.R.D. 274 (D.N.M.1969), the class was characterized as all people with Spanish surnames having Spanish, Mexican, or Indian ancestry who spoke Spanish as a primary or secondary language. It would take enormous effort to ascertain who was in that class because the membership characteristics are so complex. The district court allowed the class description to be amended to include all people with Mexican or Spanish surnames. Although this created a much larger class, the result avoided the managerial and administrative difficulties of ascertaining who satisfied all three original conditions.

The second prerequisite is that the class representative must be a member of the class. This is essentially a standing requirement. Again, the requirement may sound self-evident, but there have been cases in which the named plaintiff turned out not to be a member of the class. For example, if a class action is brought on behalf of prisoners or inmates at a mental hospital, the representative must be a current prisoner or inmate. The fact that he is a former prisoner is irrelevant; he must be a present member of the class. See White v. Sullivan, 474 F.2d 16 (5th Cir. 1973).

The first of the four express prerequisites is Rule 23(a)(1), which requires that the class be so numerous that joinder of all members is "impracticable." In most instances this requirement is mechanical. If a class has more than forty members, "numerosity" usually is satisfied; if the class numbers less than twenty-five, "numerosity" usually is lacking. When the class is between twenty-five and forty members, variables such as the geographic dispersion of class members and the size of their individual claims become important. Joinder generally is impracticable if the claims are small, because people are not likely to become involved in litigation if only a small amount of money is at stake. On the other hand, joinder usually is feasible if each individual's stake is relatively large.

The second and third express prerequisites are embodied in Rule 23(a)(2) and Rule 23(a)(3). Neither has created many difficulties for the courts. Rule 23(a)(2), the "commonality" requirement, mandates that the action raise questions of law or fact common to the class. One significant common question is enough. Rule 23(a)(3), the "typicality" prerequisite, requires that the claims of the representative party be typical of those of the class. This provision does not seem to have any independent purpose since any objective it might serve already will be achieved by the commonality requirement and the "adequacy" requirement of Rule 23(a)(4), discussed below. Few courts focus on typicality, and it tends to be discussed in almost conclusory terms.

The final express prerequisite, Rule 23(a)(4), is that the court find that the representative party will fairly and adequately protect the interests of the class. This is probably the single most important requirement, and the one most heavily litigated. It derives its importance from two factors. First, on a philosophical level, Rule 23(a)(4) embodies the due process concerns that animated the Supreme Court's decision in Hansberry v. Lee, p. 677, infra. The class action seeks to bind parties who have not *literally* had their "day in court." However, as members of a defined group with similar claims and proper representation, they have had a *figurative* day in court. It is Rule 23(a)(4) that ensures the quality of that representation. Second, on a pragmatic level, a defect in the adequacy of representation in an action might leave the judgment vulnerable to collateral attack. See Gonzales v. Cassidy, p. 681, infra. It would be an extremely wasteful expenditure of time and effort to go through the certification process, complete extensive discovery, negotiate and approve a settlement or actually adjudicate the merits of the case, and draft and enter a judgment, only to have everything unravelled years later by someone who does not want to be bound by the result and claims that the adequacy requirement was not met.

What constitutes adequacy of representation? It has three elements. First, the representative parties themselves must be adequate. The court should ascertain whether the named plaintiffs have a substantial stake in the litigation, or if there is any reason to believe that they are motivated by factors unrelated to the case itself, such as greed, vindictiveness, or pursuit of a competitive advantage. The court also should examine the relationship between the representative party and the lawyer. The two should be different people and have no strong family or financial relationship that would undermine the party's independent judgment about matters relating to the conduct of the action.

Second, the court should inquire into the adequacy of the class' lawyer. As with the party, much of the inquiry will focus on the lawyer's bona fides, but technical competence also is important. All of the lawyer's resources must be evaluated—professional experience, motivation, support personnel, and other professional commitments. Class actions usually are highly complex, protracted, and technical lawsuits, and the district judge must satisfy himself that the lawyer will be able to meet the challenges they pose.

Third, the court has an affirmative responsibility to examine the class itself, to see if it is beset by any internal antagonism. A conflict within the class that goes to the matter in litigation will defeat the party's claim of representative status. The seminal Supreme Court decision in HANSBERRY v. LEE, 311 U.S. 32, 61 S.Ct. 115, 85 L.Ed. 22 (1940), p. 677, infra, illustrates this situation. In that case the plaintiff sought to enforce a racially restrictive covenant on behalf of a class of landowners, some of whom were not in favor of enforcing it. To alleviate the problem of internal antagonism, the court must divide the class into sub-classes, often aligning a sub-class with the defendant, or separating those issues that merit class-action treatment from those that do not.

After the district judge has determined that the suit satisfies the six prerequisites already discussed, she must decide that it falls within one of the three categories of class actions enumerated in Rule 23(b). The first category, Rule 23(b)(1), which might be referred to as the "prejudice" class action, contains two clauses. Both ask whether individual actions might cause prejudice that can be avoided by using the class-action device. Subdivision (A) looks for prejudice to the non-class party; subdivision (B) inquires into prejudice to members of the class.

Subdivision (A) deals with the risk that individual actions would create "incompatible standards of conduct" for the party opposing the class. It is important to note that the rule does *not* refer to the situation in which the defendant in a series of actions would have to pay damages to some claimants but not to others. Rather, the rule applies when different results in individual actions would place the non-class party in a position of total uncertainty, not knowing how to treat the class as a whole. For example, consider a voting rights dispute involving a question of eligibility for registration. If applicants sue individually, some may win and others may lose. The election board then would be in the position of not knowing whether to register all the individuals similarly situated who have not brought suit. If a class action is brought, the judgment will bind all of the class members, and the board can take appropriate action.

Subdivision (B) requires that individual actions "substantially impair or impede" the ability of class members to protect their interests. The classic example is a case in which there are multiple claimants to a limited fund, such as the proceeds of an insurance policy. If litigants are allowed to proceed individually, there is a risk that those who sue first will deplete the fund and leave nothing for the latecomers; thus, the latter group would "as a practical matter" be prejudiced by individual actions.

The second class-action category includes suits for injunctive or declaratory relief under Rule 23(b)(2). More cases have been brought under this provision than under either of the two other. Its primary application is to injunction suits such as employment discrimination, consumer, or environmental cases. Note that for an action to fall within Rule 23(b)(2), the defendant's conduct need only be "generally applicable" to the class; there is no requirement that the conduct be damaging or offensive to every class member. Thus, a suit to enjoin the enforcement of a school dress code can be instituted under Rule 23(b)(2) even though a majority of the students are not offended by the code and are willing to comply with it, since the defendant school, by trying to enforce the code, acts in a manner generally applicable to the entire student body.

Finally, Rule 23(b)(3) describes the "damage" class action, so called because the only tie among the members of the class is that they claim to have been injured in the same way by the defendant. Two special prerequisites govern the application of this provision. First, questions of law or fact common to the class members must "predominate" over any questions affecting only individual class members. Second, the court must find that a "class action is superior to other available methods for the fair and efficient adjudication of the controversy." These special requirements are designed to ensure that the efficiency and economy objectives of Rule 23(b)(3) are met.

Although it is easy to state the Rule 23(b)(3) tests, the district courts have not applied them with any degree of uniformity. Questions of predominance and superiority have become highly individualistic and fact dependent, and since the ruling on the certification question is interlocutory, and not subject to immediate appellate review, we have limited guidelines from the Courts of Appeals. Nevertheless, a reading of Rule 23(b)(3) cases does suggest several recurring problems associated with its application.

The first problem is the meaning of "predominance." It is unclear whether the district judge is to count the issues and see whether a majority are common, or to evaluate the issues and see if the most important are common. Furthermore, in some cases common and individual issues seem to be in equilibrium no matter which method of determining predominance is followed. The key to resolving this difficulty lies in ascertaining whether the efficiency and economy of common adjudication outweigh the interest each class member may have in individual adjudication. For example, if the case involves a discriminatory practice in hiring or promotion, there probably is predominance. On the other hand, in a case brought by a group of securities investors who are claiming that a broker has unnecessarily multiplied transactions in their accounts, there probably is no predominance because what constitutes this so-called "churning" of one investor's account may not for another. This is particularly true since people have different investment objectives.

The "superiority" prerequisite obliges the court to compare other adjudicative possibilities. The most obvious include leaving the disputants to individual actions, administrative proceedings, or an agreement to be bound by the result in a single "test" case.

Rule 23(b)(3) outlines four factors that the court should consider in deciding the superiority and predominance questions. The fourth, difficulties likely to be encountered in the management of a class action, generally is viewed as the key to the two requirements. Matters such as the size or contentiousness of the class, the number of class members who seek to intervene and participate in the action, or the onerousness of the Rule 23(c)(2) notice requirement are to be considered when deciding if the class action is manageable. See Eisen v. Carlisle & Jacquelin, p. 683, infra.

b. The Certification Decision

A judge can draw upon several sources in evaluating whether a proposed class meets the requirements for certification. There is the paper record—the complaint, the briefs supporting and opposing class certification, and any other affidavits or papers submitted to the court. In addition, there may be a hearing on the certification motion. If a court chooses to hold a hearing, it must be careful to limit its inquiry to the appropriateness of class certification; the Supreme Court has ruled that courts may not make a preliminary inquiry into the merits of the underlying substantive claim in considering whether to certify a class action. See Eisen v. Carlisle & Jacquelin, p. 683, infra. And, finally, there may be discovery to ascertain information about the nature of the class.

Ultimately, a court may certify the class as proposed; may deny the certification motion; or may certify a modified class. It is the last option that is most interesting. Rule 23(c) gives judges the power to amend certification decisions at any time before a decision on the merits. Some judges, when granting certification, highlight the tentative character of their decisions by certifying classes conditionally.

In issuing a certification order, the judge defines the terms on which the class-action suit will proceed. First, the order approves a particular description of the class—that is, it defines who is included in it. For example, the court might certify a class consisting of all female employees of the Widget Company from 1986 to the present. The court has broad power to divide a proposed class into smaller constituent subclasses, each with its own named representatives. Thus, for example, it could choose to certify several classes, each consisting of female employees of the Widget Company working at separate plants.

Second, the certification order defines the substantive issues the suit will consider. For instance, a class suit might entertain a broad range of issues (such as allegations of company-wide gender discrimination in hiring, promotion, and pay, as well as allegations of sexual harassment by foremen in all of the company's factories), or it might take a more narrow approach (limiting the class issues to allegations of gender discrimination in a single plant's promotion decisions). A judge even may decide to certify a "partial class action"—that is, considering on a class basis only a limited number of factual issues relevant to a larger cause of action. For example, in a products liability suit, a judge could create a "partial class action" by certifying only the issue of whether a pharmaceutical manufacturer knew of a drug's potentially lethal side effects before introducing it on the market. In such a case, individual suits, litigated simultaneously or subsequently, would be pursued on the other issues.

Third, and finally, the certification order appoints a class representative. In plaintiff class actions, the parties seeking certification normally will nominate themselves as class representatives. In defendant class actions the plaintiff, who would be the party most likely to seek class treatment, nominates particular members of the defendant class to serve in the representative capacity. It is important to note, however, that the parties' nominations are not dispositive. Judges have discretion in appointing class representatives, and are free to accept, reject, or modify the parties' suggestions. Judges even may choose to supplement the parties' nominations by appointing as class representatives individuals who are not before the court.

c. The Importance of Certification

Certification is perhaps the most critical stage in the life of a class action. The papers, hearings, and discovery inevitably presented force the court to analyze the nature of the parties and the issues involved in the case.

The certification process is even more critical from the parties' point of view. Most importantly, the certification decision dictates the relative leverage that the parties can bring to settlement negotiations. The value of settlement leverage cannot be underestimated, because most class suits are settled before trial. Moreover, for the party opposing the class, a certification order means more than a loss of leverage; the threat that a class may be certified may be a danger in itself, because the certification of a class may create unfavorable publicity.

The tactical importance of the certification stage is increased because certification orders generally are not appealable. In the federal system, appeals typically are available only from a final judgment. See 28 U.S.C. § 1291. At first, some federal Courts of Appeals had held that some orders denying class certification were appealable under 28 U.S.C. § 1291 on the theory that they, in effect, were final decisions. These courts felt that, especially when the individual class members' claims were small, the denial of certification signaled the "death knell" of the litigation. In COOPERS & LYBRAND v. LIVESAY, 437 U.S. 463, 98 S.Ct. 2454, 57 L.Ed.2d 351 (1978), the Supreme Court rejected the death knell doctrine. In so doing, the Court noted that the order granting or denying class status to a group is subject to redetermination. The decision is not a final order and it does not affect the merits. The holding in *Coopers & Lybrand* did not make it impossible to obtain review of a certification order, however, because the Court noted that in some situations it might be possible to obtain review of a denial of certification under the provisions of 28 U.S.C. § 1292(b), which permits appeals from orders involving a "controlling question of law as to which there is a substantial ground for difference of opinion and [when] an immediate appeal from the order may materially advance the ultimate termination of the litigation."

For a discussion of individual, class, and systemic concerns that factor into the certification decision, especially in mass accident cases, see Note, *Class Certification in Mass Accident Cases Under Rule 23(b)(1)*, 96 Harv.L. Rev. 1143 (1983); see also *The Supreme Court, 1977 Term*, 92 Harv.L.Rev. 5, 234 (1978).

4. NOTICE

The question of notice to absent class members has tremendous theoretical and practical importance to class actions, and will be considered many times during this chapter. At this point we discuss only the mechanical aspects of the notice question: who prepares it, what information must be included in the notice, who should receive notice, and who should bear its cost.

a. *Preparation*

Ambiguity in the language of Rule 23 makes it unclear whether the court or the parties should prepare the notice forms. Charging the class representatives with this responsibility introduces the possibility that the notice will be used for improper purposes, such as solicitation for a litigation fund. Yet, because drafting and production can be time-consuming, most courts direct the class representative to draft the notice and permit the opposing party to make objections. This limits the court's role to mediating disputes between the parties and insuring that notice is provided.

b. *Content of Notice and Who Should Receive Notice*

Rule 23's notice requirement depends on the category of class action involved. There are relatively specific notice requirements for Rule 23(b) (3) class actions. In Rule 23(b)(1) and Rule 23(b)(2) class actions, however, courts have tremendous discretion in ordering notice.

Rule 23(c) dictates who should receive notice in a Rule 23(b)(3) class action. The language of the Rule itself is somewhat unclear as to whether individual notice to each class member is always required. However, the

Supreme Court has held that Rule 23(c) does require such notice in every Rule 23(b)(3) class action.

Rule 23(c) unambiguously lists the required content of notice for a Rule 23(b)(3) class action. In addition, the notice usually provides the class members with a description of the class claim, as well as any counterclaims that may have been filed against the class. Many courts require the notice to include a disclaimer stating that the notice of the pending action does not indicate that the court believes the class will prevail on the merits.

Rule 23(c) applies only to suits brought under Rule 23(b)(3); the court's power to shape the form of the notice in Rule 23(b)(1) and (b)(2) suits derives from Rule 23(d)—and that Rule contains no specific directives regarding notice. Thus, in many Rule 23(b)(1) and (b)(2) suits, judges decide that no notice is necessary. In other situations, judges may conclude that only general notice is needed, such as notice by publication.

c. Costs

The Supreme Court has held that the costs of providing notice must be borne by the party seeking class treatment. If the class suit is successful, the costs of sending notice may be subtracted from the class recovery, thus making each class member share the costs on a pro-rata basis.

The costs of producing a mailing list often constitute a large part of the overall expense of providing notice. In some class actions the defendant's records will be the best, if not the only, source of information from which a list can be constructed. In the past, some litigants sought to use the discovery process to obtain a plaintiff-class mailing list. This shifted to the defendant a major portion of the expenses of providing notice, because in federal discovery practice the party producing discovery requests must bear the costs of production. The Supreme Court disapproved this practice in OPPENHEIMER FUND, INC. v. SANDERS, 437 U.S. 340, 98 S.Ct. 2380, 57 L.Ed.2d 253 (1978), in which it emphasized that the costs of class notice must be borne by the class representative. *Oppenheimer* did not prohibit the representative from requesting the business records of the defendant that might aid in preparing the class mailing list; it merely required that the class representative bear the cost of producing such lists.

5. ORDERS REGULATING THE CONDUCT OF PRETRIAL AND TRIAL PROCEEDINGS

In addition to certification and notice orders, various other orders are possible under Rule 23(d). For example, the court may create a timetable for discovery and for the presentation of issues at trial; set time limits on oral presentations made by counsel; establish a committee of counsel (consisting of the attorneys representing various members of the class) to make decisions about the prosecution of the class' case; and, regulate the substantive aspects of discovery (for example, by determining the parties from whom discovery may be sought and the items which may be requested). Frequently, courts will issue these management orders after they have held a pretrial conference.

It is unclear whether nominal parties, those who are part of the class but who do not participate in the management of the suit, can be subject to a discovery order. Complying with a discovery request can be onerous, and failure to respond can result in severe sanctions. For this reason, typically only named parties are required to submit to a discovery request. However, courts have permitted discovery from unnamed parties in class-action suits. Compare Brennan v. Midwestern Union Life Ins. Co., 450 F.2d 999 (7th Cir.1971), certiorari denied 405 U.S. 921, 92 S.Ct. 957, 30 L.Ed.2d 792 (1972) (nominal parties must comply with a discovery order), and Dellums v. Powell, 566 F.2d 167 (D.C.Cir.1977) (same), with Wainwright v. Kraftco Corp., 54 F.R.D. 532 (N.D.Ga.1972) (nominal parties need not comply with discovery order).

It also is unclear how counterclaims against absent class members should be handled, or if they should be handled at all. The majority of federal district courts simply have assumed that such counterclaims are acceptable. Those courts which have considered the question in depth are split on the issue. In rejecting the counterclaim, one court asserted the absent class member's right "passively to await the outcome of the principal suit." See Donson Stores, Inc. v. American Bakeries Co., 58 F.R.D. 485 (S.D.N.Y.1973). Others have refused to entertain such counterclaims on the ground that it would encourage members to opt out of the suit. On the other hand, some courts have found persuasive the argument that since the absent members will reap the benefits of the judgment if favorable, they should be subject to its adverse effects. See National Super Spuds, Inc. v. New York Mercantile Exchange, 75 F.R.D. 40 (S.D.N.Y.1977); Wolfson v. Artisans Savings Bank, 83 F.R.D. 552 (D.Del.1979).

6. PROVING CLASS CLAIMS AND ADMINISTERING CLASS RELIEF

The fundamental characteristic of the class-action device is that the class representative serves as a proxy for the absent class members, thus making it possible to adjudicate the claims of the entire class by evaluating the claims of the class representative. A proxy is appropriate because the class-certification decision ensures congruity between the injuries and the interests of the class representative and those of the absent class members. Whether the class representative can serve as a complete proxy for the absent class members, however, depends on the nature of the underlying cause of action. In many situations, it may be necessary to supplement treatment of the class representative's claims with proceedings designed to evaluate some aspect of each class member's individual claims.

The necessity of supplementary proceedings to "individualize" aspects of a class suit may vary with the relief sought. Class suits for injunctive relief closely resemble individual suits for injunctive relief. The problems involved in proving the defendant's liability, of determining the proper relief, and of administering relief are all quite formidable, but are not materially increased by class treatment. In suits for monetary relief, however, courts entertaining class actions inevitably face problems not present in traditional litigation. In these class suits, the court must complete three analytically separate tasks: it must determine if the defendant is liable; it must calculate the amount of damages to the plaintiff class; and, it must distribute the proper share of the award to individual class members. Often, one or more of these tasks demands fragmentation or "individualization" of the class.

Courts have approached the task of individualization in different ways. One approach is to use a single trial to determine both the defendant's liability (if any) and the amount of damages. These determinations are based on the representative's individual claims, which in some cases are supplemented by statistics and expert testimony. When liability and the amount of damages are set, the court determines how to distribute the class award among individual class members.

A second approach used by courts to individualize class suits is the bifurcated trial. The first trial considers only the issue of liability, using the same evidence techniques as would be used in an ordinary proceeding. The second trial, which occurs only if the defendant is found liable, addresses the amount of damages. This second proceeding may be a highly individualized one (involving, for example, mini-trials on individual damages claims, or administrative proceedings on individual claims), or it may be a general proceeding designed to calculate the damages to the class as a whole.

In cases in which the costs of identifying and distributing the award exceed the award due each class member, or when the amount of money that can be economically distributed to class members does not exhaust the amount of the defendant's liability as determined at trial, courts sometimes utilize a third approach—the "fluid class recovery." In such cases, the class' award is used to provide a general benefit to class members rather than to compensate them individually. In an antitrust suit, for example, when it often is impossible to identify precisely all of the victims of the violation, courts sometimes will order the defendant company to lower its prices for a specified amount of time.

An award of damages in a class action suit does not end the matter because the court must set a method of distribution. Some class members may not be aware of the suit. Others may not know of its outcome. For whatever reason, these class members may fail to claim damages. The fluid class recovery is often employed in these cases to insure that the damage award is spread evenly and benefits all the members of the class.

7. SETTLEMENT

Rule 23(e) provides that a class action cannot be dismissed or compromised without court approval and that notice of any proposed dismissal or compromise must be given to all class members. In this regard the Rule is virtually unique in American law, as it is inconsistent with the general principle that litigants are free to settle or terminate a lawsuit as they see fit. Underlying Rule 23(e) is the same philosophy discussed in connection with adequacy of representation. See pp. 664–65, supra. First, due process demands that the absent class members be protected from an unfair settlement made because the representative parties have lost their enthusiasm for the litigation. In addition, the efficiency and economy objectives of Rule 23 would be subverted if the judgment produced by the settlement proves to be vulnerable to collateral attack, a situation that might arise if the settlement does not take proper account of the rights of the absent class members.

In evaluating a settlement proposal a court must consider whether it is fair, reasonable, and in the best interests of the individuals to be affected by it. Those proposing settlement have the burden of showing that this standard has been met. Whether the class as a whole favors the proposed settlement is an extremely important factor for courts to weigh in deciding whether to approve the settlement. The will of any particular class member, however, is not dispositive. Settlements can be approved over the objections of the class representatives, as well as over the objections of absent class members who received and responded to the notice of settlement. Of course, these objecting class members are free to appeal the court's decision approving the settlement when a judgment is entered.

Several problems involving class-action settlements have surfaced. First, it is unclear when the requirements of Rule 23(c) become applicable. Are court approval and notice of the proposed settlement necessary if the representatives reach a settlement before the suit is certified as a proper class action? There is considerable disagreement over this question.

One school of thought argues that a settlement never should be allowed prior to certification because the district judge does not have sufficient information to discharge his responsibilities under Rule 23(c). Without completing the seven-part certification process, he does not know whether the representation is adequate, whether there are conflicts within the class, or whether the economics of the case dictate the proposed settlement. On the other hand, by going through the certification process, the district judge will be educated and in a better position to assess the bona fides of any settlement that subsequently is proposed.

The other school of thought is that the judicial system should encourage settlement whenever it is possible to do so. Since the certification question is an extremely difficult one and often takes years to resolve, the litigants should not be inhibited from settling by artificially declaring that the certification process must be completed first. Furthermore, a court may order a hearing on the proposed settlement, at which it can satisfy itself that there has been no abuse of the settlement procedure and that the agreement would not prejudice putative class members. This school of thought emphasizes the need to give trial judges discretion, and argues that it is pointless to require a class-certification determination if that process' essential function can be served by less burdensome proceedings.

8. ROLE OF ATTORNEYS

Two features of the traditional conception of the attorney-client relation are that (1) the attorney gives advice to the client and the client makes final decisions about litigation strategy, and (2) the attorney acts with virtually unmitigated loyalty to the client's best interest. Class-action litigation strains both of these notions. Class-action attorneys exercise significant control over decisions made on behalf of the class, because class representatives generally provide less supervision and guidance than do other types of clients. And, it is difficult to define "loyalty to the client" when it is not clear who the "client" is. Should the attorney give complete loyalty to the interests and wishes of the class representative? To those of each member of the class? To the attorney's conception of the best interests of the class as a whole? These questions are difficult ones, and current ethical rules offer attorneys little help in resolving them. Moreover, the class-action device challenges the traditional notions of the lawyer's role because, frequently, class suits involve a large number of independent lawyers (or legal teams) representing interests that sometimes are in tension. The role of the individual lawyer in this context is not easy to define.

Some courts use their authority under Rule 23(d) to issue orders designed to foster orderly interaction among class attorneys and between the class attorneys and the court. For instance, a court may order the counsel representing the various class members to elect a committee, empowered to make decisions on behalf of the class. Such committees usually are governed by majority rule, though the court may provide that dissenting class attorneys can bring significant and material grievances to the attention of the court. Courts creating committees of this type frequently select two attorneys to play a special role in facilitating its operation. One attorney serves the role of "lead counsel," with responsibility for chairing meetings, drafting papers, and making arguments in court. Another serves as "liaison counsel," with responsibility for coordinating the flow of paper among the class attorneys and between the committee of counsel and the members of the class.

9. ATTORNEYS' FEES

Although there is no reference in Rule 23 to the power of the court to award attorneys' fees, the attorney for the successful representative parties typically will be awarded a fee. The rationale for this practice is that since his work on behalf of the representatives has conferred a benefit on all the class members, fairness demands that counsel be compensated out of the fund awarded them. In many contexts the fee is awarded pursuant to a specific statutory provision designed to provide an incentive for "private attorneys general." In other contexts, courts award attorneys' fees out of the common fund created by the recovery from the defendant. The Supreme Court has rejected the argument that fee awards are prohibited by the traditional American rule that the losing party shall not be forced to bear the winning parties' legal expenses.

Boeing Co. v. Van Gemert, 444 U.S. 472, 100 S.Ct. 745, 62 L.Ed.2d 676 (1980).

Traditionally, the factor most relied upon in setting the amount of the attorneys' fees was the amount of benefit that the lawsuit produced. Because this guideline was easily abused, however, most courts now use a more complicated method for calculating fee awards. Under a formula now accepted in many circuits, petitioning attorneys must present the district judge with detailed time records of the hours expended by each lawyer on the case. The records must be broken down to give some indication of the nature of the work that was done (pleading, research, discovery, negotiation, or trial) and the status of each lawyer who worked on the case (senior or junior partner, or senior or junior associate). The time records enable the district judge to make a detailed appraisal of precisely what kind of work each attorney did and how long it took to do it. This has several consequences. It virtually eliminates any possibility of misrepresentation concerning the amount of time counsel spent on any facet of the case; it provides the court with an indication of the character and quality of plaintiffs' lawyers; and it offers a benchmark for deciding how efficiently the work was performed.

Once the time records are presented to the judge, a "normal billing rate" is then attributed to each of the lawyers for each of the tasks done. This means differentiating in terms of hourly rates among different lawyers and different tasks requiring various levels of legal skill. With both time and rate figures before the court, the judge then engages in what has been called a "lodestar" computation—multiplying every lawyer's time by the rate for each of the functions performed. This produces the basic working figure for fixing the final fee.

This "lodestar" can then be modified on two grounds by the district judge. The first permits the amount of the fee to be enlarged or reduced in light of the "contingency" factor. Simply put, how risky was the case? In contexts such as antitrust or securities regulation, was there a prior government prosecution or something else that facilitated plaintiff's class action? Did the plaintiff have to break new substantive or procedural ground to maintain the action? Basically, the contingency factor gives the district judge discretion to adjust the fee to compensate lawyers who pursue cases that redress improper conduct or perform some social benefit on a contingent fee basis with no assurance they would be compensated. However, in Pennsylvania v. Delaware Valley Citizens' Council, 483 U.S. 711, 107 S.Ct. 3078, 97 L.Ed.2d 585 (1987), the Court curtailed federal judges' ability to award risk multipliers. The Court stated that risk enhancement is to be discouraged because it is difficult to administer and the reasonable hourly rate should be adequate to compensate the attorney. Only when there is a real risk of not prevailing in the case may a court increase the award, and then only by one-third of the lodestar amount.

The second factor is the "quality" of the lawyers' performance. It focuses on the manner in which each lawyer actually functioned in the particular case. Was she helpful in moving the litigation toward resolution? Was she prepared? Did she do a good job for the client? Did she work efficiently? Again, this factor gives the district judge great discretion in fixing the final fee.

The time-rate computation gives the impression of mathematical precision, but there are several inherent ambiguities making it neither a stable measure nor an easily applied one. First, courts disagree regarding which hours may be included in the fee computation. Can time expended in preparing the fee application itself be included? Compare City of Detroit v. Grinnell Corp., 560 F.2d 1093 (2d Cir.1977), with Miller v. Mackey Int'l, Inc., 70 F.R.D. 533 (S.D.Fla.1976). Second, the notion that there are fixed hourly rates that can be attributed to all lawyers in all situations and used as objective markers of their worth is illusory. For lawyers who ordinarily operate on a contingent fee basis, "normal billing rate" has no meaning. Even in corporate practice the rates generally are not fixed, but depend upon a wide range of variables and geographic locations. And when the lawyers in a large, multiparty case come from many different parts of the country, what normal billing rate should be used? And, third, the lodestar approach does not encourage attorneys to manage their time well and to avoid duplicative work.

Courts have developed the practice of appointing lead counsel or management committees in order to encourage efficiency. This "solution" has problems of its own, as is illustrated by In re Fine Paper Antitrust Litigation, 98 F.R.D. 48 (E.D.Pa.1983), affirmed in part, reversed in part 751 F.2d 562 (3d Cir.1984). Forty-one law firms submitted fee petitions totalling $21 million, forty percent of the total recovery.

> In discussing why the attorneys' fees applications were so excessive, Judge McGylnn [sic] describes how the lawyers had established an organizational structure of committees and subcommittees to handle each task in the case, and how that very structure caused mismanagement. "It was inevitable that this type of structure would generate wasted hours on useless tasks, propagate duplication and mask outright padding." One of the worst examples was a charge of approximately fifteen hundred hours by nine law firms for preparing and taking the deposition of one third-party witness.

Kane, *Of Carrots and Sticks: Evaluating the Role of the Class Action Lawyer,* 66 Tex.L.Rev. 385, 390 (1987). Professor Kane goes on to describe possible prescriptions:

> Cases like *Fine Paper* finally provoked the judiciary to force lawyers to become more efficient. The 1983 amendments to the Federal Rules provide judicial authority and guidance for pretrial management on an expansive scale. By exercising tight control early in the litigation, courts may be able to compel class action lawyers to stay abreast of these cases, keep fees down, and most importantly, to keep the cases moving along.
> * * *
> * * * To force litigating attorneys to learn the lessons of ill-managed litigation, courts are encouraging more economical management through their control of attorney fee awards. Courts now often carefully

assess attorney fee petitions and disallow fees for work that is duplicative or unproductive.

Id. at 390–92.

The Supreme Court has grappled with other questions that affect the availability of attorneys' fees in class-action suits. The first question involved the availability of statutory attorneys' fees. To encourage suits to redress civil rights deprivations, Congress passed the Civil Rights Attorney's Fees Awards Act, 42 U.S.C. § 1988, which makes it easier for victims to find attorneys by authorizing fee-shifting. In MAREK v. CHESNY, 473 U.S. 1, 105 S.Ct. 3012, 87 L.Ed.2d 1 (1985), the Court held it proper to deny recovery of costs, including attorneys' fees, when plaintiffs rejected a settlement offer higher than that ultimately obtained at trial. The Court reasoned that its holding would encourage plaintiffs to accept reasonable settlement offers, sparing themselves and the system the burden of time-consuming litigation. In so doing, however, the Court made it more risky for plaintiffs to press claims once any reasonable settlement offer had been made.

In 1986, the Court returned to Section 1988, this time to address the propriety of simultaneous negotiations for the class recovery and attorneys' fees. In EVANS v. JEFF D., 475 U.S. 717, 106 S.Ct. 1531, 89 L.Ed.2d 747 (1986), the Court permitted an attorney to waive his Section 1988 fee in order to obtain a favorable recovery for the class. The dissent argued that permitting linkage between recoveries and attorneys' fees in settlement negotiations would shrink the pool of attorneys willing to try civil rights cases.

SECTION C. DUE PROCESS CONSIDERATIONS

HANSBERRY v. LEE

Supreme Court of the United States, 1940.
311 U.S. 32, 61 S.Ct. 115, 85 L.Ed. 22.

[This suit was brought in an Illinois state court on behalf of a class of landowners to enforce a racially restrictive covenant involving land in the City of Chicago. The covenant provided that it was not effective unless signed by the "owners of 95 per centum of the frontage." Plaintiff alleged that Hansberry, a black, had purchased some of the restricted land from an owner who had signed the agreement and that suit was being brought to enjoin the sale as a breach of the covenant. He further alleged that the binding effect of the covenant had been established in an earlier Illinois state court action holding that 95 percent of all the landowners involved had signed the agreement. In response, defendants pleaded that they were not bound by the res judicata effect of the earlier judgment as they had not been parties to that suit and were not successors in interest or in privity with any of the parties to that action. Thus they argued it would be a denial of due process to hold them to the first decree.

The Illinois Circuit Court held that the issue whether the covenant was valid was res judicata, even though it found that only about 54 percent of the owners actually had signed the agreement and that the previous judgment rested on a "false and fraudulent" stipulation of the parties. The Supreme Court of Illinois affirmed. It found that although the stipulation was untrue it was not fraudulent or collusive. The Illinois court then went on to conclude that the first action had been a "class" or "representative" suit, that as such it was binding on all the class members unless reversed or set aside on direct proceedings, and that Hansberry and the persons who had sold the land to him were members of the class represented in the first action and consequently were bound by the decree in that suit.]

Certiorari to the Supreme Court of the State of Illinois.

MR. JUSTICE STONE delivered the opinion of the Court.

* * *

* * * [W]hen the judgment of a state court, ascribing to the judgment of another court the binding force and effect of *res judicata*, is challenged for want of due process it becomes the duty of this Court to examine the course of procedure in both litigations to ascertain whether the litigant whose rights have thus been adjudicated has been afforded such notice and opportunity to be heard as are requisite to the due process which the Constitution prescribes. * * *

It is a principle of general application in Anglo-American jurisprudence that one is not bound by a judgment *in personam* in a litigation in which he is not designated as a party or to which he has not been made a party by service of process. Pennoyer v. Neff * * * [p. 66, supra]. A judgment rendered in such circumstances is not entitled to the full faith and credit which the Constitution and statute of the United States * * * prescribe * * * and judicial action enforcing it against the person or property of the absent party is not that due process which the Fifth and Fourteenth Amendments requires. * * *

To these general rules there is a recognized exception that, to an extent not precisely defined by judicial opinion, the judgment in a "class" or "representative" suit, to which some members of the class are parties, may bind members of the class or those represented who were not made parties to it. * * *

The class suit was an invention of equity to enable it to proceed to a decree in suits where the number of those interested in the subject of the litigation is so great that their joinder as parties in conformity to the usual rules of procedure is impracticable. Courts are not infrequently called upon to proceed with causes in which the number of those interested in the litigation is so great as to make difficult or impossible the joinder of all because some are not within the jurisdiction or because their whereabouts is unknown or where if all were made parties to the suit its continued abatement by the death of some would prevent or unduly delay a decree. In such cases where the interests of those not joined are of the same class as the interests of those who are, and where it is considered that the latter fairly represent the former in the prosecution of the litigation of the issues in which all have a common interest, the court will proceed to a decree. * * *

It is evident that the considerations which may induce a court thus to proceed, despite a technical defect of parties, may differ from those which must be taken into account in determining whether the absent parties are bound by the decree or, if it is adjudged that they are, in ascertaining whether such an adjudication satisfies the requirements of due process and of full faith and credit. Nevertheless there is scope within the framework of the Constitution for holding in appropriate cases that a judgment rendered in a class suit is *res judicata* as to members of the class who are not formal parties to the suit. * * * With a proper regard for divergent local institutions and interests * * *, this Court is justified in saying that there has been a failure of due process only in those cases where it cannot be said that the procedure adopted, fairly insures the protection of the interests of absent parties who are to be bound by it.
* * *

It is familiar doctrine of the federal courts that members of a class not present as parties to the litigation may be bound by the judgment where they are in fact adequately represented by parties who are present, or where they actually participate in the conduct of the litigation in which members of the class are present as parties * * * or where the interest of the members of the class, some of whom are present as parties, is joint, or where for any other reason the relationship between the parties present and those who are absent is such as legally to entitle the former to stand in judgment for the latter. * * *

In all such cases, * * * we may assume for present purposes that such procedure affords a protection to the parties who are represented though absent, which would satisfy the requirements of due process and full faith and credit. * * * Nor do we find it necessary for the decision of this case to say that, when the only circumstance defining the class is that the determination of the rights of its members turns upon a single issue of fact or law, a state could not constitutionally adopt a procedure whereby some of the members of the class could stand in judgment for all, provided that the procedure were so devised and applied as to insure that those present are of the same class as those absent and that the litigation is so conducted as to insure the full and fair consideration of the common issue. * * * We decide only that the procedure and the course of litigation sustained here by the plea of res judicata do not satisfy these requirements.

The restrictive agreement did not purport to create a joint obligation or liability. If valid and effective its promises were the several obligations of the signers and those claiming under them. The promises ran several-ly to every other signer. It is plain that in such circumstances all those alleged to be bound by the agreement would not constitute a single class in any litigation brought to enforce it. Those who sought to secure its benefits by enforcing it could not be said to be in the same class with or represent those whose interest was in resisting performance, for the agreement by its terms imposes obligations and confers rights on the owner of each plot of land who signs it. If those who thus seek to secure the benefits of the agreement were rightly regarded by the state Supreme

Court as constituting a class, it is evident that those signers or their successors who are interested in challenging the validity of the agreement and resisting its performance are not of the same class in the sense that their interests are identical so that any group who had elected to enforce rights conferred by the agreement could be said to be acting in the interest of any others who were free to deny its obligation.

Because of the dual and potentially conflicting interests of those who are putative parties to the agreement in compelling or resisting its performance, it is impossible to say, solely because they are parties to it, that any two of them are of the same class. Nor without more, and with the due regard for the protection of the rights of absent parties which due process exacts, can some be permitted to stand in judgment for all.

It is one thing to say that some members of a class may represent other members in a litigation where the sole and common interest of the class in the litigation, is either to assert a common right or to challenge an asserted obligation. * * * It is quite another to hold that all those who are free alternatively either to assert rights or to challenge them are of a single class, so that any group, merely because it is of the class so constituted, may be deemed adequately to represent any others of the class in litigating their interests in either alternative. Such a selection of representatives for purposes of litigation, whose substantial interests are not necessarily or even probably the same as those whom they are deemed to represent, does not afford that protection to absent parties which due process requires. The doctrine of representation of absent parties in a class suit has not hitherto been thought to go so far. * * * Apart from the opportunities it would afford for the fraudulent and collusive sacrifice of the rights of absent parties, we think that the representation in this case no more satisfies the requirements of due process than a trial by a judicial officer who is in such situation that he may have an interest in the outcome of the litigation in conflict with that of the litigants. * * *

The plaintiffs in the [first] case sought to compel performance of the agreement in behalf of themselves and all others similarly situated. They did not designate the defendants in the suit as a class or seek any injunction or other relief against others than the named defendants, and the decree which was entered did not purport to bind others. In seeking to enforce the agreement the plaintiffs in that suit were not representing the petitioners here whose substantial interest is in resisting performance. The defendants in the first suit were not treated by the pleadings or decree as representing others or as foreclosing by their defense the rights of others, and even though nominal defendants, it does not appear that their interest in defeating the contract outweighed their interest in establishing its validity. For a court in this situation to ascribe to either the plaintiffs or defendants the performance of such functions on behalf of petitioners here, is to attribute to them a power that it cannot be said that they had assumed to exercise, and a responsibility which, in view of their dual interests it does not appear that they could rightly discharge.

Reversed.

Notes and Questions

1. In what way does the Due Process Clause apply in the class-action context? Generally, it requires that the defendant be given notice of the lawsuit and an opportunity to be heard. See Mullane v. Central Hanover Bank & Trust Co., p. 174, supra; Fuentes v. Shevin, p. 209, supra. In *Hansberry,* however, the Supreme Court focused on the adequacy of the class representation, rather than on the notice provided or the opportunity to be heard. See 7A Wright, Miller & Kane, *Federal Practice and Procedure: Civil 2d* § 1765 (1986).

2. At what point should the adequacy of the representation be judged? The Fifth Circuit allowed a collateral attack upon a class-action judgment in GONZALES v. CASSIDY, 474 F.2d 67 (5th Cir.1973). In that case, the original class action had challenged the constitutionality of a Texas statute and sought an injunction against its enforcement. The representative in the original action, an uninsured motorist, had been involved in an accident in Texas. Pursuant to statute, his driver's license and vehicle registration were suspended without a hearing on liability because he did not post security—as required by the statute—for the damages claimed by the other party in the accident. Ultimately the statute was held to be unconstitutional, but the relief asked for was applied retroactively to the representative plaintiff and prospectively to all other class members. The collateral attack in *Gonzales* charged that the original representative was inadequate for failing to appeal on the issue of retroactivity as to the class. The Fifth Circuit outlined a two-part test for reviewing whether the named plaintiff adequately represented the class so as to make the judgment in the suit binding on the absent class members:

> * * * (1) Did the trial court in the first suit correctly determine, initially, that the representative would adequately represent the class? and (2) Does it appear, after the termination of the suit, that the class representative adequately protected the interest of the class? * * *

Id. at 72. The court held that the original plaintiff's failure to appeal the initial judgment rendered him an inadequate representative of the class, since "he was representing approximately 150,000 persons, who, although having had their licenses and registration receipts suspended without due process, were denied any relief by the * * * [trial] court's prospective * * * application of its decision." Id. at 76. The court remanded the case to the District Court for reconsideration of the retroactivity question.

Implicit in the two prongs of *Gonzales* is the notion that adequacy of representation will be examined more than once: first by the court certifying the class, and second by the court called upon to evaluate the binding effect of the first action. Ultimately, a final determination on the adequacy of representation in a class action can only be made through subsequent challenges to the res judicata effect of the suit—some of which may be collateral attacks. Id. at 74.

3. If the adequacy of representation provided by class representation is important to safeguarding the due process rights of class members, courts must be vigilant in examining potential conflicts of interest among class members. The conflict of interest between the class members in the *Hansberry* case unquestionably was enough to preclude adequate representation. In

most cases, however, the conflict of interest among class members is less sharply defined than it was in *Hansberry*.

Some proposed classes might include people who prefer not to sue. For example, although certain employees might favor initiating an employment discrimination suit, others may fear that either management or coworkers will retaliate against them. Or, for another example, some potential class members may feel that the benefits of institutional reform sought in a suit do not outweigh the possibility that the suit will force the institution to close.

Proposed class members also might differ on how to remedy a particular wrong. For example, some parents challenging discrimination in public schools may believe that improving the quality of education is the most crucial goal, while other parents might see integration, and its long-term social effects, as the key objective.

What if the majority of the class members simply does not care whether suit is brought or not? In such circumstances, should the judicial system invest the additional resources inherent in adjudicating class disputes?

How much conflict should courts permit in cases in which the disagreement among class members is not attitudinal (as in the examples just cited) but results from the fact that the class is composed of parties who, by the nature of who they are, find themselves in different, or potentially different, positions with regard to the subject of the litigation. Consider whether, as a trial court judge, you would certify the following proposed classes:

(i) The complaint alleges discrimination in hiring, promotion, and conditions of employment; the proposed class includes current minority employees, minorities whose employment applications were denied, and future minority applicants and employees; the sole class representative is a current employee of the company.

(ii) Would your answer to (i) be any different if there were a second class representative who the defendant arguably had failed to hire because of discrimination?

(iii) An airline has a practice of discharging stewardesses who become pregnant. A suit for injunctive relief is brought on behalf of female airline cabin attendants, including those stewardesses who still are employed. Reinstatement of the former stewardesses, with no loss of seniority, would leapfrog them over the less senior stewardesses who still are actively employed.

(iv) Members of the proposed class in a products-liability suit reside in all parts of the nation, and there are significant differences in the products-liability laws of the various states. Should the class be certified as a single class? Suppose the injured parties can be divided into two groups for whom the applicable laws are substantially the same? What if four groupings are needed? Sixteen? At what point would this subclassing create intolerable management problems?

4. Theoretically, three entities have responsibility for protecting the interests of the class: the class representative or representatives, the class attorneys, and the court. It is not clear, however, that any of these three has a sufficient combination of incentive and information to guard the interests of absent class members.

Courts attach great importance to selecting a class representative who will adequately represent the interests of a proposed class or subclass. Many class representatives fulfill their duties admirably by actively guiding and closely supervising the conduct of the class counsel. But such supervision can entail a considerable amount of time and effort. Furthermore, surfacing conflicts within a class may threaten some of the advantages that the representative may gain from class treatment (such as the prospect of reduced attorneys' fees). Thus, the likelihood that the class representative will adequately protect absent class members' interests depends in large part on individual conscience. Similarly, practical considerations can encourage class attorneys to overlook the best interests of the class when they make tactical decisions. For instance, the prospect of a generous award of fees may tempt a class attorney to recommend a course of action regarding settlement that arguably is not in the class' interest.

Ultimately, it is the court's duty to ensure that the interests of absent class members are protected during a class suit. Nonetheless, although the court is a disinterested party, practical considerations limit its capacity to discharge this function. First, heavy caseloads diminish the ability and desire of judges to spend the time required to supervise class suits, and the same factors make it unlikely that courts will issue orders that will drastically increase the complexity of the proceedings. Second, in large part judges derive their view of a lawsuit from information provided by the parties; in this sense, their knowledge of class conflicts can be no better than that of the parties and in most instances it is more limited.

The party opposing the class may be an important source of information about class conflicts, but objections raised by class opponents are looked on with suspicion by courts fearful that class opponents are seeking to achieve tactical delays. Furthermore, if those opposing the class believe they can win on the merits, they will want a broadly defined class so as to achieve maximum res judicata effect; if the class opponents believe they will lose on the merits, they will want to raise all possible class conflicts in hopes of avoiding class certification altogether. And, whatever their motivations, class opponents cannot be relied on to protect the absentees' interests because often they will have little information about the nature of the proposed class.

5. In EISEN v. CARLISLE & JACQUELIN, 417 U.S. 156, 94 S.Ct. 2140, 40 L.Ed.2d 732 (1974), the Supreme Court relied upon the language and history of Rule 23 to hold that in a Rule 23(b)(3) class action (but not in class actions brought under other sections of the Rule), individual notice must be sent to all class members. In reaching its conclusion about what the Rule requires, the Court rejected a more general argument based on the representational quality of class actions:

> Petitioner further contends that adequate representation, rather than notice, is the touchstone of due process in a class action and therefore satisfies Rule 23. We think this view has little to commend it. To begin with, Rule 23 speaks to notice as well as to adequacy of representation and requires that both be provided. Moreover, petitioner's argument proves too much, for it quickly leads to the conclusion that no notice at all, published or otherwise, would be required in the present case. This cannot be so, for quite apart from what due process might require, the command of Rule 23 is clearly to the contrary. We therefore

conclude that Rule 23(c)(2) requires that individual notice be sent to all class members who can be identified by reasonable effort.

417 U.S. at 176–77, 94 S.Ct. at 2151–52, 40 L.Ed.2d at 748. Is *Eisen* constitutionally mandated or merely the Court's interpretation of Rule 23?

6. If notice is to serve its function, it must be intelligible to the person who receives it. Only then can a potential class member make an informed decision about opting out of the class. Is it likely that non-lawyers will understand the notice they receive? Is the possibility that the notice will not be understood likely to be greatest in those cases where class members are most in need of protection? Consider the following examples:

Dear Sir:

I received your pamphlet on drugs, which I think will be of great value to me in the future.

Due to circumstances beyond my control I will not be able to attend this class at the time prescribed on your letter due to the fact that my working hours are from 7:00 until 4:30.

Dear Sir:

Our son is in the Navy, stationed in the Caribbean some place. Please let us know exactly what kind of drugs he is accused of taking.

From a mother who will help if properly informed.

A worried mother,

Jane Doe

Dear Attorney General:

* * * I received a card from you and I don't understand it, and my husband can't read his. Most of the time all I buy is olive oil for healing oil after praying over it, it is anointed with God's power and ain't nothing like dope.

Rhode, *Class Conflicts in Class Actions,* 34 Stan.L.Rev. 1183, 1235 (1983).

SECTION D. CLASS–ACTION PRACTICE

Class action rules such as Rule 23 are designed to address many of the due process concerns discussed in the previous section. As you read the cases in this section, ask which of the requirements embodied in Rule 23 are mandated by the Due Process Clause.

WETZEL v. LIBERTY MUTUAL INSURANCE COMPANY

United States Court of Appeals, Third Circuit, 1975.
508 F.2d 239, certiorari denied 421 U.S. 1011, 95 S.Ct. 2415,
44 L.Ed.2d 679 (1976).

[Sandra Wetzel and Mari Ross were employed as claims representatives in the Pittsburgh office of the Liberty Mutual Insurance Company. Both wanted to be claims adjusters—a position similar to that of claims representative. Both positions were entry level positions open to college graduates, but claims adjusters were paid more and had greater opportunity for promotion. However, claims adjusters were primarily men; claims representatives were primarily women. When Wetzel and Ross applied for adjusters' positions, the company informed them that the position was not open to women.

Wetzel and Ross filed charges with the Pennsylvania Human Rights Commission (PHRC) and the Equal Employment Opportunity Commission (EEOC). After the charges were filed, the company decided to recruit women as claims adjusters, and reviewed its roster of claims representatives for qualified, interested applicants. Approximately 10% of the women claims representatives were hired as claims adjusters.

Both Wetzel and Ross were offered positions as claims adjusters. They rejected the offers because they believed, partly on the basis of information provided by the PHRC, that the offer included unacceptable conditions. Since the PHRC failed to resolve the claims, the EEOC issued letters to sue. Wetzel and Ross commenced a class action alleging that the company's hiring and promotion policies and its pregnancy-related policies as to the female technical employees in its claims department violated Title VII of the Civil Rights Act of 1964, 42 U.S.C. § 2000e et seq. (1970). They further alleged that the company's policy of paying higher salaries to claims adjusters than to claims representatives violated the Equal Pay Act of 1963, 29 U.S.C. § 206(d) (1970).

In response to Wetzel's and Ross's motions, the District Court certified a Rule 23(b)(2) class, which included "all present and future female technical employees in the defendant's claim department without limitation to territory in the entire geographic location in which the defendant does business." The court later refused to require that notice be sent to the nationwide class. The court's final certification order amended the class to include former, as well as future, female technical employees. Although reaffirming its decision to certify a Rule 23(b)(2) class, it acknowledged that the class was maintainable under Rule 23(b)(3) as well. The court saw no need to order the class-action notice required under Rule 23(b)(3).

In response to a summary-judgment motion, the court held that the pregnancy-related policies of the company violated Title VII. That order was appealed. The District Court later found the hiring and promotion policies also violated Title VII, but denied injunctive relief because the evidence showed that the defendant had discontinued the discriminatory practices. Liberty Mutual appealed this second ruling as well, asking the Third Circuit to review the District Court's management of the class action and its decision to grant summary judgment against the challenged hiring and promotion policies.

In its opinion on this latter appeal, the Third Circuit considered whether the requirements for Rule 23(a) had been met, and concluded that they had been satisfied. It then went on to consider the application of Rule 23(b).]

ROSENN, CIRCUIT JUDGE.

* * *

III

* * *

In the usual class action, the determination of whether the action should proceed as a 23(b)(2) or as a 23(b)(3) action offers little difficulty. In the present case, however, the order of the district court finding injunctive relief unnecessary as to Liberty Mutual's hiring and promotional practices in its claims department, because the Company's practices as to these issues have ceased, presents complications. Whether (b)(2) or not (b)(2) is indeed *the* question.

In the instant case, the district court found that the class could be maintained under either 23(b)(2) or 23(b)(3), but exercising its discretion decided to maintain the class under 23(b)(2). Liberty Mutual vigorously contends that the class could only be maintained under (b)(3), and that the procedural prerequisites for maintaining a (b)(3) suit have not been met. We find no error in the district court's determination * * *.

* * * By its very nature, a (b)(2) class must be cohesive as to those claims tried in the class action. * * * Any resultant unfairness to the members of the class was thought to be outweighed by the purposes behind class actions: eliminating the possibility of repetitious litigation and providing small claimants with a means of obtaining redress for claims too small to justify individual litigation.

Rule 23(b)(3) permits a class action where the questions of law or fact common to the class predominate over questions only affecting individual members and the "class action is superior to other available methods for the fair and efficient adjudication of the controversy." * * *

[The court then summarized the res judicata effect of pre-1966 federal class actions.]

Binding all members of a (b)(3) class, however, was not thought by the Advisory Committee to be as fair as binding all members of a (b)(2) class. By the very nature of a heterogeneous (b)(3) class, there would be many instances where a particular individual would not want to be included as a member of the class.[16] To respect these individual interests, Rule 23(c) (2) was written to afford an opportunity to every potential member to opt out of the class. * * * For the opt out procedure to be effective, 23(c)(2) also provides for notice to be sent to all potential members prior to the final determination of the class. Eisen v. Carlisle & Jacquelin, [p. 683, supra] * * *.

With the potential unfairness to members of the (b)(3) class eliminated by the opt out procedure, 23(c)(3) contemplates that all members of the

---

16. An excellent example is the situation found in Katz v. Carte Blanche Corp., [496 F.2d 747 (3d Cir.1974)]. Assume, contrary to the decision, that a (b)(3) class was allowed to be maintained. Carte Blanche might have counterclaimed against the members of the class for amounts owing from use of the credit card. A delinquent account debtor might have decided that a judgment for amounts owing would outweigh any benefits he might obtain from a favorable judgment resulting from the Truth in Lending Act violation.

(b)(3) class, as well as members of the (b)(2) class, will be bound by the res judicata effect of the judgment. * * *

B. APPROPRIATENESS OF (b)(2) FOR THIS ACTION

Liberty Mutual contends that this suit could not have been maintained as a class action under (b)(2) because such class actions are limited to only those suits in which final injunctive relief is found to be appropriate. * * *

The district court, after discovery and extensive briefing, considered whether the action here was properly maintained under (b)(2) three separate times. In its last memorandum order of December 6, 1973, the court indicated that maintenance under (b)(2) was proper because Liberty Mutual had " 'acted or refused to act on grounds generally applicable to the class' and the representative plaintiffs seek among other remedies, 'final injunctive relief or corresponding declaratory relief.' " In his opinion of January 9, 1974, Judge Weber noted:

> Because the evidentiary materials show that at certain times subsequent to the filing of the administrative charge or the within Complaint the Defendant has ceased or discontinued the discriminatory practices, injunctive relief is not appropriate as to those practices.

372 F.Supp. at 1163.

The precise issue before us then is whether a district court, having determined that a Title VII suit brought in good faith for injunctive relief may be maintained under (b)(2), is required to redetermine that the suit be maintained under (b)(3) and comply with its procedural requirements once it concludes on a motion for summary judgment that changed conditions make injunctive relief no longer appropriate. We decline to so hold.

First, a Title VII suit against discriminatory hiring and promotion policies is necessarily a suit to end discrimination because of a common class characteristic, in this case sex. The conduct of the employer is actionable "on grounds generally applicable to the class," and the relief sought is "relief with respect to the class as a whole." The class, all sharing a common characteristic subjected to discrimination, is cohesive as to the claims alleged in the complaint. Thus, a Title VII action is particularly fit for (b)(2) treatment, and the drafters of Rule 23 specifically contemplated that suits against discriminatory hiring and promotion policies would be appropriately maintained under (b)(2). * * * Since a Title VII suit is essentially equitable in nature, it cannot be characterized as one seeking exclusively or predominantly money damages. * * *

The basic nature of a Title VII suit is not altered merely because the employer's change of discriminatory policy prior to the motion for summary judgment has obviated the need for injunctive relief. The conduct of the employer is still answerable "on grounds generally applicable to the class," and the relief sought is still "relief with respect to the class as a whole." The cohesive characteristics of the class are the vital core of a (b)(2) action. Functionally, these characteristics of the class are still intact in the suit. Nothing has changed to require the procedural protections of (b)(3) to determine the presence or absence of liability. The class is still appropriately maintained under (b)(2).

Second, the language of (b)(2) does not support the contention that (b)(2) actions are limited to final injunctive relief or declaratory judgments only. Rather, the language describes the type of conduct by the party opposing the class which is subject to equitable relief by class action under (b)(2). * * * Liberty Mutual's policies at the time these charges were made were such that final injunctive relief was appropriate. This satisfies the language of the rule. The nature of these policies, and the nature of the class opposing these policies, does not change merely because subsequent action by Liberty Mutual eliminates the need for final injunctive relief.

Moreover, although the court found that injunctive relief was unnecessary, it did determine the presence of liability on the part of Liberty Mutual. The court did not preclude the possibility of directing affirmative action, in addition to back pay, to remedy conditions caused by the offensive discriminatory practices. Such affirmative action ultimately would, in effect, constitute final injunctive or declaratory relief. * * *

Courts have held that a (b)(2) class is appropriate in a Title VII suit where both final injunctive and monetary relief are granted. * * * Maintenance of a class action under (b)(2) in a Title VII action has also been held to be appropriate when the actions of the defendant after the complaint had been filed had obviated the need for final injunctive relief. * * *

Additionally, only with the benefit of hindsight do we now know that injunctive relief against the Company's hiring and promotion practices was not necessary in this case. At the (c)(1) hearing, the district court specifically found that the conduct of Liberty Mutual made appropriate final injunctive relief. Requiring the court to reconsider and possibly redetermine the class at the time of the summary judgment application and redirect the course of the litigation with notice and other procedural requirements would inevitably complicate a type of litigation which by its nature is complex at its best. For this court to compel a redetermination of the class at that point probably would require the district court to consider the merits of the case, and ultimately would lead to a practice of holding a preliminary hearing on the merits at the time of the initial (c)(1) class determination. This, of course, the Supreme Court has made clear the district court may not do * * *. Eisen v. Carlisle & Jacquelin * * *. It is at the (c)(1) hearing that the class must be shown to possess the characteristics required by (b)(2). Of course, the district court may amend its determination at a later date. See 23(c)(1). But we decline to hold that a court must reconsider its determination when, at the decision for summary judgment, it finds injunctive relief to be inappropriate.

Finally, we have reviewed the (b)(2) issue on this appeal as if the action in the district court involved only the hiring and promotion policies of Liberty Mutual. Wetzel and Ross, however, also attacked in the district court Liberty Mutual's pregnancy related policies, and its policy of paying higher salaries to claims adjusters than to claims representatives.

Due to the piecemeal nature of the appeals from the district court, the only substantive issue before us involves the hiring and promotion policies, but in the absence of the argument by Liberty Mutual that different classes should have been created for different issues, we must consider the propriety of the class determination in the light of all the substantive issues raised in the district court. Liberty Mutual has changed, as a result of the charges brought by Wetzel and Ross, neither its pregnancy related policies, nor its higher salary policy to claims adjusters. In the event these policies are found to be violative of Title VII, final injunctive relief will be necessary as redress. The (b)(2) nature of the class, while visible as to the promotion and hiring issues, becomes translucent when viewed in the light of the multifaceted attack upon Liberty Mutual's policies.

Liberty Mutual also contends that if the requirements of both (b)(2) and (b)(3) are met, the court should certify the class under (b)(3) to provide the procedural protections, namely notice and opting out, which (b)(3) affords members of the class. Virtually every class action meeting the requirements of 23(b)(2) will also meet the less severe requirements of 23(b)(3). * * * If the actions are classified under (b)(3), members of the class could elect to opt out and thereby not be bound by the judgment. This would permit the institution of separate litigation and would defeat the fundamental objective of (b)(2), to bind the members of the class with one conclusive adjudication. * * * As discussed above, the procedural protections of (b)(3), opting out and notice, are necessary because of the heterogeneity of the (b)(3) class. They are unnecessary for the homogeneous (b)(2) class.

The recent Supreme Court decision in Eisen v. Carlisle & Jacquelin, * * * does not support the Company's contention. *Eisen* does not extend the (b)(3) notice requirement to (b)(2) actions, nor to actions maintainable under either (b)(2) or (b)(3). We therefore agree with the * * * principle that an action maintainable under both (b)(2) and (b)(3) should be treated under (b)(2) to enjoy its superior res judicata effect and to eliminate the procedural complications of (b)(3) which serve no useful purpose under (b)(2). This principle has been widely adopted in the federal courts. * * *

* * *

IV

Liberty Mutual contends that if the action is maintainable under (b)(2), we should hold that notice should have been given prior to determination of liability to all members of the class, either under our supervisory powers over the circuit district courts or under the requirements of due process.

Suits brought by private employees are the cutting edge of the Title VII sword which Congress has fashioned to fight a major enemy to continuing progress, strength, and solidarity in our nation, discrimination in employment. * * * The imposition of notice and the ensuing costs often discourage such suits. * * * Therefore, we are reluctant to impose notice requirements under our supervisory power for Title VII (b)

(2) actions unless Rule 23 so requires or unfairness will result to the parties.

The due process problem surfaces because the class action judgment binds all members of a (b)(2) class. * * *.

The Supreme Court [in Mullane v. Central Hanover Bank & Trust Co. (p. 174, supra)], plainly stated that it had not committed itself to any formula in achieving a balance between the interests of the State and the interests of the individual parties in the litigation or in "determining when constructive notice may be utilized or what test it must meet. Personal notice has not in all circumstances been regarded as indispensable to the process due to residents, and it has more often been held unnecessary as to nonresidents." * * * Because the Court linked the requirement of notice to the particular circumstances of each case, it is important to note that the situation in *Mullane* is significantly different from the situation in a (b)(2) class action. First, *Mullane* dealt with the established interests of individuals in specific property, a common trust fund. Second, the interests of all the beneficiaries in that fund were not identical; some were entitled to interest income, while others were concerned with capital growth. These interests were represented by different guardians, but the personal interests of the guardians functionally differed from the interests of the beneficiaries. Therefore, a significant possibility existed that they did not adequately represent the beneficiaries in the action. Third, the beneficiaries had a resident fiduciary as a caretaker of their interest in the trust "[b]ut it is their caretaker who in the accounting becomes their adversary." * * * Under these circumstances, the possibility that parties having conflicting interests in specific property could be bound by an action of which they had no actual notice and brought by parties who possibly represented those interests inadequately does violate due process. This possibility could not occur in a (b)(2) action.

The very nature of a (b)(2) class is that it is homogeneous without any conflicting interests between the members of the class. Since the class is cohesive, its members would be bound either by the collateral estoppel or the stare decisis effect of a suit brought by an individual plaintiff. Thus, as long as the representation is adequate and faithful, there is no unfairness in giving res judicata effect to a judgment against all members of the class even if they have not received notice. Adequacy of representation of the class is a mandatory requirement for the maintenance of a class action under Rule 23(a). * * * Of course, there may be circumstances when the court, in its discretion, believes that notice to the absent members of the class is necessary for the fair conduct of the action. Rule 23(d)(2) anticipates such situations and permits the court to then require such notice. * * * We decline, therefore, to hold that due process ineluctably requires notice in all (b)(2) class actions.

* * *

We believe that if there is truly adequate representation, the interests of absent parties to a (b)(2) class are protected. We thus agree with the framers of the rule, several district courts that have expressly considered the question, and several of the commentators that notice to absent members of a (b)(2) class is not an absolute requisite of due process. For the foregoing reasons, we have concluded that there was no denial of due process in this case.

Notes and Questions

1. How hermetic are the three categories of class actions created by Rule 23(b)? It has been argued that courts treat anti-discrimination class actions differently from other suits—that courts are willing to permit backpay awards to be made in suits prosecuted under Rule 23(b)(2), even though backpay awards arguably are outside the scope of injunctive relief authorized by Rule 23(b)(2). Note, *Antidiscrimination Class Actions Under the Federal Rules of Civil Procedure: The Transformation of Rule 23(b)(2)*, 88 Yale L.J. 868 (1979). Is it possible that, by treating anti-discrimination suits differently, courts in fact have created a fourth category of class actions—one combining the characteristics of Rule 23(b)(2) and Rule 23(b)(3) suits?

The Advisory Note to Rule 23 states that "[Rule 23(b)(2)] does not extend to cases in which the appropriate final relief relates exclusively or predominantly to money damages." Is it possible to argue that in anti-discrimination suits backpay awards do not predominate?

2. When evaluating the binding effect of a class-action judgment, should a court review both notice and representation? Should adequate representation ever be allowed to cure inadequate notice? Can adequate notice ever cure inadequate representation? See generally Note, *Collateral Attack on the Binding Effect of Class Action Judgments*, 87 Harv.L.Rev. 589 (1978).

In JOHNSON v. GENERAL MOTORS CORP., 598 F.2d 432 (5th Cir.1979), the plaintiffs alleged claims of racial discrimination. In an earlier racial discrimination class suit involving the same factory, the plaintiffs had sought both injunctive and compensatory relief. The injunction was granted, and damages were awarded to the class representatives, but not to the absent class members. The plaintiff in the subsequent suit, Johnson, claimed that he had not received notice of the first suit, and attempted to prosecute his own suit for damages. The Fifth Circuit panel said:

> In light of these developments, we have previously suggested that when both monetary and injunctive relief are sought in an action certified under Rule 23(b)(2), notice may be mandatory if absent class members are to be bound. * * * [But w]hen only equitable relief is sought in an action involving a cohesive plaintiff group such as a class of black employees at an assembly plant, the due process interests of absent members will usually be safeguarded by adequate representation alone. As the Advisory Committee on Rule 23 stated, "[i]n the degree that there is cohesiveness or unity in the class and the representation is effective, the need for notice to the class will tend toward a minimum." * * * Where, however, individual monetary claims are at stake, the balance swings in favor of the provision of some form of notice. It will not always be necessary for the notice in such cases to be equivalent to that required in (b)(3) actions. * * * In some cases it may be proper to delay notice until a more advanced stage of the litigation; for example, until after class-wide liability is proven. * * * Before an absent class member

may be forever barred from pursuing an individual damage claim, however, due process requires that he receive some form of notice that the class action is pending and that his damage claims may be adjudicated as part of it.

Id. at 437–38.

———

Is the class in a class-action suit as homogeneous as Judge Rosenn suggests? Consider the following case.

GENERAL TELEPHONE CO. v. FALCON, 457 U.S. 147, 102 S.Ct. 2364, 72 L.Ed.2d 740 (1982). Mariano Falcon was passed over for a promotion to field inspector at the same time several white employees with less seniority were granted promotions. He filed charges with the Equal Employment Opportunity Commission (EEOC), stating his belief that he had been denied promotion because of his national origin and that General Telephone's promotion policy operated against Mexican-Americans as a class. The EEOC issued a right-to-sue letter, and Falcon instituted this action under Title VII of the Civil Rights Act of 1964.

Falcon's complaint alleged that General Telephone maintained a policy of discriminating against Mexican-Americans with respect to compensation and conditions of employment and a policy of subjecting Mexican-Americans to continuous employment discrimination. He claimed that as a result of this policy less qualified whites with lower evaluation scores than him and other Mexican-Americans had been promoted more rapidly. The complaint contained no factual allegations concerning General Telephone's hiring practices.

Falcon moved to certify a class of "all hourly Mexican-American employees who had been employed, were employed, or who were to apply for employment, or who had applied or who would have applied had not petitioner practiced racial discrimination in its employment practices." Without conducting an evidentiary hearing, the court certified a class including Mexican-American employees and Mexican-American applicants who had not been hired in the division of the company in which Falcon was employed. The court denied two decertification motions made by General Telephone.

At trial, the District Court found that General Telephone had not discriminated against Falcon in hiring, but that it did discriminate against him in its promotion practices. As to the class, the court found no discrimination in promotion, but did conclude General Telephone had discriminated against Mexican-Americans in its hiring practices. Relief was ultimately awarded to 13 Mexican-Americans who had applied for employment.

Appeal was taken to the Fifth Circuit. The panel rejected Falcon's claim that the class should be broadened to include employees at and applicants to all of General Telephone's plants. It concurrently rejected General Telephone's claim that the class was too broad. On the merits, the Fifth Circuit upheld Falcon's claim of disparate treatment in promotion, but held that the District Court's findings relating to disparate impact in hiring were insufficient to support recovery on behalf of the class. The Supreme Court reversed the Fifth Circuit's affirmance of the certification order.

hardline on

class A

We have repeatedly held that "a class representative must be part of the class and 'possess the same interest and suffer the same injury' as the class members." * * *

* * * We * * * [recognize] the theory behind the Fifth Circuit's across-the-board rule, noting our awareness "that suits alleging racial or ethnic discrimination are often by their very nature class suits, involving classwide wrongs," and that "[c]ommon questions of law or fact are typically present." * * * In the same breath, however, we reiterated that "careful attention to the requirements of Fed.Rule Civ.Proc. 23 remains nonetheless indispensable" and that the "mere fact that a complaint alleges racial or ethnic discrimination does not in itself ensure that the party who has brought the lawsuit will be an adequate representative of those who may have been the real victims of that discrimination." * * *

We cannot disagree with the proposition underlying the across-the-board rule—that racial discrimination is by definition class discrimination. But the allegation that such discrimination has occurred neither determines whether a class action may be maintained in accordance with Rule 23 nor defines the class that may be certified. Conceptually, there is a wide gap between (a) an individual's claim that he has been denied a promotion on discriminatory grounds, and his otherwise unsupported allegation that the company has a policy of discrimination, and (b) the existence of a class of persons who have suffered the same injury as that individual, such that the individual's claim and the class claims will share common questions of law or fact and that the individual's claim will be typical of the class claims. For respondent to bridge that gap, he must prove much more than the validity of his own claim. Even though evidence that he was passed over for promotion when several less deserving whites were advanced may support the conclusion that respondent was denied the promotion because of his national origin, such evidence would not necessarily justify the additional inferences (1) that this discriminatory treatment is typical of petitioner's promotion practices, (2) that petitioner's promotion practices are motivated by a policy of ethnic discrimination that pervades petitioner's Irving division, or (3) that this policy of ethnic discrimination is reflected in petitioner's other employment practices, such as hiring, in the same way it is manifested in the promotion practices. These additional inferences demonstrate the tenuous character of any presumption that the class claims are "fairly encompassed" within respondent's claim.

Respondent's complaint provided an insufficient basis for concluding that the adjudication of his claim of discrimination in promotion would require the decision of any common question concerning the failure of petitioner to hire more Mexican-Americans. Without any specific presentation identifying the questions of law or fact that were common to the claims of respondent and of the members of the class he sought to represent, it was error for the District Court to presume that respondent's claim was typical of other claims against petitioner by Mexican-American employees and applicants.

Id. at 156–59, 102 S.Ct. at 2370–71, 72 L.Ed.2d at 749–51.

Notes and Questions

1. Does *Falcon* overrule *Wetzel*? *Falcon* can be understood as requiring only greater specificity in pleading, and merely holding that the pleadings must show a clear and specific link between the individual and class claims. The Court, after all, did conclude the "[t]he District Court's error in this case, and the error inherent in the across-the-board rule, is the failure to evaluate carefully the legitimacy of the named plaintiff's claim that he is a proper class representative under Rule 23(a)." On the other hand, *Falcon* can be read as in tension with *Wetzel*'s notion that some differences between class members are permissible. The *Falcon* Court, for instance, did frame the question presented in rather general terms as "whether respondent Falcon, who complained that petitioner did not *promote* him because he is a Mexican-American, properly was permitted to maintain a class action on behalf of Mexican-American applicants for employment whom petitioner did not *hire*." (Emphasis in original.) The Court's answer to this question was that their claims were not fairly encompassed within Falcon's claim. 457 U.S. at 149, 102 S.Ct. at 2366, 72 L.Ed.2d at 745. This language sounds like a substantive requirement that the class be unified in interest. See Chayes, *Foreword: Public Law Litigation and the Burger Court,* 96 Harv.L.Rev. 4, 38 (1982).

2. *Wetzel* and *Falcon* illustrate that the interests of class members are often not identical. The more tenuous the links that bind the class, the greater the chance that individual members will have conflicting aims. Hence, the suit becomes more difficult to litigate and resolve. See Rhode, *Class Conflicts in Class Actions,* 34 Stan.L.Rev. 1183 (1983).

3. The class-action device places the named parties and the class attorneys in a fiduciary relation to the unnamed class members. Unfortunately, some attorneys have abused this relationship. The *Manual for Complex Litigation* § 1.41, at 27–28 n. 43 (5th ed.1982), catalogues a wide range of abuses, such as: misrepresenting the status, purpose, or effects of the class suit; soliciting agreements to pay expenses or soliciting actual payments from potential or actual class members who are not formal parties to the class suit; contacting class members to encourage them to opt out of a Rule 23(b)(3) class suit; and, serving process that appeared to be issued by a court in order to influence a class member to enter into an attorneys' fees contract, submit to discovery, or opt out of a class suit.

Following the suggestions contained in an early edition of the *Manual,* courts sought to minimize such abuses by issuing "gag" orders that limited and controlled communications with class members. In GULF OIL CO. v. BERNARD, 452 U.S. 89, 101 S.Ct. 2193, 68 L.Ed.2d 693 (1981), however, the Supreme Court struck down the imposition of automatic, blanket restrictions on attorney-class communications as being inconsistent with the general policies embodied in Rule 23. It held that such orders "should be based on a clear record and specific findings that reflect a weighing of the need for a limitation and the potential interference with the rights of the parties." Id. at 101, 101 S.Ct. at 2200, 68 L.Ed.2d at 703. Because it resolved the case through statutory interpretation, the Court did not reach the question of whether the First Amendment prohibited orders restricting attorney-class communications.

———

Perhaps the best way to explore the complexities of class action practice is to apply Rule 23 to some concrete examples. In that spirit, try your hand with the following examples.

The Peace Movement

During the United States' involvement in the Vietnam War, Dr. DeBremaecker and his daughter engaged in handing out leaflets critical of the United States' actions in Southeast Asia on public sidewalks in Houston, Texas. Several times they were approached by members of the Houston Police Department and asked to produce a permit to distribute handbills or face arrest. DeBremaecker filed a class action to enjoin the Texas Police Department from harassing people distributing leaflets. The action was filed on behalf of all Texas residents "active in the peace movement who have been harassed and intimidated as well as those who feared harassment and intimidation in exercising the First Amendment right of free expression in the form of passing out leaflets in furtherance of their cause." Should such a class be certified? What problems arise in certifying a class whose membership depends on the state of mind of the potential members? See DeBremaecker v. Short, 433 F.2d 733 (5th Cir. 1970).

Dalkon Shield

In 1970, the A.H. Robins Company placed an intrauterine contraceptive device on the market. Many women who used the device developed an infection which caused infertility or sustained other injuries. Some evidence existed that A.H. Robins knew that the device would have these effects. A class action was brought by 2.2 million women who had been adversely affected by the device, suing for compensatory damages well over $500 million and punitive damages in excess of $2.3 billion. Should the plaintiff class be certified? How? Do the inevitable differences in the plaintiffs' medical and sexual histories affect your decision? How should punitive damages be handled? Should they be awarded to one plaintiff or divided amongst them? If the award should be divided, should it be in equal allotments or according to the amount of compensatory damages that each can prove? See In re Northern District of California, Dalkon Shield IUD Products Liability Litigation, 693 F.2d 847 (9th Cir.1982), certiorari denied 459 U.S. 1171, 103 S.Ct. 817, 74 L.Ed.2d 1015 (1983).

Agent Orange Litigation

While fighting the Vietnam War, the United States Army and Marine Corps used a defoliant called Agent Orange to clear the brush in the Vietnamese forests. Later, suspicion grew that Agent Orange caused various illnesses in those who were exposed to the chemical, and caused birth defects in their children. A class-action suit based on negligence and products liability was brought on behalf of a plaintiff class consisting of "all persons who were in the United States, New Zealand or Australian Armed Forces at any time from 1962 to 1971 who were injured in or near Vietnam by exposure to Agent Orange or other phenoxy herbicides, [including] spouses, parents and children of veterans born before January 1, 1984, directly or derivately injured as a result of the exposure." There were over 15,000 named plaintiffs and nearly 2.5 million potential class members. The plaintiffs sought to press individual damage claims as well as their class claims.

Should a plaintiff class be certified? If so, should it be a (b)(1) or (b)(2) or (b)(3) class? If it should be a (b)(3) class, does clause (D) present problems? Are there other problems in certifying the class? Should the judge consider that the chemical companies may go bankrupt from an extremely large judgment? See In re Agent Orange Product Liability Litigation, 100 F.R.D. 718 (E.D.N.Y.1983), 597 F.Supp. 740, 837–42 (E.D. N.Y.1984), affirmed 818 F.2d 145 (2d Cir.1987), certiorari denied ___ U.S. ___, 108 S.Ct. 695, 98 L.Ed.2d 648 (1988).

The Problem of the Mass Tort Case

Dalkon Shield and *Agent Orange* are examples of what are known as "mass tort" cases. The class-action device has been used in mass tort situations, but the debate over its appropriateness continues.

> When personal injury and death claims are involved, a strong feeling prevails that everyone enmeshed in the dispute should have his own day in court and be represented by a lawyer of his own choice. Thus, the possibility that a class action might be used to adjudicate the claims arising out of a mass tort is particularly unattractive to those who believe the device to be inconsistent with the time-honored practice in personal injury cases and to others who fear that use of this procedure may encourage the unseemly solicitation of legal business. Furthermore, the alleged tortfeasor's defenses may depend on facts peculiar to each plaintiff, creating a risk that they may be submerged by the overall magnitude of the litigation or that individual issues actually may predominate so that a class action really would not be economical or expeditious.

7B Wright, Miller & Kane, *Federal Practice and Procedure: Civil 2d* § 1783, at 71–72 (1986).

In fact, in the *Dalkon Shield* case, the judge refused to certify the plaintiff class for just this reason. A class was certified in the *Agent Orange* litigation. Are different results in these two cases defensible? The plaintiffs in *Agent Orange* were members of the armed services and therefore subject to common government-immunity defenses. Is this fact dispositive?

SECTION E.   CLASS ACTIONS AND JURISDICTION

1.   SUBJECT–MATTER JURISDICTION

A class action based upon a federal question does not raise any special problems of subject-matter jurisdiction. A class action based upon diversity, however, does raise two special questions: first, to which class members should the court look in determining whether there is diversity of citizenship and, second, to which class members should the court look in calculating the jurisdictional-amount requirement? The Supreme Court answered the first of these questions in SUPREME TRIBE OF BEN–HUR v. CAUBLE, 255 U.S. 356, 41 S.Ct. 338, 65 L.Ed. 673 (1921), holding that determinations of diversity of citizenship in class actions should be based on the citizenship of the named parties only. See generally 7A Wright, Miller & Kane, *Federal Practice and Procedure: Civil 2d* § 1755 (1986). The Court addressed the second question—calculating the jurisdictional amount—in SNYDER v. HARRIS, 394 U.S. 332, 89 S.Ct. 1053, 22 L.Ed.2d 319 (1969), and ZAHN v. INTERNATIONAL PAPER CO., 414 U.S. 291, 94 S.Ct. 505, 38 L.Ed.2d 511 (1973).

In *Snyder,* Mrs. Margaret E. Snyder, a shareholder of Missouri Fidelity Union Trust Life Insurance Company, brought suits against members of the company's board of directors alleging that they had sold their shares of the company's stock for an amount far in excess of its fair market value, that this excess represented payment to these particular directors to obtain complete control of the company, and that under Missouri law the excess should properly be distributed among all the shareholders of the company and not merely to a few of them. The suit was brought in the United States District Court for the Eastern District of Missouri, diversity of citizenship being the basis for federal jurisdiction. Since petitioner's allegations showed that she sought for herself only $8,740 in damages, respondent moved to dismiss on the ground that the matter in controversy did not exceed $10,000 (the requisite jurisdictional amount at the time). Petitioner contended, however, that her claim should be aggregated with those of the other members of her class, approximately 4,000 shareholders of the company stock. If all 4,000 potential claims were aggregated, the amount in controversy would be approximately $1,200,000. The Supreme Court held that separate and distinct claims could not be aggregated. It noted that "[a]ggregation has been permitted only (1) in cases in which a single plaintiff seeks to aggregate two or more of his claims against a single defendant and (2) in cases where two or more plaintiffs unite to enforce a single title or right in which they have a common or undivided interest." 394 U.S. at 335, 89 S.Ct. at 1056, 22 L.Ed.2d at 323. The Court noted Rule 82's prohibition against using the Federal Rules to expand district-court jurisdiction. It also noted that Congress recently had reenacted the jurisdictional-amount requirement, and in doing so implicitly had taken the judicial rules on aggregation into account.

Justice Fortas, in a dissent joined by Justice Douglas, wrote: "The fundamental change in the law of class actions requires that prior subsidiary doctrines developed for application to the [old class action procedural rules] be harmonized with the new procedural law." Id. at 350, 89 S.Ct. at 1064, 22 L.Ed.2d at 332. The old Rule had depended on confusing concepts of jural relations such as whether claims were common or joint. The 1966 amendments specifically replaced these conceptual categorizations with more functional ones.

In *Zahn,* the petitioners, asserting that they were owners of property fronting on Lake Champlain in Orwell, Vermont, brought a diversity action in the District Court on behalf of a class consisting of themselves and 200 lakefront property owners and lessees. They sought damages from International Paper Co., a New York corporation, for allegedly having permitted discharges from its pulp and paper-making plant, located in New York, to flow into Ticonderoga Creek and to be carried by that stream into Lake Champlain, thereby polluting the waters of the lake and damaging the value and utility of the surrounding properties. The claim of all of the named plaintiffs was found to satisfy the $10,000 jurisdictional amount, but the District Court was convinced "to a legal certainty" that not every individual owner in the class had suffered pollution damages in excess of $10,000. The Supreme Court held that each plaintiff in a Rule 23(b)(3) class action must satisfy the jurisdictional-amount requirement. The majority opinion rested on the traditional rules that courts had used for aggregating claims. It cited BANK OF TROY v. G.A. WHITEHEAD & CO., 222 U.S. 39, 32 S.Ct. 9, 56 L.Ed. 81 (1911), as the "classic statement" of this traditional rule:

> When two or more plaintiffs, having separate and distinct demands, unite for convenience and economy in a single suit, it is essential that the demand of each be of the requisite jurisdictional amount; but when several plaintiffs unite to enforce a single title or right, in which they have a common and undivided interest, it is enough if their interests collectively equal the jurisdictional amount.

Id. at 40–41, 32 S.Ct. at 9, 56 L.Ed. at 82.

The Court also believed that its holding was compelled by the *Snyder* case, which it characterized as "unmistakably reject[ing] the notion that the 1966 amendments to Rule 23 were intended to effect, or effected, any change in the meaning and application of the jurisdictional-amount requirement insofar as class actions are concerned." 414 U.S. at 299, 94 S.Ct. at 511, 38 L.Ed.2d at 518.

Justice Brennan wrote a dissenting opinion, joined by Justices Douglas and Marshall, pointing out that

> petitioners * * * [had made] no argument inconsistent with the Court's holding that the theory of "joint" claims or interests will not support jurisdiction over nonappearing members of their class. Their contention is rather that a second theory, ancillary jurisdiction, supports a determination that those claims may be entertained. * * *
>
> * * * [R]ules developed to control the exercise of * * * jurisdiction * * * are * * * accommodations that take into account the

impact of the adjudication on parties and third persons, the susceptibility of the dispute or disputes in the case to resolution in a single adjudication, and the structure of the litigation as governed by the Federal Rules of Civil Procedure.

Id. at 305, 94 S.Ct. at 514, 38 L.Ed.2d at 521.

Notes and Questions

1. Many commentators have criticized *Snyder* and *Zahn* as unnecessarily hostile to federal class actions. Upon which of the three kinds of federal class actions—Rule 23(b)(1), (b)(2), or (b)(3)—do you think *Snyder* and *Zahn* will have the greatest impact?

2. Are not the Supreme Court holdings on determining diversity of citizenship and on calculating jurisdictional amount in class suits somewhat contradictory? In the former, the status of unnamed class members is irrelevant; a suit can be accorded class treatment even if the citizenship of absent class members would, if considered, have destroyed complete diversity. In calculating jurisdictional amount, on the other hand, the Court instructed lower federal courts to look to the individual claims of each member of the proposed class to see if federal jurisdictional-amount requirements are met; class status is appropriate only when all class members, both the class representatives and the absent class members, individually have satisfied the jurisdictional-amount requirement.

3. Class suits based on diversity but involving unincorporated associations pose unique questions. When unincorporated associations are sued in federal court, the court usually looks to the citizenship of each member of the association to determine whether there is diversity of citizenship. This has made it difficult for unincorporated associations to sue under diversity jurisdiction in federal courts. Some unincorporated associations have sought to circumvent this rule by using the class-action device—naming only carefully selected association members as class representatives. Should this circumvention be permitted? See Patrician Towers Owners, Inc. v. Fairchild, 513 F.2d 216 (4th Cir.1975) (citizenship of the association's members will be considered when association is named as party but not as the class representative).

2. PERSONAL JURISDICTION

The use of the class-action device raises interesting problems related to personal jurisdiction. For example, must the requirements of International Shoe Co. v. Washington, p. 82, supra, and World-Wide Volkswagen Corp. v. Woodson, p. 107, supra, be satisfied in order for the class-action judgment to bind a particular member of a defendant class? In Hansberry v. Lee, p. 677, supra, the Court said that due process is satisfied and the judgment is binding on all class members when the interests of the class are represented adequately during the suit. *Hansberry* involved a state-court judgment. Should it matter whether it is a state court or a federal court that is attempting to assert jurisdiction over the class? See generally Note, *Personal Jurisdiction and Rule 23 Defendant Class Actions,* 53 Indiana L.J. 841 (1978).

Must the requirements of *International Shoe* and *World-Wide Volkswagen* be met before a court can bind any individual member of the plaintiff class? Do the traditional doctrines of personal jurisdiction apply to non-representative members of a plaintiff class? The following case addresses this inquiry.

PHILLIPS PETROLEUM CO. v. SHUTTS

Supreme Court of the United States, 1985.
472 U.S. 797, 105 S.Ct. 2965, 86 L.Ed.2d 628.

[During the 1970's, Phillips Petroleum produced or purchased natural gas from leased land located in 11 States. Shutts and several other royalty owners possessing rights to leases from which Phillips Petroleum produced the gas brought a class action against the company in a Kansas state court, seeking to recover interest on royalty payments that had been delayed. The trial court certified a class consisting of 33,000 royalty owners. The royalty owners provided each class member with a notice by first-class mail describing the action and informing each member that he could appear in person or by counsel, that otherwise he would be represented by the named royalty owners, and that class members would be included in the class and bound by the judgment unless they "opted out" of the action by returning a "request for exclusion." The final class consisted of some 28,100 members, who resided in all 50 States, the District of Columbia, and several foreign countries. Notwithstanding that over 99% of the gas leases in question and some 97% of the plaintiff class members had no apparent connection to Kansas except for the lawsuit, the trial court applied Kansas contract and equity law to every claim and found Phillips Petroleum liable for interest on the suspended royalties to all class members. The Kansas Supreme Court affirmed over the company's contentions that the Due Process Clause of the Fourteenth Amendment prevented Kansas from adjudicating the claims of all the class members, and that that Clause and the Full Faith and Credit Clause prohibited application of Kansas law to all of the transactions between it and the class members.]

Certiorari to the Supreme Court of Kansas.

JUSTICE REHNQUIST delivered the opinion of the Court.

* * *

I

* * *

* * * As a class-action defendant petitioner is in a unique predicament. If Kansas does not possess jurisdiction over this plaintiff class, petitioner will be bound to 28,100 judgment holders scattered across the globe, but none of these will be bound by the Kansas decree. Petitioner could be subject to numerous later individual suits by these class members because a judgment issued without proper personal jurisdiction over an absent party is not entitled to full faith and credit elsewhere and thus has no res judicata effect as to that party. Whether it wins or loses on the merits, petitioner has a distinct and personal interest in seeing the entire plaintiff class bound by res judicata just as petitioner is bound. The only way a class action defendant like petitioner can assure itself of this binding effect of the judgment is to ascertain that the forum court has jurisdiction over every plaintiff whose claim it seeks to adjudicate, sufficient to support a defense of res judicata in a later suit for damages by class members.

While it is true that a court adjudicating a dispute may not be able to predetermine the res judicata effect of its own judgment, petitioner has alleged that it would be obviously and immediately injured if this class-action judgment against it became final without binding the plaintiff class. We think that such an injury is sufficient to give petitioner standing on its own right to raise the jurisdiction claim in this Court.

* * *

II

Reduced to its essentials, petitioner's argument is that unless out-of-state plaintiffs affirmatively consent, the Kansas courts may not exert jurisdiction over their claims. Petitioner claims that failure to execute and return the "request for exclusion" provided with the class notice cannot constitute consent of the out-of-state plaintiffs; thus Kansas courts may exercise jurisdiction over these plaintiffs only if the plaintiffs possess the sufficient "minimum contacts" with Kansas as that term is used in cases involving personal jurisdiction over out-of-state defendants. * * * Since Kansas had no prelitigation contact with many of the plaintiffs and leases involved, petitioner claims that Kansas has exceeded its jurisdictional reach and thereby violated the due process rights of the absent plaintiffs.

In *International Shoe* we were faced with an out-of-state corporation which sought to avoid the exercise of personal jurisdiction over it as a defendant by Washington state court. We held that the extent of the defendant's due process protection would depend "upon the quality and nature of the activity in relation to the fair and orderly administration of the laws * * *." We noted that the Due Process Clause did not permit a State to make a binding judgment against a person with whom the State had no contacts, ties, or relations. * * * If the defendant possessed certain minimum contacts with the State, so that it was "reasonable and just, according to our traditional conception of fair play and substantial justice" for a State to exercise personal jurisdiction, the State could force the defendant to defend himself in the forum, upon pain of default, and could bind him to a judgment. * * *

The purpose of this test, of course, is to protect a defendant from the travail of defending in a distant forum, unless the defendant's contacts with the forum make it just to force him to defend there. As we explained in *Woodson* * * *, the defendant's contacts should be such that "he should reasonably anticipate being haled" into the forum. * * * In Insurance Corp. of Ireland v. Compagnie des Bauxites de Guinee, * * * we explained that the requirement that a court have personal jurisdiction comes from the Due Process Clause's protection of the defendant's personal liberty interest, and said that the requirement "represents a restriction on judicial power not as a matter of sovereignty, but as a matter of individual liberty." * * *

Although the cases like *Shaffer* and *Woodson* which petitioner relies on for a minimum contacts requirement all dealt with out-of-state defendants or parties in the procedural posture of a defendant, * * * petitioner claims that the same analysis must apply to absent class-action plaintiffs. In this regard petitioner correctly points out that a chose in action is a constitutionally recognized property interest possessed by each of the plaintiffs. * * * An adverse judgment by Kansas courts in this case may extinguish the chose in action forever through res judicata. Such an adverse judgment, petitioner claims, would be every bit as onerous to an absent plaintiff as an adverse judgment on the merits would be to a defendant. Thus, the same due process protections should apply to absent plaintiffs: Kansas should not be able to exert jurisdiction over the plaintiffs' claims unless the plaintiffs have sufficient minimum contacts with Kansas.

We think petitioner's premise is in error. The burdens placed by a State upon an absent class-action plaintiff are not of the same order or magnitude as those it places upon an absent defendant. An out-of-state defendant summoned by a plaintiff is faced with the full powers of the forum State to render judgment *against* it. The defendant must generally hire counsel and travel to the forum to defend itself from the plaintiff's claim, or suffer a default judgment. The defendant may be forced to participate in extended and often costly discovery, and will be forced to respond in damages or to comply with some other form of remedy imposed by the court should it lose the suit. The defendant may also face liability for court costs and attorney's fees. These burdens are substantial, and the minimum contacts requirement of the Due Process Clause prevents the forum State from unfairly imposing them upon the defendant.

A class-action plaintiff, however, is in quite a different posture. The Court noted this difference in Hansberry v. Lee * * *, which explained that a "class" or "representative" suit was an exception to the rule that one could not be bound by judgment *in personam* unless one was made fully a party in the traditional sense. * * * As the Court pointed out in *Hansberry,* the class action was an invention of equity to enable it to proceed to a decree in suits where the number of those interested in the litigation was too great to permit joinder. The absent parties would be bound by the decree so long as the named parties adequately represented the absent class and the prosecution of the litigation was within the common interest. * * *

Modern plaintiff class actions follow the same goals, permitting litigation of a suit involving common questions when there are too many plaintiffs for proper joinder. Class actions also may permit the plaintiffs to pool claims which would be uneconomical to litigate individually. For example, this lawsuit involves claims averaging about $100 per plaintiff; most of the plaintiffs would have no realistic day in court if a class action were not available.

In sharp contrast to the predicament of a defendant haled into an out-of-state forum, the plaintiffs in this suit were not haled anywhere to defend themselves upon pain of a default judgment. As commentators have noted, from the plaintiffs' point of view a class action resembles a "quasi-administrative proceeding, conducted by the judge." * * *

A plaintiff class in Kansas and numerous other jurisdictions cannot first be certified unless the judge, with the aid of the named plaintiffs and defendant, conducts an inquiry into the common nature of the named plaintiffs' and the absent plaintiffs' claims, the adequacy of representation, the jurisdiction possessed over the class, and any other matters that will bear upon proper representation of the absent plaintiffs' interest. * * * Unlike a defendant in a civil suit, a class-action plaintiff is not required to fend for himself. * * * The court and named plaintiffs protect his interests. Indeed, the class-action defendant itself has a great interest in ensuring that the absent plaintiffs' claims are properly before the forum. In this case, for example, the defendant sought to avoid class certification by alleging that the absent plaintiffs would not be adequately represented and were not amenable to jurisdiction. * * *

The concern of the typical class-action rules for the absent plaintiffs is manifested in other ways. Most jurisdictions, including Kansas, require that a class action, once certified, may not be dismissed or compromised without the approval of the court. In many jurisdictions such as Kansas the court may amend the pleadings to ensure that all sections of the class are represented adequately. * * *

Besides this continuing solicitude for their rights, absent plaintiff class members are not subject to other burdens imposed upon defendants. They need not hire counsel or appear. They are almost never subject to counterclaims or cross-claims, or liability for fees or costs. Absent plaintiff class members are not subject to coercive or punitive remedies. Nor will an adverse judgment typically bind an absent plaintiff for any damages, although a valid adverse judgment may extinguish any of the plaintiff's claim which was litigated.

Unlike a defendant in a normal civil suit, an absent class-action plaintiff is not required to do anything. He may sit back and allow the litigation to run its course, content in knowing that there are safeguards provided for his protection. In most class actions an absent plaintiff is provided at least with an opportunity to "opt out" of the class, and if he takes advantage of that opportunity he is removed from the litigation entirely. This was true of the Kansas proceedings in this case. The Kansas procedure provided for the mailing of a notice to each class member by first-class mail. The notice, as we have previously indicated, described the action and informed the class member that he could appear in person or by counsel, in default of which he would be represented by the named plaintiffs and their attorneys. The notice further stated that class members would be included in the class and bound by the judgment unless they "opted out" by executing and returning a "request for exclusion" that was included in the notice.

Petitioner contends, however, that the "opt out" procedure provided by Kansas is not good enough, and that an "opt in" procedure is required to satisfy the Due Process Clause of the Fourteenth Amendment. Insofar as plaintiffs who have no minimum contacts with the forum State are concerned, an "opt in" provision would require that each class member affirmatively consent to his inclusion within the class.

Because States place fewer burdens upon absent class plaintiffs than they do upon absent defendants in nonclass suits, the Due Process Clause need not and does not afford the former as much protection from state-court jurisdiction as it does the latter. The Fourteenth Amendment does protect "persons," not "defendants," however, so absent plaintiffs as well as absent defendants are entitled to some protection from the jurisdiction of a forum State which seeks to adjudicate their claims. In this case we hold that a forum State may exercise jurisdiction over the claim of an absent class-action plaintiff, even though that plaintiff may not possess the minimum contacts with the forum which would support personal jurisdiction over a defendant. If the forum State wishes to bind an absent plaintiff concerning a claim for money damages or similar relief at law,[3] it must provide minimal procedural due process protection. The plaintiff must receive notice plus an opportunity to be heard and participate in the litigation, whether in person or through counsel. The notice must be the best practicable, "reasonably calculated, under all the circumstances, to apprise interested parties of the pendency of the action and afford them an opportunity to present their objections." * * * The notice should describe the action and the plaintiffs' rights in it. Additionally, we hold that due process requires at a minimum that an absent plaintiff be provided with an opportunity to remove himself from the class by executing and returning an "opt out" or "request for exclusion" form to the court. Finally, the Due Process Clause of course requires that the named plaintiff at all times adequately represent the interests of the absent class members. * * *

We reject petitioner's contention that the Due Process Clause of the Fourteenth Amendment requires that absent plaintiffs affirmatively "opt in" to the class, rather than be deemed members of the class if they do not "opt out." We think that such a contention is supported by little, if any, precedent, and that it ignores the differences between class action plaintiffs, on the one hand, and defendants in non-class civil suits on the other. Any plaintiff may consent to jurisdiction. * * * The essential question, then, is how stringent the requirement for a showing of consent will be.

We think that the procedure followed by Kansas, where a fully descriptive notice is sent first-class mail to each class member, with an explanation of the right to "opt out," satisfies due process. Requiring a plaintiff to affirmatively request inclusion would probably impede the prosecution of those class actions involving an aggregation of small

3. Our holding today is limited to those class actions which seek to bind known plaintiffs concerning claims wholly or predominately for money judgments. We intimate no view concerning other types of class action lawsuits, such as those seeking equitable relief. Nor, of course, does our discussion of personal jurisdiction address class actions where the jurisdiction is asserted against a *defendant* class.

individual claims, where a large number of claims are required to make it economical to bring suit. * * * The plaintiff's claim may be so small, or the plaintiff so unfamiliar with the law, that he would not file suit individually, nor would he affirmatively request inclusion in the class if such a request were required by the Constitution. If, on the other hand, the plaintiff's claim is sufficiently large or important that he wishes to litigate it on his own, he will likely have retained an attorney or have thought about filing suit, and should be fully capable of exercising his right to "opt out."

In this case over 3,400 members of the potential class did "opt out," which belies the contention that "opt out" procedures result in guaranteed jurisdiction by inertia. Another 1,500 were excluded because the notice and "opt out" form was undeliverable. We think that such results show that the "opt out" procedure provided by Kansas is by no means *pro forma,* and that the Constitution does not require more to protect what must be the somewhat rare species of class member who is unwilling to execute an "opt out" form, but whose claim is nonetheless so important that he cannot be presumed to consent to being a member of the class by his failure to do so. Petitioner's "opt in" requirement would require the invalidation of scores of state statutes and of the class-action provision of the Federal Rules of Civil Procedure, and for the reasons stated we do not think that the Constitution requires the State to sacrifice the obvious advantages in judicial efficiency resulting from the "opt out" approach for the protection of the *rara avis* portrayed by petitioner.

We therefore hold that the protection afforded the plaintiff class members by the Kansas statute satisfies the Due Process Clause. The interests of the absent plaintiffs are sufficiently protected by the forum State when those plaintiffs are provided with a request for exclusion that can be returned within a reasonable time to the court. * * * Both the Kansas trial court and the Supreme Court of Kansas held that the class received adequate representation, and no party disputes that conclusion here. We conclude that the Kansas court properly asserted personal jurisdiction over the absent plaintiffs and their claims against petitioner.

III

The Kansas courts applied Kansas contract and Kansas equity law to every claim in this case, notwithstanding that over 99% of the gas leases and some 97% of the plaintiffs in the case had no apparent connection to the State of Kansas except for this lawsuit. Petitioner protested that the Kansas courts should apply the laws of the States where the leases were located, or at least apply Texas and Oklahoma law because so many of the leases came from those States. The Kansas courts disregarded this contention and found petitioner liable for interest on the suspended royalties as a matter of Kansas law, and set the interest rates under Kansas equity principles.

Petitioner contends that total application of Kansas substantive law violated the constitutional limitations on choice of law mandated by the Due Process Clause of the Fourteenth Amendment and the Full Faith and Credit Clause of Article IV, § 1. We must first determine whether

Kansas law conflicts in any material way with any other law which could apply. There can be no injury in applying Kansas law if it is not in conflict with that of any other jurisdiction connected to this suit.

Petitioner claims that Kansas law conflicts with that of a number of States connected to this litigation, especially Texas and Oklahoma. These putative conflicts range from the direct to the tangential, and may be addressed by the Supreme Court of Kansas on remand under the correct constitutional standard. * * *

* * *

The conflicts on the applicable interest rates, alone—which we do not think can be labeled "false conflicts" without a more thorough-going treatment than was accorded them by the Supreme Court of Kansas— certainly amounted to millions of dollars in liability. We think that the Supreme Court of Kansas erred in deciding on the basis that it did that the application of its laws to all claims would be constitutional.

Four Terms ago we addressed a similar situation in Allstate Ins. Co. v. Hague * * *. In that case we were confronted with two conflicting rules of state insurance law. Minnesota permitted the "stacking" of separate uninsured motorist policies while Wisconsin did not. Although the decedent lived in Wisconsin, took out insurance policies and was killed there, he was employed in Minnesota and after his death his widow moved to Minnesota for reasons unrelated to the litigation, and was appointed personal representative of his estate. She filed suit in Minnesota courts, which applied the Minnesota stacking rule.

The plurality in *Allstate* noted that a particular set of facts giving rise to litigation could justify, constitutionally, the application of more than one jurisdiction's laws. The plurality recognized, however, that the Due Process Clause and the Full Faith and Credit Clause provided modest restrictions on the application of forum law. These restrictions required "that for a State's substantive law to be selected in a constitutionally permissible manner, that State must have a significant contact or significant aggregation of contacts, creating state interests, such that choice of its law is neither arbitrary nor fundamentally unfair." * * * The dissenting Justices were in substantial agreement with this principle. * * *

The plurality in *Allstate* affirmed the application of Minnesota law because of the forum's significant contacts to the litigation which supported the State's interest in applying its law. * * * Kansas' contacts to this litigation, as explained by the Kansas Supreme Court, can be gleaned from the opinion below.

Petitioner owns property and conducts substantial business in the State, so Kansas certainly has an interest in regulating petitioner's conduct in Kansas. * * * Moreover, oil and gas extraction is an important business to Kansas, and although only a few leases in issue are located in Kansas, hundreds of Kansas plaintiffs were affected by petitioner's suspension of royalties; thus the court held that the State has a real interest in protecting "the rights of these royalty owners both as individual residents of [Kansas] and as members of this particular class of plaintiffs." * * *

* * *

Kansas must have a "significant contact or aggregation of contacts" to the claims asserted by each member of the plaintiff class, contacts "creating state interests" in order to ensure that the choice of Kansas law is not arbitrary or unfair. * * * Given Kansas' lack of "interest" in claims unrelated to that State, and the substantive conflict with jurisdictions such as Texas, we conclude that application of Kansas law to every claim in this case is sufficiently arbitrary and unfair as to exceed constitutional limits.

When considering fairness in this context, an important element is the expectation of the parties. There is no indication that when the leases involving land and royalty owners outside of Kansas were executed, the parties had any idea that Kansas law would control. Neither the Due Process Clause nor the Full Faith and Credit Clause requires Kansas "to substitute for its own [laws], applicable to persons and events within it, the conflicting statute of another state," * * * but Kansas "may not abrogate the rights of parties beyond its borders having no relation to anything done or to be done within them." * * *

Here the Supreme Court of Kansas took the view that in a nationwide class action where procedural due process guarantees of notice and adequate representation were met, "the laws of the forum should be applied unless compelling reasons exist for applying a different law." * * * Whatever practical reasons may have commended this rule to the Supreme Court of Kansas, for the reasons already stated we do not believe that it is consistent with the decisions of this Court. We make no effort to determine for ourselves which law must apply to the various transactions involved in this lawsuit, and we reaffirm our observation in *Allstate* that in many situations a state court may be free to apply one of several choices of law. But the constitutional limitations laid down in cases such as *Allstate* * * * must be respected even in a nationwide class action.

We therefore affirm the judgment of the Supreme Court of Kansas insofar as it upheld the jurisdiction of the Kansas courts over the plaintiff class members in this case, and reverse its judgment insofar as it held that Kansas law was applicable to all of the transactions which it sought to adjudicate. We remand the case to that court for further proceedings not inconsistent with this opinion.

JUSTICE POWELL took no part in the decision of this case.

[JUSTICE STEVENS wrote an opinion concurring in Parts I & II of the Court's opinion and dissenting from Part III.]

Notes and Questions

1. On remand to the Kansas courts after the Supreme Court's decision in *Shutts,* Phillips Petroleum continued to press the argument that the laws of five states (Louisiana, New Mexico, Oklahoma, Texas, and Wyoming) differed in important respects from the law of Kansas—in particular on the issue of

liability for interest on suspended royalties and on the issue of the applicable interest rate where liability is found. These two issues constituted the heart of the legal controversy in the case, and the five identified states embraced 97% of the leases involved. In addressing this argument, the Kansas Supreme Court first analyzed the Supreme Court's decision in *Shutts*:

> * * * As to the choice of law question, however, it was ruled the application of Kansas law to all of the investors' claims for interest violated the due process and full faith and credit clauses. In its analysis, the Court first noted that if the law of Kansas was not in conflict with any of the other jurisdictions connected to the suit, then there would be no injury in applying the law of Kansas. * * * The Court then cited differences in the laws of Kansas, Texas, and Oklahoma which Phillips *contended* existed. It appears, however, no analysis was made by the Court to determine whether these differences existed in fact. * * *

Shutts v. Phillips Petroleum Co., 240 Kan. 764, 767, 732 P.2d 1286, 1291 (1987), certiorari denied ___ U.S. ___, 108 S.Ct. 2883, 101 L.Ed.2d 918 (1988) (emphasis in original). The Kansas court then examined the laws of the five states—only to find that *none* of the five was in conflict with the law of Kansas. It therefore entered a new judgment reflecting no change in the original outcome of the case regarding liability and the applicable prejudgment interest rate.

2. In Shaffer v. Heitner, p. 150, supra, the Supreme Court stated that "all assertions of state-court jurisdiction must be evaluated according to the standards set forth in *International Shoe* and its progeny." Does *Shutts* mean that class plaintiffs are not entitled to this protection? Or is *Shutts* based upon the inference of consent from the class member's failure to opt out of the class? Is this reasoning justified only for plaintiffs with small claims that would not be adjudicated but for the inference of consent through silence? Is the inference of consent equally appropriate when the rights of a large claimant are affected?

3. In formulating the due process requirements, the Court in *Shutts* states that each claimant in a multistate class action "must receive notice." Is the Court imposing a requirement that notice actually be received? Insistence on actual notice would go beyond due process requirements for defendants, who can be held to a judgment in a case initiated upon notice "reasonably calculated" to reach them, even if it is never received.

4. Before *Shutts,* not every class action was subject to notice and opt-out requirements. Rule 23 imposes these requirements only in (b)(3) class actions. Does the concept, articulated in *Shutts,* that the right to opt out is a fundamental due process requirement mean that there is a right to opt out of class suits brought as (b)(1) or (b)(2) class actions?

5. See generally Miller & Crump, *Jurisdiction and Choice of Law in Multistate Class Action After Phillips Petroleum Co. v. Shutts,* 96 Yale L.J. 1 (1986).

3. VENUE

In applying venue rules to class actions, should courts look to the residence of every member of the class, including absent class members? Or should courts look to the residence of the class representatives alone?

Courts have adopted the latter approach, thus making class-action venue rules resemble class-action personal-jurisdiction rules. Only the residences of the class representatives are important for purposes of venue; the residences of absent class members and intervenors are irrelevant. See 7A Wright, Miller & Kane, *Federal Practice and Procedure: Civil 2d* § 1757 (1986).

Chapter 8

PRETRIAL DEVICES FOR OBTAINING INFORMATION: DEPOSITIONS AND DISCOVERY

SECTION A. THE GENERAL SCOPE OF AND DISCRETIONARY LIMITS ON DISCOVERY

1. INTRODUCTION

Read Federal Rules of Civil Procedure 26(a), 26(b), 27(a)(1), and 32(a) and the accompanying materials in the Supplement.

The development of pretrial techniques for obtaining information has roughly paralleled the increasing complexity of litigation. Expansion of discovery also has provided a partial response to the call for new procedures to supplant, or at least augment, the pleadings, which have proven increasingly inadequate as a device for defining for the parties and the court the precise issues in controversy. The roots of discovery are found in early English equity practice, but the evolution of modern procedures did not begin until the merger of law and equity in the nineteenth century and progressed slowly until the adoption of the Federal Rules of Civil Procedure in 1938. Federal Rules 26 through 37, which are the basic discovery provisions, not only authorize the use of all the discovery techniques known at the time the rules were promulgated but also increase greatly the scope of permissible inquiry. So attractive are these provisions that they have been adopted by a large majority of the states, including a number of states that have rejected the federal pleading rules.

Modern discovery has three major purposes. The first, and least controversial, is the preservation of relevant information that might not be available at trial. Basically, this objective relates to the testimony of witnesses who are aged or ill or who will be out of the jurisdiction at the time the trial commences. See Federal Rules 27 and 32(a). The earliest discovery procedures in the federal courts were designed primarily for this

710

purpose. See *Developments in the Law—Discovery,* 74 Harv.L.Rev. 940, 949 (1961).

The second purpose is to <u>ascertain and isolate those issues that</u> <u>actually are in controversy between the parties.</u> There is little dispute that it is appropriate for one party to ask whether another party contests the existence or nonexistence of a fact that the pleadings formally have put in issue. See Federal Rule 36. However, it is not entirely clear precisely how far the discovery devices may be utilized to force a party to set out in detail his factual and legal contentions when the rules of pleading do not require that this be done. <u>The same arguments for and</u> <u>against detailed pleadings as to the law and facts may be made with</u> <u>regard to the appropriate use and scope of discovery.</u> See pp. 712–22, infra.

The final major purpose of discovery is to find out <u>what testimony and</u> <u>other evidence is available on each of the disputed factual issues.</u> Prior to discovery, a party could ascertain these matters only through private investigation; if, for example, a witness refused to discuss a matter with a party, there was no way to learn the substance of that witness' testimony in advance of trial. As a result, cases often turned on the parties' relative access to the facts and their ability to keep certain facts secret until the trial.

To the extent that the person to be questioned is a known eyewitness to the event in controversy, there is little dispute over the propriety of discovery to ascertain what will be said at trial. But the matter is far more complex if a witness, who may be a party or an attorney, obtains evidence during the investigation of the case in preparation for trial. In this context there is a sharp division between those who favor broad discovery to obviate all traces of surprise and those who allege the need for privacy of investigation and development of evidence. Under one thesis it is argued that broad discovery will eliminate the advantage that a wealthy party enjoys over a poorer opponent, whereas others claim that such discovery will induce a lazy litigant to sit back while the opposing party investigates diligently and then, by simple use of discovery, to obtain all the fruits of that investigation.

The argument rages not only as to which witnesses may be questioned before trial, but what questions may be asked. For example, should a witness be interrogated not only as to what she would be permitted to say at trial but also as to other matters such as rumors and the like, which, although inadmissible in themselves, might lead to admissible evidence? In connection with this question, read the language of Federal Rule 26(b) (1) carefully and compare it with the rules for discovery set out in Kelly v. Nationwide Mut. Ins. Co., the case following this Note.

Even if widespread discovery is assumed to be beneficial, however, a question still remains regarding the extent to which its benefits outweigh <u>the increased expenditure of time and money that results from its use.</u> Some discovery devices generally cost very little, but they are the least likely to produce highly significant information. On the other hand, those devices that are most apt to produce substantial results are costly since they require the participation and close supervision of the attorneys. Furthermore, all of the devices are susceptible of abuse, particularly by a wealthy litigant who may engage a less affluent opponent in so much discovery that it becomes cheaper to concede the case. The typical discovery system contains a number of provisions calling for judicial intercession to avoid abuse, but resort to these methods in itself involves some cost; moreover, the results of judicial involvement are not always satisfactory, since judges are reluctant to find that discovery that would be considered appropriate if both parties were of equal financial strength is somehow improper if one of the parties has more limited resources than the other. Yet, if firm control cannot effectively be exercised, discovery ceases to be a means of promoting justice and becomes a tactical weapon for harassment. Because of the imperfections in discovery, many people believe that the scope of discovery should be curtailed at the outset to eliminate the opportunities for abuse, even though this might result in the loss of substantial benefits. In reading the materials that follow, keep in mind the outlines of the philosophical dispute over the proper scope of discovery.

2. THE SCOPE OF DISCOVERY

KELLY v. NATIONWIDE MUT. INS. CO.

Ohio Court of Common Pleas, Ashtabula County, 1963.
23 Ohio Op.2d 29, 188 N.E.2d 445.

PONTIUS, JUDGE. Plaintiff sued to recover damages to a motor vehicle under the terms of a comprehensive insurance policy, claiming that the damages arose because someone put sugar in the fuel tank of plaintiff's truck "during the latter part of April, 1961." The defendant denies that such an insurance policy was in effect on April 19, 1961 and otherwise its answer amounts to a general denial. To defendant's answer was attached a list of forty-two interrogatories directed to plaintiff. Plaintiff answered the interrogatories but defendant moved to require more complete answers by plaintiff.

The issue presented by defendant's motion brings into question the proper use by a defendant of interrogatories under R.C. § 2309.43, which reads as follows:

> A party may annex to his pleading, other than a demurrer, interrogatories pertinent to the issue made in the pleadings, which interrogatories, if not demurred to, shall be plainly and fully answered under oath by the party to whom they are propounded, or if such party is a corporation, by the president, secretary, or other officer thereof, as the party propounding requires.

Although the old Common Law Bill in Equity for discovery has been largely supplanted in Ohio by this code section as well as R.C. § 2317.07, the question still remains as to whether some of the equitable principles are still in force. * * *

Defendant's answer sets up no affirmative defense. The defendant therefore has assumed no burden of proof. The issue at first instance, at least, would seem to be narrowed to the question, may a defendant who has pleaded only a general denial attach to his answer and have answered by the plaintiff interrogatories which only pry into the evidence by which the plaintiff may sustain his own case, as distinguished from inquiring for ultimate facts within plaintiff's own knowledge which may be pertinent to the issue. In other words, does the plaintiff have to reveal to the defendant in advance of trial evidence which plaintiff hopes to establish in support of his own case?

In some of the older cases in Ohio, trying to interpret this section (R.C. § 2309.43) there seems to have been established the principle that the general purpose of the discovery procedure was to aid a plaintiff in *establishing his case* or a defendant to *establish his defense.* * * * The proper use of interrogatories did not seem to extend to aiding an adversary to destroy his opponent's case. Ward v. Mutual Trucking Company, Ohio Com.Pl., 1 Ohio Supp. 42. In this case Judge Carpenter pointed out that the Ohio statute, which was passed in 1857, was very similar to the English Procedural Act passed in 1854 and quoted with approval at page 44 from the opinion in Whatley v. Crowder, 119 Rep. 645 as follows:

> I think the interrogatories must be confined to matters which might be discovered by a bill of discovery in equity. I adopt the rule in the very terms used by Sir James Wigram (Wigram on Discovery, 261 (2nd Ed.): 'The right of a plaintiff in equity to the benefit of the defendant's oath, is limited to a discovery of such material facts as relate to the plaintiff's case—and does not extend to a discovery of the manner in which the defendant's case is to be established, or to evidence which relates exclusively to his case.' *You may inquire into all that is material to your own case, though it should be in common with that of your adversary; but you may not inquire into what is exclusively his case.* (Italics supplied.)
>
> * * *

Likewise, it has been held that interrogatories are not proper where the information sought is not within the personal knowledge of the other party and is not pertinent to an issue raised by the pleading of the inquirer. * * * It has been held that interrogatories are not proper where the answer calls for mere opinion of the party, * * * nor where the information sought is not within the personal knowledge of the party interrogated. * * *

In more recent cases it has been held that this statute and likewise its counterpart must be liberally construed and that interrogatories are proper if they are designed to seek information *pertinent to the action* as distinguished from being merely *pertinent to an issue* raised by the *pleading of the inquirer.* See Sloan v. S.S. Kresge Company, Ohio Com. Pl., 97 N.E.2d 238; * * * Feinstein v. Cleveland, 67 Ohio Law Abst. 518, "Interrogatories may seek information relevant to any *issue of the action* and to all sides of the case." (Italics supplied.)

Parenthetically, it also may be observed that this same philosophy is to prevail when the information is sought by way of deposition and the inspection and production of documents is sought under R.C. § 2317.32. * * * Many states have liberalized their statutory procedure, pointing toward, if not actually adopting, the very extreme liberal rules of discovery as provided by rules 26 through 37 of the Federal Rules of Civil Procedure. * * *

Certainly the Ohio statute of 1857, regardless of what interpretation may be put upon it, does not go as far nor is it as liberal as the Federal Rules of Practice, at least because two additional factors are present:— one, that the interrogatory must be pertinent to the issue made in the pleadings, and two, if admissible in evidence, the answer may be read by either party. (R.C. § 2309.45).

This Court is inclined to the more liberal and later construction of the Ohio statutes as disclosed by Sloan v. S.S. Kresge, rather than the older rule indicated in such cases as * * * Ward v. Mutual Trucking Company; and this Court holds to the view that interrogatories, whether filed with a pleading under favor of R.C. § 2309.43 or separately under R.C. § 2317.07, are proper when:

    1. Relevant to an *issue in the action* as distinguished from merely being relevant to an *issue in the pleading* of the inquirer,

    2. They do not seek privileged information,

    3. The information sought would also be admissible as evidence in the action.

The rule is limited, however, by the further rule that interrogatories may not seek discovery of the manner whereby the opponent's case is to be established nor evidence which relates exclusively to his case, nor to what his witnesses will testify.

In this Court's opinion, there is a marked distinction between records kept by a party in the regular course of his business operations and those amassed by him only after an incident has arisen out of which his lawsuit or defense arises. The former may be ordered produced, if pertinent to an issue in the action; the latter may not. * * *

With these rules in mind further inquiry directed toward the interrogatories of defendant and answers by plaintiff must be made.

The issue in the case as presented by the petition and the answer as distinguished from issues in only one pleading or the other would seem to be:

    1. Did the plaintiff hold a comprehensive insurance policy issued by the defendant, which policy was in force in the latter part of April, 1961?

    2. Did the policy cover a 1955 White tractor (owned by plaintiff)?

    3. Was sugar placed in the mechanism of this tractor?

    4. Was the tractor damaged thereby and if so, to what extent?

Defendant's interrogatory number 2 calls upon plaintiff to state whether she was the sole proprietor of a trucking business or whether same was a partnership or corporation at the time of plaintiff's claim. This interrogatory has a direct bearing on the question of truck ownership and policy coverage. The plaintiff's answer to the interrogatory is equivocal. The plaintiff therefore will be directed to answer the interrogatory fully and completely, stating whether she owned the business as a sole proprietor or as a member of a partnership and if so, the other members thereof, or whether the business was incorporated.

Interrogatory number 6 calls for plaintiff to state where the truck was at the time the sugar allegedly got into the mechanism of the truck. The answer given is "Don't personally know." Bearing in mind that previous interrogatories and answers thereto reveal the fact that the truck in question was under the care and custody of someone else other than plaintiff, it would seem as though plaintiff's answer to this interrogatory is full and complete. The motion with respect to interrogatory and answer number 6 is therefore overruled.

Interrogatories numbers 10, 12, and 15 through 33 all deal with matters arising at the time of or after plaintiff's alleged claim arose. None deal with information or records maintained in the normal operation of plaintiff's business. On the contrary, they call for information as to the manner in which the plaintiff may attempt to establish her cause of action and do not countenance information presumably within plaintiff's own personal knowledge. They call for information which plaintiff may or may not be able to produce through testimony of witnesses upon trial. In other words, they call for hearsay or mere opinion evidence if plaintiff's answer of "Don't personally know" is true. Certainly upon trial if plaintiff were so inquired of and should so answer the same or similar interrogatories, she could not then be called upon to give her opinion or an answer which was obviously mere hearsay.

The same objection is true with interrogatories 36 and 37 and the answers given thereto; and likewise interrogatories 39 through 42 and Plaintiff's answers thereto. An additional objection to interrogatory number 42 exists, namely, assuming that a record of a test was made, it calls for the furnishing of information solely in support of plaintiff's cause of action and obviously arises after the claim arose and in connection with plaintiff's preparation for presentation of her claim and her lawsuit. This last mentioned objection is likewise true with many of the other interrogatories heretofore above covered.

Defendant's motion therefore will be overruled in all respects except with reference to the answer given by plaintiff to interrogatory number 2, and plaintiff is directed to file a complete answer as above indicated.

* * *

Notes and Questions

1. In 1970, seven years after *Kelly* was decided, Ohio adopted a set of discovery regulations almost identical with the Federal Rules. What purposes are served by extensive discovery under Rule 26 that are not served by the decision in *Kelly*? Are any particular groups of litigants, such as insurance companies or plaintiffs in negligence actions, favored or prejudiced by broad discovery? Note the limitations on the scope of discovery in Rule 26(b). Do they make the Rule too restrictive? In that connection, reconsider Boldt v. Sanders, p. 34, supra, which involved the Minnesota equivalent of Federal Rule 26. Are there certain categories or types of information not expressly mentioned in Rule 26 that should be beyond the scope of discovery or certain

classes of litigation in which discovery should be prohibited or sharply curtailed?

2. One major reason for permitting widespread discovery of the facts before trial is the elimination of surprise. Does full knowledge by one party of all the evidence to be presented by the opposing party lead to a better result at trial, or can justice sometimes be better served if a litigant is surprised by the evidence presented at trial? Compare Hawkins, *Discovery and Rule 34: What's So Wrong About Surprise?*, 39 A.B.A.J. 1075 (1953), with Holtzoff, *The Elimination of Surprise in Federal Practice,* 7 Vand.L.Rev. 576 (1954). Does discovery actually reduce surprise? See Glaser, *Pretrial Discovery and the Adversary Process* 105–09 (1968).

3. In 1977, an American Bar Association committee suggested that the language of Rule 26(b)(1) permitting discovery "relevant to the subject matter involved in the pending action" be altered to permit discovery only of nonprivileged information "relevant to the issues raised by the claims and defenses" of the parties. Report of the Special Committee for the Study of Discovery Abuse, Section on Litigation, American Bar Association, October 1977, p. 3. Would the suggested change have any negative effect? Would the change actually curb excessive discovery? See Brazil, *The Adversary Character of Civil Discovery: A Critique and Proposals for Change,* 31 Vand.L.Rev. 1295, 1332 (1978).

SIMPSON v. TRAUM, 63 A.D.2d 583, 404 N.Y.S.2d 619 (1st Dep't 1978). Petitioner applied for an order for a deposition under New York Civil Practice Law and Rules § 3102(c), providing that pre-suit "disclosure to aid in bringing an action, to preserve information or to aid in arbitration, may be obtained, but only by court order." The trial judge granted the application, but the appellate court reversed, stating:

Pre-action disclosure under CPLR 3102(c) is not available to determine if a cause of action exists. A prima facie cause of action must be demonstrated * * *. An examination to frame a complaint will not be permitted where what is sought is to ascertain or determine whether facts supporting a cause of action exist * * *, nor where petitioner "possesses sufficient information to frame a complaint without the examination which is sought" (New Rochelle Precision Grinding Corp. v. Marino, 9 A.D.2d 685, 191 N.Y.S.2d 561). Nor is it permitted "to explore the feasibility of framing a complaint" (Cotler v. Retail Credit Co., 18 A.D.2d 898, 237 N.Y.S.2d 781).

Here it is clear [from the affidavits submitted in support of the discovery order] that petitioners have sufficient information to frame a complaint. * * * Moreover, the examination sought here is much broader in scope than the limited deposition contemplated by the statute. What is sought is a full-blown deposition of the type appropriate after commencement of an action. * * *

Notes and Questions

1. Why shouldn't there be a specific provision permitting a prospective plaintiff to discover facts to aid in deciding whether or not a legal action is justified and in ascertaining against whom it should be brought? See general-

ly In re Lewis, 11 N.C.App. 541, 181 S.E.2d 806 (1971); 3 Weinstein, Korn & Miller, *New York Civil Practice* ¶¶ 3102.11–.12.

Does a pre-action discovery provision have any practical effect when given a narrow interpretation, as in the *Simpson* case? Consider KEELY v. PRICE, 27 Cal.App.3d 209, 103 Cal.Rptr. 531 (2d Dist.1972), in which defendant successfully demurred to the complaint on the ground that it failed to state a cause of action. The appellate court upheld the demurrer, but reversed the trial court's denial of leave to amend, ordering that plaintiff be afforded sufficient time and opportunity for discovery to assist in making any amendment. Contra, State v. Braunstein, 66 A.D.2d 885, 411 N.Y.S.2d 673 (2d Dep't 1978).

2. The only Federal Rule permitting pre-action discovery is Rule 27, which provides that a person, with court approval, may take a deposition of himself or any other person for the purpose of perpetuating testimony for a contemplated action that cannot presently be brought. The court must be satisfied that perpetuating the testimony may prevent a failure or delay of justice. It has been held consistently that Rule 27 cannot be used as a means to determine whether a cause of action exists and, if so, against whom it should be brought. See, e.g., In re Boland, 79 F.R.D. 665 (D.D.C.1978). Should the scope of a deposition before action be limited to evidence that would be material and admissible at trial or should its scope be the same as that allowed by Rule 26(b)? See Martin v. Reynolds Metals Corp., 297 F.2d 49 (9th Cir.1961) (court refused to limit discovery to admissible evidence but left open the question whether the full scope of Rule 26(b) applies).

Fed rules only permit pre-action discovery when perpetuating testimony for a contemplated action not to decide if caus of action exists

Rule 27

GRANT v. HUFF, 122 Ga.App. 783, 178 S.E.2d 734 (1970). Plaintiff, in a personal injury case, attempted to discover defendant's ability to pay a possible judgment by asking for information as to defendant's income, ownership of property, and the limits of a liability insurance policy. This inquiry was held improper on the ground that the information would not lead to admissible evidence at trial. In addition plaintiff sought discovery of the names and addresses of those witnesses defendant intended to use at the trial. This too was rejected on the ground that although plaintiff was entitled to discover who the eyewitnesses were, she was not entitled to know which witnesses defendant in fact would call to the stand.

Δ's income & insurance

reasonably calculated to lead to admissible evidence? (I don't think so)

Notes and Questions

1. In what way would the decision in Grant v. Huff have been altered if Georgia had adopted Federal Rule 26(b)(2)? Over the years there has been considerable controversy regarding the discoverability of liability insurance. What are the competing arguments on this question? See the comments of the Advisory Committee on Rule 26(b)(2) set forth in the Supplement. See also the discussion in Cook v. Welty, 253 F.Supp. 875, 877 (D.D.C.1966), in which the court said: "It is not to be doubted that information concerning liability insurance coverage and its extent is conducive to fair negotiations and to just settlements." Is this statement accurate in all contexts? When might the reverse be true? For a general review of the authorities, see 8 Wright & Miller, *Federal Practice and Procedure: Civil* § 2010 (1970).

deep pocket, so look for more than is "just"

2. In RENSHAW v. RAVERT, 82 F.R.D. 361 (E.D.Pa.1979), a suit in which plaintiff sought punitive as well as compensatory damages, the court required defendant to answer an interrogatory seeking information concerning his financial status. Can the decision be distinguished from Grant v. Huff and other cases in which permission to discover defendant's general financial status is refused?

3. In ROY v. MONITOR–PATRIOT CO., 112 N.H. 80, 290 A.2d 207 (1972), plaintiff sued defendant newspaper for libel, due to the publication of an article written by columnist Drew Pearson. Under the applicable law, plaintiff could recover only by proving defendant acted maliciously. Prior to trial, plaintiff was permitted to discover the existence and nature of any agreement by which Pearson had promised to indemnify the paper for defamation actions that might result from publication of his columns. Should the discovery have been allowed? Of what consequence would it be that defendant intended to call Pearson to testify on its behalf? See also Maule Industries, Inc. v. Rountree, 264 So.2d 445 (Fla.App.1972).

4. What reasons justify the decision in Grant v. Huff refusing to permit discovery of the names of witnesses whom defendant intended to call at trial? Would it make a difference if the witnesses were scientific experts hired by defendant to aid in the preparation of the case? See Federal Rule 26(b)(4)(a), which is discussed in detail at pp. 787–91, infra.

LINDBERGER v. GENERAL MOTORS CORP.

United States District Court, Western District of Wisconsin, 1972.
56 F.R.D. 433.

JAMES E. DOYLE, DISTRICT JUDGE. Plaintiff, Gordon C. Lindberger, a citizen of Wisconsin, filed a complaint against the defendants, General Motors Corporation and a division thereof, which are not citizens of Wisconsin. Plaintiff alleges that he suffered personal injuries proximately caused by the negligence of the defendants in manufacturing and designing a front end loader which was sold to the plaintiff's employer.

*   *   *

Attorneys for the defendants have refused to answer interrogatories 23, 25 and 26, which were propounded by the plaintiffs pursuant to Rule 33, Fed.R.Civ.P. Plaintiffs have filed a motion to compel discovery.

Interrogatory 23 requests the defendants to state whether any changes have been made, and if so to describe such changes, subsequent to the date when the loader in question was produced, in either the design of the braking system or in the warning system for brake malfunctions. Interrogatory 25 requests the defendants to state how any such changes affect the utility of the loader. Interrogatory 26 requests the names of persons responsible for such design changes.

*   *   *

[Defendants refused to respond to the questions, arguing that the information sought was "privileged" because evidence of subsequent alterations is inadmissible at trial. The court first held that the term "privilege" in Rule 26(b) embraces only those matters traditionally covered by that term under the law of evidence and thus did not apply to this case.]

The * * * question is whether the subject-matter of the interrogatories falls within the scope of examination permitted under Rule 26(b) * * *. [T]he plaintiff need not, at this stage of the proceedings, establish that the evidence sought would be admissible at trial. * * * It is clear that the information sought in the challenged interrogatories is relevant to the subject-matter of this action. The feasibility of the installation of a better brake system and of more adequate warning systems for brake malfunctions may be significant with respect to * * * [defendants' liability]. Furthermore, the knowledge of the defendants about the adequacy of the design of the loader as well as any information on this subject which may have been passed to the employer of the plaintiff may be relevant on the issues of negligence and contributory negligence.

In conclusion, I find that the defendants' refusal to answer interrogatories 23, 25, and 26, is without justification. Accordingly, on the basis of the entire record herein, it is hereby ordered, pursuant to Rule 37 * * *, that the defendants answer interrogatories 23, 25 and 26, within 30 days from the date of entry of this order.

Note

Claims as to what is or is not "relevant" within the meaning of Federal Rule 26(b) and its state counterparts have been as varied as the imaginations of the attorneys who practice under these rules. Consider the propriety of the following decisions:

(a) **CORNET STORES v. SUPERIOR COURT**, 108 Ariz. 84, 492 P.2d 1191 (1972). Plaintiff, a former manager of one of defendant's stores, sued for wrongful discharge, alleging that under his contract he could be fired only for misconduct, but that in fact he was fired because the contract called for higher pay than that received by the other managers. Plaintiff sought to discover the amount of pay that the other managers received. Defendant, who wished to keep its employee contracts confidential, objected that the inquiry was irrelevant since defendant was willing to stipulate that plaintiff had been the highest paid manager in its system. The court upheld discovery, stating:

> We think, however, that a party to litigation has the right to prove its case in the fashion it deems most satisfactory and may not be compelled by the court to accept an offer to stipulate, the effect of which may not have the same impact upon a jury as the evidence which establishes the fact.

(b) **MUTUAL OF OMAHA INS. CO. v. GARRIGAN**, 31 Ohio Misc. 1, 285 N.E.2d 395 (C.P.1971). Plaintiff insurance company brought an action against the widow of its insured, asking for a declaration that the insured's death by carbon monoxide poisoning had not been accidental and hence was not covered by the policy. The company sought to discover the corpse, which would have required disinterment. The court refused, stating:

> While liberal discovery rules are to be encouraged and are generally accepted, it's questionable that they should be used to override the long standing common law and statutory limitations on disinterment. Historically, disinterment has been ordered in only rare instances and then only

after the insurance company has presented evidence to show it is "reasonably certain that an examination may reveal something that will show fraud or mistake * * *." It is the opinion of this court that the plaintiffs have failed to meet that burden of proof. * * * Absent express statutory authorization, this court is not willing to extend the liberal discovery rules of Ohio into the grave.

(c) WILLIAMS v. THOMAS JEFFERSON UNIVERSITY, 343 F.Supp. 1131 (E.D.Pa.1972). Plaintiff, in a medical malpractice action involving abortion, sought to discover the names of women who had previously had abortions at defendant hospital. The stated purpose was to gather evidence to impeach testimony expected to be given by defendant doctor. Discovery was denied. The court said:

> * * * In the abstract, abortion is discussed openly and with fervor. Nevertheless, it is an extremely personal thing to each woman who has had an abortion. The consequences of allowing revelation and examination when considered in terms of family relationships and individual friendships could be disastrous to the subjects of an inquiry of the type plaintiff wants to make. A collateral attack for impeachment purposes does not weigh very heavily in a balancing of interests when opposed to such obvious reasons for privacy.

ZINSKY v. NEW YORK CENT. R. CO., 36 F.R.D. 680 (N.D.Ohio 1964). Plaintiff brought suit under the Federal Employers' Liability Act, alleging that his duties were in furtherance of interstate commerce. Defendant denied all allegations in the complaint. Plaintiff then sent the following interrogatory to defendant:

> At the time of the accident, was the plaintiff engaged in duties which were in furtherance of interstate commerce or which directly and substantially affected interstate commerce?

The court upheld defendant's objection that the question improperly called for "a legal analysis of one of the factual issues" in the case, quoting United States v. Selby, 25 F.R.D. 12, 14 (N.D.Ohio 1960), as follows:

> The assertion and discussion of legal theories, and the classification of facts in support thereof, should be by the lawyers at trial and in whatever pre-trial procedures the court may require.

Notes and Questions

1. The *Zinsky* case was decided prior to the 1970 amendment to Federal Rule 33, which added the second paragraph of Rule 33(b). Read the Advisory Committee's Note on Rule 33(b) in the Supplement. Would *Zinsky* have been decided any differently under the amended rule? Compare JOSEPH v. NORMAN'S HEALTH CLUB, INC., 336 F.Supp. 307, 319 (E.D.Mo.1971), in which the court upheld an interrogatory asking whether one defendant had ever assigned any promissory notes to another. In overruling an objection that the interrogatory called for a legal conclusion, the court held:

> The final sentence of Rule 33(b) added by amendment in 1970 * * * does not authorize interrogatories calling for legal conclusions as such.

* * * [T]he only kind of interrogatory that is objectionable without more as a legal conclusion is one that extends to "legal issues unrelated to the facts of the case."

What is a legal conclusion unrelated to the facts of the case? Does it encompass the cases upon which a party intends to rely? See Fishermen & Merchants Bank v. Burin, 11 F.R.D. 142 (S.D.Cal.1951). Consider ROGERS v. TRI–STATE MATERIALS CORP., 51 F.R.D. 234, 246 (N.D.W.Va.1970), in which defendant sought to discover any "presumption of law or fact" upon which plaintiff intended to rely. The court upheld the interrogatory as follows:

> Plaintiff may not be schooled on the meaning of the term "res ipsa loquitur" but counsel, largely responsible for preparation of answers to interrogatories, will be able to explain that a state of facts may speak for itself under certain circumstances.

Compare Estate of May v. Zorman, 5 Wash.App. 368, 487 P.2d 270 (1971) (defendants held not required to answer questions asking whether their conduct was negligent).

2. The 1970 amendments also added a provision to Federal Rule 36(a) extending the scope of requests to admit to matters "that relate to statements or opinions of fact or of the application of law to fact." See the Advisory Committee's Note on Rule 36 in the Supplement. Why should the changes as to conclusions appear only in Rules 33 and 36 and not in Rule 26(b)?

3. To what extent should a party's ability to discover the contentions of an adversary be affected by federal decisions upholding as a sufficient pleading under Rule 8 any statement that possibly can be read to state a valid claim for relief or a defense? See pp. 477–82, supra. For example, in a negligence case in which only general allegations of negligence have been made, is it proper to inquire as to the specific acts or omissions upon which the allegations are based? An inquiry of this type was upheld in Brandenberg v. El Al Israel Airlines, 79 F.R.D. 543 (S.D.N.Y.1978).

4. For an interesting discussion of the use of discovery to ascertain an adverse party's contentions, see James, *The Revival of Bills of Particulars Under the Federal Rules*, 71 Harv.L.Rev. 1473, 1481–83 (1958). As the author states:

> The real objection to requiring detailed statements of contentions is that they tie a party down in such a way that he may be deprived of his substantive rights. This is so because even astute counsel are unable always to forecast the vicissitudes of litigation. Time and again some evidence, or some combination of evidence, will emerge for the first time on trial, or will be perceived in its full significance for the first time on trial by the party concerned, or by the tribunal.
>
> * * *
>
> Administrative efficiency will, to be sure, be promoted by the narrowing of issues, at least if they stay narrow. * * * If, however, the pleader has failed to specify some particular contention which would have been within the compass of a generalized pleading and which finds unexpected support or appreciation at trial, then the court is frequently put in a dilemma: It must either refuse to decide the case on the true

facts and applicable law, or it must disrupt administrative efficiency to allow a continuance. Either resolution of the dilemma represents an evil.

How does the duty to update discovery under Federal Rule 26(e) affect the argument that a party may be too closely bound by his responses?

3. DISCRETIONARY LIMITS ON THE SCOPE OF DISCOVERY

———

Read Federal Rule of Civil Procedure 26(c), (d) and the accompanying material in the Supplement.

———

MARRESE v. AMERICAN ACADEMY OF ORTHOPAEDIC SURGEONS

United States Court of Appeals, Seventh Circuit, 1984 (en banc).
726 F.2d 1150, reversed on other grounds 470 U.S. 373, 105 S.Ct. 1327, 84
L.Ed.2d 274 (1985).

[Two orthopaedic surgeons initially sued in state court alleging that they were refused membership in the Academy without a hearing. Although membership in the Academy is not necessary to practice as an orthopaedic surgeon, it was alleged to confer some degree of professional advantage. Finding membership in the Academy was not an "economic necessity," the state court dismissed the complaint on the ground that no valid state law claim was stated. Plaintiffs then sued in federal court, alleging violations of the antitrust laws. In the course of discovery, plaintiffs demanded production by the Academy of correspondence and other documents relating to denials of membership applications between 1970 and 1980. The court ordered the Academy to produce the documents pursuant to an order protecting their confidentiality. The Academy refused to comply with the order, and was held in criminal contempt and fined $10,000. It appealed.]

POSNER, CIRCUIT JUDGE.

* * *

A motion under Rule 26(c) to limit discovery requires the district judge to compare the hardship to the party against whom discovery is sought, if discovery is allowed, with the hardship to the party seeking discovery if discovery is denied. He must consider the nature of the hardship as well as its magnitude and thus give more weight to interests that have a distinctively social value than to purely private interests; and he must consider the possibility of reconciling the competing interests through a carefully crafted protective order. He must go through the same analysis under Rule 26(d) except that an order merely postponing a particular discovery request obviously should be granted more freely than one denying the request altogether.

* * *

* * * [T]here is in this case, if not a First Amendment right, at least a First Amendment interest, which the discovery sought by the plaintiffs would impair and which differentiates this case from the usual antitrust case, where discovery is sought of invoices or salesmen's reports or the minutes of a board of directors' meeting. * * *

* * * [O]ne does not have to be a student of Aristotle and de Tocqueville to know that voluntary associations are important to many people, Americans in particular, and that voluntary professional associations are important to American professionals (the premise of the plaintiffs' antitrust suit, as it was of their Illinois suits). Since an association would not be genuinely voluntary if the members were not allowed to consider applications for new members in confidence, the involuntary disclosure of deliberations on membership applications cannot but undermine the voluntary character of an association and therefore harm worthy interests, whether or not those interests derive any additional dignity from the First Amendment. The threat to such interests is more than speculative in this case. Dr. Marrese's counsel said at the rehearing en banc that he wants to use the membership files as a source of names of Academy members to depose in an effort to find out the motives behind their opposition to his client's application. It is hard to believe that after members of the Academy find themselves deposed for this purpose they will still be willing to offer candid evaluations of prospective members.

The other side of the coin is that barring the plaintiffs or their counsel from all access to the membership files would probably make it impossible for them to prove their antitrust case. But there were various devices that the district judge could have used to reconcile the parties' competing needs. For example, he could have examined the membership files himself *in camera,* a procedure described by the Supreme Court in a related context as "a relatively costless and eminently worthwhile method to insure that the balance between petitioners' claims of irrelevance and privilege and plaintiffs' asserted need for the documents is correctly struck." Kerr v. United States District Court, 426 U.S. 394, 405, 96 S.Ct. 2119, 2125, 48 L.Ed.2d 725 (1976). We are told the membership files may be voluminous. No doubt the files in *all* cases between 1970 and 1980 where applications for membership in the Academy were refused are voluminous, but the place to start an *in camera* examination would be with the files on Drs. Marrese and Treister. If the judge found no evidence in those files of any anticompetitive purpose attributable to the Academy, he would not have to look at any other files. This is not a class action; the plaintiffs are not suing as the representatives of other orthopaedic surgeons who have been denied membership in the Academy.

Better yet, the judge might have followed the procedure discussed in this court's recent decision in EEOC v. University of Notre Dame Du Lac, 715 F.2d 331, 338–39 (7th Cir.1983). There we ordered the files of faculty tenure deliberations edited ("redacted") to remove the names of the deliberating faculty members and any other information that might enable them to be identified, and we directed that on remand the redaction be reviewed *in camera* by the district judge, who would have the originals before him to compare with (and thereby assure the accuracy of) the redactions. Had the same procedure been followed here, the plaintiffs' counsel would have been able to read the files personally. If the files had turned out to contain evidence or leads to evidence of anticompetitive conduct, the plaintiffs' counsel could then have requested the judge to order names revealed to counsel so that the relevant individuals could be deposed. We do not think that only universities should be entitled to such consideration.

The protective order that the judge did enter ("which draws on each party's submission but parallels neither," in his words) was not well designed to protect the privacy of the Academy's members. It not only allowed the plaintiffs themselves—two disappointed applicants for membership—to read the files on their own applications; it allowed the plaintiffs' counsel "to discuss with plaintiffs the general contents" of all of the other files and to depose anyone whose name they found in the files. The order was not calculated to allay the Academy's justifiable anxiety for the confidentiality of its membership deliberations.

Rule 26(d) (control of the sequence and timing of discovery) provided another method of accommodating the competing interests here with minimal damage to either. If there is other discovery that a plaintiff must complete in order to be able to resist a motion by the defendant for summary judgment, and thus a significant probability that his case will fail regardless of what the internal files he is seeking may show, the district judge has the power under Rule 26(d) to require the plaintiff to complete the other, nonsensitive discovery first. See Wright & Miller, *Federal Practice and Procedure* §§ 2040, 2047. And in an appropriate case he has the duty. "As a threshold matter, the court should be satisfied that a claim is not frivolous, a pretense for using discovery powers in a fishing expedition. In this case, plaintiff should show that it can establish jury issues on the essential elements of its case not the subject of the contested discovery." Bruno & Stillman, Inc. v. Globe Newspaper Co., 633 F.2d 583, 597 (1st Cir.1980). * * *

Of course, if the plaintiffs do not need anything beyond the contents of the Academy's membership files to prove their case, they cannot be asked to do any other discovery before getting access to the files. At oral argument we asked Dr. Marrese's counsel whether his discovery would be complete after he saw the membership files and followed up any leads the files contained. He answered that at that point he would file a motion for summary judgment arguing that the Academy had committed a per se violation of the Sherman Act, but that if the motion was denied he would conduct additional discovery, which he admitted would be necessary to prove a Rule of Reason violation. It is unlikely that the district judge would allow him to proceed in so piecemeal a fashion. The judge probably would tell him to complete discovery before moving for summary judgment. See 10 Wright, Miller & Kane, *Federal Practice and Procedure* § 2717 at p. 666 (1983). Assuming discovery would not be at an end when the files were turned over and any leads contained in them were tracked down, Rule 26(d) could have been used to schedule the sensitive discovery last.

We do not hold that all files of all voluntary associations are sacrosanct; we do not even hold that the membership files of an association of medical professionals are sacrosanct. They are discoverable in appropriate circumstances, subject to appropriate safeguards. But we may not ignore as judges what we know as lawyers—that discovery of sensitive documents is sometimes sought not to gather evidence that will help the party seeking discovery to prevail on the merits of his case but to coerce his opponent to settle regardless of the merits rather than have to produce the documents. * * *

* * * There is at least a hint of predatory discovery in this case in the fact that the plaintiffs did not seek access to the federal court system with its liberal discovery rules till after they had lost their state-court suit, and in the determination expressed by Dr. Marrese's counsel to use the Academy's membership files as the basis for deposing the individuals who voted against his client's membership application.

There are so many ways in which Judge Shadur could have prevented the plaintiffs from abusing the discovery process, without denying them any information essential to developing their case, that we are left with the firm conviction that the discovery order he issued, when he issued it, was erroneous. Our conclusion is consistent with the evolving concept of the district judge's managerial responsibility in complex litigation. Although amended Fed.R.Civ.P. 26(b)(1), which expands that responsibility, did not take effect until August 1, 1983, after the discovery order in issue here was issued, the Advisory Committee's Note indicates that the purpose of the amended rule is in part to remind federal district judges of their broad powers—and, we believe, correlative responsibilities—under Rule 26.

* * *

HARLINGTON WOOD, JR., CIRCUIT JUDGE, with whom CUMMINGS, CHIEF JUDGE, and CUDAHY, CIRCUIT JUDGE, join, dissenting.

* * *

Judge Posner's opinion now finds fault in the district court's failure to incorporate other protective devices for resolving the discovery dispute, such as an in camera inspection of the Academy's files or production of a redacted version of the files. I, too, believe that the trial judge could have improved on his discovery order. First, he could have been well-served by taking a look in camera at the Academy files on plaintiffs to see whether the files contained what plaintiffs claimed to need so badly, and whether the Academy had good reason to fight so desperately to keep the files out of sight.

The Supreme Court has commended an in camera view of documents in a discovery dispute to insure the striking of a proper balance between the interests in confidentiality and disclosure. Kerr v. United States District Court, * * *. Failure to make an in camera inspection, however, is not in itself an abuse of discretion. While the district court did not view the Academy's files, it apparently was aware that the state trial court had conducted an in camera inspection of the files in the earlier state court litigation between the same parties. After viewing the files, the state court ordered production over the Academy's objections. * * * Thus, one judge had viewed these materials and determined that the contents were relevant and disclosure was appropriate. We should not ignore the state court's first-hand determination. Further, the Academy has maintained that an in camera inspection would not improve the discovery order. In the Academy's view, as I understand it, an in camera inspection could lead to a discovery order which, even if including redaction of the files, would be an abuse of discretion at this stage of the litigation.

The propriety of the district court's order to produce the unredacted files also must be considered in light of the surrounding circumstances. In the early stages of this litigation, plaintiffs expressed their willingness to accept a redacted version of the Academy's files, at least as the first phase of discovery. The Academy refused plaintiffs' early offer to enter a redaction agreement, and plaintiffs later rescinded the offer. Both sides submitted proposed protective orders to the district court; apparently neither provided for redaction.

The Academy's participation in later court proceedings suggested its general approval of the protective order as it was developing. However, the Academy meanwhile continued to press its effort to avoid any discovery of its files. At oral argument, counsel for Dr. Treister stated that his client now would accept a redaction order if this would not limit the right to seek sanctions against the Academy. The Academy's position at oral argument was that any disclosure of its files, even after excision of names and other identifying information, would enable plaintiffs to determine the source of comments, thereby chilling participation in the Academy's admissions process. The Academy steadfastly maintained that no modification of the district court's protective order would be acceptable to it, and any forced disclosure of confidential information prior to the establishment of a jury issue on antitrust injury would be an abuse of discretion. Although the Academy's stonewalling now has paid off, I do not find an abuse of discretion in the district court's failure to order redaction under these circumstances.

Judge Posner's opinion suggests that the district court should have used its Rule 26(d) powers to control the sequence of discovery in this case. Discovery usually may proceed in any sequence, but the court upon motion, for the convenience of parties and in the interests of justice, may schedule the order of discovery on different issues. Fed.R.Civ.P. 26(d). Judge Posner's opinion correctly notes that the district court's power to order sequential discovery may rise to a duty in some cases, citing Bruno & Stillman, Inc. v. Globe Newspaper Co., 633 F.2d 583 (1st Cir.1980), a reporter's privilege case. The present case does not begin to fit into the *Bruno & Stillman* mold. The interests in the confidentiality of the Academy's files do not require such delicate treatment as do those involved in the case of a reporter seeking to protect confidential news sources from discovery. The district court considered and rejected the Academy's motion to bifurcate discovery. The court was satisfied that plaintiffs' claim was not frivolous, having withstood a motion to dismiss once, and again upon reconsideration. The Academy's proposal for sequential discovery would have required piecemeal discovery, which the district court found would burden plaintiffs unnecessarily since the Academy's confidentiality interests could be preserved adequately through a protective order. I would hold that the district court did not abuse its discretion by refusing to order sequential discovery.

Judge Posner's opinion discusses the misuse of discovery tools to coerce settlement, and apparently concludes that the district court's discovery order failed to prevent plaintiffs from abusing the discovery process. The opinion finds two "hints" of predatory discovery here: first, that plaintiffs sought access to federal court—and its liberal discovery rules—only after losing in the state court; and further, that plaintiffs planned to use information from the Academy's files as the basis for further discovery. The first hint merely returns us to the res judicata issue in the context of a dual court system. The second hint, plaintiffs' plan to follow up leads found in the files, is one of the conventional purposes of discovery.

Upon questioning at oral argument, counsel for the Academy labeled plaintiffs' suit a "fishing expedition," an attempt to gain access to otherwise unavailable information. Under the circumstances, however, plaintiffs' pursuit of the files and plan to seek further discovery using leads from the files were within the bounds of appropriate discovery. The discovery record in this case evidences not the slightest abuse, harassment, or coercion to pressure a settlement. Judicial concern about discovery abuse is always legitimate, but such arguments are gratuitous in the context of this case. The abuse of discovery here instead is the Academy's obstinate defiance of the trial court, which now is sanctioned by this court.

Although not condemning any one omission as an abuse of discretion, the discovery majority is left with the "firm conviction" that the district court's discovery order was erroneous. I am not. The district court sought and received proposed protective orders from the parties, and mediated negotiations on this issue. Bifurcation of discovery was not mandatory in this case, and the court reasonably provided for the Academy's confidentiality concerns through the protective order. The Academy should not now reap a windfall from reversal of the discovery order because the order did not incorporate certain provisions that the Academy still would refuse to accept. The Academy treated the trial judge's reasonable discovery order with contempt and its contempt should be recognized by this court.

*   *   *

Although the discovery order could have been improved, the district court's fashioning of the terms was not an abuse of discretion under the circumstances of this case. What the merits of this case would have turned out to be, we now will never know; but we must not let a prejudgment on the merits cloud our review of the discovery order. Plaintiffs * * * deserve the opportunity within reasonable limits to develop their case, and then the opportunity to try it before a judge and jury. I would affirm the district court's contempt holding, but on remand I would direct the court to view the Academy's files in camera and to

consider possible redaction before actually enforcing the discovery order.
* * *

Notes and Questions

1. As noted in the *Marrese* decision, Rule 26(b)(1) was amended in 1983 to add a sentence that directs the district courts to restrict discovery in certain circumstances. In addition, Rule 26(a) was amended at the same time to delete the last sentence, which stated that "the frequency of use" of the various discovery devices was not to be limited unless the court ordered otherwise under Rule 26(c).

2. The discovery rules originally were designed to operate with minimal judicial supervision, but Rule 26 as amended in 1983 "contemplates greater judicial involvement in the discovery process and thus acknowledges the reality that it cannot always operate on a self-regulating basis." Advisory Committee Note, 97 F.R.D. 165, 218 (1983). As you review the material in this chapter, consider how much judicial supervision is likely to be required to make the discovery rule work.

3. * * * [The] list of circumstances [in amended Rule 26(b)(1)] invokes cost-benefit principles which contemplate both achieving an optimal level of discovery beyond which additional discovery would not be cost-effective and restricting discovery when the dollar amount or values at stake are low. * * *

A potential difficulty with this approach is in finding principled criteria for differentiating between various types of cases. What values should be used in deciding whether, for example, the plaintiff in a $10,000 personal injury case should be limited in the number of depositions he may take, or the plaintiff seeking reinstatement in an employment discrimination case should be prohibited from discovering documents only tangentially related to the claim, or the defendant in a $10,000,000 product liability case should be allowed to require answers to voluminous interrogatories involving the most searching details of the plaintiff's past life? Where, one may ask, are judges expected to find the criteria and analytical structure for making such judgments?

Sherman & Kinnard, *Federal Court Discovery in the 80's—Making the Rules Work,* 95 F.R.D. 245, 276 (1983).

4. What weight should a court give to "limitations on the parties' resources" in setting limits on discovery? Is a discovery request that otherwise would be barred as disproportionate to the needs of a case permissible simply because the party from which the discovery is sought has a "deep pocket"? On the other hand, should a relatively wealthy litigant be able to buy additional discovery by offering to pay the expenses of a financially weak litigant? Should relatively wealthy antagonists be permitted to stipulate to unlimited discovery?

5. How amenable should courts now be to motions to limit the number of persons to be deposed if the same information is sought from each? In HOGAN v. ULTRONIC SYSTEMS CORP., 8 Fed.R.Serv.2d 45b.31, Case 1 (S.D.N.Y.1964), the court granted a limiting order with the caveat that if at a later time the examining party could show "some real necessity therefor," additional witnesses could be deposed. Does this approach put too much

emphasis on the first stages of discovery since a court may preclude later discovery because it appears duplicative or burdensome or because it appears that a party already has had ample opportunity to obtain the information?

6. To what extent should the court's assessment of the likelihood of a party prevailing on the merits enter, if at all, into a decision about the scope of discovery? In CABLE ELECTRIC PRODUCTS, INC. v. GENMARK, INC., 586 F.Supp. 1505 (N.D.Cal.1984), vacated on other grounds 770 F.2d 1015 (Fed. Cir.1985), the court granted summary judgment to the defendant in an unfair-competition action brought by the manufacturer of a light-sensitive "night light." It rejected the plaintiff's request that the court not rule on the motion until it had the opportunity to complete discovery concerning actual confusion that may be occurring in the marketplace as a result of alleged similarities in labeling and packaging the products, since the court thought that the probability was "vanishingly small" that the plaintiff could uncover such evidence. Is the decision correct?

SEATTLE TIMES CO. v. RHINEHART

Supreme Court of the United States, 1984.
467 U.S. 20, 104 S.Ct. 2199, 81 L.Ed.2d 17.

[Rhinehart and the Aquarian Foundation, a religious group of which he was spiritual leader, brought an action for defamation and invasion of privacy in a Washington state court against the publishers and authors of several critical articles. Pursuant to state discovery rules modeled on the Federal Rules of Civil Procedure, the trial court issued an order compelling the plaintiffs to identify donors and the amounts each contributed, and to produce a list of the foundation's members. However, the court also issued a protective order prohibiting the defendants from publishing the information or otherwise using it except as necessary to prepare for and try the case. The plaintiffs had submitted affidavits showing that public release of donor and membership lists would adversely affect foundation membership and subject its members to harassment. Both sides appealed and the Washington Supreme Court affirmed both orders. The state Supreme Court held that the protective order served the interest of the judiciary in protecting the integrity of its discovery processes, an interest sufficient to sustain it against the claim that it infringed on First Amendment rights.]

Certiorari to the Supreme Court of Washington.

JUSTICE POWELL delivered the opinion of the Court.

*   *   *

* * * The Washington Civil Rules enable parties to litigation to obtain information "relevant to the subject matter involved" that they believe will be helpful in the preparation and trial of the case. Rule 26, however, must be viewed in its entirety. Liberal discovery is provided for the sole purpose of assisting in the preparation and trial, or the settlement, of litigated disputes. Because of the liberality of pretrial discovery permitted by Rule 26(b)(1), it is necessary for the trial court to have the authority to issue protective orders conferred by Rule 26(c). It is clear from experience that pretrial discovery by depositions and interrogatories has a significant potential for abuse. This abuse is not limited to matters of delay and expense; discovery also may seriously implicate privacy interests of litigants and third parties. The Rules do not distinguish between public and private information. Nor do they apply only to parties to the litigation, as relevant information in the hands of third parties may be subject to discovery.

There is an opportunity, therefore, for litigants to obtain—incidentally or purposefully—information that not only is irrelevant but if publicly released could be damaging to reputation and privacy. The government clearly has a substantial interest in preventing this sort of abuse of its processes. * * * The prevention of the abuse that can attend the coerced production of information under a state's discovery rule is sufficient justification for the authorization of protective orders.[22]

We also find that the provision for protective orders in the Washington rules requires, in itself, no heightened First Amendment scrutiny. To be sure, Rule 26(c) confers broad discretion on the trial court to decide when a protective order is appropriate and what degree of protection is required. The legislature of the State of Washington, following the example of the Congress in its approval of the Federal Rules of Civil Procedure, has determined that such discretion is necessary, and we find no reason to disagree. The trial court is in the best position to weigh fairly the competing needs and interests of parties affected by discovery.[23] The unique character of the discovery process requires that the trial court have substantial latitude to fashion protective orders.

The facts in this case illustrate the concerns that justifiably may prompt a court to issue a protective order. As we have noted, the trial court's order allowing discovery was extremely broad. It compelled respondents—among other things—to identify all persons who had made donations over a five-year period to Rhinehart and the Aquarian Foundation, together with the amounts donated. In effect the order would compel disclosure of membership as well as sources of financial support. The Supreme Court of Washington found that dissemination of this information would "result in annoyance, embarrassment and even oppression." * * * It is sufficient for purposes of our decision that the highest court in the state found no abuse of discretion in the trial court's decision to issue a protective order pursuant to a constitutional state law. We therefore hold that where, as in this case, a protective order is entered on a showing of good cause as required by Rule 26(c), is limited to the context of pretrial civil discovery, and does not restrict the dissemination of the

22. The Supreme Court of Washington properly emphasized the importance of ensuring that potential litigants have unimpeded access to the courts: "[A]s the trial court rightly observed, rather than expose themselves to unwanted publicity, individuals may well forego the pursuit of their just claims. The judicial system will thus have made the utilization of its remedies so onerous that the people will be reluctant or unwilling to use it, resulting in frustration of a right as valuable as that of speech itself." 654 P.2d, at 689. * * *

23. In addition, heightened First Amendment scrutiny of each request for a protective order would necessitate burdensome evidentiary findings and could lead to time-consuming interlocutory appeals, as this case illustrates. * * *

information if gained from other sources, it does not offend the First Amendment.

The judgment accordingly is

Affirmed.

[The concurring opinion of JUSTICE BRENNAN, with whom JUSTICE MARSHALL joined, is omitted.]

Notes and Questions

1. What is "good cause" for a protective order under Rule 26(c)? The courts generally have required the moving party to demonstrate that "disclosure will work a clearly defined and very serious injury." Citicorp v. Interbank Card Ass'n, 478 F.Supp. 756, 765 (S.D.N.Y.1979). The movant must make a showing by "a particular and specific demonstration of fact, as distinguished from stereotyped and conclusory statements." General Dynamics Corp. v. Selb Mfg. Corp., 481 F.2d 1204, 1212 (8th Cir.1973). If the movant sustains its burden, the court then considers the interests of the nonmoving party, of nonparties, and of the public in not restricting disclosure. Does all this suggest that a district judge's decision to grant or deny a protective order is not controlled by legal rules or standards, but is left to the judge's unfettered discretion? Does the degree of discretion left to district judges make the application of the discovery rules unpredictable and uneven? Does it foster discovery disputes, or encourage lawyers to negotiate and settle their disputes?

To what extent is it relevant that a suit is brought chiefly for the purpose of obtaining for public disclosure private information of the defendant? Suppose a third person, desirous of obtaining such private information, finances the plaintiff's suit? *seems like abuse*

2. What standard should a court apply if asked to modify an existing protective order limiting the disclosure of sensitive information? In PALMIERI v. NEW YORK, 779 F.2d 861 (2d Cir.1985), the court sustained a magistrate's refusal to grant the State's Attorney General, in connection with an on-going investigation into possible criminal antitrust violations, access to the settlement agreement in a private antitrust suit and to other documents when the magistrate believed that meaningful discovery would not have occurred and the case would not have been settled absent a provision specifically barring the Attorney General from seeing the documents. The court held that a party seeking to modify the order must show that it was granted improvidently or must demonstrate some extraordinary circumstance or compelling need for disclosure of the information. Is this burden too demanding? Does it contravene the commitment to openness embodied in the discovery rules?

3. It has become commonplace in large cases for parties to stipulate to protective orders negotiated by opposing counsel. And judges generally assent to these agreements, in large part to move cases along and avoid controversy. The stipulations typically provide for "umbrella" protection for confidential information, which is defined as any information that is designated "confidential" by the producing party. As Judge Becker observed in ZENITH RADIO CORP. v. MATSUSHITA ELEC. INDUS. CO., 529 F.Supp. 866, 889 (E.D.Pa.1981): "We are unaware of any case in the past half-dozen

years of even a modicum of complexity where an umbrella protective order has not been agreed to by the parties and approved by the court." The result of such orders is that virtually all nonpublic documents are designated confidential without any individualized review. Why have these orders become so common? What is the strategic significance for a defendant of a confidentiality order? Does disclosure to third persons open the door to misuse of the court system for blackmail or extortion through the threat of suits involving sensitive issues? What does a plaintiff's attorney gain by agreeing to a broad protective order? Are such orders consistent with the Supreme Court's analysis in *Seattle Times*? Or is some degree of judicial review necessary? Should umbrella orders be enforced as written? What standard should a court apply if asked to modify an existing protective order to permit the disclosure of discovered material to non-parties?

4. Review the sample protective order governing discovery and the protection and exchange of confidential information that is reproduced in the Supplement. What problems do the provisions of the order attempt to address? Are the solutions satisfactory? Are there other possibilities that might better protect a company's trade secrets and other confidential information?

5. On protective orders generally, see Marcus, *Myth and Reality in Protective Order Litigation,* 69 Cornell L.Rev. 1 (1983); McLaughlin & Raskin, "Disputed Areas in Discovery: Developments in Protective Orders and Confidentiality," in *Civil Practice and Litigation in Federal and State Courts,* Vol. I, 493 (ALI–ABA, 4th ed. 1987).

SECTION B.   THE MECHANICS OF THE DISCOVERY DEVICES

1. DEPOSITIONS

Study Federal Rules of Civil Procedure 26(d), 30, and 31 in the Supplement.

An oral deposition allows an attorney for a party to question any person, whether a party or not, regarding the subject matter of the case. That person (the "deponent") is placed under oath by an officer who is in charge of the deposition; this can be anyone who is authorized to administer oaths or anyone upon whom the parties agree. Invariably the parties designate as officer the reporter who records the questions, the answers, and any objections made by the parties or by the witness. When the deposition is concluded, the reporter prepares a transcript, which the deponent then is called upon to sign.

Under modern discovery rules, an attorney schedules a deposition merely by serving a notice on the opposing attorney. The notice must include the name and address of the deponent, if known, and the date, time and the place of the deposition. No court order is required except when plaintiff seeks to take a deposition prior to the time when the defendant must file an answer to the plaintiff's complaint. If the deponent is a party, the notice is sufficient to require the party's appearance, and a subpoena is unnecessary. The notice may include a demand that the party produce documents and other items of evidence at the deposition, in which case the procedure of Rule 34 applies (although it is not clear whether the 30-day period of Rule 34 applies to a demand for production under Rule 30(b)(5)).

If the deponent is not a party, the notice of deposition may not be sufficient to compel the non-party's appearance. There is no requirement that a non-party be subpoenaed to a deposition. However, a non-party is not subject to any sanction if he is not subpoenaed and does not appear, or if he appears but fails to bring requested documents or other items. A person who fails to respond to a subpoena will be subject to a citation for contempt of court. In addition, if a party notices a deposition, but does not subpoena the witness, and, if the witness fails to appear, that party may be ordered to pay the reasonable expenses, including attorneys' fees, of any other party for wasting time appearing at the place where the deposition was to be taken. Thus, unless full cooperation of the non-party witness is certain, the use of a subpoena is advisable.

An attorney may notice the deposition of a corporation or association, requiring the latter to produce the person or persons having knowledge of the subject matter upon which the deposition is to be taken. Of course, the party seeking the information must detail the issues that are to be explored in order that the organization can ascertain which of its personnel has the relevant knowledge. This form of corporate depositions is useful particularly when the party taking the deposition is unaware of which individual or individuals within a large organization has the information that is needed.

Most commonly, the details as to a deposition are worked out among all of the attorneys in order to accommodate their schedules and that of the person to be deposed. If the parties cannot agree on the time, place, or details of the examination, then a court order may be obtained with respect to the disputed matters.

The usual expectation is that a deposition will proceed without court involvement. The deponent usually will answer even those questions to which counsel object, unless the deponent's counsel instructs him not to answer. Counsel interpose objections at depositions to preserve their right to object to another party's use of the deposition's transcript at trial. Counsel must object at the deposition if the ground for the objection is one that might be corrected at the time. For example, an attorney who is aware that the deposition officer omitted swearing the witness cannot object at trial, because a timely objection at the deposition would have given the officer the opportunity to correct the oversight.

Depositions are usually conducted in an adversarial but cooperative atmosphere, and thus it is rarely necessary to involve the court. Most litigators take seriously their duty of good faith in participating in the discovery process. The lawyer tempted to disrupt may be deterred by the prospects of reciprocal treatment from opposing counsel and sanctions from the court.

Suplee, *Depositions: Objectives, Strategies, Tactics, Mechanics and Problems*, 2 Rev.Litigation 255, 282 (1982). Still, problems arise, and some attorneys adopt abusive tactics.

Notes and Questions

1. The most important of the discovery devices is the oral deposition. * * * It is the only significant discovery device that may be directed against any person, and is not confined to parties to the action. It is the only discovery device that permits examination and cross-examination of a live witness by counsel, where there is no opportunity to reflect and carefully shape the information given. Thus, despite its expense, it is the most valuable device if the deponent has important information.

Wright, *Federal Courts* §§ 84–85, at 416 (4th ed. 1983).

2. One of the most significant features of federal deposition procedure is that it is designed to function by private arrangement among the parties and without need for judicial intervention. Although the rules as to when, how, before whom, and on what notice as to time and place a deposition may be taken are spelled out in detail (see Federal Rules 28, 30, 31, and 32(d) respectively), Rule 29 permits the parties to stipulate in writing to take a deposition "before any person, at any time or place, upon any notice, and in any manner." Some stipulations have become so commonplace that the reporter at the start of a deposition is likely to ask whether the attorneys agree to "the usual stipulations." A fairly common formulation of the usual stipulations is the following:

> Signing, certification, sealing, and filing are waived; all objections except as to the form of the question are reserved until the time of trial.

Which parts of the deposition rules do the stipulations modify? Should an attorney agree to the usual stipulations? What are the advantages? Disadvantages?

3. Rule 30(c) states that "[e]vidence objected to shall be taken subject to the objections." Is Rule 30(c) necessary to expedite the process of taking depositions? How strictly should it be enforced? Are there circumstances when it is proper for an attorney to instruct a deposition witness to refuse to answer a question notwithstanding the rule? See Eggleston v. Chicago Journeymen Plumbers' Local Union No. 130, 657 F.2d 890 (7th Cir.1981); International Union of Electrical, Radio & Machine Workers v. Westinghouse Elec. Corp., 91 F.R.D. 277 (D.D.C.1981).

4. Misconduct during pretrial depositions includes "speaking objections," namely, objections made in a manner that intentionally or unintentionally instruct the witness as to the answer to be given or desired by the objecting counsel, as well as blatant coaching during private discussions between the witness and his attorney during the deposition. Are these abuses amenable to judicial control? Read Standing Orders 12 and 13 of the Court on Effective Discovery in Civil Cases, United States District Court for the Eastern District of New York, which are reproduced in the Supplement. Are the orders likely to be effective? What tactics might counsel taking the deposition use to prevent or control such abuses?

5. Ever since modern discovery rules first appeared, courts have been faced with the situation in which the parties are vying to take the first

deposition, each attempting to pin down the opponent or the opponent's key witness before submitting himself or his own witnesses to the discovery process. Is there really a substantial advantage to deposing first? Does this advantage exist for an honest party as well as for an unscrupulous party who will deliberately color his testimony? See generally *Developments in the Law—Discovery*, 74 Harv.L.Rev. 940, 954–58 (1961), and review Boldt v. Sanders, p. 34, supra.

Prior to the adoption of Rule 26(d) in 1970, the federal courts generally had held that the party who first served a notice of a deposition was entitled to priority as to that deposition. This is still the situation in many states. See, e.g., N.Y.C.P.L.R. 3106. The problem is complicated by the fact that in most of these jurisdictions plaintiff is prohibited, without leave of court, from serving a notice of deposition for a specific period of time in order to permit defendant to learn of the suit and employ counsel. Cf. Federal Rule 30(a). Leave of court normally has been permitted only under exceptional circumstances. Since there is no comparable restriction on defendant, he will receive priority merely by serving notice during the period plaintiff must wait. Would elimination of plaintiff's waiting period eliminate the priority problem? If one party normally is to have priority if that party wants it, who should it be, plaintiff or defendant? Is there any satisfactory way to solve the priority question?

At the same time that Federal Rule 26(d) was adopted, Rules 30(a) and (b) were altered to include a number of related changes with regard to the timing of depositions. First, plaintiff's waiting period (30 days) was declared to run from the date defendant was served; formerly it ran from the date the complaint was filed with the clerk. Second, two significant qualifications were imposed: (1) the waiting period applies only until defendant formally seeks discovery; (2) if a plaintiff legitimately fears that a deponent is about to depart to a place where he cannot be served with process, plaintiff, upon stating the facts in the notice of deposition, can ignore the waiting period. Insofar as written depositions are concerned, Rule 31(a) has been altered to permit them by any party at any time after commencement of the action.

What evils were these alterations designed to correct? How effective do you think they are? Taken together do they end the priority problem? In its Note to Rule 26(d), the Advisory Committee states that a comprehensive study revealed that in only 16 per cent of the cases do defendants move for discovery within plaintiff's waiting period and that obviously in some of these cases priority is not a motive. Do these figures indicate that the amendments were unnecessary?

For extensive discussions of the priority problem see 8 Wright & Miller, *Federal Practice and Procedure: Civil* §§ 2045–47 (1970); *Developments in the Law—Discovery*, 74 Harv.L.Rev. 940, 954–58 (1961).

6. The practical problems involved in taking and defending depositions are discussed in Suplee, *Depositions: Objectives, Strategies, Tactics, Mechanics and Problems*, 2 Rev.Litigation 255 (1982). Useful sources on the strategic and tactical uses of the discovery devices generally, including depositions, are M. Dombroff, *Discovery* (1966); and R. Haydock, D. Herr & J. Stempel, *Fundamentals of Pretrial Discovery* 120–391 (1985).

Read Federal Rules of Civil Procedure 37(d), and 45(d), (e), and (f) in the Supplement.

———

LESS v. TABER INSTRUMENT CORP.

United States District Court, Western District of New York, 1971.
53 F.R.D. 645.

CURTIN, DISTRICT JUDGE. Teledyne, Inc., a non-party foreign corporation concededly doing business in this judicial district, was properly served by plaintiff with a subpoena commanding it to appear in this district for examination through "Henry E. Singleton, Chairman and Chief Executive Officer and * * * Edmund M. Kaufman, Assistant Secretary." Kaufman is no longer employed by Teledyne, and plaintiff concedes that his presence may not be compelled. Singleton, who is presently Chairman of Teledyne's Board of Directors and based at its Los Angeles, California, headquarters, was not personally served with a subpoena. The questions before the court are whether Singleton, a non-party director of a non-party corporation, may be required to submit to examination and, if so, shall he be so required and under what conditions.

Under the present discovery provisions of the Federal Rules of Civil Procedure, the deposition of a corporate party may be taken from a director named in the notice given to the corporation. The director need not be personally subpoenaed, and the corporation must produce him or risk the imposition of sanctions under Rule 37(d). * * * Teledyne argues that a different rule should apply to the director of a non-party corporation.

*   *   *

The Rules do not suggest that a different principle applies to discovery from a party corporation than applies to discovery from a non-party corporation. Rule 30(a), which governs the taking of depositions upon oral examination, does not distinguish between parties and non-parties; it simply provides that "any party may take the testimony of *any person, including a party,* by deposition upon oral examination." Fed.R.Civ.P. 30(a) (emphasis added). The provision that "[t]he attendance of witnesses may be compelled by subpoena as provided in Rule 45," Fed.R.Civ.P. 30(a), also connotes no operative distinction between parties and non-parties. The provision is merely intended to assure that the non-party whose testimony is sought submits to examination. There is no necessity for requiring service of a subpoena upon a party since adequate sanctions are provided in Rule 37 in the event that the party fails to respond to a notice to take a deposition.

* * * [A] non-party witness, even more than a party, must be protected against undue burden and expense. * * * Therefore, the court does not choose to depart from the ordinary rules that a mere witness will not be required to leave his residence and business and travel great distances for the convenience of the parties * * * and that the deposition of a corporation should be taken at its principal place of business. * * *

It is therefore the order of this court that the deposition upon oral examination of Henry E. Singleton be taken at the principal place of business of Teledyne, Inc. * * *.

Notes and Questions

1. Should the court in the *Less* case have discussed Federal Rule 30(b)(6)? Doesn't that provision clearly provide that a corporation has the right to choose who shall testify on its behalf? Are there reasons why the choice should be left to the corporation? See generally the Advisory Committee's Notes on the 1970 amendments to Rule 30, which appear in the Supplement. Even in the absence of a rule comparable to Rule 30(b)(6) some courts have held that the selection is to be made by the corporation, at least until it becomes apparent that the person chosen does not possess all the relevant facts known to the corporation. E.g., Fernandez v. St. John's Episcopal Hospital, 70 A.D.2d 627, 416 N.Y.S.2d 638 (2d Dep't 1979). Compare Atlantic Cape Fisheries v. Hartford Fire Ins. Co., 509 F.2d 577 (1st Cir.1975), holding that Rule 30(b)(6) does not alter the right of a party who takes the deposition of a corporation that is also a party to designate which officer, managing agent, or director shall appear to answer on behalf of the corporation.

2. The party who gives notice of the taking of a deposition is not required to subpoena even a nonparty witness whose testimony is sought. If no subpoena is issued, however, and the witness fails to attend, Federal Rule 30(g)(2) permits certain sanctions to be imposed upon the party who failed to use a subpoena. What tactical reasons might motivate a party to refrain from serving a subpoena on a witness? Note that under Rule 45(d)(2), if a witness refuses to cooperate, so that she must be subpoenaed, the deposition may have to be held in a district other than the one in which the case has been filed. Suppose the witness disobeys the subpoena. If she appears but refuses to answer questions properly put to her, the parties may seek assistance under Rule 37(a). According to Rule 37(a)(1) application for judicial assistance must be made to the court where the deposition is being held as opposed to the court where the action is filed. What is the purpose of this provision? Note that if the witness is a party, Rule 37(a)(1) permits either the court where the action is pending or the one where the deposition is being taken to issue orders relating to the deposition. Is there any reason for distinguishing between party and nonparty witnesses? See 62 Colum.L.Rev. 187 (1962).

———

CARSON v. BURLINGTON NORTHERN INC., 52 F.R.D. 492 (D.Neb. 1971). Plaintiff was injured when a steel press he was operating came down on his hand, allegedly due to defendant's negligence. Defendant moved to take plaintiff's deposition at the scene of the accident using video tape. Plaintiff objected that this procedure could only produce a staged, unnatural re-creation. The court granted the motion, holding that the 1970 amendment to Federal Rule 30(b)(4) specifically provided for video taping. The court, however, did hold that plaintiff would not be required to touch or operate the press; he only would be required to use a pointer to show the manner in which he operated the machine on the day of the accident.

Notes and Questions

1. Traditionally, depositions have been recorded by stenographic means only. See *Bailey v. Superior Court,* 19 Cal.3d 970, 140 Cal.Rptr. 669, 568 P.2d 394 (1977) (in absence of specific statutory provision or agreement among the parties, videotape recording is prohibited). What are the advantages to be gained from audio and video tape-recorded depositions? See *Lester v. Lester,* 69 Misc.2d 528, 330 N.Y.S.2d 190 (Sup.Ct.1972); Mich.Ct.Rules 2.306(C); 8 Wright & Miller, *Federal Practice and Procedure: Civil* § 2115, at 426 (1970).

2. Does the use of tape-recorded depositions raise any special problems? Who should provide and be in charge of the recording equipment? Is there ever a need for more than one recording machine? See *Colonial Times, Inc. v. Gasch,* 509 F.2d 517 (D.C.Cir.1975); *Champagne v. Hygrade Food Products, Inc.,* 79 F.R.D. 671 (E.D.Wash.1978); *Barham v. IDM Corp.,* 78 F.R.D. 340 (N.D.Ohio 1978).

3. What uses might be made of television during pretrial discovery? Does the availability of this technology solve any of the practical problems associated with discovery? For example, would a videotape of a deposition aid a court in deciding disputes over the propriety of particular questions or the sufficiency of certain answers? For practical suggestions concerning the conduct of videotape depositions, see Balabanian, *Medium v. Tedium: Video Depositions Come of Age,* 7 Litigation 25, 26–27 (1980).

Rule 31 authorizes the taking of depositions upon written questions. In what circumstances might an attorney find a written deposition more useful than an oral one? In what circumstances is a written deposition preferable to Rule 33 interrogatories? See Schmertz, *Written Depositions Under the Federal and State Rules as Cost-Effective Discovery at Home and Abroad,* 16 Vill.L.Rev. 7 (1970).

2. INTERROGATORIES TO PARTIES

Read Federal Rule of Civil Procedure 33 in the Supplement.

Written interrogatories allow one party to send to another a series of questions, to be answered under oath within a specific time. The procedure is extremely simple. No court order is required and no officers need be appointed; the entire exchange is accomplished by mail. If a question is thought to be improper, the responding party may say so rather than answering. The interrogating party then has the option of seeking a court order requiring an answer.

A party has the duty to respond to interrogatories not only on the basis of her own knowledge but also with regard to the knowledge of other persons that reasonably can be obtained through investigation. Thus, a party must consult with her attorney, employees, and other agents who have or might have knowledge.

In addition to the duty to investigate, some jurisdictions require the responding party to state her opinions or contentions as to the facts that are relevant to the subject matter of the action. Under this approach, it would be appropriate to ask a defendant whether he was negligently driving his vehicle at the time of the accident. The defendant would be free to answer the question "No," but he could not refuse to answer on the ground that it was somehow inappropriate.

Special rules have been adopted regarding a party's duty to respond to interrogatories requiring an investigation of its business records. When the answer may be derived from the answering party's business records, and when it would be just as easy for the requesting party to search those records as it would be for the responding party, then the responding party, instead of answering, may specify the records from which the answers may be obtained and give the inquiring party a reasonable opportunity to look at them. This does not mean that the responding party can simply say, "The answer is in our records," and then turn all records over to the inquiring party, knowing full well that the latter never will be able to locate the appropriate documents. The responding party must designate with some specificity just what documents contain the information in order that the inquiring party can find it. Further, if there would be a far greater burden on the inquiring party to ascertain the information than there would be on the responding party, then the latter must ascertain the answer itself.

Interrogatories may not be used to obtain information from a nonparty. Information from a nonparty may be obtained by deposition.

Notes and Questions

1. Since interrogatories can be prepared by an attorney in his own office and at his leisure, thereby avoiding the expense of oral depositions and the time consumed therein, they may be very effectively employed where a thorough-going deposition is not necessary. * * * Illustrative of this type of use is the situation encountered in reference to an attempt to ascertain the names of persons having knowledge of relevant facts concerning the matter in litigation. * * * If the "adverse party" is a partnership, association, or corporation, one single interrogatory directed to the group covers the information in the hands of all members, agents, employees, etc. * * * If such information were sought by depositions * * * this would necessitate the taking of numerous depositions and the costs incurred therewith, with no assurance that all persons who might have knowledge would be questioned.

Feirich & Feirich, *Interrogatories to Parties and Demands to Admit*, 1959 U.Ill.L.F. 733, 734. Did the adoption of Federal Rule 30(b)(6) in 1970 affect the validity of this statement? In what ways are written interrogatories under Rule 33 less effective than an oral examination under Rule 30? See 8 Wright & Miller, *Federal Practice and Procedure: Civil* § 2163 (1970).

2. How extensive should the duty of investigation be under Rule 33(a)? Should a corporate party be charged with the responsibility of finding out what is known by each of its employees regardless of the size and nature of the business? Should the duty extend to information known to employees of

subsidiary corporations that are not parties? See Sol. S. Turnoff Drug Distributors Inc. v. N.V. Nederlandsche Combinatie Voor Chemische Industrie, 55 F.R.D. 347 (E.D.Pa.1972). To what extent should the duty include former employees? See Heng Hsin Co. v. Stern Morgenthau & Co., 20 Fed.R. Serv. 509 (S.D.N.Y.1954).

Should the first sentence of Rule 33 be construed as not requiring an individual party to make an investigation into matters that are outside that party's personal knowledge? See Hickman v. Taylor, p. 766, infra, in which the Supreme Court said that a party cannot refuse to answer interrogatories merely because an attorney, rather than the party, knows the facts. Should the obligation to inquire extend beyond the party's employees and agents, perhaps to a spouse or other members of the party's immediate family?

3. Prior to 1970 Federal Rule 33 only permitted interrogatories to be served on an adverse party. This requirement, which still exists in some states, was a source of confusion and controversy. Some courts held that parties were adverse only if the pleadings formally established an issue between them; others held that an actual conflict of interest was sufficient. See generally Gorman Rupp Industries, Inc. v. Superior Court, 20 Cal.App.3d 28, 97 Cal.Rptr. 377 (2d Dist.1971); 8 Wright & Miller, *Federal Practice and Procedure: Civil* § 2171 (1970).

4. Should Federal Rule 33 be further altered to permit service of interrogatories on nonparty witnesses? See *Developments in the Law— Discovery,* 74 Harv.L.Rev. 940, 1020–22 (1961).

5. Must a party in response to an interrogatory disclose information it has, regardless of its reliability or credibility? In RILEY v. UNITED AIR LINES, INC., 32 F.R.D. 230 (S.D.N.Y.1962), the plaintiff served interrogatories, asking the defendant to state in detail how the accident occurred. In holding insufficient the defendant's response that it had "no knowledge sufficient to answer the interrogatories because all the crew members died in the accident," the court said:

> * * * It is apparent from the opposing affidavit that defendant has already obtained certain information from third persons relating to some of the interrogatories * * *. In this situation, defendant should furnish whatever information it now has, regardless of when or from whom it acquired it. * * *

> Defendant may state in its answers what the source of the information is, if it so desires, [but when] * * * the information has been obtained by persons under defendant's control solely from [questions addressed to] third persons, defendant is not required to admit its accuracy. * * *

Id. at 233. Assuming the information is disclosed, may a party be required to answer a further interrogatory that asks the party's opinion as to whether the information is true or not? See Shapiro, *Some Problems of Discovery in an Adversary System,* 63 Minn.L.Rev. 1055, 1072–77 (1979).

6. One response to abuses of interrogatories is found in Rule 46 of the Local Rules of Civil Procedure of the Southern District of New York, which is reproduced in the Supplement. What assumptions about discovery abuse are

reflected in the local rule's separate treatment of "identification interrogatories," "substantive interrogatories," and "contention interrogatories"?

————

RICH v. MARTIN MARIETTA CORP., 522 F.2d 333, 343–45 (10th Cir. 1975). The plaintiffs sued on behalf of themselves and the class of persons allegedly affected by the defendant's discrimination in promotions at its plant in Colorado. The trial court sustained the defendant's objections to 69 interrogatories that requested statistical information as to the numbers of Blacks, Hispanos, and women hired, fired, promoted, and demoted in each department of the plant, and the work records of the employees in these departments. At the conclusion of the trial, the court dismissed the plaintiffs' action for lack of evidence. The Tenth Circuit reversed the judgment and remanded, in part, because of the trial court's order limiting the scope of discovery:

> It is plain that the scope of discovery through interrogatories and requests for production of documents is limited only by relevance and burdensomeness, and in an [equal employment opportunity] case the discovery scope is extensive. This is a factor which the court should balance on the benefit side as against the burden to the defendant in answering the interrogatories. * * * If the information sought promises to be particularly cogent to the case, the defendant must be required to shoulder the burden. There is a remedy, of course, if the effort fizzles. The costs can finally be assessed to the interrogating parties.
>
> * * *
>
> The plaintiffs' requested information as to hiring, firing, promotion and demotion of blacks, Hispanos and women on a plant-wide basis and within individual departments was relevant in either an individual or class action. Particularly in light of the contention of the defendant and the findings of the court that the circumstantial evidence was ambiguous, it became the more necessary for the plant-wide statistics and facts to be obtained and presented, for they very likely would prove crucial to the establishing or failure to establish a prima facie case.
>
> In Woods v. North American Rockwell Corp., 480 F.2d 644 (10th Cir. 1973), the plaintiff contended that he was given an examination which was irrelevant in relationship to the job he was seeking. The court held that since the plaintiff made no showing that the test itself produced a discriminatory result, plaintiff had failed to establish a prima facie case. The court went on to hold that the plaintiff was required to demonstrate with statistics or otherwise the discriminatory effect of the promotion test. We think it is plain, therefore, that the plaintiffs had a right to the information and statistics from which they could have compiled trends and policies on the numbers of white persons receiving promotions during the relevant time periods in the departments and throughout the plant opposed to the number of blacks, Hispanos and women who received promotions. If it is true that the immediate evidence and circumstances pertaining to the plaintiffs are not sufficient to constitute a prima facie case, plant-wide statistics and department statistics are of the highest relevance.

If the plaintiffs do establish a prima facie case and if the defendant is able to rebut it by showing a business necessity, such information or statistics would also be relevant to an attempt by the plaintiffs to show that the business necessity was pretextual. * * *

Under the facts and circumstances of this case, taking into account that defendant was allowed to defend with plant-wide statistics, the relevance of the information sought by the plaintiffs both in support of their initial case and for the purpose of rebuttal has a high degree of relevance and cannot be ruled out as burdensome. In all likelihood the defendant already has the figures isolated and computed. If not, it ought to proceed forthwith compiling them or at least compiling information from which the plaintiffs can prepare their evidentiary tables or statistics. The fact that they might have been generally invited to peruse the defendant's documents does not fill the bill. Such an approach does not compel the defendant to come forward with everything demanded as does an interrogatory.

Notes and Questions

1. It has been said that a party ordinarily cannot be forced to prepare his opponent's case. See Kainz v. Anheuser-Busch, Inc., 15 F.R.D. 242, 252 (N.D.Ill.1954). Consequently, interrogatories that require a party to make extensive investigations, research, compilation, or evaluation of data for the adversary are in many circumstances improper. E.g., Halder v. International Tel. & Tel. Co., 75 F.R.D. 657 (E.D.N.Y.1977). Yet, it also has been held that the fact that answering interrogatories will require a party to expend considerable time, effort, and expense, or may interfere with its business operations, is not reason enough to disallow them if the information sought is relevant. E.g., Roesberg v. Johns-Manville Corp., 85 F.R.D. 292 (E.D.Pa.1980). How can these positions be reconciled?

2. Federal Rule 33(c) as amended in 1970 addressed the problem of burdensome interrogatories by expressly providing a party the option of producing its business records in lieu of answering. It was adapted from Cal. Code Civ.Proc. § 2030(f)(2), which appears in the Supplement. The Federal Rule differs in that it adds the requirement that "the burden of deriving or ascertaining the answer" must be "substantially the same for the party serving the interrogatory as for the party served." What is the justification for this additional requirement?

An informative discussion of Rule 33(c) is found in IN RE MASTER KEY ANTITRUST LITIGATION, 53 F.R.D. 87 (D.Conn.1971):

> * * * Since a respondent is required to answer proper interrogatories, it is not plausible to assume that a response that an answer may (or may not) be found in its records, accompanied by an offer to permit their inspection is sufficient. This is little more than an offer to play the discredited game of blindman's bluff at the threshold level of discovery. * * *

> I conclude that the option afforded by Rule 33(c) is not a procedural device for avoiding the duty to give information. It does not shift to the interrogating party the obligation to find out *whether* sought after information is ascertainable from the files tendered, but only permits a shift of

the burden to dig it out once the respondents have specified the records from "where the answer" can be derived or ascertained. If the answers lie in the records of the defendants, they should say so; and if, on the other side, they do not, they should say that. * * *

Id. at 90.

3. In 1980, Rule 33(c) was amended to require a party exercising the option to produce its business records to specify the records from which the answer can be found in sufficient detail to permit the interrogating party to locate and to identify them as readily as can the party served. The clarification sought to prevent the party served from directing the interrogating party to a mass of business records or by offering to make all their records available. Just how specific must a party be?

4. Interrogatories have been cited as the most abused of the available discovery devices. In response, many federal district courts have adopted local rules providing that, except on leave of court, no party shall serve on any other party more than a fixed number of interrogatories, often 20. See, e.g., Local Rule 9(g), Northern District of Illinois, adopted June 20, 1975. For an interesting opinion explaining and defending one such rule, see Crown Center Redevelopment Corp. v. Westinghouse Elec. Corp., 82 F.R.D. 108 (W.D.Mo. 1979).

In 1978, the Advisory Committee on Civil Rules considered but rejected a proposal to limit the number of interrogatories, but there is continuing pressure to adopt a numerical limitation on a nationwide basis. Schroeder & Frank, *Discovery Reform: Long Road to Nowheresville,* 68 A.B.A.J. 572, 574 (1982). What are the advantages and disadvantages of such a rule?

3. DISCOVERY AND PRODUCTION OF PROPERTY

———

Read Federal Rules of Civil Procedure 34 and 45(d) in the Supplement.

———

Rule 34 and its state counterparts give a party the right to compel an opponent to produce documents and other tangible things for inspection and copying, and to allow the party entry to land or property in the possession or control of the opponent in order to inspect, measure, survey, photograph, test or sample the property, or to observe an operation taking place on the property. A party wanting to inspect documents and things or to enter property simply serves a notice on the opponent stating what the party wants to see, and when, where, and how the party would like to see it. When first promulgated, Rule 34 required a discovering party to obtain a court order based upon a showing of good cause. That requirement, which proved to be quite costly, was eliminated in 1970, leaving it to the responding party to seek a protective order, if and when discovery is inappropriate. A few states still retain the requirement of an advance court order.

A request must describe the items to be discovered "with reasonable particularity," a flexible standard that varies with circumstances. Most courts allow discovery of general categories of items if the description is easily understood (e.g., all written communications between plaintiff and defendant between July 1 and August 1, 1988). Many attorneys combine Rule 33 interrogatories that ask the opposing party to identify documents with a Rule 34 request that the party produce "all documents identified" in the opposing party's answers to the interrogatories.

A request must specify a reasonable time, place, and manner for the inspection. The time usually is set at least 30 days after service of the request because the opposing party generally has at least 30 days to respond. The place typically designated for production of documents is the office of the requesting party's attorney, unless it is more convenient to examine the documents where they are kept or to have them copied at some other place. The manner depends on the kind of items requested. In practice, attorneys negotiate the time, place, and manner of production.

The party that gets a request serves a written response on the requesting party, as well as any other parties to the lawsuit, within the time specified by the rule. The response states the responding party's objections, if any, to part or all of the requested production or inspection. Absent objection, the responding party must produce the documents as requested, or admit counsel to its premises for the scheduled inspection.

In federal courts and in most state courts, a party cannot use a request for production to discover documents or other property in the custody or control of a nonparty. Instead, a litigant must take the nonparty's deposition and in connection with the deposition serve a subpoena duces tecum ordering the nonparty to bring the designated items to the deposition. Rule 45(d)(1) makes explicit a litigant's right to examine and copy documents and other items produced in response to a subpoena duces tecum, but in some states the inquiring party cannot inspect the property but is limited to asking the nonparty questions about it. Most discovery rules make no provision for the inspection of a nonparty's land or place of business, although an attorney sometimes can get access by fixing the land or place of business as the place for taking the nonparty's deposition.

Most discovery provisions specifically preserve the traditional equity suit for discovery, a separate action that can be brought against a nonparty. Although independent actions generally have fallen into disuse, they sometimes are useful for solving problems with discovery from non-parties.

Notes and Questions

1. Prior to the amendment of Federal Rule 34 in 1970, it provided for document discovery only on motion to the court granted upon a showing of good cause. Although many states have adopted the 1970 changes, some have retained the good-cause requirement. Compare Ohio Civ.Proc.Rule 34(a) (good cause eliminated), with N.M.Civ.Proc. Rule 34 (good cause retained). What justifications are there for the good-cause requirement? What advantages result from its elimination? See the Notes of the Advisory Committee

accompanying the 1970 amendment to Federal Rule 34, which appear in the Supplement.

2. Courts are divided on what constitutes a showing of good cause. On the one hand, there are a number of federal decisions rendered prior to the 1970 amendments in which the good-cause requirement was held satisfied by a showing that the requested documents were "relevant" within the meaning of Rule 26(b), provided that copies of the documents were not already in the hands of the party seeking discovery. See, e.g., Houdry Process Corp. v. Commonwealth Oil Refining Co., 24 F.R.D. 58 (S.D.N.Y.1959). On the other hand, most courts, both state and federal, have required a showing that the information sought is not available from another source. See, e.g., Guilford Nat. Bank v. Southern Ry. Co., 297 F.2d 921, 923–25 (4th Cir.1962), certiorari denied 375 U.S. 985, 84 S.Ct. 518, 11 L.Ed.2d 473 (1964); Alseike v. Miller, 196 Kan. 547, 412 P.2d 1007 (1966).

3. In BELCHER v. BASSETT FURNITURE INDUSTRIES, INC., 588 F.2d 904 (4th Cir.1978), an employment discrimination case, the Fourth Circuit reversed the District Court's grant of permission to plaintiff's experts to conduct a five-day inspection of a factory, coupled with interviews of workers selected at random. The purported purpose of the inspection was to uncover evidence relating to an allegation that blacks had been relegated to less attractive jobs than had whites. The court found that the inspection had a great potential for disruption of the factory's activities, while the benefits to be derived seemed slight. Is the decision correct? Consider the court's observation that "since entry upon a party's premises may entail greater burdens and risks than mere production of documents, a greater inquiry into the necessity for inspection would seem warranted." Id. at 908. Do you agree?

4. Under the Rules, a party does not have to turn over a document, including even the "smoking gun," unless the other side asks for it, and lawyers are tempted to interpret a request narrowly to avoid having to make a damaging disclosure. For example, attorneys for General Motors in a personal injury action involving the design of the fuel storage system in a 1973 Oldsmobile Omega argued that a request for "any report dated between January 1, 1966 and January 13, 1978 which pertains to any alternative fuel system design proposed, suggested, investigated, studied, considered, analyzed, and/or tested" "for possible incorporation in the 1969 through 1975 X-body series of cars" did not require it to produce reports that did not specifically mention X-body cars. Its interpretation of the request became apparent when GM was forced to explain why it had not disclosed reports of test data referred to in one of the documents it had disclosed:

> From the context of the documents that have been produced by GM, it is apparent that GM was crash testing alternative fuel storage systems in anticipation of the enactment of more stringent government safety standards for fuel system integrity. In other words, GM's goal was general product improvement. It is sophistic for GM to assert that the tests do not fall within plaintiff's document request because they relate to overall product improvement as opposed to the improvement of a particular product, i.e., 1969 through 1975 X-body vehicles. The scope of plaintiffs' document request * * * is manifestly broad and it was unreasonable for GM to construe it so narrowly. The Court is convinced that any

modifying language is likely to be interpreted by GM in such a manner so as to result in further disagreement as to the scope of the document request which would in turn involve more judicial involvement in adjudicating the dispute, and so on. Consequently, GM will be ordered to produce within 60 days any report dated between January 1, 1966 and January 13, 1978 which pertains to any fuel system design proposed, suggested, investigated, studied, considered, analyzed, and/or tested by GM.

SELLON v. SMITH, 112 F.R.D. 9, 13–14 (D.Del.1986). The court went on to award attorney's fees against the manufacturer for this and other discovery misconduct. Why would GM's counsel pursue such tactics, given the substantial likelihood of being caught? Was it a situation in which a defendant was willing to risk the imposition of sanctions because the stakes were so high? What are an attorney's professional obligations in such a situation? What should be the attorney's obligations?

5. Consider the following description of the practice of document discovery under Rule 34, at least in more complex cases:

* * * The Rule requires that the demand [for documents] be made for "designated documents," but since the party making the demand typically lacks sufficient information to describe the documents with specificity and knows only the subject matters as to which he expects the opposing party's documents to relate, his Rule 34 demand calls for all documents relating to those subject matters. Since he also expects that the opposing party will narrowly construe the language of his demand so as to avoid producing damaging materials, he attempts, in the first instance, to make that language all-encompassing, and considerable time and expense is generally expended in the very drafting of those requests.

The opposing party customarily objects to the breadth and burden of the demand—again expending great effort in his submission. Lawyers and company personnel are often dispatched to estimate the volume of documents involved and the number of man-days required for file searches and production. Negotiations are then held regarding the objections, and the party seeking production files a Rule 37 motion with a supporting (and, again, typically extensive) memorandum. The opposing party files his papers consisting of an equally long memorandum and affidavits particularizing the burdensomeness of the demands. Hearings are held on the objections—often before a magistrate with appeals to the court. Rulings are finally made and the production goes forward. The demanding party then moves under Rule 37 to compel the production of documents he believes were improperly withheld; hearings are then held on that motion; possibly depositions in aid of the motion will be taken; and hearings may be required for rulings regarding the propriety of questions asked on such depositions. The opposing party will, of course, serve his own Rule 34 demand, and in a suit between two companies that will double the work involved.

Second Circuit Commission on the Reduction of Burdens and Costs in Civil Litigation (Draft, Sept. 18, 1978).

6. The 1970 amendment to Rule 34 requires that data be produced in a "reasonably usable form." In KOZLOWSKI v. SEARS, ROEBUCK & CO., 73 F.R.D. 73 (D.Mass.1976), an action for damages for injuries suffered when

pajamas manufactured by the defendant caught fire, Sears objected to the plaintiff's discovery of prior complaints about the flammability of its pajamas; "because of its longstanding practice of indexing claims alphabetically by name of claimant, rather than by type of product, there is no practical way for anyone to determine whether there also have been any complaints similar" to plaintiff's. Id. at 75–76. The court rejected the argument, stating that the fact that compliance with the request would be costly or time-consuming ordinarily is not a valid objection. In the court's view, to permit Sears to "frustrate discovery by creating an inadequate filing system, and then claiming undue burden, would defeat the purposes of the discovery rule." Id. at 76. Rule 34(b) was amended in 1980 to permit the responding party to turn over the documents either in the order that they are kept in the ordinary course of business or in an organized fashion with proper labeling to correspond with the categories set forth in the request. Would *Kozlowski* have to be decided differently today in light of the 1980 amendment to Rule 34(b)? In light of the 1983 amendment to Rule 26(b)(1) mandating restrictions on discovery under certain circumstances?

Does a business, having created a document that might be used by an adversary in future litigation, have an obligation to keep the record? How should a court respond to a business that destroys documents in anticipation of litigation, or after litigation has begun but before the adversary has served a discovery request? How should it respond to the destruction of documents pursuant to a written plan that appears neutral on its face, but effectively denies a litigant useful evidence? See Oesterle, *A Private Litigant's Remedies for an Opponent's Inappropriate Destruction of Documents*, 61 Texas L.Rev. 1185 (1983); Fedders & Guttenplan, *Document Retention and Destruction: Practical, Legal and Ethical Considerations*, 56 Notre Dame Law. 5 (1980).

HART v. WOLFF

Supreme Court of Alaska, 1971.
489 P.2d 114.

CONNOR, JUSTICE. Plaintiff Victor Hart has appealed from the dismissal of his complaint for failure to comply with an order to produce certain documents for defendant's inspection. * * *

On December 12, 1963, Hart filed suit against Wolff alleging that on two occasions Wolff had made statements defaming Hart. The statements concerned an alleged misappropriation of funds by Hart in the formation of Arctic Bowl, Inc., an Alaska corporation which Hart and Wolff, along with others, had organized in 1958 to operate a bowling alley in Fairbanks.

Wolff was vice-president of the corporation from 1958 until September 1959, when Metropolitan Mortgage and Securities Co., Inc., a Washington corporation, purchased a controlling interest in Arctic Bowl, Inc. Following this change in corporate control, Wolff ceased to be vice-president of the corporation. Hart, who had served as president in 1958 and 1959, remained with the corporation as a manager of the bowling alley.

* * *

Hart argues on appeal that the superior court could not properly order the production of records of Arctic Bowl, Inc., under Civil Rule 34, because the records were not in the possession, custody, or control of a party to the pending action. It is true that an order issued pursuant to Civil Rule 34 may be directed only against a party having possession, custody or control of the records. The order in question here was directed against Hart. Thus, the question which faces us is whether Hart had control over the records sought to be produced.

A prima facie case of control is all that need be established to justify issuance of an order under Civil Rule 34. Norman v. Young, 422 F.2d 470 (10th Cir.1970) (construing Rule 34, F.R.Civ.P., which was then nearly identical to Alaska's Civil Rule 34) * * *. We believe that Wolff made a prima facie showing that Victor Hart had sufficient control over these records to justify the court's order of December 15, 1969.

The record in this case indicates that while Hart was no longer an officer of Arctic Bowl, Inc., at the time the motions to produce were made he was employed by that corporation in a position of authority and trust. Further, he was also employed during the same time by Metropolitan Mortgage, the controlling shareholder in Arctic Bowl, to handle Metropolitan's business affairs in Fairbanks.

This court in the past has favored liberal construction of the civil rules governing discovery. * * * While Rule 34 certainly has proper limits, the concept of "control" should not be given a hypertechnical construction that will undermine the policy favoring liberal pretrial discovery. As the United States Supreme Court stated in Societe Internationale Pour Participations Industrielles Et Commerciales S.A. v. Rogers, 357 U.S. 197, 206, 78 S.Ct. 1087, 1092, 2 L.Ed.2d 1255 (1958):

> Rule 34 [F.R.Civ.P.] is sufficiently flexible to be adapted to the exigencies of particular litigation. The propriety of the use to which it is put depends upon the circumstances of a given case * * *.

Thus, though Hart may not have had the authority to *force* Metropolitan to produce the records for Wolff's inspection, we believe the nature of Hart's relationships with Arctic Bowl and with Metropolitan Mortgage were such that the court could infer that he had some influence over Metropolitan with respect to Arctic Bowl, Inc., and could have used that influence to produce the records. In fact, following the issuance of the production order, at the hearing on the motion to strike, Hart himself testified that he imagined he did have some influence over Metropolitan.

In opposition to defendant's motions to produce, Hart merely stated that he was not an officer or director of Arctic Bowl, Inc., and that he did not have the records in his possession, custody or control. At no time did he deny that he had a close employee-employer relationship with the corporation and with the corporation's major shareholder. We hold on this record that plaintiff failed to rebut the prima facie showing of control made by Wolff. The order to produce the records was, therefore, proper.

* * *

There is support in the record that plaintiff Victor Hart willfully refused to obey the December 15, 1969, order in that he himself testified that he made no efforts to produce the records of Arctic Bowl during the thirty days following that order. Nor did he make any satisfactory explanation to the court why they had not been produced. * * * In these circumstances, we cannot say that the superior court abused its discretion in dismissing plaintiff's complaint. The order is affirmed.

* * *

RABINOWITZ, JUSTICE (concurring in part, dissenting in part).

* * * I find the record devoid of any factual basis for the majority's conclusion that Wolff made out a prima facie case of Hart's "possession, custody, or control" of Arctic Bowl's records. I cannot perceive any policy considerations, or precedential bases, for the majority's adoption of an "influence" test, either actual or potential, in substitution for the "possession, custody, or control" standards of Civil Rule 34. Nor can I agree that notions of "influence" and of liberal pretrial discovery policies furnish an adequate foundation for the discovery order and subsequent sanction which were entered.

* * *

One further comment. It strikes me as rather unusual that Wolff's battery of attorneys took approximately five years to obtain a decision on the Civil Rule 34 motion to require Hart to produce the records of Arctic Bowl, Inc. Equally extraordinary is the fact that Wolff's counsel never attempted to employ any other available discovery procedures, such as a subpoena duces tecum directed to a nonparty under Civil Rule 45(d)(1), to obtain the records of Arctic Bowl, Inc.

* * *

Notes and Questions

1. In Societé Internationale v. Rogers, quoted in *Hart*, plaintiff argued that it did not have "control" over documents it had been ordered to produce under Rule 34, because the production of the documents, which were in plaintiff's physical possession in Switzerland, would be in violation of the criminal laws of that country. The Supreme Court rejected the argument, stating that "[p]etitioner is in a most advantageous position to plead with its own sovereign for relaxation of penal laws or for adoption of plans which will at the least achieve a significant measure of compliance with the production order * * *." See generally Note, *Foreign Nondisclosure Laws and Domestic Discovery Orders in Antitrust Litigation*, 88 Yale L.J. 612 (1979).

2. As the dissenting judge in Hart v. Wolff noted, items in the possession or control of a nonparty may be sought pursuant to Rule 45(d)(1). Under Rule 30(f)(1), and subject to the right of the witness to demand a court order under Rule 45(d)(1), any party has the right to inspect and copy any materials produced by a witness at a deposition. Should a court be able to go even further and, upon a showing of good cause, order possession of property to be turned over to an inquiring party? Cf. State ex rel. Crawford v. Moody, 477 S.W.2d 438 (Mo.App.1972), indicating "no," and giving as one reason the possibility that a party might fraudulently destroy the items so produced. Is this a valid reason?

To what extent should a nonparty be able successfully to object to a subpoena ordering it to produce items for discovery? Clearly, an objection is proper on the ground of privilege, for example, if a lawyer is asked to reveal confidential information received from a client. But suppose the nonparty wishes to challenge on the ground that the evidence sought is not relevant to the underlying controversy between the parties or desires to protect other nonparties from harm that would result from revelation of nonprivileged material received in confidence? Consider Dade Cty. Medical Ass'n v. Hlis, 372 So.2d 117 (Fla.App.1979), in which the court stated that although a nonparty could not object to discovery as not relevant, it could raise objections based on its own interest in preserving confidentiality or even based on similar interests of "unrepresented strangers" to the action.

3. Discovery from nonparties under the Rules is permitted only in connection with the taking of a deposition. In some circumstances in which a party seeks to inspect items in the hands of a nonparty, a deposition is useless. Why shouldn't Rule 45 be amended to provide for production of items for pretrial inspection without the artificial deposition requirement? N.Y.C.P. L.R. 3120(b) provides that "a person not a party may be directed by order to do whatever a party may be directed to do" with respect to production of documents or other items and also with respect to entry on land for the purpose of inspecting any object or operation thereon.

Federal Rule 34(c) was added in 1970 to make it clear that Rule 34 does not preclude independent proceedings for discovery under traditional equitable principles. According to the substantive equity provisions of at least some jurisdictions, such a proceeding could result in an order allowing a party to an action to enter the property of a nonparty for purposes of discovery. See the Advisory Committee Note to the amendment adding Rule 34(c). Suppose that an equitable remedy is unavailable and that a party feels it must enter the property of a nonparty to inspect the premises or to view a large machine that cannot be removed to the lawyer's office during the course of a deposition. Is there any way under the current Federal Rules to obtain the necessary information? Cf. Carson v. Burlington Northern Inc., 52 F.R.D. 492 (D.Neb. 1971), p. 737, supra.

————

COALITION OF BLACK LEADERSHIP v. DOORLEY, 349 F.Supp. 127 (D.R.I.1972). Plaintiffs brought a civil-rights action against the city police department alleging that during the course of an arrest plaintiffs were beaten, kicked, and otherwise subject to harassment. At trial, defendants sought to introduce photographs of plaintiffs taken on the night of the arrest, presumably to show that there were no signs of physical abuse. Plaintiffs objected on the ground that defendants had failed to produce the photographs upon a request under Rule 34 asking for:

> All case records, incident reports, police log book entries and other related documents, memoranda, and reports regarding, involving, or referring to the arrests and jailing of * * * [plaintiffs].

The court held:

> Defendants, who had the photographs made pursuant to the arrests * * * attached to case files, produced the files but not the photographs. They argue that plaintiffs did not ask for photographs, so they were under no compulsion to produce them. I note that in Rule 34(a) * * * the term "documents" is expressly stated to include photographs. The photographs were within the scope of the discovery request. The failure to

produce them would be sufficient to warrant their exclusion [at trial] under Fed.R.Civ.P. 37 ＊ ＊ ＊.

Note and Questions

Rule 34(a) permits discovery of "designated documents." Was the court in *Coalition* too liberal regarding the designation requirement? Why shouldn't the designation be as precise as the circumstances permit? Should the party who seeks production have a duty to utilize other methods of discovery first, in order to learn what items exist, in order that a precise designation can be made? See Rios v. Donovan, 21 A.D.2d 409, 250 N.Y.S.2d 818 (1st Dep't 1964).

4. PHYSICAL AND MENTAL EXAMINATIONS

———

Read Federal Rule of Civil Procedure 35 in the Supplement.

———

In many lawsuits, a party will need to have its own medical professionals physically examine an adverse party whose condition is in controversy. However, a compelled medical examination involves an intrusion on a person's privacy, and some medical tests can entail discomfort and pain.

Rule 35 requires a court order for an examination and imposes strict standards. A court can force a party to submit to examination or to make persons under their legal custody or control available for examination. But the person's physical or mental condition must be in controversy, and the movant must show "good cause" to compel the examination. The determination of good cause involves weighing the pain, danger, or intrusiveness of the examination against the need for, or usefulness of, the information to be gained.

In practice, most physical and mental examinations occur as a result of agreements between attorneys. The primary effect of Rule 35 is to encourage parties to stipulate to examinations. Examinations are routine in personal injury actions, as well as in litigation involving issues of paternity, incompetence, and undue influence. Of course, the Rule is available in those cases in which the parties cannot agree. Stipulations typically address questions concerning the time and place of the examination, and the procedures to be used. Rule 35 gives the examined party the right to a copy of the examining physician's report, even if the party submitted to an examination without the compulsion of a court order.

SCHLAGENHAUF v. HOLDER
Supreme Court of the United States, 1964.
379 U.S. 104, 85 S.Ct. 234, 13 L.Ed.2d 152.

Certiorari to the United States Court of Appeals for the Seventh Circuit.

MR. JUSTICE GOLDBERG delivered the opinion of the Court.

This case involves the validity and construction of Rule 35(a) of the Federal Rules of Civil Procedure as applied to the examination of a defendant in a negligence action. * * *

An action based on diversity of citizenship was brought in the District Court seeking damages arising from personal injuries suffered by passengers of a bus which collided with the rear of a tractor-trailer. The named defendants were The Greyhound Corporation, owner of the bus; petitioner, Robert L. Schlagenhauf, the bus driver; Contract Carriers, Inc., owner of the tractor; Joseph L. McCorkhill, driver of the tractor; and National Lead Company, owner of the trailer. Answers were filed by each of the defendants denying negligence.

Greyhound then cross-claimed against Contract Carriers and National Lead for damage to Greyhound's bus, alleging that the collision was due solely to their negligence in that the tractor-trailer was driven at an unreasonably low speed, had not remained in its lane, and was not equipped with proper rear lights. Contract Carriers filed an answer to this cross-claim denying its negligence and asserting "[t]hat the negligence of the driver of the * * * bus [petitioner Schlagenhauf] proximately caused and contributed to * * * Greyhound's damages."

* * *

Contract Carriers and National Lead then petitioned the District Court for an order directing petitioner Schlagenhauf to submit to both mental and physical examinations by one specialist in each of the following fields:

(1) Internal medicine;

(2) Ophthalmology;

(3) Neurology; and

(4) Psychiatry.

For the purpose of offering a choice to the District Court of one specialist in each field, the petition recommended two specialists in internal medicine, ophthalmology, and psychiatry, respectively, and three specialists in neurology—a total of nine physicians. The petition alleged that the mental and physical condition of Schlagenhauf was "in controversy" as it had been raised by Contract Carriers' answer to Greyhound's cross-claim. This was supported by a brief of legal authorities and an affidavit of Contract Carriers' attorney stating that Schlagenhauf had seen red lights 10 to 15 seconds before the accident, that another witness had seen the rear lights of the trailer from a distance of three-quarters to one-half mile, and that Schlagenhauf had been involved in a prior accident.

* * *

While disposition of this petition was pending, National Lead filed its answer to Greyhound's cross-claim and itself "cross-claimed" against Greyhound and Schlagenhauf for damage to its trailer. * * *

The District Court, on the basis of the petition filed by Contract Carriers, and without any hearing, ordered Schlagenhauf to submit to nine examinations—one by each of the recommended specialists—despite the fact that the petition clearly requested a total of only four examinations.

Petitioner applied for a writ of mandamus in the Court of Appeals against the respondent, the District Court Judge, seeking to have set aside the order requiring his mental and physical examinations. The Court of Appeals denied mandamus, one judge dissenting * * *.

We granted certiorari to review undecided questions concerning the validity and construction of Rule 35. * * *

Rule 35 on its face applies to all "parties," which under any normal reading would include a defendant. Petitioner contends, however, that the application of the Rule to a defendant would be an unconstitutional invasion of his privacy, or, at the least, be a modification of substantive rights existing prior to the adoption of the Federal Rules of Civil Procedure and thus beyond the congressional mandate of the Rules Enabling Act.

These same contentions were raised [and rejected] in Sibbach v. Wilson & Co., [p. 373, supra] * * *, by a plaintiff in a negligence action who asserted a physical injury as a basis for recovery. * * * Petitioner does not challenge the holding in *Sibbach* as applied to plaintiffs. He contends, however, that it should not be extended to defendants. We can see no basis * * * for such a distinction. * * * Issues cannot be resolved by a doctrine of favoring one class of litigants over another.

We recognize that, insofar as reported cases show, this type of discovery in federal courts has been applied solely to plaintiffs, and that some early state cases seem to have proceeded on a theory that a plaintiff who seeks redress for injuries in a court of law thereby "waives" his right to claim the inviolability of his person.

* * * [The Court then rejected the "waiver" theory on the basis of language in the *Sibbach* case.] The chain of events leading to an ultimate determination on the merits begins with the injury of the plaintiff, an involuntary act on his part. Seeking court redress is just one step in this chain. If the plaintiff is prevented or deterred from this redress, the loss is thereby forced on him to the same extent as if the defendant were prevented or deterred from defending against the action.

* * *

Petitioner contends that even if Rule 35 is to be applied to defendants, which we have determined it must, nevertheless it should not be applied to him as he was not a party in relation to Contract Carriers and National Lead—the movants for the mental and physical examinations—at the time the examinations were sought. * * * While it is clear that the person to be examined must be a party to the case,[12] we are of the view that * * * Rule 35 only requires that the person to be examined be a

---

12. Although petitioner was an agent of Greyhound, he was himself a party to the action. He is to be distinguished from one who is not a party but is, for example, merely the agent of a party. * * * It is not now necessary to determine to what extent, if any, the term "party" includes one who is a "real party in interest" although not a named party to the action. Cf. Beach v. Beach, 72 App.D.C. 318, 114 F.2d 479, 131 A.L.R. 804.

party to the "action," not that he be an opposing party *vis-à-vis* the movant. There is no doubt that Schlagenhauf was a "party" to this "action" by virtue of the original complaint. * * * Insistence that the movant have filed a pleading against the person to be examined would have the undesirable result of an unnecessary proliferation of cross-claims and counterclaims and would not be in keeping with the aims of a liberal, nontechnical application of the Federal Rules. * * *

While the Court of Appeals held that petitioner was not a party *vis-à-vis* National Lead or Contract Carriers at the time the examinations were first sought, it went on to hold that he had become a party *vis-à-vis* National Lead by the time of a second order entered by the District Court and thus was a party within its rule. This second order, identical in all material respects with the first, was entered on the basis of supplementary petitions filed by National Lead and Contract Carriers. These petitions gave no new basis for the examinations, except for the allegation that petitioner's mental and physical condition had been additionally put in controversy by the National Lead answer and cross-claim, which had been filed subsequent to the first petition for examinations. Although the filing of the petition for mandamus intervened between these two orders, we accept, for purposes of this opinion, the determination of the Court of Appeals that this second order was the one before it and agree that petitioner was clearly a party at this juncture under any test.

Petitioner next contends that his mental or physical condition was not "in controversy" and "good cause" was not shown for the examinations, both as required by the express terms of Rule 35.

* * *

It is notable * * * that in none of the other discovery provisions is there a restriction that the matter be "in controversy," and only in Rule 34 is there Rule 35's requirement that the movant affirmatively demonstrate "good cause." [a]

This additional requirement of "good cause" was reviewed by Chief Judge Sobeloff in Guilford National Bank of Greensboro v. Southern Ry. Co., 297 F.2d 921, 924 (C.A.4th Cir.), in the following words:

> * * * The specific requirement of good cause would be meaningless if good cause could be sufficiently established by merely showing that the desired materials are relevant, for the relevancy standard has already been imposed by Rule 26(b). Thus, by adding the words " * * * good cause * * *," the Rules indicate that there must be greater showing of need under Rules 34 and 35 than under the other discovery rules.

The courts of appeals in other cases have also recognized that Rule 34's good-cause requirement is not a mere formality, but is a plainly expressed limitation on the use of that Rule. This is obviously true as to the "in controversy" and "good cause" requirements of Rule 35. They are not met by mere conclusory allegations of the pleadings—nor by mere relevance to the case—but require an affirmative showing by the movant

---

a. The "good cause" requirement was eliminated from Rule 34 in 1970. See Note 1, p. 744, *supra*.

that each condition as to which the examination is sought is really and genuinely in controversy and that good cause exists for ordering each particular examination. Obviously, what may be good cause for one type of examination may not be so for another. The ability of the movant to obtain the desired information by other means is also relevant.

Rule 35, therefore, requires discriminating application by the trial judge, who must decide, as an initial matter in every case, whether the party requesting a mental or physical examination or examinations has adequately demonstrated the existence of the Rule's requirements of "in controversy" and "good cause," which requirements, as the Court of Appeals in this case itself recognized, are necessarily related. 321 F.2d, at 51. * * *

Of course, there are situations where the pleadings alone are sufficient to meet these requirements. A plaintiff in a negligence action who asserts mental or physical injury * * * places that mental or physical injury clearly in controversy and provides the defendant with good cause for an examination to determine the existence and extent of such asserted injury. This * * * applies equally to a defendant who asserts his mental or physical condition as a defense to a claim, such as, for example, where insanity is asserted as a defense to a divorce action. * * *

Here, however, Schlagenhauf did not assert his mental or physical condition either in support of or in defense of a claim. His condition was sought to be placed in issue by other parties. Thus, under the principles discussed above, Rule 35 required that these parties make an affirmative showing that petitioner's mental or physical condition was in controversy and that there was good cause for the examinations requested. This, the record plainly shows, they failed to do.

The only allegations in the pleadings relating to this subject were the general conclusory statement in Contract Carriers' answer to the cross-claim that "Schlagenhauf was not mentally or physically capable of operating" the bus at the time of the accident and the limited allegation in National Lead's cross-claim that, at the time of the accident, "the eyes and vision of * * * Schlagenhauf was [sic] impaired and deficient."

The attorney's affidavit attached to the petition for the examinations provided:

> That * * * Schlagenhauf, in his deposition * * * admitted that he saw red lights for 10 to 15 seconds prior to a collision with a semi-tractor trailer unit and yet drove his vehicle on without reducing speed and without altering the course thereof.

> The only eye-witness to this accident known to this affiant * * * testified that immediately prior to the impact between the bus and truck that he had also been approaching the truck from the rear and that he had clearly seen the lights of the truck for a distance of three-quarters to one-half mile to the rear thereof.

> * * * Schlagenhauf has admitted in his deposition * * * that he was involved in a [prior] similar type rear end collision. * * *

This record cannot support even the corrected order which required one examination in each of the four specialties of internal medicine, ophthalmology, neurology, and psychiatry. Nothing in the pleadings or affidavit would afford a basis for a belief that Schlagenhauf was suffering from a mental or neurological illness warranting wide-ranging psychiatric or neurological examinations. Nor is there anything stated justifying the broad internal medicine examination.

The only specific allegation made in support of the four examinations ordered was that the "eyes and vision" of Schlagenhauf were impaired. Considering this in conjunction with the affidavit, we would be hesitant to set aside a visual examination if it had been the only one ordered. However, as the case must be remanded to the District Court because of the other examinations ordered, it would be appropriate for the District Judge to reconsider also this order in light of the guidelines set forth in this opinion.

* * *

Accordingly, the judgment of the Court of Appeals is vacated and the case remanded to the District Court to reconsider the examination order in light of the guidelines herein formulated and for further proceedings in conformity with this opinion.

Vacated and remanded.

MR. JUSTICE BLACK, with whom MR. JUSTICE CLARK joins, concurring in part and dissenting in part.

* * *

In a collision case like this one, evidence concerning very bad eyesight or impaired mental or physical health which may affect the ability to drive is obviously of the highest relevance. It is equally obvious, I think, that when a vehicle continues down an open road and smashes into a truck in front of it although the truck is in plain sight and there is ample time and room to avoid collision, the chances are good that the driver has some physical, mental or moral defect. When such a thing happens twice, one is even more likely to ask, "What is the matter with that driver? Is he blind or crazy?" Plainly the allegations of the other parties were relevant and put the question of Schlagenhauf's health and vision "in controversy." * * *

MR. JUSTICE DOUGLAS, dissenting in part.

* * * When the defendant's doctors examine plaintiff, they are normally interested only in answering a single question: did plaintiff in fact sustain the specific injuries claimed? But plaintiff's doctors will naturally be inclined to go on a fishing expedition in search of *anything* which will tend to prove that the defendant was unfit to perform the acts which resulted in the plaintiff's injury. And a doctor for a fee can easily discover something wrong with any patient—a condition that in prejudiced medical eyes might have caused the accident. Once defendants are turned over to medical or psychiatric clinics for an analysis of their physical well-being and the condition of their psyche, the effective trial will be held there and not before the jury. There are no lawyers in those clinics to stop the doctor from probing this organ or that one, to halt a further inquiry, to object to a line of questioning. And there is no judge to sit as arbiter. The doctor or the psychiatrist has a holiday in the privacy of his office. The defendant is at the doctor's (or psychiatrist's) mercy; and his report may either overawe or confuse the jury and prevent a fair trial.

* * *

Neither the Court nor Congress up to today has determined that any person whose physical or mental condition is brought into question during some lawsuit must surrender his right to keep his person inviolate. Congress did, according to *Sibbach*, require a plaintiff to choose between his privacy and his purse; but before today it has not been thought that any other "party" had lost this historic immunity. Congress and this Court can authorize such a rule. But a rule suited to purposes of discovery against defendants must be carefully drawn in light of the great potential of blackmail.

* * *

[JUSTICE HARLAN'S dissenting opinion is omitted.]

Notes and Questions

1. In CRIDER v. SNEIDER, 243 Ga. 642, 256 S.E.2d 335 (1979), a wrongful-death case arising from an automobile accident, defendant, during discovery, argued that he could not recall any of the events surrounding the accident because of "traumatic amnesia." Plaintiff thereupon moved unsuccessfully to require defendant to submit to a mental and physical examination. The Georgia Supreme Court held that the trial court's refusal to grant the motion was not an abuse of discretion in that plaintiff had failed to show good cause since it appeared that the facts and circumstances of the collision could be established by other sources of evidence. If no other sources had existed, could the court have properly granted the motion?

2. In WINTERS v. TRAVIA, 495 F.2d 839 (2d Cir. 1974), the court refused to order the plaintiff to submit to a physical or mental examination. The plaintiff was a Christian Scientist seeking damages on the ground that forced medication administered to her during involuntary hospitalization violated her right to freedom of religion. The court ruled that her present condition was not in controversy since plaintiff was willing to abandon any claim that any present or anticipated physical or mental disability or condition was caused by the medical treatment on which the case was based.

3. In 1970 Federal Rule 35(a) was amended to encompass persons "in the custody or under the legal control of a party." "Agents of a party" are not included in the Rule, although this had been recommended by the Advisory Committee in 1955. What reasons are there for not including agents? The 1970 amendment also redefined "physical condition" specifically to include blood type. For a general discussion of the need for the 1970 changes see Note, *Physical Examination of Non-Parties Under the Federal Rules of Civil Procedure,* 43 Iowa L.Rev. 375 (1958). See also 8 Wright & Miller, *Federal Practice and Procedure: Civil* §§ 2231–39 (1970).

4. N.Y.C.P.L.R. 3121 provides for physical examinations to be taken upon notice without a prior court order or showing of "good cause." Although in 1970 Federal Rule 34 was amended to eliminate the good-cause require-

ment as to discovery of documents and other items, the good-cause requirement in Rule 35 was retained. Is there more reason for a showing of good
cause as a prerequisite when a physical examination is desired than there is
when discovery of documents is sought?

5. The courts are called upon to exercise considerable discretion in
determining the extent of the examination to be permitted, the place of the
examination, see Annot., 71 A.L.R.2d 973 (1960), and the persons who may be
present, see Annot., 64 A.L.R.2d 497 (1959). What justification is there for
permitting the party to be examined to bring a lawyer and personal physician
with him? What arguments can be made that these "outsiders" should not be
permitted to attend?

———

BENNING v. PHELPS, 249 F.2d 47 (2d Cir.1957). Prior to suit,
plaintiff voluntarily submitted to a physical examination by defendant's
physician. Thereafter plaintiff refused to submit to another examination
and defendant moved the trial court to order plaintiff to do so. The court
granted the motion and ordered defendant to provide plaintiff with a copy
of the report of the examining physician. In compliance with the court's
order, defendant delivered to plaintiff a copy of the physician's report, and
then moved, under Rule 35(b)(1), to require plaintiff to give defendant the
reports of plaintiff's doctors. The trial court denied the motion and the
appellate court affirmed as follows:

> * * * [D]efendant is entitled to receive copies of the plaintiff's
> medical reports only if the plaintiff has previously requested and received
> copies of medical reports from the defendant. * * * Here the plaintiff
> received copies of the defendant's reports pursuant to an order of the
> court, and not pursuant to his own request. Since the trial court might
> properly have concluded that "good cause" had not been shown, * * *
> and hence might have refused to compel the plaintiff to submit to the
> second examination requested by the defendant, we cannot find that it
> erred in the condition which it placed upon its order.

———

In CHASTAIN v. EVENNOU, 35 F.R.D. 350 (D.Utah 1964), plaintiff
voluntarily submitted to a physical examination by a physician designated
by defendants, and plaintiff received a copy of the report in exchange for
copies of certain reports by his own physicians. But plaintiff specifically
withheld one physician's report, arguing that Rule 35(b) was inapplicable
since no court-ordered examination had ever taken place. The court
ordered production of the withheld report on the ground that the spirit of
Rule 35 so demanded.

Notes and Questions

1. What means other than Rule 35(b)(1) might the defendant in *Benning*
have used to discover the contents of the reports of plaintiff's doctors? Does
the availability of other means make Rule 35(b)(1) unnecessary?

2. Rule 35(b)(3) was added in 1970, in recognition of the fact that much
discovery takes place by agreement of the parties without resort to court

appearances.   How far does this new provision go?   Would it alter the result in *Benning*?

LEWIN v. JACKSON, 108 Ariz. 27, 492 P.2d 406 (1972).   Plaintiff sued for slander, alleging as damages the fact that she had been disinherited by her parents.   Defendant sought to take the deposition of plaintiff's father, who had become incompetent and had been placed under the guardianship of plaintiff.   Plaintiff objected, asking for a protective order under Rule 26(c) on the ground that her father was not physically or mentally able to give a deposition.   The court stayed the deposition but ordered the father to undergo a medical examination for the purpose of determining whether or not he could be deposed.   Plaintiff objected on the ground that Arizona Rule 35 (identical to Federal Rule 35) did not permit the examination in question.   The court concluded that although the father was a person under the "custody" and "legal control of plaintiff," Rule 35 did not apply because the action had not been brought on his behalf.   Nonetheless the court held the examination to be proper as part of the inherent power of a court "to assure itself not only that a witness' testimony will be accurate and lucid, but also that the act of testifying will not endanger the health of the proposed witness."

Questions

1.   Is the court in *Lewin* correct in holding that the requested medical examination did not fall within the scope of Rule 35?   Can the examination be justified as part of an order under Rule 26(c) controlling the course of a deposition?   Should Rule 35 be considered the exclusive source of power by which a court can require a nonparty to submit to an examination?

2.   How far does the inherent power invoked by the *Lewin* court extend?   For example, can the court order a person who witnessed an event upon which the suit is based to submit to an eye examination to determine if that person can see well enough to be considered a competent witness at a deposition or at trial?   If so, how effective is the limitation of Rule 35 to parties?

5.   REQUESTS TO ADMIT

Read Federal Rule of Civil Procedure 36 in the Supplement.

Rule 36 authorizes a party to serve on another party written requests to admit the truth of certain matters of fact or of the application of law to fact, or the genuineness of a document or other evidence that may be used at trial.   Rule 36 is not a true discovery device since it does not require the responding party to disclose information.   Requests for admissions are used to shape information already known into statements that expedite the trial by limiting the issues in dispute and by obviating some of the formalities that control the introduction of evidence at trial.   Although responses to other discovery devices are not conclusive proof and may be contradicted at trial, responses to Rule 36 requests constitute conclusive evidence, unless withdrawn, and cannot be contradicted at trial. However, requests for admissions may function as a discovery device if a party uses them early enough in the litigation to help identify the issues not in dispute and to target the remaining issues for discovery.

A request for admission may be served at any time without the necessity of a court order, although usually not later than thirty days before a fixed trial date. Rule 36 says that each matter of admission must be set forth separately, but says nothing else about the format for requests. However, Form 25 appended to the Federal Rules of Civil Procedure, which is reproduced in the Supplement, provides an illustration.

The party who receives a request to admit must respond under oath and in timely fashion, admitting or denying each matter for which an admission is requested, or providing a detailed explanation why it cannot admit or deny the matter. The responding party may also object to a request because improperly phrased (as "vague," "ambiguous," "a compound sentence," or otherwise defectively drafted), or because it seeks privileged or protected information. The responding party may request a court to extend its time to respond. Although Rule 29 does not permit counsel to stipulate as between or among themselves to an extension, most courts readily ratify a stipulation by counsel to an extension.

If the party who receives a request to admit does nothing, the party has admitted the matter in the request. Rule 36, unlike other discovery rules, is self-executing. Once the time to respond has passed, the requesting party can rely on the matters admitted and take no further discovery on those issues. If a party serves a late response, and the opponent refuses to accept it, a court may excuse the party's failure to respond in a timely manner. Likewise, a court may permit a party to withdraw or modify an admission in a timely response. In either situation, the court's decision turns on the degree of prejudice the requesting party will suffer because of its reliance on the admission. Because courts so frequently granted a responding party's request for relief from its failure to respond, leaving requesting parties uncertain about the validity of the admission, and, hence, the necessity of developing evidence for trial, Rule 36(a) was specifically amended in 1970 to permit a requesting party to move for an order deeming the matter to be admitted.

Although Rule 36 and its state counterparts can be enormously useful, in practice requests for admissions are the least used of the discovery devices. See F. Connolly, F. Holleman & M. Kuhlman, *Judicial Controls and the Civil Litigation Process: Discovery* 28 (1978). Attorneys tend to think of requests to admit as part of trial preparation, not discovery. They postpone their use to the very end, and frequently fail to file requests before the time fixed by the court to complete discovery runs out. M. Dombroff, *Discovery* 260 (1986).

Notes and Questions

1. Rule 36 formerly limited requests for admissions to matters of "fact." As amended in 1970, the Rule permits requests for admissions to inquire into matters relating to "statements or opinions of fact or of the application of law to fact, including the genuineness of any document described in the request." Does the amended provision authorize requests for admissions of law unrelated to the facts of the case? See 8 Wright & Miller, *Federal Practice and Procedure: Civil* §§ 2254–56 (1970).

Although a number of jurisdictions have amended their rules to accord with the current version of Federal Rule 36, see, e.g., Ariz.R.Civ.P. 36; Fla.R. Civ.P. 1.370, other states, like New York, have made no changes, despite restrictive interpretations by their courts. See REID SAND & GRAVEL, INC. v. BELLEVUE PROPERTIES, 7 Wash.App. 701, 502 P.2d 480 (1972), in which the court stated: "It is not a proper use of CR 36 to request an adversary to admit, in effect, the truth of the assertion that he should lose the lawsuit."

Why do some courts appear so wary of requests to admit? Is there any justification for holding improper requests to admit facts that are "in controversy" or that are the ultimate facts in issue? Doesn't it make more sense to permit the request to admit to be made so that the responding party can deny it, if untrue? See Comment, *The Dilemma of Federal Rule 36*, 56 Nw.U.L. Rev. 679, 684–85 (1961).

2. What is a "reasonable inquiry" and when is information not "readily obtainable" by an answering party? In LUMPKIN v. MESKILL, 64 F.R.D. 673 (D.Conn.1974), the court held that the defendants in a school desegregation case were required to admit or deny the accuracy of statistics concerning the racial composition of schools that were derived from the random sampling techniques used by the plaintiff's expert. Note that it is well established under Rule 33 that a party has a duty to investigate to ascertain and disclose information that is not within its personal knowledge but reasonably within its power to obtain. Should the standards for investigation be as extensive under Rule 36?

3. Is a party required to admit a matter he believes to be true? Or only a matter that he reasonably believes, on the basis of the admissible evidence known to him, that the proponent who is seeking the admission can prove at trial? Suppose an individual sues a corporation for injuries sustained in a motor vehicle accident, allegedly caused by the negligent driving of defendant's employee. The employee, apparently the only eyewitness, when asked, states that she unlawfully went through a traffic signal. Must the corporate defendant, if requested to do so, admit the unlawful act, even though it suspects that its employee, motivated by compassion for the victim, might not be telling the truth? Suppose that ten impartial witnesses all tell the same story as the employee. Could defendant legitimately deny the request to admit on the theory that all of them could possibly be lying or mistaken? See generally Finman, *The Request for Admissions in Federal Civil Procedure*, 71 Yale L.J. 371, 404–09 (1962); Shapiro, *Some Problems of Discovery in an Adversary System*, 63 Minn.L.Rev. 1055, 1078–92 (1979).

4. If a party serves a denial of the matters in the request to admit and at trial the matter is proved by the party requesting the admission, then Rule 37(c) provides that the latter may collect from the other party the reasonable

expenses incurred in making the proof. How useful is this sanction? How can a party show that a given matter has been "proved"?

5. In 1970 a new last paragraph was added to Federal Rule 36(a) specifically allowing a motion for a determination that unanswered or improperly answered requests "stand admitted"; previously, some courts had rejected such a motion because there was no express authority for it. Compare United States v. New Orleans Chapter, Associated General Contractors of America, Inc., 41 F.R.D. 33 (E.D.La.1966), affirmed without opinion 396 U.S. 115, 90 S.Ct. 398, 24 L.Ed.2d 308 (1969) (court has no power to strike inadequate responses and deem requests admitted), with Heng Hsin Co. v. Stern, Morgenthau & Co., 20 Fed.R.Serv. 586 (S.D.N.Y.1954) (ordering responding party to give more satisfactory answers). Why is it necessary to provide for a court ruling that requests stand admitted? Isn't it enough that a failure to respond results in an admission and that an untruthful response permits sanctions under Rule 37(c)?

6. THE DUTY TO SUPPLEMENT RESPONSES

———

Read Federal Rule of Civil Procedure 26(e) and the accompanying Advisory Committee's Notes in the Supplement.

———

Rule 26(e), adopted in 1970, was designed to eliminate inconsistent decisions regarding the existence and scope of the duty to update discovery answers. Note that the Rule is not all-encompassing. What information obtained subsequent to the original responses is not covered by it? How should the word "knows" in subdivision (e)(2) be interpreted? See 8 Wright & Miller, *Federal Practice and Procedure: Civil* § 2049, at 323 (1970).

Why should there be any duty to supplement answers given in the course of discovery? Some states have refused to impose it. See, e.g., Clay v. McCarthy, 73 Ill.App.3d 462, 30 Ill.Dec. 38, 392 N.E.2d 693 (3d Dist.1979). Doesn't this duty constitute an undue burden on a responding party? Why isn't it enough that the discovering party simply can send a later set of interrogatories or engage in discovery immediately before trial if it wants up-to-date replies from another party? Would it be wise to limit the duty to the giving of names of any newly discovered witnesses? See *Developments in the Law—Discovery,* 74 Harv.L.Rev. 940, 961–63 (1961). Should the duty continue until and even during trial? See Everett v. Morrison, 478 S.W.2d 312 (Mo.1972) (party must disclose identity of witness discovered after trial was in progress).

The final subdivision of Rule 26(e) spells out the circumstances in which a duty may be imposed beyond that created by the Rule, and grants the district courts considerable latitude to require supplementation of responses. Is the duty to supplement responses better addressed on a case-by-case basis, rather than by rule, and resolved in an appropriately drafted pretrial order?

What is the appropriate sanction for a breach of a duty to supplement answers? Most courts merely have prohibited the admission of the undisclosed evidence or prohibited the undisclosed witnesses from giving testimony. The language of Rule 37 does not seem to permit this sanction. Should it? See Note, *Proposed 1967 Amendments to the Federal Discovery Rules,* 68 Colum.L.Rev. 271, 293 (1968). Since Rule 26(e) also says nothing regarding the matter, courts must justify the imposition of sanctions on their inherent powers of control over the discovery process. See 8 Wright & Miller, *Federal Practice and Procedure: Civil* § 2050 (1970).

As an alternative to imposing sanctions upon the offending party, a court usually has the option of postponing the trial of a case, or granting a continuance or recess, so that the other side may complete discovery and prepare to meet any new testimony. See, e.g., Shelak v. White Motor Co., 581 F.2d 1155, 1159 (5th Cir.1978) (defendant permitted additional time to prepare for trial when interrogatory answers were supplemented three days before trial); Washington Hospital Center v. Cheeks, 129 U.S.App.D.C. 339, 394 F.2d 964 (D.C.Cir.1968) (trial recessed to permit the taking of the deposition of expert witness whose name had not been previously given). Is this procedure ordinarily better than sanctions?

7. USE OF DISCOVERY AT TRIAL

———

Read Federal Rules of Civil Procedure 32, 36(b), and 30(e) in the Supplement.

Attorneys can use the discovery devices simply to find out information, but commonly they anticipate using an adversary's or a witness's answers at trial: as admissions, to refresh a witness's recollection, or to provide a basis for cross-examination or impeachment. And sometimes a response to discovery can be used in lieu of or in addition to live testimony. The use of discovery responses at trial is governed by two sets of rules: the rules of procedure and the rules of evidence. As you read the following material, consider how the possibility that discovery responses may be used at trial should affect conduct of discovery before trial. Are there circumstances in which the objective of obtaining discovery and the objective of using discovery responses at trial conflict?

———

RICHMOND v. BROOKS
United States Court of Appeals, Second Circuit, 1955.
227 F.2d 490.

CLARK, CHIEF JUDGE. Plaintiff, residing with her present husband in California, brought suit in the New York Supreme Court against defendant, her former husband, now divorced and a resident of New York, to collect loans she had made to him. It also appears—although the court below held it immaterial—that she conducts a business in Beverly Hills, California, in merchandising women's used garments, known as "Gowns of

<image type="handwriting" location="left margin">to oral deposition
written Qs</image>

the Stars." Defendant removed the action to the district court below and the case went to trial to a jury some three and a half years later after the taking of various depositions of the defendant in New York and the plaintiff in California, the latter by interrogatories and cross interrogatories. At the trial plaintiff offered her deposition as her proof, but the court refused to receive it and later dismissed her action for failure of proof, refusing to grant her motion for a mistrial and for adjournment. Her appeal challenges these rulings.

In excluding the deposition the trial judge held that the defendant was entitled to require the presence of the plaintiff as a part of her case and the opportunity to cross-examine her before the jury. Certain cases cited to him as differently construing [Federal Rule 32(a)] * * *, the governing rule, he distinguished as applying only to a *defendant's* proof. * * *.

F.R. [32(a)] * * * is quite clear in its terms, which apply without exception equally to plaintiffs and defendants. * * *

In * * * Hyam v. American Export Lines, 2 Cir., 213 F.2d 221 * * *, libellant, a resident of Bombay, India, sued in the court below for cargo damage on a shipment carried by respondent from Philadelphia to Bombay; and the parties were at issue preliminarily as to whether libellant's deposition in Bombay should be taken by written interrogatories, as he sought, or by "open commission," with the entire cost thereof paid by him, as sought by the respondent. The district court's solution was to deny the libellant's application and to order him to appear for oral examination in New York. When he failed to comply, his action was dismissed. We reversed, suggesting the "unusually and seriously burdensome" character of the requirement made below and finding error of law on the part of the district judge in failing to exercise discretion to accord the protection invoked by libellant pursuant to [what is now Federal Rule 26(c)] * * * and in proceeding erroneously on the theory that the respondent had the right to have the suing party in New York for oral examination. We said, * * * 213 F.2d 221, 223: "The federal courts are open to foreign suitors as to others, and procedural rules are not to be construed in such fashion as to impose conditions on litigants which in their practical effect amount to a denial of jurisdiction."

Applying this principle as a touchstone, we can find no occasion to add something to the rule which is not there and which effectually distorts its purpose and utility. The tactical burden assumed by the plaintiff in proceeding to trial in her absence, to which the first judge below called attention, is likely to limit frequent resort to this course; but a suitor not able to afford a New York trip should not be denied all remedy here. There is nothing in the general law to demand such a result. * * *

The defendant relies further on the limiting provision of F.R. [32(a)(3)(B)], * * * *viz.,* "unless it appears that the absence of the witness was procured by the party offering the deposition"; and he points out that the plaintiff was in New York City with her husband during the Christmas holidays some two weeks prior to the start of the trial on January 17,

1955. The district court did not consider this issue, rejecting as immaterial plaintiff's business interests in California; and hence we have no finding as to it. But no reason is apparent to justify a requirement that plaintiff must live in New York City—of course expensively, since that is the only mode of life there—awaiting the uncertain call of a case for trial or be penalized for a normal Christmas trip. * * *

It is suggested, as in 4 Moore's Federal Practice 1195–1197 (2d Ed. 1950), that the "unless" clause just quoted may present an issue of construction as to whether the "absence" in question is from the territory embraced within the 100-mile radius or is from the trial itself, and that only the former interpretation (which is favored) permits a California resident as such to use his own deposition. Perhaps too much is made of this assumed dichotomy; it is not apparent why in this carefully defined context absence from the trial should not be tested for the validity of the excuse on the same principles as absence from the territory. Be that as it may, the language used, referring to different stages of trial *or hearing,* and obviously pointing back to the defining clause which sets forth the basic reasons for admissibility, makes it quite clear that the former is meant.

* * *

Reversed and remanded.

Notes and Questions

1. The court in COLONIAL REALTY CORP. v. BRUNSWICK CORP., 337 F.Supp. 546 (S.D.N.Y.1971), questioned whether the *Brooks* decision ought to apply automatically to a case in which plaintiff showed no hardship whatever and in which her credibility was a vital factor. Does Rule 32(a) provide the trial court with any discretion in such a case? See Gianetti v. Fenwick, 166 N.J.Super. 491, 400 A.2d 103 (App.Div.1979).

2. Suppose plaintiff in *Brooks* had sought to introduce her answers to a set of interrogatories served on her by defendant. In CALLAWAY v. PERDUE, 238 Ark. 652, 658–59, 385 S.W.2d 4, 8–9 (1964), the court stated that the answers were "self-serving declarations," and were inadmissible under the rules of evidence. In what ways do answers to interrogatories differ from the transcript of a deposition for purposes of using them at trial under Federal Rule 32(a)?

Suppose that a party, pursuant to its duty to update responses under Federal Rule 26(e), sends a supplementary set of answers much more favorable to itself than the original replies to deposition questions. May the adverse party introduce the original replies at trial? The court in MANGUAL v. PRUDENTIAL LINES, INC., 53 F.R.D. 301 (E.D.Pa.1971), held "yes," in accordance with normal evidence rules, which allow an adverse party to utilize any statement of its opponent. The court in *Mangual* went on to hold, however, that the party who made the responses was entitled to put in its subsequent answers, arguing that this was consistent with the policy of Rule 32(a)(4) providing that if only part of a deposition is introduced, the court, in the interests of justice, may order other portions to be introduced as well. Is the court's analogy a sound one?

3.   Rule 36(b) was amended in 1970 to make clear that admissions under that Rule are conclusive for purposes of the pending action unless the court, on motion, permits the admission to be withdrawn or amended. Prior to the change a few courts had held that an admission was merely an item of evidence that could be rebutted at trial. See generally Finman, *The Request for Admissions in Federal Civil Procedure,* 71 Yale L.J. 371, 421–22 (1962). Should the application of Rule 36(b) be automatic or should it apply only when the party who wishes to rely on an admission offers it into evidence? See National Bank of Georgia v. Hill, 148 Ga.App. 688, 252 S.E.2d 192 (1979) (court will ignore admission not offered into evidence).

4.   Federal Rule 33 contains no provision comparable to Rule 36(b). Should an answer to an interrogatory also be binding at trial? How does Federal Rule 26(e), which deals with the duty to supplement responses, affect your answer? See pp. 762–63, supra.

5.   Florida Rule of Civil Procedure 1.330(a) is identical to Federal Rule 32(a) with one exception, which is spelled out in Rule 1.390(b) as follows:

> The testimony of an expert or skilled witness may be taken at any time before the trial in accordance with the rules for taking depositions and may be used at trial, regardless of the place of residence of the witness or whether he is within the distance prescribed by Rule 1.330(a) (3). No special form of notice need be given that the deposition will be used for trial.

What is the purpose of this rule? Should Federal Rule 32(a) be amended to include a similar provision? See also Mich.Ct.Rules 2.302(B)(4)(d), 2.308(A)(1)(c).

SECTION C. SPECIAL PROBLEMS REGARDING THE SCOPE OF DISCOVERY

1. MATERIALS PREPARED IN ANTICIPATION OF TRIAL

Read Federal Rule of Civil Procedure 26(b)(3) and the accompanying materials in the Supplement.

HICKMAN v. TAYLOR

Supreme Court of the United States, 1947.
329 U.S. 495, 67 S.Ct. 385, 91 L.Ed. 451.

Certiorari to the Circuit Court of Appeals for the Third Circuit.

MR. JUSTICE MURPHY delivered the opinion of the Court.

This case presents an important problem under the Federal Rules * * * as to the extent to which a party may inquire into oral and written statements of witnesses, or other information, secured by an adverse party's counsel in the course of preparation for possible litigation after a claim has arisen. Examination into a person's files and records, including those resulting from the professional activities of an attorney, must be judged with care. It is not without reason that various safeguards have been established to preclude unwarranted excursions into the privacy of a man's work. At the same time, public policy supports reasonable and necessary inquiries. Properly to balance these competing interests is a delicate and difficult task.

On February 7, 1943, the tug "J.M. Taylor" sank while engaged in helping to tow a car float of the Baltimore & Ohio Railroad across the Delaware River at Philadelphia. The accident was apparently unusual in nature, the cause of it still being unknown. Five of the nine crew members were drowned. Three days later the tug owners and the underwriters employed a law firm, of which respondent Fortenbaugh is a member, to defend them against potential suits by representatives of the deceased crew members and to sue the railroad for damages to the tug.

A public hearing was held on March 4, 1943, before the United States Steamboat Inspectors, at which the four survivors were examined. This testimony was recorded and made available to all interested parties. Shortly thereafter, Fortenbaugh privately interviewed the survivors and took statements from them with an eye toward the anticipated litigation; the survivors signed these statements on March 29. Fortenbaugh also interviewed other persons believed to have some information relating to the accident and in some cases he made memoranda of what they told him. At the time when Fortenbaugh secured the statements of the survivors, representatives of two of the deceased crew members had been in communication with him. Ultimately claims were presented by representatives of all five of the deceased; four of the claims, however, were settled without litigation. The fifth claimant, petitioner herein, brought suit in a federal court under the Jones Act on November 26, 1943, naming as defendants the two tug owners, individually and as partners, and the railroad.

One year later, petitioner filed 39 interrogatories directed to the tug owners. The 38th interrogatory read: "State whether any statements of the members of the crews of the Tugs 'J.M. Taylor' and 'Philadelphia' or of any other vessel were taken in connection with the towing of the car float and the sinking of the Tug 'John M. Taylor'. Attach hereto exact copies of all such statements if in writing, and if oral, set forth in detail the exact provisions of any such oral statements or reports."

Supplemental interrogatories asked whether any oral or written statements, records, reports or other memoranda had been made concerning any matter relative to the towing operation, the sinking of the tug, the salvaging and repair of the tug, and the death of the deceased. If the answer was in the affirmative, the tug owners were then requested to set forth the nature of all such records, reports, statements or other memoranda.

The tug owners, through Fortenbaugh, answered all of the interrogatories except No. 38 and the supplemental ones just described. While admitting that statements of the survivors had been taken, they declined to summarize or set forth the contents. They did so on the ground that such requests called "for privileged matter obtained in preparation for litigation" and constituted "an attempt to obtain indirectly counsel's private files." It was claimed that answering these requests "would involve practically turning over not only the complete files, but also the telephone records and, almost, the thoughts of counsel."

In connection with the hearing on these objections, Fortenbaugh made a written statement and gave an informal oral deposition explaining the circumstances under which he had taken the statements. But he was not expressly asked in the deposition to produce the statements. The District Court for the Eastern District of Pennsylvania, sitting en banc, held that the requested matters were not privileged. 4 F.R.D. 479. The court then decreed that the tug owners and Fortenbaugh, as counsel and agent for the tug owners forthwith "Answer Plaintiff's 38th interrogatory and supplemental interrogatories; produce all written statements of witnesses obtained by Mr. Fortenbaugh, as counsel and agent for Defendants; state in substance any fact concerning this case which Defendants learned through oral statements made by witnesses to Mr. Fortenbaugh whether or not included in his private memoranda and produce Mr. Fortenbaugh's memoranda containing statements of fact by witnesses or to submit these memoranda to the Court for determination of those portions which should be revealed to Plaintiff." Upon their refusal, the court adjudged them in contempt and ordered them imprisoned until they complied.

The Third Circuit Court of Appeals, also sitting en banc, reversed the judgment of the District Court. 153 F.2d 212. It held that the information here sought was part of the "work product of the lawyer" and hence privileged from discovery under the Federal Rules of Civil Procedure. The importance of the problem, which has engendered a great divergence of views among district courts, led us to grant certiorari. * * *

There is an initial question as to which of the deposition-discovery rules is involved in this case. Petitioner, in filing his interrogatories, thought that he was proceeding under Rule 33.

* * * [I]t does not appear from the record that petitioner filed a motion under Rule 34 for a court order directing the production of the documents in question. Indeed, such an order could not have been entered as to Fortenbaugh since Rule 34, like Rule 33, is limited to parties to the proceeding, thereby excluding their counsel or agents.

Thus to the extent that petitioner was seeking the production of the memoranda and statements gathered by Fortenbaugh in the course of his activities as counsel, petitioner misconceived his remedy. Rule 33 did not permit him to obtain such memoranda and statements as adjuncts to the interrogatories addressed to the individual tug owners. A party clearly cannot refuse to answer interrogatories on the ground that the information sought is solely within the knowledge of his attorney. But that is not this case. Here production was sought of documents prepared by a party's attorney after the claim has arisen. Rule 33 does not make provision for such production, even when sought in connection with permissible interrogatories. Moreover, since petitioner was also foreclosed from securing them through an order under Rule 34, his only recourse was to take Fortenbaugh's deposition under Rule 26 and to attempt to force Fortenbaugh to produce the materials by use of a subpoena *duces tecum* in accordance with Rule 45. * * * But despite petitioner's faulty choice of action, the District Court entered an order, apparently under Rule 34, commanding the tug owners and Fortenbaugh, as their agent and counsel, to produce the materials in question. Their refusal led to the anomalous result of holding the tug owners in contempt for failure to produce that which was in the possession of their counsel and of holding Fortenbaugh in contempt for failure to produce that which he could not be compelled to produce under either Rule 33 or Rule 34.

But under the circumstances we deem it unnecessary and unwise to rest our decision upon this procedural irregularity, an irregularity which is not strongly urged upon us and which was disregarded in the two courts below. * * * [T]he basic question at stake is whether any of those devices may be used to inquire into materials collected by an adverse party's counsel in the course of preparation for possible litigation. The fact that the petitioner may have used the wrong method does not destroy the main thrust of his attempt. * * * [I]n the present circumstances, for the purposes of this decision, the procedural irregularity is not material. * * *

In urging that he has a right to inquire into the materials secured and prepared by Fortenbaugh, petitioner emphasizes that the deposition-discovery portions of the Federal Rules of Civil Procedure are designed to enable the parties to discover the true facts and to compel their disclosure wherever they may be found. It is said that inquiry may be made under these rules, epitomized by Rule 26, as to any relevant matter which is not privileged; and since the discovery provisions are to be applied as broadly and liberally as possible, the privilege limitation must be restricted to its narrowest bounds. On the premise that the attorney-client privilege is the one involved in this case, petitioner argues that it must be strictly confined to confidential communications made by a client to his attorney. And since the materials here in issue were secured by Fortenbaugh from third persons rather than from his clients, the tug owners, the conclusion is reached that these materials are proper subjects for discovery under Rule 26.

As additional support for this result, petitioner claims that to prohibit discovery under these circumstances would give a corporate defendant a tremendous advantage in a suit by an individual plaintiff. Thus in a suit by an injured employee against a railroad or in a suit by an insured person against an insurance company the corporate defendant could pull a dark veil of secrecy over all the pertinent facts it can collect after the claim arises merely on the assertion that such facts were gathered by its large staff of attorneys and claim agents. At the same time, the individual plaintiff, who often has direct knowledge of the matter in issue and has no counsel until some time after his claim arises could be compelled to disclose all the intimate details of his case. By endowing with immunity from disclosure all that a lawyer discovers in the course of his duties, it is said, the rights of individual litigants in such cases are drained of vitality and the lawsuit becomes more of a battle of deception than a search for truth.

But framing the problem in terms of assisting individual plaintiffs in their suits against corporate defendants is unsatisfactory. Discovery concededly may work to the disadvantage as well as to the advantage of individual plaintiffs. Discovery, in other words, is not a one-way proposition. It is available in all types of cases at the behest of any party, individual or corporate, plaintiff or defendant. The problem thus far transcends the situation confronting this petitioner. And we must view that problem in light of the limitless situations where the particular kind of discovery sought by petitioner might be used.

We agree, of course, that the deposition-discovery rules are to be accorded a broad and liberal treatment. No longer can the time-honored cry of "fishing expedition" serve to preclude a party from inquiring into the facts underlying his opponent's case. Mutual knowledge of all the relevant facts gathered by both parties is essential to proper litigation. To that end, either party may compel the other to disgorge whatever facts he has in his possession. The deposition-discovery procedure simply advances the stage at which the disclosure can be compelled from the time of trial to the period preceding it, thus reducing the possibility of surprise. But discovery, like all matters of procedure, has ultimate and necessary boundaries. As indicated by Rules 30(b) and (d) and 31(d), limitations inevitably arise when it can be shown that the examination is being conducted in bad faith or in such a manner as to annoy, embarrass or oppress the person subject to the inquiry. And as Rule 26(b) provides, further limitations come into existence when the inquiry touches upon the irrelevant or encroaches upon the recognized domains of privilege.

We also agree that the memoranda, statements and mental impressions in issue in this case fall outside the scope of the attorney-client privilege and hence are not protected from discovery on that basis.

* * *

But the impropriety of invoking that privilege does not provide an answer to the problem before us. Petitioner has made more than an ordinary request for relevant, non-privileged facts in the possession of his adversaries or their counsel. He has sought discovery as of right of oral and written statements of witnesses whose identity is well known and whose availability to petitioner appears unimpaired. He has sought production of these matters after making the most searching inquiries of his opponents as to the circumstances surrounding the fatal accident, which inquiries were sworn to have been answered to the best of their information and belief. Interrogatories were directed toward all the events prior to, during and subsequent to the sinking of the tug. Full and honest answers to such broad inquiries would necessarily have included all pertinent information gleaned by Fortenbaugh through his interviews with the witnesses. Petitioner makes no suggestion, and we cannot assume, that the tug owners of Fortenbaugh were incomplete or dishonest in the framing of their answers. In addition, petitioner was free to examine the public testimony of the witnesses taken before the United States Steamboat Inspectors. We are thus dealing with an attempt to secure the production of written statements and mental impressions contained in the files and the mind of the attorney Fortenbaugh without any showing of necessity or any indication or claim that denial of such production would unduly prejudice the preparation of petitioner's case or cause him any hardship or injustice. For aught that appears, the essence of what petitioner seeks either has been revealed to him already through the interrogatories or is readily available to him direct from the witnesses for the asking.

* * *

In our opinion, neither Rule 26 nor any other rule dealing with discovery contemplates production under such circumstances. That is not because the subject matter is privileged or irrelevant, as those concepts are used in these rules. Here is simply an attempt, without purported necessity or justification, to secure written statements, private memoranda and personal recollections prepared or formed by an adverse party's counsel in the course of his legal duties. As such, it falls outside the arena of discovery and contravenes the public policy underlying the orderly prosecution and defense of legal claims. Not even the most liberal of discovery theories can justify unwarranted inquiries into the files and the mental impressions of an attorney.

Historically, a lawyer is an officer of the court and is bound to work for the advancement of justice while faithfully protecting the rightful interests of his clients. In performing his various duties, however, it is essential that a lawyer work with a certain degree of privacy, free from unnecessary intrusion by opposing parties and their counsel. Proper preparation of a client's case demands that he assemble information, sift what he considers to be the relevant from the irrelevant facts, prepare his legal theories and plan his strategy without undue and needless interference. That is the historical and the necessary way in which lawyers act within the framework of our system of jurisprudence to promote justice and to protect their clients' interests. This work is reflected, of course, in interviews, statements, memoranda, correspondence, briefs, mental impressions, personal beliefs, and countless other tangible and intangible ways—aptly though roughly termed by the Circuit Court of Appeals in this case [153 F.2d 212, 223] as the "work product of the lawyer." Were such materials open to opposing counsel on mere demand, much of what is now put down in writing would remain unwritten. An attorney's thoughts, heretofore inviolate, would not be his own. Inefficiency, unfairness and sharp practices would inevitably develop in the giving of legal advice and in the preparation of cases for trial. The effect on the legal profession would be demoralizing. And the interests of the clients and the cause of justice would be poorly served.

We do not mean to say that all written materials obtained or prepared by an adversary's counsel with an eye toward litigation are necessarily free from discovery in all cases. Where relevant and non-privileged facts remain hidden in an attorney's file and where production of those facts is essential to the preparation of one's case, discovery may properly be had. Such written statements and documents might, under certain circumstances, be admissible in evidence or give clues as to the existence or location of relevant facts. Or they might be useful for purposes of impeachment or corroboration. And production might be justified where the witnesses are no longer available or can be reached only with difficulty. Were production of written statements and documents to be precluded under such circumstances, the liberal ideals of the deposition-discovery portions of the Federal Rules of Civil Procedure would be stripped of much of their meaning. But the general policy against invading the privacy of an attorney's course of preparation is so well recognized and so essential to an orderly working of our system of legal procedure that a burden rests on the one who would invade that privacy to establish adequate reasons to justify production through a subpoena or court order. That burden, we believe, is necessarily implicit in the rules as now constituted.

Rule 30(b), as presently written, gives the trial judge the requisite discretion to make a judgment as to whether discovery should be allowed as to written statements secured from witnesses. But in the instant case there was no room for that discretion to operate in favor of the petitioner. No attempt was made to establish any reason why Fortenbaugh should be forced to produce the written statements. There was only a naked, general demand for these materials as of right and a finding by the District Court that no recognizable privilege was involved. That was insufficient to justify discovery under these circumstances and the court should have sustained the refusal of the tug owners and Fortenbaugh to produce.

But as to oral statements made by witnesses to Fortenbaugh, whether presently in the form of his mental impressions or memoranda, we do not believe that any showing of necessity can be made under the circumstances of this case so as to justify production. Under ordinary conditions, forcing an attorney to repeat or write out all that witnesses have told him and to deliver the account to his adversary gives rise to grave dangers of inaccuracy and untrustworthiness. No legitimate purpose is served by such production. The practice forces the attorney to testify as to what he remembers or what he saw fit to write down regarding witnesses' remarks. Such testimony could not qualify as evidence; and to use it for impeachment or corroborative purposes would make the attorney much less an officer of the court and much more an ordinary witness. The standards of the profession would thereby suffer.

Denial of production of this nature does not mean that any material, nonprivileged facts can be hidden from the petitioner in this case. He need not be unduly hindered in the preparation of his case, in the discovery of facts or in his anticipation of his opponents' position. Searching interrogatories directed to Fortenbaugh and the tug owners, production of written documents and statements upon a proper showing and direct interviews with the witnesses themselves all serve to reveal the facts in Fortenbaugh's possession to the fullest possible extent consistent with public policy. Petitioner's counsel frankly admits that he wants the oral statements only to help prepare himself to examine witnesses and to make sure that he has overlooked nothing. That is insufficient under the circumstances to permit him an exception to the policy underlying the privacy of Fortenbaugh's professional activities. If there should be a rare situation justifying production of these matters, petitioner's case is not of that type.

We fully appreciate the wide-spread controversy among the members of the legal profession over the problem raised by this case. It is a problem that rests on what has been one of the most hazy frontiers of the discovery process. But until some rule or statute definitely prescribes otherwise, we are not justified in permitting discovery in a situation of this nature as a matter of unqualified right. When Rule 26 and the other discovery rules were adopted, this Court and the members of the bar in general certainly did not believe or contemplate that all the files and mental processes of lawyers were thereby opened to the free scrutiny of their adversaries. And we refuse to interpret the rules at this time so as to reach so harsh and unwarranted a result.

We therefore affirm the judgment of the Circuit Court of Appeals.

Affirmed.

MR. JUSTICE JACKSON, concurring.

* * *

To consider first the most extreme aspect of the requirement in litigation here, we find it calls upon counsel, if he has had any conversations with any of the crews of the vessels in question or of any other, to "set forth in detail the exact provision of any such oral statements or reports." Thus the demand is not for the production of a transcript in existence but calls for the creation of a written statement not in being. But the statement by counsel of what a witness told him is not evidence when written. Plaintiff could not introduce it to prove his case. What, then, is the purpose sought to be served by demanding this of adverse counsel?

Counsel for the petitioner candidly said on argument that he wanted this information to help prepare himself to examine witnesses, to make sure he overlooked nothing. He bases his claim to it in his brief on the view that the Rules were to do away with the old situation where a law suit developed into "a battle of wits between counsel." But a common law trial is and always should be an adversary proceeding. Discovery was hardly intended to enable a learned profession to perform its functions either without wits or on wits borrowed from the adversary.

The real purpose and the probable effect of the practice ordered by the district court would be to put trials on a level even lower than a "battle of wits." I can conceive of no practice more demoralizing to the Bar than to require a lawyer to write out and deliver to his adversary an account of what witnesses have told him. Even if his recollection were perfect, the statement would be his language permeated with his inferences. Every one who has tried it knows that it is almost impossible so fairly to record the expressions and emphasis of a witness that when he testifies in the environment of the court and under the influence of the leading question there will not be departures in some respects. Whenever the testimony of the witness would differ from the "exact" statement the lawyer had delivered, the lawyer's statement would be whipped out to impeach the witness. Counsel producing his adversary's "inexact" statement could lose nothing by saying, "Here is a contradiction, gentlemen of the jury. I do not know whether it is my adversary or his witness who is not telling the truth, but one is not." Of course, if this practice were adopted, that scene would be repeated over and over again. The lawyer who delivers such statements often would find himself branded a deceiver afraid to take the stand to support his own version of the witness's conversation with him, or else he will have to go on the stand to defend his own credibility—perhaps against that of his chief witness, or possibly even his client.

Every lawyer dislikes to take the witness stand and will do so only for grave reasons. This is partly because it is not his role; he is almost invariably a poor witness. But he steps out of professional character to do it. He regrets it; the profession discourages it. But the practice advocated here is one which would force him to be a witness, not as to what he has seen or done but as to other witnesses' stories, and not because he wants to do so but in self-defense.

And what is the lawyer to do who has interviewed one whom he believes to be a biased, lying or hostile witness to get his unfavorable statements and know what to meet? He must record and deliver such statements even though he would not vouch for the credibility of the witness by calling him. Perhaps the other side would not want to call him either, but the attorney is open to the charge of suppressing evidence at the trial if he fails to call such a hostile witness even though he never regarded him as reliable or truthful.

Having been supplied the names of the witnesses, petitioner's lawyer gives no reason why he cannot interview them himself. If an employee-witness refuses to tell his story, he, too, may be examined under the Rules. He may be compelled on discovery as fully as on the trial to disclose his version of the facts. But that is his own disclosure—it can be used to impeach him if he contradicts it and such a deposition is not useful to promote an unseemly disagreement between the witness and the counsel in the case.

It is true that the literal language of the Rules would admit of an interpretation that would sustain the district court's order. * * * But all such procedural measures have a background of custom and practice which was assumed by those who wrote and should be by those who apply them. * * * Certainly nothing in the tradition or practice of discovery up to the time of these Rules would have suggested that they would authorize such a practice as here proposed.

The question remains as to signed statements or those written by witnesses. Such statements are not evidence for the defendant. * * * Nor should I think they ordinarily could be evidence for the plaintiff. But such a statement might be useful for impeachment of the witness who signed it, if he is called and if he departs from the statement. There might be circumstances, too, where impossibility or difficulty of access to the witness or his refusal to respond to requests for information or other facts would show that the interests of justice require that such statements be made available. Production of such statements are governed by Rule 34 and on "Showing good cause therefor" the court may order their inspection, copying or photographing. No such application has here been made; the demand is made on the basis of right, not on showing of cause.

I agree to the affirmance of the judgment of the Circuit Court of Appeals which reversed the district court.

MR. JUSTICE FRANKFURTER joins in this opinion.

Notes and Questions

1. In 1970, Federal Rule 26(b)(3) was added specifically to deal with the discovery of work-product. In what ways does the work-product doctrine in the Rule differ from that stated in *Hickman*? Does *Hickman* survive the codification of the work-product doctrine in the Rule in any way? See Clermont, *Surveying Work Product*, 68 Cornell L.Rev. 755 (1983).

2. Prior to the adoption of Rule 26(b)(3) many of the states that had adopted federal discovery rules already had added special provisions to deal with work-product and related problems. These provisions vary from state to state. See Friedenthal, *Discovery and Use of an Adverse Party's Expert Information*, 14 Stan.L.Rev. 455, 474–79 (1962). Compare Federal Rule 26(b)(3), with N.Y.C.P.L.R. § 3101.

3. Courts have split on the question whether and when Rule 26(b)(3) covers documents containing the results of a party's investigations made prior to hiring an attorney or the initiation of litigation. An example of a case in which discovery was permitted is THOMAS ORGAN CO. v. JADRANSKA SLOBODNA PLOVIDBA, 54 F.R.D. 367 (N.D.Ill.1972), involving a claim for damaged goods. Some seven months prior to the time plaintiff hired an attorney, its insurer conducted an investigation of the facts regarding the loss. The court held that the report of the investigation was made in the ordinary course of business and not for litigation, noting that in the vast majority of situations involving insurance claims, matters are settled without litigation. But discovery was denied in ALMAGUER v. CHICAGO, R.I. & P. R. CO., 55 F.R.D. 147 (D.Neb.1972), in which a railroad employee brought suit against his employer for injuries incurred on the job. Plaintiff was not allowed to obtain a copy of a statement of an eyewitness taken by defendant's claims agent two months before plaintiff had employed a lawyer. The court said that whenever a railroad employee claims to have been injured on the job "the expectation of litigation * * * is a reasonable assumption."

Should the determination whether a report written prior to any legal action is discoverable be decided in terms of the likelihood that a lawsuit ultimately would be filed? See Abel Investment Co. v. United States, 53 F.R.D. 485, 489 (D.Neb.1971) (Internal Revenue Service field agent reports regarding plaintiff's tax liabilities held to be routine, and hence discoverable, since only a few such reports result in litigation). Should work-product protection be denied to any material prepared as part of an organization's normal course of business even if the probability of litigation is overwhelming? A New York court apparently so ruled, holding that subdivision (g) of N.Y.C.P.L.R. § 3101, which requires disclosure of "any written report of an accident prepared in the regular course of business operations," supersedes subdivision (d)(2) of that section which protects writings "created * * * in preparation for litigation." Pataki v. Kiseda, 80 A.D.2d 100, 437 N.Y.S.2d 692 (2d Dep't 1981). Could a federal court reach the same result under Rule 26(b)(3)?

4. Rule 26(b)(3) refers only to "discovery of documents and tangible things." May a party ask by way of interrogatory what a specific document says? See PETERSON v. UNITED STATES, 52 F.R.D. 317, 320 (S.D.Ill.1971): "It is clear to this court that discovery of a detailed description of the contents of documents through interrogatories is equivalent to discovery of the documents themselves. The discovery sought by plaintiff through the interrogatories is therefore covered by rule 26(b)(3)." Is the court correct? Suppose plaintiff merely asked a question regarding a relevant fact, the answer to which was known to defendant only through documents uncovered by investigations of his attorney. Would such a question fall within the scope of the Rule? Should it? Should work product encompass the names of eyewitnesses uncovered by an attorney or her client during pretrial investigation? Would it make a difference if a party seeks only the names of the witnesses the opposing party will call at trial? See Grant v. Huff, p. 717, supra. For a general discussion of the distinction between "documents and tangible things" and facts learned from them, see 8 Wright & Miller, *Federal Practice and Procedure: Civil* § 2023, at 194 (1970).

5. Rule 26(b)(3) allows discovery of material otherwise protected "only upon a showing that the party seeking discovery has substantial need of the materials in the preparation of the case and that he is unable without undue hardship to obtain the substantial equivalent of the materials by other means." In SNEAD v. AMERICAN EXPORT–ISBRANDTSEN LINES, INC., 59 F.R.D. 148, 151 (E.D.Pa.1973), plaintiff, who had brought suit to recover for personal injuries, moved for a court order requiring defendant to answer interrogatories as to whether defendant had possession of any secret motion pictures taken of plaintiff that would tend to bear on the scope of plaintiff's injuries. The court held as follows:

> * * * The only time there will be a substantial need to know about surveillance pictures will be in those instances where there would be a major discrepancy between the testimony the plaintiff will give and that which the films would seem to portray. By the same token this would be the only instance where there is a substantial need to withhold that information from plaintiff's counsel. If the discrepancy would be the result of the plaintiff's untruthfulness, the substantial need for his counsel to know of the variance can hardly justify making the information available to him. On the other hand, if the discrepancy would result from misleading photography, the necessary background information should be made available to the plaintiff's attorney so the fraud can be exposed. It goes without saying that the means to impeach should not be the exclusive property of the defense. * * *

I conclude these purposes can best be achieved by requiring the defense to disclose the existence of surveillance films or be barred from showing them at trial. If the defense has films and decides it wants to use them, they should be exhibited to the plaintiff and his counsel. * * *

Before any of these disclosures, however, the defense must be given an opportunity to depose the plaintiff fully as to his injuries, their effects, and his present disabilities. Once his testimony is memorialized in deposition, any variation he may make at trial to conform to the surveillance films can be used to impeach his credibility, and his knowledge at deposition that the films may exist should have a salutary effect on any tendency to be expansive. * * *

Isn't it true that whenever a document or other item is to be introduced into evidence by one party, the requisite need for discovery will be satisfied at least for the purposes of determining whether such an item has been forged, distorted, or altered in some way?

6. Rule 26(b)(3) states that the court shall "protect against" disclosure of the mental impressions, conclusions, and opinions of an attorney or other representative of a party. How can this provision be harmonized with Rules 33(b) and 36(a), which, as amended in 1970, allow interrogatories and requests for admissions involving opinions or contentions that relate to fact or the application of law to fact?

7. Courts are divided on the degree of protection to be given "opinion" work product. In an important case, the Fourth Circuit has held that "no showing of relevance, substantial need or undue hardship should justify compelled disclosure of an attorney's mental impressions, conclusions, opinions or legal theories." DUPLAN CORP. v. MOULINAGE ET RETORDERIE DE CHAVANOZ, 509 F.2d 730, 734 (4th Cir.1974), certiorari denied 420 U.S. 997, 95 S.Ct. 1438, 43 L.Ed.2d 680 (1975). But in XEROX CORP. v. INTERNATIONAL BUSINESS MACHS. CORP., 64 F.R.D. 367 (S.D.N.Y.1974), the court ordered the production of counsel's notes of interviews with defendant's employees who could not recall crucial information at their depositions even if it was not feasible to excise the portions containing the attorney's mental impressions. "A party should not be allowed to conceal critical, non-privileged, discoverable information, which is uniquely within the knowledge of the party and which is not obtainable from any other source, simply by imparting the information to its attorney and then attempting to hide behind the work product doctrine after the party fails to remember the information." Id. at 381–82.

The plaintiffs in SHELTON v. AMERICAN MOTORS CORP., 805 F.2d 1323 (8th Cir.1986), were the parents of a sixteen-year-old who was killed in a "roll-over" accident while driving a Jeep CJ–5 manufactured by the defendant. They brought suit against the manufacturer, A.M.C., alleging negligence, strict liability and failure to warn. Plaintiffs sought and a magistrate allowed them to depose various A.M.C. personnel, including A.M.C.'s in-house litigation counsel, Rita Burns. However, during Burns' deposition, she refused to answer questions concerning the existence or nonexistence of documents, including any list of lawsuits filed against A.M.C. that involved the Jeep CJ–5, records of roll-over propensity tests other than those previously disclosed, any documents, films, prints, or memoranda that had been suppressed for the purposes of previous Jeep overturn cases, documents and videotapes of the Jeep Celebrity Challenge Races, computer modeling data, and several other items. Ms. Burns asserted that disclosure of her knowledge of the existence or nonexistence of any documents would reveal her mental impressions and that therefore the information sought by plaintiffs was protected work product. Should the court have ordered Ms. Burns to answer the questions?

8. Rule 26(b)(3) excludes from protection a party's own prior statement concerning the action. Why? See the Advisory Committee's Note to Rule 26(b)(3) set out in the Supplement. The rule also permits a nonparty witness to obtain a copy of his statement upon request. Are the reasons for allowing a witness to obtain his own statement the same for a nonparty as they are for a party? Might a court usefully postpone release of the statement of a witness until after she has been deposed?

9. The work-product doctrine has been the subject of a considerable number of comments, debates, and judicial decisions in state as well as federal courts. See generally Cohn, *The Work-Product Doctrine: Protection, Not Privilege,* 71 Geo.L.J. 917 (1983); Taine, *Discovery of Trial Preparations in the Federal Courts,* 50 Colum.L.Rev. 1026 (1950); Tolman, *Discovery Under the Federal Rules: Production of Documents and the Work Products of the Lawyer,* 58 Colum.L.Rev. 498 (1958); Note, *The Work Product Doctrine,* 68 Cornell L.Rev. 760 (1983); *Developments in the Law—Discovery,* 74 Harv.L. Rev. 940, 1027–46 (1961); Comment, *The Work Product Doctrine in the State Courts,* 62 Mich.L.Rev. 1199 (1964).

2. PRIVILEGED MATTER

Rule 26(b)(1) limits discovery to matter that is "not privileged," and the usual view has been that the same rules of privilege apply to discovery as apply at the trial. A rule of privilege gives a person a right to refuse to disclose information that he otherwise would be required to provide. It also may give a person the right to prevent someone else from disclosing information, or it may give its possessor a right to refuse to become a witness. A rule of privilege is a counterweight to the general power of courts to compel testimony. Modern pretrial discovery involves an extension of the judicial power to compel disclosure and has been met by the expansion of old privileges and the creation of new ones that will check this power.

One rule of privilege that all American courts recognize is the attorney-client privilege. They also agree on its basic contours. For the privilege to attach to a communication, four elements must be present:

(1) [T]he asserted holder of the privilege is or sought to be a client; (2) the person to whom the communication was made (a) is a member of the bar of a court, or his subordinate and (b) in connection with this communication is acting as a lawyer; (3) the communication relates to a fact of which the attorney was informed (a) by his client (b) without the presence of strangers (c) for the purpose of securing primarily either (i) an opinion on law or (ii) legal services or (iii) assistance in some legal proceeding, and not (d) for the purpose of committing a crime or tort; and (4) the privilege has been (a) claimed and (b) not waived by the client.

United States v. United Shoe Machinery Corp., 89 F.Supp. 357, 358–59 (D.Mass.1950).

Because the attorney-client privilege results in the suppression of relevant facts, courts tend to construe it narrowly and to resolve doubtful cases against a finding of privilege. One observer has said that "[w]hile often unexpressed, the crucial factor limiting the privilege's availability is not the past law of the privilege but the developing rules of liberal discovery. * * * At least when precedent is not absolutely clear, whether a party can assert the privilege will often depend less on the jurisdiction's law of privilege than on the particular judge's attitude toward liberal discovery." L. Bartell, "The Attorney–Client Privilege and the Work–Product Doctrine," in *ALI–ABA Civil Procedure and Litigation in Federal and State Courts,* vol. I, at 507 (1987).

UPJOHN CO. v. UNITED STATES

Supreme Court of the United States, 1981.
449 U.S. 383, 101 S.Ct. 677, 66 L.Ed.2d 584.

Certiorari to the United States Court of Appeals for the Sixth Circuit.

JUSTICE REHNQUIST delivered the opinion of the Court.

We granted certiorari in this case to address important questions concerning the scope of the attorney-client privilege in the corporate context and the applicability of the work-product doctrine in proceedings to enforce tax summonses. With respect to the privilege question the parties and various *amici* have described our task as one of choosing between two "tests" which have gained adherents in the courts of appeals. We are acutely aware, however, that we sit to decide concrete cases and not abstract propositions of law. We decline to lay down a broad rule or series of rules to govern all conceivable future questions in this area, even were we able to do so. We can and do, however, conclude that the attorney-client privilege protects the communications involved in this case from compelled disclosure and that the work-product doctrine does apply in tax summons enforcement proceedings.

I

Petitioner Upjohn manufactures and sells pharmaceuticals here and abroad. In January 1976 independent accountants conducting an audit of one of petitioner's foreign subsidiaries discovered that the subsidiary made payments to or for the benefit of foreign government officials in order to secure government business. The accountants, so informed Mr. Gerard Thomas, petitioner's Vice-President, Secretary, and General Counsel. * * * He consulted with outside counsel and R.T. Parfet, Jr., petitioner's Chairman of the Board. It was decided that the company would conduct an internal investigation of what were termed "questionable payments." As part of this investigation the attorneys prepared a letter containing a questionnaire which was sent to "all foreign general and area managers" over the Chairman's signature. The letter began by noting recent disclosures that several American companies made "possibly illegal" payments to foreign government officials and emphasized that the management needed full information concerning any such payments made by Upjohn. The letter indicated that the Chairman had asked Thomas, identified as "the company's General Counsel," "to conduct an investigation for the purpose of determining the nature and magnitude of any payments made by the Upjohn Company or any of its subsidiaries to any employee or official of a foreign government." The questionnaire sought detailed information concerning such payments. Managers were instructed to treat the investigation as "highly confidential" and not to discuss it with anyone other than Upjohn employees who might be helpful in providing the requested information. Responses were to be sent directly to Thomas. Thomas and outside counsel also interviewed the recipients of the questionnaire and some 33 other Upjohn officers or employees as part of the investigation.

On March 26, 1976, the company voluntarily submitted a preliminary report to the Securities and Exchange Commission on Form 8–K disclosing certain questionable payments. A copy of the report was simultaneously submitted to the Internal Revenue Service, which immediately began an investigation to determine the tax consequences of the payments. Special agents conducting the investigation were given lists by Upjohn of all those interviewed and all who had responded to the questionnaire. On November 23, 1976, the Service issued a summons pursuant to 26 U.S.C. § 7602 demanding production of:

> All files relative to the investigation conducted under the supervision of Gerard Thomas to identify payments to employees of foreign governments and any political contributions made by the Upjohn Company or any of its affiliates since January 1, 1971 and to determine whether any funds of the Upjohn Company had been improperly accounted for on the corporate books during the same period.

> The records should include but not be limited to written questionnaires sent to managers of the Upjohn Company's foreign affiliates, and memoranda or notes of the interviews conducted in the United States and abroad with officers and employees of the Upjohn Company and its subsidiaries. App. 17a–18a.

The company declined to produce the documents specified in the second paragraph on the grounds that they were protected from disclosure by the attorney-client privilege and constituted the work product of attorneys prepared in anticipation of litigation. On August 31, 1977, the United States filed a petition seeking enforcement of the summons under 26 U.S.C. §§ 7402(b) and 7604(a) in the United States District Court for the Western District of Michigan. That court adopted the recommendation of a magistrate who concluded that the summons should be enforced. Petitioner appealed to the Court of Appeals for the Sixth Circuit which rejected the magistrate's finding of a waiver of the attorney-client privilege, * * * but agreed that the privilege did not apply "to the extent the communications were made by officers and agents not responsible for directing Upjohn's actions in response to legal advice * * * for the simple reason that the communications were not the 'client's.' " * * * The court reasoned that accepting petitioner's claim for a broader application of the privilege would encourage upper-echelon management to ignore unpleasant facts and create too broad a "zone of silence." Noting that petitioner's counsel had interviewed officials such as the Chairman and President, the Court of Appeals remanded to the District Court so that a determination of who was within the "control group" could be made. In a concluding footnote the court stated that the work-product doctrine "is not applicable to administrative summonses issued under 26 U.S.C. § 7602." * * *

II

Federal Rule of Evidence 501 provides that "the privilege of a witness * * * shall be governed by the principles of the common law as they may be interpreted by the courts of the United States in light of reason and experience." The attorney-client privilege is the oldest of the privileges for confidential communications known to the common law. 8 Wigmore, Evidence § 2290 (McNaughton rev. 1961). Its purpose is to encourage full and frank communication between attorneys and their clients and thereby promote broader public interests in the observance of law and administration of justice. The privilege recognizes that sound legal advice or advocacy serves public ends and that such advice or advocacy depends upon the lawyer being fully informed by the client. * * * Admittedly complications in the application of the privilege arise when the client is a corporation, which in theory is an artificial creature of the law, and not an individual; but this Court has assumed that the privilege applies when the client is a corporation. * * *

The Court of Appeals, however, considered the application of the privilege in the corporate context to present a "different problem," since the client was an inanimate entity and "only the senior management, guiding and integrating the several operations, * * * can be said to possess an identity analogous to the corporation as a whole." * * * Such a view, we think, overlooks the fact that the privilege exists to protect not only the giving of professional advice to those who can act on it but also the giving of information to the lawyer to enable him to give sound and informed advice. * * * The first step in the resolution of any legal problem is ascertaining the factual background and sifting through the facts with an eye to the legally relevant. * * *

In the case of the individual client the provider of information and the person who acts on the lawyer's advice are one and the same. In the corporate context, however, it will frequently be employees beyond the control group as defined by the court below—"officers and agents * * * responsible for directing [the company's] actions in response to legal advice"—who will possess the information needed by the corporation's lawyers. Middle-level—and indeed lower-level—employees can, by actions within the scope of their employment, embroil the corporation in serious legal difficulties, and it is only natural that these employees would have the relevant information needed by corporate counsel if he is adequately to advise the client with respect to such actual or potential difficulties. * * *

The control group test adopted by the court below thus frustrates the very purpose of the privilege by discouraging the communication of relevant information by employees of the client to attorneys seeking to render legal advice to the client corporation. The attorney's advice will also frequently be more significant to noncontrol group members than to those who officially sanction the advice, and the control group test makes it more difficult to convey full and frank legal advice to the employees who will put into effect the client corporation's policy. * * *

The narrow scope given the attorney-client privilege by the court below not only makes it difficult for corporate attorneys to formulate sound advice when their client is faced with a specific legal problem but also threatens to limit the valuable efforts of corporate counsel to ensure their client's compliance with the law. In light of the vast and complicated array of regulatory legislation confronting the modern corporation, corporations, unlike most individuals, "constantly go to lawyers to find out how to obey the law[.]" * * * [I]f the purpose of the attorney-client privilege is to be served, the attorney and client must be able to predict with some degree of certainty whether particular discussions will be protected. An uncertain privilege, or one which purports to be certain but results in widely varying applications by the courts, is little better than no privilege at all. The very terms of the test adopted by the court below suggest the unpredictability of its application. The test restricts the availability of the privilege to those officers who play a "substantial role" in deciding and directing a corporation's legal response. * * *

The communications at issue were made by Upjohn employees to counsel for Upjohn acting as such, at the direction of corporate superiors in order to secure legal advice from counsel. * * * Information, not available from upper-echelon management, was needed to supply a basis for legal advice concerning compliance with securities and tax laws, foreign laws, currency regulations, duties to shareholders, and potential litigation in each of these areas. The communications concerned matters within the scope of the employees' corporate duties, and the employees themselves were sufficiently aware that they were being questioned in order that the corporation could obtain legal advice. The questionnaire identified Thomas as "the company's General Counsel" and referred in its opening sentence to the possible illegality of payments such as the ones on which information was sought. * * * A statement of policy accompanying the questionnaire clearly indicated the legal implications of the investigation. The policy statement was issued "in order that there be no uncertainty in the future as to the policy with respect to the practices which are the subject of this investigation." It began "Upjohn will comply with all laws and regulations," and stated that commissions or payments "will not be used as a subterfuge for bribes or illegal payments" and that all payments must be "proper and legal." Any future agreements with foreign distributors or agents were to be approved "by a company attorney" and any questions concerning the policy were to be referred "to the company's General Counsel." * * * This statement was issued to Upjohn employees worldwide, so that even those interviewees not receiving a questionnaire were aware of the legal implications of the interviews. Pursuant to explicit instructions from the Chairman of the Board, the communications were considered "highly confidential" when made, * * * and have been kept confidential by the company. Consistent with the underlying purposes of the attorney-client privilege, these communications must be protected against compelled disclosure.

The Court of Appeals declined to extend the attorney-client privilege beyond the limits of the control group test for fear that doing so would entail severe burdens on discovery and create a broad "zone of silence" over corporate affairs. Application of the attorney-client privilege to communications such as those involved here, however, puts the adversary in no worse position than if the communications had never taken place. The privilege only protects disclosure of communications; it does not protect disclosure of the underlying facts by those who communicated with the attorney * * *. Here the Government was free to question the employees who communicated with Thomas and outside counsel. Upjohn has provided the IRS with a list of such employees, and the IRS has already interviewed some 25 of them. While it would probably be more convenient for the Government to secure the results of petitioner's internal investigation by simply subpoenaing the questionnaires and notes taken by petitioner's attorneys, such considerations of convenience do not overcome the policies served by the attorney-client privilege. As Justice Jackson noted in his concurring opinion in Hickman v. Taylor * * *: "Discovery was hardly intended to enable a learned profession to perform its functions * * * on wits borrowed from the adversary."

* * *

III

Our decision that the communications by Upjohn employees to counsel are covered by the attorney-client privilege disposes of the case so far as the responses to the questionnaires and any notes reflecting responses to interview questions are concerned. * * * To the extent that the material subject to the summons is not protected by the attorney-client privilege as disclosing communications between an employee and counsel, we must reach the ruling by the Court of Appeals that the work-product doctrine does not apply to summonses issued under 26 U.S.C. § 7602.[6]

The Government concedes, wisely, that the Court of Appeals erred and that the work-product doctrine does apply to IRS summonses. * * * This doctrine was announced by the Court over 30 years ago in Hickman v. Taylor. * * * In that case the Court rejected "an attempt, without purported necessity or justification, to secure written statements, private memoranda, and personal recollections prepared or formed by an adverse party's counsel in the course of his legal duties." * * * The Court noted that "it is essential that a lawyer work with a certain degree of privacy" * * *. The "strong public policy" underlying the work-product doctrine * * * has been substantially incorporated in Federal Rule of Civil Procedure 26(b)(3).

* * * Nothing in the language of the IRS summons provisions or their legislative history suggests an intent on the part of Congress to preclude application of the work-product doctrine. Rule 26(b)(3) codifies the work-product doctrine, and the Federal Rules of Civil Procedure are made applicable to summons enforcement proceedings by Rule 81(a)(3).

---

6. The following discussion will also be relevant to counsels' notes and memoranda of interviews with the seven former employees should it be determined that the attorney-client privilege does not apply to them. * * *

* * * While conceding the applicability of the work-product doctrine, the Government asserts that it has made a sufficient showing of necessity to overcome its protections. * * * The Government stresses that interviewees are scattered across the globe and that Upjohn has forbidden its employees to answer questions it considers irrelevant. The above-quoted language from *Hickman,* however, did not apply to "oral statements made by witnesses * * * whether presently in the form of [the attorney's] mental impressions or memoranda." * * * As to such material the Court did "not believe that any showing of necessity can be made under the circumstances of this case so as to justify production * * *." * * * Forcing an attorney to disclose notes and memoranda of witnesses' oral statements is particularly disfavored because it tends to reveal the attorney's mental processes * * *.

Rule 26 accords special protection to work product revealing the attorney's mental processes. The Rule permits disclosure of documents and tangible things constituting attorney work product upon a showing of substantial need and inability to obtain the equivalent without undue hardship. * * * Rule 26 goes on, however, to state that "[i]n ordering discovery of such materials when the required showing has been made, the court shall protect against disclosure of the mental impressions, conclusions, opinions or legal theories of an attorney or other representative of a party concerning the litigation." Although this language does not specifically refer to memoranda based on oral statements of witnesses, the *Hickman* court stressed the danger that compelled disclosure of such memoranda would reveal the attorney's mental processes. It is clear that this is the sort of material the draftsmen of the Rule had in mind as deserving special protection. * * *

* * * It is clear that the magistrate applied the wrong standard when he concluded that the Government had made a sufficient showing of necessity to overcome the protections of the work-product doctrine. The magistrate applied the "substantial need" and "without undue hardship" standard articulated in the first part of Rule 26(b)(3). The notes and memoranda sought by the Government here, however, are work product based on oral statements. If they reveal communications, they are, in this case, protected by the attorney-client privilege. To the extent they do not reveal communications, they reveal the attorneys' mental processes in evaluating the communications. As Rule 26 and *Hickman* make clear, such work product cannot be disclosed simply on a showing of substantial need and inability to obtain the equivalent without undue hardship.

While we are not prepared at this juncture to say that such material is always protected by the work-product rule, we think a far stronger showing of necessity and unavailability by other means than was made by the Government or applied by the magistrate in this case would be necessary to compel disclosure. * * *

Accordingly, the judgment of the Court of Appeals is reversed, and the case remanded for further proceedings.

[The concurring opinion of Chief Justice Burger is omitted.]

Notes and Questions

1. In state courts, the attorney-client privilege is a creation of state law (state common law or statute), not of federal law. For state courts, the *Upjohn* decision is not binding authority, and several have not found its reasoning to be persuasive. See, e.g., Consolidated Coal Co. v. Bucyrus–Erie Co., 89 Ill.2d 103, 59 Ill.Dec. 666, 432 N.E.2d 250 (1982) (rejecting *Upjohn* and adopting the "control group" test).

In federal courts, the privilege is solely a matter of federal law, except that Federal Rule of Evidence 501 directs a federal district court sitting in a diversity case to apply the privilege law that would be applied by the courts of the state in which the federal court sits. When federal and state law claims are joined, federal law may govern the attorney-client privilege, Valente v. Pepsico, Inc., 68 F.R.D. 361, 366 n. 10 (D.Del.1975), unless the allegedly privileged communication relates solely to the state law claims.

2. The *Upjohn* opinion did not announce a set of rules controlling the attorney-client privilege. How, then, can a corporation predict whether or not a communication will be found to be privileged? It has been suggested that the following rules underlie the *Upjohn* analysis: 1) the communication must be one that would not have been made but for the contemplation of legal services; 2) the content of the communication must relate to the legal services being rendered; 3) the information-giver must be an employee, agent, or independent contractor with a significant relationship to the corporation and the corporation's involvement in the transaction that is the subject of legal services; 4) the communication must be made in confidence; and 5) the privilege may be asserted either by the corporation or by the information-giver. Sexton, *A Post-Upjohn Consideration of the Corporate Attorney-Client Privilege*, 57 N.Y.U.L.Rev. 443 (1982). Do you agree?

For more on *Upjohn*, see Waldman, *Beyond Upjohn: The Attorney–Client Privilege in the Corporate Context*, 28 Wm. & Mary L.Rev. 473 (1987); Saltzburg, *Corporate and Related Attorney–Client Privilege Claims: A Suggested Approach*, 12 Hofstra L.Rev. 279 (1984); Williams, *The Scope of the Corporate Attorney–Client Privilege in View of Reason and Experience*, 25 Howard L.J. 425 (1982).

3. Does the employee or the former employee who speaks to the corporation's attorney enjoy the protection of the attorney-client privilege? Suppose, for example, that a corporation conducts an internal investigation concerning its accounting practices and an employee or a former employee, in the course of describing how sloppy the practices are, admits to embezzling funds. Can the employee invoke the attorney-client privilege to prevent disclosure of the admission? Can the corporation authorize its attorney to disclose the admission? In UNITED STATES v. STUCKEY, No. 81 Cr. 35 (S.D.N.Y.1981), affirmed per curiam 671 F.2d 494 (2d Cir.1981), certiorari denied 455 U.S. 1017, 102 S.Ct. 1711, 72 L.Ed.2d 134 (1982), the Second Circuit affirmed the conviction of a corporate manager who revealed incriminating material to special counsel for the corporation during an intra-corporate investigation. The District Court had concluded that the manager failed to demonstrate the existence of an attorney-client relationship between himself and counsel, and the corporation had waived its privilege with respect to the conversation. In this light, how far must a corporation's attorney go to make clear to an

employee the nature of their relationship, and to warn the employee of the risks of using counsel for the corporation as the employee's personal counsel?

4. The attorney-client privilege is waived if a protected communication is disclosed voluntarily to third persons, and once waived, a party can be forced to disclose not only the specific communication but all communications involving the same subject matter. See Duplan Corp. v. Deering Milliken, Inc., 397 F.Supp. 1146 (D.S.C.1974). The possibility of waiving the attorney-client privilege strongly influences a lawyer's handling of discovery disputes. Any slip in screening materials that are produced in discovery can result in waiver. Disclosure to non-parties can destroy the privilege. Showing privileged materials to a prospective witness or expert in advance of a deposition or of trial can forfeit the privilege's protection. What might be the costs of such broad waiver rules for litigants? For the courts? Are the costs justified by the cases in which the waiver rules result in making evidence available— sometimes critical evidence, that would not otherwise be heard? See Marcus, *The Perils of Privilege: Waiver and the Litigation,* 84 Mich.L.Rev. 1605 (1986). See also *Developments in the Law—Privileged Communications,* 98 Harv.L.Rev. 1450, 1629–65 (1985); Davison & Voth, *Waiver of the Attorney-Client Privilege,* 64 Or.L.Rev. 635 (1986).

5. Should any voluntary disclosure of work product waive its protection? A majority of courts have held that the disclosure of work product to third persons waives the immunity only if the disclosure substantially increases the opportunity for potential adversaries to obtain the information. See, e.g., GAF Corp. v. Eastman Kodak Co., 85 F.R.D. 46, 51–52 (S.D.N.Y.1979). A majority of courts also have held that a voluntary disclosure of work product to an adversary waives the protection, but the waiver is limited to the material actually disclosed and does not extend to all work-product materials on the same subject matter. See Duplan Corp. v. Deering Milliken, Inc., 540 F.2d 1215, 1222–23 (4th Cir.1976). What accounts for the different waiver rules for work product compared with the attorney-client privilege?

6. The attorney-client privilege is an example of an "absolute" privilege. If the privilege attaches to a communication, a court cannot compel its disclosure no matter how compelling the adversary's need for the information. Some privileges are "qualified." Like the protection afforded attorney work product, the privilege will yield to a party's showing of need for the materials. How might this difference affect the courts' handling of the two privileges?

7. The attorney-client privilege is just one of the privileges that affect the scope of discovery. The Constitution is the source of several privileges— for example, the Fifth Amendment privilege against self-incrimination. Other privileges are founded on common law and statutes. Among the widely recognized privileges are the privileges for communications between husband and wife, priest and penitent, and physician and patient. Other privileges struggle for recognition—for example, a privilege for communications between accountants and their clients. See generally *Developments in the Law— Privileged Communications,* 98 Harv.L.Rev. 1450 (1985).

3. EXPERT INFORMATION

Read Federal Rule of Civil Procedure 26(b)(4) and the Advisory Committee's Notes on it, which appear in the Supplement.

PERRY v. W.S. DARLEY & CO.

United States District Court, Eastern District of Wisconsin, 1971.
54 F.R.D. 278.

MYRON L. GORDON, DISTRICT JUDGE. The plaintiff Robert Perry, a volunteer fireman, seeks damages for injuries allegedly sustained when he was struck by a fire truck as he attempted to activate a pump manufactured and installed on the truck by the defendant. The defendant has moved for an order compelling disclosure of the names of certain experts who examined the truck and pump shortly after the accident; the refusal to disclose the names occurred during the oral deposition of Ward Johnson, an employee of the workmen's compensation carrier for the fire department for which Mr. Perry works.

Counsel for the plaintiffs objected to disclosure of the experts' names on the basis that such information "constitutes both privileged communication and work product." However, the defendant argues in its brief that the experts are potential witnesses who "have knowledge of relevant facts" and that it is entitled, pursuant to Rule 26(b)(1), to the "identity and location of persons having knowledge of any discoverable matter."

The plaintiffs state that

> It should be noted that the [defendant's] question did not seek the disclosure of the identity of experts which plaintiffs expect to call as witnesses upon the trial, which disclosure is explicitly required by the July 1, 1970, amendment to the Federal Rules. Federal Rule 26(b)(4)(A). However, significantly, no similar requirement is made for the disclosure of identity of experts not retained or specially employed for purposes of testifying at trial. See Rule 26(b)(4)(B).

Some courts recently have refused to adopt the position taken in earlier cases in which discovery of facts known by an expert was allowed but discovery of the expert's opinions and conclusions was refused. In United States v. Meyer, 398 F.2d 66, 73 (9th Cir.1968), the court stated:

> No fact-opinion distinction is found in the discovery rules, Rule 26(b) extends discovery broadly to "any matter, not privileged, which is relevant to the subject matter involved in the pending action." In 1946 the Supreme Court rejected a proposal to amend the rules to restrict discovery of writings reflecting the conclusions of experts. The nearly contemporaneous use of the word "fact" in certain passages in the opinion in Hickman v. Taylor, * * * cannot be taken as an implicit adoption of the rejected limitation.

See also 8 Wright & Miller, *Federal Practice and Procedure: Civil* § 2029, at 247 (1970).

In addition, the Advisory Committee note to Rule 26(b)(4) states, in part:

It should be noted that the subdivision does not address itself to the expert whose information was not acquired in preparation for trial but rather because he was an actor or viewer with respect to transactions or occurrences that are part of the subject matter of the lawsuit. Such an expert should be treated as an ordinary witness. 48 F.R.D. 487, 503 (1970).

The plaintiffs concede, as stated above, that they have a duty to disclose the identity of any expert whom they expect to call as a witness at the trial. As to experts who have been engaged "in anticipation of litigation or preparation for trial," however, the plaintiffs point to the provisions of Rule 26(b)(4)(B) to the effect that, when such experts are "not expected to be called as * * * [witnesses] * * * at trial," facts known or opinions held by them are discoverable

* * * only as provided in Rule 35(b) or upon a showing of exceptional circumstances under which it is impracticable for the party seeking discovery to obtain facts or opinions on the same subject by other means.

No means are provided by Rule 26(b) by which it may be determined that an expert is a person whom a party expects to call as a witness at trial. However, Rule 26(e) provides, in part * * * [that a party must supplement its discovery responses with regard to]

* * * the identity of each person expected to be called as an expert witness at trial, the subject matter on which he is expected to testify, and the substance of his testimony.

Furthermore, the final pretrial order regularly used by this court requires each party to provide the "names and addresses of each side's prospective expert witnesses, together with a narrative statement of each such expert's background and experience."

Rule 26(b)(4)(B) makes no distinction between the identity of an expert and facts known or opinions held by him, although it is stated in 8 Wright & Miller, *Federal Practice and Procedure: Civil* § 2032, at 255 (1970), that, "Apparently one party can find out the names of experts specially retained by another party who are not to be called." However, in an affidavit attached to the defendant's motion, the attorney for the defendant states that, because the experts viewed the fire truck well before the commencement of the present action, "this in and of itself is sufficient cause to require the plaintiff to turn over not only the names of the expert or experts but the reports of said expert or experts."

In my opinion, no showing of "exceptional circumstances" has been made by the defendant in the case at bar, nor is there any evidence to indicate that the experts were actors or viewers "with respect to [the] transactions or occurrences that are part of the subject matter of the lawsuit." Rule 26(b)(4) imposes a more rigorous standard upon the discovery of facts known and opinions held by an expert than is imposed with regard to other witnesses * * *.

Therefore, it is ordered that the defendant's motion for an order compelling answers to certain questions propounded to Ward Johnson be and hereby is denied.

Notes and Questions

1. Is the court in *Perry* correct that the experts who examined the fire truck and pump shortly after the accident were not viewers of the occurrences that gave rise to the lawsuit? And did these experts acquire their information in preparation for trial? One district court, without any special showing, ordered a defendant to disclose the names, reports, notes, and data compilations of outside experts engaged by defendant to assist its post-accident investigation into the sinking of a barge, and of defendant's regular employees who assisted in the investigation. In re Sinking of Barge "Ranger I", 92 F.R.D. 486 (S.D.Tex.1981). What factors should a court consider to determine that an expert has been retained or specially employed in anticipation of litigation or preparation for trial?

2. Is the protection of the work-product doctrine for material prepared "in anticipation of litigation or for trial" adequate to protect from discovery the facts known and opinions held by a retained expert who is not expected to testify at trial, and the identity of such experts?

3. Rule 26(b)(4)(B) permits discovery of facts and opinions from an expert employed in anticipation of trial and who will not be called to testify, but only upon a showing of special circumstances. What circumstances justify discovery under this provision? See Wasmuth v. Hinds-Toomey Auto Corp., 39 A.D.2d 723, 331 N.Y.S.2d 804 (2d Dep't 1972). Assuming that special circumstances are not shown for discovery of the facts known and opinions of such an expert, is the expert's identity nonetheless discoverable? Is any special showing required to compel the disclosure of such an expert's identity? AGER v. JANE C. STORMONT HOSPITAL & TRAINING SCHOOL FOR NURSES, 622 F.2d 496 (10th Cir.1980), was an action by a father against a hospital and a doctor for allegedly causing the death of his wife during labor and injuries to his infant daughter that left her brain damaged and paralyzed. During discovery, the doctor's counsel asked plaintiff, in interrogatories, to disclose the names and addresses of any experts that plaintiff had contacted about the case, but who were not going to testify. Plaintiff's counsel refused to answer the interrogatories. Is this discovery request governed by Rule 26(b)(4)(B)? What factors should the court have considered in deciding whether or not to compel plaintiff to disclose the names of the nonwitness experts? Can the court resolve the dispute without knowing what the expert knows or her opinions about the case? How should the court have ruled?

4. Federal Rule 26(b)(4)(A)(i) provides for limited discovery regarding information of experts who will be called to testify. How extensive must the opposing party's answers be under this provision? See WILSON v. RESNICK, 51 F.R.D. 510, 511 (E.D.Pa.1970):

> * * * [P]laintiff served interrogatories on defendant, requesting that he state the identity of his expert witnesses, the subject matter on which they were expected to testify, the substance of the facts and opinions to which they were expected to testify and a summary of the grounds for each opinion. Defendant responded that Dr. Blaker was one of his expert witnesses; that he would testify on the question of whether plaintiff was treated in accordance with good, sound medical practice; that as to plaintiff's condition, it appears that reinnervation is occurring; that any residual complaint would be more annoying than anything else;

that there is no functional disability; that the care and treatment by Dr. Resnick was in accordance with good, sound medical practice. ∗ ∗ ∗

The court held that the answers were sufficient. Do you agree? Compare Rupp v. Vock & Weiderhold, Inc., 52 F.R.D. 111 (N.D.Ohio 1971). Under what circumstances will discovery under Rule 26(b)(4)(A)(ii) be permitted? What justification is there for Rule 26(b)(4)(C) regarding the payment of fees and expenses?

5. The results of the survey indicate that the actual practice of discovery of expert witnesses expected to be called at trial varies widely from the two-step procedure of Rule 26(b)(4)(A). The interrogatory overwhelmingly is recognized as a totally unsatisfactory method of providing adequate preparation for cross-examination and rebuttal. In practice, full discovery is the rule, and practitioners use all available means of disclosure including both the discovery of expert's reports and depositions.

Graham, *Discovery of Experts Under Rule 26(b)(4) of the Federal Rules of Civil Procedure: Part Two, An Empirical Study and a Proposal,* 1977 U.Ill.L.F. 169, 172.

6. In GRINNELL CORP. v. HACKETT, 70 F.R.D. 326 (D.R.I.1976), the defendant union sought to depose an expert witness retained by the plaintiff concerning the "inception, initiation, conduct, finalization, financing and publication" of a study the expert had made prior to the events that gave rise to the lawsuit. The study had been introduced as an exhibit at a previous stage of the litigation and was likely to be introduced into evidence at trial. Is discovery concerning the expert's study governed by Rule 26(b)(4)? Is the information discoverable independently of Rule 26(b)(4)? Does it matter if plaintiff was not going to call the expert as a witness at the trial?

7. May a party obtain discovery of an expert who is not employed by any of the parties to the lawsuit? Richard Snyder, a research scientist, had conducted research and published a report that concluded that "utility vehicles, particularly the Jeep CJ–5, experience a disproportionately high roll over rate in accidents." In two personal injury cases involving utility vehicles, the manufacturer sought to take Snyder's deposition and to compel him to produce all background notes and materials pertaining to his report. Snyder had not been retained by any party to the suit, but other expert witnesses had used Snyder's research report as a basis for their opinions. Snyder moved to quash the subpoenas in both cases. How should the courts have ruled? Compare Buchanan v. American Motors Corp., 697 F.2d 151 (6th Cir.1983) (quashing the subpoena), with Wright v. Jeep Corp., 547 F.Supp. 871 (E.D. Mich.1982) (enforcing subpoena but requiring the manufacturer to pay Snyder a reasonable fee, costs, and part of the expenses of the original research). Is the discovery of an expert such as Snyder just a matter of compensation? What other considerations might prompt a court to bar such discovery? See Rule 26(b)(4)(C); see also Deitchman v. E.R. Squibb & Sons, Inc., 740 F.2d 556 (7th Cir.1984).

8. A comprehensive and influential analysis of the discovery of expert information under the Federal Rules is Graham, *Discovery of Experts Under Rule 26(b)(4) of the Federal Rules of Civil Procedure: Part One, An Analytical Study,* and *Part Two, An Empirical Study and a Proposal,* 1976 U.Ill.L.F. 895; 1977 U.Ill.L.F. 169.

9. State provisions regarding discovery of expert information vary considerably. For example, N.Y.C.P.L.R. 3101(d), which accompanies Rule 26 in the Supplement, appears more restrictive than Federal Rule 26(b)(4). And a different approach is taken in N.J. Civil Practice Rule 4:10–2(d), which provides that a party not only must identify experts who will testify and summarize the nature of their testimony but must also produce copies of any reports the experts have submitted. Furthermore, the New Jersey rule goes on to provide: "Unless the court otherwise orders, * * * [such an expert] may be deposed as to his opinions at a time and place convenient for him."

SECTION D. SANCTIONS AND JUDICIAL SUPERVISION OF DISCOVERY

Read Federal Rules of Civil Procedure 26(g) and 37 in the Supplement.

CINE FORTY–SECOND STREET THEATRE CORP. v. ALLIED ARTISTS PICTURES CORP.

United States Court of Appeals, Second Circuit, 1979.
602 F.2d 1062.

IRVING R. KAUFMAN, CHIEF JUDGE.

* * *

I

Appellee Cine * * * has operated a movie theater in New York City's Times Square area since July 1974. It alleges that those owning neighboring theaters on West Forty-Second Street * * * entered into a conspiracy with certain motion picture distributors to cut off its access to first-run, quality films. Bringing suit on August 1, 1975, Cine claimed $3,000,000 in treble damages under the antitrust laws, and sought an injunction against the defendants' alleged anticompetitive practices.

On November 6, 1975, the eleven defendants served plaintiff with a set of consolidated interrogatories. Cine thereupon secured its adversaries' consent to defer discovery on the crucial issue of damages until it could retain an expert to review the rival exhibitors' box office receipts. Not until four months after the deadline upon which the parties had agreed, however, did Cine file its first set of answers to the remaining interrogatories. Moreover, even casual scrutiny reveals the patent inadequacy of these responses. Many were bare, ambiguous cross-references to general answers elsewhere in the responses. Highly specific questions concerning the design of Cine's theater were answered with architectural drawings that did not even purport to show the dimensions requested.

Although Cine now complains bitterly that these interrogatories amounted to pure harassment, it never moved to strike them as irrelevant or as harassing. Rather, it filed supplemental answers, which were similarly deficient, and then failed to obey two subsequent orders from

Magistrate Gershon compelling discovery. At a hearing in October of 1977, the magistrate found Cine's disobedience to have been willful, and assessed $500 in costs against it. Soon afterwards, she further warned plaintiff that any further noncompliance would result in dismissal.

By the summer of 1978, as this conflict was coming to a head, Cine had still not retained the expert it claimed was necessary to respond to the damages interrogatories. Magistrate Gershon quite reasonably and leniently ordered Cine merely to produce a plan to answer, but this yielded no result. The magistrate then directed Cine to answer the damages interrogatories, admonishing its counsel that future nonfeasance would be viewed in light of past derelictions. Cine did file two sets of answers, one over two months late and both seriously deficient.

* * *

At a formal hearing on October 19, 1978, * * * after noting plaintiff's history of disobedience in the face of her own repeated warnings, the magistrate concluded that Cine's present non-compliance was willful. "[T]he plaintiff," she stated, "has decided when it will be cooperative and when it will not be cooperative, and that it does not have any right to do." She thereupon recommended to the district court that Cine be precluded from introducing evidence with respect to damages. This sanction was, of course, tantamount to a dismissal of Cine's damage claim, but left standing its claim for injunctive relief.

Judge Goettel, the district judge to whom Magistrate Gershon's order was submitted for approval, reacted to Cine's behavior as did Magistrate Gershon. He wrote, "[i]f there were ever a case in which drastic sanctions were justified, this is it." But Judge Goettel could not fully accept the magistrate's finding of willfulness. * * * [He] apparently believed it possible that Cine's counsel, confused as to the precise terms of Magistrate Gershon's oral orders, could have thought in good faith that the answers were not due. Action taken upon that baseless belief, however, was, at the very least, grossly negligent. The district court "regretfully" concluded that under Flaks v. Koegel, 504 F.2d 702 (2d Cir.1974), it lacked the power, absent a finding of willfulness, to impose the extreme sanction recommended by the magistrate. Instead, the court merely assessed costs in the amount of $1,000.[6] But, recognizing that he might have "misperceive[d] the controlling law of this circuit," Judge Goettel certified this interlocutory appeal on his own motion under 28 U.S.C. § 1292(b).

* * *

II

The question before us is whether a grossly negligent failure to obey an order compelling discovery may justify the severest disciplinary measures available under Fed.R.Civ.P. 37. This rule provides a spectrum of sanctions[8] * * * [that] serve a threefold purpose. Preclusionary orders ensure that a party will not be able to profit from its own failure to

---

6. Defendants estimate that their actual costs in seeking to compel discovery total at least $50,000.

8. Rule 37 was amended in 1970 to permit the imposition of a broader range of sanctions. By deleting the word "wilfully"

comply. * * * Rule 37 strictures are also specific deterrents and, like civil contempt, they seek to secure compliance with the particular order at hand. * * * Finally, although the most drastic sanctions may not be imposed as "mere penalties," Hammond Packing Co. v. Arkansas, 212 U.S. 322, 29 S.Ct. 370, 53 L.Ed. 530 (1909) * * *, courts are free to consider the general deterrent effect their orders may have on the instant case and on other litigation, provided that the party on whom they are imposed is, in some sense, at fault. National Hockey League v. Metropolitan Hockey Club, Inc., 427 U.S. 639, 96 S.Ct. 2778, 49 L.Ed.2d 747 (1976) (per curiam); Societe Internationale pour Participations Industrielles et Commerciales v. Rogers, 357 U.S. 197, 78 S.Ct. 1087, 2 L.Ed.2d 1255 (1958).

Where the party makes good faith efforts to comply, and is thwarted by circumstances beyond his control—for example, a foreign criminal statute prohibiting disclosure of the documents at issue—an order dismissing the complaint would deprive the party of a property interest without due process of law. See *Societe Internationale,* supra, 357 U.S., at 212, 78 S.Ct. 1087. It would, after all, be unfair and irrational to prevent a party from being heard solely because of a nonculpable failure to meet the terms of a discovery order. * * *

* * * Judge Goettel apparently believed that Cine's counsel simply did not understand the exact requirements of the magistrate's unwritten order compelling discovery. If so, Cine's failure to answer the damages interrogatories might not rise to the level of "willfulness" or "bad faith" for both of these conditions imply a deliberate disregard of the lawful orders of the court. * * * The question, then, is whether gross negligence amounting to a "total dereliction of professional responsibility," but not a conscious disregard of court orders, is properly embraced within the "fault" component of *Societe Internationale's* triple criterion.

Fault, of course, is a broad and amorphous concept, and the Courts of Appeals have had considerable difficulty construing it in this context. Indeed, one court defined "fault" by the apparent oxymoron "intentional negligence." *Bon Air Hotel, Inc.,* * * * 376 F.2d at 120. Thus, commentators have opined that an element of willfulness or conscious disregard of the court's orders is a prerequisite to the harsher categories of Rule 37 sanctions. * * * But the appellate cases commonly cited for this proposition hold only that dismissal is an abuse of discretion where failure to comply was not the result of the fault of any party. * * *

Unless we are to assume that the Court chose its words carelessly, we must accord the term "fault" a meaning of its own within the *Societe Internationale* triad. And plainly, if "fault" has any meaning not subsumed by "willfulness" and "bad faith," it must at least cover gross negligence of the type present in this case. The holding in Edgar v. Slaughter, 548 F.2d 770, 773 (8th Cir.1977), which contains the apparent suggestion that dismissal is appropriate only for actions taken "deliberately or in bad faith," does not conflict with this conclusion. Counsel's action

from subsection (d) of the Rule, the drafters intended "that wilfullness [be] relevant only to the selection of sanctions, if any, to be imposed." Advisory Committee Note * * *.

in that case at worst amounted to simple negligence and indeed may have been partially excusable, id. at 773 n. 4. Flagrant negligence of the type involved in the case at bar was simply not at issue.

In the only case that actually presented the question now before us, Affanato v. Merrill Bros., 547 F.2d 138 (1st Cir.1977), the First Circuit implicitly adopted the view we have expressed. There, the district court had entered a default judgment after what the appellant court characterized as "a series of episodes of nonfeasance which amounted, in sum, to a near total dereliction of professional responsibility" on the part of defendant's counsel. Id. at 141. The Court of Appeals affirmed, noting that counsel's failures "went well beyond ordinary negligence"—but without finding willfulness or bad faith. Id.

In the final analysis, however, this question cannot turn solely upon a definition of terms. We believe that our view advances the basic purposes of Rule 37, while respecting the demands of due process. The principal objective of the general deterrent policy of *National Hockey* is strict adherence to the "responsibilities counsel owe to the Court and to their opponents," 427 U.S. at 640, 96 S.Ct. at 2780. Negligent, no less than intentional, wrongs are fit subjects for general deterrence, see G. Calabresi, *The Costs of Accidents,* 133–173 (1970). And gross professional incompetence no less than deliberate tactical intransigence may be responsible for the interminable delays and costs that plague modern complex lawsuits. An undertaking on the scale of the large contemporary suit brooks none of the dilation, posturing, and harassment once expected in litigation. See Herbert v. Lando, 441 U.S. 153, 175–77, 99 S.Ct. 1635, 1649, 60 L.Ed.2d 115, 134, * * *. The parties, and particularly their lawyers, must rise to the freedom granted by the Rules and cooperate in good faith both in question and response.

Considerations of fair play may dictate that courts eschew the harshest sanctions provided by Rule 37 where failure to comply is due to a mere oversight of counsel amounting to no more than simple negligence * * *. But where gross professional negligence has been found—that is, where counsel clearly should have understood his duty to the court—the full range of sanctions may be marshalled. Indeed, in this day of burgeoning, costly and protracted litigation courts should not shrink from imposing harsh sanctions where, as in this case, they are clearly warranted.

A litigant chooses counsel at his peril, Link v. Wabash Railroad Co., 370 U.S. 626, 82 S.Ct. 1386, 8 L.Ed.2d 734 (1962), and here, as in countless other contexts, counsel's disregard of his professional responsibilities can lead to extinction of his client's claim. * * *

Plaintiff urges that because it has at last filed answers to the damage interrogatories, it should be permitted to prove its losses at trial. But it forgets that sanctions must be weighed in light of the full record in the case, *National Hockey,* supra, 427 U.S. at 642, 96 S.Ct. 2778. Furthermore, "[i]f parties are allowed to flout their obligations, choosing to wait to make a response until a trial court has lost patience with them, the effect will be to embroil trial judges in day-to-day supervision of discovery, a result directly contrary to the overall scheme of the federal discovery rules," *Dellums*, * * * 184 U.S.App.D.C. at 343–44, 566 F.2d at 235–36. Moreover, as we have indicated, compulsion of performance in the particular case at hand is not the sole function of Rule 37 sanctions. Under the deterrence principle of *National Hockey*, plaintiff's hopelessly belated compliance should not be accorded great weight. Any other conclusion would encourage dilatory tactics, and compliance with discovery orders would come only when the backs of counsel and the litigants were against the wall.

In light of the fact that plaintiff, through its undeniable fault, has frozen this litigation in the discovery phase for nearly four years, we see no reason to burden the court below with extensive proceedings on remand. Judge Goettel's opinion makes it abundantly clear that but for his misinterpretation of the governing law in this circuit, he would have wholeheartedly adopted Magistrate Gershon's original recommendation. Accordingly, the judge's order declining to adopt the magistrate's recommendation that proof of damages be precluded is reversed.

OAKES, CIRCUIT JUDGE (concurring):

I concur in the result. It may be that the fault for the inexcusable delays in compliance with the discovery requests and orders lay with the client or with the complexity of the interrogatories and requests of opposing counsel. If the latter, remedy lay with an application under Fed. R.Civ.P. 26(c). If the former, then the magistrate's recommendation of preclusion strikes at the proper party. It would be with the greatest reluctance, however, that I would visit upon the client the sins of counsel, absent client's knowledge, condonation, compliance, or causation.

Notes and Questions

1. Discovery disputes get to court in two ways. First, a party confronting a discovery request might seek a protective order under Rule 26(c) or Rule 30(d). Alternatively, a party confronting a discovery request might refuse to comply and the party seeking discovery would have to make a motion, pursuant to Rule 37(a), "for an order compelling discovery." Is there any reason for a party objecting to a discovery request to shoulder the burden of making a motion for a protective order, instead of waiting for the other party to move for an order to compel? Are there any sanctions in Rule 37 for failing to comply with a discovery request before a court issues an order to compel?

2. Many local court rules require attorneys to attempt to resolve discovery disputes informally before the counsel seeking discovery can file a motion to compel discovery. See, e.g., Rule 230–4 of the United States District Court for the Northern District of California, and Rule 12(d) of the General Rules of the United States District Court for the Northern District of Illinois, reproduced in the Supplement. Why would a court require such consultation?

3. Although the Federal Rules went into effect in 1938, until recently judges were extremely reluctant to apply available sanctions to curb violations of the discovery rules. Renfrew, *Discovery Sanctions: A Judicial Perspective,* 67 Calif.L.Rev. 264, 271–78 (1979); Note, *The Emerging Deterrence*

Orientation in the Imposition of Discovery Sanctions, 91 Harv.L.Rev. 1033, 1034, 1038–44 (1978).

> The typical pattern of sanctioning that emerges from the reported cases is one in which the delay, obfuscation, contumacy, and lame excuses on the part of litigants and their attorneys are tolerated without any measured remedial action until the court is provoked beyond endurance. At that point the court punishes one side or the other with a swift and final termination of the lawsuit by dismissal or default. This "all or nothing" approach to sanctions results in considerable laxity in the day-to-day application of the rules. Attorneys are well aware that sanctions will be imposed only in the most flagrant situations.

Rodes, Ripple & Mooney, *Sanctions Imposable for Violations of the Federal Rules of Civil Procedure* 85 (Fed.Jud.Center 1981).

In the last several years, however, a notable change has taken place. Spurred in part by the Supreme Court's opinions in NATIONAL HOCKEY LEAGUE v. METROPOLITAN HOCKEY CLUB, INC., 427 U.S. 639, 96 S.Ct. 2778, 49 L.Ed.2d 747 (1976), and ROADWAY EXPRESS, INC. v. PIPER, 447 U.S. 752, 100 S.Ct. 2455, 65 L.Ed.2d 488 (1980), which strongly supported the use of sanctions, judges have applied and upheld sanctions in a much wider variety of situations. See American Bar Association, *Sanctions: Rule 11 and Other Powers* 34–36, 46–48, 61–70, 79–82, 97–101, 115–16, 128–29, 138–42, 158–60, 170, 175–77, 182, 186–87 (2d ed. 1988) (surveying recent decisions). Nonetheless, although the number of reported decisions suggests that sanctions have become routine, there is a lingering sense that many judges remain reluctant to impose sanctions for discovery abuse. What factors might account for this continued reluctance? Does it suggest that there are significant institutional limitations that effectively preclude heavy reliance on sanctions to curb discovery abuses?

4. The Supreme Court in *Societe Internationale,* cited in *Cine,* addressed itself to constitutional limitations on discovery sanctions and held that a plaintiff's action could not be dismissed for failure to comply with discovery orders when compliance required the cooperation of a foreign government and when plaintiff appeared to be making a good-faith effort to obtain that cooperation. See generally 8 Wright & Miller, *Federal Practice and Procedure: Civil* § 2283 (1970). Do the decisions in *Societe Internationale* and *Cine* render most of the nonmonetary sanctions in Rule 37(b) and (d) unavailable for routine use in curbing discovery abuse?

On the issue of the standard for the imposition of severe sanctions for discovery abuse, see generally Epstein, Corcoran, Krieger & Carr, *An Up-Date on Rule 37 Sanctions After National Hockey League v. Metropolitan Hockey Clubs, Inc.,* 84 F.R.D. 145 (1980); Note, *Federal Rules of Civil Procedure: Defining a Feasible Culpability Threshold for the Imposition of Severe Discovery Sanctions,* 65 Minn.L.Rev. 137 (1980).

5. When the discovery rules were amended in 1970, it was thought that one reason judges were reluctant to impose sanctions was that the sanctions then described in Rule 37 were too drastic. The amended Rule sought to overcome this objection by making more generally available the sanction of requiring a party or his attorney to pay to his opponent the reasonable expenses incurred by the failure to make discovery. Rules 37(a)(4), 37(b), 37(d). Nonetheless, it was found in one survey that "a decided majority of the

judges reported that they 'seldom' or 'almost never' award the costs of bringing or opposing a discovery-related motion." Ellington, *A Study of Sanctions for Discovery Abuse* 8 (1979). But see Werner, *Survey of Discovery Sanctions,* 1979 Arizona St.L.J. 299, 316 (evidence that judges may be less reluctant now to exercise a literal application of Rule 37's expense sanction). Is the appropriate answer to make the award of expenses mandatory? See Shroeder & Frank, *Discovery Reform: Long Road to Nowheresville,* 68 A.B. A.J. 572, 574 (1982).

6. Rule 26(g), which was added in 1983, grants the federal courts new authority to impose sanctions to deter both excessive discovery and evasion. The rule imposes on each attorney the duty, before proceeding with respect to any discovery matter, to make a reasonable inquiry and to certify that certain standards have been met, and it mandates sanctions against attorneys, their clients, or both, who violate this duty. What is a "reasonable inquiry" under the new Rule?

Does Rule 26(g) impose upon the lawyer an obligation that is inconsistent with his traditional role in the adversary process and the ethical obligation of undivided allegiance to his client? "It is incongruous to require a lawyer to advise his client that although the information is relevant, material, and may be helpful in formulating his case, the information should not be sought because it would be too burdensome on the other party. It would be equally incongruous to require him to certify that this is the case." Fishbein, *New Federal Rule 26: A Litigator's Perspective,* 57 St. John's L.Rev. 739, 745–46 (1983). Assuming this is to be the case, is it really a problem?

7. If a court must determine whether an attorney or his client should be sanctioned, don't the attorney and client become adversaries? Would the attorney have to withdraw as counsel in order to avoid the conflict? What if the attorney's defense to the sanction depends on a privileged communication with the client? Or the disclosure of work product? Is the best answer to leave the resolution of the question of who pays the sanction to the attorney and the client?

8. What procedures must be followed before a sanction for discovery abuse can be imposed? Due process requires at least prior notice and an opportunity to be heard. See Roadway Express, Inc. v. Piper, 447 U.S. 752, 767 & n. 14, 100 S.Ct. 2455, 2464 & n. 14, 65 L.Ed.2d 488, 501–02 & n. 14 (1980). Might an evidentiary hearing also be required? In what circumstances would discovery relating to sanctions issues be appropriate? Could the sanctioning process itself clog the courts with satellite litigation, or become a tool for harassment or abuse? In MIRANDA v. SOUTHERN PACIFIC TRANSPORTATION CO., 710 F.2d 516 (9th Cir.1983), the court held that two attorneys facing court-imposed sanctions for violating local court rules regarding a pretrial conference were entitled to an opportunity to request a hearing and to show cause why the sanctions should not be imposed.

9. In J.M. CLEMINSHAW CO. v. CITY OF NORWICH, 93 F.R.D. 338 (D.Conn.1981), the court fined the defendant's attorney $150 for unnecessary delay in filing his client's answers to discovery requests of the plaintiff and of the court. These fines were payable to the court, and were in addition to costs and attorney's fees to the opposing party. The court deemed it necessary to impose the additional penalty because an award of expenses to the opposing party alone was too low to punish adequately the violation. Is the additional

sanction authorized by Rule 26(g) or Rule 37? If not, is it authorized by Section 1927 of Title 28 of the United States Code or the inherent power of a court to regulate the conduct of the attorneys who practice before it? See generally Note, *Sanctions Imposed by Courts on Attorneys Who Abuse the Judicial Process,* 44 U.Chi.L.Rev. 619 (1977).

SOFAER, SANCTIONING ATTORNEYS FOR DISCOVERY ABUSE UNDER THE NEW FEDERAL RULES: ON THE LIMITED UTILITY OF PUNISHMENT, 57 St. John's L.Rev. 680, 696–98, 720–29 (1983):

Empirical studies demonstrate that discovery presents no significant problem in most cases in the federal courts. One study, conducted for the Federal Judicial Center (FJC) and based on 3,000 cases from six metropolitan districts, showed that no discovery requests were filed in 50% of all cases, and only 5% of all cases contained 10 or more discovery initiatives. The cases involving 10 or more discovery initiatives, however, had an average of 17.47 requests each, accounting for about 60% of all discovery enforcement motions in the entire sample. Moreover, the average number of enforcement motions per discovery request was twice as high in the cases having high levels of discovery as in all other cases combined. Nine enforcement motions were made in each of the few cases with over 31 discovery requests. Similarly, in Professor Ellington's study on sanctions for discovery abuse, more than 6,000 cases, over 50% of the total studied, involved no discovery activity; and of those cases which did involve discovery activity, over 70% had no recorded discovery problem. As the FJC discovery study concluded, "discovery abuse, to the extent it exists, does not permeate the vast majority of federal filings."

On the other hand, discovery abuse may at least partially explain the intensive discovery activity and disputes that exist in the small proportion of cases involving high levels of discovery. Moreover, subjective evidence of widespread concern over discovery abuse suggests that, although such abuse may be confined to a relatively small proportion of all cases, those cases are so intensively litigated that they have a significant impact on the federal judicial system. ∗ ∗ ∗

∗ ∗ ∗

Attorneys abuse the discovery process by seeking evidence that is unnecessary, or by seeking evidence for an improper purpose, or by imposing unnecessary costs in seeking necessary material. Some familiar examples are the documentary request that calls for every paper that relates to a corporation's policies and activities on safety, hiring, firing, or pricing; the set of interrogatories with multipage introductory definitions, followed by questions that would require thousands of hours to answer, calling for all the evidence relating to each of the respondent's legal positions; and the series of largely if not entirely aimless depositions intended to impose huge costs and pressures upon an opponent.

Failures to make or to cooperate in discovery are, however, at least as prevalent a source of abuse as unnecessary or oppressive demands. Prior to the adoption of the federal rules in 1938, relatively little discovery was possible, and thus virtually all discovery abuse took the form of opposition to discovery, even when it was reasonable and limited. * * * [F]ailures [to cooperate in discovery] * * * remain widespread. Here, also, shocking conduct, though still rare, has become too familiar: documents are purged on concocted claims of privilege, destroyed, secretly withheld, produced in unusable form, or buried in truckloads of irrelevant paper; answers to interrogatories are flatly refused for improper reasons or for no reason at all; deponents are repeatedly instructed not to answer on grounds other than privilege, and depositions are delayed or terminated upon the unilateral decision of a party's attorney.

* * *

Discovery abuse exists because some litigation is itself abusive. An examination of some of the categories of cases that generate the greatest amount of discovery conflict shows that a large proportion are ultimately found to lack merit. Class actions of all kinds, for example, have high rates of dismissal. Even where recoveries are obtained through settlement, as in many securities and antitrust cases, there is often evidence that the costs and risks of litigation, rather than any merit to the claims, prompted the defendant's willingness to settle. Meritless claims or defenses generate controversy in discovery; one side will argue that little or no discovery is necessary, while the other will seek as much discovery and delay as possible.

The present system imposes only nominal costs for the right to sue. and to consume the public resources expended in running the federal courts. If a valuable commodity can be obtained at nominal cost, or, as with *in forma pauperis* litigation, for nothing, the commodity will be consumed without the restraint and responsibility that a higher, though still subsidized, cost would encourage. Furthermore, litigation incentives also exist in many cases, because of the low rates of prejudgment interest awarded in the federal courts. A party who owes money, or knows that he will eventually have to satisfy a claim, will consider the cost of contesting the claim as against the cost of paying it. * * * The prejudgment interest rate must be raised to a point that will discourage litigation, not engender it.

Massive discovery also occurs because Congress and the Executive permit the use of the federal courts as the forum for litigating highly complex, political, and social issues. For example, the recent cases of United States v. IBM and United States v. AT&T generated discovery costs equal to the costs generated by hundreds or thousands of ordinary cases. In cases such as these, in which the issues are so vague and conceptually seamless, and the stakes are so high, the parties involved will press to discover every conceivably useful piece of evidence, while at the same time vigorously opposing discovery by their opponents. Large, dynamic corporations do not lightly accept efforts by the government or private persons to subject them to damages that reach the hundreds of millions and threaten their very existence. Controversies touching the public, such as suits to correct the effects of discrimination, or to improve conditions in jails or mental institutions, or to implement school desegregation, are often hard-fought by both sides at all stages.

Discovery is also made costly because of the legal theories on which courts have permitted suits to proceed, and because many standards of law on important issues have been left unsettled by appellate courts for long periods of time. Expanded notions of strict liability, for example, enable plaintiffs to file complaints in which they need do little more than allege an injury that is believed to have resulted from some dangerous instrumentality or activity, and this will generally entitle them to search for an explanation through discovery. Civil rights claims permit persons of any race, sex, or religion, people over 40 years old, handicapped persons, and prisoners, to litigate on mere subjective belief, or on totally unsupported allegations. Once deemed properly commenced, these cases generate substantial costs, including discovery costs, which often fall upon public and quasi-public entities such as universities and hospitals, in addition to private defendants. The standards imposed on trial courts in ruling on motions for summary judgment make the granting of such motions rare events, and consequently require claims with little or no merit to be fully litigated.[b] Further, many statutes and common-law rules turn on state of mind or other subjective evidence; these generate more discovery than those which rest on objective standards. In some very intensely litigated areas, especially under the securities and antitrust laws, it is unclear which of two or more standards will apply, and parties are forced to discover and litigate on all possible theories to make a complete record.

* * *

Perhaps the mightiest catalyst for discovery abuse is the so-called American Rule, under which unsuccessful litigants do not pay their opponent's attorney's fees, even those made necessary by their failure to drop or settle a losing cause. The effect of this rule on discovery is profound: a party can have as much discovery as it wants by paying only the costs of *seeking* that discovery; the costs of compliance are generally borne without recompense by the opposing party. This means that a party can inflict the costs of collecting, organizing, duplicating, and delivering documents simply by asking for them; or can impose the costs of obtaining answers to burdensome interrogatories simply by asking questions; or can trigger the costs of depositions, simply by demanding the presence of witnesses and examining them. No express authority exists that would enable courts to require parties to pay in advance for the discovery they claim is necessary, although in egregious cases courts occasionally impose such a condition. * * *

The relatively low cost of seeking discovery leads all parties, not just plaintiffs, to engage in excessive discovery. Attorneys may seek unnecessarily broad discovery simply as a means of self-defense against the economic coercion of discovery by opponents. By seeking massive discovery against a party that has already sought extensive discovery, the attorney conveys a message to his opponent that he intends to make the costs of litigating equal, thereby tending to deter broad requests. Alternatively, resistance to discovery may be the most effective means for

---

b. The statement in the text concerning motions for summary judgment no longer may be accurate in light of later developments in the case law. See pp. 821–29, 839–46, infra.

defending against excessive discovery. A vigorous defense will tend to deter excessive demands, albeit also increasing the costs of reasonable demands. * * *

The economic incentives for discovery abuse have also been increased by hourly billing practices. The incentive for abuse, paradoxically, is greatest in cases in which an attorney has no paying client to whom to answer. For example, the government's only constraints on how much it can spend on discovery are political. Attorneys for plaintiffs in class action suits and in contingency fee situations must often finance discovery, operating as a constraint on the types of cases they will commence. Once a judgment is made that a recovery is likely, however, the incentives for unnecessary discovery in such cases become even greater than usual, since discovery costs are recoverable out of the settlement or award. In fact, unnecessary discovery is encouraged by [an] * * * approach for computing attorney's fees in class actions and other cases [, which] * * * virtually [guarantees that the costs of discovery will be recovered] * * *, at least to the extent that the amount sought falls between 20 and 30% of the total recovery. This approach in effect pays attorneys for all discovery, including as a practical matter most unnecessary attempts to obtain or to resist disclosures.

Nor can we look to defense counsel for protection against abusive practices in such cases, since extensive discovery may also be attractive to them. As Milton Gould recently wrote:

> Many years ago, I heard an eminent defense lawyer compare the lawyers for plaintiffs to the Apaches who harassed the wagon trains in the Old West. But now, the defense lawyers seem to welcome the derivative suit as an opportunity for young partners and associates to sit in endless depositions, while the clock ticks away the golden hours.

An important part of the judicial response to discovery abuse is reflected in recent amendments to the Rules that contemplate active judicial supervision of the discovery process. In 1980, Rule 26(f) was adopted to provide for the discovery conference, but, as indicated in the Advisory Committee Notes, it was not contemplated as a routine procedure. Then, in 1983, Rule 16 was amended to encourage district courts to schedule early pretrial conferences and to require them to issue scheduling orders limiting the time of the parties, among other things, to complete discovery. The Rule assures that a judge (or magistrate) takes early action on discovery matters, while the scheduling order acts to counter the procrastination and delay that is natural to busy lawyers. The following chapter takes up questions concerning the changed role of judges generally in managing the pretrial phase of litigation, including discovery.

Chapter 9

PRETRIAL MANAGEMENT AND THE PRETRIAL CONFERENCE

SECTION A.   CASE MANAGEMENT

Read Federal Rule of Civil Procedure 16 and the material accompanying it in the Supplement.

MILLER, THE ADVERSARY SYSTEM: DINOSAUR OR PHOENIX, 69 Minn.L.Rev. 201, 219–21 (1984):

But given the tremendous frustration throughout the legal profession and the public at large with the current state of affairs, one must ask seriously whether the adversary system as we know it has become too costly and inefficient a device for resolving civil disputes.   There is a growing feeling that the only means of preserving any substantial portion of the system may be to control the excesses of lawyer hyperactivity through the infusion of active judicial management from institution of a case to its termination.   This approach flies in the face of the traditional vision of our system as one in which lawyers conduct cases and judges preside from a neutral distance, stepping in only to decide questions and disputes that are framed by the advocates.   There has been understandable reluctance to tinker with, let alone jeopardize or fundamentally alter, the basic tenets of a system so entrenched and venerated.

Fortunately, the mood of the profession seems to be changing, largely because of increased caseloads.   *   *   *

In short, the notion that judges should leave cases to the lawyers has been compromised substantially by the widespread frustration with the present situation and the resulting recognition of the need for effective management.   The Federal Judicial Center's 1977 study of district court case management procedures revealed that all the courts visited had procedures designed to manage and control cases starting at their early stages.   The differences among the courts studied lay not in their willingness to adopt methods to manage cases, for each court had such procedures, but rather in the means employed, their effectiveness in moving cases along expeditiously, and the number of cases each judge could handle.   The impact of case management was dramatic, with courts employing strong management controls having an average disposition time for cases that was approximately half of the average figure for courts using few such controls.

Moreover, the impression that judges are unwilling to depart from their traditional role as passive and detached arbiters appears to be mistaken.   To the contrary, there seems to be a strong spirit of willingness among judges to assume the role of active managers and to experiment with procedures designed to enhance their effectiveness in that role, although in some quarters, particularly at the state level, the flesh of experience and training may yet be weak.   Significantly, follow-ups to another Federal Judicial Center study found that participating districts whose efficiency had been low already had adopted procedures found to be common in the more efficient courts.

Even attorneys, usually seen as jealous guardians of control over their cases, are not averse to a stronger judicial hand.   Ironically, this is due in part to the natural tendency to define abuse as what the opposition is doing to one.   Lawyers do not tend to see abusers when they look in the mirror, but rather only when they look across the negotiating table or the courtroom.   Given the frustration felt by many litigators about the atmosphere of lawlessness that often bogs down actions through hyperactivity, missed deadlines, and repeated rescheduling, the judge is seen as an ally against a common enemy—the abusive opponent.   Thus, the bar may not be a major obstacle to more aggressive management and enforcement of the rules, even at the expense of a measure of its independence and autonomy.

————

RESNIK, MANAGERIAL JUDGES, 96 Harv.L.Rev. 374, 376–85 (1982):

Until recently, the American legal establishment embraced a classical view of the judicial role.   Under this view, judges are not supposed to have an involvement or interest in the controversies they adjudicate.   Disengagement and dispassion supposedly enable judges to decide cases fairly and impartially.   The mythic emblems surrounding the goddess Justice illustrate this vision of the proper judicial attitude.   Justice carries scales, reflecting the obligation to balance claims fairly;   she possesses a sword, giving her great power to enforce decisions;   and she wears a blindfold, protecting her from distractions.

Many federal judges have departed from their earlier attitudes;   they have dropped the relatively disinterested pose to adopt a more active, "managerial" stance.   In growing numbers, judges are not only adjudicating the merits of issues presented to them by litigants, but also are meeting with parties in chambers to encourage settlement of disputes and to supervise case preparation.   Both before and after the trial, judges are playing a critical role in shaping litigation and influencing results.

* * *

* * * Today, federal district judges are assigned a case at the time of its filing and assume responsibility for shepherding the case to completion. Judges have described their new tasks as "case management"— hence my term "managerial judges." As managers, judges learn more about cases much earlier than they did in the past. They negotiate with parties about the course, timing, and scope of both pretrial and posttrial litigation. These managerial responsibilities give judges greater power. Yet the restraints that formerly circumscribed judicial authority are conspicuously absent. Managerial judges frequently work beyond the public view, off the record, with no obligation to provide written, reasoned opinions, and out of reach of appellate review.

This new managerial role has emerged for several reasons. One is the creation of pretrial discovery rights. The 1938 Federal Rules of Civil Procedure embodied contradictory mandates: a discovery system ("give your opponent all information relevant to the litigation") was grafted onto American adversarial norms ("protect your client zealously" and therefore "withhold what you can"). In some cases, parties argued about their obligations under the discovery rules; such disputes generated a need for someone to decide pretrial conflicts. Trial judges accepted the assignment and have become mediators, negotiators, and planners—as well as adjudicators. Moreover, once involved in pretrial discovery, many judges became convinced that their presence at other points in a lawsuit's development would be beneficial; supervision of discovery became a conduit for judicial control over all phases of litigation and thus infused lawsuits with the continual presence of the judge-overseer.

Partly because of their new oversight role and partly because of increasing case loads, many judges have become concerned with the volume of their work. To reduce the pressure, judges have turned to efficiency experts who promise "calendar control." Under the experts' guidance, judges have begun to experiment with schemes for speeding the resolution of cases and for persuading litigants to settle rather than try cases whenever possible. During the past decade, enthusiasm for the "managerial movement" has become widespread; what began as an experiment is likely soon to become obligatory. * * *

* * *

Until recently, federal judges rarely paid much attention to the filing of lawsuits. Complaints were "file stamped" by court clerks, plaintiffs' checks were credited to the United States, and marshals were dispatched to serve process on defendants. Once served, defendants were supposed to answer or seek dismissal within twenty days. The time limit was an artifice, however, because parties commonly stipulated to extend the deadline; months would pass before a defendant filed a responsive pleading. Once an answer was filed, issue was "joined"; but again, a judge would take no notice. Unless and until one of the parties requested some sort of judicial action (granting a motion for summary judgment, a date for trial, a pretrial conference), most judges did not intervene during the pretrial stage. The parties might undertake discovery, negotiate settlement, or let the case lie dormant for years—all without judicial scrutiny.

Even when federal judges were brought into cases, they were not responsible for the development of the cases. Although judges occasionally conducted pretrial conferences, the scope and subject matter of these conferences were limited; judges were not supposed to stress the desirability of settlement. As one court explained, for the judge to "persist" at settlement efforts and then to "hear the case and render judgment * * * inevitably raises * * * suspicion as to the fairness of the court's administration of justice." Yet despite the absence of judges' involvement, the vast majority of cases ended without trial.

* * * As late as 1958, Professors Kaplan and von Mehren and Judge Schaefer marveled at the vigorous efforts of German judges to convince parties to settle. Ironically, their description of the German judge—"constantly descending to the level of the litigants, as an examiner, patient or hectoring, as counselor and adviser [and] as insistent promoter of settlements"—now seems apt for the American judge as well. Federal judges who passively await parties' pretrial requests are out of step with colleagues who have implemented a new regime of procedures designed to speed case disposition. These procedures bring cases to judges' attention shortly after filing and encourage judges both to supervise case development before trial and to manage decree implementation after trial.

MILLER & CULP, THE NEW RULES OF CIVIL PROCEDURE: MANAGING CASES, LIMITING DISCOVERY, Nat.L.J., 23–25, Dec. 5, 1983:

Federal Rule 16 was the first major pretrial conference rule in American procedural history and remained unchanged between 1938 and 1983. But its effectiveness became increasingly limited in recent years.

The original rule called for an eve-of-trial conference designed to organize the evidence, the witnesses and the documents to make the trial as efficient as possible. Unfortunately, Rule 16 missed the heart of today's pretrial problem.

Since more than 90 percent of the civil cases do not reach trial, former Rule 16, at most, spoke to only a small portion of the cases. Of those cases that reach trial, most of them are so simple that they do not need a pretrial conference to facilitate the trial. Many of the remaining cases are so complicated they need more than an eve-of-trial conference— they need management from the outset of the pretrial process.

The advisory committee's explicit goal in revising Rule 16 was to legitimize judicial management and to encourage district judges to recognize it as part of their duties. * * *

* * *

Reducing the time frame from institution to pretrial termination certainly would be socially desirable. Since the cost of a significant amount of litigation is tax deductible, taxpayers end up footing much of the bill. Moreover, every frivolous or unnecessary motion consumes valuable public resources, such as judges and courtrooms, and drains human resources.

Furthermore, many of our most talented young lawyers may spend up to one-fifth of their legal careers on pretrial proceedings in enormous cases that often are competitive wars rather than legitimate legal disputes. By any standard, allowing litigants to play expensive dilatory games in our courts is socially costly. Thus, the advisory committee felt that the expenditure of some judge power to accelerate and improve pretrial proceedings was desirable.

* * *

Perhaps the most critical element, indeed, the most controversial feature, of new Rule 16 is Subdivision (b). It states that unless a lawsuit falls within a category of cases specifically exempted by local rule, a scheduling order "shall" be issued within 120 days of the filing of the complaint. It is anticipated that most districts will exempt cases involving review of administrative decisions, many Social Security matters, forfeitures, prisoner petitions and odometer cases. In many ways, the rule asks for something in the nature of a status conference, which most judges currently require; however, it goes further and demands the issuance of a *scheduling order*.

Many judges dislike the mandatory scheduling order because it affirmatively requires action and because they fear that the obligation will consume considerable time. * * *

The mandated scheduling order should have significant impact in complex, intractible and intransigent cases that have become a heavy millstone on the backs of federal judges during the past two decades. A district judge must intervene and take affirmative action within 120 days in every case on his docket, except those exempted by local rule.

The mandatory scheduling order *must* dictate the time frames for completing such matters as the pleadings, joinder of parties, jurisdictional, class action and joinder motions, and perhaps motions relating to threshold affirmative defenses. Finally, the order should schedule the discovery phase and perhaps pretrial conferences and the trial itself.

* * *

The goal of the advisory committee was to galvanize each judge into action. In a sense the notion is that by showing the flag, judges will energize the lawyers and start the case moving toward adjudication. But Rule 16 does not require that any pretrial conference take place. Only the issuance of a scheduling order is mandated—whether to hold *any* conference is left to the discretion of the judge.

Subdivision (c) of the Rule lists various matters that can be raised at any conference that might be held. * * *

Rule 16(c)(1), for example, suggests that conference participants may consider the formulation and simplification of the issues, including the elimination of frivolous claims or defenses. This passage attempts to address the intense battle that has been raging between the plaintiff and the defense bars for at least 15 years.

The latter contends that too many claims brought against their clients are vague, ill-defined and baseless. [D]efense counsel [argue] that they are left in the dark and subjected to discovery that is imprecise, overly broad, intrusive, disruptive, and expensive, leading them to "pay-off" unjustified claims simply to get rid of them.

The reference to "formulation" in Rule 16(c)(1) is designed to encourage beginning the process of shaping the action and limiting the issues as early as possible to those that are truly litigable. Granted, there are cases in which an attempt to do this at a threshold pretrial conference would be premature. Indeed, the risk of prematurity is greatest in antitrust, stock fraud and technologically complex cases. In these types of actions, a certain amount of discovery is necessary in order to reach the point at which one can begin to think about defining the issues. But even in these cases, the rule serves to remind the judge and the litigants to think about "shaping" the action as soon as practical.

Another recognition of the legitimacy of judicial involvement is the reference in Rule 16(c) to "the possibility of settlement." * * * Although we now treat settlement as an obvious objective of the pretrial conference, that is a relatively modern phenomenon.

Historically, there was considerable resistance to judicial participation in settlement discussions, let alone judicial pressure towards settlement. The judge was viewed as an impartial arbiter sitting on a high bench in a black robe speaking only when spoken to; the case belonged to the lawyers, including whether to settle.

But reality and practicality have changed the thinking of most in the profession. District judges now understand that in many ways they are system managers, administrators, negotiators and mediators. New Rule 16(c) reflects this change in attitude; it instructs judges that promoting settlement is part of their job and that a Rule 16 conference is a good vehicle for pursuing that objective.

*   *   *

The extent of judicial involvement in settlement is a much debated subject: Where does facilitation end and undue pressure begin? Does it matter if it is a jury or nonjury trial? Should district judges team up, one judge doing the settlement conferencing for a colleague and vice versa? The advisory committee decided that it would be premature to include anything in the Rule suggesting how a judge should or should not behave.

The other agenda items for pretrial conferences listed in Rule 16(c) are relatively straightforward. A number of them are based on the Manual for Complex Litigation. Indeed, since several of the practices described in the manual have proven effective in the crucible of actual practice, there was every reason to incorporate them into Rule 16(c).

Two new provisions in Rule 16(c) are designed to give the pretrial conference process a legitimacy and seriousness of purpose. If there is to be a conference under Rule 16, the lawyers are directed to attend with authority to stipulate and make admissions, although authority to settle is not mandatory.

This passage is the advisory committee's answer to the recurring complaint that many lawyers do not take pretrial conferences seriously and tend to deny they have authority to stipulate, admit or settle. Now, every attorney attending a conference represents that he or she has authority to stipulate and to admit regarding anything one reasonably should anticipate could come up.

A related new requirement is that the final pretrial conference, which assures that there is at least one conference, must be attended on each side by at least one attorney who actually will conduct the trial. This eliminates the problem of one lawyer appearing at the pretrial conference and a different lawyer trying the case, the latter refusing to abide by the trial plan established at the pretrial conference.

Finally, Rule 16(f) provides that an attorney may be sanctioned for various violations of Rule 16. Sanctions are available when an attorney fails to attend a scheduled conference, disobeys a pretrial order, fails to participate in good faith or is substantially unprepared to participate in the conference. The sanctions follow the pattern established under Rules 7 and 11 of leaving the matter to the court's discretion, with cost-shifting likely to become the norm.

* * *

There are three significant apprehensions regarding new Rule 16. The first is * * * if a judge is not disposed to manage, will he or she pay attention to Rule 16? Certainly there are federal judges who do not manage their dockets aggressively; they have various reasons for this attitude, which by and large reflect their own style or conception of judging. But since younger judges seem more in tune with the need for management, the number of reluctant judges is dwindling as new judges are elevated to the bench.

Another concern about Rule 16 is that it says to a heavily burdened district judge, who may be facing a docket of 500 cases, "Judge, Rule 16 asks for a portion of your valuable work time. That is time that you cannot sit in your courtroom and try cases. But, we honestly believe that time expended in scheduling and management will be offset by time economies you will experience later on in these cases."

Once again, we lack empiric evidence on the subject, but the available data indicate that management conducted early in the action will produce efficiencies later in the proceedings.

"Runaway" discovery often results because a judge who knows very little about a case is in no position to limit or terminate the process. Early management forces the judge to acquire a working knowledge of the larger cases on his docket. That can be useful in scheduling, in shaping discovery and in moving the dispute toward trial. The hope is that by robbing Peter to pay Paul in terms of allocating time, there will be a net savings for all concerned.

A third concern is worth mentioning—a somewhat abstract but nonetheless global one. True disciples of the adversary system believe that litigation should be controlled by the parties through their lawyers. The dogma is that each lawyer has carte blanche to do what he or she thinks is in the best interests of the client—to settle or not, to proceed with dispatch or delay, to pursue one procedure or another.

New Rule 16 rejects this conception because it directs the sharing of power in handling the processing of a lawsuit. A case belongs to the system as much as it does to the litigants and their attorneys. Thus, Rule 16 is a potential threat to the adversary system as it has existed for hundreds of years since it formally calls for a significant change in the relationship between judges and lawyers.

Notes and Questions

1. A judge may employ any of several techniques to "manage" a case. Some, such as the scheduling order and the pretrial order, are mentioned in Rule 16. Others may be authorized in local court rules. And still others may be developed by the judge herself as she performs the function of case manager.

For example, some courts require counsel to submit, prior to discovery, pretrial statements listing: (1) the witnesses that the party plans to call at trial, along with a brief description of each witness's expected testimony; and, (2) anticipated claims of privilege or work-product immunity. For a discussion of the managerial techniques that have been incorporated into local court rules, see generally Note, *Pretrial Conference: A Critical Examination of Local Rules Adopted by Federal Courts,* 64 Va.L.Rev. 467 (1978).

2. Some criticize the imposition of time limits as unrealistic, particularly in complex cases. Pretrial orders frequently are modified in these cases even though Rule 16 provides that a schedule may be modified only on a showing of good cause. These changes can generate additional paperwork and delay, thereby causing inefficiency in the name of efficiency. Some district courts have dealt with the problem by exempting complex cases from the requirement of a scheduling conference and order. See Local Rule 9, D.Alaska; Rule 1–15, D.D.C.; Rule 2.4.1, N.D. and S.D.Iowa; Order, M.D.Ala. Read the sample scheduling order set out in the Supplement.

3. In the late 1960's a committee of federal judges, known as the Coordinating Committee for Multiple Litigation of the United States District Courts, together with legal scholars and representatives of the bar, drafted a manual of suggested procedures for dealing with the so-called "big case." This manual, which has been revised and updated from time to time, and is now the *Manual for Complex Litigation 2d* (1985), suggests a series of four pretrial conferences: the first to assume control of the case and to handle preliminary matters such as pleading and the joinder of parties and claims; the second to plan discovery; the third to control the discovery process and provide for pretrial briefs; and the last to plan the details of the trial. The *Manual* recognizes that these procedures must be altered to fit the needs of each case.

For an analysis of the successes and problems faced by the courts in cases in which some of the *Manual*'s procedures have been utilized, see Note, *The*

Judicial Panel and the Conduct of Multidistrict Litigation, 87 Harv.L.Rev. 1001 (1974).

4. Is there a danger that managerial techniques employed by judges might be viewed as advocacy? The intimation by Professor Resnik that the increased managerial role assumed by judges has led to an abandonment of their disinterested stance has become the subject of sharp debate. Steven Flanders, the Circuit Executive for the United States Court of Appeals for the Second Circuit, argues that judicial activism has not led to an abuse of power, nor is it too great an intrusion into the adversarial process:

> In general, federal judges are circumspect and selective in their discussions of settlement. It is my experience that virtually all are keenly aware of the dangers Resnik identifies, dangers that have been widely discussed and understood for many years.

> Most judges regard their primary role in the settlement process as that of an indirect facilitator.

> * * *

> While most federal judges are alert to the risks created by their involvement in the settlement process, they also are, and must be, sensitive to the obstacles to settlement sometimes imposed by the adversary relationship.

Flanders, *Blind Umpires—A Response to Professor Resnik,* 35 Hastings L.J. 505, 511–13 (1984).

5. What is it that makes managerial judging effective? Is it the informal character of the communication between the parties, and between the parties and the judge? Or is it the range of evidence made available to the judge? Or is it simply the pressure created by imposing deadlines?

Do judicial attempts to encourage settlement inevitably affect the judge's ability to preside over a trial in that dispute? Does your answer depend on whether the trial is to a jury or to the bench? Because they fear that a judge who participates in settlement talks might be perceived as partial, some courts ask a second judge, magistrate, or master to help the parties negotiate a settlement. For discussions of the proper judicial role in the settlement process, see generally Craig & Christenson, *The Settlement Process,* 59 F.R.D. 252 (1973); Will, Merhige & Rubin, *The Role of the Judge in the Settlement Process,* 75 F.R.D. 203 (1978).

> 6. We must also remind ourselves that encouraging settlements is a policy problem of paramount importance. In a system founded upon the adversary relationship, in which lawyers are trained to fight, not to negotiate, suggestion of settlement is often taken as a sign of weakness. A settlement is in many respects the closest thing to a truly final judgment that can emerge from litigation. A settlement is not normally appealable, and it normally embodies a commitment by the parties to work together in some manner, a stance that may forestall future litigation.

Flanders, *Blind Umpires—A Response to Professor Resnik,* 35 Hastings L.J. 505, 513–14 (1984).

7. Note that Rule 16(b) empowers district courts to promulgate local rules exempting classes of cases from Rule 16. What kinds of cases are suitable for exemption? For example, should routine contract disputes or

personal-injury cases be excepted from Rule 16? Isn't it the facts of each case, not its subject matter, that determine whether the case is suitable for pretrial management?

8. State court attitudes toward pretrial management vary tremendously. A useful summary of many state pretrial procedures appears in Note, *Pretrial Conference Procedures,* 26 S.C.L.Rev. 481 (1974).

Other general treatments of pretrial management include: Brazil, *Improving Judicial Controls Over the Pretrial Development of Civil Actions: Model Rules for Case Management and Sanctions,* 1981 Am.B.Found. Research J. 873; Ebner, *Court Efforts to Reduce Pretrial Delay* (1981); Flanders, *Blind Umpires—A Response to Professor Resnik,* 35 Hastings L.J. 505 (1984); Peckham, *The Federal Judge as Case Manager: The New Role in Guiding a Case from Filing to Disposition,* 69 Calif.L.Rev. 770 (1981); Rosenberg, *The Pretrial Conference and Effective Justice* (1964).

SECTION B. EXTRAJUDICIAL PERSONNEL: MASTERS AND MAGISTRATES

Masters   Magistrates

Read Federal Rules of Civil Procedure 53 and 72 through 76 and the material accompanying them in the Supplement.

In recent years there has been increasing interest in utilizing extrajudicial personnel to perform a wide variety of judicial functions, including negotiating settlements, monitoring discovery, holding evidentiary hearings, and determining the proper size and allocation of a damage award in cases in which liability has been determined. It is argued that extrajudicial personnel sometimes can perform these tasks more competently and expeditiously than judges. For example, an expert in a particular area can serve the court well in such technically complex fields as antitrust and products liability. And, more generally, extrajudicial personnel often can interact with the parties in a more informal way than some judges— and the frank exchanges that are part of this informality may move the parties towards a resolution of a dispute. In addition, it is easier for a judge to maintain her impartiality if the pretrial conference or conference is referred to a magistrate.

The Anglo-American legal system long has used extrajudicial personnel to help process disputes. See generally Silberman, *Masters and Magistrates, Part I: The English Model,* 50 N.Y.U.L.Rev. 1070 (1975); Silberman, *Masters and Magistrates, Part II: The American Analogue,* 50 N.Y.U.L.Rev. 1297 (1975). Traditionally, however, their use in civil cases was disfavored. Thus, under former Federal Equity Rule 59, resort to masters was noted as the exception, not the rule. It was believed that resort to such personnel merely increased costs and created delays— without producing any measurable improvement in the quality of adjudication. Though some contemporary commentators still question the value of extrajudicial personnel, crowded dockets and complex cases have led to greater willingness to employ them to handle disputes.

Professor Silberman, who in the past argued vigorously for the use of special masters and magistrates, now believes that courts delegate too much to them. She argues that judicial adjuncts have unnecessarily bureaucratized the judiciary and perhaps even expanded the discovery process. "With the stadium built, the discovery game is then ready to be played." Even more troublesome, according to Professor Silberman, is the potentially unconstitutional delegation of authority to magistrates and special masters to make substantive rulings. See Silberman, *The Proliferation of New Institutions Under the Federal Rules,* ___ U.Pa.L.Rev. ___, ___ (1989).

Notes and Questions

1. What is the difference between a master and a magistrate in the federal system? When a magistrate hears pretrial motions, does she do so in her capacity as a magistrate, a special master, or both?

2. The Federal Magistrates Act of 1968 created a system of magistrates. It placed them under the control of district judges and authorized those judges to assign them "duties [that] are not inconsistent with the Constitution and laws of the United States." This language was so vague, however, that it created controversy over the proper scope of the magistrates' authority and over the weight to be given their determinations. Thus, the Act was amended in 1976 and again in 1979. Under the 1979 amendments, when both parties consent, a magistrate may "conduct any and all proceedings in a jury or non-jury civil matter and order the entry of judgment in the case, when specially designated to exercise such jurisdiction by the district court in which he serves." The 1983 amendments to the Federal Rules established procedures for cases in which magistrates are used. For the most part, these amendments simply traced the relevant portions of the Federal Magistrates Act.

Does the Magistrates Act grant so much power to magistrates as to make it unconstitutional? Article III grants life tenure and salary protections to judges to ensure that those invested with the judicial power of the United States will not be subject to political pressure. Magistrates do not enjoy these protections. Yet magistrates perform many (and, with the consent of the parties, all) of the functions normally reserved for Article III judges. Is this grant of power inconsistent with the mandate of Article III? Congress considered this question at length before passing the magistrates' bill; the consensus of the expert witnesses that appeared was that the legislation was constitutional. See generally McCabe, *The Federal Magistrate Act of 1979,* 16 Harv.J.Legis. 343, 365–79 (1979). Yet, some commentators still believe the grants to be unconstitutional. See Note, *Article III Constraints and the Expanding Jurisdiction of Federal Magistrates: A Dissenting View,* 88 Yale L.J. 1023 (1979); Note, *Article III Limits on Article I Courts: The Constitutionality of the Bankruptcy Court and the 1979 Magistrate Act,* 80 Colum.L. Rev. 560 (1980).

3. How can a magistrate's decision be appealed? How do the procedures for appealing a magistrate's decision differ from the procedures for appealing the judgment of a district-court judge? See 12 Wright & Miller, *Federal Practice and Procedure: Civil* §§ 3077.1–80 (1973).

4.   General materials relating to special masters and magistrates include: 6 Wright & Miller, *Federal Practice and Procedure: Civil* §§ 1521–40 (1971); 12 Wright & Miller, *Federal Practice and Procedure: Civil* §§ 3076–80 (1973); Kaufman, *Masters in the Federal Courts: Rule 53*, 58 Colum.L.Rev. 452 (1958); McCabe, *The Federal Magistrate Act of 1979*, 16 Harv.J.Legis. 343 (1979); Silberman, *Masters and Magistrates, Part II: The American Analogue*, 50 N.Y.U.L.Rev. 1297 (1975); Note, *The Expanding Influence of the Federal Magistrate*, 14 J.Marshall L.Rev. 465 (1981).   A fascinating set of reflections about the use of special masters, based largely on the experience of the AT&T antitrust litigation, can be found in Brazil, Hazard & Rice, *Managing Complex Litigation: A Practical Guide to the Use of Special Masters* (1983).

SECTION C.   THE FINAL PRETRIAL ORDER

———

Read the sample final pretrial order set out in the Supplement.

———

PAYNE v. S.S. NABOB

United States Court of Appeals, Third Circuit, 1962.
302 F.2d 803.

McLaughlin, Circuit Judge.   In this personal injury admiralty action libellant filed a pretrial memorandum stating that he was relying upon the condition of a winch to prove his cause of action.   The judge's pretrial report noted that.   Sometime later the suit went to trial.   Libellant's attorney included in his opening the fact that the loading had been handled improperly as an important element of his proof of unseaworthiness.   The impleaded stevedore employer objected as it was outside the scope of the pretrial memorandum and report.   The trial court sustained the objection.   Two witnesses on behalf of the libellant, not listed in his pretrial memorandum, were not allowed to testify.   Libellant's attorney moved for a continuance and this was denied.

* * *

Appellant * * * would have it that the Standing Order [local rule adopting Rule 16] did not furnish any ground for the court's barring of the unseaworthy allegation and of the witnesses not mentioned in the appellant's pretrial memorandum or the court's pretrial report.   This seems to be founded on the thought that a pretrial memorandum is merely preparatory to the conference and that the court's pretrial order is the sole proof of the results of the pretrial procedure.   In this instance, goes the contention, the function of appellant's memorandum was exhausted at the conference and since no pretrial "order" was made there were no binding results of the pretrial steps.   [Padovani v. Bruchhausen, 293 F.2d 546 (2d Cir.1961)] * * * is cited for this, where it states:

Nothing in the rule [16] affords basis for clubbing the parties into admissions they do not willingly make; but it is a way of advancing the trial ultimately to be had by setting forth points on which the parties are agreed after a conference directed by a trained judge.

Appellant was not clubbed into admissions he did not willingly make. It was his own voluntary statement of the basis of his claim that was included in the pretrial report of the judge. The report was never objected to as incorrectly outlining appellant's pretrial statement.

The position now taken that the pretrial report of the trial judge because it is not titled as an "order" does not comply with Rule 16 is without merit. Appellant's pretrial memorandum was filed. In accordance with the Standing Order it contained a "brief summary statement of both the facts of this case and counsel's contention as to the liability of defendant." It also contained "The names and addresses of all witnesses (except rebuttal) whom the plaintiff expects to call to testify at the time of trial." The pretrial conference was held in due course and attended by the attorneys for the parties. Based on the pretrial memoranda and the conference, the district judge drew and filed his report. There was no complaint concerning it or any part of it down to and including the trial until libellant's attorney was stopped in his opening as he went beyond his pretrial outline of alleged liability. The pretrial "report" [2] drawn, signed and filed by the pretrial judge properly and fully (having the particular litigation and its requirements in mind) complies with the requirements of Rule 16. It, including its references to the pretrial memoranda, succinctly fulfilled the letter and spirit of pretrial. It reduced the action to essentials, eliminated surplusage, enabled the parties and the court to prepare for a trial of stated issues, named witnesses and contained no hidden charms. The argument to the contrary, depending as it does on a quibble over the word "report", is rootless.

It is asserted on behalf of the appellant that the Standing Order can only be construed as a request to stipulate, that counsel had no intention of stipulating and that no warning or notice was given by the Standing Order that failure to list the requirements ordered would constitute a stipulation or a waiver of all other theories. Rule 16 gives as the first purpose of pretrial "The simplification of issues". Under the Standing Order counsel were asked to furnish "A brief summary of both the facts of

---

2. "Pre-Trial Report of Judge Van Dusen

Date Pre-Trial Held: 9/21/59 No. on Consolidated List: 2109 303 of 1958 in Admiralty

Case Title: Hosea Payne v. S.S. Nabob & North German Lloyd v. Lavino Shipping Co.

1. Trial Counsel: L—Philip Dorfman, Esq. & Saul C. Waldbaum, Esq.

          R—Robert A. Hauslohner, Esq. (T. Mount will try)

          IR—F. Hastings Griffin, Jr., Esq. (P. Price will try)

2. Amendments: If IR wishes to amend pre-trial memo, notice to be given to undersigned.

3. Discovery: Respondent will answer impleaded respondent's interrogatories (unexecuted copies to be furnished counsel by September 23).

4. L's Claim: Ship unseaworthy due to improper port winch on after side at # 2 hatch. Brakes would not hold when set in neutral. Port winch on house-fall did not work from early hours of morning. See pretrial memo.

5. R's Claim: Sole cause of injuries was L's negligence and that of his fellow workmen. Two men pushed draft into L and 2 other men said nothing was defective in winches. See pre-trial memo. IR's position—see pre-trial memo.

6. Stipulations:

7. Issues:

8. Legal Issues:

9. Trial Time: 6 days

          Francis L. Van Dusen, J."

          Francis L. Van Dusen, J."

the case and counsel's contentions as to the liability of the defendant." That was done. Libellant's contentions as to the liability of the defendant were inserted into the Court's Report with the note "See pre-trial memo". The Report was filed September 28, 1959. The trial did not commence until March 14, 1960, a five and a half months interval during which no effort was made to change the signed and filed contentions of the libellant regarding the liability of the defendant or to add names of witnesses. The facts that the situation was plain on its face and that the practice was well settled by then, (the Standing Order having been in effect since October 23, 1958), set the tone for this contention on behalf of appellant. Krieger v. Ownership Corporation, 270 F.2d 265 (3 Cir.1959), relied upon by appellant is inapposite. We there held that disputed issues of fact *actually raised* at the pretrial stage could not be resolved by the trial court on motion for summary judgment. It has long been the law that attorneys at the pretrial stage "owe a duty to the court and opposing counsel to make a full and fair disclosure of their views as to what the real issues at the trial will be." Cherney v. Holmes, 185 F.2d 718, 721 (7 Cir.1950) * * *. It is through such disclosure at pretrial that trial prejudice can be avoided. The awareness of appellant's attorney to the trial situation is apparent in his request for a continuance when he told the court "I think under the circumstances I would move for a continuance of the case to give *the other side* ample time, because actually this is a question of surprise." (Emphasis supplied).

It is argued also that the court abused its discretion by refusing to permit amendment of the pretrial memorandum. This was not an easy decision for the trial judge. His inclination clearly, as is habitual with judges, was to help. And help he would have if, in his opinion, he could have done so fairly. But he was confronted with the realization that if he granted the request or allowed a continuance of the trial he was repudiating the whole pretrial theory and system as understood and followed in the Eastern District at a crucial period of its existence. Pretrial was finally on a firm foundation there. The judges had all given it generous and complete attention. This, with the gradual realization of the bar that pretrial was here to stay as a vital element of litigation practice and its resultant full cooperation, had made pretrial procedure routine in the Eastern District. One consequence was that directly and indirectly enormous relief was given the badly clogged trial list. It was admittedly vitally important to make sure that pretrial procedure would continue to function properly. One necessary phase of attaining that objective was, as expressed by the trial judge, "We have come to the point of enforcing it very strictly." In the circumstances he considered himself obliged to deny the motions to amend the pretrial memorandum with respect to liability allegations and witnesses. The refusal of appellant's motion for a continuance is in the same category.

Beyond all doubt the judge acted entirely within his discretion. It was difficult for him, it took courage but it was what this sound, experienced judge had to do as he saw it, in accordance with his judicial obligation.

The decree of the district court will be affirmed.

SMITH CONTRACTING CORP. v. TROJAN CONSTRUCTION CO.

United States Court of Appeals, Tenth Circuit, 1951.
192 F.2d 234.

PHILLIPS, CHIEF JUDGE. The Trojan Construction Company, Inc., brought this action against Smith Contracting Corporation to recover damages, in excess of normal wear and tear, to equipment leased by Trojan to Smith, occurring during the use of the equipment by Smith.

The leases were in writing and the two provisions thereof, here material, in each lease, read as follows:

"2. Determination of Rental Charges. * * *.

"(a) *Monthly Rental Rates* shall not be subject to any deductions on account of any non-working time in the month, but the amount of rent payable for any fraction of a month at the beginning or end of the Rental Period shall be the monthly rental rate, prorated according to the number of calendar days in such fraction.

* * *

"8. Damage to Equipment. The Lessee shall indemnify the Lessor against all loss and damage to equipment during the Rental Period and the appraisal of any such loss or damage shall be based on the equipment values shown by the List of Equipment. Any shortage or damage claim of either party shall be made known to the other party within seven (7) days after receipt of equipment, or such claim shall be void."

A pretrial conference was held and the parties agreed that the action was predicated upon a claim that Smith returned the equipment in a damaged condition not resulting from normal wear and tear; that Smith denied there was any damage other than that resulting from normal wear and tear; and that the only question for determination was such issue of fact.

During the introduction of the testimony of the first witness of Trojan the leases were introduced in evidence. Smith then sought to prove that it paid rental for a full month at the end of the rental period, and that the equipment was returned before the end of the last monthly rental period; asserted that it was entitled to a counterclaim under the provisions of paragraph 2(a) of the leases; and asked leave to amend its answer to conform to such proof. The trial court ruled that Smith might make the proof and that it would take under advisement the question of whether the amendment would be permitted.

The trial court found that the equipment suffered damages, resulting other than from ordinary wear and tear during its use by Smith, aggregating $5,208.50. That finding is supported by substantial evidence, is not clearly erroneous, and is, therefore, binding on this court.

Trojan introduced proof that it verbally notified Craig, Superintendent of Smith, in charge of the work where the equipment was being used, of the damages to the equipment shortly before it was returned and that

Craig agreed to have the equipment repaired. It will be observed that the leases did not require notice in writing or other formality in the giving of the notice. They merely provided that any damage claim should be made known to the other party within seven days after receipt of the equipment. The trial court ruled that the verbal notice to Craig was sufficient notice of the damage required by paragraph 8 of the leases. Craig was the agent of Smith in charge of the work where the equipment was being used. We are of the opinion Craig had apparent authority to receive the notice and that the notice was sufficient. Moreover, the agreement at the pretrial conference eliminated the issue of notice.

The trial court refused to permit Smith to amend its answer to set up a counterclaim for overpayment of rental.

The provisions of the leases are plain. The time when the equipment was returned and the amounts of overpayment of rental could have been readily determined. Trojan did not dispute the claim or assert that it was not prepared to meet it. The trial was before the court and if Trojan needed additional time to check the facts, that time could have been granted. On the record, it seems clear that Smith was entitled to a counterclaim for overpayment of rental and that failure of Smith's counsel to assert it earlier resulted in no prejudice to Trojan.

* * *

It will be observed that the clause [in Rule 13(f)] "or when justice requires," is an independent ground upon which the court may grant leave to set up the counterclaim by amendment.

That portion of Rule 15(a) of the Federal Rules * * *, dealing with amendments to pleadings by leave of court provides that "leave shall be freely given when justice so requires."

We are not unmindful that the agreement arrived at during the pretrial conference as to the issues of fact to be presented did not embrace the issues of fact raised by this counterclaim. We are of the opinion, however, that rigid adherence to pretrial conference agreements should not be exacted, especially where so to do will result in injustice to one party and relaxing of such agreement will not cause prejudice to the other party. Requiring rigid adherence to pretrial conference agreements will tend to discourage cooperation of counsel and their willingness to agree at the pretrial conference as to the real and substantial issues to be presented, and will impair the effectiveness of the pretrial conference procedure.

Upon the facts presented on this record, we think justice required the granting of leave to amend the answer to set up the counterclaim and that denial thereof was an abuse of discretion.

* * *

Notes and Questions

1. Courts normally treat the final pretrial order—the stipulations, agreements, and statements of counsel made at the final pretrial conference—as binding for purposes of trial. The final pretrial order supersedes the pleadings. How binding should this order be? Many of the benefits associated with the use of the pretrial order depend upon its binding effect. But given

the exigencies that are an inevitable part of litigation, particularly at the trial level, is strict finality reasonable?

2. Compare the standards for modifying scheduling orders and final pretrial orders found in Rules 16(b) and 16(d). What justifies the difference? Consider briefly the standards for amending pleadings contained in Rule 15. Pay particular attention to which party has the burden of proof. Which Rule is more sympathetic to amendments? Why?

3. The pretrial order sometimes has been used to widen consideration of issues beyond those listed in the pleadings. In Howard v. Kerr Glass Manufacturing Co., 699 F.2d 330 (6th Cir.1983), the Sixth Circuit ruled that the final pretrial order prevailed over the original pleadings and that the trial judge had erred in refusing to admit evidence on issues included in the final pretrial order but not in the pleadings.

4. How should courts penalize the failure to cooperate in the pretrial process? Should the failure to abide by a pretrial order ever result in dismissal of the suit, or in summary judgment? See Delta Theatres, Inc. v. Paramount Pictures, Inc., 398 F.2d 323 (5th Cir.1968), certiorari denied 393 U.S. 1050, 89 S.Ct. 688, 21 L.Ed.2d 692 (1969); Wirtz v. Hooper-Holmes Bureau, Inc., 327 F.2d 939 (5th Cir.1964). Does Rule 41(b) provide an answer to this question? When would a lesser remedy—such as preclusion of an issue or exclusion of evidence—be appropriate? Do you agree that it was appropriate in *Payne*?

Is the remedy (monetary penalties) provided by the new Rule 16 preferable to the relatively drastic remedies discussed above? Does Rule 16 provide a compensatory remedy (designed to deter and to reimburse the opposing party and the court for the cost of any deviations from a pretrial order made by a party)? Or, does the Rule provide a punitive remedy (designed to encourage compliance with the court order)? An analysis of the use of monetary penalties for noncompliance with pretrial orders can be found in Brazil, *Improving Judicial Controls over the Pretrial Development of Civil Actions: Model Rules for Case Management and Sanctions,* 1981 Am.B.Found.Research J. 873, 921–55; Peckham, *The Federal Judge as Case Manager: The New Role of Guiding a Case from Filing to Disposition,* 69 Calif.L.Rev. 770, 800–04 (1981). A more general discussion of penalties for noncompliance with judicial rules and orders can be found in Rodes, Ripple & Mooney, *Sanctions Imposable for Violations of the Federal Rules of Civil Procedure* (Fed.Jud. Center 1981).

5. What are the differences between Rule 16 sanctions and Rule 11 sanctions?

> [T]he coverage of Rules 11 and 16 are by no means co-extensive. Rule 11 deals with all motions, pleadings and documents signed by an attorney or party in a lawsuit; Rule 16 relates to all aspects of pre-trial management, including numerous procedures and discussions not necessarily memorialized in a writing.

HARRIS v. MARSH, 679 F.Supp. 1204, 1389 n. 278 (E.D.N.C.1987), modified 123 F.R.D. 204 (E.D.N.C.1988). There are other differences. First, the imposition of attorneys' fees as a sanction is discretionary in Rule 11 and mandatory in Rule 16(f). Second, although Rule 11 punishes acts done for an improper purpose, Rule 16 punishes certain acts regardless of purpose.

The two rules are similar in some respects, as well.

    * * * If an allegation or contention is offered in a final pre-trial order without a reasonable factual or legal basis, much like Rule 11, it violates Rule 16. A meritless or frivolous claim, asserted with knowledge that opposing counsel will heighten his final preparation for trial of the claim on the basis of its appearance in the final pre-trial order, is not one alleged in good faith. Thus, with respect to final pre-trial orders, there is no reason to suggest the standards for professional responsibility and, therefore, liability under Rule 16 differ from those previously set forth for Rule 11. Improper motive, bad faith, even reckless behavior, is not a prerequisite for finding a violation of the rule.

Id. at 1389.

Chapter 10

ADJUDICATION WITHOUT TRIAL OR BY SPECIAL PROCEEDING

SECTION A. SUMMARY JUDGMENT

Read Federal Rule of Civil Procedure 56 and the accompanying materials in the Supplement.

ADICKES v. S.H. KRESS & CO., 398 U.S. 144, 90 S.Ct. 1598, 26 L.Ed. 2d 142 (1970). Adickes, a white female teacher at a "freedom school" for black children, entered Kress's restaurant with six of her black students. The waitress took the children's orders but refused service to Adickes because she was a white person in the company of blacks. The police then arrested Adickes on a charge of vagrancy.

Adickes sued Kress for damages under 42 U.S.C. § 1983. She charged that Kress's refusal to serve her was a state-enforced "custom of the community" that denied her civil rights and that Kress's act and the arrest, taken together, constituted a conspiracy between Kress and the police to violate her constitutional right to equal protection. On the conspiracy count, the complaint alleged that a police officer had been in the restaurant and had seen Adickes and her group before Adickes was denied service, and that, given the officer's presence in the store, there was circumstantial evidence from which a jury could infer a conspiracy between the Kress employee and the police to "set up" the arrest for vagrancy by denying Adickes service.

Kress moved for summary judgment and supplied affidavits from the store manager, the chief of police, and the arresting officers denying the existence of a pre-arranged scheme. Adickes responded by pressing her circumstantial case. She noted the allegation in the complaint that the policeman who arrested her had earlier been in the store. She adduced her sworn deposition testimony that "one of [her] students saw a police-man come in," and she offered an unsworn statement by a Kress employee (given by Kress to Adickes in discovery) stating that the officer who later arrested Adickes outside the restaurant had been in the store before Adickes was refused service. However, since the statements were hearsay assertions (and probably inadmissible at trial), the District Court ruled that Adickes had failed to allege any fact from which a conspiracy might be inferred. And, the Court of Appeals affirmed unanimously. The Supreme Court reversed:

> * * * [W]e conclude that respondent [Kress] failed to fulfill its initial burden of demonstrating what is a critical element in this aspect of the case—that there was no policeman in the store. If a policeman were present, we think it would be open to a jury, in light of the sequence that followed, to infer from the circumstances that the policeman and a Kress employee had a "meeting of the minds" and thus reached an understanding that petitioner should be refused service. Because "[o]n summary judgment the inferences to be drawn from the underlying facts contained in [the moving party's] materials must be viewed in the light most favorable to the party opposing the motion," * * * we think respondent's failure to show there was no policeman in the store requires reversal.

* * *

> * * * "[W]here the evidentiary matter in support of the motion does not establish the absence of a genuine issue, summary judgment must be denied *even if no opposing evidentiary matter is presented.*" Because respondent did not meet its initial burden of establishing the absence of a policeman in the store, petitioner here was not required to come forward with suitable opposing affidavits.

> If respondent had met its initial burden by, for example, submitting affidavits from the policemen denying their presence in the store at the time in question, Rule 56(e) would then have required petitioner to have done more than simply rely on the contrary allegation in her complaint. To have avoided conceding this fact for purposes of summary judgment, petitioner would have had to come forward with either (1) the affidavit of someone who saw the policeman in the store or (2) an affidavit under Rule 56(f) explaining why at that time it was impractical to do so. Even though not essential here to defeat respondent's motion, the submission of such an affidavit would have been the preferable course for petitioner's counsel to have followed. * * *

398 U.S. at 158–61, 90 S.Ct. at 1609–10, 26 L.Ed.2d at 155–56.

————

CELOTEX CORP. v. CATRETT

Supreme Court of the United States, 1986.
477 U.S. 317, 106 S.Ct. 2548, 91 L.Ed.2d 265.

Certiorari to the United States Court of Appeals for the District of Columbia Circuit.

JUSTICE REHNQUIST delivered the opinion of the Court.

* * *

Respondent commenced this lawsuit in September 1980, alleging that the death in 1979 of her husband, Louis H. Catrett, resulted from his exposure to products containing asbestos manufactured or distributed by 15 named corporations. Respondent's complaint sounded in negligence, breach of warranty, and strict liability.

* * *

Petitioner's summary judgment motion, which was first filed in September 1981, argued that summary judgment was proper because respondent had "failed to produce evidence that any [Celotex] product * * * was the proximate cause of the injuries alleged within the jurisdictional limits of [the District] Court." In particular, petitioner noted that respondent had failed to identify, in answering interrogatories specifically requesting such information, any witnesses who could testify about the decedent's exposure to petitioner's asbestos products. In response to petitioner's summary judgment motion, respondent then produced three documents which she claimed "demonstrate that there is a genuine material factual dispute" as to whether the decedent had ever been exposed to petitioner's asbestos products. The three documents included a transcript of a deposition of the decedent, a letter from an official of one of the decedent's former employers whom petitioner planned to call as a trial witness, and a letter from an insurance company to respondent's attorney, all tending to establish that the decedent had been exposed to petitioner's asbestos products in Chicago during 1970–1971. Petitioner, in turn, argued that the three documents were inadmissible hearsay and thus could not be considered in opposition to the summary judgment motion.

In July 1982, almost two years after the commencement of the lawsuit, the District Court granted [the motion] * * * because "there [was] no showing that the plaintiff was exposed to the defendant Celotex's product in the District of Columbia or elsewhere within the statutory period." * * * Respondent appealed * * *. The majority of the Court of Appeals held that petitioner's summary judgment motion was rendered "fatally defective" by the fact that petitioner "made no effort to adduce *any* evidence, in the form of affidavits or otherwise, to support its motion." * * * According to the majority, Rule 56(e) of the Federal Rules of Civil Procedure, and this Court's decision in Adickes v. S.H. Kress & Co., * * * establish that "the party opposing the motion for summary judgment bears the burden of responding *only after* the moving party has met its burden of coming forward with proof of the absence of any genuine issues of material fact." * * * The majority therefore declined to consider petitioner's argument that none of the evidence produced by respondent in opposition to the motion for summary judgment would have been admissible at trial. * * *

We think that the position taken by the majority of the Court of Appeals is inconsistent with the standard for summary judgment set forth in Rule 56(c) of the Federal Rules of Civil Procedure. * * * In our view, the plain language of Rule 56(c) mandates the entry of summary judgment, after adequate time for discovery and upon motion, against a party who fails to make a showing sufficient to establish the existence of an element essential to that party's case, and on which that party will bear the burden of proof at trial. * * *

Of course, a party seeking summary judgment always bears the initial responsibility of informing the district court of the basis for its motion, and identifying those portions of "the pleadings, depositions, answers to interrogatories, and admissions on file, together with the affidavits, if any," which it believes demonstrate the absence of a genuine issue of material fact. But unlike the Court of Appeals, we find no express or implied requirement in Rule 56 that the moving party support its motion with affidavits or other similar materials *negating* the opponent's claim. On the contrary, Rule 56(c), which refers to "the affidavits, *if any*" (emphasis added), suggests the absence of such a requirement. And if there were any doubt about the meaning of Rule 56(c) in this regard, such doubt is clearly removed by Rules 56(a) and (b), which provide that claimants and defendants, respectively, may move for summary judgment *"with or without supporting affidavits"* (emphasis added). The import of these subsections is that, regardless of whether the moving party accompanies its summary judgment motion with affidavits, the motion may, and should, be granted so long as whatever is before the district court demonstrates that the standard for the entry of summary judgment, as set forth in Rule 56(c), is satisfied. One of the principal purposes of the summary judgment rule is to isolate and dispose of factually unsupported claims or defenses, and we think it should be interpreted in a way that allows it to accomplish this purpose.

Respondent argues, however, that Rule 56(e), by its terms, places on the nonmoving party the burden of coming forward with rebuttal affidavits, or other specified kinds of materials, only in response to a motion for summary judgment "made and supported as provided in this rule." According to respondent's argument, since petitioner did not "support" its motion with affidavits, summary judgment was improper in this case. But as we have already explained, a motion for summary judgment may be made pursuant to Rule 56 "with or without supporting affidavits." In cases like the instant one, where the nonmoving party will bear the burden of proof at trial on a dispositive issue, a summary judgment motion may properly be made in reliance solely on the "pleadings, depositions, answers to interrogatories, and admissions on file." Such a motion, whether or not accompanied by affidavits, will be "made and supported as provided in this rule," and Rule 56(e) therefore requires the nonmoving party to go beyond the pleadings and by her own affidavits, or by the "depositions, answers to interrogatories, and admissions on file," designate "specific facts showing that there is a genuine issue for trial."

* * *

The Court of Appeals in this case felt itself constrained, however, by language in our decision in Adickes v. S.H. Kress & Co. * * *. In the course of its opinion, the *Adickes* Court said that "both the commentary on and the background of the 1963 Amendment conclusively show that it was not intended to modify the burden of the moving party * * * to show initially the absence of a genuine issue concerning any material fact." * * * We think that this statement is accurate in a literal sense, since we fully agree with the *Adickes* Court that the 1963 Amendment to Rule 56(e) was not designed to modify the burden of making the showing generally required by Rule 56(c). It also appears to us that, on the basis of the showing before the Court in *Adickes,* the motion for summary judgment in that case should have been denied. But we do not think the *Adickes* language quoted above should be construed to mean that the burden is on the party moving for summary judgment to produce evidence showing the absence of a genuine issue of material fact, even with respect to an issue on which the nonmoving party bears the burden of proof. Instead, as we have explained, the burden on the moving party may be discharged by "showing"—that is, pointing out to the District Court—that there is an absence of evidence to support the nonmoving party's case.

The last two sentences of Rule 56(e) were added, as this Court indicated in *Adickes,* to disapprove a line of cases allowing a party opposing summary judgment to resist a properly made motion by reference only to its pleadings. While the *Adickes* Court was undoubtedly correct in concluding that these two sentences were not intended to *reduce* the burden of the moving party, it is also obvious that they were not adopted to *add to* that burden. Yet that is exactly the result which the reasoning of the Court of Appeals would produce; in effect, an amendment to Rule 56(e) designed to *facilitate* the granting of motions for summary judgment would be interpreted to make it *more difficult* to grant such motions. Nothing in the two sentences themselves requires this result, for the reasons we have previously indicated, and we now put to rest any inference that they do so.

* * *

Respondent commenced this action in September 1980, and petitioner's motion was filed in September 1981. The parties had conducted discovery, and no serious claim can be made that respondent was in any sense "railroaded" by a premature motion for summary judgment. Any potential problem with such premature motions can be adequately dealt with under Rule 56(f), which allows a summary judgment motion to be denied, or the hearing on the motion to be continued, if the nonmoving party has not had an opportunity to make full discovery.

In this Court, respondent's brief and oral argument have been devoted as much to the proposition that an adequate showing of exposure to petitioner's asbestos products was made as to the proposition that no such showing should have been required. But the Court of Appeals declined to address either the adequacy of the showing made by respondent in opposition to petitioner's motion for summary judgment, or the question whether such a showing, if reduced to admissible evidence, would be sufficient to carry respondent's burden of proof at trial. We think the Court of Appeals with its superior knowledge of local law is better suited than we are to make these determinations in the first instance.

The Federal Rules of Civil Procedure have for more than 50 years authorized motions for summary judgment upon proper showings of the lack of a genuine, triable issue of material fact. Summary judgment procedure is properly regarded not as a disfavored procedural shortcut, but rather as an integral part of the Federal Rules as a whole, which are designed "to secure the just, speedy and inexpensive determination of every action." * * * Before the shift to "notice pleading" accomplished by the Federal Rules, motions to dismiss a complaint or to strike a defense were the principal tools by which factually insufficient claims or defenses could be isolated and prevented from going to trial with the attendant unwarranted consumption of public and private resources. But with the advent of "notice pleading," the motion to dismiss seldom fulfills this function any more, and its place has been taken by the motion for summary judgment. Rule 56 must be construed with due regard not only for the rights of persons asserting claims and defenses that are adequately based in fact to have those claims and defenses tried to a jury, but also for the rights of persons opposing such claims and defenses to demonstrate in the manner provided by the Rule, prior to trial, that the claims and defenses have no factual basis.

The judgment of the Court of Appeals is accordingly reversed, and the case is remanded for further proceedings consistent with this opinion.

It is so ordered.

JUSTICE WHITE, concurring.

I agree that the Court of Appeals was wrong in holding that the moving defendant must always support his motion with evidence or affidavits showing the absence of a genuine dispute about a material fact. I also agree that the movant may rely on depositions, answers to interrogatories and the like to demonstrate that the plaintiff has no evidence to prove his case and hence that there can be no factual dispute. But the movant must discharge the burden the rules place upon him: It is not enough to move for summary judgment without supporting the motion in any way or with a conclusory assertion that the plaintiff has no evidence to prove his case.

* * *

Petitioner Celotex does not dispute that if respondent has named a witness to support her claim, summary judgment should not be granted without Celotex somehow showing that the named witness' possible testimony raises no genuine issue of material fact. * * * It asserts, however, that respondent has failed on request to produce any basis for her case. Respondent, on the other hand, does not contend that she was not obligated to reveal her witnesses and evidence but insists that she has revealed enough to defeat the motion for summary judgment. Because the Court of Appeals found it unnecessary to address this aspect of the case, I agree that the case should be remanded for further proceedings.

JUSTICE BRENNAN, with whom THE CHIEF JUSTICE and JUSTICE BLACKMUN join, dissenting.

This case requires the Court to determine whether Celotex satisfied its initial burden of production in moving for summary judgment on the ground that the plaintiff lacked evidence to establish an essential element of her case at trial. I do not disagree with the Court's legal analysis. The Court clearly rejects the ruling of the Court of Appeals that the defendant must provide affirmative evidence disproving the plaintiff's case. Beyond this, however, the Court has not clearly explained what is required of a moving party seeking summary judgment on the ground that the non-moving party cannot prove its case. This lack of clarity is unfortunate: district courts must routinely decide summary judgment motions, and the Court's opinion will very likely create confusion. For this reason, even if I agreed with the Court's result, I would have written separately to explain more clearly the law in this area. However, because I believe that Celotex did not meet its burden of production under Federal Rule of Civil Procedure 56, I respectfully dissent from the Court's judgment.

I

     * * * The burden of establishing the nonexistence of a "genuine issue" is on the party moving for summary judgment. * * * This burden has two distinct components: an initial burden of production, which shifts to the nonmoving party if satisfied by the moving party; and an ultimate burden of persuasion, which always remains on the moving party. * * * The court need not decide whether the moving party has satisfied its ultimate burden of persuasion unless and until the court finds that the moving party has discharged its initial burden of production.

* * *

The manner in which this showing can be made depends upon which party will bear the burden of persuasion on the challenged claim at trial. If the *moving* party will bear the burden of persuasion at trial that party must support its motion with credible evidence—using any of the material specified in Rule 56(c)—that would entitle it to a directed verdict if not controverted at trial. * * * Such an affirmative showing shifts the burden of production to the party opposing the motion and requires that party either to produce evidentiary materials that demonstrate the exis-tence of a "genuine issue" for trial or to submit an affidavit requesting additional time for discovery. * * *

If the burden of persuasion at trial would be on the *non-moving* party, the party moving for summary judgment may satisfy Rule 56's burden of production in either of two ways. First, the moving party may submit affirmative evidence that negates an essential element of the nonmoving party's claim. Second, the moving party may demonstrate to the Court that the nonmoving party's evidence is insufficient to establish an essen-tial element of the nonmoving party's claim. * * * If the nonmoving party cannot muster sufficient evidence to make out its claim, a trial would be useless and the moving party is entitled to summary judgment as a matter of law. * * *

Where the moving party adopts this second option and seeks summa-ry judgment on the ground that the nonmoving party—who will bear the burden of persuasion at trial—has no evidence, the mechanics of discharg-ing Rule 56's burden of production are somewhat trickier. Plainly, a conclusory assertion that the nonmoving party has no evidence is insuffi-cient. * * * Such a "burden" of production is no burden at all and would simply permit summary judgment procedure to be converted into a tool for harassment. * * * Rather, as the Court confirms, a party who moves for summary judgment on the ground that the nonmoving party has no evidence must affirmatively show the absence of evidence in the record. * * * This may require the moving party to depose the non-moving party's witnesses or to establish the inadequacy of documentary evidence. If there is literally no evidence in the record, the moving party may demonstrate this by reviewing for the court the admissions, interrogatories and other exchanges between the parties that are in the record. Either way, however, the moving party must affirmatively demonstrate that there is no evidence in the record to support a judgment for the nonmoving party.

If the moving party has not fully discharged this initial burden of production, its motion for summary judgment must be denied, and the Court need not consider whether the moving party has met its ultimate burden of persuasion. Accordingly, the nonmoving party may defeat a motion for summary judgment that asserts that the nonmoving party has no evidence by calling the Court's attention to supporting evidence already in the record that was overlooked or ignored by the moving party.

* * *

II

I do not read the Court's opinion to say anything inconsistent with or different than the preceding discussion. My disagreement with the Court concerns the application of these principles to the facts of this case.

* * *

On these facts, there is simply no question that Celotex failed to discharge its initial burden of production. Having chosen to base its motion on the argument that there was no evidence in the record to support plaintiff's claim, Celotex was not free to ignore supporting evidence that the record clearly contained. Rather, Celotex was required, as an initial matter, to attack the adequacy of this evidence. Celotex' failure to fulfill this simple requirement constituted a failure to discharge its initial burden of production under Rule 56, and thereby rendered summary judgment improper.

* * *

[A dissenting opinion by JUSTICE STEVENS is omitted.]

Notes and Questions

1. On remand to the Court of Appeals, a divided panel found that the plaintiff had produced sufficient evidence of exposure and, therefore, that summary judgment was still inappropriate. Catrett v. Johns–Manville Sales Corp., 826 F.2d 33 (D.C.Cir.1987). The majority opinion on remand described the three documents on which plaintiff Catrett based her argument—a transcript of Louis Catrett's testimony in a workmen's compensation claim, in which he indicated his exposure to a product called "Firebar" while working for a company named Anning–Johnson; the letter from T.R. Hoff, the Assistant Secretary of Anning–Johnson, to an Aetna insurance agent reporting on Mr. Catrett's employment with Anning–Johnson; and a letter from the Aetna agent to Mrs. Catrett's counsel essentially restating the contents of Hoff's letter. Catrett argued that, since Celotex supplied the asbestos used by Anning–Johnson, all three documents tended to establish exposure to defen-

dant's product. Celotex countered that the three documents were inadmissible hearsay, out-of-court statements that are inadmissible at trial, and thus should not be considered on the summary-judgment motion. Judge Starr, writing for the majority, stated:

> In the circumstances of this case, we believe that the Hoff letter [a potentially damning piece of evidence] should be considered. The inadmissibility of the letter, despite Celotex's contention to the contrary, is by no means obvious (although we need not and do not pass judgment on its admissibility). Mrs. Catrett argues that the letter is admissible * * *, asserting that the Hoff letter is admissible as falling within the business records exception to the hearsay rule. See Fed.R.Evid. 803(6). *More importantly, Celotex never objected to the District Court's consideration of the Hoff letter.* * * * Since it is well established that "inadmissible documents may be considered by the court if not challenged [at trial]," * * * we are satisfied that the Hoff letter is properly (at this stage) to be considered in assessing whether a genuine issue of fact exists.

> [Moreover, i]n her supplemental interrogatory responses, Mrs. Catrett listed Hoff as a witness. There can, of course, be no doubt that this response is properly considered in ruling on a summary judgment motion. * * * Taking this response together with the Hoff letter, the record, dispassionately viewed, reflects the existence of a witness who can testify with respect to Mr. Catrett's exposure to Firebar. Thus, even if the Hoff letter itself would not be admissible at trial, Mrs. Catrett has gone on to indicate that the substance of the letter is reducible to admissible evidence in the form of trial testimony. * * *

Id. at 37–38 (emphasis in original).

Judge Bork, in dissent, wrote:

> * * * [P]laintiff has not identified "specific facts" that would indicate such exposure occurred, and I certainly think that plaintiff has not made the kind of showing necessary to defeat a directed verdict motion. I would therefore grant defendant's motion for summary judgment.

> * * * [T]he mere listing of a potential witness, without more, does not constitute setting forth specific facts. Here plaintiff has never claimed that Mr. Hoff has any personal knowledge that her husband was exposed to asbestos during his year of work at this company, and indeed did not specify the grounds of his possible testimony at all, except to say that he would be able to testify about "facts relevant to the subject matter of this lawsuit." * * * On the other hand, plaintiff has failed ever to answer interrogatories served by defendant that asked for a variety of specific items of information she might have about her husband's possible exposure to asbestos on any occasion. * * *

> The majority concludes, however, that we should interpret plaintiff's listing of Mr. Hoff as a witness in light of his letter to the insurance company, thereby finding enough evidence to stave off the equivalent of a motion for directed verdict on causation. This conclusion is incorrect for two reasons. First, the sum total of all this "evidence" falls far short of showing, or even suggesting, that anyone has been identified who can testify from personal knowledge about any asbestos exposure. That lack alone requires that defendant's motion for summary judgment be granted.

In addition, and also dispositive, the letter itself is inadmissible as evidence and thus cannot be considered by this court in evaluating the summary judgment motion. ∗ ∗ ∗ It is settled law that the judge may consider only these specific materials or other evidence that would be admissible at trial. Inadmissible evidence is not to be considered unless, like an affidavit, it is "otherwise provided for" in Rule 56.

Id. at 41.

2. Examine the language of Federal Rule 56(e) and Cal.Code Civ.Proc. § 437c, which accompanies the text of the Federal Rule in the Supplement, dealing with the character and content of the affidavits required to support or oppose a summary-judgment motion. Should a federal court, in ruling upon a summary-judgment motion, be required to disregard completely all affidavits containing only hearsay or other matters to which the affiant would not be permitted to testify at trial? Compare Trionfo & Sons, Inc. v. Board of Educ., 41 Md.App. 103, 395 A.2d 1207 (1979) (fact "conclusions" must be ignored).

Suppose A and B were killed in an automobile accident, and A's executor brings suit against B's executor alleging wrongful death. Plaintiff moves for summary judgment on the basis of a deposition of an impartial eyewitness who testified that B drove through a red light. Defendant counters with an affidavit of a police officer who avers that at the scene, shortly after the accident, another impartial eyewitness, now deceased, informed the officer that it was A rather than B who had disobeyed the traffic signal. Should any attention be paid to defendant's affidavit? Should a different test be applied to affidavits on a summary-judgment motion in a case that will be tried by a court than in one that will be heard by a jury?

3. For a helpful discussion of *Celotex,* see Kennedy, *Federal Summary Judgment: Reconciling Celotex v. Catrett with Adickes v. Kress and the Evidentiary Problems Under Rule 56,* 6 Rev. Litigation 227 (1987). On summary judgment generally, see Risinger, *Another Step in the Counter– Revolution: A Summary Judgment on the Supreme Court's New Approach to Summary Judgment,* 54 Brooklyn L.Rev. 35 (1988); Schwarzer, *Summary Judgment: A Proposed Revision of Rule 56,* 110 F.R.D. 213 (1986); Louis, *Federal Summary Judgment Doctrine: A Critical Analysis,* 83 Yale L.J. 745 (1974); 10 and 10A Wright, Miller & Kane, *Federal Practice and Procedure* §§ 2711–42 (1983).

LUNDEEN v. CORDNER

United States Court of Appeals, Eighth Circuit, 1966.
354 F.2d 401.

GIBSON, CIRCUIT JUDGE. ∗ ∗ ∗

Appellant, plaintiff below, (hereinafter referred to as plaintiff) is a former wife of one Joseph Cordner, deceased. During their marriage two children were born, Maureen Joan Cordner and Michael Joseph Cordner. Prior to the time of his death Joseph Cordner was working in Libya. Mr. Cordner's employer Socony Mobil Oil Company, Inc. (Socony) carried a group life insurance contract with Metropolitan Life Insurance Company, (Metropolitan) under which Mr. Cordner as the insured had in 1956 designated his children, Maureen and Michael, as equal beneficiaries. In 1958 Joseph Cordner, having been divorced by plaintiff, married intervener, France Jeanne Cordner. In April 1960 a child was born of this second marriage. On October 3, 1962 Joseph Cordner died. During all periods above mentioned Mr. Cordner was in the employ of Socony stationed in Libya. The insurance policy and the annuity were in effect and due proof of loss was made. The contest for the proceeds arises between adverse claimants; the original designated beneficiaries, Maureen Joan and Michael Joseph Cordner; and France Jeanne Cordner, the second wife of assured, and Northwestern, as Trustee under the Last Will and Testament of Joseph F. Cordner, deceased.

On November 5, 1963, plaintiff as guardian and on behalf of her two children Maureen and Michael Cordner, the named beneficiaries, sued the insurer, Metropolitan, to recover the proceeds of the policy. Metropolitan answered that there were adverse claims to the policy benefits. Thereafter, Northwestern as the Trustee under the Last Will and Testament of the deceased, Joseph Cordner, was interpleaded as an additional defendant. Appellee, France J. Cordner, then intervened in the action. Both intervener and Northwestern allege that sometime in 1961 the decedent effected a change of beneficiaries [in favor of intervener]. * * *

It is clear that the first two children of decedent, Maureen and Michael, are the named beneficiaries. However, it is asserted that Joseph Cordner did everything within his power to effect a change of beneficiaries as alleged by intervener. Intervener presented affidavits and exhibits in support of her position and moved for summary judgment. The motion was granted and plaintiff contests this ruling on the ground that a summary judgment is not proper at this point in the litigation and that there remains a genuine issue on a material fact. It is now our task to determine if the summary judgment was properly granted.

* * * Plaintiff accepts as controlling the general rule of law that an insured's attempt to change his beneficiary will be given effect if all that remains to be done is a ministerial duty on the part of the insurer. * * *

Therefore, if deceased completed all the necessary steps required of him to change the beneficiary in his policy, intervener would be entitled to judgment. Furthermore, if intervener can demonstrate this fact so clearly that there is no longer a genuine issue of fact, summary judgment may be properly granted under provisions of Rule 56(c) of the Fed.R.Civ.P. * * *

We are of the opinion that the affidavits and exhibits introduced by intervener clearly and undeniably indicate that deceased made a change in his policy's beneficiaries. First, it appears that after deceased's marriage in 1958 to intervener he amended his group hospitalization and employee savings plan to include intervener. Furthermore, certain correspondence conclusively indicates that a change in the life insurance was actually made.

Mr. Iten, an employee of Socony in Libya, whose duties included administration of company benefit plans, * * * prepared a letter to the New York office, dated April 19, 1961, stating that Joseph Cordner desired information as to who were his present beneficiaries under the company benefit plans and that Mr. Cordner had married for a second time and was not certain whether he had changed his beneficiary. * * *

Mr. Iten was transferred from Libya shortly thereafter and his duties were assumed by Mr. Burks. Burks by affidavit stated that early in 1961 Mr. Cordner came to him with a request to change his beneficiaries; that Burks issued the necessary forms to Cordner and gave him instructions on how to complete the forms, at which time Cordner produced a copy of his Will made in North Dakota while vacationing from Libya in 1960. They discussed the form of beneficiary designation which might be appropriate under the terms of the Will. Mr. Cordner personally completed the forms, endorsed the beneficiary changes he wished to make on the back of each form, signed the forms in Burks' presence, (the latter acting as a witness to the signature) and then left the completed forms with Burks for transmittal. Since Burks was unfamiliar with the type of beneficiary changes endorsed on the forms he made a thermofax copy of Cordner's Will and sent this reproduction together with the completed change of beneficiary forms to the New York office in a letter dated May 11, 1961, which letter in part reads as follows:

> Please review the enclosed employee change of beneficiary forms and advise us if this designation is acceptable under the plan.

The Home Office responded by stating in a letter dated June 1, 1961:

> We are processing the Change of Beneficiary forms completed by the above employee [J.F. Cordner] and forwarded to us. * * * We see no reason why the designation will not be acceptable.

Mr. Burks in his earlier affidavit of March 30, 1963 states that to the best of his recollection the change of beneficiary requested by Cordner was as follows:

> "One-fourth of the proceeds to my wife France Jeanne Cordner and the balance to the Northwestern National Bank of Minneapolis, Minnesota in trust for the uses and purposes set forth in my Last Will and Testament."

Burks in his second affidavit prepared for the purpose of the summary judgment proceeding confirmed the factual statements in his earlier affidavit and detailed the discussion and the procedures employed in the requested change of beneficiary by Cordner. He further stated that since the New York office had the Certificate for endorsement and since the Home Office stated in its letter of June 1, 1961 that they were processing the change of beneficiary forms he had no reason to believe that the processing of the changes had not proceeded to completion in the normal course. He was in the New York office at the time when a search of the files was made for the change of beneficiary forms, which, of course, they were unable to locate. When he returned to Tripoli, with instructions from the New York office to continue the search and to forward to New York all company papers having to do with Mr. Cordner's employment, he found a copy of a letter addressed to Cordner by his attorney suggesting the form of beneficiary designation required to effect the provisions of his Will. Burks then recalled that Mr. Cordner had referred to this same letter when discussing beneficiary changes in 1961 and that Cordner had used the suggested language in completing his change of beneficiary forms. After stating that he cannot restate from memory the text of the changes, he said that "I can and do reconfirm, upon my own direct knowledge and positive recollection that beneficiary changes so made by Joseph Franklin Cordner were in the form suggested by his attorney's letter and quoted verbatim from that letter in my prior affidavit."

Further correspondence indicates that the change of beneficiary forms were forwarded to the employer's Annuity and Insurance Department. A search of the department, however, never uncovered the form or the exact language used therein. It also appears by affidavit that all of the above related correspondence was properly identified and was prepared, mailed, received and kept as part of the business records of the company.

Plaintiff presents no counter evidence nor in any way indicates that intervener's evidence is not worthy of belief. Therefore, we believe there is no genuine issue of fact on this point. It is clear that Joseph Cordner actually made a change in the beneficiaries of his life insurance policy.

However, to entitle intervener to summary judgment, it must not only be clear that a change was made, but the wording of that change must be shown beyond any reasonable and genuine dispute. This point, too, was well covered in intervener's supporting papers.

* * *

From the affidavit of the attorney concerning the discussion of deceased's desires, from the letter written by the attorney explaining how the beneficiaries should be changed to effectuate these desires, and from the wording of the Last Will and Testament it is clear that Joseph Cordner intended to change the beneficiaries of his insurance policy by giving one-fourth to intervener and the balance to Northwestern in trust. We can presume that this intent remained with Mr. Cordner during the intervening ten months between the Will's execution and the date of the beneficiary change. * * *

However, in addition to this presumption we have the uncontested affidavits of a non-interested third party who was in a position to be aware of the actual wording of the change. The affiant, Mr. Harold Burks, was a fellow employee of Mr. Cordner in Libya, and supervised Mr. Cordner in filling out the required change of beneficiary forms. Mr. Burks is probably the only person that was in a position to be aware of the wording of the document. His affidavits are entitled to considerable weight in determining the merits of a summary judgment motion, especially where there is no indication of any counter-evidence. Moreover, Mr. Burks' assistance in processing the change in beneficiary was done in the regular course of business of Socony, and pursuant to his assigned duties. It has been held that the clear affidavits from the only persons in a position to be aware of a factual situation can well serve as the basis for a summary judgment. Dyer v. MacDougall, 201 F.2d 265 (2 Cir.1952).

* * *

So, in support of intervener's claim there is undisputed proof that Mr. Cordner had manifested an intent to give intervener one-fourth of his insurance proceeds with the balance going into the trust established by his Will. It is likewise clear beyond any shadow of doubt that Mr. Cordner subsequently made a change in his insurance beneficiaries. The logical conclusion is clear. He made the change in accordance with his prior expressed intent. This presumption is supported by the two affidavits of Mr. Burks which recite from direct and positive recollection that the beneficiary changes were copied from Mr. Cordner's letter from his attorney and were in form exactly as alleged by intervener.

In response to the overwhelming documentary evidence supported by affidavits all of which consistently showed that Cordner had requested a change of beneficiary in accordance with his lawyer's letter and his own Last Will and Testament, the plaintiff submitted her own counter-affidavit to the effect that Mr. Cordner was very much interested in the welfare of his first two children (the named beneficiaries) and was aware of the future financial difficulties they would face. No further information was offered. The Court, therefore, was not presented with a situation where it was asked to weigh conflicting affidavits. The problem was only, did the affidavits and exhibits of intervener sustain the necessary burden in order to allow a summary judgment? The trial court felt the burden was sustained, and from the above related facts we agree with the trial court's conclusion. * * *

We are of the opinion that if this information were presented at trial, intervener would be entitled to a directed verdict in her favor, and it has been said that if the information presented entitles one to a directed verdict, a summary judgment is in order. * * * Intervener having made a sufficient showing, it then rests upon the plaintiff to specify at least some evidence which could be produced at trial. * * * Plaintiff apparently is of the opinion that, since she makes a prima facie case by merely introducing the Certificate showing her children as designated beneficiaries, she is entitled to a trial on the issue of (1) whether any change of beneficiary was made, and (2) if so, what changes were actually made. This we do not feel is a correct view of the law.

The counter-affidavit of the plaintiff does not meet the issues raised and supported by the intervener. This leaves no genuine issue as to any material fact, and presents a predicate for a summary judgment under Rule 56(c), Fed.R.Civ.P.

* * *

The real gravamen of plaintiff's objection is not that there is conflicting evidence but rather that the summary judgment rests upon the affidavits of Harold Burks. His testimony being so vital to intervener's cause, it is asserted that the case should proceed to trial in order that the demeanor of the witness could be observed and his testimony subjected to the test of cross-examination.

In passing on this contention it might be well to make four preliminary observations. First, affiant Burks appears to be an unbiased witness. He has no financial or personal interest in the outcome of this litigation. Second, there is no doubt but what his testimony is competent both in regard to his mental capacity and his being in a position to directly observe the facts related in his affidavits. Third, his participation in the change of beneficiaries was in the regular course of his duties with Socony. Finally, both affidavits are positive, internally consistent, unequivocal, and in full accord with the documentary exhibits. Therefore, even though cross-examination is a trial right which must be carefully protected, in this case, unlike many others there is no obvious advantage to be gained from a cross-examination. If there were, a summary judgment might arguably be improper. But where there is no indication that the affiant was biased, dishonest, mistaken, unaware or unsure of the facts, the cases declaring that cross-examination is necessary when one of the above is present, have no application here. There being no positive showing that this witness's testimony could be impeached or that he might have additional testimony valuable to plaintiff, summary judgment was properly granted. The opposing party cannot as a matter of course force a trial merely in order to cross-examine such an affiant, nor must the Court deny the motion for summary judgment on the basis of a vague supposition that something might turn up at the trial. * * *

There is absolutely no showing that a trial would produce any different or additional evidence. It appears that Burks is now stationed in Singapore, far beyond the subpoena powers of the trial court. Neither party would be able to compel his attendance before the trial court. Since this witness is out of the jurisdiction, any of the parties, on the other hand, would be free to introduce Burks' testimony by use of a deposition. Therefore, in all likelihood Burks would never have to appear in open court. What would plaintiff have to gain by forcing a trial under these circumstances? We feel very little, if anything. A full trial would not give plaintiff an opportunity to cross-examine Burks in open court, nor would it unveil his demeanor to the trier of fact.

In the event of a trial plaintiff would only be free to obtain Burks' sworn testimony by deposition or upon written interrogatories pursuant to Rule 28(b) or Rule 31, Fed.R.Civ.P. and by 28 U.S.C.A. § 1783(a)(1). Plaintiff, however, was free to take this action even prior to the present motion for summary judgment but chose not to do so. When the motion for summary judgment was presented, plaintiff, if she felt Burks had information valuable to her cause, was again free to move for a delay in judgment and secure Burks' deposition. Again plaintiff took no action. Apparently plaintiff felt she had nothing to gain by a deposition, yet under the circumstances of this case that is probably the most she could expect even if this case went to trial. Therefore, we do not feel that plaintiff is in a position at this time to force a trial. A trial would not secure Burks' presence, it would only force the taking of his deposition, a course previously open to plaintiff which she elected not to pursue.

* * *

The position declaring that a party opposed to a summary judgment based upon affidavits must assume some initiative in showing that a factual issue actually exists is perfectly sound in the light of Rule 56, Fed. R.Civ.P., which specifically allows the use of affidavits in summary judgment proceedings. For if plaintiff's position is correct that an affiant's credibility is always an issue for the trial court, then the granting of a summary judgment would be virtually impossible when it is based in any way upon an affidavit. Rule 56 would be nullified by the prevailing party's use of one affidavit and the bald objection by the opposing party to the affiant's credibility. The reference in this rule to "affidavits" would therefore be of no effect.

This does not mean that an affiant's credibility cannot properly be put in issue by a litigant, but in doing so specific facts must be properly produced. At this point the 1963 amendment to Rule 56(e) comes into play requiring the opposing party to respond or suffer the fate of a summary judgment, if otherwise appropriate. Plaintiff failed to respond to the adequate and substantial showing of intervener, so the trial court properly granted the summary judgment. Keeping in mind that the purpose of the summary judgment is to avoid useless trials, from the circumstances of this case we believe a trial would indeed be a useless waste of time and expense to the parties as well as a needless inconvenience to the Court.

*   *   *

Judgment affirmed.

Notes and Questions

1. Of what consequence is it that at trial the intervenor would have had the burden of persuading the trier of fact that it was more probable than not that decedent had changed the names of the beneficiaries? Did the appellate court erroneously assume that the burden was on plaintiff to show that the beneficiaries had not been changed? If so, should the decision below have been reversed?

Consider the paragraph in Cal.Code Civ.Proc. § 437c, which is set out in the Supplement, dealing with matters of credibility and lack of an opportunity for cross-examination. What is the objective of this paragraph? Should it be added to Federal Rule 56?

2. In DYER v. MacDOUGALL, 201 F.2d 265, 268–69 (2d Cir.1952), plaintiff brought suit for slander; defendant was granted summary judgment on the basis of the affidavits of all the persons present when the slanderous statements allegedly had been made. All of the affidavits denied plaintiff's allegations. The appellate court affirmed:

> *   *   * [I]f the cause went to trial, the plaintiff would have no witnesses by whom he could prove the slanders alleged *   *   * except the two defendants, *   *   * and they would all deny that the slanders had been uttered. On such a showing how could he escape a directed verdict? It is true that the carriage, behavior, bearing, manner and appearance of a witness—in short, his "demeanor"—is a part of the evidence. The words used are by no means all that we rely on in making up our minds about the truth of a question that arises in our ordinary affairs, and it is abundantly settled that a jury is as little confined to them as we are. They may, and indeed they should, take into consideration the whole nexus of sense impressions which they get from a witness. This we have again and again declared, and have rested our affirmance of findings of fact of a judge, or of a jury, on the hypothesis that this part of the evidence may have turned the scale. Moreover, such evidence may

satisfy the tribunal, not only that the witness' testimony is not true, but that the truth is the opposite of his story; for the denial of one, who has a motive to deny, may be uttered with such hesitation, discomfort, arrogance or defiance, as to give assurance that he is fabricating, and that, if he is, there is no alternative but to assume the truth of what he denies.

Nevertheless, although it is therefore true that in strict theory a party having the affirmative might succeed in convincing a jury of the truth of his allegations in spite of the fact that all the witnesses denied them, we think it plain that a verdict would nevertheless have to be directed against him. This is owing to the fact that otherwise in such cases there could not be an effective appeal from the judge's disposition of a motion for a directed verdict. He, who has seen and heard the "demeanor" evidence, may have been right or wrong in thinking that it gave rational support to a verdict; yet, since that evidence has disappeared, it will be impossible for an appellate court to say which he was. Thus, he would become the final arbiter in all cases where the evidence of witnesses present in court might be determinative.

CROSS v. UNITED STATES

United States Court of Appeals, Second Circuit, 1964.
336 F.2d 431.

MOORE, CIRCUIT JUDGE: In this income tax refund suit, plaintiffs-appellees claim that they were entitled to a deduction of $1,300 on their joint return for the year 1954 because of expenses incurred by Professor Ephraim Cross in connection with his summer travel to various Mediterranean and European countries. Upon appellees' motion for summary judgment, the district court, whose examination of the facts included the affidavits of several professors tending to indicate the desirability of foreign travel for a teacher of languages as well as the pre-trial deposition of Professor Cross, concluded that there was no genuine issue as to any material fact, and granted appellees' motion. * * * The Government opposed the summary judgment procedure, claiming a right to cross-examine appellees as to the nature of their expenses and the educational benefits allegedly sought and also to cross-examine the affiant professors. On this appeal the only issue is whether there are triable issues of fact which render the award of summary judgment erroneous.

In 1954 Professor Cross was an Assistant Professor at City College in New York where he taught French, Spanish and romance linguistics (described by him as the study of the development of Latin into the romance languages, the study of the various dialects and the historic stages of those dialects). He, his wife and a pet dog sailed from New York on June 30, 1954 aboard a French freighter. The ship put in briefly in Portugal, Morocco, Tangiers, Oran, Algiers, Naples and Genoa and appellees spent a day or so in each place. When the freighter arrived at Marseilles, twenty-one days after leaving New York, appellees separated. Mrs. Cross joined a friend and continued touring while Professor Cross and their pet dog travelled to Paris. Although he did not pursue a formal course of study or engage in research, Professor Cross did visit schools, courts of law, churches, book publishers, theaters, motion pictures, restaurants, cafes and other places of amusement, read newspapers, listen to radio broadcasts, converse with students and teachers and attend political meetings. He rejoined his wife in this country on September 23, 1954 after his return aboard a French passenger liner.

Section 162(a), Int.Rev.Code of 1954 permits a deduction for "all the ordinary and necessary expenses paid or incurred * * * in carrying on any trade or business * * *." The Regulations promulgated under that section, Treas.Reg. 1.162–5, state:

Expenses for education—(a) Expenditures made by a taxpayer for his education are deductible if they are for education (including research activities) undertaken primarily for the purpose of:

(1) Maintaining or improving skills required by the taxpayer in his employment or trade or business, * * *

* * *

Whether or not education is of the type referred to in subparagraph (1) of this paragraph shall be determined upon the basis of all the facts of each case. If it is customary for other established members of the taxpayer's trade or business to undertake such education, the taxpayer will ordinarily be considered to have undertaken this education for the purposes described in subparagraph (1) of this paragraph.

* * *

(c) In general, a taxpayer's expenditures for travel (including travel while on sabbatical leave) as a form of education shall be considered as primarily personal in nature and therefore not deductible.

Appellees claim, and the district court held, that all of Professor Cross's expenses are deductible. Professor Cross asserted in his deposition, which was taken for discovery purposes and did not include cross-examination,

My purpose [in making the trip] was to maintain my contacts with my foreign languages for the purpose of maintaining and improving my skill as a linguist and teacher of languages, and to make my general teaching more effective, and to extend my contacts with foreign culture which I have to teach in connection with my teaching of foreign languages per se, and this can be done effectively and properly only by going into a foreign language area.

The Government disputes this explanation. It contends that all or at least part of Professor Cross's travel was a vacation and thus a personal living expense for which a deduction is not allowed under Section 162 * * *. Moreover, the Government challenges the amount of the claimed deduction and questions whether any portion of that sum was expended on behalf of Mrs. Cross.

We believe that summary judgment was improvidently granted and that the Government is entitled to a trial at which all the circumstances may be developed for the consideration of the trier of fact. Rule 56(c), Fed.R.Civ.P. permits summary judgment only where "there is no genuine issue as to any material fact," a state of affairs not normally encountered where the problem is whether expenses are ordinary and necessary in carrying on a taxpayer's trade or business. * * * Before travelling expenses can be allowed as deductible, there must be a factual determination of what parts, if any, are to be attributed to vacation travel or to educational advancement.

The essentially factual character of the issue is particularly apparent here, where the ultimate facts were warmly contested. While there was no dispute that Professor Cross was a teacher of languages and that he travelled abroad, many of the facts remain largely within his own knowledge and the Government should have the opportunity to test his credibility on cross-examination. Summary judgment is particularly inappropriate where "the inferences which the parties seek to have drawn deal with questions of motive, intent and subjective feelings and reactions." Empire Electronics Co. v. United States, 311 F.2d 175, 180 (2d Cir.1962) * * *. "'A judge may not, on a motion for summary judgment, draw fact inferences. * * * Such inferences may be drawn only on a trial.'" Bragen v. Hudson County News Co., 278 F.2d 615, 618 (3d Cir.1960). While we have recently emphasized that ordinarily the bare allegations of the pleadings, unsupported by specific evidentiary data, will not alone defeat a motion for summary judgment, Dressler v. M/V Sandpiper, 331 F.2d 130 (2d Cir.1964), this principle does not justify summary relief where, as here, the disputed questions of fact turn exclusively on the credibility of movants' witnesses.

To the teacher of modern languages, particularly in a country far removed from the European continent, it is highly important that his linguistic ear be returned as frequently as possible to the ways in which a foreign language is expressed. Moreover, a thorough familiarity with the current social, political and cultural climate of a country properly may be regarded as a prerequisite to effective classroom presentation of its language. * * *

On the other hand, a mere pleasure trip through various countries by a professor who has some fluency with the language of each country might well not fall within the deductible category. * * *

Who can doubt that the alert American trial lawyer as a part of a summer vacation might not profit greatly by spending some time at the Old Bailey listening to British barristers exhibit their skills. The surgeon, too, might be benefitted in his profession by observing some delicate operation conducted by a European surgeon of renown. Yet it is questionable whether such tangible evidences of constant interest in one's profession entitle a taxpayer to deduct all his summer vacation expenses.

In addition to determining whether the trip was devoted in whole or in part to educational advancement, the trier of the facts will have to ascertain such amounts as are to be attributed to such purpose. Were the preliminary twenty-one days prior to the Marseilles landing all part of an educational program? What part, if any, was allocable to Mrs. Cross? What charges were incurred by the dog? Although probably *de minimis,* the Treasury frequently watches every penny and might not be generously inclined even though the dog were a French poodle.

The district court reasoned that summary judgment should be granted because the Government did not adduce facts to refute Professor Cross's claims as to the purpose of his trip, and that the Government had an opportunity to cross-examine when taking his deposition. The "right to use depositions for discovery * * * does not mean that they are to supplant the right to call and examine the adverse party * * * before the jury. * * * '[W]e cannot very well overestimate the importance of having the witness examined and cross-examined in presence of the court and jury.'" Arnstein v. Porter, 154 F.2d 464, 470 (2d Cir.1946). By the same process, Professor Cross will have an opportunity to show with greater particularity that his more modern approach to the problem of linguistic improvement is far superior to the old-fashioned classroom lecture method.

Reversed and remanded for trial.

Notes and Questions

1. Can the *Cross* case be reconciled with *Celotex* and *Lundeen*? Didn't the court in *Cross* blatantly ignore the express language of Federal Rule 56(e)? Why wasn't the government at least required to cross-examine Professor Cross at the deposition as to the truth of his assertions?

2. Should evidence of "interested witnesses" be considered in a motion for summary judgment? Is the credibility of that evidence inherently factual? For a discussion whether matters of inference and credibility are questions of fact for summary-judgment purposes, see Sonenshine, *State of Mind and Credibility in the Summary Judgment Context: A Better Approach,* 78 N.W. U.L.Rev. 774 (1978); Louis, *Federal Summary Judgment Doctrine: A Critical Analysis,* 83 Yale L.J. 745, 749 (1974).

3. Some courts take the position that summary judgment is inappropriate whenever a person's state of mind is at issue. See Petro v. McCullough, 179 Ind.App. 438, 385 N.E.2d 1195 (1979). Contra, Vern Walton Motors v. Taylor, 121 Ariz. 463, 591 P.2d 555 (Ct.App.1978). Does it ever make sense to permit a moving party to use his own affidavit to establish his own intent?

4. What did the court in *Cross* mean when it stated that the trial judge was not entitled to "draw fact inferences"? Could more than a single inference be drawn from the facts presented by plaintiff through affidavits and deposition? For an interesting discussion as to whether matters of inference and credibility are questions of fact for summary-judgment purposes, see Note, *Summary Judgment Under Federal Rule of Civil Procedure 56—A Need for a Clarifying Amendment,* 48 Iowa L.Rev. 453, 461–63, 468–69 (1963).

ANDERSON v. LIBERTY LOBBY, INC.

Supreme Court of the United States, 1986.
477 U.S. 242, 106 S.Ct. 2505, 91 L.Ed.2d 202.

[Willis Carto, a right-wing publisher, and Liberty Lobby, the organization he headed, filed a libel suit against *The Investigator* magazine, its president and its publisher, columnist Jack Anderson, for articles that portrayed the plaintiffs as neo-Nazi, anti-Semitic, racist, and fascist.

Following discovery, the defendants moved for summary judgment on the ground that the plaintiffs could not prove by clear and convincing evidence that the defendants acted with actual malice—with knowledge that the statements were false or with reckless disregard of whether they were true or false—the standard required by New York Times v. Sullivan and its progeny for libel suits brought by public figures. In support of the motion, the defendants submitted an affidavit from Charles Bermant, the employee who had written the allegedly libelous articles, that stated that he had spent a substantial amount of time researching and writing the articles. His affidavit also detailed the sources for each of the statements in the article, and affirmed that he believed the facts he reported to be true. Plaintiffs responded to the motion by pointing to numerous claimed inaccuracies in the articles. On the issue of malice, plaintiffs showed that one of Bermant's sources was a twelve-year-old article published in *Time* magazine that had been the subject of an earlier libel suit by the plaintiff, which resulted in a settlement under which *Time* paid Carto a sum of money and published a favorable article about Liberty Lobby, and that one of the co-authors of the *Time* article was an editor of *The Investigator*. Plaintiffs also showed that another source was a free-lance journalist whom Bermant never met and who was not asked to, and never identified, his sources. Finally, they showed that another editor of *The Investigator* had told the magazine's president that the articles were "terrible" and "ridiculous."

The District Court granted the motion for summary judgment. The Court of Appeals reversed as to some of the allegedly defamatory statements, holding that "a jury could reasonably conclude that the * * * allegations were defamatory, false, and made with actual malice." The Court of Appeals ruled that it was irrelevant on a motion for summary judgment that the standard for proving actual malice was clear and convincing evidence, rather than a preponderance of evidence.]

Certiorari to the United States Court of Appeals for the District of Columbia Circuit.

JUSTICE WHITE delivered the opinion of the Court.

* * *

II

A

Our inquiry is whether the Court of Appeals erred in holding that the heightened evidentiary requirements that apply to proof of actual malice in this *New York Times* case need not be considered for the purposes of a motion for summary judgment. * * * By its very terms, [Rule 56(c)] provides that the mere existence of *some* alleged factual dispute between the parties will not defeat an otherwise properly supported motion for summary judgment; the requirement is that there be no *genuine* issue of *material* fact.

As to materiality, the substantive law will identify which facts are material. Only disputes over facts that might affect the outcome of the suit under the governing law will properly preclude the entry of summary judgment. Factual disputes that are irrelevant or unnecessary will not be counted. * * *

More important for present purposes, summary judgment will not lie if the dispute about a material fact is "genuine," that is, if the evidence is such that a reasonable jury could return a verdict for the nonmoving party. * * *

Our prior decisions may not have uniformly recited the same language in describing genuine factual issues under Rule 56, but is clear enough from our recent cases that at the summary judgment stage the judge's function is not himself to weigh the evidence and determine the truth of the matter but to determine whether there is a genuine issue for trial. As [the cases] indicate, there is no issue for trial unless there is sufficient evidence favoring the nonmoving party for a jury to return a verdict for that party. * * * If the evidence is merely colorable, * * * or is not significantly probative, * * * summary judgment may be granted.

That this is the proper focus of the inquiry is strongly suggested by the Rule itself. Rule 56(d) provides that, when a properly supported motion for summary judgment is made, the adverse party "must set forth specific facts showing that there is a genuine issue for trial." And, as we noted above, Rule 56(c) provides that the trial judge shall then grant summary judgment if there is no genuine issue as to any material fact and if the moving party is entitled to judgment as a matter of law. There is no requirement that the trial judge make findings of fact. The inquiry performed is the threshold inquiry of determining whether there is the need for a trial—whether, in other words, there are any genuine factual issues that properly can be resolved only by a finder of fact because they may reasonably be resolved in favor of either party.

The petitioners suggest, and we agree, that this standard mirrors the standard for a directed verdict under Federal Rule of Civil Procedure 50(a), which is that the trial judge must direct a verdict if, under the governing law, there can be but one reasonable conclusion as to the verdict. * * * If reasonable minds could differ as to the import of the evidence, however, a verdict should not be directed. * * * As the Court long ago said in Improvement Co. v. Munson, 14 Wall. 442, 448, 20 L.Ed. 867 (1872), and has several times repeated:

> Nor are judges any longer required to submit a question to a jury merely because some evidence has been introduced by the party having the burden of proof, unless the evidence be of such a character that it would warrant the jury in finding a verdict in favor of that party. Formerly it was held that if there was what is called a *scintilla* of evidence in support of a case the judge was bound to leave it to the jury, but recent decisions of high authority have established a more reasonable rule, that in every case, before the evidence is left to the jury, there is a preliminary question for the judge, not whether there is literally no evidence, but whether there is any upon which a jury could properly proceed to find a verdict for the party producing it, upon whom the *onus* of proof is imposed. * * *

* * *

The Court has said that summary judgment should be granted where the evidence is such that it "would require a directed verdict for the moving party." Sartor v. Arkansas Gas Corp., 321 U.S. 620, 624, 64 S.Ct. 724, 727, 88 L.Ed. 967 (1944). And we have noted that the "genuine issue" summary judgment standard is "very close" to the "reasonable jury" directed verdict standard: "The primary difference between the two motions is procedural; summary judgment motions are usually made before trial and decided on documentary evidence, while directed verdict motions are made at trial and decided on the evidence that has been admitted." Bill Johnson's Restaurants, Inc. v. NLRB, 461 U.S. 731, 745, n. 11, 103 S.Ct. 2161, 2171, n. 11, 76 L.Ed.2d 277 (1983). In essence, though, the inquiry under each is the same: whether the evidence presents a sufficient disagreement to require submission to a jury or whether it is so one-sided that one party must prevail as a matter of law.

B

Progressing to the specific issue in this case, we are convinced that the inquiry involved in a ruling on a motion for summary judgment or for a directed verdict necessarily implicates the substantive evidentiary standard of proof that would apply at the trial on the merits. If the defendant in a run-of-the-mill civil case moves for summary judgment or for a directed verdict based on the lack of proof of a material fact, the judge must ask himself not whether he thinks the evidence unmistakably favors one side or the other but whether a fair-minded jury could return a verdict for the plaintiff on the evidence presented. The mere existence of a scintilla of evidence in support of the plaintiff's position will be insufficient; there must be evidence on which the jury could reasonably find for the plaintiff. The judge's inquiry, therefore, unavoidably asks whether reasonable jurors could find by a preponderance of the evidence that the plaintiff is entitled to a verdict—"whether there is [evidence] upon which a jury can properly proceed to find a verdict for the party producing it, upon whom the *onus* of proof is imposed." *Munson,* supra, 14 Wall., at 448.

* * * [W]here the First Amendment mandates a "clear and convincing" standard, the trial judge in disposing of a directed verdict motion should consider whether a reasonable factfinder could conclude, for example, that the plaintiff had shown actual malice with convincing clarity.

* * * [Similarly], it is relevant in ruling on a motion for summary judgment. When determining if a genuine factual issue as to actual malice exists in a libel suit brought by a public figure, a trial judge must bear in mind the actual quantum and quality of proof necessary to support liability under *New York Times.* For example, there is no genuine issue if the evidence presented in the opposing affidavits is of insufficient caliber or quantity to allow a rational finder of fact to find actual malice by clear and convincing evidence.

Thus, in ruling on a motion for summary judgment, the judge must view the evidence presented through the prism of the substantive evidentiary burden. This conclusion is mandated by the nature of this determination. The question here is whether a jury could reasonably find *either* that the plaintiff proved his case by the quality and quantity of evidence required by the governing law *or* that he did not. Whether a jury could reasonably find for either party, however, cannot be defined except by the criteria governing what evidence would enable the jury to find for either the plaintiff or the defendant: It makes no sense to say that a jury could reasonably find for either party without some benchmark as to what standards govern its deliberations and within what boundaries its ultimate decision must fall, and these standards and boundaries are in fact provided by the applicable evidentiary standards.

Our holding that the clear-and-convincing standard of proof should be taken into account in ruling on summary judgment motions does not denigrate the role of the jury. It by no means authorizes trial on affidavits. Credibility determinations, the weighing of the evidence, and the drawing of legitimate inferences from the facts are jury functions, not those of a judge, whether he is ruling on a motion for summary judgment or for a directed verdict. The evidence of the non-movant is to be believed, and all justifiable inferences are to be drawn in his favor. * * * Neither do we suggest that the trial courts should act other than with caution in granting summary judgment or that the trial court may not deny summary judgment in a case where there is reason to believe that the better course would be to proceed to a full trial. * * *

In sum, we conclude that the determination of whether a given factual dispute requires submission to a jury must be guided by the substantive evidentiary standards that apply to the case. This is true at both the directed verdict and summary judgment stages. Consequently, where the *New York Times* "clear and convincing" evidence requirement applies, the trial judge's summary judgment inquiry as to whether a genuine issue exists will be whether the evidence presented is such that a jury applying that evidentiary standard could reasonably find for either the plaintiff or the defendant. Thus, where the factual dispute concerns actual malice, clearly a material issue in a *New York Times* case, the appropriate summary judgment question will be whether the evidence in the record could support a reasonable jury finding either that the plaintiff has shown actual malice by clear and convincing evidence or that the plaintiff has not.

III

Respondents argue, however, that whatever may be true of the applicability of the "clear and convincing" standard at the summary judgment or directed verdict stage, the defendant should seldom if ever be granted summary judgment where his state of mind is at issue and the jury might disbelieve him or his witnesses as to this issue. * * * We do not understand * * *, however, * * * that a plaintiff may defeat a defendant's properly supported motion for summary judgment in a conspiracy or libel case, for example, without offering any concrete evidence from which a reasonable juror could return a verdict in his favor and by merely asserting that the jury might, and legally could, disbelieve the defendant's denial of a conspiracy or of legal malice. The movant has the burden of showing that there is no genuine issue of fact, but the plaintiff is not thereby relieved of his own burden of producing in turn evidence that would support a jury verdict. * * * We repeat, however, that the plaintiff, to survive the defendant's motion, need only present evidence from which a jury might return a verdict in his favor. If he does so, there is a genuine issue of fact that requires a trial.

IV

In sum, a court ruling on a motion for summary judgment must be guided by the *New York Times* "clear and convincing" evidentiary standard in determining whether a genuine issue of actual malice exists—that is, whether the evidence presented is such that a reasonable jury might find that actual malice had been shown with convincing clarity. Because the Court of Appeals did not apply the correct standard in reviewing the District Court's grant of summary judgment, we vacate its decision and remand the case for further proceedings consistent with this opinion.

It is so ordered.

JUSTICE BRENNAN, dissenting.

* * * This case is about a trial court's responsibility when considering a motion for summary judgment, but in my view, the Court, while instructing the trial judge to "consider" heightened evidentiary standards, fails to explain what that means. In other words, how does a judge assess how one-sided evidence is, or what a "fair-minded" jury could "reasonably" decide? The Court provides conflicting clues to these mysteries, which I fear can lead only to increased confusion in the district and appellate courts.

The Court's opinion is replete with boilerplate language to the effect that trial courts are not to weigh evidence when deciding summary judgment motions * * *.

But the Court's opinion is also full of language which could surely be understood as an invitation—if not an instruction—to trial courts to assess and weigh evidence much as a juror would * * *.

I simply cannot square the direction that the judge "is not himself to weigh the evidence" with the direction that the judge also bear in mind the "quantum" of proof required and consider whether the evidence is of sufficient "caliber or quality" to meet that "quantum." I would have thought that a determination of the "caliber and quality," i.e., the importance and value, of the evidence in light of the "quantum," i.e., amount required could *only* be performed by weighing the evidence.

If in fact, this is what the Court would, under today's decision, require of district courts, then I am fearful that this new rule—for this surely would be a brand new procedure—will transform what is meant to provide an expedited "summary" procedure into a full blown paper trial on the merits. It is hard for me to imagine that a responsible counsel, aware that the judge will be assessing the "quantum" of the evidence he is presenting, will risk either moving for or responding to a summary judgment motion without coming forth with *all* of the evidence he can muster in support of his client's case. Moreover, if the judge on motion for summary judgment really is to weigh the evidence, then in my view grave concerns are raised concerning the constitutional right of civil litigants to a jury trial.

It may well be, as JUSTICE REHNQUIST suggests * * *, that the Court's decision today will be of little practical effect. I, for one, cannot imagine a case in which a judge might plausibly hold that the evidence on motion for summary judgment was sufficient to enable a plaintiff bearing a mere preponderance burden to get to the jury—i.e., that a *prima facie* case had been made out—but insufficient for a plaintiff bearing a clear and convincing burden to withstand a defendant's summary judgment motion. Imagine a suit for breach of contract. If, for example, the defendant moves for summary judgment and produces one purported eyewitness who states that he was present at the time the parties discussed the possibility of an agreement, and unequivocally denies that the parties ever agreed to enter into a contract, while the plaintiff produces one purported eyewitness who asserts that the parties did in fact come to terms, presumably that case would go to the jury. But if the defendant produced not one, but 100 eyewitnesses, while the plaintiff stuck with his single witness, would that case, under the Court's holding, still go to the jury? After all, although the plaintiff's burden in this hypothetical contract action is to prove his case by a mere preponderance of the evidence, the judge, so the Court tells us, is to "ask himself * * * whether a fair minded jury could return a verdict for the plaintiff on the evidence presented." * * * Is there, in this hypothetical example, "a sufficient disagreement to require submission to a jury," or is the evidence "so one-sided that one party must prevail as a matter of law"? * * * Would the result change if the plaintiff's one witness were now shown to be a convicted perjurer? Would the result change if, instead of a garden variety contract claim, the plaintiff sued on a fraud theory, thus requiring him to prove his case by clear and convincing evidence? * * *

In my view, if a plaintiff presents evidence which either directly or by permissible inference (and these inferences are a product of the substantive law of the underlying claim) supports all of the elements he needs to prove in order to prevail on his legal claim, the plaintiff has made out a *prima facie* case and a defendant's motion for summary judgment must fail regardless of the burden of proof that the plaintiff must meet. In other words, whether evidence is "clear and convincing," or proves a point by a mere preponderance, is for the factfinder to determine. As I read the case law, this is how it has been, and because of my concern that today's decision may erode the constitutionally enshrined role of the jury, and also undermine the usefulness of summary judgment procedure, this is how I believe it should remain.

JUSTICE REHNQUIST, with whom THE CHIEF JUSTICE joins, dissenting.

* * *

There is a large class of cases in which the higher standard imposed by the court today would seem to have no effect at all * * * if the Court means what it says, when it states: "Credibility determinations * * * are jury functions, not those of a judge, whether he is ruling on a motion for summary judgment or for a directed verdict. The evidence of the nonmovant is to be believed, and all justifiable inferences are to be drawn in his favor." * * *

* * * But if the application of the standards makes no difference in [cases involving credibility determinations], one may fairly ask in what sort of case *does* the difference in standards make a difference in outcome? * * *

Notes and Questions

1. Is *Anderson* consistent with Rule 56 as construed and applied in *Lundeen* and *Cross?*

2. The law distinguishes two types of evidence: direct and indirect. A witness' statement that "I saw the light and it was green" is direct evidence that the light was green. The inferences required to credit the testimony are that the witness is speaking honestly and accurately recalls the incident. A witness' statement that "I saw the car in the next lane go through the intersection without slowing down" is indirect or circumstantial evidence that the light was green, but is also consistent with the conclusion that "the car in the next lane also ran the red light." The inferences required to believe that the light was green depend not only on the assumption that the witness is worthy of belief, but also on some implicit generalizations about how well drivers obey the law and the probability of two drivers simultaneously running a red light. Is it any more or less appropriate for a judge in deciding a summary judgment motion to "weigh" direct evidence than indirect evidence? Does *Anderson* have any application to cases involving conflicts of direct evidence? What kind of evidence is involved in Justice Brennan's breach-of-contract hypothetical?

3. Under a preponderance-of-evidence standard, a jury returns a verdict for the plaintiff if it believes that the probability of his claims being true, given the evidence, is above 50%. After *Anderson,* what standard must a judge use in deciding a motion for summary judgment? See Collins, *Summary Judgment and Circumstantial Evidence,* 40 Stan.L.Rev. 491 (1988); Freidenthal, *Cases on Summary Judgment: Has There Been a Material Change in Standards?,* 63 Notre Dame L.Rev. 770 (1988); Risinger, *Another Step in the Counter-Revolution: A Summary Judgment on the Supreme Court's New Approach to Summary Judgment,* 54 Brooklyn L.Rev. 35 (1988).

4. A directed verdict is based on admissible evidence developed at a trial that produces a clearly defined and complete record, but a summary-judgment motion comes before evidentiary rulings have been made and before the record is defined with finality. Are there other respects in which the procedural differences between directed verdict and summary judgment make inappropriate the utilization of the same standard? See Stempel, *A Distorted Mirror: The Supreme Court's Shimmering View of Summary Judgment, Directed Verdict, and the Adjudication Process,* 49 Ohio St.L.J. 96 (1988); Currie, *Directed Verdict and Summary Judgment,* 45 U.Chi.L.Rev. 72, 79 (1977); Louis, *Federal Summary Judgment Doctrine: A Critical Analysis,* 83 Yale L.J. 745, 748 (1974).

ROSENTHAL v. RIZZO

United States Court of Appeals, Third Circuit, 1977.
555 F.2d 390, certiorari denied 434 U.S. 892, 98 S.Ct. 268, 54 L.Ed.2d 178.

JAMES HUNTER, III, CIRCUIT JUDGE:

* * *

Harold Rosenthal was appointed to a \$14,257–a-year position as an Administrative Assistant II in the Commercial and Industrial Relocation Department of the Redevelopment Authority of Philadelphia on October 24, 1972. When Augustine Salvitti took over as the Authority's Executive Director in January, 1974, he fired Rosenthal. * * * On January 29, 1975, Rosenthal filed an action in the Eastern District of Pennsylvania against the Authority, Salvitti, Frank Rizzo (the Mayor of Philadelphia), and Phillip Carroll (the Deputy Director of Philadelphia). * * * His primary allegations [were] that he had been discharged because of his political affiliation, in violation of his First Amendment rights of political association. He set forth factual allegations in support of [the claim]. On April 30, 1976, the district court granted summary judgment against Rosenthal as to all defendants, and he appealed.

* * *

In general, a state may not condition hiring or discharge of an employee in a way which infringes his right of political association. An exception to this First Amendment protection exists in the case of state employees who formulate policy. This exception is designed to ensure "that representative government not be undercut by tactics obstructing the implementation of policies of the new administration, policies presumably sanctioned by the electorate." Elrod [v. Burns, 427 U.S. 347, 367, 96 S.Ct. 2673, 2687, 49 L.Ed.2d 547 (1976)].

For Rosenthal to obtain relief on his First Amendment claim, then, he had to show that he was a non-policymaking employee. * * * Evidence as to the nature of Rosenthal's duties, in the form of depositions, was imprecise and cut both ways. On the one hand, there was testimony that Rosenthal was merely a "soldier," that he merely oversaw bidding practices to uncover corruption and to make sure policies implemented by others were carried out * * *; indeed, defendant Salvitti himself declared that Rosenthal's primary duty was to act as a spy for the former Director of the Authority; * * * that he had no power to decide which bids for relocation work would be accepted; * * * that he merely worked for the actual policymaker in his department. * * * On the other hand, there was testimony to the effect that he helped rewrite the relocation code; * * * that Rosenthal was a "top line" employee; * * * that he oversaw work and reviewed bids. * * *

Thus, * * * Rosenthal's status represented a genuine issue of material fact. Nevertheless, the district court took it upon itself to weigh the conflicting evidence and resolve the issue against Rosenthal on a motion for summary judgment. This was error. * * *[5]

---

5. Examination of the *Elrod* plurality's criteria for determinations of policy-making status reveals how difficult the job of weighing evidence on that issue can be and, conse-

* * * While the court below might have been inclined, as is the dissent, to resolve the evidentiary conflict in defendant's favor and conclude that Rosenthal had no duties apart from ones involving policy formulation, "a motion for summary judgment should not be granted on the ground that if a verdict were rendered for the adverse party the court would set it aside as against the weight of the evidence." 6 J. Moore, Federal Practice ¶ 56.04[2], at 2067 (2d ed. 1976).

In the case *sub judice*, Rosenthal was improperly deprived of a full trial on the issue of his status as a policymaker; consequently, his claim that he was fired because of his political affiliations, in violation of the First Amendment, was not considered. Therefore, the judgment of the district court will be reversed as to all defendants and remanded for proceedings consistent with this opinion.

ALDISERT, CIRCUIT JUDGE, dissenting.

I would affirm the judgment of the district court. * * * [S]ummary judgment was the proper disposition since no dispute existed among the parties as to the actual, historical or narrative facts of this case. * * *

In granting summary judgment, the district court properly treated the issue of whether Rosenthal was a "policymaking" employee as a matter of law. There existed no real dispute as to the historical or narrative facts. Rosenthal held the position of Administrative Assistant to the Director of Commercial and Industrial Relocation for the Redevelopment Authority of Philadelphia. He was hired by his stepsister Lynn Abraham, then Executive Director of the Authority, to report to her on the activities of the Commercial and Industrial Relocation Department of the Authority. * * * Abraham explained that she wanted somebody whom she could "trust" to tell her what was happening in that department, which, according to Abraham, was operating in an allegedly questionable fashion. * * * Appellee Salvitti described Rosenthal's hiring

quently, how inappropriate it is on a Rule 56 motion.

No clear line can be drawn between policymaking and nonpolicymaking positions. While nonpolicymaking individuals usually have limited responsibility, that is not to say that one with a number of responsibilities is necessarily in a policymaking position. The nature of the responsibilities is critical. Employee supervisors, for example, may have many responsibilities but those responsibilities may have only limited and well-defined objectives. An employee with responsibilities that are not well defined or are of broad scope more likely functions in a policymaking position. In determining whether an employee occupies a policymaking position, consideration should also be given to whether the employee acts as an adviser or formulates plans for the implementation of broad goals. Thus a matter political loyalty "justification is a matter

of proof, or at least argument, directed at particular kinds of jobs." * * * Since, as we have noted, it is the Government's burden to demonstrate an overriding interest in order to validate an encroachment on protected interests, the burden of establishing this justification as to any particular respondent will rest on the [state] on remand, cases of doubt being resolved in favor of the particular [employee].

427 U.S. at 367–68, 96 S.Ct. at 2687. Thus, the determination of status as a policymaker *vel non* presents a difficult factual question. Where there is evidence to support the employee's claim that he does not make policy, as there is here, he is entitled to a full trial on the issue. Indeed, the state bears the burden of persuasion on that question at trial. Certainly, then, it was improper for the district court to weigh the evidence and rule against Rosenthal on this issue on a Rule 56 motion.

as being "for one specific reason, that was to spy on the department for Lynn Abraham." * * *

Behind such emotive linguistic tags as "someone to trust", or "a spy", there lies a consensus which belies the majority's concern that the "conflicting evidence" should have precluded summary judgment: namely, all parties agreed that Rosenthal was hired as Lynn Abraham's personal investigator. Since there was agreement on what Rosenthal actually did—the "basic" facts—the only remaining question was how to characterize his job. Whether it should be characterized as a policymaking position was not a remaining issue of basic fact, but an issue of *ultimate* fact, and therefore a matter of law for the court, and not the jury. "The ultimate finding is a conclusion of law or at least a determination of a mixed question of law and fact. It is to be distinguished from the findings of primary, evidentiary or circumstantial facts." Helvering v. Tex–Penn Oil Co., 300 U.S. 481, 491, 57 S.Ct. 569, 574, 81 L.Ed. 755 (1937). Justice Frankfurter's explanation in Watts v. Indiana, 338 U.S. 49, 51, 69 S.Ct. 1347, 1348, 93 L.Ed. 1801 (1949), has particular significance here:

> But "issue of fact" is a coat of many colors. It does not cover a conclusion drawn from uncontroverted happenings, when that conclusion incorporates standards of conduct or criteria for judgment which in themselves are decisive of constitutional rights. Such standards and criteria, measured against the requirements drawn from constitutional provisions, and their proper applications, are issues for this Court's adjudication * * *. [It is] important to distinguish between issues of fact that are here foreclosed and issues which, though cast in the form of determination of fact, are the very issues to review which this Court sits.

> * * *

The district court here did not shirk its responsibility in meeting the question of law. Nor should this court.

* * * In the present case, ample information in the record supports the district court's characterization of Rosenthal's job as a policymaking one. Along with the undisputed fact that Rosenthal "act(ed) as an advisor" to Abraham, considerations supporting the district court's ultimate finding include Rosenthal's exercise of supervisory responsibilities, * * * his actions as liaison between two Authority departments, * * * his recommendations regarding bid acceptances, * * * and his participation in the revision of the moving and relocation code. * * *

Notes and Questions

1. Do the subsequent decisions of the Supreme Court in *Celotex* and *Anderson* vindicate Judge Aldisert's dissent in *Rosenthal?* Judge Hunter criticizes the district court (and Judge Aldisert) for weighing the conflicting evidence. Is this criticism consistent with *Anderson?* Even if *Anderson* makes clear that Judge Hunter was wrong for making this criticism, does it follow that he reached the wrong outcome?

2. One commentator has observed:

> When the evidence submitted by the proponent and opponent of the ultimate fact differs rather than conflicts, the dispute is only over the

ultimate fact to be derived from the totality of the evidence.   *   *   *
Faced with such a dispute over an ultimate fact, the court must decide
whether, for purposes of Rule 56, the issue is one of fact or law. [The
substance of the question] is not whether an ultimate fact is in dispute,
but whether it is to be decided by the judge or by the jury. If it is not a
jury issue, and the underlying historical facts are undisputed, the issue is
appropriate for summary judgment.

Schwarzer, *Summary Judgment Under the Federal Rules: Defining Genuine
Issues of Material Fact,* 99 F.R.D. 465, 471 (1984). What arguments favor
judges, rather than juries, deciding the question of Rosenthal's status as a
"policymaking employee"?

3. Courts in almost every American jurisdiction adhere to the doctrine
that the jury normally decides whether a person's conduct should be characterized as negligence, even when the historic facts are not in dispute. Whether a party has acted as a reasonably prudent person would act under the same
or similar circumstances is usually a question of fact for the jury. See, e.g.,
Gross v. Southern Ry. Co., 414 F.2d 292, 296 (5th Cir.1969). Why is a jury
better qualified than a judge to determine whether the conduct in question
meets the reasonable person standard? Is a jury any less qualified to decide
whether a discharged employee held a "policymaking" position? See Weiner,
The Civil Jury Trial and the Law–Fact Distinction, 54 Calif.L.Rev. 1867
(1966). What implications for the availability of summary judgment are
contained in the decision normally to relegate such matters to juries?

Partial Summary Judgment

Rules and statutes permitting summary judgment normally provide
that in circumstances in which judgment cannot be granted on the entire
action, the court at least may withdraw from trial those aspects of the
case that are established in the summary-judgment proceeding. See, e.g.,
Federal Rule 56(d). Furthermore, in a substantial number of jurisdictions
the trial court may enter judgment with regard to any single claim that
has been fully determined. See, e.g., Federal Rule 54(b). A major
question remains, however, whether a party may secure the entry of
summary judgment as to part of a claim that has not been fully adjudicated. For example, if plaintiff salesperson alleges that defendant employer
owes him five items of back salary, and plaintiff conclusively establishes a
right to two of those items, should plaintiff be entitled to a judgment on
the amount of the two items in order to collect immediately from defendant? Do Federal Rules 56(a) and 56(b) answer the problem? A number
of federal courts have denied relief by reading Rule 56(a) in light of Rule
54(b) or Rule 56(d). What justification, if any, exists for these decisions?
See 10A Wright, Miller & Kane, *Federal Practice and Procedure: Civil 2d*
§ 2737 (1983); 6 Moore, *Federal Practice* ¶ 56.20 (2d ed.); Comment,
Partial Summary Judgments Under Rule 56(a), 32 U.Chi.L.Rev. 816 (1965).

SECTION B. DISMISSAL OF ACTIONS

―――――

Read Federal Rule of Civil Procedure 41 and the materials accompanying it in the Supplement.

―――――

1. VOLUNTARY DISMISSAL

The voluntary dismissal allows the moving party to extricate himself from the lawsuit without affecting his legal rights before significant judicial resources are spent. Generally, a voluntary dismissal places the parties in the positions they occupied before the lawsuit began; it does not, in general, have the effect of an adjudication on the merits. Because voluntary dismissal might be used to harass defendants, if a party attempts to dismiss after previously doing so with respect to the same cause of action, the dismissal is granted, but is viewed as being an adjudication on the merits.

―――――

McCANTS v. FORD MOTOR CO., 781 F.2d 855 (11th Cir.1986). Johnny McCants, a member of the United States Army Reserve on a two-week active duty training mission, was killed while riding in a military jeep built by Ford. His administratrix commenced a wrongful death suit in federal district court in Alabama. After discovery proceeded for about a year, interrogatories were served and answered, and defendant had moved for summary judgment based on Alabama's one-year general statute of limitations, the plaintiff moved for an order pursuant to Rule 41(a)(2) for voluntary dismissal of the action without prejudice. The plaintiff sought to dismiss the suit so that she could file a new suit in Mississippi, where the controlling statute of limitations had not expired. The District Court granted the motion to dismiss, and simultaneously denied Ford's motion for summary judgment.

Notes and Questions

1. At common law, plaintiff was permitted, at any time prior to judgment, to dismiss a case voluntarily and without prejudice to refiling the action at a later date. Today the right to dismiss voluntarily generally is governed by a rule or statute that typically permits a dismissal before "trial" or "commencement" of trial. These provisions have raised many problems of interpretation regarding the meaning of the words "trial" and "commencement." A few courts have held that "before trial" means at any time prior to submission to the jury or court for decision. See generally Annot., 1 A.L.R.3d 711 (1965). What justification is there for this construction?

2. In *McCants,* the plaintiff moved to dismiss after the defendant had made a motion for summary judgment. Could any plaintiff simply move to dismiss before losing such a motion and refile in another, possibly more sympathetic, court? Could the plaintiff do this repeatedly?

3. What effect does a voluntary dismissal have on the statute of limitations? Is the statute tolled while the initial complaint is active? Or does the notion that the dismissal returns the parties to the position they occupied before the action require the court to refuse to consider the previous action for purposes of applying the statute of limitations? See DeLong's, Inc. v. Stupp Bros. Bridge & Iron Co., 40 F.R.D. 127 (E.D.Mo.1965).

4. Under Rule 41(a)(1) any dismissal is with prejudice if plaintiff previously has dismissed the same action. Should this restriction apply as well when the second dismissal is sought under Rule 41(a)(2)? See American Cyanamid Co. v. McGhee, 317 F.2d 295 (5th Cir.1963).

2. DISMISSAL FOR FAILURE TO PROSECUTE

Courts long have been regarded as possessing inherent discretionary power to dismiss an action if the plaintiff does not proceed to trial with "due diligence." Exactly when this power should be invoked has been a matter about which judges have disagreed. Should simple delay by plaintiff be sufficient to justify dismissal, or should prejudice to defendant also be required? In MESSENGER v. UNITED STATES, 231 F.2d 328, 331 (2d Cir.1956), the court said: "The operative condition of the Rule is lack of due diligence on the part of the plaintiff—not a showing by the defendant that it will be prejudiced by denial of its motion. * * * It may well be that the latter factor may be considered by the court, especially in cases of moderate or excusable neglect, in the formulation of its discretionary ruling." Does this standard make sense? Does it have any practical utility as a guide for the trial judge? What is its effect on appellate-court review of the trial court's exercise of discretion?

Some jurisdictions control dismissals for want of prosecution by statute. Thus, California permits dismissal only after the passage of three years from the filing of the complaint, but makes dismissal mandatory when five years have elapsed. Cal.Code Civ.Proc. §§ 583, 420. What justification, if any, is there for this statutory arrangement? Is it superior to a system that leaves the decision solely within the court's discretion? Compare Indiana Rule of Trial Procedure 41(E), which permits dismissal "when no action has been taken in a civil case for a period of sixty [60] days." See also N.Y.C.P.L.R. 3216. In view of the fact that, by definition, cases in which there is a failure to prosecute are not consuming judicial time or energy, why is a formal dismissal procedure necessary?

LINK v. WABASH R. CO., 370 U.S. 626, 629–30, 633–34, 82 S.Ct. 1386, 1388, 1390–91, 8 L.Ed.2d 734, 737–38, 739–40 (1962). Petitioner appealed a *sua sponte* dismissal of his diversity negligence action after petitioner and his counsel failed to attend a pretrial conference. The trial date had been set some six years after the action had been commenced, during which two other fixed trial dates had been postponed. The Seventh Circuit affirmed, after which the Supreme Court, in an opinion by Justice Harlan, affirmed, holding:

> The authority of a federal trial court to dismiss a plaintiff's action with prejudice because of his failure to prosecute cannot seriously be

doubted. The power to invoke this sanction is necessary in order to prevent undue delays in the disposition of pending cases and to avoid congestion in the calendars of the District Courts. The power is of ancient origin, having its roots in judgments of *nonsuit* and *non prosequitur* entered at common law, e.g., 3 Blackstone, Commentaries (1768), 295–296, and dismissals for want of prosecution of bills in equity * * *. It has been expressly recognized in Federal Rule of Civil Procedure 41(b) * * *.

* * *

Accordingly, when circumstances make such action appropriate, a District Court may dismiss a complaint for failure to prosecute even without affording notice of its intention to do so or providing an adversary hearing before acting. Whether such an order can stand on appeal depends not on power but on whether it was within the permissible range of the court's discretion.

On this record we are unable to say that the District Court's dismissal of this action for failure to prosecute, as evidenced only partly by the failure of petitioner's counsel to appear at a duly scheduled pretrial conference, amounted to an abuse of discretion. * * *

There is certainly no merit to the contention that dismissal of petitioner's claim because of his counsel's unexcused conduct imposes an unjust penalty on the client. Petitioner voluntarily chose this attorney as his representative in the action, and he cannot now avoid the consequences of the acts or omissions of this freely selected agent. Any other notion would be wholly inconsistent with our system of representative litigation, in which each party is deemed bound by the acts of his lawyer-agent and is considered to have "notice of all facts, notice of which can be charged upon the attorney." * * *

We need not decide whether unexplained absence from a pretrial conference would *alone* justify a dismissal with prejudice if the record showed no other evidence of dilatoriness on the part of the plaintiff. For the District Court in this case relied on *all* the circumstances that were brought to its attention, including the earlier delays.

In his dissent, Justice Black argued that it was unfair to impose such a harsh penalty upon the plaintiff for the misconduct of his attorney. The Justice suggested that numerous other sanctions were available in this instance that could have served the purpose of penalizing the attorney without resorting to a dismissal of the action, thus barring forever the plaintiff's right to recovery for his injuries.

Notes and Questions

1. If the court has power, under Rule 41(b), to dismiss the action, does it have an implied authority to fashion other, less onerous sanctions? In J.M. CLEMINSHAW CO. v. CITY OF NORWICH, 93 F.R.D. 338, 355 (D.Conn.1981), the court said:

> Fines may be imposed upon offending attorneys under Rule 41(b) even though that rule, by its terms, specifically provides only for the sanction of dismissal of the action. Indeed, fines are an appropriate sanction under Rule 41(b) precisely because dismissal is the only sanction

specified by that rule. That is, the district courts have been directed to avoid the harsh result of dismissal in cases where the delays or disobedience have been the fault of counsel rather than their clients. In these cases, the courts may draw on their inherent authority to control the course of litigation to impose on counsel the less severe sanction of a fine. * * * Cf. Schwarz v. United States, 384 F.2d 833, 836 (2d Cir.1967) (affirming dismissal pursuant to Rule 41(b); "suggest[ing] that the [district] court keep in mind the possibility, in future cases of inexcusable neglect by counsel, of imposing substantial costs and attorney's fees payable by offending counsel personally to the opposing party, as an alternative to the drastic remedy of dismissal.") * * *.

2. If her claim has been dismissed under Rule 41(b), can the plaintiff sue in state court on the same claim? In ADCOX v. SOUTHERN RY. CO., 182 Tenn. 6, 184 S.W.2d 37 (1944), the court held that a state court could hear the action even if it would be barred in federal court. If Rule 41(b) is designed to protect the defendant, doesn't the Tennessee result frustrate the operation of Rule 41(b)? Or is it that Rule 41(b) is designed merely to control the use of the resources of a particular court?

SECTION C. DEFAULT JUDGMENT

———

Read Federal Rule of Civil Procedure 55 and the accompanying materials in the Supplement.

———

COULAS v. SMITH
Supreme Court of Arizona, 1964.
96 Ariz. 325, 395 P.2d 527.

UDALL, CHIEF JUSTICE. This is an appeal from an order of the Superior Court of Pima County, denying a motion to set aside a judgment entered against the appellant.

* * *

The plaintiff filed a complaint against the defendant and cross-claimant on two counts. The first count was for $669.32 on an open account. The second count was on a promissory note upon which $3,666.67 was alleged to be due. The cross-claimant answered individually by his attorney and denied any liability to the plaintiff on either count and thereafter filed a cross-claim against the defendant in which he sought judgment against the defendant for any sums or amounts which the plaintiff may obtain against him by virtue of the judgment; for the sum of $4,000 on a debt alleged to be owed by the defendant to him, and $500 attorney's fees. The defendant appeared individually by his attorneys and answered the complaint of the plaintiff, answered the cross-claim of the cross-claimant, and counterclaimed against the plaintiff, seeking damages in the sum of $18,000. The plaintiff replied to the defendant's counterclaim.

On July 11, 1958, the lower court made an order setting the case for trial on October 10, 1958. All counsel were notified by the clerk of the court. On October 6, 1958, counsel for the plaintiff and counsel for the cross-claimant stipulated that the trial be set for December 10, 1958. The lower court ordered that the prior trial date be vacated and the case be reset for trial on December 10, 1958. All counsel were regularly notified by the clerk of the new trial setting. The defendant's counsel was not present before the court on October 6, 1958, and did not participate in the stipulation vacating the original trial setting and resetting the case for trial on December 10, 1958. The defendant and defendant's counsel deny ever receiving any notice from the clerk concerning the new trial date.

On December 10, 1958, the new trial date, the case came on regularly to be heard. The defendant did not appear either in person or by counsel. The court made the following minute entry during the course of the trial:

* * *

The plaintiff Smith and the defendant Bray announce ready for trial.

William J. Bray is sworn, cross-examined, and examined.

Plaintiff's Exhibit 1, being a promissory note in the sum of $4,000.00 dated February 14, 1955, is marked for identification and admitted in evidence.

Nicholas Coulas having failed to appear at this time either in person or by counsel, and it further appearing that this case was previously set for trial both as to the issues framed by the complaint and answer thereto of the defendant Nicholas Coulas and as to the cross-claim filed by the defendant William J. Bray, Jr., against the defendant Nicholas Coulas,

IT IS HEREBY ORDERED that the default of the said defendant Nicholas Coulas be entered as to said complaint and as to said cross-claim and the court proceeding to hear evidence pertaining to said complaint and cross-claim and being fully advised in the premises,

IT IS THEREFORE ORDERED that judgment is hereby rendered * * * against the defendant Nicholas Coulas * * *.

The plaintiff obtained judgment against the defendant on both counts and against the cross-claimant as to count two (the promissory note). The cross-claimant obtained judgment against the defendant on the promissory note. The judgment was entered on December 11, 1958.

On October 29, 1960, nearly two years later, the defendant filed a motion to set aside and vacate the judgment. The trial court denied this motion. * * *

The defendant subsequently filed this appeal.

The defendant contends that the "default" judgment entered against him was void, since he did not receive 3 days' notice of the application for judgment by default pursuant to Rule 55(b) of the Arizona Rules of Civil Procedure * * *. The defendant's contention would be valid if the judgment below was a judgment by default. A default judgment obtains when a defendant fails to plead or otherwise defend. Rule 55. If he has made an appearance in the case, he must be given 3 days' notice of application for judgment by default. * * *

However, the defendant's contention is invalid here since the judgment below was not a default judgment. It should be noted that the defendant did plead to the merits. He answered the complaint and filed a counterclaim. He then failed to appear at the trial in person or by counsel. The trial proceeded, evidence was heard, and a judgment on the merits of the plaintiff's and counter-claimant's claims was entered. The judgment was not by default within the meaning of Rule 55. Therefore Rule 55(b) with its 3-day notice requirement is not applicable. In fact, the trial court would have erred if a default was entered, since the case was at issue. Bass v. Hoagland, 172 F.2d 205 (5th Cir.1949), cert. denied, 338 U.S. 816, 70 S.Ct. 57, 94 L.Ed. 494 (1949) * * *.

The following language is from Bass v. Hoagland * * * concerning the applicability of Rule 55:

"Rule 55(a) authorizes the clerk to enter a default 'When a party against whom a judgment for affirmative relief is sought has failed to plead or otherwise defend as provided by these rules.' This does not require that to escape default the defendant must not only file a sufficient answer to the merits, but must also have a lawyer or be present in court when the case is called for a trial. The words 'otherwise defend' refer to attacks on the service, or motions to dismiss, or for better particulars, and the like, which may prevent default without presently pleading to the merits. *When Bass by his attorney filed a denial of the plaintiff's case neither the clerk nor the judge could enter a default against him. The burden of proof was put on the plaintiff in any trial. When neither Bass nor his attorney appeared at the trial, no default was generated;* the case was not confessed. The plaintiff might proceed, but he would have to prove his case." 172 F.2d p. 210 (emphasis added).

And note this language from Klein v. Rappaport, * * * [90 A.2d 834 (D.C.Mun.Ct.1952)]:

A more serious question is whether the trial court could properly enter a judgment by default on the then state of the record. It must be remembered that defendant had not defaulted in pleading. She had filed an answer and a counterclaim. Plaintiff having replied to the counterclaim, the case was at issue not only on the original claim but on the counterclaim as well. With the litigation in that posture and the judge having decided that there should be no further continuance, he should have proceeded to take proof and enter judgment on the merits. It was not proper to enter a judgment by default. *Absence of a defendant when a case is called for trial after it is at issue does not warrant a judgment against him by default,* but a trial or hearing on the issues is necessary and the judgment which follows is based on the proof adduced. * * *

The defendant relies heavily on the case of Phoenix Metals Corporation v. Roth * * * on page 109 of 79 Ariz., on page 647 of 284 P.2d:

Under the provisions of this rule [Rule 55], no judgment by default may be entered against a defendant who has appeared—as by timely filing an answer—unless he is given notice of the application for judgment.

To the extent the above language implies that a default judgment is proper where a defendant has answered to the merits, it is incorrect. The peculiar fact situation in that case made the above language somewhat misleading. * * * [T]he defendant had filed an answer in fact, but through clerical error the answer was attached to the wrong file and thus it appeared that the defendant had failed to answer and upon application to the clerk the default was erroneously entered and judgment granted thereon. This court held that judgment wholly void. It should therefore be stated that once an answer on the merits is filed and the case is at issue, a default judgment is not proper, and if the defendant fails to appear at the trial a judgment on the merits may be entered against him upon proper proof.

* * *

The contention of the defendant that he did not receive notice of the new trial date is not substantiated by the minutes. The record indicates that the clerk of the superior court notified all counsel of all of the orders and judgment pursuant to Rule 77(h), Arizona Rules of Civil Procedure. It is well settled that in the absence of a showing to the contrary a public officer, such as the clerk of the court in this case, is presumed to have performed the duty imposed upon him by law. * * * In addition, if the defendant's counsel did not receive the notice of the change of the trial date to December 10, 1958, he certainly would have learned of the change in the trial date when he appeared for trial on the earlier date, October 10, 1958.

Since the judgment of the lower court is merely voidable, at most, Rule 60(c) of the Arizona Rules of Civil Procedure prevents the defendant from attacking the judgment more than six months after it was entered. The defendant attempted to attack the judgment nearly two years after it was entered. * * * The lower court properly denied defendant's motion to set aside and vacate the judgment.

Judgment affirmed.

Notes and Questions

1. In BASS v. HOAGLAND, which is relied upon in *Coulas,* a default judgment was rendered in favor of plaintiff after defendant's counsel, who had filed an answer, had withdrawn from the case. The judgment recited that defendant had been informed of the withdrawal. Defendant did not appeal but collaterally attacked the judgment when enforcement was sought against him in another jurisdiction. Defendant claimed that he did not know of the counsel's withdrawal from the case and was not aware that the adverse judgment had been rendered. A majority of the Fifth Circuit held that, since an answer had been filed, defendant was not in default under Rule 55, that the entry of judgment without trial by jury, which had been demanded, was a violation of the Due Process Clause of the Fifth Amendment, and that the judgment was void. The court indicated that even if the case fell within Rule 55, the failure to give notice under Rule 55(b)(2) might render the judgment void, although in that event no jury trial would be required. The dissenting judge took the position that defendant, by not attending trial, was in default, no jury trial was required and therefore the decision was not void and not subject to collateral attack. The case is discussed in 62 Harv.L.Rev. 1400 (1949) and 59 Yale L.J. 345 (1950). Compare Sheepscot Land Corp. v. Gregory,

383 A.2d 16, 22 (Me.1978) (failure of defendant to appear for trial justifies default even though answer was filed).

2. Federal Rule 54(c) provides that a plaintiff may recover all the relief to which he is entitled except that plaintiff is limited to the amount prayed for in the case of a default judgment. Suppose at trial in Coulas v. Smith plaintiff's evidence showed that defendant was liable for $10,000, although only $4,000 had been claimed. Would the court have been justified in awarding plaintiff the full amount?

3. What activities of a defendant, short of a formal challenge to the jurisdiction or the pleadings, constitute an "appearance" within the meaning of Federal Rule 55(b)(2)? In RHODES v. RHODES, 3 Mich.App. 396, 142 N.W.2d 508 (1966), plaintiff, in a divorce action, obtained a default judgment against defendant without giving the notice required by the then applicable Michigan General Court Rule 520.2(2), which was analogous to Federal Rule 55(b)(2). Defendant claimed that by signing a property settlement agreement and stipulating that it be incorporated in the divorce judgment, he "appeared" in the action. The court held that defendant had not shown that these acts were intended to constitute an "appearance" and refused to set aside the judgment. For differing views as to what constitutes an appearance, see Wilson v. Moore & Associates, Inc., 564 F.2d 366 (9th Cir.1977), and Petty v. Weyerhaeuser Co., 272 S.C. 282, 251 S.E.2d 735 (1979).

4. Federal Rule 55(c) distinguishes between the setting aside of an "entry of default" ("for any good cause shown") and the setting aside of a "judgment by default" ("in accordance with Rule 60(b)").

* * * [T]he clerk or the court may enter a default upon the application of the nondefaulting party. The entry simply is an official recognition of the fact that one party is in default * * *.

In sharp contrast, a final default judgment is not possible against a party in default until the measure of recovery has been ascertained, which typically requires a hearing, in which the defaulting party may participate * * *.

* * * Not surprisingly, the federal courts are willing to grant relief from a default entry more readily and with a lesser showing than they are in the case of a default judgment.

10A Wright, Miller & Kane, *Federal Practice and Procedure: Civil 2d* § 2692 (1983).

It is important to recognize that although relief-from-judgment rules do not distinguish between default and other judgments, the courts, in exercising discretion, are far more willing to set aside default judgments in order that cases may be decided on their merits. This is particularly true when the default is due to the carelessness of counsel. See, e.g., Eastman Kodak Co. v. Guasti, 68 Ill.App.3d 484, 25 Ill.Dec. 20, 386 N.E.2d 291 (1st Dist.1979). It is exceedingly rare in such a case that an appellate court will find that a trial court has abused its discretion in setting aside a default judgment. Nevertheless such decisions are reached from time to time. See, e.g., Benjamin v. Dalmo Mfg. Co., 31 Cal.2d 523, 190 P.2d 593 (1948). For a general discussion of the power to set aside judgments, see pp. 1014–25, infra. Why shouldn't the default judgment be left unopened and the losing party be remitted to a negligence action against a careless attorney?

5. A special type of default judgment is one that is imposed on a party who has appeared and contested the matters at issue but has willfully violated the rules of procedure or disobeyed an order of the court. Such a "penalty" is invoked normally against parties who are defending claims; if the complaining party is guilty of comparable violations, the most typical remedy is to dismiss the case with prejudice. See, e.g., Federal Rule 41(b). The penalty default most frequently is rendered in cases in which a defending party willfully refuses to comply with orders for pretrial discovery. Federal Rules 37(b)(2)(C) and 37(d) and their state counterparts specifically permit default judgments in these situations. Should "penalty" defaults fall within the scope of Federal Rule 55? Compare Wilver v. Fisher, 387 F.2d 66 (10th Cir.1967) (notice provisions of Rule 55(b)(2) apply to default under Rule 37), with Vitale v. Elliott, 120 R.I. 328, 387 A.2d 1379, 1382 (1978) (Rule 55 does not govern defaults under Rule 37). Are "penalty" defaults subject to the limitation on recovery in Federal Rule 54(c)? In TRANS WORLD AIRLINES, INC. v. HUGHES, 32 F.R.D. 604, 607–08 (S.D.N.Y.1963), modified 332 F.2d 602 (2d Cir.1964), certiorari dismissed 380 U.S. 248, 85 S.Ct. 934, 13 L.Ed.2d 817 (1965), the court, after granting plaintiff's motion for entry of a default judgment on the ground of defendant's failure to produce the owner of 100% of its stock for a deposition, held:

> That branch of the [plaintiff's] motion seeking to increase the *ad damnum* clause from $105,000,000 to $135,000,000 is granted. This is not a case where a party has defaulted in appearance. Here issue was joined and adversary proceedings continued in the pretrial stages of this litigation. The damages originally asserted were unliquidated and TWA is entitled to recover for whatever damage it can show it suffered. Furthermore, Toolco [a defendant] will be represented at the hearings necessary to assess damages under rule 55(b)(2).

Compare Fong v. United States, 300 F.2d 400, 412–13 (9th Cir.), certiorari denied 370 U.S. 938, 82 S.Ct. 1584, 8 L.Ed.2d 807 (1962). Suppose TWA's suit had been on a contract and the damages were for a liquidated sum that plaintiff had erroneously understated in its complaint. Would the result have been different?

6. Consider C & H TRANSP. CO. v. WRIGHT, 396 S.W.2d 443 (Tex.Civ. App.1965). Plaintiff brought suit against a former employer, alleging that the latter erroneously had deducted the sum of $470.55 from the amount due plaintiff upon termination of the employment. Defendant did not answer or appear and a default judgment was entered. Defendant then appealed on the ground that the complaint failed to allege a cause of action. The court reversed, holding that a default judgment must be supported by a statement of a cause of action in the complaint and that plaintiff's complaint was insufficient because it contained mere conclusions of law.

Suppose defendant in *Wright* had not appealed but instead had challenged the judgment collaterally after it had become final. Should relief have been granted? Should it make a difference if the defective complaint clearly cannot be remedied by an amendment? See Comment, *Attacking a Judgment in California on the Grounds that the Complaint Failed to State a Cause of Action,* 1 U.C.L.A.L.Rev. 195 (1954); 36 Texas L.Rev. 243 (1957); 49 Mich.L. Rev. 446 (1951).

7. In Trans World Airlines, Inc. v. Hughes, Note 5, p. 859, supra, after the Supreme Court dismissed certiorari, the case was referred by the District Court to a master for a determination of damages. In the hearing on the confirmation of the master's report, defendants sought to establish "as a matter of law that facts essential to establish * * * violations [of the antitrust laws], although alleged in the complaint, are in fact untrue and could not have been proved by TWA at trial." The District Court rejected this effort:

> * * * TWA did not have to present any evidence to support the well-pleaded allegations of the complaint, and defendants may not offer evidence to controvert such allegations. That opportunity was forfeited by defendants as a result of the default.

> Defendants may show, however, that an allegation is not well pleaded, but only in very narrow, exceptional circumstances [as when] allegations * * * are contrary to facts of which the court will take judicial notice.

Trans World Airlines, Inc. v. Hughes, 308 F.Supp. 679, 683 (S.D.N.Y.1969), affirmed 449 F.2d 51 (2d Cir.1971). The Supreme Court reversed on the ground that defendants' actions were immune from the antitrust laws under 49 U.S.C. §§ 1378, 1384, because they were under the regulatory control of the Civil Aeronautics Board; the Court held that it was not precluded from considering this issue by its earlier dismissal of certiorari, because there had been no final judgment at that time. Hughes Tool Co. v. Trans World Airlines, Inc., 409 U.S. 363, 93 S.Ct. 647, 34 L.Ed.2d 577 (1973).

Chapter 11

TRIAL

SECTION A. THE NATURE OF THE TRIAL PROCESS

1. SETTING THE CASE FOR TRIAL

In theory a case should be tried once the pleadings are filed, discovery completed, settlement explored and rejected, and all pretrial motions decided. Normally, however, trial will not take place until one of the parties takes affirmative action to have the case placed on the appropriate trial calendar and the court disposes of all the cases previously on that calendar. As pointed out earlier, see pp. 802–13, supra, the wait can be long, often as much as four or five years when the case is to be tried before a jury.

The technique for placing a case on a waiting list for trial will vary from jurisdiction to jurisdiction. Generally it requires only a simple motion. But how is it possible to set a trial date in advance? Is it possible to know when the previous case assigned to a trial judge will be completed so that he and his courtroom will be available? How can one be certain that the lawyers will be free of other pressing obligations, or that crucial witnesses will not be indisposed? The answer, of course, is that there is no such certainty. Any scheduled trial date is at best tentative and is likely to be postponed a number of times.

The jockeying by the courts and the lawyers to bring a case to trial is an art. When sloppily done, it can lead to last minute alterations and result in unused courtrooms, unreasonable delays, and great logjams of cases waiting for trial. Even with the most careful and conscientious cooperation between court and counsel there may be difficulty. Ideally, if the court finds its own schedule altered so that the originally selected date for trial cannot be adhered to, it will inform the parties as far in advance as possible to enable them to readjust their schedules. Similarly, when a lawyer for one of the parties recognizes that a date for trial conflicts with another and more pressing obligation, that attorney will inform the court in advance to obtain a change in schedule. Adjustment usually is feasible for most lawyers who spend relatively little time in active trial practice. But for an attorney who spends the bulk of his time in litigation, accommodation is most difficult, since a change in the trial date for one case probably will raise a conflict with a trial date for another.

Perhaps courts should require every trial attorney to have a sufficient staff to ensure that some lawyer in the firm will be available to handle a case whenever it is called. Would such a requirement be fair to the attorney or to the clients who have confided in him and relied on his expertise? See Gorman, *Excessive Delay in the Courts,* 21 Clev.St.L.Rev. 118 (1972).

Should modern management techniques and systems theory be applied to rationalize the flow of business through the courts? What risks might there be? Of what assistance might computers be to judicial administration? See Adams, *The Move Toward Modern Data Management in the Courts,* 23 U.Fla.L.Rev. 217 (1971); Nagel, Neef & Munshaw, *Bringing Management Science to the Courts to Reduce Delay,* 62 Judicature 128 (1978).

2. TACTICAL CONSIDERATIONS IN DECIDING BETWEEN TRIAL BY JUDGE OR BY JURY

As will be discussed later, the right to trial by jury is limited; the scope of the right usually is based upon a constitutional provision, augmented to some extent by statute. Unless the right is invoked properly by one of the parties, the case will be decided by the trial judge sitting alone, as are cases in which the right does not exist. In many jurisdictions the judge has the power in a nonjury case or when a jury-trial right is waived to impanel an advisory jury whose verdict the court has discretion either to embrace or ignore. See, e.g., Federal Rule 39(c).

a. *Institutional Factors*

Even when an attorney feels that a client's chances of winning on the merits are the same whether the case is tried by judge or by jury, there may be a decided tactical advantage in choosing one form of trial over another. Suppose, for example, that plaintiff in a personal-injury action is in serious financial difficulty. Obviously she will want to pursue the fastest litigation route possible in order to obtain a recovery at an early date. In many jurisdictions there is a substantial backlog of cases on the jury-trial calendar and a long wait is inevitable, whereas the judge-trial calendar is practically current and the case may be heard within a few months. If the suit has been brought in a jurisdiction in which this type of imbalance between the jury and nonjury calendars exists, plaintiff probably will waive the jury. On the other hand, a defendant who knows plaintiff's plight will demand a jury trial, hoping to force plaintiff into a quick settlement favorable to defendant.

Similar considerations exist when time may ameliorate the extent of plaintiff's injuries. For example, if a young unmarried girl is seriously injured in an accident so that her physician will testify that there is a chance she may never be able to have children, a substantial verdict is likely. But she will be awarded far less if her case is not heard for a number of years and she has married and had a family in the interim. In cases of serious injury defendant usually has little to lose and much to gain by delay, except when the injuries are of a degenerative nature.

Also significant is the difference in cost between a jury and nonjury trial. On the average, a jury trial takes considerably more time than does a court trial. Jurors must be selected and instructed, more witnesses are called to testify, final arguments are longer, and more recesses are required. The result usually is higher counsel fees, more extensive payments to experts, and increased trial costs in the form of fees for jurors and witnesses. Although the witness fees often ultimately will be paid by the losing party, jury trial increases the financial gamble by a party who is uncertain as to his chances for success.

b. *Psychological Factors*

When is a jury more likely to give a favorable verdict than a judge? Are there substantial differences between judge and jury attitudes on questions of liability? On measuring damages? Every trial lawyer has a number of personal theories regarding these matters. Only a few empiric studies have been made and they are limited in scope. The available evidence indicates, however, that the similarities between judge and jury cases tend to outweigh the differences. As to the question of liability, statistics indicate that the judge and jury would agree in upwards of 80 percent of the cases. On the other hand, juries do seem to have a greater tendency to find against corporate and government defendants both as to liability and the amount of awards. See Broeder, *The University of Chicago Jury Project,* 38 Neb.L.Rev. 744, 750–51 (1959). But see Bledsoe, *Jury or Nonjury Trial—A Defense Viewpoint,* in 5 *Am.Jur. Trials* 123, 129, 139 (1966) (amount of jury awards on the average do not exceed awards by judges).

In making the choice between judge and jury, a lawyer has much more to go on in the context of a particular case than these generalized comparisons between judge and jury trials. An attorney will consider the nature of the case, the characteristics of the parties and the witnesses, the passions that may surround the trial, the type of jurors who are likely to be chosen, and the background and predilections of the trial judge, if the judge's identity is known in advance, which often is not the case. Each of these factors is important in deciding whether the judge or the jury is most likely to identify with and be sympathetic to a lawyer's client. For an interesting empirical study regarding jury attitudes toward various types of witnesses, attorneys, and parties, see Sonaike, *The Influence of Jury Deliberation on Juror Perception of Trial, Credibility, and Damage Awards,* 1978 Brigham Young U.L.Rev. 889.

Finally, the decision to demand a jury may depend on counsel's assessment of whether he is more effective in a judge or jury trial. In presenting a case to jurors the attorney must be a showman; he must be entertaining or their attention will wander; he must know how to excite their interest so that presentation of crucial testimony appears as a triumphant climax; and he must establish rapport with each and every juror, taking pains not to antagonize any of them by his actions or his appearance. By contrast, a lawyer in a nonjury trial need not concentrate heavily on the form of presentation since the judge will look for and pick out the significant aspects of the testimony even if they are not presented dramatically.

Rarely during the course of a jury case will an attorney have any clear sense of his success or failure in convincing the jury. He only can follow the planned presentation and hope that it was properly conceived. A sudden shift of tactics or a change of emphasis will tend to confuse and alienate the jurors. On the other hand, in a nonjury case, the judge, through statements during conferences, questions from the bench, and rulings on minor points, is constantly supplying the lawyers with clues as to her impressions of the case and the testimony. A sensitive attorney, upon detecting that things are not going well, may be able to salvage the case by changing the focus or direction of the testimony. For an interesting discussion of the different levels of involvement in the trial process as between the judge, sitting as a trier of fact, and the jury, see Wolf, *Trial by Jury: A Sociological Analysis,* 1966 Wis.L.Rev. 820.

3. THE SELECTION OF "FAVORABLE" JURORS

The first step in a jury trial is the selection of the jurors. The mechanics of selection are treated in detail in Section B of this Chapter. See pp. 923–33, infra. For present purposes it is sufficient to note that the attorneys have some control over the type of person who is chosen, since, in addition to the power to eliminate all persons who are in fact biased, each attorney may reject a small number of prospective jurors peremptorily, merely because counsel believes they will tend to react unfavorably to the client's case.

The process of trying to choose people who will make favorable jurors is extremely complex. Not only is it important to assess the way in which each individual juror is likely to view the case, but it also is necessary to analyze what effect each juror may have on the others during the course of deliberations. For example, one study indicates that as to issues involving scientific or technical information, a juror who has some relevant expertise wields considerable influence over the other jurors and often may control the verdict. Broeder, *Occupational Expertise and Bias as Affecting Juror Behavior: A Preliminary Look,* 40 N.Y.U.L.Rev. 1079 (1965). See also Bevan, Albert, Loiseaux, Mayfield & Wright, *Jury Behavior as a Function of the Prestige of the Foreman and the Nature of His Leadership,* 7 J.Pub.L. 419 (1958).

As a general rule a lawyer will seek jurors who will identify and sympathize with his client. Practically speaking, however, the lawyer only can guess at who they are, since he cannot possibly be aware of all of an individual juror's biases and hostilities. But see Suggs & Sales, *Using Communication Clues To Evaluate Prospective Jurors During the Voir Dire,* 20 Ariz.L.Rev. 629 (1978). Consider, for example, a case brought by a young mother for the wrongful death of her husband. One would think that her attorney would be overjoyed if the jury contained a woman who also had been widowed and left with small children to raise. But the lawyer would not be pleased to learn that the juror in question, after a short period of mourning, had happily remarried, since that would greatly affect her attitude as to the proper amount of damages. Even if the juror had not remarried, her presence would be less desirable if her own marriage had been so unhappy that she preferred her present status. See generally Broeder, *Plaintiff's Family Status as Affecting Jury Behavior: Some Tentative Insights,* 14 J.Pub.L. 131 (1965). For an interesting discussion of the potential impact of the age of jurors on verdicts, see Zeigler, *Young Adults as a Cognizable Group in Jury Selection,* 76 Mich.L. Rev. 1045 (1978).

4. THE SCOPE AND ORDER OF TRIAL

a. Jury Cases

Although the courts invariably have discretion to determine the order of trial, they usually do not deviate from standard practice, which is as follows:

1. Plaintiff's opening statement
2. Defendant's opening statement
3. Plaintiff's presentation of direct evidence
4. Defendant's presentation of direct evidence
5. Plaintiff's presentation of rebuttal evidence
6. Defendant's presentation of rebuttal evidence
7. Opening final argument by plaintiff
8. Defendant's final argument
9. Closing final argument by plaintiff
10. Giving instructions to the jury.

b. Nonjury Cases

Although generally jury and nonjury cases are handled in the same way, there are a number of significant differences in scope. For example, the court often will dispense with the opening statement and the closing argument, and, of course, there is never a need to give instructions. Some jurisdictions provide that an attorney has an absolute right to argue, even in nonjury cases. Rarely will such a right be exercised, however, if the judge, as is often the situation, makes clear that she believes an argument to be unnecessary.

5. TACTICAL CONSIDERATIONS REGARDING THE OPENING STATEMENT

Normally a case begins with plaintiff's opening statement. In the rare situation in which defendant has the burden of proof on *all* issues, such as when defendant admits plaintiff's allegations and goes to trial solely on his own affirmative defenses, the position of the parties is reversed throughout the trial and defendant has the right to open. Most lawyers regard the right to deliver the opening statement as so important that when they represent plaintiff they include some allegations in the complaint that defendant must deny in order to preserve the right. The reasons for viewing the right to open as substantial are fairly obvious. At the outset of the case the jurors are fresh, attentive, and impressionable. A carefully constructed statement laying out plaintiff's case in a positive, coherent fashion can convince the jurors that plaintiff's version of the facts is the correct one, which will force defendant to fight an uphill battle to offset plaintiff's initial advantage. On experimental studies of the advantages in order of argument and proof, see Walker, Thibaut & Andreoli, *Order of Presentation at Trial,* 82 Yale L.J. 216 (1972). See also Lawson, *Order of Presentation as a Factor in Jury Presentation,* 56 Ky.L.J. 523 (1968).

At common law, defendant did not make his opening statement until plaintiff had presented the affirmative case. Today, in most jurisdictions, however, defendant has the option of making an opening statement immediately after plaintiff has done so. Most trial lawyers recommend that defendant open at the earliest opportunity. If defendant waits, the initial impression created by plaintiff's opening statement may be so fortified by the opening evidence that the case is lost by the time defendant begins presenting the opposing evidence. Defendant may be able to neutralize plaintiff's initial advantage if the former immediately sets out a contrary version of the facts. For an opposite view, see Stramondo & Goodspeed, *Defendant's Presentation,* 57 Mass.L.Q. 179 (1972), in which the authors take the position that defendant's opening argument is more effective when it refutes plaintiff's evidence.

One of the most difficult tactical questions regarding the opening argument is whether or not a party should avoid mentioning an important issue or a dramatic piece of evidence in the hope of gaining an advantage through surprise. With the availability of modern discovery techniques, it has become increasingly difficult to surprise one's opponent; moreover opposing counsel, by raising and disposing of the issue in his own opening argument, will insulate the jury from a dramatic shock. Nevertheless, with some items of evidence the less said about them in advance, the greater their impact. This occurs, for example, in cases in which defendant suddenly displays a movie of plaintiff, allegedly crippled for life as a result of defendant's negligence, playing tennis on the day before trial. However, since most items of evidence are not of such caliber, it generally is considered unsound to keep them secret, for to do so weakens the effectiveness of the opening statement and gives significant advantage to the opposition. For some interesting views on the tactics and style of opening argument, see Colley, *Opening Statement: Structure, Issues, Techniques,* 18 Trial 52 (Nov.1982); Fuchsberg, *Opening Statements—Plaintiff's View,* in 5 Am.Jur. Trials 285 (1966); Stern, *Opening Statements—Defense View,* in 5 Am.Jur. Trials 305 (1966).

Just as an attorney's opening statement may advance a client's cause, it also may reveal fatal flaws in the claim or defense. If this occurs, in most jurisdictions the opposing party may move immediately for the entry of a judgment. The theory of this motion is the same as the philosophy underlying the demurrer and summary judgment—the court is not required to try a case once it becomes clear that one of the parties *must* prevail.

6.   THE PRESENTATION OF EVIDENCE

a.   *The Problems of Admissibility*

The admissibility of evidence at trial is determined by a large and complex set of rules. Each lawyer must plan carefully and in advance of trial to make certain that the evidence considered to be important will be accepted. Often, if an item of evidence cannot be admitted under one rule, it can come in under another. Moreover, except in rare circumstances, no proffered item of evidence will be excluded unless the opposing party objects to its introduction. As a result an attorney often will offer otherwise inadmissible evidence in the hope that it will not be challenged. A lawyer must be careful, however, not to do this unsuccessfully too often as it may antagonize the judge or jury. Similarly, in many circumstances the opposing party will be well advised not to challenge inadmissible evidence that is not seriously prejudicial. An attorney who constantly objects may antagonize the jury by appearing to be an obstructionist. Even if the objections are sustained, the jurors may begin to believe something is being hidden from them, and will assume that the answers, had they been permitted, would have been unfavorable to the lawyer's client.

In some situations even the most diligent attorney is powerless to keep inadmissible, highly prejudicial statements from the jurors. For example, a witness simply may blurt out such a statement voluntarily without having been asked a question pertaining to it. In such cases the court has a choice. It may admonish the jury not to consider the evidence or it may declare a mistrial. In the latter case the jury is dismissed and the trial must begin anew before an entirely different panel. Obviously such drastic action is taken only when the error is severely prejudicial. Yet, is it realistic to expect jurors to ignore completely something they have heard and are told to forget?

b.   *The Technique of Presentation*

Much has been written concerning the way in which evidence should be presented. Most of this commentary can be distilled into one basic observation: the better the preparation before trial, the better the presentation.

Usually most evidence is presented at trial through the examination and cross-examination of witnesses. A party should call witnesses in a logical order so that the jury will know, at every step of the way, what part of the case is being explored. Usually the most important witnesses are called first to put the jurors in a favorable frame of mind. The testimony of less important witnesses will then be understood by the jury as backing and fortifying that party's version of the facts. There are, of course, many factors that interfere with a planned presentation. First, the opposition, through cross-examination, will attempt to upset the pattern not only by raising questions as to the witnesses' accuracy but also by injecting new considerations that tend to confuse the jurors. Second, a party who wishes to stay on the good side of witnesses, particularly experts, may be forced to accommodate their interests by calling them when it is convenient for them to testify rather than at the most logical point in the trial. Finally, no matter how fine the preparation, every trial produces a number of surprises to which the lawyer must react immediately. If, for example, during cross-examination of an opposition witness, the interrogating attorney receives a surprise favorable response, he must press forward on the issue immediately, before the witness and the opposing attorney have the time and opportunity to soften the impact by planning an explanation.

Cross-examination is a potent trial weapon. With it a clever attorney can raise doubts concerning the accuracy of even the most accomplished and prepared witness, let alone an unsophisticated witness who actually is trying to cover up the facts. Consider, for example, the effect on the trier of fact of the following exchange from an actual cross-examination of a woman as reported in *Saturday Review,* August 19, 1967, p. 12, col. 2:

Q: Did you ever stay all night with this man in New York?

A: I refuse to answer that question.

Q: Did you ever stay all night with this man in Chicago?

A: I refuse to answer that question.

Q: Did you ever stay all night with this man in Miami?

A: No.

There are two ways to minimize the effects of cross-examination. The first is to make certain that the witness is clear as to the story and is telling the truth. This requires the attorney and the witness to go over the facts in detail shortly before the trial begins. Even after this precaution the excitement of the trial may so unnerve the witness that he forgets even the most basic facts. Consider the following actual exchange (with the names changed), again as reported in *Saturday Review,* August 19, 1967, p. 12, col. 2:

Q: What is your brother-in-law's name?

A: Borofkin.

Q: What's his first name?

A: I can't remember.

Q: He's been your brother-in-law for forty-five years and you can't remember his first name?

A: No, I tell you I'm too excited! (Rising from the witness chair and pointing to Borofkin.) Nathan, for God's sake tell them your first name!

The second method of limiting the effectiveness of cross-examination is for the attorney on direct examination to raise and dispense with any matter that might cast doubt on a witness' veracity if it were raised for the first time on cross-examination. For example, in most jurisdictions an attorney may impugn the credibility of an opposition witness by introducing evidence showing that the witness previously has been convicted of a felony. If the fact that the witness had once been convicted of a felony is raised at the very beginning of his testimony by the attorney who called him, the jury will tend to think of the witness as a person willing to suffer embarrassment to tell the truth; but if the matter is first raised on cross-examination, the jurors may tend to consider the witness a person who is trying to hide important facts. For a detailed treatment of tactical considerations in the presentation of evidence, see generally Keeton, *Trial Tactics and Methods* (2d ed. 1973).

c. The Role of the Trial Judge in the Presentation of Evidence

Suppose that an attorney's presentation of a case appears inadequate. To what extent should the trial judge take over the trial by interrogating the witness herself and perhaps by calling new witnesses she believes should be heard? Does it make a difference if the case is before a jury? These questions raise some fundamental considerations regarding the role of the trial judge: Is the court a mere umpire who must stand aloof except when called upon to make decisions or a participant with the right to supervise the conduct of the trial to help ensure a just result?

Although there is general agreement that judges do have some power to call and interrogate witnesses, there is considerable controversy as to the extent of the power. For example, in some jurisdictions it has been held that a case may be reversed if the trial judge frequently interrupts counsel's presentation or engages in extensive examination of the witnesses. See Laub, *Trial and Submission of a Case From a Judge's Standpoint,* 34 Temple L.Q. 1, 5–6 (1960). In other jurisdictions, however, the power apparently is unlimited and the only question is how it is to be exercised. See Gitelson & Gitelson, *A Trial Judge's Credo Must Include His Affirmative Duty to be an Instrumentality of Justice,* 7 Santa Clara Law. 7 (1966).

In recent years judges generally have tended to increase their active participation in the trial process. It even has been suggested that they *must* take a hand when the failure to do so will result in a miscarriage of justice, but as yet judgments have not been reversed on this ground.

d. The Power of Jurors to Question Witnesses

What if a juror is dissatisfied with the evidence? Should he be permitted to ask a witness questions that were not asked by the attorneys? Would it be feasible, tactically, for an attorney to object to the question if it called for inadmissible evidence? Is there some means by which this latter problem could be avoided?

7. THE CLOSING ARGUMENT

a. The Nature of the Argument

Closing argument is important because it is the only time when the attorneys can organize the evidence in the case for the trier of fact in a coherent fashion, without interruption, and when the logical implications of the evidence can be spelled out in detail.

Normally, final argument is in three parts, with plaintiff having the benefit of speaking both first and last. If, however, the only issues in the case are those upon which defendant has the burden of proof, the roles of the parties are reversed and defendant speaks first and last. Often the court will limit the amount of time available to each party. See Annot., 3 A.L.R.3d 1341 (1965). Whether or not such limits are imposed, the arguments should be brief, concise, sincere, and easily understood, and they should emphasize the vital points of the case. See Sisson, *The Closing Argument,* 57 Mass.L.Q. 319 (1972).

b. *Proper Versus Improper Argument*

A proper argument is one that follows from the facts of the case as supported by the evidence or inferences that properly can be drawn from the evidence. An argument is improper when it is based upon matters not in evidence, appeals to passion or racial or religious prejudice, contains references to the financial ability of the parties or includes remarks as to whether defendant is insured against the claimed liability, requests that the jurors treat the attorney's client as they would wish to be treated were they in the party's position, or distorts the evidence in order to arrive at unjustified inferences. See, e.g., Klein v. Herring, 347 So.2d 681 (Fla.App.1977). In practice lawyers are permitted considerable leeway in argument, with limitations being imposed only in certain easily defined circumstances. Opposing counsel will be reluctant to challenge an improper argument for fear of appearing weak, particularly if there is any chance that the challenge will not be upheld by the trial judge. At the same time many courts have been hesitant to interfere on their own motion, unless the argument gets completely out of hand. Is there any justification for such judicial reluctance? Shouldn't judges take a more active role in preventing abuse of the trial process? See Rinehart, *Final Argument,* 28 F.R.D. 235 (1960).

It often is difficult to detect an improper argument that is introduced subtly. Consider, for example, a case in which plaintiff, injured in a hit-run auto collision, is attempting to prove that defendant was the driver of the other car. Plaintiff's only evidence is that the accident occurred on Sunday and that the other car involved belonged to a neighbor of defendant who had permitted defendant to borrow it every Sunday for several months prior to the collision. In trying to convince the jury of the importance of this circumstantial evidence, plaintiff's attorney might say: "Suppose I were to tell you that defendant's fresh fingerprints were found on the steering wheel of the car shortly after the accident and that defendant's sweater was found near the accident. Surely there would be no doubt in your minds after that as to who was driving, even though no one saw defendant." Obviously such an argument, though proper on its face, should not be permitted since members of the jury might well believe that the fingerprints and the sweater were indeed found at the scene, although nothing in the evidence so indicates. For an excellent discussion of this and other similar problems of improper argument, see Levin & Levy, *Persuading the Jury with Facts Not in Evidence: The Fiction-Science Spectrum,* 105 U.Pa.L.Rev. 139 (1956).

8. INSTRUCTIONS TO THE JURY

Before it retires to deliberate and decide, the court instructs the jury as to the law to be applied and the manner in which it is to reach a decision. The most significant legal controversy regarding the proper sequence of this phase of a jury trial is whether the instructions should come *before* or *after* the final arguments by counsel. In most jurisdictions the courts take the position that the judge, as the impartial umpire in the case, should have the last word in order that partisan appeals by counsel will be tempered by a dispassionate statement of the law to be applied. Those who favor instructions prior to argument ask: "How can any rational argument be made if the jurors have not yet been told about the law they must apply?" Can this question be satisfactorily answered? Note that it also might be argued that the jury cannot properly understand the opening statements of counsel or evaluate evidence as it is introduced unless they have prior knowledge of the legal significance of the facts presented. Why then are the instructions not given by the court at the beginning rather than at the end of trial? Would it make sense to give two sets of instructions, one at the beginning of trial and the other at the end?

Normally the court requires the attorneys to submit proposed instructions at some point during the trial, usually after the evidence has been completed. The court then determines which of these instructions to give and which of its own to add. Under the rules of most jurisdictions a party cannot appeal the failure to give an instruction that he did not request or the giving of an erroneous instruction to which he made no immediate objection. See, e.g., Federal Rule 51. What is the purpose of rules such as these? Why should an instruction be requested or challenged prior to the time the jury commences its deliberations? Review Alexander v. Kramer Bros. Freight Lines, Inc., p. 41, supra.

From a tactical point of view, the drafting of proposed instructions poses a serious dilemma. On the one hand, every attorney wants a set of instructions that is as favorable to his client as possible. On the other hand, the more slanted the instructions proposed, the less likely they are to be given and the more probable the judge will be antagonized by them since they will be of little assistance. Moreover, there is always the danger that the judge will accept an instruction so prejudicial that a judgment based upon it will be reversed on appeal. This not only is against the interests of the client but also harms the reputation of the attorney in the eyes of the trial judge who will hesitate to trust the attorney in future cases. See generally Powers, *Requests for Instructions*, 28 F.R.D. 239 (1960). Even if the instructions are favorable in substance, they will be totally ignored if they are so long and technical that the jurors cannot understand them. Thus an attorney often is wise to seek a simple, favorable instruction on a point, even though a more complex charge might be framed in much more favorable terms.

9. SUBMISSION OF THE CASE TO THE JURY

After final arguments are completed and the instructions given, the jurors are placed in the custody of a bailiff or similar court official who guards them during deliberations. It is the bailiff's duty to make certain that the jurors remain together and have no contact with other persons except by court order.

In some cases the jurors will find it difficult to agree on a verdict. If this is due to uncertainty as to the content of the instructions, they may ask the court to reread the instructions, and, if necessary, to augment them. See, e.g., Diniero v. United States Lines Co., p. 44, supra. If the major difficulty is due to disagreement as to what one or more of the witnesses said, the jurors may request that the testimony of those witnesses be read to them. See Annot., 50 A.L.R.2d 176 (1956). Whenever the jury reenters the courtroom, whether for further instructions or for the reading of testimony, it is wise to notify both parties and their attorneys in advance. Otherwise the verdict may be subject to reversal on appeal. What is the purpose of a rule requiring notice? How rigidly should it be enforced?

Suppose after lengthy deliberations the jurors still are unable to agree. How long may they be kept in session? At what point does a court abuse its discretion by forcing them to continue their discussions? When a court does order an end to a session, must it then dismiss the jury and order a new trial? If not, must the jurors be locked up, free from all contact with outsiders, or should they be allowed to go home until such time as they are ordered to reassemble? See Kramer v. Kister, p. 1000, infra; Annot., 77 A.L.R.2d 1086 (1961), for a detailed discussion of these matters.

At some point, of course, if the jurors continue to be unable to agree, they will have to be discharged and a mistrial declared. Courts are extremely reluctant to discharge a jury without its having reached a verdict because of the cost and delay of a new trial. Thus, as already noted, see Note 6, p. 48, supra, a court often will urge a stalemated jury to make a further attempt to arrive at a verdict. Although some jurisdictions still require the traditional unanimous jury verdict, a substantial number have tried to cut down the number of stalemates by permitting a verdict to be based on something less than unanimity in civil cases. See, e.g., Cal.Code Civ.Proc. § 618 (three-fourths of jurors must agree); Mich. Ct.Rule 2.512(A) (five-sixths of jurors must agree). In Minnesota a less than unanimous verdict is permitted after the jury has deliberated for a certain length of time. Minn.Stat.Ann. § 546.17. Is there any reason why the requirement of unanimity should not be universally abolished?

In some cases the jury is able to arrive at a verdict almost immediately. Indeed, it may be possible for the jurors to agree without even leaving the jury box. Should a verdict in a complex case ever be subject to attack because it was rendered quickly? Invariably, the courts have said "no." See Annot., 91 A.L.R.2d 1220 (1963). Why should this be so?

10. DELIVERY OF THE VERDICT

The verdict of a jury is delivered by the foreman in open court. Traditionally the verdict was announced orally. Today, however, most juries render written verdicts on forms provided by the court. Once the verdict is formally announced or read by the judge or his clerk, any of the parties may demand that each of the jurors be polled to determine whether or not the verdict in fact has been agreed upon by the required number of jurors. This simply entails each of the jurors being asked whether the verdict as read reflects his or her decision. In many jurisdictions a poll is a matter of right; in others it is within the court's discretion to grant or deny. Under what circumstances would a court be inclined not to allow jurors to be polled?

Suppose a poll reveals that the announced verdict was improperly arrived at or does not reflect the views of the jurors. Should the court dismiss the action and order a new trial? In most cases the court will send the jury back for further deliberations. Is there any danger that resubmission of the case to the jury might be prejudicial to one of the parties?

Sometimes the jury will reach a verdict that is improper on its face. For example, the jury might render a verdict for defendant even though it has been instructed to find for plaintiff and confine its deliberations to the amount of damages. Again, the court will have to decide whether to send the jury back for more discussion or to order a new trial. What factors should the court consider in making its determination?

11. CHALLENGES TO THE VERDICT; ENTRY OF JUDGMENT

In the usual case when a verdict is in proper form, the trial judge or clerk will enter judgment in accordance with it. Before this is done, however, the parties will be given an opportunity to challenge the verdict on the basis of errors committed during the trial or on the ground that the evidence does not support it. The nature of these challenges and the consequences of a successful challenge are discussed in detail in Section F of this Chapter. See pp. 963–1031, infra. Serious errors that are not corrected at the trial-court level, of course, will lead to a reversal of a judgment on appeal. Why then is it necessary to give the trial judge a prior opportunity to upset the verdict? In actuality, the power of the trial judge to upset a verdict exceeds that of an appellate court to grant a reversal. Why should this be the case?

SECTION B. TRIAL BY JURY

1. THE INSTITUTION OF TRIAL BY JURY

During its formative period the jury was an activist group that not only judged the evidence but acquired much of it through its own investigation. An example of this drawn from twelfth century English history is the "jury" used to compile the famous Domesday Book, which contained an inventory of William the Conqueror's realm. The Domesday "jury" viewed the land and formed its own judgments without using witnesses.

Today, of course, the jury is a passive, disinterested body that renders its decisions on the basis of the information placed before it.

The revered status of jury trial at common law is evidenced by Blackstone's statement that the right "has been, and I trust ever will be, looked upon as the glory of the English law * * * and * * * that it is the most transcendent privilege which any subject can enjoy or wish for, that he not be affected either in his property, his liberty, or his person, but by unanimous consent of twelve of his neighbors and equals." 3 Blackstone, *Commentaries* *378. Yet, in modern English practice, the jury is used comparatively infrequently.

In this country the jury system has been eulogized by the United States Supreme Court on many occasions. For example, in SIOUX CITY & P.R. CO. v. STOUT, 84 U.S. (17 Wall.) 657, 664, 21 L.Ed. 745, 749 (1873), the Court commented:

> * * * Twelve men of the average of the community, comprising men of education and men of little education, men of learning and men whose learning consists only in what they have themselves seen and heard, the merchant, the mechanic, the farmer, the laborer; these sit together, consult, apply their separate experience of the affairs of life to the facts proven, and draw a unanimous conclusion. This average judgment thus given it is the great effort of the law to obtain. It is assumed that twelve men know more of the common affairs of life than does one man, that they can draw wiser and safer conclusions from admitted facts thus occurring than can a single judge.

But not all commentators eulogize our jury system. Perhaps the most outspoken critic of jury trial during the century was the late Judge Jerome N. Frank of the Second Circuit. His opinion of the institution is illustrated by the following passage from his book *Law and the Modern Mind* 180–81 (1930):

> The [jurors] * * * are hopelessly incompetent as fact-finders. It is possible, by training, to improve the ability of our judges to pass upon facts more objectively. But no one can be fatuous enough to believe that the entire community can be so educated that a crowd of twelve men chosen at random can do, even moderately well, what painstaking judges now find it difficult to do. * * * The jury makes the orderly administration of justice virtually impossible.

An excellent summary of Judge Frank's views is found in Paul, *Jerome Frank's Views on Trial by Jury,* 22 Mo.L.Rev. 28 (1957). More recently, the jury system has come under increasing attack from commentators claiming that the system is expensive and slow and that juries cannot understand the complex cases that, today, comprise a large part of courts' dockets. Thus, former Chief Justice Burger has listed several problems associated with jury trials in civil cases:

> *First,* do we really have truly representative juries? Experienced business executives, bankers, professional people, accountants, professors of economics, statisticians, teachers, and others arguably more competent than most to cope with complex economic or scientific questions, rarely survive to sit in the box. Peremptory challenges in the jury selection

process eliminate them and more often they are excused for cause, including the cause that they are too busy! We must stop deluding ourselves. The juries actually selected in most protracted cases are rarely true cross-sections, as we are so fond of repeating.

* * *

Second, the factual issues in protracted cases are often of enormous complexity. The analysis of documents, of expert testimony, of charts, graphs and other visual aids, and the comprehension of such evidence, present problems which often only a sophisticated business executive, an economist, or another expert could grasp; some cases would baffle even them.

Third, the legal issues, which must be explained to jurors by the trial judge, may take not hours, but a whole day or several days, by way of instructions.

Fourth, there is a limit to the capacity of any of us—jurors or judges—to understand and remember the mass of complicated transactions, documents, and legal principles usually described in the course of a long trial.

Fifth, quite apart from these considerations, there is an enormous—and inordinate—impact on the life of each of twelve jurors, and alternate jurors, thrust for months into a totally strange environment, and then confronted with the burden of decisions in areas in which few, if any of them, have any experience.

Burger, *Thinking the Unthinkable,* 31 Loyola L.Rev. 205, 210–11 (1985).

As you study the remainder of this Section try to formulate judgments on the following questions: To what extent is the jury-trial institution an anachronism? Can we reform it to make it work more effectively in the twentieth century or should we eliminate it entirely? Have the courts been overly concerned with preserving jury trial even though it has been shown to be cumbersome and uneconomical? If we abandon jury trial, what other devices and procedures are available that might provide a more modern but democratic substitute? Why is it that even opponents of the civil jury simply assume, as does Justice Peck, that jury trial must be preserved in "serious criminal cases"? Is jury trial less of an anachronism in criminal than in civil cases? Does it serve any function in the criminal-law context that it doesn't on the civil-law side?

Excellent historical material on the jury can be found in 1 Holdsworth, *A History of English Law* 298–350 (3d ed. 1922); 1 Pollock & Maitland, *The History of English Law* 138–49 (2d ed. 1911); 2 *id.* 616–32, 641–59. See also Thayer, *The Jury and Its Development,* 5 Harv.L.Rev. 249, 295, 357 (1892), substantially reprinted in *A Preliminary Treatise on Evidence at the Common Law* 47–182 (1898). For discussions of civil jury trial in other countries, see Devlin, *Trial by Jury* (3d imp. 1966); Smith, *Civil Jury Trial: A Scottish Assessment,* 50 Va.L.Rev. 1076 (1964).

2. THE NATURE OF THE RIGHT TO TRIAL BY JURY

a. Sources of the Right

Examine the Seventh Amendment to the United States Constitution and the state jury-trial guarantees set out in the Supplement. In what ways are they substantively different from each other? What reasons underlie these differences?

The federal Constitution and most state constitutions do not "create" a right to jury trial. Rather, they "preserve" the right as it existed at common law, either in 1791, the date of the Seventh Amendment's ratification, or, in the case of some states, as of the time the state constitution was adopted. Because the Seventh Amendment was assumed to incorporate the jury-trial practice as of 1791, federal judges frequently have been called upon to determine the actual availability of jury trial as of that date.

> * * * Inevitably this calls for some historical inquiry. If the issue in the context in which it arises would have been heard at common law in 1791, when the Seventh Amendment was adopted, or, more accurately, in 1938 when law and equity were merged, it is now triable of right to a jury. There is no right to jury trial if viewed historically the issue would have been tried in the courts of equity or if otherwise it would have been tried without a jury.

> * * *

> [The historical test] * * * proved difficult to apply, particularly for a generation to which the distinctions between law and equity are ancient, and largely unlearned, history. Courts have complained of being held in "historical bondage" and have apologized for an analysis that "may seem to reek unduly of the study." Even if the history were known, it often could shed but dim light as novel kinds of actions were developed and as modern procedure permitted a hybrid form of lawsuit that could never have existed in the ancient days. A vast and controversial literature developed as scholars sought to solve what were essentially insoluble problems.

9 Wright & Miller, *Federal Practice and Procedure: Civil* § 2302 (1971). For an insight into the difficulties posed by the historical test, see the majority and dissenting opinions in Damsky v. Zavatt, 289 F.2d 46 (2d Cir. 1961).

Notes and Questions

1. The significance of the Seventh Amendment's reference to "suits at common law" is described in PARSONS v. BEDFORD, 28 U.S. (3 Pet.) 433, 447, 7 L.Ed. 732, 737 (1830), as follows:

> * * * [By "common law," the framers of the Constitution meant] suits in which legal rights were to be ascertained and determined, in contradistinction to those where equitable rights alone were recognized, and equitable remedies were administered; or where, as in the admiralty, a mixture of public law, and of maritime law and equity, was often found in the same suit. Probably, there were few, if any, states in the Union, in which some new legal remedies, differing from the old common-law forms,

were not in use; but in which, however, the trial by jury intervened, and the general regulations in other respects were according to the course of the common law. * * * In a just sense, the amendment then may well be construed to embrace all suits, which are not of equity and admiralty jurisdiction, whatever may be the peculiar form which they may assume to settle legal rights. * * *

See Henderson, *The Background of the Seventh Amendment,* 80 Harv.L.Rev. 289 (1966). Does the "suits at common law" limitation make any sense now that law and equity have been merged? Consider this question in connection with Beacon Theatres, Inc. v. Westover, p. 879, infra.

Under existing constitutional doctrine, the Seventh Amendment does not generally apply to proceedings in state courts. See Walker v. Sauvinet, 92 U.S. (2 Otto) 90, 23 L.Ed. 678 (1875). Yet the Supreme Court has held that other parts of the Bill of Rights, such as the freedom of speech and expression in the First Amendment, the protection against searches and seizures in the Fourth Amendment, and the privilege against self-incrimination in the Fifth Amendment apply to the states. In what ways does the Seventh Amendment differ from these provisions? What are the arguments for applying the federal jury-trial guarantee to state-court actions? Are there any state-court actions in which a Seventh Amendment or "federal" jury trial is required at the present time?

2. If "common law" in 1791 was understood by the framers of the seventh amendment as a process, rather than as a set of perpetually static rules, then one must ask whether, with the passage of time, the historical test has caused the amendment to diverge from the original conception. * * * During the centuries of their coexistence, the jurisdiction of the law courts and the chancellor * * * were subject to an unstatic process of accretion and erosion. * * * What remains constant over the history of this process, however, is the tendency toward expansion and enrichment of the remedies provided by the law courts. * * *

If future development was contemplated—and if it is correct to view that development as largely one of the expansion of the remedies available at "common law"—then it would seem to follow that the "common law" of the seventh amendment was intended to have a changing meaning over time.

Wolfram, *The Constitutional History of the Seventh Amendment,* 57 Minn.L. Rev. 639, 738, 744 (1973). If the framers of the Amendment understood "common law" as a process in which the remedies available in common-law courts would increase, is it likely that they viewed the right of jury trial as one that would expand or one that would contract?

3. In APPLICATION OF SMITH, 381 Pa. 223, 230, 112 A.2d 625, 629 (1955), the Pennsylvania Supreme Court upheld the constitutionality of a statute that provided for compulsory arbitration in certain circumstances. The court said that a statute would not contravene the Pennsylvania constitution's provision on the jury trial unless it

closes the courts to litigants and makes the decision of the arbitrators the final determination of the rights of the parties; therefore there is no denial of the right of trial by jury if the statute preserves that right to each of the parties by the allowance of an appeal from the decision of the arbitrators or other tribunal. * * *

See also Capitol Traction Co. v. Hof, 174 U.S. 1, 19 S.Ct. 580, 43 L.Ed. 873 (1899). There are other inhibitions on securing a jury trial that have been held not to violate the constitutional mandate. For example, a party who requests a jury trial can be required to pay jury fees that ultimately are taxable as costs against the party who loses the action. What if the indexing or docketing fee for a jury trial is higher than the comparable fee for a nonjury trial? See Klein, *Jury Fees and Compensation of Jurors in the State Courts,* 26 F.R.D. 539 (1960).

4. McELRATH v. UNITED STATES, 102 U.S. (12 Otto) 426, 440, 26 L.Ed. 189, 192 (1880), held that suits against the government in the Court of Claims are not controlled by the Seventh Amendment because they are not suits at common law within its true meaning. "The government cannot be sued, except with its own consent. It can declare in what court it may be sued, and prescribe the forms of pleading and the rules of practice to be observed in such suits." Is the conclusion of the Court in *McElrath* consistent with the spirit of the jury-trial guarantee? If McElrath had not sued the government but the government had initiated suit against him, would he then have had a right to jury trial on any legal issues that might have been raised? Absent any provision in the statute authorizing suit against the government as to whether there is a right to jury trial, the legislative history is controlling. See United States v. Pfitsch, 256 U.S. 547, 41 S.Ct. 569, 65 L.Ed. 1084 (1921) (action under Lever and War Risk Insurance Acts held to be part of district court's general jurisdiction over actions at law and trial by jury held an incident thereto).

b. The Effect of the Merger of Law and Equity

Review the materials on pp. 449–58, supra.

Long before merger, equity developed the clean-up doctrine as a partial response to the problems of the bifurcation of law and equity. Under this doctrine, once an equity court obtained jurisdiction of a suit primarily of an equitable character, the court could decide any incidental legal issues that arose in the course of the litigation.

Sound considerations of policy lay behind * * * [the] "clean-up" rule, considerations which loom large and real against the background of two entirely independent systems of trial courts. The plaintiff entitled to both legal and equitable remedies needed relief from the burden of two days in court. Even worse was the plight of the litigant who had legitimately but vainly sought the chancellor's aid. The statute of limitations threatened him with total loss of remedy on an admittedly valid claim. It was the more dangerous a choice when crowded dockets and cumbersome procedure made the equitable process less than speedy. In any event, the dangers of a wrong choice of forum involved delay and all-consuming expense of litigation.

Here then was plaintiff's dilemma: to turn first to law might, as a simple matter of res judicata, lose him the more-desired chancellor's remedy; to turn to equity would often invite decision by an unpredictable conscience and perhaps the loss of all remedy. Equities had to be weighed on an imprecise balance and hardships measured by a rule the fine divisions of which were often known only to the chancellor himself. Small wonder then that the clean-up rule, the disposition of incidental questions legal in nature, was often applied even where all equitable relief was denied.

The cost of this efficiency was, however, substantial, for it involved the denial of trial by jury on all legal issues so adjudicated. In some situations this price was considered too heavy to pay for the trial convenience achieved. In others, where equity viewed a plaintiff's conduct as sufficiently reprehensible, the chancellor was pleased not to afford him aid by rapid disposition of a remaining issue.

Levin, *Equitable Clean-up and the Jury: A Suggested Orientation,* 100 U.Pa.L.Rev. 320, 320–21 (1951).

Although the codes and the Federal Rules abolish the procedural distinctions between law and equity and substitute a single form of action, they do not abrogate the differences between the substantive and remedial rules of the two systems. See pp. 458–69, supra. Undoubtedly the greatest obstacle to complete unification of law and equity has been the presence of a jury-trial right in actions that would have been triable in a law court under the bifurcated system. Indeed, Professor Chafee, in an unpublished lecture, characterized jury trial as "the sword in the bed that prevents the complete fusion of law and equity." In many ways merger actually has complicated the application of the jury-trial right because a party now may enter a single court with both legal and equitable claims. The problem of defining the contours of the right and the significance of the clean-up doctrine in these "mixed" actions, especially when the legal and the equitable claims overlap, has proven to be of considerable complexity. The problem has been further enhanced by new statutes that create new rights of action with innovative remedies. Frequently, it is difficult to classify such a new remedy as legal or equitable. The Supreme Court has itself struggled with the problem, as shown by the following line of cases.

(i) Jury Trial in the Federal Courts

BEACON THEATRES, INC. v. WESTOVER

Supreme Court of the United States, 1959.
359 U.S. 500, 79 S.Ct. 948, 3 L.Ed.2d 988.

Certiorari to the United States Court of Appeals for the Ninth Circuit.

MR. JUSTICE BLACK delivered the opinion of the Court.

Petitioner, Beacon Theatres, Inc., sought by mandamus to require a district judge in the Southern District of California to vacate certain orders alleged to deprive it of a jury trial of issues arising in a suit brought against it by Fox West Coast Theatres, Inc. The Court of Appeals for the Ninth Circuit refused the writ, holding that the trial judge had acted within his proper discretion in denying petitioner's request for a jury. * * *

Fox had asked for declaratory relief against Beacon alleging a controversy arising under the Sherman Antitrust Act, 26 Stat. 209, as amended, 15 U.S.C. §§ 1, 2, and under the Clayton Act, 38 Stat. 731, 15 U.S.C. § 15, which authorizes suits for treble damages against Sherman Act violators. According to the complaint Fox operates a movie theatre in San Bernardino, California, and has long been exhibiting films under contracts with movie distributors. These contracts grant it the exclusive right to show "first run" pictures in the "San Bernardino competitive area" and provide for "clearance"—a period of time during which no other theatre can exhibit the same pictures. After building a drive-in theatre about 11 miles from San Bernardino, Beacon notified Fox that it considered contracts barring simultaneous exhibitions of first-run films in the two theatres to be overt acts in violation of the antitrust laws. Fox's complaint alleged that this notification, together with threats of treble damage suits against Fox and its distributors, gave rise to "duress and coercion" which deprived Fox of a valuable property right, the right to negotiate for exclusive first-run contracts. Unless Beacon was restrained, the complaint continued, irreparable harm would result. Accordingly, while its pleading was styled a "Complaint for Declaratory Relief," Fox prayed both for a declaration that a grant of clearance between the Fox and Beacon theatres is reasonable and not in violation of the antitrust laws, and for an injunction, pending final resolution of the litigation, to prevent Beacon from instituting any action under the antitrust laws against Fox and its distributors arising out of the controversy alleged in the complaint. Beacon filed an answer, a counterclaim against Fox, and a cross-claim against an exhibitor who had intervened. These denied the threats and asserted that there was no substantial competition between the two theatres, that the clearances granted were therefore unreasonable, and that a conspiracy existed between Fox and its distributors to manipulate contracts and clearances so as to restrain trade and monopolize first-run pictures in violation of the antitrust laws. Treble damages were asked.

Beacon demanded a jury trial of the factual issues in the case as provided by Federal Rule * * * 38(b). The District Court, however, viewed the issues raised by the "Complaint for Declaratory Relief," including the question of competition between the two theatres, as essentially equitable. Acting under the purported authority of Rules 42(b) and 57, it directed that these issues be tried to the court before jury determination of the validity of the charges of antitrust violations made in the counterclaim and cross-claim. A common issue of the "Complaint for Declaratory Relief," the counterclaim, and the cross-claim was the reasonableness of the clearances granted to Fox, which depended, in part, on the existence of competition between the two theatres. Thus the effect of the action of the District Court could be, as the Court of Appeals believed, "to limit the petitioner's opportunity fully to try to a jury every issue which has a bearing upon its treble damage suit," for determination of the issue of clearances by the judge might "operate either by way of res judicata or collateral estoppel so as to conclude both parties with respect thereto at the subsequent trial of the treble damage claim." * * *

The District Court's finding that the Complaint for Declaratory Relief presented basically equitable issues draws no support from the Declaratory Judgment Act, 28 U.S.C. §§ 2201, 2202; Fed.Rules Civ.Proc. 57. * * * That statute, while allowing prospective defendants to sue to establish their nonliability, specifically preserves the right to jury trial for both parties. It follows that if Beacon would have been entitled to a jury trial in a treble damage suit against Fox it cannot be deprived of that right merely because Fox took advantage of the availability of declaratory relief to sue Beacon first. Since the right to trial by jury applies to treble damage suits under the antitrust laws, and is, in fact, an essential part of the congressional plan for making competition rather than monopoly the rule of trade * * *, the Sherman and Clayton Act issues * * * were essentially jury questions.

Nevertheless the Court of Appeals * * * held that the question of whether a right to jury trial existed was to be judged by Fox's complaint read as a whole. In addition to seeking a declaratory judgment, the court said, Fox's complaint can be read as making out a valid plea for injunctive relief, thus stating a claim traditionally cognizable in equity. A party who is entitled to maintain a suit in equity for an injunction, said the court, may have all the issues in his suit determined by the judge without a jury regardless of whether legal rights are involved. The court then rejected the argument that equitable relief, traditionally available only when legal remedies are inadequate, was rendered unnecessary in this case by the filing of the counterclaim and cross-claim which presented all the issues necessary to a determination of the right to injunctive relief. Relying on American Life Ins. Co. v. Stewart, 300 U.S. 203, 215, 57 S.Ct. 377, 380, 81 L.Ed. 605, decided before the enactment of the Federal Rules * * *, it invoked the principle that a court sitting in equity could retain jurisdiction even though later a legal remedy became available. In such instances the equity court had discretion to enjoin the later lawsuit in order to allow the whole dispute to be determined in one case in one court. Reasoning by analogy, the Court of Appeals held it was not an abuse of discretion for the district judge, acting under Federal Rule * * * 42(b), to try the equitable cause first even though this might, through collateral estoppel, prevent a full jury trial of the counterclaim and cross-claim which were as effectively stopped as by an equity injunction.[6]

Beacon takes issue with the holding of the Court of Appeals that the complaint stated a claim upon which equitable relief could be granted. As initially filed the complaint alleged that threats of lawsuits by petitioner against Fox and its distributors were causing irreparable harm to Fox's

---

6. 252 F.2d at page 874. In Ettelson v. Metropolitan Life Ins. Co., 317 U.S. 188, 192, 63 S.Ct. 163, 164, 87 L.Ed. 176, this Court recognized that orders enabling equitable causes to be tried before legal ones had the same effect as injunctions. In City of Morgantown, W.Va. v. Royal Ins. Co., 337 U.S. 254, 69 S.Ct. 1067, 93 L.Ed. 1347, the Court denied at least some such orders the status of injunctions for the purposes of appealability. It did not, of course, imply that when the orders came to be reviewed they would be examined any less strictly than injunctions. * * *

business relationships. The prayer for relief, however, made no mention of the threats but asked only that pending litigation of the claim for declaratory judgment, Beacon be enjoined from beginning any lawsuits under the antitrust laws against Fox and its distributors arising out of the controversy alleged in the complaint. Evidently of the opinion that this prayer did not state a good claim for equitable relief, the Court of Appeals construed it to include a request for an injunction against threats of lawsuits. * * * But this fact does not solve our problem. Assuming that the pleadings can be construed to support such a request and assuming additionally that the complaint can be read as alleging the kind of harassment by a multiplicity of lawsuits which would *traditionally* have justified equity to take jurisdiction and settle the case in one suit, we are nevertheless of the opinion that, under the Declaratory Judgment Act and the Federal Rules * * *, neither claim can justify denying Beacon a trial by jury of all the issues in the antitrust controversy.

The basis of injunctive relief in the federal courts has always been irreparable harm and inadequacy of legal remedies. At least as much is required to justify a trial court in using its discretion under the Federal Rules to allow claims of equitable origins to be tried ahead of legal ones, since this has the same effect as an equitable injunction of the legal claims. And it is immaterial, in judging if that discretion is properly employed, that before the Federal Rules and the Declaratory Judgment Act were passed, courts of equity, exercising a jurisdiction separate from courts of law, were, in some cases, allowed to enjoin subsequent legal actions between the same parties involving the same controversy. This was because the subsequent legal action, though providing an opportunity to try the case to a jury, might not protect the right of the equity plaintiff to a fair and orderly adjudication of the controversy. * * * Under such circumstances the legal remedy could quite naturally be deemed inadequate. Inadequacy of remedy and irreparable harm * * * today must be determined, not by precedents decided under discarded procedures, but in the light of the remedies now made available by the Declaratory Judgment Act and the Federal Rules.

Viewed in this manner, the use of discretion by the trial court under Rule 42(b) to deprive Beacon of a full jury trial on its counterclaim and cross-claim, as well as on Fox's plea for declaratory relief, cannot be justified. Under the Federal Rules the same court may try both legal and equitable causes in the same action. * * *

Thus any defenses, equitable or legal, Fox may have to charges of antitrust violations can be raised either in its suit for declaratory relief or in answer to Beacon's counterclaim. On proper showing, harassment by threats of other suits, or other suits actually brought, involving the issues being tried in this case, could be temporarily enjoined pending the outcome of this litigation. Whatever permanent injunctive relief Fox might be entitled to on the basis of the decision in this case could, of course, be given by the court after the jury renders its verdict. In this way the issues between these parties could be settled in one suit giving Beacon a full jury trial of every antitrust issue. * * * By contrast, the holding of the court below while granting Fox no additional protection unless the avoidance of jury trial be considered as such, would compel Beacon to split his antitrust case, trying part to a judge and part to a jury. Such a result, which involves the postponement and subordination of Fox's own legal claim for declaratory relief as well as of the counterclaim which Beacon was compelled by the Federal Rules to bring, is not permissible.

Our decision is consistent with the plan of the Federal Rules and the Declaratory Judgment Act to effect substantial procedural reform while retaining a distinction between jury and nonjury issues and leaving substantive rights unchanged. Since in the federal courts equity has always acted only when legal remedies were inadequate, the expansion of adequate legal remedies provided by the Declaratory Judgment Act and the Federal Rules necessarily affects the scope of equity. Thus, the justification for equity's deciding legal issues once it obtains jurisdiction, and refusing to dismiss a case, merely because subsequently a legal remedy becomes available, must be re-evaluated in the light of the liberal joinder provisions of the Federal Rules which allow legal and equitable causes to be brought and resolved in one civil action. Similarly the need for, and therefore, the availability of such equitable remedies as Bills of Peace, *Quia Timet* and Injunction must be reconsidered in view of the existence of the Declaratory Judgment Act as well as the liberal joinder provision of the Rules. * * *

If there should be cases where the availability of declaratory judgment or joinder in one suit of legal and equitable causes would not in all respects protect the plaintiff seeking equitable relief from irreparable harm while affording a jury trial in the legal cause, the trial court will necessarily have to use its discretion in deciding whether the legal or equitable cause should be tried first. Since the right to jury trial is a constitutional one, however, while no similar requirement protects trials by the court, that discretion is very narrowly limited and must, wherever possible, be exercised to preserve jury trial. * * * [O]nly under the most imperative circumstances, circumstances which in view of the flexible procedures of the Federal Rules we cannot now anticipate, can the right to a jury trial of legal issues be lost through prior determination of equitable claims. * * *

As we have shown, this is far from being such a case.

* * *

The judgment of the Court of Appeals is reversed.

Reversed.

MR. JUSTICE FRANKFURTER took no part in the consideration or decision of this case.

MR. JUSTICE STEWART, with whom MR. JUSTICE HARLAN and MR. JUSTICE WHITTAKER concur, dissenting.

* * *

I.

The Court suggests that "the expansion of adequate legal remedies provided by the Declaratory Judgment Act * * * necessarily affects the scope of equity." Does the Court mean to say that the mere availability of an action for a declaratory judgment operates to furnish "an adequate remedy at law" so as to deprive a court of equity of the power to act? That novel line of reasoning is at least implied in the Court's opinion. But the Declaratory Judgment Act did not "expand" the substantive law. That Act merely provided a new statutory remedy, neither legal nor equitable, but available in the areas of both equity and law. When declaratory relief is sought, the right to trial by jury depends upon the basic context in which the issues are presented. * * * If the basic issues in an action for declaratory relief are of a kind traditionally cognizable in equity, e.g., a suit for cancellation of a written instrument, the declaratory judgment is not a "remedy at law." If, on the other hand, the issues arise in a context traditionally cognizable at common law, the right to a jury trial of course remains unimpaired, even though the only relief demanded is a declaratory judgment.

Thus, if in this case the complaint had asked merely for a judgment declaring that the plaintiff's specified manner of business dealings with distributors and other exhibitors did not render it liable to Beacon under the antitrust laws, this would have been simply a "juxtaposition of parties" case in which Beacon could have demanded a jury trial. But the complaint * * * presented issues of exclusively equitable cognizance, going well beyond a mere defense to any subsequent action at law. Fox sought from the court protection against Beacon's allegedly unlawful interference with its business relationships—protection which this Court seems to recognize might not have been afforded by a declaratory judgment, unsupplemented by equitable relief. The availability of a declaratory judgment did not, therefore, operate to confer upon Beacon the right to trial by jury with respect to the issues raised by the complaint.

II.

* * * [T]he Court holds, quite apart from its reliance upon the Declaratory Judgment Act, that Beacon by filing its counterclaim and cross-claim acquired a right to trial by jury of issues which otherwise would have been properly triable to the court. Support for this position is found in the principle that, "in the federal courts equity has always acted only when legal remedies were inadequate. * * *" Yet that principle is not employed in its traditional sense as a limitation upon the exercise of power by a court of equity. This is apparent in the Court's recognition that the allegations of the complaint entitled Fox to equitable relief— relief to which Fox would not have been entitled if it had had an adequate remedy at law. Instead, the principle is employed today to mean that because it is possible under the counterclaim to have a jury trial of the factual issue of substantial competition, that issue must be tried by a jury, even though the issue was primarily presented in the original claim for equitable relief. This is a marked departure from long-settled principles.

It has been an established rule "that equitable jurisdiction existing at the filing of a bill is not destroyed because an adequate legal remedy may have become available thereafter." American Life Ins. Co. v. Stewart * * *. It has also been long settled that the District Court in its discretion may order the trial of a suit in equity in advance of an action at law between the same parties, even if there is a factual issue common to both. * * *

III.

The Court today sweeps away these basic principles as "precedents decided under discarded procedures." It suggests that the Federal Rules of Civil Procedure have somehow worked an "expansion of adequate legal remedies" so as to oust the District Courts of equitable jurisdiction, as well as to deprive them of their traditional power to control their own dockets. But obviously the Federal Rules could not and did not "expand" the substantive law one whit.

Like the Declaratory Judgment Act, the Federal Rules preserve inviolate the right to trial by jury in actions historically cognizable at common law, as under the Constitution they must. They do not create a right of trial by jury where that right "does not exist under the Constitution or statutes of the United States." Rule 39(a). Since Beacon's counterclaim was compulsory under the Rules, see Rule 13(a), it is apparent that by filing it Beacon could not be held to have waived its jury rights. * * * But neither can the counterclaim be held to have transformed Fox's original complaint into an action at law. * * *

The Rules make possible the trial of legal and equitable claims in the same proceeding, but they expressly affirm the power of a trial judge to determine the order in which claims shall be heard. Rule 42(b). Certainly the Federal Rules were not intended to undermine the basic structure of equity jurisprudence, developed over the centuries and explicitly recognized in the United States Constitution.

For these reasons I think the petition for a writ of mandamus should have been dismissed.

Notes and Questions

1. Consider the relevance of *Beacon Theatres* to the jury-trial right in the following situations:

(a) An action in which plaintiff seeks redress for a single wrong but asks for both legal and equitable relief. An example would be a copyright infringement action in which damages for past infringement (legal) and injunctive relief against future infringement (equitable) are sought. See Bruckman v. Hollzer, 152 F.2d 730 (9th Cir.1946).

(b) A situation in which plaintiff is entitled to either legal or equitable relief but not both. For example, a breach of contract action in which plaintiff sues for specific performance or damages in the alternative. If plaintiff demands a jury, will the resolution of the question depend on which relief he prefers and on the extent of the common issues? See Ford v. C.E. Wilson & Co., 30 F.Supp. 163 (D.Conn.1939), affirmed 129 F.2d 614 (2d Cir.

1942). If defendant demands a jury trial and plaintiff opposes it, does this mean that plaintiff elects equitable relief?

(c) A case in which a legal counterclaim is asserted against a claim for equitable relief or an equitable counterclaim is asserted against a legal claim. Compare Bendix Aviation Corp. v. Glass, 81 F.Supp. 645 (E.D.Pa.1948), with Liberty Oil Co. v. Condon Nat. Bank, 260 U.S. 235, 43 S.Ct. 118, 67 L.Ed. 232 (1922). Should the permissive or compulsory nature of the counterclaim be relevant in determining whether there is a jury-trial right?

(d) A situation in which an issue that was determined without a jury in an equitable proceeding arises in a subsequent action at law under circumstances in which the doctrine of collateral estoppel normally would bar relitigation. See pp. 1186–99, infra. How should the court rule if one of the parties demands a jury trial in the second action? See Parklane Hosiery Co. v. Shore, p. 1199, infra.

For an excellent analysis of many *Beacon Theatres* problems, see McCoid, *Procedural Reform and the Right to Jury Trial*, 116 U.Pa.L.Rev. 1 (1967).

2. Because of the crowded condition of jury dockets in many parts of the country, application of the *Beacon Theatres* decision may delay the adjudication of cases that would progress more rapidly on a nonjury docket. The delay may cause commercial injury to the litigants. For example, in the *Beacon Theatres* context some parties might hesitate to deal with Fox pending the outcome of the litigation, thereby adversely affecting Fox's commercial relationships during this period. This problem is partially alleviated by Rule 57, which permits the trial court to advance all declaratory-judgment actions on the calendar for speedy determination. Can the procedure in Federal Rule 42(b) be used to mitigate some of the detrimental effects of the litigation on the parties?

———

DAIRY QUEEN, INC. v. WOOD, 369 U.S. 469, 82 S.Ct. 894, 8 L.Ed.2d 44 (1962), arose out of a licensing agreement entered into by respondents, owners of the trademark "DAIRY QUEEN," under which petitioner agreed to pay $150,000 for the exclusive right to use that trademark in certain parts of Pennsylvania. The contract provided for a small initial payment, with the remaining payments to be made at the rate of 50% of all amounts received by petitioner on sales and franchises to deal with the trademark; minimum annual payments were to be made regardless of petitioner's receipts. In August, 1960, respondents wrote petitioner a letter in which they claimed that the latter had committed "a material breach of that contract" by defaulting on the contract's payment provisions and notified petitioner that the contract would be terminated unless the claimed default was remedied immediately. When petitioner continued to deal with the trademark, respondents brought an action for breach of contract praying for: (1) temporary and permanent injunctions to restrain petitioner from any future use of or dealing in the franchise and the trademark; (2) an accounting to determine the exact amount of money owed by petitioner and a judgment for that amount; and (3) an injunction pending an accounting to prevent petitioner from collecting any money from "Dairy Queen" stores in the territory.

The Eastern District of Pennsylvania granted a motion to strike petitioner's demand for a jury trial on the alternative grounds that either the action was "purely equitable" or, if not purely equitable, the legal issues were "incidental" to equitable issues, and, in either case, no right to trial by jury existed. The Third Circuit refused to mandamus the district judge to vacate this order. The Supreme Court reversed.

The Court first disposed of the District Court's conclusion that there is no right to jury trial on legal issues that are "incidental" to equitable issues.

> * * * The holding in *Beacon Theatres* * * * applies whether the trial judge chooses to characterize the legal issues presented as "incidental" to equitable issues or not. Consequently, * * * *Beacon Theatres* requires that any legal issues for which a trial by jury is timely and properly demanded be submitted to a jury. * * *

Id. at 472–73, 82 S.Ct. at 897, 8 L.Ed.2d at 48.

As to the lower court's conclusion that the action was "purely equitable," the Court said:

> * * * The most natural construction of the respondents' claim for a money judgment would seem to be that it is a claim that they are entitled to recover whatever was owed them under the contract as of the date of its purported termination plus damages for infringement of their trademark since that date. * * * As an action on a debt allegedly due under a contract, it would be difficult to conceive of an action of a more traditionally legal character. And as an action for damages based upon a charge of trademark infringement, it would be no less subject to cognizance by a court of law.

> The respondents' contention that this money claim is "purely equitable" is based primarily upon the fact that their complaint is cast in terms of an "accounting," rather than in terms of an action for "debt" or "damages." But the constitutional right to trial by jury cannot be made to depend upon the choice of words used in the pleadings. The necessary prerequisite to the right to maintain a suit for an equitable accounting, like all other equitable remedies, is, as we pointed out in *Beacon Theatres*, the absence of an adequate remedy at law. Consequently, in order to maintain such a suit on a cause of action cognizable at law, as this one is, the plaintiff must be able to show that the "accounts between the parties" are of such a "complicated nature" that only a court of equity can satisfactorily unravel them. In view of the powers given to District Courts by Federal Rule * * * 53(b) to appoint masters to assist the jury in those exceptional cases where the legal issues are too complicated for the jury adequately to handle alone, the burden of such a showing is considerably increased and it will indeed be a rare case in which it can be met. * * * A jury, under proper instructions from the court, could readily determine the recovery, if any, to be had here, whether the theory finally settled upon is that of breach of contract, that of trademark infringement, or any combination of the two. * * *

Id. at 476–79, 82 S.Ct. at 899–900, 8 L.Ed.2d at 50–52.

KATCHEN v. LANDY, 382 U.S. 323, 86 S.Ct. 467, 15 L.Ed.2d 391 (1966). Petitioner filed two claims in bankruptcy for sums allegedly due him from an insolvent corporation. The trustee in bankruptcy responded by asserting that certain payments from corporate assets to petitioner and others were "voidable preferences" under the Bankruptcy Act and could be recouped by the trustee in summary bankruptcy proceedings. Despite petitioner's objections, judgment was rendered for the trustee on the preferences and it was ordered that petitioner's claims remain unpaid until after the judgment in favor of the trustee had been satisfied. The Tenth Circuit affirmed.

In the Supreme Court, petitioner argued that a creditor who has received a preference can hold the property under a substantial adverse claim without filing a claim in the bankruptcy proceeding, thereby forcing the trustee to recover the preference by a plenary action under Section 60 of the Act, 11 U.S.C. § 96; in such a plenary action the creditor could demand a jury trial. Petitioner also contended that the situation is the same when a creditor files a claim and the trustee not only objects to its allowance but also demands surrender of the preference; petitioner's theory was that the Bankruptcy Act does not give the bankruptcy court summary jurisdiction to order preferences surrendered; petitioner contended that if it did, it would violate the Seventh Amendment.

After an extensive analysis of the "structure and purpose" of the Bankruptcy Act, the Court held that the Act does confer summary jurisdiction to compel a claimant to surrender preferences. As to the jury-trial issue, the Court said:

> * * * [A]lthough petitioner might be entitled to a jury trial on the issue of preference if he presented no claim in the bankruptcy proceeding and awaited a federal plenary action by the trustee * * *, when the same issue arises as part of the process of allowance and disallowance of claims, it is triable in equity. The Bankruptcy Act, * * * converts the creditor's legal claim into an equitable claim to a pro rata share of the res * * *, a share which can neither be determined nor allowed until the creditor disgorges the alleged voidable preference he has already received. * * * As bankruptcy courts have summary jurisdiction to adjudicate controversies relating to property over which they have actual or constructive possession * * * and as the proceedings of bankruptcy courts are inherently proceedings in equity * * * there is no Seventh Amendment right to a jury trial for determination of objections to claims * * *.

Petitioner's final reliance is on the doctrine of Beacon Theatres v. Westover * * * and Dairy Queen v. Wood * * *.

The argument here is that the same issues—whether the creditor has received a preference and, if so, its amount—may be presented either as equitable issues in the bankruptcy court or as legal issues in a plenary suit and that the bankruptcy court should stay its own proceedings and direct the bankruptcy trustee to commence a plenary suit so as to preserve petitioner's right to a jury trial. * * *

* * * [P]etitioner's argument would require that in every case where a § 57g objection [a] is interposed and a jury trial is demanded the proceedings on allowance of claims must be suspended and a plenary suit initiated, with all the delay and expense that course would entail. Such a result is not consistent with the equitable purposes of the Bankruptcy Act nor with the rule of *Beacon Theatres* and *Dairy Queen* * * *. In neither *Beacon Theatres* nor *Dairy Queen* was there involved a specific statutory scheme contemplating the prompt trial of a disputed claim without the intervention of a jury. We think Congress intended the trustee's § 57g objection to be summarily determined * * *. Both *Beacon Theatres* and *Dairy Queen* recognize that there might be situations in which the Court could proceed to resolve the equitable claim first even though the results might be dispositive of the issues involved in the legal claim. * * *

Id. at 336–40, 86 S.Ct. at 476–78, 15 L.Ed.2d at 401–03. Justice Black and Justice Douglas dissented for the reasons stated in the dissenting opinion of Judge Phillips in the Court of Appeals. 336 F.2d 535, 540 (10th Cir. 1964).

Questions

In what ways does *Dairy Queen* clarify or go beyond the *Beacon Theatres* decision? Is *Katchen* a retreat from *Beacon Theatres* and *Dairy Queen*? Compare the Supreme Court's decision in FITZGERALD v. UNITED STATES LINES CO., 374 U.S. 16, 83 S.Ct. 1646, 10 L.Ed.2d 720 (1963), discussing a Jones Act claim, which is under the aegis of a statutory jury-trial right, and a maintenance-and-cure claim, which traditionally has been a nonjury admiralty question. The Court held that the two claims, which arose out of a single occurrence, had to be tried together before a jury. Should the Court have reached that result?

ROSS v. BERNHARD, 396 U.S. 531, 90 S.Ct. 733, 24 L.Ed.2d 729 (1970). Plaintiffs brought a derivative suit in federal court against the directors of a closed-end investment company of which they were shareholders and joined the company's brokers, alleging that the company had been charged excessive brokerage fees. Plaintiffs' demand for jury trial, granted by the trial court but set aside by the Second Circuit, was upheld by the Supreme Court in a five-to-three decision:

The common law refused * * * to permit stockholders to call corporate managers to account in actions at law. * * * Early in the 19th century, equity provided relief both in this country and in England. * * * The remedy made available in equity was the derivative suit, viewed in this country as a suit to enforce a *corporate* cause of action against officers, directors, and third parties. As elaborated in the cases, one precondition for the suit was a valid claim on which the corporation could have sued; another was that the corporation itself had refused to proceed after suitable demand, unless excused by extraordinary condi-

----

a. Section 57g of the former Bankruptcy Act forbade the allowance of a claim when the creditor received or acquired a prefer- ence that was void or voidable under the Act if he did not surrender the preference.

tions. Thus the dual nature of the stockholder's action: first, the plaintiff's right to sue on behalf of the corporation and, second, the merits of the corporation's claim itself.

Derivative suits posed no Seventh Amendment problems where the action against the directors and third parties would have been by a bill in equity had the corporation brought the suit. Our concern is with cases based upon a legal claim of the corporation against directors or third parties. Does the trial of such claims at the suit of a stockholder and without a jury violate the Seventh Amendment?

* * * The heart of the action is the corporate claim. If it presents a legal issue, one entitling the corporation to a jury trial under the Seventh Amendment, the right to a jury is not forfeited merely because the stockholder's right to sue must first be adjudicated as an equitable issue triable to the court. *Beacon* and *Dairy Queen* require no less.

If under older procedures, now discarded, a court of equity could properly try the legal claims of the corporation presented in a derivative suit, it was because irreparable injury was threatened and no remedy at law existed as long as the stockholder was without standing to sue and the corporation itself refused to pursue its own remedies. * * *

* * * Actions are no longer brought as actions at law or suits in equity. Under the Rules there is only one action—a "civil action"—in which all claims may be joined and all remedies are available. Purely procedural impediments to the presentation of any issue by any party, based on the difference between law and equity, were destroyed. In a civil action presenting a stockholder's derivative claim, the court after passing upon the plaintiff's right to sue on behalf of the corporation is now able to try the corporate claim for damages with the aid of a jury. * * * The "expansion of adequate legal remedies provided by * * * the Federal Rules necessarily affects the scope of equity." Beacon Theatres, Inc. v. Westover, 359 U.S., at 509.

Thus, for example, before-merger class actions were largely a device of equity, and there was no right to a jury even on issues that might, under other circumstances, have been tried to a jury. * * * [I]t now seems settled in the lower federal courts that class action plaintiffs may obtain a jury trial on any legal issues they present. * * *

Justice Stewart, dissenting, responded:

* * * Since, as the Court concedes, a shareholder's derivative suit could be brought only in equity, it would seem to me to follow by the most elementary logic that in such suits there is no constitutional right to trial by jury. * * *

* * * [T]he Court's effort to force the facts of this case into the mold of *Beacon Theatres* and *Dairy Queen* simply does not succeed. Those cases involved a combination of historically separable suits, one in law and one in equity. * * *

But the present case is not one involving traditionally equitable claims by one party, and traditionally legal claims by the other. Nor is it a suit in which the plaintiff is asserting a combination of legal and equitable claims. For, as we have seen, a derivative suit has always been conceived of as a single, unitary, equitable cause of action. It is for this reason, and not because of "procedural impediments," that the courts of equity did not transfer derivative suits to the law side. * * *

If history is to be so cavalierly dismissed, the derivative suit can, of course, be artificially broken down into separable elements. But so then can any traditionally equitable cause of action, and the logic of the Court's position would lead to the virtual elimination of all equity jurisdiction. An equitable suit for an injunction, for instance, often involves issues of fact which, if damages had been sought, would have been triable to a jury. Does this mean that in a suit asking only for injunctive relief these factual issues *must* be tried to the jury, with the judge left to decide only whether, given the jury's findings, an injunction is the appropriate remedy? * * *

Id. at 534–35, 539–41, 544, 549–50, 90 S.Ct. at 736, 738–39, 741, 743–44, 24 L.Ed.2d at 733–34, 736–37, 739, 742.

Notes and Questions

1. A footnote in the majority opinion in *Ross* provides some guidance regarding the categorization of issues as legal or equitable for Seventh Amendment purposes:

> As our cases indicate, the "legal" nature of an issue is determined by considering, first, the pre-merger custom with reference to such questions; second, the remedy sought; and, third, the practical abilities and limitations of juries. * * *

396 U.S. at 538 n. 10, 90 S.Ct. at 738 n. 10, 24 L.Ed.2d at 736 n. 10. The significance of the third factor mentioned by the Court—the practical abilities and limitations of juries—is unclear. Should it give the trial judge discretion to limit the jury trial right to issues that are well suited for lay jury determination? Or should it be construed to deny a jury trial on complex issues or whenever there is community bias? Or is it merely a reformulation of the traditional basis for equity jurisdiction—absence of an adequate remedy at law? Kane, *Civil Jury Trial: The Case for Reasoned Iconoclasm*, 28 Hastings L.J. 1, 11, 34 (1976), offers one interpretation of the Court's cryptic comment:

> * * * The seventh amendment itself makes no mention of factors other than history that should be considered. Policy considerations or practical concerns were never openly considered in prior Supreme Court jury decisions * * *. Thus, assuming this language can be taken seriously, the use of the issue test [for determining the availability of jury trial] (a more vague, and hence more flexible, means of deciding seventh amendment questions) and the injection of policy considerations into this inquiry appear to represent a movement toward a truly functional jury trial test. * * *

The language and purpose of the seventh amendment does not prevent the Supreme Court from adopting a functional, nonhistorical approach both to expand and to contract the right to a civil jury trial. The right to a civil jury symbolizes, among other things, notions of fair trial. The decision whether an action falls within the language of the constitutional guarantee may depend upon whether jury trial provides an adequate legal remedy. Thus, if the seventh amendment is read as a rigid historical rule, it not only may be dysfunctional, but in some instances it actually may pose a threat to justice.

But compare Redish, *Seventh Amendment Right to Jury Trial: A Study in the Irrationality of Rational Decision Making,* 70 Nw.U.L.Rev. 486 (1975).

2. Some lower federal courts have read the third "consideration" mentioned in the *Ross* footnote as a basis for denying a jury trial in cases in which the number of parties, complexity of the issues, or conceptual sophistication of the evidence and applicable substantive law support a finding that a jury would not be a rational and capable fact-finder. In re Japanese Electronics Prods. Antitrust Litigation, 631 F.2d 1069 (3d Cir.1980), affirmed in part and reversed in part on other grounds following summary judgment 723 F.2d 238, 319 (3d Cir.1983), reversed on other grounds 475 U.S. 574, 106 S.Ct. 1348, 89 L.Ed.2d 538 (1986). Other federal courts have rejected this approach as too great an incursion on the Seventh Amendment. See, e.g., In re United States Financial Secs. Litigation, 609 F.2d 411 (9th Cir.1979), certiorari denied 446 U.S. 929, 100 S.Ct. 1866, 64 L.Ed.2d 281 (1980). This issue arises most frequently in major securities and antitrust suits, which present issues of a technical and esoteric nature arguably outstripping the capacity of even the most intelligent jurors. Further, these suits often consume months or even years in pretrial discovery and weeks or months in trial, and generate thousands of pages of testimony, exhibits, and supporting documents.

The argument for the "complexity exception" is threefold. First, because this exception was recognized at common law at the time of the drafting and adoption of the Seventh Amendment, it is said to be consistent with that provision. See Arnold, *A Historical Inquiry into the Right to Trial by Jury in Complex Civil Litigation,* 128 U.Pa.L.Rev. 829 (1980); Campbell, *Complex Cases and Jury Trials: A Reply to Professor Arnold,* 128 U.Pa.L.Rev. 965 (1980); Arnold, *A Modest Replication to a Lengthy Discourse,* 128 U.Pa.L.Rev. 986 (1980). Second, because there are practical limitations on jurors' knowledge, experience, and ability, it is argued that complex and esoteric cases, such as *Japanese Electronics* or *U.S. Financial Securities,* are best entrusted to the fact-finding capacity of an experienced trial judge. Third, it is contended that to submit to a jury issues exceeding its capacity for rational and sound decisionmaking constitutes a denial of the litigants' due process rights.

In *U.S. Financial Securities,* the District Court on its own motion struck the demands for jury trial because of the complexity of the factual and legal issues involved, the daunting bulk of the evidence ("the equivalent of reading the first 90 volumes of the Federal Reporter, 2d Series"), and the expected duration of the trial (two years). On interlocutory appeal, the Ninth Circuit rejected all three proffered justifications for the complexity exception. The court held that the *Ross* footnote was too casual and cursory and lacked sufficient support to serve as the foundation for a major restriction of the Seventh Amendment right. The court also pointed out that, in its Seventh Amendment cases following *Ross,* the Supreme Court never had addressed the issue of the abilities or competence of jurors. Third, the court maintained that litigants are responsible for presenting their legal claims and supporting materials in comprehensible form and that they and the trial judge have available to them numerous procedural remedies to reshape the litigation into a form comprehensible to jurors.

In *Japanese Electronics*, the Third Circuit reversed the District Court's [*strike jury trial*] decision to reject the parties' motions to strike demands for jury trial in Zenith Radio Corp. v. Matsushita Elec. Industrial Co., 478 F.Supp. 889 (E.D. Pa.1979). The court rejected the historical justification and the "juror capacity" argument for the complexity exception, although tentatively accepting the due process argument.

> Although no specific precedent exists for a finding [of] a due process violation in the trial of any case to a jury, the principles that define the procedural requirements of due process would seem to impose some limitations on the range of cases that may be submitted to a jury. The primary value promoted by due process in factfinding procedures is "to minimize the risk of erroneous decisions." * * * A jury that cannot understand the evidence and the legal rules to be applied provides no reliable safeguard against erroneous decisions. Moreover, in the context of a completely adversary proceeding, like a civil trial, due process requires that "the decisionmaker's conclusion * * * rest[s] solely on the legal rules and evidence adduced at the hearing." * * * Unless the jury can understand the legal rules and evidence, we cannot realistically expect that the jury will rest its decision on them.

631 F.2d at 1084.

The Third Circuit maintained that if a jury could not rationally reach a verdict because of the complexity of the case, a court should balance the interests protected by the Fifth and Seventh Amendments. A court would then be justified in finding, as the Third Circuit did here, that considerations of procedural due process outweigh the constitutional right to a jury trial.

The Third Circuit cautioned that a jury trial should be denied only in [*How decide too complex?*] exceptional circumstances. Before concluding that a lawsuit is too complex to be understood by a jury, a court should conduct a multi-level inquiry. First, a court should examine the factors contributing to the lawsuit's complexity. Second, a court should explore possible methods of reducing the complexity of the case or of augmenting the jury's abilities to comprehend it. Third, a court should consider the unique advantages offered by presenting a complex lawsuit to jury scrutiny.

Judge Gibbons dissented, pointing out that, even though the case was complex, the "manifestations of complexity are for the most part products of the liberal joinder rules of the Federal Rules of Civil Procedure and of the district court's ruling consolidating two multi-court cases for trial"; none of these rules is constitutionally required. The solution, Judge Gibbons maintained, is to use the provisions of the Federal Rules providing for separate trials to reduce the case to a form that jurors can understand.

Therefore, a plaintiff who requests a jury trial cannot liberally join parties and claims if these actions contribute to the overly complex nature of the case. Similarly, a defendant who demands a jury trial must seek to prevent a plaintiff from joining many separate claims and creating a complex lawsuit.

On the merits, Judge Gibbons criticized the majority's test for determining whether denial of a jury-trial demand is appropriate, maintaining that: [*arg for judicial restraint*]

> * * * [Because,] in the end the factors which are identified will permit the exercise of trial court discretion * * * [,] the exercise of that

discretion will sometimes be influenced by unarticulated sympathies for or hostilities toward the underlying policies sought to be advanced in the lawsuit. Trial court discretion, moreover, in any practical sense will be completely unreviewable. * * *

Id. at 1093. Judge Gibbons concluded that his difference with the majority was based in part on differing perceptions "of the nature of the judicial process and the role of juries in that process." Id. Because the jury performs a critical role in the legitimizing of the legal system, "any erosion of citizen participation in [that] system is in the long run likely, in my view, to result in a reduction in the moral authority that supports the process."

The court in *Japanese Electronics* suggested the use of "special trial techniques to increase a jury's capabilities"? What techniques might a court employ? Should the trial or appellate court have the most to say about the complexity of a particular case? The capabilities of a particular jury? Would this lead, in complex cases, to trial by a jury of intellectuals, rather than trial by a jury of peers? Is this constitutional?

The Supreme Court has yet to pass on this issue. *Japanese Electronics* and *U.S. Financial Securities* have provoked a spirited debate over the significance of the *Ross* footnote and the relationship between complex litigation and the Seventh Amendment's guarantee of jury trial in suits at common law: Kane, *Suing Foreign Sovereigns,* 34 Stan.L.Rev. 385 (1982); Lempert, *Civil Juries and Complex Cases: Let's Not Rush to Judgment,* 80 Mich.L.Rev. 68 (1981); Loo, *Rationale for an Exception to the Seventh Amendment Right to a Jury Trial: In re Japanese Electronics Products Antitrust Litigation,* 30 Clev.St.L.Rev. 647 (1981). On strategies and procedural devices for easing the jury's confusion and unfamiliarity with the subjects of and concepts at issue in complex litigation, see Luneberg & Nordenberg, *Specially Qualified Juries and Expert Nonjury Tribunals: Alternatives for Coping with the Complexities of Modern Civil Litigation,* 67 Va.L.Rev. 887 (1981).

3. Is there a constitutional right to a nonjury trial on issues that historically were considered equitable and therefore were tried by the chancellor? What is the significance of the statement in *Beacon Theatres* that "the right to jury trial is a constitutional one * * * while no similar requirement protects trials by the court." In MICHAELSON v. UNITED STATES ex rel. CHICAGO, ST. P., M. & O. R. CO., 291 Fed. 940, 946 (7th Cir.1923), the court remarked that "Congress cannot constitutionally deprive the parties in an equity court of the right of trial by the chancellor." The Supreme Court reversed on other grounds, 266 U.S. 42, 45 S.Ct. 18, 69 L.Ed. 162 (1924), and simply acknowledged the importance of the question.

Courts in at least seven states—Michigan, Wisconsin, Montana, New Jersey, South Carolina, South Dakota, and Utah—have declared that there is a constitutional right to a nonjury trial. The judicial reasoning is described in Van Hecke, *Trial by Jury in Equity Cases,* 31 N.C.L.Rev. 157, 173 (1953), as follows:

> The courts which have asserted that there is a constitutional right in equity cases to a trial of the facts by the judge alone, appear to have been motivated by (a) tradition, (b) respect for the chancellor's professional skill as a trier of facts, (c) a consciousness that the need for a court of equity had arisen in part from the limitation that jury trial had imposed upon the adequacy of various common-law actions, (d) an over-literal

application of state constitutional provisions relating to the structure of state courts, (e) unsympathetic reaction to early legislative attempts to fuse the administration of law and equity into one procedural system, and (f) an uninformed fear of how jury trial would work in equity cases.

Are any of these reasons of sufficient magnitude to counter the policy in favor of jury trials apparent in *Byrd, Beacon Theatres,* and *Dairy Queen?*

(ii) Jury Trial in the State Courts

In Georgia, North Carolina, Tennessee, and Texas, there is a right to jury trial in equity cases, which eliminates the problem presented by *Beacon Theatres* and *Dairy Queen.* In most states that have merged law and equity, however, issues similar to those in the federal courts have arisen since the adoption of the codes.

The Commissioners who prepared the original New York Code of Civil Procedure (1848) were aware of the problem presented by abolishing the distinction between law and equity at a time when the state constitution continued to guarantee "trial by jury in all cases in which it has been heretofore used."[b] But they may have underestimated the difficulty. Not content to leave the issue solely one of constitutional interpretation as it has been in the federal courts, they attempted to solve it by specific provisions:

> § 208. Whenever, in an action for the recovery of money only, or of specific real or personal property, there shall be an issue of fact, it must be tried by a jury, unless a jury trial be waived * * *.

> § 209. Every other issue is triable by the court, which, however, may order the whole issue, or any specific question of fact involved therein, to be tried by a jury * * *.

These provisions were copied in a great many states. But "in most jurisdictions * * * the courts, while occasionally giving the statute some weight, have regarded it generally as merely restating the law-equity dichotomy, and have proceeded to make their determination on historical grounds." Note, *The Right to Jury Trial Under Merged Procedures,* 65 Harv.L.Rev. 453, 454 (1952). In civil actions in which damages alone are sought, there has been little difficulty in finding that a jury is required, and of course in traditional equity cases, such as those involving trusts or injunctions, no jury has been allowed. In most states, there has been a reluctance to allow a mixed form of trial, with some issues being tried by the court and some by a jury. When there have been "legal" and "equitable" issues in the same case, the tendency has been to find one or the other the "predominant" concern and try the case accordingly. Perhaps most frequently the decision has been to find the case "predominantly" equitable, with jury trial denied on the "legal" issues on the grounds

b. This language appeared in the New York Constitutions of 1777, 1821, 1846, and 1894. Because it was interpreted to mean that each successive constitution guaranteed jury trial in any case to which it had been extended by the legislature since the adoption of the preceding constitution, it was changed in the constitution of 1938 to guarantee jury trial only "in all cases in which it has heretofore been guaranteed by constitutional provision." See 4 Weinstein, Korn & Miller, *New York Civil Practice* ¶¶ 4101.07–.08.

that they are "incidental," or that a jury trial is waived by joining a legal claim in an equitable action. Id. at 454–55.

The Supreme Court's decisions in *Beacon Theatres* and *Dairy Queen* have not had a broad impact on the state courts, and in the state cases in which those decisions have been discussed, the reception has been mixed. Compare Adams v. Citizens Bank, 248 So.2d 682 (Fla.App.1971), with Phoenix Mut. Life Ins. Co. v. Conway, 11 N.Y.2d 367, 229 N.Y.S.2d 740, 183 N.E.2d 754 (1962).

HIATT v. YERGIN

Indiana Court of Appeals, Second District, 1972.
152 Ind.App. 497, 284 N.E.2d 834.

[Plaintiffs alleged that they had simultaneously entered into two contracts with defendants. Under the first contract, plaintiffs agreed to sell their one-half interest in Henry County Beverage Company to defendants; under the second contract, defendants agreed to resell the interest to plaintiffs under the same terms if plaintiffs were unable to obtain a Federal Basic Permit and state Alcoholic Beverage Commission approval for their operation of another liquor distributorship. Plaintiffs further alleged that they had performed the first contract and the conditions precedent to the second contract, but that defendants had refused their demand for reconveyance of the Henry County Company stock. They claimed $500,000 damages for the withholding of the stock, and also demanded an accounting for the period during which the stock was withheld. Finally they alleged that they would sustain irreparable injury unless defendants were compelled to return the stock.

Plaintiffs demanded "trial by jury of the action herein and the issues formed on the pleadings herein." The trial court denied the motion, and after a trial found that plaintiffs had not used due diligence in seeking the permit for the operation of the second distributorship, and that they had not applied for the necessary permits for the retransfer of the Henry County Company stock. "If the specific performance requested * * * was granted," said the court, "an operating business would be closed, causing irreparable harm to the owner of the other [half-interest]." The trial court entered judgment against plaintiffs.]

BUCHANAN, JUDGE.

* * * It is our opinion that the trial court did not err in overruling Hiatt's request for a trial by jury because Rules TR. 38(A) and (C) deny a party a jury trial if the cause is of exclusive equitable jurisdiction; the main theory of this cause is equitable.

* * *

Rules TR. 38 and 39 of the Indiana Rules of Trial Procedure respectively govern Jury Trial of Right and Trial by Jury or by the Court. Pertinent parts of each provide:

Trial Rule 38
Jury trial of right

(A) *Causes triable by court and by jury. Issues of law and issues of fact in causes* that prior to the eighteenth day of June, 1852, were of exclusive equitable jurisdiction shall be tried by the court; issues of fact *in all other causes* shall be triable as the same are now triable. In case of the *joinder of causes of action* or defenses which, prior to said date, were of exclusive equitable jurisdiction with *causes of action* or defenses which prior to said date were designated as actions at law and triable by jury— the former shall be triable by the court, and the latter by a jury, unless waived; the trial of both may be at the same time or at different times, as the court may direct.

* * *

(C) *Same: Specification of issues.* In his demand a party may specify the *issues* which he wishes so tried; otherwise he shall be deemed to have demanded trial by jury for all *issues* triable as of right by jury. * * *

The emphasis supplied to the above excerpted portions exhibits to us a semantic cloud hovering over the repeated use of the word "issues" in Rules TR. 38(C) and 39(A)(1) and (2). "Issues" do not exist in a vacuum; they result from factual allegations in civil actions consisting of one or more claims which may or may not be triable by jury because they are "of exclusive equitable jurisdiction." While Rule TR. 38(A) concerns itself with issues in "causes" and "causes of action," subsections (B) and (C) and Rule TR. 39(A)(2) speak only of "issues" which a party may demand be tried by jury. At first blush, it appears that it is "issues" rather than "causes" which determine a party's right to a jury trial. This is not our construction of these Rules.

We thus conclude that * * * a party's right to trial by jury depends upon the nature of the claim(s) stated and not upon the issues that may arise within such claim(s). * * *

[O]ur courts have had little difficulty in determining when a party is entitled to a jury trial as a matter of right, if the cause was either exclusively equitable or exclusively legal, or even if there was a joinder of equitable causes of action with legal causes of action. Reichert v. Krass, (1895) 13 Ind.App. 348, 40 N.E. 706 (foreclosure of a mechanic's lien and matters contained in a counterclaim for damages on breach of contract found to be an exclusively equitable proceeding); * * * Towns v. Smith, (1888) 115 Ind. 480, 16 N.E. 811 (creditor's bill to set aside and cancel a fraudulent conveyance with additional relief seeking to recover a personal judgment on a promissory note deemed an exclusively equitable action); * * * Fish v. Prudential Ins. Co., (1947) 225 Ind. 448, 75 N.E.2d 57 (action to rescind and cancel a life insurance policy with a cross-complaint for full recovery on the policy found to be an essentially equitable cause of action).

* * *

We now turn to the Indiana precedents specifically determining the right to jury trial in causes where one or more of the issues of fact are of exclusive equitable jurisdiction and others are not. The cases are confusing. However, the tendency to deny jury trial in these circumstances is a common thread that runs through most of them.

Typical is Towns v. Smith, supra, where the court announced as early as 1888 that "*if any essential part of a cause* is exclusively of equitable cognizance, the *whole* is drawn into equity" (emphasis supplied) and tried without a jury. * * *

In further support of the proposition that the whole is drawn into equity when any essential part of a cause is exclusively equitable, is this language in Carmichael v. Adams, * * * [91 Ind. 526 (1883)] :

> *The court, having acquired jurisdiction of * * * a suit in equity * * * was not bound to dissect the suit into separate members,* and try each separately, one member as a matter of law, and the other as a matter of equity, but had a right to *treat the case as a unity,* and as one of exclusive equitable jurisdiction.
>
> * * *
>
> It would lead to confusion and injustice to direct separate trials in such cases. Should a jury find there was no right to recover on the [legal cause of action], and the court adjudge that there was a right to recover on the [equitable cause of action], there would then be a conflict not easily overcome. To be sure, the court might set aside the verdict and grant a new trial, but this, after all, would leave the control with the court, and it might just as well be there in the first instance. (Emphasis supplied.)

* * *

The repetitious use of the word "issues" in Rule TR. 38(C) * * * lends credence to holdings of the United States Supreme Court to the effect that the existence of an issue, not of equitable jurisdiction, even though incidental, in a cause that is otherwise equitable in character requires a jury trial of such issue and, further, that the legal issue must be tried first. Beacon Theatres, Inc. v. Westover * * *; Dairy Queen, Inc. v. Wood * * *. When these cases were decided, the Federal Rules of Civil Procedure contained provisions substantially similar to our Rules * * *.

As the Seventh Amendment to the United States Constitution applies only to civil trials in federal courts, the states are free to develop their own body of law concerning the right to trial by jury in civil matters.

The dissent in Beacon Theatres v. Westover, supra, provides [an additional] reason why we should reject the majority holding that as long as there is any incidental issue of fact not equitable in character for which a jury trial has been demanded, it must be submitted to the jury. The three dissenters potently argued that to adopt the majority view was to "undermine the basic structure of equity jurisprudence, developed over the centuries." * * *

The dissenters expressed the prophetic fear that to adopt the majority approach results in clogging of court calendars with frivolous or dilatory demands for jury trials and leads to administrative impasse. Rules of procedure should not oust equity of "Jurisprudence developed over the centuries and explicitly recognized in the U.S. Constitution * * * The court today sweeps away these basic principles * * *"

Hardly an inviting approach for Indiana to adopt.

* * * [W]e turn to Hiatt's one paragraph Complaint to see if he was improperly denied a jury trial.

An overview of the pleadings indicates a blending of issues of fact predominately of equitable jurisdiction with others not of such character so that the cause is in the nature of a bill in equity.

The choice of the pleader was to plead breach of contract and out of that same transaction or set of circumstances, allege substantive facts the primary object of which was equitable relief. The main theory outlined by the facts pleaded is not for damages, but for specific performance of the agreement(s) between Hiatt and Yergin with an attendant accounting and an injunction as to the manner of the future operation of the Henry County Beverage Company * * *.

* * * While the amount of damages sought, i.e., $500,000.00, is not inconsequential, the recovery of damages appears to be incidental to the main theory of the action. We note that Hiatt's last allegation is that the "Plaintiffs [Hiatt] are without an adequate remedy at law."

The decision of the trial court is therefore affirmed.

[A concurring opinion of WHITE, P.J., is omitted.]

c. Statutory Actions

CURTIS v. LOETHER

Supreme Court of the United States, 1974.
415 U.S. 189, 94 S.Ct. 1005, 39 L.Ed.2d 260.

Certiorari to the United States Court of Appeals for the Seventh Circuit.

MR. JUSTICE MARSHALL delivered the opinion of the Court.

Section 812 of the Civil Rights Act of 1968, 82 Stat. 88, 42 U.S.C. § 3612, authorizes private plaintiffs to bring civil actions to redress violations of Title VIII, the fair housing provisions of the Act * * *. The question presented in this case is whether the Civil Rights Act or the Seventh Amendment requires a jury trial upon demand by one of the parties in an action for damages and injunctive relief under this section.

Petitioner, a Negro woman, brought this action under § 812, claiming that respondents, who are white, had refused to rent an apartment to her because of her race * * *. In her complaint she sought only injunctive relief and punitive damages; a claim for compensatory damages was later added. After an evidentiary hearing, the District Court granted preliminary injunctive relief, enjoining the respondents from renting the apartment in question to anyone else pending the trial on the merits. This injunction was dissolved some five months later with the petitioner's consent, after she had finally obtained other housing, and the case went to trial on the issues of actual and punitive damages.

Respondents made a timely demand for jury trial in their answer. The District Court * * * denied the jury request. * * * After trial on the merits, the District Judge found that respondents had in fact discriminated against petitioner on account of her race. Although he found no actual damages, * * * he awarded $250 in punitive damages, denying petitioner's request for attorney's fees and court costs.

The Court of Appeals reversed on the jury trial issue. * * * In view of the importance of the jury trial issue in the administration and enforcement of Title VIII and the diversity of views in the lower courts on the question, we granted certiorari * * *. We affirm.

The legislative history on the jury trial question is sparse, and what little is available is ambiguous. There seems to be some indication that supporters of Title VIII were concerned that the possibility of racial prejudice on juries might reduce the effectiveness of civil rights damages actions. On the other hand, one bit of testimony during committee hearings indicates an awareness that jury trials would have to be afforded in damages actions under Title VIII. Both petitioner and respondents have presented plausible arguments from the wording and construction of § 812. We see no point to giving extended consideration to these arguments, however, for we think it is clear that the Seventh Amendment entitles either party to demand a jury trial in an action for damages in the federal courts under § 812.

* * * Although the thrust of the Amendment was to preserve the right to jury trial as it existed in 1791, it has long been settled that the right extends beyond the common-law forms of action recognized at that time. * * *

Petitioner nevertheless argues that the Amendment is inapplicable to new causes of action created by congressional enactment. As the Court of Appeals observed, however, we have considered the applicability of the constitutional right to jury trial in actions enforcing statutory rights "as a matter too obvious to be doubted." * * * Although the Court has apparently never discussed the issue at any length, we have often found the Seventh Amendment applicable to causes of action based on statutes. * * * Whatever doubt may have existed should now be dispelled. The Seventh Amendment does apply to actions enforcing statutory rights, and requires a jury trial upon demand, if the statute creates legal rights and remedies, enforceable in an action for damages in the ordinary courts of law.

NLRB v. Jones & Laughlin Steel Corp., 301 U.S. 1, 57 S.Ct. 615, 81 L.Ed. 893 (1937), relied on by petitioner, lends no support to her statutory-rights argument. The Court there upheld the award of back pay without jury trial in an NLRB unfair labor practice proceeding, rejecting a Seventh Amendment claim on the ground that the case involved a "statutory proceeding" and "not a suit at common law or in the nature of such a suit." Id., at 48, 57 S.Ct. at 629. *Jones & Laughlin* merely stands for the proposition that the Seventh Amendment is generally inapplicable in administrative proceedings, where jury trials would be incompatible with the whole concept of administrative adjudication and would substantially interfere with the NLRB's role in the statutory scheme. Katchen v. Landy * * *, also relied upon by petitioner, is to like effect. There the Court * * * recognized that a bankruptcy court has been traditionally viewed as a court of equity, and that jury trials would "dismember" the statutory scheme of the Bankruptcy Act. * * * See also Guthrie National Bank v. Guthrie, 173 U.S. 528, 19 S.Ct. 513, 43 L.Ed. 796 (1899).

These cases uphold congressional power to entrust enforcement of statutory rights to an administrative process or specialized court of equity free from the strictures of the Seventh Amendment. But when Congress provides for enforcement of statutory rights in an ordinary civil action in the district courts, where there is obviously no functional justification for denying the jury trial right, a jury trial must be available if the action involves rights and remedies of the sort typically enforced in an action at law.

We think it is clear that a damages action under § 812 is an action to enforce "legal rights" within the meaning of our Seventh Amendment decisions. See, e.g., Ross v. Bernhard * * *; Dairy Queen, Inc. v. Wood, * * *. A damages action under the statute sounds basically in tort— the statute merely defines a new legal duty, and authorizes the courts to compensate a plaintiff for the injury caused by the defendant's wrongful breach. As the Court of Appeals noted, this cause of action is analogous to a number of tort actions recognized at common law.[10] More important, the relief sought here—actual and punitive damages—is the traditional form of relief offered in the courts of law.

We need not, and do not, go so far as to say that any award of monetary relief must necessarily be "legal" relief. * * * A comparison of Title VIII with Title VII of the Civil Rights Act of 1964, where the courts of appeals have held that jury trial is not required in an action for reinstatement and back pay, is instructive, although we of course express no view on the jury trial issue in that context. In Title VII cases the courts of appeals have characterized back pay as an integral part of an equitable remedy, a form of restitution. But the statutory language on which this characterization is based—

> [T]he court may enjoin the respondent from engaging in such unlawful employment practice, and order such affirmative action as may be appropriate, which may include, but is not limited to, reinstatement or hiring of employees, with or without back pay * * *, or any other equitable relief as the court deems appropriate, 42 U.S.C. § 2000e–5(g) (1970 ed., Supp. II)—

contrasts sharply with § 812's simple authorization of an action for actual and punitive damages. In Title VII cases, also, the courts have relied on the fact that the decision whether to award back pay is committed to the discretion of the trial judge. There is no comparable discretion here: if a plaintiff proves unlawful discrimination and actual damages, he is entitled to judgment for that amount. Nor is there any sense in which the award here can be viewed as requiring the defendant to disgorge funds

---

10. For example, the Court of Appeals recognized that Title VIII could be viewed as an extension of the common-law duty of innkeepers not to refuse temporary lodging to a traveler without justification, a duty enforceable in a damages action triable to a jury, to those who rent apartments on a long-term basis. See 467 F.2d at 1117. An action to redress racial discrimination may also be likened to an action for defamation or intentional infliction of mental distress. Indeed, the contours of the latter tort are still developing, and it has been suggested that "under the logic of the common law development of a law of insult and indignity, racial discrimination might be treated as a dignitary tort." C. Gregory & H. Kalven, Cases and Materials on Torts 961 (2d ed. 1969).

wrongfully withheld from the plaintiff. Whatever may be the merit of the "equitable" characterization in Title VII cases, there is surely no basis for characterizing the award of compensatory and punitive damages here as equitable relief.

We are not oblivious to the force of petitioner's policy arguments. Jury trials may delay to some extent the disposition of Title VIII damages actions. But Title VIII actions seeking only equitable relief will be unaffected, and preliminary injunctive relief remains available without a jury trial even in damages actions, Dairy Queen, Inc. v. Wood * * *. Moreover, the statutory requirement of expedition of § 812 actions * * * applies equally to jury and nonjury trials. We recognize, too, the possibility that jury prejudice may deprive a victim of discrimination of the verdict to which he or she is entitled. Of course, the trial judge's power to direct a verdict, to grant judgment notwithstanding the verdict, or to grant a new trial provides substantial protection against this risk, and respondents' suggestion that jury trials will expose a broader segment of the populace to the example of the federal civil rights laws in operation has some force. More fundamentally, however, these considerations are insufficient to overcome the clear command of the Seventh Amendment. The decision of the Court of Appeals must be affirmed.

Affirmed.

Notes and Questions

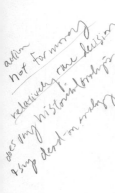

1. In a case decided the same term as *Curtis,* PERNELL v. SOUTHALL REALTY, 416 U.S. 363, 94 S.Ct. 1723, 40 L.Ed.2d 198 (1974), the Court, again speaking through Justice Marshall, decided that because a landlord's right to recover possession of real property was a right protected at common law, the Seventh Amendment jury trial guarantee applies in a summary process action for repossession under the District of Columbia Code.

2. The principal case referred to in the opinion as denying jury trial in actions for reinstatement with back pay under Title VII is Johnson v. Georgia Highway Express, Inc., 417 F.2d 1122 (5th Cir.1969). To the same effect, in districts outside the Fifth Circuit, are cases from federal courts in Connecticut, Maryland, Massachusetts, and Virginia. See cases cited in Ochoa v. American Oil Co., 338 F.Supp. 914, 923 n. 6 (S.D.Tex.1972), a scholarly opinion that quarrels with the ruling of the Fifth Circuit in *Johnson,* although adhering to it.

3. Today, plaintiffs often join civil rights claims under 42 U.S.C. § 1981 or 1983 (either of which carry a right to jury trial) with a similar claim under Title VII (which does not carry a right to jury trial). The two claims usually involve similar issues. As a result, the court in Lincoln v. Board of Regents, 697 F.2d 928, 934 (11th Cir.1983), concluded that, when a jury trial right exists as to a legal issue, "the judge is of course bound by the jury's determination of that issue as it affects his disposition of an accompanying equitable claim."

TULL v. UNITED STATES

Supreme Court of the United States, 1987.
481 U.S. 412, 107 S.Ct. 1831, 95 L.Ed.2d 365.

Certiorari to the United States Court of Appeals for the Fourth Circuit.

JUSTICE BRENNAN delivered the opinion of the Court.

The question for decision is whether the Seventh Amendment guaranteed petitioner a right to a jury trial on both liability and amount of penalty in an action instituted by the Federal Government seeking civil penalties and injunctive relief under the Clean Water Act * * *

I

The Clean Water Act prohibits discharging, without a permit, dredged or fill material into "navigable waters," including the wetlands adjacent to the waters. * * * "Wetlands" are "swamps, marshes, bogs and similar areas." * * * The Government sued the petitioner, a real estate developer, for dumping fill on wetlands on the island of Chincoteague, Virginia. The Government alleged in the original complaint that the petitioner dumped fill on three sites: Ocean Breeze Mobile Homes Sites, Mire Pond Properties, and Eel Creek. The Government later amended the complaint to allege that the petitioner also placed fill in a man-made waterway, named Fowling Gut Extended, on the Ocean Breeze property.

Section 1319 enumerates the remedies available under the Clean Water Act. Subsection (b) authorizes relief in the form of temporary or permanent injunctions. Subsection (d) provides that violators of certain sections of the Act "shall be subject to a civil penalty not to exceed $10,000 per day" during the period of the violation. The Government sought in this case both injunctive relief and civil penalties. When the complaint was filed, however, almost all of the property at issue had been sold by the petitioner to third parties. Injunctive relief was therefore impractical except with regard to a small portion of the land. * * * The Government's complaint demanded the imposition of the maximum civil penalty of $22,890,000 under subsection (d). * * *

Petitioner's timely demand for a trial by jury was denied by the District Court. During the 15-day bench trial, the petitioner did not dispute that he had placed fill at the locations alleged and did not deny his failure to obtain a permit. Petitioner contended, however, that the property in question did not constitute "wetlands." * * * The Government concedes that triable issues of fact were presented by disputes between experts involving the composition and nature of the fillings. * * *

The District Court concluded that the petitioner had illegally filled in wetland areas on all properties in question, but drastically reduced the amount of civil penalties sought by the Government. * * *

The Court of Appeals affirmed over a dissent, rejecting petitioner's argument that, under the Seventh Amendment, he was entitled to a jury trial. * * *

II

* * * The Court has construed [the Seventh Amendment] * * * to require a jury trial on the merits in those actions that are analogous to "Suits at common law." Prior to the Amendment's adoption, a jury trial was customary in suits brought in the English *law* courts. In contrast, those actions that are analogous to 18th-century cases tried in courts of equity or admiralty do not require a jury trial. * * * This analysis applies not only to common law forms of action, but also to causes of action created by congressional enactment. * * *

To determine whether a statutory action is more similar to cases that were tried in courts of law than to suits tried in courts of equity or admiralty, the Court must examine both the nature of the action and of the remedy sought. First, we compare the statutory action to 18th-century actions brought in the courts of England prior to the merger of the courts of law and equity. * * * Second, we examine the remedy sought and determine whether it is legal or equitable in nature. * * *

A

The petitioner analogizes this Government suit under § 1319(d) to an action in debt within the jurisdiction of English courts of law. Prior to the enactment of the Seventh Amendment, English courts had held that a civil penalty suit was a particular species of an action in debt that was within the jurisdiction of the courts of law. * * *

After the adoption of the Seventh Amendment, federal courts followed this English common law in treating the civil penalty suit as a particular type of an action in debt, requiring a jury trial. * * * Actions by the Government to recover civil penalties under statutory provisions historically have been viewed as one type of action in debt requiring trial by jury.

* * *

In the instant case, the Government sought penalties of over 22 million dollars for violation of the Clean Water Act and obtained a judgment in the sum of $325,000. This action is clearly analogous to the 18th-century action in debt, and federal courts have rightly assumed that the Seventh Amendment required a jury trial.

The Government argues, however, that—rather than an action in debt—the closer historical analogue is an action to abate a public nuisance. In 18th-century English law, a public nuisance was "an act or omission 'which obstructs or causes inconvenience or damage to the public in the exercise of rights common to all Her Majesty's subjects.'" * * * The Government argues that the present suit is analogous to two species of public nuisances. One is the suit of the sovereign in the English courts of equity for a "purpresture" to enjoin or order the repair of an enclosure or obstruction of public waterways; the other is the suit of the sovereign to enjoin "offensive trades and manufactures" that polluted the environment. * * *

It is true that the subject matter of this Clean Water Act suit—the placement of fill into navigable waters—resembles these two species of public nuisance. Whether, as the Government argues, a public nuisance action is a better analogy than an action in debt is debatable. But we need not decide the question. * * * [T]he fact that the subject matter of a modern statutory action and an 18th-century English action are close equivalents "is irrelevant for Seventh Amendment purposes," because "that Amendment requires trial by jury in actions unheard of at common law." It suffices that we conclude that both the public nuisance action and the action in debt are appropriate analogies to the instant statutory action.

The essential function of an action to abate a public nuisance was to provide a civil means to redress "a miscellaneous and diversified group of minor criminal offenses, based on some interference with the interests of the community, or the comfort or convenience of the general public." * * * Similarly, the essential function of an action in debt was to recover money owed under a variety of statutes or under the common law. Both of these 18th-century actions, then, could be asserted by the sovereign to seek relief for an injury to the public in numerous contexts.

We need not rest our conclusion on what has been called an "abstruse historical" search for the nearest 18th-century analogue. * * * We reiterate our previously expressed view that characterizing the relief sought is "[m]ore important" than finding a precisely analogous common law cause of action in determining whether the Seventh Amendment guarantees a jury trial. * * *

B

A civil penalty was a type of remedy at common law that could only be enforced in courts of law. Remedies intended to punish culpable individuals, as opposed to those intended simply to extract compensation or restore the status quo, were issued by courts of law, not courts of equity. * * * The action authorized by subsection 1319(d) is of this character. Subsection (d) does not direct that the "civil penalty" imposed be calculated solely on the basis of equitable determinations, such as the profits gained from violations of the statute, but simply imposes a maximum penalty of $10,000 per day of violation. The legislative history of the Act reveals that Congress wanted the district court to consider the need for retribution and deterrence, in addition to restitution, when it imposed civil penalties. * * * A court can require retribution for wrongful conduct based on the seriousness of the violations, the number of prior violations, and the lack of good-faith efforts to comply with the relevant requirements. * * * It may also seek to deter future violations by basing the penalty on its economic impact. * * * Subsection 1319(d)'s authorization of punishment to further retribution and deterrence clearly evidences that this subsection reflects more than a concern to provide equitable relief. In the present case, for instance, the District Court acknowledged that the petitioner received no profits from filling in properties in Mire Pond and Eel Creek, but still imposed a $35,000 fine. * * * Thus, the District Court intended not simply to disgorge profits but also to impose punishment. Because the nature of the relief authorized by subsection 1319(d) was traditionally available only in a court of law, the petitioner in this present action is entitled to a jury trial on demand.

The punitive nature of the relief sought in this present case is made apparent by a comparison with the relief sought in an action to abate a public nuisance. A public nuisance action was a classic example of the kind of suit that relied on the injunctive relief provided by courts in equity. * * * The Government, in fact, concedes that public nuisance cases brought in equity sought injunctive relief, not monetary penalties. * * * Indeed, courts in equity refused to enforce such penalties. * * *

The Government contends, however, that a suit enforcing civil penalties under the Clean Water Act is similar to an action for disgorgement of improper profits, traditionally considered an equitable remedy. It bases this characterization upon evidence that the District Court determined the amount of the penalties by multiplying the number of lots sold by the petitioner by the profit earned per lot. * * * An action for disgorgement of improper profits is, however, a poor analogy. Such an action is a remedy only for restitution—a more limited form of penalty than a civil fine. Restitution is limited to "restoring the status quo and ordering the return of that which rightfully belongs to the purchaser or tenant." * * * As the above discussion indicates, however, subsection 1319(d)'s concerns are by no means limited to restoration of the status quo.

The Government next contends that, even if the civil penalties under subsection 1319(d) are deemed legal in character, a jury trial is not required. A court in equity was empowered to provide monetary awards that were incidental to or intertwined with injunctive relief. The Government therefore argues that its claim under subsection 1319(b), which authorizes injunctive relief, provides jurisdiction for monetary relief in equity. * * * This argument has at least three flaws. First, while a court in equity may award monetary restitution as an adjunct to injunctive relief, it may not enforce civil penalties. * * * Second, the Government was aware when it filed suit that relief would be limited primarily to civil penalties, since the petitioner had already sold most of the properties at issue. App. 110, 119. A potential penalty of $22 million hardly can be considered incidental to the modest equitable relief sought in this case.

Finally, the Government was free to seek an equitable remedy in addition to, or independent of, legal relief. Section 1319 does not intertwine equitable relief with the imposition of civil penalties. Instead each kind of relief is separably authorized in a separate and distinct statutory provision. Subsection (b), providing injunctive relief, is independent of subsection (d), which provides only for civil penalties. In such a situation, if a "legal claim is joined with an equitable claim, the right to jury trial on the legal claim, including all issues common to both claims, remains intact. The right cannot be abridged by characterizing the legal claim as 'incidental' to the equitable relief sought." * * * Thus, the petitioner has a constitutional right to a jury trial to determine his liability on the legal claims.

III

The remaining issue is whether the petitioner additionally has a Seventh Amendment right to a jury assessment of the civil penalties. At the time this case was tried, § 1319(d) did not explicitly state whether juries or trial judges were to fix the civil penalties. The legislative history of the 1977 Amendments to the Clean Water Act shows, however, that Congress intended that trial judges perform the highly discretionary calculations necessary to award civil penalties after liability is found. * * * We must decide therefore whether Congress can, consistent with the Seventh Amendment, authorize judges to assess civil penalties.

The Seventh Amendment is silent on the question whether a jury must determine the remedy in a trial in which it must determine liability.[9] The answer must depend on whether the jury must shoulder this responsibility as necessary to preserve the "substance of the common-law right of trial by jury." * * * Is a jury role necessary for that purpose? We do not think so. " 'Only those incidents which are regarded as fundamental, as inherent in and of the essence of the system of trial by jury, are placed beyond the reach of the legislature.' " * * * The assessment of a civil penalty is not one of the "most fundamental elements." Congress' authority to fix the penalty by statute has not been questioned, and it was also the British practice. * * * In the United States, the action to recover civil penalties usually seeks the amount fixed by the Congress. * * * The assessment of civil penalties thus cannot be said to involve the "substance of a common-law right to a trial by jury," nor a "fundamental element of a jury trial."

Congress' assignment of the determination of the amount of civil penalties to trial judges therefore does not infringe on the constitutional right to a jury trial. Since Congress itself may fix the civil penalties, it may delegate that determination to trial judges. In this case, highly discretionary calculations that take into account multiple factors are necessary in order to set civil penalties under the Clean Water Act. These are the kinds of calculations traditionally performed by judges. * * * We therefore hold that a determination of a civil penalty is not an essential function of a jury trial, and that the Seventh Amendment does not require a jury trial for that purpose in a civil action.

IV

We conclude that the Seventh Amendment required that the petitioner's demand for a jury trial be granted to determine his liability, but that the trial court and not the jury should determine the amount of penalty, if

---

9. Nothing in the Amendment's language suggests that the right to a jury trial extends to the remedy phase of a civil trial. Instead, the language "defines the kind of cases for which jury trial is preserved, namely 'suits at common law.' " * * * Although " '[w]e have almost no direct evidence concerning the intention of the framers of the seventh amendment itself,'

the historical setting in which the Seventh Amendment was adopted highlighted a controversy that was generated * * * by fear that the civil jury itself would be abolished." * * * We have been presented with no evidence that the Framers meant to extend the right to a jury to the remedy phase of a civil trial.

any. The judgment of the Court of Appeals is therefore reversed, and the case is remanded for further proceedings consistent with this opinion.

It is so ordered.

JUSTICE SCALIA, with whom JUSTICE STEVENS joins, concurring in part and dissenting in part.

I join the Court's disposition, and Parts I and II of its opinion. I do not join Part III because in my view the right to trial by jury on whether a civil penalty of unspecified amount is assessable also involves a right to trial by jury on what the amount should be. The fact that the legislature could elect to fix the amount of penalty has nothing to do with whether, if it chooses not to do so, that element comes within the jury-trial guarantee. Congress could, I suppose, create a private cause of action by one individual against another for a fixed amount of damages, but it surely does not follow that if it creates such a cause of action *without* prescribing the amount of damages, that issue could be taken from the jury.

While purporting to base its determination (quite correctly) upon historical practice, the Court creates a form of civil adjudication I have never encountered. I can recall no precedent for judgment of civil liability by jury but assessment of amount by the court. Even punitive damages are assessed by the jury when liability is determined in that fashion. One is of course tempted to make an exception in a case like this, where the government is imposing a non-compensatory remedy to enforce direct exercise of its regulatory authority, because there comes immediately to mind the role of the sentencing judge in a criminal proceeding. If criminal trials are to be the model, however, determination of liability by the jury should be on a standard of proof requiring guilt beyond a reasonable doubt. Having chosen to proceed in civil fashion, with the advantages which that mode entails, it seems to me the government must take the bitter with the sweet. Since, as the Court correctly reasons, the proper analogue to a civil-fine action is the common-law action for debt, the government need only prove liability by a preponderance of the evidence; but must, as in any action for debt, accept the amount of award determined not by its own officials but by twelve private citizens. If that tends to discourage the government from proceeding in this fashion, I doubt that the Founding Fathers would be upset.

I would reverse and remand for jury determination of both issues.

Notes and Questions

1. Reread Notes 1–2, pp. 891–94, supra. Notice that the majority in *Tull* omits the third factor listed in the *Ross* footnote when it lists the considerations that determine the existence of a right to jury trial. Does that imply the Supreme Court now believes that the complexity of a trial is not a basis for denying the Seventh Amendment right to a jury trial?

2. The majority in *Tull* declares that the relief sought is the most important factor in determining whether the action is legal or equitable in nature. How can the Court hold that one is not entitled to a jury trial on the

question of the amount of relief, when the nature of the relief sought is the very factor that renders the action legal rather than equitable?

ATLAS ROOFING CO. v. OCCUPATIONAL SAFETY & HEALTH REVIEW COMMISSION, 430 U.S. 442, 97 S.Ct. 1261, 51 L.Ed.2d 464 (1977). Petitioners were cited for violations of the Occupational Safety and Health Act (OSHA) and fines were imposed on them after hearings before administrative law judges of the Occupational Safety and Health Review Commission (OSHRC). Two Courts of Appeals upheld the Commission's orders and rejected the petitioners' claim that the enforcement scheme violated the Seventh Amendment. In an opinion by Justice White, the Supreme Court affirmed:

> * * * At least in cases in which "public rights" are being litigated—e.g., cases in which the Government sues in its sovereign capacity to enforce public rights created by statutes within the power of Congress to enact—the Seventh Amendment does not prohibit Congress from assigning the factfinding function and initial adjudication to an administrative forum with which the jury would be incompatible.

> * * * [Petitioners also argue] that the right to jury trial was never intended to depend on the identity of the forum to which Congress has chosen to submit a dispute; otherwise, it is said, Congress could utterly destroy the right to a jury trial by always providing for administrative rather than judicial resolution of the vast range of cases that now arise in the courts. The argument is well put, but it overstates the holdings of our prior cases and is in any event unpersuasive. Our prior cases support administrative factfinding in only those situations involving "public rights," e.g., where the Government is involved in its sovereign capacity under an otherwise valid statute creating enforceable public rights. Wholly private tort, contract, and property cases, as well as a vast range of other cases, are not at all implicated.

> More to the point, it is apparent from the history of jury trial in civil matters that factfinding, which is the essential function of the jury in civil cases, * * * was never the exclusive province of the jury under either the English or American legal systems at the time of the adoption of the Seventh Amendment; and the question whether a fact would be found by a jury turned to a considerable degree on the nature of the forum in which a litigant found himself. * * * The question whether a particular case was to be tried in a court of equity—without a jury—or a court of law—with a jury—did not depend on whether the suit involved factfinding or on the nature of the facts to be found. * * * Rather, as a general rule, the decision turned on whether courts of law supplied a cause of action and an adequate remedy to the litigant. If it did, then the case would be tried in a court of law before a jury. * * * Thus, suits for damages for breach of contract, for example, were suits at common law with the issues of the making of the contract and its breach to be decided by a jury; but specific performance was a remedy unavailable in a court of law and where such relief was sought the case would be tried in a court of equity with the facts as to making and breach to be ascertained by the court.

The Seventh Amendment was declaratory of the existing law, for it required only that jury trial in suits at common law was to be "preserved." It thus did not purport to require a jury trial where none was required before. Moreover, it did not seek to change the factfinding mode in equity or admiralty or to freeze equity jurisdiction as it existed in 1789, preventing it from developing new remedies where those available in courts of law were inadequate. Ross v. Bernhard * * * held that a jury trial is required in stockholder derivative suits where * * * a jury trial would have been available to the corporation. It is apparent, however, that prior to the 1938 Federal Rules of Civil Procedure merging the law and equity functions of the federal courts, the very suit involved in *Bernhard* would have been in a court of equity sitting without a jury, not because the underlying issue was any different at all from the issue the corporation would have presented had it sued, but because the stockholder plaintiff who was denied standing in a court of law to sue on the issue was enabled in proper circumstances, starting in the early part of the 19th century, to sue in equity on behalf of the company.

The point is that the Seventh Amendment was never intended to establish the jury as the exclusive mechanism for factfinding in civil cases. It took the existing legal order as it found it, and there is little or no basis for concluding that the Amendment should now be interpreted to provide an impenetrable barrier to administrative factfinding under otherwise valid federal regulatory statutes. We cannot conclude that the Amendment rendered Congress powerless—when it concluded that remedies available in courts of law were inadequate to cope with a problem within Congress' power to regulate—to create new public rights and remedies by statute and commit their enforcement, if it chose, to a tribunal other than a court of law—such as an administrative agency—in which facts are not found by juries. * * *

* * * [H]istory and our cases support the proposition that the right to a jury trial turns not solely on the nature of the issue to be resolved but also on the forum in which it is to be resolved. Congress found the common-law and other existing remedies for work injuries resulting from unsafe working conditions to be inadequate to protect the Nation's working men and women. It created a new cause of action, and remedies therefor, unknown to the common law, and placed their enforcement in a tribunal supplying speedy and expert resolutions of the issues involved. The Seventh Amendment is no bar to the creation of new rights or to their enforcement outside the regular courts of law.

*   *   *

Id. at 450, 457–61, 97 S.Ct. at 1266, 1270–72, 51 L.Ed.2d at 472, 476–79.

Notes and Questions

1. Could the Court have reached the result in *Atlas* by invoking the doctrine of Katchen v. Landy, p. 888, supra, rather than creating a new "public rights" exception?

2. Does *Atlas* only create a "public rights" exception to the jury-trial guarantee? Justice White relied on a number of prior cases, including Justice Marshall's dicta in *Curtis* and *Pernell* interpreting NLRB v. Jones & Laughlin Steel Corp., 301 U.S. 1, 57 S.Ct. 615, 81 L.Ed. 893 (1937), as support for the

proposition that Congress may avoid the jury-trial guarantee by entrusting enforcement of statutory rights to administrative proceedings in which the Seventh Amendment generally is inapplicable. But neither of those cases indicated that there are any limits on Congress' power to replace common-law actions with statutory actions and assign their adjudication to administrative tribunals, as was done with OSHA and workmen's compensation. Could the legislature provide that ordinary personal-injury actions be decided by such a tribunal? See In re Opinion of the Justices, 87 N.H. 492, 179 A. 344 (1935); Brown, *Administrative Commissions and the Judicial Power,* 19 Minn.L.Rev. 261 (1935).

3. In LEHMAN v. NAKSHIAN, 453 U.S. 156, 101 S.Ct. 2698, 69 L.Ed.2d 548 (1981), the respondent brought suit against the Navy under the Age Discrimination in Employment Act, 29 U.S.C. §§ 621–34 (ADEA). The Act had been amended to permit suits by civilian employees against government agencies such as the Navy, 29 U.S.C. § 633a(a), and the Supreme Court had held in Lorillard v. Pons, 434 U.S. 575, 98 S.Ct. 866, 55 L.Ed.2d 40 (1978), that jury trials were permitted in suits against private employers under Section 626(c) of the ADEA. The respondent maintained that Section 626(c) also permitted jury trials of suits against the government. The Navy moved to strike the respondent's demand for jury trial, but the District Court and Court of Appeals refused to grant its motion.

The Supreme Court reversed, holding that the right to jury trial was not available in suits against the Government under the ADEA. The Court based its ruling on the traditional principles that the United States, as sovereign, is immune from suit except as it consents to be sued and that, even when it consents to be sued, the terms of its consent bind the federal courts. The Court held, further, that the common law in 1791 did not permit jury trials in suits against the sovereign. The Court rejected arguments based on the legislative history of the ADEA and held also that Federal Rule 38(a) "requires an affirmative grant of the right [to jury trial] where, as in this case, the Seventh Amendment does not apply."

Dissenting for himself and Justices Marshall, Blackmun, and Stevens, Justice Brennan contended that when immunity is waived, Congress must act *explicitly* to restrict consents to suit by forbidding them to be tried to a jury. Relying on the legislative history and emphasizing that ADEA suits against the government are to be brought in the district courts, in which jury trial generally is available, rather than the Court of Claims, in which jury trial never is available, Justice Brennan concluded that by fair implication Congress intended to allow jury trials in ADEA suits against the government.

d. The Six-Member Jury

In PATTON v. UNITED STATES, 281 U.S. 276, 288, 50 S.Ct. 253, 254, 74 L.Ed. 854, 858 (1930), a criminal case, the Court said that the phrase "trial by jury"

> includes all the essential elements as they were recognized in this country and England when the Constitution was adopted * * *. Those elements were: (1) That the jury should consist of twelve men, neither more nor less; (2) that the trial should be in the presence and under the superintendence of a judge having power to instruct them as to the law

and advise them in respect of the facts; and (3) that the verdict should be unanimous.

But in WILLIAMS v. FLORIDA, 399 U.S. 78, 90 S.Ct. 1893, 26 L.Ed.2d 446 (1970), the Court held that a state might constitutionally use a jury with six (or perhaps fewer) members in a criminal case. Because the Court had held in DUNCAN v. LOUISIANA, 391 U.S. 145, 88 S.Ct. 1444, 20 L.Ed.2d 491 (1968), that the Sixth Amendment guarantee of jury trial in criminal cases applied to the states through "incorporation" in the Fourteenth Amendment, the result in *Williams* required the Court to recognize that such a jury would also satisfy the constitutional guarantee in federal criminal cases, a recognition it made explicit.[c]

Seizing upon the holding in *Williams* and transferring it to the civil-jury guarantee in the Seventh Amendment, numerous federal district courts through their Rule 83 power to make local rules have provided that ordinary civil actions shall be tried by six-member juries only.

COLGROVE v. BATTIN, 413 U.S. 149, 93 S.Ct. 2448, 37 L.Ed.2d 522 (1973). Petitioner sought mandamus to compel a federal district judge to impanel a twelve-member jury, notwithstanding Local Rule 13(d)(1) of the District Court for the District of Montana, which provided for a six-member jury in all civil cases. Petitioner argued that the Local Rule violated the Seventh Amendment, the Enabling Act, 28 U.S.C. § 2072, and Federal Rule 48. The Ninth Circuit denied mandamus, and the Supreme Court affirmed, five to four:

> * * * [T]he historical setting in which the Seventh Amendment was adopted highlighted a controversy that was generated not by concern for preservation of jury characteristics at common law but by fear that the civil jury itself would be abolished unless protected in express words. * * *

> * * * We can only conclude, therefore, that by referring to the "common law," the Framers of the Seventh Amendment were concerned with preserving the *right* of trial by jury in civil cases where it existed at common law, rather than the various incidents of trial by jury. In short, what was said in *Williams* with respect to the criminal jury is equally applicable here: constitutional history reveals no intention on the part of the Framers "to equate the constitutional and common-law characteristics of the jury." * * *

> * * * In *Williams,* we rejected the notion that "the reliability of the jury as a factfinder * * * [is] a function of its size," * * * and nothing has been suggested to lead us to alter that conclusion. * * *

c. "The decision evinces, I think, a recognition that the 'incorporationist' view * * * which underlay *Duncan* * * * must be tempered to allow the States more elbow room in ordering their own criminal systems. With that much I agree. But to accomplish this by diluting constitutional protections within the federal system itself is something to which I cannot possibly subscribe. Tempering the rigor of *Duncan* should be done forthrightly, by facing up to the fact that at least in this area the 'incorporation' doctrine does not fit well with our federal structure, and by the same token that *Duncan* was wrongly decided." Williams v. Florida, 399 U.S. 78, 118, 90 S.Ct. 1893, 1915, 26 L.Ed.2d 446, 464 (1970) (Harlan, J., concurring).

* * * Significantly, our determination that there was "no discernible difference between the results reached by the two different-sized juries" * * * drew largely upon the results of studies of the operations of juries of six in civil cases. * * * Thus, while we express no view as to whether any number less than six would suffice, we conclude that a jury of six satisfies the Seventh Amendment's guarantee of trial by jury in civil cases.

Id. at 152, 155–56, 157, 158–60, 93 S.Ct. at 2450, 2452, 2453–54, 37 L.Ed.2d at 526, 528, 529, 530–31.

The Court further found that the Montana Local Rule did not violate the Enabling Act, since it concluded that the Congress in saying that the rules "shall preserve the right of trial by jury as at common law and as declared by the Seventh Amendment" had not intended to go beyond the Seventh Amendment guarantee itself. Finally, it held that the Local Rule was not in conflict with Federal Rule 48, saying that the latter was only concerned with numbers stipulated by the parties, and was inapplicable when a number was imposed regardless of the parties' consent.

Note

The majority and dissenting opinions in *Colgrove* cite a number of studies of the six-member jury, including Devitt, *The Six-Man Jury in the Federal Court,* 53 F.R.D. 273 (1971), and Zeisel, *And Then There Were None: The Diminution of the Federal Jury,* 38 U.Chi.L.Rev. 710 (1970), which are two excellent presentations of opposing views. For an interesting critique of the Court's use of empirical data in *Colgrove,* see Zeisel & Diamond, *"Convincing Empirical Evidence" on the Six Member Jury,* 41 U.Chi.L.Rev. 281 (1974). See also Sperlich, * * * *And Then There Were Six: The Decline of the American Jury,* 63 Judicature 262 (1980). Local rules providing for six-member juries in federal civil actions are now common.

3. THE PROVINCE OF JUDGE AND JURY

SLOCUM v. NEW YORK LIFE INS. CO., 228 U.S. 364, 382, 33 S.Ct. 523, 530, 57 L.Ed. 879, 888 (1913), p. 983, infra:

In the trial by jury * * * both the court and the jury are essential factors. To the former is committed a power of direction and superintendence, and to the latter the ultimate determination of the issues of fact. Only through the cooperation of the two, each acting within its appropriate sphere, can the constitutional right be satisfied. And so, to dispense with either, or to permit one to disregard the province of the other, is to impinge on that right.

———

JERKE v. DELMONT STATE BANK, 54 S.D. 446, 456–59, 223 N.W. 585, 589–90 (1929):

* * * We frequently see the phrase, "It is for the jury to say what the facts are." Historically speaking, this may have been true in the sixteenth century, but it has long since ceased to be true. The power and right and duty of the jury is not "to *say* what the facts are," but to adjudge and determine what the facts are by the usual and ordinary intellectual processes; that is, by applying the thinking faculties of their minds to the evidence received and the presumptions existing in the case, if any, and thereby forming an opinion or judgment. * * *

Jurors do not determine all questions of ultimate fact, even in jury cases. They determine the existence or nonexistence of those facts, and those only, with reference to the existence of which the judgment of reasonable men might differ as a result of the application of their intellectual faculties to the evidence. If the proof offered by the party having the burden in support of the existence of ultimate issuable facts is so meager that a reasonable mind could not therefrom arrive at the existence of such ultimate fact, there is nothing for the jury, and the judge not only may, but should, direct a verdict against the party having the burden of proof.[d] * * *

WEINER, THE CIVIL JURY AND THE LAW–FACT DISTINCTION, 54 Calif.L.Rev. 1867, 1867–68 (1966):

The categories of "questions of law" and "questions of fact" have been the traditional touchstones by which courts have purported to allocate decision-making between judge and jury. * * * Many statutes in effect today echo * * * [the] dichotomy, utilizing the law and fact terminology to identify the respective provinces of the judge and the jurors in a civil case. None of these statutes, however, attempts to define what is meant by a question of law or a question of fact. Nor have the courts shown any inclination to fashion definitions which can serve as useful guidelines. Indeed, when faced with a dispute as to whether a specific issue should be resolved by the judge or the jury, the typical appellate opinion today does no more than label the question as one of law or of fact, perhaps citing some authorities which are equally devoid of any more detailed consideration of the point. * * * A question of law or a question of fact is a mere synonym for a judge question or a jury question.

DOBSON v. MASONITE CORP.

United States Court of Appeals, Fifth Circuit, 1966.
359 F.2d 921.

HUTCHESON, CIRCUIT JUDGE: * * *

Masonite desired to rid its Mississippi lands * * * of all oak timber and undesirable and unwanted species of tree. In March, 1963, Dobson orally agreed to undertake cutting operations on Masonite's lands. Neither party disputes the existence of the oral agreement; nor is there any real quarrel regarding the basic terms of the agreement. Under the contract Dobson was (1) to cut all oak * * *; (2) to have complete control over the entire cutting operation and the timber cut; (3) to sell so

---

d. There is substantial evidence that during the colonial period and the first part of the nineteenth century the jury determined questions of law in some jurisdictions and that the law-fact dichotomy was a later development. See Scott, *Trial by Jury and the Reform of Civil Procedure,* 31 Harv.L.Rev. 669, 675–78 (1918); Note, *The Changing Role of the Jury in the Nineteenth Century,* 74 Yale L.J. 170 (1964).

much of the cut timber as he could; and (4) to pay Masonite initially twelve dollars, and subsequently ten dollars, per thousand log feet of oak actually sold, and to retain all amounts received in excess thereof as compensation for his services. Dobson incurred rather heavy expenditures in preparing for operations, found buyers for much of the oak to be cut, and commenced clearing the lands.

During the period in question the stumpage value of oak was approximately twenty dollars per thousand log feet; thus by selecting and selling the merchantable oak from that which he cut, Dobson was able to realize profits from his operations. Dobson continued clearing operations from March, 1963, to December, 1963, at which time Masonite unilaterally terminated the agreement and ordered Dobson to discontinue his operations. Dobson during this time cleared 4,000 acres of land, and realized a net profit, after all expenses, including payments to Masonite, of $9,383.02.

This suit was initiated by Dobson to recover the amount of net profits he would have realized had he been permitted to complete the clearing of Masonite's lands. Dobson interpreted the contract as one for services; he argued that the agreement was for clearing the land of unwanted oak trees. Masonite denied liability, interpreting the contract as one for the sale of standing timber, and invoking the Mississippi Statute of Frauds to bar Dobson's claim. At the close of the evidence Masonite moved for a directed verdict. The court denied this motion and submitted the case to the jury on special interrogatories inquiring (1) whether the contract was for services or for the sale of timber; and (2) whether the agreement could have been completed within the permissible period under the Statute of Frauds. The jury answered the interrogatories in favor of Dobson and assessed damages at $26,500.

Masonite then moved for judgment notwithstanding the verdict under Fed.R.Civ.P. 50(b). The district court sustained this motion, stating that only "the legal analysis and legal effect of that done" was in question, ruling that as a matter of law Dobson by virtue of the contract acquired an interest in standing timber, and holding that recovery under the contract was therefore barred by the Statute of Frauds.

The district court quite properly observed that under the Mississippi Statute of Frauds, an oral contract for the sale of standing timber is unenforceable. * * * Counsel for Dobson is also correct in his statement of Mississippi law; an agreement for services in cutting and clearing land of timber is not within the Statute. * * *

But this [is] of little assistance in determining *which type* of contract—sales or service—was here involved. This calls for an interpretation of the agreement between the parties to determine what they meant by the terms of that agreement. Interpretation is always a question of fact. * * * As a question of fact, this issue was properly presented to, and determined by, the jury; and unless there was no evidence which, if believed, would authorize the jury's conclusions, they must stand.

* * *

Plainly what the parties meant by the language of the contract was uncertain and at the heart of this controversy; just as plainly, this was the very issue presented to the jury through special interrogatories. On the record before us, there is certainly ample evidence from which the jury could conclude that the contract between Dobson and Masonite was for the rendition of services, rather than for the sale of standing timber. In drawing the ultimate conclusion as to the meaning of the parties, we believe the jury was fulfilling its traditional function as the finder of the facts. * * *

The district court, apparently because there was no dispute regarding the existence of the oral contract or its terms, felt that only a legal question, what was the legal effect of the contract, was involved. But "legal effect" is the result of applying rules of law to the facts; necessarily this determination must await a determination of all the facts. And, as we have stated, deciding what is the meaning of the contract is a question of fact.

* * *

Reversed and remanded with directions.

Notes and Questions

1. In RANKIN v. FIDELITY TRUST & SAFE DEPOSIT CO., 189 U.S. 242, 23 S.Ct. 553, 47 L.Ed. 792 (1903), the existence or nonexistence of a contract depended upon the effect given to a series of letters that were contradictory in many respects. The Supreme Court held that the question whether a contract existed was for the jury subject to the court's instruction. In HOLTMAN v. BUTTERFIELD, 51 Cal.App. 89, 196 P. 85 (1st Dist.1921), plaintiff alleged that an undisputed unambiguous letter constituted a contract. The court held that there being no contradictory evidence, the question was for the court. Can the two cases be harmonized? Is either case inconsistent with *Dobson?* In what way is it relevant that in *Dobson* the contract was oral? What difficulties in differentiating questions of law from questions of fact do these cases suggest? See generally 3 Corbin, *Contracts* § 554, at 222–23 (1960).

2. * * * The statement that jurors are the judges of the facts and the weight of evidence must be qualified by a recognition of the admitted powers of the court (1) to find in certain cases the existence or nonexistence of facts as a necessary basis for the determination of the competency of proffered witnesses or written evidence; (2) under certain circumstances to direct a nonsuit or particular verdict at the close of plaintiff's or defendant's evidence, or at the close of all the evidence; (3) to charge or instruct the jury on the facts in the Federal courts and some state courts; and (4) to set aside the verdict of the jury for error of law, or if contrary to the manifest weight of the evidence; and (a) to grant a new trial, or (b) condition the overruling of a new trial upon the entry of a remittitur or (c) to enter a judgment contrary to and notwithstanding the verdict.

Busch, *Law and Tactics in Jury Trials* 238 (1949). Many of these powers will be discussed later in Parts E and F of this Chapter.

3. To what extent should the categorization of a particular issue as one of fact or law depend on whether the question should be decided with

reference to a fixed standard that applies to all members of the community impartially or as an ad hoc matter in particular cases? When an issue is classified as one of "law," the rule binds litigants in subsequent cases. Of course, the crucial question is: When is the need for a precise legal standard sufficient to justify withdrawing the matter from the jury? In many contexts the answer depends on whether the system has accumulated enough experience on the issue to justify announcing a standard that will be binding in future cases. Another basis for differentiation is whether the issue involves a sensitive area that warrants a "popular" or "communal" judgment. Consider, for example, the case of a prosecution of a publisher for distributing an allegedly obscene book. Shouldn't the decision to give the question of obscenity to a judge or a jury depend on whether the need for certainty on that issue outweighs the desirability of a judgment by the community as reflected by several juries passing on the question in different locales? Shifting to another context, should the interpretation of the words of an unambiguous contract be left to the jury or to the court? In that connection, re-examine *Dobson, Rankin,* and *Holtman.* What about the issue of negligence? See the classic discussion in Holmes, *The Common Law* 123–26 (1881).

4. Juries frequently have been accused of invading the province of the judge by ignoring his instructions, fabricating their own rules of law, and applying them to the facts. E.g., Frank, *Courts on Trial* 110–11 (1949). Consider the situations described in the following excerpt in terms of whether the jury really is abusing its function:

> In tort actions, especially negligence cases, where the jury functions at its best, it knocks off many rough edges of the law. Although the law may state that a plaintiff who has been guilty of contributory negligence, no matter how slight, cannot recover, the general verdict has often times refused to leave the plaintiff remediless. There is considerable evidence that juries are now making defendants in Federal Employers' Liability and Jones Act cases absolutely liable for injury; and this is probably also true as to defendants in motor accident cases, especially where the defendant is a common carrier. In theory this is a sorry way to correct the law of contributory negligence or to extend the law of absolute liability, but practice cannot always wait upon the proper development of legal theories. * * * Legislatures and courts are often laggards in the process of synchronization. Jury legislation narrows the length of time required for synchronization. It is akin to a private bill. * * *

5 Moore, *Federal Practice* ¶ 38.02[1], at 15–17 (2d ed.). See also James, *Functions of Judge and Jury in Negligence Cases,* 58 Yale L.J. 667 (1949); Kalven, *The Dignity of the Civil Jury,* 50 Va.L.Rev. 1055, 1062–68 (1964). Does the fact that the law often lags behind social reality justify the jury stepping outside its historical bounds and "taking the law into its own hands"? Isn't the jury's invasion of the court's province and its knocking "off many rough edges of the law" likely to inhibit change in the law by making legislative and judicial innovation "unnecessary"?

5. To what extent does our willingness to permit juries to modify the legal rules described by the judge depend on the particular substantive issues and the parties involved in the case? Should the jury have a different degree of freedom in criminal cases than in civil cases, especially in light of the fact that a verdict of acquittal in a criminal case cannot be set aside? Consider

the following passage from Professor Howe's review of Kalven & Zeisel, *The American Jury*, in *Scientific American*, vol. 215, pp. 295, 298, Sept., 1966.

    * * * As the study shows, juries commonly tend to disregard a fundamental axiom of our jurisprudence that the only parties to litigation in the criminal law are the state and the defendant. Thanks to this sloppy indifference, many jurors allow the contributory negligence or the viciousness of the victim of the crime to enter into their weighing of the culpability of the defendant. In other words, the jurors confound the clear distinction between the civil and the criminal law and look on the action charged to the defendant as a tort rather than a crime. "The cases," we are told, "show a bootlegging of tort concepts of contributory negligence and assumption of risk into the criminal law."

    * * * Many will ask the same question James Fenimore Cooper asked more than a century ago: In a society that has been foolish enough to establish an elective judiciary and wise enough to make judicial tenure subject to good behavior, does a jury serve any more useful purpose than that of a symbol of freedom? On Patriot's Day we celebrate the fortitude of the juries that set William Penn and John Peter Zenger free. On what days shall we celebrate the courage of those solid yeoman who, in our own day, saw fit to let * * * [those accused of killing] Medgar Evers, Mrs. Viola Liuzzo and Jonathan Daniels go free? There are surely occasions on which one is tempted to suggest that the time has come to amend our constitutions so as to allow the abolition of the jury even in criminal cases. * * *

    Before that happens, however, I hope that someone will undertake a study no less extensive than the Chicago-Ford jury project to determine whether or not our judges are to be trusted with the power that would be theirs were they to go it alone. I confess *The American Jury* seems infected by an excessive respect for the vision, wisdom and integrity of American judges. I have too often heard practicing lawyers from our large cities insist that the one reason—and that a compelling one—for preserving jury trial is that it is our best safeguard against the corruption of judges.

    Doesn't the fact that it is very rare for a jury verdict to be overturned despite certain acts of "misconduct" or even when it appears to be against the weight of the evidence demonstrate that our judicial system is fully prepared to allow, and often encourages, the jury to manipulate the legal standards offered by the trial judge? In this connection, reread Texas Employers' Ins. Ass'n v. Price, p. 49, supra, and Lavender v. Kurn, p. 53, supra; consider this question again in connection with the material on jury misconduct on pp. 1026–31, infra.

4. DEMAND AND WAIVER OF TRIAL BY JURY

SEGAL v. AMERICAN CAS. CO.

United States District Court, District of Maryland, 1966.
250 F.Supp. 936.

    NORTHROP, DISTRICT JUDGE. This case involves defendants' motion to strike plaintiffs' demand for a jury trial. * * *

In essence, plaintiffs claim that they are entitled to a jury trial, notwithstanding the fact that this action was removed from the Circuit Court of Worcester County on April 3, 1963, that the answer was filed on November 25, 1964, and that a demand for a jury trial in this court was not made until June 29, 1965. The demand, urge the plaintiffs, was filed for the sole purpose of informing the court and counsel for the defendants that plaintiffs did not consent to trial without a jury. Thus, they claim that they would be entitled to a jury trial even in the absence of the June 1965 demand.

* * *

It is the contention of plaintiffs that the time limitations of Rule 38(b) are not applicable in this case, inasmuch as Rule 81(c) removes the necessity for a demand when no demand would have been necessary, under state law, in the court from which the case was removed. * * *

I

Plaintiffs claim that "state law" did not require that a demand for jury trial be made in the Circuit Court for Worcester County, and that, therefore, they were not required to demand a jury trial in this court, but were entitled to trial by jury without demand. This claim must be rejected.

Section 2 of Rule VII of the court from which this case was removed reads as follows:

> On the Saturday of the second week preceding each jury term at 10 o'clock A.M., there shall be a preliminary call by the clerk of cases on the civil docket appearing on the trial calendar. As each case is called the litigants, in proper person or by attorneys, will indicate by proper order whether the respective cases will be tried or continued at the first available trial date under these rules, *and if to be tried whether a jury will be required.* * * * The election of a jury at the preliminary call shall be final for the next ensuing jury session of the court unless the parties shall agree and the court consent otherwise, or unless the case shall be settled, continued or removed by order of court. * * * (Emphasis added.)

In the Circuit Court for Worcester County, if a request for a jury trial is not made at the preliminary call of the docket, a jury trial cannot be had. Thus, by rule of the court, if the party seeking trial by jury does not signify this election, his case is not tried before a jury. This procedure in Worcester County is different from that in certain other counties in the state of Maryland; in these other counties, the filing of a case on the law side of the court automatically results in the setting of the case for jury trial, with no further action being required of the litigants. The issue, then, is whether the rule of court in Worcester County is "state law in the court from which the case is removed." This court concludes that it is.

* * *

The rule in the Circuit Court for Worcester County is not contrary to or conflicting with any statute or any rule of the Maryland Court of Appeals. Nor does the rule contravene section 6 of Article XV of the Maryland Constitution, preserving the *right* to jury trial. Rather, the local rule, like the corresponding federal rules, merely states the manner in which the *right* to a jury trial must be *exercised*. The local rule, having the force and effect of law, * * * is "state law" within the meaning of Federal Rule 81(c).

II

* * *

Admittedly, at the time of removal this case was in the early stages. The time for the preliminary call of the docket in the state court, and, therefore, the time at which an election for a jury trial would have to be made, were a long way off. This situation is similar to that in McRae v. Arabian American Oil Co., 34 F.R.D. 513 (S.D.N.Y.1964). There, state law required a demand for a jury trial at a stage in the proceedings subsequent to the stage reached by the time of removal. The plaintiffs in that case claimed that since, at the stage reached by the time of removal, they were not required to make formal demand for a jury trial, Rule 81(c) obviated the necessity for a demand after removal. * * * [T]he court replied:

> * * * The answer to that contention is that the plain language of the amendment does not so provide; it merely obviates the necessity of a demand after removal in the absence of *any* state requirement for a demand. 34 F.R.D. at 515. [Emphasis added.]

This court agrees with the reasoning of the *McRae* case and concludes that under Rule 81(c) a party seeking a jury must, after removal, make a formal demand for a jury trial if, in the court from which the case was removed, he would have had to take some action to exercise his right to a jury trial. This court finds, as did the court in *McRae,* that the necessity for a demand after removal is obviated only where the case automatically would have been set for jury trial in the court from which removed, without the necessity for any action on the part of the party desiring jury trial. * * *

Since the benefits of Rule 81(c) are not available to plaintiffs in this case, the successful exercise of their right to trial by jury depends upon their compliance with the provisions of Rule 38(b). Inasmuch as the demand in the present case was not made until many months after removal and after the answer had been filed, those time limitations have not been met. Plaintiffs, therefore, are not entitled to claim trial by jury as of right.

III

Although this court, in the exercise of its discretion under Rule 39(b), might allow a jury trial notwithstanding the lateness of the demand, it declines to do so.

In Washington County Ins. Co. v. Wilkinson, 19 F.R.D. 177, 178–179 (D.Md.1956), also involving an appeal to the court's discretion where the demand for jury trial had not been timely made, Judge Chesnut remarked:

> In my opinion the determining factor in such cases should be wheth-er, despite the failure to comply with the rule, the nature of the case is

such that one or the other of the parties is likely to be really prejudiced by the failure to have a jury trial. Where the issues are predominantly factual rather than legal there is more reason for the liberal exercise of the discretion to grant a jury trial. * * *

There is still another consideration to be weighed. * * * I think rule 38 providing for the waiver of a jury trial unless specifically demanded within the time mentioned, is an illustration of the general policy of interpretation announced in rule 1. It is a matter of common experience that in civil cases, particularly those of a contractual nature, a nonjury trial can fairly and properly be concluded in substantially less time than is usually required in a jury case. And it should also not be overlooked that, especially where there is a considerable number of cases pending on the docket ready for trial, the time unnecessarily consumed in the trial of a particular case delays the trial of subsequent cases. And it is also to be remembered that needlessly longer trials usually involve more expense to litigants and to the government which freely provides the courts for the litigants.

On similar grounds, this court declines to exercise its discretion to grant a jury trial:

1. There are ten similar cases pending, each arising from the same storm in Ocean City and each involving a similar clause in the insurance policies.

2. In nine of the ten similar cases, as in this one, the demand for a jury trial was made a number of months after removal and after the filing of the answer.

3. In a case tried earlier, involving the same storm and the same contractual clause, a jury trial consumed two weeks; there is no indication that any of the pending cases would take less time if tried before a jury.

4. The docket of this court is overcrowded, as is the case with most courts today.

5. The expert testimony in each of these cases will be lengthy and complex. * * *

6. The court can see no possible prejudice which would result from a trial before the court without a jury.

7. There will be much less expense for all parties if the cases are tried without a jury.

Therefore, the motion to strike plaintiffs' demand for a jury trial is granted. * * *

Notes and Questions

1. The "discretion" given the district court by Federal Rule 39(b) to permit a jury trial despite the absence of a demand is exercised sparingly. E.g., Canister Co. v. National Can Corp., 8 F.R.D. 408, 409 (D.Del.1948) (the fact that the equitable relief originally sought with legal relief no longer was available was not a basis for exercising discretion when plaintiff failed to ask for a jury trial for over five years). Is the negligence of an attorney in failing

to demand jury trial a proper ground for exercising discretion to grant an untimely demand? See Supplies, Inc. v. Aetna Cas. & Sur. Co., 18 F.R.D. 226 (W.D.Pa.1955); Krussman v. Omaha Woodmen Life Ins. Soc'y, 2 F.R.D. 3 (D.Idaho 1941). Rather than deny a party a jury trial, shouldn't the attorney be punished in a way that does not adversely affect the client? How can this be done?

Does the following passage from BECKSTROM v. COASTWISE LINE, 14 Alaska 190, 13 F.R.D. 480, 483 (D.Alaska 1953), explain the restrictive application of Rule 39(b)?

> * * * For more than two years past, the Court has uniformly denied such requests by reason of the volume of litigation—more than 850 cases a year—coming before this Court for determination. This is more than three times the average number of cases per judge in the 86 * * * District Courts of the United States. The granting of trials by jury in such cases, where demand is not seasonably made, inevitably results in further delay and consequent further "denial of justice" to other litigants, who are presumed to have equally meritorious causes. Until an additional judge is authorized and appointed for this Division the practice will be adhered to. * * *

Is the attitude expressed in *Beckstrom* consistent with this country's commitment to jury trial? Should a constitutional right be used as a pawn in a struggle for more adequately staffed courts?

2. Are automatic waiver provisions constitutional? In AETNA INS. CO. v. KENNEDY, 301 U.S. 389, 57 S.Ct. 809, 81 L.Ed. 1177 (1937), the Court said that "as the right of jury trial is fundamental, courts indulge every reasonable presumption against waiver." Nonetheless, the constitutionality of waiver provisions has been upheld.

The early code provisions relating to jury trial required an express waiver or a failure to perform certain procedural acts before a party lost his jury-trial right. Practice under these provisions became cumbersome and the affirmative-demand procedure came into vogue, although a few states still require an express waiver. See generally Clark, *Code Pleading* § 17 (2d ed. 1947); 4 Weinstein, Korn & Miller, *New York Civil Practice* ¶¶ 4102.01–.22. Courts in many states that have rules patterned after the Federal Rules appear to be more lenient than the federal courts in exercising discretion to relieve a party's failure to make a timely demand. See, e.g., Wood v. Warriner, 62 So. 2d 728 (Fla.1953) (jury demand granted even though plaintiff did not request jury until the first day of trial). But see Bloch v. Bentfield, 1 Ariz.App. 412, 403 P.2d 559 (1965) (waiver by failure to appear at trial).

Should a contractual waiver of jury trial be honored? See N.Y. Real Property Law § 259–c. Suppose the waiver is challenged because of fraud or on some other basis; is there a right to jury trial on the issues raised by the challenge?

3. In BERESLAVSKY v. CAFFEY, 161 F.2d 499 (2d Cir.), certiorari denied 332 U.S. 770, 68 S.Ct. 82, 92 L.Ed. 355 (1947), plaintiff sought an injunction against patent infringement. Subsequently he amended the complaint by striking the request for equitable relief and asking for money damages. The court held that plaintiff was entitled to trial by jury even though the Rule 38(b) time period had expired. The court reasoned that

although the original complaint carried no right to jury trial, a later amendment changing the claim from equitable to legal relief renewed the right and gave plaintiff an additional ten days to demand a jury. The demand period was not extended in ALCOA S.S. CO. v. RYAN, 211 F.2d 576 (2d Cir.1954), apparently because plaintiff's claim under certain insurance policies remained substantially the same after the amendment, which simply eliminated allegations requesting rescission of an agreement canceling the policies. Does anything turn on whether the party who seeks a jury trial is the same party who amended the pleadings? If plaintiff in *Alcoa* felt that a jury trial on the issues in the amended complaint was tactically important, could it have obtained it by taking a voluntary dismissal under Federal Rule 41, reinstituting the suit, and making a new demand for jury trial? Cf. Noonan v. Cunard S.S. Co., 375 F.2d 69 (2d Cir.1967).

4. In LOCAL 783, ALLIED INDUSTRIAL WORKERS v. GENERAL ELECTRIC CO., 471 F.2d 751 (6th Cir.), certiorari denied 414 U.S. 822, 94 S.Ct. 120, 38 L.Ed.2d 55 (1973), plaintiff, who originally had asked only for injunctive relief, filed a motion to amend the complaint by adding a legal claim for damages nine months after the original claim and only eight days before trial. The Court of Appeals held that the trial judge had erred in permitting the amendment only on the condition that jury trial be waived.

Should the court consider whether the late request in *Local 783* is being made for a proper purpose? Given the time required to prepare for a jury trial, late requests could be an effective means of delaying the trial. What should a court do when an amendment is sought to change a claim for legal relief, on which jury trial has been demanded, to a claim for equitable relief? In ruling on the motion to amend, should the court take into account that a loss of jury trial may be entailed?

5. SELECTION AND COMPOSITION OF THE JURY

Jury selection is a two-stage process. First, a list of potential jurors is compiled and they are assembled. A number of them, equal to the number who will serve, usually twelve or six, are then selected at random to sit as a tentative jury. Second, these tentative jurors are questioned by the judge and/or by the attorneys to determine whether each of them can fairly and appropriately decide the case. If one of them is dismissed, his or her place is taken by another member of the venire, selected at random, who is in turn subject to questioning. This process continues until the final panel is in place.

THIEL v. SOUTHERN PAC. CO.

Supreme Court of the United States, 1946.
328 U.S. 217, 66 S.Ct. 984, 90 L.Ed. 1181.

Certiorari to the United States Court of Appeals for the Ninth Circuit.

MR. JUSTICE MURPHY delivered the opinion of the Court.

Petitioner, a passenger, jumped out of the window of a moving train operated by the respondent * * *. He filed a complaint in a California state court to recover damages, alleging that the respondent's agents knew that he was "out of his normal mind" and should not be accepted as a passenger or else should be guarded and that, having accepted him as a passenger, they left him unguarded and failed to stop the train before he finally fell to the ground. At respondent's request the case was removed to the federal district court at San Francisco on the ground of diversity of citizenship, respondent being a Kentucky corporation. * * *

After demanding a jury trial, petitioner moved to strike out the entire jury panel, alleging inter alia that "mostly business executives or those having the employer's viewpoint are purposely selected on said panel, thus giving a majority representation to one class or occupation and discriminating against other occupations and classes, particularly the employees and those in the poorer classes who constitute, by far, the great majority of citizens eligible for jury service." * * * [T]he motion was denied. Petitioner then attempted to withdraw his demand for a jury trial but the respondent refused to consent. A jury of twelve was chosen. Petitioner thereupon challenged these jurors upon the same grounds previously urged in relation to the entire jury panel and upon the further ground that six of the twelve jurors were closely affiliated and connected with the respondent. The court denied this challenge. The trial proceeded and the jury returned a verdict for the respondent.

Petitioner renewed his objections in his motion to set aside the verdict or, in the alternative, to grant a new trial. In denying this motion the court orally found that five of the twelve jurors "belong more closely and intimately with the working man and employee class than they do with any other class" and that they might be expected to be "sympathetic with the experiences in life, the affairs of life, and with the economic views, of people who belong to the working or employee class." The Ninth Circuit Court of Appeals affirmed * * *.

The American tradition of trial by jury, considered in connection with either criminal or civil proceedings, necessarily contemplates an impartial jury drawn from a cross-section of the community. * * * This does not mean, of course, that every jury must contain representatives of all the economic, social, religious, racial, political and geographical groups of the community; frequently such complete representation would be impossible. But it does mean that prospective jurors shall be selected by court officials without systematic and intentional exclusion of any of these groups. Recognition must be given to the fact that those eligible for jury service are to be found in every stratum of society. Jury competence is an individual rather than a group or class matter. That fact lies at the very heart of the jury system. To disregard it is to open the door to class distinctions and discriminations which are abhorrent to the democratic ideals of trial by jury.

The choice of the means by which unlawful distinctions and discriminations are to be avoided rests largely in the sound discretion of the trial courts and their officers. * * *

The undisputed evidence in this case demonstrates a failure to abide by the proper rules and principles of jury selection. Both the clerk of the court and the jury commissioner testified that they deliberately and intentionally excluded from the jury lists all persons who work for a daily wage. They generally used the city directory as the source of names of prospective jurors. In the words of the clerk, "If I see in the directory the name of John Jones and it says he is a longshoreman, I do not put his name in, because I have found by experience that that man will not serve as a juror, and I will not get people who will qualify. The minute that a juror is called into court on a venire and says he is working for $10 a day and cannot afford to work for four, the Judge has never made one of those men serve, and so in order to avoid putting names of people in who I know won't become jurors in the court, won't qualify as jurors in this court, I do leave them out. * * *" The jury commissioner corroborated this testimony, adding that he purposely excluded "all the iron craft, bricklayers, carpenters, and machinists" because in the past "those men came into court and offered that [financial hardship] as an excuse, and the judge usually let them go." The evidence indicated, however, that laborers who were paid weekly or monthly wages were placed on the jury lists, as well as the wives of daily wage earners.

It was further admitted that business men and their wives constituted at least 50% of the jury lists, although both the clerk and the commissioner denied that they consciously chose according to wealth or occupation. Thus the admitted discrimination was limited to those who worked for a daily wage, many of whom might suffer financial loss by serving on juries at the rate of $4 a day and would be excused for that reason.

This exclusion of all those who earn a daily wage cannot be justified by federal or state law. * * * A juror, to be competent, need only be a citizen of the United States over the age of 21, a resident of the state and county for one year preceding selection, possessed of his natural faculties and of ordinary intelligence and not decrepit, and possessed of sufficient knowledge of the English language. California Code of Civil Procedure, § 198. * * *

Moreover, the general principles underlying proper jury selection clearly outlaw the exclusion practiced in this instance. Jury competence is not limited to those who earn their livelihood on other than a daily basis. One who is paid $3 a day may be as fully competent as one who is paid $30 a week or $300 a month. * * * Wage earners, including those who are paid by the day, constitute a very substantial portion of the community, a portion that cannot be intentionally and systematically excluded in whole or in part without doing violence to the democratic nature of the jury system. Were we to sanction an exclusion of this nature we would encourage whatever desires those responsible for the selection of jury panels may have to discriminate against persons of low economic and social status. We would breathe life into any latent tendencies to establish the jury as the instrument of the economically and socially privileged. That we refuse to do.

It is clear that a federal judge would be justified in excusing a daily wage earner for whom jury service would entail an undue financial hardship. But that fact cannot support the complete exclusion of all daily wage earners regardless of whether there is actual hardship involved. Here there was no effort, no intention, to determine in advance which individual members of the daily wage earning class would suffer an undue hardship by serving on a jury at the rate of $4 a day. All were systematically and automatically excluded. In this connection it should be noted that the mere fact that a person earns more than $4 a day would not serve as an excuse. Jury service is a duty as well as a privilege of citizenship; it is a duty that cannot be shirked on a plea of inconvenience or decreased earning power. Only when the financial embarrassment is such as to impose a real burden and hardship does a valid excuse of this nature appear. Thus a blanket exclusion of all daily wage earners, however well-intentioned and however justified by prior actions of trial judges, must be counted among those tendencies which undermine and weaken the institution of jury trial. * * *

It follows that we cannot sanction the method by which the jury panel was formed in this case. The trial court should have granted petitioner's motion to strike the panel. That conclusion requires us to reverse the judgment below in the exercise of our power of supervision over the administration of justice in the federal courts. * * * On that basis it becomes unnecessary to determine whether the petitioner was in any way prejudiced by the wrongful exclusion or whether he was one of the excluded class. * * * It is likewise immaterial that the jury which actually decided the factual issue in the case was found to contain at least five members of the laboring class. The evil lies in the admitted wholesale exclusion of a large class of wage earners in disregard of the high standards of jury selection. To reassert those standards, to guard against the subtle undermining of the jury system, requires a new trial by a jury drawn from a panel properly and fairly chosen.

Reversed.

MR. JUSTICE JACKSON took no part in the consideration or decision of this case.

MR. JUSTICE FRANKFURTER, with whom MR. JUSTICE REED concurs, dissenting.

* * * [I]t is not suggested that the jury was selected so as to bring property prejudice into play in relation to this specific case or type of case, nor is there the basis for contending that the trial judge allowed the selective process to be manipulated in favor of the particular defendant. * * * Neither is it claimed that the district judges for the Northern District of California, with the approval of the circuit judges, designed racial, religious, social, or economic discrimination to influence the make-up of jury panels, or that such unfair influence infused the selection of the panel, or was reflected in those who were chosen as jurors in this case. Nor is there any suggestion that the method of selecting the jury in this case was an innovation. What is challenged is a long standing practice adopted in order to deal with the special hardship which jury service entails for workers paid by the day. What is challenged, in short, is not a covert attempt to benefit the propertied but a practice designed, wisely or unwisely, to relieve the economically least secure from the financial burden which jury service involves under existing circumstances.

No constitutional issue is at stake. The problem is one of judicial administration. * * *

Trial by jury presupposes a jury drawn from a pool broadly representative of the community as well as impartial in a specific case. Since the color of a man's skin is unrelated to his fitness as a juror, negroes cannot be excluded from jury service because they are negroes. * * * A group may be excluded for reasons that are relevant not to their fitness but to competing considerations of public interest, as is true of the exclusion of doctors, ministers, lawyers, and the like. * * * But the broad representative character of the jury should be maintained, partly as assurance of a diffused impartiality and partly because sharing in the administration of justice is a phase of civic responsibility. * * *

It is difficult to believe that this judgment would have been reversed if the trial judge had excused, one by one, all those wage earners whom the jury commissioner, acting on the practice of trial judges of San Francisco, excluded. For it will hardly be contended that the absence of such daily wage earners from the jury panel removed a group who would act otherwise than workers paid by the week or the wives of the daily wage earners themselves. * * *

No doubt, in view of the changes in the composition and distribution of our population and the growth of metropolitan areas, a reexamination is due of the operation of the jury system in the federal courts. * * * The object is to devise a system that is fairly representative of our variegated population, exacts the obligation of citizenship to share in the administration of justice without operating too harshly upon any section of the community, and is duly regardful of the public interest in matters outside the jury system. This means that the many factors entering into the manner of selection, with appropriate qualifications and exemptions, the length of service and the basis of compensation must be properly balanced. These are essentially problems in administration calling for appropriate standards flexibly adjusted.

* * *

The Court now deals by adjudication with one phase of an organic problem and does so by nullifying a judgment which, on the record, was wholly unaffected by difficulties inherent in a situation that calls for comprehensive treatment, both legislative and administrative. * * * To reverse a judgment free from intrinsic infirmity and perhaps to put in question other judgments based on verdicts that resulted from the same method of selecting juries, reminds too much of burning the barn in order to roast the pig.

I would affirm the judgment.

Notes and Questions

1. Read 28 U.S.C. §§ 1861–66 in the Supplement. The *Report of the Committee on the Operation of the Jury System of the Judicial Conference of the United States*, on which the present federal jury-selection statute is based, appears at 42 F.R.D. 353 (1967).

How representative of the community is a federal jury in view of the substantial classes of people who are exempt or may be exempted under Section 1863(b)(6) or who may be excused under Section 1863(b)(5)? Qualifications for jury service vary from state to state and include such factors as citizenship, local residence, ownership of property, health, and payment of taxes.

2.   A number of different methods are used to select names for jury lists. The person responsible for compiling the list (usually called the jury commissioner) may pick names from his own knowledge, rely on names referred by others, use telephone and city directories, voter lists, census reports, property tax lists, club lists, or other sources.

The "key number" system, which is based on the voter registration list, is a recommended method of compiling a jury list.   Under it, the commissioner calculates the number of jurors needed for the year, draws names, and sends questionnaires to those whose names are drawn.   Prospective jurors are then examined and if finally selected their names are placed in a box for weekly drawing.   The term of service usually is two weeks.

The so-called "key man" system consists of sending a letter to certain select individuals with a "high sense of civic responsibility" and asking them "to furnish a stated number of prospective jurors 'with a good reputation for honesty and morality, with sufficient education to understand the problems involved in a lawsuit and who are worthy representatives of your county and favor proper enforcement of the law.'   *   *   * The key-men are requested to include in their lists, so far as reasonably practicable, women, Negroes, and other representatives of all economic or social classes, and from every walk of life."   Wicker, *Jury Panels in Federal Courts,* 22 Tenn.L.Rev. 203, 212–13 (1952).

Does it make any difference how the names for jury lists are selected? How much discretion should the jury commissioner have in making up jury lists?   Would any of the methods mentioned above discriminate against any class or groups?   Would there be any advantage in having a uniform system for the selection of jury lists for all federal courts?   For the states?

3.   The special or "blue ribbon" jury, which is composed of people who are specially selected because of their above-average intelligence, is an attempt to meet the contention that the ordinary juror is incompetent to deal with the complex problems of modern litigation.   In FAY v. NEW YORK, 332 U.S. 261, 67 S.Ct. 1613, 91 L.Ed. 2043 (1947), the Supreme Court upheld the constitutionality of a New York statute that gave the trial court discretion to empanel a "blue ribbon" jury upon application of either party.   Would the Supreme Court uphold a federal statute that provided for "blue ribbon" juries in federal courts?   Are "blue ribbon" juries consistent with the Seventh Amendment or the idea that a person should be "judged by peers" or by a group that represents a cross-section of society?   See Oldham, *Origins of the Special Jury,* 50 U.Chi.L.Rev. 137 (1983).

4.   The use of questionnaires, personal interviews, and psychological tests has been suggested for ascertaining the competence of prospective jurors.   To what extent is the following passage from Note, *Psychological Tests and Standards of Competence for Selecting Jurors,* 65 Yale L.J. 531, 541 (1956), wishful thinking?

*   *   * A more competent jury may force a change in the tactics of advocacy, so that attorneys will put greater emphasis on rational rather than emotional appeals.   Parties may also be dissuaded from taking weak

cases to court in the hope of achieving an unjustified result. Exclusionary rules of evidence, evolved to protect litigants from inept juries, can be liberalized. Juries held in higher esteem will restore respect for the right of trial by jury, and even, perhaps, for jury duty.

Wouldn't psychological testing of jurors result in the erosion of our traditional views of jury composition? Would they be permissible under *Thiel*?

FLOWERS v. FLOWERS

Court of Civil Appeals of Texas, 1965.
397 S.W.2d 121.

CHAPMAN, JUSTICE. The subject matter of this suit involves a question of the disqualification of a juror in a child custody contest tried to a jury * * *.

This case was tried in a town and county of very small population where the record shows many members of the jury panel had heard what they referred to as gossip or rumors concerning the case. The parties to the suit are Billie Charlene Flowers, plaintiff below, the mother; and R.A. Flowers, Jr., the father. The victims of the unfortunate broken home are three little girls ranging in ages from two to ten at the time of the filing of divorce by their mother in January 1964.

* * *

The jurors were told on voir dire examination that the evidence would show that plaintiff drank some socially and on one or two occasions had consumed alcoholic beverages to excess. They were questioned as to whether that fact standing alone would prejudice them against her as a fit and proper person to have custody of the children.

The record preserved upon examination of Mrs. Schmidt as a prospective juror shows that she first testified she was well acquainted with the Flowers family, belonged to the same Baptist church they did in the little town of Miami, and that she had no opinion formed in the case at all. Then when counsel said to her the evidence will show "that Billie does drink upon social occasions with the crowd at a dance, or something of that sort, she would have a highball or cocktail, and it will show on one occasion that she had too much, or two times had too much, what is your attitude—," she answered:

A. I am against drinking in any manner, any kind.

Q. Any way or any fashion at all?

A. Any type.

Q. Mrs. Schmidt, that would definitely affect your judgment in the case wouldn't it?

A. If the evidence was true.

Q. Could you enter the—you would take a seat as a juror with a positive feeling that any drinking whatsoever is wrong, and it is bad so far as the mother of these little girls is concerned,—

A. Anybody else.

Q. If the evidence shows Billie has had one drink or two—drinks at a social occasion, you would hold that against her?

A. I don't approve.

The court then took over the examination and asked her a number of questions, one of which was:

Q. Well, are you saying by that, Mrs. Schmidt, that you wouldn't grant either party to this law suit custody of their children if they drank?

A. I am.

The court then turned to leading questions to the juror as to her attitude about passing upon whether the mother was a fit person to have the custody of the girls, saying:

Q. Dependent upon the testimony you hear in a trial; the mere fact that she got drunk a few times and threw a conniption fit or something, you wouldn't hold that against her and think she wasn't—

A. Not especially.

The court then overruled the challenge of the juror for cause.

The record also shows by affidavit of a lady juror panelist who sat next to Mrs. Schmidt during voir dire examination that Mrs. Schmidt stated " * * * she felt sorry for R.A. Flowers, Jr. and that you had to admire a man that would go on to Sunday School and church after what had happened to him." Mrs. Philpot's affidavit also affirmed that Mrs. Schmidt made a statement to one of the other prospective jurors sitting next to her before the jury was selected that Billie Flowers had run off and left R.A. Flowers, Jr. once before and that both of such statements were made before she was selected and sworn to serve as a juror.

At both the motion for mistrial and motion for new trial based partly upon the proceedings just related, the court declined to hear Mrs. Philpot's tendered testimony as a witness in support of her affidavit. Upon the hearing of the motion for new trial Mrs. Flowers' attorney testified there were eleven jurors, including Mrs. Schmidt, who were undesirable to the plaintiff and that if Mrs. Schmidt on voir dire had correctly stated her attitude reflected by Mrs. Philpot's affidavit, they would have exercised a peremptory challenge as to her rather than as to some other juror.

* * *

Article 2134, Vernon's Ann.Tex.Civ.St., provides as one of the disqualifications: "Any person who has a bias or prejudice in favor of or against either of the parties."

This disqualification for bias or prejudice extends not only to the parties personally, but also to the subject matter of the litigation. * * * Compton v. Henrie, Tex., 364 S.W.2d 179.

In defining the terms "bias" and "prejudice" as used in Article 2134 our Supreme Court in the HENRIE case just cited has said:

Bias, in its usual meaning, is an inclination toward one side of an issue rather than to the other, but to disqualify, it must appear that the state of mind of the juror leads to the natural inference that he will not or did not act with impartiality. Prejudice is more easily defined for it means pre-judgment, and consequently embraces bias; the converse is not true. * * *

Mrs. Schmidt's statements indicate to us both bias and prejudice factually and such a prejudgment of the case as to indicate she could not have acted with impartiality. If we are correct in this factual conclusion then under the authorities just cited her disqualification is not a matter of discretion with the trial court but a matter of law. * * *

Even if we are in error in our pronouncements in the preceding paragraphs, it cannot be gainsaid that the record shows bias and prejudice on the part of Mrs. Schmidt toward plaintiff and toward her alcoholic consumption her attorney admitted would be shown before the examination of the jury on voir dire. From the viewpoint of this writer, such feelings on the part of Mrs. Schmidt are to her credit even if it did disqualify her as a juror. But even if under the facts of this case bias or prejudice was a fact to be determined by the trial court, those feelings having been clearly established, her answer of "Yes, sir" to a leading question to the effect that she would be able to decide the case on the evidence submitted, should be disregarded. * * * In any event we believe the court abused its discretion in refusing to hold the juror disqualified.

* * *

The judgment of the trial court is reversed and remanded for a new trial.

Notes and Questions

1. Challenges to individual jurors—sometimes called challenges to the polls—are of two kinds: for cause and peremptory. Challenges for cause permit a prospective juror to be rejected when partiality can be shown. Peremptory challenges permit rejection of jurors without any statement of reason and usually are based on an assumed partiality that may not be susceptible of proof. Thiel v. Southern Pac. Co., supra, involved a third type of challenge: a challenge to the composition and selection of the entire panel, frequently called a challenge to the array.

An unlimited number of challenges for cause are permitted each party. These challenges are determined by the trial judge, although some states have experimented with so-called "triers"—independent officials who have the responsibility of determining challenges for cause. On what grounds should a juror be challenged for cause? Can the judge disqualify a prospective juror on the court's own motion or must he wait for a motion from one of the parties? May jurors be interrogated as to possible racial, religious, economic, or political prejudice? Is it relevant that the plaintiff or defendant is an individual or an organization espousing an unpopular viewpoint or cause? What if plaintiff or defendant merely happens to be a member of a group of this type? See Casey v. Roman Catholic Archbishop, 217 Md. 595, 143 A.2d 627 (1958).

The number of peremptory challenges allowed each side varies among the states. The general range is from two to six. In the federal courts each side is permitted three. See 28 U.S.C. § 1870. Should the number be increased if there are multiple parties on one or both sides? Since the number of peremptory challenges is limited, they usually are carefully husbanded. Can the use of the peremptory challenge be reconciled with the principle that a jury should be composed of a representative sampling of the community?

In BATSON v. KENTUCKY, 476 U.S. 79, 106 S.Ct. 1712, 90 L.Ed.2d 69 (1986), a criminal case involving a black defendant, the Supreme Court held, on Sixth Amendment grounds, that a prosecutor cannot use his peremptory challenges to excuse black jurors solely on account of their race or on the assumption that black jurors as a group will be unable impartially to consider the state's case against a black defendant. Thus, in certain circumstances, courts are instructed to evaluate a prosecutor's motivation in dismissing a juror with a peremptory challenge. To what extent does this holding undermine the notion of the peremptory challenge? The applicability of *Batson* to civil cases is unclear.

2. Rules concerning who may participate in *voir dire* vary from jurisdiction to jurisdiction. Federal Rule 47(a) leaves the entire matter to the trial judge's discretion in federal cases. Some states have held that the judge may conduct the entire examination subject to suggestions from counsel. Others have held it error not to allow each juror to be examined by counsel prior to the exercise of challenges. See Babcock, *Voir Dire: Preserving Its Wonderful Power*, 27 Stan.L.Rev. 545 (1975).

Consider the arguments of the Supreme Court of Nevada, which held that denying counsel the opportunity to conduct *voir dire* examination constituted reversible error:

> Under the federal rule, the decision to allow attorneys to directly examine prospective jurors is left to the sound discretion of the trial judge. * * *
>
> We concur with those states that reject the federal approach. The importance of a truly impartial jury, whether the action is criminal or civil, is so basic to our notion of jurisprudence that its necessity has never really been questioned in this country. * * * The voir dire process is designed to ensure—to the fullest extent possible—that an intelligent, alert, and impartial jury which will perform the important duty assigned to it by our judicial system is obtained. * * * The purpose of voir dire examination is to determine whether a prospective juror can and will render a fair and impartial verdict on the evidence presented and apply the facts, as he or she finds them, to the law given. * * * We are convinced that prohibiting attorney-conducted voir dire altogether may seriously impede that objective.
>
> Usually, trial counsel are more familiar with the facts and nuances of a case and the personalities involved than the trial judge. Therefore, they are often more able to probe delicate areas in which prejudice may exist or pursue answers that reveal a possibility of prejudice. Moreover, while we do not doubt the ability of trial judges to conduct voir dire, there is concern that on occasion jurors may be less candid when responding with personal disclosures to a presiding judicial officer. Finally, many trial attorneys develop a sense of discernment from participation in voir dire that often reveals favor or antagonism among prospective jurors. The likelihood of perceiving such attitudes is greatly attenuated by a lack of dialogue between counsel and the individuals who may ultimately judge the merits of the case. In that regard, we expressly disapprove of

any language or inferences in *Frame* that tend to minify the importance of counsel's voir dire as a source of enlightenment in the intelligent exercise of peremptory challenges.

We have said or implied nothing in this opinion that detracts from the absolute right of a trial judge to reasonably control and limit an attorney's participation in voir dire. Indeed, we encourage the trial bench not to tolerate the desultory excursions of unprepared counsel who show little regard for judicial economy. Both the scope of voir dire and the method by which voir dire is pursued remain within the discretion of the district court.

WHITLOCK v. SALMON, ___ Nev. ___, 752 P.2d 210 (1988). Do you agree? What are the respective advantages and disadvantages to permitting *voir dire* to be conducted by the trial judge? See Jones, *Judge- Versus Attorney-Conducted Voir Dire: An Empirical Investigation of Juror Candor,* 11 Law & Human Behav. 131 (1987).

3. How far can an attorney go in relating the *voir dire* examination to the lawsuit that the jury will hear? Would it be prejudicial for the lawyer to state hypothetical questions based on the actual facts of the case or to ask how the juror would apply certain legal principles to those facts?

Should a juror's relationship with an insurance company be a proper subject for inquiry by plaintiff's counsel on *voir dire*? What about her willingness to be fair in assessing damages even though she knows defendant is insured? In KING v. WESTLAKE, 264 Ark. 555, 572 S.W.2d 841 (1978), counsel, on *voir dire,* after referring to recent insurance advertisements in national magazines saying that high jury verdicts resulted in higher insurance premiums for everyone, asked the following questions:

> It is improper for either side to imply or suggest that the defendant does or does not have insurance, and the questions I will now direct to you have nothing to do with whether or not the defendant has insurance. The questions I will ask concern your insurance premiums, not insurance in this case. How many of you believe that jury verdicts affect insurance premiums?

> Your insurance premiums may not be affected greatly one way or the other, but will not the verdicts that you render have some effect on your insurance rates?

[A:] Yes

> The question I have been building up to is this: Assuming that the verdict you render could cost you a little more or a little less money on your insurance premiums, can you listen to the testimony, the statements of counsel, and the instructions and then put aside the financial interest you have in this case because of your insurance premiums and render a verdict? (All jurors raised their hands.)

What effect will such questions have upon the jury? Are they proper for *voir dire*? Does this line of questioning give the attorney a back door opportunity to raise an impermissible topic? Should insurance be an impermissible topic? For a colorful debate on the question of insurance and *voir dire,* read the four opinions in Fosness v. Panagos, 376 Mich. 485, 138 N.W.2d 380 (1965).

SECTION C. THE LAW OF EVIDENCE

1. THE NATURE AND PURPOSES OF EVIDENCE

The law of evidence is concerned with one of the most complex undertakings in the entire litigation process—the reconstruction of past events in an effort to arrive at "the truth." Truth is not sought in an absolute sense; in a civil case, for example, the existence or nonexistence of a fact usually need only be shown to be "more probable than not." Even so, the task of finding truth is difficult, in large part because the adversary nature of the trial process effectively discourages the presentation of evidence in a scientific manner under laboratory conditions. Instead, each attorney attempts to construct the strongest possible case in favor of his client, with tactics and personalities often determining which items of evidence are presented and stressed and which items are omitted or de-emphasized. The search for truth is weakened further by the fact that evidence presented is not analyzed and appraised by experts, especially in a jury case; so that emotion or "hunch" may play a large part in the evaluation of evidence and the ultimate decision.

One may ask why the law does not embrace a more efficient system— one that takes advantage of modern advances in medicine, science, and engineering. Why, for example, shouldn't factual determinations be made by a panel of scientific experts who employ "truth sera," hypnosis, psychoanalysis, and similar techniques to question every person who might have relevant knowledge? Why, in an age of high-speed analog and digital computers, aren't we gathering, analyzing, and making judgments about information electronically rather than by archaic and imprecise manual methods? What would be wrong with using such procedures in the judicial process? In Sweden, experts at assessing the testimony of others may be called to give their views of the evidence. What should be the criteria for a satisfactory system of arriving at "truth"?

Within the framework of the current system of trial, an elaborate set of rules has been devised to control the presentation of evidence. Generally speaking, the rules have three basic purposes: (1) to avoid prejudicing the trier of fact by prohibiting presentation of evidence that is inherently unreliable, (2) to expedite trial by eliminating worthless evidence, and (3) to protect the privacy of individuals when social policy places a higher value on that privacy than it does on learning the truth for purposes of litigation. Those rules that are designed to avoid prejudice are aimed primarily, if not solely, at jurors. Thus, they generally are ignored in nonjury litigation, although technically there is but one law of evidence and it is applicable in all cases. Does it make sense to keep evidence from the jury that may help it to reach a sound decision, on the ground that the jury may misuse the evidence? Why can't we rely on jurors to weigh each item of evidence in light of its inherent weaknesses?

Some of the major aspects of evidence law are discussed in the material that follows, although the analysis is far from exhaustive. The function of this description is to demonstrate generally the types of problems lawyers face in attempting to prove their cases. Since the law of evidence is best understood in the context of the factual issues in a particular dispute, we shall consider the subject in light of the following situation:

> Plaintiff, Patsy, has filed suit for slander, alleging that she was falsely branded a prostitute by Dolly, defendant. As the case goes to trial there are three matters in dispute: (1) Is the Hill Club, where Patsy admits she lives, a house of prostitution; (2) if the answer to (1) is "yes," is Patsy merely a boarder at the club, unaware of the activities around her; and (3) if Dolly's alleged statement is false and Patsy is entitled to collect, what is the extent of the damage to her reputation?

2. RELEVANCY

An item of evidence will not be admitted unless it has some logical connection with an issue sought to be proved. Suppose, for example, that in our hypothetical, Dolly's attorney calls a witness to testify solely that Patsy had leased a room at the Hill Club. Although such evidence would tend to prove that Patsy did live at the Hill Club, that fact has been admitted; it is not an issue in the case and unless the evidence is relevant for some other purpose, it should be excluded.

Not all questions of relevancy are quite that easy, however. Suppose, for example, that a witness is called to testify that Patsy is friendly with Marie who lives at the Hill Club and who has been arrested and convicted of prostitution three times within the past eight months. What inferences can be drawn from this testimony regarding Patsy's behavior? Does the mere fact that Marie lives at the Hill Club tend to establish that it is a brothel? Does Patsy's association with Marie lead to the conclusion that Patsy shares the same occupation? Isn't it equally possible that Patsy is a religious or social missionary who cultivated a friendship with Marie in an effort to "save her soul"? If so, should the evidence be excluded as irrelevant because it does not, of itself, tend to prove or disprove the existence of a fact in issue?

In answering the latter question consider the impact of exclusion on the ability of an attorney, in this case Dolly's attorney, to build a case for her client. Isn't it necessary to define evidence as irrelevant only if it could not, either by itself or in association with other evidence, show the existence or nonexistence of a fact in dispute? See McCormick, *Evidence* § 185 (3d ed. 1984). Doesn't this mean that most evidence will be considered relevant? Is that desirable? Indeed, why are the courts even concerned with the exclusion of irrelevant evidence? After all, the trier of fact is asked to do many difficult tasks: choose among competing inferences, analyze credibility, reject perjury, and apply difficult legal rules, to name just a few. Why is it too much to ask that the trier also disregard evidence that can have no logical bearing on the decision?

Even if evidence is logically probative of a material fact, it still may be excluded as not being "legally" relevant for other reasons. Thus, Uniform Rule of Evidence 45 provides:

* * * [T]he judge may in his discretion exclude evidence if he finds that its probative value is substantially outweighed by the risk that its admission will (a) necessitate undue consumption of time, or (b) create substantial danger of undue prejudice or of confusing the issues or of misleading the jury, or (c) unfairly and harmfully surprise a party who has not had reasonable opportunity to anticipate that such evidence would be offered.

What are the justifications for such a rule? How should it be applied? Suppose, for example, that in our hypothetical suit seven of the twelve jurors are nonunion workers in a factory owned and operated by Smythe, who, to the surprise of everyone, takes the witness stand to testify that he owns the Hill Club. Should the court exclude as unduly prejudicial Smythe's testimony that he personally supervised operation of the Club and, as an honest citizen, would never permit its use as a house of prostitution?

[margin handwritten note: it does have probative value — Smythe knows about workers already I think so let it thru]

3. HEARSAY

One of the basic rules of evidence is the rejection of hearsay testimony. Generally speaking, hearsay may be defined as the repetition (or description) by a witness of an out-of-court statement (or writing or action) by another person (or occasionally by the witness himself) regarding the existence of a fact in issue when the statement is sought to be used to prove that fact. See Federal Rules of Evidence 801–02. The asserted deficiency of hearsay testimony is the inability to test the credibility of the out-of-court declarant. For example, suppose that Dolly's attorney, in an attempt to prove that the Hill Club is a house of prostitution, calls as a witness an undercover detective to testify that upon entering a local taxi, the driver said: "If you want some action, I'll take you to the Hill Club. It's the only place in town the police allow prostitutes to operate unmolested." Before cavalierly permitting such testimony, shouldn't we be concerned as to the source of the cab driver's information and the possibility that he might have been mistaken or lying? Is it clear exactly what was meant by the words "operate unmolested"? Obviously it would be much more satisfactory if the driver were called to testify so that he could be examined and cross-examined. But why should the availability of a better source render the testimony of the detective inadmissible? Unless it is totally unreliable, why don't we trust the trier of fact to evaluate the detective's testimony in light of its inherent weaknesses?

Sometimes it is difficult to determine whether evidence is or is not hearsay. Suppose, for example, that our undercover detective testified he had shared his taxicab with plaintiff, Patsy, and that when the driver made his statement she replied, "That's the place I'm headed for. Let's go." Note that these facts may impart new significance to the words of the taxicab driver; they may now be important merely because they were uttered without regard to their truth; if so, they would no longer be hearsay. Why should this be true? If we permit the detective to testify that the driver's statement was made in Patsy's presence, however, how do we avoid the danger that the trier of fact may not only consider the statement for purposes of determining whether it was made but also as an indication of the truth of its content? Often a court will counsel a jury to consider evidence only for a certain purpose. How effective is such an instruction? Does this practice cast doubt on the validity of the basic rule excluding hearsay?

4. EXCEPTIONS TO THE HEARSAY RULE

The rule excluding hearsay testimony is riddled with formal exceptions, which, generally speaking, are based (1) on the fact that there are special circumstances tending to make a particular item of hearsay reliable and (2) on the fact that the evidence is likely to be of importance. In analyzing a few of the more significant exceptions set out below, consider the extent to which they cast doubt on the validity of the hearsay rule itself.

a. *Admissions of a Party*

Suppose a witness is called to testify that our plaintiff, Patsy, said that "she is one of the fun-girls at the Hill Club." Such relevant out-of-court statements by a party universally are admitted when presented by an opposing party, even though technically they may fall within the definition of hearsay. Why? Isn't witness repetition of a party's out-of-court statement subject to the same hearsay dangers as the statement of a nonparty? Is there any significance to the fact that a party is able to testify in his or her own behalf but a nonparty may be unavailable as a witness?

b. *Declarations Against Interest*

Suppose our undercover detective is prepared to testify that the cab driver confessed that he was a panderer who procured customers for Patsy. Should this evidence be admitted? Is it significant that pandering is a criminal act? In some jurisdictions the driver's statement would be excluded and in others it would be admitted under an exception to the hearsay rule for statements against interest; until recently most courts would apply the exception only if the statement would be against the pecuniary interests of the cab driver, for example, if he admitted that he owed Patsy money collected on her behalf. Does a distinction between pecuniary and penal interests make any sense? Suppose that Jones, a well respected member of the community and a family man, tells the detective that he knows Patsy is a prostitute because he has been one of her clients. Should this statement be admissible? Testimony constituting declarations against interest is allowed only if the declarant is unavailable to testify in person.

c. *Spontaneous and Contemporaneous Statements*

Suppose a young lady in search of a room enters the Hill Club only to emerge a few minutes later, screaming: "Good gracious, it's full of prostitutes; they thought I was one!" Should a passerby be permitted to testify as to what she said? Courts usually admit a hearsay statement made spontaneously under emotional stress. Why? *b/c bcasume she isn't lieing*

What difference, if any, should it make if the statement was made by the young lady to a police officer some twenty minutes after the event? Suppose that upon entering the Hill Club and seeing that it was a brothel, she had calmly borrowed the Club phone and informed the police of the illegal activities? A few courts, at least, would permit the police officer who received the call to relate her dispassionate description of the ongoing events.

d. Written Records

Suppose that our plaintiff, Patsy, claims that she has been attending college every evening during the hours when the Hill Club allegedly opens its doors for its "business activities." In order to prove her whereabouts Patsy seeks to introduce the school attendance records, which reveal that she has not missed a class for two years. These records consist of the absentee lists filed by each of her teachers at the conclusion of each class. The school secretary who keeps the records testifies as to the routine by which they are prepared and filed, but, of course, he cannot vouch for their accuracy. In effect, the records are statements of Patsy's teachers and are hearsay.

Courts permit the introduction of such routine business reports, however, when they are made soon after the events detailed by a person having firsthand knowledge, and when there is no reason to suspect that the reports are inaccurate. Is such an exception justifiable? Recognize that if it were not permitted, Patsy would be required to call her teachers to testify as to the attendance records. Assuming the teachers are available to testify, how likely are they to remember the extent to which Patsy was or was not present over the two-year period? The law recognizes the inability of individuals to recall such details. Therefore, if a witness testifies that he cannot remember a certain event, but presents a written account, which he made shortly after the event, that account may be admitted, even if it is not a business record; of course, there must be no reason to suspect that the account is inaccurate.

5. PRIVILEGE

The rules regarding privilege have been mentioned briefly in connection with the materials on pretrial discovery, see pp. 778–86, supra. They differ markedly from other evidence rules in that they are not designed to aid the trier of fact to reach a just decision with dispatch. Instead they are designed to withhold valid, nonprejudicial evidence for reasons of external policy.

Assume, for example, that in the hypothetical case our defendant, Dolly, informs her attorney that she has no information whatsoever to support her public statements that plaintiff is a prostitute. May defendant's attorney be called as a witness to testify as to this admission by the client? The answer is "no." Statements made by a client to an attorney for the purpose of obtaining legal advice are privileged, and cannot be revealed without the client's consent. What justification is there for this rule? In many jurisdictions, although not all, there is a privilege for

complete free admitting everything

statements made by a patient to a medical doctor for purposes of receiving treatment. There are similar privileges for confidential statements made by one spouse to another and by a parishioner to his clergyman. Are all of these privileges justifiable? Should privileges be extended to cover confidential statements made to accountants, investment counselors, bankers, newsmen, and close relatives such as parents or children? [e]

What if the taxicab driver is called to the witness stand and asked whether or not he is a panderer? The law clearly provides that a witness need not answer any question that might tend to incriminate him of illegal activities. Note the significant difference between this type of privilege and that which protects confidential communications. In this context we are not merely prohibiting one person from revealing second-hand information received in confidence from another; instead, we are allowing an individual with direct, first-hand knowledge to remain silent. How can such a rule be justified? Note that the privilege against self-incrimination is not the same thing as the right of a defendant in a criminal case to refuse to take the witness stand. A litigant in a civil action cannot refuse to testify, even though the testimony will be detrimental to the party's interests, unless it can be shown that the testimony might lead to a criminal conviction.

6. RELIABILITY OF DOCUMENTARY EVIDENCE

Suppose that plaintiff, Patsy, in order to show the damages she has suffered, offers into evidence a letter, purportedly from the dean of a local law school, rejecting her application for admission on the ground that there is a serious question whether she is of good character. Before the letter will be admitted, Patsy must make some showing that the document is genuine. See Federal Rule of Evidence 901. This may be done in a number of ways: by calling the dean himself; by calling someone who can testify that the signature is, in fact, that of the dean; or by showing that the letter was in response to a letter sent to the dean. What reason is there for a rule requiring a preliminary showing of validity before the evidence is admitted? If the letter is admitted and the opposing party believes it to be a forgery, that party is free to introduce evidence to that effect, in order to convince the trier of fact to disregard the letter. Isn't the opposing party's right to challenge the letter a sufficient safeguard against fraudulent evidence?

What if Patsy attempts to introduce a copy of the dean's letter rather than the original? The so-called best-evidence rule requires that a party either furnish the original of a document or provide an explanation as to why the original is unavailable. The fact that the original is lost or destroyed is enough to permit the copy to be introduced but only if it can be authenticated as a true copy of a genuine original.

e. Many civil-law jurisdictions have extremely broad evidentiary privileges and render a number of groups of potential witnesses incompetent to testify. See generally Miller, *International Cooperation in Litigation Between the United States and Switzerland: Unilateral Procedural Accommodation in a Test Tube*, 49 Minn.L.Rev. 1069, 1092–93 (1965).

Note that analogous problems of authentication exist with regard to other types of nontestimonial evidence. Suppose, for example, that defendant wishes to introduce a motion picture allegedly taken of activities in the Hill Club. Defendant must call to the witness stand the photographer who took the pictures and the people who had custody of the film thereafter to testify that the pictures were not faked or altered prior to trial.

7. RELIABILITY OF ORAL TESTIMONY

a. Competency of Witnesses

What if defendant calls as a witness a four-year-old child to testify as to activities allegedly observed on the grounds of the Hill Club, which is adjacent to the child's home? What possible damages or risks do you see in permitting a small child to testify? Would it make any difference if the child were testifying on a less sensitive subject? How do the problems differ if the witness is a physically handicapped or mentally ill adult?

The law does not exclude the relevant testimony of any person who has the capacity to observe and remember the matters on which that person testifies, the ability to communicate this knowledge, and an understanding of the obligation to tell the truth. When any of these factors are in doubt, it is up to the trial judge, by preliminary examination of the witness, to determine whether the witness can meet these requirements.

b. Opinion

As a general proposition, a witness is not permitted to include opinions in his testimony. Thus a person would not be allowed to conclude, "From what I've seen of the Hill Club, the way people go in and out at all hours of the night, and the noise, in my opinion it's a house of prostitution." What is the reason for this rule? Is testimony of this type unreliable? As one might suspect, the line between fact and opinion hardly is clear cut. By way of example, is it improper for a witness to testify that he often sees plaintiff emerge from the Hill Club in a "drunken stupor"? Could the statement be framed in a different way so as to avoid any claim that it contained opinion? Is it helpful to the trier of fact if the witness is permitted to give such an opinion?

The major exception to the proscription against opinions involves the expert witness who is called for the express purpose of rendering an opinion. Why is the exception justified? What kind of opinions should the expert be permitted to give? If, for example, Patsy is examined by a gynecologist, undoubtedly she could testify as to whether in her opinion Patsy had ever engaged in acts of sexual intercourse. Could she go on to testify that Patsy had done so frequently? Could the doctor give an opinion as to whether Patsy was a prostitute? Should the court permit Patsy's psychiatrist to testify that she is psychologically incapable of sexual activity?

c. *Form of Examination*

Suppose defendant's attorney, in our hypothetical case, begins her examination of a witness with the following question: "Isn't it true that just three weeks ago, at 10 p.m., you entered the Hill Club, asked the desk clerk for a girl, paid $25, were directed to a small room containing a bed, waited for a short period until plaintiff in this case entered the room, and then engaged in an act of sexual intercourse with her?" This is referred to as a "leading question" and normally is improper for use on direct examination. Why? However, if the witness is the opposing party or any other witness who is hostile to the interests of the examining attorney's client, the attorney may then resort to leading questions. Furthermore, such questions universally are permitted on cross-examination. What justifications are there for these exceptions? Shouldn't the proper form of the question depend on the nature of the evidence sought to be elicited? For example, wouldn't the use of leading questions be appropriate and save a great deal of time in obtaining routine information such as the name, address, and occupation of the witness?

8. IMPEACHMENT

There are many ways by which an attorney can overcome unfavorable testimony. The lawyer may present new evidence to contradict what has been said, may cross-examine unfavorable witnesses and force them to change their original testimony, and, finally, may show that the unfavorable witnesses are unreliable and hence not to be believed.

Assume that Patsy's attorney is faced with the task of discrediting the taxicab driver's testimony that Patsy was a prostitute for whom he procured customers. Her attorney will be permitted to introduce into evidence a prior statement made to a detective by the driver that the latter had known Patsy all her life and that she was of high moral character. Note, however, that in most courts the statement may be used only to impugn the driver's credibility; it is normally considered improper to introduce it to prove the truth of the statement because this would violate the hearsay rule. Does this make any sense when the statement is introduced during cross-examination of the driver who is present to explain exactly what he meant by the prior statement? Should there be a special exception to the hearsay rule to cover this situation?

A witness' reliability also may be weakened by showing that the witness is biased. For example, Patsy's attorney would be permitted to introduce evidence showing that the taxicab driver had become extremely angry with her when she rejected his advances. Or the attorney might show that the driver was in the part-time employ of Dolly, our hypothetical defendant.

A final method of impeachment is through the use of character evidence. Basically there are three permissible methods of attacking a witness' character. First, in most, but not all, jurisdictions a witness may be asked questions on cross-examination regarding personal associations and history. The courts tend to keep tight control over such questioning, limiting it to important witnesses and to matters that have a direct

relationship to their reliability at the present time. Second, as has previously been pointed out, see pp. 868–69, supra, an attorney may bring out on cross-examination that the witness has previously been convicted of a serious crime, at least if the conviction was fairly recent. Finally, an attorney may impeach a witness by calling another person who will testify that he is aware of the witness' reputation for truth and veracity in the community in which the witness lives, and that it is bad. Is there any ground upon which this method of attack can be justified? Does application of such a rule make more sense in some communities than in others?

9. JURISDICTIONAL VARIATIONS

In attempting to evaluate the law of evidence several things should be remembered. First, the foregoing review of the basic rules of evidence is skeletal and far from complete. Second, every jurisdiction has its own evidence rules and there are marked differences among them, although serious efforts are being made to bring some degree of uniformity to the subject. See, e.g., Uniform Rules of Evidence. Finally, the law of evidence has been changing radically and rapidly in an effort to eliminate archaic rules based on assumptions shown to be erroneous by modern behavioral and scientific study.

One final point should be noted. The Federal Rules of Evidence, a uniform set of regulations for the federal courts, became effective on January 2, 1975. The Rules were formally approved by Congress after a tortuous process of drafting. One major question that arose during their preparation was the extent to which these uniform Rules should apply in diversity cases or in other cases to issues decided under state law. See generally Degnan, *The Law of Federal Evidence Reform,* 76 Harv.L.Rev. 275, 287 (1962). In general it was decided that the Rules should apply to all issues and all actions except that as to matters of privilege and the competency of witnesses, when the matter concerns "a claim or defense as to which State law supplies the rule of decision," such questions of privilege and competency "shall be determined in accordance with State law." Federal Rules of Evidence 501, 601. Is there any justification for applying state evidentiary rules regarding privilege and competency and ignoring state practices as to hearsay, relevancy, and prejudice?

SECTION D. THE BURDEN OF PROOF: PRODUCTION AND PERSUASION

KNOWLES v. GILCHRIST CO.

Supreme Judicial Court of Massachusetts, 1972.
362 Mass. 642, 289 N.E.2d 879.

TAURO, CHIEF JUSTICE. The plaintiff (bailor) in an action of tort and contract in the Municipal Court against the defendant Gilchrist Company (bailee) seeks to recover damages for loss of certain articles of furniture in the bailee's possession pursuant to an agreement by the bailee to reupholster and return furniture to the bailor. [It was agreed that the furniture was destroyed by fire while in the bailee's possession.] There was a finding for the bailor in the amount of $800. * * * The Appellate Division vacated the Municipal Court's finding for the bailor and ordered judgment for the bailee. The bailor appeals.

The Appellate Division rested its decision on the basis of our cases which have held that the bailor has the burden of proving by a fair preponderance of the evidence that the bailee broke the bailment contract by its negligence in caring for the goods. * * * Well established case authority in Massachusetts and in most other States has followed this rule despite the obvious problems in situations where, because the property was in the bailee's exclusive possession, the bailor has no knowledge of or access to the facts concerning its loss.

Originally, Massachusetts case law made a distinction between tort and contract actions in deciding where the burden of proof would be fixed. In Cass v. Boston & Lowell R.R., 14 Allen 448 (1867), the plaintiff bailor brought a contract action against a warehouseman to recover for the bailee's failure to return the goods entrusted to it. This court held that when the bailor alleged and proved that the bailee had received the bailor's property and failed to deliver it upon timely demand, the bailee had the burden of proving that the goods had been lost without any fault on its part. The pleadings were held to be decisive on the issue of burden of proof. * * * Since the bailor had sued in *contract,* he had not alleged that the bailee was negligent. The *Cass* opinion placed the burden of proving the absence of negligence on the party who alleged it in its pleadings, namely, the bailee. This line of reasoning led the court to conclude that the burden of proof lies on the *bailor* in tort actions because the bailor must allege negligence in his pleadings. * * *

Thus, the majority opinion in the *Cass* case created a rule predicated on the art of pleading. * * *

* * *

Chief Justice Bigelow in his dissenting opinion in the *Cass* case also relied on a pleading rationale to allocate the burden of proof. His position was that ultimately the plaintiff bailor had to show a want of due care on the bailee's part to prove that the bailee breached his contract. * * *

Just twenty years later, this court adopted Chief Justice Bigelow's dissent as the law and in effect overruled the *Cass* case in [Willet v. Rich, 142 Mass. 356, 7 N.E. 776 (1886)]. * * * Thus, the *Willett* case established the rule, which is followed by most other jurisdictions, that the bailor has the burden of proving the bailee's negligence, regardless of whether the bailor's action sounds in tort or contract.

* * * Under this rule, since the bailor has the burden of proving the bailee's negligence, the bailee can simply plead impossibility as a defence, introduce evidence of a fire and rest as the bailee did in the instant case, even though the bailee may be the only party with access to the facts surrounding the loss.

In response to the obvious inequities and difficulties created by fixing the burden of proof on the bailor, recent decisions by State and Federal courts have held that the bailor can establish an inference or presumption of negligence merely by showing a bailment and failure to deliver by the bailee. Once the bailor makes this showing, the burden of *production* shifts to the bailee to go forward with evidence to rebut this presumption. * * * [However the burden of *persuasion* does not shift, therefore, if the bailee does go forward with evidence enough to raise doubts as to the validity of the inference of negligence on the bailee's part, the bailor must convince the trier of fact that the bailee was negligent.]

* * * [I]t appears that our cases have adopted the rule followed by a majority of the States that the bailee may satisfy his burden of production and rebut the presumption of negligence arising from his failure to return goods entrusted to him by proof of loss arising from a fire or other extraordinary event. * * *

The irrational result of this holding is that evidence of a fire is sufficient evidence of due care on the bailee's part to overcome the bailor's inference of negligence. Moreover, it leaves the bailor in the same position of having to produce evidence of the bailee's negligence although it may have no access to such information. The imposition of such a minimal burden of production on the bailee defeats the rule's basic purpose because the bailee can simply note that a theft or a fire of unknown origin made delivery of the bailed goods impossible and rest his case.

Realizing the obvious defects of such a rule, many State courts have recently imposed a more stringent burden of production on the bailee. The Alaska Supreme Court's decision in Harris v. Deveau, 385 P.2d 283, reflects this modern trend in bailment cases. * * * "[T]he bailee must not only prove that the damage or loss occurred by reason of theft, fire or other cause beyond his control, but produce further evidence in explanation of the actual damage or loss which would indicate exercise of care on his part in the protection of the property. * * * He should disclose, to the extent that he is able, the manner in which the damage or loss occurred, the facts and circumstances attending such damage or loss and the precautions taken to prevent it." * * *

However, we feel that defining the bailee's burden of production in this manner resolves only in part the problem created by fixing the ultimate risk of nonpersuasion (or burden of proof by a fair preponderance of the evidence) on the bailor. A stringent burden of production on the bailee mitigates but does not cure the evil of imposing the burden of proof (or persuasion) on the party who has little or no access to the facts surrounding the loss or damage of the bailed property. * * * This essential unfairness is even more pronounced in cases, like the instant one, where the bailor is a consumer. The consumer's unfamiliarity with the bailee's trade practices and commercial customs *aggravates* the difficult task that all bailors face in trying to rebut the inference of due care which the bailee has created by selecting the most favorable facts from all the information exclusively available to him.

* * * As we have already noted, this court has justified placing the burden of proof on the bailor by relying on a pleading rationale. * * * The obvious problem with this rule is that it begs the essential question,

which party should bear the *ultimate* burden of proving that the bailee was negligent. Until the burden of proof has been allocated to one of the parties, the fact of negligence is no less essential to one side than the other. Moreover, the fact that the bailor may have to affirmatively plead negligence does not justify placing the burden of proof on him. * * *

Since negligence is the determinative issue in the ordinary bailment case, the burden of proof should rest on the party who is in the best position to determine what actually happened to the goods and what safeguards existed both before and after the precipitating event that destroyed or damaged the bailed property. Clearly, the bailee has greater access to the information needed to show negligence or due care.

* * *

Therefore, we hold that once the bailor proves delivery of the property to the bailee in good condition and the failure to redeliver upon timely demand, the burden of proof is irrevocably fixed upon the bailee to prove by a fair preponderance of the evidence that he has exercised due care to prevent the property's loss or destruction. * * *

The order of the Appellate Division is reversed. * * *

[Opinion of BRAUCHER, J., dissenting in part, is omitted.]

Notes and Questions

1. In a jury case, who decides whether the burden of production on a particular issue has been met, the judge or the jury? What happens if a party fails to meet the burden of production?

2. Under the decision in *Knowles,* will a plaintiff in a similar case have any burden of production? Will plaintiff have the burden of persuasion on any issue? Describe the course of the trial in terms of the burden of production. What would have been the course of the trial before *Knowles*? What will the jury be told about the burden of persuasion after *Knowles*?

3. In civil cases, the burden of persuasion usually is defined as requiring proof by a preponderance of the evidence, with the additional caution that this does not mean simply the volume of the evidence or the number of witnesses. In some civil cases, particularly those involving allegations of fraud, many courts impose a heavier burden of persuasion—"proof by clear and convincing evidence." In criminal cases, "proof beyond a reasonable doubt" is constitutionally required. In re Winship, 397 U.S. 358, 90 S.Ct. 1068, 25 L.Ed.2d 368 (1970). See generally McCormick, *Evidence* §§ 339–41 (3d ed.1984). Can the jury's degree of certainty on a particular point meaningfully be divided into these three categories?

SECTION E.   INSTRUCTIONS AND VERDICTS

1.   INSTRUCTIONS

———

Read Federal Rule of Civil Procedure 51 and the accompanying materials in the Supplement.

———

GRIFFIN v. CITY OF CINCINNATI

Court of Appeals of Ohio, 1952.
92 Ohio App. 492, 111 N.E.2d 31.

PER CURIAM. On March 3, 1949, at about 7 p.m., the plaintiff, a man 37 years of age and in good health, approached the intersection of Sycamore and Eighth streets in the city of Cincinnati, going eastwardly on the north sidewalk of Eighth street. He was walking at a "normal pace," and, as he neared the intersection, he did not glance down at the sidewalk, but constantly looked straight ahead. * * * The sidewalk was constructed of concrete blocks and on a line with the north building line of Eighth street and about the middle of the Sycamore street sidewalk an offset of about one and one-half inches existed and a small section of one of the blocks was missing, making a shallow depression of undetermined depth. The plaintiff did not see either the offset or the depression before he fell while in the act of turning to go north on Sycamore street. It was either the offset or the depression, or both, that caused him to fall. His foot caught on this defect in the sidewalk.

* * * The jury found for the plaintiff. * * *

It is urged * * * that the court erred in the giving and refusal of certain special charges.

The court refused to give this special charge, requested by defendant:

If you find from the evidence that the plaintiff was guilty of negligence in failing to look where he walked at the time and place as alleged in the petition filed herein, and if you find that such negligence was a proximate cause of and directly contributed in the slightest degree to the accident, you must bring a verdict for the defendant, the city of Cincinnati, even though you find that the defendant was guilty of a violation of its statutory duty.

It is urged in support of this refusal that the special charge assumed that the plaintiff failed to look where he was walking. Authorities are cited to sustain this position holding that a charge which assumes a controverted fact is an invasion of the province of the jury and is erroneous. There is no doubt about that rule. Its inapplicability here results from the fact that the fact assumed was not controverted. The plaintiff testified that he did not look. He, of course, was bound by his own testimony. The only issuable fact left, therefore, was whether such failure constituted negligence * * *. We hold that the special charge was a correct statement of the law applicable to the controverted facts and that the court erred in refusing to give it.

But it is urged that no prejudice resulted because of the giving of other special charges at defendant's request. We have examined the special charges relating to the duty of the plaintiff and find that none of them submitted to the jury the specific issue of whether the admitted failure to devote at least some of his sense of vision to the sidewalk upon which he was walking was a failure to exercise reasonable care—whether it was negligence.

We, therefore, conclude that the failure to give the special charge was prejudicial.

At the plaintiff's request, the court gave this special charge:

> The court charges you that, if you find that the sidewalk in question was not in a state of repair at the time plaintiff fell and that this condition existed for a time sufficient to have given the city of Cincinnati constructive notice of its condition, then it was the duty of the city to notify the abutting property owner to repair it and if said property owner failed to do so within a reasonable time it was the duty of the city to make the repairs and to recover the costs thereof from such property owner.

The defendant excepted to the giving of this charge, and now assigns this as error.

The duty of the abutting property owner was entirely irrelevant to the issues in this case between a pedestrian on the sidewalk and the municipality. Whether it was the duty of the municipality to notify the property owner was immaterial. This irrelevant and immaterial issue was coupled with a positive vice in the charge that gave the municipality more than a reasonable time to repair the sidewalk. It permitted the municipality to notify the property owner to repair and then wait a reasonable time for him to repair the defect before proceeding to perform its duty. This gave the municipality more than a reasonable time after notice of the existence of the defect. While part of the charge was favorable to defendant and part unfavorable, we are of the opinion it was prejudicial error to give this charge.

* * *

Judgment reversed.

Ross, Judge (dissenting). * * *

Here is a cleverly designed pitfall for the jury. It is true that the trained legal mind is able to dissect the language employed and arrive at the conclusion that the jury is not told that failure to look is negligence as a matter of law, but the average layman would so construe such instruction and the court properly refused it. It is more than apparent that the attention of the jury was intended to be directed to the words, "guilty of negligence in failing to look where he walked."

Technically, and from a pure academic standpoint, the words, "if you find from the evidence," may be said to stabilize the charge as correct. In this particular case, where as stated in the opinion of the majority "the plaintiff's attention was more dispersed while turning than it would have been while walking in a straight line with his view unobstructed in any way by the abutting building," the jury should be presented an instruction which in no way may be construed to state that failure to look directly at a defect in the sidewalk is negligence, and that is exactly what a jury of laymen would infer from the charge refused, although that is not what is actually stated.

I think that this special instruction should receive the definite disapproval of the court, and that in no case should it be given. It contains a correct statement of law which will always mislead the jury into a misapprehension of what is the applicable rule.

* * *

Now as to the special instruction given by the court, quoted in the majority opinion, requested by the plaintiff, and objected to by the defendant: The "vice" in this instruction * * * is one of which the plaintiff might have complained, but certainly the city may not complain * * *.

The instruction did deal with matters extraneous to the issues involved. But was the jury misled to the prejudice of the defendant? * * *

I think the judgment should be affirmed.

Notes and Questions

1. Assuming that the dissenting judge in *Griffin* is correct in deciding that the instruction refused below was improper in form (and that the other challenged instruction was not prejudicial), does it necessarily follow that the judgment below should be affirmed? To what extent would Federal Rule 51 bear on the answer if the case had been brought in a federal court? Reread pp. 41–43, supra. See TURNER CONSTRUCTION CO. v. HOULIHAN, 240 F.2d 435, 439 (1st Cir.1957):

> The first sentence of Rule 51 permits, but does not require, the filing of requests for instructions. If none are filed, the court must nevertheless charge the jury on the broad general fundamental rules of law applicable to the principal issues of fact in the case. * * * If, however, counsel want the jury instructed specifically on particular matters, requests for such instructions must be filed.

Compare OUILLE v. SALIBA, 246 Miss. 365, 368–69, 149 So.2d 468, 469 (1963), stating the law in Mississippi: "Appellant did not request any instructions in accordance with the counterclaim * * *. If appellant desired instructions on her counterclaim, she should have requested them. The judge cannot instruct the jury on his own motion."

Why shouldn't there be a positive duty on the court to give proper instructions, regardless of the aid of counsel? In North Carolina it is not enough that the judge charge generally on the issues involved; even in the absence of a request therefor the court must go further and relate the law to the evidence that has been introduced. Horne v. Wall, 27 N.C.App. 373, 219 S.E.2d 288 (1975). What dangers do you see in such a rule?

2. Suppose defendant in *Griffin* had failed to challenge the alleged erroneous instruction. Would it be more sensible to be lenient with an attorney who fails to request a vital instruction than with one who sits back and permits an erroneous instruction to be given? Compare Turner Constr. Co. v. Houlihan, quoted in Note 1, supra, with Crespo v. Fireman's Fund Indem. Co., 318 F.2d 174 (9th Cir.1963) (even "plain error" will not justify an attack on an instruction not challenged at trial). See WIRTZ v. INTERNATIONAL HARVESTER CO., 331 F.2d 462 (5th Cir.), certiorari denied 379 U.S. 845, 85 S.Ct. 36, 13 L.Ed.2d 50 (1964), in which the court reversed a judgment on the ground that a vital instruction, not challenged below, clearly was

incorrect. The appellate court stated that *both* parties have a duty to ensure that important instructions are properly phrased, not just the party who would be injured if the improper instruction were to be given.

3. Why shouldn't instructions be the sole responsibility of the trial judge? Federal Rule 51 and its state counterparts usually are justified on the ground that a court should be told of its errors and omissions in time to correct them in order to avoid the costs and delays of a new trial. Is there some other reason? Note that Rule 51 requires the trial judge to inform the lawyers prior to their closing arguments as to what instructions will be given. What purpose does this serve?

Doesn't rigid application of rules requiring a party to object to erroneous or omitted instructions simply result in decisions, erroneous as a matter of law, that cannot successfully be appealed? Are such rules consistent with provisions allowing a complaint to be challenged at any time for failure to state a claim, or with cases setting aside default judgments based on such complaints, see Notes 6 and 7, pp. 859–60, supra?

4. Rule 51 spells out the manner and timing in which requests for instructions and objections are to be made. Why should requests for instructions be made in writing? Note that objections are to be made before the jury retires but out of its hearing. What purposes do these provisions serve?

Formal objections are not required under most modern procedural rules. See, e.g., Federal Rule 46. All that is necessary is that the complaining party make clear the nature of the error. It is not sufficient, however, for a party simply to make a general objection to an instruction without pointing out the specific defect. See RATAY v. LINCOLN NAT. LIFE INS. CO., 378 F.2d 209 (3d Cir.1967), in which the court admonishes trial judges who have permitted and even encouraged use of general objections to the instructions. Why should an appellate court be so concerned about the format of an objection? Is there any argument in favor of permitting general objections?

5. What if a trial court erroneously gives or refuses an instruction? Does this necessarily mean that the decision must be reversed? Suppose, for example, in the *Griffin* case the trial court had given an instruction, correct in form and substance, regarding the general duty of plaintiffs with respect to contributory negligence. Should this render harmless the failure to give a requested instruction relating directly to the evidence in the case? Or suppose the issue of whether plaintiff had looked where he was walking had been in dispute. Does the *Griffin* decision make it clear that the trial court would then have been reversed had it given the special instruction? Would it make any difference if prior to giving such a special instruction, the trial court had charged the jury that one of the issues to be decided was whether plaintiff had looked where he was going and properly had placed the burden of proof of that issue on plaintiff? See Peterson v. Brune, 273 S.W.2d 278, 284 (Mo.1954) (incorrect instruction harmless when all instructions, read together, are not misleading).

6. Lawyers and judges always will be seriously concerned with the precise wording of jury instructions as long as technical inaccuracies may lead to reversal on appeal. The irony is that many jurors do not even understand the basic aspects of the instructions, let alone the fine distinctions that often are drawn. Part of the problem is due to the manner in which the instructions are given. All too often the judge reads the instructions in disjointed

fashion in a nearly inaudible monotone using technical terms without any regard for the fact that the statements are incomprehensible. Much of this evil could be corrected if trial judges made an effort to improve the way in which they deliver the charge. But even then, it is a great deal to ask of a juror, even in a simple case, to grasp the fine points of the applicable law. As already discussed, see Notes 4 and 5, pp. 917–18, supra, the value of the jury may lie in the fact that it does not, and is not expected to, apply the law in strict fashion. If this is true, would it not be possible to eliminate instructions or at least limit them to a short generalized statement? Is preservation of appellate review of the technical wording of jury instructions necessary to the proper development and growth of the law? See Charrow & Charrow, *Making Legal Language Understandable: A Psycholinguistic Study of Jury Instruction,* 79 Colum.L.Rev. 1306 (1979); Farrell, *Communication in the Courtroom: Jury Instructions,* 85 W.Va.L.Rev. 5 (1982).

7. In recent years there has been a strong tendency for courts and lawyers to resort to the use of standard or "pattern" instructions. In a number of jurisdictions such instructions have been developed by courts and judges to cover a wide variety of common legal issues. What advantages and disadvantages are there to the use of standard instructions? Should use of such instructions be required? See Ill.Stat.Ann. ch. 110A, § 239.

a. Commenting on the Evidence by Judges

NUNLEY v. PETTWAY OIL CO., 346 F.2d 95 (6th Cir.1965). Plaintiff brought suit for personal injuries received when a truck fell off a grease rack in a gas station. The jury found plaintiff to be a licensee rather than an invitee at the time of the accident, and, applying the applicable law, the court entered judgment for defendant. On appeal plaintiff contended that the court had improperly commented to the jury on the licensee-invitee question. During their initial deliberations the jurors were unable to agree on this issue, whereupon the judge called them into the courtroom and urged them to try to arrive at a decision as follows:

Now, the jury of course is the sole and exclusive judge of the facts in this lawsuit. It is appropriate that the Court in an effort to be possibly of some help to the jury may comment upon the evidence. I refrain from doing that and have refrained until this time from doing it in this case. However, in an effort to be of some possible assistance to you I think that I should under these circumstances make some comment upon the evidence upon this issue of invitee-licensee. I want you to understand, however, that in making these comments that you are not in any degree, in any respect, obligated to receive or accept or agree with what I may say. It is your duty to accept what I say with regard to the law in the case, but it is not your duty to accept any comment that I may make or any evaluation that I may make or conclusion that I might reach on the evidence. That is solely your responsibility and solely your duty. *But, with that understanding, it is the opinion of the Court in this case that, from all the evidence upon the issue of invitee or licensee, that the evidence will establish that at the time and place of the accident the plaintiff was a licensee and not an invitee.* Now, I say that just for the purpose, as I say, of possibly being of some help to you, but I want you to understand that in making that comment you are not obligated whatsoever to accept that comment as your comment or as your opinion in the case, because it is your job and your responsibility to resolve that issue. I only make that with the thought and the hope that it may be of some possible assistance to you. At any rate, I want to ask you once again to retire and consider your verdict and see if you cannot come to some agreement, some verdict that will reflect the views of all of the jurors. * * *

Id. at 98. The Court of Appeals reversed, stating:

We recognize that the right of a District Judge to comment on the evidence is firmly established in the federal system. See Quercia v. United States, 289 U.S. 466, 53 S.Ct. 698, 77 L.Ed. 1321 (1933) * * *.

Nonetheless, we believe that under the circumstances enumerated, the trial judge's opinion on the licensee-invitee issue was an opinion on an ultimate fact question peculiarly for jury consideration and amounted to an instructed verdict as to defendant Pettway Oil Company.

In Quercia v. United States, supra, Chief Justice Hughes commented:

This privilege of the judge to comment on the facts has its inherent limitations. His discretion is not arbitrary and uncontrolled, but judicial, to be exercised in conformity with the standards governing the judicial office. In commenting upon testimony he may not assume the role of a witness. He may analyze and dissect the evidence, but he may not either distort it or add to it. His privilege of comment in order to give appropriate assistance to the jury is too important to be left without safeguards against abuses.

* * *

Nor do we think that the error was cured by the statement of the trial judge that his opinion of the evidence was not binding on the jury and that if they did not agree with it they should find the defendant not guilty. His definite and concrete assertion of fact, which he had made with all the persuasiveness of judicial utterance, as to the basis of his opinion, was not withdrawn. * * *

Id. at 98–99.

Notes and Questions

1. In *Quercia,* a *criminal* case, the Supreme Court reversed a conviction because the following charge was given to the jury:

And now I am going to tell you what I think of the defendant's testimony. You may have noticed, Mr. Foreman and gentlemen, that he wiped his hands during his testimony. It is rather a curious thing, but that is almost always an indication of lying. Why it should be so we don't know, but that is the fact. I think that every single word that man said, except when he agreed with the Government's testimony, was a lie.

Now, that opinion is an opinion of evidence and is not binding on you, and if you don't agree with it, it is your duty to find him not guilty.

Is the court in *Nunley* justified in relying on *Quercia*? Aren't there substantial differences between the two cases?

2. In light of the decision in *Nunley,* what is the meaning of the court's statement: "We recognize that the right of a District Judge to comment on

the evidence is firmly established in the federal system'"? The trial judge's common-law power to comment on the evidence, as retained in a minority of jurisdictions, includes the power to express an opinion regarding both evidentiary issues and the credibility of witnesses.

Those federal decisions that appear to limit the common-law practice are in line with limitations in a majority of states, which take two basic forms: (1) the trial judge is confined to a statement of the applicable law and deprived of power even to mention the evidence (see Colorado Rule of Civil Procedure 51), or (2) the court is limited to presenting an impartial summary of the evidence (see, e.g., Belk v. Schweizer, 268 N.C. 50, 149 S.E.2d 565 (1966)). It has been suggested that the latter approach is not feasible. Wright, *Instructions to the Jury: Summary Without Comment,* 1954 Wash.U.L.Q. 177. Why? *Former evidence*

3. The *Nunley* opinion emphasizes that the judge's comment was on an "ultimate fact question." The Fifth Circuit holds that comments are proper on "evidentiary matters," but not on "ultimate factual issues." Travelers Ins. Co. v. Ryan, 416 F.2d 362, 364 (5th Cir.1969). Is there any sound basis for this distinction?   *What inferences drawn*

4. What are the arguments for and against allowance of a broad judicial power to comment on the evidence? Professor Wigmore passionately advocated restoration of the broad power, and severely criticized the federal approach exemplified in *Quercia.*   9 Wigmore on Evidence § 2551, at 669–70 n. 7 (Chadbourn rev. 1981). See also Weinstein, *The Power and Duty of Federal Judges to Marshall and Comment on Evidence in Jury Trials and Some Suggestions on Charging Juries,* 118 F.R.D. 161 (1988) (favoring permissiveness with respect to judicial comments).

5. Jurisdiction in the *Nunley* case was based on diversity of citizenship. Suppose that the law of the state permits the trial judge to express an opinion as to whether the evidence is sufficient to establish the ultimate facts in the case. To what extent is the federal court bound by the state practice? See Byrd v. Blue Ridge Rural Elec. Coop., Inc., p. 359, supra.

b. Permitting Instructions to Be Taken Into the Jury Room

A substantial number of state and federal courts either require or permit written instructions to be taken into the jury room. See California Law Revision Commission, *Recommendation and Study Relating to Taking Instructions into the Jury Room,* pp. C–15–C–17 (1956) (Tabular Summary of the Law of Other States). The Study speaks about the merits of these provisions as follows:

> Much can be said, it is believed, for giving a copy of the instructions to the jury, either as a matter of routine or upon the request of a party or of the jury. The instructions are intended to guide the jury's deliberations. Yet, even in a relatively simple case they are usually lengthy and complex. It is hardly reasonable to suppose that the jury, composed as it is of persons unfamiliar with either law or legal language and having heard the instructions but once as given orally by the court, will be able to remember them in detail as it ponders the matters committed to it for decision.

Are there any effective arguments against allowing the jury to possess the written instructions during its deliberations? What effect does the possession of written instructions have on the focus of the jury's discussion? Does possession of written instructions tend to affect the amount of influence some jurors have on the rest of the panel?

In many jurisdictions jurors are permitted and even encouraged to take notes throughout the trial for use during the deliberations. See State ex rel. Dep't of Highways v. Lehman, 462 P.2d 649 (Okl.1969). Does this obviate any need for written instructions? Is there any reason why note-taking should not be permitted?

Should the complexity of the litigation or the length of the trial affect the rules on taking written instructions or notes into the jury room? See Burger, *Can Juries Cope With Multi-Month Trials?*, 3 Am.J. of Trial Advocacy 448 (1980).

2. THE FORM OF THE VERDICT

Read Federal Rule of Civil Procedure 49 in the Supplement.

The traditional form of the jury decision, used almost exclusively in the great majority of courts, is the general verdict. No matter how complex the case and how long and involved the instructions were, all a jury need do to render a general verdict is to announce which party wins, and, if it is plaintiff, the amount that should be recovered. This type of verdict has two major deficiencies. First, there is no way to tell how the jurors decided specific issues, which, in turn, can result in the unnecessary retrial of the entire case. For example, suppose a defendant raises a number of defenses, any one of which, if established, would require a verdict for defendant. Then the court, in an otherwise faultless charge, erroneously instructs the jury on one of these defenses in a manner detrimental to plaintiff, after which the jury finds for defendant. On appeal the court will be required to reverse since it has no way of telling whether the verdict was based solely on the tainted defense. If, however, the jury had been required to render a verdict on each one of the defenses, the court would know at once the bases of the jury decision and whether the error in the instruction was harmless. See, e.g., Castilleja v. Southern Pacific Co., 445 F.2d 183 (5th Cir.1971). The second major drawback to the general verdict is the fact that there is no way of knowing whether the jury actually focused its attention on every major aspect of the case as required by the instructions, or whether it ignored the instructions altogether and rendered a decision based solely on sentiment, public opinion, bias, or similar emotion.

To avoid these objections, many writers have advocated use of the special verdict, which requires the jury to answer a series of questions regarding each facet of the case. For example, in Frank, *Courts on Trial* 141–42 (1950), the following argument is advanced:

A special verdict would seem to do away with some of the most objectionable features of trial by jury. The division of functions between jury and judge is apparently assured, the one attending to the facts alone, the other to the legal rules alone. The jury seems, by this device, to be shorn of its power to ignore the rules or to make rules to suit itself. As one court said, special verdicts "dispel * * * the darkness visible of general verdicts." The finding of facts, says Sunderland, "is much better done by means of the special verdict. Every advantage which the jury is popularly supposed to have over the [judge] as a trier of facts is retained, with the very great additional advantage that the analysis and separation of the facts in the case which the court and the attorney must necessarily effect in employing the special verdict, materially reduce the chance of error. It is easy to make mistakes in dealing at large with aggregates of facts. The special verdict compels detailed consideration. But above all it enables the public, the parties and the court to see what the jury has really done * * *. The morale of the jury also is aided by throwing off the cloak of secrecy, for only through publicity is there developed the proper feeling of responsibility in public servants. So far, then, as the facts go, they can be much more effectively, conveniently, and usefully tried by abandoning the general verdict * * *." [Sunderland, *Verdicts General and Special*, 29 Yale L.J. 253 (1920).]

* * * It is suggested, too, that a special verdict "searches the conscience of the individual juror, as a general verdict does not," because "such are the contradictions in human nature that many a man who will unite in a general verdict for a large and unwarranted sum of money will shrink from a specific finding against his judgment of right and wrong." [Clementson, *Special Verdicts and Special Findings by Juries* 15 (1905).]

This view has been strongly opposed on the ground that the special verdict improperly subverts the fundamental nature of the jury decision. See 5 Moore, *Federal Practice* ¶ 49.05, at 2217 (2d ed.):

* * * [T]he general verdict, at times, achieves a triumph of justice over law. The jury is not, nor should it become, a scientific fact finding body. Its chief value is that it applies the "law," oftentimes a body of technical and refined theoretical principles and sometimes edged with harshness, in an earthy fashion that comports with "justice" as conceived by the masses, for whom after all the law is mainly meant to serve. The general verdict is the answer from the man in the street. If on occasion the trial judge thinks the jury should be quizzed about its overall judgment as evidenced by the general verdict, this can be done by interrogatories accompanying the general verdict. But if there is sufficient evidence to get by a motion for directed verdict, then the problem is usually best solved by an overall, common judgment of the jurors—the general verdict.

And see the statement of Justices Black and Douglas issued in connection with the 1963 amendment of Rule 49, 374 U.S. 865, 867–68, 83 S.Ct. 43, 44–45 (1963):

* * * Rule 49 should be repealed. * * * Such devices are used to impair or wholly take away the power of a jury to render a general verdict. One of the ancient, fundamental reasons for having general jury verdicts was to preserve the right of trial by jury as an indispensable part of a free government. Many of the most famous constitutional controversies in England revolved around litigants' insistence, particularly in seditious libel cases, that a jury had the right to render a general verdict without being compelled to return a number of subsidiary findings to support its general verdict. Some English jurors had to go to jail because they insisted upon

their right to render general verdicts over the repeated commands of tyrannical judges not to do so. Rule 49 is but another means utilized by courts to weaken the constitutional power of juries and to vest judges with more power to decide cases according to their own judgments.

See also 9 Wright & Miller, *Federal Practice and Procedure: Civil* § 2505 (1971).

A third, intermediate approach is the general verdict with answers to interrogatories, which permits the jury to give a general verdict but also requires it to provide answers to a series of questions that usually are less extensive than those used with the special verdict. Although this form alleviates some of the concerns about the general verdict, problems arise when the answers to the interrogatories are inconsistent with the general verdict or with each other.

NOLLENBERGER v. UNITED AIR LINES, INC.
United States District Court, Southern District of California, 1963.
216 F.Supp. 734.
Vacated 335 F.2d 379 (9th Cir.).
Certiorari dismissed 379 U.S. 951, 85 S.Ct. 452, 13 L.Ed.2d 549 (1964).

HALL, CHIEF JUDGE. [This is a wrongful-death action in which the jury, pursuant to Rule 49(b), rendered a general verdict accompanied by interrogatories. The plaintiffs allege that the answers to the interrogatories are inconsistent with the general verdict. They request that the court either submit additional interrogatories to the jury, or calculate the verdict on the basis of the answers to the questions given, or grant a new trial.]

* * *

The first task of the Court is to determine whether or not the Findings of Fact in the answers, given by the jury to the special interrogatories, are consistent with each other and whether one or more, if consistent with each other, are inconsistent with the general verdict fixing the total sum of damages to the plaintiffs resulting from the death of the decedent. And in doing so, Gallick v. Baltimore & Ohio R.R. Co., 372 U.S. 108, 83 S.Ct. 659, 9 L.Ed.2d 618 (1963), "it is the duty of the courts to attempt to harmonize the answers, if it is possible under a fair reading of them * * *."

The text of the special verdict on damages in the Nollenberger case is as follows:

We, the Jury in the above entitled case, unanimously find as follows:

QUESTIONS	ANSWERS
1. Which one of the following named persons, viz.: William Edward Nollenberger, 45 years of age on April 21, 1958; Catherine B. Nollenberger, his widow, age 47 on April 21, 1958; William Edward Nollenberger, Jr., son, age 20 on April 21, 1958; Lawrence P. Nollenberger, son, age 11 on April 21, 1958; had the shortest life expectancy?	 Wm. E. Nollenberger (Name)

QUESTIONS	ANSWERS

2. How many years was that life expectancy on April 21, 1958?

25
(Total number of years)

3. How many years was decedent's work and earning expectancy from and after April 21, 1958?

15 yrs
(Total number of years)

4. From and after April 21, 1958, what total sum of money do you find the decedent would have earned during the period of his work and earning expectancy stated in your answer to No. 3 above?

$235,210
(Total)

5. From and after the end of his work and earning expectancy, and during the remainder of his life, if any such remained, what total sum of money do you find decedent would have received as a result of his government employment?

$100,200
(Total sum)

6. What is the total reasonable value of services susceptible of being furnished by others which you find it was reasonably probable that decedent would have provided under my instructions to you to the plaintiffs during his lifetime?

$25,000
(Total value)

7. What percentage of his annual earnings, had he lived, from and after April 21, 1958, would have been used by decedent for his own personal expenses which were eliminated by his death?

25%
(Percentage of annual earnings)

8. What percentage of his income would be paid as annual income tax had he lived after April 21, 1958?

15%

9. What percentage of the income from the award will be paid by plaintiffs as income tax?

11%

10. In determining the present reasonable value of services as defined in No. 6 above, what annual rate of inflation, if any, do you find should be allowed?

1%

QUESTIONS	ANSWERS

11. What discount rate should be applied in arriving at the total sum of general damages?

4%
(Discount rate)

12. What sum of money do you find plaintiffs' general damages to be which you assess against Defendant United Air Lines?

$114,655.00

DATED: At Los Angeles, California, January 16, 1963.

S/ Burford A. Reynold
Foreman"

The answers to the Special Interrogatories No. 1 to No. 11 are plainly consistent with each other and are amply supported by the evidence.

But, in repeated efforts to "harmonize" and "reconcile" the answers to the 11 special interrogatories with the general verdict of $114,655.00, I have been unable to do so. And hence I must and do conclude that they are not harmonious or reconcilable.

While Rule 49(b) * * * under such circumstances permits, as one of three alternatives, the Court to re-submit the matter to the jury for further consideration, the plaintiffs desire the Court to go further and to submit additional interrogatories * * *. [H]ad it been the intention to permit *additional interrogatories* to be submitted *after* the general verdict and answers to the special interrogatories submitted with the verdict, the rule would have so provided, and the rule would not have contained the restrictive language of the second sentence of Rule 49(b) that the Court " * * * shall direct the jury both to make written answers and to render a general verdict," or the language in the fourth sentence of Rule 49(b) (applicable here) that the Court, as one alternative, " * * * may return the jury for *further consideration of its answers and verdict.*"

It could be argued from the portion of the rule last quoted that if that procedure were followed the jury could change both its answers and general verdict, or only the answers and not the general verdict. * * * That such action by the jury was not intended by the Rule is evidenced from the citation in the note to Rule 49 by the Advisory Committee of the case of Victor-American Fuel Co. v. Peccarich (C.C.A.1913) 209 F. 568, cert. den. 232 U.S. 727, 34 S.Ct. 603, 58 L.Ed. 817. In that case the Court stated, at page 571: " * * * these special findings must control when they clearly compel a different judgment from that which would follow the general verdict" * * *.

I conclude (1) that the findings of fact of the jury in answer to special interrogatories control over the general verdict; (2) that it is not within the power of the court under F.R.Civ.P. 49(b) to submit additional interrogatories after the jury has returned its verdict answering special interrogatories and at the same time returned a general verdict; (3) that in * * * Nollenberger * * * the answers to the special interrogatories are consistent with each other and inconsistent with and cannot be reconciled or harmonized with the general verdict; (4) that before granting a new trial, it is the duty of the Court to make calculations from the special interrogatories, and enter a judgment thereon. Which latter, I shall now do.

[The court then calculated the damages at $171,702.00 and entered judgment for that amount.]

* * *

Notes and Questions

1. In overturning the *Nollenberger* decision, the Court of Appeals held as follows (335 F.2d at 407–09):

The district court stated that after repeated efforts, by mathematical calculation, to harmonize and reconcile the answers to the eleven special interrogatories with the general verdict, no harmony resulted. This may be so. But nothing in the law compelled the jury to calculate its damage awards according to a fixed mathematical formula using only the factors contained in the eleven special findings. * * *

The jury was admonished to award damages in accordance with all the instructions of the court. No party specifies as error the giving of any of the instructions set forth in the margin.[43]

* * * Suffice it to say that the answers to the eleven special interrogatories do not exhaust all of the factors of damage included within the instructions, and therefore no square conflict exists between the answers and the general verdict. We are not called upon to consider either whether the jury should not have been permitted to consider one or more of the italicized factors or whether the damage awards manifest such passion or prejudice as would render them inadequate. We hold that the court's utilization of the provisions of Rule 49(b) did not render proper its increase of damages in accordance with mathematical computations based upon the special findings.

2. Is the appellate-court decision in *Nollenberger* realistic? If so, what possible justification was there for the trial court's decision to present the jury with special interrogatories? The appellate court gave plaintiff the option of accepting the jury's general verdict or of having the case returned to the trial court for a ruling on plaintiff's motion for a new trial. Should the Court of Appeals itself have decided whether there should be a new trial in the event that plaintiff decided not to accept the jury award?

3. Just how far should a court go in attempting to reconcile a jury's answers to specific interrogatories, either among themselves or with a general

43.

* * *

"You should award the plaintiffs herein such sum as, *under all of the circumstances of the case, may be fair and just compensation* for the pecuniary loss which the [widow and child(ren)] have suffered by reason of the death of [decedent].

"

* * *

"In weighing these matters, you may consider * * * *the disposition of the deceased, whether it was kindly, affectionate or other-*

wise; whether or not he showed an inclination to contribute to the support of the plaintiffs or any of them; the earning capacity of the deceased; and *such other facts shown by the evidence as throw light upon the pecuniary value of the support, society, care, comfort and protection* other than the loss of consortium between husband and wife, which the plaintiffs reasonably might have expected to receive from the deceased had he lived. * * *" (Emphasis added.)

verdict? In POPHAM v. CITY OF KENNESAW, 820 F.2d 1570 (11th Cir.1987), plaintiff sued to recover for violations of his civil rights alleging that the police used excessive force to arrest him, falsely arrested him, and arrested him in order to deprive him of his First Amendment rights. The trial court submitted special interrogatories, including one asking whether the police used excessive force and another asking whether the officers held qualified immunity. The jury answered both in the affirmative, yet awarded damages to plaintiff. The Court of Appeals, in upholding the jury verdict, held that the trial judge had an obligation to interpret apparently conflicting interrogatories so as to sustain the jury's general verdict. Applying the principle to the facts of the case, the court found that the jury's answer about immunity was made only with respect to the false arrest and First Amendment claims, citing the trial judge's instructions as support for its holding.

3. FINDINGS AND CONCLUSIONS IN NONJURY CASES

Read Federal Rule of Civil Procedure 52 in the Supplement.

ROBERTS v. ROSS

United States Court of Appeals, Third Circuit, 1965.
344 F.2d 747.

MARIS, CIRCUIT JUDGE. The plaintiff, Herbert J. Roberts, appeals from a judgment entered in the District Court of the Virgin Islands dismissing his action brought to recover the sum of $3,087.50 which he alleged the defendant Norman M. Ross, Jr. promised to pay him for services rendered in producing a buyer for a dwelling house which the defendant had built in St. Thomas. The defendant answered, denying any such promise and, subsequently, with leave of court, he filed an amended answer in which he interposed the special defense of the Statute of Frauds.

* * *

On December 30, 1963, the trial judge entered an order stating that he had found for the defendant on the issues presented and directing counsel for the defendant within 10 days to file proposed findings of fact, conclusions of law and draft of judgment. Counsel for the plaintiff was given leave within 10 days thereafter to file objections thereto, which he did. On January 14, 1964 the findings of fact, conclusions of law, and judgment prepared and filed by counsel for the defendant were signed by the trial judge without change. It was concluded as a matter of law that "plaintiff has failed to prove by a preponderance of the evidence that the sale of said property by the defendant was procured through the agency of plaintiff," and that "in any event, said alleged promise not being in writing is within the Statute of Frauds." The plaintiff appealed from the judgment entered thereon dismissing his complaint.

* * *

The defendant * * * argues that * * * the plaintiff failed to prove the alleged agreement by a preponderance of the evidence, and the trial judge was accordingly justified in concluding that any discussion relating to compensating plaintiff for alleged sale of the property was at most the offer of a gratuity on the part of the defendant not specifically enforceable for indefiniteness. The fallacy in defendant's argument is that the trial judge failed to make any such findings. There is no finding as to whether the defendant agreed to pay the plaintiff a commission for producing a customer for the sale of the property—a question which was the crucial issue in the case. And there is no support in the record for the conclusion as a matter of law that "plaintiff has failed to prove by a preponderance of the evidence that the sale of said property by the defendant was procured through the agency of plaintiff." For it was undisputed that the plaintiff brought [the buyer] * * * to the property and introduced him to the defendant as a prospective purchaser. Perhaps the term "agency" in the quoted conclusion is intended to mean that the plaintiff, in doing so, did not act as agent for the defendant, thus possibly implying that the defendant did not agree to pay plaintiff a commission if he producd [sic] a buyer for the property. The trial judge's conclusion is, however, so inadequate as to afford this court no indication of the legal standard under which the evidence was considered.

This Court has had occasion to point out that Rule 52(a) of the Federal Rules of Civil Procedure requires the trier of the facts to find the facts specially and state his conclusions of law thereon with clarity. The findings of fact and conclusions of law must be sufficient to indicate the bases of the trial judge's decision. * * * The findings and conclusions in the present case do not meet this requirement.

Moreover we have observed in this case and in a number of others which have been brought here from the district court for review that the judge of the court has followed the practice of announcing his decision for the plaintiff or the defendant substantially in the form of a general verdict, either in a written order or by communication to counsel, and of thereupon directing counsel for the prevailing party to prepare and submit findings of fact, conclusions of law and a form of judgment. The trial judge's order has not been accompanied by an opinion setting out, even summarily, the facts and legal conclusions which have brought him to his decision. Obviously the judge must have dealt with the questions of fact and law involved in the case in the course of the reasoning by which he has reached his ultimate conclusion, even though his reasoning has not been articulated and put on paper. But counsel who is called upon to articulate and write out the findings and conclusions must do so without any knowledge of the fact findings and reasoning processes through which the judge has actually gone in reaching his decision.

We strongly disapprove this practice. For it not only imposes a well-nigh impossible task upon counsel but also flies in the face of the spirit and purpose, if not the letter, of Rule 52(a). The purpose of that rule is to require the trial judge to formulate and articulate his findings of fact and conclusions of law in the course of his consideration and determination of the case and as a part of his decision making process, so that he himself may be satisfied that he has dealt fully and properly with all the issues in the case before he decides it and so that the parties involved and this court on appeal may be fully informed as to the bases of his decision when it is made. Findings and conclusions prepared ex post facto by counsel, even though signed by the judge, do not serve adequately the function contemplated by the rule. At most they provide the judge with an opportunity to reconsider the bases of his original decision but without affording the parties any information as to what those bases were or which of them are being reconsidered. At worst they are likely to convict the judge of error because, as here, they are inadequate to support his decision or because, as we have observed in other cases, they are loaded down with argumentative over-detailed partisan matter much of which is likely to be of doubtful validity or even wholly without support in the record.

    * * * We * * * do not * * * mean to suggest that a trial judge should not have the right to invite counsel for both parties to submit to him proposed findings of fact and conclusions of law, accompanied by briefs if he desires them, to assist him in formulating his own findings and conclusions and reaching his decision. In the process of studying the facts and the law, findings and conclusions formulated and proposed by the parties may be most helpful to the judge in sharpening the issues and may serve a very useful purpose in aiding him in drafting his own findings and conclusions. In most cases it will appear that many of the findings proposed by one or the other of the parties are fully supported by the evidence, are directed to material matters and may be adopted verbatim and it may even be that in some cases the findings and conclusions proposed by a party will be so carefully and objectively prepared that they may all properly be adopted by the trial judge without change. But it should be remembered that findings and conclusions prepared by a party and adopted by the trial judge without change are likely to be looked at by the appellate court more narrowly and given less weight on review than if they are the work product of the judge himself or at least bear evidence that he has given them careful study and revision. For the latter procedure would assure the appellate court, as Judge Wisdom pointed out in Louis Dreyfus & Cie. v. Panama Canal Company, 5 Cir., 1962, 298 F.2d 733, 738, "that the trial judge did indeed consider all the factual questions thoroughly and would guarantee that each word in the finding is impartially chosen." It has been the general practice of the district judges of the Third Circuit in the past under Rule 52(a) to formulate their findings of fact and conclusions of law in the course of and as a part of their decision-making process and to articulate and file them at the time of announcing the decision, either in an opinion if filed at that time or in a separate document. * * * [W]e strongly approve this practice and direct it to be followed * * * by the court below.

* * *

Notes and Questions

    1. Roberts v. Ross is discussed in 51 Cornell L.Q. 567 (1966), in which it is noted that on remand, the trial court, without a new hearing, reversed its earlier decision, and entered judgment for the party against whom it ruled

initially. Compare HETEROCHEMICAL CORP. v. UNITED STATES RUB-
BER CO., 368 F.2d 169, 172 (7th Cir.1966):

> After post-trial briefing and oral arguments, the district court invited
> findings and conclusions from both parties and ordered an exchange of
> the proposals. * * * The court thereafter adopted the proposals of
> United States Rubber.

> This court has termed the adoption of proposed findings a "practical
> and wise custom," in view of the obligation of a prevailing party to assist
> a busy court. * * * This is particularly true in a case where the
> evidence is highly technical, so long as the trial court's procedure is fair
> to both parties and the findings reveal insight and understanding of the
> basic issue. * * * In view of the district court's procedure in adopting
> findings of fact and conclusions of law, we are not persuaded that they
> were "mechanically adopted"; nor can we agree that they do not reveal
> insight and understanding of the basic issue. * * *

See Shlensky v. Dorsey, 574 F.2d 131 (3d Cir.1978) (adoption of a party's
predecision proposed findings invites more careful examination on appeal).

2. In LEIGHTON v. ONE WILLIAM STREET FUND, INC., 343 F.2d
565, 567 (2d Cir.1965), the court discussed Federal Rule 52(a) as follows:

> The purpose of Rule 52(a), as it is applied to a non-jury case, is
> usually stated to be three-fold: (1) to aid the appellate court by affording
> it a clear understanding of the ground or the basis of the decision of the
> trial court; (2) to make definite just what is decided by the case to enable
> the application of *res judicata* and estoppel principles to subsequent
> decisions; and (3) to evoke care on the part of the trial judge in ascertain-
> ing the facts.

Which of the listed purposes of Rule 52(a) do you find most important?

3. Rule 52(a) states that the findings of fact by a lower court shall not be
set aside unless "clearly erroneous." In 1987, Rule 52(a) was amended to
include the phrase "whether based on oral or documentary evidence" because
there was confusion among the courts concerning whether the same standard
of review existed for findings of fact based on credibility evidence and those
based on documentary evidence. Why might courts have drawn this distinction?

Anticipating the change in the rule, the Supreme Court addressed the
issue in ANDERSON v. CITY OF BESSEMER CITY, 470 U.S. 564, 105 S.Ct.
1504, 84 L.Ed.2d 518 (1985), although the holding is somewhat cloudy. Justice
White, speaking for the majority, explains:

> [The clearly erroneous standard applies] * * * even when the district
> court's findings do not rest on credibility determinations, but are based
> instead on physical or documentary evidence or inferences from other
> facts. * * * That the rule goes on to emphasize the special deference to
> be paid credibility determinations does not alter its clear command: Rule
> 52(a) "does not make exceptions or purport to exclude certain categories
> of factual findings unless clearly erroneous." * * *

> The rationale for deference of the original finder of fact is not limited
> to the superiority of the trial judge's position to make determinations of
> credibility. The trial judge's major role is the determination of fact, and
> with experience in fulfilling that role comes expertise. Duplication of the

trial judge's efforts in the court of appeals would very likely contribute only negligibly to the accuracy of fact determination at a huge cost in diversion of judicial resources. In addition, the parties to a case on appeal have already been forced to concentrate their energies and resources on persuading the trial judge that their account of the facts is the correct one; requiring them to persuade three more judges at the appellate level is requiring too much. * * * For these reasons, review of factual findings under the clearly-erroneous standard—with its deference to the trier of fact—is the rule, not the exception.

When findings are based on determinations regarding the credibility of witnesses, Rule 52(a) demands even greater deference to the trial court's findings; for only the trial judge can be aware of the variations in demeanor and tone of voice that bear so heavily on the listener's understanding of and belief in what is said. * * * This is not to suggest that the trial judge may insulate his findings from review by denominating them credibility determinations, for factors other than demeanor and inflection go into the decision whether or not to believe a witness. Documents or objective evidence may contradict the witness' story; or the story itself may be so internally inconsistent or implausible on its face that a reasonable factfinder would not credit it. Where such factors are present, the court of appeals may well find clear error even in a finding purportedly based on a credibility determination. * * * But when a trial judge's finding is based on his decision to credit the testimony of one of two or more witnesses, each of whom has told a coherent and facially plausible story that is not contradicted by extrinsic evidence, that finding, if not internally inconsistent, can virtually never be clear error.

470 U.S. at 574, 105 S.Ct. at 1511–12, 84 L.Ed.2d at 528–30.

What standard did the Supreme Court adopt? Does the additional language in the 1987 version of the rule settle the issue? See Childress, *"Clearly Erroneous": Judicial Review Over District Courts in the Eighth Circuit and Beyond,* 51 Mo.L.Rev. 93 (1986).

Review Hicks v. United States, p. 58, supra. Would the new language of Rule 52(a) have altered the outcome in that case? Would the Court's language in *Anderson* have altered the outcome?

SECTION F. ATTACKS ON VERDICTS AND JUDGMENTS

1. TESTING THE SUFFICIENCY OF THE EVIDENCE: DIRECTED VERDICTS, JUDGMENTS NOTWITHSTANDING THE VERDICT, AND NEW TRIALS

a. *The Constitutional Issues*

GALLOWAY v. UNITED STATES

Supreme Court of the United States, 1943.
319 U.S. 372, 63 S.Ct. 1077, 87 L.Ed. 1458.

Certiorari to the United States Circuit Court of Appeals for the Ninth Circuit.

MR. JUSTICE RUTLEDGE delivered the opinion of the Court.

Petitioner seeks benefits for total and permanent disability by reason of insanity he claims existed May 31, 1919. On that day his policy of yearly renewable term insurance lapsed for nonpayment of premium.

* * * At the close of all the evidence the District Court granted the Government's motion for a directed verdict. Judgment was entered accordingly. The Circuit Court of Appeals affirmed. * * * Both courts held the evidence legally insufficient to sustain a verdict for petitioner. He says this was erroneous and, in effect, deprived him of trial by jury, contrary to the Seventh Amendment.

* * *

I.

Certain facts are undisputed. Petitioner worked as a longshoreman in Philadelphia and elsewhere prior to enlistment in the Army November 1, 1917. He became a cook in a machine gun battalion. His unit arrived in France in April, 1918. He served actively until September 24. From then to the following January he was in a hospital with influenza. He then returned to active duty. He came back to the United States, and received honorable discharge April 29, 1919. He enlisted in the Navy January 15, 1920, and was discharged for bad conduct in July. The following December he again enlisted in the Army and served until May, 1922, when he deserted. Thereafter he was carried on the Army records as a deserter.

In 1930 began a series of medical examinations by Veterans' Bureau physicians. On May 19 that year his condition was diagnosed as "Moron, low grade; observation, dementia praecox, simple type." In November, 1931, further examination gave the diagnosis, "Psychosis with other diseases or conditions (organic disease of the central nervous system—type undetermined)." In July, 1934, still another examination was made, with diagnosis: "Psychosis-manic and depressive insanity incompetent * * *."

Petitioner concededly is now totally and permanently disabled by reason of insanity and has been for some time prior to institution of this suit. It is conceded also that he was sound in mind and body until he arrived in France in April, 1918.

The theory of his case is that the strain of active service abroad brought on an immediate change, which was the beginning of a mental breakdown that has grown worse continuously through all the later years. Essential in this is the view it had become a total and permanent disability not later than May 31, 1919.

[Petitioner's evidence was as follows: Two witnesses who had served with him in France testified to conduct on petitioner's part there that evinced a disturbed mind. A boyhood friend, one O'Neill, testified that in 1919 petitioner "was a wreck compared to what he was before he went away; * * * [his] mind was evidently unbalanced." A chaplain testified that he had observed a Private Galloway in an Army mental ward in 1920 who appeared insane; his identification of petitioner, however, was less than positive. Petitioner's naval commanding officer deposed that petitioner had caused trouble by disobedience and absence without leave, and his Army commanding officer in 1921 deposed that he was sometimes "one of the very best soldiers," and at other times undependable, that he had alternate periods of gaiety and depression, talked incoherently at times, but seemed to get along well with other soldiers. A physician who first saw petitioner shortly before trial testified as to his conclusion, based upon his own observation as well as the other testimony and petitioner's documentary medical history, that petitioner was born with an inherent instability, that he had "gone to pieces" in France, and that he was insane at all times subsequent to July 1918.]

Sounds like Ct is disbelieving ✓ expert

II.

* * *

But if the record is taken to show that some form of mental disability existed in 1930, which later became total and permanent, petitioner's problem remains to demonstrate by more than speculative inference that this condition itself began on or before May 31, 1919 and continuously existed or progressed through the intervening years to 1930.

To show origin before the crucial date, he gives evidence of two abnormal incidents occurring while he was in France, one creating the disturbance before he came near the fighting front, the other yelling that the Germans were coming when he was on guard duty at the Marne. There is no other evidence of abnormal behavior during his entire service of more than a year abroad.

* * *

O'Neill's testimony apparently takes no account of petitioner's having spent 101 days in a hospital in France with influenza just before he came home. But, given the utmost credence, as is required, it does no more than show that petitioner was subject to alternating periods of gaiety and depression for some indefinite period after his return, extending perhaps as late as 1922. But because of its vagueness as to time, dates, frequency of opportunity for observation, and specific incident, O'Neill's testimony concerning the period from 1922 to 1925 is hardly more than speculative.

We have then the two incidents in France followed by O'Neill's testimony of petitioner's changed condition in 1919 and its continuance to 1922.[11] There is also the testimony of Commander Platt and Lt. Col. James E. Matthews as to his service in the Navy and the Army, respectively, during 1920–1922. Neither thought petitioner was insane or that his conduct indicated insanity. Then follows a chasm of eight years.

* * *

11. Chaplain Mathews' testimony would be highly probative of insanity existing early in 1920, if petitioner were sufficiently identified as its subject. However, the bare inference of identity which might otherwise be drawn from the mere identity of names cannot be made reasonably in view of its overwhelming contradiction by other evidence presented by petitioner and the failure to produce records from Fort MacArthur Hospital or the Army or from persons who knew the fact that petitioner had been there at any time. The omission eloquently testifies in a manner which no inference could overcome that petitioner never was there. The chaplain's testimony therefore should have been stricken, had the case gone to the jury * * *.

This period was eight years of continuous insanity, according to the inference petitioner would be allowed to have drawn. If so, he should have no need of inference. Insanity so long and continuously sustained does not hide itself from the eyes and ears of witnesses. The assiduity which produced the evidence of two "crazy" incidents during a year and a half in France should produce one during eight years or, for that matter, five years in the United States.

Inference is capable of bridging many gaps. But not, in these circumstances, one so wide and deep as this. Knowledge of petitioner's activities and behavior from 1922 or 1925 to 1930 was peculiarly within his ken and that of his wife, who has litigated this cause in his and presumably, though indirectly, in her own behalf. His was the burden to show continuous disability. What he did in this time, or did not do, was vital to his case. Apart from the mere fact of his marriage, the record is blank for five years and almost blank for eight. For all that appears, he may have worked full time and continuously for five and perhaps for eight, with only a possible single interruption.

No favorable inference can be drawn from the omission. It was not one of oversight or inability to secure proof. That is shown by the thoroughness with which the record was prepared for all other periods, before and after this one, and by the fact petitioner's wife, though she married him during the period and was available, did not testify. The only reasonable conclusion is that petitioner, or those who acted for him, deliberately chose, for reasons no doubt considered sufficient (and which we do not criticize, since such matters including tactical ones, are for the judgment of counsel) to present no evidence or perhaps to withhold evidence readily available concerning this long interval, and to trust to the genius of expert medical inference and judicial laxity to bridge this canyon.

In the circumstances exhibited, the former is not equal to the feat, and the latter will not permit it. No case has been cited and none has been found in which inference, however expert, has been permitted to make so broad a leap and take the place of evidence which, according to all reason, must have been at hand. To allow this would permit the substitution of inference, tenuous at best, not merely for evidence absent because impossible or difficult to secure, but for evidence disclosed to be available and not produced. This would substitute speculation for proof. Furthermore, the inference would be more plausible perhaps if the evidence of insanity as of May, 1919, were stronger than it is, such for instance as Chaplain Mathews' testimony would have furnished if it could be taken as applying to petitioner. But, on this record, the evidence of insanity as of that time is thin at best, if it can be regarded as at all more than speculative.

Beyond this, there is nothing to show totality or permanence.

* * *

III.

What has been said disposes of the case as the parties have made it. For that reason perhaps nothing more need be said. But objection has been advanced that, in some manner not wholly clear, the directed verdict practice offends the Seventh Amendment.

It may be noted, first, that the Amendment has no application of its own force to this case. The suit is one to enforce a monetary claim against the United States. It hardly can be maintained that under the common law in 1791 jury trial was a matter of right for persons asserting claims against the sovereign. Whatever force the Amendment has therefore is derived because Congress * * * has made it applicable. Even so, the objection made on the score of its requirements is untenable.

If the intention is to claim generally that the Amendment deprives the federal courts of power to direct a verdict for insufficiency of evidence, the short answer is the contention has been foreclosed by repeated decisions made here consistently for nearly a century. More recently the practice has been approved explicitly in the promulgation of the Federal Rules of Civil Procedure. * * * The objection therefore comes too late.

Furthermore, the argument from history is not convincing. It is not that "the rules of the common law" in 1791 deprived trial courts of power to withdraw cases from the jury, because not made out, or appellate courts of power to review such determinations. The jury was not absolute master of fact in 1791. Then as now courts excluded evidence for irrelevancy and relevant proof for other reasons. The argument concedes they weighed the evidence, not only piecemeal but *in toto* for submission to the jury, by at least two procedures, the demurrer to the evidence and the motion for a new trial. The objection is not therefore to the basic thing, which is the power of the court to withhold cases from the jury or set aside the verdict for insufficiency of the evidence. It is rather to incidental or collateral effects, namely, that the directed verdict as now administered differs from both those procedures because, on the one hand, allegedly higher standards of proof are required and, on the other, different consequences follow as to further maintenance of the litigation. Apart from the standards of proof, the argument appears to urge that in 1791, a litigant could challenge his opponent's evidence, either by the demurrer, which when determined ended the litigation, or by motion for a new trial which, if successful, gave the adversary another chance to prove his case; and therefore the Amendment excluded any challenge to which one or the other of these consequences does not attach.

The Amendment did not bind the federal courts to the exact procedural incidents or details of jury trial according to the common law in 1791, any more than it tied them to the common-law system of pleading or the specific rules of evidence then prevailing. Nor were "the rules of the common law" then prevalent, including those relating to the procedure by which the judge regulated the jury's role on questions of fact, crystalized in a fixed and immutable system. On the contrary, they were constantly changing and developing during the late eighteenth and early nineteenth centuries.[23] In 1791 this process already had resulted in widely divergent common-law rules on procedural matters among the states, and between them and England. * * *

This difficulty, no doubt, accounts for the amorphous character of the objection now advanced, which insists, not that any single one of the features criticized, but that the cumulative total or the alternative effect of all, was embodied in the Amendment. The more logical conclusion, we think, and the one which both history and the previous decisions here support, is that the Amendment was designed to preserve the basic institution of jury trial in only its most fundamental elements, not the great mass of procedural forms and details, varying even then so widely among common-law jurisdictions.

Apart from the uncertainty and the variety of conclusion which follows from an effort at purely historical accuracy, the consequences flowing from the view asserted are sufficient to refute it. It may be doubted that the Amendment requires challenge to an opponent's case to be made without reference to the merits of one's own and at the price of all opportunity to have it considered. On the other hand, there is equal room for disbelieving it compels endless repetition of litigation and unlimited chance, by education gained at the opposing party's expense, for perfecting a case at other trials. The essential inconsistency of these alternatives would seem sufficient to refute that either or both, to the exclusion of all others, received constitutional sanctity by the Amendment's force. The first alternative, drawn from the demurrer to the evidence, attributes to the Amendment the effect of forcing one admission because another and an entirely different one is made,[28] and thereby compels conclusion of the litigation once and for all. The true effect of imposing such a risk would not be to guarantee the plaintiff a jury trial. It would be rather to deprive the defendant (or the plaintiff if he were the challenger) of that right; or, if not that, then of the right to challenge the

---

23. E.g., during the eighteenth and nineteenth centuries, the nonsuit was being transformed in practice from a device by which a plaintiff voluntarily discontinued his action in order to try again another day into a procedure by which a defendant could put in issue the sufficiency of the plaintiff's evidence to go to the jury, differing from the directed verdict in that respect only in form. * * * The nonsuit, of course, differed in consequence from the directed verdict, for it left the plaintiff free to try again. * * *

Similarly the demurrer to the evidence practice was not static during this period as a comparison of Cocksedge v. Fanshaw, 1779, 1 Doug. 118, with Gibson v. Hunter, 1793, 2 H.Bl. 187, and the American practice on the demurrer to the evidence reveals * * *. Nor was the conception of directing a verdict entirely unknown to the eighteenth century common law. * * * While there is no reason to believe that the notion at that time even approximated in character the

present directed verdict, the cases serve further to show the plastic and developing character of these procedural devices during the eighteenth and nineteenth centuries.

28. By conceding the full scope of an opponent's evidence and asserting its insufficiency in law, which is one thing, the challenger must be taken * * * also to admit he has no case, if the other's evidence is found legally sufficient, which is quite another thing. In effect, one must stake his case, not upon its own merit on the facts, but on the chance he may be right in regarding his opponent's as wanting in probative content. If he takes the gamble and loses, he pays with his own case, * * * without opportunity for the jury to consider it. To force this choice and yet deny that afforded by the directed verdict would be to imbed in the Constitution the hypertechnicality of common-law pleading and procedure in their heyday. * * *

legal sufficiency of the opposing case. The Amendment was not framed or adopted to deprive either party of either right. It is impartial in its guaranty of both. To posit assertion of one upon sacrifice of the other would dilute and distort the full protection intended. The admitted validity of the practice on the motion for a new trial goes far to demonstrate this.[29] It negatives any idea that the challenge must be made at such a risk as the demurrer imposed. As for the other alternative, it is not urged that the Amendment guarantees another trial whenever challenge to the sufficiency of evidence is sustained. * * * That argument, in turn, is precluded by the practice on demurrer to the evidence.

Each of the classical modes of challenge, therefore, disproves the notion that the characteristic feature of the other, for effect upon continuing the litigation, became a part of the Seventh Amendment's guaranty to the exclusion of all others. * * * Alternatives so contradictory give room, not for the inference that one or the other is required, but rather for the view that neither is essential.

Finally, the objection appears to be directed generally at the standards of proof judges have required for submission of evidence to the jury. But standards, contrary to the objection's assumption, cannot be framed wholesale for the great variety of situations in respect to which the question arises. * * * The matter is essentially one to be worked out in particular situations and for particular types of cases. Whatever may be the general formulation, the essential requirement is that mere speculation be not allowed to do duty for probative facts, after making due allowance for all reasonably possible inferences favoring the party whose case is attacked. The mere difference in labels used to describe this standard * * * cannot amount to a departure from "the rules of the common law" which the Amendment requires to be followed. * * *

Judged by this requirement, or by any standard other than sheer speculation, we are unable to conclude that one whose burden, by the nature of his claim, is to show continuing and total disability for nearly twenty years supplies the essential proof of continuity when he wholly omits to show his whereabouts, activities or condition for five years, although the record discloses evidence must have been available, and, further, throws no light upon three additional years, except for one vaguely described and dated visit to his former home. * * * The words "total and permanent" are the statute's, not our own. They mean something more than incipient or occasional disability. We hardly need add that we give full credence to all of the testimony. But that cannot cure its inherent vagueness or supply essential elements omitted or withheld.

29. Under that practice the moving party receives the benefit of jury evaluation of his own case and of challenge to his opponent's for insufficiency. If he loses on the challenge, the litigation is ended. But this is not because, in making it, he is forced to admit his own is insufficient. It is rather for the reasons that the court finds the opposite party's evidence is legally sufficient and the jury has found it outweighs his own. There is thus no forced surrender of one right from assertion of another.

On the other hand, if the challenger wins, there is another trial. But this is because he has sought it, not because the Amendment guarantees it.

Accordingly, the judgment is

Affirmed.

MR. JUSTICE BLACK, with whom MR. JUSTICE DOUGLAS and MR. JUSTICE MURPHY concur, dissenting.

* * *

The Court here re-examines testimony offered in a common law suit, weighs conflicting evidence, and holds that the litigant may never take this case to a jury. * * * Today's decision marks a continuation of the gradual process of judicial erosion which in one hundred fifty years has slowly worn away a major portion of the essential guarantee of the Seventh Amendment.

I.

Alexander Hamilton in The Federalist emphasized his loyalty to the jury system in civil cases and declared that jury verdicts should be re-examined, if at all, only "by a second jury, either by remanding the cause to the court below for a second trial of the fact, or by directing an issue immediately out of the Supreme Court."

* * * The first Congress expected the Seventh Amendment to meet the objections of men like Patrick Henry to the Constitution itself. Henry, speaking in the Virginia Constitutional Convention, had expressed the general conviction of the people of the Thirteen States when he said, "* * * We are told that we are to part with that trial by jury with which our ancestors secured their lives and property. * * * I hope we shall never be induced, by such arguments, to part with that excellent mode of trial. No appeal can now be made as to fact in common law suits. *The unanimous verdict of impartial men cannot be reversed.*" * * *

In 1789, juries occupied the principal place in the administration of justice. They were frequently in both criminal and civil cases the arbiters not only of fact but of law. Less than three years after the ratification of the Seventh Amendment, this Court called a jury in a civil case brought under our original jurisdiction. There was no disagreement as to the facts of the case. Chief Justice Jay, charging the jury for a unanimous Court, three of whose members had sat in the Constitutional Convention, said: "For as, on the one hand, it is presumed, that juries are the best judges of facts; it is, on the other hand, presumable, that the court[s] are the best judges of law. But still, both objects are lawfully within your power of decision." State of Georgia v. Brailsford, 3 Dall. 1, 4, 1 L.Ed. 483. * * *

The principal method by which judges prevented cases from going to the jury in the Seventeenth and Eighteenth Centuries was by the demurrer to the evidence. * * * This practice fell into disuse in England in 1793, Gibson v. Hunter, 2 H.Bl. 187, and in the United States federal courts in 1826, Fowle v. Alexandria, 11 Wheat. 320, 6 L.Ed. 484. The power of federal judges to comment to the jury on the evidence gave them additional influence. * * * The right of involuntary nonsuit of a plaintiff, which might have been used to expand judicial power at jury expense was at first denied federal courts. * * *

As Hamilton had declared in The Federalist, the basic judicial control of the jury function was in the court's power to order a new trial. In 1830, this Court said: "The only modes known to the common law to re-examine such facts, are the granting of a new trial by the court where the issue was tried, or to which the record was properly returnable; or the award of a venire facias de novo, by an appellate court, for some error of law which intervened in the proceedings." Parsons v. Bedford, * * * 3 Pet. at page 448, 7 L.Ed. 732. * * *

A long step toward the determination of fact by judges instead of by juries was the invention of the directed verdict.[11] In 1850, what seems to have been the first directed verdict case considered by this Court, Parks v. Ross, 11 How. 362, 374, 13 L.Ed. 730, was presented for decision. The Court held that the directed verdict serves the same purpose as the demurrer to the evidence, and that since there was "no evidence whatever" on the critical issue in the case, the directed verdict was approved. The decision was an innovation, a departure from the traditional rule restated only fifteen years before in Greenleaf v. Birth, 1835, 9 Pet. 292, 299, 9 L.Ed. 132, in which this Court had said: "Where there is no evidence tending to prove a particular fact, the court[s] are bound so to instruct the jury, when requested; but they cannot legally give any instruction which shall take from the jury the right of weighing the evidence and determining what effect it shall have."

This new device contained potentialities for judicial control of the jury which had not existed in the demurrer to the evidence. In the first place, demurring to the evidence was risky business, for in so doing the party not only admitted the truth of all the testimony against him but also all reasonable inferences which might be drawn from it; and upon joinder in demurrer the case was withdrawn from the jury while the court proceeded to give final judgment either for or against the demurrant. * * * Imposition of this risk was no mere technicality; for by making withdrawal of a case from the jury dangerous to the moving litigant's cause, the early law went far to assure that facts would never be examined except by a jury. * * * The litigant not only takes no risk by a motion for a directed verdict, but in making such a motion gives himself two opportunities to avoid the jury's decision; for under the federal variant of judgment notwithstanding the verdict, the judge may reserve opinion on the motion for a directed verdict and then give judgment for the moving party after the jury was formally found against him. In the second place, under the directed verdict practice the courts soon abandoned the "admission of all facts and reasonable inferences" standard referred to, and created the so-called "substantial evidence" rule which

11. I do not mean to minimize other forms of judicial control. In a summary of important techniques of judicial domination of the jury, Thayer lists the following: control by the requirement of a "reasonable judgment"—i.e., one satisfactory to the judge; control of the rules of "presumption" * * *; the control of the "definition of language"; the control of rules of practice, and forms of pleading ("It is remarkable how judges and legislatures in this country are unconsciously travelling back towards the old result of controlling the jury, by requiring special verdicts and answers to specific questions. * * *"); the control of "mixed questions of law and fact"; the control of factual decisions by appellate courts. Thayer on Evidence (1898 ed.) p. 208 et seq.

permitted directed verdicts even though there was far more evidence in the case than a plaintiff would have needed to withstand a demurrer.

The substantial evidence rule did not spring into existence immediately upon the adoption of the directed verdict device. For a few more years federal judges held to the traditional rule that juries might pass finally on facts if there was "any evidence" to support a party's contention. The rule that a case must go to the jury unless there was "no evidence" was completely repudiated in Schuylkill and Dauphin Improvement Co. v. Munson, 1871, 14 Wall. 442, 447, 448, 20 L.Ed. 867, upon which the Court today relies in part. There the Court declared that "some" evidence was not enough—there must be evidence sufficiently persuasive to the judge so that he thinks "a jury can properly proceed." The traditional rule was given an ugly name, "the scintilla rule", to hasten its demise. * * * The same transition from jury supremacy to jury subordination through judicial decisions took place in State courts.

Later cases permitted the development of added judicial control. * * * [J]ury verdicts on disputed facts have been set aside or directed verdicts authorized so regularly as to make the practice commonplace while the motion for directed verdict itself has become routine. * * * Today the Court comes dangerously close to weighing the credibility of a witness and rejecting his testimony because the majority do not believe it.

* * *

The call for the true application of the Seventh Amendment is not to words, but to the spirit of honest desire to see that Constitutional right preserved. Either the judge or the jury must decide facts and to the extent that we take this responsibility, we lessen the jury function. Our duty to preserve this one of the Bill of Rights may be peculiarly difficult, for here it is our own power which we must restrain. * * * As for myself, I believe that a verdict should be directed, if at all, only when, without weighing the credibility of the witnesses, there is in the evidence no room whatever for honest difference of opinion over the factual issue in controversy. * * *

II.

* * * It is undisputed that the petitioner's health was sound in 1918, and it is evidently conceded that he was disabled at least since 1930. When in the intervening period, did the disability take place?

* * * There is substantial testimony from which reasonable men might conclude that the petitioner was insane from the date claimed.

Two witnesses testify as to the petitioner's mental irresponsibility while he was in France. * * * The Court disposes of this testimony, which obviously indicates some degree of mental unbalance, by saying no more than that it "does not prove he was insane." No reason is given, nor can I imagine any, why a jury should not be entitled to consider this evidence and draw its own conclusions.

* * * The Court analyzes O'Neill's testimony for internal consistency, criticizes his failure to remember the details of his association with the petitioner fifteen years before his appearance in this case, and concludes

that O'Neill's evidence shows no more than that "petitioner was subject to alternating periods of gaiety and depression for some indefinite period." This extreme emotional instability is an accepted symptom of the disease from which the petitioner suffers. If he exhibited the same symptoms in 1922, it is, at the minimum, probable that the condition has been continuous since an origin during the war. O'Neill's testimony coupled with the petitioner's present condition presents precisely the type of question which a jury should resolve.

* * * The testimony of his Commanding Officer while he was in the Army, Col. Matthews, is that the petitioner had "periods of gaiety and exhilaration" and was then "depressed as if he had had a hangover"; that petitioner tried to create disturbances and dissatisfy the men; that he suffered from a belief that he was being treated unfairly; and that generally his actions "were not those of a normal man". The Colonel was not a doctor and might well not have recognized insanity had he seen it; as it was, he concluded that the petitioner was an alcoholic and a narcotic addict. However, the officer was unable, upon repeated investigations, to discover any actual use of narcotics. A jury fitting this information into the general pattern of the testimony might well have been driven to the conclusion that the petitioner was insane at the time the Colonel had him under observation.

All of this evidence, if believed, showed a man healthy and normal before he went to the war suffering for several years after he came back from a disease which had the symptoms attributed to schizophrenia and who was insane from 1930 until his trial. Under these circumstances, I think that the physician's testimony of total and permanent disability by reason of continuous insanity from 1918 to 1938 was reasonable. The fact that there was no direct testimony for a period of five years, while it might be the basis of fair argument to the jury by the government, does not, as the Court seems to believe, create a presumption against the petitioner so strong that his case must be excluded from the jury entirely. Even if during these five years the petitioner was spasmodically employed, we could not conclude that he was not totally and permanently disabled. * * * It is not doubted that schizophrenia is permanent even though there may be a momentary appearance of recovery.

* * *

This case graphically illustrates the injustice resulting from permitting judges to direct verdicts instead of requiring them to await a jury decision and then, if necessary, allow a new trial. The chief reason given for approving a directed verdict against this petitioner is that no evidence except expert medical testimony was offered for a five to eight year period. Perhaps, now that the petitioner knows he has insufficient evidence to satisfy a judge even though he may have enough to satisfy a jury, he would be able to fill this time gap to meet any judge's demand. * * * If, as the Court believes, insufficient evidence has been offered to sustain a jury verdict for the petitioner, we should at least authorize a new trial. * * *

Notes and Questions

1. Traditional rules, still followed today in some jurisdictions, require a party to assume a risk in order to move for a directed verdict. What policy is served by a rule requiring entry of judgment against a party whose motion is denied? Or by a rule to the effect that before moving for a directed verdict at the end of plaintiff's case, defendant must waive the right to produce evidence if the motion fails? Cf. Morley v. Liverpool & London & Globe Ins. Co., 85 Mich. 210, 48 N.W. 502 (1891); Bartholomew v. Impastato, 12 So.2d 700 (La. App.1943). Or by providing that if plaintiff and defendant both move for a directed verdict at the close of the evidence, they waive the right to jury trial in the event that both motions are denied? See Estes v. Hancock Cty. Bank, 259 Ind. 542, 289 N.E.2d 728 (1972); Bunch v. Davidson, 242 Or. 635, 409 P.2d 910 (1966), overruled by Godell v. Johnson, 244 Or. 587, 418 P.2d 505 (1966); Annot., 68 A.L.R.2d 300 (1959). To what extent are the policies underlying such rules dictated by the same considerations that support jury trial? Are these rules consistent with rules and decisions in other areas of procedure that have reduced the part played by formal requirements and technical errors? How does Federal Rule 50 treat these questions?

2. What do you think of the following argument as addressed to a case such as *Galloway*?

> It seems to me that in this case the strongest argument in favor of submitting the cause to the jury is the widely divergent views among the members of this court, not only as to the conclusions which may properly be drawn from the testimony, but as to the testimony itself. If the judges of this court so differ in the proportion of four to three, can it be said that there is but one inference to be drawn, or that different minds may not honestly draw different conclusions? If the minds of the members of this court may so honestly differ, why may not the minds of jurors just as honestly differ? The logical deduction from the opinion of the court is that minority judges, and jurors generally, either do not have rational minds, or that they may not honestly reach a conclusion differing from the majority.

NUCCI v. COLORADO & S. RY. CO., 63 Colo. 582, 602, 169 P. 273, 281 (1917) (dissenting opinion).

———

HERRON v. SOUTHERN PAC. CO., 283 U.S. 91, 51 S.Ct. 383, 75 L.Ed. 857 (1931). The Arizona Constitution, Article 18, Section 5, provides that the defenses of contributory negligence and assumption of risk "shall, in all cases whatsoever, be a question of fact and shall, at all times, be left to the jury." Does this provision prevent a federal court in Arizona, hearing a diversity case, from directing a verdict for defendant on the ground that as a matter of law plaintiff was guilty of contributory negligence? Chief Justice Hughes, writing for the Supreme Court, said it does not.

> It does not appear to be insisted by the appellant, and it could not be maintained, that this constitutional provision must be followed by the federal courts by virtue of the Conformity Act * * *. The State, without violating the requirements of due process, may provide such a

rule for its own courts, * * * but in view of its nature and effect, the rule cannot be regarded as one that relates merely to practice or to a "form" or "mode of proceeding." The provision "cuts deep into the right, observed at common law, by which a defendant can obtain a decision by the court upon a proven state of facts." Atchison, Topeka & Santa Fé Railway Company v. Spencer (C.C.A.) 20 F.2d 714, 718. * * *

Nor is the [Rules of Decision Act] applicable * * *. The controlling principle governing the decision of the present question is that state laws cannot alter the essential character or function of a federal court. The function of the trial judge in a federal court is not in any sense a local matter, and state statutes which would interfere with the appropriate performance of that function are not binding upon the federal court * * *.

In a trial by jury in a federal court, the judge is not a mere moderator, but is the governor of the trial for the purpose of assuring its proper conduct and of determining questions of law. This discharge of the judicial function as at common law is an essential factor in the process for which the Federal Constitution provides. * * *

Id. at 93–95, 51 S.Ct. at 384, 75 L.Ed. at 859–60.

Notes and Questions

1. Would the issue in the *Herron* case have been decided differently after Erie R. Co. v. Tompkins, p. 346, supra? Why?

2. Could Congress deprive the federal courts of the authority to direct verdicts on the issue of contributory negligence in a case based upon a state cause of action? In a case based upon a federal cause of action? Does the latter possibility present a different issue than would be posed if Congress abolished the defense of contributory negligence in a federal cause of action?

3. The constitutional provision involved in the *Herron* case has not escaped restrictive interpretation by the courts of Arizona. See, e.g., Franco v. Vakares, 35 Ariz. 309, 277 P. 812 (1929) ("independent" negligence of plaintiff required directed verdict for defendant); Sax v. Kopelman, 96 Ariz. 394, 396 P.2d 17 (1964) (directed verdict *for* plaintiff on issue of contributory negligence required when no evidence of contributory negligence introduced).

b. Standards for the Directed Verdict and Judgment Notwithstanding the Verdict

Read Federal Rule of Civil Procedure 50 in the Supplement.

DENMAN v. SPAIN

Supreme Court of Mississippi, 1961.
242 Miss. 431, 135 So.2d 195.

LEE, PRESIDING JUSTICE. Betty Denman, a minor, * * * sued * * * [the] executrix of the estate of Joseph A. Ross, deceased, to recover damages for personal injuries sustained by her, allegedly resulting from the negligence of the decedent in the operation of an automobile. The issue was submitted to a jury on the evidence for the plaintiff—no evidence being offered for the defendant—and there was a verdict and judgment for the plaintiff in the sum of $5,000. However, on motion of the defendant, a judgment *non obstante veredicto* * * * was sustained and entered. From that action, the plaintiff has appealed.

* * *

The appellant contends that the evidence offered by her, together with the reasonable inferences therefrom, was sufficient to make an issue for the jury as to whether the alleged negligence of the deceased driver, Ross, proximately caused or contributed to the collision and the consequent damage * * *.

A careful scrutiny and analysis of the evidence is therefore necessary:

Sunday, March 23, 1958, was a rainy, foggy day. About six o'clock that afternoon, at dusk, Mrs. Eva B. Denman, accompanied by her granddaughter, Betty, the plaintiff, was driving her Ford car southward on U.S. Highway 49E. At that time, Joseph A. Ross, accompanied by Miss Euna Tanner and Mrs. J.L. Haining, was driving his Plymouth car northward on said highway. Just south of the Town of Sumner, the cars collided. Mrs. Denman, Miss Tanner and Ross were killed. Betty, nearly seven years of age at the time, and Mrs. Haining were injured. Neither had any recollection of what had happened at the time of the collision.

* * *

Plaintiff's father, Stuart Denman, who went to the scene shortly after the collision, described the situation substantially as follows: The Ford car was about seven yards off the paved surface on the east side in a bar pit "heading back towards the railroad track, which is in an easterly direction." The engine and transmission were on the opposite side of the road, out of the car and about fifty yards apart. The Plymouth was also on the east side, facing west, about fifteen yards north of the Ford.

No proof was offered as to skid marks, or other evidence to show the point of contact between these two vehicles. Eleven photographs of the damaged Plymouth, taken from various positions, and thirteen pictures of the damaged Ford, also taken from various positions, other than being mute evidence of a terrible tragedy, depict no reasonable or plausible explanation as to why this collision occurred, or who was responsible for it. * * *

Over objection by the defendant, John Barnett testified that he was driving a Dodge pickup north of [sic] highway 49E on his way to Tutwiler; that he was traveling at a speed of fifty or fifty-five miles per hour; that the Plymouth, which was in the wreck, passed him about three-fourths of a mile south of where the collision occurred, going at a speed of about seventy miles per hour; that when it passed, it got back in its lane, and neither wavered nor wobbled thereafter; that he followed and observed it for a distance of forty or fifty yards, and that it stayed in its proper lane as long as he saw it. Although another car was on the road ahead of him, he could have seen as far as the place of the accident except for the rain and fog.

Over objection by the defendant, Hal Buckley, a Negro man, testified that he was also traveling north on 49E on his way to Tutwiler at a speed of forty to fifty miles per hour. About two hundred yards south of the place where the collision occurred, a light green Plymouth, which he later saw at the scene of the accident, passed him at a speed of seventy-five or eighty miles an hour. He could see its taillights after it passed, and "he was just steady going; he wasn't doing no slowing up." He saw it until it ran into the other car. On cross-examination, he said that, after this car passed him, it got back on its side of the road, drove straight, and he did not notice that it ever went back over the center. Also on cross-examination, in an effort at impeachment, a part of the transcript in the other trial,[f] containing this question and answer, was read to him as follows: "What do you estimate the speed of that car was when it passed you—the one that was going the same direction that you were?," and the answer was: "Well, I don't have no idea." * * * He then admitted that when the car passed him, it got back on its side and drove straight ahead, and that he could see the accident, but he could not tell anything about it or on which side of the road it happened. He also did not notice the other car, which came from the other direction.

Since Barnett did not see the car any more after it had gone forty or fifty yards beyond him, and his knowledge of speed was based on what he saw about three-fourths of a mile south of the place where the collision occurred, this evidence was inadmissible * * *. On the contrary, since Buckley testified the speed of this car, when it passed him, was seventy-five to eighty miles an hour and that it did not slow down in the remaining distance of two hundred yards before the collision, such evidence was competent and admissible * * *. The attempted impeachment went to its credibility and not its admissibility.

From this evidence, the plaintiff reasons that the jury could, and did, find that the Ross car was being operated, under inclement weather conditions, at an unlawful and negligent rate of speed, and that, if Ross had had his car under adequate and proper control, in all probability the collision could have been avoided. She voices the opinion that the physical facts, including the pictures of the wrecked vehicles, indicated that the Ford car was probably across the highway at an angle of perhaps forty-five degrees at the time of the collision.

But the testimony of Buckley showed only that the Plymouth was being operated at an excessive and negligent rate of speed. It otherwise showed that the car was in its proper lane. He did not notice it go over the center at any time, but it was driven straight down the road. No eyewitness claimed to have seen what happened. There was no evidence to indicate the place in the road where the vehicles came in contact with each other. There was no showing as to the speed of the Ford, whether fast or slow; or as to whether it was traveling on the right or wrong side of the road; or as to whether it slid or was suddenly driven to the wrong

f. Plaintiff had separately sued the estate of her grandmother. Trial in that case resulted in a directed verdict for defendant, which was affirmed. Denman v. Denman, 242 Miss. 59, 134 So.2d 457 (1961).

side of the road into the path of the Plymouth. The cars were so badly damaged that the pictures afford no reasonable explanation as to what person or persons were legally responsible for their condition. In other words, just how and why this grievous tragedy occurred is completely shrouded in mystery.

The burden was on the plaintiff to prove by a preponderance of the evidence, not only that the operator of the Plymouth was guilty of negligence but also that such negligence proximately caused or contributed to the collision and consequent damage. By the use of metaphysical learning, speculation and conjecture, one may reach several possible conclusions as to how the accident occurred. However such conclusions could only be classed as possibilities; and this Court has many times held that verdicts cannot be based on possibilities. At all events, there is no sound or reasonable basis upon which a jury or this Court can say that the plaintiff met that burden.

The judgment must be affirmed.

Affirmed.

Notes and Questions

1. At this point I am going to say something which you may find very shocking. [The judge] * * * is supposed to submit an issue to the jury if, as the judges say, the jury can decide reasonably either way. But to say that I can decide an issue of fact reasonably either way is to say, I submit, that I cannot, by the exercise of reason, decide the question. That means that the issue which we typically submit to juries is an issue which the jury cannot decide by the exercise of its reason.

The decision of an issue of fact in cases of closely balanced probabilities, therefore, must, in the nature of things, be an emotional rather than a rational act * * *.

Michael, *The Basic Rules of Pleading*, 5 Record of N.Y.C.B.A. 175, 199–200 (1950). Do you agree with Professor Michael? What is the relevance of this comment to the opinion in the *Denman* case?

2. Do you believe a jury could properly have found for plaintiff in the *Denman* case? What inferences would have to be drawn from the evidence to reach such a conclusion? How would you support the proposition that these inferences could reasonably be found to be stronger than other inferences that would not lead to a verdict for plaintiff?

3. Is the *Denman* case contrary to Lavender v. Kurn, p. 53, supra? In PLANTERS MFG. CO. v. PROTECTION MUT. INS. CO., 380 F.2d 869 (5th Cir.1967), the Court of Appeals concluded that the two cases are inconsistent, and thus had to confront squarely the question whether a state standard for directing a verdict is controlling under *Erie*, a question the United States Supreme Court has found unnecessary to answer in two cases that raised it. Dick v. New York Life Ins. Co., 359 U.S. 437, 79 S.Ct. 921, 3 L.Ed.2d 935 (1959), and Mercer v. Theriot, 377 U.S. 152, 84 S.Ct. 1157, 12 L.Ed.2d 206 (1964). How should the question be resolved? It has been argued that while "federal courts may appropriately follow their own standards * * * with respect to at least most of the problems surrounding jury evaluation of

witness credibility * * * problems of jury freedom with respect to drawing inferences from the evidence and applying the law to the facts * * * should almost invariably be referred to state standards." Cooper, *Directions for Directed Verdicts: A Compass for Federal Courts,* 55 Minn.L.Rev. 903, 975–76 (1971). But cf. 9 Wright & Miller, *Federal Practice and Procedure: Civil* § 2303 (1971).

4. Cases like *Denman,* which involve head-on vehicular collisions, present a difficult problem with regard to the control of jury verdicts. The circumstances of these collisions ordinarily suggest that at least one driver was negligent but may not indicate which driver it was, and direct evidence often is lacking because all witnesses are dead. See Annot., 77 A.L.R.2d 580 (1961). Can you suggest a solution to the problem?

5. In KIRCHER v. ATCHISON, TOPEKA & SANTA FE RY. CO., 32 Cal. 2d 176, 195 P.2d 427 (1948), plaintiff sued for the loss of a hand, which had been run over by defendant's train. A judgment for plaintiff was affirmed. Justice Carter, for the court, said:

> * * * In the light of all the circumstances * * * it cannot be held as a matter of law, that plaintiff's version was such as to contravene the laws of nature, or as to render the jury's acceptance of it unreasonable. * * * Although he stated quite frankly that he was unable to explain with certainty the manner in which his left hand came to be placed on the east rail * * *, the jury had before it evidence indicating that * * * there was a hole in the depot platform * * * and the ultimate fact that defendant's train ran over his hand at the time and place in question. In these circumstances the jury was not compelled to find against him because he could not with certainty relate the exact manner in which his left hand came to be on the east rail. It could reasonably have inferred that his failure to explain this circumstance was due to the fact that in the critical few minutes he was under the train he was unconscious, or substantially so, from the blow on his head as the outcome of stepping into the hole.

Id. at 184, 195 P.2d at 433.

Justice Traynor, dissenting, said:

> It is my opinion that although the accident as described by plaintiff is not outside the realm of possibility, his version, which is that of an interested and impeached witness, involves so extraordinary and improbable a sequence of events that without corroboration it does not warrant belief by a reasonable jury.

Id. at 189, 195 P.2d at 436.

Does the *Kircher* case present the same kind of issue as the *Denman* case? Should a verdict ever be directed for the party having the burden of producing evidence on an issue when the evidence in that party's favor is testimonial rather than documentary? As previously noted, see pp. 936–38, supra, hearsay evidence is excluded on objection because it is not regarded as a reliable basis for a jury's decision. If hearsay evidence comes in without objection, and the party against whom that evidence militates subsequently moves for a directed verdict, should the hearsay evidence be taken into account in determining whether there is sufficient evidence to support a jury verdict for the other party?

ROGERS v. MISSOURI PACIFIC R. CO.

Supreme Court of the United States, 1957.
352 U.S. 500, 77 S.Ct. 443, 1 L.Ed.2d 493.

Certiorari to the Supreme Court of Missouri.

MR. JUSTICE BRENNAN delivered the opinion of the Court.

A jury in the Circuit Court of St. Louis awarded damages to the petitioner in this action under the Federal Employers' Liability Act. The Supreme Court of Missouri reversed upon the ground that the petitioner's evidence did not support the finding of respondent's liability. * * *

Petitioner was a laborer in a section gang, working on July 17, 1951, along a portion of respondent's double-track line which, near Garner, Arkansas, runs generally north and south. The tracks are on ballast topping the surface of a dirt "dump" with sloping sides, and there is a path about a yard wide bordering each side of the surface between the crest of the slope and the edge of the ballast. Weeds and vegetation, killed chemically preparatory to burning them off, covered the paths and slopes. Petitioner's foreman assigned him to burn off the weeds and vegetation—the first time he was given that task in the two months he had worked for the respondent. He testified that it was customary to burn off such vegetation with a flame thrower operated from a car running on the tracks. Railroad witnesses testified, however, that the respondent discontinued the use of flame throwers at least a year earlier because the fires started by them sometimes spread beyond the railroad right of way.

Petitioner was supplied with a crude hand torch and was instructed to burn off the weeds and vegetation along the west path and for two or three feet down the west slope. The events leading to his mishap occurred after he proceeded with the work to a point within thirty to thirty-five yards of a culvert adjoining the path.

Petitioner testified, without contradiction, that the foreman instructed him and other members of the section gang to stop what they were doing when a train passed and to take positions off the tracks and ties to observe the journals of the passing train for hot boxes. The instructions were explicit not to go on either of the tracks or to stand on or near the ends of the ties when a train was passing on a far track. This was a safety precaution because "the sound of one train would deaden the sound of another one that possibly would come from the other way."

On this day, petitioner heard the whistle of a train which was approaching from behind him on the east track. He promptly "quit firing" and ran north to a place on the path near the mentioned culvert. He was standing a few feet from the culvert observing the train for hotboxes when he became enveloped in smoke and flames. The passing train had fanned the flames of the burning vegetation and weeds, carrying the fire to the vegetation around his position. He threw his arm over his face, retreated quickly back on the culvert and slipped and fell from the top of the culvert, suffering the serious injuries for which he sought damages in this suit.

* * *

We think that the evidence was sufficient to support the jury finding for the petitioner. The testimony that the burning off of weeds and vegetation was ordinarily done with flame throwers from cars on the tracks and not, as here, by a workman on foot using a crude hand torch, when that evidence is considered with the uncontradicted testimony that the petitioner was where he was on this narrow path atop the dirt "dump" in furtherance of explicit orders * * *, supplied ample support for a jury finding that respondent's negligence played a part in the petitioner's injury. These were probative facts from which the jury could find that respondent was or should have been aware of conditions which created a likelihood that petitioner, in performing the duties required of him, would suffer just such an injury as he did. Common experience teaches both that a passing train will fan the flames of a fire, and that a person suddenly enveloped in flames and smoke will instinctively react by retreating from the danger and in the process pay scant heed to other dangers which may imperil him. In this view, it was an irrelevant consideration whether the immediate reason for his slipping off the culvert was the presence of gravel negligently allowed by respondent to remain on the surface, or was some cause not identified from the evidence.

The Missouri Supreme Court based its reversal upon its finding of an alleged admission by the petitioner that he knew it was his primary duty to watch the fire. From that premise the Missouri court reasoned that petitioner was inattentive to the fire and that the emergency which confronted him "was an emergency brought about by himself." It said that if, as petitioner testified, the immediate cause of his fall was that loose gravel on the surface of the culvert rolled out from under him, yet it was his inattention to the fire which caused it to spread and obliged petitioner "to move blindly away and fall," and this was "something extraordinary, unrelated to, and disconnected from the incline of the gravel at the culvert."

We interpret the foregoing to mean that the Missouri court found as a matter of law that the petitioner's conduct was the sole cause of his mishap. But when the petitioner agreed that his primary duty was to watch the fire he did not also say that he was relieved of the duty to stop to watch a passing train for hotboxes. Indeed, no witness testified that the instruction was countermanded. At best, uncertainty as to the fact arises from the petitioner's testimony, and in that circumstance not the court, but the jury, was the tribunal to determine the fact.

We may assume that the jury could properly have reached the court's conclusion. But, as the probative facts also supported with reason the verdict favorable to the petitioner, the decision was exclusively for the jury to make. The jury was instructed to return a verdict for the respondent if it was found that negligence of the petitioner was the sole cause of his mishap. We must take it that the verdict was obedient to the trial judge's charge and that the jury found that such was not the case but that petitioner's injury resulted at least in part from the respondent's negligence.

The opinion may also be read as basing the reversal on another ground, namely, that it appeared to the court that the petitioner's conduct was at least as probable a cause for his mishap as any negligence of the respondent, and that in such case there was no case for the jury. But that would mean that there is no jury question in actions under this statute, although the employee's proofs support with reason a verdict in his favor, unless the judge can say that the jury may exclude the idea that his injury was due to causes with which the defendant was not connected, or, stated another way, unless his proofs are so strong that the jury, on grounds of probability, may exclude a conclusion favorable to the defendant. That is not the governing principle defining the proof which requires a submission to the jury in these cases. The Missouri court's opinion implies its view that this is the governing standard by saying that the proofs must show that "the injury would not have occurred but for the negligence" of his employer, and that "[t]he test of whether there is causal connection is that, absent the negligent act the injury would not have occurred." * * *

Under this statute the test of a jury case is simply whether the proofs justify with reason the conclusion that employer negligence played any part, even the slightest, in producing the injury or death for which damages are sought. It does not matter that, from the evidence, the jury may also with reason, on grounds of probability, attribute the result to other causes, including the employee's contributory negligence. Judicial appraisal of the proofs to determine whether a jury question is presented is narrowly limited to the single inquiry whether, with reason, the conclusion may be drawn that negligence of the employer played any part at all in the injury or death. Judges are to fix their sights primarily to make that appraisal and, if that test is met, are bound to find that a case for the jury is made out whether or not the evidence allows the jury a choice of other probabilities. The statute expressly imposes liability upon the employer to pay damages for injury or death due "in whole or *in part*" to its negligence. (Emphasis added.)

* * *

The Congress when adopting the law was particularly concerned that the issues whether there was employer fault and whether that fault played any part in the injury or death of the employee should be decided by the jury whenever fair-minded men could reach these conclusions on the evidence. Originally, judicial administration of the 1908 Act substantially limited the cases in which employees were allowed a jury determination. That was because the courts developed concepts of assumption of risk and of the coverage of the law, which defeated employee claims as a matter of law. Congress corrected this by the 1939 amendments and removed the fetters which hobbled the full play of the basic congressional intention to leave to the fact-finding function of the jury the decision of the primary question raised in these cases—whether employer fault played any part in the employee's mishap. * * *

The judgment is reversed. * * *

MR. JUSTICE BURTON concurs in the result.

MR. JUSTICE REED would affirm the judgment of the Supreme Court of Missouri.

[Dissenting opinions of JUSTICE FRANKFURTER and JUSTICE HARLAN are omitted.]

Notes and Questions

1. Is the nature of the issue that the Court said should have been left to the jury in *Rogers* different from that in *Lavender, Denman,* and *Kircher?* If so, is the difference significant to the formulation of a standard? Might a directed verdict be more readily sustained on one type of issue than the other?

2. A municipal ordinance permitted an authorized emergency vehicle to proceed past a stop signal or exceed the speed limit "when the driver of such vehicle sounds a siren, bell or exhaust whistle to the extent reasonably necessary." A police car in rush-hour traffic, on call to a robbery then in progress, proceeded at excessive speed through a red light, and struck plaintiff. In LO CICERO v. COLUMBIA CAS. CO., 268 F.2d 440 (5th Cir.), certiorari denied 361 U.S. 917, 80 S.Ct. 261, 4 L.Ed.2d 187 (1959), the court held that the jury should have been instructed that the policeman was negligent as a matter of law in failing to sound the siren. Is this distinguishable from directing a verdict on the issue of negligence when no statute is involved? Cf. Note 3, p. 916–17, supra.

3. Justice Frankfurter dissented in the *Rogers* case on the ground that certiorari had been "improvidently granted"; the Justice declined to express himself on the merits. The case is one of many in which he argued that the Supreme Court should not take time to review cases in which the only issue was the sufficiency of the evidence to take a case to the jury. See pp. 1140–43, infra.

c. Judgment Notwithstanding the Verdict in the Federal Courts—A Procedural Muddle

------

Read Federal Rules of Civil Procedure 50(b), (c), and (d) and the accompanying material in the Supplement.

SLOCUM v. NEW YORK LIFE INSURANCE CO.

Supreme Court of the United States, 1913.
228 U.S. 364, 33 S.Ct. 523, 57 L.Ed. 879.

Certiorari to the United States Circuit Court of Appeals for the Third Circuit.

MR. JUSTICE VAN DEVANTER delivered the opinion of the court.

* * * The case made by the evidence, in that view of it which is most favorable to the plaintiff, was as follows: [Defendant insurer issued a policy of life insurance to plaintiff's decedent on November 27, 1899;

[handwritten margin notes: "8 yr policy", "got payment made only in part", "Appct should have directed a new trial"]

death occurred December 31, 1907. The annual premium due November 27, 1907, was not paid, but on the last day of the grace period, December 27, plaintiff paid a portion of it in cash and received a note, to be signed by the decedent, for the balance; plaintiff told the agent that her husband was ill and might not be able to sign the note for several days and was told to mail the note as soon as she could. Decedent died before signing the note. Plaintiff brought suit on the policy in a federal circuit court; defendant's motion for a directed verdict at the close of the evidence was denied. The jury returned a verdict for plaintiff. In accordance with Pennsylvania practice, defendant moved for judgment notwithstanding the verdict which was also denied. On writ of error, the circuit court of appeals reversed the judgment for plaintiff with instructions to sustain the motion for judgment n.o.v. "on the ground that the evidence did not legally admit of the conclusion that the policy was a subsisting contract of insurance at the date of the insured's death."] * * *

We are * * * of opinion that the evidence did not admit of a finding that the policy was in force at the time of the insured's death, and therefore that the circuit court should have granted the company's request that a verdict in its favor be directed. As that request was denied, the circuit court of appeals did not err in reversing the judgment.

It becomes necessary, therefore, to consider whether that court should have directed a new trial instead of a judgment on the evidence contrary to the verdict.

* * * [T]he circuit court of appeals directed a judgment for one party when the verdict was for the other, and did this on the theory, not that the judgment was required by the state of the pleadings, but that it was warranted by the evidence. It will be perceived, therefore, that the court * * * did not order a new trial, but assumed to pass finally upon the issues of fact presented by the pleadings and to direct a judgment accordingly. If this was an infraction of the 7th Amendment, it matters not that it was in conformity with the state statute, or with the practice thereunder in the courts of the state, for neither the statute nor the practice could be followed in opposition to the Amendment, which, although not applicable to proceedings in the courts of the several states, is controlling in the Federal courts.

* * *

* * * [It is] plain, first, that the action of the circuit court of appeals in setting aside the verdict and assuming to pass upon the issues of fact, and to direct a judgment accordingly, must be tested by the rules of the common law; second, that while under those rules that court could set aside the verdict for error of law in the proceedings in the circuit court, and order a new trial, it could not itself determine the facts; and, third, that when the verdict was set aside there arose the same right of trial by jury as in the first instance. How, then, can it be said that there was not an infraction of the 7th Amendment? When the verdict was set aside the issues of fact were left undetermined, and until they should be determined anew no judgment on the merits could be given. The new determination, according to the rules of the common law, could be had

only through a new trial, with the same right to a jury as before. Disregarding those rules, the circuit court of appeals itself determined the facts, without a new trial. Thus, it assumed a power it did not possess, and cut off the plaintiff's right to have the facts settled by the verdict of a jury.

While it is true * * * that the evidence produced at the trial was not sufficient to sustain a verdict for the plaintiff, and that the circuit court erred in refusing so to instruct the jury, this does not militate against the conclusion just stated. According to the rules of the common law, such an error, like other errors of law affecting a verdict, could be corrected on writ of error only by ordering a new trial. * * * And this procedure was regarded as of real value, because, in addition to fully recognizing that right, it afforded an opportunity for adducing further evidence rightly conducing to a solution of the issues.

* * * [W]hile it is the province of the court to aid the jury in the right discharge of their duty, even to the extent of directing their verdict where the insufficiency or conclusive character of the evidence warrants such a direction, the court cannot dispense with a verdict, or disregard one when given, and itself pass on the issues of fact. In other words, the constitutional guaranty operates to require that the issues be settled by the verdict of a jury, unless the right thereto be waived. * * *

* * * At the trial the defendant requested that a verdict in its favor be directed, and had the court indicated its purpose to do that, it would have been open to the plaintiff, under the then prevailing practice, to take a voluntary nonsuit, which would have enabled her to make a fuller and better presentation of her case, if the facts permitted, at another trial in a new suit. * * *

The judgment of the Circuit Court of Appeals is accordingly modified by eliminating the direction to enter judgment for the defendant notwithstanding the verdict, and by substituting a direction for a new trial.

MR. JUSTICE HUGHES, dissenting:

I concur in the decision of the court so far as it holds that the circuit court of appeals was right in reversing the judgment; but I am unable to agree with the conclusion that the circuit court of appeals was bound to order a new trial * * *.

The serious and far-reaching consequences of this decision are manifest. Not only does it overturn the established practice of the Federal courts in Pennsylvania in applying, under the conformity act, the provisions of the state law, but it erects an impassable barrier—unless the Constitution be amended—to action by Congress along the same line for the purpose of remedying the mischief of repeated trials, and of thus diminishing in a highly important degree the delays and expense of litigation. It cannot be gainsaid that such a conclusion is not to be reached unless the constitutional provision compels it. I cannot see that it does compel it.

* * * [W]herein has any matter of fact tried by a jury been reexamined? Concededly, there was no fact to be tried by a jury; the case

as made was barren of any such fact; and there being none, there has been no reexamination of it. How can it be said that the circuit court of appeals has determined the facts or has passed upon issues of fact? Whether there was any evidence for the jury was a question of law. The trial court, in wrongly deciding it, did not convert it into a question of fact; it was not altered by the verdict, but remained the same in its nature,—a question for the determination of the court. That, it seems to me, is the substance of the matter, and all else is form and procedure. * * * [I]t is not a matter withdrawn from legislative control by the constitutional provision for trial by jury, which is concerned with the settlement of disputes of fact, and not with the determination of legal questions, or with the consequences, which should ensue when that determination is decisive of the right of recovery on the case made.

* * *

The dominating idea, in overturning the practice below, seems to be that at common law, if there was an issue of fact upon the pleadings, the plaintiff was entitled to have a verdict taken in any event; that is, if he did not voluntarily take a nonsuit, it was essential that a verdict be rendered, notwithstanding that upon the evidence there was no question of fact for the jury.

* * *

It is said, however, that a new trial affords opportunity to a plaintiff to better his case by presenting evidence which may not have been available before. But we are not dealing with an application for a new trial upon the ground of newly discovered evidence, or with the principles controlling an application of that sort. We are concerned with the question whether a party has a constitutional right to another trial, simply because the trial court erred in its determination of a question of law which was decisive of the case made. Had the trial court done what this court says it should have done, it would have directed a verdict for the defendant; and if the jury, simply following the instruction of the trial court, had so found, final judgment would have been entered and no new trial would now be granted. Still the jury would not have passed upon any question of fact, but would simply have obeyed the judge. The opportunity to better the case on a second trial would probably be as welcome, but it would not be accorded. I am unable to see any basis for a constitutional distinction which raises a constitutional right to another trial in the one case and not in the other.

* * *

I am authorized to say that MR. JUSTICE HOLMES, MR. JUSTICE LURTON, and MR. JUSTICE PITNEY concur in this dissent.

Notes and Questions

1. Under the Federal Rules, does a plaintiff have a right to a voluntary nonsuit that would allow the action to be recommenced? See Wall v. Connecticut Mut. Life Ins. Co., 2 F.R.D. 244 (N.D.Ga.1941). See also pp. 851–52, supra.

2.   How do the Federal Rules provide for the case in which a jury refuses to return a verdict as directed? Is this procedure consistent with the majority opinion in *Slocum?*

———

BALTIMORE & CAROLINA LINE, INC. v. REDMAN, 295 U.S. 654, 656, 658–60, 55 S.Ct. 890, 891–93, 79 L.Ed. 1636, 1637–40 (1935) (opinion by Justice Van Devanter):

This was an action in a federal court in New York to recover damages for personal injuries allegedly sustained by the plaintiff through the defendant's negligence. The issues were tried before the court and a jury. At the conclusion of the evidence, the defendant moved for a dismissal of the complaint because the evidence was insufficient to support a verdict for the plaintiff, and also moved for a directed verdict in its favor on the same ground. The court reserved its decision on both motions, submitted the case to the jury subject to its opinion on the questions reserved, and received from the jury a verdict for the plaintiff. No objection was made to the reservation or this mode of proceeding. Thereafter the court held the evidence sufficient and the motions ill grounded, and accordingly entered a judgment for the plaintiff on the verdict.

The defendant appealed to the Circuit Court of Appeals, which held the evidence insufficient and reversed the judgment with a direction for a new trial. The defendant urged that the direction be for a dismissal of the complaint. But the Court of Appeals ruled that under our decision in Slocum v. New York Life Insurance Company the direction must be for a new trial. * * *

A very different situation [from *Slocum*] is disclosed in the present case. The trial court expressly reserved its ruling on the defendant's motions to dismiss and for a directed verdict, both of which were based on the asserted insufficiency of the evidence to support a verdict for the plaintiff. Whether the evidence was sufficient or otherwise was a question of law to be resolved by the court. The verdict for the plaintiff was taken pending the court's rulings on the motions and subject to those rulings. No objection was made to the reservation or this mode of proceeding, and they must be regarded as having the tacit consent of the parties. * * *

At common law there was a well-established practice of reserving questions of law arising during trials by jury and of taking verdicts subject to the ultimate ruling on the questions reserved; and under this practice the reservation carried with it authority to make such ultimate disposition of the case as might be made essential by the ruling under the reservation, such as nonsuiting the plaintiff where he had obtained a verdict, entering a verdict or judgment for one party where the jury had given a verdict to the other, or making other essential adjustments.

Fragmentary references to the origin and basis of the practice indicate that it came to be supported on the theory that it gave better opportunity for considered rulings, made new trials less frequent, and commanded such general approval that parties litigant assented to its application as a matter of course. But whatever may have been its origin or theoretical basis, it undoubtedly was well established when the Seventh Amendment was adopted, and therefore must be regarded as a part of the common-law rules to which resort must be had in testing and measuring the right of trial by jury as preserved and protected by that amendment.

Notes and Questions

1. How critical is the fact, emphasized by the Court, that plaintiff in the *Redman* case did not object to the reservation of the decision on the motion for a directed verdict? Does Federal Rule 50(b) require the nonmoving party's consent?

2. In LO CICERO v. COLUMBIA CAS. CO., p. 983, supra, plaintiff had not asked that the jury be charged that the policeman was guilty of negligence as a matter of law in failing to sound a siren nor did plaintiff object to the failure so to charge. Although the jury returned a verdict for defendant, the Court of Appeals reversed, holding that the policeman was negligent as a matter of law, and remanded the case for a determination of the issues of proximate cause, contributory negligence, and last clear chance. Is this result consistent with the requirement that before judgment n.o.v. can be entered for a party, by a trial or an appellate court, the party must have moved for a directed verdict? Is that requirement inapplicable to any ruling that forecloses jury determination of a factual issue that does not by itself dispose of the entire claim?

3. If defendant moves for a directed verdict at the close of plaintiff's case, may defendant, without renewing the directed-verdict motion, move for judgment n.o.v. after verdict? May defendant seek a new trial by raising the denial of the earlier motion as error on appeal? Are your answers to these questions related to the doctrine that defendant may not move for a directed verdict without resting his case? See Columbia & P.S.R.R. v. Hawthorne, 144 U.S. 202, 12 S.Ct. 591, 36 L.Ed. 405 (1892).

NEELY v. MARTIN K. EBY CONSTRUCTION CO.

Supreme Court of the United States, 1967.
386 U.S. 317, 87 S.Ct. 1072, 18 L.Ed.2d 75.

Certiorari to the United States Court of Appeals for the Tenth Circuit.

MR. JUSTICE WHITE delivered the opinion of the Court.

Petitioner brought this diversity action in the United States District Court for the District of Colorado alleging that respondent's negligent construction, maintenance, and supervision of a scaffold platform used in the construction of a missile silo near Elizabeth, Colorado, had proximately caused her father's fatal plunge from the platform during the course of his employment as Night Silo Captain for * * * an engineering firm engaged in the construction of a missile launcher system in the silo. At the close of the petitioner's evidence and again at the close of all the evidence, respondent moved for a directed verdict. The trial judge denied both motions and submitted the case to a jury, which returned a verdict for petitioner for $25,000.

Respondent then moved for judgment notwithstanding the jury's verdict or, in the alternative, for a new trial * * *. The trial court denied the motions and entered judgment for petitioner on the jury's verdict. * * *

The Court of Appeals held that the evidence at trial was insufficient to establish either negligence by respondent or proximate cause and reversed the judgment of the District Court "with instructions to dismiss the action." * * * [P]etitioner then sought a writ of certiorari, presenting the question whether the Court of Appeals could, consistent with the 1963 amendments to Rule 50 * * * and with the Seventh Amendment's guarantee of a right to jury trial, direct the trial court to dismiss the action. Our order allowing certiorari directed the parties' attention to whether Rule 50(d) and our decisions in Cone v. West Virginia Pulp & Paper Co., 330 U.S. 212, 67 S.Ct. 752, 91 L.Ed. 849; Globe Liquor Co. v. San Roman, 332 U.S. 571, 68 S.Ct. 246, 92 L.Ed. 177; and Weade v. Dichmann, Wright & Pugh, Inc., 337 U.S. 801, 69 S.Ct. 1326, 93 L.Ed. 1704, permit this disposition by a court of appeals despite Rule 50(c)(2), which gives a party whose jury verdict is set aside by a trial court 10 days in which to invoke the trial court's discretion to order a new trial. We affirm.

* * *

The question here is whether the Court of Appeals, after reversing the denial of a defendant's Rule 50(b) motion for judgment notwithstanding the verdict, may itself order dismissal or direct entry of judgment for defendant. As far as the Seventh Amendment's right to jury trial is concerned, there is no greater restriction on the province of the jury when an appellate court enters judgment n.o.v. than when a trial court does; consequently, there is no constitutional bar to an appellate court granting judgment n.o.v.

* * * Federal Rules 50(c) and 50(d) * * * were added to Rule 50 in 1963 to clarify the proper practice under this Rule. Though Rule 50(d) is more pertinent to the facts of this case, it is useful to examine these interrelated provisions together. * * * As the Advisory Committee's Note to Rule 50(c) makes clear, Rule 50(c)(1) contemplates that the appellate court will review on appeal both the grant of judgment n.o.v. and, if necessary, the trial court's conditional disposition of the motion for new trial. This review necessarily includes the power to grant or to deny a new trial in appropriate cases.

Rule 50(d) is applicable to cases such as this one where the trial court has denied a motion for judgment n.o.v. Rule 50(d) expressly preserves to the party who prevailed in the district court the right to urge that the court of appeals grant a new trial should the jury's verdict be set aside on appeal. Rule 50(d) also emphasizes that "nothing in the rule precludes" the court of appeals "from determining that the appellee is entitled to a new trial, or from directing the trial court to determine whether a new trial shall be granted." Quite properly, this Rule recognizes that the appellate court may prefer that the trial judge pass first upon the appellee's new trial suggestion. Nevertheless, consideration of the new

trial question "in the first instance" is lodged with the court of appeals.
* * *

Rule 50(c)(2) * * * is on its face inapplicable to the situation presented here. That Rule regulates the verdict winner's opportunity to move for a new trial if the *trial court* has granted a Rule 50(b) motion for judgment n.o.v. In this case, the trial court denied judgment n.o.v. and respondent appealed. Jurisdiction over the case then passed to the Court of Appeals, and petitioner's right to seek a new trial in the trial court after her jury verdict was set aside became dependent upon the disposition by the Court of Appeals under Rule 50(d).

* * * In Cone v. West Virginia Pulp & Paper Co., supra, the defendant moved for directed verdict, but the trial judge sent the case to the jury. After a jury verdict for the plaintiff, the trial court denied defendant's motion for a new trial. On appeal, the Court of Appeals reversed and ordered the entry of judgment n.o.v. This Court reversed the Court of Appeals on the ground that the defendant had not moved for judgment n.o.v. in the trial court, but only for a new trial, and consequently the Court of Appeals was precluded from directing any disposition other than a new trial. * * * In Johnson v. New York, N.H. & H.R.R., 344 U.S. 48, 73 S.Ct. 125, 97 L.Ed. 77, this Court held that a verdict loser's motion to "set aside" the jury's verdict did not comply with Rule 50(b)'s requirement of a timely motion for judgment n.o.v. and therefore that the Court of Appeals could not direct entry of judgment n.o.v. And in Weade v. Dichmann, Wright & Pugh, Inc., supra, where a proper motion for judgment n.o.v. was made and denied in the trial court, we modified a Court of Appeals decision directing entry of judgment n.o.v. because there were "suggestions in the complaint and evidence" of an alternative theory of liability which had not been passed upon by the jury and therefore which might justify the grant of a new trial. * * *

The opinions in the above cases make it clear that an appellate court may not order judgment n.o.v. where the verdict loser has failed strictly to comply with the procedural requirements of Rule 50(b), or where the record reveals a new trial issue which has not been resolved. Part of the Court's concern has been to protect the rights of the party whose jury verdict has been set aside on appeal and who may have valid grounds for a new trial, some or all of which should be passed upon by the district court, rather than the court of appeals, because of the trial judge's first-hand knowledge of witnesses, testimony, and issues—because of his "feel" for the overall case. These are very valid concerns to which the court of appeals should be constantly alert. * * *

But these considerations do not justify an ironclad rule that the court of appeals should never order dismissal or judgment for defendant when the plaintiff's verdict has been set aside on appeal. Such a rule would not serve the purpose of Rule 50 to speed litigation and to avoid unnecessary retrials. * * *

There are, on the one hand, situations where the defendant's grounds for setting aside the jury's verdict raise questions of subject matter jurisdiction or dispositive issues of law which, if resolved in defendant's favor, must necessarily terminate the litigation. * * *

On the other hand, where the court of appeals sets aside the jury's verdict because the evidence was insufficient to send the case to the jury, it is not so clear that the litigation should be terminated. Although many of the plaintiff-appellee's possible grounds for a new trial, such as inadequacy of the verdict, will not survive a decision that the case should not have gone to the jury in the first place, there remain important considerations which may entitle him to a new trial. The erroneous exclusion of evidence which would have strengthened his case is an important possibility. Another is that the trial court itself caused the insufficiency in plaintiff-appellee's case by erroneously placing too high a burden of proof on him at trial. But issues like these are issues of law with which the courts of appeals regularly and characteristically must deal. The district court in all likelihood has already ruled on these questions in the course of the trial and, in any event, has no special advantage or competence in dealing with them. They are precisely the kind of issues that the losing defendant below may bring to the court of appeals without ever moving for a new trial in the district court. * * *

A plaintiff whose jury verdict is set aside by the trial court on defendant's n.o.v. motion may ask the trial judge to grant a voluntary nonsuit to give plaintiff another chance to fill a gap in his proof. * * * The plaintiff-appellee should have this same opportunity when his verdict is set aside on appeal. Undoubtedly, in many cases this question will call for an exercise of the trial court's discretion. However, there is no substantial reason why the appellee should not present the matter to the court of appeals, which can if necessary remand the case to permit initial consideration by the district court.

* * *

In our view, therefore, Rule 50(d) makes express and adequate provision for the opportunity—which the plaintiff-appellee had without this rule—to present his grounds for a new trial in the event his verdict is set aside by the court of appeals. If he does so in his brief—or in a petition for rehearing if the court of appeals has directed entry of judgment for appellant—the court of appeals may make final disposition of the issues presented, except those which in its informed discretion should be reserved for the trial court. If appellee presents no new trial issues in his brief or in a petition for rehearing, the court of appeals may, in any event, order a new trial on its own motion or refer the question to the district court, based on factors encountered in its own review of the case. * * *

In the case before us, petitioner won a verdict in the District Court which survived respondent's n.o.v. motion. In the Court of Appeals the issue was the sufficiency of the evidence and that court set aside the verdict. Petitioner, as appellee, suggested no grounds for a new trial in the event her judgment was reversed, nor did she petition for rehearing in the Court of Appeals, even though that court had directed a dismissal of her case. Neither was it suggested that the record was insufficient to present any new trial issues or that any other reason required a remand to the District Court. Indeed, in her brief in the Court of Appeals, petitioner stated, "this law suit was fairly tried and the jury was properly instructed." It was, of course, incumbent on the Court of Appeals to consider the new trial question in the light of its own experience with the case. But we will not assume that the court ignored its duty in this respect, although it would have been better had its opinion expressly dealt with the new trial question.

* * *

Affirmed.

MR. JUSTICE DOUGLAS and MR. JUSTICE FORTAS, while agreeing with the Court's construction of Rule 50, would reverse the judgment because in their view the evidence of negligence and proximate cause was sufficient to go to the jury.

MR. JUSTICE BLACK, dissenting.

I dissent from the Court's decision in this case for three reasons: First, I think the evidence in this case was clearly sufficient to go to the jury on the issues of both negligence and proximate cause. Second, I think that under our prior decisions and Rule 50, a court of appeals, in reversing a trial court's refusal to enter judgment n.o.v. on the ground of insufficiency of the evidence, is entirely powerless to order the trial court to dismiss the case, thus depriving the verdict winner of any opportunity to present a motion for new trial to the trial judge who is thoroughly familiar with the case. Third, even if a court of appeals has that power, I find it manifestly unfair to affirm the Court of Appeals' judgment here without giving this petitioner a chance to present her grounds for a new trial to the Court of Appeals as the Court today for the first time holds she must.

* * *

Since the adoption of Rule 50, our cases have consistently and emphatically preserved the right of a litigant whose judgment—whether it be a judgment entered on the verdict or judgment n.o.v.—is set aside to invoke the discretion of the trial court in ruling on a motion for new trial. The first of these cases was Montgomery Ward & Co. v. Duncan, 311 U.S. 243, 61 S.Ct. 189, 85 L.Ed. 147, where the trial judge, unlike here, granted the defendant's motion for judgment n.o.v., but in doing so failed to rule on his alternative motion for a new trial. The Court of Appeals reversed the trial court's grant of judgment n.o.v. to the defendant and remanded the case with directions to enter judgment on the verdict for the plaintiff. * * * Holding that the trial judge should have initially ruled on this alternative motion, this Court remanded the case to the trial judge for the purpose of passing on that motion. In explaining this result the Court said:

> The rule contemplates that either party to the action is entitled to the trial judge's decision on both motions, if both are presented. * * *

* * *

This issue of whether a new trial is justified after a verdict is set aside either by a trial or an appellate court is a new issue which it was not necessary to decide in the original trial. It is a factual issue and that the trial court is the more appropriate tribunal to determine it has been almost universally accepted by both federal and state courts throughout the years. * * * Appellate tribunals are not equipped to try factual issues as trial courts are. A trial judge who has heard the evidence in the original case has a vast store of information and knowledge about it that the appellate court cannot get from a cold, printed record. Thus, as we said in *Cone,* the trial judge can base the broad discretion granted him in determining factual issues of a new trial on his own knowledge of the evidence and the issues "in a perspective peculiarly available to him alone." * * *

Notes and Questions

1. In JOHNSON v. NEW YORK, N.H. & H.R. CO., discussed in the *Neely* case, defendant's lawyer moved "to set aside the verdict on the ground that it is contrary to the law and contrary to the evidence and contrary to the weight of the evidence and excessive." The motion was denied, but the Court of Appeals directed that judgment n.o.v. for defendant be entered. The Supreme Court reversed, holding that the Court of Appeals could not order such a judgment in the absence of a motion for judgment n.o.v. after the return of the jury verdict and that the motion defendant's lawyer made could not be considered to constitute such a motion. Why not? How technically perfect must a motion for judgment n.o.v. be? Courts continue to disagree. See Note, 31 Okl.L.Rev. 208, 216–17 (1978).

If a motion for directed verdict is made and denied, and the jury returns a verdict for the nonmoving party, may the trial court grant judgment n.o.v. for the party who asked for the directed verdict even if that party makes no motion for one? Should it make any difference how long after the verdict the court acts? Should it make any difference whether the trial judge has "expressly" reserved decision on the motion for a directed verdict? See First Safe Deposit Nat. Bank v. Western Union Tel. Co., 337 F.2d 743 (1st Cir.1964); Shaw v. Edward Hines Lumber Co., 249 F.2d 434 (7th Cir.1957).

2. If a motion for a directed verdict is made and denied, and subsequent to the verdict a motion for judgment n.o.v. is made but a new trial is not requested, may the trial court, if it denies the judgment n.o.v., grant a new trial more than ten days after the judgment? See Jackson v. Wilson Trucking Corp., 243 F.2d 212 (D.C.Cir.1957). See also pp. 1015–25, infra.

2. CHALLENGING ERRORS: NEW TRIAL

a. *The Nature and the Scope of the Power to Grant a New Trial*

———

Read Federal Rules of Civil Procedure 59 and 61 and the accompanying materials in the Supplement. Note particularly the grounds for new trial listed in Minnesota Rule of Civil Procedure 59.01.

———

The Range of the Trial Court's Discretion

1. Errors committed during the course of a trial may be categorized as follows: (i) those that would result in reversal if the case were to be appealed; (ii) those that may have had an impact on the verdict, but do not justify reversal of the case on appeal, and (iii) those that did not significantly affect the outcome. Obviously errors that do not have any impact on the decision are harmless and it would be an abuse of discretion for the trial court to predicate a new trial on them. On the other hand, errors that would justify a reversal by an appellate court demand remedial measures at the trial level. A judge should not force a litigant to pay the costs of prosecuting an appeal as well as the costs of the new trial to which he is entitled.

2. Theoretically, it is only with regard to errors that affect the result in the case but would not lead to reversal on appeal that the trial court has discretion to decide whether or not a new trial is appropriate. As a practical matter, however, the almost unlimited power of the court with regard to the granting of new trials is far greater than it might otherwise seem to be. First, an aggrieved litigant may decide to stand or fall on the motion for new trial since the case simply may not be worth the added cost of an appeal or the litigant may not have sufficient funds to continue fighting. Second, in many jurisdictions, the grant of a new trial, not being a final judgment, cannot be appealed. Thus the cost of a new trial will have to be absorbed before an appeal is even possible. Third, the very question of what constitutes reversible error on appeal often is affected by the ruling of the trial judge on the motion for new trial. In those jurisdictions in which a motion for a new trial is a prerequisite for appeal, see, e.g., Martin v. Opdyke Agency, 156 Colo. 316, 398 P.2d 971 (1965) (applying former Colorado Rule 59(f)); Evans v. Wilkinson, 419 P.2d 275 (Okl.1966), the denial of a new trial certainly will influence the appellate court in deciding whether the error is harmless for purposes of appeal if the effect of the error in question can better be determined by the trial judge. Even when a motion for a new trial is not required, and when, theoretically, the appellate court should not penalize a litigant for having so moved, knowledge that the trial judge has rejected the alleged error as harmless may have an impact on the appellate-court decision. Finally, in some jurisdictions the trial judge may grant a new trial without specifying or without actually relying on any precise grounds. Obviously this narrows the scope of review of such decisions.

———

GINSBERG v. WILLIAMS, 270 Minn. 474, 135 N.W.2d 213 (1965). Plaintiff brought suit for damages received in an automobile accident. The jury rendered a verdict for defendant and plaintiff moved for a new trial. The court granted the motion "in the interests of justice," giving no other basis for its ruling. Defendant sought a writ of prohibition to restrain enforcement of the ruling, claiming that the trial court is empowered to grant a new trial only for one of the grounds specifically set forth in Rule 59.01 of the Minnesota Rules of Civil Procedure. The Minnesota Supreme Court granted the writ, holding as follows:

> * * * The causes enumerated in Rule 59.01 are so comprehensive that they include every conceivable reason for which a new trial ought to be ordered. Those causes requiring the exercise of discretion, such as 59.01(1) (irregularities depriving the moving party of a fair trial) and 59.01(8) (insufficiency of the evidence), vest the broadest possible discretionary power in the trial court. To permit granting a new trial "in the interests of justice" would invite an arbitrary exercise of power over which appellate review is not now available. Even if it were, it would be difficult to fashion any effective rules to control arbitrary action since the basis for such an order would necessarily be subjective, varying from judge to judge. Further, each of the causes enumerated is designed to promote justice and prevent injustice. It is one thing to order a new trial "on the ground that on the evidence substantial justice has not been done" or in the interest of justice on the ground that the evidence does not justify the verdict, and quite another thing to order a new trial simply "in the interests of justice." It is difficult to conceive how such a general ground would add anything to the grounds enumerated in our rules unless it is desirable to restore the common-law power of granting a new trial when the judge is personally dissatisfied with the verdict.

Id. at 483–84, 135 N.W.2d at 220.

Notes and Questions

1. In COPPO v. VAN WIERINGEN, 36 Wash.2d 120, 123–24, 217 P.2d 294, 297 (1950), the court stated:

> One of the reasons assigned by the trial judge in the instant cases for granting new trials is that "substantial justice has not been done." The statutes which enumerate the grounds on which new trials may be granted * * * make no mention of such a ground for a new trial; but we have always upheld the right of the trial judge to grant a new trial when he is convinced that substantial justice has not been done, on the theory that it is an exercise of the trial court's inherent power. * * *

> Actually, of course, when a trial judge says that "substantial justice has not been done," he is stating a conclusion for which there must be a reason or reasons. * * * The reason we have barred any review of an order granting a new trial based on this conclusion * * * was expressed by the supreme court of Wisconsin in the case of McLimans v. City of Lancaster, 57 Wis. 297, 15 N.W. 194, 195: "The judge before whom the cause was tried heard the testimony, observed the appearance and bearing of the witnesses and their manner of testifying, and was much better qualified to pass upon the credibility and weight of their testimony than this court can be. *There are many comparatively trifling appearances and incidents, lights and shadows, which are not preserved in the record, which may well have affected the mind of the judge as well as the jury in forming opinions of the weight of the evidence, the character and credibility of the witnesses, and of the very right and justice of the case.* These considerations cannot be ignored in determining whether the judge exer-

cised a reasonable discretion or abused his discretion in granting or refusing a motion for a new trial." (Italics ours.)

For subsequent developments in Washington, see Knecht v. Marzano, 65 Wash.2d 290, 396 P.2d 782 (1964); Trautman, *Serving Substantial Justice—A Dilemma,* 40 Wash.L.Rev. 270 (1965).

2. Suppose a party moves for a new trial based on a number of specific errors, no one of which alone would be sufficiently prejudicial to justify a new trial. May the court under Ginsberg v. Williams grant the motion on the ground that all of the errors, taken together, deprived the losing party of a fair trial? Cf. Walker v. Holiday Lanes, Inc., 196 Kan. 513, 413 P.2d 63 (1966); Miller v. Staton, 64 Wash.2d 837, 394 P.2d 799 (1964).

3. To what extent does the decision in *Ginsberg* provide significant appellate-court control over the "arbitrary exercise" of power by the trial judge? What more can the exercise of discretion mean than that the trial judge can decide that errors, trivial in appearance, have resulted in manifest injustice to the party seeking a new trial because of "lights and shadows which are not preserved in the record"?

4. Under what circumstances, if any, should errors during trial justify a new trial in a nonjury case? In the much-quoted opinion in BUILDERS STEEL CO. v. COMMISSIONER, 179 F.2d 377, 379 (8th Cir.1950), the court said:

> In the trial of a nonjury case, it is virtually impossible for a trial judge to commit reversible error by receiving incompetent evidence, whether objected to or not. An appellate court will not reverse a judgment in a nonjury case because of the admission of incompetent evidence, unless all of the competent evidence is insufficient to support the judgment or unless it affirmatively appears that the incompetent evidence induced the court to make an essential finding which would not otherwise have been made. * * * On the other hand, a trial judge who, in the trial of a nonjury case, attempts to make strict rulings on the admissibility of evidence, can easily get his decision reversed by excluding evidence which is objected to, but which, on review, the appellate court believes should have been admitted. * * *

Is the attitude of the court proper? To what extent should the court's reasoning apply to errors other than the improper admission of evidence?

b. Incoherent Jury Verdicts

MAGNANI v. TROGI

Appellate Court of Illinois, Second District, 1966.
70 Ill.App.2d 216, 218 N.E.2d 21.

CORYN, PRESIDING JUSTICE. * * *

Plaintiff's complaint states two separate causes of action. In Count I she seeks recovery of $30,000.00, as Administratrix, for the wrongful death of her decedent, pursuant to the Wrongful Death Act (Ill.Rev.Stats., ch. 70, §§ 1 & 2). By the second count of the complaint she seeks reimbursement, in her individual capacity, for medical and funeral expenses necessarily incurred by her as the result of the injury and death to her husband, pursuant to the Family Expense Statute (Ill.Rev.Stats., ch. 68, § 15).

The Wrongful Death Act provides that any recovery thereunder shall be distributed by the court in which the cause was heard to the widow and next of kin of the decedent, in proportion, as determined by the trial court, "that the percentage of dependency of each such person upon the deceased person bears to the sum of the percentages of dependency of all such persons upon the deceased person." Here, any award of the jury, for a wrongful death, would be apportioned by the trial court to the widow and minor son of decedent. There would be no apportionment of any award made under the provisions of the Family Expense Statute.

* * *

In the instant case, there can be no doubt that the recovery sought under each count of plaintiff's complaint was based on separate causes of action, that is, one action for wrongful death, and the other under the Family Expense Statute. Unfortunately, neither party to this suit tendered separate forms of verdict for each of these counts. Rather, a single form of verdict was submitted by the court to the jury without objection from plaintiff or defendant. Using this form the jury returned the following verdict: "We, the jury, find in favor of the plaintiff and against the defendant. We assess the damages in the sum of $19,000.00." The trial judge, in his memorandum of opinion allowing a new trial, properly expressed the dilemma this verdict created for him by stating: "In the case at bar, there were two counts. Does the single verdict all apply to just one count, or to both counts? It might be that the verdict was all for the wrongful death action, and non-liability as to the medical expense cause of action." After making this observation, the trial judge then concluded that the verdict must be set aside and a new trial ordered as to both the liability and damage aspects of the case. Although other points have been raised in this appeal, we believe the determinative issue to be whether the trial judge, when faced with this situation, abused his discretion by granting a new trial.

The purpose of vesting the trial judge with power to grant a new trial is to permit him, before losing jurisdiction of the case, to correct errors that he or the jury might have made during the course of the trial. Courts of review have repeatedly stated that they will not disturb the decision of a trial court on a motion for new trial unless a clear abuse of discretion is affirmatively shown. The reason for this rule is that the trial court has had the opportunity to consider the conduct of the trial as a whole, and therefore is in a superior position to consider the effects of errors which occurred, the fairness of the trial to all parties, and whether substantial justice was accomplished. * * * Greater latitude is allowed a trial court in granting a new trial than in denying a new trial. * * *

Plaintiff argues that defendant has waived his right to complain of the form of verdict because he did not object to the giving of this form to the jury, but raised the issue for the first time in his post-trial motion. In most instances this would be a valid argument. Here, however, because of the single form of verdict, the jury's determination of liability and damages on each of the two causes of action was not made known. It appears that the jury found liability against the defendant on the wrongful death action, but any conclusion about what the jury's verdict was regarding liability on the family expense action is pure conjecture. Also, the language of the verdict returned gives no indication of the jury's determination as to what portion of the total verdict of $19,000.00 it attributed to damages for wrongful death, and what portion, if any, to damages for medical and funeral expenses. The determination of liability and damages, in the first instance, is to be made by the jury.

The jury returned its verdict on December 21, 1962, and the defendant filed his post-trial motion on January 15, 1963, thereby raising this issue for the first time. It was impossible, then, for the court to re-assemble the jury and instruct them to correct the error in the form of verdict. * * * We are not holding, by this opinion, that the failure to submit to the jury separate forms of verdict in cases involving multiple causes of action should, in every instance, result in the granting of a new trial, but rather, that in the situation presented here it was not an abuse of discretion for the trial judge to grant a new trial.

The order of the Circuit Court of Lake County, granting defendant's motion for new trial, vacating and setting aside the verdict and judgment, and denying defendant's motion for judgment notwithstanding the verdict, is affirmed.

Affirmed.

STOUDER, JUSTICE (dissenting). I do not agree with the opinion of the majority. The record before us clearly shows that Plaintiff waived any individual interest in the verdict. The verdict, then being within the range of the evidence and the law, any possible dilemma facing the trial court was thereby solved.

As was succinctly stated in Hall v. Chicago and Northwestern Ry. Company, 349 Ill.App. 175, 110 N.E.2d 654 "We are not unmindful of the rule and cases which hold that the trial judge is allowed broad discretion in granting motions for a new trial, and that his actions will not be reversed on appeal except in cases of clear abuse of such discretion; but this rule, like all others, has its limitations. A judge is not empowered to set aside a verdict in any case simply because he does not agree with it. * * *" In the instant case the trial court's granting of a new trial was based upon a finding that the forms of verdict submitted to the jury were improper. It therefore should be our duty to examine the propriety of this finding in order to determine the limits which were self-imposed upon the discretion of the trial court.

Upon thorough examination of the record before us I am unable to find that Defendant made any objection to the forms of verdict at the conference on instructions or at any time prior to his post-trial motion. * * * Defendant's failure to object to the forms at the proper time as well as his later failure to show that he was in fact prejudiced compels me in the instant case to find that the trial court's finding was erroneous and Defendant's motion for a new trial should have been denied.

* * *

ROBB v. JOHN C. HICKEY, INC.

Circuit Court of New Jersey, Morris County, 1941.
19 N.J.Misc. 455, 20 A.2d 707.

LEYDEN, JUDGE.   The issues presented by the pleadings were the negligence of the defendants and the contributory negligence of the plaintiff's decedent.   The jury was instructed concerning the applicable principles of law, in the course of which it was pointed out that if contributory negligence upon the part of the plaintiff's decedent had been established, the comparative degrees of the negligence of the parties was immaterial.

The jury returned a verdict in the absence of the judge and it was recorded at the clerk's desk as follows: "The jury finds that there was negligence on the part of both parties involved—The evidence shown is that the defendant was more negligent than the plaintiff—We therefore recommend an award of $2,000.00 to the plaintiff Clyde J. Robb and against the defendants John C. Hickey, Inc., a New Jersey Corporation and Roger W. King."

Both parties are dissatisfied with the verdict; the plaintiff with its substance and the defendants with its form.   Plaintiff has a rule to set aside the verdict upon the ground that it is ambiguous, inconsistent, inadequate and contrary to the charge of the court.   Defendants, upon notice, move to mould the verdict into one in favor of the defendants and against the plaintiff, urging that it is merely informal and the intent of the jury to find for the defendants is clearly indicated * * *.

It is true that a verdict must be responsive to the issues and recommendations of the jury dehors the issues submitted by the court, such as the suggestion of the equal division of another fund between the parties * * * or the amount claimed in the suit be donated to the American Red Cross * * * or each party (plaintiff being unsuccessful) pay his own cost * * * or of leniency in a criminal case * * * may be treated as surplusage and properly disregarded.

However, such is not the situation in the instant case.   Here the verdict finds both parties guilty of negligence, erroneously compares the degrees of their negligence and recommends an award of $2,000 in favor of the plaintiff and against both defendants.   What then did the jury agree upon and intend?   Did it find in favor of the defendants as is legally indicated by the first sentence, or in favor of plaintiff in the sum of $2,000 as is clearly indicated by the last sentence?   The recommendation of an award to the plaintiff is pertinent to the issues, for basically the liability of defendants to plaintiff in damages was in question.   It cannot be treated as surplusage and disregarded.   Reading the verdict as a whole, it is self-contradictory, inconsistent and ambiguous.   One is left to conjecture and surmise as to the real purpose of the jury.   It is defective in substance, not merely in form.

The court may, in fact should, mould an informal verdict to render it formal, effective and to coincide with the substance of the verdict as agreed upon and intended by the jury, but this power is only exercised where the real purpose and intent of the jury clearly, sufficiently and convincingly appears. * * * Where, as here, the verdict is uncertain or ambiguous, it cannot be moulded. The court will not substitute its verdict in place thereof. * * *

This leads to the denial of defendants' motion to mould and is also dispositive of the plaintiff's rule. The latter will be made absolute and a new trial granted.

Notes and Questions

1. Why is the verdict in *Robb* different from a verdict that recommends that the amount claimed be donated to the American Red Cross? Can't a strong argument be made in favor of a new trial in the latter situation? See Rusidoff v. DeBolt Transfer, Inc., 251 Pa.Super. 208, 380 A.2d 451 (1977), in which the trial judge's denial of a new trial was reversed when the jury verdict for defendant was rendered "with reservations due to the evidence provided."

2. Suppose plaintiff brings suit for injuries suffered in an accident allegedly due to defendant's negligence. The jury renders a verdict in favor of plaintiff but assesses damages at zero, although it is clear from the evidence that plaintiff has been badly hurt. May the judge enter judgment on the verdict? See Wingerter v. Maryland Cas. Co., 313 F.2d 754 (5th Cir.1963), and Pitcher v. Rogers, 259 F.Supp. 412 (N.D.Miss.1966), in which the courts answered "yes." Can these decisions be reconciled with *Robb*? To what extent does the answer depend upon the nature of the evidence regarding the causation of damages? There are a number of decisions holding that such a verdict cannot stand. See, e.g., Fugitt v. Jones, 549 F.2d 1001 (5th Cir.1977).

3. How far should a trial court go in attempting to ascertain the "true intent" of the jury in order to be able to "mould" a verdict? Should the court be permitted to ask the jurors what they intended? Why shouldn't all but the clearest cases be returned for a new trial? Compare Hanolt v. Mlakar, 421 Pa. 136, 218 A.2d 750 (1966), with Gilday v. Hauchwit, 91 N.J.Super. 233, 219 A.2d 873 (App.Div.1966), reversed in part on other grounds 48 N.J. 557, 226 A.2d 834 (1967). Is there any way to avoid the costs and delays of a new trial if the verdict cannot be moulded?

———

KRAMER v. KISTER, 187 Pa. 227, 233–36, 40 A. 1008, 1008–10 (1898):

[The jury agreed to a sealed verdict and separated. When the verdict was opened the next morning, one juror dissented from it; the jury was sent out again and returned shortly with the same verdict, which was entered.]

* * * At common law the jury were kept together from the time they were sworn, as is still the general rule in criminal cases involving life. After they had retired to consider their verdict, they were kept without food, drink, fire, or light until they agreed; and Blackstone says, "It has been held that, if the jurors do not agree in their verdict before the judges are about to leave the town, though they are not to be threatened or imprisoned, the judges are not bound to wait for them, but may carry them round the circuit, from town to town, in a cart." 3 Bl.Comm. 376.

From the manner of this mention, it is to be inferred that this latter practice was at least unusual in Blackstone's day; and he says expressly that the deprivation of food, fire, and light was subject to the indulgence of the court. * * * With the prolongation of trials in the more complicated issues of modern times, and especially with the amelioration of manners, the treatment of jurors has gradually become less harsh, and changes of practice have been made in their relief. It is no longer the custom to keep them together and secluded during the whole trial, though I apprehend that the judge may do so in any case where public excitement or other exceptional reason may make it advisable, in the interest of the proper administration of justice, to do so * * *. After the retirement of the jury to consider their verdict, this indulgence terminates, and they are kept together and apart from others until verdict rendered. But, if the adjournment of the court is to such time or under such circumstances as seem likely to lead to serious inconvenience to the jurors, the practice of allowing them to seal a verdict grew up. * * * When a juror dissents from a sealed verdict, there is a necessary choice of evils,—a mistrial, or a verdict finally delivered under circumstances that justly subject it to suspicion of coercion or improper influences. * * * If the dissenting juror was honest in his declaration that he had not agreed to the first verdict, except because he thought he was obliged to, then his agreement to the second without having been instructed as to his rights cannot be freed from a well-founded appearance of coercion. If, on the other hand, the second verdict had been for the defendant, contrary to the first, the inference could hardly have been escaped that the change was produced by new evidence, or information illegally acquired by the dissenting juror, or by even more reprehensible means. The only safe way out of such a situation is to treat it as a mistrial, and discharge the jury. * * *

Notes and Questions

1. Note that very few jurisdictions today require jurors constantly to remain together once the case has been submitted to them. See Annot., 77 A.L.R.2d 1086 (1961). Before allowing the jurors to separate, however, the court normally will warn them not to discuss the case with anyone outside the jury room and not to inspect sites referred to in the testimony or otherwise to obtain evidence. See Steckler, *Management of the Jury*, 28 F.R.D. 190, 191 (1960). What effect should the failure to give such cautionary instructions have on the validity of the verdict?

2. Do you agree with the reasoning of the court in *Kramer* as to why the resubmission was improper? To what extent does the case turn upon the time at which the resubmission was made? Suppose, for example, that the original verdict had been an oral one, rendered at the end of the deliberations. Would an immediate resubmission have been justifiable? If so, in light of modern practice permitting jurors to separate during their deliberations, isn't *Kramer* outmoded? See Annot., 164 A.L.R. 1265, 1276–79 (1946).

To what extent should the validity of resubmission depend upon whether the jury has been discharged from the case? Suppose the error in the verdict is first noticed after the jurors have been discharged but while they are still present in the courtroom? See generally Annot., 66 A.L.R. 536 (1930).

3. To what extent may a court resubmit a verdict for defects other than the lack of unanimity or a proper majority?

(a) Suppose, for example, the error is one that the court could correct itself by moulding a proper verdict. Wouldn't it be preferable to resubmit the case to the jury? See Gilday v. Hauchwit, 91 N.J.Super. 233, 219 A.2d 873 (App.Div.1966), reversed in part on other grounds 48 N.J. 557, 226 A.2d 834 (1967).

(b) What if the error was similar to that in Robb v. John C. Hickey, Inc., in which the court held that it could not correct the verdict itself. Would a resubmission to the jury have been improper? See Sigel v. Boston & Me. R. Co., 107 N.H. 8, 216 A.2d 794 (1966) (resubmission held appropriate). Isn't resubmission always preferable to a new trial?

c. New Trial Because the Verdict Is Against the Weight of the Evidence

AETNA CASUALTY & SURETY CO. v. YEATTS

United States Circuit Court of Appeals, Fourth Circuit, 1941.
122 F.2d 350.

PARKER, CIRCUIT JUDGE. This is the second appeal in a suit originally instituted to obtain a declaratory judgment with respect to the coverage of a policy of indemnity insurance. * * * The company denied liability on the ground that the defendant Yeatts was engaged in the performance of a criminal abortion at the time he incurred the liability for which the recovery was had against him, and that such liability was expressly excluded from the coverage of the policy. The question as to whether the defendant Yeatts was engaged in such criminal conduct was submitted to the jury, and from verdict and judgment in his favor the plaintiff brings this appeal.

There was testimony below from which the jury would have been amply justified in finding in favor of the plaintiff insurance company on the issue submitted; but the defendant himself was examined as a witness and, if his testimony is believed, he was guilty of no criminal act. No motion for directed verdict was made by the plaintiff, nor was the sufficiency of the evidence to sustain a finding in favor of the defendant challenged in any other way before verdict. After verdict, plaintiff moved for judgment non obstante veredicto and also for a new trial, on the ground that the verdict was contrary to the credible evidence in the case; and exceptions directed to denial of these motions constitute the only points presented by the appeal.

Even if a motion for directed verdict had been made by plaintiff, it is clear that same should have been denied as should also, any motion for judgment non obstante veredicto based thereon * * *.

The motion to set aside the verdict and grant a new trial was a matter of federal procedure, governed by Rule * * * 59 and not subject in any way to the rules of state practice. On such a motion it is the duty of the judge to set aside the verdict and grant a new trial, if he is of opinion that the verdict is against the clear weight of the evidence, or is based upon evidence which is false, or will result in a miscarriage of justice, even though there may be substantial evidence which would prevent the direction of a verdict. The exercise of this power is not in derogation of the right of trial by jury but is one of the historic safeguards of that right. * * * The matter was well put by Mr. Justice Mitchell, speaking for the Supreme Court of Pennsylvania in Smith v. Times Publishing Co., * * * [178 Pa. 481, 36 A. 298], as follows: "The authority of the common pleas in the control and revision of excessive verdicts through the means of new trials was firmly settled in England before the foundation of this colony, and has always existed here without challenge under any of our constitutions. It is a power to examine the whole case on the law and the evidence, with a view to securing a result, not merely legal, but also not manifestly against justice,—a power exercised in pursuance of a sound judicial discretion, *without which the jury system would be a capricious and intolerable tyranny,* which no people could long endure. This court has had occasion more than once recently to say that it was *a power the courts ought to exercise unflinchingly."* (Italics supplied).

In the same case, Mr. Justice Williams, in a concurring opinion, traces the history of the exercise of this power and sums up his conclusion as follows:

* * *

As early * * * as 1665, the courts at Westminster did precisely what we have done in this case, and for the same reason. The right of trial by jury was not then supposed to give to a successful party the right to insist on an advantage due to the mistake or the willful misconduct of the jury, no matter how grossly unjust and oppressive the result might be; but the supervisory control of the court in banc, sitting as a court of review, was promptly exercised to relieve against the miscarriage of justice. The exercise of this power was then thought to be in aid of trial by jury. * * *

* * *

The distinction between the rules to be followed in granting a new trial and directing a verdict were stated by us with some care in Garrison v. United States, 4 Cir., 62 F.2d 41, 42, * * * as follows: "Where there is substantial evidence in support of plaintiff's case, the judge may not direct a verdict against him, even though he may not believe his evidence or may think that the weight of the evidence is on the other side; for, under the constitutional guaranty of trial by jury, it is for the jury to weigh the evidence and pass upon its credibility. He may, however, set aside a verdict supported by substantial evidence where in his opinion it is contrary to the clear weight of the evidence, or is based upon evidence which is false; for, even though the evidence be sufficient to preclude the direction of a verdict, it is still his duty to exercise his power over the proceedings before him to prevent a miscarriage of justice. * * *"

It is equally well settled, however, that the granting or refusing of a new trial is a matter resting in the sound discretion of the trial judge, and that his action thereon is not reviewable upon appeal, save in the most exceptional circumstances. * * * The rule and the reason therefor is thus stated by Mr. Justice Brandeis in Fairmont Glass Works v. Cub Fork

Coal Co., * * * [287 U.S. 474, 53 S.Ct. 254, 77 L.Ed. 439]: "The rule that this Court will not review the action of a federal trial court in granting or denying a motion for a new trial for error of fact has been settled by a long and unbroken line of decisions * * *. The rule precludes likewise a review of such action by a Circuit Court of Appeals. Its early formulation by this Court was influenced by the mandate of the Judiciary Act of 1789, which provided in section 22 that there should be 'no reversal in either (circuit or Supreme) court on such writ of error * * * for any error in fact.' Sometimes the rule has been rested on that part of the Seventh Amendment which provides that 'no fact tried by a jury, shall be otherwise reexamined in any court of the United States than according to the rules of the common law'. More frequently the reason given for the denial of review is that the granting or refusing of a motion for a new trial is a matter within the discretion of the trial court."

While an examination of the record has led us to the conclusion that the trial judge might very properly have granted the motion for new trial, we cannot say that his denial of the motion amounted to an abuse of discretion on his part or that there are present any of the special circumstances which would subject his action to review by this court. The judgment appealed from will accordingly be affirmed.

Affirmed.

Notes and Questions

1. In MARSH v. ILLINOIS CENT. R. CO., 175 F.2d 498, 500 (5th Cir. 1949), the district judge had granted judgment notwithstanding the verdict, but had denied an alternative motion for new trial, saying: "It is my judgment that the evidence was insufficient to go to the jury, but if I am wrong in that, then I do not think a new trial should be granted as there were no other errors of law." The Court of Appeals reversed:

> * * * While it is not our function to weigh the evidence, we do agree with the trial judge's first expressed opinion that the weight of the evidence is "overwhelmingly against the plaintiff". But we do not agree that the grant of a judgment notwithstanding the verdict was therefore justified. There was evidence of the appellant, not very explicit or positive, which if believed might authorize a jury to conclude he was hurt in the manner he claims. Because the trial judge does not believe it, because of appellant's own contradictions and conduct and of opposing evidence which seem to overwhelm it, is not ground for a judgment notwithstanding the verdict, and we must reverse that judgment. * * *

> But it is ground for the trial judge to grant a new trial, though the trial was free of other error. He has in strong terms disapproved the verdict as contrary to the evidence * * *. We have reversed the entering of a final judgment, but it is evident that the new trial ought to be granted and would have been except for the misconception that absence of other error prevented it. The full discretion vested in the trial judge not having been exercised, we will remand the case with direction to the judge to grant a new trial * * * if he continues to think the verdict to be against the overwhelming weight of the evidence.

2.   In cases such as Lavender v. Kurn, p. 53, supra, and Denman v. Spain, p. 975, supra, when there is a lack of proof of what happened rather than a conflict of proof, would the grant of a new trial be any more appropriate than the direction of a verdict? See also McClam v. New York Life Ins. Co., 9 F.Supp. 415, 415–16 (E.D.S.C.1935).

3.   In DYER v. MacDOUGALL, 201 F.2d 265, 271 (2d Cir.1952), Judge Frank, concurring, said:

> * * * The well-settled rule is that, in passing on a motion for a directed verdict, the trial judge always must utterly disregard his own views of witnesses' credibility, and therefore of their demeanor; that he believes or disbelieves some of the testimony is irrelevant. When asked to direct a verdict for the defendant, the judge must assume that, if he lets the case go to the jury, the jurymen will believe all evidence— including "demeanor evidence"—favorable to the plaintiff. In other words, the judge must not deprive plaintiff of any advantage that plaintiff might derive from having the jury pass upon the oral testimony. Indeed, the important difference between a trial judge's power on a motion for a new trial and on a motion for a directed verdict is precisely that on a new-trial motion he may base his action on his belief or disbelief in some of the witnesses, while on a directed-verdict motion he may not.

Compare BOWDITCH v. BOSTON, 101 U.S. (11 Otto) 16, 18, 25 L.Ed. 980, 980–81 (1879): "It is now a settled rule in the courts of the United States that whenever, in the trial of a civil case, it is clear that the state of the evidence is such as not to warrant a verdict for a party, and that if such a verdict were rendered the other party would be entitled to a new trial, it is the right and duty of the judge to direct the jury to find according to the views of the court." The *Bowditch* case is but one of many with language of this kind. For an excellent discussion of the standards for granting a directed verdict and a new trial on the weight of the evidence, see the scholarly opinion of Judge (later Justice) Lurton, in MT. ADAMS & E.P. INCLINED RY. CO. v. LOWERY, 74 Fed. 463 (6th Cir.1896).

4.   On the unreviewability of orders denying new trials, see Taylor v. Washington Terminal Co., 133 U.S.App.D.C. 110, 409 F.2d 145, 148 (D.C.Cir.), certiorari denied 396 U.S. 835, 90 S.Ct. 93, 24 L.Ed.2d 85 (1969); Wright, *The Doubtful Omniscience of Appellate Courts*, 41 Minn.L.Rev. 751, 758–63 (1957).

5.   Suppose a verdict has been set aside and a new trial granted. If the jury in the second trial returns a verdict similar to the one rendered in the first action, may the court again order a new trial on the ground that the verdict is against the weight of the evidence? Compare Palmer v. Miller, 60 F.Supp. 710 (W.D.Mo.1945) (yes), with Mo.Rev.Stat. (V.A.M.S.) § 510.330, which appears in the Supplement following Federal Rule 59. See 6A Moore, *Federal Practice* ¶ 59.08[5], at 3816–17 (2d ed.): "While there is probably no fixed limit at common law upon the number of new trials which the trial court may grant, solely because the verdict is against the weight of the evidence, the trial court must, nevertheless, realize that the successive grants of a new trial, on that ground, cannot be limitless without violating the constitutional right of jury trial."

DYER v. HASTINGS, 87 Ohio App. 147, 149–50, 94 N.E.2d 213, 215 (1950):

No judgment may be vacated or set aside and new trial granted upon the ground that the verdict is against the weight of the evidence except as a matter of law; and a judgment will not be vacated or set aside and a new trial granted upon such ground where the verdict is supported by competent, substantial and apparently credible evidence which goes to all the essential elements of the case. * * *

In formulating this rule the word, "substantial," modifying the word, "evidence," is used in the sense of "constituting more than a scintilla of," and the word, "apparently," as used to modify the word "credible," is used to indicate that the court does not undertake to judge the credibility of the evidence, but only to judge whether it has the semblance of credibility.

The evidence in the instant case is in direct and sharp conflict on many essential elements of the case and is such that a verdict for either party would be supported by competent, substantial and apparently credible evidence.

In this situation it was the sole function of the jury to determine the credibility of the evidence, which it did by returning a verdict in favor of the defendant.

IN RE GREEN'S ESTATE, 25 Cal.2d 535, 542–43, 154 P.2d 692, 695–96 (1944):

It is next contended by contestant that the court erred in granting proponent's motion for a new trial on the ground "that the evidence as a whole was insufficient as a matter of law to support a verdict for respondents." The rules of law applicable to an appeal from an order of the trial court granting a motion for a new trial on the ground of the insufficiency of the evidence are well settled and, as stated in one of our most recent decisions, are as follows: "* * * When the motion is granted, as here, for insufficiency of the evidence, it is only in rare cases showing abuse of discretion that an appellate court will interfere because the trial judge must weigh all the evidence and determine the just conclusion to be drawn therefrom. * * * It cannot be held that a trial court has abused its discretion where there is a conflict in the evidence or where there is any evidence which would support a judgment in favor of the moving party." Hames v. Rust, 14 Cal.2d 119, 123, 124, 92 P.2d 1010, 1012.

* * *

We may not agree with the determination reached by the trial judge or with any of his conclusions. That is not the question before us. It is his duty to weigh the evidence and to pass upon any and all conflicts existing therein. * * * If after such an examination of the evidence he concludes that it is insufficient to support the verdict, his duty is to grant the motion and a reviewing court may not set aside his conclusion unless a showing of abuse of discretion is made out by appellant. * * * As we have seen, if there is any substantial evidence in the case supporting the trial court's action, then we should not interfere with its order granting said motion.

Notes and Questions

1. As for equating the test for directing a verdict to that for setting aside a verdict and granting a new trial, the matter is complicated by the wide range among the tests used in different jurisdictions for setting a verdict aside. * * * [T]he equation is more nearly valid in some jurisdictions than it is in others, but the differences are rather because of variations in the new trial test than because of any variation in the directed verdict test.

James, *Sufficiency of the Evidence and Jury-Control Devices Available Before Verdict,* 47 Va.L.Rev. 218, 233–34 (1961).

2. It is difficult to ascertain the standard for granting a new trial in a particular jurisdiction and to compare it with the standard applied in another jurisdiction because of peculiarities regarding the appealability, reviewability, and scope of review of a decision on a motion for a new trial. In many jurisdictions the grant of a new trial may be unappealable because it is not a "final order"; even if appealable, a grant or denial of the motion may not be disturbed on appeal except upon a showing of an abuse of discretion by the trial court, which is rarely found. The result is that the new-trial standard actually is formulated and controlled by trial, not appellate courts; inasmuch as the standard is shaped by courts whose opinions are infrequently reported and therefore will not provide a guideline for other courts, or establish a body of precedent, the standard may vary widely from case to case.

In GREEN v. ACACIA MUT. LIFE INS. CO., 156 Ohio St. 1, 100 N.E.2d 211 (1951), the Ohio Supreme Court held unconstitutional the statute under which the Ohio Court of Appeals in Dyer v. Hastings had reviewed the grant of a new trial, because it conferred authority on the Ohio Courts of Appeals to review nonfinal judgments. In AID INVESTMENT & DISCOUNT, INC. v. YOUNKIN, 66 Ohio L.Abs. 514, 118 N.E.2d 183 (Ct.App.1951), another court of appeals, reviewing a grant of a new trial, held that by reason of *Green* it could reverse only if it found an abuse of discretion, and, that, although it regarded the trial court's order as erroneous, it could not say it was an abuse of discretion. Do *Green* and *Younkin* affect the standard for granting a new trial in Ohio announced in Dyer v. Hastings?

3. In In re Green's Estate, is the California Supreme Court discussing a standard for granting the motion for a new trial or a standard for reviewing the grant of the motion?

A trial judge's decision to grant a new trial is much more likely to be upheld on appeal than a decision to deny a new trial. One reason is that appellate courts recognize that the trial judge is in the best position to have seen errors that may have occurred at trial and to gauge whether those errors may have affected the fairness of the first trial. See Magnani v. Trogi, p. 996, supra.

d. The Power to Grant Conditional and Partial New Trials

FISCH v. MANGER

Supreme Court of New Jersey, 1957.
24 N.J. 66, 130 A.2d 815.

JACOBS, J. The plaintiff suffered serious injuries in an automobile accident and, after trial, received a jury verdict in the sum of $3,000. He applied for a new trial because of the inadequacy of the verdict but his application was denied when the defendants consented that the damages awarded to the plaintiff be increased to the sum of $7,500. The plaintiff appealed and we thereafter certified on our own motion.

* * *

The plaintiff's actual expenditures to doctors and nurses and for drugs and hospitalization exceeded $2,200. And although he received most of his normal earnings despite his temporary incapacity, there was a loss of wages approximating $620. While the jury's verdict of $3,000 just about took care of the plaintiff's actual monetary losses, it awarded substantially nothing for his suffering and permanent injuries. Its gross inadequacy was recognized by the trial judge who pointed out that "there was no dispute but that the plaintiff suffered excruciating pain, and was rendered totally helpless for a considerable period of time." On June 28, 1956 the trial judge wrote to the parties advising that unless the defendants filed a consent in writing that the verdict be increased from $3,000 to $7,500, "then the verdict heretofore rendered will be set aside and a new trial granted limited to damages only." The consent was filed by the defendants and on June 30, 1956 a formal order was entered dismissing the plaintiff's motion for a new trial. * * *

The first point which he urges in support of his appeal is that once the trial court had concluded that the damages awarded by the verdict were inadequate it had no legal power whatever to condition the grant of a new trial upon the defendants' failure to consent to a prescribed increase in the verdict. * * * Much has appeared in the law reviews in support of the practices of *remittitur* and *additur* as enlightened aids in securing substantial justice between the parties without the burdensome costs, delays and harassments of new trials. See Carlin, *"Remittiturs and Additurs,"* 49 W.Va.L.Q. 1 (1942); Note, "Correction of Damage Verdicts by *Remittitur* and *Additur,"* 44 Yale L.J. 318 (1934) * * *. The term *remittitur* is used to describe an order denying the defendant's application for new trial on condition that the plaintiff consent to a specified reduction in the jury's award, whereas the term *additur* is used to describe an order denying the plaintiff's application for a new trial on condition that the defendant consent to a specified increase in the jury's award. While it is now recognized that the two practices are logically and realistically indistinguishable, *remittiturs* have been recognized almost everywhere, whereas *additurs* are still outlawed in some, though by no means all, of the states. * * *

The English precedents prior to the American Revolution are somewhat obscure and they are discussed in the majority and minority opinions in Dimick v. Schiedt, 293 U.S. 474, 55 S.Ct. 296, 302, 79 L.Ed. 603

(1935).   There Justice Sutherland, speaking for a majority of five (with Justice Stone, joined by Chief Justice Hughes and Justices Brandeis and Cardozo, dissenting) held that although *remittitur* is permissible in the federal courts, *additur* is prohibited by * * * the Seventh Amendment * * *.   In Belt v. Lawes (1884), 12 Q.B. 356, the court sustained the denial of a new trial upon the plaintiff's consent to accept a lesser amount than that awarded by the jury; on appeal, Brett, M.R. not only approved the practice followed below but suggested that the court would also have power "to say that the damages given are too small, but that if the defendant will agree to their being increased to such a sum as may be stated, a new trial shall be refused." * * * In the later case of Watt v. Watt (1905), A.C. 115 the court took an opposite position and rejected the view that a court could condition a denial of a new trial on the plaintiff's acceptance of a reduced verdict. * * * However, Justice Sutherland in the Dimick case did not follow the result in the Watt case and declined to upset the *remittitur* practice, first approved by Justice Story in Blunt v. Little, 3 Fed.Cas.No. 1,578 (C.C.Mass.1822), and since reaffirmed in many federal decisions. * * *

In his dissenting opinion in the Dimick case, Justice Stone pointed out that the Seventh Amendment was concerned with substance rather than form and that the Supreme Court had often declined to construe it as perpetuating in changeless form the minutiae of trial practice as it existed in the English courts in 1791; he referred to the many jury procedures unknown to the common law but now well established in federal practice; he considered wholly impersuasive the suggested differentiation between the settled *remittitur* practice which the majority continued and the *additur* practice which it rejected; and he concluded with the following remarks * * *:

> To me it seems an indefensible anachronism for the law to reject the like principle of decision, in reviewing on appeal denials of motions for new trial, where the plaintiff has consented to decrease the judgment or the defendant has consented to increase it by the proper amount, or to apply it in the one case and reject it in the other.   It is difficult to see upon what principle the denial of a motion for a new trial, which for centuries has been regarded as so much a matter of discretion that it is not disturbed when its only support may be a bad or inadequate reason, may nevertheless be set aside on appeal when it is supported by a good one: That the defendant has bound himself to pay an increased amount of damages which the court judicially knows is within the limits of a proper verdict.

The majority opinion in Dimick has been the subject of much criticism and it is doubtful whether the Supreme Court would still subscribe to it;[g] in any event, the Seventh Amendment differs somewhat from our constitutional provision and has no application to proceedings in our state courts. * * * We must look primarily to our own history and precedents in ascertaining whether the highly desirable practices of *remittitur* and *additur* may be adhered to in our State * * *.

g. But see Novak v. Gramm, 469 F.2d 430 (8th Cir.1972).

The *remittitur* practice has been recognized in New Jersey since early days. * * * [In 1917] the Court of Errors and Appeals had occasion to deal with a negligence case in which the practice of *additur* had been invoked. * * * Chancellor Walker, speaking for the entire court, had this to say ([Gaffney v. Illingsworth,] 90 N.J.L. at page 492, 101 A. at page 243):

> The power of the court in granting a new trial upon the ground that the damages are *excessive*, upon terms that a new trial shall be had unless the plaintiff will accept a certain sum named, less than that awarded by a verdict, is too well established to be questioned. It would seem to follow, by parity of reasoning, that when a new trial is granted because the damages are inadequate, the court may impose like terms, that is, terms to the effect that if the defeated party will pay a certain sum, greater than that awarded by the verdict, the rule will be discharged, subject, doubtless, to the power of an appellate court to vacate any such terms when they appear to be an abuse of discretion. * * *

* * *

Shortly after the adoption of the 1947 Constitution our courts had occasion to deal anew with the practices of *remittitur* and *additur*. In Esposito v. Lazar * * * [2 N.J. 257, 66 A.2d 172 (1949)] the jury returned a verdict for plaintiff in the sum of $1,200; the trial court found the damages inadequate and ordered a new trial limited to damages unless the defendant consented to increasing the award to $3,500. The defendant refused and on retrial the jury awarded $3,000. On appeal, this court, in an opinion by Justice Ackerson, approvingly cited Gaffney v. Illingsworth, supra, and expressly recognized that a trial court has discretionary power to deny a new trial upon the plaintiff's consent to accept a reduced amount or upon the defendant's consent to pay a larger amount. See 2 N.J. at page 259, 66 A.2d at page 173. It held, however, that in the case before it the new trial should not have been limited to damages because the original jury verdict appeared to represent a compromise finding on the issue of liability. * * *

In the light of all of the foregoing, we are satisfied that the practices of *remittitur* and *additur* violate none of our constitutional interdictions and, if fairly invoked, serve the laudable purpose of avoiding a further trial where substantial justice may be attained on the basis of the original trial. * * * Accordingly, we reject the first point urged by the plaintiff and come now to his meritorious contention that, in any event, the prescribed increase to $7,500 was "grossly inadequate and should be set aside." * * * In the instant matter, we believe that the trial judge had a mistaken notion of the evidence which led to his prescribing the scanty sum of $7,500. He stated that the plaintiff was not entitled to a "great sum, because he certainly did have a back condition before this accident occurred"; but the evidence in the record points to the view that whatever "back condition" the plaintiff had as a result of the 1950 accident had cleared up and had no relation to the very severe injuries resulting from the 1953 accident. Under these highly special circumstances, we believe that the trial court's action should not be permitted to stand and that the interests of justice will best be served by permitting a second jury to pass on the issue of damages. The separable issue of liability was clearly and properly decided against the defendants; under the evidence it could hardly have been determined otherwise and need not be submitted for redetermination. * * *

Reversed, with direction for a new trial on the issue of damages.

HEHER, J. (concurring in result). * * *

As is shown by Justice Sutherland's analysis of the case history in Dimick v. Schiedt * * *, there was no power in the English courts at the time of the adoption of the New Jersey Constitution of 1776 to increase, either absolutely or conditionally, the damages fixed by a jury in a case such as this. * * *

* * * Justice Sutherland concluded, and with unquestionable authority, that "while there was some practice to the contrary in respect of *decreasing* damages, the established practice and the rule of the common law, as it existed in England at the time of the adoption of the Constitution, forbade the court to *increase* the amount of damages awarded by a jury in actions such as that here under consideration." He observed that "this court in a very special sense is charged with the duty of construing and upholding the Constitution; and in the discharge of that important duty, it ever must be alert to see that a doubtful precedent [involving *remittitur*] be not extended by mere analogy to a different case if the result will be to weaken or subvert what it conceives to be a principle of the fundamental law of the land"; and that "the power to conditionally increase the verdict of a jury does not follow as a necessary corollary from the power to conditionally decrease it," since in the case of a conditional *remittitur* "a jury has already awarded a sum in excess of that fixed by the court as a basis for a *remittitur*, which at least finds some support in the early English practice, while in the second case, no jury has ever passed on the increased amount, and the practice has no precedent according to the rules of the common law."

The "controlling distinction between the power of the court and that of the jury," said Justice Sutherland, "is that the former is the power to determine the law and the latter to determine the facts," and while the *remittitur* practice in the case of an excessive verdict "is not without plausible support in the view that what remains is included in the verdict along with the unlawful excess,—in the sense that it has been found by the jury,—and that the *remittitur* has the effect of merely lopping off an excrescence," yet where an inadequate verdict is increased by the court there is a "bald addition of something which in no sense can be said to be included in the verdict," and if that be done with the consent of the defendant alone, the plaintiff is compelled to forego his "constitutional right to the verdict of a jury and accept 'an assessment partly made by a jury which has acted improperly, and partly by a tribunal which has no power to assess.'"

* * *

There can be no doubt that the *additur* practice sanctioned here contravenes the essence of the common-law right of trial by jury at the time of the adoption of the 1776 Constitution, then and ever since a basic right under the law of England; and this is the very substance of our own constitutional guaranty. * * *

POWERS v. ALLSTATE INS. CO., 10 Wis.2d 78, 102 N.W.2d 393 (1960). Plaintiff received a jury award for permanent injuries in the amount of $5,000. The award was excessive and called for a remittitur. The question before the state supreme court was what standard should determine the amount to which the damages should be reduced. The court noted that since its decision in Heimlich v. Tabor, 123 Wis. 565, 102 N.W. 10 (1905), Wisconsin judges had been required to set damages at the lowest amount that a reasonable jury could have awarded. This rule was contrary to the practice in most jurisdictions, in which "the courts follow the practice of allowing the plaintiff the option of avoiding a new trial by remission of the excess above an amount which the court considers reasonable." The court went on to point out that the Wisconsin rule tended to limit the effectiveness of the remittitur practice.

> * * * We are firmly of the opinion that if the plaintiff were granted the option of accepting a reasonable amount as determined by the trial or appellate court, instead of the least amount that an unprejudiced jury properly instructed might award, the number of instances in which the plaintiff would be likely to refuse such option and elect a new trial would be greatly reduced.

The court then specifically overruled *Heimlich* and adopted the standard rule.

Notes and Questions

1. Should a trial court have discretion to set a reasonable remittitur figure somewhere between the highest and lowest possible verdicts? Would it make more sense to require, as the alternative to a new trial, the highest amount an unprejudiced jury could properly have awarded plaintiff?

2. Suppose the federal courts had adopted the rule in the *Heimlich* case, which was overruled in *Powers*. Would application of an analogous rule to additur have permitted its use without violation of the Seventh Amendment?

3. In an action under the Federal Employers' Liability Act, 45 U.S.C. § 51, the California Supreme Court held that the trial court could order an additur. Jehl v. Southern Pac. Co., 66 Cal.2d 821, 59 Cal.Rptr. 276, 427 P.2d 988 (1967). In light of *Dimick*, is this holding consistent with Dice v. Akron, Canton & Youngstown R. Co., p. 414, supra?

4. If defendant appeals from a judgment for plaintiff, who has consented to a remittitur, may plaintiff cross-appeal on the ground that the verdict should not have been reduced? See Jangula v. Klocek, 284 Minn. 477, 170 N.W.2d 587 (1969), 54 Minn.L.Rev. 1096 (1970).

DOUTRE v. NIEC

Michigan Court of Appeals, 1965.
2 Mich.App. 88, 138 N.W.2d 501.

T.G. KAVANAGH, JUDGE. Defendants operate a beauty shop in Flint. On April 19, 1962 plaintiff was given a bleach and color treatment by defendants without a pretreatment patch test. Plaintiff received head and facial injuries as a result of the treatment and sued for damages.

During the trial defendants were not allowed to testify as to the standard of care observed by beauty shops in the Flint area when administering such treatment. The jury awarded plaintiff $10,000. Defendants filed a motion for a new trial. Such motion was granted and a new trial ordered but limited to the question of liability.

Both parties appeal.

The plaintiff alleges error in granting the new trial as to liability on the theory that the court was correct in the first place when he ruled at the trial that the proffered testimony on the standard of care was not admissible. The defendants allege the court erred in limiting the new trial to the issue of liability on the theory that the questions of liability and damages are so closely intertwined that they should be tried together.

As to the plaintiff's claim we find little merit. His objection is based on the theory that the defendants could know of the practices of the trade in Flint only by hearsay. This is not supported by the record.

The record shows that one of the defendants had been in the business for 24 years and the other for 14 years; they had attended conventions of beauticians and observed their practices and said they were abreast of the practices of other beauticians in Genesee County.

We agree with the trial court's last ruling that these witnesses should have been allowed to testify and that to exclude their testimony was error requiring a new trial. Such testimony is admissible because no one is held to a higher standard of care than the average in the industry.

* * *

The limitation of the trial to the issue of liability only poses a more difficult problem.

It has long been recognized that the questions of liability and damages are so closely intertwined that they may not usually be separated. The only exception the Michigan Supreme Court has so far recognized is in the case wherein "liability is clear" a retrial of the issue of damage alone may be permitted. * * *

In this case the court reiterated its position that despite the court rule authorizing it (GCR 1963, 527.1), limited new trials are not favored.

No compelling reason moves us to extend the rule.

The trial judge's opinion states: "This ruling (on the evidentiary question) may have materially influenced the jury on the liability issue. It could not, however, by any stretch of the imagination have affected the issue of damages." This bespeaks an assurance we do not share.

In the case before us the damages are not liquidated and the liability was determined pursuant to a trial in which an admitted error touching on liability was committed.

Under these circumstances it seems to us that justice requires that the jury which determines the liability or lack of it should have the responsibility for measuring any damages.

The trial court's order for a new trial shall be extended to all of the issues.

Costs are awarded defendants.

Notes and Questions

1. Compare the dissenting opinion of Judge Freedman in HUTTON v. FISHER, 359 F.2d 913, 920 (3d Cir.1966):

> * * * [A]s a matter of practical justice the damage verdict should not be permitted to stand where the question of liability is to be retried. It is the great and saving virtue of the jury system in accident cases that it permits laymen guided by the courts on questions of law to work out in a worldly way an accommodation between the strict requirements of law and their everyday view of justice. That a defendant therefore suffers disadvantage when a trial is limited to damages and liability is conceded is a fact of life, acknowledged everywhere but in courtrooms. * * * The limitation of a new trial by excluding some of the issues decided is exceptional, and the power to grant a partial new trial must be "exercised with caution." Geffen v. Winer, 100 U.S.App.D.C. 286, 244 F.2d 375, 376 (1947). A retrial of liability will be less than the full relief the defendants are entitled to have, for its effect will be insulated from the damage question into which it ordinarily percolates.

See also Vizzini v. Ford Motor Co., 569 F.2d 754, 760 (3d Cir.1977) (reversing decision to limit new trial to amount of damages).

2. In LARIMER v. PLATTE, 243 Iowa 1167, 53 N.W.2d 262 (1952), in which plaintiff's decedent was killed in a motor-vehicle collision, plaintiff sought damages for wrongful death and defendant counterclaimed for damage to his vehicle and the loss of its use during repair. Based on stipulation of the parties, the court instructed the jury that if it found for defendant on the counterclaim, it must find damages for repairs in the amount of $2205.49. In addition the jury was instructed it could find damages for loss of use not to exceed $600. The jury found for defendant and awarded him $600. Plaintiff's motion for a new trial was overruled on the ground that only defendant was prejudiced by the jury verdict. On appeal the court reversed and granted a new trial on the counterclaim. Plaintiff also requested a new trial on his claim for wrongful death. Should the request have been granted?

3. To what extent should the court, in deciding whether to grant a partial new trial, consider the extra cost to the court and the parties of a new trial on all of the issues?

e. The Power to Set Aside a Judgment on Grounds Discovered After It Was Rendered

Read Federal Rule of Civil Procedure 60 in the Supplement.

(i) Mistake and Excusable Neglect—Timeliness of Requests for New Trial

HULSON v. ATCHISON, TOPEKA & SANTA FE RY.

United States Court of Appeals, Seventh Circuit, 1961.
289 F.2d 726.
Certiorari denied 368 U.S. 835, 82 S.Ct. 61, 7 L.Ed.2d 36.

HASTINGS, CHIEF JUDGE. This is an action for damages alleged to have resulted from personal injuries sustained in an accident on December 22, 1957.

Edward T. Hulson and Walter A. Christensen (plaintiffs) were employed by the United States Post Office as postal transportation clerks. On December 22, 1957, together with other clerks, they began their work at 9:10 o'clock a.m. inside a railroad car, half of which was constructed and designed as a railway post office, while such car was standing on a track at the Kansas City, Missouri terminal. This car was moved from that location and coupled with other cars of The Atchison, Topeka and Santa Fe Railway Company (defendant) as a part of defendant's train No. 12. About noon that day while defendant was engaged in a switching operation wherein certain cars of this train were being moved, plaintiffs were injured as a result of being thrown against various parts of the inside of the car in which they were working.

Plaintiffs commenced this action by filing a complaint against defendant in the Circuit Court of Cook County, Illinois. * * * Defendant removed the cause to the United States District Court for the Northern District of Illinois, Eastern Division, on diversity grounds.

Defendant answered denying generally the allegations in the complaint. The cause was set for trial on the sole issue of liability. * * *

On June 7, 1960, after the close of all the evidence, plaintiffs moved for a directed verdict. The motion was denied at that time.

On June 7, 1960, the jury returned a verdict finding defendant "not guilty" as to both plaintiffs. On the same day judgment was entered on the verdict against plaintiffs and favorable to defendant.

On June 16, 1960, plaintiffs served on defendant and filed with the clerk of the district court a written notice that they would appear before the trial court on June 17, 1960 and present a motion (copy of which was attached) praying that the plaintiffs be "granted a reasonable time *to amend their motion for a new trial* by making specific objections to specific instructions." (Emphasis added.) An affidavit was attached to the motion by plaintiffs' counsel in which counsel stated that he had been diligent in his efforts to secure a transcript of the jury instructions and that it would be impossible to set out the specific instructions to which he objected and to state the objections thereto "unless the Court sees fit to permit him to amend his Motion for a new trial within a reasonable time." At that time no motion for a new trial had been filed by plaintiffs.

On June 17, 1960, counsel for all parties were present in court, and plaintiffs' attorney orally moved the court for an order extending the time in which to file plaintiffs' motion for a new trial. Plaintiffs' counsel stated that defendant's counsel had no objection to the motion. At that time the following colloquy took place between the court and counsel in open court:

* * *

The Court: * * * Would you be available later this afternoon?

Mr. Patterson [plaintiffs' attorney]: Yes, Your Honor, but counsel has no objection. I am merely asking for an extension of time in which to file my motion for a New Trial.

The Court: All right, if that is all you are asking, why the motion is granted.

Mr. Patterson: You will extend the time for what period, your Honor?

* * *

Mr. Svolos [defendant's attorney]: There is only one thing I would like to point out to the Court; I will be gone for the next two months. I will be out on the West Coast. It would be impossible for me to argue this orally this summer.

On the same day the court entered the following order:

On motion of plaintiffs, time to file motion for judgment notwithstanding the verdict or, in the alternative, for a new trial extended for a period of ten days, briefs to follow.

On June 27, 1960, for the first time, plaintiffs filed their motion for judgment notwithstanding the verdict, or in the alternative, for a new trial. The motion set out eight grounds for entry of a judgment n.o.v. and twenty-four grounds for granting a new trial. * * *

On July 15, 1960, defendant filed its written motion to strike plaintiffs' motion for judgment n.o.v., or in the alternative, for a new trial. The ground for this motion to strike was that plaintiffs' motion was not filed within the time and limits prescribed by Rule 50(b) and Rule 59(b), (d) and (e) of the Federal Rules * * *. It was further stated that the trial court was prohibited from enlarging the time in which to file such motion by the provisions of Rule 6(b). * * *

On August 23, 1960, plaintiffs filed their motion for relief under Rule 60(b). Following briefs addressed to this latter motion, on September 7, 1960, the trial court entered an order granting defendant's motion to strike plaintiffs' motion for judgment n.o.v., or in the alternative, for a new trial; and such motion was stricken. In a memorandum opinion filed on September 13, 1960 the trial court held that it could not grant relief to plaintiffs under Rule 60(b).

Plaintiffs filed their notice of appeal on October 4, 1960 stating that they were appealing from:

1.   The judgment on the verdict finding the defendant not guilty, entered in this action on June 7, 1960;

2.   The order denying the plaintiffs' motion for a directed verdict at the close of all of the evidence, entered in this action on June 7, 1960;

3.   The order extending for a period of 10 days the time to file a motion for judgment notwithstanding the verdict, or in the alternative, for a new trial, entered in this action on June 17, 1960;

4.   The order allowing the defendant's motion to strike the motion of the plaintiffs for judgment notwithstanding the verdict or in the alternative for a new trial, and striking the plaintiffs' said motion, entered in this action on September 7, 1960.

Defendant moved in this court "to dismiss paragraphs 1, 2 and 3 of the [above] notice of appeal," and we ordered the motion continued without prejudice and to be taken with the case on its merits as to the above paragraph 4.

We shall first consider defendant's motion to dismiss this appeal as to paragraphs 1, 2 and 3 in the notice of appeal.

As applied to this case, under Rule 73(a) plaintiffs were permitted to take an appeal within "30 days from the entry of the judgment appealed from." [h]   The jury verdict was received and judgment entered thereon finding defendant not guilty on June 7, 1960.   The notice of appeal was filed on October 4, 1960.

Under Rule 50(b) plaintiffs were required to move for motion for judgment n.o.v. "[w]ithin 10 days after the reception of a verdict * * *." Plaintiffs' said motion was not filed until June 27, 1960, or 20 days thereafter.

* * *

Under Rule 6(b) the trial court "may not extend the time for taking any action under rules * * * 50(b), * * * 59(b), (d) and (e), 60(b), and 73(a) and (g), except to the extent and under the conditions stated in them."

Thus, it is quite clear that plaintiffs' motion for judgment n.o.v. was not made within 10 days after the reception of the verdict and is not within the limitation imposed by Rule 50(b).   Under such circumstances "the rule forbids the trial judge or an appellate court to enter such a judgment."   Johnson v. New York, N.H. & H.R. Co., 1952, 344 U.S. 48, 50, 73 S.Ct. 125, 127, 97 L.Ed. 77 * * *.

Further, Rule 59(b), (d) and (e) prohibits a trial court from granting a motion for a new trial made after the expiration of 10 days after entry of judgment.   * * *.   If the motion for new trial is untimely, the trial court has no choice but to deny the motion; and *the tardy motion will not toll the time for taking an appeal.*   * * *

h.   Federal Rule of Civil Procedure 73(a), as it read at the time the *Hulson* case was decided, provided that the 30-day period runs from the time of entry of judgment unless a "timely" motion under Rule 50(b), Rule 52(b), or Rule 59 is made, in which case the period runs from the date of the ruling on the motion.   See Federal Rule of Appellate Procedure 4(a).

The 10 day limit for filing a motion for new trial fixed in Rule 59(b) cannot be enlarged under Rule 6(b), except as provided in subsection (c) of Rule 59, and such exception has no application to the situation before us here. * * *

In order to avoid the application of the foregoing rules, plaintiffs urge this court to treat the motion for extension "to amend their motion for a new trial," served on June 16, 1960, as a motion for a new trial. The trial court did not err in rejecting this contention. Plaintiffs' motion "cannot be measured by its unexpressed intention or wants." It "should be treated as nothing but what it actually was," one to amend a motion for a new trial which was not on file and was never timely filed. * * *

In light of the foregoing, we hold that defendant's motion to dismiss this appeal as to paragraphs 1, 2 and 3 of the notice of appeal must be sustained for lack of jurisdiction, pursuant to Rules 73(a) and 6(b).

The question raised in paragraph 4 of the notice of appeal and the denial of relief under Rule 60(b) is properly before us. This concerns the appeal from the order of the district court entered on September 7, 1960. * * *

Plaintiffs point to the fact that defendant's counsel agreed to the extension of time for filing their motion for judgment n.o.v., or in the alternative, for a new trial and thereby, in effect, waived plaintiffs' failure to comply with the rules. However, it is quite clear that counsel cannot waive the strict requirements of the rules. * * *

Plaintiffs candidly admit that they were mistaken in understanding the requirements of the rules, but urge that counsel for all parties and the trial court in good faith believed at the time that granting the extension of time was proper and permissible under the rules. Ignorance of the rules resulting in an agreement for an unauthorized extension of time cannot serve to furnish grounds for relief under Rule 60(b), under the facts before us in this appeal.

Plaintiffs rely heavily on the following statement made by the district court in its memorandum opinion:

> It is with a great deal of reluctance that I arrive at the conclusion that defendant's motion to strike must be allowed. There is considerable merit in plaintiffs' motion for a new trial and if the Court had jurisdiction, I would set aside the verdict and the judgment entered thereon, and allow the plaintiffs a new trial on the ground that the verdict was against the overwhelming weight of the evidence * * *.
>
> * * *

We think the statement made by Judge Maris in John E. Smith's Sons Co. v. Lattimer Foundry & Mach. Co., 3 Cir., 1956, 239 F.2d 815, 817–818, is dispositive of the issue raised under Rule 60(b):

> * * * Conceding that under appropriate circumstances the district court may entertain under Rule 60(b) a motion for a new trial which is untimely under Rule 59(b) it is perfectly plain that it may do so only if a showing is made which complies with the requirements of that rule, clause (1) of which requires a showing of "mistake, inadvertence, surprise,

or excusable neglect" and clause (6) a showing of "any other reason justifying relief from the operation of the judgment." As we pointed out in Federal Deposit Insurance Corp. v. Alker, 3 Cir., 1956, 234 F.2d 113, 117, Rule 60(b) provides for extraordinary relief and may only be invoked upon a showing of exceptional circumstances. * * *

[handwritten: this just exceptional]

Since the motion for a new trial was untimely served under Rule 59(b) and no showing was made of exceptional circumstances calling for extraordinary relief under Rule 60(b) the district court did not err in striking the motion.

We hold the trial court did not err in striking plaintiffs' motion for judgment n.o.v., or in the alternative, for a new trial, and in denying plaintiffs relief under Rule 60(b).

* * *

Appeal dismissed in part and affirmed in part.

Notes and Questions

1. In THOMPSON v. IMMIGRATION & NATURALIZATION SERV., 375 U.S. 384, 84 S.Ct. 397, 11 L.Ed.2d 404 (1964), petitioner's motion for new trial was served 12 days after entry of judgment but only 10 days from receipt of notice of entry of judgment by his lawyers who had not been in court when the judgment was entered. Respondent raised no objection as to the timeliness of the motion and the trial court specifically declared it to have been made "in ample time." The motion was denied on the merits and petitioner appealed. Under former Federal Rule 73 the appeal was timely if the filing period was measured from the date the motion was denied but not timely if measured from the date of the entry of judgment. The Supreme Court held (5 to 4) that petitioner was entitled to rely upon the trial court's statement that the new-trial motion was timely and, therefore, the appeal also was timely.

To what extent does *Thompson* cast doubt on the rigid application of the 10-day time limit in Rule 59(b)? Does the case indicate that *Hulson* is incorrect in holding that plaintiff was not entitled to relief under clauses (1) and (6) of Rule 60(b)?

[handwritten: I think so]

2. (a) Under Federal Rule 7(b) a motion in the federal courts normally must be in writing and state the grounds on which it is based. Suppose a party serves a timely motion for new trial but fails to specify a ground upon which he intends to rely. May he amend his motion subsequent to the 10-day period? Although there is some authority to the contrary, a large majority of cases have held "no." See 6A Moore, *Federal Practice* ¶ 59.09[2] (2d ed.); 5 Wright & Miller, *Federal Practice and Procedure: Civil* § 1195 (1969). What justification is there for a rigid application of the time limit?

[handwritten: rule incentive to get it right / no prejudice to other side / certainty]

(b) Rule 59(d) provides that a court may order a new trial on its own initiative, but again, there is a 10-day limit. Suppose a party serves a timely motion but fails to include as a ground an error that the court believes should result in a new trial. May the court order a new trial on such a ground subsequent to the 10-day period? Prior to the 1966 amendment to Federal Rule 59(d) the answer was generally held to be "no." The amendment, adding what is now the second sentence of that Rule, was designed specifically to give the trial courts such power. See Steinberg v. Indemnity Ins. Co., 36 F.R.D. 253 (E.D.La.1964). As a practical matter doesn't this amendment take the

[handwritten: standard flexible special circum...]

sting out of the rule that a party cannot amend a motion once the 10-day period has elapsed?

(c) Note that the time limit in Rule 59(b) is geared to the time a motion is served on the parties rather than to the time the motion is filed with the court. The only provision as to filing is contained in Rule 5(d) requiring a motion to be filed within a reasonable time after service. If the motion was served within the 10-day limit, it should be sufficient if the filing takes place within a reasonable time thereafter. See Claybrook Drilling Co. v. Divanco, Inc., 336 F.2d 697 (10th Cir.1964). Suppose a motion is filed within the 10-day period but served thereafter? Should it be dismissed? See Sutherland v. Fitzgerald, 291 F.2d 846 (10th Cir.1961).

3. The decision in *Hulson* raises the question of what type of cases do fall within the scope of Rule 60(b)(1). In almost every instance they involve situations in which a party was prevented from obtaining any trial whatsoever, such as a default judgment, see Rooks v. American Brass Co., 263 F.2d 166 (6th Cir.1959) (defendant's illness prevented a proper defense), an erroneous stipulation by counsel that resulted in a summary judgment against the client, see Griffin v. Kennedy, 344 F.2d 198 (D.C.Cir.1965), or a dismissal for failure of plaintiff to prosecute the action, see Leong v. Railroad Transfer Serv., Inc., 302 F.2d 555 (7th Cir.1962). Should the Rule specifically be limited to such matters of default? That the courts generally disfavor default judgments and readily set them aside is abundantly clear. In such cases it is often said that the errors of counsel should not be attributed to clients. See, e.g., Mieszkowski v. Norville, 61 Ill.App.2d 289, 209 N.E.2d 358 (2d Dist.1965).

4. The proper scope of Rule 60(b)(6) has been the subject of considerable litigation. It frequently has been held that the Rule must have been intended to cover only matters outside the scope of Rules 60(b)(1)–(5). E.g., Costa v. Chapkines, 316 F.2d 541 (2d Cir.1963); Federal Deposit Ins. Corp. v. Alker, 30 F.R.D. 527, 532 (E.D.Pa.1962), affirmed 316 F.2d 236 (3d Cir.), certiorari denied 375 U.S. 880, 84 S.Ct. 150, 11 L.Ed.2d 111 (1963). Otherwise the specific time limits on motions under Rules 60(b)(1), (2), and (3) would be meaningless. But it is the existence of these very limits that have pressured many courts, in the interests of justice, to find that errors ostensibly falling within Rules 60(b)(1), (2), or (3), are somehow so special that they come within Rule 60(b)(6) and hence are not subject to a specific time limitation. Can a strained interpretation of Rule 60(b) be justified by the fact that otherwise few if any cases would fall within Rule 60(b)(6)? See United States v. Karahalias, 205 F.2d 331, 333 (2d Cir.1953). For a comprehensive analysis of Rule 60(b)(6), see Kane, *Relief from Federal Judgments: A Morass Unrelieved by a Rule,* 30 Hastings L.J. 41 (1978).

Note that although Rule 60(b)(6) (and Rules 60(b)(4) and (5)) has no specific time limitation, the motion still must be made within a reasonable time. Is a motion under Rules 60(b)(1), (2), or (3) always timely as long as it is filed within the one-year period? See Di Vito v. Fidelity & Deposit Co., 361 F.2d 936, 939 (7th Cir.1966) (failure to move within four and one-half months from discovery of fraud held to bar relief); Schildhaus v. Moe, 335 F.2d 529, 531 (2d Cir.1964) (motion filed within 8 months held untimely).

(ii) Newly Discovered Evidence; Fraud

PATRICK v. SEDWICK, 413 P.2d 169 (Alaska 1966). Plaintiff brought an action for medical malpractice, alleging permanent physical injuries. The case was tried in October 1961 without a jury. In February 1962, the trial judge rendered findings on the issues of liability. These findings were subject to a lengthy appeal and it was not until more than two years later that the appellate court directed the trial court to enter findings for plaintiff on all issues of liability and to proceed to determine damages. The trial judge fixed the amount of damages on the basis of the evidence that had been presented at the trial and entered judgment on January 12, 1965. On January 22, 1965, defendant moved for a new trial on the ground that in 1963 a Dr. Robert Lewy had devised a new treatment that would ameliorate plaintiff's injuries and therefore should reduce his damages. The trial court denied the motion. The judge rejected the significance of the new treatment since there was no assurance that any improvement it might bring would be permanent.

The appellate court affirmed the denial of a new trial with the following explanation:

> * * * [A] motion for new trial on the grounds of newly discovered evidence must meet the following requirements before it [can] be granted:
>
> (1) must be such as would probably change the result on a new trial; (2) must have been discovered since the trial; (3) must be of such a nature that it could not have been discovered before trial by due diligence; (4) must be material; (5) must not be merely cumulative or impeaching.
>
> In addition to the foregoing requirements, it is established that for any evidence to come within the category of "newly discovered" such evidence must relate to facts which were in existence at the time of the trial. * * *
>
> We hold, under the authorities referred to, that the trial court did not abuse its discretion in denying appellee's motion for a new trial on the grounds of newly discovered evidence. It is clear from the record that Dr. Lewy's discovery of the Teflon technique did not occur until a considerable period of time had elapsed after the case was tried in October 1961. Thus, the Lewy technique was not in existence at the time the trial took place and under the above authorities would not qualify as newly discovered evidence.

Id. at 177.

Notes and Questions

1. In SWIFT AGRICULTURAL CHEMICAL CORP. v. USAMEX FERTILIZERS, INC., 27 Fed.R.Serv.2d 930 (E.D.La.1979), the trial court originally held for plaintiff in a patent-infringement suit regarding the manufacture of a chemical compound. The basic issue was the time in which a key reaction took place. It initially appeared that the reaction time for both plaintiff's and defendant's processes was less than one second. Subsequently, defendant moved for relief under Rule 60(b)(2), claiming that new methods of measurement, developed after the judgment was rendered, showed that defendant's

process had a far greater reaction time than that of plaintiff's process and hence there was no infringement. Plaintiff argued that relief was unavailable because the evidence had not been in existence at the time of trial. The court rejected this position on the ground that the reaction time had been in existence and only the means of measuring it had not. Does this decision make any sense? Can it be reconciled with Patrick v. Sedwick?

2. Suppose a plaintiff obtains damages based on testimony that her injuries will prevent her from bearing children. Shortly thereafter plaintiff becomes pregnant and delivers a normal, healthy child. Should the trial court grant a motion by defendant to reopen the case? Cf. Anshutz v. Louisville Ry. Co., 152 Ky. 741, 154 S.W. 13 (1913). See generally Annot., 31 A.L.R.2d 1236 (1953).

3. To what extent, if any, should Rule 60(b) permit a case to be reopened for consideration of a change in the applicable law? In TITLE v. UNITED STATES, 263 F.2d 28, 31 (9th Cir.), certiorari denied 359 U.S. 989, 79 S.Ct. 1118, 3 L.Ed.2d 978 (1959), appellant sought to set aside a judgment of denaturalization on the ground that some two years thereafter the United States Supreme Court, in a different case, interpreted the immigration act in such a way as to demonstrate that the original decision in *Title* was erroneous. Appellant relied on Rules 60(b)(4) and (5). The trial court denied the motions and the Court of Appeals affirmed: "Rule 60(b) was not intended to provide relief for error on the part of the court or to afford a substitute for appeal. * * * Nor is a change in the judicial view of applicable law after a final judgment sufficient basis for vacating such judgment entered before announcement of the change." See also Berryhill v. United States, 199 F.2d 217 (6th Cir.1952); Loucke v. United States, 21 F.R.D. 305 (S.D.N.Y.1957).

What does Rule 60(b)(5) mean when it allows relief from a judgment when "a prior judgment upon which it is based has been reversed or otherwise vacated"? See Jackson v. Jackson, 276 F.2d 501 (D.C.Cir.), certiorari denied 364 U.S. 849, 81 S.Ct. 94, 5 L.Ed.2d 73 (1960).

———

SMITH v. GREAT LAKES AIRLINES, INC., 242 Cal.App.2d 23, 51 Cal.Rptr. 1 (2d Dist.1966). The airline originally brought an action for breach of contract against Smith, the current plaintiff. The airline claimed that it had purchased a plane from Smith; that Smith promised to turn over documents showing that the plane had been overhauled pursuant to the regulations of the Civil Aeronautics Administration; that Smith failed to produce the necessary documents; and that, as a result, the airline was required by the Administration to make a major overhaul. At trial, an official of the agency testified that the required major overhaul had been completed. As a result, the airline was awarded substantial damages.

This action was instituted by Smith to set aside the original decision on the ground of fraud. Smith contended that in fact a major overhaul was neither required nor made. Allegedly, the government official who testified had conspired with the airline to perjure himself. Smith had not challenged the substance of this testimony at the trial, but had relied on the official status of the witness.

The trial judge sustained a demurrer to Smith's complaint and Smith appealed. The appellate court affirmed on the ground that the fraud alleged was "intrinsic," and that an action can be set aside only on the basis of "extrinsic" fraud. Extrinsic fraud was defined as that which prevents a litigant from making a claim or defense, for example, when one party fraudulently induces the opposing party not to file suit until the statute of limitations has become a bar. On the other hand, intrinsic fraud was said to be that which the trial itself is designed to discover, that is, which witnesses are lying. The court held that Smith should have been ready to meet all the issues in the case, and could not set the decision aside because he had not been prepared.

Notes and Questions

1. The current attitude in the federal courts is demonstrated by the opinion in PEACOCK RECORDS, INC. v. CHECKER RECORDS, INC., 365 F.2d 145, 147 (7th Cir.1966), certiorari denied 385 U.S. 1003, 87 S.Ct. 707, 17 L.Ed.2d 542 (1967), in which the court reversed as an abuse of discretion a denial of a motion under Rule 60(b):

> * * * We hold that where it appears that perjured testimony may have played some part in influencing the court to render a judgment, the perjury will not be *weighed,* on a motion to set aside the judgment. This seems self evident. * * * [If the judgment was obtained in part by the use of perjury] then it was clearly the duty of the district court to set aside the judgment, because poison had permeated the fountain of justice.

2. In BROWN v. PENNSYLVANIA R. CO., 282 F.2d 522 (3d Cir.1960), certiorari denied 365 U.S. 818, 81 S.Ct. 690, 5 L.Ed.2d 696 (1961), plaintiff brought suit under the Federal Employers' Liability Act against the railroad, his employer. Plaintiff's doctor testified that plaintiff's condition was such as to make it increasingly difficult if not impossible for him to work in the future. Defendant's medical witnesses testified that plaintiff had fully recovered from any injuries received in the accident. A verdict was rendered for plaintiff, but in an amount less than had been sought. Shortly after the trial, defendant discharged plaintiff, relying on the testimony given by plaintiff's doctor at the trial. Plaintiff moved for a new trial on damages under Rule 60(b)(3). The motion was denied and the appellate court affirmed. Is the decision sound? Is it consistent with the *Peacock Records* case? Compare *Rozier v. Ford Motor Co.*, 573 F.2d 1332 (5th Cir.1978).

3. Note that Rule 60(b) distinguishes between fraud perpetrated by one party on an opponent and fraud on the court. What is the reason for the distinction? What effect does it have? In HAZEL–ATLAS GLASS CO. v. HARTFORD–EMPIRE CO., 322 U.S. 238, 245–46, 64 S.Ct. 997, 1001, 88 L.Ed. 1250, 1255–56 (1944), plaintiff brought an action in the Court of Appeals to set aside a judgment rendered against it some nine years earlier. The first action had turned on the validity of a patent held by defendant. Both the issuance of that patent by the Patent Office and the determination of its validity by the federal Court of Appeals in the prior action had been affected by an article offered by defendant, ostensibly written by a disinterested expert, but actually prepared by defendant's own officials, to the effect that the machine under patent was a "revolutionary device." One of the attorneys who presented

defendant's case in the first action also had participated in the scheme to prepare and publish the fraudulent article. The Court of Appeals refused to set aside the judgment; the Supreme Court reversed:

> Every element of the fraud here disclosed demands the exercise of the historic power of equity to set aside fraudulently begotten judgments. This is not simply a case of a judgment obtained with the aid of a witness who, on the basis of after-discovered evidence, is believed possibly to have been guilty of perjury. Here, even if we consider nothing but Hartford's sworn admissions, we find a deliberately planned and carefully executed scheme to defraud not only the Patent Office but the Circuit Court of Appeals. * * *

Submitted for J ct

> The Circuit Court did not hold that Hartford's fraud fell short of that which prompts equitable intervention, but thought Hazel had not exercised proper diligence in uncovering the fraud and that this should stand in the way of its obtaining relief. We cannot easily understand how, under the admitted facts, Hazel should have been expected to do more than it did to uncover the fraud. But even if Hazel did not exercise the highest degree of diligence, Hartford's fraud cannot be condoned for that reason alone. This matter does not concern only private parties. There are issues of great moment to the public in a patent suit. * * * Furthermore, tampering with the administration of justice in the manner indisputably shown here involves far more than an injury to a single litigant. It is a wrong against the institutions set up to protect and safeguard the public, institutions in which fraud cannot complacently be tolerated consistently with the good order of society. Surely it cannot be that preservation of the integrity of the judicial process must always wait upon the diligence of litigants. The public welfare demands that the agencies of public justice be not so impotent that they must always be mute and helpless victims of deception and fraud.

Does *Hazel-Atlas* stand for the proposition that a court on its own motion may set aside a judgment obtained by fraud on the court? Was it proper for the Court to find that there had been a fraud on the lower court? See Toscano v. Commissioner, 441 F.2d 930 (9th Cir.1971); Hawkins v. Lindsley, 327 F.2d 356, 359 (2d Cir.1964); Lockwood v. Bowles, 46 F.R.D. 625, 632 (D.D.C.1969). If so, wouldn't ordinary perjury also qualify? Should the notion of fraud on the court apply only to situations such as bribery or corruption of a member of the court or jury?

4. Many jurisdictions, including the federal courts under Rule 60(b), permit an independent action in equity to set aside a judgment, which is discussed after these Notes. As seen in Smith v. Great Lakes Airlines, Inc., fraud is one of the substantive grounds upon which relief may be granted in such an action. Can the distinction between extrinsic and intrinsic fraud be justified when the judgment is attacked collaterally in a separate action as opposed to being attacked directly under a Rule 60(b) type motion? See Maschhoff v. International Union, UAW, 23 Fed.R.Serv.2d 1204 (E.D.Mich. 1977) (only extrinsic fraud justifies relief in independent action). Did the acts of the defendants in the *Hazel-Atlas* case qualify as extrinsic fraud? The majority did not discuss the issue; Justice Roberts, in a dissenting opinion, stated that the fraud was extrinsic. 322 U.S. at 261 n. 18, 64 S.Ct. at 1009 n. 18, 88 L.Ed. at 1264 n. 18.

Suppose that instead of putting forth false information, a party merely conceals facts of which she has direct knowledge that would have a definite bearing on the outcome of the case. Does this constitute fraud? If so, is it extrinsic? See Buice v. T. & B. Builders, Inc., 219 Ga. 259, 132 S.E.2d 784 (1963); Jennings v. Bridgeford, 218 Tenn. 287, 403 S.W.2d 289 (1966).

(iii) The Independent Action to Obtain Relief from a Prior Judgment

1. Federal Rule 60(b) expressly preserves the right of the trial court to entertain an independent action to relieve a party from a prior judgment. What conceivable justification is there for retaining this procedure? Shouldn't Rules 60(b)(1)–(6) be read to cover all possible grounds? Can an independent action be anything more than a method of avoiding the time limits set out in Rule 60(b)? See CAPUTO v. GLOBE INDEM CO., 41 F.R.D. 239 (E.D.Pa.1966), in which the court held that the denial of relief under Rule 60(b)(1) because the motion was filed more than a year after judgment did not bar an independent action to set the judgment aside on the same grounds that had been alleged on the motion. Compare LOCKLIN v. SWITZER BROS., INC., 335 F.2d 331 (7th Cir.1964), certiorari denied 379 U.S. 962, 85 S.Ct. 652, 13 L.Ed.2d 557 (1965), in which plaintiff filed a separate action in the Northern District of Illinois to set aside a judgment rendered in a federal court in California. Previously, plaintiff had made a timely but unsuccessful motion in the latter court under Rule 60(b) to set aside its judgment, advancing the same grounds subsequently alleged in the independent action. The Seventh Circuit affirmed a denial of relief on the ground that the prior decision under Rule 60(b) barred relief in an independent action by way of res judicata. It rejected an argument based on California state decisions that a denial of a post-trial motion should not bar a later independent action to set aside the judgment on the same grounds.

2. In the *Locklin* case the independent action was brought in a jurisdiction other than the one in which the judgment was rendered and the court accepted the case, although it denied relief. Is there any argument that would justify refusal by the second court to accept jurisdiction? See LAPIN v. SHULTON, INC., 333 F.2d 169 (9th Cir.), certiorari denied 379 U.S. 904, 85 S.Ct. 193, 13 L.Ed.2d 177 (1964), which "remanded" the parties for relief to the court issuing the initial judgment. Compare Bankers Mortgage Co. v. United States, 423 F.2d 73 (5th Cir.), certiorari denied 399 U.S. 927, 90 S.Ct. 2242, 26 L.Ed.2d 793 (1970). There is ancillary jurisdiction over an independent action brought in the court that entered the initial judgment. Crosby v. Mills, 413 F.2d 1273 (10th Cir.1969). Reread pp. 282–88, supra.

3. Suppose a party brings an action in a federal court, based on diversity-of-citizenship jurisdiction, to set aside a judgment rendered in a state court. If the state itself would provide a means of challenging the judgment, should the federal court refuse to hear the case? If the federal court does hear the case, what law should apply in determining whether relief is appropriate?

3. JURY MISCONDUCT AND THE INTEGRITY OF THE VER-DICT

The general rule that jurors' affidavits cannot be utilized to attack the verdict already has been noted. See Note 2, pp. 51–52, supra. The rule's validity has vigorously been challenged. For example in SOPP v. SMITH, 59 Cal.2d 12, 27 Cal.Rptr. 593, 377 P.2d 649 (1963), an auto accident case, a motion for new trial was based on affidavits of several jurors stating that during the trial they had visited the scene of the accident personally to check driver visibility, road conditions, and distances about which testimony had been produced. The California Supreme Court upheld a denial of a new trial on the ground that the affidavits were inadmissible. Justice Peters dissented:

> The majority, following the rule of stare decisis, adhere to a court created doctrine first announced by Judge Mansfield in Vaise v. Delaval, 1 Term R. 11, 99 Eng.Rep. 944 (K.B.1785). That rule is that affidavits of jurors may not be used to impeach their verdict.

> * * * At least 12 jurisdictions, by judicial decision, have [followed the lead of Iowa in modifying] * * * the strict Mansfield rule. * * *

> The Iowa rule is based upon the distinction between extrinsic or overt acts which may be corroborated or disproved, such as access to improper matter or an illegal method of reaching a verdict, and intrinsic matters which "inhere in the verdict itself" and hence are known only to the individual juror, such as misunderstanding or prejudice. Because matters which "inhere" in the verdict, including the thought processes and motives of the juror in reaching his decision, are not readily capable of being either corroborated or disproved they should be excluded.

> * * *

> In spite of the fact that the legal scholars in this field are practically unanimous in their opinion that the Iowa rule is sound, it must be conceded that the majority of the states still adhere to the Mansfield rule. The reason for this has been several times noted. Justice Learned Hand stated it as follows: " * * * judges again and again repeat the consecrated rubric which has so confused the subject; it offers an easy escape from embarrassing choices." (Jorgensen v. York Ice Machinery Corp., * * * (2nd Cir.1947) 160 F.2d 432, 435, cert. denied, 332 U.S. 764, 68 S.Ct. 69, 92 L.Ed. 349.) * * *

> Generally speaking, * * * the courts cite one or more of the following reasons for continuing to invoke the strict rule of exclusion: (1) The need for stability of verdicts; (2) the need to protect jurors from fraud and harassment by disappointed litigants; (3) the desire to prevent prolonged litigation; (4) the need to prevent verdicts from being set aside because of the subsequent doubts or change of attitude by a juror; (5) the concept of the sanctity of the jury room.

> Wigmore has completely demolished these arguments (8 Wigmore on Evidence (McNaughton rev. 1961) § 2353, pp. 697–699). In 47 Colum.L. Rev. 1373, 1375, it is stated * * * "It is anomalous that the best and usually the only evidence of which the case admits should be excluded [citation]. The objection that admission of this evidence would allow undue tampering with jurors is greatly exaggerated; courts in early

decisions before the rule was adopted were apparently not troubled by fear of excessive jury corruption [citations]. The argument that uncertainty of jury verdicts would result from a more liberal rule of admissibility is misdirected since the acceptance of jurors' testimony does not mean that any jury irregularity warrants a new trial, but only that such evidence may be considered in determining whether or not a new trial is required [citation]. The real problem, therefore, is substantive rather than procedural; namely, what kind of jury misbehavior should be considered grounds for reversal."

[handwritten margin note: Wigmore thinks Q should be asked]

The fear that under the Iowa rule a juror might have doubts about his verdict and subsequently seek to upset it by an affidavit on motion for new trial is unfounded. This is so because a juror's testimony or affidavit is and should be admissible only when it concerns overt acts. Furthermore, admissibility of the evidence does not a fortiori mean reversal—prejudice must be proved. * * *

* * * The trial court held, as a matter of law, that the affidavits of the offending jurors could not be considered by it. Such testimony was obviously the best evidence available on the issue. Had the wife of one of the offending jurors who accompanied him while he made the improper measurements filed the affidavit to the effect that she had observed her husband, such affidavit would admittedly have been admissible. * * * Yet here where it is admitted that misconduct occurred, the majority say that even though such misconduct may have deprived the plaintiff of a fair trial we will not permit him to show that by the affidavit of the very man that committed the overt act that constituted the misconduct. This is logically absurd. * * *

[handwritten margin note: affidavit of jury that did/act is not trustworthy]

Id. at 15–20, 27 Cal.Rptr. at 595–98, 377 P.2d at 651–54.

Notes and Questions

1. In 1969 the California Supreme Court in PEOPLE v. HUTCHINSON, 71 Cal.2d 342, 78 Cal.Rptr. 196, 455 P.2d 132 (1969), reversed its prior stance and accepted Justice Peters' position in Sopp v. Smith. For an example of the difficulties that can arise when the court accepts affidavits of dissenting jurors alleging misconduct of the majority (when only a majority verdict is required), see Johns v. City of Los Angeles, 78 Cal.App.3d 983, 144 Cal.Rptr. 629 (2d Dist. 1978) (hearing denied by 4–3 vote of the California Supreme Court).

2. Suppose the jurors agree upon a verdict but through the mistake of the jury foreman, judge, or court clerk a different verdict is entered. Should affidavits of jurors be admissible to correct the error? Is this "impeachment" within the meaning of the common law? If so, would the case fall within the exceptions permitted by the Iowa rule? See FORD MOTOR CREDIT CO. v. AMODT, 29 Wis. 441, 139 N.W.2d 6 (1966), in which the court refused to accept affidavits of eight of twelve jurors to the effect that a "No" rather than a "Yes" answer had been improperly reported as to a crucial interrogatory.

[handwritten margin note: I think should be allowed]

May affidavits be used when a verdict for plaintiff was rendered, but the amount of damages found was omitted? See Hodgkins v. Mead, 119 N.Y. 166, 23 N.E. 559 (1890).

3. Rule 606(b) of the Federal Rules of Evidence provides:

Inquiry into validity of verdict or indictment. Upon an inquiry into the validity of a verdict or indictment, a juror may not testify as to any matter or statement occurring during the course of the jury's deliberations or to the effect of anything upon his or any other juror's mind or emotions as influencing him to assent to or dissent from the verdict or indictment or concerning his mental processes in connection therewith, except that a juror may testify on the question whether extraneous prejudicial information was improperly brought to the jury's attention or whether any outside influence was improperly brought to bear upon any juror. Nor may his affidavit or evidence of any statement by him concerning a matter about which he would be precluded from testifying be received for these purposes.

For a thorough analysis of the problems of impeachment and the role of the Federal Rule, see Mueller, *Juror's Impeachment of Verdicts and Indictments in Federal Court Under Rule 606(b),* 57 Neb.L.Rev. 920 (1978).

HUKLE v. KIMBLE

Supreme Court of Kansas, 1952.
172 Kan. 630, 243 P.2d 225.

SMITH, JUSTICE. This was an action for damages alleged to have been sustained when plaintiff was caught between a truck driven by one of defendants and a pillar in the driveway of an elevator where plaintiff was employed. Judgment was for the plaintiff. Defendants have appealed.

* * *

Defendants * * * argue that the trial court erred in overruling their motion for a new trial. One of the grounds of this motion was misconduct of the jury. On the hearing of the motion for a new trial testimony of various members of the jury was heard on the question of whether the verdict was a quotient verdict. One of the jurors testified as follows:

Q. Without giving any of the other deliberations—in other words, without telling what was in your mind—I would like to ask you how this verdict was arrived at, the amount of this verdict? A. Mr. Brann was the foreman of the jury and he asked that—or suggested that if the—there was a judgment, which he thought there should be, if we would all put down an amount on a piece of paper, which we did, then someone in the group added it up and divided it by 12 and arrived at the $5,208.33, and then Mr. Brann said, 'Is there anyone that feels this is an unfair amount? Is this the amount that all of us wish, if you don't feel that way why speak up now,' and we all agreed that that would be the amount that we felt was right.

Q. And there had been something said before the quotient was taken, before you divided by 12 to do that to arrive at a verdict? A. I think so. I think it was. I think it was agreed that, before we wrote down those amounts that that would be the fair way, if one person said one amount and someone else said something higher and not knowing any better way, we agreed that an average would be right, and we discussed the average after we took it.

The foreman of the jury testified as follows:

Q. You have heard the testimony of these two other jurors? A. Yes, sir.

Q. Is that what occurred there at the time? A. That is correct.

Q. Do you have anything to add to it at all? A. I don't know as there is anything I could add. I thought it was fair and square.

Q. You suggested that you add their respective figures together and then divide the sum by 12 and that that would be adopted as the verdict; is that right? A. Well, yes.

Plaintiff realizes the potency of this evidence and seeks to counteract it by claiming that on cross-examination these jurors testified that they were asked after the quotient had been reached whether they believed the amount to be fair and all the jury members said it was. The fact remains, however, that the evidence is uncontradicted, that the jury members all agreed that the quotient would be the verdict and it was. * * * The result is the trial court erred in overruling the defendant's motion for a new trial.

Notes and Questions

1. As a practical matter does reversal in the *Hukle* case make any sense? Is the quotient verdict really all that evil? Would it be of significance if the jurors had taken a quotient verdict before deliberating the question of liability? What difference, if any, would it have made had the jury, after arriving at the quotient figure, discussed at length its propriety in light of the evidence? In SCHULZ v. CHADWELL, 558 S.W.2d 183, 186 (Ky.App.1977), the jurors used the quotient method to set an amount for each element of the claimed damage. The court rejected the appellant's claim that the verdict was thus an invalid quotient verdict: "The average of the jurors' views was obtained merely as a basis for further deliberation." For an extensive general discussion of the problems of quotient verdicts, see Annot., 8 A.L.R.3d 335 (1966).

2. There are many forms of jury misconduct, some of which were discussed in Chapter One, see pp. 49–52, supra. Often the question is not whether the conduct was improper but whether the error is so serious that the verdict must be overturned. Assuming that a trial court has before it the following sets of facts, what rulings should it make on motions for a new trial?

(a) The jury, after deliberation, was deadlocked seven to five for defendant, but because, during trial, one juror had learned of the death of a son and wished to return home, the jurors agreed to abide by the vote of the majority, and therefore, without further discussion, rendered a verdict for defendant. See Jorgensen v. York Ice Mach. Corp., 160 F.2d 432 (2d Cir.), certiorari denied 332 U.S. 764, 68 S.Ct. 69, 92 L.Ed. 349 (1947). Suppose the jury, although properly instructed, erroneously believed that a majority verdict was all that was necessary? Cf. Hoffman v. French, Ltd., 394 S.W.2d 259, 266 (Tex.Civ.App.1965).

(b) On *voir dire* in a personal-injury action, the prospective jurors had been asked whether they had ever had any claims arising from the alleged negligence of another person. Four members of the panel had asserted such claims, and they had been paid cash settlements without filing suit. Nonetheless they remained silent, believing the question to relate only to actual lawsuits. These four were not challenged and thus sat on the jury that rendered a verdict for plaintiff. Compare Photostat Corp. v. Ball, 338 F.2d 783 (10th Cir.1964) (denial of new trial reversed), with Derr v. St. Louis Pub. Serv. Co., 399 S.W.2d 241 (Mo.App.1965) (denial of new trial affirmed). Suppose the jurors had understood the question but nevertheless concealed the fact of their prior claims. Should the motives of the jurors bear on the question? See Pierce v. Altman, 147 Ga.App. 22, 248 S.E.2d 34 (1978) (denial of new trial reversed).

(c) After the case was submitted to the jury and the jury deliberated for more than an hour without reaching a verdict the bailiff, on instruction of the court, took the jurors to lunch in a local hotel and supplied them with alcoholic beverages in moderate amounts. Shortly thereafter the jurors returned to the court and, after a half hour of deliberation, rendered a verdict. See Kealoha v. Tanaka, 45 Hawaii 457, 370 P.2d 468 (1962) (denial of new trial affirmed by 3–2 decision). What difference would it make if one juror had become intoxicated? See generally Annot., 6 A.L.R.3d 934 (1966).

(d) During a court recess plaintiff entered an elevator containing three jurors on their way to lunch. The plaintiff initiated a friendly conversation with one of the jurors regarding the fact that some of plaintiff's relatives lived in the area where the juror owned and operated a drugstore. The conversation was short and nothing was said about the case. See United States v. Harry Barfield Co., 359 F.2d 120 (5th Cir.1966) (denial of new trial reversed by a 2-to-1 decision).

There are many cases in which jurors have been charged with misconduct for holding unauthorized conversations concerning the case. See Annot., 62 A.L.R.2d 298 (1958) (contact with a party to the case or his attorney); Annot., 52 A.L.R.2d 182 (1957) (contact with witnesses); Annot., 41 A.L.R.2d 288 (1955) (contact with judges, court officials, and attendants); Annot., 64 A.L.R.2d 158 (1959) (contact with outsiders generally). Most of the decisions turn on the nature of the conversation regarding the case and the extent to which the juror might have been influenced in his decision. See, e.g., Adams v. Davis, 578 S.W.2d 899 (Ky.App.1979). Does it make sense conclusively to presume prejudice in contexts such as United States v. Harry Barfield Co., above? Should every contact between a juror and a party or attorney, or between a juror and a witness, be considered prejudicial? See Printed Terry Finishing Co. v. City of Lebanon, 247 Pa.Super. 277, 299–300, 372 A.2d 460, 469 (1977) (unexplained contact requires new trial). See generally Note, 4 Houston L.Rev. 583 (1966).

In McDONOUGH POWER EQUIPMENT, INC. v. GREENWOOD, 464 U.S. 548, 104 S.Ct. 845, 78 L.Ed.2d 663 (1984), the respondent was injured in an accident involving a power mower manufactured by the petitioner. During the *voir dire* before the empanelling of the six-member jury, the respondents' attorney asked prospective jurors whether they or any member of their immediate family had sustained any severe injury. The jury ultimately found for the petitioner. After judgment was entered for the petitioner, the respondents' attorney questioned the jurors and discovered that the son of the foreman of the jury had been injured some time before by the explosion of a truck tire, sustaining a broken leg. During the post-judgment interview, the foreman said that "having accidents are [sic] a part of life," and that "all his children have been involved in accidents." Id. at 553 n. 3, 104 S.Ct. at 848 n. 3, 78 L.Ed.2d at 669 n. 3. The District Court, which did not have these details before it, refused the respondents' motion for a new trial. The Tenth Circuit held (based in part on the information quoted above but not presented to the District Court) that the juror's failure to respond to the question during the *voir dire* proceeding constituted juror misconduct requiring a new trial. The Supreme Court reversed:

> To invalidate the result of a 3-week trial because of a juror's mistaken, though honest, response to a question, is to insist on something closer to perfection than our judicial system can be expected to give. A trial represents an important investment of private and social resources, and it ill serves the important end of finality to wipe the slate clean simply to recreate the peremptory challenge process because counsel lacked an item of information which objectively he should have obtained from a juror on *voir dire* examination. * * * We hold that to obtain a new trial in such a situation, a party must first demonstrate that a juror failed to answer honestly a material question on *voir dire,* and then further show that a correct response would have provided a valid basis for a challenge for cause. The motives for concealing information may vary, but only those reasons that affect a juror's impartiality can truly be said to affect the fairness of a trial.

Id. at 555–56, 104 S.Ct. at 849–50, 78 L.Ed.2d at 671.

Justice Blackmun, joined by Justices Stevens and O'Connor, concurred, stressing that the decision should not be understood as "foreclos[ing] the normal avenue of relief available to a party who is asserting that he did not have the benefit of an impartial jury." Id. at 556, 104 S.Ct. at 850, 78 L.Ed.2d at 672. Justice Brennan, joined by Justice Marshall, concurred in the judgment, proposing a different legal standard:

> * * * In my view, the proper focus when ruling on a motion for new trial in this situation should be on the bias of the juror and the resulting prejudice to the litigant. More specifically, to be awarded a new trial, a litigant should be required to demonstrate that the juror incorrectly responded to a material question on *voir dire,* and that, under the facts and circumstances surrounding the particular case, the juror was biased against the moving litigant. * * *

> * * * [F]or a court to determine properly whether bias exists, it must consider at least two questions: are there any facts in the case suggesting that bias should be conclusively presumed; and, if not, is it more probable than not that the juror was actually biased against the litigant. Whether the juror answered a particular question on *voir dire* honestly or dishonestly, or whether an inaccurate answer was inadvertent or intentional, are simply factors to be considered in this latter determination of actual bias. * * *

Id. at 557–58, 104 S.Ct. at 851, 78 L.Ed.2d at 672–73.

Chapter 12

SECURING AND ENFORCING JUDGMENTS

The commencement of a lawsuit or, for that matter, even the entry of a judgment, does not necessarily mean that plaintiff actually will secure the objectives of the action. A victorious plaintiff's ability to collect a judgment depends primarily on defendant's capacity and willingness to pay at the time the award is made and secondarily on the effectiveness of the court's judgment-enforcement procedures in the event the judgment debtor is capable of paying but is being recalcitrant. For example, plaintiff's efforts may be frustrated if defendant has become insolvent during the litigation or has secreted his assets or fraudulently conveyed them to third persons. In short, the arduous litigation process often proves to be a preliminary to the equally protracted travail of collecting the award.

The attempts to enforce a libel judgment against a New York Congressman, the late Adam Clayton Powell, illustrate some of the problems that often face a judgment creditor. In the case of Powell, the creditor was Mrs. Ethel James whose efforts to claim her due are a study in the breakdown of the enforcement process. Mrs. James originally was awarded a $46,000 libel judgment in April, 1963 and that judgment was affirmed by the New York Court of Appeals in July, 1964. Employing a number of tactics, including transfers of property to relatives and invocations of congressional immunity from arrest and process, Powell avoided collection for 32 months. His maneuvers frustrated Mrs. James' attempts to discover Powell's assets in New York and Puerto Rico and resulted in her bringing suit against the Congressman again, basing her claim on the little used common-law tort of evasion of a judgment. After Powell failed to appear for examination in the second suit, his answer was stricken and compensatory damages were set at $75,000 and punitive damages were assessed at $500,000. These were reduced to $56,000 and $100,000 respectively in James v. Powell, 26 A.D.2d 525, 270 N.Y.S.2d 789 (1st Dep't 1966). Pursuit of Powell continued into 1967, but so did his appeals and in early March, 1967, the New York Court of Appeals reversed the verdict in the evasion-of-judgment suit because Puerto Rican law should have been applied to the compensatory-damage claim and New York law, which governed the remainder of the claim, apparently did not permit punitive damages under the circumstances of the case. 19 N.Y.2d 249, 279 N.Y.S.2d 10, 225 N.E.2d 741 (1967). Thus, Mrs. James was left with the original libel judgment and a cause of action under Puerto Rican law. See "No Home in the House," *Time,* March 10, 1967.

At one point Powell was paying off Mrs. James' libel judgment through the proceeds from a long-playing album, "Keep the Faith, Baby," part of which was recorded live at his Caribbean island retreat on Bimini. Mrs. James, apparently disillusioned by the entire episode, decided there must be a better way to make a living than collecting judgments. She followed Powell's example and recorded an album of her own. Fittingly, in some eyes at least, one number on that album exclaims:

> There was once a man
> who said that he
> Would like to retire to Bimini,
> But that was before he
> broke the law,
> And now the people are going
> haw-haw-haw.

Who had the last laugh is not clear, but it certainly was not the courts. Other reports of the pursuit of the Congressman include "Hooking a Catfish," *Newsweek,* December 27, 1965; "Man May Come and Man May Go (But Powell Goes on Forever)," *National Review,* June 29, 1965; and "Monstrous Mackerel," *Time,* December 24, 1965.

SECTION A.   METHODS OF SECURING THE JUDGMENT—PROVISIONAL REMEDIES

Most states attempt to maximize a plaintiff's chances for collecting the judgment ultimately secured by providing a series of security devices that operate during the action. These so-called "provisional" remedies primarily are creatures of statute and their character and effectiveness vary considerably from state to state. Thus, in a creditor-oriented state, it is not surprising to find that provisional remedies generally are available in almost all actions, whereas in a debtor-oriented jurisdiction they will be restricted to particular types of actions and be subjected to a variety of procedural restrictions. By virtue of Federal Rule 64, a federal court may use the provisional remedies available to the courts of the state in which it is sitting to the extent the state remedies are not inconsistent with any other federal rule or statute.

Articles 60 through 65 of New York's Civil Practice Law and Rules provide a claimant with the remedies of attachment and garnishment of property and debts, injunction, receivership, and notice of pendency.[a] Since New York's provisional-remedies scheme is one of the most fully developed systems in the United States, the description that follows will

a. In 1979, New York repealed N.Y.C.P. L.R. Article 61, which had provided for the provisional remedy of civil arrest.

use it as a model. For a general discussion of provisional remedies, see Millar, *Civil Procedure of the Trial Court in Historical Perspective* 481–515 (1952). Federal practice is described in 11 & 12 Wright & Miller, *Federal Practice and Procedure: Civil* §§ 2931–36, 2941–62, 2981–90 (1973); 7 Moore, *Federal Practice* ¶¶ 64.01–.10, 65.03–.08, 66.01–.10 (2d ed.). On the practice in particular states, see, e.g., 7 & 7A Weinstein, Korn & Miller, *New York Civil Practice* ¶¶ 6001.01–6515.07; Brewer, *Illuminating a Gray Area: Prejudgment Attachment in Arkansas After Springdale Farms Inc. v. McIlroy Bank & Trust,* 38 Ark.L.Rev. 881 (1985).

Although the need to provide creditors with expeditious remedies against recalcitrant debtors seems clear, there is no doubt that from time to time some of the provisional remedies have been used as a bludgeon to collect money that occasionally was not actually due plaintiff. In a series of cases that began in 1969 with Sniadach v. Family Finance Corp., 395 U.S. 337, 89 S.Ct. 1820, 23 L.Ed.2d 349 (1969), p. 219, supra, the United States Supreme Court has significantly modified the availability of pretrial "provisional" remedies. The Court's decisions have been based on the theory that any interference with the property of a defendant prior to an adjudication of the merits of plaintiff's claim is an unconstitutional invasion of defendant's rights, unless certain procedural safeguards are provided. See generally Countryman, *The Bill of Rights and the Bill Collector,* 15 Ariz.L.Rev. 521 (1973). The state courts have been prompted by the Supreme Court's decisions to construe the scope of provisional remedies narrowly, and to be especially wary of ex parte procedures. Accordingly, in considering the material that follows, the reader must constantly be aware of these dramatic shifts in judicial thinking about provisional remedies.

1. ATTACHMENT

The use of attachment for securing jurisdiction in rem or quasi-in-rem when the court cannot acquire jurisdiction over the person of the defendant was examined in Chapter Two. Reread the cases and notes on pp. 147–65, supra. Attachment also is valuable as a provisional remedy because it prevents defendant from selling or otherwise disposing of any real or personal property that has been taken into the custody of the attaching officer. Since attachment deprives defendant of the use and enjoyment of property long before liability is established (and, of course, in many cases no liability will be found), most jurisdictions limit its availability to certain classes of actions. Further limitations on the remedy's availability have resulted from restrictive judicial construction of attachment statutes. See, e.g., Arcturus Mfg. Corp. v. Superior Court, 223 Cal.App.2d 187, 35 Cal.Rptr. 502 (2d Dist.1963). How can the remedy of attachment be harmonized with our traditional notion that plaintiff's right to relief depends upon his establishment of the elements of his claim?

The procedure for invoking the remedy of prejudgment garnishment has been significantly affected by the Supreme Court's decision in SNIADACH v. FAMILY FINANCE CORP., p. 219, supra, which held the

Wisconsin prejudgment garnishment procedure unconstitutional. Under it, a summons issued at the request of the creditor's lawyer who served the garnishee to freeze the debtor's wages during the period before trial of the main suit without the wage earner having any opportunity to be heard. Initially, the effect of *Sniadach* on other provisional remedies was unclear. However, in FUENTES v. SHEVIN, p. 209, supra, the Court held unconstitutional state statutes providing for the replevin of chattels without a prior opportunity to be heard. State courts applying *Sniadach* also have invalidated prejudgment garnishment of accounts receivable without notice and a statute permitting a prejudgment writ of immediate possession by a landlord pending a hearing on the merits. See generally Clark & Landers, *Sniadach, Fuentes and Beyond: The Creditor Meets the Constitution*, 59 Va.L.Rev. 355 (1973); Note, *Procedural Due Process—The Prior Hearing Rule and the Demise of Ex Parte Remedies*, 53 B.U.L.Rev. 41 (1973).

Uncertainty about the requirements of due process surfaced again after the Court in MITCHELL v. W. T. GRANT CO., p. 220, supra, upheld the Louisiana sequestration statute permitting the creditor to obtain the writ on ex parte application without giving the debtor either notice or a prior opportunity for a hearing. The Court reasoned that the risk of a wrongful taking was minimized by the creditor's interest in the property prior to the lawsuit, the judicial authorization of the writ, and the immediate availability of a post-seizure hearing.

[handwritten margin note: Mitchell held Const—]

In a more recent case, NORTH GEORGIA FINISHING, INC. v. DI–CHEM, INC., p. 222, supra, the Court relied on *Fuentes* to invalidate the Georgia garnishment statute, which permitted the writ to be issued on the basis of conclusory allegations by the plaintiff without providing the defendant with an opportunity for an "early" hearing "or other safeguard against mistaken repossession." The opinion for the Court stressed the need for statutes to guard against the risk of initial error resulting in irreparable injury to the defendant even when the debt arises in a commercial context between parties of equal bargaining power, two corporations in this case.

[handwritten margin note: N. Georgia Unconst—]

As you proceed through this Chapter, consider whether the various remedies discussed are valid in light of these Supreme Court cases. See generally Alderman, *Default Judgments and Prejudgment Remedies Meet the Constitution: Effectuating Sniadach and Its Progeny*, 65 Geo.L.J. 1 (1976).

New York's attachment statute, N.Y.C.P.L.R. 6201, permits prejudgment attachment (1) when the defendant is a nondomiciliary residing outside the state or an unlicensed foreign corporation, (2) when the defendant is within the state but diligent efforts to personally serve her have failed, or (3) when the defendant's conduct in connection with the property indicates her intent to defraud creditors or frustrate the enforcement of a potentially unfavorable judgment. In contrast to the New York approach, some states provide that attachment is available in all contract actions, whether against residents or nonresidents, and in any action against a nonresident. What is the logic behind the distinction between the treatment accorded residents and nonresidents?

All nonexempt tangible and intangible property in which defendant has a recognizable interest is subject to attachment for purposes of securing the enforcement of the prospective judgment. New York permits the attachment of income, whether already earned or to be earned in the future, claims under insurance policies, bank accounts, and assignable choses in action and judgments. Certain property is exempt from attachment in order to permit defendant to maintain his standard of living during the pendency of the action. The elaborate, and somewhat archaic, New York exemptions are set out in N.Y.C.P.L.R. 5205–06. See also pp. 1043–50, infra.

When property of or a debt owed to defendant is in the hands of a third person, that person (the garnishee) may be prohibited from selling, assigning, or interfering with any property in which defendant has an interest or from paying or discharging any debt except as directed by the sheriff or a court order. The garnishee also may be ordered to turn the property or proceeds of the debt over to the court at the conclusion of the action for application to the final judgment.

Even if the statutory requirements for attachment are met and even if plaintiff is willing to post a bond to protect defendant, the court still has discretion to deny the remedy if it believes that the harm to defendant outweighs the risk that plaintiff's judgment will be unenforceable. Thus when the value of the property sought to be attached is significantly greater than defendant's potential liability or when the property is part of an ongoing business, the remedy may be denied. See generally Gray v. American Sur. Co., 129 Cal.App.2d 471, 277 P.2d 436 (3d Dist.1954).

The mechanics of attachment are relatively simple. A writ of attachment is directed to the appropriate law-enforcement officer, usually the sheriff, who serves the writ on defendant and seizes property equal in value to the amount set forth in the writ. The attachment remains in force for a limited period—usually until the action is concluded or for a fixed period long enough to permit the final determination of plaintiff's claim. In cases of hardship or special circumstances, the court may alter the length of time the attachment remains in force. For further information on the remedy of attachment, see Kheel, *New York's Amended Attachment Statute: A Prejudgment Remedy in Need of Further Revision*, 44 Brooklyn L.Rev. 199 (1978); Comment, *Abuse of Process and Attachment: Toward a Balance of Power*, 30 U.C.L.A.L.Rev. 1218 (1983).

2. PRELIMINARY INJUNCTIONS AND TEMPORARY RE-STRAINING ORDERS

A preliminary injunction is available when defendant is acting or threatening to act in a manner that would irreparably injure plaintiff or render the judgment in the action ineffectual. Since a preliminary injunction is granted before there has been a trial on the merits and it often has the same effect as the ultimate relief requested by plaintiff, it may have an extremely adverse impact on defendant; as a result, the

courts use preliminary injunctions only in the most appealing and neces- *bond*
sary circumstances. Rule 65(c) requires that before an injunction may
issue, a bond must be posted under which the defendant may recover if a
court later determines that he was "wrongfully enjoined." Moreover,
because of the "extraordinary" character of the remedy, the moving party *@ other*
traditionally has been required to show that none of the less drastic *no other alternatives*
provisional remedies provides an adequate alternative. For example, in
CRAMOND v. AFL–CIO, 267 Minn. 229, 126 N.W.2d 252 (1964), plaintiff
sought equitable relief and damages to correct his wrongful removal from
office in a labor union. The court required plaintiff to demonstrate that
there was no alternative to a preliminary injunction and that final relief
would be ineffective unless a temporary injunction was issued against a
scheduled election. According to the court, the grant or denial of a
preliminary injunction depends upon a balancing of the relative harm to
each party. See also Los Angeles Memorial Coliseum Comm'n v. National
Football League, 634 F.2d 1197 (9th Cir.1980). Is this balancing technique
objectionable because it amounts to a trial on the merits and thus is
wasteful of judicial time? Are there ways of avoiding this duplication?
See Federal Rule 65(a). See generally 11 Wright & Miller, *Federal
Practice and Procedure: Civil* §§ 2947–50 (1973); Leubsdorf, *The Standard
for Preliminary Injunctions,* 91 Harv.L.Rev. 525 (1978).

When plaintiff believes that immediate relief is essential, most states
will entertain an application for a temporary restraining order (TRO),
which will issue upon a showing that irreparable harm will occur absent
the order. Unlike the preliminary injunction, an application for a restraining order usually is made ex parte since time considerations do not
permit the giving of formal notice. Because of a concern over the
potential unfairness of ex parte proceedings, a number of special conditions, such as those set out in Federal Rule 65(b), usually are imposed
when notice is not given to all parties. See 11 Wright & Miller, *Federal
Practice and Procedure: Civil* §§ 2951–53 (1973). When an injunction
may infringe on fundamental rights guaranteed by the Constitution,
issuance of the injunction may be contingent on notice. Carroll v.
President & Commissioners of Princess Anne, 393 U.S. 175, 89 S.Ct. 347,
21 L.Ed.2d 325 (1968). Are temporary restraining orders consistent with
the *Sniadach* requirements of notice and an opportunity to defend? To
what extent does the imposition of special conditions such as those
described in Rule 65(b) satisfy due process considerations? A temporary
restraining order generally will remain effective only for a relatively brief
period or until a hearing is held on plaintiff's request for a preliminary
injunction. See generally Curtis v. Tozer, 374 S.W.2d 557 (Mo.App.1964);
Note, *Duration of Temporary Restraining Orders in Federal Courts,* 12
U.Balt.L.Rev. 276 (1983):

Despite the judicial hesitancy in issuing preliminary injunctions and
temporary restraining orders, these remedies are among the most useful
weapons in the procedural arsenal. Injunctions are extremely flexible
and can be molded to restrain or compel the performance of a wide variety
of acts. Because the primary purpose of these orders is to preserve the
status quo pending a full hearing on the merits, they usually will be

negative or prohibitory in character and restrain defendant from acting in a particular fashion. On the other hand, when property must be maintained or a course of conduct continued in order to preserve the status quo or prevent irreparable injury, the court will grant a request that defendant undertake or continue certain activities or honor a given standard of care. Such an order generally is referred to as mandatory or affirmative. A classic discussion of mandatory injunctions appears in then-Judge William Howard Taft's opinion in TOLEDO, A. A. & N.M. RY. v. PENNSYLVANIA CO., 54 Fed. 730, 741 (C.C.N.D.Ohio 1893):

> The office of a preliminary injunction is to preserve the status quo until, upon final hearing, the court may grant full relief. Generally this can be accomplished by an injunction prohibitory in form, but it sometimes happens that the status quo is a condition not of rest, but of action, and the condition of rest is exactly what will inflict the irreparable injury upon complainant, which he appeals to a court of equity to protect him from. In such a case courts of equity issue mandatory writs before the case is heard on its merits. * * *

In addition to the requirement that defendant's conduct violate plaintiff's rights and tend to render the ultimate judgment ineffectual, the act to be restrained must affect the subject matter of the action. Thus, a preliminary injunction or temporary restraining order relating to defendant's conduct is unavailable in an ordinary tort or contract action for money damages, since money is not considered the "subject" of the action. The objective of the action must be the preservation or a change in the status of property or a right. See generally Eastern Rock Products, Inc. v. Natanson, 239 App.Div. 529, 269 N.Y.S. 435 (3d Dep't 1933). As to the notion that defendant must be endangering the effectiveness of the final judgment, see, e.g., Maine Products Co. v. Alexander, 115 App.Div. 109, 112, 114, 100 N.Y.S. 709, 711, 712 (1st Dep't 1906) (three cases).

Even if plaintiff demonstrates a need for a preliminary injunction or temporary restraining order, the remedy will not necessarily be granted. The court's discretion will be exercised in light of the same principles of equity that influence a judicial determination as to whether a permanent injunction should issue. These factors include the availability of an adequate legal remedy, the difficulties of administering and enforcing the order, whether the injunction will prove effective, the possibility of irreparable harm, and whether the applicant has "unclean hands" or is guilty of laches. See Comment, *Formulating a Theory for Preliminary Injunctions: American Hospital Supply Corp. v. Hospital Products, Ltd.*, 72 Iowa L.Rev. 1157 (1987); Rendleman, *Inadequate Remedy at Law Prerequisite for an Injunction*, 33 U.Fla.L.Rev. 346 (1981); Laycock, *Injunctions and the Irreparable Injury Rule*, 57 Texas L.Rev. 1065 (1979).

Preliminary injunctions and temporary restraining orders usually bind only the parties to the action, their agents and servants, and anyone acting in collusion with or for the benefit of a party. In determining who is bound by the order, a great deal of caution is exercised to insure that anyone affected by the injunction has had a day in court and that the freedom of individual action and the right to voice personal opinions are not impaired simply because that person is a member of a group or unincorporated organization that has been enjoined by the court. Many courts inquire into the association's control over its members as an aid in determining whether or not individual members should be bound by an order issued against the group. See generally Rendleman, *Beyond Contempt: Obligors to Injunctions*, 53 Texas L.Rev. 873 (1975).

A problem that presents a particularly difficult question is whether a preliminary injunction or temporary restraining order should be used to prohibit parties from commencing or continuing an action in another court or from enforcing a judgment issued by another court. The problem becomes bound up with questions of jurisdiction and conflict of laws when a state court is asked to enjoin the parties from proceeding in an action pending in another state or in a federal court. For an illustration, see MERRITT–CHAPMAN & SCOTT CORP. v. MUTUAL BENEFIT LIFE INS. CO., 237 App.Div. 70, 73, 260 N.Y.S. 374, 378 (1st Dep't 1932), in which the court said it would not interfere with an action in another court "unless it has clear priority of jurisdiction, or exceptional circumstances are shown to exist which require such drastic remedy." See McClintock, *Equity* § 37 (2d ed. 1948); 7A Weinstein, Korn & Miller, *New York Civil Practice* ¶ 6301.27. What factors are relevant to the question whether a federal court should enjoin parties from proceeding in a state court? See Moore, *Conflict of Jurisdiction*, 23 La.L.Rev. 29 (1962). Are the considerations different when a state-court order purports to direct the parties not to proceed in a federal court? See Donovan v. City of Dallas, 377 U.S. 408, 84 S.Ct. 1579, 12 L.Ed.2d 409 (1964). See generally 17 Wright, Miller & Cooper, *Federal Practice and Procedure: Jurisdiction and Related Matters 2d* §§ 4211–12, 4221–26, 4251–55 (1988).

3. RECEIVERSHIP

Because the remedy originated in equity and therefore can be characterized as "extraordinary," a number of courts refuse to appoint a receiver to act as a custodian or manager of disputed property pendente lite whenever the movant is shown to have an adequate remedy at law or an alternative remedy. See, e.g., State ex rel. Larry C. Iverson, Inc. v. District Court, 146 Mont. 362, 406 P.2d 828 (1965). Even today, however, this hesitancy is both understandable and appropriate since in many instances the remedy will deprive defendant of the control and enjoyment of property without a hearing on the merits or will subject him to the high cost of a receivership. Courts sometimes may prefer receivership when the alternative is the potentially more draconian and expensive remedy of civil arrest. See First National State Bank v. Kron, 190 N.J.Super. 510, 464 A.2d 1146 (App.Div.1983).

Defendant's actual or potential insolvency is the primary reason for the appointment of a receiver. Another appropriate use of the remedy is to preserve property pending litigation when there is a substantial danger that the property will be removed from the state, lost, materially injured, or destroyed. See, e.g., Cafadaris v. Bulow, 138 Misc. 301, 244 N.Y.S. 600 (Sup.Ct.1930) (receiver appointed when immigration visa of person in possession of property about to expire). See also Gunther v. Gunther, 283 S.W.2d 826 (Tex.Civ.App.1955) (court stated that receivership may be used when it is incidental to an injunction or *lis pendens*).

In most states only plaintiff can secure the appointment of a receiver and the receivership extends only to property actually involved in the litigation. New York, however, gives its courts the power to appoint a receiver upon the motion of any person having an "apparent interest" in the property. N.Y.C.P.L.R. 6401. What possible justification is there for such a provision? New York practice also requires any person who moves for the appointment of a receiver to be joined as a party, thereby permitting the movant to protect her interest in the property in the previously commenced action; of course, this practice occasionally may prove burdensome to the person seeking the appointment of the receiver. See 7A Weinstein, Korn & Miller, *New York Civil Practice* ¶ 6401.14. Doesn't this unnecessarily complicate and proliferate the litigation?

A temporary receiver must be disinterested and owes primary allegiance to the appointing court and not to the parties or the person who sought the appointment. Because of this status, virtually all of a receiver's official acts are subject to the approval of the appointing court. When the debtor requests the appointment of a receiver, the court will look to see whether the debtor is manipulating the receivership to hinder and delay recovery by the creditors. See Shapiro v. Wilgus, 287 U.S. 348, 53 S.Ct. 142, 77 L.Ed. 355 (1932).

A temporary receiver's powers are found in the statute or rule authorizing the appointment or in the court order naming the receiver. He usually is required to take possession of the property as soon as possible after the appointing order has been entered. In VANDER VORSTE v. NORTHWESTERN NAT. BANK, 81 S.D. 566, 138 N.W.2d 411 (1965), the basic obligation of a receiver is described as the duty of preserving and protecting the property and assets of the estate that have been placed in protective custody. Although the receiver is not given title to the property, he generally is given the responsibility of managing or disposing of the property and the power to take any action necessary to maintain or improve it. See, e.g., Knickerbocker Fed. Sav. & Loan Ass'n v. 531 E. 144th St., Inc., 39 Misc.2d 23, 240 N.Y.S.2d 112 (Sup.Ct.1963).

In order to prevent dereliction in the performance of his duties, a temporary receiver normally is required to execute and file an undertaking before any official duties are initiated. The undertaking protects the integrity of the court and the litigants by guaranteeing that injuries caused by any defalcation by the receiver can be indemnified.

The appointment of receivers in the federal courts is governed by Federal Rule 66. Section 959(b) of Title 28 of the United States Code defines the receiver's substantive rights, duties, and liabilities. See 12 Wright & Miller, *Federal Practice and Procedure: Civil* §§ 2981–86 (1973), for a discussion of federal receivers.

4. CIVIL ARREST

The provisional remedy of civil arrest had its genesis in the common-law practice of commencing an action by taking into custody and imprisoning defendant until judgment was rendered or bail was posted. Although incarceration effectively prevented defendant from rendering the potential judgment unenforceable, its Draconian quality made it a frequent source of abuse. The debtor's prison strikingly portrayed by Dickens in the *Pickwick Papers* illustrates the unpleasant consequences of the remedy. Consequently, courts and legislatures have sharply restricted the availability of civil arrest in most jurisdictions. For an historical discussion of the development and use of civil arrest see Freedman, *Imprisonment for Debt,* 2 Temple L.Q. 330 (1928). See also Morris & Wiener, *Civil Arrest: A Medieval Anachronism,* 43 Brooklyn L.Rev. 383 (1976).

The availability of civil arrest varies widely from state to state. Some state constitutions (Mississippi Const., Art. III, § 30 and Texas Const., Art. 1, § 18) prohibit imprisonment for debt and thus render civil arrest unavailable; a number of states simply have not enacted legislation authorizing civil arrest, although their constitutions would not prohibit use of the remedy. Other states allow civil arrest only in limited types of actions, such as those based on fraud, deceit, or conversion and those in which injunctive relief is sought.[b]

Even when civil arrest has been authorized by statute, certain public policy exemptions generally limit its application. For example, some courts have exempted all public servants from civil arrest. States granting immunity from service of process to nonresident witnesses also generally extend that immunity to cover civil arrest.

A motion for civil arrest is addressed to the court's discretion, which, in view of the severity of the remedy, is exercised with a great degree of caution. This is exemplified by the following statement from SUMMERS v. DISTRICT COURT, 68 Nev. 99, 227 P.2d 201 (1951):

> The legislative authorization of such a remedy based upon probability is an extraordinary grant of power to the courts and carries with it extraordinary judicial responsibilities. The extensive discretion so granted assumes the highest of judicial wisdom and, accordingly, demands the highest degree of consideration in its exercise.

Furthermore, plaintiff usually must file an "undertaking" guaranteeing the payment of any legal costs and damages that defendant may sustain if the arrest proves to have been wrongful. The undertaking protects

---

b. Civil arrest is available in many states in actions involving extremely violent or cruel batteries and other "malicious torts." See generally Shatz v. Paul, 7 Ill.App.2d 223, 129 N.E.2d 348 (1st Dist.1955), which contains an excellent historical discussion of the use of arrest. Traditionally, women have been exempted from civil arrest in many states. In 1976, New York modified its statute by deleting the word "women" and substituting the language "parent, guardian or other person * * * whose principal responsibility is * * * the daily care and supervision of [a child under sixteen or an incompetent of any age] * * *." After further restricting the availability of civil arrest, the 1978 amendment eliminated the exemption altogether, N.Y.C.P.L.R. 6101. New York abolished the remedy of civil arrest in 1979.

defendant and insures that those thinking about invoking the remedy will "look before they leap."

An arrested defendant will be released if bail is posted in an amount designated by the court; the bail then serves as security for any judgment plaintiff ultimately may recover. Bail usually is set high enough to cover the prospective judgment, although the court will avoid setting bail at a figure that makes it impossible for defendant to secure his release. See People v. Tweed, 5 Hun 382 (App.Div.), appeal dismissed 63 N.Y. 202 (1875). But for a grievous example of the possible consequences of civil arrest, see In re Harris, 69 Cal.2d 486, 72 Cal.Rptr. 340, 446 P.2d 148 (1968).

5. NOTICE OF PENDENCY

Although not strictly a provisional remedy, the notice of pendency is included in this discussion because of its similarity to the four provisional remedies already described. The genesis of the notice of pendency is found in the common-law doctrine of *lis pendens,* which sought to guarantee the effectiveness of a judgment in an action involving specific tangible property by charging any purchaser or encumbrancer of the property with knowledge that an action involving it had been instituted. Thus, at common law a prospective purchaser or encumbrancer not only had to check all of the conveyance records to be certain of the vendor's good title but also had to investigate whether the vendor was involved in any pending litigation that might affect the property—often a practical impossibility. Today, this burdensome aspect of the *lis pendens* doctrine generally has been restricted by statute. See White, *Lis Pendens in the District of Columbia: A Need for Codification,* 35 Cath.U.L.Rev. 703 (1987). See, e.g., Picerne v. Redd, 72 R.I. 4, 47 A.2d 906 (1946). For a history of the common-law procedure, see Bennett, *Lis Pendens* (1887).

The statutory notice of pendency is designed to protect prospective purchasers and encumbrancers by requiring plaintiff to file a notice of the litigation before the protection of constructive notice can be claimed. Thus, if plaintiff fails to file a notice of pendency and properly index it, he will not be protected against a purchaser or encumbrancer who does not have actual knowledge of the litigation involving the property. In some states, such as New York, notice-of-pendency statutes apply only to real property, which may mean that the harsher *lis pendens* doctrine is still applicable to actions involving personalty. More likely, the common-law practice has been eliminated by negative implication.

Statutory notice of pendency differs from other provisional remedies because it usually does not involve judicial discretion; the right to file a notice is absolute in any litigation falling within the classes enumerated in the notice-of-pendency statute. The only question on which the court must exercise its judgment usually is whether the action affects real property. Obviously, however, the court's power over this issue can be used to restrict or contract the availability of the remedy considerably. See the discussion in Braunston v. Anchorage Woods, Inc., 10 N.Y.2d 302,

222 N.Y.S.2d 316, 178 N.E.2d 717 (1961).   Why shouldn't the courts be able to handle notice-of-pendency applications on a discretionary basis?

6.   A POSTSCRIPT

Despite their obvious practical importance to the proper functioning of a judicial system, little effort has been devoted to the rationalization of provisional remedies and their integration into the total procedural picture.   Indeed many practitioners are ill-informed as to the availability and operation of provisional remedies in their jurisdiction and often miss an opportunity to protect their clients against debilitating and frustrating post-judgment enforcement procedures.   What better evidence of the second-class treatment accorded the subject of provisional remedies is there than the cavalier incorporation of state provisional-remedy practice by Federal Rule 64 and the reference to federal receivership practice "heretofore followed" in Rule 66?   With the goals and the structure of federal procedure as a background, see if you can formulate a comprehensive provisional-remedies rule for the federal courts; make certain that it will be consistent with contemporary notions of due process as set forth in the United States Supreme Court cases described on pages 1034–35, supra.   In what ways are the availability or unavailability of post-judgment enforcement techniques relevant to framing a provisional-remedies rule?   Reconsider this question after studying the remaining materials in this Chapter.

SECTION B.   METHODS OF COLLECTING AND ENFORCING THE JUDGMENT

1.   EXECUTION

GRIGGS v. MILLER
Supreme Court of Missouri, 1963.
374 S.W.2d 119.

WALTER H. BOHLING, SPECIAL COMMISSIONER.   Bill Griggs, on January 19, 1961, sued W. A. Brookshire in ejectment for the possession of a 322 acre farm in Boone County, Missouri, and for damages for withholding possession.   Plaintiff had purchased the farm for $20,600 on January 16, 1961, at a public sale under a general execution against defendant. * * * Defendant's answer was a general denial, and his counterclaim sought to set aside the sheriff's execution sale and deed. * * * The cause was considered and treated by the parties and the court "as one of 'equitable cognizance.' "   The court found the issues for the plaintiff and against the defendant on plaintiff's petition; for the plaintiff and the third-party defendant [the sheriff] on defendant's counterclaim; and that plaintiff was entitled to $2,483.24 damages by reason of defendant's withholding of possession of said farm from January 18, 1961, to November 15, 1961, the date of said judgment and decree, and that plaintiff recover $250 per month from and after November 15, 1961, for so long as defendant withheld possession from plaintiff.   Defendant Brookshire, after filing his notice of appeal, was incarcerated in the Missouri Penitentiary. * * * Miller was appointed trustee of the Estate of W. A. Brookshire, and substituted as a party litigant for said Brookshire.

* * *

Ray Crouch recovered a judgment against W. A. Brookshire, defendant, in the Circuit Court of Henry County, Missouri, on July 15, 1959, for $1,966.69. Said judgment was affirmed on December 5, 1960 * * *. The right to an execution follows immediately upon the rendition of a judgment. * * * No supersedeas bond was given to stay an execution. * * * A general execution was issued on said judgment to the Sheriff of Boone County on December 10, 1960. The Sheriff levied on defendant's 322 acre farm December 14, 1960, filed a notice of his levy in the office of the Recorder of Deeds of Boone County, and advertised and sold said real estate at public sale on January 16, 1961.

Dorothy Contestible, Administratrix of the Estate of Ralph Burton Collings, Deceased, recovered a judgment of $17,000 against William Albert Brookshire, defendant, in a wrongful death action in the Circuit Court of Audrain County, Missouri, on July 29, 1960. A general execution issued on said $17,000 judgment to the Sheriff of Boone County on December 23, 1960. This execution was mailed to Mrs. Contestible's attorneys in Columbia and was delivered to Sheriff Powell January 10, 1961. He levied upon defendant's 322 acres under said execution on January 11, 1961.

Defendant contends it was error to sell his 322 acre farm without attempting to make the judgment debt, interest and costs out of a portion of said farm.

* * * [A] judgment debtor is to be afforded reasonable protection in levying on and selling his property under execution. Civil Rule 76.21 (§ 513.095) provides in effect that if a judgment debtor gives the officer a list of his property sufficient to satisfy the execution, "the officer shall levy upon the property and, no other, if in his opinion it is sufficient; if not, then upon such additional property as shall be sufficient."

Civil Rule 76.24 (§ 513.210) provides: "When an execution shall be levied upon real estate, the officer levying the same shall divide such property, if susceptible of division, and sell so much thereof as will be sufficient to satisfy such execution, unless the debtor in the execution shall desire the whole of any tract or lot of land to be sold together, in which case it shall be sold accordingly."

And Rule 76.25 (§ 513.100) provides: "The person whose goods, chattels and real estate are taken in execution may elect what part thereof shall be first sold; and if he shall deliver to the officer having charge thereof a statement, in writing, of such election, three days before the day appointed for the sale, stating specifically what goods, chattels and real estate he desires to be first sold, and so on, until the execution be satisfied, the officer shall proceed according to such election, until sufficient money shall be made to satisfy the amount in the execution specified and costs."

It is stated in 21 Am.Jur., Execution, § 380, that an execution is not "leviable upon all the debtor's property, but only upon sufficient property owned by the debtor within the jurisdiction to satisfy the debt, interest, and costs"; and, while the officer is left to his own judgment, he "must exercise the care and discretion which a reasonably prudent man would exercise under like conditions and circumstances." And, with respect to the property to be sold when more than enough to satisfy the debt is seized, it is stated in § 384: "The general rule is that the execution officer may make a division of the property, if that is practicable, and sell only so much of it as is necessary to satisfy the debt." * * * A failure to divide real estate and sell only enough to satisfy the execution [has been] considered an abuse of discretion * * * and a constructive fraud * * *.

* * *

Defendant wrote Sheriff Powell under date of January 11, 1961, re the Crouch judgment, levy and sale, stating, among other things, that his land was worth in excess of $100 an acre; and: "I am restricting the amount which you can sell to the northeast 40 acres of said tract of land. This land is clear. There is no mortgage or encumbrance of any kind against it."

Defendant protested the execution sale to those assembled for the sale and stated in effect that the judgment involved had been obtained in Henry County and the case was on appeal and the judgment was not final; that: "After the judgment becomes final it will be paid"; that Crouch had in his possession cattle belonging to defendant worth $10,000 against which there was no lien; that "I have notified the sheriff that this farm is clear of any mortgages whatsoever; that it is worth approximately $50,000.00; that one forty acre sold would be more than adequate. I have pointed out the forty acres * * * to be sold"; that he was certain the $17,000 judgment against him in the Contestible case would be reversed; that a supersedeas bond would be given; that this sale would be illegal and whoever bought the farm would buy a law suit. (The Contestible judgment, however, was affirmed January 8, 1962, in Contestible v. Brookshire, Mo., 355 S.W.2d 36.)

Sheriff Powell, who had been sheriff for about twenty years, admitted 40 acres of defendant's farm "might have been" worth far in excess of $2,000. Asked why he had not told defendant the 40 acres would not be sufficient, he would take 80 acres, Sheriff Powell answered: "I didn't intend to take 80 acres." He testified he had levied on and held three or four execution sales of defendant's 322 acre farm. He stated he did not know it was illegal to sell $50,000 worth of property to satisfy a $2,000 judgment; and there was testimony he had levied on the 322 acres to collect a $13.00 judgment, and to collect a $600 judgment. He stated "I checked the record and there was several thousand dollars" against all of the farm, and that is why "I levied on all of it." He also stated "I never checked the records." He did not levy on personal property because "It was much easier to do it this way." He knew defendant had stocks in various corporations and had more than 200 head of Hereford cattle on the farm; that they might have sold for at least $200 a head on the market and as registered cattle would have brought more, and that 20 head of the cattle "might have" been sufficient to more than pay the Crouch judgment, interest and costs.

Ray Crouch, the judgment creditor, testified he wanted to and asked his attorney to levy on defendant's farm, and that he knew defendant had collateral * * * to take care of the Crouch judgment. Sheriff Powell testified that Crouch had told him defendant had deposited sufficient collateral with the Hartford Insurance Company to take care of the Crouch judgment.

* * *

A sheriff conducting an execution sale is the agent of the property owner and the judgment creditor, and his duty is to protect the interests of both and to see that the property is not sacrificed. * * * Forced sales of property usually do not bring full value.

Sheriff Powell's advertisement of the sale of defendant's 322 acre farm was to "sell all of said real estate or as much thereof as *it* be necessary to pay the judgment of $1,966.69," in the Henry County Circuit Court, which, with interest and costs, amounted to $2,308.16 on the day of sale.

Defendant's farm was never advertised for sale under the Audrain County (Contestible) execution. Defendant first knew of the levy on his farm under the $17,000 Audrain County judgment about 30 minutes before its sale under the Crouch judgment. Sheriff Powell testified that he sold under the Henry County, and not under the Audrain County, execution.

Defendant's 322 acres was not divided for the purpose of selling but was sold as a whole to plaintiff for $20,600.00. The only bidders were Ed Orr, one of the attorneys for Mrs. Contestible, and Ralph Alexander, a bondsman and attorney for the sheriff. Plaintiff Griggs testified he heard the farm would bring enough to satisfy the two judgments about 15 or 20 minutes before the sale; that about 5 or 10 minutes before it was sold he decided to buy it because "it didn't bring any more than it did," and that he asked Mr. Alexander to bid for him. * * *

It is not questioned but that this 322 acre farm, consisting of approximately eight forties, could have been offered for sale in parcels. Rule 76.24 (§ 513.210) contemplates that the officer "divide such property, if susceptible of division, and sell so much thereof as will be sufficient to satisfy such execution." This was not done, and we hold that it should have been so divided. In Brookshire v. Powell, Mo., 335 S.W.2d 176, 181, the disparity between the market value of this farm and a bid of $2,300 was considered so great as to require setting aside that execution sale and sheriff's deed. In the case at bar the Henry County judgment, interest and costs amounted to $2,308.16; and for that amount under said execution and the constructive levy of the Audrain County execution, but without an advertisement for sale under Rule 76.36, supra, under said Audrain County execution, it is sought to justify this forced sale for $20,600 of property valued at about $46,000. This record calls for the result reached in Brookshire v. Powell * * *

Defendant is entitled to relief upon doing equity. * * * Accordingly, if defendant will, within thirty days, deposit in this court, for the use and benefit of those entitled thereto, the sum of $20,600 with interest at the rate of 6% per annum from the date of sale until the same is paid, the decree appealed from will be reversed and the cause remanded with directions to cancel the sheriff's sale and the sheriff's deed to plaintiff made pursuant thereto; otherwise the decree will stand affirmed. In either event the costs are assessed against the estate of defendant Brookshire.

PER CURIAM. The foregoing opinion by BOHLING, Special Commissioner, is adopted as the opinion of the court.

All of the Judges concur.

[The court's opinion on a motion to modify and for a rehearing and the court's supplemental opinion are omitted.]

Notes and Questions

1. Execution is the traditional method of enforcing a money judgment. It applies to both personal and real property. In contemplating the effectiveness of the device, consider the following questions. What is the territorial reach of an execution? In what order should various types of property be levied upon and sold by the officer to whom the execution is delivered? How are priorities determined as between competing executions? Use of the execution in particular situations and the interrelationship between execution and other judgment-enforcement devices are discussed in Heiserman, *Procedures Available for Implementation of a Judgment in Iowa*, 42 Iowa L.Rev. 265 (1957); Walker, *The Collection of Debts From Insolvent and Fully-Mortgaged Debtors*, 43 Tenn.L.Rev. 399 (1976). For further information, see Woodward, *Collecting Money Judgments: Priorities and Procedure*, in T. Eisenberg, *Debtor-Creditor Law*, vol. 9, ch. 37 (1988).

2. The text of Federal Rule 69 and the cases decided under it indicate that the procedures of the state in which the federal court is sitting are to be followed in enforcing federal-court judgments. See United States v. Hackett, 123 F.Supp. 106 (W.D.Mo.1954). By way of exception to the use of state practice, Rule 69 provides that "any statute of the United States governs to the extent that it is applicable." In addition, a judgment creditor who wishes to examine the judgment debtor or any other person as to the debtor's assets may proceed under either state supplementary-proceeding practice or under the Federal Rules relating to depositions and discovery. See generally 12 Wright & Miller, *Federal Practice and Procedure: Civil* §§ 3011–15 (1973).

3. One form of execution used to attach intangible property is garnishment. The most common subject is wages, although bank accounts also may be garnished. State law generally exempts part of the judgment debtor's income and real and personal property from enforcement procedures such as execution and garnishment. See generally Abrahams & Feldman, *The Exemption of Wages from Garnishment: Some Comparisons and Comments*, 3 De Paul L.Rev. 153 (1954). The percentage of income exempted from execution varies from little or nothing to a high of ninety percent. What accounts for this disparity? An excellent critique of garnishment appears in Brunn, *Wage Garnishment in California: A Study and Recommendations*, 53 Calif.L.Rev.

1214 (1965). After an analysis of the existing garnishment pattern, the author concludes:

> The time when a family had few, if any, debts except perhaps a home purchase mortgage may be remembered nostalgically, but it has passed. The years following the end of World War II saw the development of what might be called the American way of debt. * * * Consumer credit has become a major industry and consumer debt consumes a major slice of many a family's income. * * *

> Individual debt, not so long ago discouraged and regarded with suspicion, is now encouraged. * * *

> Even with sales managers named Jesse James, one may grant that the contribution of consumer credit to the economy and to the standard of living of many families is substantial. But when personal debt is no longer unusual, no longer a sign of improvidence, when debt has instead become a mass production, hard-sell item that citizens are widely encouraged to "buy," one may doubt the continued appropriateness of a device such as wage garnishment. * * * Today this harsh remedy, humiliating at best, disastrous to the debtor and his family at worst, seems far less justifiable than in an age when personal debt was uncommon and disfavored. It is time that our attitude toward wage garnishment—which is, after all, a drastic form of intervention by government on behalf of creditors—caught up with our attitude toward debt.

* * *

> Collection agencies find wage garnishment a useful tool, not only because of the debtor's earnings actually reached by levies, but because the threat of garnishment encourages the debtor to make payments. Whether one views this effect as persuasive or coercive depends to some extent on one's point of view. In any event, the encouragement is due to the debtor's fear that he will lose his job if there are more garnishments. The fear is real. Discharges because of repeated wage levies are not uncommon. Employers dislike the added work and expense brought by levies and often limit the number of levies they will permit without discharge. Labor organizations have apparently not been able to bargain effectively on this issue.[c]

> The employee who is threatened with discharge, and who cannot pay, sometimes chooses bankruptcy as a means of saving his job. The expansion of consumer credit in the postwar years has been accompanied by a sharp rise in bankruptcies, particularly in nonbusiness bankruptcies. Bankruptcy rates tend to be lower in states that do not permit wage garnishment or that sharply restrict its use. * * *

> Wage garnishment is costly. Its immediate costs include official fees—chargeable to debtors—expense to employers, and the community's subsidy of the garnishment process. There are other costs in terms of distress and economic hardship when the family whose earnings are garnished spirals into bankruptcy or unemployment. And there are losses to creditors from garnishment-triggered no-asset bankruptcies.

---

c. New York has attempted to solve this problem by statute. See N.Y.C.P.L.R. 5252. Since the publication of the article in text, California has enacted a statute preventing an employee from being discharged because his wages have been garnished. See Cal. Stats.1971, ch. 1607.

> Hardship is not limited to bankruptcy and unemployment; a debtor who avoids both is faced with a * * * wage exemption, [in] an amount that in the great bulk of cases is grossly inadequate.

Id. at 1243–47.

A 1970 amendment to the Consumer Credit Protection Act of 1968 establishes a nationwide limit on the amount of an employee's wages that are subject to garnishment and affords an employee some protection against being discharged as a result of garnishment. 15 U.S.C. §§ 1673–74 (1983).

Real and personal-property exemptions from execution usually are defined by statute on an item-by-item basis rather than by percentage of property value. The failure to revise these statutes over long periods of time has led to some incredibly outdated provisions. By way of illustration, see the lists of property exempted from execution by Section 5205 (personal) and Section 5206 (real) of New York's Civil Practice Law and Rules. In some instances the result of a failure to revise these statutes is far from amusing. For example, New York exempts from execution a lot of land that is being used as the principal residence by a householder or a woman, but only up to a value of $10,000. N.Y.C.P.L.R. 5206(a). For many years, the exemption was limited to $2,000. If the purpose of homestead exemptions is to permit the judgment debtor and family to maintain a minimum standard of living, this exemption may be woefully inadequate. See Dean, *Economic Relations Between Husband and Wife in New York,* 41 Cornell L.Q. 175, 213–14 (1956). See generally 6 Weinstein, Korn & Miller, *New York Civil Practice* ¶¶ 5205.01–5206.29.

Since one of the primary purposes of exemption statutes is to protect the judgment debtor's dependents against an overzealous judgment holder, nearly every state provides that the exemptions do not apply when the attaching creditor is the spouse or a dependent of the debtor, who typically sue for alimony or child support payments. See Fischer v. Fischer, 13 N.J. 162, 98 A.2d 568 (1953). In SCHLAEFER v. SCHLAEFER, 112 F.2d 177, 185 (D.C.Cir. 1940), the court said:

> * * * [T]he usual purpose of exemption is to relieve the person exempted from the pressure of claims hostile to his dependents' essential needs as well as his own personal ones, not to relieve him of familial obligations and destroy what may be the family's last and only security, short of public relief. * * *

Various types of real and personal property also are exempt from execution. Exempt property typically is defined by dollar amount and type of property, both of which vary greatly from state to state. Perhaps the most important exemption is the homestead exemption, which protects the family house up to a certain dollar amount. For background on the sources of modern homestead laws, see McKnight, *Protection of the Family Home from Seizure by Creditors: The Sources and Evolution of a Legal Principle,* 86 S.W. Hist.L.Q. 364 (1983).

4. In an attempt to reduce the cost of enforcing a spouse's duty of support, the National Conference of Commissioners on Uniform State Laws adopted in 1950 the Uniform Reciprocal Enforcement of Support Act, 9B Uniform Laws Annotated 381 (1987). In a Prefatory Note, the Act's operation is described as follows:

The Act itself creates no duties of family support but leaves this to the legislatures of the several states. The Act is concerned solely with the enforcement of the already existing duties when the person to whom a duty is owed is in one state and the person owing the duty is in another state (or under the Act as it has been adopted in a few states is in a different county of the same state).

Over the years many thousands of cases have been brought under the Act and many millions of dollars have been recovered. As a result, the duty of family support is placed where it belongs, on the shoulders of the one who, under state law, owes the duty. The state is thus relieved from keeping on its relief rolls those, often in destitute circumstances, to whom the duty is owed.

The amendments of 1968, like previous ones, are designed to plug loop holes and cure defects in the enforcement procedure. Machinery for enforcement in many states is efficient. In a few states it is less so. Sometimes local officials have not fulfilled their duties. The present Act seeks to create ways and means of filling this gap (Sections 12, 18 and 29). Improved machinery for finding the obligor has been written into the Act (Section 17). The new Act has guidelines for the conduct of the trial in the responding state (Sections 21 and 23), for cases where paternity is in issue (Section 27) or where there has been interference with visitation rights (Section 23) or where it may be desirable to take an appeal (Section 34). The procedure for registering and enforcing out-of-state support orders has been simplified (Sections 39 and 40).

Would this type of a system cure some of the deficiencies in the existing procedures for collecting a judgment by execution or garnishment? See generally Note, *Constitutional Implications of the Child Support Enforcement Amendments of 1984,* 24 J.Fam.L. 301 (1986).

2. SUPPLEMENTARY PROCEEDINGS

COHEN, COLLECTION OF MONEY JUDGMENTS IN NEW YORK: SUPPLEMENTARY PROCEEDINGS, 35 Colum.L.Rev. 1007, 1012–14, 1030–34 (1935):

* * * [S]upplementary proceedings existed at common law, although under a different trade name. After the return of execution unsatisfied a creditor was empowered to proceed in equity by way of a judgment creditor's bill for two primary purposes: (a) to reach "equitable" assets beyond the scope of legal execution, and (b) to uncover property owned by the judgment debtor but deviously concealed and "transferred."

The judgment creditor's suit fitted itself into a finely grooved routine in its course through the court of chancery. * * *

* * * [T]he net result of the judgment creditor's bill was an examination of the debtor, a disclosure by him of his property, and the assignment thereof under order of the court to a receiver who acted as the agent of the court in converting the judgment debtor's property into currency, rendering it applicable to the payment of the original claim. * * * [T]he creditor's bill finally became a highly formalized procedure * * *. In their labors to provide a new and simpler scheme for judgment collection the [New York] Code Commissioners devised a prac-

tice which was expressly intended to be a substitute for the old creditors' bill: the "supplementary proceedings."

There would be an examination of the judgment debtor. This might disclose: (a) debts due to the judgment debtor, (b) tangible personal property of the judgment debtor in his own possession or in the possession of a third party, (c) real property owned by the judgment debtor. Real property could be reached by execution. For third party debtors there was devised the third party order, and for tangible personal property in the hands of the debtor or third persons there was created an order directing such property to be applied in satisfaction of the judgment. * * * In addition, * * * the Code Commissioners provided that the judge could appoint a receiver of the property of the judgment debtor.

* * *

The effectiveness of the remedy granted by way of supplementary proceedings depends in large part upon the efficiency with which the instrument may be used to discover property of the debtor and have it applied upon the judgment. Conceivably the proceeding may be so broad as to permit all issues as to title to be adjudicated therein with finality. That this has not happened in most Code states is one of the prime causes of the ineffectiveness of the modern judgment collection system. Under the [New York] Field-Throop Code, and under the [New York] Civil Practice Act, the examination is not a trial. It merely affords the creditor an opportunity to question the debtor in an attempt to discover assets.

At the outset the creditor is faced with the problem of obtaining personal service of the order on the debtor. In plenary suits jurisdiction may be obtained by substitution upon debtors who evade service, but no similar provision is available in supplementary proceedings, although these constitute a new proceeding and would seem analogous to a plenary suit. Should the judgment debtor desire to dodge service the creditor can do little but spend time and money trying to catch him. * * *

Having obtained service the creditor will find that the court facilities afforded for the examination are quite meagre. The debtor is not examined in the presence of the Court, nor is the testimony officially transcribed. * * * The * * * statute provides that upon the consent of the debtor or his attorney the examination may be taken before a notary public or commissioner of deeds at any place mutually agreeable to the parties. And it also specifies, in what may be a helpful reform, that the Appellate Division may assign official referees to preside at examinations, although it is to be regretted that the statute did not incorporate the reform * * * that the examination be held immediately after the trial and before the justice then presiding.

* * * Where there is no official supervision, constant disputes arise as to the scope of the examination and the accuracy with which it was transcribed. This tends to hamper the investigation and affords evasive debtors opportunities to change their testimony. Thus the absence of satisfactory judicial facilities, at least in New York City, often results in defeating creditors' efforts at collection.

This situation has been aggravated by some judicially evolved rules defining the creditor's rights. After examining the debtor the creditor naturally desires to adjourn the examination so that he may have an opportunity to investigate the debtor's testimony. Prior to the new statute, such adjournments were denied as a matter of right, and rested solely in the consent of the debtor or the discretion of the justice at Special Term. Moreover the creditor was denied the power to investigate the debtor's books and records. He could subpoena them, but he could not examine them; they could be used solely to "refresh" the debtor's recollection.

The current reforms have attempted to remedy some of these difficulties. Reexaminations of the debtor at stated intervals are permitted. In certain cases the creditor may examine witnesses within six months after the debtor's examination has been closed. * * * And finally, perjury is now punishable as a contempt. However, since the statute predicates the applicability of this sanction upon the "materiality" of the testimony in question, the effectiveness of this sanction will rest largely upon what the court feels is "material" evidence.

These, however, are minor matters. As it stands today the examination merely affords the creditor an opportunity to discover that the debtor's assets do not belong to him, but to his wife and kindred, and that they were transferred to pay long standing obligations to the spouse, as to which no records exist. The scope of the examination is not such as to permit a trial of title; whenever a question of title is raised, the dispute may not be settled within the supplementary proceeding. For any real relief the creditor must start a separate action to set aside transfers obviously made to prevent judgment collection.

Notes and Questions

1. New York extensively revised the supplementary procedures described in the quoted passage in 1935. See Cohen, *Collection of Money Judgments: Experimentation with Supplementary Proceedings,* 36 Colum.L. Rev. 1061 (1936), which outlines these changes and comments on the practice in many other states. New York's judgment-collection procedures were revamped again in 1963. Present New York practice is described in Volume Six of Weinstein, Korn & Miller, *New York Civil Practice.* Because modernization of enforcement procedures generally has lagged throughout the country, the excerpt from the Cohen article provides a good statement of the supplementary proceedings presently in force in many states. See also Note, *Supplementary Proceedings in Illinois: The Uncertain Remedy,* 1979 U.Ill.L.F. 241. However, because discovery within the execution process is now more widely available than it once was, judgment creditors have less occasion to resort to supplementary proceedings. Federal Rule 60 permits broad discovery in aid of execution. Additionally, of the many states that have loosened or eliminated restrictions on pre-execution discovery of assets, most have followed the pattern of Federal Rule 69. See Woodward, *Enforcement of Money Judgments: Objectives and Restrictions,* in T. Eisenberg, *Debtor-Creditor Law,* vol. 9, ch. 37, ¶ 37.02 (1988).

2. Should supplementary proceedings be treated as a separate action or merely an adjunct to the action in which the judgment was recovered? On this question compare Arnold v. National Union of Marine Cooks & Stewards Ass'n, 42 Wash.2d 648, 257 P.2d 629 (1953) (part of main action), with Riley v. Fatt, 47 So.2d 769 (Fla.1950) (separate action). What turns on the answer to this question?

3. Suppose A recovers a judgment from B and during supplementary proceedings B claims that C is in possession of property belonging to B. When A attempts to have the property applied to the judgment, C contests B's interest. How is the dispute between B and C as to the ownership of the property to be determined? If the supplementary proceeding is under the control of a judge, can the court determine the dispute between B and C and, if it finds in B's favor, apply the property to the satisfaction of A's judgment? What objections are there to the judge making such a determination? Compare Letz v. Letz, 123 Mont. 494, 215 P.2d 534 (1950), with Mewes v. Jacobson, 70 Idaho 427, 220 P.2d 681 (1950). In THOMAS v. THOMAS, 192 Cal.App.2d 771, 13 Cal.Rptr. 872 (2d Dist.1961), defendant's former wife brought an action for support payments and tried to reach defendant's pension installments. What effect might a good-faith denial by defendant's employer of any indebtedness to the employee have on the original trial-court's jurisdiction to determine whether the ex-wife had any right in future installments? In *Thomas,* defendant's employer contended that it was a denial of due process to proceed with the supplementary proceeding and that an independent action was necessary. How should that question have been resolved?

4. When a judgment is reversed on appeal, what is the status of the enforcement proceedings already undertaken? Is the prevailing party liable for damages caused by the attempt to enforce the judgment? In HARP v. BROOKSHIRE, 197 Ky. 794, 248 S.W. 177 (1923), H sued B for a declaration that he had a right of way over B's farm. H obtained a temporary injunction to prevent B from interfering with the claimed right of way. The trial court held that H had no right of way and dissolved the injunction. During the pendency of H's appeal, B refused to let H cross the land. The lower court's decision ultimately was reversed and H's right of way upheld. In a subsequent suit by H for damages caused by B's excluding him from the land, the court held that although a party generally is not liable for the consequences of acts performed in obedience to a judgment that later is reversed, B would be held liable since the acts were not directly or expressly authorized by the judgment. But didn't the trial court's decision effectively declare B's ownership of the land and give him the right to control access to it? How could B have protected himself pending H's appeal?

3. CONTEMPT AND BODY EXECUTION

REEVES v. CROWNSHIELD

Court of Appeals of New York, 1937.
274 N.Y. 74, 8 N.E.2d 283.

FINCH, JUDGE. The uncollectibility of money judgments has ever been a subject of concern to bench and bar. A large part of the statute law of this state is designed to enable a judgment creditor to obtain satisfaction upon his money judgment. That a large percentage of these money judgments have remained uncollectible has been confirmed by statistical surveys. Johns Hopkins University Institute of Law, Survey of Litigation in New York (1931). Many debtors who were in a position to pay have evaded their legal obligations by unlawful and technical means. Discontent with this situation resulted in agitation for reform in collection procedure. * * * Finally, in 1935, upon the recommendation of the Judicial Council, a law was enacted creating a new mode of enforcing the payment of judgments. * * *

Section 793 of the Civil Practice Act [currently N.Y.C.P.L.R. 5226] now provides that, in addition to the garnishee provisions of the old law, the court may make an order directing a judgment debtor to make payments in installments out of the income which he receives. Such orders must be made upon notice to the judgment debtor and after he has had an opportunity to show inability to pay, and with due regard to the reasonable requirements of the judgment debtor and his family, as well as of payments required to be made by him to other creditors. Section 801 of the Civil Practice Act [now found in N.Y.C.P.L.R. 5251] provides that refusal to pay after such an order of the court is punishable as a contempt. * * *

This new procedure was invoked against the appellant, in an attempt to collect a judgment for approximately $400. The examination in supplementary proceedings disclosed that he was employed by the Federal Government as a steamship inspector at a salary of $230 per month, less a small pension deduction. He has no children, and the whereabouts of his wife are unknown. Aside from $48 a month paid as rent and his living expenses, he has no financial obligations. The court ordered the appellant to pay installments of $20 per month until the judgment was satisfied. Upon his failure to pay, he was held in contempt and fined the sum of $20, commitment being provided for in default of payment.

An appeal was taken directly to this court from the City Court of New York City on the ground that a constitutional question was involved.

* * *

The judgment debtor challenges the constitutionality of section 793 and section 801 on the ground that in effect they provide for imprisonment for debt. It is admitted that neither the State nor the Federal Constitutions contain provisions expressly prohibiting imprisonment for debt, and that the statutory provision forbidding imprisonment for debt found in section 21 of the New York Civil Rights Law excepts cases otherwise specially prescribed by law. It is asserted, however, that imprisonment for debt is barred by the due process clauses of the State and Federal Constitutions (Const.N.Y. art. 1, § 6; Const.U.S. Amend. 14). No cases so holding are cited * * *. Whatever doubt there may exist as to whether imprisonment for debt without regard to ability to pay may be treated as a deprivation of liberty without due process of law * * *, there can be no doubt that imprisonment for failure to obey an order of a court to make payment out of income, which order is made with due regard to the needs of the debtor and his family, is not violative of the due process clause.

* * *

In the case at bar the judgment debtor has not complained that the order directing the payment of $20 per month is unjust, inequitable, or harsh. His position is an arbitrary refusal to pay. It is based upon the ground that the courts are powerless to compel him to pay out of his income an amount fixed after deducting the sum necessary for his reasonable needs.

The Legislature has seen fit to provide a creditor with a direct remedy for the collection of his just debts. A refusal to recognize such an order by the judgment debtor entitles the creditor to move to have him punished for contempt. Without this right, there would be no power in the court to enforce its order. To compel the judgment debtor to obey the order of the court is not imprisonment for debt, but only imprisonment for disobedience of an order with which he is able to comply. His refusal is contumacious conduct, the same as a refusal to obey any other lawful order of the court.

It also is asserted that the application of this law to the appellant is unconstitutional, since it interferes with the operation of a federal instrumentality. To sustain this contention, reference is made to the cases declaring State laws taxing the salaries of federal officers unconstitutional. * * * Analysis shows that these cases are not in point. The true basis for declaring a state tax on the salaries of federal officers unconstitutional is that since the Federal Government presumably finds it necessary to pay its officers a salary based upon the value of their services, the state should not be permitted to tax the salaries thereby reducing the compensation and making it necessary for the Federal Government to increase the salaries paid by it.

* * *

It is true that the wages of a federal employee cannot be garnisheed, but once his wage has been paid to him a state is not prohibited from ordering him to apply a portion of such income towards the payment of his just debts. The moment the salary is received it becomes a part of the general income of the owner. If he should therewith purchase property the property could be taken under execution for the payment of a judgment against the owner. No reason appears for exempting the income while still held as money and not exempting it when it has been converted into property. * * *

* * *

Orders affirmed.

Notes and Questions

1. Compare the principal case with PEOPLE ex rel. SARLAY v. POPE, 230 App.Div. 649, 650, 246 N.Y.S. 414, 416 (3d Dep't 1930), in which the court said that the "imprisonment of the defendants until the payment of a fine in the amount of the judgment recovered in the contract action would be, in effect, imprisonment for a civil debt." In the absence of an express constitutional provision forbidding imprisonment for debt, is there any theory under which it can be held unconstitutional? If contempt or body execution is

aimed at the recalcitrant or dilatory judgment debtor, how is the good faith, but penniless, debtor protected against being caught in the contempt trap? Is it sufficient simply to require that the judgment debtor's failure be "willful" in order to punish for contempt? See generally Note, *Body Attachment and Body Execution: Forgotten But Not Gone,* 17 Wm. & Mary L.Rev. 543 (1976).

2. What are the differences between body execution and contempt? Should courts in jurisdictions that have prohibited or severely limited body execution use contempt proceedings to circumvent the restrictions on body execution? See Note, *Present Status of Execution Against the Body of the Judgment Debtor,* 42 Iowa L.Rev. 306 (1957). See also the distinctions between contempt and body execution drawn in Zeitinger v. Mitchell, 244 S.W.2d 91 (Mo.1951).

3. Doesn't the *Reeves* case suggest that the problems that frequently arise during supplementary proceedings could be cured by an order to disclose all hidden or undiscovered assets reinforced by the contempt sanction? How would the court determine whether or not the judgment debtor is telling the truth when he claims to have no leviable property? What types of post-judgment defaults other than the one involved in *Reeves* properly are punishable by contempt? See generally 6 Weinstein, Korn & Miller, *New York Civil Practice* ¶¶ 5251.10–.21.

4. LIENS AND PRIORITIES

MATTER OF FORNABAI

United States District Court, District of New Jersey, 1964.
227 F.Supp. 928.

SHAW, DISTRICT JUDGE. This matter comes before the Court * * * on Petition for Review of an order by the Referee in Bankruptcy. The order of the Referee in Bankruptcy dated June 4, 1963 determined that two judgment liens were entitled to priority in satisfaction over tax liens of the United States of America out of a real estate fund being administered by the Court.

The pertinent facts may be recited briefly as follows: On May 2, 1962 Nicholas Fornabai individually and doing business as Fornaby Equipment Co. was adjudicated a bankrupt in a Chapter XI proceeding. The realty of the bankrupt was sold and valid liens against the realty transferred to the proceeds of the sale. The amount thereof held by the Trustee in Bankruptcy is insufficient for full satisfaction of all valid liens.

* * * The lien of the United States is for taxes assessed against the bankrupt pursuant to provisions of the Internal Revenue Code of 1954. Truck Equipment Corporation recovered a judgment in the Superior Court of New Jersey against the bankrupt on December 8, 1960. The amount is $13,716.85 plus interest. Pak-Mor Manufacturing Co. recovered its judgment against the bankrupt in the United States District Court for the District of New Jersey on March 10, 1961. The amount of this judgment is $18,199.61 plus interest. Both judgments were docketed as of the dates of recovery thereof. The United States filed notice of tax liens against the bankrupt. * * *

The precise question presented is whether the liens of the two judgment creditors above mentioned were perfected in the sense that they became choate liens on the realty of the bankrupt prior to the date when the United States filed its notice of tax liens. If so, the judgment liens are entitled to priority.

A judgment docketed in the Superior Court of New Jersey is a lien upon all real estate of the judgment debtor located within the State of New Jersey from the date the judgment is docketed. N.J.S.A. 2A:16–1.
* * *

By federal statute it is provided with respect to judgments of the United States District Court that:

> Every judgment rendered by a district court within a State shall be a lien on the property located in such State in the same manner, to the same extent and under the same conditions as a judgment of a court of general jurisdiction in such State, and shall cease to be a lien in the same manner and time. * * * 28 U.S.C.A. § 1962.

Taxes assessed against a taxpayer pursuant to the provisions of the Internal Revenue Code of 1954 become liens in favor of the United States upon all property and rights to property belonging to the taxpayer. 26 U.S.C.A. § 6321. But the lien for taxes is not valid "as against any mortgagee, pledgee, purchaser, or *judgment creditor* until notice thereof has been filed." (Emphasis supplied.) 26 U.S.C.A. § 6323. As noted above, the earliest date on which the Government filed notice of a tax lien was April 10, 1961.

Federal law determines which secured creditors are judgment creditors for purposes of protection under Section 6323. * * *

In the case of United States v. Gilbert Associates, Inc., [345 U.S. 361, 73 S.Ct. 701, 97 L.Ed. 1071 (1953)] * * * the Supreme Court stated:
* * *

> A cardinal principle of Congress in its tax scheme is uniformity, as far as may be. Therefore, a 'judgment creditor' should have the same application in all the states. In this instance, we think Congress used the words 'judgment creditor' in § 3672 [now 26 U.S.C.A. § 6323] in the usual, conventional sense of a judgment of a court of record, since all states have such courts.

The priority of a lien created by state law over a tax lien of the federal government depends on the time it attached to the property in question and became choate. It is perfected to the point of being a choate lien "when the identity of the lienor, the property subject to the lien, and the amount of the lien are established." United States v. Pioneer American Insurance Co., 374 U.S. 84, 88, 89, 83 S.Ct. 1651, 1655, 10 L.Ed.2d 770 (1963).

Each of the judgments here were recovered in a court of record and docketed therein. The identity of each judgment lienor, the property subject to the judgment lien and the amount thereof has been established. Nevertheless, the Government contends that neither of the judgments imposed a choate lien upon realty of the bankrupt because neither of the judgment creditors caused a writ of execution to issue against the real estate of the bankrupt. In support of its argument, the Government cites N.J.S.A. 2A:17–39 * * *. [The cited statute gives the purchaser of real property good title as against a judgment creditor who has not issued an execution against the property.]

The effect and purpose of the above cited statutory provision is misconstrued. A writ of execution on a judgment does not create the lien; it is merely the procedural means by which the judgment creditor obtains satisfaction out of the proceeds of the sale of realty. * * *

It is clear from the language of the statutory provision upon which the Government relies, and the judicial interpretation of it over many years that its provisions were intended to apply only to priority inter se among those holding liens by judgment or recognizance and that it has no effect in the determination of priority of lien holders other than those mentioned. It creates an exception to the Common Law rule of "the first in time is the first in right," in favor of a subsequent judgment creditor who has issued execution on the judgment and the reason for the exception is clearly stated in the statute. In the early case of Clement v. Kaighn, 15 N.J.Eq. 47 (Chancery 1862), the Court stated that a judgment shall bind the lands of a defendant from the time of actual entry of the judgment on the record of the Court, but that the purpose of the statutory exception among judgment creditors was to give a junior judgment creditor whose execution was first sued out the "proper effect and fruits thereof." * * *

It would be manifestly inequitable if a senior judgment creditor were permitted to stand by while a junior judgment creditor incurred the expense in issuance of a writ of execution, levy upon, and sale of lands of a defendant, and then step in to share first in the proceeds. This would deny the junior lien holder who proceeded with diligence "the proper effect and fruits thereof." It was this inequity in procedural enforcement affecting judgment creditors and liens attaching by recognizance that the State Legislature recognized and sought to correct. Application of the provisions of the statute to priority status of liens other than those existing by virtue of judgment or recognizance would rest upon an interpretation which the plain language of the statutory provision does not support and one which finds no sanction by weight of judicial precedent in the state courts.

There is no rational basis upon which the Government can equate its tax lien in this instance with a judgment lien or recognizance for purposes of claiming the benefit of the provisions of N.J.S.A. 2A:17–39. Its position might be analogous to that of a judgment creditor who had issued execution on a judgment, if it had been *first* to take action to enforce the tax lien against realty of the taxpayer pursuant to the provisions of Title 26 U.S.C.A. § 7403. But that is not the case here. The mere filing of its notice of tax lien without further action to subject property of the taxpayer to payment of the tax liability, does not give the Government a status analogous to that of a judgment creditor who has issued a writ of execution to satisfy a judgment. Accordingly, as between the Government holding a tax lien by virtue of assessment and notice filed and a judgment creditor who has not issued a writ of execution, the common law rule of "the first in time is the first in right," is the applicable rule. * * *

Moreover, it might be stated as a matter of practical observation, that if the provisions of 26 U.S.C.A. § 6323 in favor of prior judgment creditors were to have no application until the property in question was in the process of sale to satisfy a judgment, the limited effect thereof on judgment liens generally would render the intended benefits sterile. This indeed would be a narrow interpretation of a remedial statute with emphasis upon local procedures to enforce satisfaction of a lien rather than upon the substantive right created by the lien.

* * * A judgment entered in the Superior Court of New Jersey is a lien upon all real estate within the jurisdiction of the court from the date of entry thereof. * * * The judgment creates the substantive right of lien, not the writ of execution.

Accordingly, the determination by order of the Referee in Bankruptcy that the two judgment creditors have priority of lien over the federal tax liens is affirmed. An appropriate order in accordance herewith will be submitted.

Notes and Questions

1. Lien and priority-of-lien problems are among the most complex in the law of judgment enforcement. The traditional "lien" situation involves the judgment creditor's right to a particular piece of property as against the judgment debtor or someone claiming under the latter, such as an assignee or purchaser of the property. The judgment creditor's rights against a transferee are based on the purchaser's or assignee's having actual or constructive notice of the creditor's rights in the property. Questions of "priority of liens," as in the *Fornabai* case, involve a dispute between two or more judgment creditors over the debtor's property. As a general rule, the rights of one creditor *vis à vis* another are based on the equitable principle of "diligence," which seeks to prevent a creditor from refraining from enforcing a judgment while maintaining priority of lien. What factors should determine whether one judgment creditor is more "diligent" than another?

Because courts often confuse "priority-of-lien" and "lien" situations, the line between the two has been somewhat obscured. The New York practice is analyzed in 6 Weinstein, Korn & Miller, *New York Civil Practice* ¶ 5202.02. The terminology is further analyzed in Distler & Schubin, *Enforcement Priorities and Liens: The New York Judgment Creditor's Rights in Personal Property,* 60 Colum.L.Rev. 458 (1960). For illustrations of some of the many problems that arise in this context, see Burroughs, *The Choate Lien Doctrine,* 1963 Duke L.J. 449; Comment, *Priorities of Creditors Under Judgment Creditor's Bills,* 42 Yale L.J. 919 (1933).

2. Section 5202 of New York's Civil Practice Law and Rules expressly provides that an execution creditor's rights in the judgment debtor's personal property are superior to those of anyone who acquires an interest after the delivery of an execution to a sheriff except: (1) transferees who acquire the debt or property for fair consideration before levy and (2) transferees who acquire the debt or property, when it is not capable of delivery, for fair

consideration after it was levied upon but without knowledge of the levy. What are the purposes of these two exceptions? See 6 Weinstein, Korn & Miller, *New York Civil Practice* ¶¶ 5202.11–.12. The judgment creditor's lien remains in effect as long as the execution is in force but once it expires the judgment creditor's lien terminates and the transfer of any property that was not actually levied upon under the execution made while the execution was in force will be effective as against the judgment creditor.

3. An execution creditor can lose her lien or priority of lien if she allows the execution to become "dormant," which permits the rights of a diligent creditor to be advanced over those of a creditor who is not pursuing the enforcement of a claim. A classic definition of dormancy is found in EXCELSIOR NEEDLE CO. v. GLOBE CYCLE WORKS, 48 App.Div. 304, 310, 62 N.Y.S. 538, 541 (4th Dep't 1900):

> The law * * * seems to be settled that any direction by the execution creditor to the sheriff, which suspends the lien or delays the enforcement of the levy, renders the execution dormant against subsequent creditors or *bona fide* purchasers. However veiled may be the direction; however much it may be founded on a humane desire to protect the debtor; if it is tantamount to a mandate or instruction to the sheriff to withhold the execution of his process during the interim that he accedes to this demand, the levy ceases to be effective. That doctrine rests on public policy and is necessary to prevent fraud and it should receive a fairly rigorous enforcement.

What justification is there for the dormancy doctrine? Should a judgment creditor's execution or attachment become dormant when he directs the sheriff not to levy out of a hope that the judgment debtor will become financially stable if the property and business are not disturbed and the latter is not besieged by creditors?

Chapter 13

APPELLATE REVIEW

SECTION A. THE PRINCIPLE OF FINALITY

1. INTRODUCTION: THE HISTORICAL BACKGROUND

CRICK, THE FINAL JUDGMENT AS A BASIS FOR APPEAL, 41 Yale L.J. 539, 541–43, 545–48, 550 (1932):

From very early times in England the method whereby a litigant came into the king's court and attacked a decision rendered in a feudal or manorial court was the complaint of false judgment. It was early decided, however, that the king's courts could not be charged with a false judgment, and the means whereby the King's Bench corrected errors in the other common law courts was by writ of error, the method destined to survive in many jurisdictions to our own day. The common law decisions involving writ of error are clearly the origin of our rule that only final judgments are appealable. The real factors in the establishment of this practice must go back to the very beginning of the history of the writ of error, and it is impossible at this time to give more than an explanation which is merely plausible.

* * * The matter seems to be connected in some way with the "record" by which the proceedings in the lower court are made known to the King's Bench, for counsel in [John de Ralegh's Case, Y.B. 17 Ed. 3 (R.S.) 234 (1343)] * * * says, "You have no warrant to try this record for the record is not fully here, because the case is still pending in another Court. * * * It is impossible that on one and the same original writ there should be two records in different courts." * * *

If we combine with this conception of the record, the fact that a proceeding on a writ of error seems to have been regarded as a new action, and not merely a continuation of the suit in the inferior court, we see how it may have been that the record could not be sent up until the suit below had been completed. Suing out a writ of error before final judgment would result in two actions in different courts, to the procedure of each of which the formal record was essential. To remove it while the case was pending below "would disturb the proceedings" there, while the reviewing court could not proceed until it was informed of what had happened below.

*   *   *

We see, then, that [in Blackstone's time] there were three types of pronouncements made during the course of a case [in equity]. First, orders, second, interlocutory decrees, and third, final decrees. Unlike the common law, however, which * * * required a case to go to final judgment before the decisions of the court might be questioned, equity gave relief from all three types of pronouncements. * * *

Thus we see that equity practice never knew the rule of the common law that only final judgments were appealable. Not only could interlocutory decrees be taken to the House of Lords, but also those decisions which had not even attained the dignity of decrees, that is, orders. As to the reason for this, we may tentatively assign two factors. First, appeals to the House of Lords from the Lord Chancellor were established comparatively late in legal history. * * * During the intervening centuries, therefore, a given case had its beginning and ending in the same court, and the only method by which a decision could be altered was by rehearing before the chancellor. * * *

When the House of Lords finally asserted appellate jurisdiction over proceedings in chancery, therefore, it found a system whereby the chancellor passed on all decrees issued, as well as on interlocutory orders, and we need not be surprised that appeals were taken to the Lords from interlocutory decrees because in chancery there was no particular magic in a final decree. * * *

Second, when we consider the character of litigation handled in chancery we see how much more convenient it was to review intermediate decisions as the case progressed. * * * [M]uch of its litigation was of a complicated type unsuited to the more simple common law forms of action. There was a much greater use of subordinate officials than in the common law courts, and the requirement of documentation of evidence introduced difficulties unknown to the King's courts. In equity, judgments were not compelled to follow stereotyped forms, and this made possible dealing with the case by as many orders, decrees, and modifications of the same as were necessary in the particular case. Thus, equity had a more elastic procedure, and also required a less rigid practice on appeal to review the many and varied steps taken below.

When we pass to the American scene we are at once confronted with confusion. * * * However, two main trends seem to have characterized the process.

First, there has been a general tendency to take the common law rule that error lay only after final judgment and to apply it to equity procedure. Second, hampered by this restriction in both law and equity, the courts have gone through elaborate logical exercises in order to escape from the strict application of the restriction * * *.

Another factor which may have had some effect was the failure to keep distinct the practice of law and equity, particularly on appeal. Very commonly one appellate court was established to hear appeals in both law and equity, and in some states, at least, the common law writ of error was the method of appeal in equity cases as well as at law. * * *

2. APPLICATION OF THE BASIC CONCEPT

———

Read 28 U.S.C. §§ 1291 and 1292 in the Supplement.

———

COOPER, EXTRAORDINARY WRIT PRACTICE IN CRIMINAL CASES: ANALOGIES FOR THE MILITARY COURTS, 98 F.R.D. 593, 594–596 (1983):

A truly final judgment is one that marks the completion of all the events that will occur in a trial court. Nothing more remains to be done, unless it be execution of a judgment against the defendant.

The advantages that may be gained by deferring appeals until entry of a truly final judgment are familiar, and can be summarized in short order. Immediate review of every ruling made by a trial court could not be tolerated. Repeated interruptions and delays could put the trial process beyond any reasonable control, even if appeals were taken only when there was a good faith and reasonable belief that the court was wrong. The opportunities for less honorable delay and harassment of an adversary also would not go entirely unexploited. More limited opportunities for interlocutory review would not be so disastrous, but would carry some part of the same costs. The possible advantages to be set against these costs arise from the opportunity to correct a wrong ruling. These advantages, however, are reduced by the prospects that most trial court rulings are correct; that wrong rulings often are corrected by the trial court; and that uncorrected wrong rulings will not, in the end, taint the final judgment.

The price that is paid for a final judgment rule, however, can be high. An erroneous ruling may taint everything that follows. If appeal must be delayed until final judgment, it may become necessary to repeat the entire trial proceeding. The costs of repeating the trial go beyond the obvious costs of expense and anxiety. The further proceedings will be held later, and may suffer from lapses of memory, inconsequential inconsistencies that are blown into exaggerated importance, and actual loss of evidence. Beyond these defects, the retrial proceedings often will be affected by lessons learned at the first trial. * * * The problem is more than one of boredom; strategies have been revealed and must be revised, opportunities to sustain truth by impeachment are diminished, and so on.

* * *

Beyond the impact on individual cases, loss of the opportunity for interlocutory review means that some areas of law must develop without much opportunity for appellate guidance. Questions of discovery, for example, may confuse and divide trial courts for years without the guidance and uniformity that appeals could provide.

LIBERTY MUTUAL INSURANCE CO. v. WETZEL

Supreme Court of the United States, 1976.
424 U.S. 737, 96 S.Ct. 1202, 47 L.Ed.2d 435.

Certiorari to the United States Court of Appeals for the Third Circuit.

MR. JUSTICE REHNQUIST delivered the opinion of the Court.

Respondents filed a complaint in the United States District Court for the Western District of Pennsylvania in which they asserted that petitioner's employee insurance benefits and maternity leave regulations discriminated against women in violation of Title VII of the Civil Rights Act of 1964 * * *. The District Court ruled in favor of respondents on the issue of petitioner's liability under that Act, and petitioner appealed to the Court of Appeals for the Third Circuit. That court held that it had jurisdiction of petitioner's appeal under 28 U.S.C. § 1291, and proceeded to affirm on the merits the judgment of the District Court. We granted certiorari * * * and heard argument on the merits. Though neither party has questioned the jurisdiction of the Court of Appeals to entertain the appeal, we are obligated to do so on our own motion if a question thereto exists. * * *

Respondents' complaint, after alleging jurisdiction and facts deemed pertinent to their claim, prayed for a judgment against petitioner embodying the following relief:

(a) requiring that defendant establish non-discriminatory hiring, payment, opportunity, and promotional plans and programs;

(b) enjoining the continuance by defendant of the illegal acts and practices alleged herein;

(c) requiring that defendant pay over to plaintiffs and to the members of the class the damages sustained by plaintiffs and the members of the class by reason of defendant's illegal acts and practices, including adjusted backpay, with interest, and an additional equal amount as liquidated damages, and exemplary damages;

(d) requiring that defendant pay to plaintiffs and to the members of the class the costs of this suit and a reasonable attorneys' fee, with interest; and

(e) such other and further relief as the Court deems appropriate. App. 19.

After extensive discovery, respondents moved for partial summary judgment only as to the issue of liability. * * * The District Court * * *, finding no issues of material fact in dispute, entered an order to the effect that petitioner's pregnancy-related policies violated Title VII of the Civil Rights Act of 1964. It also ruled that Liberty Mutual's hiring and promotion policies violated Title VII. Petitioner thereafter filed a motion for reconsideration which was denied by the District Court. * * *

It is obvious from the District Court's order that respondents, although having received a favorable ruling on the issue of petitioner's liability to them, received none of the relief which they expressly prayed for in the portion of their complaint set forth above. They requested an injunction, but did not get one; they requested damages, but were not awarded any; they requested attorneys' fees, but received none.

Counsel for respondents when questioned during oral argument in this Court suggested that at least the District Court's order of February 20 amounted to a declaratory judgment on the issue of liability pursuant to the provisions of 28 U.S.C. § 2201. Had respondents sought *only* a declaratory judgment, and no other form of relief, we would of course have a different case. But even if we accept respondents' contention that the District Court's order was a declaratory judgment on the issue of liability, it nonetheless left unresolved respondents' requests for an injunction, for compensatory and exemplary damages, and for attorneys' fees. It finally disposed of none of respondents' prayers for relief.

The District Court and the Court of Appeals apparently took the view that because the District Court made the recital required by Fed.Rule Civ. Proc. 54(b) that final judgment be entered on the issue of liability, and that there was no just reason for delay, the orders thereby became appealable as a final decision pursuant to 28 U.S.C. § 1291. We cannot agree with this application of the Rule and statute in question.

Rule 54(b) "does not apply to a single claim action * * *. It is limited expressly to multiple claims actions in which 'one or more but less than all' of the multiple claims have been finally decided and are found otherwise to be ready for appeal." Sears, Roebuck & Co. v. Mackey, 351 U.S. 427, 435, 76 S.Ct. 895, 899, 100 L.Ed. 1297, 1306 (1956). Here, however, respondents set forth but a single claim: that petitioner's employee insurance benefits and maternity leave regulations discriminated against its women employees in violation of Title VII of the Civil Rights Act of 1964. They prayed for several different types of relief in the event that they sustained the allegations of their complaint, see Fed.Rule Civ.Proc. 8(a)(3), but their complaint advanced a single legal theory which was applied to only one set of facts. Thus, despite the fact that the District Court undoubtedly made the findings required under the Rule had it been applicable, those findings do not in a case such as this make the order appealable pursuant to 28 U.S.C. § 1291. * * *

We turn to consider whether the District Court's order might have been appealed by petitioner to the Court of Appeals under any other theory. The order, viewed apart from its discussion of Rule 54(b), constitutes a grant of partial summary judgment limited to the issue of petitioner's liability. Such judgments are by their terms interlocutory, see Fed.Rule Civ.Proc. 56(c), and where assessment of damages or awarding of other relief remains to be resolved have never been considered to be "final" within the meaning of 28 U.S.C. § 1291. * * * Thus the only possible authorization for an appeal from the District Court's order would be pursuant to the provisions of 28 U.S.C. § 1292.

If the District Court had granted injunctive relief but had not ruled on respondents' other requests for relief, this interlocutory order would have been appealable under § 1292(a)(1). But, as noted above, the court did not issue an injunction. It might be argued that the order of the

District Court, insofar as it failed to include the injunctive relief requested by respondents, is an interlocutory order refusing an injunction within the meaning of § 1292(a)(1). But even if this would have allowed *respondents* to then obtain review in the Court of Appeals, there was no denial of any injunction sought by *petitioner* and it could not avail itself of that grant of jurisdiction.

Nor was this order appealable pursuant to 28 U.S.C. § 1292(b). Although the District Court's findings made with a view to satisfying Rule 54(b) might be viewed as substantial compliance with the certification requirement of that section, there is no showing in this record that petitioner made application to the Court of Appeals within the 10 days therein specified. And that court's holding that its jurisdiction was pursuant to § 1291 makes it clear that it thought itself obliged to consider on the merits petitioner's appeal. There can be no assurance that had the other requirements of § 1292(b) been complied with, the Court of Appeals would have exercised its discretion to entertain the interlocutory appeal.

Were we to sustain the procedure followed here, we would condone a practice whereby a district court in virtually any case before it might render an interlocutory decision on the question of liability of the defendant, and the defendant would thereupon be permitted to appeal to the court of appeals without satisfying any of the requirements that Congress carefully set forth. We believe that Congress, in enacting present §§ 1291 and 1292 of Title 28, has been well aware of the dangers of an overly rigid insistence upon a "final decision" for appeal in every case, and has in those sections made ample provision for appeal of orders which are not "final" so as to alleviate any possible hardship. We would twist the fabric of the statute more than it will bear if we were to agree that the District Court's order of February 20, 1974, was appealable to the Court of Appeals.

The judgment of the Court of Appeals is therefore vacated, and the case is remanded with instructions to dismiss the petitioner's appeal.

It is so ordered.

MR. JUSTICE BLACKMUN took no part in the consideration or decision of this case.

———

JETCO ELECTRONIC INDUSTRIES, INC. v. GARDINER, 473 F.2d 1228 (5th Cir.1973). Plaintiff Jetco filed suit against three defendants, ETL, Gardiner, and Gardiner Electronics. The trial court granted ETL's motion to dismiss for lack of personal jurisdiction and for failure to state a claim for relief, and an appeal was taken from that order. Several months after the order involving ETL, the trial court entered a second order disposing of Jetco's claims against Gardiner and Gardiner Electronics. On ETL's motion to dismiss the appeal, the Court of Appeals held as follows:

> The March order dismissing appellants' suit against ETL * * * said nothing about appellants' rights as against the other two defendants, Gardiner and Gardiner Electronics * * *. That order is thus not a

final judgment * * *. Nor was the later order entering an agreed judgment disposing of appellants' claim against Gardiner and Gardiner Electronics a final judgment [since] * * * it did not adjudicate appellants' rights as against ETL. Nevertheless, these two orders, considered together, terminated this litigation just as effectively as would have been the case had the district judge gone through the motions of entering a single order formally reciting the substance of the earlier two orders. Mindful of the Supreme Court's command that practical, not technical, considerations are to govern the application of principles of finality * * * we decline appellee's invitation to exalt form over substance by dismissing this appeal. We hold that the March order dismissing appellants' suit against ETL is, under the circumstances of this case, within our appellate jurisdiction. * * *

Id. at 1231.

Notes and Questions

1. *Liberty Mutual* illustrates the proposition that the question whether a court may hear an appeal—with its constituent issues of finality, timeliness, and mode—is almost without exception viewed as involving "jurisdiction over the subject matter." See also Collins v. Miller, 252 U.S. 364, 40 S.Ct. 347, 64 L.Ed. 616 (1920); United States v. Girault, 52 U.S. (11 How.) 22, 13 L.Ed. 587 (1850). All the doctrinal overtones of that concept are present. For example, a lower appellate-court's decision will be reversed for lack of appellate jurisdiction and the appeal will be ordered dismissed even though the issue of the propriety of the appeal was not raised in the lower court; the parties may not waive the requirements for an appeal; neither the trial nor appellate court can supply the defects or depart from the rigid rules of law regarding appeals. What are the reasons for this approach? Are the same dangers present when an appellate court conducts a premature review as when a trial court hears a cause that is not within its competence? The rigidity of the traditional view is cogently criticized in 6 Moore, *Federal Practice* ¶ 54.43 (2d ed.). See also 15 Wright, Miller & Cooper, *Federal Practice and Procedure: Jurisdiction and Related Matters* § 3905 (1976).

2. Does the *Jetco* decision represent a departure from the traditional approach discussed in Note 1 above? Would your answer be different if the trial court's second order, dismissing the case against Gardiner and Gardiner Electronics, had been rendered prior to the time Jetco's appeal was filed? Compare Oak Constr. Co. v. Huron Cement Co., 475 F.2d 1220 (6th Cir.1973) (subsequent trial-court action cannot save appeal that was inappropriate at the time it was filed). Should Jetco be free to file a separate appeal challenging the court's second order?

3. THE NEW YORK APPROACH

New York has taken a different approach than that taken by the federal courts, allowing appeals to the State's appellate divisions in a great many situations in which no final judgment has been rendered. Read the New York provision, N.Y.C.P.L.R. 5701, which is found in the Supplement following 28 U.S.C. § 1292. What benefits and burdens does the New York system contain that the federal system does not?

In PEART v. PEART, 48 Hun 79 (N.Y.Sup.Ct.1888), the defendant's motion to require plaintiff to make her complaint more definite and certain was denied, and the defendant appealed. A motion to dismiss the appeal was denied:

The order is appealable. It is definitely settled so far as this court is concerned, that orders made at a Special Term involving questions as to the form of the pleadings and whether they contain irrelevant, redundant or scandalous matter, or are so indefinite and uncertain that the precise meaning or application of an allegation therein is not apparent, may be reviewed by this court on appeal, and if any error has been committed it may be corrected.

KORN, CIVIL JURISDICTION OF THE NEW YORK COURT OF APPEALS AND APPELLATE DIVISIONS, 16 Buffalo L.Rev. 307, 330, 332 (1967):

It is generally recognized that this broad authority for appeal as of right from almost every kind of intermediate determination is a prime source of delay and expense in litigation and imposes an undue burden on the Appellate Divisions. Nevertheless, the proposal of the CPLR revisers to eliminate the broad catch-all language met with substantial opposition from some segments of the bar. The result was a compromise limited only to orders on motions to require a more definite statement or to strike scandalous or prejudicial matter in a pleading; as to these CPLR 5701(b) now requires permission to appeal.

* * *

Today * * * it is well known that there is hardly a question of practice that cannot be appealed; and, if a matter is said to be addressed to the court's discretion or favor, this may mean a more limited scope of review but will rarely affect appealability. Appeals on practice matters are legion, ranging far and wide over questions of venue, parties, consolidation and joint trial, pleading and pre-trial disclosure. The only meaningful method of inquiry as to the content of the present standards is to examine the types of orders that have been held *not* to involve some part of the merits or affect a substantial right.

Notes and Questions

1. What are the advantages of freely allowing appeals from interlocutory orders? The disadvantages? Is it better to resolve the question of allowing an interlocutory appeal by weighing these advantages and disadvantages against each other in the abstract or by considering them as they apply in each case? See generally Crick, *The Final Judgment as a Basis for Appeal*, 41 Yale L.J. 539 (1932); Note, *Appealability in the Federal Courts*, 75 Harv.L. Rev. 351 (1961).

2. In refusing to allow an appeal from an interlocutory order, we may avoid an unnecessary appellate hearing; in allowing an appeal, we may avoid an unnecessary trial, either by disposing of the case at that stage or by correcting in advance of trial an error that might otherwise require a new trial. Is there any basis for supposing that the appellate hearing is more

likely to prove unnecessary than the trial? Is it relevant that the trial judge, hopefully, will be correct in his rulings more often than he is wrong?

Even if we assume that a reversal of the trial court's order by the appellate court is as probable as its affirmance and we also take into consideration that trial may demand more time of lawyers and judges than an appeal, does it follow that interlocutory appeals should be freely allowed? Consider the effect of the following factors. (1) In the course of a single lawsuit there may be many interlocutory orders from which one of the parties would like to appeal; thus, if finality is required, several appeals may be saved for every trial that would be saved under the other approach. (2) Not every reversal of an interlocutory order will terminate the case without trial. (3) The number of appellate courts cannot be increased as readily as can the number of trial courts in order to take care of heavier calendars. There will be a serious problem as long as it is the function of appellate courts not only to review trial-court decisions but to establish and maintain a degree of uniformity in the law.

The debate over the relative merits of a final-judgment rule and an interlocutory-appeal system is intertwined with the larger problem of court congestion at the appellate level. See Project, *The Appellate Division of the Supreme Court of New York: An Empirical Study of Its Powers and Functions as an Intermediate State Court,* 47 Fordham L.Rev. 929, 1006–08 (1979). The attention given to crowding at the trial level has obscured the fact that a comparable problem exists in many reviewing courts.

3. Appeals are expensive. See Willcox, Karlen & Roemer, *Justice Lost— By What Appellate Papers Cost,* 33 N.Y.U.L.Rev. 934 (1958); Note, *Cost of Appeal,* 27 Mont.L.Rev. 49 (1965). Preparation of the necessary briefs and records demands a substantial amount of the lawyer's time, and duplication of these documents is costly, although some progress has been made in recent years by reducing the need to reproduce certain parts of the record and by using cheaper processes than printing for duplicating records and briefs. Substantial travelling costs often are involved because an appellate court usually is not as proximate to the attorneys as is the trial court. Because of expense and the delay caused by congestion, the availability of appeal often presents a tactical opportunity to one of the parties. Is there any effective sanction against the use of appeal for purely tactical reasons? See Kamine, *Frivolous Appeals,* 47 Calif.St.B.J. 307 (1972). In what ways might modern communications and duplication technology reduce the cost of appeals?

4. Should the avoidance of extra expense, delay, and needless hearings be the only consideration in deciding whether to permit appeals from interlocutory orders? Is the trial judge's independence and discretion threatened by too frequent a review? Is a party who has been ordered to answer questions in a deposition interested in obtaining immediate review solely in order to save time or money?

4. DEPARTURES FROM THE FINAL–JUDGMENT RULE IN THE FEDERAL COURTS

a. *Amelioration of the Basic Concept*

(i) *Cases involving multiple claims*

———

Read Federal Rule of Civil Procedure 54(b) in the Supplement, with the accompanying material.

SEARS, ROEBUCK & CO. v. MACKEY, 351 U.S. 427, 76 S.Ct. 895, 100 L.Ed. 1297 (1956). Mackey brought suit for damages against Sears, Roebuck under the Sherman Antitrust Act (Counts I & II) and under common law for unlawfully inducing a breach of contract (Count III) and unfair competition and patent infringement (Count IV). The District Court dismissed only those claims presented in Counts I and II. On appeal to the Court of Appeals for the Seventh Circuit, the court upheld its appellate jurisdiction under 28 U.S.C. § 1291. The Supreme Court affirmed.

The Court noted that before the promulgation of the Federal Rules, no appeal would have been allowed from the final determination of Counts I and II since the District Court's judgment was not a final decision of the whole case. However, with the adoption of the Federal Rules and the subsequent increase in multiple-claim actions, the promulgators recognized the need to ameliorate the standard that "*all* claims had to be finally decided before an appeal could be entertained from a final decision upon any of them." Id. at 434, 76 S.Ct. at 899, 100 L.Ed. at 1305. Consequently, Rule 54(b) was adopted.

* * * [Rule 54(b), as amended in 1946,] does not relax the finality required of each decision, as an individual claim, to render it appealable, but it does provide a practical means of permitting an appeal to be taken from one or more final decisions on individual claims, in multiple claims actions, without waiting for final decisions to be rendered on *all* the claims in the case. * * *

To meet the demonstrated need for flexibility, the District Court is used as a "dispatcher." It is permitted to determine, in the first instance, the appropriate *time when each "final decision"* upon "one or more but less than all" of the claims in a multiple claims action is ready for appeal. This arrangement already has lent welcome certainty to the appellate procedure. Its "negative effect" has met with uniform approval. The effect so referred to is the rule's specific requirement that for "one or more but less than all" multiple claims to become appealable, the District Court must make both "an express determination that there is no just reason for delay" and "an express direction for the entry of judgment." A party adversely affected by a final decision thus knows that his time for appeal will *not* run against him until this certification has been made.

* * *

In the case before us, there is no doubt that each of the claims dismissed is a "claim for relief" within the meaning of Rule 54(b), or that their dismissal constitutes a "final decision" on individual claims. Also, it cannot well be argued that the claims stated in Counts I and II are so inherently inseparable from, or closely related to, those stated in Counts III and IV that the District Court has abused its discretion in certifying that there exists no just reason for delay. They certainly *can* be decided independently of each other.

Petitioner contends that amended Rule 54(b) attempts to make an unauthorized extension of § 1291. We disagree. It could readily be argued here that the claims stated in Counts I and II are sufficiently independent of those stated in Counts III and IV to satisfy the requirements of Rule 54(b) even in its original form. * * *

* * * The District Court *cannot,* in the exercise of its discretion, treat as "final" that which is not "final" within the meaning of § 1291. But the District Court *may,* by the exercise of its discretion in the interest of sound judicial administration, release for appeal final decisions upon one or more, but less than all, claims in multiple claims actions. The timing of such a release is, with good reason, vested by the rule primarily in the discretion of the District Court as the one most likely to be familiar with the case and with any justifiable reasons for delay. * * *

* * * [Rule 54] does not supersede any statute controlling appellate jurisdiction. It scrupulously recognizes the statutory requirement of a "final decision" under § 1291 as a basic requirement for an appeal to the Court of Appeals. It merely administers that requirement in a practical manner in multiple claims actions and does so by rule instead of by judicial decision. By its negative effect, it operates to restrict in a valid manner the number of appeals in multiple claims actions.

We reach a like conclusion as to the validity of the amended rule where the District Court acts affirmatively and thus assists in properly timing the release of final decisions in multiple claims actions. The amended rule adapts the single judicial unit theory so that it better meets the current needs of judicial administration. Just as Rule 54(b), in its original form, resulted in the release of some decisions on claims in multiple claims actions before they otherwise would have been released, so amended Rule 54(b) now makes possible the release of more of such decisions subject to judicial supervision. The amended rule preserves the historic federal policy against piecemeal appeals in many cases more effectively than did the original rule.

Id. at 435–38, 76 S.Ct. at 899–901, 100 L.Ed. at 1306–07.

On the same day it decided *Mackey,* the Supreme Court in COLD METAL PROCESS CO. v. UNITED ENGINEERING & FOUNDRY CO., 351 U.S. 445, 76 S.Ct. 904, 100 L.Ed. 1311 (1956), held that an appeal by defendant was appropriate under Section 1291 and Rule 54(b) even though a counterclaim arising out of the same transaction had not yet been decided. Justice Frankfurter, who concurred in *Mackey,* dissented in *Cold Metal:*

The Court does indicate that what has been the core of the doctrine of finality as applied to multiple claims litigation—that only that part of a litigation which is separate from, and independent of, the remainder of the litigation can be appealed before the completion of the entire litigation—is no longer to be applied as a standard, or at least as an exclusive standard, for deciding what is final for purposes of § 1291. The Court does not, however, indicate what standards the district courts and the courts of appeals are now to apply in determining when a decision is final. It leaves this problem in the first instance to the district courts, subject to review by the courts of appeals for an abuse of discretion. In other instances where a district court's ruling can be upset only for an abuse of its discretion, the scope of review is necessarily narrow. Here, in regard to the present problem, what is to come under review is a newly modified requirement of finality. But the requirement continues to be based upon a statute * * * and that statute defines and constricts the jurisdiction of the courts of appeals. Therefore the issue of compliance with this congressional command would, I should suppose, cast upon the courts of appeals a duty of independent judgment broader than is implied by the usual flavor of the phrase "abuse of discretion."

For me, the propositions emerging from analysis of the relationship of Rule 54(b) to 28 U.S.C. § 1291 are clear.

1. 28 U.S.C. § 1291 is left intact by Rule 54(b). * * *

2. 28 U.S.C. § 1291 is not a technical rule in a game. It expresses not only a deeply rooted but a wisely sanctioned principle against piece-meal appeals governing litigation in the federal courts. * * * The great importance of this characteristic feature of the federal judicial system * * * is made luminously manifest by considering the evils where, as in New York, piecemeal reviews are allowed.

3. * * * What have been called exceptions are not exceptions at all in the sense of inroads on the principle. They have not qualified the core, that is, that there should be no premature, intermediate appeal.

* * *

4. The expansion by the Federal Rules of the allowable content of a proceeding and the range of a litigation inevitably enlarged the occasions for severing one aspect or portion of a litigation from what remains under the traditional test of a "final decision." On the basis of prior cases, we held that it was not a departure from the policy against piecemeal appeals to permit an appeal with respect to that part of a multiple claims litigation based on a set of facts separate and independent from the facts on which the remainder of the litigation was based. * * *

The principles which this Court has heretofore enunciated over a long course of decisions under § 1291 furnish ready guides for deciding the appealability of the certified parts of the litigation in the two cases now before the Court. Count II in Sears, Roebuck & Co. v. Mackey * * * is appealable since the transactions and occurrences involved in it do not involve any of those embraced in Counts III and IV. Count I involves at least two transactions which are also the subject matter of Counts III and IV but is appealable under § 1292(1) as an interlocutory order denying an injunction. In *Cold Metal* * * * the counterclaim, even if not compulsory, is based in substantial part on the transactions involved in the main litigation and hence not appealable.

Id. at 439–43, 76 S.Ct. at 902–04, 100 L.Ed. at 1308–10.

Notes and Questions

1. In CURTISS–WRIGHT CORP. v. GENERAL ELEC. CO., 446 U.S. 1, 100 S.Ct. 1460, 64 L.Ed.2d 1 (1980), Curtiss-Wright brought a diversity action, seeking damages and reformation with regard to a series of contracts between it and General Electric. General Electric counterclaimed. As to one of Curtiss-Wright's affirmative claims—for $19 million due on the contracts

already performed—the District Court granted summary judgment for Curtiss-Wright. When Curtiss-Wright requested certification of this judgment as a final judgment under Rule 54(b), the court granted the motion—after determining, as required by the Rule, that there was "no just reason for delay." The Third Circuit reversed on the ground that the existence of a nonfrivolous counterclaim limited the power of the District Court to enter a final judgment on the original claim. In the view of the Court of Appeals, the District Court had abused its discretion by granting the Rule 54(b) certification.

The Supreme Court agreed with the District Court:

> * * * The mere presence of [nonfrivolous counterclaims] * * * does not render a Rule 54(b) certification inappropriate. If it did, Rule 54(b) would lose much of its utility. * * * [C]ounterclaims, whether compulsory or permissive, present no special problems for Rule 54(b) determinations; counterclaims are not to be evaluated differently from other claims. * * * Like other claims, their significance for Rule 54(b) purposes turns on their interrelationship with the claims on which certification is sought. Here, the District Judge determined that General Electric's counterclaims were severable from the claims which had been determined in terms of both the factual and the legal issues involved. The Court of Appeals did not conclude otherwise.

> What the Court of Appeals found objectionable about the District Judge's exercise of discretion was the assessment of the equities involved. The Court of Appeals concluded that the possibility of a setoff required that the status quo be maintained unless petitioner could show harsh or unusual circumstances; it held that such a showing had not been made in the District Court.

> This holding reflects a misinterpretation of the standard of review for Rule 54(b) certifications and a misperception of the appellate function in such cases. * * *

> There are thus two aspects to the proper function of a reviewing court in Rule 54(b) cases. The court of appeals must, of course, scrutinize the district court's evaluation of such factors as the interrelationship of the claims so as to prevent piecemeal appeals in cases which should be reviewed only as single units. But once such juridical concerns have been met, the discretionary judgment of the district court should be given substantial deference, for that court is "the one most likely to be familiar with the case and with any justifiable reasons for delay." * * * The reviewing court should disturb the trial court's assessment of the equities only if it can say that the judge's conclusion was clearly unreasonable. Plainly, sound judicial administration does not require that Rule 54(b) requests be granted routinely. That is implicit in commending them to the sound discretion of a district court. Because this discretion "is, with good reason, vested by the rule primarily" in the district courts, * * * and because the number of possible situations is large, we are reluctant either to fix or sanction narrow guidelines for the district courts to follow. We are satisfied, however, that on the record here the District Court's assessment of the equities was reasonable.

Id. at 9–11, 100 S.Ct. at 1465–66, 64 L.Ed.2d at 11–13.

2. Why did the Supreme Court indicate in *Mackey* that Rule 54(b) would be an unauthorized Rule if it extended the scope of 28 U.S.C. § 1291? Reread 28 U.S.C. § 2072 in the Supplement.

3. Is the purpose of Rule 54(b) the same as that underlying 28 U.S.C. § 1292(b), which allows interlocutory appeals at the joint discretion of the district judge and the court of appeals? Will the appeal of separate claims speed up or delay the final resolution of the entire case?

4. If the trial judge determines that there is no reason for delay and orders judgment entered on a separate claim, and no immediate appeal is taken from that order, may the judgment on the separate claim be attacked on an appeal from the final judgment on the entire case? May the propriety of entering judgment on the separate claim be challenged at that time?

5. If the trial judge, in accordance with Rule 54(b), directs entry of judgment on a separate claim that "certainly *can* be decided independently," may the court of appeals nonetheless refuse to hear the appeal? In PANICHELLA v. PENNSYLVANIA R. CO., 252 F.2d 452 (3d Cir.1958), the court held that the district judge had abused his discretion in directing the separate entry of judgment against defendant on his claim against an impleaded third party, because (1) the whole matter would be moot if defendant prevailed against plaintiff, (2) the legal effect of the same release was in question both on the third-party claim and the principal claim and thus would have to be determined twice by the Court of Appeals if this appeal were allowed, and (3) the claimed advantage of allowing the appeal—that the two claims could be tried together if the appeal were successful—would necessitate delaying the trial of the principal claim. Does the fact that a third-party claim was involved affect the weight to be given the court's third point?

(ii) Decisions involving "collateral orders"

In COHEN v. BENEFICIAL INDUSTRIAL LOAN CORP., 337 U.S. 541, 69 S.Ct. 1221, 93 L.Ed. 1528 (1949), Cohen brought a shareholder's derivative suit in a New Jersey federal court. The District Court denied Beneficial's motion to require Cohen to post security for costs pursuant to a New Jersey statute, holding the statute inapplicable to an action in a federal court. The Court of Appeals reversed, and the Supreme Court affirmed that decision. The Justices addressed the question of appealability in the following passage:

> * * * Appeal gives the upper court a power of review, not one of intervention. So long as the matter remains open, unfinished or inconclusive, there may be no intrusion by appeal. But the District Court's action upon this application was concluded and closed and its decision final in that sense before the appeal was taken.
>
> Nor does the statute permit appeals, even from fully consummated decisions, where they are but steps towards final judgment in which they will merge. The purpose is to combine in one review all stages of the proceeding that effectively may be reviewed and corrected if and when final judgment results. But this order of the District Court did not make any step toward final disposition of the merits of the case and will not be merged in final judgment. When that time comes, it will be too late effectively to review the present order and the rights conferred by the statute, if it is applicable, will have been lost, probably irreparably. We conclude that the matters embraced in the decision appealed from are not

of such an interlocutory nature as to affect, or to be affected by, decision of the merits of this case.

This decision appears to fall in that small class which finally determine claims of right separable from, and collateral to, rights asserted in the action, too important to be denied review and too independent of the cause itself to require that appellate consideration be deferred until the whole case is adjudicated. The Court has long given this provision of the statute this practical rather than a technical construction. * * *

We hold this order appealable because it is a final disposition of a claimed right which is not an ingredient of the cause of action and does not require consideration with it. * * * Here it is the right to security that presents a serious and unsettled question. If the right were admitted or clear and the order involved only an exercise of discretion as to the amount of security, a matter the statute makes subject to reconsideration from time to time, appealability would present a different question.

Id. at 545, 69 S.Ct. at 1225, 93 L.Ed. at 1536.

Notes and Questions

1. In LAURO LINES S.R.L. v. CHASSER, ___ U.S. ___, 109 S.Ct. ___, ___ L.Ed.2d ___ (1989), the plaintiffs were passengers or representatives of former passengers aboard the Achille Lauro when it was hijacked by terrorists of the Palestine Liberation Organization. The passengers were held captive and terrorized, and filed consolidated actions to recover damages for physical and psychological injuries and for the wrongful death of Leon Klinghoffer. Defendant moved to dismiss on several grounds, including that a forum-selection clause in each passenger ticket required plaintiffs to bring suit in Naples. The District Court denied the motions to dismiss, concluding that the clause on the ticket did not reasonably communicate the importance of the provision: "[I]t does not give fair warning to the American citizen passenger that he or she is renouncing and waiving his or her opportunity to sue in a domestic forum over a contract made and delivered in the United States." Id. at 51–52. Defendant sought to appeal the District Court's orders. The Second Circuit dismissed the appeal on the ground that the orders were interlocutory and did not fall into the exception for collateral orders established in *Cohen*. The Supreme Court affirmed, pointing out that, to satisfy the *Cohen* exception, an order must conclusively determine the disputed question, resolve an important issue completely separate from the merits of the action, and be effectively unreviewable on appeal from a final judgment. The Court found that the third condition was not satisfied:

* * * Petitioner's claim that it may be sued only in Naples, while not perfectly secured by appeal after final judgment, is adequately vindicable at that stage—surely as effectively vindicable as a claim that the trial court lacked personal jurisdiction over the defendant—and hence does not fall within the third prong of the collateral order doctrine.

In Van Cauwenberghe v. Biard, ___ U.S. ___, ___, 108 S.Ct. 1945, 1947, 100 L.Ed.2d 517, 521 (1988), the Supreme Court unanimously held that the denial of a motion to dismiss on the ground that an extradited person is immune from civil process, or on grounds of *forum non conveniens,* is not a collateral order subject to immediate appeal as a final judgment under Section 1291.

If a motion to dismiss is denied in circumstances such as those in *Chasser* and *Biard,* jurisdiction over the person is asserted and the defendant must bear the full costs of trial and wait for final judgment to appeal. Is this fair to the defendant? Does he have any remedy in the event that an appellate court later finds that jurisdiction was not present? Note that it may be in the interest of plaintiff as well as defendant to have such motions decided before a costly, perhaps meaningless, trial takes place. Should the parties be permitted to obtain an immediate appeal if they make a joint request therefor?

2.   In STRINGFELLOW v. CONCERNED NEIGHBORS IN ACTION, 480 U.S. 370, 107 S.Ct. 1177, 94 L.Ed.2d 389 (1987), Concerned Neighbors in Action (CNA) sought to intervene in an action by the United States and the State of California against the Stringfellow Acid Pits. The complaint alleged that Stringfellow had created a substantial danger to the area surrounding the pit, and it sought injunctive relief requiring Stringfellow to abate the release of harmful substances from the site, to take remedial steps to correct the unsafe conditions, and to reimburse the costs of bringing about the cleanup. CNA claimed that it was entitled to intervene as a matter of right pursuant to Federal Rule of Civil Procedure 24(a), since it had a substantial interest in the litigation. Alternatively, CNA claimed that it should be allowed to intervene by permission pursuant to Rule 24(b).

The District Court denied CNA's request to intervene as of right, but granted its application under Rule 24(b). However, it conditioned CNA's intervention on certain limitations. First, CNA could assert no claim for relief that had not already been requested by one of the parties. Second, CNA could not intervene in the government's claim for recovery of the clean-up costs. Finally, CNA could not file any motions or conduct its own discovery unless it first conferred with all the original parties, and then obtained permission to go forward from at least one of these litigants. CNA appealed. The Ninth Circuit dismissed the appeal, finding that the District Court order was not a "final decision" within the meaning of 28 U.S.C. § 1291. The court subsequently withdrew its opinion, however, concluding that the holding was inconsistent with Ninth Circuit precedent holding that denial of intervention as of right is a final appealable order, despite the grant of permissive intervention.

Stringfellow obtained review in the Supreme Court which held that a district court order granting permissive intervention but denying intervention as of right was not immediately appealable. The Court found first that such an order was not a "collateral order." As a party to the suit by virtue of permissive intervention, the intervenor (here, CNA) can obtain effective review of its claims on appeal from the final judgment. In the Court's view, "[a]lthough it may be difficult for CNA to show that the harm from the intervention order is sufficiently great to overturn the final judgment, this has little bearing on whether CNA has the right to an interlocutory appeal under the collateral order doctrine." 480 U.S. at 376–77, 107 S.Ct. at 1182, 94 L.Ed.2d at 399.

The Court refused to accept CNA's argument that the onerous limitations on their right to participate in the case constituted a complete denial of the right to intervention. The Court held that it was sufficient that CNA was a "participant in the proceeding and had alternative means for challenging the order." 480 U.S. at 377, 107 S.Ct. at 1183, 94 L.Ed.2d at 399. CNA's right to an appeal was not impaired.

The Court also rejected CNA's contention that the District Court order fell within the statutory exception to finality in 28 U.S.C. § 1291(a) which provides for interlocutory appeals. The Court stated that it had

> made it clear that not all denials of injunctive relief are immediately appealable: a party seeking review also must show that the order will have a "serious, perhaps irreparable, consequence," and that the order can be "effectually challenged" only by immediate appeal.

Id. at 379, 107 S.Ct. at 1184, 94 L.Ed.2d at 400, citing Carson v. American Brands, Inc., 450 U.S. 79, 84, 101 S.Ct. 993, 996, 67 L.Ed.2d 59 (1981).

The Court concluded by stressing that the "finality doctrine protected the strong interest in allowing trial judges to supervise pretrial and trial procedures without undue interference." Id. at 380, 107 S.Ct. at 1184, 94 L.Ed.2d at 401.

Does the Court's decision in *Stringfellow* make sense? Justice Brennan concurred, finding two more reasons for the result:

> First, it would be inconsistent to afford a permissive intervenor a right to appeal that would be denied an intervenor of right or an original party on whose participation severe restrictions had been placed. Second, if the conditions imposed on a party would have the practical effect of denying that party the right to participate in the litigation, and if postjudgment appeal is likely to prove ineffective, the available means of relief include a petition to the Court of Appeals for a writ of mandamus.

Id. at 381, 107 S.Ct. at 1185, 94 L.Ed.2d at 402. Are Justice Brennan's reasons for the result persuasive?

3. While observing that most discovery orders are not "sufficiently separable from the merits of the underlying dispute" to fall within the *Cohen* standard, the First Circuit has said that denials of protective orders may be immediately appealable under *Cohen,* if resolution of the matter turns on whether irreparable harm will result to appellants, "not from the district court order itself, but from a delay in obtaining appellate review of that order." In re San Juan Star Co., 662 F.2d 108, 112 (1st Cir.1981), quoting In re Continental Investment Corp., 637 F.2d 1, 5 (1st Cir.1980). Thus, the court concluded that it could review interlocutory orders prohibiting the attorneys in a civil rights suit arising out of the shooting of two suspected terrorists from disclosing any evidence obtained through depositions to the press and public, or by plaintiff's counsel to their clients.

4. In UNITED STATES v. RYAN, 402 U.S. 530, 91 S.Ct. 1580, 29 L.Ed.2d 85 (1971), and COBBLEDICK v. UNITED STATES, 309 U.S. 323, 60 S.Ct. 540, 84 L.Ed. 783 (1940), petitioners had moved unsuccessfully in the District Court to quash subpoenas directing them to appear and produce documents before a grand jury. In each case the Supreme Court held that the Court of Appeals was required to dismiss the appeal from the District Court order. According to the Supreme Court, if petitioners disobeyed the order and were found in contempt, their situation would become "so severed from the main proceeding as to permit an appeal." The Court distinguished PERLMAN v. UNITED STATES, 247 U.S. 7, 38 S.Ct. 417, 62 L.Ed. 950 (1918), in which an appeal was

allowed from an order denying a motion to prohibit turning over to a grand jury property already in the custody of the court, on the ground that the person making the motion in that case was otherwise "powerless to avert the mischief of the order." Are the cases really distinguishable? Consider the fact that a grand-jury proceeding has no defined litigants and that it renders no "final judgments" in the same sense as does a court.

In UNITED STATES v. NIXON, 418 U.S. 683, 690–92, 94 S.Ct. 3090, 3098–99, 41 L.Ed.2d 1039, 1053–55 (1974), the President of the United States had been ordered to produce certain tape recordings for examination by a federal district judge. The Supreme Court said that an appeal would lie under the doctrine of the *Perlman* case. It explained that "the traditional contempt avenue to immediate appeal is peculiarly inappropriate due to the unique setting in which the question arises. To require a President of the United States to place himself in the posture of disobeying an order of a court merely to trigger the procedural mechanism for review of the ruling would be unseemly, and would present an unnecessary occasion for constitutional confrontation between two branches of the Government."

5. May a person always obtain review of an interlocutory order by disobeying it and being found in contempt? In what type of case might even this Spartan tactic be unavailable? When it is available, is this method of obtaining review an adequate or rational substitute for allowing an appeal from the interlocutory order in the first place? Hickman v. Taylor, p. 766, supra, was a case in which review was obtained of an interlocutory discovery order through disobedience and contempt. In that case, defendants and their lawyer were found in criminal contempt, and an appeal was allowed. Had they been found in civil contempt—that is, if the contempt citation were intended only to coerce compliance with the order and not to punish their disobedience of it—the lawyer, but not defendants themselves, would have been able to appeal because an adjudication of civil contempt is not regarded as a final order as to the parties. See Fox v. Capital Co., 299 U.S. 105, 57 S.Ct. 57, 81 L.Ed. 67 (1936). See also Fenton v. Walling, 139 F.2d 608 (9th Cir.1943).

In UNITED STATES CATHOLIC CONFERENCE v. ABORTION RIGHTS MOBILIZATION, INC., ___ U.S. ___, 108 S.Ct. 2268, 101 L.Ed.2d 69 (1988), Abortion Rights Mobilization, Inc. and others (ARM) filed suit against government officials and the United States Catholic Conference and the National Conference of Catholic Bishops (USCC) to revoke the Roman Catholic Church's tax-exempt status on the ground that the Church had violated the anti-electioneering provision of 26 U.S.C. § 501(c)(3). USCC was later dismissed from the suit, and only the government defendants remained. Nevertheless, ARM served subpoenas on USCC in order to obtain evidence to support its claims. USCC refused to comply with the subpoenas and moved to quash the subpoenas on the ground that the District Court lacked subject-matter jurisdiction over the dispute between ARM and the government defendants. The District Court refused to quash the subpoena. Subsequently, USCC was held in civil contempt. The court assessed fines of $50,000 per day for each day of noncompliance.

The Court of Appeals upheld the contempt citations. It held that a nonparty witness can resist discovery by challenging the trial court's subject-matter jurisdiction in defense of a civil contempt citation only if it can show that there is no colorable basis for exercising subject-matter jurisdiction.

The Supreme Court reversed, holding that

a nonparty witness can challenge the court's lack of subject-matter jurisdiction in defense of a civil contempt citation, notwithstanding the absence of a final judgment in the underlying action. * * * [While] a District Court [has] the power to issue subpoenas as to witnesses and documents, * * * the subpoena power of a court cannot be more extensive than its jurisdiction. * * * Therefore, a nonparty witness may attack a civil contempt citation by asserting that the issuing court lacks jurisdiction over the case.

The right of a nonparty to appeal an adjudication of contempt cannot be questioned. The order finding a nonparty witness in contempt is appealable notwithstanding the absence of a final judgment in the underlying action. * * * Once the right to appeal a civil contempt order is acknowledged, arguments in its legitimate support should not be so confined that the power of the issuing court remains untested. * * *

The challenge in this case goes to the subject matter jurisdiction of the court and hence its power to issue the order. The distinction between subject-matter jurisdiction and waivable defenses is not a mere nicety of legal metaphysics. It rests instead on the central principle of a free society that courts have finite bounds of authority, some of constitutional origin, which exist to protect citizens from the very wrong asserted here, the excessive use of judicial power. The courts, no less than the political branches of the government, must respect the limits of their authority.

* * *

Additionally, the Court of Appeals was concerned that permitting the nonparty witness to challenge the jurisdiction of the court would invite collusion, allowing parties to avoid restrictions on interlocutory appeals and to test jurisdiction by proxy. * * * We are not persuaded that such considerations should alter the rule we apply in this case. To begin with, the objection does not meet the fundamental premise that the nonparty should not be denied the right to object to the very jurisdictional exercise that causes injury. Further, we conclude that there are ample protections against collusive appeals. If the Court of Appeals finds that the witness and a party acted in collusion to appeal in order to gain an interlocutory ruling on jurisdiction, it can decline to treat the witness as a nonparty for purposes of the question. * * * Additionally, there remain the usual provisions for sanctioning frivolous appeals or abuse of court processes. * * *

* * * Nothing we have said puts in question the inherent and legitimate authority of the court to issue process and other binding orders, including orders of discovery directed to nonparty witnesses, as necessary for the court to determine and rule upon its own jurisdiction, including jurisdiction over the subject matter.

* * * It is a recognized and appropriate procedure for a court to limit discovery proceedings at the outset to a determination of jurisdictional matters * * *, but that was not the objective of this discovery order, even by implication.

Id. at ___, 108 S.Ct. at 2270–72, 101 L.Ed.2d at 76–79. Is the Court correct in its determination that there are "ample protections against collusive appeals?" Are the procedural rules working properly when a nonparty witness, such as USCC, is permitted to take an interlocutory appeal, but a party to the case, such as ARM, must wait for final judgment?

6. Would the orders in *Ryan* and *Cobbledick* have been appealable in New York? Would a discretionary appeal be available under 28 U.S.C. § 1292(b) to test a discovery order in a federal court? See pp. 1096–99, infra.

7. In FORGAY v. CONRAD, 47 U.S. (6 How.) 201, 203, 12 L.Ed. 404, 405 (1848), the trial court, upon finding that a fraudulent conveyance had been made, ordered property delivered to an assignee in bankruptcy and directed an accounting before a master. The order to deliver was held appealable even before the conclusion of the accounting because of the irreparable injury that might be sustained if the property were disposed of by the assignee in bankruptcy while the accounting was in progress. Chief Justice Taney said: "Undoubtedly, [the decree] * * * is not final, in the strict, technical sense of that term. But this court has not heretofore understood the words 'final decrees' in this strict and technical sense, but has given to them a more liberal, and, as we think, a more reasonable construction, and one more consonant to the intention of the legislature." See also Altschuler v. Altschuler, 399 Ill. 559, 78 N.E.2d 225 (1948); Annot., 3 A.L.R.2d 342 (1949).

In BROWN SHOE CO. v. UNITED STATES, 370 U.S. 294, 82 S.Ct. 1502, 8 L.Ed.2d 510 (1962), the District Court found defendant had violated the antitrust laws and directed divestiture of a subsidiary, but it reserved its ruling on a specific plan of divestiture. On a direct appeal by the Shoe Company under the Expediting Act, 15 U.S.C. § 29, the Supreme Court held the divestiture decree was sufficiently final to be appealable even though a specific plan had not been formulated. Its own past practice, said the Court, had been to hear such appeals in antitrust cases; the substantive aspects of the case had been fully determined and to delay decision on the merits would chill the "careful, and often extended, negotiation and formulation" of the final divestiture order.

Should an appeal from an order such as those in *Cohen, Forgay, and Brown* be subject to the requirements of Rule 54(b)? See 10 Wright, Miller & Kane, *Federal Practice and Procedure: Civil 2d* § 2658.4, at 67–75 (1983).

In which of the cases thus far considered would it be practical for the proceedings in the lower court to continue while the appeal was being determined? Is this factor relevant to the decision whether to allow appeal? See Note, *Appealability in the Federal Courts*, 75 Harv.L.Rev. 351, 365 (1961).

Does the *Brown Shoe* decision reflect the operation of the same considerations that Crick found to have been influential in the history of appeals in English equity? See pp. 1061–63, supra.

8. What are the procedural distinctions between 28 U.S.C. § 1291 and § 1292? What is the degree of discretion that is available to a trial court in each? To an appellate court? What variables might influence a judge's decision? What policies are implicated? An appeal from a non-final order may be heard, pursuant to § 1292(b), as long as the district court and the appellate court both give their consents. Why the need for dual consent?

COOPERS & LYBRAND v. LIVESAY

Supreme Court of the United States, 1978.
437 U.S. 463, 98 S.Ct. 2454, 57 L.Ed.2d 351.

Certiorari to the United States Court of Appeals for the Eighth Circuit.

MR. JUSTICE STEVENS delivered the opinion of the Court.

The question in this case is whether a district court's determination that an action may not be maintained as a class action pursuant to Fed. Rule Civ.Proc. 23 is a "final decision" within the meaning of 28 U.S.C. § 1291 and therefore appealable as a matter of right. Because there is a conflict in the Circuits over this issue, we granted certiorari and now hold that such an order is not appealable under § 1291.

Petitioner, Coopers & Lybrand, is an accounting firm that certified the financial statements in a prospectus issued in connection with a 1972 public offering of securities in Punta Gorda Isles for an aggregate price of over $18 million. Respondents purchased securities in reliance on that prospectus. In its next annual report to shareholders, Punta Gorda restated the earnings that had been reported in the prospectus for 1970 and 1971 by writing down its net income for each year by over $1 million. Thereafter, respondents sold their Punta Gorda securities and sustained a loss of $2,650 on their investment.

* * * [Respondents] alleged that petitioner and other defendants had violated various sections of the Securities Act of 1933 and the Securities Exchange Act of 1934. The District Court first certified, and then, after further proceedings, decertified the class.

Respondents did not request the District Court to certify its order for interlocutory review under 28 U.S.C. § 1292(b). Rather, they filed a notice of appeal pursuant to § 1291. The Court of Appeals regarded its appellate jurisdiction as depending on whether the decertification order had sounded the "death knell" of the action. After examining the amount of respondents' claims in relation to their financial resources and the probable cost of the litigation, the court concluded that they would not pursue their claims individually. The Court of Appeals therefore held that it had jurisdiction to hear the appeal and, on the merits, reversed the order decertifying the class. * * *

Federal appellate jurisdiction generally depends on the existence of a decision by the District Court that "ends the litigation on the merits and leaves nothing for the court to do but execute the judgment." * * * An order refusing to certify, or decertifying, a class does not of its own force terminate the entire litigation because the plaintiff is free to proceed on his individual claim. Such an order is appealable, therefore, only if it comes within an appropriate exception to the final-judgment rule. In this case respondents rely on the "collateral order" exception articulated by this Court in Cohen v. Beneficial Industrial Loan Corp., * * * and on the "death knell" doctrine adopted by several Circuits to determine the appealability of orders denying class certification.

I

*   *   *

To come within the "small class" of decisions excepted from the final-judgment rule by *Cohen,* the order must conclusively determine the disputed question, resolve an important issue completely separate from the merits of the action, and be effectively unreviewable on appeal from a final judgment. *   *   * An order passing on a request for class certification does not fall in that category. First, such an order is subject to revision in the District Court. Fed.Rule Civ.Proc. 23(c)(1). Second, the class determination generally involves considerations that are "enmeshed in the factual and legal issues comprising the plaintiff's cause of action." *   *   * Finally, an order denying class certification is subject to effective review after final judgment at the behest of the named plaintiff or intervening class members. United Airlines, Inc. v. McDonald, 432 U.S. 385, 97 S.Ct. 2464, 53 L.Ed.2d 423. For these reasons, as the Courts of Appeals have consistently recognized, the collateral-order doctrine is not applicable to the kind of order involved in this case.

II

Several Circuits, including the Court of Appeals in this case, have held that an order denying class certification is appealable if it is likely to sound the "death knell" of the litigation. The "death knell" doctrine assumes that without the incentive of a possible group recovery the individual plaintiff may find it economically imprudent to pursue his lawsuit to a final judgment and then seek appellate review of an adverse class determination. Without questioning this assumption, we hold that orders relating to class certification are not independently appealable under § 1291 prior to judgment.

*   *   *

There are special rules relating to class actions and, to that extent, they are a special kind of litigation. Those rules do not, however, contain any unique provisions governing appeals. The appealability of any order entered in a class action is determined by the same standards that govern appealability in other types of litigation. Thus, if the "death knell" doctrine has merit, it would apply equally to the many interlocutory orders in ordinary litigation—rulings on discovery, on venue, on summary judgment—that may have such tactical economic significance that a defeat is tantamount to a "death knell" for the entire case.

Though a refusal to certify a class is inherently interlocutory, it may induce a plaintiff to abandon his individual claim. On the other hand, the litigation will often survive an adverse class determination. What effect the economic disincentives created by an interlocutory order may have on the fate of any litigation will depend on a variety of factors.[15] Under the "death knell" doctrine, appealability turns on the court's perception of that impact in the individual case. Thus, if the court believes that the

15. *E.g.,* the plaintiff's resources; the size of his claim and his subjective willingness to finance prosecution of the claim; the probable cost of the litigation and the possibility of joining others who will share that cost; and the prospect of prevailing on the merits and reversing an order denying class certification.

plaintiff has adequate incentive to continue, the order is considered interlocutory; but if the court concludes that the ruling, as a practical matter, makes further litigation improbable, it is considered an appealable final decision.

* * *

A threshold inquiry of this kind may, it is true, identify some orders that would truly end the litigation prior to final judgment; allowing an immediate appeal from those orders may enhance the quality of justice afforded a few litigants. But this incremental benefit is outweighed by the impact of such an individualized jurisdictional inquiry on the judicial system's overall capacity to administer justice.

The potential waste of judicial resources is plain. The district court must take evidence, entertain argument, and make findings; and the court of appeals must review that record and those findings simply to determine whether a discretionary class determination is subject to appellate review. And if the record provides an inadequate basis for this determination, a remand for further factual development may be required. Moreover, even if the court makes a "death knell" finding and reviews the class-designation order on the merits, there is no assurance that the trial process will not again be disrupted by interlocutory review. For even if a ruling that the plaintiff does not adequately represent the class is reversed on appeal, the district court may still refuse to certify the class on the ground that, for example, common questions of law or fact do not predominate. Under the "death knell" theory, plaintiff would again be entitled to an appeal as a matter of right pursuant to § 1291. And since other kinds of interlocutory orders may also create the risk of a premature demise, the potential for multiple appeals in every complex case is apparent and serious.

Perhaps the principal vice of the "death knell" doctrine is that it authorizes *indiscriminate* interlocutory review of decisions made by the trial judge. The Interlocutory Appeals Act of 1958 * * * was enacted to meet the recognized need for prompt review of certain nonfinal orders. However, Congress carefully confined the availability of such review. Nonfinal orders could never be appealed as a matter of right. Moreover, the discretionary power to permit an interlocutory appeal is not, in the first instance, vested in the courts of appeals. A party seeking review of a nonfinal order must first obtain the consent of the trial judge. This screening procedure serves the dual purpose of ensuring that such review will be confined to appropriate cases and avoiding time-consuming jurisdictional determinations in the court of appeals. Finally, even if the district judge certifies the order under § 1292(b), the appellant still "has the burden of persuading the court of appeals that exceptional circumstances justify a departure from the basic policy of postponing appellate review until after the entry of a final judgment." * * * The appellate court may deny the appeal for any reason, including docket congestion. By permitting appeals of right from class-designation orders after jurisdictional determinations that turn on questions of fact, the "death knell" doctrine circumvents these restrictions.

Additional considerations reinforce our conclusion that the "death knell" doctrine does not support appellate jurisdiction of prejudgment orders denying class certification. First, the doctrine operates only in favor of plaintiffs even though the class issue—whether to certify, and if so, how large the class should be—will often be of critical importance to defendants as well. Certification of a large class may so increase the defendant's potential damages liability and litigation costs that he may find it economically prudent to settle and to abandon a meritorious defense. Yet the Courts of Appeals have correctly concluded that orders granting class certification are interlocutory. Whatever similarities or differences there are between plaintiffs and defendants in this context involve questions of policy for Congress. Moreover, allowing appeals of right from nonfinal orders that turn on the facts of a particular case thrusts appellate courts indiscriminately into the trial process and thus defeats one vital purpose of the final-judgment rule—"that of maintaining the appropriate relationship between the respective courts . . . This goal, in the absence of most compelling reasons to the contrary, is very much worth preserving."

Accordingly, * * * the judgment of the Court of Appeals is reversed with directions to dismiss the appeal.

It is so ordered.

Notes and Questions

1. Why aren't the occasional needs for appeal in such cases adequately met by 28 U.S.C. § 1292(b), enacted in 1958 to allow discretionary appeals from interlocutory orders when both the trial and appellate courts agree that an appeal is appropriate? See pp. 1096–99, infra.

2. Should the fact that defendant in a class suit has no right to appeal the grant of certification influence the decision whether plaintiff is able to appeal a denial of class status? Aren't the considerations quite different? See Note, 27 U.Kan.L.Rev. 529, 535–36 (1979). See also Comment, *The Appealability of Orders Denying Motions for Disqualification of Counsel in the Federal Courts,* 45 U.Chi.L.Rev. 450, 464 (1978).

FIRESTONE TIRE & RUBBER CORP. v. RISJORD, 449 U.S. 368, 101 S.Ct. 669, 66 L.Ed.2d 571 (1981). Risjord was lead counsel for the plaintiffs in four consolidated product-liability suits in federal district court against Firestone and other manufacturers. Firestone moved to disqualify him from representing the plaintiffs because his law firm occasionally had represented Firestone's liability insurer (thereby allegedly creating a conflict of interest). However, after Risjord obtained the consent of the plaintiffs and the insurer, the District Court allowed him to continue to represent the plaintiffs. On appeal, the Eighth Circuit held that district-court orders denying disqualification motions were not immediately appealable under 28 U.S.C. § 1291; nonetheless, because it was overruling prior cases, the court made its decision prospective only, reached the merits, and affirmed the District Court's order permitting Risjord to continue to represent the plaintiffs.

The Supreme Court agreed that orders denying motions to disqualify counsel are not appealable final decisions under Section 1291, but went on to vacate the judgment of the Court of Appeals and remand the case with instructions that the appeal be dismissed for lack of jurisdiction. Justice Marshall delivered the opinion of the Court:

> * * * We have consistently interpreted * * * [Section 1291] as indicating that a party may not take an appeal under this section until there has been "a decision by the District Court that 'ends the litigation on the merits and leaves nothing for the court to do but execute the judgment.'" Coopers & Lybrand v. Livesay, * * * quoting Catlin v. United States, 324 U.S. 229, 233, 65 S.Ct. 631, 633, 89 L.Ed. 911 (1945).
>
> * * *
>
> Our decisions have recognized, however, a narrow exception to the requirement that all appeals under § 1291 await final judgment on the merits. In Cohen v. Beneficial Industrial Loan Corp. * * * we held that a "small class" of orders that did not end the main litigation were nevertheless final and appealable pursuant to § 1291. * * * *Cohen* did not establish new law; rather, it continued a tradition of giving § 1291 a "practical rather than a technical construction." * * *
>
> Because the litigation from which the instant petition arises had not reached final judgment at the time the notice of appeal was filed, the order denying petitioner's motion to disqualify respondent is appealable under § 1291 only if it falls within the *Cohen* doctrine. The Court of Appeals held that it does not, and 5 of the other 10 Circuits have also reached the conclusion that denials of disqualification motions are not immediately appealable "collateral orders." We agree with these courts that under *Cohen* such an order is not subject to appeal prior to resolution of the merits.
>
> An order denying a disqualification motion meets the first part of the "collateral order" test. It "conclusively determine[s] the disputed question," because the only issue is whether challenged counsel will be permitted to continue his representation. In addition, we will assume, although we do not decide, that the disqualification question "resolve[s] an important issue completely separate from the merits of the action," the second part of the test. Nevertheless, petitioner is unable to demonstrate that an order denying disqualification is "effectively unreviewable on appeal from a final judgment" within the meaning of our cases.
>
> * * *
>
> An order refusing to disqualify counsel plainly falls within the large class of orders that are indeed reviewable on appeal after final judgment, and not within the much smaller class of those that are not. The propriety of the district court's denial of a disqualification motion will often be difficult to assess until its impact on the underlying litigation may be evaluated, which is normally only after final judgment. The decision whether to disqualify an attorney ordinarily turns on the peculiar factual situation of the case then at hand, and the order embodying such a decision will rarely, if ever, represent a final rejection of a claim of fundamental right that cannot effectively be reviewed following judgment on the merits. In the case before us, petitioner has made no showing that its opportunity for meaningful review will perish unless immediate ap-

peal is permitted. On the contrary, should the Court of Appeals conclude after the trial has ended that permitting continuing representation was prejudicial error, it would retain its usual authority to vacate the judgment appealed from and order a new trial. That remedy seems plainly adequate should petitioner's concerns of possible injury ultimately prove well founded. * * * [T]he potential harm that might be caused by requiring that a party await final judgment before it may appeal even when the denial of its disqualification motion was erroneous does not "diffe[r] in any significant way from the harm resulting from other interlocutory orders that may be erroneous, such as orders requiring discovery over a work-product objection or orders denying motions for recusal of the trial judge." * * * But interlocutory orders are not appealable "on the mere ground that they may be erroneous." * * * Permitting wholesale appeals on that ground not only would constitute an unjustified waste of scarce judicial resources, but also would transform the limited exception carved out in *Cohen* into a license for broad disregard of the finality rule imposed by Congress in § 1291. This we decline to do.

We hold that a district court's order denying a motion to disqualify counsel is not appealable under § 1291 prior to final judgment in the underlying litigation. Insofar as the Eighth Circuit reached this conclusion, its decision is correct. But because its decision was contrary to precedent in the Circuit, the court went further and reached the merits of the order appealed from. This approach, however, overlooks the fact that the finality requirement embodied in § 1291 is jurisdictional in nature. If the appellate court finds that the order from which a party seeks to appeal does not fall within the statute, its inquiry is over. A court lacks discretion to consider the merits of a case over which it is without jurisdiction, and thus, by definition, a jurisdictional ruling may never be made prospective only. We therefore hold that because the Court of Appeals was without jurisdiction to hear the appeal, it was without authority to decide the merits. * * *

Id. at 373–79, 101 S.Ct. at 673–76, 66 L.Ed.2d at 578–82.

Notes and Questions

1. In footnote 13 of his opinion, Justice Marshall noted:

In the proper circumstances, the moving party may seek sanctions short of disqualification, such as a protective order limiting counsel's ability to disclose or to act on purportedly confidential information. If additional facts in support of the motion develop in the course of the litigation, the moving party might ask the trial court to reconsider its decision. Ultimately, if dissatisfied with the result in the District Court and absolutely determined that it will be harmed irreparably, a party may seek to have the question certified for interlocutory appellate review pursuant to 28 U.S.C. § 1292(b) * * * and, in the exceptional circumstances for which it was designed, a writ of mandamus from the court of appeals might be available.

449 U.S. at 378–79, 101 S.Ct. at 676, 66 L.Ed.2d at 581. Is Justice Marshall correct in suggesting that these alternative means will adequately safeguard the interests of the litigants? Is a writ of mandamus a viable means to

overcome the possible irreparable harm arising out of the nonappealability of denials of disqualification motions?

2. In RICHARDSON–MERRELL, INC. v. KOLLER, 472 U.S. 424, 105 S.Ct. 2757, 86 L.Ed.2d 340 (1985), the Supreme Court reaffirmed its position on disqualification motions, stating that orders disqualifying counsel in civil cases, like orders disqualifying counsel in criminal cases and orders denying motions to disqualify in civil cases, are not collateral orders subject to appeal as final orders. The Court explained:

> * * * One purpose of the final judgment rule embodied in § 1291 is to avoid the delay that inherently accompanies time-consuming interlocutory appeals. * * * When an appellate court accepts jurisdiction of an order disqualifying counsel, the practical effect is to delay proceedings on the merits until the appeal is decided. * * *

> The delay accompanying an appeal results not only when counsel appeals "injudicious use of disqualification motions," but also when counsel appeals an entirely proper disqualification order. Most pretrial orders of district judges are ultimately affirmed by appellate courts. * * * Given an attorney's personal and financial interest in the disqualification decision, orders disqualifying counsel may be more likely to lead to an interlocutory appeal than other pretrial rulings, whether those rulings are correct or otherwise. To be sure, an order granting disqualification itself leads to delay. Alternate counsel must often be retained. Even in cases like this one where competent alternate counsel had already entered appearances and participated in the litigation, such counsel will need time to gain the knowledge of the disqualified attorneys. But where the disqualification decision of the trial court is correct, this delay is unavoidable. We do not think that the delay resulting from the occasionally erroneous disqualification outweighs the delay that would result from allowing piecemeal appeal of every order disqualifying counsel.

Id. at 434, 105 S.Ct. at 2762–63, 86 L.Ed.2d at 348–49.

3. When a disqualification order of the type at issue in *Richardson-Merrell* is granted it can cripple the party whose attorney is disqualified—the attorney may have spent months or even years preparing the case, and replacing her in some instances may be a practical impossibility. Consider the parallel problem raised by IN RE CEMENT ANTITRUST LITIGATION, 673 F.2d 1020 (9th Cir.1981), affirmed sub nom. Arizona v. Ash Grove Cement Co., 459 U.S. 1190, 103 S.Ct. 1172, 75 L.Ed.2d 425 (1983). That case, a complex antitrust suit against cement producers brought by a nationwide class of public and private purchasers of cement and cement-containing products and two state-wide classes of governmental purchasers, was assigned by the Judicial Panel on Multi-District Litigation to the chief judge of the District of Arizona. After two years of coordinated pretrial proceedings, the judge certified the litigation to proceed as a class action, after which the plaintiffs filed a master class list of 210,235 entities. Two years later, defendants moved that the judge recuse himself because his wife owned shares of stock in seven of the 210,235 entities, none of which had requested exclusion from the litigation. The judge recused himself under 28 U.S.C. § 455(b)(4). The Ninth Circuit refused to disturb the judge's decision to grant the recusal motion, holding that an order granting a motion to recuse is neither a final decision within the meaning of Section 1291 nor a collateral

order fitting within the *Cohen* exception. The Ninth Circuit held, relying on Hampton v. City of Chicago, 643 F.2d 478 (7th Cir.1981), that the erroneous grant of a motion to recuse does not deprive the litigant opposing the motion of any recognizable interest and rejected the appellants' sweeping arguments that allowing the trial judge's order to stand effectively would disqualify any federal district judge from hearing the case:

> * * * There may well be exceptional situations in which the costs of familiarizing a new judge, in terms of delay, will prove to be very great. However, there will also be situations in which, although the original judge's participation greatly exceeds that of the judge in *Hampton,* the effect of recusal on the course of litigation will be nonexistent or insignificant. It is not necessary to create a general rule permitting immediate appeal of all recusal decisions in order to resolve the exceptional situations. * * * Ultimately, if dissatisfied with the district judge's decision and confident that the litigation will be greatly disrupted, a party may seek a writ of mandamus from the court of appeals. It is for just such an exceptional circumstance that the writ was designed. * * * Plaintiffs have done so here and that petition will be reviewed on the merits.

673 F.2d at 1025. Because only five Justices of the Supreme Court were not disqualified from hearing the case, a quorum of the Court did not exist and the Ninth Circuit's decision was summarily affirmed under 28 U.S.C. § 2109. On the mandamus proceeding, see pp. 1090–96, infra.

Do you agree with the Ninth Circuit's refusal to formulate a definite, "bright-line" rule for review of recusal motions? Are the costs of losing a judge fully familiar with the record developed in the case and the legal issues involved significant enough to warrant inclusion of review of recusal orders within the *Cohen* exception? Are recusal orders distinguishable from disqualification orders?

4. In PALMER v. CITY OF CHICAGO, 806 F.2d 1316 (7th Cir.1986), the City of Chicago appealed an order that it pay $113,000 in interim attorney's fees to the plaintiffs in this civil rights case. Although the case was effectively completed, no final judgment had been entered. Judge Posner found that the court did have jurisdiction to hear the appeal, since the order fell within the *Cohen* doctrine. Judge Posner explained:

> [A]n order is collateral if an appeal would not interfere with the litigation in the district court. We interpreted "collateral" in this functional, pragmatic sense in United States v. Dorfman, 690 F.2d 1230, 1231–32 (7th Cir.1982), decided before *Koller.* An order that is collateral in this sense is appealable immediately if postponing appellate review till the end of the case would cause substantial irreparable harm to the party against whom the order was directed. The interim fee order in this case thus was collateral, and we shall therefore concentrate our attention on the question whether the city would have been irrevocably harmed by being forced to pay the interim fees and to wait till the end of the entire litigation before seeking their recovery through an appeal.

806 F.2d at 1319. The court found that the city would have been irrevocably harmed since there was a danger that the fees would have disappeared into insolvent hands and the city might not have been able to get its money back.

Is Judge Posner correct in interpreting the collateral-order doctrine in this "pragmatic" way? Is there too much room for abuse under the Seventh Circuit's formulation of the collateral-order doctrine, or is this interpretation a more creative way of dealing with hard cases?

The Third Circuit was faced with a similar question in BECKWITH MACHINERY CO. v. TRAVELERS INDEMNITY CO., 815 F.2d 286 (3d Cir. 1987). Plaintiff brought an action against its insurer alleging breach of an insurance contract when Travelers withdrew its defense of Beckwith in an underlying lawsuit. The District Court entered an order granting Beckwith's motion for summary judgment and entered a judgment on behalf of Beckwith for reimbursement in the amount of settlement of the underlying action and for attorney's fees and costs for the breach-of-contract trial. The District Court did not quantify these fees. The dominant issue on appeal was whether a district court's order awarding, but not quantifying, attorney's fees is a final order from which an appeal may be taken when the fee award arises not as a collateral matter under a separate statutory provision, but instead results from the underlying cause of action which forms the basis of the dispute between the parties. The court did not question that a claim for attorney's fees under 42 U.S.C. § 1988 "raised legal issues collateral to the main cause of action" and "is uniquely separable from the cause of action to be proved at trial." Id. at 288. But here, the question of attorney's fees was integrally related to part of the merits of the dispute. After surveying the differing approaches the circuits have taken, some recognizing the distinctions in the two types of cases, others adopting a bright-line test, Judge Garth rejected the bright-line approach and held that:

> [W]hen the award of attorney's fees arises out of and is part of the claimant's cause of action and is not separately authorized by a statute providing for such an award, an order does not become final until the attorney's fees are quantified.
>
> * * * [W]e can find no basis in logic for distinguishing the case before us from that of a breach of contract action which, among other damages claimed, involves liquidated damages. * * *
>
> [U]ntil the attorney's fee aspect of the order is quantified, the order, as in the hypothetical contract case, necessarily lacks finality as it has not ended the litigation on the merits and there is still more for the court to do. * * *
>
> [T]he fee award is an integral part of the damage award and arises directly out of the initial determination of liability. * * *
>
> [T]he value of having a bright-line rule is severely compromised when the generality of the rule masks important underlying differences. * * *
>
> [T]he order from which Travelers appealed is not a final order which will vest jurisdiction in this court.

Id. at 290–91. Chief Judge Gibbons dissented on the grounds that standards of appellate review should establish clear rules as to when review may be sought, provide workable rules to avoid unnecessary or premature adjudications and avoid multiplicity of disputes. He maintained that the decision of the court thwarts these aims and called for a congressional response to the problem.

Do the same concerns motivate the Third Circuit in *Beckwith* as the Seventh Circuit in *Palmer*? What about the dissent's concerns about judicial efficiency and workable standards for review? Do these concerns cast doubt on the wisdom of the approaches adopted in *Beckwith* and *Palmer*?

b. Avoidance or Evasion of the Basic Concept—Mandamus

Read 28 U.S.C. § 1651(a) in the Supplement.

LA BUY v. HOWES LEATHER CO.

Supreme Court of the United States, 1957.
352 U.S. 249, 77 S.Ct. 309, 1 L.Ed.2d 290.

Certiorari to the United States Court of Appeals for the Seventh Circuit.

Mr. Justice Clark delivered the opinion of the Court.

These two consolidated cases present a question of the power of the Courts of Appeals to issue writs of mandamus to compel a District Judge to vacate his orders entered under Rule 53(b) * * * referring antitrust cases for trial before a master. The petitioner, a United States District Judge * * *, contends that the Courts of Appeals have no such power and that, even if they did, these cases were not appropriate ones for its exercise. The Court of Appeals for the Seventh Circuit has decided unanimously that it has such power and, by a divided court, that the circumstances surrounding the references by the petitioner required it to issue the mandamus about which he complains. * * *

History of the Litigation.—These petitions for mandamus * * * arose from two antitrust actions instituted in the District Court in 1950. Rohlfing involves 87 plaintiffs * * * [and] six named defendants * * *. Shaffer involves six plaintiffs * * * and six defendants * * *.

The record indicates that the cases had been burdensome to the petitioner. In Rohlfing alone, 27 pages of the record are devoted to docket entries reflecting that petitioner had conducted many hearings on preliminary pleas and motions. * * * It is reasonable to conclude that much time would have been saved at the trial had petitioner heard the case because of his familarity with the litigation.

* * * The cases were called on February 23, 1955, on a motion to reset them for trial. * * * The petitioner announced that "it has taken a long time to get this case at issue. I remember hearing more motions, I think, in this case than any case I have ever sat on in this court." The plaintiffs estimated that the trial would take six weeks, whereupon petitioner stated he did not know when he could try the case "if it is going to take this long." He asked if the parties could agree "to have a Master hear" it. The parties ignored this query and at a conference in chambers the next day petitioner entered the orders of reference *sua sponte*. The

orders declared that the court was "confronted with an extremely congested calendar" and that "exception [*sic*] conditions exist for this reason" requiring the references. The cases were referred to the master "to take evidence and to report the same to this Court, together with his findings of fact and conclusions of law." * * *

Upon petitioner's refusal to vacate the references, these mandamus actions were filed in the Court of Appeals seeking the issuance of writs ordering petitioner to do so. These applications were grounded on 28 U.S.C. § 1651(a), the All Writs Act. * * * Declaring that the references amounted to * * * "a refusal on his [petitioner's] part, as a judge, to try the causes in due course," the Court of Appeals concluded that "in view of the extraordinary nature of these causes" the references must be vacated "if we find that the orders were beyond the court's power under the pertinent rule." * * * And, it being so found, the writs issued under the authority of the All Writs Act. * * *

The Power of the Courts of Appeals.—Petitioner contends that the power of the Courts of Appeals does not extend to the issuance of writs of mandamus to review interlocutory orders except in those cases where the review of the case on appeal after final judgment would be frustrated. * * * The question of naked power has long been settled by this Court. As late as Roche v. Evaporated Milk Association, 1943, 319 U.S. 21, 25, 63 S.Ct. 938, 941, 87 L.Ed. 1185, Mr. Chief Justice Stone reviewed the decisions and, in considering the power of Courts of Appeals to issue writs of mandamus, the Court held that "the common-law writs, like equitable remedies, may be granted or withheld in the sound discretion of the court." * * * Since the Court of Appeals could at some stage of the antitrust proceedings entertain appeals in these cases, it has power in proper circumstances, as here, to issue writs of mandamus reaching them. * * *

The Discretionary Use of the Writs.—It appears from the docket entries to which we heretofore referred that the petitioner was well informed as to the nature of the antitrust litigation * * *. Nevertheless, he referred both suits to a master on the general issue. Furthermore, neither the existence of the alleged conspiracy nor the question of liability *vel non* had been determined in either case. These issues, as well as the damages, if any, and the question concerning the issuance of an injunction, were likewise included in the references. Under all of the circumstances, we believe the Court of Appeals was justified in finding the orders of reference were an abuse of the petitioner's power under Rule 53(b). They amounted to little less than an abdication of the judicial function depriving the parties of a trial before the court on the basic issues involved in the litigation.

The use of masters is "to aid judges in the performance of specific judicial duties, as they may arise in the progress of a cause," Ex parte Peterson, 1920, 253 U.S. 300, 312, 40 S.Ct. 543, 547, 64 L.Ed. 919, and not to displace the court. The exceptional circumstances here warrant the use of the extraordinary remedy of mandamus. * * *

It is also contended that the Seventh Circuit has erroneously construed the All Writs Act as "conferring on it a 'roving commission' to supervise interlocutory orders of the District Courts in advance of final decision." Our examination of its opinions in this regard leads us to the conclusion that the Court of Appeals has exercised commendable self-restraint. It is true that mandamus should be resorted to only in extreme cases, since it places trial judges in the anomalous position of being litigants without counsel other than uncompensated volunteers. However, there is an end of patience and it clearly appears that the Court of Appeals has [since 1938] * * * admonished the trial judges of the Seventh Circuit that the practice of making references "does not commend itself" and " * * * should seldom be made, and if at all only when unusual circumstances exist." * * * Still the Court of Appeals did not disturb the reference practice by reversal or mandamus until this case was decided in October 1955. * * * The record does not show to what extent references are made by the full bench of the District Court in the Northern District; however, it does reveal that petitioner has referred 11 cases to masters in the past 6 years. But even "a little cloud may bring a flood's downpour" if we approve the practice here indulged, particularly in the face of presently congested dockets, increased filings, and more extended trials. * * * [B]e that as it may, congestion in itself is not such an exceptional circumstance as to warrant a reference to a master. If such were the test, present congestion would make references the rule rather than the exception. Petitioner realizes this, for in addition to calendar congestion he alleges that the cases referred had unusual complexity of issues of both fact and law. But most litigation in the antitrust field is complex. It does not follow that antitrust litigants are not entitled to a trial before a court. On the contrary, we believe that this is an impelling reason for trial before a regular, experienced trial judge rather than before a temporary substitute appointed on an *ad hoc* basis and ordinarily not experienced in judicial work. * * * We agree that the detailed accounting required in order to determine the damages suffered by each plaintiff might be referred to a master after the court has determined the over-all liability of defendants, provided the circumstances indicate that the use of the court's time is not warranted in receiving the proof and making the tabulation.

* * *

Affirmed.

MR. JUSTICE BRENNAN, with whom MR. JUSTICE FRANKFURTER, MR. JUSTICE BURTON and MR. JUSTICE HARLAN join, dissenting.

* * * The case before the Court of Appeals was "not a case where a court has exceeded or refused to exercise its jurisdiction * * *." Rule 53(b) * * * vested Judge La Buy with discretionary power to make a reference if he found, and he did, that "some exceptional condition" required the reference. * * * If Judge La Buy erred in finding that there was an "exceptional condition" requiring the reference or did not give proper weight to the caveat of the Rule that a "reference to a master

shall be the exception and not the rule," that was mere error "in ruling on matters within [the District Court's] jurisdiction." * * *

But, regrettable as is this Court's approval of what I consider to be a clear departure by the Court of Appeals from the settled principles governing the issuance of the extraordinary writs, what this Court says in reaching its result is reason for particularly grave concern. I think this Court has today seriously undermined the long-standing statutory policy against piecemeal appeals. My brethren say: "Since the Court of Appeals could at some stage of the antitrust proceedings entertain appeals in these cases, it has power in proper circumstances, as here, to issue writs of mandamus reaching them. * * *" I understand this to mean that proper circumstances are present for the issuance of a writ in this case because, if the litigants are not now heard, the Court of Appeals will not have an opportunity to relieve them of the burden of the added expense and delay of decision alleged to be the consequence of the reference. But that bridge was crossed by this Court in *Roche* * * *.

What this Court is saying, therefore, is that the All Writs Act confers an independent appellate power in the Courts of Appeals to review interlocutory orders. I have always understood the law to be precisely to the contrary. * * *

The power of the Courts of Appeals to issue extraordinary writs stems from § 14 of the Judiciary Act of 1789. Chief Judge Magruder, in In re Josephson, 1 Cir., 218 F.2d 174, provides us with an invaluable history of this power and of the judicial development of its scope. He demonstrates most persuasively that "[t]he all writs section does not confer an independent appellate power; the power is strictly of an auxiliary nature, in aid of a jurisdiction granted in some other provision of law * * *."

The focal question posed for a Court of Appeals by a petition for the issuance of a writ is whether the action of the District Court tends to frustrate or impede the ultimate exercise by the Court of Appeals of its appellate jurisdiction granted in some other provision of the law. The answer is clearly in the affirmative where, for example, the order of the District Court transfers a cause to a District Court of another circuit for decision. That was Josephson, where * * * "the effect of the order is that the district judge has declined to proceed with the determination of a case which could eventually come to this court by appeal from a 'final decision'." * * * In contrast, a District Court order denying a transfer would not come under the umbrella of power under the All Writs Act, since retention of the cause by the District Court can hardly thwart or tend to defeat the power of the Court of Appeals to review that order after final decision of the case. * * *

The view now taken by this Court that the All Writs Act confers an independent appellate power, although not so broad as "to authorize the indiscriminate use of prerogative writs as a means of reviewing interlocutory orders," in effect engrafts upon federal appellate procedure a standard of interlocutory review never embraced by the Congress throughout our history, although it is written into the English Judicature Act and is followed in varying degrees in some of the States. That standard allows interlocutory appeals by leave of the appellate court. * * *

Notes and Questions

1. In SCHLAGENHAUF v. HOLDER, 379 U.S. 104, 85 S.Ct. 234, 13 L.Ed.2d 152 (1964), the substantive aspects of which are set out at p. 751, supra, the Court upheld the use of mandamus to review an order requiring a defendant to submit to a physical and mental examination:

It is, of course, well settled that the writ is not to be used as a substitute for appeal * * * even though hardship may result from delay and perhaps unnecessary trial * * *. The writ is appropriately issued, however, when there is "usurpation of judicial power" or a clear abuse of discretion * * *.

[T]he challenged order * * * appears to be the first of its kind in any reported decision in the federal courts under Rule 35 * * *.

* * * It is thus appropriate for us to determine on the merits the issues presented and to formulate the necessary guidelines in this area. * * *

This is not to say, however, that following the setting of guidelines in this opinion, any future allegation that the District Court was in error in applying these guidelines to a particular case makes mandamus an appropriate remedy.

Id. at 110–12, 85 S.Ct. at 238–39, 13 L.Ed.2d at 156–60.

Do the decisions in *LaBuy* and *Schlagenhauf* give sufficient guidance as to when mandamus is an appropriate means of review? Note that both cases involve significant problems regarding application of the Federal Rules. It has been suggested that the *LaBuy* holding might "possibly be limited to issues of judicial administration which have broad significance beyond the particular case." Note, *Appealability in the Federal Courts,* 75 Harv.L.Rev. 351, 377 (1961). Compare WILL v. UNITED STATES, 389 U.S. 90, 88 S.Ct. 269, 19 L.Ed.2d 305 (1967), a criminal case in which the government sought mandamus to overturn a District Court order granting discovery for the defendant. The Court of Appeals granted the writ. The Supreme Court reversed, stating that the facts did not reveal an extraordinary situation for which the writs must be reserved. The Court did not discuss the fact that without mandamus the government cannot obtain guidance on discovery matters since it cannot appeal an acquittal.

Relying heavily on *Will,* the Supreme Court in KERR v. UNITED STATES DISTRICT COURT, 426 U.S. 394, 96 S.Ct. 2119, 48 L.Ed.2d 725 (1976), affirmed a denial of mandamus by a court of appeals in a civil case in which the trial judge had ordered defendants, state correction officers, to turn over to plaintiff a number of prisoner personnel files. Defendants argued that such discovery should be compelled only after a determination by the trial judge that plaintiff's need for the information outweighs its confidentiality. In a cogent opinion the Court reiterated the reasons for limiting use of writs to avoid piecemeal appeals and also recognized that restricting the use of writs to matters of "jurisdiction" in the technical sense would be too narrow. The Court "assumed" that the trial judge would now accept its "suggestion" to review each of the personnel files *in camera* to determine if discovery should be permitted, thus making a writ unnecessary. Isn't such an opinion self-defeating in that it encourages litigants to continue to file for mandamus in the hope that even if it is rejected the Court's opinion will effectively order the relief sought?

2. In LYONS v. WESTINGHOUSE ELEC. CORP., 222 F.2d 184 (2d Cir. 1955), certiorari denied 350 U.S. 825, 76 S.Ct. 52, 100 L.Ed. 737 (1955), the district judge had stayed an antitrust case pending the determination of a related state-court action. The Court of Appeals held that if a state judgment would have a collateral estoppel effect on the federal action, it would not,

> literally speaking, end the jurisdiction of the district court; but it will do so in substance, if it is an estoppel at all, for it will conclude any further consideration of the existence of the conspiracy, and on that all else depends. For this reason, we hold * * * that the question whether a final judgment will be an estoppel so nearly touches the jurisdiction of the district court, as to make it proper for us to entertain the petition for mandamus.

Id. at 186.

In light of the court's holding on the merits that the state-court judgment "can have no effect upon the decision of the action at bar," was the court justified in directing the District Court to vacate the stay? What would the court have directed if it had ruled the other way on the merits? The Court of Appeals did not in fact issue a writ of mandamus. Its order reads: "Writ of mandamus to go thirty days after the filing of this opinion * * * unless [the stay] * * * has been vacated theretofore." Such conditional orders are common in mandamus cases. Why?

3. In IN RE CEMENT ANTITRUST LITIGATION, 688 F.2d 1297 (9th Cir.1982), a later stage of the controversy over the recusal order described at pp. 1087–88, supra, the Ninth Circuit refused to issue a writ of mandamus compelling the district judge to revoke his order granting the defendants' motion that he recuse himself:

> In order to confine the use of mandamus to its proper office, we enunciated five general guidelines * * * to assist in the determination of whether mandamus is the appropriate remedy in a particular case. The guidelines are: (1) whether the party seeking the writ has no other adequate means, such as direct appeal, to attain the relief he desires; (2) whether the petitioner will be damaged or prejudiced in a way that is not correctable on appeal; (3) whether the district court's order is clearly erroneous as a matter of law; (4) whether the district court's order is an oft repeated error or manifests persistent disregard for the federal rules; and (5) whether the district court's order raises new and important problems or issues of law of first impression. * * * Related considerations include: whether the injury alleged by petitioners, although not correctable on appeal, is the kind that justifies invocation of our mandamus authority; whether the petition presents an issue of law which may repeatedly evade appellate review; and whether there are other compelling factors relating to the efficient and orderly administration of the district courts.

* * * The guidelines are not susceptible of mechanical application; they are not meant to supplant reasoned and independent analysis by appellate courts. In sum, the guidelines serve only as a useful starting point, an analytic framework for determinations regarding the propriety of mandamus relief.

Id. at 1301. Although the Ninth Circuit held that the exercise of supervisory mandamus authority was appropriate in this case because the issue raised was an important issue of first impression capable of evading review because of its collateral nature, it also held that the grant of the recusal motion was not erroneous and that, even if erroneous, it was harmless error. Because only five Justices of the Supreme Court were not disqualified from hearing the appeal, a quorum of the Court did not exist and the Ninth Circuit's decision was affirmed summarily under 28 U.S.C. § 2109. Arizona v. United States District Court, 459 U.S. 1191, 103 S.Ct. 1173, 75 L.Ed.2d 425 (1983).

4. In NIXON v. SIRICA, 487 F.2d 700, 707 (D.C.Cir.1973), a district judge ordered the President of the United States to produce certain tape recordings for the judge's inspection prior to a determination whether the recordings were subject to a grand jury subpoena. The President petitioned for a writ of mandamus, and the Court of Appeals, although denying the petition on the merits, held that it was an appropriate mode of review:

From the viewpoint of mandamus * * * the central question that the President raises—whether the District Court exceeded its authority in ordering an *in camera* inspection of the tapes—is essentially jurisdictional. It is, too, a jurisdictional problem of "first impression" involving a "basic, undecided question." And if indeed the only avenue of direct appellate review open to the President requires that he first disobey the court's order, appeal seems to be "a clearly inadequate remedy." These circumstances * * * warrant the exercise * * * of our review power under the All Writs Act, particularly in light of the great public interest in prompt resolution of the issues * * *.

See also the Supreme Court's discussion of the order involved in this case in United States v. Nixon, p. 1078, supra.

c. *Displacement of the Basic Concept—Discretionary Appeals*

Read 28 U.S.C. § 1292(b) in the Supplement.

ATLANTIC CITY ELEC. CO. v. GENERAL ELEC. CO.
United States Court of Appeals, Second Circuit, 1964.
337 F.2d 844.

PER CURIAM. The district court has certified pursuant to section 1292(b) * * * that its order, sustaining objections to interrogatories designed to discover whether damages were actually sustained by plaintiffs who may have shifted such damages, if any, to their customers of electricity, involves a controlling question of law in these litigations and that there is substantial ground for differences of opinion. * * *

In sustaining the objections to the interrogatories posed, the district court has, in effect, foreclosed defendants from pre-trial discovery of facts relating to a defense that plaintiffs have "passed-on" to their customers any damages incurred by plaintiffs and hence are not entitled to recover to the extent that defendants can prove such passing-on.

Upon this application for leave to appeal it would not be appropriate to isolate and endeavor to decide before an appeal from any final judgment this particular question of law. Pre-trial leave to appeal applications must be decided against the background of the entire case. Many important questions of law will undoubtedly arise in these cases but the problem now confronting us is the feasibility and advisability of trying to decide this particular question in advance of trial.

If pre-trial discovery were allowed as defendants request it could easily develop into a multitude of full scale rate cases which could dwarf in time and testimony the already extensive pre-trial proceedings. If the district court is in error * * * defendants will have full opportunity in the event of an adverse judgment, if based in whole or in part upon this error, to have it corrected upon appeal together with any other errors which may be urged. It is doubtful that any discoveries or hearings required to establish the extent of any damages, if the passing-on-doctrine applies, would be more burdensome then than now. Since defendants' rights to this defense are not being taken away or prejudiced on any ultimate appeal by denial of the pre-trial appeal now sought, we believe that the ultimate disposition of these cases would be delayed rather than advanced by granting this application.

Application denied.

Notes and Questions

1. In COMMONWEALTH EDISON CO. v. ALLIS CHALMERS MFG. CO., 335 F.2d 203 (7th Cir.1964), having accepted an appeal under Section 1292(b) on the same issue involved in the principal case, the Seventh Circuit held that the passing-on defense was not available, and hence affirmed an order sustaining objections to similar interrogatories. Which of the courts of appeals followed the sounder procedure? Should the Second Circuit have ruled differently if the district judge had directed plaintiffs to answer the interrogatories? See generally Note, *The Final Judgment Rule and Appellate Review of Discovery Orders in Nebraska,* 35 Neb.L.Rev. 469 (1956).

Suppose the trial court in *Atlantic City Elec. Co.* had ruled directly on the applicability of the passing-on defense. Would the Court of Appeals have had less justification for rejecting the appeal? Compare Obron v. Union Camp Corp., 477 F.2d 542 (6th Cir.1973) (allowing appeal).

2. Is Section 1292(b) a solution to the type of problem raised in *Ryan* or *Cobbledick,* p. 1077, supra? In UNITED STATES v. WOODBURY, 263 F.2d 784 (9th Cir.1959), the court declined to review an order granting discovery even though the District Court had ordered defendant's answer and counterclaim stricken if it did not comply. But in GROOVER, CHRISTIE & MERRITT v. LoBIANCO, 336 F.2d 969, 973–74 (D.C.Cir.1964), a malpractice action, the court allowed an appeal from an order granting discovery of a letter by

defendant to an insurer, detailing defendant's investigation of the case. The court then reversed, finding that "good cause" had not been adequately established under Rule 34, and directed the trial judge to make further findings and to consider whether the letter was privileged under Hickman v. Taylor, p. 766, supra. Judge Wright dissented vigorously, stating: "This case is a graphic illustration of the mischief that results when [Section 1292(b)] * * * is misused. * * * And rather than advance the ultimate termination of this litigation, the dilatory tactics * * *, including this interlocutory appeal, have already been the cause of significant delay." Compare Judge Clark, dissenting, in MATTHIES v. SEYMOUR MFG. CO., 271 F.2d 740 (2d Cir.1959), certiorari denied 361 U.S. 962, 80 S.Ct. 591, 4 L.Ed.2d 544 (1960): "In passing I might note that this seems to me another illustration of the unfortunate tendency of the new interlocutory appeals statute * * * to overemphasize strict pleading and in so doing to throw our procedure out of line with the liberal spirit fostered by the civil rules." Why should Section 1292(b) have this effect? Cf. Clark, *Special Problems in Drafting and Interpreting Procedural Codes and Rules,* 3 Vand.L.Rev. 493, 498 (1950).

3. Would Section 1292(b) be a satisfactory device in *LaBuy* or *Lyons?* See Lear Siegler, Inc. v. Adkins, 330 F.2d 595 (9th Cir.1964). Should the court of appeals be given power to hear appeals from orders fulfilling the requirements described in Section 1292(b) without the certificate of the district judge? Compare Leasco Data Processing Equip. Corp. v. Maxwell, 468 F.2d 1326, 1344 (2d Cir.1972) (court of appeals cannot order trial court to issue certificate).

4. The courts of appeals have not been markedly hospitable to interlocutory appeals under Section 1292(b). Decisions during the 1950's placing strong emphasis on the exceptional nature of the relief, e.g., In re Heddendorf, 263 F.2d 887 (1st Cir.1959); Milbert v. Bison Labs, Inc., 260 F.2d 431 (3d Cir. 1958), have not lost their precedential force. In the fiscal year 1966, the courts of appeals considered 68 applications and allowed only 36; in subsequent years the figures were 80 and 41 (1967); 122 and 58 (1968); 105 and 64 (1969). In 1970, both figures increased markedly: 290 applications considered, and 225 allowed. Annual Report of the Director of the Administrative Office of the United States Courts, 1966, p. 160; id. 1967, p. 191; id. 1968, p. 185; id. 1969, p. 195; id. 1970, p. 221. More recent reports have not included these figures.

5. In NICKERT v. PUGET SOUND TUG & BARGE CO., 480 F.2d 1039 (9th Cir.1973), a wrongful-death case, one defendant, A, cross-claimed for indemnity against another defendant, B. Prior to trial on the cross-complaint, the trial court granted a "partial summary judgment" for B stating that if at trial it were to be found that A had negligently contributed to the wrongful death, indemnity would not be permitted. The trial judge thereupon issued a certificate under Section 1292(b)(2) allowing A to appeal. The Court of Appeals admitted that the issue was important and controversial, but nevertheless dismissed the appeal, stating:

> * * * The trial court's announcement of its opinion on this question of law * * * is nothing more * * * than an hypothetical, advisory opinion. It is subject to revision or reversal at any time by the trial judge to the point where a definitive action has been taken on the question; for examples, an instruction to the jury, or the adoption of a conclusion of law in a trial to the court. Similarly, an announcement by

this Court of its opinion of the trial judge's tentative opinion would be purely advisory * * *.

Id. at 1041. Do you agree with the appellate court's decision? Does it undercut the policy upon which Section 1292(b) is based? Is it consistent with Rule 56(a), which permits partial summary judgment?

6. For a comprehensive analysis of Section 1292(b), see Note, *Interlocutory Appeals in the Federal Courts Under 28 U.S.C. § 1292(b)*, 88 Harv.L.Rev. 607 (1975).

GILLESPIE v. UNITED STATES STEEL CORP.

Supreme Court of the United States, 1964.
379 U.S. 148, 85 S.Ct. 308, 13 L.Ed.2d 199.

Certiorari to the United States Court of Appeals for the Sixth Circuit.

MR. JUSTICE BLACK delivered the opinion of the Court.

The petitioner, administratrix of the estate of her son Daniel Gillespie, brought this action in federal court against the respondent shipowner-employer to recover damages for Gillespie's death, which was alleged to have occurred when he fell and was drowned while working as a seaman on respondent's ship docked in Ohio. She claimed a right to recover for the benefit of herself and of the decedent's dependent brother and sisters under the Jones Act, which subjects employers to liability if by negligence they cause a seaman's injury or death. She also claimed a right of recovery under the Ohio wrongful death statute because the vessel allegedly was not seaworthy as required by the "general maritime law." The complaint in addition sought damages for Gillespie's pain and suffering before he died, based on the Jones Act and the general maritime law, causes of action which petitioner said survived Gillespie's death by force of the Jones Act itself and the Ohio survival statute, respectively. The District Judge, holding that the Jones Act supplied the exclusive remedy, on motion of respondent struck all parts of the complaint which referred to the Ohio statutes or to unseaworthiness. He also struck all reference to recovery for the benefit of the brother and sisters of the decedent, who respondent had argued were not beneficiaries entitled to recovery under the Jones Act while their mother was living.

Petitioner immediately appealed to the Court of Appeals. Respondent moved to dismiss the appeal on the ground that the ruling appealed from was not a "final" decision of the District Court * * *. Thereupon petitioner administratrix, this time joined by the brother and sisters, filed in the Court of Appeals a petition for mandamus or other appropriate writ commanding the District Judge to vacate his original order and enter a new one * * *. Without definitely deciding whether mandamus would have been appropriate in this case or deciding the "close" question of appealability, the Court of Appeals proceeded to determine the controversy "on the merits as though it were submitted on an appeal"; this the court said it felt free to do since its resolution of the merits did not prejudice respondent in any way, because it sustained respondent's contentions by denying the petition for mandamus and affirming the District Court's order. * * *

In this Court respondent joins petitioner in urging us to hold that 28 U.S.C. § 1291 does not require us to dismiss this case * * *. We agree. * * * [A]s this Court often has pointed out, a decision "final" within the meaning of § 1291 does not necessarily mean the last order possible to be made in a case. * * * It is true that the review of this case by the Court of Appeals could be called "piecemeal"; but it does not appear that the inconvenience and cost of trying this case will be greater because the Court of Appeals decided the issues raised instead of compelling the parties to go to trial with them unanswered. * * * And it seems clear now that the case is before us that the eventual costs, as all the parties recognize, will certainly be less if we now pass on the questions presented here rather than send the case back with those issues undecided. Moreover, delay of perhaps a number of years in having the brother's and sisters' rights determined might work a great injustice on them, since the claims for recovery for their benefit have been effectively cut off so long as the District Judge's ruling stands. And while their claims are not formally severable so as to make the court's order unquestionably appealable as to them, * * * there certainly is ample reason to view their claims as severable in deciding the issue of finality, particularly since the brother and sisters were separate parties in the petition for extraordinary relief. * * * Furthermore, in United States v. General Motors Corp., 323 U.S. 373, 377, 65 S.Ct. 357, 359, 89 L.Ed. 311, this Court contrary to its usual practice reviewed a trial court's refusal to permit proof of certain items of damages in a case not yet fully tried, because the ruling was "fundamental to the further conduct of the case." * * * We think that the questions presented here are equally "fundamental to the further conduct of the case." It is true that if the District Judge had certified the case to the Court of Appeals under 28 U.S.C. § 1292(b), the appeal unquestionably would have been proper; in light of the circumstances we believe that the Court of Appeals properly implemented the same policy Congress sought to promote in § 1292(b) by treating this obviously marginal case as final and appealable * * *.

[The opinion of Justice GOLDBERG, concurring in part and dissenting in part, is omitted.]

Mr. Justice HARLAN, dissenting.

* * * The Court substantially affirms the judgment of the Court of Appeals and the parties are remanded to a trial on the merits, but only after they have incurred needless delay and expense in consequence of the loose practices sanctioned by the Court of Appeals and in turn by this Court. This case thus presents a striking example of the vice inherent in a system which permits piecemeal litigation of the issues in a lawsuit.

* * * The justifications given by the Court for tolerating the lower court's departure from the requirements of § 1291 are, with all respect, unsatisfactory.

1. The Court relies on the discretionary right of a district court to certify an interlocutory order to the court of appeals under § 1292(b) when the "order involves a controlling question of law," but the District Court in its discretion—and rightly it turns out—did not make such a

certification in this case, and the Court of Appeals, equally correctly in my judgment, refused to order it to do so. * * *

2. Cohen v. Beneficial Industrial Loan Corp. * * * does not support a different result. * * * It is clear in this case that had petitioner proceeded to trial and won on her Jones Act claim, her asserted cause of action for unseaworthiness would have merged in the judgment. * * * Conversely, her claim would have been preserved for appeal had she lost on her Jones Act claim. Surely the assertion that petitioner is entitled to submit her unseaworthiness theory to the jury is not collateral to rights asserted in her action * * *.

3. Finally, the Court's suggestion that "it seems clear now that the case is before us that the eventual costs, as all the parties recognize, will certainly be less if we now pass on the questions presented here rather than send the case back with those issues undecided," * * * furnishes no excuse for avoidance of the finality rule. Essentially such a position would justify review here of any case decided by a court of appeals whenever this Court, as it did in this instance, erroneously grants certiorari and permits counsel to brief and argue the case on the merits. That, I believe, is neither good law nor sound judicial administration.

* * *

[A memorandum by JUSTICE STEWART is omitted.]

Notes and Questions

1. Is the majority or Justice Harlan correct on the appealability under Section 1292(b) of the District Court's order in *Gillespie*?

2. Is *Gillespie* still good law after *Coopers & Lybrand,* p. 1081, supra?

d. An Historical Footnote to the Basic Concept—Injunctions

———

Read 28 U.S.C. § 1292(a)(1) and Federal Rules of Civil Procedure 65(a) and (b) in the Supplement.

———

SMITH v. VULCAN IRON WORKS, 165 U.S. 518, 525, 17 S.Ct. 407, 410, 41 L.Ed. 810, 812 (1897):

The manifest intent of this provision, read in the light of the previous practice in the courts of the United States, contrasted with the practice in courts of equity of the highest authority elsewhere, appears to this court to have been, not only to permit the defendant to obtain immediate relief from an injunction, the continuance of which throughout the progress of the cause might seriously affect his interests, but also to save both parties from the expense of further litigation, should the appellate court be of opinion that the plaintiff was not entitled to an injunction because his bill had no equity to support it.

Notes and Questions

1. Is the Supreme Court's ruling that an appeal under the predecessor of Section 1292(a)(1) allows the reviewing court to consider not only the question whether the injunction should have been issued, but the merits of the whole case, supported by the traditional doctrines regarding the character of equitable relief? Review pp. 878–79, supra.

2. What are the reasons for allowing appeals from interlocutory orders granting or refusing injunctions? Do these reasons apply to orders granting or denying preliminary, as opposed to permanent, injunctions? Could these reasons be served as well by relegating the parties to discretionary appeals under Section 1292(b)?

3. Is the grant or denial of a temporary restraining order appealable under Section 1292(a)(1)? See Grant v. United States, 282 F.2d 165 (2d Cir. 1960). In close cases it may be difficult to tell the difference between a preliminary injunction and a temporary restraining order. See Connell v. Dulien Steel Products, Inc., 240 F.2d 414 (5th Cir.1957), 71 Harv.L.Rev. 550 (1958) (28-day temporary restraining order). Are the differences between preliminary injunctions and temporary restraining orders relevant to the question whether appeal should be permitted in the case of the former and not permitted in the case of the latter?

In UNITED STATES v. WOOD, 295 F.2d 772 (5th Cir.1961), certiorari denied 369 U.S. 850, 82 S.Ct. 933, 8 L.Ed.2d 9 (1962), a Black man who was active in voter registration in Mississippi was arrested for disturbing the peace and ordered to trial in fifteen days. Two days before trial, the United States, moving under 42 U.S.C. § 1971 and alleging that the prosecution would intimidate Blacks in the exercise of their voting rights, brought suit to restrain the criminal action. A temporary restraining order was denied and the government appealed. The Court of Appeals held that it had jurisdiction under Section 1291. Inasmuch as the case would quickly become moot if the restraining order was not issued, the court said, its denial was "a final disposition of the * * * claimed right. * * * [T]o call this de facto dismissal a nonappealable interlocutory order is to preclude review altogether."

4. In SAMPSON v. MURRAY, 415 U.S. 61, 94 S.Ct. 937, 39 L.Ed.2d 166 (1974), the respondent, a probationary federal employee, filed an action to enjoin temporarily her dismissal pending her pursuit of an administrative appeal to the Civil Service Commission. The District Court granted the temporary restraining order and, after an adversary hearing, extended the interim relief until the respondent's supervisor testified about the reasons for her dismissal. The United States Court of Appeals for the District of Columbia Circuit affirmed. The Supreme Court reversed, holding that the Court of Appeals had correctly treated the extension order as a preliminary injunction, but that the order in question failed to meet the standards for such injunctions set by Rule 65. In the Court's view, the respondent had failed to demonstrate irreparable harm. Neither the temporary loss of income (ultimately to be recovered) nor the humiliation and damage to the respondent's reputation were sufficient to constitute irreparable injury justifying the granting of a preliminary injunction.

Justices Douglas, Marshall, and Brennan dissented. Justice Douglas agreed with the majority that the extension order at issue was an appealable order; however, he maintained that the order was a valid stay designed to preserve the status quo until the District Court was able to hold a hearing on the issue of whether the respondent had suffered an irreparable injury justifying the issuing of the order as a preliminary injunction. Justices Marshall and Brennan, on the other hand, argued that the order was not appealable. In their view, because the temporary restraining order at issue did not meet any of the requirements for interlocutory injunctions set forth in Rule 52(a), "no valid preliminary injunction was ever issued." Thus, it did not make sense for the Court to review the District Court's order as the grant of a preliminary injunction. They continued:

> * * * Even if the order entered by the District Court is appealable, it should be appealable only for the purposes of holding it invalid for failure to comply with Rule 52(a). * * *

In addition, the Government had other courses it could have taken in this case. In view of the District Court's error in granting a restraining order of unlimited duration without complying with the requirements for a preliminary injunction, the Government could have moved the District Court to dissolve its order indefinitely continuing the temporary restraining order. Rule 65(b) expressly provides for such a motion. Had the Government followed this course, the District Court could have corrected its error and gone on to resolve the issues presented by the application for a preliminary injunction. The end result would have been the grant or denial of a preliminary injunction, with findings of fact and conclusions of law, which we could meaningfully review.

Here, instead, we find the Supreme Court determining that although the District Court had jurisdiction to grant injunctive relief, the equities of Mrs. Murray's case did not support a preliminary injunction, when neither the District Court nor the Court of Appeals has yet confronted the latter issue. I do not believe this makes for sound law.

Id. at 99–100, 94 S.Ct. at 957, 39 L.Ed.2d at 191–92.

GULFSTREAM AEROSPACE CORP. v. MAYACAMAS CORP.

Supreme Court of the United States, 1988.
485 U.S. 271, 108 S.Ct. 1133, 99 L.Ed.2d 296.

Certiorari to the United States Court of Appeals for the Ninth Circuit.

JUSTICE MARSHALL delivered the opinion of the Court.

The primary issue in this case is whether a district court order denying a motion to stay or dismiss an action when a similar suit is pending in state court is immediately appealable.

* * *

[Gulfstream sued Mayacamas in state court for breach of contract. Mayacamas did not remove the action to federal court, but, one month later, filed a diversity action against petitioner in the Federal District Court for breach of the same contract. The District Court denied Gulfstream's motion to stay or dismiss the action before it, finding that the facts of the case fell short of those necessary to justify the requested discontinuance of the federal-court action under Colorado River Water Conservation Dist. v. United States, 424 U.S. 800, 96 S.Ct. 1236, 47 L.Ed.2d 483 (1976), which held that, in "exceptional" circumstances, a district court may stay or dismiss an action because of the pendency of similar state-court litigation. The Court of Appeals dismissed petitioner's appeal for lack of jurisdiction, holding that neither 28 U.S.C. § 1291 nor § 1292(a)(1) allowed an immediate appeal from the District Court's order. The court also declined to treat petitioner's notice of appeal as an application for a writ of mandamus under the All Writs Act.

The Supreme Court first rejected petitioner's contention that the District Court's order denying the motion to stay or dismiss the federal-court litigation was immediately appealable under § 1291. The Court reasoned that such an order does not end the litigation but rather ensures that it will continue in the District Court. The Court added that such an order does not fall within the collateral-order exception to § 1291, since it fails to satisfy the exception's "conclusiveness" requirement in that it is inherently tentative and not made with the expectation that it will be the final word on the subject addressed: "[A] district court usually will expect to revisit and reassess an order denying a stay in light of events occurring in the normal course of litigation."

After disposing of the § 1291 issue, the Court considered whether such an order constituted an injunction appealable under § 1292(a)(1).]

Petitioner argues in the alternative that the District Court's order in this case is immediately appealable under § 1292(a)(1), which gives the courts of appeals jurisdiction of appeals from interlocutory orders granting or denying injunctions. An order by a federal court that relates only to the conduct or progress of litigation before that court ordinarily is not considered an injunction and therefore is not appealable under § 1292(a)(1). * * * Under the *Enelow-Ettelson* doctrine, however, certain orders that stay or refuse to stay judicial proceedings are considered injunctions and therefore are immediately appealable. Petitioner asserts that the order in this case, which denied a motion for a stay of a federal-court action pending the resolution of a concurrent state-court proceeding, is appealable under § 1292(a)(1) pursuant to the *Enelow-Ettelson* doctrine.

The line of cases we must examine to resolve this claim began some fifty years ago, when this Court decided Enelow v. New York Life Ins. Co., 293 U.S. 379, 55 S.Ct. 310, 79 L.Ed. 440 (1935). At the time of that decision, law and equity remained separate jurisprudential systems in the federal courts. The same judges administered both these systems, however, so that a federal district judge was both a chancellor in equity and a judge at law. In *Enelow,* the plaintiff sued at law to recover on a life insurance policy. The insurance company raised the affirmative defense that the policy had been obtained by fraud and moved the District Court to stay the trial of the law action pending resolution of this equitable defense. The District Court granted this motion, and the plaintiff appealed. This Court likened the stay to an injunction issued by an equity court to restrain an action at law. The Court stated:

[T]he grant or refusal of * * * a stay by a court of equity of proceedings at law is a grant or refusal of an injunction within the meaning of [the statute.] And, in this aspect, it makes no difference that the two cases, the suit in equity for an injunction and the action at law in which proceedings are stayed, are both pending in the same court, in view of the established distinction between "proceedings at law and proceedings in equity in the national courts. * * *"

* * *

It is thus apparent that when an order or decree is made * * * requiring, or refusing to require, that an equitable defense shall first be tried, the court, exercising what is essentially an equitable jurisdiction, in effect grants or refuses an injunction restraining proceedings at law precisely as if the court had acted upon a bill of complaint in a separate suit for the same purpose. Id., at 382–383, 55 S.Ct., at 311.

The Court thus concluded that the District Court's order was appealable under § 1292(a)(1).

In Ettelson v. Metropolitan Life Ins. Co., 317 U.S. 188, 63 S.Ct. 163, 87 L.Ed. 176 (1942), the Court reaffirmed the rule of *Enelow,* notwithstanding that the Federal Rules of Civil Procedure had fully merged law and equity in the interim. The relevant facts of *Ettelson* were identical to those of *Enelow*, and the Court responded to them in the same fashion. In response to the argument that the fusion of law and equity had destroyed the analogy between the stay ordered in the action and an injunction issued by a chancellor of a separate proceeding at law, the Court stated only that the plaintiffs were "in no different position than if a state equity court had restrained them from proceeding in the law action." * * * Thus, the order granting the stay was held to be immediately appealable as an injunction.

The historical analysis underlying the results in *Enelow* and *Ettelson* has bred a doctrine of curious contours. Under the *Enelow-Ettelson* rule, most recently restated in Baltimore Contractors, Inc. v. Bodinger, 348 U.S. 176, 75 S.Ct. 249, 99 L.Ed. 233 (1955), an order by a federal court staying or refusing to stay its own proceedings is appealable under § 1292(a)(1) as the grant or denial of an injunction if two conditions are met. First, the action in which the order is entered must be an action that, before the merger of law and equity, was by its nature an action at law. Second, the order must arise from or be based on some matter that would then have been considered an equitable defense or counterclaim. If both conditions are satisfied, the historical equivalent of the modern order would have been an injunction, issued by a separate equity court, to restrain proceedings in an action at law. If either condition is not met, however, the historical analogy fails. When the underlying suit is historically equitable and the stay is based on a defense or counterclaim that is historically legal, the analogy fails because a law judge had no power to issue an injunction restraining equitable proceedings. And when both the underlying suit and the defense or counterclaim on which the stay is based are historically equitable, or when both are historically legal, the analogy fails because when a chancellor or a law judge stayed an action in his own court, he was not issuing an injunction, but merely arranging matters on his docket. Thus, unless a stay order is made in a historically legal action on the basis of a historically equitable defense or counterclaim, the order cannot be analogized to a pre-merger injunction and therefore cannot be appealed under § 1292(a)(1) pursuant to the *Enelow-Ettelson* doctrine.

The parties in this case dispute whether the *Enelow-Ettelson* rule makes the District Court's decision to deny a stay immediately appealable under § 1292(a)(1). Both parties agree that an action for breach of contract was an action at law prior to the merger of law and equity. They vigorously contest, however, whether the stay of an action pending the resolution of similar proceedings in a state court is equitable in the requisite sense. * * *

We decline to address the issue of appealability in these terms; indeed, the sterility of the debate between the parties illustrates the need for a more fundamental consideration of the precedents in this area. This Court long has understood that the *Enelow-Ettelson* rule is deficient in utility and sense. In the two cases we have decided since *Ettelson* relating to the rule, we criticized its perpetuation of "outmoded procedural differentiations" and its consequent tendency to produce incongruous results. * * * We refrained then from overruling the *Enelow* and *Ettelson* decisions, but today we take that step. A half century's experience has persuaded us, as it has persuaded an impressive array of judges and commentators, that the rule is unsound in theory, unworkable and arbitrary in practice, and unnecessary to achieve any legitimate goals.

As an initial matter, the *Enelow-Ettelson* doctrine is, in the modern world of litigation, a total fiction. Even when the rule was announced, it was artificial. Although at that time law and equity remained two separate systems, they were administered by the same judges. When a single official was both chancellor and law judge, a stay of an action at law on equitable grounds required nothing more than an order issued by the official regulating the progress of the litigation before him, and the decision to call this order an injunction just because it would have been an injunction in a system with separate law and equity judges had little justification. With the merger of law and equity, which was accomplished by the Federal Rules of Civil Procedure, the practice of describing these stays as injunctions lost all connection with the reality of the federal courts' procedural system. As Judge Charles Clark, the principal draftsman of the Rules, wrote:

> "[W]e lack any rationale to explain the concept of a judge enjoining himself when he merely decides upon the method he will follow in trying the case. The metamorphosis of a law judge into a hostile chancellor on the other 'side' of the court could not have been overclear to the lay litigant under the divided procedure; but if now without even that fictitious sea change one judge in one form of action may split his judicial self at one instant into two mutually antagonistic parts, the litigant surely will think himself in Alice's Wonderland." Beaunit Mills, Inc. v. Eday Fabric Sales Corp., 124 F.2d 563, 565 (CA2 1942).

The *Enelow* rule had presupposed two different systems of justice administered by separate tribunals, even if these tribunals were no more than two "sides" to the same court; with the abandonment of that separation, the premise of the rule disappeared. The doctrine, and the distinctions it drew between equitable and legal actions and defenses, lost all moorings to the actual practice of the federal courts.

* * *

Most important, the *Enelow-Ettelson* doctrine is "divorced from any rational or coherent appeals policy." * * * Under the rule, appellate jurisdiction of orders granting or denying stays depends upon a set of considerations that in no way reflects or relates to the need for interlocutory review. There is no reason to think that appeal of a stay order is more suitable in cases in which the underlying action is at law and the stay is based on equitable grounds than in cases in which one of these conditions is not satisfied. The rule's focus on historical distinctions thus produces arbitrary and anomalous results. * * * Two orders may involve similar issues and produce similar consequences, and yet one will be appealable whereas the other will not.

For these reasons, the lower federal courts repeatedly have lambasted the *Enelow-Ettelson* doctrine. The rule has been called "a remnant from the jurisprudential attic," * * * "an anachronism wrapped up in an atavism," * * * and a "Byzantine peculiarit[y]" * * *. With the exception of the Federal Circuit, which apparently has not yet confronted an *Enelow-Ettelson* appeal, every Circuit is on record with criticism of the doctrine. One Circuit Judge has urged his court to reject the doctrine outright. * * * Although a majority of the panel declined to do so, it agreed that the *Enelow-Ettelson* rule was " 'artificial,' " " 'medieval,' " and " 'outmoded.' " * * * Another Circuit Judge, in a majority opinion, recently wrote an extensive and scholarly critique of the doctrine and concluded only with great reluctance that repudiating the doctrine would be improper. * * *

Commentators have been no less scathing in their evaluations of the *Enelow-Ettelson* rule. Professor Moore and his collaborators have noted the difficulty of applying archaic labels to modern actions and defenses and expressed the wish that "the Supreme Court will accept the first opportunity offered to decide that the reason for the *Enelow-Ettelson* rule having ceased, the rule is no more." * * * Professor Wright and his collaborators have gone further, arguing that the extensive experience that the courts of appeals have had in attempting to rationalize and apply the rule would justify them in rejecting it. * * *

The case against perpetuation of this sterile and antiquated doctrine seems to us conclusive. We therefore overturn the cases establishing the *Enelow-Ettelson* rule and hold that orders granting or denying stays of "legal" proceedings on "equitable" grounds are not automatically appealable under § 1292(a)(1). This holding will not prevent interlocutory review of district court orders when such review is truly needed. Section 1292(a)(1) will, of course, continue to provide appellate jurisdiction over orders that grant or deny injunctions and orders that have the practical effect of granting or denying injunctions and have " 'serious, perhaps irreparable, consequence.' " * * * As for orders that were appealable under § 1292(a)(1) solely by virtue of the *Enelow-Ettelson* doctrine, they may, in appropriate circumstances, be reviewed under the collateral-order doctrine of § 1291, see Moses H. Cone Memorial Hospital v. Mercury Construction Corp., 460 U.S. 1, 103 S.Ct. 927, 74 L.Ed.2d 765 (1983), and the permissive appeal provision of § 1292(b), as well as by application for writ of mandamus. Our holding today merely prevents interlocutory review of district court orders on the basis of historical circumstances that have no relevance to modern litigation. Because we repudiate the *Enelow-Ettelson* doctrine, we reject petitioner's claim that the District Court's order in this case is appealable under § 1292(a)(1) pursuant to that doctrine.

[The Court also rejected petitioner's contention that the Court of Appeals should have issued a writ of mandamus directing the District Court to grant the requested stay or dismissal of the federal-court action.]

* * * Accordingly, the judgment of the Court of Appeals is affirmed.

It is so ordered.

JUSTICE KENNEDY took no part in the consideration or decision of this case.

[A concurring opinion by JUSTICE SCALIA is omitted.]

Notes and Questions

1. Does Section 1292(a)(1) apply to an order denying a motion for summary judgment in an action in which a permanent injunction is sought? This question, which had plagued the courts of appeals for years, was resolved in SWITZERLAND CHEESE ASS'N, INC. v. E. HORNE'S MARKET, INC., 385 U.S. 23, 25, 87 S.Ct. 193, 195, 17 L.Ed.2d 23, 25 (1966):

* * * [T]he denial of a motion for summary judgment because of unresolved issues of fact does not settle or even tentatively decide anything about the merits of the claim. It is strictly a pre-trial order that decides only one thing—that the case should go to trial. Orders that in no way touch on the merits of the claim but only relate to pre-trial procedures are not in our view "interlocutory" within the meaning of § 1292(a)(1). We see no other way to protect the integrity of the congressional policy against piecemeal appeals.

2. In CARSON v. AMERICAN BRANDS, INC., 450 U.S. 79, 101 S.Ct. 993, 67 L.Ed.2d 59 (1981), petitioners brought a class action against the respondent employers, charging violations of Title VII of the Civil Rights Act of 1964 and seeking injunctive and declaratory relief and damages. The parties settled and together moved for entry of a proposed consent decree enjoining further discrimination and implementing an affirmative action plan for hiring and seniority preferences. The District Court denied the motion, holding that, since there was no showing of present or past discrimination, the proposed decree illegally granted racial preferences to the petitioner class and also illegally provided relief to all present and future black employees rather than only to the actual victims of the alleged discrimination. The Fourth Circuit dismissed the petitioners' appeal for want of jurisdiction, holding that the District Court's order was not appealable under Section 1292(a)(1). The

Supreme Court unanimously reversed, holding that the order, although not explicitly refusing an injunction, had the practical effect of doing so. The Court also found that the petitioners had satisfied the requirement that the order might have "serious, perhaps irreparable consequences" which could be "effectually challenged" only by immediate appeal. If the District Court order were allowed to stand, the petitioners might lose their opportunity to settle on the negotiated terms. Because consent decrees are the product of lengthy and detailed negotiations and are based upon the express or implied desire of the parties to avoid the costs and uncertainties of litigation, a district court's rejection of that agreement might force litigation when neither party wanted it and might have the serious, perhaps irreparable, consequence of denying the parties their right to compromise their dispute on mutually agreeable terms.

3. If an appeal is not taken from an interlocutory order that is made appealable by Section 1292(a)(1), are matters adjudged therein foreclosed on an appeal from the final judgment? See Victor Talking Mach. Co. v. George, 105 F.2d 697 (3d Cir.), certiorari denied 308 U.S. 611, 60 S.Ct. 176, 84 L.Ed. 511 (1939).

SECTION B.   THE TIME TO APPEAL

Read Federal Rule of Civil Procedure 58 and Rules 3, 4, and 5 of the Federal Rules of Appellate Procedure.

The time limit for appeal is treated as a matter of jurisdiction and cannot be altered by consent of the parties. See 16 Wright, Miller, Cooper & Gressman, *Federal Practice and Procedure: Jurisdiction and Related Matters* § 3949 (1977). It may be extended by the district court only, not by an appellate court, for 30 days upon a showing of "excusable neglect." The time limitation is triggered when the district court clerk enters a judgment conforming to the requirements of Fed.R.Civ.P. 58. The clerk is required to mail notice of entry of judgment to the parties but a party may elect to serve notice formally on his opponent. Fed.R.Civ.P. 77(d).

UNITED STATES v. F. & M. SCHAEFER BREWING CO.

Supreme Court of the United States, 1958.
356 U.S. 227, 78 S.Ct. 674, 2 L.Ed.2d 721.

Certiorari to the United States Court of Appeals for the Second Circuit.

MR. JUSTICE WHITTAKER delivered the opinion of the Court.

* * * Respondent sued the Government for $7,189.57, alleged to have been illegally assessed and collected from it as federal stamp taxes, and for interest thereon from the date of payment. After issue was joined, respondent moved for summary judgment. The district judge, after hearing the motion, filed an opinion on April 14, 1955 * * * in which, after finding that respondent had paid stamp taxes to the Government in the amount of $7,012.50 and interest in the amount of $177.07, but making no finding of the date or dates of payment, he referred to an earlier decision of the same legal question by his colleague * * * and concluded, saying: "I am in agreement with Judge Leibell's analysis and, accordingly, the plaintiff's motion is granted." Thereupon, the clerk made the following notation in the civil docket: "April 14, 1955. Rayfiel, J. Decision rendered on motion for summary judgment. Motion granted. See opinion on file."

Thereafter, on May 24, 1955, counsel for *respondent* presented to the judge, and the latter signed and filed, a formal document captioned "Judgment," which referred to the motion and the hearing of it and to the "opinion" of April 14, and then,

> Ordered, adjudged and decreed that the plaintiff, The F. & M. Schaefer Brewing Co., recover of the defendant, United States of America, the sum of $7189.57 and interest thereon from February 19, 1954 in the amount of $542.80, together with costs as taxed by the Clerk of the Court in the sum of $37, aggregating the sum of $7769.37, and that plaintiff have judgment against defendant therefor.

On the same day the clerk stamped the document "Judgment Rendered: Dated: May 24th, 1955," and made the following notation in the civil docket:

> May 24, 1955. Rayfiel, J. Judgment filed and docketed against defendant in the sum of $7,189.57 with interest of $542.80 together with costs $37 amounting in all to $7,769.37. Bill of Costs attached to judgment.

On July 21, 1955, the Government filed its notice of appeal from the order "entered in this action on May 25th, 1955 * * *." Thereafter, respondent moved to dismiss the appeal upon the ground that the opinion of April 14 constituted the "judgment," that the clerk's entry of that date constituted "entry of the judgment," and that the appeal was not taken within 60 days from the "entry of the judgment," as required by [former Civil] Rule 73(a). The Court of Appeals, holding that the opinion of April 14 was a "decisive and complete act of adjudication," and that the notation made by the clerk in the civil docket on that date constituted "entry of the judgment" within the meaning of Rule 58 and adequately disclosed the "substance" of the judgment as required by Rule 79(a), sustained the motion and dismissed the appeal as untimely. * * *

At the outset the Government contends that practical considerations—namely, certainty as to what judicial pronouncements are intended to be final judgments in order to avoid both premature and untimely appeals, to render certain the date of judgment liens, and to enable the procurement of writs of execution, transcripts and certified copies of judgments—require that a judgment be contained in a separate document so labeled, and urges us so to hold. Whatever may be the practical needs in these respects, the answer is that no present statute or rule so requires, as the Government concedes, and the decisional law seems settled that "[n]o form of words * * * is necessary to evince [the] rendition [of a judgment]." United States v. Hark, 320 U.S. 531, 534, 64 S.Ct. 359, 361, 88 L.Ed. 290. * * *

While an opinion may embody a *final decision,* the question whether it does so depends upon whether the judge has or has not clearly declared his intention in this respect in his opinion. Therefore, when, as here, the action is for money only * * * it is necessary to determine whether the language of the opinion embodies the essential elements of a judgment for money and clearly evidences the judge's intention that it shall be his final act in the case. If it does so, it constitutes his final judgment and, under Rule 58, it "directs that a party recover [a sum of] money," and, "upon receipt by [the clerk] of the [opinion]," requires him to "enter judgment forthwith" against the party found liable for the amount awarded, which is to be done by making a brief "notation of [the] judgment in the civil docket [showing the substance of the judgment of the court] as provided by Rule 79(a)." When all of these elements clearly appear final judgment has been both pronounced and entered, and the time to appeal starts to run * * *. And as correctly held by the Court of Appeals, the later filing and entry of a more formal judgment could not constitute a second final judgment in the case nor extend the time to appeal. * * *

But, on the other hand, if the opinion leaves doubtful whether the judge intended it to be his final act in the case—and, in an action for money, failure to determine either expressly or by reference the amount to be awarded is strong evidence of such lack of intention—one cannot say that it "directs that a party recover [a sum of] money"; * * * nor can one say that the clerk's "notation * * * in the civil docket"—if it sets forth no more substance than is contained or directed in the opinion, and being only a ministerial act * * * it may do no more—"show[s] * * * the substance of [a] judgment" of the court * * *.

But respondent argues, as the Court of Appeals held, that the opinion stated the amount of money illegally collected from respondent and, therefore, adequately determined the amount awarded, and that inasmuch as the clerk's entry incorporated the opinion by reference, it, too, adequately stated the amount of the judgment. This contention might well be accepted were it not for the fact that the action also sought recovery of interest on the amount paid by respondent from the date of payment to the date of judgment, and for the fact that the opinion does not state the date or dates of payment and, hence, did not state facts necessary to compute the amount of interest to be included in the judgment. * * * In an effort to counter the effect of these omissions, respondent states that a search of the record, which it urges we should make, would show that the Government's answer admitted the date of payment, and thus would furnish the information necessary to compute the amount of interest to be included in the judgment. * * * This argument cannot be accepted under the facts here for the reason that Rule 79(a) expressly requires that the clerk's entry "shall show * * * the substance of [the] judgment of the court * * *." Surely the amount of a judgment for money is a vital part of its substance. To hold that one must search the whole record to determine the amount, or the facts necessary to compute the amount, of a final judgment for money would be to ignore the quoted provision of Rule 79(a).

The actions of all concerned—of the judge in not stating in his opinion the amount, or means for determining the amount, of the judgment; of the clerk in not stating the amount of the judgment in his notation on the civil docket; of counsel for the Government in not appealing from the "opinion"; of counsel for respondent in preparing and presenting to the judge a formal "judgment" on May 24; and, finally, of the judge himself in signing and filing the formal "judgment" on the latter date—clearly show that none of them understood the opinion to be the judge's final act or to constitute his final judgment in the case.   *   *   *

Reversed.

[The dissenting opinions of JUSTICE FRANKFURTER and JUSTICE HARLAN omitted.]

Notes and Questions

1. Read the Advisory Committee's 1963 Note to Rule 58 in the Supplement. Do the changes made in 1963 substantially ameliorate the problem presented by *Schaefer?* In FOILES v. UNITED STATES, 465 F.2d 163, 168 (7th Cir.1972), the Court of Appeals held that "when the jury verdict is clear and unequivocal, setting forth a general verdict with reference to the sole question of liability and where nothing remains to be decided and when no opinion or memorandum is written, as is the situation described in clause (1) of Rule 58, there is no requirement for a separate document to start the time limits for appeal running." The Supreme Court reversed sub nom. United States v. Indrelunas, 411 U.S. 216, 93 S.Ct. 1562, 36 L.Ed.2d 202 (1973). Should the trial judge be required to direct the entry of a judgment expressly? What changes in Rule 58 short of that might be made?

2. In RICHERSON v. JONES, 551 F.2d 918 (3d Cir.1977), plaintiff brought suit alleging employment discrimination based on race. He sought retroactive promotion, back pay, interest, and attorneys' fees. After the case was heard, the trial court, on December 18, 1975, issued an order incorporating its findings of fact and conclusions of law and simply stating, "judgment is entered for plaintiff and against defendant." On March 12, 1976, the court issued a second order awarding plaintiff retroactive promotion, back pay, and interest. In a third order, issued April 29, 1976, the court granted plaintiff his counsel fees and expenses of litigation. Under Rule 58, which of the orders was the final judgment from which an appeal could properly be taken?

The appeals court held that the April 29 order was the final order since it was the one that disposed of the last of the relief demanded by plaintiff in his complaint. The court went on to hold that defendant's "premature" appeal of the March 12 order would be considered as an appeal from the April 29 order in the absence of any prejudice to plaintiff. Compare STATE FARM MUT. AUTO. INS. CO. v. PALMER, 350 U.S. 944, 76 S.Ct. 321, 100 L.Ed. 823 (1956), reversing 225 F.2d 876 (9th Cir.1955). See also Comment, *Ad Hoc Relief for Untimely Appeals,* 65 Colum.L.Rev. 97 (1965). Review Thompson v. Immigration & Naturalization Serv., p. 1019, supra.

3. Consider how the Federal Rules of Civil Procedure and the Federal Rules of Appellate Procedure function together. Federal Rule of Civil Procedure 59(e) concerns motions to alter or amend the judgment, and specifies a ten-day period. It is invoked only to support reconsideration of matters properly encompassed in a decision on the merits. Federal Rule of Appellate Procedure 4(a)(4) provides that if any party files a timely motion under Rule 59, the time for an appeal shall run from the entry of the order granting or denying such a motion. The rule specifically states that a notice of appeal filed before the disposition of such a motion shall have no effect but a new notice of appeal must be filed within the prescribed time.

In BUCKANAN v. STANSHIPS, INC., 485 U.S. 265, 108 S.Ct. 1130, 99 L.Ed.2d 289 (1988), the District Court entered judgment in favor of Stanships on the merits but did not mention costs. Buckanan filed an appeal. Stanships then filed an application for costs, described as a motion to alter or amend the judgment, which was granted by the District Court. Buckanan did not file a second notice of appeal. Stanships moved to dismiss for failure to file a timely notice of appeal. The Supreme Court, in a per curiam decision, held that the postjudgment motion for costs did not imply a change in the judgment but merely sought what was due because of the judgment:

> * * * Assessment of such costs does not involve reconsideration of any aspect of the decision on the merits. Under Rule 54(d), the "prevailing party" automatically is entitled to costs "unless the court otherwise directs." * * * [A] district judge need not take up the issue at all unless the losing party makes a timely motion for judicial review.
> * * *
> * * * [A] motion for costs filed pursuant to Rule 54(d) does not seek to "alter or amend the judgment" within the meaning of Rule 59(e). Instead, such a request for costs raises issues wholly collateral to the judgment in the main cause of action, issues to which Rule 59(e) was not intended to apply. * * * Because respondents' motion, properly viewed, was a Rule 54(d) motion for costs rather than a Rule 59 motion to alter or amend a judgment, petitioners' notice of appeal was timely under the Federal Rules of Appellate Procedure.

Id. at ___, 108 S.Ct. at 1131–32, 99 L.Ed.2d at 294.

4. Jurisdictional questions often arise when a party fails to comply specifically with statutory requirements for appeal. CHATHAS v. SMITH, 848 F.2d 93 (7th Cir.1988), involved a motion by Chathas in a civil rights case to amend a notice of appeal to include the name of one defendant who was unintentionally omitted. Rule 3(c) of the Federal Rules of Appellate Procedure prescribes the contents of the notice of appeal and requires the notice to specify the appellant, the judgment appealed from and the court to which the appeal is taken. The rule does not require the appellant to list the appellees. The court noted that the purpose of the rule is to provide notice to the opposing party that an appeal has been taken and to facilitate a determination whether the appeal was timely. Judge Posner found that:

> The notice of appeal notifies the opposite party that the judgment in his favor is being appealed. Ordinarily it does this just by naming the judgment, but where it names all but one of the defendants the omitted defendant may reasonably believe that he is off the hook and need not hire a lawyer to defend the appeal. * * * This is not such a case, since

all the defendants are represented by the same counsel at no expense to themselves * * *. * * * The omission of [the party's] name from the notice of appeal was thus a harmless error.

* * * [T]he only reason that occurs to us for a motion to amend a notice of appeal is, by dispelling confusion in the appellees' minds * * *, to forestall their arguing that they were misled. If this function could be performed only by such a motion, no doubt we could find jurisdiction under the All-Writs Act, 28 U.S.C. § 1651, to amend what is functionally a part of the appellate process though it is formally a filing in the district court. * * * But the doubt-dispelling function can be performed by a letter to the appellees' counsel. * * *

Id. at 94. Isn't the court, in effect, ordering the relief the appellant requested? If so, why deny the motion?

In TORRES v. OAKLAND SCAVENGER CO., ___ U.S. ___, 108 S.Ct. 2405, 101 L.Ed.2d 285 (1988), the Supreme Court resolved the jurisdictional issue implicated when Federal Rule of Appellate Procedure 3(c) is not followed specifically. Torres was one of sixteen plaintiffs who intervened in an employment discrimination suit against Oakland Scavenger. The intervenors claimed to act in their own behalf and on behalf of all persons similarly situated. The District Court dismissed the complaint for failure to state a cause of action. A notice of appeal was filed, but the notice and the order of the Court of Appeals omitted Torres' name. Oakland Scavenger moved for partial summary judgment on the ground that the prior judgment of dismissal was final as to Torres by virtue of his failure to appeal. The District Court granted the motion and the Court of Appeals affirmed on the ground that if the party is not named, the appellate court lacks jurisdiction over him. Rule 4 prescribes the time limits for filing a notice of appeal. The Supreme Court, resolving a split in the circuits, affirmed:

* * * Permitting courts to exercise jurisdiction over unnamed parties after the time for filing a notice of appeal has passed is equivalent to permitting courts to extend the time for filing a notice of appeal. * * * [T]he Advisory Committee Note following Rule 3 * * * makes no distinction among the various requirements of Rule 3 and Rule 4; rather it treats the requirements of the two rules as a single jurisdictional threshold. * * * [But] if a litigant files papers in a fashion that is technically at variance with the letter of a procedural rule, a court may nonetheless find that the litigant has complied with the rule if the litigant's action is the functional equivalent of what the rule requires. * * * Applying these principles to the instant case, we find that petitioner failed to comply with the specificity requirement of Rule 3(c), even liberally construed. Petitioner did not file the functional equivalent of a notice of appeal; he was never named or otherwise designated * * * in the notice of appeal * * *. Nor did petitioner seek leave to amend the notice of appeal within the time limits set by Rule 4. * * * Permitting [the use of et al. to signify other appellants] would leave the appellee and the court unable to determine with certitude whether a losing party not named in the notice of appeal should be bound by an adverse judgment * * *. The specificity requirement of Rule 3(c) is met

only by some designation that gives fair notice of the specific individual or entity seeking to appeal.

Id. at ___, 108 S.Ct. at 2408–09, 101 L.Ed.2d at 290–92.

5.   The timely filing of certain motions tolls the time clock for an appeal. If a party files a timely motion in a district court for a judgment notwithstanding the verdict under Rule 50(b), to amend or make additional findings under Rule 52(b), to alter or amend the judgment under Rule 59, or for a new trial under Rule 59, any notice of appeal filed before the disposition of any of the above motions will not be given effect.   A new notice of appeal must be filed after the motion is decided.   Fed.Rule App.P. 4(a)(4).   See also Griggs v. Provident Consumer Discount Co., 459 U.S. 56, 103 S.Ct. 400, 74 L.Ed.2d 225 (1982).

6.   In some states separate appeals lie from the judgment and an order denying a motion for new trial.   See, e.g., Minn.R.Civ.App.Proc. 103.03, which is in the Supplement following 28 U.S.C. § 1292.   The time for each appeal typically is different, and each raises certain issues not raised by the other. See Note, *Scope of Review in Minnesota and its Dependence upon the Form of Appeal Taken,* 41 Minn.L.Rev. 110 (1956).   Under provisions of this type, an appeal from either the judgment or the order cannot be treated as an appeal from the other.

SECTION C.   THE AMBIT OF REVIEW

1.   ISSUES SUBJECT TO REVIEW

There are a number of well-defined limits on the scope of appellate review.   First, the alleged errors must appear in the trial-court record. Thus it is vital during the course of pretrial preparation as well as during trial itself that an attorney make certain that all rulings and events that might form the basis for an appeal be formally recorded.   Second, an aggrieved party must have promptly objected to the trial court regarding rulings or events that the judge could have corrected or ameliorated. Normally an error is waived unless objection was taken.   Third, even if the issue that the appellant seeks to have reviewed has been presented properly below and has not been waived, it must not constitute "harmless error"—that is, it must have affected substantial rights.   Finally, an alleged error must be presented to the appellate court in appellant's brief and the relevant portions of the trial-court record must be brought to the appellate court's attention.

J.F. WHITE CONTRACTING CO. v. NEW ENGLAND TANK INDUSTRIES OF NEW HAMPSHIRE, INC.

United States Court of Appeals, First Circuit, 1968.
393 F.2d 449.

COFFIN, CIRCUIT JUDGE.   This appeal concerns a contract to build oil tanker dock facilities on the Piscataqua river.   Appellant, J.F. White Contracting Co. (White) agreed to build the dock, consisting of four cylindrical metal cells filled with sand and gravel, connected with each other and with the shore by catwalks. Appellee, New England Tank Industries of New Hampshire, Inc. (Tank), owner of the premises, sues for defective workmanship. Unlike the Piscataqua itself, the case meandered interminably for five years before a jury trial was finally reached. From an adverse verdict in the amount of $20,000 White takes this appeal.

* * *

Appellant * * * [contends] that recovery is barred by a contract provision which stipulated that approval of invoices by Tank's engineer was "final, conclusive, and binding on both parties". Without saying what effect we would give to such a provision under the factual circumstances of this case, we merely observe that we cannot consider this issue on appeal since appellant neither pleaded it as an affirmative defense nor had it "raised, considered nor passed upon in the district court." * * *

* * * White argues alternatively that it was error to have allowed the question of one of the cells being "out of round" to go to the jury. This cell had been struck in the process of installation by a ship and knocked "out of round". White undertook to repair it. This damage, being above the waterline, was visible and much less hidden or latent than the underwater ruptures.

Even if the fact that the dented cell was located some four hundred feet from shore constituted enough evidence of latency for the jury, and even if Tank had received something less than the cylindrical cell it had bargained for, there was no evidence of the extent to which it was damaged. There was no evidence that the utility or longevity of the cell was affected, nor does there seem to have been sufficient evidence regarding the cost of repairing the dent. The underwater inspection report of the diver Howard B. Pratt did mention that cell 3 was "noticeably out of round" and his original estimate of repairs to cell 3 "as per our drawing" was $43,150. This figure might conceivably be considered some evidence of the cost to repair the dented cell. Without more, however, it would seem to be an insufficient basis for the jury to make any rational determination.

While the court's action in submitting the "out-of-roundness" issue to the jury was error, we are not persuaded that there was even a remote possibility that this error affected the verdict or "the substantial rights of the parties". Fed.R.Civ.P. 61 * * *. Nor does appellant assert that it did. Briefs of both sides argue the adequacy of damages issue by reference solely to testimony of cost of repairs and value addressed to the ruptures. Counsel for Tank did not argue the issue at all to the jury while counsel for White made it clear that it ought not be considered. Finally, the court's instructions on damages were proper and emphasized that only evidence of value, which included evidence of cost of repairs, could be considered. There is no reason to suspect that the jury did not follow these instructions.

* * *

Affirmed.

Notes and Questions

1. What justification is there for a rule that a party may not raise an issue on appeal that was not raised in the trial court? Is it fair to penalize the party for what is likely a lawyer's error? Note that under Rule 60(b) a party may ask a district court to reopen a judgment on the basis of newly discovered facts.

2. What underlies a rule that an error, if "harmless," will not provide a basis for reversal? Is it possible for an appellate court to determine what would have affected a jury's determination? Does this rule give the appellate court broad latitude to disregard error below? Or does the rule make it possible for an appellate court to instruct lower courts without needlessly incurring the systemic costs of a new trial?

———

Even when the issues have been preserved properly in the trial court and presented to the appellate court for review, there is another limit on the scope of appellate review that must be considered—whether, and in what circumstances, an appellate court may entertain an appeal by the party who, at least ostensibly, won below.

ELECTRICAL FITTINGS CORP. v. THOMAS & BETTS CO.

Supreme Court of the United States, 1939.
307 U.S. 241, 59 S.Ct. 860, 83 L.Ed. 1263.

Certiorari to United States Circuit Court of Appeals for the Second Circuit.

MR. JUSTICE ROBERTS delivered the opinion of the Court.

This was a suit in equity by the respondents for alleged infringement of a patent. The District Court held claim 1 valid but not infringed and claim 2 invalid. Instead of dismissing the bill without more, it entered a decree adjudging claim 1 valid but dismissing the bill for failure to prove infringement.

The respondents did not appeal, but filed in the Patent Office a disclaimer of claim 2. The petitioners appealed to the Circuit Court of Appeals from so much of the decree as adjudicated claim 1 valid. The appeal was dismissed on the ground that the petitioners had been awarded all the relief to which they were entitled, the litigation having finally terminated in their favor. The court was of opinion that the decree would not bind the petitioners in subsequent suits on the issue of the validity of claim 1.

* * * A party may not appeal from a judgment or decree in his favor, for the purpose of obtaining a review of findings he deems erroneous which are not necessary to support the decree. But here the decree itself purports to adjudge the validity of claim 1, and though the adjudication was immaterial to the disposition of the cause, it stands as an adjudication of one of the issues litigated. We think the petitioners were entitled to have this portion of the decree eliminated, and that the Circuit

Court of Appeals had jurisdiction * * * to entertain the appeal, not for the purpose of passing on the merits, but to direct the reformation of the decree.

* * *

Reversed and remanded.

Notes and Questions

1. NEW YORK TEL. CO. v. MALTBIE, 291 U.S. 645, 54 S.Ct. 443, 78 L.Ed. 1041, 1042 (1934) (per curiam):

> The District Court * * * permanently enjoined, as confiscatory, the enforcement of the rate orders which are the subject of this suit. The injunction is unqualified. Appellant, having obtained this relief, is not entitled to prosecute an appeal from the decree in its favor, for the purpose of reviewing the portions of the decree fixing the value of appellant's property as of the years 1924, 1926, and 1928, and the rate of return to be allowed. The matters set forth in these portions of the decree are not to be regarded as res judicata in relation to subsequent legislative action by the Public Service Commission in fixing rates for the future or in any judicial proceeding relating to such rates.

2. Would the decree in *Electrical Fittings* have been res judicata of the validity of claim 1 of the patent? Why else might petitioners in that case have been concerned about the decree? The Declaratory Judgment Act, 28 U.S.C. §§ 2201–02, was not in force at the time of the *Electrical Fittings* decision. Had it been, might it have been possible to treat the District Court's decree as a declaratory judgment with respect to claim 1 and consider it as having been entered under the authority of Rule 54(c)?

3. In PARTMAR CORP. v. PARAMOUNT PICTURES THEATRES CORP., 347 U.S. 89, 74 S.Ct. 414, 98 L.Ed. 532 (1954), plaintiff leased its theater to, and entered into a franchise agreement with, defendant; the lease was to be terminable at plaintiff's option if the franchise agreement were terminated. Plaintiff sued to regain possession of the theater, alleging that it was entitled to terminate the lease because the franchise agreement was invalid under the antitrust laws; defendant counterclaimed for damages under the antitrust laws. The trial court denied plaintiff's claim, holding that the franchise agreement was not invalid because no conspiracy in violation of the antitrust laws had been established; it also dismissed the counterclaims. Defendant appealed from the dismissal of its counterclaims, and the Supreme Court held that the trial court's finding of no conspiracy on plaintiff's claim operated as collateral estoppel on the issue. See Note 4, p. 1177, infra. Could defendant have appealed from the judgment in its favor on plaintiff's claim? The majority, citing *New York Tel. Co.* and *Electrical Fittings,* held that it could.

> * * * The finding and conclusion of law * * * were essential to the determination of Paramount's claim for possession of the theatre. Paramount's position * * * was that the agreements were invalid under the federal antitrust statutes as the product of an illegal conspiracy. It is only when a finding of law or fact is not necessary for a decree that the prevailing party may not appeal and the finding does not form the basis for collateral estoppel. * * *

Id. at 99 n. 6, 74 S.Ct. at 420 n. 6, 98 L.Ed. at 541 n. 6. Chief Justice Warren, dissenting, argued:

> * * * Petitioner, as the successful party in the eviction suit, could not appeal the District Court's finding that there was no evidence of conspiracy. * * * The adverse finding was not included in the Court's decree, as in *Electrical Fittings Corp.* * * *

> * * * The Court's opinion cites no case, in this Court or any other, holding that a successful party can appeal findings which are not inserted as part of the decree. Indeed, the opinion overlooks the very holdings of this Court on which it relies for support. * * *

Id. at 109 n. 8, 74 S.Ct. at 425 n. 8, 98 L.Ed. at 546 n. 8.

STANDARD ACCIDENT INS. CO. v. ROBERTS
United States Circuit Court of Appeals, Eighth Circuit, 1942.
132 F.2d 794.

STONE, CIRCUIT JUDGE. The Standard Accident Insurance Company issued its liability policy to Herbert Roberts. Thereafter, personal injury judgments were secured against Roberts by Clyde, Pearl, George Willie and Forest Wayne Primm. Thereafter, the Standard filed this action against Roberts and the Primms to obtain a declaratory judgment that it was not liable to them on the above policy. The trial court found that the cause of the injuries to the Primms was not within the coverage of the policy but determined that the Standard, "with full knowledge of the date, place and circumstances of the injuries" had assumed and retained control of the investigation and defense of the damage suit under such circumstances that it was estopped from denying liability thereon to the detriment and prejudice of Roberts. This is an appeal by the Standard from the judgment dismissing its petition.

Appellant presents three points: (1) that there was no liability under the policy and liability cannot be extended by estoppel; (2) that no estoppel was proven; (3) that insured was not prejudiced by the acts and conduct of Standard.

Appellees contest the above points and, in addition, urge: (1) that the policy should have been reformed to express the intention of the parties thereto; (2) that the court should have allowed reasonable attorney fees and the statutory penalty; (3) that the policy covered the accident causing the injuries to the Primms. Appellant urges that none of these three additional matters presented by appellees is open here because appellees took no cross-appeal. In this situation as to contentions of the parties, it is necessary to determine just what contentions are examinable here.

Since appellees' contentions as to reformation of the policy and as to allowance of attorney fees and penalty seek to change or to add to the relief accorded by the judgment which was in their favor, they can raise here such issues only by a cross-appeal. * * * On the other hand, the contention that the policy covered the accident seeks only to sustain the judgment for a reason presented at the trial and determined adversely to appellees. The recovery is upon the policy; and it is no more than a change of reason for such recovery, whether it be under the terms of the policy or because of an estoppel to question the applicability of the terms. In such situations the rule is that "a respondent or an appellee may urge any matter appearing in the record in support of a judgment". Le Tulle v. Scofield, 308 U.S. 415, 421, 60 S.Ct. 313, 316, 84 L.Ed. 355. * * * Therefore, appellees may, in support of the decree, urge here this ground that the policy covers the accident.

* * *

Notes and Questions

1. Read Federal Rule of Appellate Procedure 4(a)(3) in the Supplement. Why is a party permitted to file a notice of appeal within 14 days after another party has noticed an appeal?

2. Plaintiff's decedent was hired by a contractor to work on defendant railroad's roadbed. Plaintiff brought an action for decedent's death against the railroad in a state court, relying on the Federal Employers' Liability Act and on common-law negligence; the railroad brought a third-party claim against the contractor for indemnity. The trial court held that FELA was not applicable because decedent was not a servant of the railroad and also that the contractor was not liable to the railroad; it submitted the case against the railroad to the jury on common-law negligence, and the jury found for the railroad on the ground of contributory negligence, which is not a defense in an FELA action. Plaintiff appealed, posting an appeal bond in favor of both the railroad and the contractor, but the railroad did not perfect an appeal against the contractor. The Texas Court of Civil Appeals affirmed the judgment, but the United States Supreme Court reversed, holding the FELA applicable. On remand, the Texas Court of Civil Appeals, in BAKER v. TEXAS & P. RY. CO., 326 S.W.2d 639, 640 (1959), held that because the "liability vel non of [the contractor] on the Railroad's cross-action centers upon the facts, which will be rehashed even in greater detail than before * * * the situation, in our opinion, justif[ies] a reversal of cause in its entirety." Compare Whitehead v. American Sec. & Trust Co., 285 F.2d 282 (D.C.Cir.1960).

3. What is the effect of a reversal upon a party who took no part in an appeal at all? See In re Barnett, 124 F.2d 1005 (2d Cir.1942).

4. Consider California's exception to the general standard of review. In WARD v. TAGGART, 51 Cal.2d 736, 336 P.2d 534 (1959), plaintiff arranged to buy a parcel of real property through defendant Taggart, who falsely had represented himself to be the exclusive real estate agent for the property. Plaintiff brought a tort action for fraud, and was awarded compensatory damages and exemplary damages.

On appeal, the California Supreme Court agreed with defendant's contention that there can be no recovery in fraud absent "out-of-pocket" loss. Here, plaintiff had suffered no loss. However, the court permitted plaintiff to recover on a theory of quasi-contract:

> Although this theory of recovery was not advanced by plaintiffs in the trial court, it is settled that a change in theory is permitted on appeal when "a question of law only is presented on the facts appearing in the record * * *." Panopulos v. Maderis, 47 Cal.2d 337, 341, 303 P.2d 738, 741 * * *. The general rule confining the parties upon appeal to the theory advanced below is based on the rationale that the opposing party

should not be required to defend for the first time on appeal against a new theory that "contemplates a factual situation the consequences of which are open to controversy and were not put in issue or presented at the trial." * * * Such is not the case here. Although the facts pleaded and proved by plaintiffs do not sustain the judgment on the theory of tort, they are sufficient to uphold recovery under the quasi-contractual theory of unjust enrichment since that theory does not contemplate any factual situation different from that established by the evidence in the trial court. Defendants were given ample opportunity to present their version of the transaction involved, and the issue of whether or not their actions constituted fraud was decided adversely to them by the trial court.

Id. at 742, 336 P.2d at 537–38.

If the Supreme Court of California had not found a quasi-contractual remedy available, and plaintiffs had shown evidence, not offered at trial, of facts, not raised at trial, supporting the existence of a fiduciary relationship between Taggart and himself, what result should have been reached by the court? Read Cal.Code Civ.Proc. § 909 in the Supplement. "Probably the most significant practical characteristic of this California exception is its sparing use, especially in situations where the additional evidence aims at reversal of the judgment instead of affirmance." Louisell & Degnan, *Rehearing in American Appellate Courts,* 44 Calif.L.Rev. 627, 629 n. 8 (1956).

5. Plaintiff brought an action for payments due on a subscription for two burial crypts. At the close of plaintiff's case, defendant moved for judgment on the ground that plaintiff had not shown that the mausoleum was constructed in accordance with the plans and specifications; the trial court denied plaintiff permission to reopen the case to supply the missing proof, and granted defendant's motion. On appeal, the Supreme Court of Arizona found that the refusal to permit plaintiff to reopen had been an abuse of discretion. At that point, should defendant have been permitted to raise for the first time plaintiff's failure to allege and prove that he was a licensed real-estate broker as required by law? See Bowman v. Hall, 83 Ariz. 56, 316 P.2d 484 (1957). See generally Millar, *New Allegation and Proof on Appeal in Anglo-American Civil Procedure,* 47 Nw.U.L.Rev. 427 (1952); Pound, *New Evidence in the Appellate Court,* 56 Harv.L.Rev. 1313 (1943).

2. SCOPE OF REVIEW OF FACTS

CORCORAN v. CITY OF CHICAGO

Supreme Court of Illinois, 1940.
373 Ill. 567, 27 N.E.2d 451.

MURPHY, JUSTICE. John F. Corcoran * * * began a suit * * * against the city of Chicago * * * to recover damages for personal injuries alleged to have been caused by the negligent acts of the defendant. The cause was tried with a jury and resulted in a verdict for the plaintiff for $5,000. A motion for new trial was overruled and judgment entered on the verdict. On appeal, the Appellate Court for the First District reversed the judgment and remanded the cause for another trial. The plaintiff filed a motion in the Appellate Court asking that the remanding part of the order be stricken. * * * The motion was granted * * *.

The negligence charged was that defendant had carelessly and negligently permitted certain streets to be and remain in an unsafe condition for travel * * *. The evidence was conflicting. The Appellate Court found the verdict was against the manifest weight of the evidence and reversed the judgment for that reason.

It is conceded the power which the Appellate Court assumed to exercise in reviewing the evidence and setting aside the verdict is found in section 92(3b) of the Civil Practice Act * * * which provides that Appellate Courts may review "error of fact, in that the judgment, decree or order appealed from is not sustained by the evidence or is against the weight of the evidence." Plaintiff's position is that such provision, as applied to facts found by a jury upon conflicting evidence, as in the instant case, is unconstitutional, in that the findings of the Appellate Court * * * take from him the right to a trial by jury as guaranteed by section 5 of article 2 of the Constitution * * *.

* * *

Prior to 1837, the law of this state was that the granting or refusal of a motion for a new trial rested in the sound discretion of the trial court and the ruling thereon could not be urged as error in the court of review. * * * In 1837, an act was passed which provided "exceptions taken to opinions or decisions of circuit court overruling motions in arrest of judgment, motions for new trials and for continuance of causes shall hereafter be allowed and the party excepting may assign for error any opinion so excepted to, any usage to the contrary notwithstanding." The substance of the act * * * has been the statutory law of this state since 1837.

* * *

The effect of the operation of the statute was considered in Chicago & Rock Island Railroad Co. v. McKean, 40 Ill. 218, a case where the trial court had overruled a motion for new trial and error was assigned on such ruling. Mr. Justice Breese, speaking for the court, said: "An appellate court was, before the passage of that act, judge of the law only * * *. The old and honored maxim once was, 'the judges respond to the law, the jury to the facts,' but now, by this innovation, the judges of an appellate court have as much power over the facts as the jury had in the first instance, for it is undeniable this court may set aside a verdict if the facts fail to satisfy it of its propriety. * * *"

Plaintiff contends that on all questions of fact where the evidence is conflicting the verdict of the jury can not be set aside as being against the weight of the evidence except by the court that tried the case, and asserts that such was the practice at common law. * * *

* * *

From the authorities cited and others which have been examined, we conclude that there was a practice at common law which authorized courts exercising appellate jurisdiction to set aside verdicts on the grounds the findings of fact were not supported by the evidence. * * *

Judgment affirmed.

Notes and Questions

1. In 1957, Professor Charles Alan Wright stated "that, so far as I can find, there is not a single case in which a federal appellate court has ever reversed and ordered a new trial on the ground that the trial court did abuse its discretion in denying a motion [for a new trial on the weight of the evidence] * * *." Wright, *The Doubtful Omniscience of Appellate Courts,* 41 Minn.L.Rev. 751, 760 (1957). At the time he was criticizing a dictum of the Court of Appeals for the District of Columbia Circuit claiming the existence of the power to reverse; but, he observed, "today's dictum claiming extended power for appellate courts is frequently the prelude to tomorrow's holding to that effect." Id. at 763.

Subsequently at least one court of appeals has acted as he prophesied. Georgia-Pac. Corp. v. United States, 264 F.2d 161 (5th Cir.1959). Is there a significant difference between an appellate court's reversing a trial court's order denying a new trial and an appellate court's ordering a new trial because the trial court has erroneously denied a motion for a directed verdict as in Slocum v. New York Life Ins. Co., p. 983, supra? Is there really a difference between reversing an order denying a new trial and reversing an order granting a new trial?

2. The power to reverse denials of new trials on the ground that the verdict is excessive or to condition affirmance upon a remittitur is now asserted by most of the courts of appeals, after "seemingly endless controversy," and in spite of the extremely strong doubts thrown on the subject by Justice Brandeis' opinion in FAIRMOUNT GLASS WORKS v. CUB FORK COAL CO., 287 U.S. 474, 53 S.Ct. 252, 77 L.Ed. 439 (1933). See also the exhaustive opinion of Judge Medina in Dagnello v. Long Island R. Co., 289 F.2d 797 (2d Cir.1961). Why should this power be more commonly found than the power discussed in Note 1?

ORVIS v. HIGGINS
United States Court of Appeals, Second Circuit, 1950.
180 F.2d 537.
Certiorari denied 340 U.S. 810, 71 S.Ct. 37, 95 L.Ed. 595.

FRANK, CIRCUIT JUDGE. [This was an action for refund of federal estate taxes. Deceased husband and his wife each had set up a trust in 1934 in which the other received a life interest. If these trusts were set up independently, the husband's estate was not chargeable with any estate tax on the property that was in the trust created by the wife. If the trusts were set up by mutual agreement, however, each trust being in consideration of the other, then the trust set up by the wife would be treated as a trust set up by the husband, and since the deceased received a life income from the trust, the value of that trust would be taxable to the estate. The trial judge had found that the trusts were set up independently.]

In opinions holding that the findings of trial judges were not "clearly erroneous" within the meaning of Rule 52(a), * * * we have often stressed the importance of a trial judge's advantage over us when he saw and heard the witnesses as they testified. We have pointed out our inability to appraise the cogency of demeanor evidence, lost to us because it cannot be captured in the witness' words as recorded on paper. In so holding, we may perhaps, at times, have overlooked distinctions described in United States v. United States Gypsum Co., 333 U.S. 364, 394–396, 68 S.Ct. 525, 542, 92 L.Ed. 746.

There the Court made it clear that Rule 52(a) merely adopted the equity practice then prevailing in the federal courts. The Court said a finding of a trial court, if it be by a judge, "is 'clearly erroneous' when although there is evidence to support it, the reviewing court on the entire evidence is left with the definite and firm conviction that a mistake has been committed." * * *

In the light of the Gypsum case, we may make approximate gradations as follows: We must sustain a general or a special jury verdict when there is some evidence which the jury might have believed, and when a reasonable inference from that evidence will support the verdict, regardless of whether that evidence is oral or by deposition. In the case of findings by an administrative agency, the usual rule is substantially the same as that in the case of a jury, the findings being treated like a special verdict. Where a trial judge sits without a jury, the rule varies with the character of the evidence: (a) If he decides a fact issue on written evidence alone, we are as able as he to determine credibility, and so we may disregard his finding. (b) Where the evidence is partly oral and the balance is written or deals with undisputed facts, then we may ignore the trial judge's finding and substitute our own, (1) if the written evidence or some undisputed fact renders the credibility of the oral testimony extremely doubtful, or (2) if the trial judge's finding must rest exclusively on the written evidence or the undisputed facts, so that his evaluation of credibility has no significance. (c) But where the evidence supporting his finding as to any fact issue is entirely oral testimony, we may disturb that finding only in the most unusual circumstances.

It follows that evidence sufficient to support a jury verdict or an administrative finding may not suffice to support a trial judge's finding. So in the instant case, perhaps, on the record evidence, we might have affirmed a jury's verdict or an administrative agency's finding in plaintiff's favor. That, however, we need not decide. For here the finding is that of a trial judge, and the evidence consists in large part of facts neither side disputes, in circumstances such that the trial judge's evaluation of credibility becomes unimportant. In short, for reasons we shall state, the undisputed facts are such that we have a "definite and firm conviction" that the trial judge was mistaken in finding that Orvis and Mrs. Orvis "each pursued an independent course" in creating the 1934 trusts, and that no reciprocity was intended. We therefore hold that finding "clearly erroneous," and hold, rather, that each of those trusts was made in consideration of the other.

In so holding we assume that, because of the "evanescent factor which cannot come before us"—i.e., the demeanor of the witnesses—the trial judge fully believed everything they said. Even so, there is nothing in the testimony which in any manner offsets what we believe to be the virtually irresistible inference drawn from the undisputed facts. To offset that inference, the trial judge relied on no positive testimony that Mr. and Mrs. Orvis acted independently but relied merely on negative testimony as to the absence of an expressed intention to act reciprocally, i.e., that "no witness even intimated that the decedent acted with Mrs. Orvis' intention in mind or she with his." The only testimony on which the trial judge relied, or could have relied * * *, is that of Mr. Merritt as to the reasons respectively given to him by husband and wife for the creation of their respective trusts. Not only were those respective reasons strikingly similar but none of them sufficed or purported to explain why each of the trusts set up a life estate; nor did the expression of those reasons at all negative the existence of an intent to make the trusts reciprocal. The finding of an absence of such an intention must, then, depend not on an inference drawn from anything positive in the testimony concerning statements of intention made by Mr. and Mrs. Orvis, but on an inference from their conduct. And that inference, in turn, must rest on a belief in the purely chance concurrence of several events, although the coincidental occurrence of those events would ordinarily be highly improbable. Such a belief ought not to be the foundation of a trial judge's finding on a fact issue, in favor of that side having (like plaintiffs here) the burden of proof as to that issue, unless the purely chance character of those events is positively confirmed by clear evidence. There is no such confirmatory evidence here.

* * *

Reversed and remanded.

CHASE, CIRCUIT JUDGE (dissenting). * * *

This is a typical instance for the application of Civil Rule 52(a). Though trial judges may at times be mistaken as to facts, appellate judges are not always omniscient.

I would affirm.

Notes and Questions

1. Consider the following views:

(a) "There is no logical reason for placing the findings of fact of a trial judge upon a substantially lower level of conclusiveness than the fact findings of a jury of laymen, or those of an administrative agency * * *. The existence of any doubt as to whether the trial court or this Court is the ultimate trier of fact issues in nonjury cases is, we think, detrimental to the orderly administration of justice, impairs the confidence of litigants and the public in the decisions of the district courts, and multiplies the number of appeals in such cases." PENDERGRASS v. NEW YORK LIFE INS. CO., 181 F.2d 136, 138 (8th Cir.1950).

(b) "[E]ven where the question is what finding of fact should be made on the basis of documentary evidence, the trial judge has the advantage of having made the initial sifting of the entire record and of having put it into logical sequence, while the appellate court has lawyers before it picking out bits and pieces of the record to attack or defend a particular finding." Wright, *The Doubtful Omniscience of Appellate Courts*, 41 Minn.L.Rev. 751, 782 (1957).

(c) "[R]eversal by a higher court is not proof justice is thereby better done. There is no doubt that if there were a super-Supreme Court, a substantial proportion of our reversals of state courts would also be reversed. We are not final because we are infallible, but we are infallible only because we are final." Justice Jackson, concurring, in BROWN v. ALLEN, 344 U.S. 443, 540, 73 S.Ct. 397, 427, 97 L.Ed. 469, 533 (1953).

2. Reread Hicks v. United States, p. 58, supra. Consider the following:

> Taking a cautious view of the propriety of directed verdicts in negligence cases tried to juries, appellate courts have warned, "Our ideas as to what would be proper care vary according to temperament, knowledge, and experience. A party should not be held to the peculiar notions of the judge as to what would be ordinary care." Curiously, most courts have failed to apply these observations to the nonjury trial. Using orthodox terminology, it makes sense to label the reasonable man standard a "question of fact" in the jury case, but a "question of law" in the nonjury case. In the nonjury negligence case, the appellate court, not the trial judge, should be analogized to the jury. * * * [O]nce the facts have been found without clear error, the group of judges on the appellate court is better qualified to decide the issue of negligence than is the trial judge acting alone, according to the teaching of jury cases.

Weiner, *The Civil Nonjury Trial and the Law-Fact Distinction*, 55 Calif.L.Rev. 1020, 1033 (1967).

PULLMAN–STANDARD v. SWINT
Supreme Court of the United States, 1982.
456 U.S. 273, 102 S.Ct. 1781, 72 L.Ed.2d 66.

Certiorari to the United States Court of Appeals for the Fifth Circuit.

JUSTICE WHITE delivered the opinion of the Court.

Respondents were black employees at the Bessemer, Alabama plant of petitioner, Pullman-Standard (the "company"), a manufacturer of railway freight cars and parts. They brought suit against the company and the union petitioners * * * alleging violations of Title VII of the Civil Rights Act of 1964 * * *. As they come here, these cases involve only the validity, under Title VII, of a seniority system maintained by the Company and USW [the United Steel Workers of America]. The District Court found "that the differences in terms, conditions or privileges of employment resulting [from the seniority system] are 'not the result of an intention to discriminate' because of race or color," * * * and held, therefore, that the system satisfied the requirements of § 703(h) of the Act. The Court of Appeals for the Fifth Circuit reversed:

> Because we find that the differences in the terms, conditions and standards of employment for black workers and white workers at Pullman-Standard resulted from an intent to discriminate because of race, we hold that the system is not legally valid under section 703(h) of Title VII, 42 U.S.C. 2000e–2(h). * * *

We granted the petitions for certiorari * * * limited to the first question presented in each petition: whether a Court of Appeals is bound by the "clearly erroneous" rule of Fed.Rules Civ.Proc. 52(a) in reviewing a

District Court's findings of fact, arrived at after a lengthy trial, as to the motivation of the parties who negotiated a seniority system; and whether the court below applied wrong legal criteria in determining the *bona fides* of the seniority system. We conclude that the Court of Appeals erred in the course of its review and accordingly reverse its judgment and remand for further proceedings.

* * *

In connection with its assertion that it was convinced that a mistake had been made, the Court of Appeals, in a footnote, referred to the clearly erroneous standard of Rule 52(a). * * * It pointed out, however, that if findings "are made under an erroneous view of controlling legal principles, the clearly erroneous rule does not apply, and the findings may not stand." Finally, quoting from East v. Romine, Inc., 518 F.2d 332, 339 (CA5 1975), the Court of Appeals repeated the following view of its appellate function in Title VII cases where purposeful discrimination is at issue:

> Although discrimination *vel non* is essentially a question of fact it is, at the same time, the ultimate issue for resolution in this case, being expressly proscribed by 42 U.S.C.A. § 2000e–2(a). As such, a finding of discrimination or nondiscrimination is a finding of ultimate fact. [Cites omitted.] In reviewing the district court's findings, therefore, we will proceed to make an independent determination of appellant's allegations of discrimination, though bound by findings of subsidiary fact which are themselves not clearly erroneous.

* * * Petitioners submit that the Court of Appeals made an independent determination of discriminatory purpose, the "ultimate fact" in this case, and that this was error under Rule 52. We agree with petitioners that if the Court of Appeals followed what seems to be the accepted rule in that circuit, its judgment must be reversed.

Rule 52 broadly requires that findings of fact not be set aside unless clearly erroneous. It does not make exceptions or purport to exclude certain categories of factual findings from the obligation of a Court of Appeals to accept a district court's findings unless clearly erroneous. It does not divide facts into categories; in particular, it does not divide findings of fact into those that deal with "ultimate" and those that deal with "subsidiary" facts.

The rule does not apply to conclusions of law. The Court of Appeals, therefore, was quite right in saying that if a District Court's findings rest on an erroneous view of the law, they may be set aside on that basis. But here the District Court was not faulted for misunderstanding or applying an erroneous definition of intentional discrimination. It was reversed for arriving at what the Court of Appeals thought was an erroneous finding as to whether the differential impact of the seniority system reflected an intent to discriminate on account of race. That question, as we see it, is a pure question of fact, subject to Rule 52's clearly erroneous standard. It is not a question of law and not a mixed question of law and fact.

* * * Rule 52 does not furnish particular guidance with respect to distinguishing law from fact. Nor do we yet know of any other rule or

principle that will unerringly distinguish a factual finding from a legal conclusion. For the reasons that follow, however, we have little doubt about the factual nature of § 703(h)'s requirement that a seniority system be free of an intent to discriminate.

* * *

* * * It would make no sense to say that the intent to discriminate required by § 703(h) may be presumed from such an impact. As § 703(h) was construed in * * * [Teamsters v. United States, 431 U.S. 324, 97 S.Ct. 1834, 52 L.Ed.2d 396 (1977)] there must be a finding of actual intent to discriminate on racial grounds on the part of those who negotiated or maintained the system. That finding appears to us to be a pure question of fact.

This is not to say that discriminatory impact is not part of the evidence to be considered by the trial court in reaching a finding on whether there was such a discriminatory intent as a factual matter. We do assert, however, that under § 703(h) discriminatory intent is a finding of fact to be made by the trial court; it is not a question of law and not a mixed question of law and fact of the kind that in some cases may allow an appellate court to review the facts to see if they satisfy some legal concept of discriminatory intent. Discriminatory intent here means actual motive; it is not a legal presumption to be drawn from a factual showing of something less than actual motive. Thus, a court of appeals may only reverse a district court's finding on discriminatory intent if it concludes that the finding is clearly erroneous under Rule 52(a). Insofar as the Fifth Circuit assumed otherwise, it erred.

Appellees do not directly defend the Fifth Circuit rule that a trial court's finding on discriminatory intent is not subject to the clearly erroneous standard of Rule 52. Rather, among other things, they submit that the Court of Appeals recognized and, where appropriate, properly applied Rule 52 in setting aside the findings of the District Court. This position has force, but for two reasons it is not persuasive.

First, although the Court of Appeals acknowledged and correctly stated the controlling standard of Rule 52, the acknowledgement came late in the court's opinion. The court had not expressly referred to or applied Rule 52 in the course of disagreeing with the District Court's resolution of the factual issues * * *. Furthermore, the paragraph in which the court finally concludes that the USW seniority system is unprotected by § 703(h) strongly suggests that the outcome was the product of the court's independent consideration of the totality of the circumstances it found in the record.

Second and more fundamentally, when the court stated that it was convinced that a mistake had been made, it then not only identified the mistake but also the source of that mistake. The mistake of the District Court was that on the record there could be no doubt about the existence of a discriminatory purpose. * * *

When an appellate court discerns that a district court has failed to make a finding because of an erroneous view of the law, the usual rule is that there should be a remand for further proceedings to permit the trial court to make the missing findings * * *. Likewise, where findings are infirm because of an erroneous view of the law, a remand is the proper course unless the record permits only one resolution of the factual issue. Kelley v. Southern Pacific Co., 419 U.S. 318, 331–332, 95 S.Ct. 472, 479–480, 42 L.Ed.2d 498 (1974). All of this is elementary. Yet the Court of Appeals, after holding that the District Court had failed to consider relevant evidence and indicating that the District Court might have come to a different conclusion had it considered that evidence, failed to remand for further proceedings * * *. Instead, the Court of Appeals made its own determination [and findings] * * * and apparently concluded that the foregoing was sufficient to remove the system from the protection of § 703(h).

Proceeding in this manner seems to us incredible unless the Court of Appeals construed its own well-established Circuit rule with respect to its authority to arrive at independent findings on ultimate facts free of the strictures of Rule 52 also to permit it to examine the record and make its own independent findings with respect to those issues on which the district court's findings are set aside for an error of law. As we have previously said, however, the premise for this conclusion is infirm: whether an ultimate fact or not, discriminatory intent under § 703(h) is a factual matter subject to the clearly erroneous standard of Rule 52. It follows that when a district court's finding on such an ultimate fact is set aside for an error of law, the court of appeals is not relieved of the usual requirement of remanding for further proceedings to the tribunal charged with the task of fact-finding in the first instance.

* * *

[JUSTICE STEVENS concurred in part.]

JUSTICE MARSHALL, with whom JUSTICE BLACKMUN joins * * *, dissenting.

* * *

As the majority acknowledges, where findings of fact "are made under an erroneous view of controlling legal principles, the clearly erroneous rule does not apply, and the findings may not stand." * * * Having found that the District Court's findings * * * were made under an erroneous view of controlling legal principles, the Court of Appeals was *compelled* to set aside those findings free of the requirements of the clearly erroneous rule. But once these two findings were set aside, the District Court's conclusion that the departmental system was bona fide within the meaning of § 703(h) also had to be rejected, since that conclusion was based at least in part on its erroneous determinations * * *.

At the very least, therefore, the Court of Appeals was entitled to remand this case to the District Court for the purpose of reexamining the bona fides of the seniority system under proper legal standards. However, as we have often noted, in some cases a remand is inappropriate where the facts on the record are susceptible to only one reasonable interpretation. * * * In such cases, "[e]ffective judicial administration" requires that the Court of Appeals draw the inescapable factual conclusion itself, rather than remand the case to the District Court for further needless proceedings. * * * Such action is particularly appropriate where the court of appeals is in as good a position to evaluate the record evidence as the district court. The major premise behind the deference to trial courts expressed in Rule 52 is that findings of fact "depend peculiarly upon the credit given to witnesses by those who see and hear them." * * *

In the cases before the Court today this usual deference is not required because the District Court's findings of fact were entirely based on documentary evidence. As we noted in United States v. General Motors Corp., supra, 384 U.S., at 141 n. 16, 86 S.Ct., at 1328 n. 16, "the trial court's customary opportunity to evaluate the demeanor and thus the credibility of the witnesses, which is the rationale behind Rule 52(a) * * *, plays only a restricted role [in] a 'paper case.'" * * *

I believe that the Court of Appeals correctly determined that a finding of discriminatory intent was compelled by the documentary record presented to the District Court. * * *

* * * Because I fail to see how the Court of Appeals erred in carrying out its appellate function, I respectfully dissent from the majority's decision to prolong respondents' 11-year quest for the vindication of their rights by requiring yet another trial.

INWOOD LABS., INC. v. IVES LABS., INC., 456 U.S. 844, 102 S.Ct. 2182, 72 L.Ed.2d 606 (1982). In a patent infringement suit brought by Ives Laboratories against Inwood Laboratories, the District Court entered judgment for Inwood, finding that Ives had not made the necessary factual showings. The Court of Appeals reversed, making its own review of the evidence, and concluding that the District Court did not give enough weight to the evidence offered by Ives. The court held that the evidence was clearly sufficient to establish a Section 32 violation. The Supreme Court reversed:

> In reviewing the factual findings of the District Court, the Court of Appeals was bound by the "clearly erroneous" standard of Rule 52(a). * * * That Rule recognizes and rests upon the unique opportunity afforded the trial court judge to evaluate the credibility of witnesses and to weigh the evidence. * * * Because of the deference due the trial judge, unless an appellate court is left with the "definite and firm conviction that a mistake has been committed," * * * it must accept the trial court's findings.
>
> * * *
>
> Each of [the Second Circuit's] conclusions is contrary to the findings of the District Court. An appellate court cannot substitute its interpretation of the evidence for that of the trial court simply because the reviewing court "might give the facts another construction, resolve the ambiguities differently, and find a more sinister cast to actions which the District Court apparently deemed innocent." * * *
>
> The Court of Appeals erred in setting aside findings of fact that were not clearly erroneous. Accordingly, the judgment of the Court of Appeals that the petitioners violated § 32 of the Lanham Act is reversed.

Id. at 855–59, 102 S.Ct. at 2186–87, 72 L.Ed.2d at 616–18. Justices White and Marshall concurred in the result only, maintaining that the Rule 52(a) issue had not been properly presented to the Court.

———

In ANDERSON v. CITY OF BESSEMER CITY, 470 U.S. 564, 105 S.Ct. 1504, 84 L.Ed.2d 518 (1985), Anderson filed discrimination charges against the City of Bessemer City, alleging that she was overlooked for a position as Recreation Director with the City on the ground of her sex, and that the position was awarded to a less qualified male applicant. When her efforts at the EEOC proved unsuccessful, petitioner obtained a right-to-sue letter and filed an action in the federal district court. The District Court found, as a matter of fact, that petitioner was the most qualified candidate, and issued further findings of fact and conclusions of law. The Court of Appeals for the Fourth Circuit reversed, holding that the District Court's findings were clearly erroneous and that the court had therefore erred in finding that petitioner had been discriminated against on account of sex.

The Supreme Court reversed. Justice White noted that the District Court did not uncritically accept the findings prepared by the prevailing party but provided a framework for its proposed findings in a preliminary memorandum. This document set forth the District Court's essential findings and directed petitioner's counsel to submit a more detailed set of findings consistent with them. Therefore, the Court concluded, there was no reason to doubt that the ultimate findings represented the court's own considered conclusions or to subject those findings to a more stringent appellate review than is called for by the applicable rules. Id. at 572–73, 105 S.Ct. at 1510–11, 84 L.Ed.2d at 527–28.

The Court then considered whether the Court of Appeals engaged in the type of inquiry required by Federal Rule of Civil Procedure 52(a) governing findings of fact:

* * * Findings of fact shall not be set aside unless clearly erroneous, and due regard shall be given to the opportunity of the trial court to judge of the credibility of the witnesses. * * *

* * * [A] finding is "clearly erroneous" when although there is evidence to support it, the reviewing court on the entire evidence is left with the definite and firm conviction that a mistake has been committed. * * * "In applying the clearly erroneous standard to the findings of a district court sitting without a jury, appellate courts must constantly have in mind that their function is not to decide factual issues *de novo.*" * * * If the district court's account of the evidence is plausible in light of the record viewed in its entirety, the court of appeals may not reverse it even though convinced that had it been sitting as the trier of fact, it would have weighed the evidence differently. Where there are two permissible views of the evidence, the factfinder's choice between them cannot be clearly erroneous. * * *

This is so even when the district court's findings do not rest on credibility determinations, but are based instead on physical or documentary evidence or inferences from other facts. * * *

The rationale for deference to the original finder of fact is not limited to the superiority of the trial judge's position to make determinations of credibility. The trial judge's major role is the determination of fact, and with experience in fulfilling that role comes expertise. Duplication of the trial judge's efforts in the court of appeals would very likely contribute only negligibly to the accuracy of fact determination at a huge cost in diversion of judicial resources. In addition, the parties to a case on appeal have already been forced to concentrate their energies and resources on persuading the trial judge that their account of the facts is the correct one * * *.

When findings are based on determinations regarding the credibility of witnesses, Rule 52(a) demands even greater deference to the trial court's findings. * * *

* * * [T]he Fourth Circuit improperly conducted what amounted to a *de novo* weighing of the evidence in the record. * * *

* * * When the record is examined in light of the appropriately deferential standard, it is apparent that it contains nothing that mandates a finding that the District Court's conclusion was clearly erroneous.

Id. at 573–77, 105 S.Ct. at 1511–13, 84 L.Ed.2d at 528–30.

———

BOSE CORP. v. CONSUMERS UNION OF UNITED STATES, INC., 466 U.S. 485, 104 S.Ct. 1949, 80 L.Ed.2d 502 (1984). Bose, a manufacturer of stereo loudspeaker systems, sued the Consumers Union for product disparagement based on statements contained in an article evaluating a loudspeaker system manufactured by Bose. The District Court found that Bose was a "public figure" under the standard of New York Times Co. v. Sullivan, 376 U.S. 254, 84 S.Ct. 710, 11 L.Ed.2d 686 (1964), and its progeny, and therefore held that Bose was required to prove by clear and convincing evidence that the respondent made a false disparaging statement with "actual malice." The court found "actual malice," however, and entered judgment for Bose. The Court of Appeals reversed, holding that its review of the "actual malice" determination was not limited by the "clearly erroneous" standard of Rule 52(a) and that it must perform a de novo review of the record to evaluate the District Court's application of the governing constitutional standard.

The Supreme Court affirmed. Writing for the Court, Justice Stevens noted that the Rule's command of deference to findings of fact made by trial courts seems to conflict with the requirement, embodied in the *New York Times* case, that appellate courts conduct a complete examination of the trial record to measure the judgment by the constitutional protection afforded by the First Amendment. He continued, however:

* * * The conflict between the two rules is in some respects more apparent than real. The *New York Times* rule emphasizes the need for an appellate court to make an independent examination of the entire record; Rule 52(a) never forbids such an examination, and indeed our seminal decision on the rule expressly contemplated a review of the entire record, stating that a "finding is 'clearly erroneous' when although there is evidence to support it, the reviewing court *on the entire evidence* is left

with the definite and firm conviction that a mistake has been committed." United States v. United States Gypsum Co. * * * (emphasis supplied). Moreover, Rule 52(a) commands that "due regard" shall be given to the trial judge's opportunity to observe the demeanor of the witnesses; the constitutionally-based rule of independent review permits this opportunity to be given its due. * * *

* * * [T]he rule of independent review assigns to judges a constitutional responsibility that cannot be delegated to the trier of fact, whether the factfinding function be performed in the particular case by a jury or by a trial judge.

Rule 52(a) applies to findings of fact, including those described as "ultimate facts" because they may determine the outcome of litigation. See Pullman-Standard v. Swint * * *. But Rule 52(a) does not inhibit an appellate court's power to correct errors of law, including those that may infect a so-called mixed finding of law and fact, or a finding of fact that is predicated on a misunderstanding of the governing rule of law. * * * Nor does Rule 52(a) "furnish particular guidance with respect to distinguishing law from fact." Pullman-Standard v. Swint * * *.

In a consideration of the possible application of the distinction to the issue of "actual malice," at least three characteristics of the rule enunciated in the *New York Times* case are relevant. First, the common law heritage of the rule itself assigns an especially broad role to the judge in applying it to specific factual situations. Second, the content of the rule is not revealed simply by its literal text, but rather is given meaning through the evolutionary process of common law adjudication; though the source of the rule is found in the Constitution, it is nevertheless largely a judge-made rule of law. Finally, the constitutional values protected by the rule make it imperative that judges—and in some cases judges of this Court—make sure that it is correctly applied. * * *

* * *

The requirement of independent appellate review reiterated in New York Times v. Sullivan is a rule of federal constitutional law. It emerged from the exigency of deciding concrete cases; it is law in its purest form under our common law heritage. It reflects a deeply held conviction that judges—and particularly members of this Court—must exercise such review in order to preserve the precious liberties established and ordained by the Constitution. The question whether the evidence in the record in a defamation case is of the convincing clarity required to strip the utterance of First Amendment protection is not merely a question for the trier of fact. * * *

Id. at 510–11, 104 S.Ct. at 1959–65, 80 L.Ed.2d at 515–23.

The Court then conducted its own *de novo* review, and found that, even accepting all of the purely factual findings of the District Court, the record did not contain clear and convincing evidence that the author of the article or his employer prepared the loudspeaker article with knowledge that it contained a false statement, or with reckless disregard of the truth. In an important passage, the Court held:

* * * We hold that the clearly erroneous standard of Rule 52(a) of the Federal Rules of Civil Procedure does not prescribe the standard of

review to be applied in reviewing a determination of actual malice in a case governed by New York Times v. Sullivan. Appellate judges in such a case must exercise independent judgment and determine whether the record establishes actual malice with convincing clarity.

Id. at 514, 104 S.Ct. at 1967, 80 L.Ed.2d at 525–26.

Chief Justice Burger concurred in the result. Justice White dissented, arguing that because the District Court found that the defamatory statement was written with actual knowledge of its falsity, the Court of Appeals erred in reversing the District Court based on its *de novo* review. Justices Rehnquist and O'Connor also dissented:

> It is * * * ironic that, in the interest of protecting the First Amendment, the Court rejects the "clearly erroneous" standard of review mandated by Federal Rule of Civil Procedure 52(a) in favor of a "*de novo*" standard of review for the "constitutional facts" surrounding the "actual malice" determination. But the facts dispositive of that determination— actual knowledge or subjective reckless disregard for truth—involve no more than findings about the mens rea of an author, findings which appellate courts are simply ill-prepared to make in any context, including the First Amendment context. Unless "actual malice" now means something different from the definition given to the term 20 years ago by this Court in *New York Times,* I do not think that the constitutional requirement of "actual malice" properly can bring into play any standard of factual review other than the "clearly erroneous" standard.

> * * *

> I think that the issues of "falsity" and "actual malice" in this case may be close questions, but I am convinced that the District Court, which heard the principal witness for the respondent testify for almost six days during the trial, fully understood both the applicable law and its role as a finder of fact. Because it is not clear to me that the de novo findings of appellate courts, with only bare records before them, are likely to be any more reliable than the findings reached by trial judges, I cannot join the majority's sanctioning of factual second guessing by appellate courts. I believe that the primary result of the Court's holding today will not be greater protection for First Amendment values, but rather only lessened confidence in the judgments of lower courts and more entirely fact-bound appeals.

> I continue to adhere to the view expressed in Pullman-Standard v. Swint * * * that Rule 52(a) "does not make exceptions or purport to exclude certain categories of factual findings from the obligation of a court of appeals to accept a district court's findings unless clearly erroneous." * * *

Id. at 515–20, 104 S.Ct. at 1968–70, 80 L.Ed.2d at 526–29.

Notes and Questions

1. Is *Bose* consistent with *Pullman-Standard* and *Inwood Labs?* Do you accept Justice Stevens' identification and resolution of the conflict between the "independent review" requirement of *New York Times* and the "clearly erroneous" standard embodied in Rule 52(a)? Or is Justice Rehnquist correct in challenging as an unwarranted extension of *New York Times* the develop-

ment by the majority in *Bose* of a special standard for the application of Rule 52(a) in defamation cases?

2.   Can you identify any other constitutional mandates that would conflict with the "clearly erroneous" standard? What of the argument that the Civil Rights Act of 1964 is the statutory embodiment of the constitutional commands on civil rights embodied in the Fourteenth Amendment? Is there a clash between constitutional requirements and Rule 52(a) that the majority disregarded in *Pullman-Standard*?

3.   Appellate courts are often not as deferential to trial court findings as the standards or the case law would indicate. Goettel, *Appellate Fact Finding—and Other Atrocities,* 13 Litigation 7 (Fall 1986). In fact, Judge Goettel notes that "[t]rial judges often can barely recognize their cases in appellate opinions, so convoluted have the facts become. With the facts so extensively revamped, reversal becomes inevitable." Id. at 7.

3.   ABUSE OF DISCRETION—REVIEW OF FACTS

In ROLAND MACHINERY CO. v. DRESSER INDUSTRIES, INC., 749 F.2d 380 (7th Cir.1984), Roland Machinery, a dealer in construction equipment, sought a preliminary injunction on its claim under the Clayton Act against Dresser, a domestic equipment manufacturer, which had cancelled their exclusive distributorship agreement. Roland Machinery also had an exclusive distributorship contract with a Japanese equipment manufacturer. The District Court issued a preliminary injunction and Dresser appealed. The Seventh Circuit reversed, holding that Dresser had a plausible argument that an exclusive dealer would promote its line more effectively than a nonexclusive dealer, and would improve the overall competition in the market.

Judge Posner and Judge Swygert disagreed on the appropriate standard of review in preliminary injunction cases. Judge Posner surveyed the different elements that a plaintiff must prove in order to obtain a preliminary injunction and determined that the following elements must be present in order for an injunction to issue:

1.   In every case in which the plaintiff wants a preliminary injunction he must show that he has "no adequate remedy at law" and (unless the statute under which he is suing excuses a showing of irreparable harm) * * * that he will suffer "irreparable harm" if the preliminary injunction is not granted. * * *

2.   [P]laintiff must show that an award of damages at the end of trial will be inadequate, * * * seriously deficient as a remedy for the harm suffered. * * *

3.   In deciding whether to grant a preliminary injunction, the court must also consider any irreparable harm that the defendant might suffer from the injunction—harm that would not be either cured by the defendant's ultimately prevailing in the trial on the merits or fully compensated by the injunction bond that Rule 65(c) of the Federal Rules of Civil Procedure requires the district court to make the plaintiff post. * * * [S]ince the defendant may suffer irreparable harm from the entry of a preliminary injunction, the court must not only determine that the plaintiff will suffer irreparable harm if the preliminary injunction is

denied—a threshold requirement for granting a preliminary injunction—
but also weigh that harm against any irreparable harm that the defendant can show he will suffer if the injunction is granted.

4. * * * [Plaintiff must show] a likelihood of succeeding on the
merits. * * *

5. If the plaintiff does show some likelihood of success, the court
must then determine how likely that success is, because this affects the
balance of relative harms (point 3 above). * * *

The idea underlying these * * * approaches is * * * for the
district judge * * * to minimize errors * * *. The judge must try to
avoid the error that is more costly in the circumstances. That cost is a
function of the gravity of the error if it occurs and the probability that it
will occur. * * *

6. Sometimes an order granting or denying a preliminary injunction
will have consequences beyond the immediate parties. If so, those interests * * * must be reckoned into the weighing process * * *.

7. The application of the above principles requires the seasoned
judgment of the district court—what is usually called the court's "discretion" * * *.

* * * The factors to be considered are few and definite; they are as
we have said spread out on a record; and they are to be compared in a
particular sequence and in accordance with a specific formula which
requires first deciding whether plaintiff has crossed specific thresholds
and then weighting the parties' likely harms from the grant and denial of
the preliminary judgment, respectively, by the strength of the plaintiff's
case.

Although there is a sense in which equitable relief is inherently
discretionary because historically, and still to a large extent, there is no
absolute right to an equitable remedy * * *, this is a different meaning
of discretion, one that actually cuts against a highly deferential standard
of review when as in this case the district court *grants* the preliminary
injunction. * * * The exercise of a power so far-reaching ought to be
subject to effective, and not merely perfunctory, appellate review.
* * *

* * * Although, considering the nature of the judge's determination and the stakes to the parties, we do not think the term abuse of
discretion can be limited to cases where the judge can be said to have
acted irrationally or fancifully * * *, we also do not think, considering
the imponderable character of the balancing process and the judge's
superior feel for the issues which a cold transcript may not fully communicate to the reviewing court, that we are entitled to substitute our
judgment for the district judge's. * * * The question for us is to
determine whether the judge exceeded the bounds of permissible choice in
the circumstances, not what we would have done had we been in his
shoes.

We need not be any more precise than this about the meaning of
"abuse of discretion" in the context of appellate review of orders granting
or denying preliminary injunctions in order to decide this case. * * *
For as we * * * see, the district judge committed a clear factual error

and a legal effort that require us to set aside his conclusion on the balance of harms, and another legal error with respect to the probable success of Roland on the merits of its antitrust claim.

749 F.2d at 386–91.

In an emphatic dissent, Judge Swygert argued that Judge Posner's new standard of review was unsatisfactory:

> * * * [P]rinciples of equity jurisprudence require the maintenance of the "abuse of discretion" standard of review. * * *

> * * * I endorse the four-part test set forth by the majority for determining the propriety of granting a preliminary injunction. I believe, however, that the formulation of that or any other test cannot replace the role of discretion in the decision to grant or deny a preliminary injunction. I further believe that the discretion must lie with the district court in the first instance.

> * * *

> * * * Determining a plaintiff's likelihood of success on the merits prior to trial is unique to interlocutory relief. To fulfill its role of softening the harshness of the law and offering relief when a legal remedy is unavailable, the rules for granting preliminary injunctive relief must remain flexible and able to account for a myriad of situations. In sum, the decision whether to grant a preliminary injunction does not lend itself to a rigid legal formulation. * * *

> Because the preliminary injunction is an extraordinary remedy that may impose a great burden on defendants and is granted before a full trial or a final determination of liability, the notion of leaving the decision to the unbridled discretion of judges is particularly troublesome. * * * Thus, I endorse the majority formulation of a coherent test to guide both the district courts and the reviewing courts. I believe, however, that within the confines of that test the district court does and must exercise a large degree of discretion. * * *

> The discretion that inheres in the decision whether to grant a preliminary injunction cannot rest with the reviewing court but must lie in the district court. First, it must be remembered that the district court has the responsibility for making a final determination on the merits of the case. * * * Second, given the flexibility of the standard for preliminary injunctive relief and the necessity for discretionary judgments, two courts could easily arrive at different although equally viable conclusions. Refusal to defer to the decision of the lower court in the first instance frequently will result in a substitution of the judgment of the reviewing court for that of the district court. This is a poor use of judicial resources. * * * Finally, and most importantly, if discretionary judgments must be made * * * in deciding to grant or deny preliminary injunctive relief, the trial court with its greater knowledge of the case and the parties * * * is in a better position than a reviewing court to make those judgments. * * *

> * * * [U]niform treatment historically has not been and should not be a goal in preliminary injunction decisions, without, of course, condoning arbitrary decisionmaking. The decision to grant or deny a preliminary injunction should depend on the unique circumstances of and

the parties in each case. I do not believe that uniform treatment is even possible under the test adopted today. The test is flexible, at least in theory. The sliding scale approach by its nature is antithetical to uniformity. Unique facts are certain to exist in each case which must be factored into the test. The decision to grant or deny injunctive relief simply defies mechanical treatment.

Finally, despite the majority's contention that a preliminary injunction hearing produces a record similar to a trial record, a reviewing court does not have the same access to evidence that the district court has or that the reviewing court has after trial. * * * We should encourage trial judges to refrain from making absolute findings that may impede a fair final resolution on the merits and at the same time to determine the appropriateness of preliminary injunctive relief on the basis of all of the evidence then available to them. I fear that the majority's refusal to defer to the judgments of the trial judge will encourage the opposite; judges will be forced either to make their conclusions explicit and absolute or disregard them. * * *

* * * [E]ven assuming that the district court has committed an isolated error of fact or an isolated mistake of law, the court's ultimate decision to grant or deny preliminary injunctive relief should be reversed only if it constitutes an abuse of discretion under the totality of the circumstances. * * *

Id. at 396–99. Who has the better argument, Judge Posner or Judge Swygert? Whose opinion is more consistent with the Supreme Court's decision in *Anderson?*

Notes and Questions

1. For an analysis of Judge Posner's standard of review in preliminary injunction cases, and of Judge Swygert's opposing view, see Silberman, *Injunctions by the Numbers: Less Than the Sum of Its Parts,* 63 Chicago–Kent L.Rev. 279 (1987).

2. The standard of review is different for declaratory judgments. In the declaratory-judgment context, an appellate court may make two inquiries. It may determine whether the trial court abused its discretion by making an arbitrary choice to hear a claim for declaratory judgment. Wilmington Chemical Corp. v. Celebrezze, 229 F.Supp. 168 (N.D.Ill.1964). Additionally, it may determine that, even if the action is properly a declaratory-judgment action, the lower court's opinion was nevertheless erroneous. National Health Federation v. Weinberger, 518 F.2d 711 (7th Cir.1975). In other words, the appellate court may engage in *de novo* review. What is it about declaratory judgments that permits *de novo* review?

SECTION D. THE VIEW AT THE TOP—COURTS ABOVE APPELLATE COURTS

———

Read 28 U.S.C. §§ 1251–54, 1257 in the Supplement and all the accompanying material.

———

1. REVIEW AS OF RIGHT

In the federal-court system and in the judicial structure of about one-third of the states, intermediate appellate courts are interposed between the trial courts of general jurisdiction and the highest court. The principal purpose in creating intermediate appellate courts has been to relieve the pressure of burgeoning appellate litigation on the highest court, leaving that tribunal free to concentrate on deciding important and novel questions of law and on maintaining uniformity in the law applied by the lower courts. To achieve this purpose fully, two conditions must be met. Most appeals must begin and end in the intermediate appellate courts, but the possibility of review by the highest court must be open in every case.

Both conditions would be satisfied if the intermediate courts heard every appeal in the first instance and the highest court had complete discretion to review the decisions of those courts. But no American system seems to have fully adopted this approach. In every state that has intermediate appellate courts, as well as in the federal courts, some matters are reviewable directly by the highest court, and, in most systems, some matters, decided in the first instance by the intermediate courts, are appealable as of right to the highest court. The systems differ markedly, however, both in the extent to which the intermediate appellate courts are bypassed and in the amount of discretion given to the highest court to choose the cases it hears.

Notes and Questions

1. Compare the provisions for direct appeal to the Supreme Court of California, the Supreme Court of Georgia, and the Court of Appeals of New York that are set out in the Supplement following 28 U.S.C. § 1254. What is the reason for each of these provisions? Which set of state provisions seems most appropriate?

2. Prior to 1988, when it repealed 28 U.S.C. § 1252, Congress had provided for direct appeal to the Supreme Court of the United States from any decision of a federal district court "holding an Act of Congress unconstitutional in any civil action * * * to which the United States or any of its agencies [or employees] * * * is a party." What might have led Congress to repeal this provision? See Brown Shoe Co. v. United States, 370 U.S. 294, 355, 364, 82 S.Ct. 1502, 1541, 1546, 8 L.Ed.2d 510, 557, 562 (1962) (sharp criticisms of direct appeals by Justice Clark and Justice Harlan). Direct appeals are still available under 28 U.S.C. § 1253. What is the justification for such a provision? Note that the Supreme Court can effect a direct appeal in any case in which certiorari would lie by taking up the case as soon as it is docketed in the court of appeals and before that court considers it, but this power has been rarely exercised. See, e.g., United States v. Nixon, 418 U.S. 683, 94 S.Ct. 3090, 41 L.Ed.2d 1039 (1974). Do the state courts mentioned in Note 1, supra, possess comparable authority?

3. A significant drawback of a provision for direct appeal is the confusion that may exist as to whether a particular case falls within the provision and as to the appropriate disposition of such case if it is appealed to the wrong court. In a case in which a United States district judge erroneously had refused to convene a three-judge district court, does the court of appeals have

jurisdiction to remand the case for determination by a three-judge court, or is the only remedy a petition for mandamus in the United States Supreme Court? See Idlewild Bon Voyage Liquor Corp. v. Epstein, 370 U.S. 713, 82 S.Ct. 1294, 8 L.Ed.2d 794 (1962); Cancel v. Wyman, 441 F.2d 553 (2d Cir.1971); Wright, *Federal Courts* § 50 (4th ed. 1983).

4. For many years, Congress had provided in 28 U.S.C. §§ 1254 and 1257 that the Supreme Court was *required* to review certain decisions of the federal courts of appeals and of state courts in situations involving the validity of state laws under the Constitution, treaties or laws of the United States. In fact, the requirement was somewhat illusory because the Court took the position that it had jurisdiction only if the case involved a "substantial federal question." Zucht v. King, 260 U.S. 174, 43 S.Ct. 24, 67 L.Ed. 194 (1922). Many such appeals were therefore dismissed because the issue was considered remote or already well-settled.

In 1988, Congress amended Sections 1254 and 1257 to provide that such decisions receive no special treatment, but shall be reviewed, as most others, only if the Supreme Court, in its discretion, grants a petition for a writ of certiorari. See pp. 1141–43, infra.

5. The most important restriction on Supreme Court review of state-court decisions of federal claims is that the judgment necessarily must turn on the federal question and that it not rest upon an independent state ground. Even if the decision is based on alternative grounds, one federal and one state, review will be denied. Zacchini v. Scripps-Howard Broadcasting Co., 433 U.S. 562, 568, 97 S.Ct. 2849, 2853–54, 53 L.Ed.2d 965, 971–72 (1977). Suppose that the highest state court, in deciding how to interpret its own law, feels bound by federal law. In such cases Supreme Court review is permitted. See ibid. Why?

In most cases a state court's judgment, based upon a state ground, will have the same effect that it would have had if the court had sustained the claim of a federal right. Should it make any difference whether the state ground is substantive or procedural? See Henry v. Mississippi, 379 U.S. 443, 85 S.Ct. 564, 13 L.Ed.2d 408 (1965). Should the Supreme Court's power be different when the effect of the state court's judgment is to defeat the claim of a federal right? See Sandalow, *Henry v. Mississippi and the Adequate State Ground: Proposals for a Revised Doctrine,* 1965 Sup.Ct.Rev. 187. See generally Wright, *Federal Courts* § 107 (4th ed.1983).

6. Appeals from courts of inferior jurisdiction, such as justice-of-the-peace courts, probate courts, and municipal courts, frequently lie to the trial courts of general jurisdiction. The organization of inferior courts differs so widely from state to state that few generalizations can be drawn. Typically, however, the jurisdictional provisions call for a *de novo* hearing in the court of general jurisdiction and, in the case of very small claims, make the determination of the latter court final and unreviewable.

2. DISCRETIONARY REVIEW

Review 28 U.S.C. §§ 1254(1), 1257(a).

DICK v. NEW YORK LIFE INS. CO., 359 U.S. 437, 448, 79 S.Ct. 921, 928, 3 L.Ed.2d 935, 943 (1959). Justice FRANKFURTER, dissenting:

Establishment of intermediate appellate courts in 1891 was designed by Congress to relieve the overburdened docket of the Court. The Circuit Courts of Appeals were to be equal in dignity to the Supreme Courts of the several States. The essential purpose of the Evarts Act was to enable the Supreme Court to discharge its indispensable functions in our federal system by relieving it of the duty of adjudication in cases that are important only to the litigants. The Act provided, therefore, that in diversity cases "the judgments or decrees of the circuit courts of appeals shall be final." * * * [However], this Court was given the discretionary power to grant certiorari in these cases, to be exercised if some question of general interest, outside the limited scope of an ordinary diversity litigation, was also involved.

* * *

Time and again in the years immediately following the passage of the Evarts Act this Court stated that it was only in cases of "gravity and general importance" or "to secure uniformity of decision" that the certiorari power should be exercised. * * *

These considerations have led the Court in scores of cases to dismiss the writ of certiorari even after oral argument when it became manifest that the writ was granted under a misapprehension of the true issues. * * *

To strengthen further this Court's control over its docket and to avoid review of cases which in the main raise only factual controversies, Congress in 1916 made cases arising under the Federal Employers' Liability Act * * * final in the Courts of Appeals, reviewable by this Court only when required by the guiding standards for exercising its certiorari jurisdiction.

In 1925 Congress enacted the "Judges' Bill," called such because it was drafted by a committee of this Court composed of Van Devanter, McReynolds, and Sutherland, JJ. At the hearings on the bill * * * Mr. Chief Justice Taft said:

> No litigant is entitled to more than two chances, namely, to the original trial and to a review, and the intermediate courts of review are provided for that purpose. When a case goes beyond that, it is not primarily to preserve the rights of the litigants. The Supreme Court's function is for the purpose of expounding and stabilizing principles of law for the benefit of the people of the country, passing upon constitutional questions and other important questions of law for the public benefit. It is to preserve uniformity of decision among the intermediate courts of appeal.

Questions of fact have traditionally been deemed to be the kind of questions which ought not to be recanvassed here unless they are entangled in the proper determination of constitutional or other important legal issues. * * * The proper use of the discretionary certiorari jurisdiction was on a later occasion thus expounded by Mr. Chief Justice Hughes:

Records are replete with testimony and evidence of facts. But the questions on certiorari are questions of law. * * * It is only when the facts are interwoven with the questions of law which we should review that the evidence must be examined and then only to the extent that it is necessary to decide the questions of law. * * *

HARRIS v. PENNSYLVANIA R. CO., 361 U.S. 15, 17–19, 80 S.Ct. 22, 24–25, 4 L.Ed.2d 1, 3–4 (1959). Justice DOUGLAS, concurring:

It is suggested that the Court has consumed too much of its time in reviewing these FELA cases. An examination of the 33 cases in which the Court has granted certiorari during the period [1949–1959] * * * reveals that 16 of these cases were summarily reversed without oral argument and without full opinions. Only 17 cases were argued during this period of more than a decade and, of these, 5 were disposed of by brief *per curiam* opinions. Only 12 cases in over 10 years were argued, briefed and disposed of with full opinions by the Court. We have granted certiorari in these cases on an average of less than 3 per year and have given plenary consideration to slightly more than 1 per year. Wastage of our time is therefore a false issue.

The difference between the majority and minority of the Court in our treatment of FELA cases concerns the degree of vigilance we should exercise in safeguarding the jury trial—guaranteed by the Seventh Amendment and part and parcel of the remedy under this Federal Act when suit is brought in state courts. * * * Whether that right has been impaired in a particular instance often produces a contrariety of views. Yet the practice of the Court in allowing four out of nine votes to control the certiorari docket is well established and of long duration. Without it, the vast discretion which Congress allowed us in granting or denying certiorari might not be tolerable. Every member of the Court has known instances where he has strongly protested the action of the minority in bringing a case or type of case here for adjudication. He may then feel that there are more important and pressing matters to which the Court should give its attention. That is, however, a price we pay for keeping our promise to Congress [3] to let the vote of four Justices bring up any case here on certiorari.

3. The "rule of four" was given as one of the reasons why the Congress thought that the increase of our discretionary jurisdiction was warranted. The House Report stated:

"Lest it should be thought that the increase of discretionary jurisdiction might impair the administration of justice and lead to partial hearings and not secure a decision by the whole court, it is proper to call attention to the very thorough and complete system by which discretionary jurisdiction is exercised. * * * [According to] Mr. Justice Van Devanter * * *:

" * * *

" ' * * * We always grant the petition when as many as four think that it should be granted and sometimes when as many as three think that way. We proceed upon the theory that, if that number out of the nine are impressed with the thought that the case is one that ought to be heard and decided by us, the petition should be granted.' " H.R.Rep. No. 1075, 68th Cong., 2d Sess., p. 3.

Notes and Questions

1.   In the early 1970's, the sharp increase in the number of petitions for review filed with the Supreme Court led some commentators to conclude that the Court was being strangled by its workload.   Some of these commentators proposed the creation of a new federal appellate court, positioned between the Supreme Court and the present courts of appeals—the so-called National Court of Appeals.   See, e.g., *Report of the Study Group on the Caseload of the Supreme Court* (1972), reprinted at 57 F.R.D. 573 (1972); Commission on Revision of the Federal Court Appellate System, *Structure and Internal Procedures: Recommendations for Change* (1975), reprinted in 67 F.R.D. 195 (1975).   Finally, in the early 1980's, Chief Justice Burger endorsed these proposals and considerable interest in them was generated.   As recently as 1987, the Senate and the House of Representatives conducted hearings on bills that would have created a temporary, experimental National Court of Appeals or Intercircuit Tribunal.   The Supreme Court would have referred cases to this new court for resolution, but would have retained power of ultimate review by writ of certiorari.   The results of the experiment would have been assessed at the end of five years, at which time the court could be made permanent or abolished.

Scholars have questioned whether the Supreme Court inevitably is faced with more cases demanding its attention than it can handle and have challenged the premise upon which the case for a national court of appeals is most often made.   See Estreicher & Sexton, *The Supreme Court's Case Selection Process and the National Court of Appeals,* 59 N.Y.U.L.Rev. 1 (1985), in which the authors examine the history and the contours of the debate over the Court's "workload problem," offer a theory of the Court's role in the federal judicial system, and present a detailed examination of the case selection process as it operated in the October 1982 Term.   Their study concludes that the unfocused nature of the criteria for case selection presented in Supreme Court Rule 17 causes the Court to "overgrant," thereby creating the illusion of overload.   Professors Estreicher and Sexton argue that revision of these criteria and other minor procedural changes would dispose of the need for a new federal appellate court.

2.   Compare United States Supreme Court Rule 17(1) with California Appellate Rule 29, both of which are set out in the Supplement following 28 U.S.C.A. § 1254.   What considerations should govern the highest court of a state in deciding whether to hear a case within its discretionary jurisdiction? See 7 Weinstein, Korn & Miller, *New York Civil Practice* ¶ 5602.04; Cuomo, *The New York Court of Appeals: A Practical Perspective,* 34 St. John's L.Rev. 197, 201 (1960); Poulos & Varner, *Review of Intermediate Appellate Court Decisions in California,* 15 Hastings L.J. 11, 15 (1963).   Should these considerations be any different from those followed by the Supreme Court of the United States in ruling on a petition for a writ of certiorari?

The Final Judgment Requirement Under Section 1257

Section 1257 limits Supreme Court review to "final judgments of the highest state court in which a decision could be had."   The question is whether and to what extent determinations as to what is a final judgment under Section 1257 should be influenced by decisions as to what is final under Section 1291. See pp. 1063–67, 1069–90, supra. In COX BROAD-CASTING CORP. v. COHN, 420 U.S. 469, 95 S.Ct. 1029, 43 L.Ed.2d 328 (1975), plaintiff brought suit for damages in a state court against the owner of a television station, alleging that the station had wrongfully invaded his privacy by revealing that his daughter had been the victim of rape and murder. Defendant claimed the broadcast was privileged under the First and Fourteenth Amendments to the federal Constitution. The trial judge granted partial summary judgment for plaintiff on liability. The state supreme court overturned the summary judgment, but held that the federal Constitution did not necessarily rule out the possibility of liability and returned the case to the trial court for further proceedings. On appeal, the United States Supreme Court, noting that the requirement of finality under Section 1257 has been applied in a "pragmatic" rather than in a "mechanical fashion," upheld immediate appeal since the state decision was final as to the federal issue, a vital issue that should be decided as soon as possible so that broadcasters would know what they could or could not publish without fear of a lawsuit. The Court cited Gillespie v. United States Steel Corp., set out at pp. 1099–1101, supra, accepting its approach even though it had been decided under Section 1291. Justice Rehnquist dissented, arguing that the policies underlying Sections 1257 and 1291 differ substantially.

Notes and Questions

1. Does the Supreme Court's decision in Coopers & Lybrand v. Livesay, see pp. 1081–84, supra, undermine the *Cox* decision?

2. Even if the policies behind Sections 1257 and 1291 differ, should that affect the interpretation given to the word "final" in each? Aren't the reasons for avoiding appeals of interlocutory orders applicable under both provisions? Shouldn't it be up to Congress to create exceptions to Section 1257 as it has with regard to Section 1291?

3. The Court in *Cox* listed four situations in which a technical definition of "final" may give way to "pragmatic" considerations:

(1) When the decision is final from a practical point of view—for example, when the interlocutory decision clearly dictates the final result.

(2) When the federal issue necessarily would survive no matter how the state courts would rule in subsequent proceedings.

(3) When, under state law, subsequent review could be prohibited—for example, in criminal or certain administrative-law cases in which an acquittal or decision against the government would not be appealable.

(4) When important federal rights are involved and when delay would erode federal policy.

How much emphasis should be placed on the last situation? Suppose in *Cox* the state supreme court merely had vacated the summary judgment and returned the case to the trial court with the admonition, "study anew the defenses based on the federal constitution which were originally treated summarily and without adequate briefing from counsel." Should an immediate appeal to the Supreme Court be permitted to avoid leaving local broadcasters uncertain about their rights? For a comprehensive review of *Cox* and of the final-judgment rule under Section 1257, see Note, *The Finality Rule for Supreme Court Review of State Court Orders,* 91 Harv.L.Rev. 1004 (1978).

Chapter 14

THE BINDING EFFECT OF PRIOR DECISIONS: RES JUDICATA AND COLLATERAL ESTOPPEL

"Courts can only do their best to determine the truth on the basis of the evidence, and the first lesson one must learn on the subject of res judicata is that judicial findings must not be confused with absolute truth." Currie, *Mutuality of Collateral Estoppel: Limits of the Bernhard Doctrine*, 9 Stan.L.Rev. 281, 315 (1957).

SECTION A. TERMINOLOGY

The effects of a former adjudication have been discussed in varying and occasionally conflicting terminology. Although the time has not yet come when courts will use a single vocabulary, substantial progress has been made toward a convention. Judge Rubin has provided a highly useful summary that sets out the major variations in current terminology:

> The rules of *res judicata*, as the term is sometimes sweepingly used, actually comprise two doctrines concerning the preclusive effect of a prior adjudication. The first such doctrine is "claim preclusion," or true *res judicata*. It treats a judgment, once rendered, as the full measure of relief to be accorded between the same parties on the same "claim" or "cause of action." * * * When the plaintiff obtains a judgment in his favor, his claim "merges" in the judgment; he may seek no further relief on that claim in a separate action. Conversely, when a judgment is rendered for a defendant, the plaintiff's claim is extinguished; the judgment then acts as a "bar." * * * Under these rules of claim preclusion, the effect of a judgment extends to the litigation of all issues relevant to the same claim between the same parties, whether or not raised at trial. * * * The aim of claim preclusion is thus to avoid multiple suits on identical entitlements or obligations between the same parties, accompanied, as they would be, by the redetermination of identical issues of duty and breach.

> The second doctrine, collateral estoppel or "issue preclusion," recognizes that suits addressed to particular claims may present issues relevant to suits on other claims. In order to effectuate the public policy in

favor of minimizing redundant litigation, issue preclusion bars the relitigation of issues actually adjudicated, and essential to the judgment, in a prior litigation between the same parties. * * * It is insufficient for the invocation of issue preclusion that some question of fact or law in a later suit was relevant to a prior adjudication between the parties; the contested issue must have been litigated and necessary to the judgment earlier rendered.

KASPAR WIRE WORKS, INC. v. LECO ENGINEERING & MACHINE, INC., 575 F.2d 530, 535–36 (5th Cir.1978).

Another useful summary is the following:

Foreclosure of matters that never have been litigated has traditionally been expressed by stating that a single "cause of action" cannot be "split" by advancing one part in a first suit and reserving some other part for a later suit. The entire cause of action was said to "merge" in a judgment for the plaintiff, leaving a new cause of action on the judgment, or to be subject to the "bar" of a judgment for the defendant. There is now a growing tendency * * * to substitute the word "claim" for the cause of action phrase. Here as in other fields of procedure the new word may help to escape uncomfortable historic legacies of thought expressed in cause of action terms. There is an additional advantage that the resulting "claim preclusion" phrase provides a clear contrast to the concept of "issue preclusion." It remains convenient, however, to supplement this phrase with the words of merger and bar.

Foreclosure of matters that have been once litigated has been described by a wide variety of phrases. For many years, the "awkward phrase" of "collateral estoppel" has been used. The estoppel is characterized as collateral because the later litigation commonly involves a different cause of action; purists accordingly have felt obliged to refer to "direct estoppel" whenever a first suit was ended in a manner that did not give rise to claim preclusion, but that did warrant preclusion of a specific issue. The more modern "issue preclusion" phrase encompasses both varieties of estoppel, and warrants the growing acceptance it has found in current federal decisions.

Finally, courts have found it convenient to identify the judgments that warrant preclusive effect as "final" or as "on the merits." Little harm is done by such phrases in themselves, but they may obscure the fundamental proposition that different requirements are appropriate to different preclusive effects. Dismissal of a suit for want of federal subject matter jurisdiction, for example, should not bar an action on the same claim in a court that does have subject matter jurisdiction, but ordinarily should preclude relitigation of the same issue of subject matter jurisdiction in a second federal suit on the same claim.

18 Wright, Miller & Cooper, *Federal Practice and Procedure: Jurisdiction and Related Matters* § 4402, at 8–11 (1981).

SECTION B. CLAIM AND DEFENSE PRECLUSION

1. CLAIM PRECLUSION

Although it is difficult to give a precise definition of the doctrine of claim preclusion, it is possible to sketch its general form. One formulation is: In certain circumstances, when a second suit is brought, the judgment in a prior suit will be considered conclusive, both on the parties to the judgment and on those in privity with them, as to matters that actually were litigated or should have been litigated in the first suit. Justice Field provided a more detailed formulation of the same basic rule:

> * * * [A] judgment, if rendered upon the merits, constitutes an absolute bar to a subsequent action. It is a finality as to the claim or demand in controversy, concluding parties and those in privity with them, not only as to every matter which was offered and received to sustain or defeat the claim or demand, but as to any other admissible matter which might have been offered for that purpose. Thus, for example, a judgment rendered upon a promissory note is conclusive as to the validity of the instrument and the amount due on it, although it be subsequently alleged that perfect defences actually existed, of which no proof was offered, such as forgery, want of consideration, or payment. * * * The judgment is as conclusive, so far as future proceedings at law are concerned, as though the defences never existed. * * *

CROMWELL v. COUNTY OF SAC, 94 U.S. (4 Otto) 351, 352–53, 24 L.Ed. 195, 197–98 (1876).

For claim preclusion to operate, three elements must be present. First, only judgments that are "final," "valid," and "on the merits" have preclusive effect. Second, the parties in the subsequent action must be identical to those in the first. This requirement is one of the most important distinctions between claim preclusion and its sister doctrine, issue preclusion. And, third, the claim in the second suit must involve matters properly considered included in the first action. Clearly, this last requirement turns on what the first action decided or should have decided.

RUSH v. CITY OF MAPLE HEIGHTS
Supreme Court of Ohio, 1958.
167 Ohio St. 221, 147 N.E.2d 599.
Certiorari denied 358 U.S. 814, 79 S.Ct. 21, 3 L.Ed.2d 57.

[Plaintiff was injured in a fall from a motorcycle. She brought an action in the Municipal Court of Cleveland for damage to her personal property; that court found that defendant city was negligent in maintaining its street and that this negligence was the proximate cause of plaintiff's damages, which were fixed at $100. Defendant appealed and the judgment was affirmed by the Ohio Court of Appeals and Supreme Court. Plaintiff also brought this action in the Court of Common Pleas of Cuyahoga County for personal injuries she incurred in the same accident; her motion to set trial on the issue of damages alone was granted on the ground that the issue of negligence was res judicata because of the Municipal Court action; judgment was entered on a verdict for $12,000, and the Court of Appeals affirmed.]

HERBERT, JUDGE. The eighth error assigned by the defendant is that "the trial and appellate courts committed error in permitting plaintiff to split her cause of action * * *."

In the case of Vasu v. Kohlers, Inc., 145 Ohio St. 321, 61 N.E.2d 707, 709, 166 A.L.R. 855, plaintiff operating an automobile came into collision with defendant's truck, in which collision he suffered personal injuries and also damage to his automobile. At the time of collision, plaintiff had coverage of a $50 deductible collision policy on his automobile. The insurance company paid the plaintiff a sum covering the damage to his automobile, whereupon, in accordance with a provision of the policy, the plaintiff assigned to the insurer his claim for such damage.

In February 1942, the insurance company commenced an action * * * against Kohlers, Inc., * * * to recoup the money paid by it to cover the damage to Vasu's automobile.

In August 1942, Vasu commenced an action in the same court against Kohlers, Inc., to recover for personal injuries which he suffered in the same collision.

In March 1943, in the insurance company's action, a verdict was rendered in favor of the defendant, followed by judgment.

Two months later an amended answer was filed in the Vasu case, setting out as a bar to the action * * * the judgment rendered in favor of defendant in the insurance company case. A motion to strike that defense * * * [was] sustained * * *. A trial of the action resulted in a verdict for plaintiff, upon which judgment was entered.

On appeal to the Court of Appeals the defendant claimed that the Court of Common Pleas erred in sustaining plaintiff's motion to strike from the defendant's answer the defense of *res judicata* claimed to have arisen by reason of the judgment in favor of the defendant in the action by the insurance company.

The Court of Appeals reversed the judgment of the Court of Common Pleas and entered final judgment in favor of defendant.

This court reversed the judgment of the Court of Appeals, holding in the syllabus, in part, as follows:

* * *

4. Injuries to both person and property suffered by the same person as a result of the same wrongful act are infringements of different rights and give rise to distinct causes of action, with the result that the recovery or denial of recovery of compensation for damages to the property is no bar to an action subsequently prosecuted for the personal injury, unless by an adverse judgment in the first action issues are determined against the plaintiff which operate as an estoppel against him in the second action.

* * *

6. Where an injury to person and to property through a single wrongful act causes a prior contract of indemnity and subrogation as to the injury to property to come into operation for the benefit of the person injured, the indemnitor may prosecute a separate action against the party causing such injury for reimbursement for indemnity monies paid under such contract.

7. Parties in privy, in the sense that they are bound by a judgment, are those who acquired an interest in the subject matter after the beginning of the action or the rendition of the judgment; and if their title or interest attached before that fact, they are not bound unless made parties.

8. A grantor or assignor is not bound, as to third persons, by any judgment which such third persons may obtain against his grantee or assignee adjudicating the title to or claim for the interest transferred unless he participated in the action in such manner as to become, in effect, a party.

* * * The sixth, seventh and eighth paragraphs deal with the factual situation which existed in the Vasu case, i.e., a prior contract of indemnity and subrogation. Although, as discussed infra, it was not actually necessary to the determination of the issue in that case, attention centers on the fourth paragraph.

* * * [Subsequent] cases, distinguishing and explaining the Vasu case, have not changed the rule established in paragraph four of the syllabus * * *.

However, it is contended here that that rule is in conflict with the great weight of authority in this country and has caused vexatious litigation. * * *

Upon examination of decisions of courts of last resort, we find that the majority rule is followed in the following cases in each of which the action was between the person suffering injury and the person committing the tort, and where insurers were not involved, as in the case here. * * * [The court cited cases from 20 states forming the majority and 5 states forming the minority.]

The reasoning behind the majority rule seems to be well stated in the case of Mobile & Ohio Rd. Co. v. Matthews * * * [115 Tenn. 172, 91 S.W. 194 (1906)], as follows:

> The negligent action of the plaintiff in error constituted but one tort. The injuries to the person and property of the defendant in error were the several results and effects of one wrongful act. A single tort can be the basis of but one action. It is not improper to declare in different counts for damages to the person and property when both result from the same tort, and it is the better practice to do so where there is any difference in the measure of damages, and all the damages sustained must be sued for in one suit. This is necessary to prevent multiplicity of suits, burdensome expense, and delays to plaintiffs, and vexatious litigation against defendants. * * *

The minority rule would seem to stem from the English case of Brunsden v. Humphrey (1884), 14 Q.B. 141. The facts in that case are set forth in the opinion in the Vasu case * * * concluding with the statement:

> The Master of the Rolls, in his opinion, stated that the test is "whether the same sort of evidence would prove the plaintiff's case in the two actions," and that, in the action relating to the cab, "it would be necessary to give evidence of the damage done to the plaintiff's vehicle. In the present action it would be necessary to give evidence of the bodily injury occasioned to the plaintiff, and of the sufferings which he has undergone, and for this purpose to call medical witnesses. This one test shows that the causes of action as to the damage done to the plaintiff's cab, and as to the injury occasioned to the plaintiff's person, are distinct."

The fallacy of the reasoning in the English court is best portrayed in the dissenting opinion of Lord Coleridge, as follows:

> * * * [I]t seems to me a subtlety not warranted by law to hold that a man cannot bring two actions, if he is injured in his arm and in his leg, but can bring two, if besides his arm and leg being injured, his trousers which contain his leg, and his coat-sleeve which contains his arm, have been torn.

There appears to be no valid reason in these days of code pleading to adhere to the old English rule as to distinctions between injuries to the person and damages to the person's property resulting from a single tort. It would seem that the minority rule is bottomed on the proposition that the right of bodily security is fundamentally different from the right of security of property and, also, that, in actions predicated upon a negligent act, damages are a necessary element of each independent cause of action and no recovery may be had unless and until actual consequential damages are shown.

Whether or not injuries to both person and property resulting from the same wrongful act are to be treated as injuries to separate rights or as separate items of damage, * * * a plaintiff may maintain only one action to enforce his rights existing at the time such action is commenced.

The decision of the question actually in issue in the Vasu case is found in paragraphs six, seven and eight of the syllabus, as it is quite apparent from the facts there that the first judgment, claimed to be *res judicata* in Vasu's action against the defendant, was rendered against Vasu's insurer in an action initiated by it after having paid Vasu for the damages to his automobile. * * *

Upon further examination of the cases from other jurisdictions, it appears that in those instances where the courts have held to the majority rule, a separation of causes of action is almost universally recognized where an insurer has acquired by an assignment or by subrogation the right to recover for money it has advanced to pay for property damage.

* * *

In the light of the foregoing, it is the view of this court that the so-called majority rule conforms much more properly to modern practice, and that the rule declared in the fourth paragraph of the syllabus in the Vasu case, on a point not actually at issue therein, should not be followed.

* * *

Judgment reversed and final judgment for defendant.

STEWART, JUDGE (concurring). * * * If it had been necessary [in *Vasu*] to decide the question whether a single tort gives rise to two causes of action as to the one injured by such tort, I would be reluctant to disturb that holding. However, neither the discussion in the Vasu case as to whether a single or double cause of action arises from one tort nor the language of the fourth paragraph of the syllabus was necessary to decide the issue presented in the case, and obviously both such language and such paragraph are obiter dicta and, therefore, are not as persuasive an authority as if they had been appropriate to the question presented.

* * *

ZIMMERMAN, JUDGE (dissenting). I am not unalterably opposed to upsetting prior decisions of this court where changing conditions and the lessons of experience clearly indicate the desirability of such course, but, where those considerations do not obtain, established law should remain undisturbed in order to insure a stability on which the lower courts and the legal profession generally may rely with some degree of confidence.

* * *

Notes and Questions

1. The *Rush* case illustrates three ways in which the adjudication in one action may affect a subsequent lawsuit. The first is one with which you are already familiar: *stare decisis*. Although neither party in *Rush* had been a party to Vasu v. Kohler's, Inc., both of the lower Ohio courts as well as the dissenting judge in the Supreme Court of Ohio regarded that case as controlling in *Rush*. Of course, as the *Rush* case itself demonstrates, the binding force of *stare decisis* is not absolute, and the parties to a later action are free to argue that the law announced in an earlier case should be changed. But a court will not lightly depart from precedent even though the parties who are before it were not represented in the case that established the precedent. The second and third ways in which adjudication in one action may affect a subsequent lawsuit involve the doctrines of claim and issue preclusion introduced in Section A. How does *stare decisis* differ from these concepts?

If the Ohio court had not found claim preclusion in *Rush*, what would have been the effect of issue preclusion? Note that both lower courts in *Rush* held that the only issue open in plaintiff's suit for her personal injuries was the amount of her damages, because the issues of negligence, proximate cause, and contributory negligence had all been conclusively determined by her judgment in the earlier action for property damage.

Among the more valuable sources on res judicata are: 1B Moore, *Federal Practice* (2d ed.); 18 Wright, Miller & Cooper, *Federal Practice and Procedure: Jurisdiction and Related Matters* § 4401 et seq. (1981); *Restatement (Second), Judgments* (1982).

2. Was the critical language in *Vasu* a holding or dictum? Compare UNITED STATES v. TITLE INS. & TRUST CO., 265 U.S. 472, 485–86, 44 S.Ct. 621, 623, 68 L.Ed. 1110, 1114 (1924), in which Justice Van Devanter said, in connection with an attempt to distinguish an earlier case:

Enough has been said to make it apparent that that case and this are so much alike that what was said and ruled in that should be equally

applicable in this. But it is urged that what we have described as ruled
there was *obiter dictum* and should be disregarded, because the Court
there gave a second ground for its decision which was broad enough to
sustain it independently of the first ground. The premise of the contention is right but the conclusion is wrong; for where there are two
grounds, upon either of which an appellate court may rest its decision,
and it adopts both, "the ruling on neither is *obiter,* but each is the
judgment of the court and of equal validity with the other."

3. What reasons might plaintiff in *Rush* have had for wishing to sue
first on the claim for property damage and then separately for the personal
injuries?

4. The tests for determining the scope of claim preclusion have undergone a significant development since the beginning of the century. The
Restatement (Second) of Judgments summarizes this transition:

> In defining claim to embrace all the remedial rights of the plaintiff
> against the defendant growing out of the relevant transaction (or series of
> connected transactions), [Section 24 of the Restatement] responds to
> modern procedural ideas which have found expression in the Federal
> Rules of Civil Procedure and other procedural systems.

> "Claim," in the context of res judicata, has never been broader than
> the transaction to which it related. But in the days when civil procedure
> still bore the imprint of the forms of action and the division between law
> and equity, the courts were prone to associate claim with a single theory
> of recovery, so that, with respect to one transaction, a plaintiff might
> have as many claims as there were theories of the substantive law upon
> which he could seek relief against the defendant. Thus, defeated in an
> action based on one theory, the plaintiff might be able to maintain
> another action based on a different theory, even though both actions were
> grounded upon the defendant's identical act or connected acts forming a
> single life-situation. In those earlier days there was also some adherence
> to a view that associated claim with the assertion of a single primary
> right as accorded by the substantive law, so that, if it appeared that the
> defendant had invaded a number of primary rights conceived to be held
> by the plaintiff, the plaintiff had the same number of claims, even though
> they all sprang from a unitary occurrence. There was difficulty in
> knowing which rights were primary and what was their extent, but a
> primary right and the corresponding claim might turn out to be narrow.
> Thus it was held by some courts that a judgment for or against the
> plaintiff in an action for personal injuries did not preclude an action by
> him for property damage occasioned by the same negligent conduct on the
> part of the defendant—this deriving from the idea that the right to be
> free of bodily injury was distinct from the property right. Still another
> view of claim looked to sameness of evidence; a second action was
> precluded where the evidence to support it was the same as that needed
> to support the first. Sometimes this was made the sole test of identity of
> claim; sometimes it figured as a positive but not as a negative test; that
> is, in certain situations a second action might be precluded although the
> evidence material to it varied from that in the first action. Even so,
> claim was not coterminous with the transaction itself.

The present trend is to see claim in factual terms and to make it coterminous with the transaction regardless of the number of substantive theories, or variant forms of relief flowing from those theories, that may be available to the plaintiff; regardless of the number of primary rights that may have been invaded; and regardless of the variations in the evidence needed to support the theories or rights. The transaction is the basis of the litigative unit or entity which may not be split.

Restatement (Second), Judgments § 24, comment *a* (1982).

5. A party may waive the benefits of preclusion by failing to raise it as an affirmative defense in the second suit. Given the systemic interest in preclusion, do you think a court should be able to raise preclusion on its own initiative?

MATHEWS v. NEW YORK RACING ASSOCIATION, INC.

United States District Court, Southern District of New York, 1961.
193 F.Supp. 293.

MacMahon, District Judge. Defendants move for summary judgment, pursuant to Rule 56(b), Federal Rules on [sic] Civil Procedure, on the ground that a judgment in a prior action in this court is res judicata as to the claim alleged in the complaint.

New York Racing Association Inc. is a New York corporation which operates Jamaica Race Track. It employs defendant Thoroughbred Racing Protective Association Inc., a private detective agency, for security purposes.

Plaintiff brings this action against the Association and Thoroughbred alleging that on April 4, 1958, at Jamaica Race Track, he was "assaulted," "kidnaped," "falsely arrested," and "falsely imprisoned" by employees of Thoroughbred. He further alleges that the defendants charged him with disorderly conduct and maliciously caused him to be prosecuted and convicted in the Magistrate's Court of the City of New York on April 10, 1958. He prays for relief in the form of money damages and an injunction restraining the defendants from interfering with his attendance at race tracks, from publication of libelous statements, and from acting as peace officers.

The prior judgment on which defendants rely was entered in this court on June 30, 1960 following a trial before Judge Palmieri sitting without a jury. The complaint in that action alleged, among other matters, that plaintiff was assaulted by the defendant's private investigators at Jamaica Race Track on April 4, 1958. It also alleged that the employees of the defendants had made libelous statements concerning the plaintiff on several occasions, including plaintiff's trial for disorderly conduct on April 10, 1958. The relief prayed for in that action was also money damages and an injunction from further interference with plaintiff's attendance at race tracks within the United States. The earlier action named three individuals as defendants. The only two properly served were employees of the defendants named in the present suit.

The doctrine of res judicata operates as a bar to subsequent suits involving the same parties, or those in privity with them, based on a claim which has once reached a judgment on the merits. * * * There can be no doubt that the parties in this action are in privity with those in the earlier suit. * * *

The classic situation in which the doctrine of res judicata comes into play is where a second claim between the same parties is based on the same operative facts as the earlier one. The issues tried in the first claim and any other issues which could have been dealt with there are forever barred by the first judgment. * * *

Thus, the question is whether the claim alleged in this complaint is the same as that in the suit concluded earlier. The term "claim" refers to a group of facts limited to a single occurrence or transaction without particular reference to the resulting legal rights. It is the facts surrounding the occurrence which operate to make up the claim, not the legal theory upon which a plaintiff relies. * * *

The facts upon which plaintiff predicates this action occurred on two days, separated by almost a week, but they are so interrelated as to constitute a single claim. The ejection from the race track on April 4, 1958 was the subject of the subsequent trial for disorderly conduct on April 10, 1958.

The facts relevant to the incident at Jamaica Race Track on April 4, 1958, along with three other separate claims based on different facts, were tried to a conclusion in the earlier suit. There, the plaintiff relied on the acts of the agents occurring on April 4, 1958 as the basis of a claim against them on the theory of assault. Now, he asserts these same acts as the basis of a claim against the agents' principals on the theory of false arrest. In the earlier action, plaintiff relied on the statements of the agents made on April 10, 1958 as the basis of a claim against them on the theory of libel. Now, he asserts those same statements as the basis of a claim against their principals on the theory of malicious prosecution. Clearly, any liability of the defendants for the acts or statements of their agents must be predicated upon the familiar principle of respondeat superior. Thus, if the agents committed no actionable wrong against the plaintiff, neither did their principals. * * *

Essentially, therefore, the same facts are the basis for liability in each suit. The testimony of the witnesses who took part in or saw the ejection of the plaintiff on April 4, 1958 is the same under any theory of liability. The evidence that agents of the defendants characterized plaintiff as undesirable is the same in each suit, whether plaintiff claims the words the agents used are actionable under a theory of libel or under a theory of malicious prosecution.

The plaintiff cannot be permitted to splinter his claim into a multiplicity of suits and try them piecemeal at his convenience. * * * "The plaintiff having alleged operative facts which state a cause of action because he tells of defendant's misconduct and his own harm has had his day in court. He does not get another day after the first lawsuit is concluded by giving a different reason than he gave in the first for recovery of damages for the same invasion of his rights. The problem of his rights against the defendant based upon the alleged wrongful acts is fully before the court whether all the reasons for recovery were stated to the court or not." * * *

The issues relating to plaintiff's ejection from Jamaica Race Track on April 4, 1958 and his trial on April 10, 1958 were tried and determined by Judge Palmieri, who found that upon the facts and law plaintiff had shown no right to relief. He specifically found that plaintiff had physically resisted removal from the track, and that the defendants' employees had used no more force than was reasonably necessary to effect his removal. Therefore, plaintiff is estopped, both directly and collaterally, from maintaining this action. * * *

The court is cognizant of the fact that plaintiff appears pro se, but as the law provides a beginning for litigation, it must also provide an end. The doctrine of res judicata is a barrier against needless multiplication of litigation. "Litigation is the means for vindicating rights, but it may also involve unwarranted friction and waste. The doctrine * * * reflects the refusal of law to tolerate needless litigation. Litigation is needless if, by fair process, a controversy has once gone through the courts to conclusion." Angel v. Bullington, supra, 330 U.S. at pages 192–193, 67 S.Ct. at page 662. * * *

Notes and Questions

1. *Rush* and *Mathews* illustrate one of the primary purposes of the claim-preclusion doctrine: to prevent the splitting of a single claim into two separate suits. In *Rush,* the plaintiff won her first suit for property damage, and the court held that any claims she had for personal injuries were "merged"—in other words, extinguished—in the first suit. In *Mathews,* the plaintiff had lost the first suit. Since the basic factual setting of the claim in the second suit was the same as in the first, the court held that the allegations were "barred" by the earlier judgment.

2. *Rush* and *Mathews* use the transaction approach to determine the scope of the first suit's preclusive effect. One of the greatest advantages of this test is its flexibility. Yet, flexibility comes at a price. Because a court may interpret the claim presented in the first lawsuit more broadly than a litigant does, the litigant unknowingly may forfeit parts of his action by failing to raise them. For this reason litigants will learn "by trial and error in the harsh school of experience" of the need to raise all possibly connected allegations in the first proceeding. Cleary, *Res Judicata Reexamined,* 57 Yale L.J. 339, 340 (1948). This well may mean that they will advance claims that they otherwise might not have brought to court.

3. In the federal system, the rules governing compulsory counterclaims and pendent jurisdiction also use a form of transaction test. Does the concept of a "transaction" vary in these different contexts?

FEDERATED DEPARTMENT STORES, INC. v. MOITIE, 452 U.S. 394, 101 S.Ct. 2424, 69 L.Ed.2d 103 (1981). Respondents Moitie and Brown were two of seven plaintiffs to file separate antitrust actions against petitioner (*Moitie I* and *Brown I*). The actions were consolidated in the District Court after which they were dismissed for failure to allege an "injury" to their "business or property" within the meaning of Section 4 of the Clayton Act. The other five plaintiffs appealed to the Ninth Circuit. Moitie and Brown, however, did not appeal, but, instead, refiled their actions in state court (*Moitie II* and *Brown II*). The actions were removed to federal court and then dismissed on res judicata grounds. Meanwhile, the five appeals cases were reversed and remanded to the District Court to be reconsidered in light of an intervening Supreme Court opinion. When *Moitie II* and *Brown II* reached the Ninth Circuit on appeal, it held that, although a strict application of res judicata would preclude the second action, an exception should be made when the dismissal rested on a case that had been effectively overruled. The Supreme Court disagreed:

> The Court of Appeals * * * rested its opinion in part on what it viewed as "simple justice." But we do not see the grave injustice which would be done by the application of accepted principles of res judicata. "Simple justice" is achieved when a complex body of law developed over a period of years is evenhandedly applied. The doctrine of res judicata serves vital public interests beyond any individual judge's ad hoc determination of the equities in a particular case. There is simply "no principle of law or equity which sanctions the rejection by a federal court of the salutary principle of *res judicata.*" * * * The Court of Appeals' reliance on "public policy" is similarly misplaced. This Court has long recognized that "[p]ublic policy dictates that there be an end of litigation; that those who have contested an issue shall be bound by the result of the contest, and that matters once tried shall be considered forever settled as between the parties." Baldwin v. Traveling Men's Association, 283 U.S. 522, 525, 51 S.Ct. 517, 518, 75 L.Ed. 1244 (1931). We have stressed that "[the] doctrine of *res judicata* is not a mere matter of practice or procedure inherited from a more technical time than ours. It is a rule of fundamental and substantial justice, 'of public policy and of private peace,' which should be cordially regarded and enforced by the courts * * *." Hart Steel Co. v. Railroad Supply Co., 244 U.S. 294, 299, 37 S.Ct. 506, 507, 61 L.Ed. 1148 (1917). * * *

Id. at 401–02, 101 S.Ct. at 2429–30, 69 L.Ed.2d at 110–11.

Notes and Questions

1. In spite of the harsh language of *Moitie*, there are situations in which considerations of justice and fairness dictate that prior judgments not be given preclusive effect. When the prior judgment was obtained by the use of fraud, courts generally will not consider it binding. See, e.g., McCarty v. First of Georgia Ins. Co., 713 F.2d 609 (10th Cir.1983). Similarly, when there was a clear and fundamental jurisdictional defect that should have prevented the first court from hearing the suit, courts often will hold that the judgment has no preclusive effect.

2. What impact should an appeal have on the preclusive effect of a trial court's judgment? Federal courts grant preclusion pending appeal of an underlying judgment, but state rules vary. What should be the effect of a remand for retrial on the preclusive effect of the underlying judgment? What if the legal underpinning of the underlying judgment is overruled? See Fed.R.Civ.P. 60(b)(5), 18 Wright, Miller & Cooper, *Federal Practice and Procedure: Jurisdiction and Related Matters* § 4433 (1981).

JONES v. MORRIS PLAN BANK OF PORTSMOUTH

Supreme Court of Appeals of Virginia, 1937.
168 Va. 284, 191 S.E. 608.

GREGORY, JUSTICE. William B. Jones instituted an action for damages against the Morris Plan Bank of Portsmouth for the conversion of his automobile. * * *

After the plaintiff had introduced all of his evidence and before the defendant had introduced any evidence on its behalf, the latter's counsel moved to strike the evidence of the plaintiff and the court sustained the motion. A verdict for the defendant resulted.

The facts are that the plaintiff purchased from J.A. Parker, a dealer in automobiles, a Plymouth sedan, agreeing to pay therefor $595. He paid a part of the purchase price by the delivery of a used car to Parker of the agreed value of $245 and after crediting that amount on the purchase price and adding a finance charge of $78.40, there remained an unpaid balance due the dealer of $428. This latter amount was payable in 12 monthly installments of $35.70 each and evidenced by one note in the principal sum of $428.40. The note contained this provision: "The whole amount of this note (less any payments made hereon) becomes immediately due and payable in the event of nonpayment at maturity of any installment thereof." The note was secured by the usual conditional sales contract * * * in which it was agreed that the title to the car would be retained by the dealer until the entire purchase price was paid in full. * * * [T]he contract was assigned to the defendant * * * and the note was indorsed by Parker and delivered to the defendant at the same time.

Installment payments due on the note for May and June were not made when payable and for them an action was instituted in the civil and police court of the city of Suffolk. No appearance was made by the defendant (Jones) in that action and judgment was obtained against him for the two payments. Execution issued upon the judgment and it was satisfied * * * by Jones * * *.

Later the defendant instituted another action against Jones in the same court for the July installment which had become due and was unpaid, and to that action Jones filed a plea of res adjudicata, whereupon the * * * [Bank] took a nonsuit.

* * * [T]he defendant * * * took possession of the automobile without the consent of the plaintiff and later sold it and applied the proceeds upon the note.

Afterwards, the plaintiff instituted the present action for conversion to recover damages for the loss of the automobile. His action in the court below was founded upon the theory that when the May and June installments became due and were unpaid, then under the acceleration clause in the note, the entire balance due thereon matured and at once became due and the defendant having elected to sue him for only two installments instead of the entire amount of the note, and having obtained a judgment for the two installments and satisfaction of the execution issued thereon, it waived its right to collect the balance. He also contends that the note was satisfied in the manner narrated and that the conditional sales contract, the sole purpose of which was to secure the payment of the note, served its purpose and ceased to exist, and, therefore, the title to the automobile was no longer retained, but upon the satisfaction of the note, passed to the plaintiff and was his property when the agent of the defendant removed it and converted it to its own use.

The position of the defendant is that * * * the title to the automobile, which was the subject of the alleged conversion, was not vested in the plaintiff at the time of the action, nor since, because the condition in the contract was that the title should be retained by the seller (whose rights were assigned to the defendant) until the entire purchase price was paid, and that the purchase price had never been paid * * *.

The defendant also contends that the note and conditional sales contract were divisible; that successive actions could be brought upon the installments as they matured; and that it was not bound, at the risk of waiving its right to claim the balance, to sue for all installments in one action.

* * *

We decide that under the unconditional acceleration provision in the note involved here and in the absence of the usual optional provision reserved to the holder, the entire amount due upon the note became due and payable when default was made in paying an installment. * * *

Was it essential that the defendant here institute an action for all of the installments then due, or could it institute its action for only two of the installments and later institute another action for other installments? The answer to that question depends upon the nature of the transaction. If a transaction is represented by one single and indivisible contract and the breach gives rise to one single cause of action, it cannot be split into distinct parts and separate actions maintained for each.

On the other hand, if the contract is divisible giving rise to more than one cause of action, each may be proceeded upon separately.

Was the contract here single and indivisible or was it divisible? Our answer is that the note and conditional sales contract constituted one single contract. The sole purpose of the conditional sales contract was to retain the title in the seller until the note was paid. When that condition was performed, the contract ended.

One of the principal tests in determining whether a demand is single and entire, or whether it is several, so as to give rise to more than one cause of action, is the identity of facts necessary to maintain the action. If the same evidence will support both actions, there is but one cause of action.

In the case at bar, all of the installments were due. The evidence essential to support the action on the two installments for which the action was brought would be the identical evidence necessary to maintain an action upon all of the installments. All installments having matured at the time the action was begun, under well-settled principles, those not embraced in that action are now barred.

* * * At the time the defendant lost its right to institute any action for the remaining installments, the title to the automobile passed to the plaintiff. He was the owner at the time the agent of the defendant took possession of it and exposed it to sale.

It follows that the judgment of the court below will be reversed, and the case will be remanded for the sole purpose of determining the quantum of damages.

Reversed and remanded.

Notes and Questions

1. Why did the court remand only for the purpose of determining damages rather than order a new trial?

2. When a debt is secured by a series of notes or when a bond includes a number of interest coupons, an action on one of the notes or coupons, even though others are due, does not bar a subsequent action on those others. *Restatement, Judgments* § 62, comment *i* (1942); *Restatement (Second), Judgments* § 24, comment *d* (1982). Cf. NESBIT v. RIVERSIDE IND. DISTRICT, 144 U.S. 610, 619, 12 S.Ct. 746, 748, 36 L.Ed. 562, 565 (1892):

> Each matured coupon is a separable promise, and gives rise to a separate cause of action. It may be detached from the bond and sold by itself. Indeed, the title to several matured coupons of the same bond may be in as many different persons, and upon each a distinct and separate action be maintained. So, while the promises of the bond and of the coupons in the first instance are upon the same paper, and the coupons are for interest due upon the bond, yet the promise to pay the coupon is as distinct from that to pay the bond as though the two promises were placed in different instruments, upon different paper.

3. It particularly is difficult to define the scope of a prior judgment in controversies involving continuing or renewed conduct. Section 24 of the *Restatement (Second) of Judgments* lists some considerations relevant to determining whether a factual grouping constitutes a single transaction, and suggests evaluating "whether the facts are related in time, space, origin, or motivation, whether they form a convenient trial unit, and whether their treatment as a unit conforms to the parties' expectations or business understanding or usage." See *Restatement (Second), Judgments,* § 24 (1982).

There are some other useful rules of thumb to be used in cases of continuing or renewed conduct. For example, if the conduct that is the subject of the first action continues after judgment in the first action, claim preclusion would not prevent a second suit. Issue preclusion may apply, however, to matters of status or to issues of fact resolved in the first action. When the purpose of the first suit is to establish general rules of legality, such as when the first suit is a declaratory-judgment action, subsequent claims involving the same conduct are precluded.

Nuisance suits commonly involve continuing conduct. Judgments involving "permanent" nuisances are considered to have full preclusive effect; those involving "temporary" nuisances are not considered to preclude later litigation involving the same behavior. Courts are not always consistent in their classification of nuisances. See 18 Wright, Miller & Cooper, *Federal Practice and Procedure: Jurisdiction and Related Matters* § 4425 (1981).

4. Often, the underlying substantive law will affect the definition of the claim for the purposes of preclusion. For example, if one party to a contract commits a material breach that neither is accompanied nor followed by a repudiation, the law of contracts teaches that the other party is free, on the one hand, to treat the contract as binding and sue for the damages or, on the other hand, to treat the contract as ended. If the aggrieved party chooses the former option, and then suffers further material breaches, she will not be barred from suing for damages not sought in the first suit. See *Restatement (Second), Judgments* § 26, comment *g* (1982).

The expectations of the parties also may be decisive in determining the scope of the prior judgment. Imagine that a wholesale distributor regularly ships goods to a retailer on credit. If the parties conceive of their relationship as a series of discrete transactions, a suit by the creditor seeking to recover any one of the payments would not bar subsequent suits for other payments. If, however, the parties believe they have a single running account, a suit by the creditor would have to seek to recover the entire balance then due.

Can you think of other situations in which substantive law might affect the scope of the prior judgment? See generally 18 Wright, Miller & Cooper, *Federal Practice and Procedure: Jurisdiction and Related Matters* § 4409 (1981).

2. DEFENSE PRECLUSION

MITCHELL v. FEDERAL INTERMEDIATE CREDIT BANK

Supreme Court of South Carolina, 1932.
165 S.C. 457, 164 S.E. 136.

[Action for an accounting against defendant bank for proceeds of a crop of potatoes. Plaintiff alleged that in order to obtain loans from defendant he had—at the behest of defendant's agent—sold his potatoes through a growers' association and assigned the proceeds as security for two notes, totalling $9,000, which had been discounted with defendant; that the potatoes had netted $18,000, but that he had never received any of this, and that the proceeds had been received by defendant or an agent of defendant. In a previous action by defendant on the notes, plaintiff had pleaded in the answer the same facts now the basis of an affirmative claim, but had not counterclaimed or asked relief; judgment had been for him in that action. In the present suit, defendant contended that plaintiff's claim was merged in the earlier judgment. This contention was upheld by the trial court.]

STABLER, J. * * *

We now come to the main question presented by the appeal, namely, Was the circuit judge in error in sustaining the plea in bar to plaintiff's action? Turning to appellant's answer in the federal court case * * * we find that the facts there pleaded by him as a defense to the bank's recovery on its notes are the same as those set out by him in his complaint as the basis of his action in the case at bar, it being alleged that the total amount paid to the bank was in excess of all sums advanced to him on the notes or otherwise, and as a result of the transaction the notes sued upon were fully paid and discharged. In addition, we find in the record of the case before us the following statement by appellant as an admission of fact on his part: "* * * The indebtedness of the bank to Mitchell arising from the embezzlement of the proceeds of the crop was used pro tanto as an offset to the claim of the bank in the Federal Court. The case at bar seeks recovery of the surplusage, over the offset, of the proceeds of the same crop lost by the same embezzlement. The appellant, however, is not seeking to recover in this action the same money that has already been used as an offset."

* * *

In support of his position * * * appellant cites certain decisions of this court, which he claims to be conclusive of the issue, relying especially upon Kirven v. Chemical Co., 77 S.C. 493, 58 S.E. 424, 426.

* * * [T]he record shows that Kirven had bought from the Chemical Company $2,228 worth of fertilizers and had given his note for that amount. The company, upon maturity of the note, brought action against him on his obligation. He at first filed an answer setting up three defenses, the third of which was that the fertilizers furnished were deleterious and destructive to the crops, and that there was an entire failure of consideration for the note. Later, he was permitted to file a supplemental answer in which he withdrew the third defense. On trial in the federal court, the jury rendered a verdict for the Chemical Company. Thereafter, Kirven brought an action against the company * * * alleging that the defendant caused damage to his crop in the sum of $1,995 by reason of the deleterious effect of the fertilizers furnished. The company set up the defense that the issues in this action were or could have been adjudicated in the [first] suit * * *. A verdict was given Kirven in the amount prayed for, and on appeal * * * it was pointed out that the question raised in the state court was not *actually* litigated and determined in the federal action, and it appears that the court, for that reason, took the view that a bar or estoppel did not exist. Mr. Justice Woods, in his concurring opinion, took the view that, as Kirven elected not to use, as a defense, the fact of *worthlessness,* which might have been available in the action of the company against him, "he was not precluded from using the very different facts of deleteriousness and positive injury caused by appellant's alleged negligence in the manufacture of the fertilizer as the basis of an independent cause of action."

We think the facts of the case at bar, however, present a different situation. * * *

O'Connor v. Varney, 10 Gray (Mass.) 231, was an action on contract to recover damages for Varney's failure to build certain additions to a house according to the terms of a written agreement between the parties. The defendant set up as a defense "a judgment recovered by O'Connor in an action brought by Varney against him on that contract to recover the price therein agreed to be paid for the work, in defence of which O'Connor relied on the same nonperformance by Varney, and in which an auditor to whom the case was referred * * * found that Varney was not entitled to recover under the agreement," as the work had been so imperfectly done that it would require a greater sum than the amount sued for to make it correspond with the contract. At the trial of the second action, the trial judge ruled that the judgment in the first suit was a bar, and directed a verdict for the defendant. The plaintiff O'Connor thereupon appealed.

Chief Justice Shaw, who rendered the opinion of the court, said: "The presiding judge rightly ruled that the former judgment was a bar to this action. A party against whom an action is brought on a contract has two modes of defending himself. He may allege specific breaches of the contract declared upon, and rely on them in defence. But if he intends to claim, by way of damages for nonperformance of the contract, more than the amount for which he is sued, he must not rely on the contract in defence, but must bring a cross action, and apply to the court to have the cases continued so that the executions may be set off. He cannot use the same defence, first as a shield, and then as a sword. * * *"

It will be noted that Varney was not entitled to recover in the first suit because his dereliction amounted to more than he sued for. This would seem to be exactly the situation in the case at bar.

* * * When the bank sued * * * [Mitchell] on his two notes, amounting to about $9,000, he had the option to interpose his claim as a defense to that suit or to demand judgment against the bank, by way of counterclaim, for the amount owing him by it. * * * The transaction out of which the case at bar arises is the same transaction that Mitchell pleaded as a defense in the federal suit. He might, therefore, "have recovered in that action, upon the same allegations and proofs which he there made, the judgment which he now seeks, if he had prayed for it." He did not do this, but attempted to split his cause of action, and to use one portion of it for defense in that suit and to reserve the remainder for offense in a subsequent suit, which, under applicable principles, could not be done. * * *

The judgment of the circuit court is affirmed.

Questions

1. Compulsory-counterclaim rules, such as Federal Rule 13(a), effectively supersede the rules of preclusion in many contexts. Generally, under Rule 13(a) compulsory counterclaims that are not raised may not be raised in subsequent litigation in federal court. In most situations the broad sweep of compulsory-counterclaim preclusion thus makes it unnecessary to consider whether and how defense preclusion might apply.

Defense preclusion does apply, however, in the many state court systems in which there is no compulsory-counterclaim rule. Moreover, even when there are compulsory-counterclaim rules, they often contain express exceptions. Rule 13(a), for example, does not require parties to include claims that already are pending in another suit. And, some courts have held Rule 13(a) inapplicable in suits in which no responsive pleading was filed because the action was terminated by default, settlement, or dismissal on motion.

2. At common law, would Mitchell's defense in the first action have been in the nature of a recoupment or a set-off? Assuming that the defense would have been one or the other, would this have made a difference as to the right to bring a later suit for the excess? See pp. 556–57, supra.

LINDERMAN MACHINE CO. v. HILLENBRAND CO., 75 Ind.App. 111, 127 N.E. 813 (1920). L sold H a machine, and subsequently sued to recover the purchase price; H answered that the contract had been obtained by fraudulent representations as to the machine's capacity to do H's work, that the machine did not perform as represented, and that H had notified L to remove the machine. Judgment was rendered against L. Subsequently H sued L to recover damages for fraud, alleging that it had incurred great expense in transporting, installing, attempting to operate, and removing the machine. L answered that the action was barred by the judgment in the first suit. The court held for H:

It is true that a party, when sued, must interpose all defenses which he has, and as to them, whether pleaded or not, the judgment is conclusive; but it is not conclusive as to an affirmative right or cause of action which he may have against the plaintiff, and of which he could have taken advantage by way of cross-complaint. He is not compelled to file his cross-complaint, and, on his failure to do so, his rights with reference thereto will not be adjudged. * * *

There was no issue in the action brought by [L] to recover the purchase price * * * as to the right of [H] to recover the expenses which it had been put to in installing the machinery, and without such issue therein, [L] is not in position now to invoke against [H] the doctrine of res adjudicata.

Id. at 118, 127 N.E. at 815.

Notes and Questions

1. Is *Linderman* consistent with *Mitchell*?

2. Problems with preclusion also may arise when a dispute involves multiple potential defendants. In FIRST ACCEPTANCE CORP. v. KENNEDY, 95 F.Supp. 861 (N.D.Iowa 1951), reversed on other grounds 194 F.2d 819 (8th Cir.1952), defendant purchased an air conditioner for an onion-drying shed under a conditional-sales agreement with a vendor who assigned the contract to plaintiff. In a suit for the balance of the purchase price, the trial court permitted defendant to raise fraud as a total defense to the contract, even though he had not rescinded the contract. The trial judge's opinion reflects the procedural difficulty that claim preclusion poses:

The defendant claims that the transaction between the United States Air Conditioning Corporation and the plaintiff placed him in a legal dilemma and that he used the defense of fraud in the only manner left open to him. It is the contention of the defendant that rescission was legally impossible for the reason that rescission could not be made with the United States Air Conditioning Corporation because the title to the subject matter of the sale was in the plaintiff; and that rescission could not be had with the plaintiff because the sum of $2,800 paid by him under the contract had been retained by the United States Air Conditioning Corporation and the plaintiff was under no obligation or duty to make refund of the $2,800 upon rescission. The defendant points out that the United States Air Conditioning Corporation was not subject to service of process in Iowa and, therefore, it could not be made a party to this action.

The defendant further claims that the damages sustained by him because of the fraud practiced upon him * * * are greatly in excess of the amount which the plaintiff seeks to recover herein; and that if he asserted part of his damages as an offset or by way of recoupment against the plaintiff's claim he would be splitting his cause of action and that he then would be unable to recover the balance of his damages from the United States Air Conditioning Corporation.

It is plain that the defendant in his pleadings very carefully refrained from attempting to use any part of his damages as an offset or by way of recoupment. The position of the defendant is that since rescission was impossible and since he could not use part of his claim as an offset or by way of recoupment without losing the balance of his claim all that he could do was to ask that the contract be not enforced against him because of fraud in its procurement.

Id. at 870–71.

3. Defense preclusion typically is raised in a subsequent action by the original plaintiff when the defendant tries to assert a defense that was not raised in the earlier action. It undoubtedly should apply if the subsequent action is a suit to enforce the first action; in other kinds of suits, however, the role of defense preclusion is more ambiguous. On the one hand, it could be argued that defense preclusion should not apply, as often defendants will have very good reasons for not raising a particular defense in the first action (for example, it may have been difficult to obtain the necessary evidence or witnesses). On the other hand, permitting a new defense to be raised may destroy the plaintiff's sense of repose.

Consider JACOBSON v. MILLER, 41 Mich. 90, 1 N.W. 1013 (1879). A landlord brought and prevailed on an action to recover unpaid installments of rent. Subsequently, the landlord brought another suit to recover later unpaid installments. Although he had made no mention of a defense in the initial proceeding, the tenant sought to defend the second suit by alleging that he had never executed the lease. Should the court have permitted the defense to be made? Remember that if the defendant had raised this claim in the first action successfully, the landlord could have taken affirmative steps to remedy the problem, and perhaps even could have found a new tenant. See generally 18 Wright, Miller & Cooper, *Federal Practice and Procedure: Jurisdiction and Related Matters* § 4414 (1981); *Restatement (Second), Judgments* § 22 (1982).

SECTION C. ISSUE PRECLUSION

One of the most frequently quoted descriptions of what is now referred to as issue preclusion was provided by the first Justice Harlan in SOUTHERN PAC. R. CO. v. UNITED STATES, 168 U.S. 1, 48–49, 18 S.Ct. 18, 27, 42 L.Ed. 355, 377 (1897):

> The general principle announced in numerous cases is that a right, question, or fact distinctly put in issue and directly determined by a court of competent jurisdiction, as a ground of recovery, cannot be disputed in a subsequent suit between the same parties or their privies; and, even if the second suit is for a different cause of action, the right, question, or fact once so determined must, as between the same parties or their privies, be taken as conclusively established, so long as the judgment in the first suit remains unmodified. This general rule is demanded by the very object for which civil courts have been established, which is to secure the peace and repose of society by the settlement of matters capable of judicial determination. Its enforcement is essential to the maintenance of social order; for the aid of judicial tribunals would not be invoked for the vindication of rights of person and property if, as between parties and their privies, conclusiveness did not attend the judgments of such tribunals in respect of all matters properly put in issue, and actually determined by them.

not overturned on appeal

As this passage reveals, there is a critical difference between claim preclusion and issue preclusion. Under the doctrine of claim preclusion, a claim may be "merged" or "barred" by a party's failure to raise the claim in a prior action. Issue preclusion, however, applies only to matters argued and decided in an earlier lawsuit.

For issue preclusion to exist, a proceeding must involve the same issue as a previous suit. The term "issue," like the term "transaction" in the context of claim preclusion, is ambiguous and subject to manipulation. And, the application *vel non* of doctrines of issue preclusion sometimes will turn on the ability of advocates to manipulate the definition of this crucial term.

To trigger the doctrines of issue preclusion, however, more than a mere duplication of issues is required. It is necessary to examine the nature of the first action and the treatment that the issue received in it. Just as for claim preclusion, the judgment in the first action must have been of a certain "quality"—that is, it must have been valid, final, and on the merits (the "on the merits" requirement does not apply if the issue being precluded is exclusively a procedural issue). Moreover, the issue raised in a second suit actually must have been litigated in the first action, and must have been decided by the first court. And, determination of that issue must have been necessary to the court's judgment.

Some courts require still more before they will allow a party to invoke issue preclusion. For example, some demand that the issue have occupied a high position in the hierarchy of legal rules applied in the first action— that it was important. Others require "mutuality"—that is, that the party invoking preclusion would have been bound by an unfavorable judgment in the first suit. Fewer and fewer courts now impose these latter two conditions, however, and the mutuality requirement in particular is now widely disregarded.

Issue preclusion can be used in a variety of ways. It can be invoked offensively, when the plaintiff in the second action seeks to preclude litigation of an issue that was decided favorably to him in a prior action. Or, it can be used defensively, when the defendant in the second suit seeks to preclude relitigation of an issue that was decided in his favor in a prior suit. Some courts and commentators further distinguish between "direct" and "collateral" preclusion or estoppel—depending upon whether the second proceeding involves the same cause of action as the first. When the two suits involve the same cause of action, issue preclusion sometimes is referred to as direct estoppel. When the second suit involves a new claim or cause of action, issue preclusion sometimes is referred to as collateral estoppel.

1. ACTUALLY LITIGATED

CROMWELL v. COUNTY OF SAC

Supreme Court of the United States, 1876.
94 U.S. (4 Otto) 351, 24 L.Ed. 195.

Error to the Circuit Court of the United States for the District of Iowa.

MR. JUSTICE FIELD delivered the opinion of the court.

This was an action on four bonds * * * each for $1,000, and four coupons for interest, attached to them, each for $100. The bonds were issued in 1860, and were made payable to bearer, in the city of New York, in the years 1868, 1869, 1870, and 1871, respectively, with annual interest at the rate of ten per cent a year.

To defeat this action, the defendant relied upon the estoppel of a judgment rendered in favor of the county in a prior action brought by one Samuel C. Smith upon certain earlier maturing coupons on the same bonds, accompanied with proof that the plaintiff Cromwell was at the time the owner of the coupons in that action, and that the action was prosecuted for his sole use and benefit.

* * *

In considering the operation of this judgment, it should be borne in mind * * * that there is a difference between the effect of a judgment as a bar or estoppel against the prosecution of a second action upon the same claim or demand, and its effect as an estoppel in another action between the same parties upon a different claim or cause of action. In the former case, the judgment, if rendered upon the merits, constitutes an absolute bar to a subsequent action. [The Court's description of claim preclusion appears at p. 1148, supra.] * * * The language * * * which is so often used, that a judgment estops not only as to every ground of recovery or defence actually presented in the action, but also as to every ground which might have been presented, is strictly accurate, when applied to the demand or claim in controversy. * * *

But where the second action between the same parties is upon a different claim or demand, the judgment in the prior action operates as an estoppel only as to those matters in issue or points controverted, upon the determination of which the finding or verdict was rendered. In all cases, therefore, where it is sought to apply the estoppel of a judgment rendered upon one cause of action to matters arising in a suit upon a different cause of action, the inquiry must always be as to the point or question actually litigated and determined in the original action, not what might have been thus litigated and determined. Only upon such matters is the judgment conclusive in another action.

The difference in the operation of a judgment in the two classes of cases mentioned is seen through all the leading adjudications upon the doctrine of estoppel. Thus, in the case of Outram v. Morewood, 3 East, 346, the defendants were held estopped from averring title to a mine, in an action of trespass for digging out coal from it, because, in a previous action for a similar trespass, they had set up the same title, and it had been determined against them. In commenting upon a decision cited in that case, Lord Ellenborough, in his elaborate opinion, said: "It is not the recovery, but the matter alleged by the party, and upon which the recovery proceeds, which creates the estoppel. The recovery of itself in an action of trespass is only a bar to the future recovery of damages for the same injury; but the estoppel precludes parties and privies from contending to the contrary of that point or matter of fact, which, having been once distinctly put in issue by them, or by those to whom they are privy in estate or law, has been, on such issue joined, solemnly found against them."

* * *

Various considerations, other than the actual merits, may govern a party in bringing forward grounds of recovery or defence in one action, which may not exist in another action upon a different demand, such as the smallness of the amount or the value of the property in controversy, the difficulty of obtaining the necessary evidence, the expense of the litigation, and his own situation at the time. A party acting upon considerations like these ought not to be precluded from contesting in a subsequent action other demands arising out of the same transaction.
* * *

If, now, we consider the main question presented for our determination * * * its solution will not be difficult. It appears from the findings in the original action of Smith, that the county of Sac, by a vote of its people, authorized the issue of bonds to the amount of $10,000, for the erection of a court-house; that bonds to that amount were issued by the county judge, and delivered to one Meserey, with whom he had made a contract for the erection of the court-house; that immediately upon receipt of the bonds the contractor gave one of them as a gratuity to the county judge; and that the court-house was never constructed by the contractor, or by any other person pursuant to the contract. It also appears that the plaintiff had become, before their maturity, the holder of twenty-five coupons, which had been attached to the bonds, but there was

no finding that he had ever given any value for them. * * * The case
coming here on writ of error, this court held that the facts disclosed by the
findings were sufficient evidence of fraud and illegality in the inception of
the bonds to call upon the holder to show that he had given value for the
coupons; and, not having done so, the judgment was affirmed. Reading
the record of the lower court by the opinion and judgment of this court, it
must be considered that the matters adjudged in that case were these:
that the bonds were void as against the county in the hands of parties who
did not acquire them before maturity and give value for them, and that
the plaintiff, not having proved that he gave such value, was not entitled
to recover upon the coupons. * * * The finding and judgment upon the
invalidity of the bonds, as against the county, must be held to estop the
plaintiff here from averring to the contrary. But as the bonds were
negotiable instruments * * * they would be held as valid obligations
against the county in the hands of a *bona fide* holder taking them for
value before maturity * * *. If, therefore, the plaintiff received the
bond and coupons in suit before maturity for value, as he offered to prove,
he should have been permitted to show that fact. There was nothing
adjudged in the former action in the finding that the plaintiff had not
made such proof in that case which can preclude the present plaintiff
from making such proof here. The fact that a party may not have shown
that he gave value for one bond or coupon is not even presumptive, much
less conclusive, evidence that he may not have given value for another
and different bond or coupon. The exclusion of the evidence offered by
the plaintiff was erroneous * * *.

Judgment reversed, and cause remanded for a new trial.

[The dissenting opinion of Justice Clifford is omitted.]

Notes and Questions

1. A physician sues a patient to collect her fee for services rendered.
The patient defaults, judgment is entered, and the judgment is satisfied.
Later, the patient sues the physician for malpractice. Does the earlier default
judgment establish that the physician's services were of value, and not
worthless or harmful? Is the fact that the patient may have had little
incentive to litigate the first suit relevant? Would it make a difference if the
malpractice claim was not foreseeable at the time of the first action? What if
the patient had strong reasons for wanting to litigate the malpractice claim in
a different jurisdiction from the one where the first suit was brought?
Compare Gwynn v. Wilhelm, 226 Or. 606, 360 P.2d 312 (1961), with Blair v.
Barlett, 75 N.Y. 150 (1878). See Annot., 77 A.L.R.2d 1410 (1961).

2. Professor Allan Vestal criticizes the actually litigated requirement on
the ground that the justifications offered on its behalf are unsound:

> * * * [One argument made in favor of the actually litigated re-
> quirement is] that an action may involve "so small an amount that
> litigation of the issue may cost more than the value of the lawsuit."
> [*Restatement (Second), Judgments* § 68, comment *e* (Tent. Draft No. 4,
> 1977).] This is a rather curious rationale. It does not support the
> "actually litigated" requirement; rather it supports a rejection of issue

preclusion under any circumstances. If there is insufficient incentive to litigate a matter, then there should be no issue preclusion. Litigation in small claims courts or prosecutions for misdemeanors cannot give rise to issue preclusion because often those actions provide litigants with inadequate incentive to litigate. Although the line is not clearly defined, it seems reasonable to conclude that prosecutions for felonies and civil litigation involving substantial amounts will give rise to issue preclusion. The burden properly falls on the presumably precluded party to show why issue preclusion should not apply.

* * * [A second argument used to justify the actually litigated requirement is] that "the forum may be an inconvenient one in which to produce the necessary evidence or in which to litigate at all." [Id.] If a valid judgment is going to be handed down, then this forum must have jurisdiction over the defendant and it is the forum of choice of the plaintiff. As the forum of choice of the plaintiff, it is proper to hold that the plaintiff should be bound by any adverse decision reached by the court. It is only in the case of the defendant that he might be able to assert that he should not be bound because it is inconvenient.

In light of (a) the present constitutional limitations on the exercise of jurisdiction over defendants, (b) the fact that the suit by definition involves a substantial interest, and (c) the availability of procedures to get and present the relevant evidence, this justification is not very persuasive. Would it not be better to hold for issue preclusion, and then permit the apparently precluded party to explain why preclusion should not apply?

The [*Restatement's*] Comment also gives as a reason for the "actually litigated" rule that a rule to the contrary "might serve to discourage compromise, to decrease the likelihood that the issues in an action would be narrowed by stipulation, and thus to intensify litigation." Id. This litigation, where there is the incentive to litigate, must involve substantial interests on the part of the parties. The issue preclusion that may flow from the judgment does not change the suit from unimportant to important. The suit is, by definition, important. If a compromise is going to be discouraged, it probably will be by the size of the present suit. If there is going to be a refusal to stipulate and thus narrow issues, in all probability it will be because of the importance of the instant suit and not because of the issue preclusion that may flow from the decision.

Vestal, *The Restatement (Second) of Judgments: A Modest Dissent,* 66 Cornell L.Rev. 464, 473–74 (1981).

3. Section 28 of the *Restatement (Second) of Judgments* adopts the actually litigated requirement. Professor Geoffrey Hazard, the Restatement's final Reporter, believes that other trends in civil procedure provide powerful arguments against relaxing the requirement:

A good case can be made for saying that if a matter is distinctly put in issue and formally admitted, the party making the admission should be bound by it in subsequent litigation. This was the old formulation of the rule of "judicial estoppel," as it was then called: "The former verdict is conclusive only as to facts directly and distinctly put in issue * * *." But how can a matter be "directly and distinctly put in issue"? Obviously, by actual litigation. Another way is through pleadings. In a pleading system where matters are "distinctly put in issue," it makes sense to say that if a proposition is clearly asserted, and if a party is called upon solemnly to admit or deny the proposition, and if the stakes are high enough to assure that the party is serious in dealing with the issue, and if the party then admits or fails to deny the proposition, then he ought to be estopped from controverting it on some other occasion, particularly if that other occasion involves essentially the same transaction. The clearest case for such an estoppel is where a defendant pleads guilty to a substantial criminal charge and then seeks in civil litigation concerning the same transaction to assert that he did not commit the criminal act. Particularly galling is the situation where a criminal convicted on his own guilty plea seeks as plaintiff in a subsequent civil action to claim redress based on a repudiation of the confession. The effrontery or, as some might say it, *chutzpah,* is too much to take. There certainly should be an estoppel in such a case.

The same principle could apply when an issue is put forward and admitted "distinctly"—that is, clearly and solemnly—in a civil case. It is therefore appropriate to impose an estoppel based on a formal admission in a civil case, and the law of evidence does so. A judicial admission is considered in subsequent litigations as prima facie evidence that the admitted matter is true.

The relation between judicial admissions and subsequent estoppel merits closer examination. In a procedural system that aims to put things "distinctly in issue" in the pre-trial stage, judicial admissions are elicited as a matter of course. This was the effect of the system of common law pleading, the Hillary Rules, and the classical form of code pleading. Admissions were an important by-product of a system of pleading designed to put things "distinctly in issue" as a preface to conducting a trial. The process of obtaining admissions in this way was so familiar that they were called "judicial admissions," treated as part of the law of judgments, and mentioned in books dealing with judgments. In a procedural system that focuses on pre-trial formulation of issues, it is appropriate to give estoppel effect to judicial admissions. If a party is confronted by a distinct allegation, is required by the procedural rules to admit or deny such assertions, has adequate incentive to litigate, and does not deny it, he should be estopped from later controverting the allegation. That apparently was the rule under the regime of code pleading.

But today we work under the Federal Rules of Civil Procedure and analogous systems. The federal rules reject issue formulation as the basis of adjudicative procedure. Pleadings under the federal rules merely give notice in broad terms that some sort of legal controversy is afoot. The federal rules' mechanism for identifying issues is not pleading, but interrogation and proof through discovery and summary judgment or trial. The technique for specifying the issues is direct immersion in evidence—actual litigation—and not issue formulation. Professor Vestal, for all his aspiration to modernity, is thus writing for the wrong century. What he sees as an imminent form of preclusion in modern procedure is a fading vestige of code pleading.

This is another instance where change in procedural rules requires modification of res judicata doctrine. Under modern civil procedure, a party is not required to put matters "distinctly in issue" before proof is formally marshalled and weighed. Moreover, in modern civil procedure a party has practically unlimited freedom, or "opportunity," to assert claims and issues. Even in a simple civil action, a plaintiff can open up any legal controversy between the parties within the subject matter jurisdiction of the court—law or equity, tort or contract, common law or statute, state or federal. In a strict sense, a plaintiff has an "opportunity" to raise every issue that could possibly be tendered in any claim the pleading and jurisdiction rules allow him to raise, regardless of the logical or evidentiary connections among them. A defendant has comparable latitude. A defendant has "opportunity" to raise every issue that would be involved in any defense, avoidance, or counterclaim that the procedural rules allow him to assert. Modern pleading allows a defendant to assert as a defense anything relevant to plaintiff's claim, and to assert as a counterclaim everything he may have against plaintiff, regardless of relevancy to plaintiff's claim.

This is the measure of "opportunity to litigate" under modern civil procedure. Does issue preclusion sweep this broad, so that "opportunity to litigate" an issue becomes the equivalent of necessity to litigate? No, of course it does not. * * *

* * *

Professor Vestal says there should be an estoppel because, where there is an incentive to deny, failure to deny constitutes an admission. This turns the notion of incentive to litigate on its head. The "incentive to litigate" formula, as used in most of the cases and in the *Restatement Second,* allows a party who *did* litigate an issue to relitigate it if the party can show that the original litigation was a side show rather than a struggle to the finish. [See *Restatement (Second) of Judgments* § 68.1(e), Comment *j* (Tent. Draft No. 4, 1977).] The *Restatement Second* allows a party to rebut the inference naturally drawn from the fact that the issue was actually litigated—the inference that the party had treated the issue with entire seriousness in the first litigation. In Professor Vestal's system, however, "incentive to litigate" allows a court to conjecture that the party probably had reason to litigate the issue in the first action, and to conjecture further that the failure to litigate is an admission of a proposition not litigated. Professor Vestal's "opportunity" theory allows the court to infer that the issue was important to a party whose behavior indicates he thought the issue was unimportant, and, having done that, to convict the party by his silence. * * *

Hazard, *Revisiting the Second Restatement of Judgments: Issue Preclusion and Related Problems,* 66 Cornell L.Rev. 564, 577–79, 584 (1981).

4. Should the actually litigated requirement eliminate the preclusive effect of a guilty plea in a criminal suit? Not surprisingly, Professor Vestal argues that a guilty plea should be given preclusive effect unless the defendant can show that he lacked an adequate opportunity or incentive to litigate. The *Restatement* contains no exception from the actually litigated requirement for guilty pleas, but it does note that guilty pleas are admissible into evidence in later civil suits. Despite the *Restatement*'s position, some courts, without always setting forth a clear rationale, have granted preclusive effect to guilty pleas in subsequent suits involving the essential elements of the

crime. See Shapiro, *Should a Guilty Plea Have Preclusive Effect?*, 70 Iowa L.Rev. 2449 (1985).

5. How should a court go about determining what was decided in a prior litigation? Will the difficulty of this task be affected by whether the case was tried to a judge or to a jury? Are there any procedural rules that can play a role in defining what a suit has decided? Consider, in particular, Rule 49 and Rule 52.

When the prior decision is ambiguous on what it actually decided, doubts should be resolved against the party seeking to assert preclusion. But it sometimes will be necessary to conduct a hearing to determine what was decided. Is it possible to use the record of the prior trial to help ascertain what issues actually were decided? Is it permissible to introduce extrinsic evidence to prove what issues were litigated? There is some authority for permitting both of these methods of proof. For a general discussion of this topic, see 18 Wright, Miller & Cooper, *Federal Practice and Procedure: Jurisdiction and Related Matters* § 4420 (1981).

2. NECESSARILY DECIDED

RUSSELL v. PLACE

Supreme Court of the United States, 1876.
94 U.S. (4 Otto) 606, 24 L.Ed. 214.

Appeal from the Circuit Court of the United States for the Northern District of New York.

MR. JUSTICE FIELD delivered the opinion of the court.

This is a suit for an infringement of a patent to the complainant for an alleged new and useful improvement in the preparation of leather * * *.

The bill of complaint sets forth the invention claimed, the issue of a patent for the same, its surrender for alleged defective and insufficient description of the invention, its reissue with an amended specification, and the recovery of judgment against the defendants for damages in an action at law for a violation of the exclusive privileges secured by the patent.

The bill then alleges the subsequent manufacture, use, and sale by the defendants, without the license of the patentee, of the alleged invention and improvement, and prays that they may be decreed to account for the gains and profits thus acquired by them, and be enjoined from further infringement.

The answer admits the issue of the patent, its surrender and reissue, and, as a defence to this suit, sets up in substance the want of novelty in the invention, its use by the public for more than two years prior to the application for the patent, and that the reissue, so far as it differs from the original patent, is not for the same invention. * * *

The action at law was brought * * * in the ordinary form of such actions for infringement of the privileges secured by a patent. The defendants pleaded the general issue, and set up, by special notice under the act of Congress, the want of novelty in the invention, and its use by the public for more than two years prior to the application for a patent. The plaintiff obtained a verdict for damages, upon which the judgment mentioned was entered; and this judgment, it is now insisted, estops the defendants in this suit from insisting upon the want of novelty in the invention patented, and its prior use by the public, and also from insisting upon any ground going to the validity of the patent which might have been availed of as a defence in that action, and, of course, upon the want of identity in the invention covered by the reissue with that of the original patent.

It is undoubtedly settled law that a judgment of a court of competent jurisdiction, upon a question directly involved in one suit, is conclusive as to that question in another suit between the same parties. But to this operation of the judgment it must appear, either upon the face of the record or be shown by extrinsic evidence, that the precise question was raised and determined in the former suit. If there be any uncertainty on this head in the record—as, for example, if it appear that several distinct matters may have been litigated, upon one or more of which the judgment may have passed, without indicating which of them was thus litigated, and upon which the judgment was rendered—the whole subject-matter of the action will be at large, and open to a new contention, unless this uncertainty be removed by extrinsic evidence showing the precise point involved and determined. * * *

Tested by these views, the question presented * * * is of easy solution. The record of that action does not disclose the nature of the infringement for which damages were recovered. The declaration only avers * * * as the infringement complained of, that the defendants have made and used the invention, and have caused others to make and use it. The patent contains two claims: one for the use of fat liquor generally in the treatment of leather, and the other for a process of treating bark tanned lamb or sheep skin by means of a compound composed and applied in a particular manner. Whether the infringement for which the verdict and judgment passed consisted in the simple use of fat liquor in the treatment of leather, or in the use of the process specified, does not appear from the record. A recovery for an infringement of one claim of the patent is not of itself conclusive of an infringement of the other claim, and there was no extrinsic evidence offered to remove the uncertainty upon the record * * *. The verdict may have been for an infringement of the first claim; it may have been for an infringement of the second; it may have been for an infringement of both. The validity of the patent was not necessarily involved, except with respect to the claim which was the basis of the recovery. A patent may be valid as to a single claim and not valid as to the others. The record wants, therefore, that certainty which is essential to its operation as an estoppel, and does not conclude the defendants from contesting the infringement or the validity of the patent in this suit.

The record is not unlike a record in an action for money had and received to the plaintiff's use. It would be impossible to affirm from such a record, with certainty, for what moneys thus received the action was brought, without extrinsic evidence showing the fact; and, of course, without such evidence the verdict and judgment would conclude nothing, except as to the amount of indebtedness established.

* * *

Decree affirmed.

MR. JUSTICE CLIFFORD dissented.

Notes and Questions

1. Plaintiff brings an action against defendant for personal injuries arising out of a collision of their automobiles. Defendant answers, denying negligence and affirmatively pleading contributory negligence. Evidence is presented on both issues, and there is a general verdict for defendant. If defendant subsequently sues plaintiff for his own injuries arising out of the same accident, may defendant rely upon the first judgment as establishing any part of the case? See *Developments in the Law—Res Judicata,* 65 Harv.L. Rev. 818, 845–46 (1952).

2. In KELLEY v. CURTISS, 16 N.J. 265, 273, 108 A.2d 431, 435 (1954), the New Jersey Supreme Court said: "The case against [defendant] having been submitted to the jury with instructions that he was entitled to a verdict of no cause of action if the jury found either that he was not negligent or that [plaintiff] was guilty of contributory negligence, the general verdict is to be considered as determining both grounds in [defendant's] favor." Is this holding consistent with Russell v. Place? If not, which case advances the better rule?

3. Should the principles embodied in *Russell* call for a different result if the jury in the first action makes specific findings of fact on each of the alternative grounds? What if the first action is a bench trial and the judge specifically discussed her findings on each of the alternative grounds? In MALLOY v. TROMBLEY, 50 N.Y.2d 46, 427 N.Y.S.2d 969, 405 N.E.2d 213 (1980), issue preclusion was allowed, even though the issue had been an alternative ground in the earlier action. The *Malloy* court's holding was based, in part, on the fact that the judge in the earlier action had provided a complete discussion of his holding on each ground.

RIOS v. DAVIS

Court of Civil Appeals of Texas, Eastland, 1963.
373 S.W.2d 386.

COLLINGS, JUSTICE. Juan C. Rios brought this suit against Jessie Hubert Davis in the District Court to recover damages * * * alleged to have been sustained as a result of personal injuries received * * * in an automobile collision. Plaintiff alleged that his injuries were proximately caused by negligence on the part of the defendant. The defendant answered alleging that Rios was guilty of contributory negligence. Also, among other defenses, the defendant urged a plea of res judicata and collateral estoppel based upon the findings and the judgment entered * * * in a suit between the same parties in the County Court at Law of

El Paso County. The plea of res judicata was sustained and judgment was entered in favor of the defendant * * *.

It is shown by the record that * * * Popular Dry Goods Company brought suit against appellee Davis * * * seeking to recover for damages to its truck in the sum of $443.97, alleged to have been sustained in the same collision here involved. Davis answered alleging contributory negligence on the part of Popular and joined appellant Juan C. Rios as a third party defendant and sought to recover from Rios $248.50, the alleged amount of damages to his automobile. The jury * * * found that Popular Dry Goods Company and Rios were guilty of negligence proximately causing the collision. However, the jury also found that Davis was guilty of negligence proximately causing the collision, and judgment was entered * * * denying Popular Dry Goods any recovery against Davis and denying Davis any recovery against Rios.

Appellant Rios in his third point contends that the District Court erred in sustaining appellee's plea of res judicata based upon the judgment of the County Court at Law because the findings on the issues regarding appellant's negligence and liability * * * were immaterial because the judgment entered in that case was in favor of appellant. We sustain this point. * * * The sole basis for the judgment * * * as between Rios and Davis was the findings concerning the negligence of Davis. The finding that Rios was negligent was not essential or material to the judgment and the judgment was not based thereon. On the contrary, the finding * * * that Rios was negligent proximately causing the accident would, if it had been controlling, led [sic] to a different result. Since the judgment was in favor of Rios he had no right or opportunity to complain of or to appeal from the finding that he was guilty of such negligence even if such finding had been without any support whatever in the evidence. The right of appeal is from a judgment and not from a finding. * * * In the case of Word v. Colley, Tex.Civ.App., 173 S.W. 629, at page 634 of its opinion (Error Ref.), the court stated as follows:

> It is the judgment, and not the verdict or the conclusions of fact, filed by a trial court which constitutes the estoppel, and a finding of fact by a jury or a court which does not become the basis or one of the grounds of the judgment rendered is not conclusive against either party to the suit.

* * *

The judgment is, therefore, reversed, and the cause is remanded.

Notes and Questions

1. The verdict in the earlier action in *Rios* reflects the consistent practice, utilized in some states, of submitting a case to the jury on "special issues." Does *Rios* suggest a reason why special verdicts should be used more often?

2. The court in *Rios* held that the judgment in the earlier case did not estop Rios from denying his own negligence. Should the earlier judgment estop Davis from denying his own negligence?

3. Suppose Davis had not cross-claimed against Rios, merely impleading the latter on a contingent claim for contribution; that Popular had then made

a claim against Rios; that at trial Davis and Rios each had argued the other was solely negligent; and that the jury had found for Popular against both of them. In a subsequent suit by Rios against Davis, would the earlier finding that each had been negligent estop Rios from denying negligence? Compare Byrum v. Ames & Webb, Inc., 196 Va. 597, 85 S.E.2d 364 (1955) (no), with Stangle v. Chicago, R.I. & P.R. Co., 295 F.2d 789 (7th Cir.1961) (yes). In both of these cases, the parties in the later action had been named as codefendants by the plaintiff in the earlier action; should it make any difference if one of them had brought the other in by impleader? Should it make any difference if, in the earlier case, the jury had found one of them negligent, and the other not negligent?

Generally, a judgment does not act as collateral estoppel between coparties unless they are adversaries, and they are considered adversaries only if there is a claim for relief by one coparty against the other. The fact that their interests clash and that they are on opposite sides of every issue does not make them adversaries for this purpose in the absence of such a claim. See Glaser v. Huette, 232 App.Div. 119, 249 N.Y.S. 374 (1st Dep't), affirmed without opinion 256 N.Y. 686, 177 N.E. 193 (1931). But see Tuz v. Edward M. Chadbourne, Inc., 310 So.2d 8 (Fla.1975).

4. The court in *Rios* supports its view by noting that Rios could not appeal the finding of his negligence in the earlier action. See also *Restatement (Second), Judgments* § 28(1) (1982). Should the prevailing party in the earlier action be permitted in a later action to attack a finding that was necessary to the judgment in the earlier action? Such a situation will not be common, but did arise in an interesting case in Missouri. Plaintiff in the first action sued for partition of an alleged tenancy in common, but defendant answered with a general denial, which in effect disclaimed "all interest or title to the land in dispute." The court found on the basis of the evidence and the pleadings that plaintiff owned the land, and ordered that "plaintiff take nothing by his writ." Subsequently plaintiff sued to eject defendant, who answered that he had title to the land. In BARTLEY v. BARTLEY, 172 Mo. 208, 72 S.W. 521 (1903), the Supreme Court of Missouri held that the finding in the earlier case could not be attacked.

5. *Rios* should be compared with HOME OWNERS FED. SAV. & LOAN ASS'N v. NORTHWESTERN FIRE & MARINE INS. CO., 354 Mass. 448, 238 N.E.2d 55 (1968), in which the majority opinion states, in what may well be dictum, that "certain findings not strictly essential to the final judgment in the prior action * * * may be relied upon if it is clear that the issues underlying them were treated as essential to the prior case by the court and the party to be bound." What advantages does this test have over the *Rios* approach? What disadvantages? Three of the seven justices dissented.

3. DEFINING AND CHARACTERIZING THE ISSUE

UNITED STATES v. MOSER, 266 U.S. 236, 45 S.Ct. 66, 69 L.Ed. 262 (1924). Moser was a captain when he retired from the Navy. In his first action, he won a ruling that service as a Naval Academy cadet during the Civil War constituted service during the war that entitled him to be retired with the rank and three-fourths of the sea pay of the next higher grade. Although the Court of Claims changed its mind about the interpretation of the pension statutes, he won his next two actions for later installments of his pay on the basis of res judicata. In his fourth action for still later installments, the Court of Claims ruled both that its initial interpretation of the statute had been correct and that in any event he was entitled to rely on res judicata. The Supreme Court affirmed solely on the res judicata ground:

> * * * The question expressly and definitely presented in this suit is the same as that definitely and actually litigated and adjudged in favor of the claimant in the three preceding suits, viz. whether he occupied the status of an officer who had served during the Civil War.

The contention of the government seems to be that the doctrine of res judicata does not apply to questions of law; and, in a sense, that is true. It does not apply to unmixed questions of law. Where, for example, a court in deciding a case has enunciated a rule of law, the parties in a subsequent action upon a different demand are not estopped from insisting that the law is otherwise, merely because the parties are the same in both cases. But a *fact, question* or *right* distinctly adjudged in the original action cannot be disputed in a subsequent action, even though the determination was reached upon an erroneous view or by an erroneous application of the law. That would be to affirm the principle in respect of the thing adjudged but, at the same time, deny it all efficacy by sustaining a challenge to the grounds upon which the judgment was based. * * *

Id. at 241–42, 45 S.Ct. at 67, 69 L.Ed. at 264.

COMMISSIONER OF INTERNAL REVENUE v. SUNNEN

Supreme Court of the United States, 1948.
333 U.S. 591, 68 S.Ct. 715, 92 L.Ed. 898.

Certiorari to the United States Circuit Court of Appeals for the Eighth Circuit.

Mr. Justice Murphy delivered the opinion of the Court.

[Under a series of agreements, a taxpayer had licensed a corporation, which he controlled, to use his patents in exchange for payment of a 10% royalty. At various times, the taxpayer assigned his interest in these agreements to his wife without consideration. Income from these agreements was reported on her income tax returns, and these taxes were paid. The Commissioner contended that the income was taxable to the taxpayer himself and a deficiency was assessed against him.]

* * * [T]he Tax Court held that, with one exception, all the royalties paid to the wife from 1937 to 1941 were part of the taxable income of the taxpayer. * * * The one exception concerned the royalties of $4,881.35 paid in 1937 under the 1928 agreement. In an earlier proceeding in 1935, the Board of Tax Appeals dealt with the taxpayer's income tax liability for the years 1929–1931; it concluded that he was not taxable on the royalties paid to his wife during those years under the 1928 license agreement. This prior determination by the Board caused the Tax Court to apply the principle of *res judicata* to bar a different result as to the royalties paid pursuant to the same agreement during 1937.

The Tax Court's decision was affirmed in part and reversed in part by the Eighth Circuit Court of Appeals. * * * Approval was given to the Tax Court's application of the *res judicata* doctrine to exclude from the taxpayer's income the $4,881.35 in royalties paid in 1937 under the 1928 agreement. But to the extent that the taxpayer had been held taxable on royalties paid to his wife during the taxable years of 1937–1941, the decision was reversed on the theory that such payments were not income to him. * * *

If the doctrine of *res judicata* is properly applicable so that all the royalty payments made during 1937–1941 are governed by the prior decision of the Board of Tax Appeals, the case may be disposed of without reaching the merits of the controversy. * * *

* * * [The concepts of res judicata and collateral estoppel] are applicable in the federal income tax field. Income taxes are levied on an annual basis. Each year is the origin of a new liability and of a separate cause of action. Thus if a claim of liability or non-liability relating to a particular tax year is litigated, a judgment on the merits is *res judicata* as to any subsequent proceeding involving the same claim and the same tax year. But if the later proceeding is concerned with a similar or unlike claim relating to a different tax year, the prior judgment acts as a collateral estoppel only as to those matters in the second proceeding which were actually presented and determined in the first suit. Collateral estoppel operates, in other words, to relieve the government and the taxpayer of "redundant litigation of the identical question of the statute's application to the taxpayer's status." Tait v. Western Md. R. Co., 289 U.S. 620, 624, 53 S.Ct. 706, 707, 77 L.Ed. 1405.

But collateral estoppel is a doctrine capable of being applied so as to avoid an undue disparity in the impact of income tax liability. A taxpayer may secure a judicial determination of a particular tax matter, a matter which may recur without substantial variation for some years thereafter. But a subsequent modification of the significant facts or a change or development in the controlling legal principles may make that determination obsolete or erroneous, at least for future purposes. If such a determination is then perpetuated each succeeding year as to the taxpayer involved in the original litigation, he is accorded a tax treatment different from that given to other taxpayers of the same class. As a result, there are inequalities in the administration of the revenue laws, discriminatory distinctions in tax liability, and a fertile basis for litigious confusion. * * * Such consequences, however, are neither necessitated nor justified by the principle of collateral estoppel. That principle is designed to prevent repetitious lawsuits over matters which have once been decided and which have remained substantially static, factually and legally. It is not meant to create vested rights in decisions that have become obsolete or erroneous with time, thereby causing inequities among taxpayers.

And so where two cases involve income taxes in different taxable years, collateral estoppel must be used with its limitations carefully in mind so as to avoid injustice. It must be confined to situations where the matter raised in the second suit is identical in all respects with that decided in the first proceeding and where the controlling facts and applicable legal rules remain unchanged. * * * As demonstrated by Blair v. Commissioner, 300 U.S. 5, 9, 57 S.Ct. 330, 331, 81 L.Ed. 465, a judicial declaration intervening between the two proceedings may so change the legal atmosphere as to render the rule of collateral estoppel inapplicable. But the intervening decision need not necessarily be that of a state court, as it was in the Blair case. While such a state court decision may be considered as having changed the facts for federal tax litigation purposes, a modification or growth in legal principles as enunciated in intervening decisions of this Court may also effect a significant change in the situation. Tax inequality can result as readily from neglecting legal modulations by this Court as from disregarding factual changes wrought by state courts. In either event, the supervening decision cannot justly be ignored by blind reliance upon the rule of collateral estoppel. * * * It naturally follows that an interposed alteration in the pertinent statutory provisions or Treasury regulations can make the use of that rule unwarranted. * * *

Of course, where a question of fact essential to the judgment is actually litigated and determined in the first tax proceeding, the parties are bound by that determination in a subsequent proceeding even though the cause of action is different. * * * And if the very same facts and no others are involved in the second case, a case relating to a different tax year, the prior judgment will be conclusive as to the same legal issues which appear, assuming no intervening doctrinal change. But if the relevant facts in the two cases are separable, even though they be similar or identical, collateral estoppel does not govern the legal issues which recur in the second case. Thus the second proceeding may involve an instrument or transaction identical with, but in a form separable from, the one dealt with in the first proceeding. In that situation, a court is free in the second proceeding to make an independent examination of the legal matters at issue. It may then reach a different result or, if consistency in decision is considered just and desirable, reliance may be placed upon the ordinary rule of *stare decisis*. Before a party can invoke the collateral estoppel doctrine in these circumstances, the legal matter raised in the second proceeding must involve the same set of events or documents and the same bundle of legal principles that contributed to the rendering of the first judgment. * * *

It is readily apparent in this case that the royalty payments growing out of the license contracts which were not involved in the earlier action before the Board of Tax Appeals and which concerned different tax years are free from the effects of the collateral estoppel doctrine. That is true even though those contracts are identical in all important respects with the 1928 contract, the only one that was before the Board, and even though the issue as to those contracts is the same as that raised by the 1928 contract. * * *

A more difficult problem is posed as to the $4,881.35 in royalties paid to the taxpayer's wife in 1937 under the 1928 contract. Here there is complete identity of facts, issues and parties as between the earlier Board proceeding and the instant one. The Commissioner claims, however, that legal principles developed in various intervening decisions of this Court have made plain the error of the Board's conclusion in the earlier proceeding, thus creating a situation like that involved in Blair v. Commissioner, supra. * * *

The principles which have * * * been recognized and developed by * * * [Helvering v. Clifford, 309 U.S. 331, 60 S.Ct. 554, 84 L.Ed. 788 (1940), and Helvering v. Horst, 311 U.S. 112, 61 S.Ct. 144, 85 L.Ed. 75, 131 A.L.R. 655 (1940)] are directly applicable to the transfer of patent license contracts between members of the same family. They are guideposts for those who seek to determine in a particular instance whether such an assignor retains sufficient control over the assigned contracts or over the receipt of income by the assignee to make it fair to impose income tax liability on him.

Moreover, the clarification and growth of these principles through the Clifford-Horst line of cases constitute, in our opinion, a sufficient change in the legal climate to render inapplicable in the instant proceeding, the doctrine of collateral estoppel relative to the assignment of the 1928 contract. True, these cases did not originate the concept that an assignor is taxable if he retains control over the assigned property or power to defeat the receipt of income by the assignee. But they gave much added emphasis and substance to that concept, making it more suited to meet the "attenuated subtleties" created by taxpayers. So substantial was the amplification of this concept as to justify a reconsideration of earlier Tax Court decisions reached without the benefit of the expanded notions, decisions which are now sought to be perpetuated regardless of their present correctness. Thus in the earlier litigation in 1935, the Board of Tax Appeals was unable to bring to bear on the assignment of the 1928 contract the full breadth of the ideas enunciated in the Clifford-Horst series of cases. And, as we shall see, a proper application of the principles as there developed might well have produced a different result, such as was reached by the Tax Court in this case in regard to the assignments of the other contracts. Under those circumstances collateral estoppel should not have been used by the Tax Court in the instant proceeding to perpetuate the 1935 viewpoint of the assignment.

* * *

The judgment below must therefore be reversed and the case remanded for such further proceedings as may be necessary in light of this opinion.

Reversed.

MR. JUSTICE FRANKFURTER and MR. JUSTICE JACKSON believe the judgment of the Tax Court is based on substantial evidence and is consistent with the law, and would affirm that judgment * * *.

Notes and Questions

1. How might you reconcile *Sunnen* and *Moser*? Both opinions, in a sense, seek to determine if the subsequent suit concerns facts that are

separable from those of the first suit. What is the proper test for this separability? Is it whether historically distinct facts are at issue? Is it whether the facts in the subsequent suit legally are indistinguishable from those of the earlier suit?

2. Is the outcome in the *Sunnen* case consistent with the underlying goals of res judicata? Doesn't its holding undermine the sense of reliance that judgments should foster? After all, if Sunnen had lost the first litigation, he probably would not have renewed the contract assigning income to his wife.

3. *Moser* held that "unmixed questions of law" are not subject to issue preclusion. More recently, however, the Supreme Court has recognized that "the *Moser* exception may be difficult to delineate." Montana v. United States, 440 U.S. 147, 163, 99 S.Ct. 970, 978, 59 L.Ed.2d 210, 223 (1979).

4. As *Sunnen* and *Moser* illustrate, the careful "delineation" of questions of pure law, and their exemption from issue preclusion, may be important especially when the government is a party. "Decisions of law in cases involving [a public agency] generally have significance beyond their immediate impact * * *. [A] 'repeat' litigant, particularly the government, ordinarily should be free to relitigate a legal issue in subsequent litigation that could result in appeal to a higher level of authority in the legal system." Hazard, *Preclusion as to Issues of Law: The Legal System's Interest*, 70 Iowa L.Rev. 81, 92 (1984).

5. How does the preclusion of pure questions of law relate to the doctrine of *stare decisis*? See Buckley, *Issue Preclusion and Issues of Law: A Doctrinal Framework Based on Rules of Recognition, Jurisdiction, and Legal History*, 24 Houston L.Rev. 875 (1987).

6. When a court makes a determination on a mixed question of law and fact, how should changes in the relevant substantive law influence whether preclusive effect is given to those determinations? The *Sunnen* opinion helps answer this question. When new historic facts are the basis of the second suit and there has been a change in legal regime since the prior suit was adjudicated, the first judgment will not preclude the second litigation.

In some situations it is easy to determine when this exception is invoked properly. When a new statute or new regulation has been enacted, or when a controlling Supreme Court precedent has been altered, the exception's application is indisputable. In other situations it is not so clear that a change in substantive law should prevent preclusion. Should preclusion be allowed if there is an inconsistent decision by the same court on similar facts?

7. The frequent changes in tax law arguably prevent any individual from developing much of a sense of repose in tax decisions, and there is a particularly urgent need to treat similarly situated taxpayers alike. These factors suggest that a narrow definition of "issue" may be appropriate in cases involving tax law. In tax, as in other areas, however, the policy considerations that underlie substantive law still must be balanced against the strong individual interests in repose and reliance that particular fact patterns may exhibit.

THE EVERGREENS v. NUNAN

United States Circuit Court of Appeals, Second Circuit, 1944.
141 F.2d 927, certiorari denied 323 U.S. 720, 65 S.Ct. 49, 89 L.Ed. 579.

[The taxpayer was a cemetery company. Its taxable gains on sale of its property depended upon its value as of March 1, 1913. The first litigation involved tax liability arising from disposition of fully improved burial lots during the tax years from 1929 through 1933. It was found that the March 1, 1913 value of the fully improved lots was $1.55 per square foot. In addition, as a matter later determined not to have been necessary to the decision, it was found that the cost of improving the partially improved lots to the status of fully improved lots was between eight and twenty cents a square foot. The second litigation involved tax liability for 1934 and 1935. As to fully improved lots, the $1.55 value found in the first proceeding was held by the Tax Court to preclude relitigation, and no appeal was taken. During these same years, however, a large tract of partially improved lots was taken over by the City of New York for municipal purposes. The cemetery argued that the March 1, 1913 value of the partially improved lots should be calculated by subtracting the modest cost of improvement from the $1.55 value of the fully improved lots. The Tax Court refused to use the finding in this way, and determined that the value of the partially improved lots was only thirty-five cents a square foot.]

L. HAND, CIRCUIT JUDGE. * * *

It is of course well-settled law that a fact, once decided in an earlier suit, is conclusively established between the parties in any later suit, provided it was necessary to the result in the first suit. * * * However, a "fact" may be of two kinds. It may be one of those facts, upon whose combined occurrence the law raises the duty, or the right, in question; or it may be a fact, from whose existence may be rationally inferred the existence of one of the facts upon whose combined occurrence the law raises the duty, or the right. The first kind of fact we shall for convenience call an "ultimate" fact; the second, a "mediate datum." "Ultimate" facts are those which the law makes the occasion for imposing its sanctions.

* * * The next question is whether, after the court in the second suit has learned what the court in the first suit actually did decide, the judgment conclusively establishes for any purpose any other facts than those which were "ultimate" in the first suit; that is to say, whether any facts decided in the first which were only "mediate data" in that suit, are conclusively established in the second suit. Some courts hold that only facts "ultimate" in the first suit are conclusively established. * * * The same notion was foreshadowed in the often quoted language of Coke: "Every estoppel * * * must be certain to every intent, and not to be taken by argument or inference." Co. Lit. 352b. * * * On the other hand, other courts refuse to distinguish between "ultimate" facts and "mediate data" decided in the first suit, so long as they were necessary to the result. * * * We need not choose between these two doctrines,

because ＊ ＊ ＊ the Board decided nothing in the first proceedings which was both a "mediate datum" in that proceeding and necessary to the result.

The important question here is not therefore whether "mediate data" in the first suit are as conclusively established as "ultimate" facts in that suit. On the contrary, we are to decide what are the purposes in the second suit for which anything decided in the first suit—whether "ultimate facts," or "mediate data" therein—are conclusively established. Do the "ultimate" facts, or the "mediate data" decided in the first suit conclusively establish in the second, anything but facts "ultimate" in that suit? Do they also establish "mediate data" in that suit: i.e. premises from which to deduce the existence of any of the facts "ultimate" in that suit?

It is, as we have said, a condition upon the conclusive establishing of any fact that its decision should have been necessary to the result in the first suit. That is a protection, for it means that the issue will be really disputed and that the loser will have put out his best efforts. It can make no difference in this regard whether the original issue was as to an "ultimate" fact or as to a "mediate datum"; the parties can have no interest in what place in the logical hierarchy the issue occupies, if only the final outcome hinges upon it. Altogether different considerations should determine whether any sort of fact, decided in the first suit, should conclusively establish "mediate data" in the second suit. Indeed, it often works very harshly inexorably to make a fact decided in the first suit conclusively establish even a fact "ultimate" in the second. The stake in the first suit may have been too small to justify great trouble and expense in its prosecution or defense; and the chance that a fact decided in it, even though necessary to its result, may later become important between the parties may have been extremely remote. It is altogether right that the judgment shall forever put an end to the first cause of action; but it is not plain that it is always fair that every fact—"ultimate" or "mediate datum"—decided in it, shall be conclusively established between the parties in all future suits, just because the decision was necessary to the result. What jural relevance facts may acquire in the future it is often impossible even remotely to anticipate. Were the law to be recast, it would therefore be a pertinent inquiry whether the conclusiveness, even as to facts "ultimate" in the second suit, of facts decided in the first, might not properly be limited to future controversies which could be thought reasonably in prospect when the first suit was tried. That is of course not the law as it stands; but if it be proposed to make any fact, decided in the first suit, an indisputable datum in the second, from which the winner may make all rational inferences, the loser's risks become enormously enlarged. It is difficult enough to know to what other possible causes of action a fact found in the first suit will later prove to be "ultimate"; but the field is at least somewhat restricted, particularly because the causes of action to which it can apply are apt to be already in existence. But it is utterly impossible to set even the widest boundaries to the situations in which facts found in the first suit may become relevant as data from which to deduce any facts, "ultimate" in all possible future causes of action. Logical relevance is of infinite possibility; there is no conceivable limit which can be put to it. Defeat in one suit might entail results beyond all calculation by either party; a trivial controversy might bring utter disaster in its train. There is no reason for subjecting the loser to such extravagant hazards; unless the decisions compel us to go so far, we will not do so.

We have been able to find very little authority upon the point * * *. Indeed, we have seen that it has not even yet become wholly settled whether facts decided in the first suit, and therein only "mediate data," conclusively establish facts "ultimate" in the second.

* * * Being free to decide, and for the reasons we have given, we do not hesitate to hold that, even assuming arguendo that "mediate data," decided in the first suit, conclusively establish facts, "ultimate" in the second, no fact decided in the first whether "ultimate" or a "mediate datum," conclusively establishes any "mediate datum," in the second, or anything except a fact "ultimate" in that suit.

Order affirmed.

Notes and Questions

1. What is the distinction between mediate and ultimate facts? Many commentators criticize this terminology as difficult to understand and even more difficult to apply. See Heckman, *Collateral Estoppel as the Answer to Multiple Litigation Problems in Federal Tax Law: Another View of Sunnen and The Evergreens,* 19 Case W.Res.L.Rev. 230 (1967); Polasky, *Collateral Estoppel—Effects of Prior Litigation,* 39 Iowa L.Rev. 217 (1954). The response of courts has been no more favorable; the vast majority simply ignore *The Evergreens* rule. Yet Judge Hand was not engaged in an exercise in hair-splitting. Can you identify the purposes his distinctions were meant to serve?

2. Consider Judge Hand's discussion of the rule that looks to the role that the issue played in the first suit. Don't the concerns embodied in this rule seem better protected by the other prerequisites for issue preclusion, such as the actually litigated and necessarily decided requirements? Alternatively, these same concerns could be reduced to a single requirement of foreseeability. For instance, Judge Wisdom recast *The Evergreens* doctrine in the following fashion in HYMAN v. REGENSTEIN, 258 F.2d 502, 510–11 (5th Cir. 1958), certiorari denied 359 U.S. 913, 79 S.Ct. 589, 3 L.Ed.2d 575 (1959): "[Issue preclusion] is applicable only when it is evident from the pleadings and record that determination of the fact in question was necessary to the final judgment and it was foreseeable that the fact would be of importance in future litigation." Is the requirement of foreseeability likely to have much practical effect on the application of issue preclusion? For example, isn't litigation growing out of the same incident or fact pattern almost always foreseeable at the time of the first litigation?

3. Judge Hand's second rule—which looks to the role that the issue will play in the second litigation—seems to embody legitimate concerns, but they have been well concealed in Judge Hand's formulation. The following excerpt may help cast some light on the purposes that underlie *The Evergreens* rule:

The valid core of the Evergreens rule might be preserved by expanding the requirement that the first action afford a full and fair opportunity to litigate the common issue. Substantial changes in the legal context or the consequences of the issue, particularly, could support the conclusion that the initial opportunity was not sufficient to support preclusion. It would be more difficult to consider the need to retry related issues on substantially the same evidence through the full and fair opportunity test. Reliance on the full and fair opportunity test would also work against relitigation because of a common reluctance to challenge directly the adequacy of a prior action. Wise administration of the full and fair opportunity test can go far; it may not go far enough.

In the end, the question can be simply put. There are strong reasons to adopt a general rule that issue preclusion is defeated by substantial changes in the legal context in which the issue arises, by substantial changes in the consequences it may entail, or by the need to retry related issues. A general rule framed in these terms would force attention to the real sources of concern. It seems likely that such a general rule would not defeat issue preclusion in any substantial portion of the cases that satisfy all of the other requirements. Even when the result is to deny preclusion, there may be little injury to the values generally served by preclusion. Nonetheless, the price might prove too high. Federal courts have not yet spun any such rule out of the Evergreens decision, and any proof of its value must await the effort and the experience.

18 Wright, Miller & Cooper, *Federal Practice and Procedure: Jurisdiction and Related Matters* § 4424, at 242 (1981).

SECTION D. THE REQUIRED QUALITY OF JUDGMENT

Only judgments of a certain quality will give rise to preclusion. For the most part, this Chapter's discussion of preclusion doctrine has assumed that the prior judgment satisfied that requirement. This section is designed to highlight some of the difficult questions the "quality of judgment" requirement raises.

The traditional words used to describe a judgment of sufficient quality to create preclusion is that the judgment must be valid, final, and on the merits. These terms are not unambiguous, however; indeed, they are somewhat misleading. It perhaps is best simply to remember that a judgment must meet certain procedural criteria before it will preclude subsequent litigation. Consider the following questions:

1. What impact should stipulations and consent judgments have on subsequent litigation? Suppose a small consumer electronics firm institutes an unfair competition suit against a large electronics company. Eventually, the suit is settled and a consent judgment entered, the larger company agreeing to pay damages and to cease and desist from certain of the allegedly illegal practices. Can this agreement between the parties be considered a court judgment, or is it more properly characterized as a contract? If it is merely a contract, should the intent of the parties as to its preclusive effect govern that issue? Would a rule that did not make

the intent of the parties dispositive have the effect of discouraging consent judgments?

Suppose that rather than settling the dispute the parties merely stipulated most of the material facts. The case went to trial, further factual findings were made, and a decision was rendered for the defendant. Should the admissions made in those stipulations be available in a subsequent suit between the parties? What if the suit is between another consumer electronics firm and the defendant, and the complaint is based upon the same allegedly unfair competition? What light does Rule 36 shed on this problem?

2. Should default judgments give rise to full preclusion? Suppose a small Massachusetts computer company contracts with a large California microchip supplier. The computer company refuses to pay for a shipment, alleging that a large percentage of the chips are defective. The supplier files suit in California to recover $2,000, the balance due on the contract. The computer company chooses not to defend the action because the liability isn't large enough to justify the cost of litigation, and a default judgment is entered against it. Subsequently, the computer company is sued for $1,000,000 by a customer whose computer exploded due to a defective chip. The computer company impleads the supplier, seeking indemnification. But the supplier argues that the judgment in the California suit determined that it had delivered chips produced to specifications. Should the default judgment be given preclusive effect in these circumstances? Would it make a difference if the second suit had been filed before the default judgment was entered?

(I think NO)

Suppose the computer company had brought the first action for rescission in Massachusetts and the supplier had defaulted. And, suppose other small computer suppliers also received defective chips. Could they use the default judgment to trigger issue preclusion in their suits against the supplier? Would it make a difference if they were not suing for rescission but were suing for huge damages based on harm to their business reputation?

3. How should the dismissal of a prior action on the ground that it was barred by a statute of limitations be treated in a subsequent suit on the same matter? Suppose a discharged employee brings a sex discrimination suit against her employer, but the case is dismissed because it was filed after the limitations period had expired. The employee then files a second suit based on breach of contract, a cause of action that would not be barred by the statute of limitations. Is the second action precluded?

(I think not preclusive)

Would your answer change if the contract action was brought in a different court system from the one in which the sex-discrimination suit had been lodged? If both jurisdictions apply the same limitations period to sex-discrimination claims, isn't it clear that the result should be the same as it would be if the second suit were brought in the same system? But, what if the second jurisdiction applies a more liberal statute of limitations to sex-discrimination claims—one that would not have barred the first suit? Is it possible in these circumstances that limitations rulings should be held to preclude only specific limitations issues and not the underlying claim?

4. How should prior criminal proceedings affect subsequent litigation? Suppose that upon trial in federal court a criminal defendant, who asserted the defense of entrapment, was acquitted of charges of knowingly engaging in the business of dealing in firearms without a license, in violation of federal law. Suppose that the government then instituted an in rem action for forfeiture of the firearms involved pursuant to a federal statute which authorizes forfeitures of any firearms used or intended to be used in violation of federal law. Can the defendant argue that the in rem proceeding is precluded by the prior acquittal? Remember, acquittal on the criminal charge merely reflected the existence of a reasonable doubt about the defendant's guilt; the jury did not find that it was more probable than not that the defendant did not have possession of the firearms with an intent to violate federal law. See United States v. One Assortment of 89 Firearms, 465 U.S. 354, 104 S.Ct. 1099, 79 L.Ed.2d 361 (1984).

SECTION E. PERSONS BENEFITTED AND PERSONS BOUND BY PRECLUSION

1. THE TRADITIONAL MODEL

RALPH WOLFF & SONS v. NEW ZEALAND INS. CO.

Court of Appeals of Kentucky, 1933.
248 Ky. 304, 58 S.W.2d 623.

STANLEY, COMMISSIONER. The opinion of Wolff v. Niagara Fire Insurance Co., 236 Ky. 1, 32 S.W.2d 548, discloses that H.C. Wolff and R.C. Wolff, partners, suffered the partial loss by fire of their candy factory in December, 1924, and that they had twelve insurance policies on the property for a total sum of $19,500. That case was a consolidation of nine suits on as many policies for the aggregate of $14,500. The verdict was for $2,500 in favor of the plaintiffs "to cover the amount of the loss and damage by fire and water." That was construed to be a finding that the total property loss was $2,500. Since the insurance involved in the consolidated action was 14500/19500 of the whole coverage, judgment was rendered for that fractional part of the total loss fixed by the jury, that is, for $1,858.90, and that judgment was affirmed.

[Plaintiffs also sued two other insurers, each of whom had insured plaintiffs for $1,000.] * * * Among the several defenses set up in each case was the plea that the policy provided the company should not be liable for a greater proportion of any loss than the amount of the policy bore to the whole insurance covering the property; that in the consolidated cases referred to it had been judicially ascertained and determined that the total loss was $2,500 and by reason thereof the amount of the loss was res judicata and plaintiffs were estopped to assert a greater damage; and that if liable at all it was only for its proportional part, or 1000/19500, to wit $128.20. A demurrer to this plea was overruled * * * and judgment for $128.20 was rendered against each company. * * *

The sole question before us, therefore, is * * * whether the plaintiffs in these suits are bound by the judgment in their cases against the other nine companies.

It is said in Jeter v. Hewitt, 22 How. 352, 364, 16 L.Ed. 345, that "res judicata renders white that which is black, and straight that which is crooked." But all will agree that there are qualifications and that is not true except when there are certain concurring elements, as where one has had a chance, either personally or by representation, to show that black is black and crooked things are crooked. It is conceded, quite naturally, that in order to render a matter res judicata, among other things, there must be identity of parties or their privies; and that is so though the judgment relied upon as a bar involved the same state of facts. * * * The defendants in these actions were not parties to the other one and in no way participated in their defense. There is nothing to show that they even had notice of the pendency of the other suits.

* * * "The fact that persons are interested in the same question or in proving the same facts * * * does not make them privies." Section 438, Freeman on Judgments. * * *

The appellees rest their argument of privity upon what they say is the contractual relation, that is, in effect that as each policy contained the apportionment or contribution clause, they were and are bound together in a common cause. * * * True it is there may be such a contractual relationship that a party becomes bound under certain conditions by the action of another in regard to the matter involved in a suit or by the judgment, such as where he is responsible over, as a warrantor, or as an indemnitor, or as a surety. * * * But we cannot see the application here. The stipulation in the respective contracts of insurance upon the appellants' property was that the company would be liable only for its proportionate share of any loss sustained if other insurance contracts should be made. This, of course, was to avoid duplication of indemnity and to prevent overinsurance. There was no contract nor privity of contract among the insurers. * * * It may be doubted that such would have been claimed had the loss been fixed by the former judgment at what the companies regarded as excessive. To bind the plaintiffs the defendants must also have been bound, for an estoppel is always mutual.

* * *

As further refuting the view that the concurrent or pro rata insurance clauses in the several policies so interlocked the contracts as to make them one in effect * * *, it is held that insurers cannot avail themselves of an adjustment by the insured with another insurer either to defeat recovery or reduce the amount of liability under their contract; and that in ascertaining a company's proportionate share of the loss no regard is to be had to the fact that some of the companies have been settled with for a less sum than they were liable for or have paid more than their share. * * * [T]here can be no difference when the settlement is pursuant to a judicial determination.

(C., F., M. & S.) Civil Proc. 5th Ed. ACB—27

* * *

It seems to the court, therefore, that the judgment holding the appellants to be bound by the judgment in the former suit is erroneous. It is accordingly reversed, and the case remanded for consistent proceedings.

Notes and Questions

1. Why should it be true, in the words of the court in the principal case, that "to bind the plaintiffs, the defendants must also have been bound"? Is this principle of mutuality based upon any of the purposes we have seen advanced in support of the doctrine of res judicata? Might plaintiff in *Ralph Wolff & Sons* have had anything to gain in trying the actions against the insurers in separate groups instead of all at once? Should the answer to the last question affect the decision whether to follow the rule enunciated by the court? Should there be one rule when plaintiff has proceeded purposefully so as to obtain separate trials and another rule when plaintiff was unable to avoid separate trials?

2. Would there have been any reasonable basis in the principal case for restricting plaintiff's total recovery to $2,500, while not restricting the possible liability of the two defendants to $128.20 each?

3. A street car and a coal wagon collided. The driver of the wagon sued the street-car company for his injuries and won, the jury finding that he had not been guilty of any want of ordinary care. Subsequently, a pedestrian, against whom the wagon had been thrown, sued the street-car company and the coal company for her injuries. Should the earlier judgment in favor of the wagon driver operate as res judicata on the issue of his lack of negligence? If a verdict is returned against both defendants, should the court order that the judgment contain a provision that execution must be first satisfied out of the property of the street-car company? See Ertel v. Milwaukee Elec. Ry. & Light Co., 164 Wis. 380, 160 N.W. 263 (1916).

4. When an action is brought against one who is entitled to be indemnified by another if he should lose, a judgment against the indemnitee will bind the indemnitor on the issue of the indemnitee's liability in the first action, if the indemnitor has been "vouched in," that is, if notified of the first action and offered an opportunity to defend. See, e.g., First Nat. Bank v. City Nat. Bank, 182 Mass. 130, 65 N.E. 24 (1902) (so holding, even though the indemnitor was not subject to personal jurisdiction in the state in which the first action was brought). See Note 2, p. 611, supra.

CITY OF ANDERSON v. FLEMING, 160 Ind. 597, 602–03, 67 N.E. 443, 445 (1903). Plaintiff suffered personal injuries by stepping into an excavation in the street. She sued the contractor responsible for the excavation, but judgment went against her. Subsequently, she sued the city for the same injuries, and the city pleaded the judgment in favor of the contractor. The Supreme Court of Indiana held for defendant city:

* * * The established rule in this state is that when a street of a municipal corporation is rendered unsafe by the wrongful acts or negli-

gence of a third person, and the corporation is compelled to pay for injuries caused by said unsafe street, it has a right of action over against the person who rendered the same unsafe, for the amount so paid, and, if properly notified of the action, such person is bound and concluded by said judgment recovered against the corporation.

* * * It is clearly established * * * that if appellee was injured, without contributory fault on her part, by reason of said excavations being negligently left open, without proper guards or signals, as alleged, appellant would be entitled to recover from the contractor whatever appellee might recover against it. Such right * * * would rest upon the principles of subrogation. Appellant would be entitled to be subrogated to appellee's right of action against the contractor, but the judgment on the merits in the contractor's favor in appellee's action against him conclusively adjudged that he was not liable to appellee, or any person claiming under her, for the same cause of action. If appellee was not entitled to recover for said injury against the contractor, she is not entitled to recover therefor against appellant.

The contractor had the right, if duly notified by appellant, to appear and set up said former judgment in his favor against appellee in bar of this action against appellant, and appellant has the same right; otherwise the contractor would have to defend the same cause twice on its merits.

Notes and Questions

1. A, an employee acting within the scope of his employment and driving the employer's, B's, car, collides with a car driven by C. C sues A, and judgment is for A. Subsequently B sues C for damages to the car. What effect should the earlier judgment for A have in B's suit against C? See Good Health Dairy Prods. Corp. v. Emery, 275 N.Y. 14, 9 N.E.2d 758 (1937).

2. Suppose on the facts of Question 1 that C had first sued B, and judgment had been for B, and C had then sued A. What effect should the earlier judgment for B have in C's suit against A? Would your answer be different if the second suit had been by A against C? Compare Emery v. Fowler, 39 Me. 326 (1855), with Elder v. New York & Penn. Motor Express, Inc., 284 N.Y. 350, 31 N.E.2d 188 (1940).

3. Suppose that in the first action, A, a real-estate broker, had sued the seller of property, B, for commissions. The trial court dismissed A's action after trial on the ground that A had not produced the person, C, who ultimately had purchased B's property and therefore was not entitled to a brokerage commission. In the second action A sues C for inducing B to breach the brokerage contract causing a loss of the commission. Can C successfully rely on the decision against A in the first action as a bar to A's action against him? See Israel v. Wood Dolson Co., 1 N.Y.2d 116, 151 N.Y.S.2d 1, 134 N.E.2d 97 (1956). The New York cases on mutuality of estoppel are discussed at length in 5 Weinstein, Korn & Miller, *New York Civil Practice* ¶¶ 5011.32–.42.

4. When a wrongful-death action for the death of a child has been brought by a personal representative and judgment was for defendant, is the mother estopped by the earlier judgment in an action for her personal injuries arising out of the same accident when she would have been one of the

beneficiaries if the first action had been successful? See Smith v. Bishop, 26 Ill.2d 434, 187 N.E.2d 217 (1962).

———

These traditional rules of preclusion have changed dramatically in recent years. As you read the remainder of this Section, consider whether it is appropriate to allow a nonparty to take advantage of a favorable judgment when that nonparty would not have been subject to preclusion if the prior judgment had been unfavorable to him. Courts have shown an increasing willingness to permit preclusion (often referred to as nonmutual estoppel) in such circumstances. Also consider whether it is appropriate to bind nonparties by an unfavorable judgment. A limited number of courts have shown a willingness to permit exceptions to the traditional rule that an individual can be bound by a court decision only when he has had his "day in court."

2. MUTUALITY

BERNHARD v. BANK OF AMERICA NAT. TRUST & SAV. ASS'N

Supreme Court of California, 1942.
19 Cal.2d 807, 122 P.2d 892.

TRAYNOR, JUSTICE. In June, 1933, Mrs. Clara Sather, an elderly woman, made her home with Mr. and Mrs. Charles O. Cook in San Dimas, California. Because of her failing health, she authorized Mr. Cook and Dr. Joseph Zeiler to make drafts jointly against her commercial account in the Security First National Bank of Los Angeles. On August 24, 1933, Mr. Cook opened a commercial account at the First National Bank of San Dimas in the name of "Clara Sather by Charles O. Cook." * * * Thereafter, a number of checks drawn by Cook and Zeiler on Mrs. Sather's commercial account in Los Angeles were deposited in the San Dimas account * * *.

On October 26, 1933, a teller from the Los Angeles Bank called on Mrs. Sather at her request to assist in transferring her money from the Los Angeles Bank to the San Dimas Bank. In the presence of this teller, the cashier of the San Dimas Bank, Mr. Cook, and her physician, Mrs. Sather signed by mark an authorization directing the Security First National Bank of Los Angeles to transfer the balance of her savings account in the amount of $4,155.68 to the First National Bank of San Dimas * * * "for credit to the account of Mrs. Clara Sather." The order was credited by the San Dimas Bank to the account of "Clara Sather by Charles O. Cook." Cook withdrew the entire balance from that account and opened a new account in the same bank in the name of himself and his wife. * * *

Mrs. Sather died in November, 1933. Cook qualified as executor of the estate and proceeded with its administration. After a lapse of several years he filed an account at the instance of the probate court accompanied by his resignation. The account made no mention of the money transferred by Mrs. Sather to the San Dimas Bank; and Helen Bernhard

* * * [and other] beneficiaries under Mrs. Sather's will, filed objections to the account for this reason. After a hearing on the objections the court settled the account, and as part of its order declared that the decedent during her lifetime had made a gift to Charles O. Cook of the amount of the deposit in question.

After Cook's discharge, Helen Bernhard was appointed administratrix with the will annexed. She instituted this action against defendant, the Bank of America, successor to the San Dimas Bank, seeking to recover the deposit on the ground that the bank was indebted to the estate for this amount because Mrs. Sather never authorized its withdrawal. In addition to a general denial, defendant pleaded two affirmative defenses: (1) That the money on deposit was paid out to Charles O. Cook with the consent of Mrs. Sather and (2) that this fact is res judicata by virtue of the finding of the probate court * * *. The trial court * * * gave judgment for defendant on the ground that Cook's ownership of the money was conclusively established by the finding of the probate court. * * *

Plaintiff contends that the doctrine of res judicata does not apply because the defendant who is asserting the plea was not a party to the previous action nor in privity with a party to that action and because there is no mutuality of estoppel.

* * *

Many courts have stated the facile formula that the plea of res judicata is available only when there is privity and mutuality of estoppel. * * * Under the requirement of privity, only parties to the former judgment or their privies may take advantage of or be bound by it. * * * A party in this connection is one who is "directly interested in the subject matter, and had a right to make defense, or to control the proceeding, and to appeal from the judgment." * * * A privy is one who, after rendition of the judgment, has acquired an interest in the subject matter affected by the judgment through or under one of the parties, as by inheritance, succession, or purchase. * * * The estoppel is mutual if the one taking advantage of the earlier adjudication would have been bound by it, had it gone against him. * * *

The criteria for determining who may assert a plea of res judicata differ fundamentally from the criteria for determining against whom a plea of res judicata may be asserted. The requirements of due process of law forbid the assertion of a plea of res judicata against a party unless he was bound by the earlier litigation in which the matter was decided. * * * He is bound by that litigation only if he has been a party thereto or in privity with a party thereto. * * * There is no compelling reason, however, for requiring that the party asserting the plea of res judicata must have been a party, or in privity with a party, to the earlier litigation.

No satisfactory rationalization has been advanced for the requirement of mutuality. Just why a party who was not bound by a previous action should be precluded from asserting it as res judicata against a party who was bound by it is difficult to comprehend. * * * Many courts have abandoned the requirement of mutuality and confined the requirement of privity to the party against whom the plea of res judicata is asserted.

* * * The commentators are almost unanimously in accord. * * * The courts of most jurisdictions have in effect accomplished the same result by recognizing a broad exception to the requirements of mutuality and privity, namely, that they are not necessary where the liability of the defendant asserting the plea of res judicata is dependent upon or derived from the liability of one who was exonerated in an earlier suit brought by the same plaintiff upon the same facts. * * * Typical examples of such derivative liability are master and servant, principal and agent, and indemnitor and indemnitee. Thus, if a plaintiff sues a servant for injuries caused by the servant's alleged negligence within the scope of his employment, a judgment against the plaintiff of [sic] the grounds that the servant was not negligent can be pleaded by the master as res judicata if he is subsequently sued by the same plaintiff for the same injuries. Conversely, if the plaintiff first sues the master, a judgment against the plaintiff on the grounds that the servant was not negligent can be pleaded by the servant as res judicata if he is subsequently sued by the plaintiff. In each of these situations the party asserting the plea of res judicata was not a party to the previous action nor in privity with such a party * * *. Likewise, the estoppel is not mutual since the party asserting the plea, not having been a party or in privity with a party to the former action, would not have been bound by it had it been decided the other way. The cases justify this exception on the ground that it would be unjust to permit one who has had his day in court to reopen identical issues by merely switching adversaries.

In determining the validity of a plea of res judicata three questions are pertinent: Was the issue decided in the prior adjudication identical with the one presented in the action in question? Was there a final judgment on the merits? Was the party against whom the plea is asserted a party or in privity with a party to the prior adjudication?

* * * Since the issue as to the ownership of the money is identical with the issue raised in the probate proceeding, and since the order of the probate court settling the executor's account was a final adjudication of this issue on the merits * * *, it remains only to determine whether the plaintiff in the present action was a party or in privity with a party to the earlier proceeding. The plaintiff has brought the present action in the capacity of administratrix of the estate. In this capacity she represents the very same persons and interests that were represented in the earlier hearing on the executor's account. In that proceeding plaintiff and the other legatees who objected to the executor's account represented the estate of the decedent. They were seeking not a personal recovery but, like the plaintiff in the present action, as administratrix, a recovery for the benefit of the legatees and creditors of the estate, all of whom were bound by the order settling the account. * * *

The judgment is affirmed.

Notes and Questions

1. In *Bernhard* Justice Traynor mentions that some courts already had recognized that exceptions to the mutuality requirement arise most often in cases involving vicarious liability. Consider these common examples:

(1) A institutes an action for negligence against B, an employee of C, for conduct occurring while B was acting in the scope of employment. If B prevails, C will be able to raise the first judgment in a suit by A to recover against C.

(2) X corporation is a general contractor liable for the proper performance of an entire contract in which Y is a subcontractor. Z, the beneficiary of the contract, sues Y for incomplete performance and loses. If Z brings a suit against X that raises the same claim as the earlier suit, X will be able to invoke the preclusive effects of this prior judgment.

These exceptions reflect the duality inherent in the vicarious liability relationship. The *Restatement (Second) of Judgments* has outlined the nature of this duality:

> * * * The injured person's claims against the primary obligor and the person vicariously responsible for his conduct are in important respects separate claims. First, neither of the obligors is ordinarily the representative of the other, so that a judgment against one of them ordinarily is not preclusive against the other. * * * Second, a release of one does not ordinarily release the other. * * * Third, one of the obligors may be immune from suit while the other is not, and different statutes of limitations may be applicable to them. Finally, the claims are separate in the sense that neither the rule against "splitting" a claim nor the usual rules of joinder of parties require that they be maintained in a single action.
>
> In an important sense, however, there is only a single claim. The same loss is involved, usually the same measure of damages, and the same or nearly identical issues of fact and law. The substantive legal basis for vicarious responsibility rests largely on the notion that the injured person should have the additional security for recovery of his loss that is represented in imposition of liability on a person other than the primary obligor. The optional additional security thus afforded by rules of vicarious responsibility should not, however, afford the injured person a further option to litigate successively the issues upon which his claim to redress is founded. He is ordinarily in a position to sue both obligors in the same action and may justly be expected to do so. Beyond this, if he is allowed to sue the second obligor after having lost an action against the first, two anomalous consequences may result. First, he may be given recovery for conduct that has already been determined not to be wrongful. Second, if the first action is unsuccessfully maintained against the primary obligor, and the second successfully maintained against the person vicariously responsible, it could happen that the latter could obtain indemnity from the primary obligor. The result would be that the primary obligor would

have to pay indirectly an obligation from which he had been directly exonerated.

Restatement (Second), Judgments § 51, comment *b* (1982).

2. In which of the following situations would preclusion be available under *Bernhard*?

(a) Three cars, driven by A, B, and C, respectively, collide in an intersection in a jurisdiction without a compulsory-joinder statute. Driver A, believing that C does not have enough money to satisfy the judgment, institutes a negligence action against B. At trial B is exonerated, the court holding that A's injuries were solely the result of A's own negligence. A then discovers that C actually does have enough money to make him worth suing, and promptly files suit against him. Can C invoke the judgment in A's prior action against B to preclude recovery by A against him?

(b) Assume the same fact pattern as above. Could C assert the judgment in the prior suit as the basis to recover on a counterclaim against A?

(c) A bus owned and driven by D is in an accident. Passenger P1 sues D, alleging that the accident was caused by D's negligent driving. The trial court finds for P1. Passenger P2 files a claim against D, also alleging damages as a result of D's negligence. Is preclusion available to P2? Can you articulate how this fact pattern differs from that of (b)?

(d) What if, on the facts of (c), the bus driver/owner had prevailed in the first suit? When P2 brought the second litigation, could D then use the first suit's judgment as a defense to the second action?

3. Many of the cases involving mutuality of collateral estoppel that have arisen since *Bernhard* are noted and briefly discussed in the appendix to Currie, *Civil Procedure: The Tempest Brews*, 53 Calif.L.Rev. 25, 38–46 (1965). Other useful discussions of mutuality include Currie, *Mutuality of Collateral Estoppel—Limits of the* Bernhard *Doctrine*, 9 Stan.L.Rev. 281 (1957); Moore & Currier, *Mutuality and Conclusiveness of Judgments*, 35 Tul.L.Rev. 301 (1961); Polasky, *Collateral Estoppel—Effects of Prior Litigation*, 39 Iowa L.Rev. 217 (1954); Semmel, *Collateral Estoppel, Mutuality and Joinder of Parties*, 68 Colum.L.Rev. 1457 (1968); Note, *A Probabilistic Analysis of the Doctrine of Mutuality of Collateral Estoppel*, 76 Mich.L.Rev. 612 (1978); Note, *Collateral Estoppel Without Mutuality: Accepting the Bernhard Doctrine*, 35 Vand.L. Rev. 1423 (1982).

BLONDER–TONGUE LABORATORIES, INC. v. UNIVERSITY OF ILLINOIS FOUNDATION, 402 U.S. 313, 91 S.Ct. 1434, 28 L.Ed.2d 788 (1971), was the case in which the Supreme Court first began to abrogate the mutuality requirement for the federal system. The University of Illinois Foundation owned, by assignment, a patent for a radio and television antenna. In an infringement action against an antenna manufacturer, a trial court had held the Foundation's patent invalid. But, in a second infringement action against a different defendant, the patent was held to be valid. In TRIPLETT v. LOWELL, 297 U.S. 638, 56 S.Ct. 645, 80 L.Ed. 949 (1936), a case decided shortly before Justice Traynor's *Bernhard* decision, the United States Supreme Court had reaffirmed the rule that a holding that a patent was invalid did not preclude a patent holder from asserting the validity of the patent in subsequent litigation against different defendants. In *Blonder-Tongue,* the Court specifically requested the parties to discuss the vitality of the *Triplett* rule.

The substance of the Court's opinion in *Blonder-Tongue* begins with a review of the seminal state and lower federal-court opinions that had abandoned the mutuality requirement in certain contexts. The Court then offered its own views on the propriety of nonmutual preclusion:

> The cases and authorities discussed above connect erosion of the mutuality requirement to the goal of limiting relitigation of issues where that can be achieved without compromising fairness in particular cases. The courts have often discarded the rule while commenting on crowded dockets and long delays preceding trial. Authorities differ on whether the public interest in efficient judicial administration is a sufficient ground in and of itself for abandoning mutuality, but it is clear that more than crowded dockets is involved. The broader question is whether it is any longer tenable to afford a litigant more than one full and fair opportunity for judicial resolution of the same issue. The question in these terms includes as part of the calculus the effect on judicial administration, but it also encompasses the concern exemplified by Bentham's reference to the gaming table in his attack on the principle of mutuality of estoppel. In any lawsuit where a defendant, because of the mutuality principle, is forced to present a complete defense on the merits to a claim which the plaintiff has fully litigated and lost in a prior action, there is an arguable misallocation of resources. To the extent the defendant in the second suit may not win by asserting, without contradiction, that the plaintiff had fully and fairly, but unsuccessfully, litigated the same claim in the prior suit, the defendant's time and money are diverted from alternative uses—productive or otherwise—to relitigation of a decided issue. And, still assuming that the issue was resolved correctly in the first suit, there is reason to be concerned about the plaintiff's allocation of resources. Permitting repeated litigation of the same issue as long as the supply of unrelated defendants holds out reflects either the aura of the gaming table or "a lack of discipline and of disinterestedness on the part of the lower courts, hardly a worthy or wise basis for fashioning rules of procedure." Kerotest Mfg. Co. v. C–O–Two Co., 342 U.S. 180, 185, 72 S.Ct. 219, 222, 96 L.Ed. 200 (1952). Although neither judges, the parties, nor the adversary system performs perfectly in all cases, the requirement of determining whether the party against whom an estoppel is asserted had a full and fair opportunity to litigate is a most significant safeguard.

> Some litigants—those who never appeared in a prior action—may not be collaterally estopped without litigating the issue. They have never had a chance to present their evidence and arguments on the claim. Due process prohibits estopping them despite one or more existing adjudications of the identical issue which stand squarely against their position. * * * Also, the authorities have been more willing to permit a defendant in a second suit to invoke an estoppel against a plaintiff who lost on the same claim in an earlier suit than they have been to allow a plaintiff in the second suit to use offensively a judgment obtained by a different plaintiff in a prior suit against the same defendant. But the case before us involves neither due process nor "offensive use" questions. Rather, it

depends on the considerations weighing for and against permitting a patent holder to sue on his patent after it has once been held invalid following opportunity for full and fair trial.

Id. at 328–33, 91 S.Ct. at 1442–43, 28 L.Ed.2d at 799–800.

Later in the opinion, the Court focused on two economic consequences of continued adherence to the *Triplett* rule. First, the costs of litigating patent suits was inordinately high. For patentees, the average fee was $50,000; for defendants, the fees often ran into the hundreds of thousands of dollars. Second, the statutory presumption in favor of the validity of patents often forced prospective defendants to settle with the patent holders rather than engage in lengthy and expensive litigation challenging the patent. The Court recognized that overturning the *Triplett* rule might serve as a check on the monopoly power that the patent statute gave to patent holders, and noted other decisions in which it had similarly tried to give inventors sufficient incentives without giving them undue protection from competition.

In the penultimate section of the opinion, the Court once again considered the question of resource allocation:

> As the preceding discussion indicates, although patent trials are only a small portion of the total amount of litigation in the federal courts, they tend to be of disproportionate length. Despite this, respondents urge that the burden on the federal courts from relitigation of patents once held invalid is *de minimis.* They rely on the figures presented in the 1961 Staff Report: during the period 1948–1959, 62 federal suits were terminated which involved relitigation of a patent previously held invalid, a figure constituting about 1% of the patent suits commenced during the same period. The same figures show that these 62 suits involved 27 patents, indicating that some patentees sue more than once after their patent has been invalidated. Respondents also urge that most of these 62 suits were settled without litigation. 1961 Staff Report 19. But, as we have suggested, this fact cuts both ways.

> Even accepting respondents' characterization of these figures as *de minimis,* it is clear that abrogation of *Triplett* will save *some* judicial time if even a few relatively lengthy patent suits may be fairly disposed of on pleas of estoppel. More fundamentally, while the cases do discuss reduction in dockets as an effect of elimination of the mutuality requirement, they do not purport to hold that predictions about the actual amount of judicial time that will be saved under such a holding control decision of that question.

Id. at 348–49, 91 S.Ct. at 1452–53, 28 L.Ed.2d at 810–11.

Ultimately, the Court overruled *Triplett* "to the extent it forecloses a plea of estoppel by one facing a charge of infringement of a patent that has once been declared invalid." Id. at 350, 91 S.Ct. at 1453, 28 L.Ed.2d at 811.

Notes and Questions

1. A close reading of the *Blonder-Tongue* opinion reveals that the holding plausibly could be limited to patent actions. Lower federal courts,

however, have freely cited it as authority for nonmutual preclusion in all types of substantive claims.

2. What effect should substantive law have on the scope of preclusion rules? Should it matter whether the issue involved is a constitutional one? Should the nature of the parties' expectations about the scope of the first decision have an effect on the reach of nonmutual estoppel?

3. In both *Bernhard* and *Blonder-Tongue* the party that was precluded in the second action was the party who had instituted the first action. Should this be an important factor in determining whether nonmutual preclusion is appropriate? Or should the only relevant consideration be whether the party against whom preclusion is being asserted had a full and fair opportunity to litigate? See Teitelbaum Furs, Inc. v. Dominion Insurance Co., 58 Cal.2d 601, 25 Cal.Rptr. 559, 375 P.2d 439 (1962) (Traynor, J.); Zdanok v. Glidden Co., 327 F.2d 944 (2d Cir.) (Friendly, J.), certiorari denied 377 U.S. 934, 84 S.Ct. 1338, 12 L.Ed.2d 298 (1964); Currie, *Civil Procedure: The Tempest Brews,* 53 Calif.L. Rev. 25 (1965).

PARKLANE HOSIERY CO. v. SHORE

Supreme Court of the United States, 1979.
439 U.S. 322, 99 S.Ct. 645, 58 L.Ed.2d 552.

Certiorari to the United States Court of Appeals for the Second Circuit.

MR. JUSTICE STEWART delivered the opinion of the Court.

* * *

The respondent brought this stockholder's class action against the petitioners in a federal district court. The complaint alleged that the petitioners * * * had issued a materially false and misleading proxy statement in connection with a merger. * * * The complaint sought damages, rescission of the merger, and recovery of costs.

Before this action came to trial, the SEC filed suit against the same defendants in a federal district court, alleging that the proxy statement that had been issued by Parklane was materially false and misleading in essentially the same respects as those that had been alleged in the respondent's complaint. Injunctive relief was requested. After a four-day trial, the District Court found that the proxy statement was materially false and misleading in the respects alleged, and entered a declaratory judgment to that effect. * * * The Court of Appeals for the Second Circuit affirmed * * *.

The respondent in the present case then moved for partial summary judgment against the petitioners, asserting that the petitioners were collaterally estopped from relitigating the issues that had been resolved against them in the action brought by the SEC. The District Court denied the motion on the ground that such an application of collateral estoppel would deny the petitioners their Seventh Amendment right to a jury trial. The Court of Appeals for the Second Circuit reversed * * *. Because of an intercircuit conflict,[3] we granted certiorari.

3. The position of the Court of Appeals for the Second Circuit is in conflict with that taken by the Court of Appeals for the Fifth Circuit in Rachal v. Hill, 435 F.2d 59.

I

The threshold question to be considered is whether, quite apart from the right to a jury trial under the Seventh Amendment, the petitioners can be precluded from relitigating facts resolved adversely to them in a prior equitable proceeding with another party under the general law of collateral estoppel. Specifically, we must determine whether a litigant who was not a party to a prior judgment may nevertheless use that judgment "offensively" to prevent a defendant from relitigating issues resolved in the earlier proceeding.[4]

* * *

B

The *Blonder-Tongue* case involved defensive use of collateral estoppel * * *. The present case, by contrast, involves offensive use of collateral estoppel—a plaintiff is seeking to estop a defendant from relitigating the issues which the defendant previously litigated and lost against another plaintiff. In both the offensive and defensive use situations, the party against whom estoppel is asserted has litigated and lost in an earlier action. Nevertheless, several reasons have been advanced why the two situations should be treated differently.

First, offensive use of collateral estoppel does not promote judicial economy in the same manner as defensive use does. Defensive use of collateral estoppel precludes a plaintiff from relitigating identical issues by merely "switching adversaries." * * * Thus defensive collateral estoppel gives a plaintiff a strong incentive to join all potential defendants in the first action if possible. Offensive use of collateral estoppel, on the other hand, creates precisely the opposite incentive. Since a plaintiff will be able to rely on a previous judgment against a defendant but will not be bound by that judgment if the defendant wins, the plaintiff has every incentive to adopt a "wait and see" attitude, in the hope that the first action by another plaintiff will result in a favorable judgment. * * * Thus offensive use of collateral estoppel will likely increase rather than decrease the total amount of litigation, since potential plaintiffs will have everything to gain and nothing to lose by not intervening in the first action.[13]

A second argument against offensive use of collateral estoppel is that it may be unfair to a defendant. If a defendant in the first action is sued for small or nominal damages, he may have little incentive to defend vigorously, particularly if future suits are not foreseeable. * * * Allowing offensive collateral estoppel may also be unfair to a defendant if the judgment relied upon as a basis for the estoppel is itself inconsistent

---

4. In this context, offensive use of collateral estoppel occurs when the plaintiff seeks to foreclose the defendant from litigating an issue the defendant has previously litigated unsuccessfully in an action with another party. Defensive use occurs when a defendant seeks to prevent a plaintiff from asserting a claim the plaintiff has previously litigated and lost against another defendant.

13. The *Restatement (Second) of Judgments* (Tent. Draft No. 2, 1975) § 88(3), provides that application of collateral estoppel may be denied if the party asserting it "could have effected joinder in the first action between himself and his present adversary."

with one or more previous judgments in favor of the defendant. Still another situation where it might be unfair to apply offensive estoppel is where the second action affords the defendant procedural opportunities unavailable in the first action that could readily cause a different result.[15]

C

We have concluded that the preferable approach for dealing with these problems in the federal courts is not to preclude the use of offensive collateral estoppel, but to grant trial courts broad discretion to determine when it should be applied. The general rule should be that in cases where a plaintiff could easily have joined in the earlier action or where, either for the reasons discussed above or for other reasons, the application of offensive estoppel would be unfair to a defendant, a trial judge should not allow the use of offensive collateral estoppel.

In the present case, however, none of the circumstances that might justify reluctance to allow the offensive use of collateral estoppel is present. The application of offensive collateral estoppel will not here reward a private plaintiff who could have joined in the previous action, since the respondent probably could not have joined in the injunctive action brought by the SEC even had he so desired.[17] Similarly, there is no unfairness to the petitioners in applying offensive collateral estoppel in this case. First, in light of the serious allegations made in the SEC's complaint against the petitioners, as well as the foreseeability of subsequent private suits that typically follow a successful government judgment, the petitioners had every incentive to litigate the SEC lawsuit fully and vigorously. Second, the judgment in the Commission action was not inconsistent with any previous decision. Finally, there will in the respondent's action be no procedural opportunities available to the petitioner that were unavailable in the first action of a kind that might be likely to cause a different result.[19]

We conclude, therefore, that none of the considerations that would justify a refusal to allow the use of offensive collateral estoppel is present

---

15. If, for example, the defendant in the first action was forced to defend in an inconvenient forum and therefore was unable to engage in full scale discovery or call witnesses, application of offensive collateral estoppel may be unwarranted. Indeed, differences in available procedures may sometimes justify not allowing a prior judgment to have estoppel effect in a subsequent action even between the same parties, or where defensive estoppel is asserted against a plaintiff who has litigated and lost. The problem of unfairness is particularly acute in cases of offensive estoppel, however, because the defendant against whom estoppel is asserted typically will not have chosen the forum in the first action. See *Restatement (Second) of Judgments* (Tentative Draft No. 2, 1975) § 88(2) and Comment *d*.

17. SEC v. Everest Management Corp., 475 F.2d 1236, 1240 (CA2) ("[T]he complicat-

ing effect of the additional issues and the additional parties outweighs any advantage of a single disposition of the common issues"). Moreover, consolidation of a private action with one brought by the SEC without its consent is prohibited by statute. 15 U.S.C. § 78u(g).

19. It is true, of course, that the petitioners in the present action would be entitled to a jury trial of the issues bearing on whether the proxy statement was materially false and misleading had the SEC action never been brought—a matter to be discussed in Part II of this opinion. But the presence or absence of a jury as factfinder is basically neutral, quite unlike, for example, the necessity of defending the first lawsuit in an inconvenient forum.

in this case. Since the petitioners received a "full and fair" opportunity to litigate their claims in the SEC action, the contemporary law of collateral estoppel leads inescapably to the conclusion that the petitioners are collaterally estopped from relitigating the question of whether the proxy statements were materially false and misleading.

II

The question that remains is whether, notwithstanding the law of collateral estoppel, the use of offensive collateral estoppel in this case would violate the petitioners' Seventh Amendment right to a jury trial.

A

* * *

Recognition that an equitable determination could have collateral estoppel effect in a subsequent legal action was the major premise of this Court's decision in Beacon Theatres v. Westover [p. 879, supra] * * *.

It is clear that the Court in the *Beacon Theatres* case thought that if an issue common to both legal and equitable claims was first determined by a judge, relitigation of the issue before a jury might be foreclosed by res judicata or collateral estoppel. * * *

B

* * * The petitioners contend that since the scope of the Amendment must be determined by reference to the common law as it existed in 1791, and since the common law permitted collateral estoppel only where there was mutuality of parties, collateral estoppel cannot constitutionally be applied when such mutuality is absent.

The petitioners have advanced no persuasive reason, however, why the meaning of the Seventh Amendment should depend on whether or not mutuality of parties is present. A litigant who has lost because of adverse factual findings in an equity action is equally deprived of a jury trial whether he is estopped from relitigating the factual issues against the same party or a new party. In either case, the party against whom estoppel is asserted has litigated questions of fact, and has had the facts determined against him in an earlier proceeding. In either case there is no further factfinding function for the jury to perform, since the common factual issues have been resolved in the previous action. * * *

The Seventh Amendment has never been interpreted in the rigid manner advocated by the petitioners. On the contrary, many procedural devices developed since 1791 that have diminished the civil jury's historic domain have been found not to be inconsistent with the Seventh Amendment. * * *

The law of collateral estoppel, like the law in other procedural areas defining the scope of the jury's function, has evolved since 1791. * * * [T]hese developments are not repugnant to the Seventh Amendment simply for the reason that they did not exist in 1791. Thus if, as we have held, the law of collateral estoppel forcloses the petitioners from relitigating the factual issues determined against them in the SEC action, nothing in the Seventh Amendment dictates a different result, even though because of lack of mutuality there would have been no collateral estoppel in 1791.

The judgment of the Court of Appeals is

Affirmed.

MR. JUSTICE REHNQUIST, dissenting.

It is admittedly difficult to be outraged about the treatment accorded by the federal judiciary to petitioners' demand for a jury trial in this lawsuit. Outrage is an emotion all but impossible to generate with respect to a corporate defendant in a securities fraud action, and this case is no exception. But the nagging sense of unfairness as to the way petitioners have been treated, engendered by the *imprimatur* placed by the Court of Appeals on respondent's "heads I win, tails you lose" theory of this litigation, is not dispelled by this Court's antiseptic analysis of the issues in the case. It may be that if this Nation were to adopt a new Constitution today, the Seventh Amendment guaranteeing the right of jury trial in civil cases in federal courts would not be included among its provisions. But any present sentiment to that effect cannot obscure or dilute our obligation to enforce the Seventh Amendment, which *was* included in the Bill of Rights in 1791 and which has not since been repealed in the only manner provided by the Constitution for repeal of its provisions.

* * *

The Seventh Amendment requires that the right of trial by jury be "preserved." Because the Seventh Amendment demands preservation of the jury trial right, our cases have uniformly held that the content of the right must be judged by historical standards. * * * If a jury would have been impaneled in a particular kind of case in 1791, then the Seventh Amendment requires a jury trial today, if either party so desires.

To be sure, it is the substance of the right of jury trial that is preserved, not the incidental or collateral effects of common-law practice in 1791. * * *

To say that the Seventh Amendment does not tie federal courts to the exact procedure of the common law in 1791 does not imply, however, that any nominally "procedural" change can be implemented, regardless of its impact on the functions of the jury. * * *

Judged by the foregoing principles, I think it is clear that petitioners were denied their Seventh Amendment right to a jury trial in this case. Neither respondents nor the Court doubt that at common law as it existed in 1791, petitioners would have been entitled in the private action to have a jury determine whether the proxy statement was false and misleading in the respects alleged. The reason is that at common law in 1791, collateral estoppel was permitted only where the parties in the first action were identical to, or in privity with, the parties to the subsequent action. * * * [D]evelopments in the judge-made doctrine of collateral estoppel, however salutary, cannot, consistent with the Seventh Amendment, contract in any material fashion the right to a jury trial that a defendant would have enjoyed in 1791. * * *

* * * [T]he Court seems to suggest that the offensive use of collateral estoppel in this case is permissible under the limited principle set forth above that a mere procedural change that does not invade the province of the jury and a defendant's right thereto to a greater extent than authorized by the common law is permissible. But the Court's actions today constitute a far greater infringement of the defendant's rights than it ever before has sanctioned. * * * The procedural devices of summary judgment and directed verdict are direct descendants of their common-law antecedents. They accomplish nothing more than could have been done at common law, albeit by a more cumbersome procedure. * * *

By contrast, the development of nonmutual estoppel is a substantial departure from the common law and its use in this case completely deprives petitioners of their right to have a jury determine contested issues of fact. * * *

Even accepting, *arguendo,* the majority's position that there is no violation of the Seventh Amendment here, I nonetheless would not sanction the use of collateral estoppel in this case. * * * In my view, it is "unfair" to apply offensive collateral estoppel where the party who is sought to be estopped has not had an opportunity to have the facts of his case determined by a jury. Since in this case petitioners were not entitled to a jury trial in the Securities and Exchange Commission (SEC) lawsuit, I would not estop them from relitigating the issues determined in the SEC suit before a jury in the private action. I believe that several factors militate in favor of this result.

First, the use of offensive collateral estoppel in this case runs counter to the strong federal policy favoring jury trials, even if it does not, as the majority holds, violate the Seventh Amendment. * * *

Second, I believe that the opportunity for a jury trial in the second action could easily lead to a different result from that obtained in the first action before the court and therefore that it is unfair to estop petitioners from relitigating the issues before a jury. * * *

The ultimate irony of today's decision is that its potential for significantly conserving the resources of either the litigants or the judiciary is doubtful at best. That being the case, I see absolutely no reason to frustrate so cavalierly the important federal policy favoring jury decisions of disputed fact questions. The instant case is an apt example of the minimal savings that will be accomplished by the Court's decision. As the Court admits, even if petitioners are collaterally estopped from relitigating whether the proxy was materially false and misleading they are still entitled to have a jury determine whether respondents were injured by the alleged misstatements and the amount of damages, if any, sustained by respondents. * * * Thus, a jury must be impaneled in this case in any event. The time saved by not trying the issue of whether the proxy was materially false and misleading before the jury is likely to be insubstantial.[24] It is just as probable that today's decision will have the

---

24. Much of the delay in jury trials is attributed to the jury selection, *voir dire* and the charge. See H. Zeisel, H. Kalven, & B. Buchholtz, Delay in the Court 79 (1959). None of these delaying factors will be avoided by today's decision.

result of coercing defendants to agree to consent orders, or settlements in agency enforcement action in order to preserve their right to jury trial in the private actions. In that event, the Court, for no compelling reason, will have simply added a powerful club to the administrative agencies' arsenals that even Congress was unwilling to provide them.

Notes and Questions

1. How should inconsistent prior adjudications affect the application of issue preclusion? This problem was posed most dramatically in the multiple-claimant anomaly developed by the late Professor Brainerd Currie after the *Bernhard* decision. See Currie, *Mutuality of Collateral Estoppel: The Limits of the Bernhard Doctrine,* 9 Stan.L.Rev. 281 (1957). A train accident injures fifty passengers, and each of these passengers files a separate negligence action against the railroad. The railroad prevails in the first twenty-five suits to reach judgment, but loses the twenty-sixth. How should the twenty-sixth judgment affect the remaining suits?

How might your answer to this question change if the prior twenty-five cases all had been litigated in a court of limited jurisdiction, such as a small-claims court, and if the twenty-sixth judgment was rendered by a court of general jurisdiction? How does this variation on the hypothetical differ from the issue, discussed in Section D, supra, of whether a judgment by a court of limited jurisdiction should itself preclude the relitigation of certain issues?

Notice the more fundamental implications that the multiple-claimant anomaly has for nonmutual estoppel. Currie's hypothetical was designed to highlight the aberrant quality of the twenty-sixth judgment. Yet there is no reason that this "aberrant" result might not have been reached in the first trial rather than the twenty-sixth. If the holding against the railroad had been rendered in the first case, nonmutual estoppel would have been available to the remaining forty-nine passengers. In short, although any single decision may be an anomaly, a single decision can still have preclusive effect. Given these observations, do you believe nonmutual estoppel is desirable?

What if before a case settles it yields a judicial finding that conflicts with a prior adjudication of the same issue? Such a finding may result, for example, when a motion to dismiss is denied before a settlement is reached. Can that finding create sufficient inconsistency to block offensive issue preclusion? In JACK FAUCETT ASSOCIATES v. AMERICAN TELEPHONE & TELEGRAPH CO., 744 F.2d 118 (D.C.Cir.1984), Judge Mikva wrote for the court: "*Parklane Hosiery* does not hold that only inconsistent final *judgments* can preclude offensive estoppel." Id. at 130. According to Judge Mikva, the issue is only whether "the inconsistency undermines the court's confidence in the correctness of the prior decision." Id.

In the *Jack Faucett* case, the court found another factor weighing against the application of offensive issue preclusion. The prior decision upon which the party seeking preclusion sought to rely had been affirmed by the Second Circuit. In the course of its affirmance, however, the Circuit Court had held that one of the trial judge's evidentiary rulings had been erroneous, though harmless. The Court of Appeals for the District of Columbia Circuit found that the presence of even "harmless" error in the rulings of the trial court upon whose findings a second court was being urged to rely constituted a "serious obstacle" to offensive issue preclusion. Id. at 128. "[W]e decline to hold that the Second Circuit's conclusion of harmless error mandates * * * that we must ignore that error in our analysis of offensive estoppel." Id. at 129.

2. What preclusive effect should be given to a compromise verdict? In TAYLOR v. HAWKINSON, 47 Cal.2d 893, 306 P.2d 797 (1957), the California Supreme Court, in an opinion by Justice Traynor, held that the *Bernhard* rule should not be applied due to evidence of a compromise verdict:

> * * * Regardless of the effectiveness of [compromise verdicts] in extinguishing the causes of action or settling the rights directly involved therein * * *, it does not constitute such a determination of the issues involved as to render them res judicata where distinct rights are sought to be litigated in a separate cause of action. * * *

Id. at 896–97, 306 P.2d at 799.

Just how far should a court go in allowing parties in subsequent litigation to prove that the earlier verdict was a compromise? KATZ v. ELI LILLY & CO., 84 F.R.D. 378 (E.D.N.Y.1979), may represent the extreme. A suit prior to *Katz* had held the defendant liable for the wrongful death of the child of a mother who had taken diethylstilbestrol (DES) during pregnancy. Plaintiff Katz sought to take advantage of this prior verdict. The defendant, noticing signs that the earlier verdict may have been a compromise, subpoenaed two members of the jury in the prior case. The plaintiff moved to quash the subpoenas on the ground that the testimony of jurors may not be used to impeach a verdict. The court denied the motion to quash. Could you justify the court's refusal to quash the subpoenas? Would allowing such testimony truly impeach the verdict of the *prior* case? Are there ways to get the jurors' testimony without impeaching the earlier verdict? Should the potential liability of the defendant if preclusion is permitted be allowed to affect the decision of whether to subpoena the jurors? At what point does the effort involved in evaluating the prior verdict outweigh the effort saved in relitigating the substantive issues at stake in the suit?

3. What kind of preclusive effect should arise between coparties to an action? Consider SCHWARTZ v. PUBLIC ADMINISTRATOR, 24 N.Y.2d 65, 298 N.Y.S.2d 955, 246 N.E.2d 725 (1969). A multiple car collision resulted in a number of deaths and serious injuries. A passenger in one of the vehicles instituted an action against all of the drivers, alleging that their negligence made them liable for the injuries the passenger had suffered. The passenger prevailed. The question before the court in *Schwartz* was whether this prior judgment should preclude the drivers in subsequent suits against each other. The New York Court of Appeals held that preclusion was appropriate:

> The present plaintiffs were full participants in the earlier cases. All of these actions involved substantial sums. They did not involve claims for property damage amounting to but a few hundred dollars so that there would be no assurance that there was a vigorous fight on the issue of liability. Moreover, each of the plaintiffs had a full opportunity to tell his story at the first trial in order to remove himself from liability or to cast it elsewhere. None claims a lack of adequate representation, and none has shown any prejudice because of the forum of the earlier action. Likewise, no prejudice is claimed because in the earlier action the passenger had any tactical advantages. Finally, there is no assertion of

any significant new evidence, which would almost certainly change the earlier result. It is, therefore, utterly fair to apply the doctrine of collateral estoppel here and to the typical case where driver sues driver following a verdict by a passenger against both.

When we turn from the specifics of these cases, we find other more general arguments which have been advanced against permitting the use of collateral estoppel in cases such as the type involved here. The contentions raise problems which are not unreal, but to which there is a simple answer. It is said, for example, that the first verdict in favor of the passenger may have been influenced by sympathy since the jury almost certainly knows that the defendants had at least some insurance. Yet where the driver interposes a counterclaim or there is a consolidation of actions, this danger is greatly mitigated and wholly eliminated if the driver's injuries are more severe than the passenger's.

In this connection, claimant Wever points out that he was not in a position to interpose a counterclaim as he was required to seek relief in arbitration pursuant to the endorsement on his insurance policy because his accident involved an uninsured automobile. This claim is not without some merit, but Wever has offered nothing which would indicate that he was actually prejudiced by his inability to join his claim to the prior action. He has not shown that the first verdict was influenced by excessive sympathy for the injured passenger or was a compromise verdict.

* * *

It is also urged against the approach we have here adopted that attorneys who represent the drivers in the earlier actions are representatives of liability insurance carriers and are not counsel of the drivers' choice. As noted before, it is not difficult to conceive of a situation where a carrier may have devoted almost all of its efforts, in defending the action by the passenger, to obtaining a partner to share in paying a recovery by the passenger. Other possible sources of inadequate representation may arise if in the first action the passenger had suffered relatively minor injuries or the claim had involved a relatively small sum of money. The carrier may not then have made a substantial investment of time and effort in defending the action. But here again, these dangers can be obviated if the driver interposes a counterclaim in the first action or consolidates his action with the passenger's. At that point he will have an attorney of his own choosing who will be protecting only his interests in the litigation.

It can be seen that the arguments against applying collateral estoppel may be effectively answered while, on the other hand, the arguments for applying it are powerful indeed. It will reduce the number of inconsistent results which are always a blemish on a judicial system. * * * [I]t is difficult to tolerate a condition where, on relatively the same set of facts, one fact-finder, be it a court or jury, may hold the driver liable, while the other exonerates him. Finally, in this day of great delays in accident litigation, a single trial of all claims growing out of the same accident will constitute a great saving of judicial manpower and time, without any true unfairness to the parties. * * *

Id. at 72–74, 298 N.Y.S.2d at 961–63, 246 N.E.2d at 729–31.

When *Schwartz* was litigated, New York was a contributory-negligence state. It later adopted comparative negligence. Are the problems of preclusion between coparties reduced when a comparative negligence rule is in force?

4. Issue preclusion can interfere with a party's right to a jury trial, as *Parklane* demonstrates. The Supreme Court has held consistently that the Seventh Amendment does not guarantee the right to relitigate an issue before a jury if the issue already has been litigated fully in an equitable action. But what happens if a party is denied a jury trial because of an erroneous trial court ruling in the prior action? The courts of appeals are split. In RITTER v. MOUNT ST. MARY'S COLLEGE, 814 F.2d 986 (4th Cir.1987), plaintiff, a teacher, filed an employment discrimination suit in federal district court involving both legal and equitable claims. The District Court dismissed the plaintiff's two legal claims and conducted a bench trial on the equitable claim, finding for the defendant. On appeal, the Fourth Circuit reversed the dismissal of the legal claims. Upon remand, the defendant petitioned the District Court for summary judgment based upon the issue preclusive effect of the prior bench trial, which had involved the same issues as the remanded legal claims. The District Court granted summary judgment, and the Circuit Court affirmed. Although recognizing that "[h]ad the district court not erroneously dismissed the appellant's legal claims, a jury, and not the court, would have determined the facts arising out of Mrs. Ritter's denial of tenure," the court held that, under *Parklane*, the denial of a jury trial was "insufficient to override the judicial interest in the speedy resolution of disputes," and the fact that the denial was erroneous in this case was "irrelevant." Id. at 990–91. The Seventh Circuit has held to the contrary. Hussein v. Oshkosh Motor Truck Co., 816 F.2d 348 (7th Cir.1987).

3. BINDING NONPARTIES

IN RE MULTIDISTRICT CIVIL ACTIONS INVOLVING THE AIR CRASH DISASTER NEAR DAYTON, OHIO, ON MARCH 9, 1967

United States District Court, Southern District of Ohio, 1972.
350 F.Supp. 757.
Reversed sub nom. HUMPHREYS v. TANN, Sixth Circuit Court of Appeals, 1973.
487 F.2d 666, certiorari denied 416 U.S. 956, 94 S.Ct. 1970, 40 L.Ed.2d 307 (1974).

MEMORANDUM OPINION AND ORDER

WEINMAN, CHIEF JUDGE. On March 9, 1967 a DC–9 passenger aircraft owned and operated by Trans World Airlines, Inc. and a Beech Baron aircraft owned and operated by the Tann Company collided in mid-air near Dayton, Ohio. As a result of this air disaster, all occupants of both planes were killed. Numerous civil actions seeking recovery for alleged wrongful death and property damage were filed in this Court, other federal district courts and in various state courts across the country. Six actions pending in other federal district courts were transferred to this Court by the Judicial Panel on Multidistrict Litigation for consolidated and coordinated pretrial proceedings pursuant to Section 1407, Title 28 U.S.C. Among the actions transferred to this Court was a passenger wrongful death action against the Tann Company captioned Humphreys

v. Herman Tann, et al. which was originally commenced in the United States District Court for the Eastern District of Michigan, Southern Division.

On July 15, 1970 this Court conducted its first pretrial conference for the purpose of scheduling consolidated discovery with respect to all actions pending before the Court arising from the mid-air collision. Thomas F. Wolcott, attorney for plaintiff Humphreys in Case No. 3834ML(F) was among the attorneys attending this first pretrial conference. On July 22, 1970 this Court issued a pretrial order which among other things set forth a schedule for the completion of consolidated discovery in these multidistrict actions.

In accordance with this Court's first pretrial order consolidated discovery was expeditiously completed in these actions. Counsel for all parties including counsel for plaintiff Humphreys was given a full and ample opportunity to participate in all consolidated discovery proceedings, to ascertain all relevant facts concerning the mid-air disaster near Dayton, Ohio and to frame the issues.

After the completion of consolidated discovery the next pretrial conference was scheduled for December 15, 1970. On November 4, 1970 this Court sent an information order to all attorneys advising them that in view of the completion of discovery all counsel shall make a statement to the Court of what he or they expect to prove and further advising all counsel that the Court was planning an early date for trial and would consider recommendations concerning the joinder of party plaintiffs and whether or not there should be separate trials on liability and damages.

The second pretrial conference was held as scheduled. At this conference Craig Spangenberg, Esq. of the Cleveland, Ohio Bar, an acknowledged specialist in the representation of plaintiffs in air disaster cases delivered a statement of the facts which the passenger plaintiffs would attempt to prove in establishing acts of negligence on the part of both Trans World Airlines and the Tann Company. Plaintiffs' counsel who were present at the pretrial conference concurred in Mr. Spangenberg's statement of facts. It was further determined at this second pretrial conference that the passenger wrongful death action captioned Downey v. Trans World Airlines, Inc. and Tann Company would be the first case to proceed for trial. No objection was voiced to the trial of the Downey case first.

For some unexplained reason, Thomas Wolcott, attorney for plaintiff Humphreys, who had received notice of the scheduled December 15 pretrial conference and this Court's desire for a statement of facts from all parties failed to attend the second pretrial conference.

From March 22, 1971 to April 7, 1971 the wrongful death action brought by Vera Downey against Trans World Airlines and Tann Company, Civil Action No. 3521ML was tried to a jury in this Court. At the trial plaintiff was represented by attorney Craig Spangenberg of the Cleveland, Ohio Bar, an extremely experienced and highly competent plaintiff's lawyer, who has a reputation among the Bar as a specialist in air disaster cases. Mr. Spangenberg who was thoroughly familiar with all the facts surrounding the mid-air disaster presented to the jury in the Downey case all the claimed acts of negligence which were acknowledged by all the plaintiffs as constituting a basis for a finding of liability on the part of the Tann Company. In addition attorney Daniel J. O'Neill, counsel for Trans World Airlines, an equally qualified and competent trial attorney who also possessed a high degree of expertise in the highly technical area of aviation law, presented evidence and vigorously attempted to persuade the jury that the sole proximate cause of the mid-air collision was the negligence of the Tann Company pilot. After receiving all relevant evidence concerning the liability of Tann Company and hearing vigorous and well reasoned arguments attempting to fix the responsibility for the mid-air disaster upon the Tann Company pilot, the jury returned a general verdict in favor of the plaintiff in the amount of $300,000 against Trans World Airlines only and found against plaintiff on her claims against the Tann Company. No appeal was filed by any party and upon the satisfaction of the judgment by defendant Trans World Airlines, the judgment in the Downey case became final.

After the judgment in the Downey case became final, a series of motions were filed in the pending Multidistrict cases against the defendant Trans World Airlines seeking to invoke the doctrine of res judicata or collateral estoppel based on the final judgment in the Downey case. In a memorandum opinion issued January 20, 1972 this Court resolved these pending motions with the exception of the motion filed by the Tann Company for summary judgment on the basis of the doctrine of collateral estoppel in all outstanding passenger actions pending against the Tann Company. * * *

* * *

On May 3, 1972, after the [other passenger] * * * actions against Tann Company were settled, this Court heard oral argument on the pending motion. Counsel for plaintiff Humphreys * * * was present and presented oral argument.

Plaintiff Humphreys was not a party to the Downey case in which the liability or responsibility of the Tann Company for the mid-air disaster was determined. Thus the pending motion for summary judgment in the passenger cases raises the interesting but difficult question of whether the doctrine of res judicata or collateral estoppel can be applied against a person who was not a party to the prior action.

* * *

The Bernhard Doctrine abandoning the requirement of strict mutuality is especially applicable to protracted multiple litigation arising from common disasters where the factual and legal issues concerning the liability of defendants are identical. * * *

* * * Had the jury in the Downey case rendered judgment against the Tann Company this Court on the basis of the judgment in the Downey case would have sustained motions for summary judgment on the issue of liability in favor of plaintiffs in the outstanding passenger cases brought against Tann Company.

Turning to the facts of the present case it is clear that two of the essential elements of the Bernhard Doctrine have been satisfied. A final judgment on the merits has been rendered and the issue of whether the Tann Company pilot was guilty of any act of negligence constituting a proximate cause of the mid-air disaster has been actually litigated. The third essential requirement for the application of the doctrine of collateral estoppel however is lacking—that is—the plaintiff Humphreys against whom the doctrine is invoked has not personally litigated the issue of Tann Company's liability. Thus the Tann Company in its motion asks this Court to carry the Bernhard Doctrine one step further and apply the collateral estoppel doctrine against a stranger to the prior action.

Reasons which are not insubstantial have been advanced for the rule denying the application of collateral estoppel against a stranger. These reasons have been aptly summarized as follows:

> The rule * * * is based upon obvious principles of justice, fairness, and requirements of due process of law. The reason for the rule lies in the fact that a stranger to an action does not have the opportunity, vouchsafed to parties, to prove or ascertain the truth of the questions in issue, and the principle that no man's right should be prejudiced without an opportunity of defending it. Indeed, it is a fundamental doctrine of the law that a party to be affected by a personal judgment must have a day in court and an opportunity to be heard. 46 Am.Jur.2d Judgments § 519, page 671.

The constitutional requirement that each person be afforded his day in court is premised upon the underlying principle that fundamental fairness guaranteed by the due process clause of the Fifth and Fourteenth Amendments dictates that no person shall be deprived of a valuable right or claim without first being afforded the right to appear and be heard.

This Court does not believe that the maxim that each man must be given his day in court is so inexorably fixed that it must mandatorily apply where a careful evaluation of the record of pretrial and trial proceedings in the prior action discloses that the absent party was given full and complete opportunity to ascertain and develop all relevant facts and to frame the issues during discovery and the liability issue was adjudicated at a trial conducted in an atmosphere free from errors in substantive, evidentiary and procedural law or trial strategy which if avoided would have changed the result.

In the limited context of these multidistrict litigation cases the Court does not believe the principles of fundamental fairness guaranteed by due process of law are violated by the application of the doctrine of collateral estoppel against plaintiff Humphreys. The Humphreys case was transferred to this Court by the Judicial Panel on Multidistrict Litigation for coordinated and consolidated pretrial proceedings. Coordinated discovery was conducted at which counsel for plaintiff Humphreys was given the opportunity to ascertain and develop all relevant facts concerning the cause of the mid-air collision. Under the coordinated discovery proceedings Humphreys' counsel received the added advantage of reaping the benefit of facts developed by other attorneys who specialize in this type of litigation. At subsequent pretrial conferences counsel for Humphreys had the opportunity to participate in the framing of issues for trial and in selecting the first case to be tried. At the trial itself all parties were represented by highly competent attorneys who can accurately be designated as specialists in aviation disaster litigation. All tenable claims of negligence on the part of Tann Company were presented not only by plaintiffs' counsel but by the equally competent counsel for Trans World Airlines who attempted to convince the jury that the sole proximate cause of the mid-air collision was the negligence of the Tann Company pilot. Well reasoned opening statements and closing arguments were presented to the jury. The Court deems it extremely significant that counsel for plaintiff Humphreys, either in his brief or during oral argument, did not assert that learned counsel for plaintiff Downey failed to introduce all relevant evidence, neglected to present all claims of negligence on the part of Tann or otherwise made errors of commission or omission with respect to substantive, procedural or evidentiary law or trial strategy which resulted or contributed to the verdict in favor of Tann Company. No errors on the part of this Court in the admission of evidence or the charge to the jury have been raised. Having had the advantage of presiding at the trial of the Downey case, this Court can truly say that the Downey case was one of the most skillfully tried cases this Court has had the pleasure of adjudicating.

Finally, this is not the type of case where there is an appreciable danger that the jury verdict in favor of the Tann Company was a compromise motivated by sympathy. The uncontradicted evidence discloses that the deceased passenger Edward Downey was an outstanding individual in terms of his business endeavors and private life. The decedent was a graduate engineer who was selected by his employer for further advancement. The decedent was active in church and civic affairs and at the time of his death left a wife and three minor children. It was obvious that plaintiff's counsel who represented the heirs of other deceased passengers was litigating his most favorable case in an attempt to test the liability and monetary responsibility of both Trans World Airlines and the Tann Company.

Upon considering all these factors the Court concludes that no principle of fundamental fairness inherent in the concept of due process will be offended by the application of the doctrine against plaintiff Humphreys to bar the relitigation of the issue of the Tann Company's liability for the mid-air disaster. In this Court's opinion unfairness will result and the effective administration of justice will be retarded if plaintiff Humphreys is permitted to relitigate an issue which has been fully and fairly adjudicated.

* * *

The Court realizes that this decision does not conform to the weight of authority and appreciates that there is room for reasonable divergence of opinion as to the validity of the result reached herein. However, in view of the great increase in the number of civil actions commenced in the federal district courts in recent years, the Court believes that the federal trial courts should not hesitate to adopt new approaches designed to terminate needless and futile litigation where identical liability issues have been fairly and truly tried in a prior action. Furthermore, the Court believes that this is a proper case in which to test the power of a transferee court in common disaster multidistrict litigation to bar relitigation in subsequent common disaster actions of identical liability issues which have been actually litigated in a prior action arising from the same incident.

Accordingly, the motion of the Tann Company for summary judgment in its favor * * * hereby is sustained and this action hereby is dismissed.

Notes and Questions

1. The Sixth Circuit reversed Chief Judge Weinman's ruling in the principal case, saying: "We share the concern of the district court for the crowded dockets of federal courts and the proper utilization of judicial time. However, we do not believe that these considerations can overcome the due process objections * * *." Humphreys v. Tann, 487 F.2d 666, 671 (6th Cir. 1973).

2. The District Court seems to base its holding on two intertwined but distinct considerations. What are they? Would either, standing alone, provide a sufficient basis for the court to hold a nonparty precluded?

3. Often, formal relationships between persons will justify nonparty preclusion. For instance, when a guardian litigates a suit on behalf of a minor, the minor will normally be bound by the suit's outcome. Can you think of other relationships that would justify nonparty preclusion? What if a party assigns her rights to a person who then sues upon them? Suppose the assignee is an insurance company and the assignor the insured?

4. Sometimes a relationship between parties need not be so formal as that between a guardian and a child in order to justify nonparty preclusion. In MONTANA v. UNITED STATES, 440 U.S. 147, 99 S.Ct. 970, 59 L.Ed.2d 210 (1979), the Supreme Court held that when nonparties assume control over litigation in which they have a direct financial or pecuniary interest, they may be precluded from subsequently relitigating issues that the earlier suit resolved. Montana gave contractors different tax treatment depending on whether they contracted to build public or private projects. A contractor on a federal construction project brought a state-court action challenging the constitutionality of this practice. The United States directed and financed the litigation for the contractor, but it also brought an action challenging the practice in federal court. After the Montana Supreme Court upheld Montana's system of taxation, the United States continued with its federal action. But Montana argued that the federal government was bound by the state-court judgment. When the case reached the Supreme Court, Justice Marshall, writing for the Court, observed that "although not a party, the United States plainly had a sufficient laboring oar in the conduct of the state-court litigation to actuate principles of estoppel." Id. at 154–55, 99 S.Ct. at 974, 59 L.Ed.2d at 217–18.

The *Montana* case suggests other types of representation that might justify nonparty preclusion. What if individuals agree that a case will serve as a test case? Some courts have held that, when sufficient evidence of an agreement exists, nonparties are precluded from relitigating the claims. See generally *Restatement (Second), Judgments* § 40 (1982).

5. A limited number of courts have been willing to permit nonparty preclusion in a narrow range of circumstances in which "virtual" representation has occurred. The theory underlying preclusion in cases of virtual representation, which is similar to the theory upon which class-action rules are based, is that once an issue has been adjudicated by a court in an adequate adversarial contest, it should be considered settled once and for all—both as to those who participated in the litigation and as to those who did not. Thus, preclusion based on virtual representation is very different from the other forms of preclusion, each of which was based upon the fact that, in some sense, the party against whom preclusion was invoked had enjoyed a day in court. See Cauefield v. Fidelity & Casualty Co., 378 F.2d 876, 879 (5th Cir.), certiorari denied 389 U.S. 1009, 88 S.Ct. 571, 19 L.Ed.2d 606 (1967).

6. Does an expansive doctrine of nonparty preclusion go beyond the bounds of fairness required by the Constitution? Traditionally, the Due Process Clause has been thought to guarantee that a litigant will have an opportunity to present his claims in court before he can be bound by a judgment. See Blonder-Tongue Labs., Inc. v. University of Illinois Foundation, p. 1196, supra ("Some litigants—those who never appeared in a prior action—may not be collaterally estopped without litigating the issue. They have never had a chance to present their evidence and arguments on their claim. Due process prohibits estopping them despite one or more existing judgments of the identical issue which stand squarely against their position.").

In MARTIN v. WILKS, ___ U.S. ___, 109 S.Ct. 2180, ___ L.Ed.2d ___ (1989), the Supreme Court returned to the suggestion, raised by Justice Harlan in Provident Tradesmens Bank & Trust Co. v. Patterson, p. 600, supra, that a nonparty to a prior lawsuit might "be bound by the previous decision because, although technically a nonparty, he had purposely bypassed an adequate opportunity to intervene." *Martin* was a suit by White firefighters against the City of Birmingham (Alabama) and the Jefferson County Personnel Board alleging that the Whites were being denied promotions illegally in favor of less qualified Blacks. The City and the Board responded that consent decrees entered in earlier suits brought by Blacks (suits in which the White employees had not participated) included goals for hiring Blacks as firefighters and for promoting them. The Supreme Court, in a 5-to-4 decision, held that the nonparty Whites were not precluded from challenging the employment decisions taken pursuant to the consent decrees. Chief Justice Rehnquist wrote for the majority:

We begin with the words of Justice Brandeis in Chase National Bank v. Norwalk, 291 U.S. 431 (1934):

"The law does not impose upon any person absolutely entitled to a hearing the burden of voluntary intervention in a suit to which he is a stranger * * *. Unless duly summoned to appear in a legal proceeding, a person not a privy may rest assured that a judgment recovered therein will not affect his legal rights." Id. at 441.

While these words were written before the adoption of the Federal Rules of Civil Procedure, we think the Rules incorporate the same principle; a party seeking a judgment binding on another cannot obligate that person to intervene; he must be joined. See [Zenith Radio Corp. v. Hazeltine Research, Inc., 395 U.S. 100, 110, 89 S.Ct. 1562, 1569, 23 L.Ed.2d 129, ___ (1969)] (judgment against Hazeltine vacated because it was not named as a party or served, even though as the parent corporation of one of the parties it clearly knew of the claim against it and had made a special appearance to contest jurisdiction). Against the background of permissive intervention set forth in *Chase National Bank,* the drafters cast Rule 24, governing intervention, in permissive terms. * * * They determined that the concern for finality and completeness of judgments would be "better [served] by mandatory joinder procedures." * * * Accordingly, Rule 19(a) provides for mandatory joinder in circumstances where a judgment rendered in the absence of a person may "leave * * * persons already parties subject to a substantial risk of incurring * * * inconsistent obligations * * *." Rule 19(b) sets forth the factors to be considered by a court in deciding whether to allow an action to proceed in the absence of an interested party.

Joinder as a party, rather than knowledge of a lawsuit and an opportunity to intervene, is the method by which potential parties are subjected to the jurisdiction of the court and bound by a judgment or decree. The parties to a lawsuit presumably know better than anyone else the nature and scope of relief sought in the action, and at whose expense such relief might be granted. It makes sense, therefore, to place on them a burden of bringing in additional parties where such a step is indicated, rather than placing on potential additional parties a duty to intervene when they acquire knowledge of the lawsuit. The linchpin of the "impermissible collateral attack" doctrine—the attribution of preclusive effect to a failure to intervene—is therefore quite inconsistent with Rule 19 and Rule 24.

Does the Supreme Court's decision in *Martin* cast doubt on any of the instances of nonparty preclusion raised in Notes 3 through 5?

SECTION F. INTERSYSTEM PRECLUSION

The preceding discussion of preclusion assumed that both the original and subsequent court were in the same judicial system. Often, however, questions of preclusion are presented to a court that is part of a judicial system different from the court that rendered the prior judgment. Should this affect the preclusive effect given the prior judgment?

Read U.S. Const. Art. IV, § 1 and 28 U.S.C. § 1738 in the Supplement.

1. INTERSTATE PRECLUSION

PARKER v. HOEFER
Court of Appeals of New York, 1957.
2 N.Y.2d 612, 162 N.Y.S.2d 13, 142 N.E.2d 194.

DYE, JUDGE.

In this appeal by our permission, we consider whether New York must give full faith and credit to a foreign judgment, notwithstanding that the underlying claim would not be enforcible in the State [of New York].

The plaintiff, a resident of Vermont, has a final judgment against the defendant, a resident of New York, in an action for alienation of her husband's affections and for criminal conversation. When such judgment could not be collected in Vermont, she commenced this action to enforce it in New York. The defendant, by her answer, interposed a defense based upon all the provisions of article 2–A of the Civil Practice Act, relating to actions against the public policy of the State of New York which, among others, includes actions "based upon alleged alienation of affections [and] criminal conversation" (§ 61–a).   *   *   *

Article 2–A of the Civil Practice Act designates various causes of action which may not be enforced in New York *   *   * but nowhere does it abolish an action on a judgment rendered in a sister State by a court having jurisdiction of the person and the subject matter.

*   *   *

Had the Legislature attempted to abolish actions for enforcement of judgments rendered by courts of competent jurisdiction in sister States, it would have incurred the risk of unconstitutionality.   *   *   *   The Supreme Court of the United States has from the beginning consistently seen to it that a "judgment of a state court should have the same credit, validity, and effect in every other court in the United States, which it had in the state where it was pronounced."   *   *   *

Because there is a full faith and credit clause, defendant may not a second time challenge the validity of plaintiff's right which has ripened into a judgment *   *   *, which is to say that a judgment of a court having jurisdiction of the parties and of the subject matter operates as *res judicata* in the absence of fraud or collusion, even if obtained upon default. "Such a judgment obtained in a sister State is, with exceptions not relevant here, *   *   * entitled to full faith and credit in another State, though the underlying claim would not be enforced in the State of the forum"   *   *   *.

*   *   * Here, the plaintiff is not attempting to enforce in the courts of New York an action for alienation of affections and criminal conversation, which have been abolished in New York but, rather, to enforce a judgment rendered in Vermont as between these parties, which was final and conclusive on the rights litigated. New York cannot retry the case or review as on appeal the Vermont judgment. The tort on which the Vermont action was based was fully merged in the judgment. The judgment became a debt which the defendant was under obligation to pay. *   *   * The present suit, then, is upon an entirely different cause of action from that merged in the judgment and may not be called a suit on an action abolished in New York.   *   *   * When so viewed, it does not contravene New York policy as enunciated in article 2–A of the Civil Practice Act. The answer raises no issues of fact requiring a trial, for the defenses relied on are insufficient as matter of law.

The judgment appealed from is affirmed, with costs.

[The dissenting opinion of JUDGE FROESSEL is omitted.]

Notes and Questions

1. Do the statutory and constitutional provisions require that states give a judgment the same preclusive effect—neither more nor less—as would the courts of the rendering state? Or do the provisions establish a minimum preclusive effect that one state must give another's judgment? There has been considerable debate over whether a court can rest non-mutual preclusion on the judgment of a court that itself would require mutuality. The more common view appears to be in favor of employing the rules of the rendering

court. This approach allows the first court the power to limit the effect of its own proceedings. See 18 Wright, Miller & Cooper, *Federal Practice and Procedure: Jurisdiction and Related Matters* § 4467 n. 54, § 4469 n. 33 (1981 and Supp.1988). The issue is left open in the *Restatement (Second) of Judgments* § 86, comment *g* (1982). Nonetheless, some courts have given non-mutual preclusive effect to a judgment that the rendering state's courts would not have treated as preclusive.

In FINLEY v. KESLING, 105 Ill.App.3d 1, 60 Ill.Dec. 874, 433 N.E.2d 1172 (1982), Finley testified in Indiana divorce proceedings that four of his children owned 40% of the stock in a family corporation, and this testimony was accepted as the basis for the division of property. Thereafter he sued his four children in Illinois for a declaration that he was the beneficial owner of the stock. The Illinois court expressed doubt whether Indiana would cling to its traditional mutuality requirement in these circumstances, but concluded that it could apply collateral estoppel without regard to what Indiana might do. In the Illinois court's view, although a second state cannot reduce the effect of a judgment below the level commanded by the law of the judgment state, it can expand its effect. The court, nonetheless, advanced an alternative ground for decision—that Illinois courts would not permit a party to contradict his sworn testimony in a prior proceeding, and that this is a matter independent of the effect of judgments or full faith and credit requirements.

In HART v. AMERICAN AIRLINES, INC., 61 Misc.2d 41, 304 N.Y.S.2d 810 (Sup.Ct.1969), a New York court reached a similar result in a case in which the findings relied upon had been made by a federal district court in Texas. In deciding to give non-mutual preclusive effect in circumstances in which the rendering court would not have done so, the court said:

> Defendant's reliance on "full faith and credit" to defeat the application of collateral estoppel herein is misplaced. This is not a situation where the judgment, as such, of the Texas court is sought to be enforced. What is here involved is a policy determination by our courts that " 'One who has had his day in court should not be permitted to litigate the question anew' " * * *, and, further, refusal "to tolerate a condition where, on relatively the same set of facts, one fact-finder, be it court or jury" may find a party liable while another exonerates him leading to the "inconsistent results which are always a blemish on a judicial system" * * *. It is in order to carry out these policy determinations in the disposition of cases in this jurisdiction that an evidentiary use is being made of a particular issue determination made in the Texas action.

> * * *

> Defendant further seeks to forestall the conclusive effect of the Texas liability determination on the ground that such may be "an aberration" stemming from local prejudice against corporate defendants or from sympathy considerations. Such conjectural musings, which significantly are in no way documented by any supporting facts, are, of course, a complete indictment of all notions of "full faith and credit" of which defendant is elsewhere so solicitous.

> Even more interesting is the argument raised by defendant which may be paraphrased in Biblical terms as "hear them not for they know not what they do." Defendant seriously suggests that the determination in the Texas action should not be accorded further conclusive effect because that action involved only a single claimant and the jury's decision

as to defendant's negligence is somehow impaired because rendered "without any awareness whatsoever by the jury that its verdict would determine the obligation of the defendant to many other persons not before it." It is apparently defendant's contention that the issue as to whether or not it was negligent in the operation of its aircraft is in some manner dependent upon the number of claims which may ultimately be asserted against it. This court is unaware of any rule of law which supports this novel rule of liability, nor has defendant cited any authority in that regard.

Id. at 42–46, 304 N.Y.S.2d at 813–15.

What limits does the Due Process Clause place on expanding the preclusive effect given a state judgment? How should the foreseeability of the expanded preclusive effect figure into this question?

2. Often a plaintiff may wish to enforce a judgment in a state other than the one that rendered the judgment. The procedures for enforcing an out-of-state judgment vary from state to state. Sometimes it is possible simply to register the existence of the out-of-state judgment with the clerk of the court in which the judgment is to be enforced. Other times the plaintiff must institute a new suit, which is then subject to abbreviated procedures. What requirements do the constitutional and statutory provisions regarding full faith and credit place on a state's treatment of enforcement proceedings?

The basic implications of full faith and credit are the same for enforcement proceedings as they are for preclusion. There are, however, some exceptions to this general rule. For example, judgments based on limited forms of personal jurisdiction—in rem and quasi-in-rem judgments—need not be honored in execution proceedings. Or, for another example, a state may refuse to entertain an enforcement proceeding on grounds that its statute of limitations for such enforcement proceedings has run, even though the statute of the rendering state would not have run. And, for a final example, state statutes often specify that certain items of personal property, such as social-security payments and the last $200 of a savings account, cannot be used to satisfy court judgments. It is not a violation of full faith and credit for a state to refuse to enforce a judgment because it would require attachment of exempt property, even though that property would not have been considered exempt in the state rendering the judgment. For more general discussions of full faith and credit, see Nadelmann, *Full Faith and Credit to Judgments and Public Acts,* 56 Mich.L.Rev. 33 (1957); Radin, *The Authenticated Full Faith and Credit Clause: Its History,* 39 Ill.L.Rev. 1 (1944).

3. Recall the problem of limited appearances discussed in Chapter Two at pages 236–37, supra. What implications does the existence of claim and issue preclusion have for limited appearances? Suppose that plaintiff P institutes a quasi-in-rem suit in jurisdiction X, which permits limited appearances. Defendant D makes the limited appearance, contesting the merits of the suit but risking only the value of the attached property. Plaintiff wins, but it turns out that the value of the property does not satisfy the judgment of the underlying claim. Can the plaintiff then institute a second suit on the same cause of action, styled either as another quasi-in-rem suit or, if possible, as an in personam suit, in a different jurisdiction, and then assert preclusion based on the earlier quasi-in-rem judgment? Would both claim and issue preclusion be available to such a plaintiff? Alternatively, suppose the defen-

dant had prevailed in the first proceeding. Could the defendant assert preclusion defensively in subsequent proceedings?

The dilemma posed is easy to state and difficult to resolve. To allow preclusion in such situations undermines the value, if not the very existence, of limited appearances. Not to allow preclusion would be inconsistent with the principles of preclusion as they normally are applied. The *Restatement (Second) of Judgments* would allow preclusion based on judgments in quasi-in-rem suits; the Reporter's Note concludes that consistency within the law of preclusion is of greater value than the existence of limited appearances. See *Restatement (Second), Judgments* § 32, comment *d* (1982).

The position taken by the *Restatement* has been criticized. See Note, *Limited Appearances and Issue Preclusion: Resetting the Trap?*, 66 Cornell L.Rev. 595 (1981). It has been argued that the rule recommended in the *Restatement* may increase use of judicial resources. If no preclusive effect would attach to quasi-in-rem judgments, a rational defendant making limited appearances would never mount a defense more costly than the value of attached property. The threat of greater preclusive effect may cause these defendants to mount more extensive defenses to quasi-in-rem suits. How do you think that this rule of preclusion will affect use of judicial resources? Do you believe that it will increase use of such resources, or merely fail to decrease their use?

2. STATE–FEDERAL PRECLUSION

Although the Full Faith and Credit Clause of the Constitution, it generally is agreed, applies only to state courts, Section 1738 (known as the Full Faith and Credit Statute) imposes the same general principles on the federal courts, requiring them to accord full faith and credit to the judgments of state courts. Because the requirement is statutory and not constitutional, however, it may be supervened. For example, the writ of habeas corpus, 28 U.S.C. §§ 2241–55, provides a federal forum in which people who have been convicted of crimes in state court may litigate constitutional claims arising out of their prosecutions. Under traditional rules of preclusion, this subsequent action would be prevented.

What other circumstances might justify departing from the usual rules of intersystem preclusion? Consider, for example, cases involving federal issues. Should a federal court give preclusive effect to a state-court determination of federal law? What about circumstances in which the federal claim arises only by way of defense, and thus the original action could not have been removed to federal court? What if that issue was an area, such as copyright, which is within the exclusive jurisdiction of the federal courts?

ALLEN v. McCURRY
Supreme Court of the United States, 1980.
449 U.S. 90, 101 S.Ct. 411, 66 L.Ed.2d 308.

[McCurry was charged with possession of heroin in a state-court proceeding. At a pretrial suppression hearing, the trial judge excluded some of the evidence on the ground that it was the product of an illegal police search, but admitted the drugs and other contraband that the officers had found "in plain view." McCurry was subsequently convicted after a jury trial. McCurry later filed a civil action for damages under 42 U.S.C. § 1983, claiming that Allen and other police officers had unconstitutionally searched his house and seized the property that had been used to convict him. The District Court granted Allen and the other defendants summary judgment, holding that McCurry already had raised the Fourth Amendment issue unsuccessfully in the state-court proceeding. The Court of Appeals reversed, holding that the issue should be allowed to go to trial unencumbered by rules of issue preclusion due to the special role of the federal courts in protecting civil rights.]

Certiorari to the United States Court of Appeals for the Eighth Circuit.

JUSTICE STEWART delivered the opinion of the Court.

*   *   *

In recent years, this Court has reaffirmed the benefits of collateral estoppel in particular, finding the policies underlying it to apply in contexts not formerly recognized at common law. Thus, the Court has eliminated the requirement of mutuality in applying collateral estoppel to bar relitigation of issues decided earlier in federal-court suits, *   *   * and has allowed a litigant who was not a party to a federal case to use collateral estoppel "offensively" in a new federal suit against the party who lost on the decided issue in the first case *   *   *. But one general limitation the Court has repeatedly recognized is that the concept of collateral estoppel cannot apply when the party against whom the earlier decision is asserted did not have a "full and fair opportunity" to litigate that issue in the earlier case. *   *   *

The federal courts generally have *   *   * consistently accorded preclusive effect to issues decided by state courts. E.g., Montana v. United States, supra; Angel v. Bullington, 330 U.S. 183, 67 S.Ct. 657, 91 L.Ed. 832. Thus, res judicata and collateral estoppel not only reduce unnecessary litigation and foster reliance on adjudication, but also promote the comity between state and federal courts that has been recognized as a bulwark of the federal system. *   *   *

Indeed, though the federal courts may look to the common law or to the policies supporting res judicata and collateral estoppel in assessing the preclusive effect of decisions of other federal courts, Congress has specifically required all federal courts to give preclusive effect to state-court judgments whenever the courts of the State from which the judgments emerged would do so *   *   * [citing 28 U.S.C. § 1738]. It is against this background that we examine the relationship of § 1983 and collateral estoppel, and the decision of the Court of Appeals in this case.

III

This Court has never directly decided whether the rules of res judicata and collateral estoppel are generally applicable to § 1983 actions. But in Preiser v. Rodriguez *   *   *, the Court noted with implicit approval the view of other federal courts that res judicata principles fully apply to civil rights suits brought under that statute. *   *   * And the virtually unanimous view of the Courts of Appeals since *Preiser* has been that § 1983 presents no categorical bar to the application of res judicata and collateral estoppel concepts.[10] These federal appellate court decisions have spoken with little explanation or citation in assuming the compatibility of § 1983 and rules of preclusion, but the statute and its legislative history clearly support the courts' decisions.

Because the requirement of mutuality of estoppel was still alive in the federal courts until well into this century, * * * the drafters of the 1871 Civil Rights Act, of which § 1983 is a part, may have had less reason to concern themselves with rules of preclusion than a modern Congress would. Nevertheless, in 1871 res judicata and collateral estoppel could certainly have applied in federal suits following state-court litigation between the same parties or their privies, and nothing in the language of § 1983 remotely expresses any congressional intent to contravene the common-law rules of preclusion or to repeal the express statutory requirements of the predecessor of 28 U.S.C. § 1738 * * *. Section 1983 creates a new federal cause of action. It says nothing about the preclusive effect of state-court judgments.

Moreover, the legislative history of § 1983 does not in any clear way suggest that Congress intended to repeal or restrict the traditional doctrines of preclusion. The main goal of the Act was to override the corrupting influence of the Ku Klux Klan and its sympathizers on the governments and law enforcement agencies of the Southern States, see Monroe v. Pape, 365 U.S. 167, 174, 81 S.Ct. 473, 477, 5 L.Ed.2d 492, and of course the debates show that one strong motive behind its enactment was grave congressional concern that the state courts had been deficient in protecting federal rights * * *. But in the context of the legislative history as a whole, this congressional concern lends only the most equivocal support to any argument that, in cases where the state courts have recognized the constitutional claims asserted and provided fair procedures for determining them, Congress intended to override § 1738 or the common-law rules of collateral estoppel and res judicata. Since repeals by implication are disfavored, * * * much clearer support than this would be required to hold that § 1738 and the traditional rules of preclusion are not applicable to § 1983 suits.

As the Court has understood the history of the legislation, Congress realized that in enacting § 1983 it was altering the balance of judicial power between the state and federal courts. * * * But in doing so, Congress was adding to the jurisdiction of the federal courts, not subtracting from that of the state courts. * * * The debates contain several references to the concurrent jurisdiction of the state courts over federal questions, and numerous suggestions that the state courts would

---

10. * * * A very few courts have suggested that the normal rules of claim preclusion should not apply in § 1983 suits in one peculiar circumstance: Where a § 1983 plaintiff seeks to litigate in federal court a federal issue which he could have raised but did not raise in an earlier state-court suit against the same adverse party. Graves v. Olgiati, 550 F.2d 1327 (CA2 1977); Lombard v. Board of Ed. of New York City, 502 F.2d 631 (CA2 1974); Mack v. Florida Bd. of Dentistry, 430 F.2d 862 (CA5 1970). These cases present a narrow question not now before us, and we intimate no view as to whether they were correctly decided.

retain their established jurisdiction so that they could, when the then current political passions abated, demonstrate a new sensitivity to federal rights.

To the extent that it did intend to change the balance of power over federal questions between the state and federal courts, the 42d Congress was acting in a way thoroughly consistent with the doctrines of preclusion. In reviewing the legislative history of § 1983, * * * the Court inferred that Congress had intended a federal remedy in three circumstances: where state substantive law was facially unconstitutional, where state procedural law was inadequate to allow full litigation of a constitutional claim, and where state procedural law, though adequate in theory, was inadequate in practice. * * * In short, the federal courts could step in where the state courts were unable or unwilling to protect federal rights. Id., at 176, 81 S.Ct., at 478. This understanding of § 1983 might well support an exception to res judicata and collateral estoppel where state law did not provide fair procedures for the litigation of constitutional claims, or where a state court failed to even acknowledge the existence of the constitutional principle on which a litigant based his claim. Such an exception, however, would be essentially the same as the important general limit on rules of preclusion that already exists: Collateral estoppel does not apply where the party against whom an earlier court decision is asserted did not have a full and fair opportunity to litigate the claim or issue decided by the first court. * * * But the Court's view of § 1983 in *Monroe* lends no strength to any argument that Congress intended to allow relitigation of federal issues decided after a full and fair hearing in a state court simply because the state court's decision may have been erroneous.

* * *

The actual basis of the Court of Appeals' holding appears to be a generally framed principle that every person asserting a federal right is entitled to one unencumbered opportunity to litigate that right in a federal district court, regardless of the legal posture in which the federal claim arises. But the authority for this principle is difficult to discern. It cannot lie in the Constitution, which makes no such guarantee, but leaves the scope of the jurisdiction of the federal district courts to the wisdom of Congress. And no such authority is to be found in § 1983 itself. For reasons already discussed at length, nothing in the language or legislative history of § 1983 proves any congressional intent to deny binding effect to a state-court judgment or decision when the state court, acting within its proper jurisdiction, has given the parties a full and fair opportunity to litigate federal claims, and thereby has shown itself willing and able to protect federal rights. And nothing in the legislative history of § 1983 reveals any purpose to afford less deference to judgments in state criminal proceedings than to those in state civil proceedings. There is, in short, no reason to believe that Congress intended to provide a person claiming a federal right an unrestricted opportunity to relitigate an issue already decided in state court simply because the issue arose in a state proceeding in which he would rather not have been engaged at all.

* * *

The only other conceivable basis for finding a universal right to litigate a federal claim in a federal district court is hardly a legal basis at all, but rather a general distrust of the capacity of the state courts to render correct decisions on constitutional issues. *   *   *

The Court of Appeals erred in holding that McCurry's inability to obtain federal habeas corpus relief upon his Fourth Amendment claim renders the doctrine of collateral estoppel inapplicable to his § 1983 suit. Accordingly, the judgment is reversed, and the case is remanded to the Court of Appeals for proceedings consistent with this opinion.

It is so ordered.

JUSTICE BLACKMUN, with whom JUSTICE BRENNAN and JUSTICE MARSHALL join, dissenting.

*   *   *

The following factors persuade me to conclude that this respondent should not be precluded from asserting his claim in federal court. First, at the time § 1983 was passed, a nonparty's ability, as a practical matter, to invoke collateral estoppel was nonexistent. One could not preclude an opponent from relitigating an issue in a new cause of action, though that issue had been determined conclusively in a prior proceeding, unless there was "mutuality." Additionally, the definitions of "cause of action" and "issue" were narrow. As a result, and obviously, no preclusive effect could arise out of a criminal proceeding that would affect subsequent *civil* litigation. Thus, the 42d Congress could not have anticipated or approved that a criminal defendant, tried and convicted in state court, would be precluded from raising against police officers a constitutional claim arising out of his arrest.

Also, the process of deciding in a state criminal trial whether to exclude or admit evidence is not at all the equivalent of a § 1983 proceeding. The remedy sought in the latter is utterly different. In bringing the civil suit the criminal defendant does not seek to challenge his conviction collaterally. At most, he wins damages. In contrast, the exclusion of evidence may prevent a criminal conviction. A trial court, faced with the decision whether to exclude relevant evidence, confronts institutional pressures that may cause it to give a different shape to the Fourth Amendment right from what would result in civil litigation of a damages claim. Also, the issue whether to exclude evidence is subsidiary to the purpose of a criminal trial, which is to determine the guilt or innocence of the defendant, and a trial court, at least subconsciously, must weigh the potential damage to the truth-seeking process caused by excluding relevant evidence. *   *   *

Notes and Questions

1. The logic of *Allen* was soon extended by the Supreme Court. In MIGRA v. WARREN CITY SCHOOL DISTRICT BOARD OF EDUCATION, 465 U.S. 75, 104 S.Ct. 892, 79 L.Ed.2d 56 (1984), the Court found that a prior state-court adjudication precluded the plaintiff from bringing a subsequent suit in federal court, even though the later proceeding was based on constitutional issues that the plaintiff failed to raise, but could have raised, in the

earlier state action. Justice Blackmun, who dissented in *Allen*, wrote for the Court:

> Petitioner suggests that to give state-court judgments full issue preclusive effect but not claim preclusive effect would enable litigants to bring their state claims in state court and their federal claims in federal court, thereby taking advantage of the relative expertise of both forums. Although such a division may seem attractive from a plaintiff's perspective, it is not the system established by § 1738. That statute embodies the view that it is more important to give full faith and credit to state-court judgments than to ensure separate forums for federal and state claims. This reflects a variety of concerns, including notions of comity, the need to prevent vexatious litigation, and a desire to conserve judicial resources.

> In the present litigation, petitioner does not claim that the state court would not have adjudicated her federal claims had she presented them in her original suit in state court. Alternatively, petitioner could have obtained a federal forum for her federal claim by litigating it first in a federal court. Section 1983, however, does not override state preclusion law and guarantee petitioner a right to proceed to judgment in state court on her state claims and then turn to federal court for adjudication of her federal claims. We hold, therefore, that petitioner's state-court judgment in this litigation has the same claim preclusive effect in federal court that the judgment would have in the Ohio state courts.

Id. at 84, 104 S.Ct. at 898, 79 L.Ed.2d at 64.

2. *Allen* and *Migra* held that Section 1983 did not imply an exception to Section 1738. Does a congressional grant of exclusive federal jurisdiction imply such an exception? For example, can an action based upon state antitrust law preclude a later action under the Sherman Antitrust Act, over which federal courts have exclusive jurisdiction? In MARRESE v. AMERICAN ACADEMY OF ORTHOPAEDIC SURGEONS, 470 U.S. 373, 105 S.Ct. 1327, 84 L.Ed.2d 274 (1985), a case arising under the Sherman Act, Justice O'Connor set forth a two-step approach for determining the preclusive effect of a state court judgment in a subsequent suit over which federal courts have exclusive jurisdiction. First, applying the Full Faith and Credit Statute, the federal court must determine whether *state* claim preclusion law would preclude the federal suit. If not, there is no preclusion. If the state would bar the federal action, then, as a second step, the federal court must determine whether the relevant federal law contains an implied or explicit exception to Section 1738. The *Marrese* Court remanded the case before it for a determination of how Illinois would have treated the second lawsuit, thereby avoiding the issue of whether the Sherman Act creates an exception to Section 1738.

In most cases *Marrese* will prevent preclusion. This is so because virtually every state follows the "prior jurisdictional competency" rule, which prohibits preclusion of a claim beyond the rendering court's jurisdiction. Since state courts cannot hear cases when the federal court's jurisdiction is exclusive, the prior jurisdictional competency rule would prevent a state court from precluding such cases; *Marrese* prohibits federal courts from precluding claims that would not be precluded under state rules.

Marrese does raise the possibility, however, of the application of state issue preclusion rules whenever a congressional grant of exclusive jurisdiction is deemed not to imply an exception to Section 1738. The application of state rules of issue preclusion often will effectively eliminate the federal action. See Murphy v. Gallagher, 761 F.2d 878 (2d Cir.1985) (state rules of issue preclusion apply in later federal securities fraud action, over which federal court has exclusive jurisdiction, even though the result is to dispose of the entire federal action).

3. In KREMER v. CHEMICAL CONSTR. CORP., 456 U.S. 461, 102 S.Ct. 1883, 72 L.Ed.2d 262 (1982), the Court held that, although the plaintiff could have sued in federal court on an employment-discrimination claim initially, once he opted to appeal a state agency determination in state court, he was subject to the usual rules of preclusion. Having litigated in state court, he could only relitigate the issues in federal court if there was reason to doubt the quality, extensiveness, or fairness of the procedures followed in the state-court action. Justice Blackmun, in dissent, argued that the nature of the state-court review was different than the review a federal district court would give the action. The standard of review in state court was whether the state agency's determination was arbitrary; a federal court would have engaged in a full adjudication on the merits of the employment-discrimination claim.

3. FEDERAL–STATE PRECLUSION

Must a state court grant preclusive effect to a prior federal-court judgment? The general requirement that federal judgments be given full faith and credit in state courts never has been challenged seriously, even though the Full Faith and Credit Clause does not apply to the situation, and even though most courts agree that Section 1738 is inapplicable as well. Commentators invoke various provisions of the Constitution (including the Supremacy Clause and the "case or controversy" doctrine) to support binding state courts to federal-court judgments. The lack of any express provision may reflect the constitutional compromise that relegated to Congress the decision of whether to establish inferior federal courts.

Notes and Questions

1. The conclusion that state courts are obliged to grant preclusive effect to federal-court judgments does not determine which rules of preclusion the state should apply. There is almost universal agreement that federal preclusion rules usually apply when the prior federal-court judgment involved a federal question. Authorities are split, however, on whether federal preclusion rules should define the effect in a subsequent action of a prior federal judgment deciding state-law claims. Arguably, the *Erie* doctrine requires the court to treat a prior federal determination of the state-law claim in the same way that it would treat a prior state determination of the claim; under Section 1738, that would mean the application of the preclusion rules of the state in which the rendering federal court sits. Professor Degnan argues, however, that federal law should define the preclusive effect of all federal judgments. In explaining his position, he writes:

> The argument in support of this conclusion is abstract, and requires a cautious statement. At its root is the constitutional provision that the federal judicial power extends only to cases and controversies. To decide

a case or controversy implies some binding effect. A judgment or decree that lacked finality would constitute something other than an exercise of the judicial power. If that principle be accepted (and it has rarely been denied), it seems inappropriate that some other sovereignty—the states—should have ultimate authority to determine *what* binding effect the judgment has and on whom.

There may have been merit, when the Conformity Act [which preceded the Federal Rules of Civil Procedure and required federal courts to employ the rules of procedure of the state in which they sat] prevailed, in following, within limits, state law on the effect of judgments. The proper scope of judgments is determined in large part by the procedures leading to their rendition. Thus it was not unreasonable to declare that federal judgments should have the same scope, neither more nor less, as judgments rendered by the courts of the states wherein they sat, if only as a matter of Congress's power to regulate the jurisdiction and procedure of federal courts. But the time of conformity is past. Except by special incorporation of state law, federal procedure under the Rules is independent of the states. That there is still some deference to state law cannot be denied. Rule 4, which serves to define who may be bound by a federal adjudication, partially incorporates state methods of service of process. But in the absence of such restraints, federal law (judge-made when the Rules do not speak) should prevail. The specter of *Erie* should be banished from this realm.

The ultimate reason for this conclusion is that it is in the nature of the judicial power to determine its own boundaries. * * * Without that power it is less than a court. The clear thrust of the Constitution is that courts created by the Congress are courts in the fullest historical sense of the word. It is for that reason that we need not look to see whether Congress has enacted an explicit rule on judgments, or even delegated a power to do so. The only possible limitation of federal courts' power to give force to their own adjudications would arise if the Congress had acted affirmatively and unequivocally to reduce it. Perhaps the Congress could, but that issue need not be faced until an attempt is made. None has been.

Degnan, *Federalized Res Judicata,* 85 Yale L.J. 741, 768–70 (1976). Are Professor Degnan's arguments weaker when applied to the judgment of a federal court sitting in a diversity suit? A much-quoted passage from an opinion by Judge Medina supports Degnan's views:

* * * One of the strongest policies a court can have is that of determining the scope of its own judgments. * * * It would be destructive of the basic principles of the Federal Rules of Civil Procedure to say that the effect of a judgment of a federal court was governed by the law of the state where the court sits simply because the source of federal jurisdiction is diversity. The rights and obligations of the parties are fixed by state law. * * * But we think it would be strange doctrine to allow a state to nullify the judgments of federal courts * * *. The Erie doctrine * * * is not applicable here.

KERN v. HETTINGER, 303 F.2d 333, 340 (2d Cir.1962).

Professor Degnan also has spoken directly to the issue:

> To treat the effect of diversity judgments as a matter amenable to rulemaking by the federal courts is not inconsistent with the command of the Rules of Decision Act that the "laws of the several states * * * be regarded as rules of decision." 28 U.S.C. § 1652 (1970). By the terms of the Act, state rules of decision are applicable only where there is no constitutional or statutory requirement to the contrary, and only "in cases where they apply." That the power to decide the force of federal adjudications is, *in extremis,* a defining element of Article III judicial power gives reason to find that even in less extreme instances the laws of the several states do not "apply" within the terms of the Rules of Decision Act itself.

Degnan, *Federalized Res Judicata,* 85 Yale L.J. 741, 770 n. 138 (1976).

Professor Burbank disagrees with Professor Degnan:

> Professor Degnan's argument is curious. Article III may be the ultimate source of the obligation to respect federal judgments. If so, article III may be thought to require a limited number of federal preclusion rules to protect the basic norm of respect. But the notion that it is also a grant of power to the federal courts initially and finally to determine all matters relating to the preclusive effects of their judgments is wishful thinking. The inherent powers of federal courts, in the sense of powers that are insulated from congressional override, are limited to those "necessary to the exercise of all others." Tested by that demanding standard, an assertion of inherent power with respect to most preclusion rules simply comes too late in the day. * * * The switch from the Conformity Act to the Federal Rules, whatever its significance for subconstitutional law, cannot transmogrify a power that was not regarded as inherent in the sense of being "shielded from direct democratic controls" into one that is so regarded.

Burbank, *Interjurisdictional Preclusion, Full Faith and Credit and Federal Common Law: A General Approach,* 71 Cornell L.Rev. 733, 753–54 (1986).

The *Restatement of Judgments* adopts the position that, although federal law ultimately must control the choice of preclusion rules, federal law should mandate the application of state rules when those rules are important to the effectuation of substantive state policies. *Restatement (Second), Judgments* § 87 (1982). See also 18 Wright, Miller & Cooper, *Federal Practice and Procedure: Jurisdiction and Related Matters* §§ 4468, 4472 (1981).

2. What happens if a state court, in attempting to apply federal preclusion rules to a prior federal judgment, makes a mistake? If the parties subsequently return to federal court to correct the error, is the federal court bound under Section 1738 to give preclusive effect to the state court's prior decision on the issue of preclusion?

In PARSONS STEEL, INC. v. FIRST ALABAMA BANK, 474 U.S. 518, 106 S.Ct. 768, 88 L.Ed.2d 877 (1986), the Supreme Court held that a state court's rejection of a claim that an earlier federal judgment precludes the state action is itself res judicata in a later federal action to enjoin the enforcement of the state-court judgment.

3. What rules of preclusion should a diversity court apply to the judgment of a prior diversity court from another state? Again, Professor Degnan argues that federal law should govern the effect of the prior federal judgment, whether or not the prior federal judgment involved a federal question. Other commentators argue that rules of preclusion are substantive, since they materially affect the outcome of a case, and that *Erie* therefore mandates the application of the rules the state court would apply. As discussed above, however, note 1, supra, state courts themselves are undecided as to the proper rules of preclusion to apply to a prior diversity judgment. See Note, *Erie and the Preclusive Effect of Federal Diversity Judgments,* 85 Colum.L.Rev. 1505 (1985).

4. If a plaintiff properly brings an action in federal court and fails to include certain related state claims that may have been heard under pendent jurisdiction, should that plaintiff be permitted to litigate those claims in a subsequent state action? The *Restatement (Second) of Judgments* recommends that preclusion result if the federal court would have exercised jurisdiction over the claims. See *Restatement (Second), Judgments* § 25, comment *e* (1982). Yet even assuming that answer, difficult questions remain. How is a court considering such preclusion going to determine whether the first court would have exercised pendent jurisdiction?

One commentator has suggested that whether the federal court would have invoked pendent jurisdiction can be determined by looking at (1) whether there was a common nucleus of operative fact between the federal and state claims, thus ensuring that the federal court would have had the power to exercise pendent jurisdiction, and (2) looking at how the prior court disposed of the federal claim. Assuming the existence of a common nucleus of operative fact, the court should determine which one of four possible ways the prior court disposed of the federal claim. When the federal claim is decided after a full trial on the merits, or when it is decided by default judgment, the state claims should be precluded from subsequent litigation. When the federal claim is dismissed for lack of jurisdiction, improper venue, or failure to join an indispensable party, preclusion should not attach. Similarly, when the federal claim is dismissed for failure to state a claim on which relief can be granted, the plaintiff should not be precluded from subsequently filing a state suit asserting the state claims. See Note, *The Res Judicata Implications of Pendent Jurisdiction,* 66 Cornell L.Rev. 608 (1981).

4. INTERSYSTEM ADMINISTRATIVE PRECLUSION

The Supreme Court has held that Section 1738 is limited in scope to the judgments of courts, and does not apply to the decisions of administrative agencies. What preclusive effect do the factual and legal decisions of agencies deserve? Discussing a federal administrative agency decision, the Supreme Court held in UNITED STATES v. UTAH CONSTRUCTION & MINING CO., 384 U.S. 394, 86 S.Ct. 1545, 16 L.Ed.2d 642 (1966): "When an administrative agency is acting in a judicial capacity and resolves disputed issues of fact properly before it which the parties have had an adequate opportunity to litigate, the courts have not hesitated to apply *res judicata* * * *." 384 U.S. at 422, 86 S.Ct. at 1560, 16 L.Ed.2d at 661. More and more, states are moving toward giving preclusive effect *within the state court system* to the decisions of state administrative agencies.

In UNIVERSITY OF TENNESSEE v. ELLIOTT, 478 U.S. 788, 106 S.Ct. 3220, 92 L.Ed.2d 635 (1986), plaintiff was discharged as an employee of the university. He commenced an action in federal court alleging that his racially motivated discharge violated Title VII of the Civil Rights Act of 1964 and 42 U.S.C. § 1983. While the federal lawsuit was pending, a state administrative law judge found that the discharge was not racially motivated, and the University moved for summary judgment in the federal action on the grounds of issue preclusion. The Sixth Circuit denied preclusion on both the Title VII and the Section 1983 claims. The Supreme Court affirmed the Court of Appeals' ruling that the agency's decision did not preclude the Title VII claim, citing a specific congressional intent that state agency findings *not* preclude later Title VII actions on the same facts. However, reversing in part, the Supreme Court found that the agency's ruling did preclude the Section 1983 claim. The Court reasoned that Congress had not expressed a desire that state-agency decisions not preclude Section 1983 claims; therefore, the general principles of Section 1738 applied. The Court conceded that Section 1738 itself did not require preclusion, because it applies only to court judgments. The Justices felt free, however, to promulgate a common-law rule of preclusion requiring federal courts to give preclusive effect to the decisions of state administrative agencies in circumstances in which the courts of the agency's state would give the decision preclusive effect in a subsequent action.

Notes and Questions

1. Once the Supreme Court found, based on legislative intent, that certain claims could not be precluded by state agency findings of fact (Title VII claims) but that others could be precluded (Section 1983 claims), the federal courts were left to decide which federal statutes fell into each category. For example, in STILLIANS v. IOWA, 843 F.2d 276 (8th Cir.1988), the court held that the plaintiff's claim under the federal Age Discrimination in Employment Act (ADEA) was precluded by earlier findings of the Iowa Merit Employment Commission. It reasoned that, under *Elliott*, Iowa issue preclusion law, which would not have permitted relitigation of the discrimination issue, bound the federal court. The Eighth Circuit found insufficient evidence in the legislative history of the ADEA to justify breaking from the common-law rule of preclusion set forth in *Elliott*.

2. What did the court in *Utah Construction* mean by the term "acting in a judicial capacity"? When is an administrative proceeding "judicial" enough to warrant preclusive effect? The courts have not set forth any clear statements of this requirement. See *Restatement (Second), Judgments* § 83(2) and comments *b* and *c* (1982); 18 Wright, Miller & Cooper, *Federal Practice and Procedure: Jurisdiction and Related Matters* § 4475 (1981).

Chapter 15

ALTERNATIVE DISPUTE RESOLUTION

SECTION A. INTRODUCTION

1. THE NEED FOR ALTERNATIVE DISPUTE-RESOLUTION MECHANISMS

The previous chapters focused on the procedures associated with one kind of dispute-resolution mechanism: courts. Courts are highly structured institutions in which technically trained representatives (lawyers) present arguments for their clients before a factfinding body (judge and/or jury). And, of course, a court's decisions are enforced by the state. But the formality that is characteristic of courts sometimes can be disadvantageous. These disadvantages have led some to conclude that in many cases courts are not the best available dispute-resolution forum. This Chapter will explore some of the other major mechanisms. First, however, some of the predominant complaints lodged against the traditional adjudicative process should be catalogued.

One complaint frequently heard is that the traditional process takes so long. In part because of a dramatic increase in the number of cases filed in the courts of our nation (the number of filings in federal court increased from 35,000 to 180,000 between 1940 and 1981, and filings in state courts also have increased sharply), it sometimes takes years for a case to work its way through the process. Delays can contribute to serious injustice—both directly, because justice delayed often is justice denied, and indirectly, because the threat of delay may create an artificial pressure on one of the litigants to settle on less than fair terms.

Another criticism of judicial dispute resolution is that it is too expensive. Given the cost of litigation, many claims are too small to pursue. And, there are times when some of our citizens cannot afford to pursue even major claims. Not only poor people but many middle-income people cannot afford legal services. And, even when they can afford legal services, they often find themselves "outlitigated" by an opponent with greater resources and experience.

By far the largest single component of the cost of litigation is the attorney's fees. Even large corporations are beginning to balk at the size of their legal bills. To some extent, reducing delays would reduce legal costs. But many people find the hourly rates charged by some lawyers unconscionable, even when the number of hours invested by the lawyer is kept to a minimum. Thus, more zealous reformers argue that more disputes should be settled without lawyers. Small claims courts, for example, were designed with simplified procedures so that disputants could handle their controversies without professional assistance.

Some reformers focus on a factor more fundamental than cost in arguing that the role of lawyers must be reduced. They argue that when legal professionals become involved in a complex human dispute they tend to recast it into legal categories. When that happens, the person with the problem may find that her central concerns are dismissed by the professionals as "irrelevant." In an informal proceeding, by contrast, when a disputant can represent herself, she can raise issues that are important to her, even if those concerns are not strictly relevant to the legal issue.

This criticism of legal professionals is closely related to a criticism that often is lodged against the adversary system itself. It is said that the adversary system simply may be inappropriate for some disputes, such as those in which the disputants have a continuing relationship. Relations among neighbors, friends, and family members may be distorted by a process that claims to derive its legitimacy from the hostility of the disputants. A process that is less dependent on combat may produce better resolution of the underlying problems and enable the disputants to continue their relationship amicably.

Proposals to address the problems with traditional adjudication just mentioned (and others not mentioned) are numerous and varied. Commentators are legion. For some, the goal is to streamline the court system. For others, it is to avoid the court system altogether, at least in certain circumstances. And still others concede that many disputes are well handled in an adversarial system, but believe that it is necessary for given classes of disputes to employ nonlegal norms (such as the "standard of practice in the industry") to resolve the controversy. Some urge that the law is poorly equipped to resolve some types of disputes; for these disputes, it is urged, greater reliance should be placed upon community values, compromise, and individualized discretion. Rather than thrusting these disputes upon the courts, we should create replacements for traditional institutions that used to play a major role in resolving disputes, such as extended family, neighborhood, community, and church. More ambitious reformers, motivated in part by a perception that the legal system is biased against the poor, argue that local dispute-resolution centers be established as part of a program to enable residents in poor communities to resolve their own disputes without recourse to the legal system.

As can be seen from this brief introduction, there are a number of independent justifications that can be offered for developing alternative techniques for resolving disputes—and the justifications are not necessarily compatible with each other.   The purpose of this Chapter is not to assess the merits of the case for alternative dispute-resolution techniques, but to explore how and when they might be used.   The following excerpt is designed to help you begin to shape your thinking on the subject.

SANDER, VARIETIES OF DISPUTE PROCESSING, 70 F.R.D. 111, 119–33 (1976):

CRITERIA

* * *

1. NATURE OF DISPUTE

Lon Fuller has written at some length about "polycentric" problems that are not well suited to an adjudicatory approach since they are not amenable to an all-or-nothing solution.   He cites the example of a testator who leaves a collection of paintings in equal parts to two museums. Obviously here a negotiated or mediated solution that seeks to accommodate the desires of the two museums is far better than any externally imposed solution.   Similar considerations may apply to other allocational tasks where no clear guidelines are provided.

At the other extreme is a highly repetitive and routinized task involving application of established principles to a large number of individual cases.   Here adjudication may be appropriate, but in a form more efficient than litigation (e.g., an administrative agency).   Particularly once the courts have established the basic principles in such areas, a speedier and less cumbersome procedure than litigation should be utilized.

* * *

With respect to many problems, there is a need for developing a flexible mechanism that serves to sort out the large general question from the repetitive application of settled principle.   I do not believe that a court is the most effective way to perform this kind of sifting task.
* * *

Perhaps a word should also be said about courts undertaking some of the complex and unorthodox tasks that they have recently been called upon to undertake.   Without going into the question of legitimacy, I am not persuaded that the courts have sufficient competence, resources or remedial power to run mental hospitals, schools or welfare departments. Yet where serious constitutional denials are at issue, they can hardly decline jurisdiction.   This seems to me an area where one can make no headway without talking about very specific cases and exploring in detail alternative dispute resolution mechanisms.   * * *

2. RELATIONSHIP BETWEEN DISPUTANTS

A different situation is presented when disputes arise between individuals who are in a long-term relationship than is the case with respect to an isolated dispute.   In the former situation, there is more potential for having the parties, at least initially, seek to work out their own solution, for such a solution is likely to be far more acceptable (and hence durable). Thus negotiation, or if necessary, mediation, appears to be a preferable approach in the first instance.   Another advantage of such an approach is that it facilitates a probing of conflicts in the underlying relationship, rather than simply dealing with each surface symptom as an isolated event.

Consider, for example, a case such as might be heard in the recently established mediation session of the Dorchester (Massachusetts) District Court. A white woman (Mrs. W.) has filed a criminal complaint for assault against her black neighbor (Mrs. B.). The facts, as they emerge at the mediation session, are that Mrs. W. has for some time gratuitously taken care of Mrs. B.'s two young children so that Mrs. B. can go to work. On the day in question one of the B. children for the second time in a row broke the expensive eyeglasses of one of the W. children, and had been generally out of control. Mrs. W., having reached the end of her rope, struck the child. When Mrs. B. heard about this, she marched over to Mrs. W. and hit her. Mrs. W. thereupon filed a criminal complaint.

Fortunately the Dorchester District Court, like a number of other courts around the country, has a program under which, if the clerk or judge deems the case appropriate, and the two parties are willing, the case can be referred to a panel of three trained mediators drawn from the local community. The panel will attempt to let each of the disputants fully state her side of the story, and then, through skillful probing, will seek to elicit points of tension in the underlying relationship * * *. Finally, the mediators will attempt to work out an agreement which seeks to alleviate the long-run tensions as well as resolve the immediate controversy * * *. Such a solution (unlike the aborted criminal adjudication) would most likely be acceptable to both parties; more significantly, it would have a therapeutic effect on the long-term relationship between these two individuals because it would permit them to ventilate their feelings, and then help them to restructure their future relationship in a way that met the expectations of both parties. In addition it would teach them how they might themselves resolve future conflicts. Thus there is a strong likelihood that future disputes would be avoided, or at least minimized.

Of course, it might be suggested that a court could also induce such a settlement. But quite aside from the unlikelihood of a busy court being able to create a climate that encourages the disputants to ventilate their underlying grievances, there is a world of difference between a coerced or semi-coerced settlement of the kind that so often results in court and a voluntary agreement arrived at by the parties.

A similar approach would appear to be feasible in a number of other areas. The grievance procedure under the typical collective bargaining agreement is based on a similar premise, in that it usually provides first for attempts to settle the dispute at the lower levels, and only then calls for an adjudicatory proceeding (arbitration) at the end of the line if the prior steps do not lead to settlement. However one difficulty is that, perhaps for reasons of economy, there is usually no mediator at the lower levels. Hence, if the parties have become too entrenched in their respective positions, there is little effective communication between them, and the early stages of the grievance procedure are often simply rote steps to be gone through before getting to arbitration. And while the arbitrator can then seek to play a mediational role, as is done by some arbitrators provided the parties give their consent, there is an obvious difficulty if the mediator-arbitrator is unsuccessful in his mediational role and then seeks to assume the role of impartial judge. For effective mediation may require gaining confidential information from the parties which they may be reluctant to give if they know that it may be used against them in the adjudicatory phase. And even if they do give it, it may then jeopardize the arbitrator's sense of objectivity. In addition it will be difficult for him to take a disinterested view of the case—and even more so to *appear* to do so—after he has once expressed his views concerning a reasonable settlement.

Another long-term (at least sometimes) relationship that may be amenable to this type of dispute resolution mechanism is the family. * * * [I]t may well be that as our courts are beginning to play less and less of a role in divorce, as a result of the pervasive adoption of no-fault statutes, a need arises for some new flexible instrument—clearly not a court—that will concern itself with the resolution of family conflicts.

* * * Of course in a sense we have developed a mediative solution for most family conflict—social work and family therapy. Still where there is a breakdown of the family as a result of death or divorce, the courts have customarily become involved and it is here that alternative dispute resolution devices—particularly mediation—need to be further explored.

3. AMOUNT IN DISPUTE

Although, generally speaking, we have acted to date in a fairly hit-or-miss fashion in determining what problems should be resolved by a particular dispute resolution mechanism, amount in controversy has been an item consistently looked to to determine the amount of process that is "due". * * * Yet the evidence now seems overwhelming that the Small Claims Court has failed its original purpose; that the individuals for whom it was designed have turned out to be its victims. Small wonder when one considers the lack of rational connection between amount in controversy and appropriate process. Quite obviously a small case may be complex, just as a large case may be simple. The need, according to a persuasive recent study, is for a preliminary investigative-conciliational stage (which could well be administered by a lay individual or paraprofessional) with ultimate recourse to the court. This individual could readily screen out those cases which need not take a court's time (e.g., where there is no dispute about liability but the defendant has no funds), and preserve the adjudicatory process for those cases where the issues have been properly joined and there is a genuine dispute of fact or law. Obviously such a screening mechanism is not limited in its utility to the Small Claims Court.

4. COST

There is a dearth of reliable data comparing the costs of different dispute resolution processes. Undoubtedly this is due in part to the difficulty of determining what are the appropriate ingredients of such a computation. It may be relatively easy to determine the costs of an ad hoc arbitration (though even there one must deal with such intangibles as the costs connected with the selection of the arbitrator(s)). But determining the comparable cost of a court proceeding would appear to pose very difficult issues of cost accounting. Even more difficult to calculate are the intangible "costs" of inadequate (in the sense of incomplete and unsatisfactory) dispute resolution. Still, until better data become available one can probably proceed safely on the assumption that costs rise as procedural formalities increase.

The lack of adequate cost data is particularly unfortunate with respect to essentially comparable processes, such as litigation and arbitration. * * * One difficulty in this connection is that we have always considered access to the courts as an essential right of citizenship for which no significant charge should be imposed, while the parties generally bear the cost of arbitration. Thus although I believe, on the basis of my own arbitration experience, that that process is, by and large, as effective as and cheaper than litigation, lawyers tend not to make extensive use of it (outside of special areas such as labor and commercial law), in part because it is always cheaper for the clients to have society rather than the litigants pay the judges. Perhaps if arbitration is to be made compulsory in certain types of cases because we believe it to be more efficient, then it should follow that society should assume the costs * * *.

5. SPEED

The deficiency of sophisticated data concerning the costs of different dispute resolution processes also extends to the factor of speed. Although it is generally assumed—rightly, I believe—that arbitration is speedier than litigation, I am not aware of any studies that have reached such a conclusion on the basis of a controlled experiment that seeks to take account of such factors as the possibly differing complexity of the two classes of cases, the greater diversity of "judges" in the arbitration group, and the possibly greater cooperation of the litigants in the arbitration setting.

IMPLICATIONS

1. At one time perhaps the courts were the principal public dispute processors. But that time is long gone. With the development of administrative law, the delegation of certain problems to specialized bodies for initial resolution has become a commonplace. Within the judicial sphere, too, we have developed specialized courts to handle family problems and tax problems, among others.

These were essentially *substantive* diversions, that is, resort to agencies having substantive expertise. Perhaps the time is now ripe for greater resort to an alternate primary *process*. As I have indicated earlier, such a step would be particularly appropriate in situations involving disputing individuals who are engaged in a long-term relationship. The process ought to consist initially of a mediational phase, and then, if necessary, of an adjudicative one. Problems that would appear to be particularly amenable to such a two-stage process are disputes between neighbors, family members, supplier and distributor, landlord and tenant. Where there is an authority relationship between the parties (such as exists between prisoner and warden or school and student) special problems may be presented, but, as indicated earlier, such relationships, too, are, with some adjustments, amenable to a sequential mediation-adjudication solution.

* * *

2. * * * I am impressed by * * * [attempts] to divert certain types of minor criminal offenses (e.g., ones like the case earlier described between Mrs. B. and Mrs. W.) to a mediational proceeding. Such a process readily fits under the general rubric described in the immediately preceding section; but it can also be seen in the larger context of a movement towards a community "moot," offering informal and supportive services to community members. * * *

* * *

4. What I am thus advocating is a flexible and diverse panoply of dispute resolution processes, with particular types of cases being assigned to differing processes (or combinations of processes), according to some of the criteria previously mentioned. Conceivably such allocation might be accomplished for a particular class of cases at the outset by the legislature; that in effect is what was done by the Massachusetts legislature for malpractice cases. * * *

* * *

5. I would be less than candid if I were to leave this idyllic picture without at least brief reference to some of the substantial impediments to reform in this area. To begin with there is always the deadening drag of status quoism. But I have reference to more specific problems. First, particularly in the criminal field, cries of "denial of due process" will undoubtedly be heard if an informal mediational process is sought to be substituted for the strict protections of the adversary process. In response to this objection it must be asserted candidly that many thoughtful commentators appear agreed that we may have over-judicialized the system, with concomitant adverse effects on its efficiency as well as its accessibility to powerless litigants. * * *

A related concern is * * * the need to retain the courts as the ultimate agency capable of effectively protecting the rights of the disadvantaged. This is a legitimate concern which I believe to be consistent with the goals I have advocated. I am not maintaining that cases asserting novel constitutional claims ought to be diverted to mediation or arbitration. On the contrary, the goal is to reserve the courts for those activities for which they are best suited and to avoid swamping and paralyzing them with cases that do not require their unique capabilities.

Finally, we are robbed of much-needed flexibility by the constitutional requirement of jury trial. For present purposes this normally means that cases initially referred to binding arbitration (or some other nonjudicial process) must have the consent of both parties or else that a de novo trial must be permitted. Obviously we can live with such restrictions and still achieve considerable constructive change, especially if * * * the price of the de novo appeal from arbitration is to require the appellant to assume the cost of the arbitration. But one is bound to wonder whether, as an original matter, the requirement of jury trial still makes sense in the run-of-the-mill civil case, particularly if one keeps in mind the attendant increase in cost and time. In view of the desperate state of some of our civil calendars, it seems to me that the burden of persuasion should shift to those who maintain that the high costs are justified by unique advantages afforded by jury trials. Here again we must try to shun the endless abstract discussions of pros and cons, and seek instead to explore whether there are specific types of cases in which juries make more or less sense, so that we might opt ultimately for a constitutional amendment that would give greater flexibility to the legislature on this question.

2. EVALUATING ALTERNATIVE DISPUTE–RESOLUTION MECHANISMS

In order to match the resolution mechanism to the dispute, we must explore the parameters along which various mechanisms vary. Methods of dispute resolution can be defined, in part, by the answers they provide to the following four questions:

Who resolves the dispute?

What is the source of the standard for resolution?

How are the disputants represented?

What is the nature and extent of fact-finding and standard-finding?

All dispute-resolution mechanisms answer these questions in a particular way; the possibilities vary from other dispute-resolution mechanisms and from adjudication to the extent that they answer them differently.

Who resolves the dispute?

Possibilities include:

— a judge, an officer of the state with professional education in the law,

— a lawyer with similar professional training,

— an expert in the field in which the dispute arose with no legal training at all,

— a representative of the community,

— the disputants with the help of a neutral third party,

— the disputants themselves.

In all categories but the last, the disputants invoke the assistance of a neutral third party to play a role in resolving the dispute. These will be referred to collectively as "third-party methods."

What is the source of the standard for resolution?

Possibilities include:

— rules established by legislatures and courts ("law"),

— the prior practice of those similarly situated,

— community values,

— the disputants themselves, determined either before or after the dispute arose.

How are the disputants represented?

Possibilities include:

— lawyers,

— persons without professional legal training,

— the disputants themselves.

What is the nature and extent of fact-finding and standard-finding?

Possibilities include:

— the disputants or their representatives could be responsible for the research and presentation of evidence to establish facts and arguments to establish the standard for resolution,

— the dispute resolver could aid the disputants in performing some or all of these tasks,

— the dispute resolver could be responsible for these tasks.

By combining answers to these four questions in various ways, a wide array of dispute-resolution mechanisms can be generated. Depending on the nature of the dispute, one mechanism or another would be the most appropriate way to resolve the dispute. Moreover, the appropriate perspective from which to evaluate the mechanisms is in their entirety, as an interconnected system of dealing with disputes. See generally Marles, Johnson & Szanton, *Dispute Resolution in America: Process in Evolution* (National Institute for Dispute Resolution, 1984). The following list is offered in an attempt to provide a sense of the wide variety of alternative dispute-resolution mechanisms that are available, but without attempting to be exhaustive.

SMALL–CLAIMS COURT:

Small-claims court is designed to handle matters in which the amount in controversy is quite low. A typical limit is $750. These disputes are unlikely to be resolved through standard adjudication because the legal fees, if they did not exceed the amount in controversy, would constitute a substantial fraction of it. A judge is the dispute resolver and the law is the source of the standard for resolution, but the disputants can represent themselves. They are not expected to research or argue the rule of law to be applied. The dispute resolver shoulders this responsibility. The disputants are responsible for researching and presenting evidence; however, the dispute resolver often takes an active role in questioning witnesses to elicit information.

ARBITRATION:

Arbitration is designed to be a less formal, less complex, and quicker means of resolving disputes than court proceedings. Typically, the disputants agree before a dispute has arisen to submit all disputes that do arise to an arbitrator, a dispute resolver who may or may not be a person with legal training who is empowered by the disputants to render a final and binding decision. Sometimes they agree to arbitration after the dispute has arisen. Similarly, the parties may name the arbitrator either before or after the dispute arises. The arbitrator often is selected because of her expertise in the field in which the dispute arose. The agreement that defines the arbitrator's powers is generally the source of the standard for resolution, although practices of the industry and general legal principles come into play as well.

Disputants often are represented by lawyers. The disputants, through the lawyers, are responsible for researching and presenting evidence and arguments. Less time need be spent on these tasks, however, because of the arbitrator's experience and expertise in the field.

Because it can take place outside of the court structure and because of the shortened fact-finding process, arbitration can be much faster than adjudication. Arbitration has been used extensively in labor-management and commercial disputes because speed is important. Arbitration also is used in these situations since it minimizes the disruption to the continuing relationship of the disputants and avoids the purely adversarial setting of adjudication. In contexts such as commercial contracts in which trade practices are an important component in determining the governing standard, the fact that an arbitrator with knowledge of the trade, rather than a judge or jury, is the dispute resolver is also a factor in its use. Arbitration is considered in more detail in Section C, pp. 1269–80, infra.

FINAL–OFFER ARBITRATION:

Final-offer arbitration is much like standard arbitration but is used typically to set the terms of contracts (such as the salaries of major league baseball players and some public employees) rather than interpret and apply contractual provisions. The dispute resolver must choose between one or the other disputants' final offers of settlement. That is, one disputant receives everything she demands in her last offer; the other is left empty-handed. Thus, the party with the most reasonable final offer gets all she requests; the party who insists upon outrageous demands runs the risk of being saddled with her adversary's only-slightly-less-outrageous demands.

Final-offer arbitration is designed to encourage serious negotiation in areas in which it is important that the disputants' dealings not be interrupted. Fact-finding can be more limited because the arbitrator need only choose between two positions rather than find and justify one particular result out of many possible.

ONE–WAY ARBITRATION:

One-way arbitration differs from standard arbitration in that only one party agrees to be bound. It is used by some corporations in response to consumer complaints. The corporation promises to abide by the arbitrator's decision; the consumer is free to pursue other legal remedies if dissatisfied with the decision.

COURT–ANNEXED ARBITRATION:

Court-annexed arbitration builds upon the standard model of arbitration described above but the parties have not agreed to arbitrate their dispute. Instead, certain disputes, usually those in which the amount in controversy is less than a certain dollar figure, are referred to an arbitrator before the court will hear them.

The arbitrator thus is less likely to have expertise in the subject area in which the conflict arose. Moreover, since the source of the standard for resolution is the law, the arbitrator typically will be a lawyer. The nature and extent of fact-finding and standard-finding are not substantially different from adjudication, although discovery may be limited and the rules of evidence may be relaxed. If dissatisfied with the arbitrator's decision, a disputant can demand a trial *de novo*.

PRIVATE JUDGING:

Private judging is utilized by disputants who can afford it in order to avoid the delays of the court system. The disputants agree, after the dispute has arisen and been filed in court, to hire a private judge, often a retired judge, to resolve the dispute. The court then refers the case to the private judge.

The source of the standard for resolution is the law and the proceedings are conducted in much the same manner as a bench trial, although in an expedited and simplified manner. Unlike the award of an arbitrator, the decision can be appealed as if the court referring it to the private judge had made the decision itself. Thus the disputants can ensure that the resolution will be in accordance with the law, while bypassing the backlog in the trial courts.

NEGOTIATED SETTLEMENT:

In a negotiated settlement, the disputants themselves resolve the conflict under whatever standards they choose. Although in the early stages the disputants typically represent themselves, once lawyers become involved they tend to handle the negotiations as well. There is no need for fact-finding or standard-finding as such, since the only facts and standards that matter are those that the disputants choose to recognize.

MEDIATION:

Mediation is a process in which the mediator, who is often but not always a human-relations professional, assists the disputants in reaching a negotiated settlement of their differences. The mediator is not empowered to render a decision. Thus the resolvers are the disputants. Since mediation ultimately seeks agreement between the disputants, a mediator does not evaluate the strengths and weaknesses of evidence and arguments. Instead, she seeks common ground between the disputants concerning facts and standards. There are, however, different forms of mediation, and mediators have differing conceptions of their proper role. Some mediators are simply communication facilitators. Others are more active, suggesting possible grounds for settlement and attempting to persuade disputants to settle. Mediators of the former type are more likely to conduct all sessions with both disputants present; mediators of the latter type are more likely to conduct both joint sessions and private sessions with each disputant.

Although the source of the standard for resolution is the disputants, when a mediator attempts persuasion, other values, such as the mediator's or the community's, also come into play. Disputants typically represent themselves; some mediators actively discourage the presence of lawyers and witnesses. Mediation is most appropriate when the disputants have equal bargaining power. This ordinarily occurs when the conflict is between individuals, rather than a conflict between an individual and a private institution or government. If successful, mediation results in a signed agreement that defines the future behavior of the parties. This agreement may be an enforceable contract.

Mediation often is used when the disputants have a continuing relationship that it is important to preserve. Rather than attempting to assess blame for past conduct, mediation focuses the disputants' attention on the future and the desirability of maintaining an amicable relationship. Disputes between neighbors and family members often are considered particularly suited to mediation. Divorce mediation is considered in greater detail in Section C, pp. 1263–69, infra.

COURT–ANNEXED MEDIATION:

Court-annexed mediation builds upon the model of mediation described above but the disputants have not agreed to mediate their dispute. Instead, certain disputes, usually those involving family matters, are referred to a mediator before the court will hear them. Lawyers are likely to be present. If the disputants do not reach an agreement, or refuse to participate in the mediation process, the case goes to trial. In some jurisdictions the mediator makes a recommendation to the court.

NEIGHBORHOOD JUSTICE CENTER:

Neighborhood Justice Center was the title given to the three local dispute-resolution centers funded by the Department of Justice in an experimental program in the mid 1970s. That experiment contributed to the start of approximately 180 local centers now operating throughout the country under the sponsorship of local and state governments, bar associations, and foundations. Neighborhood Justice Centers deal primarily with disputes between individuals with ongoing relationships. Many draw their caseloads from referrals from police, local courts, or prosecutor's offices with which they are affiliated. The goal of Neighborhood Justice Centers is to resolve disputes that otherwise never would reach the civil court system and resolve them before they escalate into matters that truly belong in the criminal courts.

Some Neighborhood Justice Centers use mediation by local residents; others use outsiders. Disputants represent themselves. To the extent that these mediators use persuasion, the source of the standard for resolution is community or personal values. Neighborhood Justice Centers are discussed in more detail in Section C, pp. 1256–63, infra.

OMBUDSPERSON:

An ombudsperson is a third party who receives and investigates complaints aimed at an institution by its constituents, clients, or employees. An ombudsperson may take actions such as bringing an apparent injustice to the attention of high-level officials, advising the complainant of available options and resources, proposing a settlement of the dispute or proposing systemic changes in the institution. An ombudsperson often is employed in a staff position in the institution against which the complaint is made. In government, an ombudsperson can serve the important function of steering a complaint through a tangled bureaucracy.

Ombudspersons are most likely to be hired in closely regulated institutions, those in which customer satisfaction is critical, and institutions concerned with resolving disputes internally. Universities frequently use ombudspersons to enforce a set of university rules that may be different than those applying to people generally. Some independent ombudspersons, however, are employed by local media and use publicity as their major tool. The disputants are responsible for resolution of the dispute, although the ombudsperson can pressure the institution to settle. The source of the standard for resolution is either internal policy or commonly shared values. The ombudsperson acts as representative of the complainant, investigating and presenting the facts for her as well as reminding the high-level officials of the policies they have set or the shared values of the community.

It often is used by retail stores and utilities since customer satisfaction is an important corporate goal. Providing an inexpensive way to "get results" enhances the institution's image. The ombudsperson, particularly with utilities, is capable of working the often complex institutional bureaucracy, whereas a complainant, on her own, easily would be discouraged by the red tape.

MINI–TRIAL:

The mini-trial is a privately developed method of helping to bring about a negotiated settlement in lieu of complex and protracted corporate litigation. The procedural contours of mini-trials are tailored individually in accordance with the desires of the disputants. A typical mini-trial is a confidential process that entails a period of limited discovery after which attorneys for each side present an abbreviated version of the case before a panel consisting of managers with authority to settle and a neutral advisor. The neutral advisor is often a retired judge or respected lawyer. The managers then enter settlement negotiations.

Thus the disputants resolve the dispute aided by the assessment of the neutral advisor as to the likely outcome should the dispute go to court. The advisor's impartial appraisal of the conflict encourages the parties to adopt more realistic goals in negotiating a settlement. The source of the standard for resolution is the disputants, despite the presence of the neutral legal advisor. Disputants are represented by lawyers, but the key to the process is that the managers see the other side's best case directly, in addition to the filtered version provided by their own lawyer. Facts and standards are researched and presented by the disputants's lawyers, although in an abbreviated way. Mini-trials have been used successfully in disputes that were bogged down in discovery and motion practice by reconverting what had become a lawyers' problem back into a business problem. See *Recent Developments in Alternative Forms of Dispute Resolution,* 100 F.R.D. 512 (1984); Lambros, *Summary Jury Trial and Other Methods of Dispute Resolution,* 103 F.R.D. 461, 467 (1984).

Notes and Questions

1. The goals of increasing speed, economy, access, and disputant control as well as reducing adversariness, professionalism, and legalism conflict in significant ways. For example, isn't reducing access the easiest way to increase speed? If few disputants could employ a dispute-resolution system, could not the system resolve the disputes brought to it rather quickly? Moreover, isn't there a danger that by reducing adversariness, professionalism, and legalism, reform could make access meaningless by removing the protections that come with professional representation governed by norms of law? For a critical assessment of alternative dispute resolution, see Brunet, *Questioning the Quality of Alternate Dispute Resolution,* 62 Tulane L.Rev. 1 (1987).

2. Consider the following proposal:

The idea that different types of disputes may be particularly amenable to particular forms of dispute resolution has led to the notion of a multifaceted Dispute Resolution Center. Such a Center, instead of having just one "door" leading to the courtroom, would have many doors directing disputants to the most appropriate dispute-resolution process. Among the doors in such a *multidoor courthouse* might be ones labelled "arbitration," "mediation," and "ombudsman." Provision might also be made for channeling disputes into existing specialized tribunals such as medical malpractice screening boards, small claims courts, or juvenile courts.

The key feature of the multidoor courthouse is the intake screening. Here disputes would be analyzed according to various criteria to determine what mechanism would be best suited for the resolution of the particular controversy. Take, for example, a case involving a minor assault by one neighbor against another growing out of increasing anger over a trespassing dog. Presently such a dispute would probably wind up in criminal court because that is the tag society has placed on this type of conflict. But since the parties really want help in resolving this interpersonal problem, not a determination of whether A struck B, the case might well be sent to mediation, at least in the first instance. Similar treatment might be accorded to a landlord-tenant dispute over the adequacy of the services provided by the landlord. But if the landlord sought to raise questions about the constitutionality of the rent-control law, then obviously that case would have to be sent to the regular court. So, too, with respect to all cases involving major crimes.

The notion thus is that a sophisticated intake officer would analyze the dispute and refer it to that process, or sequence of processes, most likely to resolve it effectively. The potential benefits of such a multifaceted mechanism are increased efficiency, possible time and cost savings, and the legitimization of various alternative dispute-resolution processes, thus decreasing citizens' frustration in attempting to locate the most appropriate mechanism. An additional benefit is that it would help us to gain a better understanding of the peculiar advantages and disadvantages of particular dispute-resolution processes for specific types of disputes. Perhaps the intake official could also refer disputants' associated nonlegal problems to appropriate social service agencies.

Sander, *The Multidoor Courthouse,* National Forum, Vol. LXIII, No. 4, Fall 1983. Doesn't the multidoor courthouse concept put enormous strain on the role of the intake specialist? Is such a concentration of power tolerable? How should the intake specialist be selected, trained, and held accountable?

3. In a multidoor courthouse, should disputants be compelled to use the alternative mechanisms instead of court? For example, should the government require or encourage corporations involved in complicated disputes to have a privately funded mini-trial before proceeding to a full, publicly funded court trial? Is it proper to offer disputants incentives designed to make it attractive for them to use the appropriate mechanism? Who decides which mechanism is appropriate in a particular case and what incentive to offer? The intake specialist? What about alternative dispute-resolution mechanisms such as mini-trials, which are now purely private and voluntary?

Consider the following argument:

Family law issues—domestic violence, equitable distribution, custody, the award and enforcement of spousal and child support—are the principal issues that bring women into the courts. They are also the issues our legal system has never valued highly and that our courts would like to be rid of. * * * Today, across the country, women pursuing family law claims are being pushed out of the courts and into mediation, where there is no record and no accountability. After decades of struggling to make the courts treat seriously the issues generated by the domestic sphere, women are once again seeing these issues privatized. Mediation can be a valuable tool, but it works best for parties equal in power. Women in these cases are often vulnerable. Fearful of violent husbands, less worldly, lacking the economic resources to press their cases in a difficult forum, these women may be easily pressured into compromises which make the mediator feel successful, but which the women come to regret.

Schafran, Women in the Courts Today; How Much Has Changed? [Paper given at Marymount College, "Women and the U.S. Constitution Program," New York, N.Y., Nov. 16, 1987].

4. Doesn't an effective channeling system threaten to close off the judiciary from certain disputes and disputants? Might this not only leave some litigants with second-class justice but also reduce judicial exposure to facts and ideas that influence the direction of legal doctrine?

5. Isn't there a danger that in the quest for the most appropriate device for each kind of dispute that we will re-invent the forms of action? Wasn't the elimination of the forms of action and the unification of law and equity designed precisely to avoid the problems of having to choose the proper device for each kind of dispute? See Carrington, *Civil Procedure and Alternative*

Dispute Resolution, 34 J.Leg.Educ. 298, 302 (1984). Should plaintiffs have the option of choosing between the court and an alternative forum?

6. For an assessment of the contention that the United States is excessively litigious, see Galanter, *Reading the Landscape of Disputes: What We Know and Don't Know (And Think We Know) About Our Allegedly Contentious and Litigious Society,* 31 U.C.L.A.L.Rev. 4 (1983). Isn't it possible that the availability of other dispute-resolution mechanisms, by providing procedures for the resolution of disputes that now simply are "lumped," might increase rather than decrease litigiousness?

7. Arbitration and private judging are quite similar in that the disputants agree to submit the matter to a third party for resolution. An arbitrator's award can be set aside only under highly unusual circumstances (such as fraud, bias, or when the arbitrator exceeded the authority granted by the parties). Errors of law are not grounds for setting aside an arbitrator's award. On the other hand, the decision of a private judge can be appealed like any other trial-court decision. Is this distinction based on the fact that a court participates in referring the case to a private judge? Or is private judging designed for disputants who would not agree to arbitration because they need to secure a legally accurate decision and, as such, is nothing more than a mechanism to reduce the congestion in the courts? For a critique of private judging, see Note, *The California Rent-A-Judge Experiment: Constitutional and Policy Considerations of Pay-As-You-Go Courts,* 94 Harv.L.Rev. 1592 (1981).

SECTION B.   NEGOTIATED SETTLEMENT

Many of the alternative dispute-resolution mechanisms described in the last Section are designed to encourage and facilitate negotiated settlements. Indeed, negotiated settlement is one of the most common forms of alternative dispute resolution; for example, over 90% of the cases filed in court are settled through negotiation.

1. THE NATURE OF NEGOTIATIONS AND THE DESIRABILITY OF ENCOURAGING SETTLEMENT

EISENBERG, PRIVATE ORDERING THROUGH NEGOTIATION: DISPUTE–SETTLEMENT AND RULEMAKING, 89 Harv.L.Rev. 637, 638, 644–45, 647–49 (1976):

* * * Adjudication is conventionally perceived as a norm-bound process centered on the establishment of facts and the determination and application of principles, rules, and precedents. Negotiation, on the other hand, is conventionally perceived as a relatively norm-free process centered on the transmutation of underlying bargaining strength into agreement by the exercise of power, horse-trading, threat, and bluff. * * *

* * *

In adjudication (or, at least, that style of adjudication prevalent in complex Western cultures) the universe and operation of norms is highly stylized and tightly controlled. Where norms conflict, a court will characteristically treat one norm as not only subordinate but totally invalid—so that a court which adopts the doctrine of contributory negligence will deny the validity of comparative negligence. Where norms collide, a court will characteristically select one as determinative of the outcome of the case and reject the other as inapplicable—so that in a case to which the norms of privacy and free speech might be applicable, a court will typically hold that the outcome is controlled by one or the other, but not both. Finally, courts tend to treat person-oriented norms as either invalid or irrelevant—so that in the United States the socially recognized principle that brothers owe each other special obligations will typically give rise to neither a cause of action nor a defense.

In contrast, the universe and operation of norms in dispute-negotiation is typically open-ended. Thus it is characteristic of dispute-negotiation that when norms collide account is taken of both, although the eventual settlement may reflect an adjustment for relative applicability and weight. Similarly, the parties in dispute-negotiation may accord partial or even full recognition to a norm that is generally deemed subordinate or even legally invalid, so that a negligent plaintiff who has no "right" to prevail in a tort action because of the doctrine of contributory negligence may nevertheless make a favorable settlement by reason of the legally invalid but socially real principle of comparative negligence. Finally, parties to dispute-negotiation can and frequently do take person-oriented norms into account as freely as act-oriented norms.

* * *

[Dispute-settlement processes, like adjudication, should be regarded as principled decision-making. This point, as well as the element of reconciliation possible in negotiation, is illustrated by a case reported by the political scientist Daniel Lev.]

[*T's Case*] In late 1960 I [Lev] agreed to accompany an American visitor on a trip across Java. In Jogjakarta we registered at the city's largest hotel * * *.

After registering, T and I went to our room. T went to the bathroom, where the toilet was an old-fashioned one with a wall tank and cord. When T pulled the cord the cover of the tank and the whole mechanism inside came down (though no water), nearly hit him and crashed onto the toilet bowl, knocking a huge chunk out of it. * * * [A] servant came to the room and handed me a note which informed us that the hotel expected Rp. 5,000 for replacement of the toilet. I was astonished at this and without thinking everything over went directly to the hotel office and asked to see the manager. * * * For half an hour or more he and I argued about the bill. I told him that it was not T's fault the tank's insides had come down and that had T been hit by the falling metal, clearly the hotel would have been responsible for damages. * * * The manager would not accept this reasoning and said that T had not been hit by the metal and, since such a thing had never happened before, T must be responsible for the damage * * *. Finally I told him that we would not pay the bill, that it was best to take the matter to court, and that I would ask Judge S [a friend] * * * to talk the problem over * * *.

[In the course of the next several hours the manager and I met at various times to establish our relative power positions by indicating which influential officials we knew, a game often played in this kind of conflict and one that involves a good deal of bluffing. As it happened, a new element was introduced into the affair when a friend from Djakarta stopped at the hotel and mentioned that not long ago another toilet tank had fallen from the wall in the hotel. When the manager was reminded of this, the situation changed somewhat.]

I finally called up Judge S, fully intending to take the case to court or at least to scare the manager into withdrawing his claim * * *. Judge S's reactions left me momentarily speechless. He agreed the civil code was on our side. Then he said, "Well, but of course you are willing to pay part of the expenses for replacing the toilet, aren't you? Offer the manager some money in payment of the damages, to show good will, and then come to a settlement somewhere between his demand and your offer." * * * Only if the manager demands full Rp. 5,000 and refuses the offer to *damai* [compromise] should you take the case to court."

Later * * * accepting Judge S's advice * * * we offered the manager a thousand rupiah. He carried on a bit but finally accepted without demanding more, we had some tea and small talk together, and the issue was never raised again.

* * *

* * * There are * * * at least two other possible interpretations of *T's Case* * * * which [are] * * * consistent with the norm-centered model of dispute-negotiation. First, the outcome may have simply reflected an accommodation of conflicting facts and norms. After all, it could not be unequivocally established that *T* was not at fault—perhaps he pulled too hard on the cord. Furthermore, even if *T* was not at fault, he was nevertheless a cause-in-fact of damage to hotel property. Although modern legal systems have adopted the principle that liability for property damage should normally be predicated on fault, the social sphere continues to recognize a subordinate principle that one is responsible for any property damage that one has caused in fact, regardless of fault. Thus the compromise settlement in *T's Case* may have reflected the likelihood that *T* was at fault and the strength, in this context, of the causation-in-fact principle.

Assume, however, that (as was probably the case) the settlement was not based on the accommodation of conflicting norms and facts * * *. The case can still be interpreted as one in which the outcome turned heavily on principle. Even if it was clear to Lev that *T* was not liable on the basis of the relevant legal rules—that is, even if Lev gave no recognition to any counter-norm or alternative facts—the manager may nevertheless have *believed in good faith* that *T* was liable. On that assumption, if Lev, as *T*'s stand-in, had refused to pay anything, he and the manager would have been left in a state of permanent opposition: The case would have been one in which a claimant had put forth a claim of right, founded, he believed, in justice, and the respondent had answered by denying that the claimant had any right whatsoever on his side—surely a slap in the face that would have made a continued relationship between the parties extremely difficult. On the other hand, if in such a case the respondent makes a payment in satisfaction of the claim, he tacitly admits that the claimant has some degree of right; while the claimant, by accepting, indicates that the books are now closed on the matter. In *T's Case* the hotel manager did not get the full amount he claimed. He was not, however, placed in a position where his claim of right was rejected out of hand. Instead his claim was accepted, but with the modification that a colliding defense was also accepted. The claim and defense were mutually accommodated, and an amicable relationship between the parties could and did continue.

Notes and Questions

1. For another articulation of the argument that the dichotomy between norm-based and normless methods of resolving disputes is too strong, see Fischer & Ury, *Getting to Yes* (1981) (advocating "principled" negotiation). Doesn't the idea of principled negotiation assume that the disputants share certain values? Is this a reasonable assumption?

2. Implicit in the attempts to encourage and facilitate settlements is an assumption that negotiated settlements are desirable. Professor Owen Fiss, on the other hand, argues that "when the parties settle, society gets less than what appears, and for a price it does not know it is paying." He claims:

> The advocates of ADR [alternative dispute resolution] are led to support such measures and to exalt the idea of settlement more generally because they view adjudication as a process to resolve disputes. They act as though courts arose to resolve quarrels between neighbors who had reached an impasse and turned to a stranger for help. Courts are seen as an institutionalization of the stranger and adjudication is viewed as the process by which the stranger exercises power. The very fact that the neighbors have turned to someone else to resolve their dispute signifies a breakdown in their social relations; the advocates of ADR acknowledge this, but nonetheless hope that the neighbors will be able to reach agreement before the stranger renders judgment. Settlement is that agreement. It is a truce more than a true reconciliation, but it seems preferable to judgment because it rests on the consent of both parties and avoids the cost of a lengthy trial.

> In my view, however, this account of adjudication and the case for settlement rest on questionable premises. I do not believe that settlement as a generic practice is preferable to judgment or should be institutionalized on a wholesale and indiscriminate basis. It should be treated instead as a highly problematic technique for streamlining dockets. Settlement is for me the civil analogue of plea bargaining: Consent is often coerced; the bargain may be struck by someone without authority; the absence of a trial and judgment renders subsequent judicial involvement troublesome; and although dockets are trimmed, justice may not be done. Like plea bargaining, settlement is a capitulation to the conditions of mass society and should be neither encouraged nor praised.

> * * *

> * * * I * * * see adjudication in more public terms: Civil litigation is an institutional arrangement for using state power to bring a recalcitrant reality closer to our chosen ideals. We turn to the courts

because we need to, not because of some quirk in our personalities. We train our students in the tougher arts so that they may help secure all that the law promises, not because we want them to become gladiators or because we take a special pleasure in combat.

Fiss, *Against Settlement,* 93 Yale L.J. 1073, 1075, 1089 (1984).

3. One of the virtues of negotiated settlements is the privacy they afford. Although this may be desirable for the parties, is it desirable for society as a whole? Or is this, in Fiss' analysis, part of the price that the public pays when the parties settle? Does the public have a stake in every dispute? See Macklin, *Promoting Settlement, Foregoing the Facts,* 14 N.Y.U.Rev.L. & Soc. Change 579 (1986) (stressing the value of judicial fact-finding as "a source of tested facts" for use in public policy discussion and planning).

4. On the contemporary American legal scene the negotiation of disputes is not an alternative to litigation. It is only a slight exaggeration to say that it is litigation. These are not two distinct processes, negotiation and litigation: there is a single process of disputing in the vicinity of official tribunals that we might call "litigotiation"; that is, the strategic pursuit of a settlement through mobilizing the court process. Full-blown adjudication of the dispute—running the whole course—might be though of as an infrequently pursued alternative to the ordinary course of litigation.

Galanter, *Using Negotiation to Teach About Legal Process,* 34 J.Leg.Educ. 268 (1984). Viewed in this light, legal rules—both substantive and procedural—are simply one set of many "bargaining chips" for the parties to use in litigation. See also Mnookin & Kornhauser, *Bargaining in the Shadow of the Law: The Case of Divorce,* 88 Yale L.J. 950 (1979).

Mark Lazerson has published a case study of the use of procedures as bargaining chips in New York City Landlord-Tenant Court. He argues that the strategy adopted by the South Bronx Legal Services Corporation of using "every available procedural technicality and objection as a defense against tenant eviction proceedings" was quite successful until the Landlord-Tenant Court was replaced by a new court, denominated the Housing Court. It began in 1973, and sought informality, conciliation, and compromise. The author concludes:

A legal system that encourages conciliation between landlords and tenants—two parties with vastly unequal resources—by curtailing the procedural rights of the weaker can only succeed in amplifying that inequality. Procedural formality recognizes inequality and attempts to compensate for it by making both parties conform to the same standards. Once formality is withdrawn the courts are transformed into collection agencies operating with the seal of the state of New York.

Lazerson, *In the Halls of Justice, the Only Justice is in the Halls,* in Abel, *The Politics of Informal Justice,* vol. I, The American Experience (1982).

2. MECHANISMS FOR ENCOURAGING AND FACILITATING NE-GOTIATED SETTLEMENT

Negotiated settlements are not favored only by advocates of alternative forms of dispute resolution. The rules of most court systems are designed to foster negotiated settlements.

———

Read Federal Rules of Civil Procedure 54(a), 54(d) and 68, and 28 U.S.C. § 1920 in the Supplement.

———

DELTA AIR LINES, INC. v. AUGUST, 450 U.S. 346, 101 S.Ct. 1146, 67 L.Ed.2d 287 (1981). Rosemary August filed suit against Delta Air Lines seeking $20,000 in back pay for violation of Title VII of the Civil Rights Act of 1964. Delta made a formal settlement offer of $450, which August rejected. At trial, judgment was for Delta and the District Court directed that each party bear its own costs. The court held that Federal Rule 68, which directs that a plaintiff who rejects a formal settlement offer must pay post-offer costs if the "judgment finally obtained by the offeree is not more favorable than the offer," was not applicable since Delta's offer of $450 was not a reasonable, good-faith attempt to settle the case. The Court of Appeals for the Seventh Circuit affirmed on the same grounds.

The Supreme Court affirmed the result, although it rejected the reasoning of the lower courts. In an opinion written by Justice Stevens, the Court held that "the plain language, the purpose, and the history of Rule 68" made clear that the words "judgment * * * obtained by the offeree" do not encompass a judgment against the offeree:

> Our interpretation of the Rule is consistent with its purpose. The purpose of Rule 68 is to encourage the settlement of litigation. In all litigation, the adverse consequences of potential defeat provide both parties with an incentive to settle in advance of trial. Rule 68 provides an additional inducement to settle in those cases in which there is a strong probability that the plaintiff will obtain a judgment but the amount of recovery is uncertain. Because prevailing plaintiffs presumptively will obtain costs under Rule 54(d), Rule 68 imposes a special burden on the plaintiff to whom a formal settlement offer is made. If a plaintiff rejects a Rule 68 settlement offer, he will lose some of the benefits of victory if his recovery is less than the offer. Because costs are usually assessed against the losing party, liability for costs is a normal incident of defeat. Therefore, a nonsettling plaintiff does not run the risk of suffering additional burdens that do not ordinarily attend a defeat, and Rule 68 would provide little, if any, additional incentive if it were applied when the plaintiff loses.

> Defendant argues that Rule 68 does provide such an incentive, because it operates to deprive the district judge of the discretion vested in him by Rule 54(d). According to this reasoning, Rule 68 is mandatory, and a district judge must assess costs against a plaintiff who rejects a

settlement offer and then either fails to obtain a judgment or recovers less than the offer. * * *

* * * If, as defendant argues, Rule 68 applies to defeated plaintiffs, any settlement offer, no matter how small, would apparently trigger the operation of the Rule. Thus any defendant, by performing the meaningless act of making a nominal settlement offer, could eliminate the trial judge's discretion under Rule 54(d). We cannot reasonably conclude that the drafters of the Federal Rules intended on the one hand affirmatively to grant the district judge discretion to deny costs to the prevailing party under Rule 54(d) and then on the other hand to give defendants—and only defendants—the power to take away that discretion by performing a token act. Moreover, if the Rule operated as defendant argues, we cannot conceive of a reason why the drafters would have given only defendants, and not plaintiffs, the power to divest the judge of his Rule 54(d) discretion. * * * When Rule 68 is read literally, however, it is even-handed in its operation. As we have already noted, it does not apply to judgments in favor of the defendant or to judgments in favor of the plaintiff for an amount greater than the settlement offer. In both of those extreme situations the trial judge retains his Rule 54(d) discretion. * * * Thus unless we assume that the Federal Rules were intended to be biased in favor of defendants, we can conceive of no reason why defendants—and not plaintiffs—should be given an entirely risk-free method of denying trial judges the discretion that Rule 54(d) confers regardless of the outcome of the litigation.

The Court of Appeals, perceiving the anomaly of allowing defendants to control the discretion of district judges by making sham offers, resolved the problem by holding that only reasonable offers trigger the operation of Rule 68. But the plain language of the Rule makes it unnecessary to read a reasonableness requirement into the Rule. A literal interpretation totally avoids the problem of sham offers, because such an offer will serve no purpose, and a defendant will be encouraged to make only realistic settlement offers. * * *

Id. at 352–55, 101 S.Ct. at 1150–52, 67 L.Ed.2d at 292–95.

Justice Rehnquist, joined by Chief Justice Burger and Justice Stewart, dissented:

* * * [T]he Court criticizes the Court of Appeals for its failure to confront "the threshold question whether Rule 68 has any application to a case in which judgment is entered against the plaintiff-offeree and in favor of the defendant-offeror." * * * The Court's resolution of the case turns on that threshold question and it finds that the answer "is dictated by the plain language, the purpose, and the history of Rule 68."
* * *

Though the ultimate result reached by the Court is the same as that of the Court of Appeals, the difference in approach of the two opinions could not be more striking. * * * To the Court of Appeals, the mandatory language of Rule 68, at least in a Title VII case, is only discretionary where the offer is not "reasonable" and in "good faith" (neither of which qualifications are found in Rule 68). But to this Court, the Court of Appeals was entirely in error in even reaching that question because Rule 68 has no applicability to a case in which a judgment is entered *against* the plaintiff-offeree and *in favor of* the defendant-offeror. Totally ignoring the common-sense maxim that the greater includes the lesser, the Court concludes that its answer is "dictated by the plain language, the purpose, and the history of Rule 68."

Two of the three reasons advanced by the Court of Appeals in support of its opinion permitting the District Court not to impose costs on respondent in this case are squarely negated by the reasoning of the Court's opinion. The "plain language" of the Rule refers neither to an exception for Title VII cases nor to a requirement that an offer be "reasonable" or made "in good faith."

* * *

In my view, there is also no basis for reading into Rule 68 any additional conditions for bringing the Rule into play other than those which are specifically contained in the provisions of the Rule itself. I assume that the Court would agree with this approach in view of its fondness for the "plain meaning" canon of statutory construction. Therefore, the best and shortest response to the Court of Appeals' suggestion that a Rule 68 offer must be "reasonable" and made in "good faith" is that Rule 68 simply does not incorporate any such requirement; it deprives a district court of its traditional discretion under Rule 54 to disallow costs to the prevailing party in the strongest verb of its type known to the English language—"must" * * *. Over a half century ago the Court of Appeals for the Sixth Circuit said "the word 'must' is so imperative in its meaning that no case has been called to our attention where that word has been read 'may.'" Berg v. Merchant, 15 F.2d 990 (1926), cert. denied, 274 U.S. 738, 47 S.Ct. 575, 71 L.Ed. 1317 (1927). To import into the mandatory language of Rule 68 a requirement that the tender of judgment must be "reasonable" or made in "good faith" not only rewrites Rule 68, but also puts a district court in the impossible position of having to evaluate such uncertain and nebulous concepts in the context of an "offer of judgment" that in many cases may have been made years past.

* * *

The Court asserts that the result reached by, if not the reasoning of, the Court of Appeals is correct because Rule 68, by its "plain language," applies only in cases in which a "judgment [is] finally obtained by the offeree." * * *

I read both the "plain language" of the Rule and its history quite differently than does the Court. According to it, a plaintiff—"offeree" under the terms of Rule 68—must *win* in the trial court in order to "obtain" a "judgment" within the meaning of that Rule. But we may call upon the various canons of statutory construction to pass before us in review as many times as we choose without being reduced to this anomalous conclusion.

The term "judgment" is defined in Rule 54(a) of the Federal Rules of Civil Procedure to mean a "decree and any order from which an appeal lies." Unquestionably, respondent "obtained" an "order from which an appeal lies" when the District Court entered its judgment in this case. Certainly, respondent did not subscribe to the Court's reasoning because she immediately sought review in the Court of Appeals of the "judgment" which had been entered against her. Rule 68, when construed to include a traditional "take nothing" judgment, * * * as well as a judgment in favor of the plaintiff but less than the amount of the offer, thus fits with the remaining parts of the Federal Rules of Civil Procedure pertaining to judgments and orders in a manner in which the drafters of the Rule surely must have intended. * * *

Obviously, the event that "triggered" the operation of the original Rule 68 was the failure of the plaintiff to obtain a judgment more favorable than that offered. Just as obviously, the plaintiff in this case did not meet her burden of obtaining a judgment more favorable than the $450 she was offered. The operation of Rule 68 was not intended to change when this part of the Rule was amended in 1948 to its present form. * * *

* * * I do think it appropriate to note that no policy argument will convince me that a plaintiff who has refused an offer under Rule 68 and then has a "take nothing" judgment entered against her should be in a better position than a similar plaintiff who has refused an offer under Rule 68 but obtained a judgment in her favor, although in a lesser amount than that which was offered pursuant to Rule 68. The construction of Rule 68 urged by the Court would place in a better position a defendant who tendered $10,000 to a plaintiff under Rule 68 in a case where the plaintiff was awarded $5,000 than where the same tender was made and the plaintiff was awarded nothing.

* * *

Id. at 367–72, 101 S.Ct. at 1157–60, 67 L.Ed.2d at 302–07.

———

MAREK v. CHESNY, 473 U.S. 1, 105 S.Ct. 3012, 87 L.Ed.2d 1 (1985). Three police officers, in answering a call on a domestic disturbance, shot and killed Alfred Chesny's son. Chesny, on his own behalf and as administrator of his son's estate, filed suit against the officers in federal district court under 42 U.S.C. § 1983 and state tort law. Prior to trial, the police officers made a timely offer of settlement of $100,000, expressly including accrued costs and attorney's fees, but Chesny did not accept the offer. The case went to trial and Chesny was awarded $5,000 on the state-law claim, $52,000 for the Section 1983 violation, and $3,000 in punitive damages. Chesny then filed a request for attorney's fees under 42 U.S.C. § 1983, which provides that a prevailing party in a Section 1983 action may be awarded attorney's fees "as part of the costs." The claimed attorney's fees included fees for work performed subsequent to the settlement offer. The District Court declined to award these latter fees pursuant to Rule 68. The Court of Appeals reversed, but the Supreme Court agreed with the District Court.

The Court held first that the officers' offer was valid under Rule 68. As the Court read it, the Rule does not require that a defendant's offer itemize the respective amounts being tendered for settlement of the underlying substantive claim and for costs. In reaching this result, Chief Justice Burger (who wrote for the majority) asserted that the drafters' concern was not so much with the particular components of offers, but with the judgments to be allowed against defendants. Whether or not the offer recites that costs are included or specifies an amount for costs, the offer allows judgment to be entered against the defendant both for damages caused by the challenged conduct and for costs. In Chief Justice Burger's view, this construction of Rule 68 furthers its objective of encouraging settlements.

Chief Justice Burger next noted that the drafters of the Rule 68 were aware of the various federal statutes that, as an exception to the "American Rule," authorize an award of attorney's fees to prevailing parties as part of the costs in particular cases. From this, he concluded that the term "costs" in the Rule was intended to refer to all costs properly awardable under the relevant substantive statute. Thus, when the underlying statute defines "costs" to include attorney's fees, the fees are to be included as costs for purposes of Rule 68. Since Section 1983 expressly includes attorney's fees as "costs" available to a prevailing plaintiff in a suit under the statute, those fees are subject to the cost-shifting provision of Rule 68. As Chief Justice Burger saw it, rather than "cutting against the grain" of Section 1983, applying Rule 68 in the context of a Section 1983 action is consistent with Section 1988's policies and objectives of encouraging plaintiffs to bring meritorious civil rights suits; Rule 68 simply encourages settlements.

Justice Brennan filed a vigorous dissent for himself and Justices Marshall and Blackmun:

> The question presented by this case is whether the term "costs" as it is used in Rule 68 of the Federal Rules of Civil Procedure and elsewhere throughout the Rules refers simply to those taxable costs defined in 28 U.S.C. § 1920 and traditionally understood as "costs"—court fees, printing expenses, and the like—or instead includes attorney's fees when an underlying fees-award statute happens to refer to fees "as part of" the awardable costs. Relying on what it recurrently emphasizes is the "plain language" of one such statute, 42 U.S.C. § 1988, the Court today holds that a prevailing civil rights litigant entitled to fees under that statute is *per se* barred by Rule 68 from recovering any fees for work performed after rejecting a settlement offer where he ultimately recovers less than the proffered amount in settlement.

> I dissent. The Court's reasoning is wholly inconsistent with the history and structure of the Federal Rules, and its application to the over 100 attorney's fees statutes enacted by Congress will produce absurd variations in Rule 68's operation based on nothing more than picayune differences in statutory phraseology. Neither Congress nor the drafters of the Rules could possibly have intended such inexplicable variations in settlement incentives. Moreover, the Court's interpretation will "seriously undermine the purposes behind the attorney's fees provisions" of the civil rights laws. * * *

Notes and Questions

1. Most litigators agree that post-offer costs excluding attorney's fees (the most significant item of litigation expense) are too small to make a

significant difference in deciding whether to settle or go to trial. See Simon, *The Riddle of Rule 68,* 54 Geo.Wash.L.Rev. 1, 55–61 (1985). The allowable items of costs set forth in 28 U.S.C. § 1920 is a short list, and the Supreme Court has cautioned that Rule 54(d) does not give district judges "unrestrained discretion to tax costs to reimburse a winning litigant for every expense he has seen fit to incur in the conduct of his case." In particular, the Court instructed, "the discretion given district judges to tax costs should be sparingly exercised with reference to expenses not specifically allowed by statute." Farmer v. Arabian American Oil Co., 379 U.S. 227, 235, 85 S.Ct. 411, 416, 13 L.Ed.2d 248, 254 (1964). See generally Bartell, *Taxation of Costs and Awards of Expenses in Federal Court,* 101 F.R.D. 553 (1984). Thus, not surprisingly, Rule 68 was rarely used before the late 1970's when defense attorneys turned to the rule as a possible device to undercut the effect of a growing number of statutes, such as 42 U.S.C. § 1988, that altered the usual American rule in favor of prevailing plaintiffs recovering their attorney's fees. But see Crawford Fitting Co. v. J.T. Gibbons, Inc., 482 U.S. 437, 107 S.Ct. 2494, 96 L.Ed.2d 385 (1987).

2. The majority in *Marek* argues that the effect of Rule 68 is neutral because settlements serve the interest of plaintiffs as well as defendants. But does Rule 68 actually encourage settlements? Or is its primary effect to force plaintiffs to accept less in settlement of cases that would settle in the absence of the rule, but on terms more favorable to plaintiffs? See Miller, *An Economic Analysis of Rule 68,* 15 J.Legal Studies 93 (1986); Rowe, *Predicting the Effects of Attorney Fee Shifting,* 47 Law & Contemp.Prob. 139 (1984).

3. The majority in *Marek* did not answer the question whether a prevailing civil rights plaintiff also must pay the losing defendant's post-offer attorney's fees if the plaintiff obtains a judgment that is not more favorable than the Rule 68 offer. How will this question be resolved in light of the Court's decision in *Marek*? Does it matter that the Court has ruled elsewhere that a prevailing civil rights defendant may not recover attorney's fees under Section 1988 unless the trial court determines that the plaintiff's action was frivolous, unreasonable, or without foundation? See Crossman v. Marcoccio, 806 F.2d 329 (1st Cir.1986), certiorari denied 481 U.S. 1029, 107 S.Ct. 1955, 95 L.Ed.2d 527 (1987).

4. Another procedure used to encourage settlements is the summary jury trial. The proceeding, which rarely lasts longer than a day, is presided over by either the judge or a magistrate. An advisory jury is selected from the same pool used for actual trials. After counsel give expedited presentations of the case, the jury renders a non-binding decision. A summary jury trial takes place shortly before the actual trial is scheduled to occur. The technique aims to give the parties a better sense of the likely outcome as a basis for reaching a mutually acceptable settlement. See generally Lambros, *The Summary Jury Trial and Other Alternative Methods of Dispute Resolution,* 103 F.R.D. 461 (1984). For a critical analysis, see Posner, *The Summary Jury Trial and Other Methods of Alternative Dispute Resolution: Some Cautionary Observations,* 53 U.Chi.L.Rev. 366 (1986).

A useful compendium of techniques of alternative dispute resolution that judges are using or encouraging is *Alternative Dispute Resolution: A Handbook For Judges* (Hartes ed. 1987).

5. What legal authority authorizes the lower federal courts to set up and require litigants to use alternative dispute-resolution techniques? In STRANDELL v. JACKSON COUNTY, 838 F.2d 884 (7th Cir.1987), the Court of Appeals held that a district court may not require litigants to participate in a non-binding summary jury trial. The court observed that, "in those areas of trial practice where the Supreme Court and the Congress, acting together, have addressed the appropriate balance between the needs for judicial efficiency and the rights of the individual litigant, innovation by the individual judicial officer must conform to that balance." Id. at 886–87. The court found nothing in Rule 16(c)(7) or (11) that authorized a mandatory summary jury trial. It also observed that a mandatory summary jury trial as a pretrial settlement device also could affect seriously the well-established rules concerning discovery and work-product privilege.

SECTION C. ALTERNATIVE SYSTEMS OF DISPUTE RESOLUTION: BEYOND ADVERSARINESS, BEYOND THE LAW

This Section examines three third-party methods of alternative-dispute resolution (ADR). Keep two points in mind as you study them:

First, no matter how informal a dispute-resolution system may be, it requires some procedural structure to enable the participants to conduct themselves and settle their disagreements in an orderly and predictable manner. To what extent are the goals of a nonadjudicative system of dispute resolution in conflict with the need for procedural safeguards?

Second, some proponents of alternative dispute resolution assume, either explicitly or implicitly, that those who choose to work out their disputes by means other than litigation *consent* to be bound by the result. But one party may decide that she does not like the result and may refuse to be bound by it. What provision can be made to bind those who refuse to abide by the results that an ADR system produces? What provision should be made for persons who are not parties to a given dispute but who will be affected by the result produced by the proceeding? To the extent that an alternative dispute-resolution system is able to function only if those who bring disputes to it can agree beforehand to abide by the result, is its practical utility severely limited? To the extent that an alternative dispute-resolution system is endowed with coercive powers to enforce the results it produces, is it merely a variant of a traditional court system?

1. NEITHER ADVERSARINESS NOR LAW: THE NEIGHBORHOOD JUSTICE CENTERS

The Neighborhood Justice Center (NJC) program was but one of several experiments in creating small, decentralized institutions to serve local communities. These experiments were attempted several times during the late 1960s and early 1970s, but a key event in the history of developing these institutions was the 1976 National Conference on the Causes of Popular Dissatisfaction with the Administration of Justice, also known as the Pound Conference. Many participants in the Conference, including Chief Justice Burger, decried the overload of the nation's courts and suggested the creation of informal tribunals or neighborhood dispute-resolution centers. As Chief Justice Burger put it:

> The notion that ordinary people want black-robed judges, well-dressed lawyers, and fine paneled courtrooms as the setting to resolve their disputes is not correct. People with problems, like people with pain, want relief, and they want it as quickly and inexpensively as possible.

Burger, *Our Vicious Legal Spiral,* 16 Judges' J. 23 (1977). Some advocates of the NJC program stressed the limited utility of adversary litigation in dispute resolution. These reformers urged the creation of such centers as a way to resolve disputes while sparing participants the agonies of litigation, to encourage involvement in government by local communities, and to decentralize government to bring it closer to the people it affected most directly—and many of them saw the NJC program as part of a larger program to effect "community control."

Drawing on the accumulated experience of earlier attempts to create neighborhood dispute-resolution projects, the Department of Justice in cooperation with various local governments and groups opened three NJCs in 1978 with annual budgets of about $135,000 and similar operating structures. The NJCs recruited mediators from the local community—generally from what students of the NJCs have called the "helping professions," the retired, and the unemployed. These mediators received training based on the approach developed by the Institute for Mediation and Conflict Resolution.

Cases were brought to the NJCs through referrals—from local courts and police, other administrative agencies, and judges—and by individuals. The Kansas City and Atlanta NJCs obtained their cases primarily through referrals; the Venice/Mar Vista, California NJC was set up primarily to deal with cases brought directly to it by individuals. The relationship of the Kansas City and Atlanta NJCs to the pre-existing court system emphasized the NJCs' role in those cities as absorbers of overflow from the local courts. By contrast, the Venice/Mar Vista NJC emphasized voluntary referrals from the community itself through an extensive media campaign and other means designed to present the option of alternative dispute resolution to the community.

The following, from a leaflet prepared by one of the NJCs to advertise its services, describes the Center's sense of its role:

Problem Solvers

Having an argument with your spouse, friend, landlord, neighbor, local merchant or employer?

Maybe the Neighborhood Justice Center can help you work out a quick, fair and lasting solution—at no cost to you!

The Center provides you with an alternative to the courts by offering a *free* mediation service.

* * *

Types of Disputes We Will Handle

Domestic problems involving family members

Neighborhood problem—noise, pets, nuisances

Landlord-tenant problems—security deposits, repairs, damages

Small claims over money, personal property

Juvenile problems—fights, vandalism

Consumer-merchant problems—faulty merchandise, deposits, refunds, exchanges

Business Related problems—employer/employee grievances

Educational problems—involving handicapped students, administrative/staff/parent conflicts

Types of Disputes We Will Not Handle

Problems requiring legal assistance—filing lawsuits, criminal defenses, divorces, wills, etc.

Disputes involving bad checks given to merchants

Problems in which one of the parties refuses to participate willingly

Problems which can't be settled by compromise

Community Handbook of the Venice/Mar Vista Neighborhood Justice Center (1982).

The methods employed by mediators at the NJCs to handle disputes were quite informal:

* * * [T]he mediator made an opening statement to explain the mediator's role and describe the mediation process. Each disputant was asked to tell his or her side of the dispute without interruption, followed by clarifying questions from the mediator. The hearing would then continue as a joint session, with the issues discussed by both parties and mediator, or as a series of individual meetings in which the mediator would shuttle back and forth between the two parties. However organized, the job of the mediator was to gather facts and review issues in an attempt to move the parties toward an agreement. In a final joint session, if some resolution was reached, a written agreement was signed by both parties and witnessed by the mediator. Alternatively, the mediator might announce that no agreement could be reached and terminate the process. Of course, there were considerable variations in this process, depending on the type of case and parties and the individual style of the mediator. Some mediators, for instance, would actively question and lecture participants, while others would consciously refrain from such activities.

Roehl & Cook, *The Neighborhood Justice Centers Field Test*, in *Neighborhood Justice: Assessment of an Emerging Idea* 91, 94–95 (Tomasic & Feeley ed. 1982).

Evaluation of the NJCs and other neighborhood dispute-resolution experiments has been inconclusive. The Atlanta NJC handled between 150 and 200 cases per month, almost half of which were referred by court clerks in the Fulton County state court and a fourth of which were referred by judges. The remainder included referrals from social-service agencies and from the community at large. The NJC disposed of about 55 of these through mediation (with an agreement rate of 81 percent) and about 25 through a conciliation process; thus, it was able to resolve disputes about half the time.

The Kansas City NJC handled about 60 cases each month. Two-thirds of these were referrals of criminal matters from the prosecutor's office, the police department, and judges. The remainder included referrals from other social-service organizations and from the community at large. The NJC resolved about 22 cases per month through mediation and another 10 per month without a hearing.

The Venice/Mar Vista NJC handled about 50 cases each month, more than half of which were brought to it by individuals from the community and the remainder of which were referred by other social-service agencies, the courts, and the police. Of these cases, about 16 each month were resolved successfully through mediation and 7 through conciliation. The NJC referred many of its unresolved matters to other agencies, largely because so many of these cases were brought to it by individual citizens.

Roehl and Cook, who prepared *The Neighborhood Justice Centers Field Test* quoted above, sought to persuade the federal government to expand the NJC experiment. Not surprisingly, therefore, they concluded that mediation—the method of dispute resolution most frequently used by NJCs—was "an effective and satisfactory method for resolving many types of minor disputes." Roehl & Cook, supra, at 97. See also Cook, Roehl & Sheppard, *Neighborhood Justice Centers Field Test: Final Evaluation Report* (1980); McGillis, *Neighborhood Justice Centers* (1981).

Other assessments of the NJCs and similar experiments are more critical. Some scholars contend that the dispute-resolution centers of whatever type were not demonstrably speedier or cheaper than the courts. They also questioned the assumption of proponents of the NJCs that NJC-supervised mediation was noncoercive as opposed to traditional adjudication and criticized the tendency of some of the NJCs to become adjuncts of the existing court system. The most comprehensive critique is Tomasic, *Mediation as an Alternative to Adjudication: Rhetoric and Reality in the Neighborhood Justice Movement,* in *Neighborhood Justice: Assessment of an Emerging Idea* 215–48 (Tomasic & Feeley ed. 1982).

On a more theoretical level, some scholars attack the ideological assumptions underlying the NJCs and other community dispute-resolution experiments. For example, some scholars question the usefulness of the NJCs in reviving a sense of "community," arguing that institutions imposed from above did very little to encourage local residents to think of themselves as a community with shared values, goals, and standards of behavior. Others argue that dispute-resolution centers, rather than providing easier access to the justice system, actually served as an exit from that system, diverting problems that otherwise would have been brought before the courts involving significant disputes over individual rights. Some critics contend that neighborhood dispute resolution is really an

institution of social control, rather than social justice: it uses professional-
ly trained mediators to cool off disputants, not to assist them in making
valid claims, and to extend social control to areas of conflict that the
courts and other institutions are incapable of regulating effectively. R.
Hofrichter, *Neighborhood Justice In Capitalist Society* (1987).

Whatever the criticisms, the experiment with neighborhood justice
centers in the 1970s led to the establishment in the 1980s of numerous
dispute-resolution programs. In 1981, New York State enacted a law that
appropriated $1.1 million for dispute-resolution programs. Twenty other
states had enacted comprehensive legislation or appropriated funds for
mediation by 1986. Nationwide, over three hundred programs are operating, many sponsored by local courts, local governments, businesses, bar
associations, and criminal justice agencies. L. Ray, P. Kestner, J.
Thweatt, M. Leffles, J. Perkins, J. O'Hara, & A. Clare, *Dispute Resolution
Program Directory* (1986).

Notes and Questions

1. The dominant themes of the NJC experiment are informality and
consent. These, of course, have significant implications for procedural issues
raised by the structure and function of the NJCs. For example, the ability of
the NJC to establish personal jurisdiction over a disputant is premised solely
upon consent. If the noncomplaining party does not agree to submit the
dispute to mediation, then the matter is not properly before the NJC. How
useful is a system that cannot hear a case unless both parties are willing to
submit the matter to it? Consider situations in which the NJC is used to
provide third-party assistance in resolving questions that are simply too small
to be brought to court. If people now know that there is an agency geared to
solve problems that they would not otherwise bring to court or otherwise
would try to solve themselves, will they end up bringing more of these
disputes to the NJC?

2. The subject-matter jurisdiction of the NJCs also is based largely upon
consent. Does this mean that the NJC can hear a dispute based upon *any*
subject so long as the parties agree? Disputants cannot confer subject-matter
jurisdiction upon courts. Why should there be a different rule for NJCs? Is
it because NJCs, in a sense, do not have any jurisdiction in that they do not
"speak the law"? Yet some NJCs have decided that they will not handle
certain disputes. For example, the Atlanta NJC will not handle disputes
involving bad checks given to merchants, divorces, and wills.

3. Some traditional procedural problems obviously are eliminated by the
consensual nature of the NJC proceedings. For example, service of process
and notice are irrelevant, since the NJC will not handle a matter unless the
nonreferring party actually is informed that the dispute has been submitted
to the NJC and agrees to participate in the process.

4. Because the NJC procedure in effect begins with what is a fusion of
the pretrial conference and trial stages of an adjudication, there is no issue of
pretrial discovery. The sole source of information is the parties themselves;
the NJC mediator engages in no independent fact-finding and concentrates on
working out a mutually acceptable solution rather than attempting to establish the facts of a given dispute. Indeed, some NJCs actually discourage

witnesses. Doesn't the absence of pleading and discovery of facts in the NJCs, so crucial to adjudication, leave disputants who do not have the information or who do not have the skill to manipulate information at a significant disadvantage vis-a-vis disputants possessing both the information and the skills necessary to use it?

5. Is a NJC mediator supposed to be a passive referee or an active participant? What rules should govern the mediator's participation in the dispute resolution process? Consider the following instructions to mediators used in one program:

Guidelines for Conducting a Successful Hearing

1. Make an initial statement that each party will have an opportunity to be fully heard without interruption. This will ease some of the tension and should help the respondent feel less defensive.

2. Attempt to secure an agreement from each party that they will remain silent while the other person is telling their side of the story.

3. Assess the emotional state of each party.

4. You are a catalyst to get the parties to arrive at a mutually agreeable resolution. Minimize guilt or innocence and maximize communication.

5. Try and keep disputants calm. If one or both is getting extremely upset, try and calm them down by asking that they lower their voice, or sit back in their chair or slow down their rate of speech. Identify the action that they are manifesting that indicated they are upset. Do not just say, "Calm down."

6. Some rules for listening that may be helpful include:

    A. Attention responses such as "Uh huh," "OK," "I understand." Do not approve or disapprove, but acknowledge person's remarks.

    B. Echo responses where you may repeat key words or phrases. This will facilitate word flow in the proper direction and limit rambling.

7. Ask questions; however, use open ended questions rather than questions that can be answered "yes" or "no". Do not ask questions that are too broad. Try and focus questions on the main problem.

8. After everyone has a basic understanding of the problems, it is time for the mediation state of the hearing.

    A. Try to encourage and guide parties toward suggesting their own solution.

    B. Do not prescribe a solution or try to impose your values on them.

    C. If all else fails, make a specific suggestion that does not favor either party if possible.

Citizen Dispute Settlement Program, *Guidelines for Conducting a Successful Program* (1979). Do these instructions imply a high degree of manipulation of the process by the mediator? Are they consistent with the notion that the disputants control the process and determine the outcome? Judges are constrained by rules of law that generally are understood by anyone observing the process. Are there comparable constraints on the conduct of a mediator? Are the participants likely to know what those constraints are?

6. A significantly large segment of the caseload of NJCs consists of referrals from other agencies, whether courts, prosecutors, the police, or other government and social service agencies. To what degree should a referral be binding on the parties, one of whom might prefer to have his or her day in court? How voluntary is any procedure that is court-annexed? Is there not a fear of a "stigma" attached to the unwilling party when the disputants return to the referring court?

7. The literature describing and assessing the NJC experiment is silent, for the most part, concerning the enforcement of NJC "decisions." As described in the materials above, these "decisions" actually are agreements drawn up by the mediator and signed by both parties. It is not clear, however, what, if any, sanctions are to be imposed should either party violate that agreement. The Dispute Settlement Center of North Carolina, a dispute-resolution center almost identical to the Atlanta NJC, adds a *caveat* to the literature distributed to the general public: "Though not legally binding, the signed resolution form [the agreement] indicates the parties' commitment to the resolution of the dispute." Should the agreement be enforceable as a contract between the disputants? To the extent that NJCs or other such dispute-resolution centers provide "justice" for disputes that will not be brought elsewhere, should the NJCs be given enforcement powers that could be imposed directly on the noncomplying disputant? Would adding coercive powers to the NJCs create the types of due process problems requiring procedural safeguards like those found in conventional courts?

8. Consider the following critical evaluation of the NJCs and alternative dispute resolution:

> * * * [T]he new mediation proposals were not oblivious to social class. The poverty line largely determined their clientele. As identifiable groups of citizens, mostly poor and black, were diverted to informal institutions, the danger that they would lose access to courts, and the opportunity for redress there, moved closer to reality. The multiplication of mediation centers made access to justice more difficult, not less, by directing people to "exit points" from judicial institutions. Those who were likely to fare poorly in court were unlikely to receive substantial protection from informal proceedings. The longer the reach of informal processes the likelier it was that certain disputes (perhaps trivial at the level of an individual grievance but with potentially broad political and social implications for all victims of discrimination if adjudicated) might be excluded from the courts altogether. In the end, the justice system was the "community" that the new mediation programs most effectively represented.
>
> Justice centers and their progeny managed to combine some of the worst features of legality *and* of informality, without incorporating many advantages of either. Government sponsorship encouraged the extension of state legal control into urban neighborhoods, bringing private disputes under official scrutiny. At the same time, however, mediation processes dispensed with due-process safeguards (representation by counsel and the right to a jury trial), making rights even more precarious than they were

in court without compensatory benefits to disputants. With relatively little at stake in any particular dispute, mediation tribunals could encourage procedural flexibility "and present the result as fair compromise." But compromise only is an equitable solution between equals; between unequals, it "inevitably reproduces inequality." Alternative dispute settlement offered mechanical remedies for political problems: the characteristic response of law reformers since the turn of the century as they struggled to neutralize political opposition to the values that the legal system protected.

Auerbach, *Justice Without Law?* 135–36 (1983).

The issue of shared community values and standards of conduct is an extremely difficult and troubling one. The sources of the NJC idea were anthropological studies of African tribal "moots" and socialist "people's courts"—models alien to Anglo-American jurisprudence and not readily adaptable to modern American society. But does this foreclose the development of alternative dispute resolution in America today? Is a small, homogeneous community with shared values and standards of conduct a necessary precondition for a successful nonadjudicative dispute resolution system? Or might it not be argued with equal plausibility that a pluralist society is peculiarly appropriate for the construction of an alternative model of dispute resolution?

2. RESOLVING DISPUTES WITHOUT ADVERSARINESS: FAMILY LAW AND ALTERNATIVES TO ADJUDICATION

Many proponents of alternative dispute resolution single out family law, particularly disputes involving divorce, property settlement, and child custody, as a fruitful area for experimentation with alternatives to court adjudication. Consider divorce mediation.

WINKS, DIVORCE MEDIATION: A NONADVERSARY PROCEDURE FOR THE NO–FAULT DIVORCE, 19 J.Fam.L. 615, 616–25, 634–40 (1981):

II. HISTORICAL BACKGROUND

A. ADVERSARY LAW, ADVERSARY PROCEDURES

* * *

The law [historically] reflected society's disapproval of divorce by setting up a succession of legal impediments which could be overcome only by the very rich or the very tenacious. As soon as the marriage institution was threatened by dissolution, the law intervened with clumsy inefficiency. As one court noted, "in every divorce suit the state is a third party whose interests take precedence over the private interests of the spouses." The desire to manage one's private affairs without the intrusion of this third party doubtless contributed to the high incidence of informal divorce: desertion, separation and the "Enoch Arden" divorce.

A divorce was granted only after exhaustive judicial inquiry into the appropriate grounds, which were narrowly defined. The process required

that there be one party desirous of divorce, the other in opposition.
* * *

* * *

Even scrupulous lawyers were placed in the difficult position of having to evade the law in order to help their clients. The tawdry machinations which were often necessary to provide adequate justification for divorce—the staged raid on a hotel room to prove adultery, the perjured testimony—contributed to the poor image of the family lawyer. Frustration and anger were displaced from the law to the lawyer, who was forced to demand the public disclosure of private affairs in an adversary legal setting.

* * *

B. NONADVERSARY LAW, ADVERSARY PROCEDURES

No-fault divorce was designed to preserve the privacy of the parties by eliminating the need for public recrimination. Wrongs no longer had to be spelled out in embarrassing personal detail. Legal vocabulary was changed: divorce became dissolution, plaintiff and defendant became petitioner and respondent. But the removal of fault from the pleadings was not accompanied by the removal of fault from the procedures.
* * *

Where there are adversary procedures, there are secrets to be disclosed. The secrets ferreted out by the divorce lawyer are now secrets of the checking account rather than secrets of the bedroom. But when custody is in dispute, defects of character and lapses in behavior continue to be brought before the court to demonstrate parental unfitness.

Ideally, adversary procedures facilitate disclosure. In theory, each side tells its own truth and uncovers the truth concealed by the other. All too often, however, the truth is suppressed, or at least distorted. Each side presents self-serving information and strives mightily to keep the other side ignorant. Attorneys have little opportunity to counteract this distortion because of the ground rules for divorce. Clients provide a picture of their marriage which lawyers cannot revise because they have no contact with the other spouse. Such contact is enjoined by the profession * * *.

Clients are often directed not to talk with the other spouse. * * * Like the child's game of "telephone," messages must be transmitted from husband to his attorney to her attorney to wife, with inevitable distortion.

Adversary lawyers may reinforce the conflict between the parties and create obstacles to settlement. * * * The assumption that divorce lawyers will escalate the hostility has led some arbitrators and attorneys to suggest that the settlement be concluded before the lawyer steps in.

An adversary family lawyer of many years' experience has identified the two crucial determinants of the divorce outcome: the opposing counsel and the presiding judge. The comment reflects perhaps the gravest defect of the adversary process—the lack of direct involvement of the divorcing parties. The removal of the parties from the sphere of controversy is regarded as a means of promoting objectivity in resolving differences.

The lawyer is the client's "affiliate." * * * Unfortunately, affiliates are not always so evenly matched. The competent lawyer pitted against an irresponsible fighter will be limited in strategy and options, and the client will be the worse for it.

Where the differences between the parties cannot be resolved through the negotiation of their attorneys, classic divorce strategy calls for each attorney to threaten to go all the way to trial, set a court date and then tell the judge more time is needed to settle. The ensuing hallway negotiations and a few minutes of the court's time decide the future of the couple. Because judges seldom question settlements, this hasty decision-making bears the stamp of finality. As a consequence, the parties may accede to open-court stipulations that they do not understand until they sign the agreement weeks later. Unfortunately, motions to set aside such agreements seldom succeed.

If the attorneys cannot reach agreement, the judge assumes an active role. A common bench tactic is to invite opposing counsel into chambers. The judge gives a cursory first look at the file when counsel walk in. The attorneys interrupt each other as each nervously urges acceptance of his client's position. On the basis of this truncated version of the issues, the judge tells them what (s)he would do. The attorneys return to their clients with the easy excuse that they made concessions in order to avoid the risk of an imposed settlement.

Another judicial ploy is the crowded calendar. At the time scheduled for trial, the parties are advised that no room is available. Because it may be months before a new date can be set, the parties are pressured to reach agreement to avoid the uncertainty of delay.

Often attorneys settle not out of reluctance to litigate but out of familiarity with the judge's rulings. * * * Domestic relations judges in the San Francisco Bay area have coauthored a booklet of guidelines that make protracted litigation foolhardy and impractical. Such guidelines encourage settlement and save the divorcing parties from the expense and emotion of the contested divorce. But implicit in the guidelines as well as in the other procedures used to arrive at agreement is the assumption that the judges and the attorneys know what the divorcing parties want or what they ought to want.

* * *

III. AN ALTERNATIVE NONADVERSARY PROCEDURE: DIVORCE MEDIATION

* * * The mediator represents neither party in a divorce action. He is what Louis Brandeis called "counsel for the situation." The mediator's task is to provide the information which will enable the parties to arrive at a fair settlement; he is counselor and advisor, but not decisionmaker.

Perhaps little real difference exists between representing both parties and representing neither party, but the distinction, however cosmetic, is perceived as important by the legal profession. The role of disinterested advisor is regarded as more consonant with the attorney's traditional function than the role of representative of two parties with clearly differing interests.

* * *

A. HOW DIVORCE MEDIATION WORKS

Communication with both parties may begin even before the first interview. When a client calls for an appointment, one mediator asks that the other spouse call to confirm. Because mediation is so uncommon, couples often have little notion of what is involved. The two telephone conversations serve to emphasize the procedure's mutuality.

The constraints of the mediation process are carefully explained at the initial interview. The couple are made aware of the necessity for full consent and disclosure, the attorney's inability to represent either party in litigation and confidentiality of all attorney-client communications. Failure to warn leaves the attorney open to the charge of legal malpractice. The parties are told that they may consult outside attorneys at any time. Both sign a consent form which explains their rights and responsibilities. They are reminded that the mediator "is not acting as attorney for either party nor as attorney for both parties." Clients are alerted to their differing interests.   *   *   *

* * *

The attorney proceeds with special care at the initial interview. Neutral, open-ended questions elicit responses that enable the interviewer to observe the dynamics of the marital relationship. Traditional legal skills of definition, clarification and summarization come into play. By summarizing what each party has said, the lawyer enables them to hear themselves more clearly and to identify problems with some detachment.

After the initial interview, the lawyer may see each client separately, then together again.   *   *   * Some spouses may unburden themselves more freely in a separate interview. The mediator learns which areas each considers important, and where concessions can be made. Then when the parties are together, negotiations can proceed more swiftly.

* * *

A single attorney must avoid being co-opted by one party, and needs to monitor his or her own reactions in order to maintain strict impartiality. This does not mean that the mediator does not take sides. In the give and take of negotiation the skilled mediator will know when and how to alter the balance. When a stalemate occurs the mediator may shift the topic of negotiation, then reopen the issue when it provides an area for compromise.

If there are children, most lawyers deal with child support, custody and visitation first. Resolution of these issues shows the couple that cooperation will be possible in other areas as well. Custodial arrangements necessarily involve financial planning.   *   *   * Shared responsibility for the resolution of the custodial issue makes resolution of other issues easier.

In helping the couple draft an agreement, the lawyer uses the therapeutic tool of having each clarify goals and objectives. Do both parties expect their children to go to college? How will this expense be taken care of? Do both expect to be self-supporting? Will one spouse need or want vocational training? * * *

The mediator does not naively assume that parties will willingly disclose financial or other secrets. Self-protection is both inevitable and desirable. The motivation for full and fair disclosure is realistic aware-ness that if the parties cannot agree, the courts will make the agreement for them. They are dependent on each other's cooperation and must bargain in good faith.

Just as the personal injury lawyer "cools the client out," or prepares the client to accept less than the anticipated windfall, so the family lawyer prepares both spouses to accept a realistic division of assets. Each party must adjust expectations. They cannot merely discard the detritus (the inconveniently present spouse and sometimes the community debts) and hold on to the fruits of the marriage. The client who dreams of "winning big" may need to be reminded that even in adversary proceed-ings no one wins big any more. Additionally, it does little good to be awarded a whopping settlement if the other spouse, understandably resentful and antagonistic, will not abide by the provisions. The statistics on alimony, child support and visitation are a sad indicator of the minimal enforcement of settlement provisions. An agreement that re-flects realistic expectations may well prevent future litigation.

* * *

The mediator may accompany the clients to court and appear as a friend of the court, or stay away entirely. One attorney pointed out that his presence is not needed, and his absence saves the clients money. The parties' appearance in court on their own behalf serves to underscore their autonomy and responsibility for the agreement.

Notes and Questions

1. What issues should be discussed in a divorce mediation? Should the disputants determine the "subject-matter jurisdiction" of the mediator? Or should a mediator decide, for example, that custody is inseparable from child support and refuse to mediate one without the other?

2. Divorce mediation raises significant questions of professional responsi-bility. Should a lawyer engage in divorce mediation at all? If so, who is the client? Doesn't representation of both spouses involve a serious conflict of interest? Is it a sufficient response to this problem simply to decide that the lawyer-mediator does not represent either disputant? Or should a lawyer only become involved in the process as a drafter of the agreement that the disputants have reached with the help of a nonlawyer mediator? On the other hand, is a nonlawyer who mediates a divorce dispute engaged in the unauthorized practice of law? See, e.g., Silberman, *Professional Responsibili-ty Problems in Divorce Mediation*, 16 Fam.L.Q. 107 (1981); Crouch, *Divorce Mediation and Legal Ethics*, 16 Fam.L.Q. 219 (1982).

3. How active a role should a mediator, whether a lawyer or not, play in shaping the agreement? Should she (1) conduct private sessions or only joint

sessions?; (2) simply try to facilitate agreement or try to achieve certain substantive goals?; or (3) try to redress inequalities in bargaining power?

4. The Standards of Practice for Lawyer Mediators in Family Disputes approved by the House of Delegates of the American Bar Association in August 1984 provide: "If the mediator believes that * * * reasonable agreement is unlikely, the mediator may suspend or terminate mediation and should encourage the parties to seek appropriate professional help. * * * The mediator shall not, however, participate in a process that the mediator believes will result in harm to a participant." *Standards of Practice for Lawyer Mediators in Family Disputes,* 18 Fam.L.Q. 363, 366–67 (1984). What is the difference between an unreasonable agreement and one that results in harm to a participant?

5. How can we guarantee that the mediator has been impartial? Should the disputants have independent counsel in order to protect their interests? Should their attorneys participate in the mediation process? Or would their participation transform the mediation into an adversarial legal proceeding? Is the disputants' knowledge that they need not reach an agreement sufficient protection? Does not the degree of protection required depend on how active the mediator is in trying to persuade a disputant to be "reasonable"?

6. Should children participate in the mediation as well? Should they have representation? Should the mediator be responsible for guaranteeing that the agreement protects the children's interests? Or should the determination of the best interests of the children be left to the parents? After all, parents are permitted wide latitude in making that determination while they are married. Why should divorce be an occasion for a third party to interfere? See Spencer & Zammit, *Mediation—Arbitration: A Proposal for Private Resolution of Disputes Between Divorced or Separated Parents,* 1976 Duke L.J. 911 (1976); Guggenheim, *The Right to be Represented But Not Heard: Reflections on Legal Representation for Children,* 59 N.Y.U.L.Rev. 76 (1984).

7. What role should a mental-health professional play in the mediation process? Should she make a recommendation to the disputants based on her professional assessment of the situation or defer to the wishes of the disputants? Should she undertake independent fact-finding to learn about the disputants and their children that otherwise might not be revealed? Should the information be revealed at the mediation sessions?

8. Should the mediation be confidential? Or, if the mediation does not produce an agreement, should the disputants be able to use the information disclosed through the mediation process in court? Should mediators be called upon to testify regarding the mediation? To give a recommendation? If the mediation is not confidential, will disputants be less likely to be frank in their discussions? Viewed from the perspective of a trial judge, however, should not all information be made available in making the difficult decision of determining the best interests of a child?

9. How does a mediator insure that all information, such as financial information, is made available? Without a mechanism for discovery, how can mediation prevent a disputant from hiding assets?

10. Should a court enforce a mediated agreement? Or, in its role as parens patriae, should a court determine for itself the best interests of the

children? Should the decision to enforce or not depend on the answers a particular mediation provided to the questions above? For example, should a court be more willing to enforce a mediated agreement if the parents consulted independent counsel before signing the agreement? If the mediator guided the discussion informed by legal standards?

11. Consider the following:

> The unequal financial and social power of men and women makes mediation an unfair means of resolving family-related disputes. Women do not have equal bargaining power and cannot assert equal power in an informal setting unrepresented by counsel. In families where domestic violence and child sexual abuse is present, the lack of legal protection offered by mediation can be life threatening for abused family members. Mediation is inappropriate with respect to any issue (be it related to violence or not) if there has been any act or threat of violence against the women or children, since the threat of violence coerces involuntary compromise.

> Standards and enforcement are just being developed by the legal system in the areas of child and spousal support, and mediation would offer no standards and enforcement. Formal discovery is crucial to property division and is lacking in the mediation process. Finally, the rights of primary caretakers and the best interests of the children are being undermined by compromise. These issues must not be relegated to closed-door proceedings.

Lefcourt, *Women, Mediation and Family Law,* Clearinghouse Review 266, 269 (July 1984).

3. THE ADVERSARY PROCESS WITHOUT LAW: ARBITRATION

a. Introduction

Arbitration is probably the most common third-party method of alternative dispute resolution. The parties select an arbitrator or arbitrators, who conduct hearings and then reach a decision. The arbitration hearing is an adversary proceeding, in which each of the parties presents its case, with full opportunity for cross-examination and rebuttal. Frequently, the decision of the arbitrator, called an "award," is then entered in court, much as a judgment in a formally adjudicated case is entered. In each case, both parties are bound to abide by the award, even though in certain limited circumstances, discussed below, either or both parties may seek to challenge, modify, or even vacate the award.

Arbitration is the method of alternative dispute resolution with which the American legal system has had the longest experience; not surprisingly, therefore, it also is the third-party method that has adapted itself most closely to work with the legal system. Arbitration developed in the commercial and the labor-management contexts. Commercial arbitration was the first to develop. Labor arbitration first appeared during the latter half of the nineteenth century in response to repeated outbreaks of labor unrest, but did not achieve widespread acceptance until after World War II:

   * * * [T]hrough the 1930s only about 10 percent of all collective bargaining agreements in the United States provided for arbitration. The mass production industries have been the principal locus for the development of this central facet of industrial jurisprudence. * * * By the mid-1940s the rate of use for arbitration had risen to 30 to 40 percent. Arbitration has continued to grow. The most recent surveys show that about 95 percent of major collective bargaining agreements now have provisions for final and binding arbitration as the last step in the grievance process.

Antoine, *Arbitration and the Law,* in *Arbitration in Practice* 9 (Zack ed. 1984).

   As a general matter, arbitration (whether commercial, labor, or otherwise) is contractual: either the parties must have agreed in writing before the dispute in question to submit disagreements to arbitration, or they must have entered into an agreement to submit an existing dispute to arbitration.

   In addition to the arbitration agreement, both federal and state statutes play a significant role in shaping the context in which arbitration occurs. The federal statute, the Federal Arbitration Act, 9 U.S.C. §§ 1 et seq., and the major state arbitration statutes were enacted in the 1920s. The Federal Arbitration Act and Article 75 of New York's Civil Practice Law and Rules are the most notable statutes of this type, and both have served as models for other states' arbitration statutes.

   Initially, the legal system viewed arbitration with distrust; in recent years, however, we have witnessed a dramatic shift from distrust of and reluctance to enforce arbitration agreements to a strong presumption in favor of arbitration as a sound, acceptable method of resolving disputes without litigation. Possibly the final, decisive step in this shift was SOUTHLAND CORP. v. KEATING, 465 U.S. 1, 104 S.Ct. 852, 79 L.Ed.2d 1 (1984).

   In *Southland,* the appellant, the owner and franchisor of 7–Eleven convenience stores, entered into franchise agreements with the individual appellees, franchisees located in the state of California. Between September 1975 and January 1977, several individual appellees sued the appellant for breach of contract, fraud, misrepresentation, breach of fiduciary duty, and violations of the California Franchise Investment Law. The California courts consolidated the various actions with the named appellees' class action alleging identical claims against the appellant. The California Supreme Court held that the appellees' claims under the Franchise Investment Law were not arbitrable under the arbitration clause, interpreting the California Investment Law to require judicial consideration of claims brought under that statute and concluding that the California statute did not contravene the Federal Arbitration Act.

   The Supreme Court reversed, holding that "in enacting Section 2 of the federal Act, Congress declared a national policy favoring arbitration and withdrew the power of the states to require a judicial forum for the resolution of claims which the contracting parties agreed to resolve by arbitration. * * * Congress has thus mandated the enforcement of arbitration agreements." The Court rejected the argument advanced in dissent by Justices O'Connor and Rehnquist that Congress intended the Act only to be a procedural restraint on federal courts; writing for the Court, the Chief Justice maintained that the possibility of forum-shopping by litigants militated in favor of reading the statute as a source of substantive law binding both federal and state courts. See also Perry v. Thomas, 482 U.S. 483, 107 S.Ct. 2520, 96 L.Ed.2d 426 (1987).

Notes and Questions

1. Different presumptions govern arbitrations in the commercial and labor-management contexts. In labor arbitrations, it is presumed that unless a matter specifically is excluded from the coverage of the arbitration clause, the parties are obligated to arbitrate their dispute under that provision. See United Steelworkers of America v. American Manufacturing Co., 363 U.S. 564, 80 S.Ct. 1343, 4 L.Ed.2d 1403 (1960); United Steelworkers of America v. Warrior & Gulf Co., 363 U.S. 574, 80 S.Ct. 1347, 4 L.Ed.2d 1409 (1960); and United Steelworkers of America v. Enterprise Wheel & Car Corp., 363 U.S. 593, 80 S.Ct. 1358, 4 L.Ed.2d 1424 (1960) (the *Steelworker Trilogy* cases). By contrast, in disputes arising under commercial contracts that do not contain a blanket provision, the clause is held not to apply unless it clearly covers the issue. See, e.g., Perkins & Will Partnership v. Sykes & Hennessy, 41 N.Y.2d 1045, 396 N.Y.S.2d 167, 364 N.E.2d 832 (1977).

Why should there be a difference between labor arbitrations and commercial arbitrations concerning the presumption of arbitrability? Is it a sound reason for the presumption of arbitrability in labor arbitration to say that it is essential to preserve the vital continuing relationships between labor and management? Is the presumption of arbitrability in the labor field a modification of the conventional common-law principle that parties should be understood to waive causes of action in a lawsuit arising out of a given dispute unless they specifically reserve them? Why, then, should there be a presumption against arbitrability in the commercial context? Does the latter presumption manifest the system's willingness to preserve the parties' right to adjudicate disputes absent a specific agreement to the contrary? Conversely, is the presumption of arbitrability in the labor context a complement to the "no-strike" clause found in many collective-bargaining agreements?

2. The *Southland* case may well be the legal system's final rejection of the old common-law suspicion of and hostility to arbitration. But is this shift desirable in all circumstances? Dissenting in part from the Court's opinion, Justice Stevens contended that certain substantive state policy concerns justify refusing to enforce arbitration clauses such as that contained in the 7–Eleven franchise agreement:

> * * * [T]he California legislature has declared all conditions purporting to waive compliance with the protections of the Franchise Disclosure Act, including but not limited to arbitration provisions, void as a matter of public policy. Given the importance to the State of franchise relationships, the relative disparity in the bargaining positions between the franchisor and the franchisee, and the remedial purposes of the California Act, I believe this declaration of State policy is entitled to some respect.

465 U.S. at 20, 104 S.Ct. at 863, 79 L.Ed.2d at 18.   Do you agree?   Justice Stevens argued that the limited objective of the Arbitration Act was to abrogate the general common-law rule against specific enforcement of arbitration agreements and not to pre-empt such state policy.

3.   Can it be said that arbitration, like other alternative dispute-resolution devices, is effective only as between parties with equal bargaining power? Given the disparity in power and resources between a nationwide franchisor such as the appellant in *Southland* and individual franchisees, is arbitration a sound way to resolve franchisees' claims against a franchisor based on violations of a state regulatory scheme?

4.   Note that in *Southland* Keating was the named plaintiff in a class action representing 800 California franchisees.   After the lower court granted the franchisor's motion to compel arbitration of most of the claims brought by the class, the California Court of Appeal ordered that all of the claims be arbitrated and issued a writ of mandamus directing the trial court to permit the arbitration to proceed on a classwide basis.   As the case developed, the United States Supreme Court did not address the propriety of superimposing class-action procedures on a contract arbitration.   The issue is an important one, however.   Is arbitration on a classwide basis feasible?   Appropriate? Which of the procedures developed for judicial treatment of class actions would be necessary or desirable in the context of arbitration?

If you believe that it would be necessary or desirable to import into the context of arbitration procedural safeguards developed in the context of fully litigated class actions, do you believe that it is necessary or desirable to import procedural devices other than the class-action rule to safeguard the interests of the parties in other types of arbitration?   For example, should rules for arbitration similar to the rules of civil procedure governing joinder, intervention, and impleader be developed?   What of res judicata and collateral estoppel?   If we impose many civil-procedure rules in the context of arbitration, are we undermining its usefulness?

b. *How Arbitration Works*

The parties may select an arbitrator in their agreement to arbitrate, or they may authorize a neutral party, such as the American Arbitration Association, to select arbitrators.   In circumstances in which the agreement does not designate an arbitrator or a method to select an arbitrator, both the federal Act and the New York statute, for example, provide that an arbitrator may be named by a court on application of one or all of the parties.   9 U.S.C. § 5;   N.Y.C.P.L.R. § 7504.

Arbitration can take place before a single arbitrator or before a panel of arbitrators (most often consisting of three members).   Usually, the agreement will specify the number.   It is common, for example, for an agreement to provide for a panel of three arbitrators—one appointed by each party and a third appointed by the American Arbitration Association.   When the agreement specifies the number of arbitrators it governs; when it does not, both the Federal Arbitration Act and the New York statute provide that the arbitration hearing shall be conducted by a single arbitrator.

Although arbitration is a form of adversary adjudication, its procedural structure depends largely on the pre-dispositions of the arbitrator or arbitrators conducting a given hearing. The arbitrator is relatively free to shape the hearing as he sees fit. The arbitrator has three broad areas of responsibility: (1) the pre-hearing phase; (2) the hearing; and (3) the award and the opinion (if an opinion is thought necessary).

The pre-hearing phase is the least structured and thus is the most governed by individual preference. For example, it is frequently the case that the parties, represented by counsel, submit briefs (often indistinguishable from those that would be submitted in a formal adjudication) and argue their case at a hearing. In other arbitrations, the parties may choose to submit their respective cases in documentary form and waive hearings entirely. And in still other arbitrations, the parties may, but are not required to (and often do not), submit written statements, presentations, and even briefs to arbitrators. Patterns of practice tend to become associated with particular types of arbitration. For example, commercial arbitrators receive written briefs frequently. By contrast, labor arbitrators tend to discourage them.

Pre-hearing discovery usually is limited to what the parties voluntarily disclose, because federal and state arbitration statutes do not grant arbitrators the authority to use discovery devices. However, arbitrators are empowered at the request of either party to subpoena documents, as well as persons, for the hearing, and counsel generally can agree on a procedure to review the subpoenaed documents in advance of the hearing. A party may ask a court for pre-arbitration discovery, but a court will order it in extreme circumstances only. See Katsoris, *The Arbitration of a Public Securities Dispute*, 53 Fordham L.Rev. 279, 287 n. 52 (1984).

The hearing phase is somewhat more structured than the pre-hearing phase. The hearing itself is an adversary proceeding; its conduct is best described by Rule 29 of the Association's Commercial Arbitration Rules:

The Arbitrator may, at the beginning of the hearing, ask for statements clarifying the issues involved.

The complaining party shall then present its claim and proofs and its witnesses, who shall submit to questions or other examination. The defending party shall then present its defense and proofs and its witnesses, who shall submit to questions or other examination. The Arbitrator has discretion to vary this procedure but shall afford full and equal opportunity to all parties for the presentation of any material or relevant proofs.

Exhibits, when offered by either party, may be received in evidence by the Arbitrator.

Although the arbitrator is the sole judge of the relevance and materiality of evidence offered and need not conform to the legal rules of evidence, some arbitrators believe that at least some compliance with traditional rules of evidence is both necessary and beneficial:

You do not have to call them the rules of evidence, but you have to have a way of sorting out information and evaluating what is happening. It cannot be denied that a large part of what goes on in hearings is people getting things off their chests, and this, of course, bears on your attitude toward evidentiary problems as they arise. The arbitrator's basic problem is to find out as much as possible about what really happened.

Jones, *Problems of Procedure and Evidence,* in *Arbitration in Practice* 48, 52 (Zack ed. 1984).

Because the arbitrator has such broad discretion to choose to admit or exclude evidence or to hear or refuse to hear witnesses (although arbitrators that have spoken to the issue counsel their colleagues to err on the side of inclusiveness), his or her power to find facts and decide questions of law virtually is unlimited.

The federal and New York arbitration statutes empower the arbitrator to administer an oath to the witnesses testifying during the proceedings. Although some states do not empower arbitrators to swear in witnesses, some arbitrators believe in administering oaths with or without such authority.

Occasionally, although both parties may consent to submit their dispute to arbitration, one party does not appear at the hearing. Although the arbitrator is not permitted either to abandon the hearing on the ground that one party is not present, he is not permitted to rule automatically in favor of the appearing party. The New York statute pertaining to evidence at arbitration hearings, N.Y.C.P.L.R. § 7506(c), as well as common arbitration practice dictate that the appearing party be permitted to put in its statements and evidence and that the arbitrator consider this material in reaching his or her decision on the issue submitted.

The final phase of an arbitration produces the award. The arbitrator's award of a dispute need not contain anything more than a statement of the rights and obligations of the parties to that dispute, and their associations discourage them from giving reasons for a decision. See R. Coulson, Business Arbitration—What You Need to Know 29 (3d ed. 1986) ("Written opinions can be dangerous because they identify targets for the losing party to attack."). Still, arbitrators frequently prepare opinions setting forth their reasoning:

> The Supreme Court in *Enterprise Wheel* * * * said that while arbitrators do not owe the Court an explanation of their decisions, "a well reasoned opinion tends to engender confidence in the integrity of the process and aids in clarifying the underlying agreement." * * * Although the parties may of course waive an opinion, except in the small minority of cases involving bench decisions, there is no demand for awards without opinions. The parties almost always want something in writing, something that will explain why we awarded as we did. * * * The parties are interested in principles and guidelines for the future. For their future guidance, they are entitled to the arbitrator's findings of fact, his or her view of the evidence, understanding of the respective contentions of the parties, and finally, the relevant interpretation and application of the parties' agreement.

Rehmus, *Writing the Opinion,* in *Arbitration in Practice* 209, 209–10 (Zack ed. 1984). Both issues of arbitrability—whether the issues submitted properly are before the arbitrator and whether the arbitration procedures have been followed correctly—and issues on the merits usually are addressed in opinions. Often, the arbitrator finds himself under the obligation to write not only for the parties (the company and the union) but also for the NLRB, other employers and unions (for opinions frequently are circulated throughout the industry), and occasionally for the courts (to ensure that, if the award is challenged in the courts, the reviewing court understands the reasoning and conclusions underlying the award).

Notes and Questions

1. Consider the following:

> * * * Arbitration provides not only a speedier form of adjudication, but its very nature lends itself to the accurate projection of reasonable, budgeted legal costs. Another singular feature offered by arbitration is the experience and expertise brought to the adjudication process by arbitrators who invariably have familiarity with the nature of the industry in which the parties to the dispute conduct business. Typically, neither the trial judge assigned to a calendar matter nor the jury has this type of in-depth background. The speed with which arbitration proceeds also encourages a timely assessment of the settlement value of a case, and concomitantly, its eventual settlement. In short, the practitioner can properly expect increasing resort to arbitration as an alternative means of dispute resolution.

DiBenedetto, *Practical Guide: An Outline for Arbitration Under the Civil Practice Law and Rules,* 48 Albany L.Rev. 763, 777–78 (1984).

2. Advocates of arbitration maintain that it is a flexible device capable of resolving more complex disputes than conventional two-party disputes, but the various structures and rules for arbitration presuppose that the dispute in question will be a two-party dispute. Are the arbitration procedures described in this section as adaptable to multi-party disputes as proponents of arbitration contend? What difficulties would an arbitrator face in adjudicating a multi-party dispute?

3. Although at first it may appear that issues of notice and service of process do not arise in the context of arbitration (just as they did not arise in the context of the Neighborhood Justice Centers), arbitration proceedings may take place *ex parte*. However, the failure of a party to participate in an arbitration hearing does not result in an automatic default judgment in favor of the party that actually appears. If a party proves that she had no notice of the arbitration, should she be allowed to challenge the award arrived at by the arbitration in the *ex parte* proceeding? See N.Y.C.P.L.R. § 7511(b)(2).

4. Most often, the parties themselves bring matters to arbitration. This is not always the case, however. Under both the federal and the New York statutes, a defendant in a civil suit may move to halt the suit pending arbitration on the basis that the parties previously had entered into an agreement to arbitrate. 9 U.S.C. § 3; N.Y.C.P.L.R. § 7503(a). Conversely, when a party to an arbitration agreement refuses to submit a dispute to arbitration, the other party may move in court to compel the dispute's submission to arbitration. 9 U.S.C. § 4; N.Y.C.P.L.R. § 7503(a).

5. In reaching her decision, the arbitrator is not required to apply rules of decision derived from federal or state statutes, common-law rules, or even rules derived from the decisions of other arbitrators, although she may draw on such sources for guidance in reaching a decision. It has become common practice for parties to arbitration proceedings to circulate arbitration awards and decisions. Considering the legal system's reluctance to disturb arbitration awards and decisions except in certain narrowly defined circumstances, is this use of arbitration awards and decisions as nonbinding precedent sound? Should later arbitrators depend on awards and decisions that may have been flawed but whose flaws were not of sufficient dimension or significance to support a challenge in court?

6. How much preclusive effect should be given to an arbitrator's award in subsequent litigation? As to claim preclusion, it seems safe to infer that most agreements to submit disputes to arbitration contemplate that the award will merge or bar all of the claims and defenses involved. If any party dissatisfied with the award were left free to pursue a judicial remedy on the same claim or defenses, arbitration would be substantially worthless. See *Restatement (Second), Judgments* § 84, and comment *b* (1982). Unless the express terms of the agreement or the peculiar custom of a trade dictate otherwise, therefore, subsequent judicial proceedings on the same claim or defenses ordinarily should be precluded. Special statutory schemes, however, may provide judicial remedies that are intended to supplement arbitration without regard to the intent of the parties. Thus, the Supreme Court has ruled that grievance arbitration under a collective-bargaining contract does not preclude an employment-discrimination claim under Title VII of the Civil Rights Act of 1964; at most, the findings of the arbitrator can be admitted in evidence with such weight as the court may find appropriate. Alexander v. Gardner-Denver Co., 415 U.S. 36, 94 S.Ct. 1011, 39 L.Ed.2d 147 (1974). Since the values of arbitration may be drastically undermined by permitting supplemental court proceedings in this fashion, should they be permitted only when compelled by an overriding public policy that cannot safely be entrusted to arbitration?

As to issue preclusion, one commentator has concluded that:

* * * it seems probable that only in a very limited situation is preclusiveness to be accorded to an issue decided by an arbitrator's award. Perhaps this is to be limited to certain industries where the arbitration has gained such stature that this is the expectation of the parties.

Vestal, *Preclusion/Res Judicata Variables,* 54 Geo.L.J. 857, 881 (1966). What considerations underlie a reluctance to grant issue-preclusive effect to arbitral awards and decisions? To what extent might issue preclusion be necessary to support the values of stability, repose, and reliance generated by an arbitrator's award?

c. Enforcement

As a general rule, once the arbitrator has issued his award and decision, the parties have a period of time during which they can apply to modify or correct the award. Under the New York statute, for example, the parties have twenty days in which to apply to the arbitrator to modify or correct the award. N.Y.C.P.L.R. § 7509. And, under both the federal Act and the New York statute, the parties have three months in which to apply to a court to modify or to correct or even to vacate the award. 9 U.S.C. § 12; N.Y.C.P.L.R. § 7511(a).

Once the award has been issued (and assuming it is not modified, corrected, or vacated), it may be submitted to the relevant court for confirmation and entry as if it were a judgment of that court. 9 U.S.C. § 9; N.Y.C.P.L.R. § 7510. Under both the federal and New York statutes, the award must be submitted within one year after its delivery by the arbitrator to the applying party. The nonapplying party may choose either to accept the award (and, thus, not to challenge the application) or to challenge the application. In New York, a failure to move to vacate or modify the award within the three months prescribed for that procedure does not deprive the nonapplying party of any recognized ground to oppose a motion to confirm the award. N.Y.C.P.L.R. § 7510.

Both statutes give judges the discretion to order re-opening of the arbitration, although the New York statute, N.Y.C.P.L.R. § 7511(d), also permits the judge to order an entirely new arbitration proceeding (but only if the time specified in the agreement to resolve the dispute has not expired).

———————

SPRINZEN v. NOMBERG, 46 N.Y.2d 623, 415 N.Y.S.2d 974, 389 N.E.2d 456 (1979). Respondent was employed as a business agent by the petitioner, a labor organization, for service in New Jersey, Connecticut, and Pennsylvania. The respondent agreed to a restrictive covenant providing that, for five years after the termination of his employment with the petitioner, he would refrain from organizing workers within New York, New Jersey, Pennsylvania, and Connecticut. The respondent also agreed to submit all complaints and disputes whatsoever of whatever kind or nature to arbitration.

After three years, the respondent changed jobs and accepted a position with another union as its business representative for an area including Manhattan and Staten Island. The petitioner demanded arbitration, seeking to enjoin the respondent from continuing his new employment. The respondent initially submitted to arbitration but, after unsuccessfully challenging the partiality of the arbitrator (who had been named by the original agreement), the respondent refused to participate in the proceedings. The arbitrator heard the petitioner's evidence and ruled for the petitioner. The New York Supreme Court, Special Term, affirmed the award, and the respondent appealed. The Appellate Division reversed, holding that the "arbitration award under the circumstances of this case [is] in contravention of public policy." The New York Court of Appeals, reversing the Appellate Division and reinstating the award, discussed the evolving nature of public policy:

> In furtherance of the laudable purposes served by permitting consenting parties to submit controversies to arbitration, the law has adopted a policy of noninterference, with few exceptions, in this mode of dispute resolution. Quite simply, it can be said that the arbitrator is not bound to abide by, absent a contrary provision in the arbitration agreement, those principles of substantive law or rules of procedure which govern the

traditional litigation process. * * * An arbitrator's paramount responsibility is to reach an equitable result, and the courts will not assume the role of overseers to mold the award to conform to their sense of justice. Thus, an arbitrator's award will not be vacated for errors of law and fact committed by the arbitrator * * * and "[e]ven where the arbitrator states an intention to apply a law, and then misapplies it, the award will not be set aside * * *.

Despite this policy of according an arbitrator seemingly unfettered discretion in matters submitted to him by the consent of the parties, it is the established law in this State that an award which is violative of public policy will not be permitted to stand. * * * The courts, however, must exercise due restraint in this regard, for the preservation of the arbitration process and the policy of allowing parties to choose a nonjudicial forum, embedded in freedom to contract principles, must not be disturbed by courts, acting under the guise of public policy, wishing to decide the dispute on its merits, for arguably every controversy has at its core some issue requiring the application, or weighing, of policy considerations. Thus, there are now but a few matters of concern which have been recognized as so intertwined with overriding public policy considerations as to either place them beyond the bounds of the arbitration process itself or mandate the vacatur of awards which do violence to the principles upon which such matters rest. * * *

Some examples would be instructive. It has been held that an arbitrator is without power to award punitive damages, a sanction reserved solely to the State * * * and that an agreement to arbitrate, when sought to be enforced by a lender, cannot divest the courts of their responsibility to determine whether a purported sales agreement is in fact a usurious loan, and thus illegal. * * * Matters involving the enforcement of our State's antitrust laws, recognized as representing "public policy of the first magnitude," cannot be left to commercial arbitration * * * and claims concerning the liquidation of insolvent insurance companies have been held to be beyond the reach of an arbitrator's discretion where a State statute bestows upon the Supreme Court exclusive jurisdiction over these proceedings. * * *

* * *

Applying these principles to this case, we now hold that disputes involving restrictive covenants of employment can be, by mutual consent of the parties, submitted to arbitration, and an arbitrator's award which specifically enforces such covenants, even to the extent of enjoining an individual from engaging in like employment for a reasonable period of years in the future, will not be vacated on public policy grounds.

While it is true that considerations of public policy militate against the enforcement of restrictive covenants of future employment * * *, these covenants are not per se unenforceable as being null and void. * * * Each case turns upon its own distinct facts. If the restrictive covenant is found, under all the circumstances, to be "reasonable in time and area, necessary to protect the employer's legitimate interests, not harmful to the general public and not unreasonably burdensome to the employee," it will be subject to specific enforcement. * * *

Here, the parties, by reason of a broad arbitration clause contained in their signed agreement, submitted the issue of the enforceability of the restrictive covenant to arbitration, clearly a proper forum for the resolution of their dispute in this private matter. By so doing, the parties placed upon the arbitrator, not the courts, the responsibility of passing upon the merits of their controversy with the expectation that a just, yet practical, result would be reached. While there may be some doubt whether we would have enforced the restrictive covenant now before us had this dispute been adjudicated in the courts, such consideration is irrelevant to the disposition of this case, for courts will not second-guess the factual findings or the legal conclusions of the arbitrator. The utility of the arbitration process itself is derived from its autonomy, and courts must honor the choice of the parties to have their controversy decided within this framework. Insofar as public policy considerations do not absolutely preclude the enforcement of restrictive covenants of future employment for a reasonable period of time or related business concerns, we conclude that the arbitrator had the power to pass upon the issue of both the reasonableness and the necessity of the restrictions imposed upon the employee. Having thus concluded, and acknowledging the wide latitude afforded arbitrators in formulating just relief, the award rendered should not now be disturbed.

Id. at 629–32, 415 N.Y.S.2d at 976–79, 389 N.E.2d at 458–60.

Notes and Questions

1. Arbitrators do not receive any in-depth professional training or briefing on their task:

> * * * The result is a dearth of written material for training new arbitrators, upgrading the skills of practicing arbitrators, or showing the parties how arbitrators think. Experienced arbitrators may reflect on how their individual cases fit into the larger patterns of conflict resolution. Unfortunately, too few take the time, or are willing to make the time, to share these thoughts with others. Some have written papers or volumes on labor relations subjects, often intended for a broader audience than those who actually participate in arbitrations. Few arbitrators have had any opportunity to write informally for other arbitrators or for practitioners on the substantive or procedural issues one confronts in daily practice.

Zack, *Preface,* in *Arbitration in Practice* v–vi (Zack ed. 1984). Given that arbitrators are afforded such broad discretion and that, as arbitrator Edgar A. Jones, Jr., has pointed out, "[t]he number of arbitrator's awards challenged in court is less than two hundred out of more than twenty-five thousand (perhaps as many as forty thousand) awards issued each year," Jones, *Problems of Procedure and Evidence,* in *Arbitration in Practice* 49 (Zack ed. 1984), is it not troubling that arbitrators' awards can be challenged only on the relatively narrow grounds set forth in *Sprinzen?*

2. Courts will rule certain contracts void as against public policy and refuse to enforce them. Is the *Sprinzen* court saying that courts will rule certain arbitration awards void as against public policy and refuse to enforce them? Does this opinion imply that parties may order their own affairs except in the narrowly defined context in which the legislature has deter-

mined that they cannot or should not determine their affairs? How is this legislative power limited in the arbitration context? Is it merely a matter of substantive contract law? Compare Southland Corp. v. Keating, p. 1270, supra, which teaches us that legislatures may not remove certain classes of dispute from the binding effect of a valid arbitration agreement.

Index

†